PHILOSOPHY

Traditional and Experimental Readings

PHILOSOPHY

Traditional and Experimental Readings

Fritz Allhoff
Ron Mallon
Shaun Nichols

New York • Oxford
OXFORD UNIVERSITY PRESS

Oxford University Press is a department of the University of Oxford.
It furthers the University's objective of excellence in research,
scholarship, and education by publishing worldwide.

Oxford   New York
Auckland   Cape Town   Dar es Salaam   Hong Kong   Karachi
Kuala Lumpur   Madrid   Melbourne   Mexico City   Nairobi
New Delhi   Shanghai   Taipei   Toronto

With offices in
Argentina   Austria   Brazil   Chile   Czech Republic   France   Greece
Guatemala   Hungary   Italy   Japan   Poland   Portugal   Singapore
South Korea   Switzerland   Thailand   Turkey   Ukraine   Vietnam

For titles covered by Section 112 of the US Higher Education Opportunity
Act, please visit www.oup.com/us/he for the latest information about
pricing and alternate formats.

Published by Oxford University Press
198 Madison Avenue, New York, New York 10016
www.oup.com

Oxford is a registered trademark of Oxford University Press.

ISBN 978-0-19-977525-5

Printing number: 9 8 7 6 5 4 3 2 1

Printed in the United States of America
on acid-free paper

To our teachers

Contents

Preface

P HILOSOPHY IS OFTEN CHARACTERIZED AS ABSTRUSE and pointless, an enterprise entirely apart from practical concerns and commonsense thinking. This estimation is very old, going back at least to the fifth century BCE when the Greek playwright Aristophanes caricatured the great philosopher Socrates as spouting pompous nonsense completely out of touch with common sense. This characterization of philosophy is far from the truth. Common sense is philosophy's starting point as well as one of its most important tools. Of course, professors in lecture engage in philosophical thinking; but so do ordinary people in bars and stores, churches and coffee shops, homes and hospitals. Even young children pose philosophical questions, such as "Where does everything come from?" or "Why does God let people get hurt?"

Many of the oldest and most important philosophical problems emerge from commonly held beliefs. For instance, on the one hand, it seems like when you bite into a slice of mango, the taste of the mango is not a physical thing in the world; the taste of mango is an *experience*. On the other hand, it seems obvious that the taste of mango is part of the physical world. Putting the mango in your mouth, the contact of the mango with your taste buds, swallowing the fruit—these are all physical events that produce a distinctive experience. The taste of mango doesn't seem like it could be physical, but it also seems like the taste of mango is part of the physical world. These are commonsense beliefs we all have, and it is unclear how to reconcile them. That is a philosophical problem, but it is one that you can understand without spending years of training in an ivory tower.

Although philosophy often starts with commonsense questions, philosophers sometimes arrive at rather complicated views. Here are the opening lines to a book by the Danish philosopher Søren Kierkegaard:

> A human being is spirit. But what is spirit? Spirit is the self. But what is the self? The self is a relation that relates itself to itself or is the relation's relating itself to itself in the relation; the self is not the relation but is the relation's relating itself to itself.[1]

We have no idea what this bewildering passage means. But we do know that the problems Kierkegaard was concerned with, questions about the nature of the self, are problems that flow naturally from common sense. What is the self? What makes a person the same person across time? What would be required in order for a person to survive biological death? These are questions that everyone can understand. They're questions that naturally arise just from reflecting on ourselves and the world.

Many of the philosophical problems represented in this volume, for example, problems of free will, the nature of morality, or the existence of God, start with common beliefs. And many of the methods that philosophers use are commonsense methods. Perhaps the most important of these philosophical methods is argument, and especially, *deductive* argument. Philosophers call deductive arguments "valid" if and only if the conclusion follows necessarily from the premises. (Or to put it another way, the truth of the premises ensures or guarantees the truth of the conclusion.) A simple example of a deductive argument is:

P1) Neil Armstrong walked on the moon in 1969.
P2) Neil Armstrong is (and always has been) a human.
C) A human walked on the moon in 1969.

This argument is valid. So, while some conspiracy theorists deny that Armstrong walked on the moon, if the conspiracy theorists are rational, even they would have to acknowledge that *if* the premises are true, then so is the conclusion.

It is worth emphasizing that an argument can be invalid even if its premises are true, and an argument can be valid even if its premises are obviously false. For instance, here is a valid argument with false premises:

P1) Neil Armstrong is a pickle.
P2) All pickles are made of wood.
C) Neil Armstrong is made of wood.

These examples illustrate what a deductive argument is, but philosophers aim to produce arguments that are more interesting than these silly illustrations. As the great philosopher Bertrand Russell once put it, "The point of philosophy is to start with something so simple as not to seem worth stating, and to end with something so paradoxical that no one will believe it."[2] In this spirit, many philosophers aim to present deductive arguments with widely accepted premises and provocative conclusions. For example, one well-known argument in philosophy of religion goes as follows:

P1) If God exists, then evil wouldn't exist.
P2) Evil does exist.
C) God doesn't exist.

This is a powerful argument that has inspired a great deal of discussion. It uses common sense in both of the ways we have mentioned: as a tool or method and as a starting point. The argument is deductively valid. If the premises are true, the conclusion has to be true. And each of the premises has some plausibility. If we think of God as all-knowing, all-powerful, and all-good, then it seems like God would stop evil before it started. And yet there seems to be plenty of evil in the world. It is therefore a valid argument with plausible premises. Some philosophers maintain that the argument shows that God doesn't exist. Other philosophers reject the argument by rejecting one of the premises. Some hold that the existence of God is compatible with evil, while others deny that evil really exists.

In the argument concerning God and evil, the premises are based in common religious beliefs, but the kinds of premises that are available for philosophical arguments are quite diverse. Sometimes, philosophers offer premises based in our everyday intuitions, like the above judgment that it *seems* like the taste of mango is not some pattern in brain matter. In still other cases, philosophers focus our attention on quite complex cases in order to see whether our everyday intuitions favor one philosophical theory or another. Philippa Foot asks you to imagine that you see a runaway trolley heading for five people who will be killed by the trolley if you do nothing.[3] In one version of the story, you notice a switch that will divert the trolley onto a side track. There is one person on the side track, and he will be killed if you divert the trolley.[4] Is it morally okay for you to switch or not? The decision to switch has a clear advantage: it saves five lives, and only one person dies. Does that make it morally permissible to do it? Judith Jarvis Thomson compares that with another version of the case:

> You are standing on a footbridge over the trolley track. You can see a trolley hurtling down the track, out of control. You turn around to see where the trolley is headed, and there are five workmen on the track.... It just so happens that standing next to you on the footbridge is a fat man, a really fat man. He is leaning over the railing, watching the trolley; all you have to do is to give him a little shove, and over the railing he will go, onto the track in the path of the trolley. Would it be permissible for you to do this?[5]

As in the first case, you can kill one to save five. Is it morally okay for you to push the man? How about this: did you offer the same answer in the second case as in the first? If you did not, what reasons could you offer for treating the cases differently? Moral philosophers use thought experiments like these to elicit moral intuitions. Such intuitions can sometimes serve as premises in arguments for principles we should live by.

In addition to intuitions and common beliefs, philosophers sometimes use scientific research as the basis for premises in their arguments. For example, consider this argument:

P1) If the mind is completely independent of the brain, then brain damage should not cause damage to the mind.
P2) Brain damage (whether from disease or injury) does cause damage to the mind.
C) The mind is not completely independent of the brain.

This argument has some currency in contemporary philosophy. Crucially, the second premise is supported by scientific findings on how brain damage is associated with deficits in memory, language, and the emotions. Perhaps the most famous case is that of Phineas Gage, a foreman on a railroad crew. He was well liked by the men who served under him, and he was regarded as an excellent foreman by his employers. However, on September 14, 1848, an explosion propelled a tamping iron through Gage's left eye and into his brain. Remarkably, he survived the accident, but it had a profound effect on Gage's personality. One of his doctors reported that after the injury, Gage was "fitful, irreverent, indulging at times in the grossest profanity (which was not previously his custom)." Indeed, the change was so great, the doctor reports, that his friends said that he was "no longer Gage."[6] Subsequent work in neuropsychology has indicated that the area of the brain that was likely destroyed in Gage (*viz.*, the ventromedial prefrontal cortex) is critical for moral emotions. Patients with tumors or strokes in that area have been shown to have significantly reduced capacities for shame and guilt. This body of evidence suggests that damage to the brain can indeed cause profound damage to the mind. Such empirical evidence on the effects of brain damage is obviously critical for supporting (P2) in the above argument. In this way, scientific evidence can make invaluable contributions to philosophical progress.

But is there really such a thing as philosophical progress? Philosophical problems tend to be old. Many questions that remain unresolved today were first articulated by ancient Greek philosophers over 2,500 years ago. The longevity of the problems leads some to despair that philosophical problems, for example, problems concerning freedom of the will, the source of morality, or the nature of linguistic meaning, raise irresolvable problems on which no genuine progress can be made. It has been a hallmark of the philosophical tradition to resist this conclusion, and instead to continuously bring new theoretical and empirical considerations to bear on old problems. For example, the late nineteenth and early twentieth centuries brought the birth of "analytic" philosophy, an intellectual movement that brought new attention to issues of language, meaning, and logic and the role these might play in addressing philosophical and metaphysical questions. The result was a period of enormous philosophical productivity and advancement. This pattern has been repeated again and again in the philosophical tradition. In the last century, philosophers incorporated ideas, methods, and findings from such diverse disciplines as mathematics, computation theory, game theory, cognitive psychology, and evolutionary theory to advance discussions in metaphysics, ethics, political theory, and the philosophy of science. Over the last fifteen years, there has been an explosion of interest in using psychological experiments to investigate how people think about philosophical issues. This emerging approach has come to be known as "experimental philosophy" since it explores philosophical judgments about philosophically important concepts by conducting experiments to elicit people's philosophical intuitions. Some experimentalists use simple surveys, while others use more sophisticated experimental techniques like fMRI or reaction time measures to understand both the contents and sources of philosophical judgments. The guiding idea is simply that, given the importance and difficulty of these kinds of questions, we need to bring everything we know to bear on resolving them.

Many of these approaches to philosophy continue to play a role in contemporary philosophy. The selections in this volume are meant to both represent older philosophical methods and reflect the increasing role that empirical (and especially scientific) considerations are playing in many philosophical arguments. The readings include theoretical arguments, scientific reports, and research that draw extensively on science to make philosophical progress.

The aim of this volume is not to impose some specific philosophical view on the reader; instead, the aim is to give you a rich sense of the opposing sides of the issues. Although we have suggested that there is good reason to be optimistic about progress in philosophy, it is equally important to emphasize that the traditional problems in philosophy have persisted for a good reason: they are deep and difficult. Do we have free will? Is the mind mortal? Is morality relative? In philosophy, careful thought has always been one of the primary means for making progress. We invite you now to think through these problems for yourself.

Notes

1. Kierkegaard, *Sickness unto Death,* trans. E. Hong and H. Hong (Princeton: Princeton University Press, 1980), 13.
2. Bertrand Russell and David Pears, *The Philosophy of Logical Atomism* (LaSalle, IL: Open Court, 1985), 53.
3. P. Foot, *Virtues and Vices and Other Essays in Moral Philosophy* (Oxford: Basil Blackwell, 1978).
4. J. Thomson, "The Trolley Problem," *Yale Law Journal* 94 (1985): 1397 (1395–1415).
5. Ibid., 1409.
6. J. M. Harlow, "Recovery from the Passage of an Iron Bar through the Head," *Publications of the Massachusetts Medical Society* 2 (1868): 327–347.

Acknowledgments

THIS HAS BEEN A HIGHLY COLLABORATIVE project, and we have many people to thank. In addition to helpful comments from several anonymous reviewers, we would like to thank the following for feedback on the manuscript: Jeff Dean; John Doris, Washington University–St. Louis; Michael Gill, University of Arizona; Harold Greenstein, State University of New York–Brockport; Daniel Jenkins, Montgomery College–Takoma Park; Christopher Lay, California State University–Northridge; Joshua May, University of California–Santa Barbara; Thomas Nadelhoffer, Dickinson College; Eddy Nahmias, Georgia State University; David Prentiss, University of Rhode Island; Adina Roskies, Dartmouth College; Walter Sinnott-Armstrong, Duke University; Mark Timmons, University of Arizona; Jonathan Weinberg, University of Arizona; and Simine Vazire, Washington University–St. Louis. At Oxford University Press, we thank our editor, Robert Miller, as well as his editorial assistants Emily Krupin, Kristin Maffei, Christina Mancuso, and Lauren Roth. Our deepest gratitude is extended to the chapter editors for their considerable efforts in bringing this volume into existence. Finally, we acknowledge the support of the National Endowment for the Humanities, which funded the summer institute at which the project was conceived.

Part I

Knowledge and Reality

CHAPTER 1

Belief in God

KEVIN TIMPE

P HILOSOPHY OF RELIGION IS, MOST GENERALLY, philosophical reflection on and examination of the central themes or claims of religion. While philosophy of religion is related to other disciplines with a similar subject matter, such as theology and religious studies, it is nevertheless distinct. One important way in which philosophy of religion is distinct from theology is that the latter must be done from within a particular religious tradition. Philosophy of religion, on the other hand, can be done by those who are not committed to the truth of any particular religion. In fact, many of the leading philosophers of religion are themselves atheists or agnostics. Philosophy of religion is also distinct from religious studies. Religious studies investigates religious beliefs, behaviors, and institutions, but it does not do so primarily by drawing upon the tools, resources, and methodologies of philosophy. Instead, it approaches the subject matter from an interdisciplinary, historical, or anthropological point of view. So, like theology or religious studies, philosophy of religion is a study of religion. But unlike theology and religious studies, which approach their subject matter by way of a specific religion or by way of historical, anthropological, and sociological methods, respectively, philosophy of religion approaches religion with an eye to logical analysis and rational consistency.

Philosophy of religion is as old as philosophy itself. The best-known and most common subspecies of philosophy of religion is *natural theology*. Natural theology is the enterprise of providing support for religious beliefs, such as the existence of God or claims about God's nature, only on the basis of human reason and without the aid of divine revelation. Thus, natural theology does not appeal to divine revelation at all, as does *revealed theology.* That is why natural theology is—despite its name—a branch of philosophy rather than theology. Philosopher William Alston described natural theology more fully as follows:

> Natural theology is the enterprise of providing support for religious belief by starting with premises that neither are nor presuppose any religious belief. We begin from the mere existence of the world, or the teleological order of the world, or the concept of God, and we try to show that when we think through the implications of our starting point we are led to recognize the existence of a being that possesses attributes sufficient to identify Him as God.[1]

Natural theology has often been taken to aim at proving (in some relevant sense of "proving") that God exists; more recently, however, much of natural theology has taken its goal to be the weaker claim of showing that belief in God can be reasonable or rationally acceptable.In contrast, we may take natural *atheology* to be the attempt to disprove the existence of God on the basis of unaided human reason. But like natural theology, natural atheology can also have a weaker goal. As Alvin Plantinga describes this weaker goal, natural atheology aims to show that "belief in God is demonstrably irrational or unreasonable."[2]

Both natural theology and natural atheology can thus be seen to have both an ontological aim (i.e., establishing whether or not a particular being exists) and an epistemological aim (i.e., establishing whether or not belief in a particular being is rational).

The unit begins with readings that attempt to provide arguments that support belief in the existence of God. Such arguments come in a number of forms. Even if no single argument gives sufficient rational support for believing in the existence of God, it is still possible that all the arguments, together, provide a cumulative case for the existence of God. For this reason, it is helpful to think of the various arguments for the existence of God as interrelated, rather than as stand-alone entities.

The wide range of arguments can be classified in a number of ways. The most common method of classification differentiates between *a posteriori* arguments and *a priori* arguments. *A posteriori* arguments have at least one premise that is based on some feature of the universe that we know via experience. For example, various versions of the design argument focus on particular facts about the nature of the universe in which we live, such as the exact strength of gravity, the electromagnetic force, or biological facts about living organisms. Similarly, one version of the cosmological argument has a crucial premise that there exists a contingent universe (i.e., a universe that does exist but doesn't have to exist). In contrast, *a priori* arguments do not rest on premises known by means of experience. *A priori* arguments for the existence of God instead focus on concepts or principles that can purportedly be known simply by reflection or introspection.

The best known type of *a priori* argument for the existence of God, the *ontological argument*, is the subject of the first reading in this unit. While there are many formulations of the ontological argument, the most famous is that presented by Saint Anselm in the *Proslogion*. (Some scholars contend that Anselm gives two distinct versions of the ontological argument in the *Proslogion*[3]; the exact numbering of them, however, need not concern us here.) Anselm takes God to be, by definition, "a being than which nothing greater can be conceived." According to Anselm, everyone—even the atheist—understands the claim that such a being exists. It is therefore the case, on Anselm's way of putting it, that God exists in the understanding. But the existence of an object in the understanding does not entail that such a being really exists. Anselm illustrates this point by pointing to works of art, which exist only in the understanding of the artist who makes them before they actually exist. The crucial next step in Anselm's argument, however, is to point out that "a being than which nothing greater can be conceived" cannot exist only in the understanding. For a being that exists in both the understanding and in reality is surely greater than a being that only exists in the understanding. (If you're not sure of this, consider the following: which is greater, a million dollars that only exists in your understanding or an actually existing million dollars?) So God must exist.

Coupled with this selection from Anselm is a reply from one of his contemporaries, Gaunilo. Though a theist himself, Gaunilo argues that Anselm's argument must be invalid. (An argument is invalid if and only if the truth of its premises does not guarantee the truth of its conclusion. Validity is therefore a function only of the form of an argument, not its content.) According to Gaunilo, if Anselm's argument is to establish the existence of "a being than which nothing greater can be conceived," then a parallel argument would establish the existence of "an island than which nothing greater can be conceived." But clearly such an argument would not prove the existence of such an island; nor would it even give us good reason for believing in the existence of it. Since the truth of the premises does not entail the truth of the conclusion, the argument must be invalid.

The next selection contains other historically influential arguments for the existence of God, Aquinas's "five ways" from the *Summa Theologiae*. The *Summa* was originally written as an introduction to Christian theology for Dominican priests. But near the beginning, Aquinas gives a rational defense of the preambles of the faith, including arguing that the existence of God can be demonstrated. Aquinas's five ways are probably the best-known part of his entire vast corpus, but their proper interpretation and role within the rest of the *Summa* of which they are a part is a matter of some dispute. As one recent commentator on the five ways has put it:

> Throughout history, the Five Ways have received widely different interpretations and evaluations. To some, they belong to the most valuable of Thomas' contributions to philosophy (although Thomas himself does not claim any originality for them); to others they may be regarded as nothing more than a preliminary clarification of what the notion "God" stands for in the context of Christian faith. The significance to be attached to the demonstration of God's existence in the context of the *scientia* of faith is a matter of discussion. One can say that, mostly, the arguments of the Five Ways are approached from a distinctly philosophical viewpoint, assuming that they are intended to be *philosophical proofs* and as such open for critical analysis and assessment of their logical validity. On this view, what the proofs of God's existence intend to provide is philosophically good evidence on the basis of which one can rationally believe that God exists.[4]

Although it is questionable that the five ways can be fully understood divorced from the wider context of the *Summa* of which they are a part, they have come to be seen as paradigmatic arguments for the existence of God. The first three ways are structurally parallel and each offers a kind of *cosmological argument* inspired by the Aristotelian metaphysic that Aquinas adopted, focusing on motion, efficient causation, and contingency. The fourth way, which focuses on degrees of goodness, truthfulness, and nobleness, however, also indicates the Platonic influence on Aquinas. The fifth way is a form of *design argument.*

The selection from Thomas Paley's *Natural Theology* gives another well-known, but this time more thorough, version of the design (or teleological) argument. Most generally, design arguments proceed as follows. First, they claim that the universe (or some part thereof) exemplifies some particular property, *P.* They then proceed to argue that the best explanation for the universe (or part thereof) having *P* is that it was intelligently designed or given this feature on purpose by an intentional agent. While some versions of the design argument are arguments by analogy, Paley's version is more complex. Paley begins his argument by considering a watch and suggests that a watch has properties that are reliable indicators of intelligent design. First, a watch performs a particular function that intelligent agents would regard as valuable. Second, the watch is only able to perform this valuable function because its various parts (e.g., the spring, gears, and glass face) have been designed to work together to make that function possible. These two properties, taken in conjunction, can be called functional complexity and give reason to believe that it was intelligently designed to perform that function. Paley then proceeds to argue (in parts of *Natural Theology* that are not reprinted here) that the universe as a whole exhibits these same two properties as does a watch: "for every indication of contrivance, every manifestation of design, which existed in the watch, exists in the works of nature; with the difference, on the side of nature, of being greater and more, and that in a degree which exceeds all computation."[5] The specific properties that he lists as showing functional complexity include, among others, the functioning of the eye and ear, the reproduction of plants and animals, the various systems of the human body, and astronomical relations.

> Wherever we see marks of contrivance, we are led for its cause to an *intelligent* author. And this transition of the understanding is founded upon uniform experience. We see intelligence constantly contriving, that is, we see intelligence constantly producing effects, marked and distinguished by certain properties; not certain particular properties, but by a kind and class of properties, such as relation to an end, relation of parts to one another, and to a common purpose.[6]

Insofar as it illustrates functional complexity, the universe thus gives one reason to believe that God exists and designed the universe and its parts thereof to perform their functions.

Blaise Pascal, a seventeenth-century French mathematician and philosopher, gives a quite different justification for believing in God's existence. Rather than focusing on arguments that attempt to prove that God exists, he gives an argument for the pragmatic value of religious belief known as "*Pascal's Wager.*" Considered the forerunner to modern decision theory, Pascal asks us to consider the following two disjuncts: either God exists or he doesn't, and either an individual believes in God's existence or she doesn't. Since these two disjuncts are orthogonal to each other, we can construct the following two-by-two matrix:

	God exists	God doesn't exist
Believe in God		
Don't believe in God		

According to Pascal, reason cannot settle whether or not we should believe in God; we must wager. Pascal then asks us to "weigh the gain and the loss in wagering that God is. Let us estimate these two chances. If you gain, you gain all; if you lose, you lose nothing." We can then fill in the payoffs of the matrix as follows:

	God exists	God doesn't exist
Believe in God	infinite reward	nothing
Don't believe in God	infinite punishment	nothing

Through considering these options, Pascal thinks that we'll see that the pragmatic thing to do is to wager for God insofar as the payout, if he exists, outweighs the risks associated with not believing in him. So what we should all do is "endeavor then to convince yourself [that God exists], not by increase of proofs of God, but by the abatement of your passions."

Having focused thus far on reasons given in support of natural theology, let us turn our attention to natural atheology. The most common atheological argument is often taken to be the problem of evil. However, despite widespread reference to "the problem of evil," there is no single argument or problem deserving of this phrase at the expense of others. Rather, there are a plethora of arguments that fall under the scope of this phrase. As Peter van Inwagen notes in his recent book on the topic,

> The word "evil" when it occurs in phrases like "the argument from evil" or "the problem of evil" means "bad things." What, then, is the problem of evil; what is the problem of bad things? It is remarkably hard to say.... I think the reason is this: there are really a lot of different problems, problems intimately related to one another but nevertheless importantly different from one another, that have been lumped together under the heading "the problem of evil." The phrase is used to refer to this family of problems collectively.... Any attempt to give a precise sense of the term "the problem of evil," any attempt to identify it with any "single, reasonably well-defined" philosophical or theological problem, or any single, reasonably well-defined problem of any sort, runs afoul of this fact.[7]

It is common, however, to differentiate two general versions of the argument from evil; these are commonly referred to under the titles *the logical problem of evil* and *the evidential problem of evil*. The logical problem of evil is a *de facto* objection to religious belief insofar as it aims to prove that the existence of God is logically incompatible with the existence of evil. Insofar as evil exists, an omnipotent, omniscient, omnibenevolent God cannot. In "The Argument from Evil," Peter van Inwagen both raises and responds to the logical problem of evil. That there is no logical contradiction between the existence of evil and the existence of God can be shown by telling a story that, if that story were true, would show why evil could exist even if an all-perfect God also existed. Such stories are commonly referred to as "defenses." Defenses aim to give a morally sufficient reason God could have for allowing evil to exist. (In contrast, theodicies aim to give the actual reason God has for allowing evil.) It is common for defenses (and theodicies) to claim that the greater good served by God's allowing evil is the good of agents having free will. Van Inwagen presents a version of the free will defense that is, as he puts it, "true for all we know." According to van Inwagen, the reason there is evil in the world is that it is a great good for rational beings to have free will. Since the existence of evil is justified by a greater good, it is not gratuitous and thus does not count against the existence or goodness of God. The evidential problem of evil, on the other hand, is a *de jure* objection to religious belief insofar as it claims not that God cannot exist given the existence of evil, but that the existence of evil makes belief in God less rational. Contemporary philosophical debates on the evidential problem of evil can become fairly complex quite quickly, and none are included here.

But philosophers are not the only ones to raise *de jure* objections to religious belief. The late nineteenth- and early twentieth-century psychologist and neurologist Sigmund Freud is well known for giving a *de jure* objection to religious belief. Freud argues in *The Future of an Illusion* that religious belief is "an illusion and it derives its strength from the fact that it falls in with our instinctual desires."[8] But note that Freud is using this term in a technical sense, not in its customary vernacular sense. Freud defines *illusions* as "fulfillments of the oldest, strongest, and most urgent wishes of mankind."[9] An illusion for Freud is a belief that is caused by and helps satisfy a psychological need or longing. What makes them illusions is not that they are false—Freud thinks there can be true illusions—but that they are acquired and maintained despite lacking evidence that supports their truth. (To prefigure, one might say that illusions, even true ones, lack warrant.) Religious belief, according to Freud, is an expression of neuroses and distress that is rooted in the childhood need for protection, which is usually initially provided by one's father. As humans grow and become more aware of death, suffering, and uncertainty, humans project this need for a father figure onto a grander, more cosmic scale: "the derivation of religious needs from the infant's helplessness and the longing for the father aroused by it seems to me incontrovertible....The origin of the religious attitude can be traced back in clear outlines as far as the feeling of infantile hopelessness."[10] But just as children both seek the protection of their fathers and yet also fear them, so too do religious believers both trust and fear God. As he writes elsewhere: "Religion is an attempt to get control over the sensory world, in which we are placed, by means of the wish-world, which we have developed inside us as a result of biological and psychological necessities."[11] Thus, according to Freud, our belief in God is unjustified because it is based on something akin to wishful thinking.

Perhaps no philosopher has done more work on religious belief than Alvin Plantinga. Prior to Plantinga, it was commonly assumed that religious belief was only justified if one could give good philosophical arguments for those religious claims. Plantinga's most recent work on religious epistemology has focused on the concept of warrant: "that property—or better, *quantity*—enough of which is what makes the difference between knowledge and mere true belief."[12] In the reading from *Warranted Christian Belief*, Plantinga argues that Freud's criticism of religious belief, as well as a similar criticism by Karl Marx, succeeds only if it is false that God exists. That is, their objections to religious belief succeed only if one has already given a satisfactory argument for the nonexistence of God. But insofar as neither Freud nor Marx has, in Plantinga's evaluation, provided a satisfactory argument against God's existence, their criticisms of religious belief fail.

The last two readings in this unit concern explanations for the prevalence of religious belief other than traditional arguments for and against the existence of God. There is a rather large body of empirical data on religious belief, both from psychology and from evolutionary theory. Such research seeks to give an account of the origin and function of religious belief in a way that does not depend on the existence of God. For instance, Canadian psychologist M. D. Faber's *The Psychological Roots of Religious Belief* aims to show that "religious matters...can be reasonably, competently, satisfactorily explained down to the nuances themselves by...psychological approaches and analyses."[13] According to Faber, the root of religious belief is completely naturalistic and can be fully explained by biological, psychological, and sociological factors, and the central thesis of his book is to "indicate in at least a preliminary way the naturalistic, psychological direction from which all such false, hallucinatory perceptions arise."[14]

While the amount and range of scientific work on religious belief is vast, included in this unit are two different, but fairly paradigmatic, selections of such research. The first selection, from developmental psychologist Deborah Kelemen, looks at a number of recent psychological studies that suggest that children are "intuitive theists"—that is, that children are somehow psychologically hardwired to believe in God. Kelemen focuses on children's disposition to engage in teleological—or goal-directed—thinking, attributing objects' behaviors and functions to intentional design. This same tendency to attribute goals or aims to things then leads to a disposition to attribute the perceived goal or purpose to a nonhuman designer—namely, a god. In an interview with science writer Elizabeth Culotta, Kelemen comments that her research "does not speak to the existence of God; it speaks to why and how we might believe. Whether God exists is a separate question, one we can't scientifically test."[15] But one wonders, if science can give an account of religious belief that is independent of the truth of those beliefs, what reason do we have for taking those beliefs to be true?

This unit's final contributor is philosopher Daniel Dennett, whose recent book *Breaking the Spell: Religion as a Natural Phenomenon* is self-described as "a forthright, scientific, no-holds-barred investigation of religion as one natural phenomenon among many."[16] He argues not only that the traditional arguments for the existence of God fail but also that one can give a naturalistic and evolutionary account of religious belief that undermines its continued rational acceptance. He begins his book by comparing religious belief with a parasitic worm that invades an ant's brain, leading it to do what would otherwise be irrational behavior—the product of an evolutionary adaptation that is good for the propagation of the worm (or religious belief) but bad for the ant (or human species). The foundation of Dennett's theory of the origin of religious belief is what he calls a "hyperactive agent detection device, or HADD"[17]—an evolutionary innovation akin to what Kelemen's research has seen in children. Religious belief has since become a meme, a term introduced by Richard Dawkins and defined as "a unit of cultural [evolutionary] transmission, or a unit of *imitation*"[18] in a parallel way to how the gene functions as a unit of biological evolutionary transmission. And Dennett agrees with Dawkins's evaluation of this particular meme:

> The survival value of the god meme in the meme pool results from its great psychological appeal. It provides a superficially plausible answer to deep and troubling questions about existence. It suggests that injustices in this world may be rectified in the next. The "everlasting arms" hold out a cushion against our own inadequacies which, like a doctor's placebo, is none the less effective for being imaginary. These are some of the reasons why the idea of God is copied so readily by successive generations in individual brains. God exists, if only in the form of a meme with high survival value, or infective power, in the environment provided by human culture.[19]

Dennett, like Dawkins, thinks that the human race would be better off if this particular meme would go extinct.

Notes

1. William Alston, *Perceiving God: The Epistemology of Religious Experience* (Ithaca, NY: Cornell University Press, 1991), 289.
2. Alvin Plantinga, *God, Freedom, and Evil* (Grand Rapids: Eerdmans, 1977), 3.
3. See, for instance, Charles Hartshorne, *The Logic of Perfection*, 3rd ed. (Chicago: Open Court, 1991).

4. Rudi te Velde, *Aquinas on God* (Aldershot: Ashgate, 2006), 37.
5. William Paley, *Natural Theology* (Boston: Gould and Lincoln, 1860), 13.
6. Ibid., 232.
7. Peter van Inwagen, *The Problem of Evil* (New York: Oxford University Press, 2006), 4.
8. Sigmund Freud, *New Introductory Lectures on Psychoanalysis* (New York: Norton, 1965), 33.
9. Sigmund Freud, *Future of an Illusion* (New York: Norton, 1961), 38.
10. Sigmund Freud, *Civilization and Its Discontents* (New York: Norton, 1961), 47.
11. Sigmund Freud, *New Introductory Lectures on Psychoanalysis* (New York: Norton, 1965), 214f.
12. Alvin Plantinga, *Warranted Christian Belief* (Oxford: Oxford University Press, 2000), xi.
13. M. D. Faber, *The Psychological Roots of Religious Belief* (Amherst, NY: Prometheus, 2004), 14.
14. Ibid., 227.
15. http://blogs.sciencemag.org/origins/2009/11/do-studies-of-the-origin-of-re.html.
16. Daniel Dennett, *Breaking the Spell: Religion as a Natural Phenomenon* (New York: Penguin, 2006), 17
17. Ibid., 109.
18. Richard Dawkins, *The Selfish Gene* (Oxford: Oxford University Press), 192.
19. Ibid., 193.

References

Alston, William. *Perceiving God: The Epistemology of Religious Experience.* Ithaca, NY: Cornell University Press, 1991.

Dawkins, Richard. *The Selfish Gene.* Oxford: Oxford University Press, 2006.

Dennett, Daniel. *Breaking the Spell: Religion as a Natural Phenomenon.* New York: Penguin, 2006.

Faber, M. D. *The Psychological Roots of Religious Belief.* Amherst, NY: Prometheus, 2004.

Freud, Sigmund. *Civilization and Its Discontents.* New York: Norton, 1961.

Freud, Sigmund. *Future of an Illusion.* New York: Norton, 1961.

Freud, Sigmund. *New Introductory Lectures on Psychoanalysis.* New York: Norton, 1965.

Hartshorne, Charles. *The Logic of Perfection.* 3rd ed. Chicago: Open Court, 1991.

Paley, William. *Natural Theology.* Boston: Gould and Lincoln, 1860.

Plantinga, Alvin. *God, Freedom, and Evil.* Grand Rapids: Eerdmans, 1977.

Plantinga, Alvin. *Warranted Christian Belief.* Oxford: Oxford University Press, 2000.

te Velde, Rudi. *Aquinas on God.* Aldershot: Ashgate, 2006.

van Inwagen, Peter. *The Problem of Evil.* New York: Oxford University Press, 2006.

Suggestions for Further Reading

Craig, William Lane. *The Cosmological Argument from Plato to Leibniz.* New York: Palgrave Macmillan, 1980.

Craig, William Lane, and J. P. Moreland, eds. *The Blackwell Companion to Natural Theology.* Malden, MA: Blackwell, 2009.

Dawkins, Richard. *The God Delusion.* New York: Houghton Mifflin, 2006.

Dennett, Daniel. *Breaking the Spell: Religion as a Natural Phenomenon.* New York: Penguin, 2006.

Evans, C. Stephen. *Natural Signs and Knowledge of God: A New Look at Theistic Arguments.* Oxford: Oxford University Press, 2010.

Faber, M. D. *The Psychological Roots of Religious Belief.* Amherst, NY: Prometheus, 2004.

Flint, Thomas, and Michael Rea, eds. *The Oxford Handbook to Philosophical Theology.* Oxford: Oxford University Press, 2009.

Ganssle, Gregory. *A Reasonable God: Engaging the New Face of Atheism.* Waco, TX: Baylor University Press, 2009.

Jordan, Jeff. *Pascal's Wager: Pragmatic Arguments and Belief in God.* Oxford: Oxford University Press, 2006.

Nietzsche, F. *On the Genealogy of Morals,* trans. Walter Kaufmann and R. J. Hollingdale, in *On the Genealogy of Morals and Ecce Homo.* New York: Random House, 1967.

Oppy, Graham. *Ontological Arguments and Belief in God.* Cambridge: Cambridge University Press, 1995.

Plantinga, Alvin. *Warranted Christian Belief.* New York: Oxford University Press, 2000.

Quinn, Philip, and Charles Taliaferro, eds. *A Companion to Philosophy of Religion.* Malden, MA: Blackwell, 1997.

Murray, Michael, and Michael Rea. *An Introduction to the Philosophy of Religion.* Cambridge: Cambridge University Press, 2008.

Timpe, Kevin, ed. *Arguing about Religion.* New York: Routledge, 2009.

Wainwright, William, ed. *The Oxford Handbook of Philosophy of Religion.* New York: Oxford University Press, 2004.

Proslogion

ANSELM OF CANTERBURY

ANSELM OF CANTERBURY (1033–1109) was a monk and perhaps the most influential Christian thinker of the eleventh century. As prior and later abbot of his monastery in Bec (outside what is now northwestern France), Anselm was in charge of instructing his fellow monks and quickly became known for his philosophical and theological insight. He later became archbishop of Canterbury and was declared saint and Doctor of the Roman Catholic Church in 1720. Below is a selection from his book the *Proslogion*, best known for the ontological argument for God's existence in which Anselm argues that God, as "a being than which nothing greater can be conceived," must exist in reality and not just in the understanding.

CHAPTER II

Truly there is a God, although the fool hath said in his heart, There is no God.

And so, Lord, do thou, who dost give understanding to faith, give me, so far as thou knowest it to be profitable, to understand that thou art as we believe; and that thou art that which we believe. And indeed, we believe that thou art a being than which nothing greater can be conceived. Or is there no such nature, since the fool hath said in his heart, there is no God? (Psalms xiv. 1). But, at any rate, this very fool, when he hears of this being of which I speak—a being than which nothing greater can be conceived—understands what he hears, and what he understands is in his understanding; although he does not understand it to exist.

For, it is one thing for an object to be in the understanding, and another to understand that the object exists. When a painter first conceives of what he will afterwards perform, he has it in his understanding, but he does not yet understand it to be, because he has not yet performed it. But after he has made the painting, he both has it in his understanding, and he understands that it exists, because he has made it.

Hence, even the fool is convinced that something exists in the understanding, at least, than which nothing greater can be conceived. For, when he hears of this, he understands it. And whatever is understood, exists in the understanding. And assuredly that, than which nothing greater can be conceived, cannot exist in the understanding alone. For, suppose it exists in the understanding alone: then it can be conceived to exist in reality; which is greater.

Therefore, if that, than which nothing greater can be conceived, exists in the understanding alone, the very being, than which nothing greater can be conceived, is one, than which a greater can be conceived. But obviously this is impossible. Hence, there is no doubt that there exists a being, than which nothing greater can be conceived, and it exists both in the understanding and in reality.

CHAPTER III

God cannot be conceived not to exist.—God is that, than which nothing greater can be conceived.—That which can be conceived not to exist is not God.

And it assuredly exists so truly, that it cannot be conceived not to exist. For, it is possible to conceive of a being which cannot be conceived not to exist; and this is greater than one which can be conceived not to exist. Hence, if that, than which nothing greater can be conceived, can be conceived not to exist, it is not that, than which nothing greater can be conceived. But this is an irreconcilable contradiction. There is, then, so truly a being than which nothing greater can be conceived to exist, that it cannot even be conceived not to exist; and this being thou art, O Lord, our God.

So truly, therefore, dost thou exist, O Lord, my God, that thou canst not be conceived not to exist; and rightly. For, if a mind could conceive of a being better than thee, the creature would rise above the Creator; and this is most absurd. And, indeed, whatever else there is, except thee alone, can be conceived not to exist. To thee alone, therefore, it belongs to exist more truly than all other beings, and hence in a higher degree than all others. For, whatever else exists does not exist so truly, and hence in a less degree it belongs to it to exist. Why, then, has the fool said in his heart, there is no God (Psalms xiv. 1), since it is so evident, to a rational mind, that thou dost exist in the highest degree of all? Why, except that he is dull and a fool?

CHAPTER IV

How the fool has said in his heart what cannot be conceived.—A thing may be conceived in two ways: (1) when the word signifying it is conceived; (2) when the thing itself is understood. As far as the word goes, God can be conceived not to exist; in reality he cannot.

But how has the fool said in his heart what he could not conceive; or how is it that he could not conceive what he said in his heart? since it is the same to say in the heart, and to conceive.

But, if really, nay, since really, he both conceived, because he said in his heart; and did not say in his heart, because he could not conceive; there is more than one way in which a thing is said in the heart or conceived. For, in one sense, an object is conceived, when the word signifying it is conceived; and in another, when the very entity, which the object is, is understood.

In the former sense, then, God can be conceived not to exist; but in the latter, not at all. For no one who understands what fire and water are can conceive fire to be water, in accordance with the nature of the facts themselves, although this is possible according to the words. So, then, no one who understands what God is can conceive that God does not exist; although he says these words in his heart, either without any or with some foreign, signification. For, God is that than which a greater cannot be conceived. And he who thoroughly understands this, assuredly understands that this being so truly exists, that not even in concept can it be non-existent. Therefore, he who understands that God so exists, cannot conceive that he does not exist.

I thank thee, gracious Lord, I thank thee; because what I formerly believed by thy bounty, I now so understand by thine illumination, that if I were unwilling to believe that thou dost exist, I should not be able not to understand this to be true.

CHAPTER V

God is whatever it is better to be than not to be; and he, as the only self-existent being, creates all things from nothing.

What art thou, then, Lord God, than whom nothing greater can be conceived? But what art thou, except that which, as the highest of all beings, alone exists through itself, and creates all other things from nothing? For, whatever is not this is less than a thing which can be conceived of. But this cannot be conceived of thee. What good, therefore, does the supreme Good lack, through which every good is? Therefore, thou art just, truthful, blessed, and whatever it is better to be than not to be. For it is better to be just than not just; better to be blessed than not blessed.

A Reply on Behalf of the Fool

GAUNILO OF MARMOUTIERS

1.1b

Included here is a reply to Anselm's argument by fellow monk Gaunilo of Marmoutiers. Gaunilo objects to Anselm's argument because a parallel argument would prove that there exists a greatest possible island. Given that there is no such island, Anselm's argument must not be valid.

1. IF ONE DOUBTS OR DENIES the existence of a being of such a nature that nothing greater than it can be conceived, he receives this answer:

The existence of this being is proved, in the first place, by the fact that he himself, in his doubt or denial regarding this being, already has it in his understanding; for in hearing it spoken of he understands what is spoken of. It is proved, therefore, by the fact that what he understands must exist not only in his understanding, but in reality also.

And the proof of this is as follows.—It is a greater thing to exist both in the understanding and in reality than to be in the understanding alone. And if this being is in the understanding alone, whatever has even in the past existed in reality will be greater than this being. And so that which was greater than all beings will be less than some being, and will not be greater than all: which is a manifest contradiction.

And hence, that which is greater than all, already proved to be in the understanding, must exist not only in the understanding, but also in reality: for otherwise it will not be greater than all other beings.

2. The fool might make this reply:

This being is said to be in my understanding already, only because I understand what is said. Now could it not with equal justice be said that I have in my understanding all manner of unreal objects, having absolutely no existence in themselves, because I understand these things if one speaks of them, whatever they may be?

Unless indeed it is shown that this being is of such a character that it cannot be held in concept like all unreal objects, or objects whose existence is uncertain: and hence I am not able to conceive of it when I hear of it, or to hold it in concept; but I must understand it and have it in my understanding; because, it seems, I cannot conceive of it in any other way than by understanding it, that is, by comprehending in my knowledge its existence in reality.

But if this is the case, in the first place there will be no distinction between what has precedence in time—namely, the having of an object in the understanding—and what is subsequent in time—namely, the understanding that an object exists; as in the example of the picture, which exists first in the mind of the painter, and afterwards in his work.

Moreover, the following assertion can hardly be accepted: that this being, when it is spoken of and heard of, cannot be conceived not to exist in the way in which even God can be conceived not to exist. For if this is impossible, what was the object of this argument against one who doubts or denies the existence of such a being?

Finally, that this being so exists that it cannot be perceived by an understanding convinced of its own indubitable existence, unless this being is afterwards conceived of—this should be proved to me by an indisputable argument, but not by that which you have advanced: namely, that what I understand, when I hear it, already is in my understanding. For thus in my understanding, as I still think, could be all sorts of things whose existence is uncertain, or which do not exist at all, if some one whose words I should understand mentioned them. And so much the more if I should be deceived, as often happens, and believe in them: though I do not yet believe in the being whose existence you would prove.

3. Hence, your example of the painter who already has in his understanding what he is to paint cannot agree with this argument. For the picture, before it is made, is contained in the artificer's art itself; and any such thing, existing in the art of an artificer, is nothing but a part of his understanding itself. A joiner, St. Augustine says, when he is about to make a box in fact, first has it in his art. The box which is made in fact is not life; but the box which exists in his art is life. For the artificer's soul lives, in which all these things are, before they are produced. Why, then, are these things life in the living soul of the artificer, unless because they are nothing else than the knowledge or understanding of the soul itself?

With the exception, however, of those facts which are known to pertain to the mental nature, whatever, on being heard and thought out by the understanding, is perceived to be real, undoubtedly that real object is one thing, and the understanding itself, by which the object is grasped, is another. Hence, even if it were true that there is a being than which a greater is inconceivable: yet to this being, when heard of and understood, the not yet created picture in the mind of the painter is not analogous.

4. Let us notice also the point touched on above, with regard to this being which is greater than all which can be conceived, and which, it is said, can be none other than God himself. I, so far as actual knowledge of the object, either from its specific or general character, is concerned, am as little able to conceive of this being when I hear of it, or to have it in my understanding, as I am to conceive of or understand God himself: whom, indeed, for this very reason I can conceive not to exist. For I do not know that reality itself which God is, nor can I form a conjecture of that reality from some other like reality. For you yourself assert that that reality is such that there can be nothing else like it.

For, suppose that I should hear something said of a man absolutely unknown to me, of whose very existence I was unaware. Through that special or general knowledge by which I know what man is, or what men are, I could conceive of him also, according to the reality itself, which man is. And yet it would be possible, if the person who told me of him deceived me, that the man himself, of whom I conceived, did not exist; since that reality according to which I conceived of him, though a no less indisputable fact, was not that man, but any man.

Hence, I am not able, in the way in which I should have this unreal being in concept or in understanding, to have that being of which you speak in concept or in understanding, when I hear the word *God* or the words, *a being greater than all other beings.* For I can conceive of the man according to a fact that is real and familiar to me: but of God, or a being greater than all others, I could not conceive at all, except merely according to the word. And an object can hardly or never be conceived according to the word alone.

For when it is so conceived, it is not so much the word itself (which is, indeed, a real thing—that is, the sound of the letters and syllables) as the signification of the word, when heard, that is conceived. But it is not conceived as by one who knows what is generally signified by the word; by whom, that is, it is conceived according to a reality and in true conception alone. It is conceived as by a man who does not know the object, and conceives of it only in accordance with the movement of his mind produced by hearing the word, the mind attempting to image for itself the signification of the word that is heard. And it would be surprising if in the reality of fact it could ever attain to this.

Thus, it appears, and in no other way, this being is also in my understanding, when I hear and understand a person who says that there is a being greater than all conceivable beings. So much for the assertion that this supreme nature already is in my understanding.

5. But that this being must exist, not only in the understanding but also in reality, is thus proved to me:

If it did not so exist, whatever exists in reality would be greater than it. And so the being which has been already proved to exist in my understanding, will not be greater than all other beings.

I still answer: if it should be said that a being which cannot be even conceived in terms of any fact, is in the understanding, I do not deny that this being is, accordingly, in my understanding. But since through this fact it can in no wise attain to real existence also, I do not yet concede to it that existence at all, until some certain proof of it shall be given.

For he who says that this being exists, because otherwise the being which is greater than all will not be greater than all, does not attend strictly enough to what he is saying. For I do not yet say, no, I even deny or doubt that this being is greater than any real object. Nor do I concede to it any other existence than this (if it should be called existence) which it has when the mind, according to a word merely heard, tries to form the image of an object absolutely unknown to it.

How, then, is the veritable existence of that being proved to me from the assumption, by hypothesis, that it is greater than all other beings? For I should still deny this, or doubt your demonstration of it, to this extent, that I should not admit that this being is in my understanding and concept even in the way in which many objects whose real existence is uncertain and doubtful, are in my understanding and concept. For it should be proved first that this being itself really exists somewhere; and then, from the fact that it is greater than all, we shall not hesitate to infer that it also subsists in itself.

6. For example: it is said that somewhere in the ocean is an island, which, because of the difficulty, or rather the impossibility, of discovering what does not exist, is called the lost island. And they say that this island has an inestimable wealth of all manner of riches and delicacies in greater abundance than is told of the Islands of the Blest; and that having no owner or inhabitant, it is more excellent than all other countries, which are inhabited by mankind, in the abundance with which it is stored.

Now if some one should tell me that there is such an island, I should easily understand his words, in which there is no difficulty. But suppose that he went on to say, as if by a logical inference: "You can no longer doubt that this island which is more excellent than all lands exists somewhere, since you have no doubt that it is in your understanding. And since it is more excellent not to be in the understanding alone, but to exist both in the understanding and in reality, for this reason it must exist. For if it does not exist, any land which really exists will be more excellent than it; and so the island already understood by you to be more excellent will not be more excellent."

If a man should try to prove to me by such reasoning that this island truly exists, and that its existence should no longer be doubted, either I should believe that he was jesting, or I know not which I ought to regard as the greater fool: myself, supposing that I should allow this proof; or him, if he should suppose that he had established with any certainty the existence of this island. For he ought to show first that the hypothetical excellence of this island exists as a real and indubitable fact, and in no wise as any unreal object, or one whose existence is uncertain, in my understanding.

7. This, in the mean time, is the answer the fool could make to the arguments urged against him. When he is assured in the first place that this being is so great that its non-existence is not even conceivable, and that this in turn is proved on no other ground than the fact that otherwise it will not be greater than all things, the fool may make the same answer, and say:

When did I say that any such being exists in reality, that is, a being greater than all others?—that on this ground it should be proved to me that it also exists in reality to such a degree that it cannot even be conceived not to exist? Whereas in the first place it should be in some way proved that a nature which is higher, that is, greater and better, than all other natures, exists; in order that from this we may then be able to prove all attributes which necessarily the being that is greater and better than all possesses.

Moreover, it is said that the non-existence of this being is inconceivable. It might better be said, perhaps, that its non-existence, or the possibility of its non-existence, is unintelligible. For according to the true meaning of the word, unreal objects are unintelligible. Yet their existence is conceivable in the way in which the fool conceived of the non-existence of God. I am most certainly aware of my own existence; but I know, nevertheless, that my non-existence is possible. As to that supreme being, moreover, which God is, I understand without any doubt both his existence, and the impossibility of his non-existence. Whether, however, so long as I am most positively aware of my existence, I can conceive of my non-existence, I am not sure. But if I can, why can I not conceive of the non-existence of whatever else I know with the same certainty? If, however, I cannot, God will not be the only being of which it can be said, it is impossible to conceive of his non-existence.

Study Questions

1. Why does Anselm think "a being than which nothing greater can be conceived" must exist?

2. Why does Anselm think one must be a fool to doubt God's existence?

3. Do you think that Gaunilo's argument for the existence of a perfect island has the same force as Anselm's argument for a perfect being?

Summa Theologiae

THOMAS AQUINAS

THOMAS AQUINAS (1225–1274) was a Catholic priest belonging to the Dominican Order. He was very influential in integrating Aristotelian philosophy with Christian theology. Like Anselm, he is a Doctor of the Catholic Church. His influential *Summa Theologiae* was intended to be a text to train other Dominican priests in theology. Early on in the *Summa*, Aquinas argues that the existence of God can be proven in an *a posteriori* manner: "the existence of God, in so far as it is not self-evident to us, can be demonstrated from those of His effects which are known to us." Though he rejects Anselm's ontological argument, he gives five arguments—often referred to as "the five ways"—for the existence of God. The first three ways are versions of the cosmological argument, and the fifth is a version of the design argument; the fourth focuses on gradations of goodness and is not easily categorized.

The existence of God can be proved in five ways.

The first and more manifest way is the argument from motion. It is certain, and evident to our senses, that in the world some things are in motion. Now whatever is in motion is put in motion by another, for nothing can be in motion except it is in potentiality to that towards which it is in motion; whereas a thing moves inasmuch as it is in act. For motion is nothing else than the reduction of something from potentiality to actuality. But nothing can be reduced from potentiality to actuality, except by something in a state of actuality. Thus that which is actually hot, as fire, makes wood, which is potentially hot, to be actually hot, and thereby moves and changes it. Now it is not possible that the same thing should be at once in actuality and potentiality in the same respect, but only in different respects. For what is actually hot cannot simultaneously be potentially hot; but it is simultaneously potentially cold. It is therefore impossible that in the same respect and in the same way a thing should be both mover and moved, i.e. that it should move itself. Therefore, whatever is in motion must be put in motion by another. If that by which it is put in motion be itself put in motion, then this also must needs be put in motion by another, and that by another again. But this cannot go on to infinity, because then there would be no first mover, and, consequently, no other mover; seeing that subsequent movers move only inasmuch as they are put in motion by the first mover; as the staff moves only because it is put in motion by the hand. Therefore it is necessary to arrive at a first mover, put in motion by no other; and this everyone understands to be God.

The second way is from the nature of the efficient cause. In the world of sense we find there is an order of efficient causes. There is no case known (neither is it, indeed, possible) in which a thing is found to be the efficient cause of itself; for so it would be prior to itself, which is impossible. Now in efficient causes it

Thomas Aquinas, *Summa Theologiae*, translated by Fathers of the English Dominican Province (Benzinger Bros ed., 1947).

is not possible to go on to infinity, because in all efficient causes following in order, the first is the cause of the intermediate cause, and the intermediate is the cause of the ultimate cause, whether the intermediate cause be several, or only one. Now to take away the cause is to take away the effect. Therefore, if there be no first cause among efficient causes, there will be no ultimate, nor any intermediate cause. But if in efficient causes it is possible to go on to infinity, there will be no first efficient cause, neither will there be an ultimate effect, nor any intermediate efficient causes; all of which is plainly false. Therefore it is necessary to admit a first efficient cause, to which everyone gives the name of God.

The third way is taken from possibility and necessity, and runs thus. We find in nature things that are possible to be and not to be, since they are found to be generated, and to corrupt, and consequently, they are possible to be and not to be. But it is impossible for these always to exist, for that which is possible not to be at some time is not. Therefore, if everything is possible not to be, then at one time there could have been nothing in existence. Now if this were true, even now there would be nothing in existence, because that which does not exist only begins to exist by something already existing. Therefore, if at one time nothing was in existence, it would have been impossible for anything to have begun to exist; and thus even now nothing would be in existence—which is absurd. Therefore, not all beings are merely possible, but there must exist something the existence of which is necessary. But every necessary thing either has its necessity caused by another, or not. Now it is impossible to go on to infinity in necessary things which have their necessity caused by another, as has been already proved in regard to efficient causes. Therefore we cannot but postulate the existence of some being having of itself its own necessity, and not receiving it from another, but rather causing in others their necessity. This all men speak of as God.

The fourth way is taken from the gradation to be found in things. Among beings there are some more and some less good, true, noble and the like. But "more" and "less" are predicated of different things, according as they resemble in their different ways something which is the maximum, as a thing is said to be hotter according as it more nearly resembles that which is hottest; so that there is something which is truest, something best, something noblest and, consequently, something which is uttermost being; for those things that are greatest in truth are greatest in being, as it is written in Metaph. ii. Now the maximum in any genus is the cause of all in that genus; as fire, which is the maximum heat, is the cause of all hot things. Therefore there must also be something which is to all beings the cause of their being, goodness, and every other perfection; and this we call God.

The fifth way is taken from the governance of the world. We see that things which lack intelligence, such as natural bodies, act for an end, and this is evident from their acting always, or nearly always, in the same way, so as to obtain the best result. Hence it is plain that not fortuitously, but designedly, do they achieve their end. Now whatever lacks intelligence cannot move towards an end, unless it be directed by some being endowed with knowledge and intelligence; as the arrow is shot to its mark by the archer. Therefore some intelligent being exists by whom all natural things are directed to their end; and this being we call God.

Study Questions

1. Of these five arguments, which do you consider to be the strongest? Why?
2. What, if anything, can be learned about God's nature from these proofs?
3. In what ways, if any, do you think scientific advances since the thirteenth century affect Aquinas's five ways?

Natural Theology

1.3

WILLIAM PALEY

WILLIAM PALEY (1743–1805) was an Anglican priest and fellow at Christ College, Cambridge. He wrote a number of books on philosophy and religion, many of which were quite influential in nineteenth-century England. Among these was *Natural Theology: or, Evidences of the Existence and Attributes of the Deity, Collected from the Appearances of Nature*, which was first published in 1802 and a part of which is reprinted below. As the title indicates, Paley's central task is to show what can be known about the nature of God by considering the natural world. In this selection, Paley advances a version of the design argument for the existence of God, arguing that nature is so well ordered and functional that "there must have existed, at some time, and at some place or other, an artificer or artificers who formed it for the purpose which we find it actually to answer; who comprehended its construction, and designed its use." This being, Paley contends, is God.

In crossing a heath, suppose I pitched my foot against a *stone*, and were asked how the stone came to be there, I might possibly answer, that for any thing I knew to the contrary it had lain there for ever; nor would it, perhaps, be very easy to show the absurdity of this answer. But suppose I had found a *watch* upon the ground, and it should be inquired how the watch happened to be in that place, I should hardly think of the answer which I had before given, that for any thing I knew the watch might have always been there. Yet why should not this answer serve for the watch as well as for the stone; why is it not as admissible in the second case as in the first? For this reason, and for no other, namely, that when we come to inspect the watch, we perceive—what we could not discover in the stone—that its several parts are framed and put together for a purpose, *e.g.* that they are so formed and adjusted as to produce motion, and that motion so regulated as to point out the hour of the day; that if the different parts had been differently shaped from what they are, or placed after any other manner or in any other order than that in which they are placed, either no motion at all would have been carried on in the machine, or none which would have answered the use that is now served by it. To reckon up a few of the plainest of these parts and of their offices, all tending to one result: We see a cylindrical box containing a coiled elastic spring, which, by its endeavor to relax itself, turns round the box. We next observe a flexible chain—artificially wrought for the sake of flexure—communicating the action of the spring from the box to the fusee. We then find a series of wheels, the teeth of which catch in and apply to each other, conducting the motion from the fusee to the balance and from the balance to the pointer, and at the same time, by the size and shape of those wheels, so regulating that

William Paley, *Natural Theology* (New York: American Tract Society, 1802).

motion as to terminate in causing an index, by an equable and measured progression, to pass over a given space in a given time. We take notice that the wheels are made of brass, in order to keep them from rust; the springs of steel, no other metal being so elastic; that over the face of the watch there is placed a glass, a material employed in no other part of the work, but in the room of which, if there had been any other than a transparent substance, the hour could not be seen without opening the case. This mechanism being observed—it requires indeed an examination of the instrument, and perhaps some previous knowledge of the subject, to perceive and understand it; but being once, as we have said, observed and understood, the inference we think is inevitable, that the watch must have had a maker—that there must have existed, at some time and at some place or other, an artificer or artificers who formed it for the purpose which we find it actually to answer, who comprehended its construction and designed its use.

I. Nor would it, I apprehend, weaken the conclusion, that we had never seen a watch made—that we had never known an artist capable of making one—that we were altogether incapable of executing such a piece of workmanship ourselves, or of understanding in what manner it was performed; all this being no more than what is true of some exquisite remains of ancient art, of some lost arts, and, to the generality of mankind, of the more curious productions of modern manufacture. Does one man in a million know how oval frames are turned? Ignorance of this kind exalts our opinion of the unseen and unknown artist's skill, if he be unseen and unknown, but raises no doubt in our minds of the existence and agency of such an artist, at some former time and in some place or other. Nor can I perceive that it varies at all the inference, whether the question arise concerning a human agent or concerning an agent of a different species, or an agent possessing in some respects a different nature.

II. Neither, secondly, would it invalidate our conclusion, that the watch sometimes went wrong, or that it seldom went exactly right. The purpose of the machinery, the design, and the designer might be evident, and in the case supposed, would be evident, in whatever way we accounted for the irregularity of the movement, or whether we could account for it or not. It is not necessary that a machine be perfect, in order to show with what design it was made: still less necessary, where the only question is whether it were made with any design at all.

III. Nor, thirdly, would it bring any uncertainty into the argument, if there were a few parts of the watch, concerning which we could not discover or had not yet discovered in what manner they conduced to the general effect; or even some parts, concerning which we could not ascertain whether they conduced to that effect in any manner whatever. For, as to the first branch of the case, if by the loss, or disorder, or decay of the parts in question, the movement of the watch were found in fact to be stopped, or disturbed, or retarded, no doubt would remain in our minds as to the utility or intention of these parts, although we should be unable to investigate the manner according to which, or the connection by which, the ultimate effect depended upon their action or assistance; and the more complex the machine, the more likely is this obscurity to arise. Then, as to the second thing supposed, namely, that there were parts which might be spared without prejudice to the movement of the watch, and that we had proved this by experiment, these superfluous parts, even if we were completely assured that they were such, would not vacate the reasoning which we had instituted concerning other parts. The indication of contrivance remained, with respect to them, nearly as it was before.

IV. Nor, fourthly, would any man in his senses think the existence of the watch with its various machinery accounted for, by being told that it was one out of possible combinations of material forms; that whatever he had found in the place where he found the watch, must have contained some internal configuration or other; and that this configuration might be the structure now exhibited, namely, of the works of a watch, as well as a different structure.

V. Nor, fifthly, would it yield his inquiry more satisfaction, to be answered that there existed in things a principle of order, which had disposed the parts of the watch into their present form and situation. He never knew a watch made by the principle of order; nor can he even form to himself an idea of what is meant by a principle of order, distinct from the intelligence of the watchmaker. [...]

VIII. Neither, lastly, would our observer be driven out of his conclusion or from his confidence in its truth, by being told that he knew nothing at all about the matter. He knows enough for his argument; he knows the utility of the end; he knows the subserviency and adaptation of the means to the end. These points being known, his ignorance of other points, his doubts concerning other points, affect not the certainty of his reasoning. The consciousness of knowing little need not beget a distrust of that which he does know. [...]

Suppose, in the next place, that the person who found the watch should after some time discover, that in addition to all the properties which he had hitherto observed in it; it possessed the unexpected property of producing in the course of its movement another watch like itself—the thing is conceivable; that it contained within it a mechanism, a system of parts—a mould, for instance, or a complex adjustment of lathes, files, and other tools—evidently and separately calculated for this purpose; let us inquire what effect ought such a discovery to have upon his former conclusion.

I. The first effect would be to increase his admiration of the contrivance, and his conviction of the consummate skill of the contriver. Whether he regarded the object of the contrivance, the distinct apparatus, the intricate, yet in many parts intelligible mechanism by which it was carried on, he would perceive in this new observation nothing but an additional reason

for doing what he had already done—for referring the construction of the watch to design and to supreme art. If that construction *without* this property, or which is the same thing, before this property had been noticed, proved intention and art to have been employed about it, still more strong would the proof appear when he came to the knowledge of this further property, the crown and perfection of all the rest.

II. He would reflect, that though the watch before him were *in some sense* the maker of the watch which was fabricated in the course of its movements, yet it was in a very different sense from that in which a carpenter, for instance, is the maker of a chair—the author of its contrivance, the cause of the relation of its parts to their use. With respect to these, the first watch was no cause at all to the second; in no such sense as this was it the author of the constitution and order, either of the parts which the new watch contained, or of the parts by the aid and instrumentality of which it was produced. We might possibly say, but with great latitude of expression, that a stream of water ground corn; but no latitude of expression would allow us to say, no stretch of conjecture could lead us to think, that the stream of water built the mill, though it were too ancient for us to know who the builder was. What the stream of water does in the affair is neither more nor less than this: by the application of an unintelligent impulse to a mechanism previously arranged, arranged independently of it and arranged by intelligence, an effect is produced, namely, the corn is ground. But the effect results from the arrangement. The force of the stream cannot be said to be the cause or the author of the effect, still less of the arrangement. Understanding and plan in the formation of the mill were not the less necessary for any share which the water has in grinding the corn; yet is this share the same as that which the watch would have contributed to the production of the new watch, upon the supposition assumed in the last section. Therefore,

III. Though it be now no longer probable that the individual watch which our observer had found was made immediately by the hand of an artificer, yet doth not this alteration in anywise affect the inference, that an artificer had been originally employed and concerned in the production. The argument from design remains as it was. Marks of design and contrivance are no more accounted for now than they were before. In the same thing, we may ask for the cause of different properties. We may ask for the cause of the color of a body, of its hardness, of its heat; and these causes may be all different. We are now asking for the cause of that subserviency to a use, that relation to an end, which we have remarked in the watch before us. No answer is given to this question, by telling us that a preceding watch produced it. There cannot be design without a designer; contrivance, without a contriver; order, without choice; arrangement, without any thing capable of arranging; subserviency and relation to a purpose, without that which could intend a purpose; means suitable to an end, and executing their office in accomplishing that end, without the end ever having been contemplated, or the means accommodated to it. Arrangement, disposition of parts, subserviency of means to an end, relation of instruments to a use, imply the presence of intelligence and mind. No one, therefore, can rationally believe that the insensible, inanimate watch, from which the watch before us issued, was the proper cause of the mechanism we so much admire in it—could be truly said, to have constructed the instrument, disposed its parts, assigned their office, determined their order, action, and mutual dependency, combined their several motions into one result, and that also a result connected with the utilities of other beings. All these properties, therefore, are as much unaccounted for as they were before.

IV. Nor is any thing gained by running the difficulty farther back, that is, by supposing the watch before us to have been produced from another watch, that from a former, and so on indefinitely. Our going back ever so far brings us no nearer to the least degree of satisfaction upon the subject. Contrivance is still unaccounted for. We still want a contriver. A designing mind is neither supplied by this supposition nor dispensed with. If the difficulty were diminished the farther we went back, by going back indefinitely we might exhaust it. And this is the only case to which this sort of reasoning applies. Where there is a tendency, or, as we increase the number of terms, a continual approach towards a limit, *there*, by supposing the number of terms to be what is called infinite, we may conceive the limit to be attained; but where there is no such tendency or approach, nothing is effected by lengthening the series. There is no difference as to the point in question, whatever there may be as to many points, between one series and another—between a series which is finite, and a series which is infinite. A chain composed of an infinite number of links can no more support itself than a chain composed of a finite number of links. And of this we are assured, though we never *can* have tried the experiment; because, by increasing the number of links, from ten, for instance, to a hundred, from a hundred to a thousand, etc., we make not the smallest approach, we observe not the smallest tendency towards self-support. There is no difference in this respect—yet there may be a great difference in several respects—between a chain of a greater or less length, between one chain and another, between one that is finite and one that is infinite. This very much resembles the case before us. The machine which we are inspecting demonstrates, by its construction, contrivance and design. Contrivance must have had a contriver, design a designer, whether the machine immediately proceeded from another machine or not. That circumstance alters not the case. That other machine may, in like manner, have proceeded from a former machine: nor does that alter the case; the contrivance must have had a contriver. That former one from one preceding it: no alteration still; a contriver is still necessary.

No tendency is perceived, no approach towards a diminution of this necessity. It is the same with any and every succession of these machines—a succession of ten, of a hundred, of a thousand; with one series, as with another—a series which is finite, as with a series which is infinite. In whatever other respects they may differ, in this they do not. In all equally, contrivance and design are unaccounted for.

The question is not simply, How came the first watch into existence? which question, it may be pretended, is done away by supposing the series of watches thus produced from one another to have been infinite, and consequently to have had no such *first*, for which it was necessary to provide a cause. This, perhaps, would have been nearly the state of the question, if nothing had been before us but an unorganized, unmechanized substance, without mark or indication of contrivance. It might be difficult to show that such substance could not have existed from eternity, either in succession—if it were possible, which I think it is not, for unorganized bodies to spring from one another—or by individual perpetuity. But that is not the question now. To suppose it to be so, is to suppose that it made no difference whether he had found a watch or a stone. As it is, the metaphysics of that question have no place; for, in the watch which we are examining, are seen contrivance, design, an end, a purpose, means for the end, adaptation to the purpose. And the question which irresistibly presses upon our thoughts is, Whence this contrivance and design? The thing required is the intending mind, the adapted hand, the intelligence by which that hand was directed. This question, this demand, is not shaken off by increasing a number or succession of substances destitute of these properties; nor the more, by increasing that number to infinity. If it be said, that upon the supposition of one watch being produced from another in the course of that other's movements, and by means of the mechanism within it, we have a cause for the watch in my hand, namely, the watch from which it proceeded—I deny, that for the design,

the contrivance, the suitableness of means to an end, the adaptation of instruments to a use, all of which we discover in the watch, we have any cause whatever. It is in vain, therefore, to assign a series of such causes, or to allege that a series may be carried back to infinity; for I do not admit that we have yet any cause at all for the phenomena, still less any series of causes either finite or infinite. Here is contrivance, but no contriver; proofs of design, but no designer.

V. Our observer would further also reflect, that the maker of the watch before him was in truth and reality, the maker of every watch produced from it: there being no difference, except that the latter manifests a more exquisite skill, between the making of another watch with his own hands, by the mediation of files, lathes, chisels, etc., and the disposing, fixing, and inserting of these instruments, or of others equivalent to them, in the body of the watch already made, in such a manner as to form a new watch in the course of the movements which he had given to the old one. It is only working by one set of tools instead of another.

The conclusion which the *first* examination of the watch, of its works, construction, and movement, suggested, was, that it must have had, for cause and author of that construction, an artificer who understood its mechanism and designed its use. This conclusion is invincible. A *second* examination presents us with a new discovery. The watch is found, in the course of its movement, to produce another watch similar to itself; and not only so, but we perceive in it a system or organization separately calculated for that purpose. What effect would this discovery have, or ought it to have, upon our former inference? What, as hath already been said, but to increase beyond measure our admiration of the skill which had been employed in the formation of such a machine? Or shall it, instead of this, all at once turn us round to an opposite conclusion, namely, that no art or skill whatever has been concerned in the business, although all other evidences of art and skill remain as they were, and this last and supreme piece of art be now added to the rest? Can this be maintained without absurdity? Yet this is atheism.

Study Questions

1. How well supported do you think Paley's comparison between a watch and the natural world is?

2. Even if his argument does establish the existence of a designer, what else can be known about the nature of this designer from the natural world?

3. Charles Darwin, the biologist known for his claim that evolution happens by means of natural selection, read Paley's *Natural Theology* at Cambridge and was quite impressed by it. What impact do you think evolution has on Paley's argument?

1.4   Pensées

 BLAISE PASCAL

BLAISE PASCAL (1623–1662) was a French mathematician and scientist. He is credited with inventing an early mechanical calculator, the hydraulic press, and the syringe. He made significant contributions to what would later be called probability theory and decision theory. Later in his life, he underwent a religious experience and was greatly influenced by Jansenism, a strain of Catholic theology that was later condemned as heretical. His most influential theological work, the *Pensées* (or "Thoughts"), was never completed and was published only posthumously. The section of *Pensées* from which the following reading comes is two pages covered front and back with handwritten thoughts, corrections, and insertions, a fact that no doubt contributes to the controversy over its proper interpretation. It is usually claimed that the key paragraph contains three different but interrelated arguments for the conclusion that rationality requires you to wager for God. What exactly it means to wager, however, is not clearly specified.

343. *Infinite. Nothing.* Our soul is tossed into the body where it finds number, time, dimensions. It argues about them, calls them nature or necessity, and cannot believe in anything else.

Unity joined to infinity does not add anything to it, any more than a foot to a measure which is infinite. The finite is annihilated in the presence of the infinite, and becomes pure nothingness. Thus it is with our mind in the presence of God; thus our justice in face of divine justice.

There is not such a great disproportion between our justice and God's as between unity and infinity.

Blaise Pascal, *Pensées*, translated by Martin Turnbull (New York: Harper and Brothers, 1962), pp. 200–7 from Pascal's *Pensées* by Blaise Pascal. Translated and with an Introduction by Martin Turnbull. Harper & Brothers New York 1962. Reprinted by permission of HarperCollins Publishers.

The justice of God must be immense like his mercy. Now justice shown to the damned is less overwhelming and must be less shocking, than mercy towards the saved.

We know that there is an infinite, but are ignorant of its nature. Since we know that it is untrue that numbers are finite, it follows that there is infinity in number. But we do not know what it is: it is untrue to say that it is even, untrue to say that it is odd; for the addition of unity does not alter its nature; yet it is a number and every number is odd or even (it is true that this applies to all finite numbers). Thus we may be sure that there is a God without knowing what he is.

Is there not one substantial truth, since there are so many true things which are not truth itself?

We therefore know the existence and nature of the finite because we are finite and like it consist of extension in space. We know the existence of the infinite and do not know its nature because it possesses extension like ourselves, but not limits like us. But we do not know either the existence or the nature of God because he has neither extension nor limits.

But through faith we know that he exists; through glory we shall come to know his nature. Now, I have already shown that we can perfectly well know the existence of something without knowing its nature.

Let us now speak according to our natural lights.

If there is a God, he is infinitely incomprehensible because having neither dimensions nor limits, he has no relation to us. We are therefore incapable of knowing either what he is, or whether he exists. That being so, who will be bold enough to attempt the solution of the problem? Not we who have no communication with him.

Who then will blame Christians for not being able to give reasons for their beliefs since they profess belief in a religion which they cannot explain? They declare, when they expound it to the world, that it is foolishness, *stultitiam*; and then you complain because they do not prove it! If they proved it, they would not keep their word; it is through their lack of proofs that they show they are not lacking in sense.

"Yes, but even if it excuses those who present it in such a way, and if it excuses them for presenting it without giving reasons, it does not excuse those who accept it."

Let us consider the point and say: "Either God exists, or he does not exist." But which of the alternatives shall we choose? Reason can determine nothing: there is an infinite chaos which divides us. A coin is being spun at the extreme point of this infinite distance which will turn up heads or tails. What is your bet? If you rely on reason you cannot settle for either, or defend either position.

Do not therefore accuse those who have made their choice of falseness because you know nothing about it.

"No, I do not blame them for their choice, but for making a choice at all because he who calls heads and he who calls tails are guilty of the same mistake, they are both wrong: the right course is not to wager." "Yes, but we have to wager. You are not a free agent; you are committed. Which will you have then? Come on. Since you are obliged to choose, let us see which interests you least. You may lose two things: the true and the good; and there are two things that you stake: your reason and your will, your knowledge and your beatitude; and your nature has two things from which to escape: error and unhappiness. Your reason is not more deeply wounded by choosing one rather than the other because it is bound to choose. That disposes of one point. But what about your beatitude? Let us measure the gain and the loss by saying: 'Heads God exists.' Let us compare the two cases; if you win, you win everything; if you lose, you lose nothing. Don't hesitate then. Take a bet that he exists."

"That's fine. Yes, I must take a bet; but perhaps I am staking too much."

"Come. Since there is an equal chance of gain and loss, if you were only to win two lives for one, you could still wager; but if there were three to be won, you would have to gamble (since you are bound to gamble), and it would be imprudent, when you are obliged to gamble, not to risk your life in order to win three lives at a game in which there is such a chance of loss and gain. But there is an eternity of life and happiness at stake. And since it is so, if there were an infinite number of chances of which only one was for you, you would still be right to risk one to win two; and you would be taking the wrong road if, being forced to gamble, you refuse to stake one life against three in a game in which, out of an infinite number of chances, one is for you, if the prize were an infinity of life which was infinitely happy. But in this game you can win eternal life which is eternally happy; you have one chance of winning against a finite number of chances of losing, and what you are staking is finite. That settles it: wherever there is infinity, and where there is not an infinity of chances of losing against the chance of winning, there is no room for hesitation: you must stake everything. And so, since you are forced to gamble, you must abandon reason in order to save your life, rather than risk it for the infinite gain which is just as likely to turn up as the loss of nothing."

For it is useless to say that it is doubtful whether we shall win, that it is certain that we are running a risk, and that the infinite distance which lies between the *certainty* of what we stake and the *uncertainty* of what we shall win, is equal to the finite good which we certainly stake against the uncertain infinite. It is not like that; every gambler risks something that is certain in the hope of winning something which is uncertain; and nevertheless he risks a finite certainty in order to win a finite uncertainty without committing a sin against reason. There is not an infinite distance between the certainty of the risk and the uncertainty of a win; that is untrue. There is, to be sure, an infinite distance between the certainty of winning and the certainty of losing. But the uncertainty of winning is proportionate to the certainty of what we risk, depending on the proportion between the chances of gain and loss.

Thus if there are as many chances on one side as on the other, the odds are equal; and then the certainty of the stake is equal to the uncertainty of the prize: it is far from being true that the distance between them is infinite. And so our argument is of overwhelming force, when the finite must be staked in a game in which the chances of gain and loss are equal, and the infinite is the prize. That can be demonstrated; and if men are capable of grasping any truth, that is one.

"I confess, I admit it. But is there still no means of seeing the reverse side of the cards?" "Yes, Scripture and the rest, etc."

"Yes, but my hands are tied and my lips sealed; I am forced to gamble and am not free; they will not let go of me. And I am made in such a way that I cannot believe. What do you expect me to do?"

"That's true. But at any rate, you must realise that since your reason inclines you to believe and yet you cannot believe, your inability to believe comes from your passions. Try then, not to convince yourself by multiplying the proofs of the existence of God, but by diminishing your passions. You want to find faith but you do not know the way; you want to cure yourself of unbelief, and you ask for the remedies: learn from the examples of those who like yourself were in bondage and who now stake their whole fortune: they are people who know the path that you would like to follow, and who have been cured of an ill of which you wish to be cured. Follow the method by which they began: it is by behaving as though they did believe, by taking holy water, by having masses said, etc. That will naturally make you inclined to believe and will calm you."

"But that's just what I'm afraid of." "But why? What have you got to lose?"

"But in order to prove to you that it works, it will diminish the passions which for you are the great stumbling-block."

End of the address. "Now, what harm will you come to if you adopt this course? You will be faithful, honest, humble, grateful, beneficent, a true friend, genuine. In truth, you will no longer find yourself submerged in poisonous pleasures, such as lust and desire for fame: but will you have no others? I tell you that you will gain in this life; and that with every step you take along this path, you will see such certainty of gain and so much of the worthlessness of what you risk, that you will have gambled on something that is certain, infinite and has cost you nothing."

"Oh, these words delight and ravish me, etc."

If the argument appeals to you and appears well founded, you must know that it was composed by a man who went down on his knees, before and after it, to pray to the infinite Indivisible Being to whom he submitted the whole of his being that God might grant the submission of the whole of your being for your own good and for his glory, and that in this way strength might be given to lowliness.

[...]

349. *Objection.* Those who hope for salvation are happy in that respect, but it is counterbalanced by the fear of hell.

Reply. Who has the greater reason to fear hell, the man who does not know whether there is a hell and who is certain of damnation if there is one; or the man who is to a certain extent convinced that there is a hell, and hopes to be saved if there is?

[...]

Fear, not the fear which comes from the fact that we believe in God, but the fear which comes from doubting whether he exists or not. The right kind of fear comes from faith: the wrong kind from doubt. The right kind linked to hope because it is born of faith, and because we hope in the God in whom we believe: wrong kind linked to despair because we fear the God in whom we do not believe. Some fear to lose him,—others fear to find him.

Study Questions

1. Do you think Pascal is correct in assigning "nothing" as the outcome of the wager if God doesn't exist?
2. What do you think Pascal means by wagering on the existence of God?
3. How do you see the fact of religious pluralism affecting Pascal's argument that it is in our best pragmatic interest to believe in God?

The Argument from Evil   1.5

PETER VAN INWAGEN

PETER VAN INWAGEN (1942–) is the John Cardinal O'Hara Professor of Philosophy at the University of Notre Dame. He is perhaps best known for his work on free will, and in particular his arguments that the existence of free will is incompatible with the truth of determinism, though he has also published extensively in numerous areas of metaphysics and the philosophy of religion. Here, van Inwagen brings together his work on free will and the problem of evil. He begins by laying out the logical problem of evil, which aims to show that there is a logical contradiction between the existence of evil and the existence of God. He then develops a defense: a story that, if true, would show God's reason for allowing evil. He argues that this story is "true for all we know."

Peter van Inwagen, "The Argument from Evil." *The Problem of Evil: The Gifford Lectures Delivered in the University of St. Andrews in 2003* (2008), pp. 209–21. By permission of Oxford University Press.

By the argument from evil, I understand the following argument (or any argument sufficiently similar to it that the two arguments stand or fall together): We find vast amounts of truly horrendous evil in the world; if there were a God, we should not find vast amounts of horrendous evil in the world; there is, therefore, no God. [. . .]

Having defended the moral propriety of critically examining the argument from evil, I will now do just that. The argument presupposes, and rightly, that two features God is supposed to have are "non-negotiable": that he is omnipotent and morally perfect. That he is omnipotent means that he can do anything that doesn't involve an intrinsic impossibility. Thus, God, if he exists, can change water to wine, since there is no intrinsic impossibility in the elementary particles that constitute the water in a cup being rearranged so as to constitute wine. But even God can't draw a round square or cause it both to rain and not to rain at the same place at the same time or change the past because these things are intrinsically impossible. To say that God is morally perfect is to say that he never does anything morally wrong—that he could not possibly do anything morally wrong. If God exists, therefore, and if you think he's done something morally wrong, you must be mistaken: either he didn't do the thing you think he did, or the thing he did that you think is morally wrong isn't. Omnipotence and moral perfection are, as I said, non-negotiable components of the idea of God. If the universe was made by an intelligent being, and if that being is less than omnipotent (and if there's no other being who is omnipotent), then the atheists are right: God does not exist. If the universe was made by an omnipotent being, and if that being has done even one thing that was morally wrong (and if there isn't another omnipotent being, one who never does anything morally wrong), then the atheists are right: God does not exist. If the Creator of the universe lacked either omnipotence or moral perfection, and if he claimed to be God, he would be either an impostor (if he claimed to be omnipotent and

morally perfect) or confused (if he conceded that he lacked either omnipotence or moral perfection and claimed to be God anyway).

To these two "non-negotiable" features of the concept of God, we must add one other that doesn't call for much comment: God, if he exists, must know a great deal about the world he has created. Now it is usually said that God is *omniscient*—that he knows *everything*. But the argument from evil doesn't require this strong assumption about God's knowledge—it requires only that God know enough to be aware of a significant amount of the evil that exists in the world. If God knew even the little that you and I know about the amount and extent of evil, that would be sufficient for the argument.

Now consider those evils God knows about. Since he's morally perfect, he must desire that these evils not exist—their non-existence must be what he *wants*. And an omnipotent being can achieve or bring about whatever he wants. So if there were an omnipotent, morally perfect being who knew about these evils—well, they wouldn't have arisen in the first place, for he'd have prevented their occurrence. Or if, for some reason, he didn't do that, he'd certainly remove them the instant they began to exist. But we observe evils, and very long-lasting ones. So we must conclude that God does not exist.

How much force has this argument? Suppose I believe in God and grant that the world contains vast amounts of truly horrible evil. What might I say in reply? I should, and do, think that the place to begin is with an examination of the word "want." Granted, in some sense of the word, the non-existence of evil must be what a morally perfect being *wants*. But we often don't bring about states of affairs we can bring about and want. Suppose, for example, that Alice's mother is dying in great pain and that Alice yearns desperately for her mother to die—today, and not next week or next month. And suppose it would be easy for Alice to arrange this—she is perhaps a doctor or a nurse and has easy access to pharmaceutical resources that would enable her to achieve this end. Does it follow that she will act on this ability that she has? It is obvious that it does not, for Alice might have *reasons* for not doing what she can do. Two obvious candidates for such reasons are: she thinks it would be morally wrong; she is afraid that her act would be discovered and that she would be prosecuted for murder. And either of these reasons might be sufficient, in her mind, to outweigh her desire for an immediate end to her mother's sufferings. So it may be that someone has a very strong desire for something and is able to obtain this thing, but does not act on this desire—because he has reasons for not doing so that seem to him to outweigh the desirability of the thing. The conclusion that evil does not exist does not, therefore, follow *logically* from the premises that the non-existence of evil is what God wants and that he is able to bring about the object of his desire—since, for all logic can tell us, God might have reasons for allowing evil to exist that, in his mind, outweigh the desirability of the non-existence of evil. But are such reasons even imaginable? What might they be?

Suppose I believe I know what God's reasons for allowing evil to exist are, and that I tell them to you. Then I have presented you with what is called a *theodicy*. This word comes from two Greek words that mean "God" and "justice." Thus, Milton, in *Paradise Lost*, tells us that the purpose of the poem is to "justify the ways of God to men"—"justify" meaning "exhibit as just." If I could present a theodicy, and if those to whom I presented it found it convincing, I'd have a reply to the argument from evil. But suppose that, although I believe in God, I *don't* claim to know what God's reasons for allowing evil are. Is there any way for someone in my position to reply to the argument from evil? There is. Consider this analogy.

Suppose your friend Clarissa, a single mother, left her two very young children alone in her flat for over an hour very late last night. Your Aunt Harriet, a maiden lady of strong moral principles, learns of this and declares that Clarissa is unfit to raise children. You spring to your friend's defense: "Now, Aunt Harriet, don't go jumping to conclusions. There's probably a perfectly good explanation. Maybe Billy or Annie took ill, and she decided to go over to St. Luke's for help. You know she hasn't got a phone or a car and no one in that neighborhood of hers would come to the door at two o'clock in the morning." If you tell your Aunt Harriet a story like this, you don't claim to know what Clarissa's reasons for leaving her children alone really were. And you're not claiming to have said anything that shows that Clarissa really is a good mother. You're claiming only to show that the fact Aunt Harriet has adduced doesn't prove that she isn't one; what you're trying to establish is that for all you and Aunt Harriet know, she had some good reason for what she did. And you're not trying to establish only that there is some remote possibility that she had a good reason. [. . .] What you're trying to convince Aunt Harriet of is that there is, as we say, *a very real possibility* that Clarissa had a good reason for leaving her children alone; and your attempt to convince her of this consists in your presenting her with an example of what such a reason *might* be.

Critical responses to the argument from evil—at least responses by philosophers—usually take just this form. A philosopher who responds to the argument from evil typically does so by telling a story, a story in which God allows evil to exist. This story will, of course, represent God as having reasons for allowing the existence of evil, reasons that, if the rest of the story were true, would be good ones. Such a story philosophers call a *defense*. A defense and a theodicy will not necessarily differ in content. A defense may, indeed, be verbally identical with a theodicy. The difference between a theodicy and a defense is simply that a theodicy is put forward as true, while nothing more is claimed for a defense than that it represents a real possibility—or a real possibility given that God exists. If I offer a story about God and evil as a defense, I hope for the following reaction from my audience: "Given that God exists, the rest of the story might well be true. I can't see any reason to rule it out."

A defense cannot simply take the form of a story about how God brings some great good out of the evils of the world, a good that outweighs those evils. At the very least, a defense will have to include the proposition that God was *unable* to bring about the greater good without allowing the evils we observe (or some other evils as bad or worse). And to find a story that can plausibly be said to have this feature is no trivial undertaking. The reason for this lies in God's omnipotence. A human being can often be excused for allowing, or even causing, a certain evil if that evil was a necessary means, or an unavoidable consequence thereof, to some good that outweighed it—or if it was a necessary means to the prevention of some greater evil. The eighteenth-century surgeon who operated without anesthetic caused unimaginable pain to his patients, but we do not condemn him because (at least if he knew what he was doing) the pain was an unavoidable consequence of the means necessary to some good that outweighed it—such as saving the patient's life. But we should not excuse a present-day surgeon who had anesthetics available and who nevertheless operated without using them—not even if his operation saved the patient's life and thus resulted in a good that outweighed the horrible pain the patient suffered. [. . .]

The general point this example is intended to illustrate is simply that the resources of an omnipotent being are unlimited—or are limited only by what is intrinsically possible—and that a defense must take account of these unlimited resources.

There seems to me to be only one defense that has any hope of succeeding, and that is the so-called free-will defense. In its simplest, most abstract, form, the free-will defense goes as follows:

> God made the world and it was very good. An indispensable part of the goodness he chose was the existence of rational beings: self-aware beings capable of abstract thought and love and having the power of free choice between contemplated alternative courses of action. This last feature of rational beings, free choice or free will, is a good. But even an omnipotent being is unable to control the exercise of the power of free choice, for a choice that was controlled would *ipso facto* not be free. In other words, if I have a free choice between x and y, even God cannot ensure that I choose x. To ask God to give me a free choice between x and y and to see to it that I choose x instead of y is to ask God to bring about the intrinsically impossible; it is like asking him to create a round square, a material body that has no shape, or an invisible object that casts a shadow. Having this power of free choice, some or all human beings misuse it and produce a certain amount of evil. But free will is a sufficiently great good that its existence outweighs the evils that result from its abuse; and God foresaw this.

The free-will defense immediately suggests several objections. The two most pressing of them are these:

> How could anyone possibly believe that the evils of this world are outweighed by the good inherent in our having free will? Perhaps free will is a good and would outweigh a certain amount of evil, but it seems impossible to believe that it can outweigh the amount of physical suffering (to say nothing of other sorts of evil) that actually exists.

> Not all evils are the result of human free will. Consider, for example, the Lisbon earthquake or the almost inconceivable loss of life produced by the hurricane that ravaged Honduras in 1997. Such events are not the result of any act of human will, free or unfree.

In my view, the simple form of the free-will defense I have presented is unable to deal with either of these objections. The simple form of the free-will defense can deal with at best the existence of *some* evil—as opposed to the vast amount of evil we actually observe—and the evil with which it can deal is only that evil that is caused by the acts of human beings. I believe, however, that more sophisticated forms of the free-will defense do have interesting things to say about the vast amount of evil in the world and about those evils that are not caused by human beings. Before I discuss these "more sophisticated" forms of the free-will defense, however, I want to examine an objection that has been raised against the free-will defense that is so fundamental that, if valid, it would refute any elaboration of the defense, however sophisticated. This objection has to do with the nature of free will. There is a school of thought—Hobbes, Hume, and Mill are its most illustrious representatives—whose adherents maintain that free will and determinism are perfectly compatible: that there could be a world in which the past determined a unique future and the inhabitants of which were nonetheless free beings. Now if this school of philosophers is right, the free-will defense fails, for if free will and determinism are compatible, then an omnipotent being can, contrary to the central premise of the free-will defense, create a person who has a free choice between x and y and ensure that that person choose x rather than y. [...]

But how plausible is this account of free will? Not very, I think. It certainly yields some odd conclusions. Consider the lower social orders in Aldous Huxley's *Brave New World*, the "deltas" and "epsilons." These unfortunate people have their deepest desires chosen for them by others—by the "alphas" who make up the highest social stratum. What the deltas and epsilons primarily desire is to do what the alphas (and the "beta" and "gamma" overseers who are appointed to supervise their labors) tell them. This is their primary desire because it is imposed on them by prenatal and postnatal conditioning. (If Huxley were writing today, he might have added genetic engineering to the alphas' list of resources for determining the desires of their slaves.) It would be hard to think of beings who better fitted the description "lacks free will" than the deltas and epsilons of *Brave New World*. And yet, if the account of free will that we are considering is

right, the deltas and epsilons are exemplars of beings with free will. Each of them is always doing exactly what he wants, after all, and who among us is in that fortunate position? What he wants is to do as he is told by those appointed over him, of course, but the account of free will we are examining says nothing about the *content* of one's desires: it requires only that there be no barrier to acting on them. [...]

Despite the fact that (I freely confess) I do not have a philosophically satisfactory account of free will, I can see that this person hasn't got it. Therefore, I contend, the atheist's attempt to show that the story that constitutes the free-will defense is false rests on a false theory about the nature of free will. Now my argument for the falsity of this theory is, I concede, inconclusive. [...] But let us remember the dialectical situation in which this inconclusive argument occurs. That is, let us remember who is trying to prove what. The atheist has opened the discussion by trying to prove the non-existence of God; the alleged proof of this conclusion is the argument from evil. The theist responds by producing the free-will defense and contends that this defense shows that evil does not prove the non-existence of God. The atheist's re-joinder is that the story called the free-will defense is false and that its falsity can be demonstrated by reflection on the nature of free will. The theist replies that the atheist has got the nature of free will wrong, and he offers a philosophical argument for this conclusion (the "Brave New World" argument), an argument that perhaps falls short of being a proof but has nevertheless seemed fairly plausible to many intelligent people. When we add up all the pluses and minuses of this exchange, it seems that the free-will defense triumphs in its limited sphere of application. When we think about it, we see that, for all the atheist has said, the story called the free-will defense *may well be true*—at least given that there is a God. One cannot show that a story involving creatures with free will is false or probably false by pointing out that the story would be false if a certain theory about free will were true. To show that, one would also have to show that the theory of free will that one has put forward was true or probably true. And the atheist hasn't shown that his theory of free will, the "no barriers" theory, is true or probably true, for the objections to the atheist's theory of free will that I have set out show that this theory faces very serious problems indeed.

The atheist's most promising course of action, I think, is to admit that the free-will defense shows that there might, for all anyone can say, be a certain amount of evil, a certain amount of pain and suffering, in a world created by an all-powerful and morally perfect being, and to stress the amounts and the kinds of evil that we find in the world as it is. The world as it is, I have said, contains vast amounts of truly horrendous evil (that's the point about amounts), and some of the kinds of evil to be found in the world as it is are not caused by human beings—wholly unforeseeable natural disasters, for example (that's the point about kinds). Can any elaboration of our simple version of the free-will defense take account of these two points in any very plausible way?

Let me suggest some elaborations toward this end. The reader must decide whether they are plausible. The free-will defense as I've stated it suggests—though it does not entail—that God created human beings with free will, and then just left them to their own devices. It suggests that the evils of the world are the more or less unrelated consequences of uncounted millions of largely unrelated abuses of free will by human beings. Let me propose a sort of plot to be added to the bare and abstract free-will defense I stated above. Consider the story of creation and rebellion and the expulsion from paradise that is told in the first three chapters of Genesis. Could this story be true—I mean literally true, true in every detail? Well, no. It contradicts what science has discovered about human evolution and the history of the physical universe. And that is hardly surprising, for it long antedates these discoveries. The story is a re-working—with much original material—by Hebrew authors (or, as I believe,

a Hebrew author) of elements found in many ancient Middle Eastern mythologies. Like the *Aeneid*, it is a literary refashioning of materials originally supplied by legend and myth, and it retains a strong mythological flavor. It is possible, nevertheless, that the first three chapters of Genesis are a mythico-literary representation of actual events of human pre-history. The following is consistent with what we know of human pre-history. Our current knowledge of human evolution, in fact, presents us with no particular reason to believe that this story is false. [...]

For millions of years, perhaps for thousands of millions of years, God guided the course of evolution so as eventually to produce certain very clever primates, the immediate predecessors of *Homo sapiens*. At some time in the last few hundred thousand years, the whole population of our pre-human ancestors formed a small breeding community—a few hundred or even a few score. That is to say, there was a time when every ancestor of modern human beings who was then alive was a member of this tiny, geographically tightly knit group of primates. In the fullness of time, God took the members of this breeding group and miraculously raised them to rationality. That is, he gave them the gifts of language, abstract thought, and disinterested love—and, of course, the gift of free will. He gave them the gift of free will because free will is necessary for love. Love, and not only erotic love, implies free will. [...]

God not only raised these primates to rationality—not only made of them what we call human beings—but also took them into a kind of mystical union with himself, the sort of union that Christians hope for in heaven and call the Beatific Vision. Being in union with God, these new human beings, these primates who had become human beings at a certain point in their lives, lived together in the harmony of perfect love and also possessed what theologians used to call preternatural powers—something like what people who believe in them today call paranormal abilities. Because they lived in the harmony of perfect love, none of them did any harm to the others. Because of their preternatural powers, they were able somehow to protect themselves from wild beasts (which they were able to tame with a word), from disease (which they were able to cure with a touch) and from random, destructive natural events (like earthquakes), which they knew about in advance and were able to avoid. There was thus no evil in their world. And it was God's intention that they should never become decrepit with age or die, as their primate forbears had. But, somehow, in some way that must be mysterious to us, they were not content with this paradisal state. They abused the gift of free will and separated themselves from their union with God.

The result was horrific: not only did they no longer enjoy the Beatific Vision, but they now faced destruction by the random forces of nature, and were subject to old age and natural death. Nevertheless, they were too proud to end their rebellion. As the generations passed, they drifted further and further from God—into the worship of false gods (a worship that sometimes involved human sacrifice), inter-tribal warfare (complete with the gleeful torture of prisoners of war), private murder, slavery, and rape. On one level, they realized, or some of them realized, that something was horribly wrong, but they were unable to do anything about it. After they had separated themselves from God, they were, as an engineer might say, "not operating under design conditions." [. . .]

When human beings had become like this, God looked out over a ruined world. It would have been just for him to leave human beings in the ruin they had made of themselves and their world. But God is more than a God of justice. He is, indeed, more than a God of mercy—a God who was merely merciful might simply have brought the story of humanity to an end at that point, like someone who shoots a horse with a broken leg. But God is more than a God of mercy: he is a God of love. He therefore neither left humanity to its own devices nor mercifully destroyed

it. Rather, he set in motion a rescue operation. He put into operation a plan designed to restore separated humanity to union with himself. This defense will not specify the nature of this plan of atonement. The three Abrahamic religions, Judaism, Christianity, and Islam, tell three different stories about the nature of this plan, and I do not propose to favor one of them over another in telling a story that, after all, I do not maintain is true. This much must be said, however: the plan has the following feature, and any plan with the object of restoring separated humanity to union with God would have to have this feature: its object is to bring it about that human beings once more love God. And, since love essentially involves free will, love is not something that can be imposed from the outside, by an act of sheer power. Human beings must choose freely to be reunited with God and to love him, and this is something they are unable to do of their own efforts. They must therefore cooperate with God. As is the case with many rescue operations, the rescuer and those whom he is rescuing must cooperate. For human beings to cooperate with God in this rescue operation, they must know that they need to be rescued. They must know what it means to be separated from him. And what it means to be separated from God is to live in a world of horrors. If God simply "canceled" all the horrors of this world by an endless series of miracles, he would thereby frustrate his own plan of reconciliation. If he did that, we should be content with our lot and should see no reason to cooperate with him. Here is an analogy. Suppose Dorothy suffers from angina, and that what she needs to do is to stop smoking and lose weight. Suppose her doctor knows of a drug that will stop the pain but will do nothing to cure the condition. Should the doctor prescribe the drug for her, in the full knowledge that if the pain is alleviated, there is no chance that she will stop smoking and lose weight? Well, perhaps the answer is yes. The doctor is Dorothy's fellow adult and fellow citizen, after all. Perhaps it would be insufferably paternalistic to refuse to alleviate Dorothy's pain in order to provide her with a motivation to do what is to her own advantage. If one were of an especially libertarian cast of mind, one might even say that someone who did that was "playing God." It is far from clear, however, whether there is anything wrong with *God's* behaving as if he were God. It is at least very plausible to suppose that it is morally permissible for God to allow human beings to suffer if the result of suppressing the suffering would be to deprive them of a very great good, one that far outweighed the suffering. But God does shield us from *much* evil, from a great proportion of the sufferings that would be a natural consequence of our rebellion. If he did not, all human history would be at least this bad: every human society would be on the moral level of Nazi Germany. But, however much evil God shields us from, he must leave in place a vast amount of evil if he is not to deceive us about what separation from him means. The amount he has left us with is so vast and so horrible that we cannot really comprehend it, especially if we are middle-class Americans or Europeans. Nevertheless, it could have been much worse. The inhabitants of a world in which human beings had separated ourselves from God and he had then simply left them to their own devices would regard our world as a comparative paradise. All this evil, however, will come to an end. At some point, for all eternity, there will be no more unmerited suffering. Every evil done by the wicked to the innocent will have been avenged, and every tear will have been wiped away. If there is still suffering, it will be merited: the suffering of those who refuse to cooperate with God's great rescue operation and are allowed by him to exist forever in a state of elected ruin—those who, in a word, are in hell.

One aspect of this story needs to be brought out more clearly than I have. If the story is true, much of the evil in the world is due to chance. There is generally no explanation of why *this* evil happened to *that* person. What there is is an explanation of why evils happen to people without any reason. And the explanation is: that is part of what being separated from God means: it means being the playthings of chance. It means living in a world in which innocent children die horribly, and it means something worse than that: it means living in a world in which innocent children die horribly *for no reason at all*. It means living in a world in which the wicked, through sheer luck, often prosper. [. . .]

Here, then, is a defense. Do I believe it? Well, I believe parts of it and I don't disbelieve any of it. [. . .] I am not at all sure about "preternatural powers," for example, or about the proposition that God shields us from much evil and that the world would be far worse if he did not. The story I have told is, I remind you, only supposed to be a defense. It is not put forward as a theodicy, as a statement of the real truth of the matter, as I see it, about the co-presence of God and evil in the world. I contend only that this story is—given that God exists—true for all we know.[. . .]

Suppose, then, for the sake of argument, that the defense I have presented is a true story. Does it justify the evils of the world? Or put the question this way. Suppose there were an omnipotent and omniscient being and that this being acted just as God has acted in the story I have told. Could any moral case be made against the actions of this being? Is there any barrier to saying that this being is not only omnipotent and omniscient but morally perfect as well? In my view, it is not self-evident that there is no barrier to saying this—but it is not self-evident that there is a barrier, either. The defense I have presented, the story I have told, should be thought of as the beginning of a conversation. If there is anyone who maintains that the story I have told, even if it is true, does not absolve a being who acts as I have supposed God to act from serious moral criticism, let that person explain why he or she thinks this is so. Then I, or some other defender of theism, can attempt to meet this objection, and the objector can reply to the rejoinder and . . . but so philosophy goes: philosophy is argument without end. As J. L. Austin said—also speaking on the topic of excuses—here I leave and commend the subject to you.

1. What are the three nonnegotiable features of the concept of God van Inwagen discusses, and why does he think that each is nonnegotiable?

2. What are the two most pressing objections to the free will defense that van Inwagen addresses?

3. How successful do you think van Inwagen's response to the existence of evil is?

The Future of an Illusion   1.6

SIGMUND FREUD

SIGMUND FREUD (1856–1939) was an Austrian psychologist and neurologist and is often considered the father of psychoanalysis. His well-known books include *The Interpretation of Dreams, Introduction to Psychoanalysis,* and *Civilization and Its Discontents.* His book *The Future of an Illusion,* part of which is reprinted here, is Freud's account of the origin, development, and future of religious belief. Religion, according to Freud, is rooted in the conflict between the individual and society. Human's natural impulses—including the "instinctual wishes...of incest, cannibalism, and lust for killing"—undermine the ability of a society to function well. Religious belief functions as a way of controlling individuals and fostering social stability by helping them deal with their feelings of helplessness, suffering, and death. More specifically, belief in the existence of God has as its prototype the childhood need for protection, which is provided by one's father. Belief in God allays human fear about the dangers of life, helps establish justice through fear of divine punishment, and provides a larger framework for the human disposition to engage in wish fulfillment.

In what does the peculiar value of religious ideas lie?

We have spoken of the hostility to civilization which is produced by the pressure that civilization exercises, the renunciations of instinct which it demands. If one imagines its prohibitions lifted—if, then, one may take any woman one pleases as a sexual object, if one may without hesitation kill one's rival for her love or anyone else who stands in one's way, if, too, one can carry off any of the other man's belongings without asking leave—how splendid, what a string of satisfactions one's life would be! True, one soon comes across the first difficulty: everyone else has exactly the same wishes as I have and will treat me with no more consideration than I treat him. And so in reality only one person could be made unrestrictedly happy by such a removal of the restrictions of civilization, and he would be a tyrant, a dictator, who had seized all the means

Sigmund Freud, *Future of an Illusion* (Pacific Publishing Studio, 2010).

to power. And even he would have every reason to wish that the others would observe at least one cultural commandment: "thou shalt not kill."

But how ungrateful, how short-sighted after all, to strive for the abolition of civilization! What would then remain would be a state of nature, and that would be far harder to bear. It is true that nature would not demand any restrictions of instinct from us, she would let us do as we liked; but she has her own particularly effective method of restricting us. She destroys us—coldly, cruelly, relentlessly, as it seems to us, and possibly through the very things that occasioned our satisfaction. It was precisely because of these dangers with which nature threatens us that we came together and created civilization, which is also, among other things, intended to make our communal life possible. For the principal task of civilization, its actual *raison d'être*, is to defend us against nature.

We all know that in many ways civilization does this fairly well already, and clearly as time goes on it will do it much better. But no one is under the illusion that nature has already been vanquished; and few dare hope that she will ever be entirely subjected to man. There are the elements, which seem to mock at all human control: the earth, which quakes and is torn apart and buries all human life and its works; water, which deluges and drowns everything in a turmoil; storms, which blow everything before them; there are diseases, which we have only recently recognized as attacks by other organisms; and finally there is the painful riddle of death, against which no medicine has yet been found, nor probably will be. With these forces nature rises up against us, majestic, cruel and inexorable; she brings to our mind once more our weakness and helplessness, which we thought to escape through the work of civilization. One of the few gratifying and exalting impressions which mankind can offer is when, in the face of an elemental catastrophe, it forgets the discordancies of its civilization and all its internal difficulties and animosities, and recalls the great common task of preserving itself against the superior power of nature.

For the individual, too, life is hard to bear, just as it is for mankind in general. The civilization in which he participates imposes some amount of privation on him, and other men bring him a measure of suffering, either in spite of the precepts of his civilization or because of its imperfections. To this are added the injuries which untamed nature—he calls it Fate—inflicts on him. One might suppose that this condition of things would result in a permanent state of anxious expectation in him and a severe injury to his natural narcissism. We know already how the individual reacts to the injuries which civilization and other men inflict on him: he develops a corresponding degree of resistance to the regulations of civilization and of hostility to it. But how does he defend himself against the superior powers of nature, of Fate, which threaten him as they threaten all the rest?

Civilization relieves him of this task; it performs it in the same way for all alike; and it is noteworthy that in this almost all civilizations act alike. Civilization does not call a halt in the task of defending man against nature, it merely pursues it by other means. The task is a manifold one. Man's self-regard, seriously menaced, calls for consolation; life and the universe must be robbed of their terrors; moreover his curiosity, moved, it is true, by the strongest practical interest, demands an answer.

A great deal is already gained with the first step: the humanization of nature. Impersonal forces and destinies cannot be approached; they remain eternally remote. But if the elements have passions that rage as they do in our own souls, if death itself is not something spontaneous but the violent act of an evil Will, if everywhere in nature there are Beings around us of a kind that we know in our own society, then we can breathe freely, can feel at home in the uncanny and can deal by psychical means with our senseless anxiety. We are still defenceless, perhaps, but we are no longer helplessly paralysed; we can at least react. Perhaps, indeed, we are not even defenceless. We can apply the same methods against these violent supermen outside that we employ in our own society; we can try to adjure them, to appease them, to bribe them, and, by so influencing them, we may rob them of a part of their power. A replacement like this of natural science by psychology not only provides immediate relief, but also points the way to a further mastering of the situation.

For this situation is nothing new. It has an infantile prototype, of which it is in fact only the continuation. For once before one has found oneself in a similar state of helplessness: as a small child, in relation to one's parents. One had reason to fear them, and especially one's father; and yet one was sure of his protection against the dangers one knew. Thus it was natural to assimilate the two situations. Here, too, wishing played its part, as it does in dream-life. The sleeper may be seized with a presentiment of death, which threatens to place him in the grave. But the dream-work knows how to select a condition that will turn even that dreaded event into a wish-fulfilment: the dreamer sees himself in an ancient Etruscan grave which he has climbed down into, happy to find his archaeological interests satisfied. In the same way, a man makes the forces of nature not simply into persons with whom he can associate as he would with his equals—that would not do justice to the overpowering impression which those forces make on him—but he gives them the character of a father. He turns them into gods, following in this, as I have tried to show, not only an infantile prototype but a phylogenetic one.

In the course of time the first observations were made of regularity and conformity to law in natural phenomena, and with this the forces of nature lost their human traits. But man's helplessness remains and along with it his longing for his father, and the gods. The gods retain their threefold task: they must exorcize the terrors of nature, they must reconcile men to the cruelty of Fate, particularly as it is shown in death, and

they must compensate them for the sufferings and privations which a civilized life in common has imposed on them.

But within these functions there is a gradual displacement of accent. It was observed that the phenomena of nature developed automatically according to internal necessities. Without doubt the gods were the lords of nature; they had arranged it to be as it was and now they could leave it to itself. Only occasionally, in what are known as miracles, did they intervene in its course, as though to make it plain that they had relinquished nothing of their original sphere of power. As regards the apportioning of destinies, an unpleasant suspicion persisted that the perplexity and helplessness of the human race could not be remedied. It was here that the gods were most apt to fail. If they themselves created Fate, then their counsels must be deemed inscrutable. The notion dawned on the most gifted people of antiquity that Moira [Fate] stood above the gods and that the gods themselves had their own destinies. And the more autonomous nature became and the more the gods withdrew from it, the more earnestly were all expectations directed to the third function of the gods—the more did morality become their true domain. It now became the task of the gods to even out the defects and evils of civilization, to attend to the sufferings which men inflict on one another in their life together and to watch over the fulfilment of the precepts of civilization, which men obey so imperfectly. Those precepts themselves were credited with a divine origin; they were elevated beyond human society and were extended to nature and the universe.

And thus a store of ideas is created, born from man's need to make his helplessness tolerable and built up from the material of memories of the helplessness of his own childhood and the childhood of the human race. It can clearly be seen that the possession of these ideas protects him in two directions—against the dangers of nature and Fate, and against the injuries that threaten him from human society itself. Here is the gist of the matter. Life in this world serves a higher purpose; no doubt it is not easy to guess what that purpose is, but it certainly signifies a perfecting of man's nature. It is probably the spiritual part of man, the soul, which in the course of time has so slowly and unwillingly detached itself from the body, that is the object of this elevation and exaltation. Everything that happens in this world is an expression of the intentions of an intelligence superior to us, which in the end, though its ways and byways are difficult to follow, orders everything for the best—that is, to make it enjoyable for us. Over each one of us there watches a benevolent Providence which is only seemingly stern and which will not suffer us to become a plaything of the overmighty and pitiless forces of nature. Death itself is not extinction, is not a return to inorganic lifelessness, but the beginning of a new kind of existence which lies on the path of development to something higher. And, looking in the other direction, this view announces that the same moral laws which our civilizations have set up govern the whole universe as well, except that they are maintained by a supreme court of justice with incomparably more power and consistency. In the end all good is rewarded and all evil punished, if not actually in this form of life then in the later existences that begin after death. In this way all the terrors, the sufferings and the hardships of life are destined to be obliterated. Life after death, which continues life on earth just as the invisible part of the spectrum joins on to the visible part, brings us all the perfection that we may perhaps have missed here. And the superior wisdom which directs this course of things, the infinite goodness that expresses itself in it, the justice that achieves its aim in it—these are the attributes of the divine beings who also created us and the world as a whole, or rather, of the one divine being into which, in our civilization, all the gods of antiquity have been condensed. The people which first succeeded in thus concentrating the divine attributes was not a little proud of the advance. It had laid open to view the father who

had all along been hidden behind every divine figure as its nucleus. Fundamentally this was a return to the historical beginnings of the idea of God. Now that God was a single person, man's relations to him could recover the intimacy and intensity of the child's relation to his father. But if one had done so much for one's father, one wanted to have a reward, or at least to be his only beloved child, his Chosen People. [. . .]

I think we have prepared the way sufficiently for an answer to both these questions. It will be found if we turn our attention to the psychical origin of religious ideas. These, which are given out as teachings, are not precipitates of experience or end-results of thinking: they are illusions, fulfilments of the oldest, strongest and most urgent wishes of mankind. The secret of their strength lies in the strength of those wishes. As we already know, the terrifying impression of helplessness in childhood aroused the need for protection—for protection through love—which was provided by the father; and the recognition that this helplessness lasts throughout life made it necessary to cling to the existence of a father, but this time a more powerful one. Thus the benevolent rule of a divine Providence allays our fear of the dangers of life; the establishment of a moral world-order ensures the fulfilment of the demands of justice, which have so often remained unfulfilled in human civilization; and the prolongation of earthly existence in a future life provides the local and temporal framework in which these wish-fulfilments shall take place. Answers to the riddles that tempt the curiosity of man, such as how the universe began or what the relation is between body and mind, are developed in conformity with the underlying assumptions of this system. It is an enormous relief to the individual psyche if the conflicts of its childhood arising from the father-complex—conflicts which it has never wholly overcome—are removed from it and brought to a solution which is universally accepted.

When I say that these things are all illusions, I must define the meaning of the word. An illusion is not the same thing as an error; nor is it necessarily an error. Aristotle's belief that vermin are developed out of dung (a belief to which ignorant people still cling) was an error; so was the belief of a former generation of doctors that *tabes dorsalis* is the result of sexual excess. It would be incorrect to call these errors illusions. On the other hand, it was an illusion of Columbus's that he had discovered a new sea-route to the Indies. The part played by his wish in this error is very clear. One may describe as an illusion the assertion made by certain nationalists that the Indo-Germanic race is the only one capable of civilization; or the belief, which was only destroyed by psychoanalysis, that children are creatures without sexuality. What is characteristic of illusions is that they are derived from human wishes. In this respect they come near to psychiatric delusions. But they differ from them, too, apart from the more complicated structure of delusions. In the case of delusions, we emphasize as essential their being in contradiction with reality. Illusions need not necessarily be false—that is to say, unrealizable or in contradiction to reality. For instance, a middle-class girl may have the illusion that a prince will come and marry her. This is possible; and a few such cases have occurred. That the Messiah will come and found a golden age is much less likely. Whether one classifies this belief as an illusion or as something analogous to a delusion will depend on one's personal attitude. Examples of illusions which have proved true are not easy to find, but the illusion of the alchemists that all metals can be turned into gold might be one of them. The wish to have a great deal of gold, as much gold as possible, has, it is true, been a good deal damped by our present-day knowledge of the determinants of wealth, but chemistry no longer regards the transmutation of metals into gold as impossible. Thus we call a belief an illusion when a wish-fulfilment is a prominent factor in its motivation, and in doing so we disregard its relations to reality, just as the illusion itself sets no store by verification.

Having thus taken our bearings, let us return once more to the question of religious doctrines. We can now repeat that all of them are illusions and insusceptible of proof. No one can be compelled to think them true, to believe in them. Some of them are so improbable, so incompatible with everything we have laboriously discovered about the reality of the world, that we may compare them—if we pay proper regard to the psychological differences—to delusions. Of the reality value of most of them we cannot judge; just as they cannot be proved, so they cannot be refuted. We still know too little to make a critical approach to them. The riddles of the universe reveal themselves only slowly to our investigation; there are many questions to which science to-day can give no answer. But scientific work is the only road which can lead us to a knowledge of reality outside ourselves. It is once again merely an illusion to expect anything from intuition and introspection; they can give us nothing but particulars about our own mental life, which are hard to interpret, never any information about the questions which religious doctrine finds it so easy to answer. It would be insolent to let one's own arbitrary will step into the breach and, according to one's personal estimate, declare this or that part of the religious system to be less or more acceptable. Such questions are too momentous for that; they might be called too sacred.

At this point one must expect to meet with an objection. "Well then, if even obdurate sceptics admit that the assertions of religion cannot be refuted by reason, why should I not believe in them, since they have so much on their side—tradition, the agreement of mankind, and all the consolations they offer?" Why not, indeed? Just as no one can be forced to believe, so no one can be forced to disbelieve. But do not let us be satisfied with deceiving ourselves that arguments like these take us along the road of correct thinking. If ever there was a case of a lame excuse we have it here. Ignorance is ignorance; no right to believe anything can be derived from it. In other matters no sensible person will behave so irresponsibly or rest content with such feeble grounds for his opinions and for the line he takes. It is only in the highest and most sacred things that he allows himself to do so. In reality these are only attempts at pretending to oneself or to other people that one is still firmly attached to religion, when one has long since cut oneself loose from it. Where questions of religion are concerned, people are guilty of every possible sort of dishonesty and intellectual misdemeanour. Philosophers stretch the meaning of words until they retain scarcely anything of their original sense. They give the name of "God" to some vague abstraction which they have created for themselves; having done so they can pose before all the world as deists, as believers in God, and they can even boast that they have recognized a higher, purer concept of God, notwithstanding that their God is now nothing more than an insubstantial shadow and no longer the mighty personality of religious doctrines. Critics persist in describing as "deeply religious" anyone who admits to a sense of man's insignificance or impotence in the face of the universe, although what constitutes the essence of the religious attitude is not this feeling but only the next step after it, the reaction to it which seeks a remedy for it. The man who goes no further, but humbly acquiesces in the small part which human beings play in the great world—such a man is, on the contrary, irreligious in the truest sense of the word.

To assess the truth-value of religious doctrines does not lie within the scope of the present enquiry. It is enough for us that we have recognized them as being, in their psychological nature, illusions. But we do not have to conceal the fact that this discovery also strongly influences our attitude to the question which must appear to many to be the most important of all. We know approximately at what periods and by what kind of men religious doctrines were created. If in addition we discover the motives which led to this, our attitude to the problem of religion will undergo a marked displacement. We shall tell ourselves that it would be very nice if there were a God who created the world and was a benevolent Providence, and if there were a moral order in the universe and an after-life; but it is a very striking fact that all this is exactly as we are bound to wish it to be. And it would be more remarkable still if our wretched, ignorant and downtrodden ancestors had succeeded in solving all these difficult riddles of the universe.

Study Questions

1. Why does Freud think that religious beliefs are insusceptible to proof?
2. To what degree do you think that Freud's account of religious belief as illusion is true?
3. How, if at all, does the origin of religious belief in illusion and wish fulfillment affect the truth of those beliefs?

Warranted Christian Belief   1.7

ALVIN PLANTINGA

ALVIN PLANTINGA (1932–) taught philosophy at Yale, Wayne State University, and Calvin College and was John A. O'Brien Professor of Philosophy at the University of Notre Dame. He has written extensively on epistemology, metaphysics, and philosophy of religion. He is perhaps best known for his work on reformed epistemology, which argues that belief in God can be properly basic—that is, that it can be epistemologically acceptable to believe in the existence of God even if that belief is not based on any other belief. More recently, Plantinga's epistemology has focused on warrant, which is the property that distinguishes knowledge from mere true belief. Recent *de jure* objections to religious belief have focused on their lacking warrant. In this reading, Plantinga examines Freud's and Marx's criticisms that religious beliefs are rationally unacceptable insofar as they originate in illusion or other cognitive dysfunction.

I. THE F&M COMPLAINT

[...] Atheologians (those who argue against Christian belief) have often claimed that Christian belief is *irrational*; so far, we have failed to find a sensible version of this claim. But perhaps we can make progress by exploring the animadversions on Christian belief proposed by Freud, Marx, and the whole cadre of their nineteenth- and twentieth-century followers.[1] We could also examine here Nietzsche's similar complaint: that religion originates in slave morality, in the *ressentiment* of the oppressed. As Nietzsche sees it, Christianity both fosters and arises from a sort of sniveling, cowardly, servile, evasive, duplicitous, and all-around contemptible sort of character, which is at the same time envious, self-righteous, and full of hate disguised as charitable kindness. (Not a pretty picture.) I've chosen not to consider Nietzsche for two reasons: first, he really has little to add to what Marx and Freud say; second, he is harder to take seriously. He writes with a fine coruscating brilliance, his outrageous rhetoric is sometimes entertaining, and no doubt

much of the extravagance is meant as overstatement to make a point. Taken overall, however, the violence and exaggeration seem pathological; for a candidate for the sober truth, we shall certainly have to look elsewhere.

Now Freud, Marx, and their many epigoni (and anticipators) *criticize* religious belief; they purport to find something *wrong* with it; they are "masters of suspicion" and (at any rate in their own view) *unmask* it. And in examining their critical comments on religious belief, I think we can finally locate a proper *de jure* question: one that is distinct from the *de facto* question, is such that the answer is nontrivial, and is relevant in the sense that a negative answer to it would be a serious point against Christian belief. The first order of business, therefore, is to try to get clear as to what the Freud-Marx critical project ("the F&M complaint," as I shall call it) really *is*.

A. Freud

There are several sides to Freud's critique of religion. For example, he was fascinated by what he saw as the Darwinian picture of early human beings coming together in packs or herds (like wolves or elk), all the females belonging to one powerful, dominant, jealous male, and he tells a dramatic story about how religion arose out of an extraordinary interaction among the members of that primal horde:

> The father of the primal horde, since he was an unlimited despot, had seized all the women for himself; his sons, being dangerous to him as rivals, had been killed or driven away. One day, however, the sons came together and united to overwhelm, kill, and devour their father, who had been their enemy but also their ideal. After the deed they were unable to take over their heritage since they stood in one another's way. Under the influence of failure and remorse they learned to come to an agreement among themselves; they banded themselves into a clan of brothers by the help of the ordinances of totemism, which aimed at preventing a repetition of such a deed, and they jointly undertook to forgo the possession of the women on whose account they had killed their father. They were then driven to finding strange women, and this was the origin of the exogamy which is so closely bound up with totemism. The Totem meal was the festival commemorating the fearful deed from which sprang man's sense of guilt (or "original sin")....
>
> ...This view of religion throws a particularly clear light upon the psychological basis of Christianity, in which, as we know, the ceremony of the totem meal still survives, with but little distortion, in the form of Communion.[2]

Strong stuff, this, displaying Freud's redoubtable imaginative powers and his ability to tell a sensational story; all the elements—sex, murder, cannibalism, remorse—of a dandy Hollywood spectacular are here. Taken as a serious attempt at a historical account of the origin of religion, though, it has little to recommend it and is at best a wild guess, much less science than science fiction. But perhaps Freud didn't intend it as sober and literal truth. (He himself calls it a "vision.") Perhaps it is something like a parable, maybe something like how some Christians understand early *Genesis* or *Job*, meant to

illustrate and present a truth in graphic but nonliteral form. (Maybe here as elsewhere Freud is under the spell of biblical ways of writing and thinking.) And just as it isn't always easy to draw the right moral from a biblical parable, so it isn't easy to see what Freud intends us to gather from this gripping if grisly little tale.

In any event, Freud offers quite a different account of the psychological origins of religious (theistic) belief:

> These [religious beliefs], which are given out as teachings, are not precipitates of experience or end-results of thinking: they are illusions, fulfillments of the oldest, strongest and most urgent wishes of mankind. The secret of their strength lies in the strength of those wishes. As we already know, the terrifying impressions of helplessness in childhood aroused the need for protection—for protection through love—which was provided by the father; and the recognition that this helplessness lasts throughout life made it necessary to cling to the existence of a father, but this time a more powerful one. Thus the benevolent rule of a divine Providence allays our fear of the dangers of life; the establishment of a moral world-order ensures the fulfillment of the demands of justice, which have so often remained unfulfilled in human civilization; and the prolongation of earthly existence in a future life provides the local and temporal framework in which these wish-fulfillments shall take place.[3]

As we see, there is more to Freud's critique than phantasmagoric fables about the primal horde. The idea is that theistic belief arises from a psychological mechanism Freud calls "wish-fulfillment"; the wish in this case is father, not to the deed, but to the belief. Nature rises up against us, cold, pitiless, implacable, blind to our needs and desires. She delivers hurt, fear, and pain; in the end, she demands our death. Paralyzed and appalled, we invent (unconsciously, of course) a Father in Heaven who exceeds our earthly fathers as much in power and knowledge as in goodness and benevolence; the alternative would be to sink into depression, stupor, paralysis, and finally death. According to Freud, belief in God is an *illusion* in a semitechnical use of the term: a belief that arises from the mechanism of wish-fulfillment. This illusion somehow becomes internalized.

An illusion (as opposed to a delusion), says Freud, is not necessarily false; and he goes on to add that it isn't possible to prove that theistic belief is mistaken. Nevertheless, there is more here than a mere antiseptic comment on the origin of religion. Although religion originates in the cognitive mechanism of wish-fulfillment, Freud apparently believes that it is within our power to resist this illusion, and that there is something condemnable, something intellectually irresponsible, in failing to do so:

> If ever there was a case of a lame excuse we have it here. Ignorance is ignorance; no right to believe anything can be derived from it. In other matters no sensible person will behave so irresponsibly or rest content with such feeble grounds for his opinions and for the line he takes....Where questions of religion are concerned, people are guilty of every possible sort of dishonesty and intellectual misdemeanour.[4]
> [...]

The fundamental theme here, therefore, is that religious belief arises from wish-fulfillment. We shall have to try to see more exactly what this amounts to and what bearing, if any, it has on the rationality of Christian belief; first, however, we should briefly note Marx's rather similar criticism.

B. Marx

Marx's most famous pronouncement on religion:

> The basis of irreligious criticism is *man makes religion*, religion does not make man. In other words, religion is the self-consciousness and the self-feeling of the man who has either not yet found himself, or else (having found himself) has lost himself once more. But man is no abstract being squatting outside the world. Man is the *world of man*, the state, society. This state, this society, produce religion, a *perverted*

world consciousness, because they are a *perverted* world....

> *Religious* distress is at the same time the *expression* of real distress and the *protest* against real distress. Religion is the sigh of the oppressed creature, the heart of a heartless world, just as it is the spirit of a spiritless situation. It is the *opium* of the people.

> The abolition of religion as the *illusory* happiness of the people is required for their *real* happiness. The demand to give up the illusions about its condition is the *demand to give up a condition which requires illusions*. The criticism of religion is therefore *in embryo the criticism of the vale of woe*, the *halo* of which is religion [Marx's emphasis].[5]

Marx suggests that religion arises from *perverted* world consciousness—perverted from a correct, or right, or natural condition. Religion involves a cognitive dysfunction, a disorder or perversion that is apparently brought about, somehow, by an unhealthy and perverted social order. Religious belief, according to Marx, is a result of cognitive dysfunction, of a lack of mental and emotional health. The believer is therefore in an etymological sense insane. Because of a dysfunctional, perverse social environment, the believer's cognitive equipment isn't working properly. If his cognitive equipment *were* working properly—if, for example, it were working more like Marx's—he would not be under the spell of this illusion. He would instead face the world and our place in it with the clear-eyed apprehension that we are alone, and that any comfort and help we get will have to be of our own devising.

And here we can see an initial difference between Freud and Marx: Freud doesn't necessarily think religious belief is produced by cognitive faculties that are malfunctioning. Religious belief—specifically belief in God—is, indeed, produced by wish-fulfillment; it is the product of illusion; still, illusion and wish-fulfillment have their functions. In this case, their function is to enable us to get along in this cold and heartless world into which we find ourselves thrown.

How then is this a *criticism* of religious belief? Freud speaks elsewhere of a "reality principle." Beliefs produced by wish-fulfillment aren't oriented toward reality; their function is not to produce *true* belief, but belief with some other property (psychological comfort, for example). So we could initially put it like this: religious belief is produced by cognitive processes whose function is not that of producing true beliefs, but rather that of producing beliefs conducive to psychological well-being. We will look into this in more detail below; for the moment, perhaps what we can say is that the Marxist criticism of religious belief is that it is produced by disordered cognitive processes, while the Freudian criticism is that it is produced by processes that are not aimed at the production of true beliefs. [...]

IV. THE F&M COMPLAINT REVISITED

[...] Marx's complaint about religion is that it is produced by cognitive faculties that are malfunctioning; this cognitive dysfunction is due to *social* dysfunction and dislocation. Besides that famous "Religion is the opium of the people" passage, however, Marx doesn't have a lot to say about religious belief—except, of course, for a number of semi-journalistic gibes and japes and other expressions of hostility.[6] I shall therefore concentrate on Freud, who holds (as we saw in the last chapter) not that theistic belief originates in cognitive malfunction, but that it is an *illusion*, in his technical sense. It finds its origin in *wish-fulfillment*, which, although it is a cognitive process with an important role to play in the total economy of our intellectual life, is nevertheless not aimed at the production of true beliefs. On Freud's view, then, theistic belief, given that it is produced by wish-fulfillment, does not have warrant; it fails to satisfy the condition of being produced by cognitive faculties whose purpose it is to produce true belief. He goes on to

characterize religious belief as "neurosis," "illusion," "poison," "intoxicant," and "childishness to be overcome," all on one page of *The Future of an Illusion*.[7] [...]

Is there any reason to believe these things? Is there any evidence for the F&M complaint? Why should anyone believe it? First, however, it is only fair to defend this complaint against a fairly common objection. The F&M style of criticizing religious (or other) belief is often improperly dismissed as an instance of the "genetic fallacy." The question, so the claim goes, is whether the theistic beliefs in question are *true*; the question is not how it is that someone comes to hold them or what the origin of the belief might be. Furthermore (so the claim continues), questions of origin are ordinarily irrelevant to questions of truth. ("Ordinarily"—of course we can think of silly exceptions. For example, we might know that Sam came to believe a proposition by accepting the testimony of someone who, on the subject of the belief in question, asserts nothing but falsehoods; in that case the origin of the belief is obviously relevant to its truth.)

This criticism of the F&M complaint is mistaken. True, questions of origin are ordinarily not relevant to the question of the *truth* of a belief; but they can be crucially relevant to the question of the *warrant* a belief enjoys. The objector fails to note that there are *de jure* questions and criticisms as well as *de facto*; his objection is relevant only if it is the *latter* sort that is at issue. But the F&M complaint is that theistic belief is not *rational* and lacks *warrant*. Unlike memory beliefs, *a priori* beliefs, or perceptual belief, theistic belief does not originate in the proper function of cognitive processes successfully aimed at the production of true belief. And if the problem, according to F&M, is that such beliefs have no *warrant*, then questions of origin may be intensely relevant; on many accounts of warrant, including the one I defend in [*Warrant and Proper Function*] the genesis of a belief *is* intimately connected with the degree of warrant, if any, it enjoys. [...]

But is Freud right: *does* theistic belief arise from wish-fulfillment, thereby failing to have warrant? Is there any reason to believe this? Does he offer argument or evidence for this claim, or (in Mill's phrase) other considerations to determine the intellect? Or is it mere assertion? Note that if the F&M complaint is to be a successful criticism, if it is to show that theistic belief lacks warrant, it must meet two conditions. First, it must show that theistic belief really *does* arise from the mechanism of wish-fulfillment; second (as I'll explain below), it must show that this *particular* operation of that mechanism is not aimed at the production of true beliefs. Consider the first. Freud offers no more than the most perfunctory argument here, and one can see why: it isn't easy to see how to argue the point. How would one argue that it is *that* mechanism, wish-fulfillment, rather than some other, that produces religious belief? Much of religious belief, after all, is not something that, on the face of it, fulfills your wildest dreams. Thus Christianity (as well as other theistic religions) includes the belief that human beings have sinned, that they merit divine wrath and even damnation, and that they are broken, wretched, in need of salvation; according to the Heidelberg Catechism, the first thing I have to know is my sins and miseries. This isn't precisely a fulfillment of one's wildest dreams. A follower of Freud might say: "Well, at any rate *theistic* belief, the belief that there is such a person as God, arises from wish-fulfillment." But this also is far from clear: many people thoroughly dislike the idea of an omnipotent, omniscient being monitoring their every activity, privy to their every thought, and passing judgment on all they do or think. Others dislike the lack of human autonomy consequent upon there being a Someone by comparison with whom we are as dust and ashes, and to whom we owe worship and obedience.

And in any event where is the evidence (empirical or otherwise) for the Freudian claim? A survey wouldn't be of much use. Hardly anyone reports believing in God out of wish-fulfillment; the usual reports are, instead, of being seized, compelled, or overwhelmed, or its just seeming right after considerable thought and agony, or its having always seemed clearly true, or its suddenly becoming obvious that it is really so. It certainly doesn't *seem* to those of us who believe in God that we do so out of wish-fulfillment. Of course that won't be taken as relevant; the beauty of Freudian explanations is that the postulated mechanisms all operate unconsciously, unavailable to inspection. The claim is that you subconsciously recognize the miserable and frightening condition we human beings face, subconsciously see that the alternatives are paralyzing despair or belief in God, and subconsciously opt for the latter. Even after careful introspection and reflection, you can't see that the proffered explanation is true: that fact won't be taken as even the slightest reason for doubting the explanation. (Just as with your indignant denial that you hate your father because you see him as a rival for your mother's sexual favors. In fact your indignation may be taken as confirmation; you are *resisting* what at some level you know or suspect is the proper diagnosis.) So suppose you subject yourself to a decade or so of psychoanalysis, but still can't see that this is the origin of your belief; well (so you'll be told), psychoanalysis isn't always successful. (In fact its cure rate, as far as scientific study can demonstrate, is about the same as no treatment at all.) Now things *could* be like this; and in the nature of the case maybe this sort of thing can't be demonstrated. Still, why should we believe it?

As far as I can see, the only evidence Freud actually offers is the claim that we see a lot of young people, nowadays, who give up religion when their father's authority breaks down:

> Psycho-analysis has made us familiar with the intimate connection between the father-complex and belief in God: it has shown us that a personal God is, psychologically, nothing other than an exalted father, and it brings us evidence every day of how young people lose their

religious beliefs as soon as their father's author- ity breaks down. Thus we recognize that the roots of the need for religion are in the parental complex: the almighty and just God, and kindly Nature, appear to us as grand sublimations of father and mother....[8]

No doubt Freud saw a good bit of that in his day (and perhaps even in his own case). [...] But how is this alleged evidence supposed to confirm the thesis that theistic belief results from wish-fulfillment? The claim is that when the father's authority (Freud doesn't say whether he means specifically with respect to religious belief or more generally) breaks down, young people often lose their religious beliefs. How is that fact, supposing that it is a fact, supposed to be evidence for the thesis that theistic belief results from wish-fulfillment? That's not at all obvious. Suppose theistic belief did result from wish-fulfillment: then wouldn't we expect some kind of correlation between serious belief and a recognition of the pitiless, indifferent char- acter of nature? On Freud's thesis, we would expect that a young person would start evinc- ing belief in God perhaps fairly soon after he comes to see that this is in fact the way the world is. But (given the thesis) why would we expect someone whose father's authority had suffered a breakdown to give up belief in God? The fact is someone who had a warm, loving, respectful relation with his father would be less likely to see the cold and indifferent face of nature than someone whose father had lost authority. As far as I can see, therefore, this alleged evidence doesn't fit well with the main Freudian thesis about the origin of theistic belief and certainly doesn't serve as evidence for it. Perhaps it shows instead that some young people like to display their maturity and independence by rejecting the religious stance of their parents, whatever that stance might be. (Thus at present we find many cases of children rejecting the *unbelief* of their parents.) But it certainly doesn't tend to show that religious or theistic belief arises out of wish-fulfillment.

Of course the thesis isn't stated exactly, or with enough detail to enable us to see just what *would* be evidence for it. One naturally thinks that there must be a deeper, more precise state- ment of the theory somewhere; sadly enough, one can't find any such thing. The evidence for the theory would perhaps have to be something like the way it fits or explains all the data, all the phenomena of religious or theistic belief. But before we could seriously assess its fit with the evidence, the theory would have to be stated much more precisely; we should have to be able to see what it does and doesn't predict much more clearly than, in fact, we can. Freudian explanations have never been strong along these lines.

Even if it were established that wish-fulfill- ment *is* the source of theistic belief, however, that wouldn't be enough to establish that the latter has no warrant. It must also be established that wish-fulfillment *in this particular manifes- tation* is not aimed at true belief. The cognitive design plan of human beings is subtle and com- plicated; a source of belief might be such that *in general* it isn't aimed at the formation of true belief, but in some special cases it is. So perhaps this is true of wish-fulfillment; in general, its purpose is not that of producing true belief, but in this special case precisely that *is* its purpose. Perhaps human beings have been created by God with a deep need to believe in his presence and goodness and love. Perhaps God designed us that way in order that we come to believe in him and be aware of his presence. Perhaps this is how God has arranged for us to come to know him. If so, then the particular bit of the cognitive design plan governing the formation of theistic belief is indeed aimed at true belief, even if the belief in question arises from wish- fulfillment. Perhaps God has designed us to know that he is present and loves us by way of creating us with a strong desire for him, a desire that leads to the belief that in fact he is there. Nor is this a mere speculative possibility; some- thing like it is embraced both by St. Augustine

("Our hearts are restless til they rest in thee, O God") and Jonathan Edwards [. . .].

And how would Freud or a follower establish that the mechanism whereby human beings come to believe in God (come to believe that there is such a person as God) is *not* aimed at the truth? This is really the crux of the matter. Freud offers no arguments or reasons here at all. As far as I can see, he simply takes it for granted that there is no God and that theistic belief is false; he then casts about for some kind of explanation of this widespread phenomenon of mistaken belief. He hits on wish-fulfillment and apparently assumes it is obvious that this mechanism is not "reality oriented"—that is, is not aimed at the production of true belief— so that such belief lacks warrant. As we have seen, this is a safe assumption if in fact theism *is* false. But then Freud's version of the *de jure* criticism really depends on his atheism: it isn't an independent criticism at all, and it won't (or shouldn't) have any force for anyone who doesn't share that atheism. [. . .]

Notes

1. Of course, it wasn't only *Christian* belief that drew their fire: Freud and Marx were equal-opportunity animadverters, attacking religion generally and without discrimination.
2. "An Autobiographical Study," in volume 20 of the *Standard Edition of the Complete Psychological Works of Sigmund Freud*. (London: Hogarth Press and the Institute of Psychoanalysis, 1953–74), p. 68.
3. *The Future of an Illusion*, tr. and ed. James Strachey (New York: W. W. Norton, 1961), p. 30. This work was originally published as *Die Zukunft einer Illusion* (Leipzig: Internationaler Psychoanalytischer Verlag, 1927).
4. *The Future of an Illusion*, p. 32.
5. "Contribution to the Critique of Hegel's Philosophy of Right, Introduction," in *On Religion*, by Karl Marx and Friedrich Engels, tr. Reinhold Niebuhr (Chico, Calif.: Scholar's Press, 1964), pp. 41–42.
6. See *On Religion* by Karl Marx and Frederick Engels, ed. Reinhold Niebuhr (Chico, Calif.: Scholars Press, 1964). This is a collection of bits of various writings on religion by Marx and Engels.
7. New York: W. W. Norton, 1961 (originally published 1927), p. 49.
8. Memoir of Leonardo da Vinci in *The Standard Edition of the Complete Psychological Works of Sigmund Freud*, ed. J. Strachey (London: Hogarth Press, 1957), vol. 11, p. 123.

Study Questions

1. To what degree do you think that the origin of religious belief affects the truth of those beliefs?
2. Why does Plantinga think that the F&M complaint is not a version of the genetic fallacy?
3. To what degree do you think that religious beliefs can have warrant?

1.8   Are Children "Intuitive Theists"?

 ### DEBORAH KELEMEN

DEBORAH KELEMEN (1967–) teaches cognitive development in the Department of Psychology at Boston University, where she also directs the Child Cognition Lab. Her research focuses on children's developing conceptions of the natural world and understanding how children reason about intentional agency and reasoning. In other research, Kelemen describes experimental evidence that by age five children have a "teleofunctional bias," that is, a tendency to see all objects and behaviors as having an intentional purpose. Furthermore, this tendency seems to be independent of children's religious or cultural background. In the present article, Kelemen canvases numerous recent studies that suggest that children are prone not only to see purpose but also to attribute this purpose to nonhuman design by age 10. She describes the natural explanatory approach of children as "intuitive theism."

PROMISCUOUS TELEOLOGY AND "CREATIONISM" IN CHILDREN

Contemporary research on teleological reasoning—the tendency to reason about entities and events in terms of purpose—was initiated in the context of the debate on the origins of biological understanding. Consistent with the view that children's reasoning about living things is constrained by teleological assumptions from a very early age, studies have found that young children attend to shared functional adaptation rather than shared overall appearance (or category membership) when generalizing behaviors to novel animals (Kelemen, Widdowson, Posner, Brown, & Casler, 2003), judge whether biological properties are heritable on the basis of their functional consequences rather than their origin (Springer & Keil, 1989), and explain body properties by reference to their self-serving functions and not their physical-mechanical cause (Keil, 1992; Kelemen, 2003).

Results like these lend support to the idea that a purpose-based teleological stance might, therefore, be humans' innate adaptation for biological reasoning (Atran, 1995; Keil, 1992). This conclusion has been complicated, however, by findings that children see not only the biological but also the nonbiological natural world in teleological terms. For example, when asked to identify unanswerable questions, American 4- and 5-year-olds differ from adults by finding the question "what's this for?" appropriate not only to artifacts and body parts, but also to whole living things like lions ("to go in the zoo") and nonliving natural kinds like clouds ("for raining"). Additionally, when asked whether they agree that, for example, raining is really just what a cloud "does" rather than what it is "made for," preschoolers demur, endorsing the view that natural entities are "made for something" and that is why they are here (Kelemen, 1999b).

These kinds of promiscuous teleological intuitions persist into elementary school, particularly

Deborah Keleman, "Are Children 'Intuitive Theists'?: Reasoning About Purposes and Design in Nature," *Psychological Science* (2004).

in relation to object properties. For instance, when asked to conduct a "science" task and decide whether prehistoric rocks were pointy because of a physical process (e.g., "bits of stuff piled up for a long period of time") or because they performed a function, American 7- and 8-year-olds, unlike adults, preferred teleological explanations whether they invoked "self-survival" functions (e.g., "so that animals wouldn't sit on them and smash them") or "artifact" functions (e.g., "so that animals could scratch on them when they got itchy"; Kelemen, 1999c; but see Keil, 1992). This bias in favor of teleological explanation for properties of both living and nonliving natural objects occurs even when children are told that adults apply physical kinds of explanation to nonliving natural entities (Kelemen, 2003). In American children, the bias begins to moderate around 9 to 10 years of age, and this pattern now has been found also with British children for both object properties and, slightly less markedly, natural object wholes. These British findings are relevant because they weigh against interpretations that promiscuous teleological intuitions are a simple reflection of the relatively pronounced cultural religiosity, or religious exceptionalism (in postindustrial, international context), of the United States (see Kelemen, 2003, for discussion of religiosity differences).

So, if ambient cultural religiosity is not the obvious explanation, what does cause this promiscuous teleology? A study of responses young children receive when asking questions about nature indicates parents generally favor causal rather than teleological explanation, so current evidence suggests the answer does not lie there, at least, not in any straightforward sense (Kelemen, Callanan, Casler, & Pérez-Granados, 2002). Another hypothesis being explored in my lab is, therefore, as follows (e.g., Kelemen, 1999b, 1999c). Perhaps children's generalized attributions of purpose are, essentially, side effects of a socially intelligent mind that is naturally inclined to privilege intentional explanation and is, therefore, oriented toward explanations characterizing

nature as an intentionally designed artifact—an orientation given further support by the artifact-saturated context of human cultures. Specifically, the proposal is that the human tendency to attribute purpose to objects develops from infants' core, and precociously developing, ability to attribute goals to agents (as discussed later): Initially, on the basis of observing agents' object-directed behavior, children understand objects as means to agents' goals, then as embodiments of agents' goals (thus "for" specific purposes in a teleological sense), and, subsequently—as a result of a growing understanding of artifacts and the creative abilities of agents—as intentionally caused by agents' goals. A bias to explain, plus a human predilection for intentional explanation, may then be what leads children, in the absence of knowledge, to a generalized, default view of entities as intentionally caused by someone for a purpose.

Details aside, the basic idea that children are disposed to view entities in terms of intentional design, or as "quasi-artifacts," is similar to one independently developed by Evans in her work on origins beliefs (Evans, 2000a, 2000b, 2001). Evans has found that regardless of the religiosity of their home background, children show a bias to endorse intentional accounts of how species originate. Thus, when asked questions like "how do you think the very first sun bear got here on earth?" 8- to 10-year-olds from both fundamentalist and nonfundamentalist American homes favored "creationist" accounts whether generating their own answers or rating agreement with the following responses: (a) God made it, (b) a person made it, (c) it changed from a different kind of animal that used to live on earth, or (d) it appeared (Evans, 2001). This preference was also found in 5- to 7-year-old children's agreement ratings for animate and inanimate entities. Indeed, it was only among 11- to 13-year-old nonfundamentalist children that divergence from the theist position emerged. Evans's results do not stand in isolation. Gelman and Kremer (1991) found that although American preschoolers recognize that artifacts rather than natural entities are human made, they favor God as the explanation of the origin of remote natural items (e.g., oceans). Petrovich (1997) found similar results with British preschoolers. [...]

Considered together, current data on children's promiscuous teleology and explanations of origins might therefore suggest an obvious affirmative answer to the question of whether children are intuitive theists: Children view natural phenomena as intentionally designed by a god. Not coincidentally, they therefore view natural objects as existing for a purpose. But before embracing, or even entertaining, this conclusion, we must look first at whether it is actually defensible. What evidence is there that children possess any of the conceptual prerequisites that intuitive theism might entail? What evidence is there that their intuitions display any coherence at all?

CONCEPTUAL PREREQUISITES TO INTUITIVE THEISM

Piaget (1929) found that when asked how natural objects originated, children frequently identified "God" as the cause. Piaget argued that these statements were simply further cases of artificialism: Unable to entertain an abstraction such as God, and egocentrically focused, children used "God" to refer to a person who was fundamentally similar to the dominant authority in children's own lives—their parent.

Once again, however, Piaget's assumptions about the concreteness of children's concepts have been challenged. Research now suggests that rather than being anthropomorphic, children's earliest concept of agency is abstract, and is invoked by a range of nonhuman entities from the time when overt signs of children's sensitivity to mental states are becoming increasingly robust. Thus, 12-month-old infants will follow the "gaze" of faceless blobs as long as they have engaged in contingent interaction with them

(S.C. Johnson, Booth, & O'Hearn, 2001) and will attribute goal directedness to computer-generated shapes (e.g., Csibra & Gergely, 1998). By 15 months, infants will complete the incomplete actions of a nonhuman agent by inferring its goals (S.C. Johnson et al., 2001). From infancy, we are, then, excellent "agency detectors" (Barrett, 2000; Guthrie, 2002).

But, although relevant, these indications that children attribute mental states to perceivable nonhuman agents while watching them are still nonevidential with respect to young children's ability to reason about the creative intentions of intangible, nonnatural agents like gods. Presumably several capacities are minimally prerequisite in order to reason about such special causal agents: first, the capacity to maintain a mental representation of such an agent despite its intangibility; second, the ability to attribute to that special agent mental states distinguishing it from more commonplace agents; and third—and particularly pertinent to the question of nonnatural artifice—the basic ability to attribute design intentions to agents and understand an object's purpose as deriving from such intentions.

CONCEPTIONS OF INTANGIBLE AGENTS

Several lines of research are suggestive of young children's abilities regarding the first two prerequisites. First, Taylor's (1999) research on children's propensity to maintain social relationships with imaginary companions suggests that by age 3 to 4 years, children are already conceptually equipped to vividly mentally represent the wants, opinions, actions, and personalities of intangible agents on a sustained basis. Like supernatural agents, such companions are found cross-culturally and are often distinguished from more commonplace agents by special biological, psychological, and physical traits beyond invisibility. Examples are animals that talk and individuals who understand gibberish, hear wishes, or live on stars (Taylor, 1999). Interestingly, ideas about imaginary companions, like ideas about gods, can be culturally transmitted, at least, within families.[1]

Imaginary companions, then, provide some indications of young children's ability to symbolically represent and reason about immaterial individuals. But research explicitly focused on children's understanding of God has also found that by 5 years of age, children can make quite sophisticated predictions as to how a more widely recognized nonnatural agent's mental states are distinguished from those of more earthly individuals. Specifically, Barrett, Richert, and Driesenga (2001) cleverly capitalized on the well-documented shift in 3- to 5-year-olds' ability to pass false-belief tasks—tests that putatively measure children's theory-of-mind understanding that beliefs are mental representations and, as such, can mismatch with physical reality. In their study, Barrett et al. used a standard form of the task: Children were shown a cracker box, asked what they believed it contained, allowed to peek inside and see the actual contents (pebbles), and then asked the test question, What would someone (who had not been shown) believe was inside the container? As is typical in such studies, Barrett et al. found that 3-year-olds failed the test, giving an answer that, in some sense, assumes that people are all-knowing; that is, 3-year-olds answered, "pebbles." In contrast, an increasing percentage of 4- and 5-year-olds passed, saying "crackers"—an answer recognizing the fallibility of beliefs. Interestingly, however, a different pattern emerged when these Protestant-raised children were asked what God would believe. At all ages tested, children treated God as all-knowing, even when they clearly understood that earthly agents would have a false belief. This developmental pattern led Barrett et al. to provocatively suggest that children may be innately attuned to "godlike" nonhuman agency but need to acquire an understanding of the limitations of human minds. Similar results have now also been obtained with Yukatec Mayan children, who discriminated not only the Christian God but also other supernatural agents as less susceptible to false belief than people (Knight, Sousa, Barrett, & Atran, 2003; also Atran, 2002, for a description).

In sum, then, these findings suggest that around 5 years of age, children possess the prerequisites to make advanced, distinctive, attributions of mental states to nonnatural agents. But are children truly conceptually distinguishing these agents from people or just representing these agents as humans augmented with culturally prescribed, superhuman properties inferred from adults' religious talk? The answer to this question is unclear. Certainly children's supernatural concepts, like those of adults, are likely to be influenced by culturally prescribed, systematically counterintuitive properties (Atran, 2002; Boyer, 2001) and may also be anthropomorphic in many ways. But, even if children's concepts of nonnatural agency do have human features, this does not undermine the claim that children conceive of such agents as distinct: We do not question adults' capacity to conceive of supernatural agents, and yet research indicates that even when adults explicitly attribute gods with properties like omnipresence, they assume, in their implicit reasoning, that gods act in accordance with human temporal, psychological, and physical constraints (Barrett, 2000).

Even so, perhaps applying the phrase "intuitive theists" to children—given all that the term "theism" implies to adults—might seem misplaced, if not irreverent. After all, although young children might conceive of nonnatural agents and hypothesize about their mental states, presumably they do not contemplate the metaphysical "truth" of which such agents can be part, or experience emotions concomitant with endorsing a particular metaphysical-religious system. Intuitively, these assumptions seem correct although, again, there are reasons to equivocate—not only because research suggests adult religious belief systems are often not particularly coherent or contemplated (e.g., Boyer, 2001), but also because the question of when children begin to develop metaphysical understanding in the adult self-reflective sense is debated (e.g., Evans & Mull, 2002; Harris, 2000; C.N. Johnson, 2000). Specifically, although children might not explicitly demarcate their musings as special, it has been found that even from very young ages, children pose questions about the nature of things that echo adult metaphysical themes (Harris, 2000; Piaget, 1929). Furthermore, we actually know little about young children's emotions concerning self-generated or culturally derived concepts of nonnatural agency, outside of their emotional relationships with imaginary companions. Gaps in our knowledge therefore preclude general conclusions as to children's capacity to entertain adultlike religious feeling.

However, for the present purpose, such issues are, to a large extent, irrelevant because in the current context the term intuitive theist embodies no claims regarding children's emotional or metaphysical commitments. All that is under question is whether children make sense of the world in a manner superficially approximating adult theism, by forming a working hypothesis that natural phenomena derive from a nonhuman "somebody" who designed them for a purpose—an intuition that may be elaborated by a particular religious culture but derives primarily from cognitive predispositions and artifact knowledge.[2] This point circles us back to the third conceptual prerequisite for intuitive theism—children's ability to understand that an object's purpose derives from the designer's goals.

CHILDREN'S UNDERSTANDING OF ARTIFACTS AND DESIGN

Adult reasoning about artifacts is anchored by intuitions about the designer's intended function (e.g., Keil, 1989; Rips, 1989), but although behavioral measures suggest that from around 3 years of age children will teleologically treat artifacts as "for" a single privileged function (Casler & Kelemen, 2003a; Markson, 2001), the question of when children adopt an adultlike teleological construal based on reasoning about the creator's intent (the "design stance") is debated (Kelemen & Carey, 2007).

One reason for the lack of consensus is studies suggesting that, until they are quite old, children apply category labels to artifacts on the basis of shared shape, not shared function (e.g., Gentner, 1978; Graham, Williams, & Huber, 1999; Landau, Smith, & Jones, 1998). Such studies have found that until around 6 years of age, children will judge that if an object looks similar to an artifact called "a wug," it is also "a wug" even though it does not do the same thing. Children's apparent indifference to what artifacts did in these categorization studies seemed to render it unlikely that the deeper principle of intended function could play much of a role in their concepts of artifacts.

However, recent findings suggest that the stimuli in earlier studies may have significantly contributed to children's categorization failures in that experimenters unnaturally dissociated artifact form from artifact function, an approach leading to uncompelling "functions" equivalent to general object properties (e.g., capacities to rattle, roll, absorb). In current research using artifacts that look designed in that their structural properties clearly relate to their functional affordances, children from around the age of 2 years have generalized labels on the basis of function rather than shape similarity (e.g., Kemler Nelson, Frankenfield, Morris, & Blair, 2000; Kemler Nelson, Russell, Duke, & Jones, 2000). Furthermore, evidence also suggests that even when children categorize artifacts by shape, rather than being a superficial perceptual strategy, this approach reflects the valid conceptual assumption that shape predicts the creator's intent. Thus, Diesendruck, Markson, and Bloom (2003) found that if 3-year-olds have the shape similarity between two artifacts pointed out to them but then hear that the objects have different intended functions, they eschew classifying them as the same kind of artifact, instead forming categories based on shared function and perceptual dissimilarity. This shift from a shape to a function strategy happens only if children hear about *intended* functions—information about possible function is not sufficient.

These findings provide suggestive evidence that young children have a sensitivity to intended function from around the age of 3 years. They are particularly interesting when considered alongside research explicitly focused on when children weigh overt information about intended design. In studies in my own lab, this tendency is increasingly evident between ages 4 and 5 years. For example, in one study, 4- and 5-year-old children were told stories about depicted novel artifacts that were intentionally designed for one purpose (e.g., squeezing lemons), given away, and then accidentally or intentionally used for another activity (e.g., picking up snails). When asked what each object was "for," the children, like adults, favored the intended function, even in experimental conditions in which the alternative use occurred frequently rather than just once (Kelemen, 1999b). A subsequent study replicated this effect using manipulable, novel artifacts. In contrast to 3-year-olds, groups of 4- and 5-year-olds not only judged the objects as "for" their designed function rather than their everyday intentional use, but also favored intended function when judging where items belonged in a house (Kelemen, 2001).

Research by Matan and Carey (2001) also reveals some early sensitivity to intended function. In their study, children were told about artifacts that were made for one purpose (e.g., to water flowers) but used for something else (to make tea in). When asked which familiar artifact category the object belonged to (e.g., watering can or teapot), 4- and 6-year-olds, like adults, had a preference for the design category. However, 4-year-olds' tendency to be influenced by the order of forced-choice response options on some trials led Matan and Carey to conclude

that an understanding of designer's intent does not organize children's artifact concepts until around 6 years of age.[3]

[...] An underlying developmental pattern does emerge across all of these studies. With some reliability, the findings suggest that beginning some time around the kindergarten period, children adopt a design-based teleological view of objects with increasing consistency. In light of this work, and the earlier-described research on children's reasoning about nonnatural agents' mental states, the proposal that children might be intuitive theists becomes increasingly viable.

However, an issue still remains: Just because children can consider objects as products of design does not mean this ability has any actual connection to children's attributions of purpose to nature. It is possible, after all, that, like some adults, children view supernatural agents as originators of nature but consider the functionality of many natural phenomena as deriving from an entirely different, nonintentional cause (e.g., evolution). Thus, although children may invoke God in their explanations of origins (e.g., Evans, 2001) and view natural phenomena as existing for a purpose (e.g., Kelemen, 1999b), the two sets of intuitions may have no systematic relation.

A recent study addressing this question suggests that this is not the case. Six- to 10-year-old British children were first asked to generate ideas about why various animals, natural objects, and events exist, and then consider other people's explanations, indicating their preference between teleological and physical explanations for each item. Subsequently, the children were also asked questions probing their ideas about intentional origins and whether they thought the earlier items originated because they "just happened" or because they were "made by someone/something." The design of the study precluded children from tracking their answers and aligning their answers to earlier and later questions in the absence of intuitions of their own. Nevertheless, the results revealed correlations between children's teleological ideas about nature and their endorsements of intentional design. Furthermore, no artificialism was found: Children identified people as the designing agents of artifacts (control items), distinguishing God as the designing agent of nature (Kelemen & DiYanni, 2005).

SUMMARY

This article began by posing a question: Given findings regarding children's beliefs about purpose and their ideas about the intentional origins of nature, is it possible that children are intuitive theists insofar as they are predisposed to develop a view of nature as an artifact of nonhuman design?

A review of recent cognitive developmental research reveals that by around 5 years of age, children understand natural objects as not humanly caused, can reason about nonnatural agents' mental states, and demonstrate the capacity to view objects in terms of design. Finally, evidence from 6- to 10-year-olds suggests that children's assignments of purpose to nature relate to their ideas concerning intentional nonhuman causation. Together, these research findings tentatively suggest that children's explanatory approach may be accurately characterized as intuitive theism—a characterization that has broad relevance not only to cognitivists or the growing interdisciplinary community studying the underpinnings of religion (Barrett, 2000), but also, at an applied level, to science educators because the implication is that children's science failures may, in part, result from inherent conflicts between intuitive ideas and the basic tenets of contemporary scientific thought.

Further research is required, of course, to clarify how well the description really holds across individuals and cultures (reliable, empirical cross-cultural research is limited), how robust the orientation to purpose and design is, and how it interacts with education over time. A significant theoretical goal is to empirically discriminate the present hypothesis that children are inherently predisposed to invoke intention-based teleological explanations of nature and find them satisfying (see Bering, 2002, for a related stance) from the milder hypothesis that children's teleological orientation arises primarily from their possession of the kind of cognitive machinery (e.g., agency detection) that renders them susceptible to the religious representations of their adult culture—a position that predicts children would not independently generate explanations in terms of designing nonnatural agency without adult cultural influence.

A proper discussion of the pros and cons of each position, along with how to empirically distinguish them, is beyond the scope of this short article. However, it is worth emphasizing that the kind of research program proposed here is one that involves focusing on adults as much as children because although the question "are children intuitive theists?" implies a dichotomy between child and adult thought, the current proposal tacitly assumes that the idea of such a fundamental dichotomy is false: If, as suggested here, the tendency to think in teleological quasi-artifact terms is a side effect of human mental design (and pan-cultural experience with artifacts) rather than socialization, it is likely to remain as a default explanatory strategy throughout life, even as other explanations are elaborated. This idea contrasts with the notion that through conceptual change (e.g., Carey, 1985), such an explanatory approach is revised and replaced by a physical-reductionist view of nature in cultures endorsing such ideas.

Several factors provide support for this suggestion of developmental continuity. First, reasoning about all aspects of nature in nonteleological physical-reductionist terms is a relatively recent development in the history of human thought (see Kelemen, 1999a, for a brief history of the "design argument"), and contemporary adults are still surprisingly bad at it. For example, evolution is generally misconstrued as a quasi-intentional needs-responsive designing force, indicating that even when adults elaborate alternative scientific explanations, signs of intention-based reasoning about nature are still in evidence (see Evans, 2000a, for review). Second, recent research with American college undergraduates has found that although such populations endorse teleological explanation in a selective, scientifically appropriate way in the evaluative context of a forced-choice "scientific" experiment, in a less evaluative environment they will more promiscuously generate teleological explanations of why animals and inanimate natural objects exist. These results suggest that even in a post-Darwinian culture, continuity rather than conceptual change may be at play in educated individuals' preference for teleological explanation (Kelemen, 2003). Finally, and significant to the conjecture that scientific educations suppress rather than replace teleological explanatory tendencies, research with scientifically uneducated Romanian Gypsy adults has found that they have promiscuous teleological intuitions much like scientifically naive British and American elementary-school children (Casler & Kelemen, 2003b). In conclusion, the question of whether children and adults are intuitive theists provides fertile ground for future research.

Notes

1. I do not intend to suggest that children's relationships with imaginary companions are akin to adults' relationships with gods. An important difference is that the latter are experienced as real (Boyer, 2001), whereas evidence suggests that (American) children's imaginary companions are experienced as fictions (Taylor, 1999).

2. Some form of folk religion appears to exist in all human cultures, but not all religions are theist (e.g., animism), raising the interesting possibility that children's intuitions may sometimes mismap with the dominant adult culture's religious ideas. However, because all known folk religions involve nonnatural agents and intentional causation—the substrate of intuitive theism—such mismappings need not represent an ongoing conceptual conflict, but instead leave children's intuitions open to coexist with and be influenced by cultural religious ideas.

3. Matan and Carey's children made fewer design-based judgments when the design category name was presented second rather than first—an effect perhaps caused by the use of familiar artifacts as stimuli and pretrial procedures for familiarizing children with these stimuli that may have subsequently prompted prepotent responding to the first function information heard, reducing design-based reasoning overall.

References

Atran, S. (1995). Causal constraints on categories. In D. Sperber, D. Premack, & A.J. Premack (Eds.), *Causal cognition: A multi-disciplinary debate* (pp. 263–265). Oxford, England: Clarendon Press.

Atran, S. (2002). *In gods we trust: The evolutionary landscape of religion.* New York: Oxford University Press.

Baillargeon, R. (1993). The object concept revisited: New directions in the investigation of infants' physical knowledge. In C.E. Granrud (Ed.), *Visual perception and cognition in infancy* (Carnegie Mellon Symposia on Cognition Vol. 23, pp. 265–315). Hillsdale, NJ: Erlbaum.

Barrett, J.L. (2000). Exploring the natural foundations of religion. *Trends in Cognitive Sciences, 4,* 29–34.

Barrett, J.L., Richert, R., & Driesenga, A. (2001). God's beliefs versus mother's: The development of non-human agent concepts. *Child Development, 72,* 50–65.

Bering, J. (2002). Intuitive conceptions of dead agents' minds: The natural foundations of afterlife beliefs as a phenomenological boundary. *Journal of Cognition and Culture, 2,* 263–308.

Boyer, P. (2001). *Religion explained: The evolutionary origins of religious thought.* New York: Basic Books.

Carey, S. (1985). *Conceptual change in childhood.* Cambridge, MA: MIT Press.

Casler, K., & Kelemen, D. (2003a). *Teleological explanations of nature among Romanian Roma (Gypsy) adults.* Unpublished manuscript, Boston University, Boston.

Casler, K., & Kelemen, D. (2003b). *Tool use and children's understanding of artifact function.* Unpublished manuscript, Boston University, Boston.

Csibra, G., & Gergely, G. (1998). The teleological origins of mentalistic action explanations: A developmental hypothesis. *Developmental Science, 1,* 255–259.

Diesendruck, G., Markson, L.M., & Bloom, P. (2003). Children's reliance on creator's intent in extending names for artifacts. *Psychological Science, 14,* 164–168.

Evans, E.M. (2000a). Beyond Scopes: Why Creationism is here to stay. In K.S. Rosengren, C.N. Johnson, & P.L. Harris (Eds.), *Imagining the impossible: The development of magical, scientific and religious thinking in contemporary society* (pp. 305–333). Cambridge, England: Cambridge University Press.

Evans, E.M. (2000b). The emergence of beliefs about the origin of species in school-age children. *Merrill Palmer Quarterly, 46,* 221–254.

Evans, E.M. (2001). Cognitive and contextual factors in the emergence of diverse belief systems: Creation versus evolution. *Cognitive Psychology, 42,* 217–266.

Evans, E.M., & Mull, M. (2002). *Magic can happen in that world (but not this one): Constructing a naïve metaphysics.* Manuscript submitted for publication.

Gelman, S.A., & Kremer, K.E. (1991). Understanding natural cause: Children's explanations of how objects and their properties originate. *Child Development, 62,* 396–414.

Gentner, D. (1978). What looks like a jiggy but acts like a zimbo? A study of early word meaning using artificial objects. *Papers and Reports on Child Language Development, 15,* 1–6.

Graham, S.A., Williams, L.D., & Huber, J.F. (1999). Preschoolers' and adults' reliance on object shape and object function for lexical extension. *Journal of Experimental Child Psychology, 74,* 128–151.

Guthrie, S. (2002). Animal animism: Evolutionary roots of religious cognition. In I. Pyysiainen & V. Anttonen (Eds.), *Current approaches in the cognitive science of religion* (pp. 38–67). London: Continuum.

Harris, P. (2000). On not falling down to earth: Children's metaphysical questions. In K.S. Rosengren, C.N. Johnson, & P.L. Harris (Eds.), *Imagining the impossible: The development of magical, scientific and religious thinking in contemporary society* (pp. 157–178). Cambridge, England: Cambridge University Press.

Johnson, C.N. (2000). Putting different things together: The development of metaphysical thinking. In K.S. Rosengren, C.N. Johnson, & P.L. Harris (Eds.), *Imagining the impossible: The development of magical, scientific and religious thinking in contemporary society* (pp. 179–211). Cambridge, England: Cambridge University Press.

Johnson, S.C., Booth, A., & O'Hearn, K. (2001). Inferring the goals of a nonhuman agent. *Cognitive Development, 16,* 637–656.

Keil, F.C. (1989). *Concepts, kinds, and cognitive development.* Cambridge, MA: MIT Press.

Keil, F.C. (1992). The origins of an autonomous biology. In M.R. Gunnar & M. Maratsos (Eds.), *Minnesota Symposia on Child Psychology: Vol. 25. Modularity and constraints in language and cognition* (pp. 103–137). Hillsdale, NJ: Erlbaum.

Kelemen, D. (1999a). Beliefs about purpose: On the origins of teleological thought. In M. Corballis & S. Lea (Eds.), *The descent of mind: Psychological perspectives on hominid evolution* (pp. 278–294). Oxford, England: Oxford University Press.

Kelemen, D. (1999b). The scope of teleological thinking in preschool children. *Cognition, 70,* 241–272.

Kelemen, D. (1999c). Why are rocks pointy? Children's preference for teleological explanations of the natural world. *Developmental Psychology, 35,* 1440–1453.

Kelemen, D. (2001, April). *Intention in children's understanding of artifact function.* Paper presented at the biennial meeting of the Society for Research in Child Development, Minneapolis, MN.

Kelemen, D. (2003). British and American children's preferences for teleo-functional explanations of the natural world. *Cognition, 88,* 201–221.

Kelemen, D., Callanan, M., Casler, K., & Pérez-Granados, D. (2002). *"Why things happen": Teleological explanation in parent-child conversations.* Manuscript submitted for publication.

Kelemen, D., & Carey, S. (2007). The essence of artifacts: Developing the design stance. In S. Laurence & E. Margolis (Eds.), *Creations of the mind: Theories of artifacts and their representation.* Oxford, England: Oxford University Press.

Kelemen, D., & DiYanni, C. (2005). Intuitions about origins: Purpose and intelligent design in children's reasoning about nature. *Journal of Cognition and Development.*

Kelemen, D., Widdowson, D., Posner, T., Brown, A., & Casler, K. (2003). Teleofunctional constraints on preschool children's reasoning about living things. *Developmental Science, 6,* 329–345.

Kemler Nelson, D.G., Frankenfield, A., Morris, C., & Blair, E. (2000). Young children's use of functional information to categorize artifacts: Three factors that matter. *Cognition, 77,* 133–168.

Kemler Nelson, D.G., Russell, R., Duke, N., & Jones, K. (2000). Two-year-olds will name artifacts by their functions. *Child Development, 71*, 1271–1288.

Knight, N., Sousa, P., Barrett, J.L., & Atran, S. (2003). Children's attributions of beliefs to humans and God: Cross cultural evidence. *Cognitive Science*.

Landau, B., Smith, L.B., & Jones, S.S. (1998). Object shape, object function, and object name. *Journal of Memory and Language, 38*, 1–27.

Markson, L.M. (2001, April). *Developing understanding of artifact function*. Paper presented at the biennial meeting of the Society for Research in Child Development, Minneapolis, MN.

Matan, A., & Carey, S. (2001). Developmental changes within the core of artifact concepts. *Cognition, 78*, 1–26.

Mead, M. (1932). An investigation of the thought of primitive children with special reference to animism. *Journal of the Royal Anthropological Institute of Great Britain and Ireland, 62*, 173–190.

Petrovich, O. (1997). Understanding of non-natural causality in children and adults: A case against artificialism. *Psyche and Geloof, 8*, 151–165.

Piaget, J. (1929). *The child's conception of the world*. London: Routledge & Kegan Paul.

Rips, L.J. (1989). Similarity, typicality and categorization. In S. Vosniadou & A. Ortony (Eds.), *Similarity and analogical reasoning* (pp. 21–59). Cambridge, England: Cambridge University Press.

Springer, K., & Keil, F.C. (1989). On the development of biologically specific beliefs: The case of inheritance. *Child Development, 60*, 637–648.

Taylor, M. (1999). *Imaginary companions and the children who create them*. New York: Oxford University Press.

Study Questions

1. What are the three capacities that are prerequisites to children being "intuitive theists"?

2. To what degree do you think Kelemen's data on children being "intuitive theists" affects the rationality of religious belief?

3. More generally, what do you think is the relationship between psychological accounts of belief and the truth of theism?

Breaking the Spell   1.9

DANIEL DENNETT

DANIEL DENNETT (1942–) is the Austin B. Fletcher Professor of Philosophy and co-director of the Center for Cognitive Studies at Tufts University. The majority of his writing focuses on the philosophy of mind, consciousness, free will, and philosophy of biology. Along with Sam Harris, Richard Dawkins, and Christopher Hitchens, he is also known as one of the "New Atheists." The New Atheists make significant use of the natural sciences both to criticize religious beliefs and to account for their origin. Rejecting the truth of religious beliefs, Dennett seeks to give a naturalist explanation of their origin. In this selection from *Breaking the Spell*, Dennett describes the need for a scientific investigation of religion given its social and political influence on our world. He then gives a sketch of the evolutionary advantage of religious belief, suggesting that it was advantageous for rulers to be able to control the behavior and beliefs of their subjects. The reading ends with Dennett's suggestions for future scientific study of religion.

Daniel Dennett, *Breaking the Spell* (New York: Penguin, 2007).

BREAKING WHICH SPELL?

[...] It is high time that we subject religion as a global phenomenon to the most intensive multi-disciplinary research we can muster, calling on the best minds on the planet. Why? Because religion is too important for us to remain ignorant about. It affects not just our social, political, and economic conflicts, but the very meanings we find in our lives. For many people, probably a majority of the people on Earth, nothing matters more than religion. For this very reason, it is imperative that we learn as much as we can about it. That, in a nutshell, is the argument of this book.

Wouldn't such an exhaustive and invasive examination damage the phenomenon itself? Mightn't it *break the spell?* That is a good question, and I don't know the answer. *Nobody knows the answer.* That is why I raise the question, to explore it carefully now, so that we (1) don't rush headlong into inquiries we would all be much better off not undertaking, and yet (2) don't hide facts from ourselves that could guide us to better lives for all. The people on this planet confront a terrible array of problems—poverty, hunger, disease, oppression, the violence of war and crime, and many more—and in the twenty-first century we have unparalleled powers for doing something about all these problems. But what shall we do?

Good intentions are not enough. If we learned anything in the twentieth century, we learned this, for we made some colossal mistakes with the best of intentions. In the early decades of the century, communism seemed to many millions of thoughtful, well-intentioned people to be a beautiful and even obvious solution to the terrible unfairness that all can see, but they were wrong. An obscenely costly mistake. Prohibition also seemed like a good idea at the time, not just to power-hungry prudes intent on imposing their taste on their fellow citizens, but to many decent people who could see the terrible toll of alcoholism and figured that nothing short of a total ban would suffice. They were proven wrong, and we still haven't recovered from all the bad effects that well-intentioned policy set in motion. There was a time, not so long ago, when the idea of keeping blacks and whites in separate communities, with separate facilities, seemed to many sincere people to be a reasonable solution to pressing problems of interracial strife. It took the civil-rights movement in the United States, and the painful and humiliating experience of Apartheid and its eventual dismantling in South Africa, to show how wrong those well-intentioned people were to have ever believed this. Shame on them, you may say. They should have known better. That is my point. We *can* come to know better if we try our best to find out, and we have no excuse for not trying. Or do we? Are some topics off limits, no matter what the consequences?

Today, billions of people pray for peace, and I wouldn't be surprised if most of them believe with all their hearts that the best path to follow to peace throughout the world is a path that runs through their particular religious institution, whether it is Christianity, Judaism, Islam, Hinduism, Buddhism, or any of hundreds of other systems of religion. Indeed, many people think that the best hope for humankind is that we can bring together all of the religions of the world in a mutually respectful conversation and ultimate agreement on how to treat one another. They may be right, but *they don't know.* The fervor of their belief is no substitute for good hard evidence, and the evidence in favor of this beautiful hope is hardly overwhelming. In fact, it is not persuasive at all, since just as many people, apparently, sincerely believe that world peace is less important, in both the short run and the long, than the global triumph of their particular religion over its competition. Some see religion as the best hope for peace, a lifeboat we dare not rock lest we overturn it and all of us perish, and others see religious self-identification as the main source of conflict and violence in the world, and believe just as fervently that religious conviction is a terrible substitute for calm, informed reasoning. Good intentions pave both roads.

Who is right? I don't know. Neither do the billions of people with their passionate religious convictions. Neither do those atheists who are sure the world would be a much better place if all religion went extinct. There is an asymmetry: atheists in general welcome the most intensive and objective examination of their views, practices, and reasons. (In fact, their incessant demand for self-examination can become quite tedious.) The religious, in contrast, often bristle at the impertinence, the lack of respect, the *sacrilege*, implied by anybody who wants to investigate their views. I respectfully demur: there is indeed an ancient tradition to which they are appealing here, but it is mistaken and should not be permitted to continue. *This* spell must be broken, and broken now. Those who are religious and believe religion to be the best hope of humankind cannot reasonably expect those of us who are skeptical to refrain from expressing our doubts if they themselves are unwilling to put their convictions under the microscope. If they are right—especially if they are obviously right, on further reflection—we skeptics will not only concede this but enthusiastically join the cause. We want what they (mostly) say they want: a world at peace, with as little suffering as we can manage, with freedom and justice and well-being and meaning for all. If the case for their path cannot be made, *this is something that they themselves should want to know*. It is as simple as that. They claim the moral high ground; maybe they deserve it and maybe they don't. Let's find out. [...]

The question is not whether good science of religion as a natural phenomenon is possible: it is. The question is whether we should do it.

2 *SHOULD* SCIENCE STUDY RELIGION?

Look before you leap.—Aesop, "The Fox and the Goat"

Research is expensive and sometimes has harmful side effects. One of the lessons of the twentieth century is that scientists are not above confabulating justifications for the work they want to do, driven by insatiable curiosity. Are there in fact good reasons, aside from sheer curiosity, to try to develop the natural science of religion? Do we need this for anything? Would it help us choose policies, respond to problems, improve our world? What do we know about the future of religion? Consider five wildly different hypotheses:

1. *The Enlightenment is long gone; the creeping "secularization" of modern societies that has been anticipated for two centuries is evaporating before our eyes.* The tide is turning and religion is becoming more important than ever. In this scenario, religion soon resumes something like the dominant social and moral role it had before the rise of modern science in the seventeenth century. As people recover from their infatuation with technology and material comforts, spiritual identity becomes a person's most valued attribute, and populations come to be ever more sharply divided among Christianity, Islam, Judaism, Hinduism, and a few other major multinational religious organizations. Eventually—it might take another millennium, or it might be hastened by catastrophe—one major faith sweeps the planet.

2. *Religion is in its death throes; today's outbursts of fervor and fanaticism are but a brief and awkward transition to a truly modern society in which religion plays at most a ceremonial role.* In this scenario, although there may be some local and temporary revivals and even some violent catastrophes, the major religions of the world soon go just as extinct as the hundreds of minor religions that are vanishing faster than anthropologists can record them. Within the lifetimes of our grandchildren, Vatican City becomes the European Museum of Roman Catholicism, and Mecca is turned into Disney's Magic Kingdom of Allah.

3. *Religions transform themselves into institutions unlike anything seen before on the planet: basically creedless associations selling self-help and enabling moral teamwork, using ceremony and tradition to cement relationships and build "long-term fan loyalty."* In this scenario, being a member of a religion becomes more and more like being a Boston Red Sox fan, or a Dallas Cowboys fan. Different colors, different songs and cheers, different symbols, and vigorous competition—would you want your daughter to marry a Yankees fan?—but aside from a rabid few, everybody appreciates the importance of peaceful coexistence in a Global League of Religions. Religious art and music flourish, and friendly rivalry leads to a degree of specialization, with one religion priding itself on its environmental stewardship, providing clean water for the world's billions, while another becomes duly famous for its concerted defense of social justice and economic equality.

4. *Religion diminishes in prestige and visibility, rather like smoking; it is tolerated, since there are those who say they can't live without it, but it is discouraged, and teaching religion to impressionable young children is frowned upon in most societies and actually outlawed in others.* In this scenario, politicians who still practice religion can be elected if they prove themselves worthy in other regards, but few would advertise their religious affiliation—or affliction, as the politically incorrect insist on calling it. It is considered as rude to draw attention to the religion of somebody as it is to comment in public about his sexuality or whether she has been divorced.

5. *Judgment Day arrives. The blessed ascend bodily into heaven, and the rest are left behind to suffer the agonies of the damned, as the Antichrist is vanquished.* As the Bible prophecies foretold, the rebirth of the nation of Israel in 1948 and the ongoing conflict over Palestine are clear signs of the End Times, when the Second Coming of Christ sweeps all the other hypotheses into oblivion.

Other possibilities are describable, of course, but these five hypotheses highlight the extremes that are taken seriously. What is remarkable about the set is that just about anybody would find at least one of them preposterous, or troubling, or even deeply offensive, but every one of them is not just anticipated but yearned for. People act on what they yearn for. We are at cross-purposes about religion, to say the least, so we can anticipate problems, ranging from wasted effort and counterproductive campaigns if we are lucky to all-out war and genocidal catastrophe if we are not.

Only one of these hypotheses (at most) will turn out to be true; the rest are not just wrong but wildly wrong. Many people think they know which is true, but nobody does. Isn't that fact, all by itself, enough reason to study religion scientifically? Whether you want religion to flourish or perish, whether you think it should transform itself or stay just as it is, you can hardly deny that whatever happens will be of tremendous significance to the planet. It would be useful to your hopes, whatever they are, to know more about what is likely to happen and why. In this regard, it is worth noting how assiduously those who firmly believe in number 5 scan the world news for evidence of prophecies fulfilled. They sort and evaluate their sources, debating the pros and cons of various interpretations of those prophecies. They think there is a reason to investigate the future of religion, and they don't even think the course of future events lies within human power to determine. The rest of us have all the more reason to investigate the phenomena, since it is quite obvious that complacency and ignorance could lead us to squander our opportunities to steer the phenomena in what we take to be the benign directions. [...]

So what I am calling for is a concerted effort to achieve a mutual agreement under which religion—all religion—becomes a proper object of scientific study.

Here I find that opinion is divided among those who are already convinced that this would be a good idea, those who are dubious and inclined to doubt that it would be of much value, and those who find the proposal evil—offensive, dangerous, and stupid. Not wanting to preach to the converted, I am particularly concerned to address those who hate this idea, in hopes of persuading them that their repugnance is misplaced. This is a daunting task, like trying to persuade your friend with the cancer symptoms that she really ought to see a doctor *now*, since her anxiety may be misplaced and the sooner she learns that the sooner she can get on with her life, and if she does have cancer, timely intervention may make all the difference. Friends can get quite annoyed when you interfere with their denial at times like that, but perseverance is called for. Yes, I want to put religion on the examination table. If it is fundamentally benign, as many of its devotees insist, it should emerge just fine; suspicions will be put to rest and we can then concentrate on the few peripheral pathologies that religion, like every other natural phenomenon, falls prey to. If it is not, the sooner we identify the problems clearly the better. Will the inquiry itself generate some discomfort and embarrassment? Almost certainly, but that is a small price to pay. Is there a risk that such an invasive examination will make a healthy religion ill, or even disable it? Of course. There are always risks. Are they worth taking? Perhaps not, but I haven't yet seen an argument that persuades me of this, and we will soon consider the best of them. The only arguments worth attending to will have to demonstrate that (1) religion provides net benefits to humankind, and (2) these benefits would be unlikely to survive such an investigation. I, for one, fear that if we *don't* subject religion to such scrutiny now, and work out together whatever revisions and reforms are called for, we will pass on a legacy of ever more toxic forms of religion to our descendants. I can't prove that, and those who are dead sure that this will not happen are encouraged to say what supports their conviction, aside from loyalty to their tradition,

which goes without saying and doesn't count for anything here. [...]

4 THE DOMESTICATION OF RELIGIONS

Folk religions emerge out of the daily lives of people living in small groups, and share common features the world over. How and when did these metamorphose into organized religions? There is a general consensus among researchers that the big shift responsible was the emergence of agriculture and the larger settlements that this made both possible and necessary. Researchers disagree, however, on what to emphasize in this major transition. The creation of non-portable food stockpiles, and the resultant shift to fixed residence, permitted the emergence of an unprecedented division of labor (Seabright, 2004, is especially clear about this), and this in turn gave rise to *markets*, and opportunities for ever more specialized occupations. These new ways for people to interact created novel opportunities and novel needs. When you find that you have to deal on a daily basis with people *who are not your close kin*, the prospect of a few like-minded people forming a coalition that is quite different from an extended family must almost always present itself, and often be an attractive option. Boyer (2001) is not alone in arguing that the transition from folk religion to organized religion was primarily one of these market phenomena.

> Throughout history, guilds and other groups of craftsmen and specialists have tried to establish common prices and common standards and to stop non-guild members from delivering comparable services. By establishing a quasi monopoly, they make sure that all the custom comes their way. By maintaining common prices and common standards, they make it difficult for a particularly skilled or efficient member to undersell the others. So most people pay a small price for being members of a group that guarantees a

minimal share of the market to each of its members. [p. 275]

The first step to such organization is the big one, but the next steps, from a guild of priests or shamans to what are, in effect, *firms* (and *franchises* and *brand names*), are an almost inevitable consequence of the growing self-consciousness and market savvy of those individuals who joined to form the guilds in the first place. *Cui bono?* When individuals start asking themselves how best to enhance and preserve the organizations they have created, they radically change the focus of the question, bringing new selective pressures into existence.

Darwin appreciated this, and used the transition from what he called "unconscious" selection to "methodical" selection as a pedagogical bridge to explain his great idea of natural selection in the opening chapter of his masterpiece. [. . .]

> At the present time, eminent breeders try by methodical selection, with a distinct object in view, to make a new strain or sub-breed, superior to any existing in the country. But for our purpose, a kind of Selection, which may be called Unconscious, and which results from every one trying to possess and breed from the best individual animals, is more important. Thus a man who intends keeping pointers naturally tries to get as good dogs as he can, and afterwards breeds from his own best dogs, but he has no wish or expectation of permanently altering the breed. Nevertheless I cannot doubt that this process, continued during centuries, would improve and modify any breed....There is reason to believe that King Charles's spaniel has been unconsciously modified to a large extent since the time of that monarch. [pp. 34–35]

Domestication of both plants and animals occurred without any farseeing intention or invention on the part of the stewards of the seeds and studs. But what a stroke of good fortune for those lineages that became domesticated! All that remains of the ancestors of today's grains are small scattered patches of wild-grass cousins, and the nearest surviving relatives of all the domesticated animals could be carried off in a few arks. How clever of wild sheep to have acquired that most versatile adaptation, the shepherd! By forming a symbiotic alliance with *Homo sapiens*, sheep could *outsource* their chief survival tasks: food finding and predator avoidance. They even got shelter and emergency medical care thrown in as a bonus. The price they paid—losing the freedom of mate selection and being slaughtered instead of being killed by predators (if that is a cost)—was a pittance compared with the gain in offspring survival it purchased. But of course it wasn't *their* cleverness that explains the good bargain. It was the blind, foresightless cleverness of Mother Nature, evolution, which ratified the free-floating rationale of this arrangement. Sheep and other domesticated animals are, in fact, significantly more stupid than their wild relatives—because they can be. Their brains are smaller (relative to body size and weight), and this is not just due to their having been bred for muscle mass (meat). Since both the domesticated animals and their domesticators have enjoyed huge population explosions (going from less than 1 percent of the terrestrial vertebrate biomass ten thousand years ago to over 98 percent today [. . .]), there can be no doubt that this symbiosis was mutualistic—fitness-enhancing to both parties.

What I now want to suggest is that, alongside the domestication of animals and plants, there was a gradual process in which the wild (self-sustaining) memes of folk religion became thoroughly domesticated. They acquired stewards. Memes that are fortunate enough to have stewards, people who will work hard and use their intelligence to foster their propagation and protect them from their enemies, are relieved of much of the burden of keeping their own lineages going. In extreme cases, they no longer need to be particularly catchy, or appeal to our sensual instincts at all. The multiplication-table memes, for instance, to say nothing of the calculus memes, are hardly crowd-pleasers, and yet they are duly propagated by hardworking teachers—meme shepherds—whose responsibility it is to keep these lineages strong. The wild memes of language and folk religion, in other words, are like rats and squirrels, pigeons and cold viruses—magnificently adapted to living with us and exploiting us whether we like them or not. The domesticated memes, in contrast, depend on help from human guardians to keep going.

People have been poring over their religious practices and institutions for almost as long as they have been refining their agricultural practices and institutions, and these reflective examiners have all had agendas—individual or shared *conceptions* of what was valuable and why. Some have been wise and some foolish, some widely informed and some naïve, some pure and saintly, and some venal and vicious. Jared Diamond's hypothesis about the practically exhaustive search by our ancestors for domesticatable species in their neighborhoods [...] can be extended. Curious practitioners will also have uncovered whatever Good Tricks are in the nearest neighborhoods in the Design Space of possible religions. Diamond sees the transition from bands of fewer than a hundred people to tribes of hundreds to chiefdoms of thousands to states of over fifty thousand people as an inexorable march "from egalitarianism to kleptocracy," government by thieves. Speaking of chiefdoms, he remarks:

> At best, they do good by providing expensive services impossible to contract for on an individual basis. At worst, they function unabashedly as kleptocracies, transferring net wealth from commoners to upper classes....Why do the commoners tolerate the transfer of the fruits of their hard labor to kleptocrats? This question, raised by political theorists from Plato to Marx, is raised anew by voters in every modern election. [1997, p. 276]

There are four ways, he suggests, that kleptocrats have tried to maintain their power: (1) disarm the populace and arm the elite, (2) make the masses happy by redistributing much of the tribute received, (3) use the monopoly of force to promote happiness, by maintaining public order and curbing violence, or (4) construct an ideology or religion justifying kleptocracy (p. 277).

How might a religion support a kleptocracy? By an alliance between the political leader and the priests, of course, in which, first of all, the leader is declared to be divine, or descended from the gods, or, as Diamond puts it, at least having "a hotline to the gods."

> Besides justifying the transfer of wealth to kleptocrats, institutionalized religion brings two other important benefits to centralized societies. First, shared ideology or religion helps solve the problem of how unrelated individuals are to live together without killing each other—by providing them with a bond not based on kinship. Second, it gives people a motive, other than genetic self-interest, for sacrificing their lives on behalf of others. At the cost of a few society members who die in battle as soldiers, the whole society becomes much more effective at conquering other societies or resisting attacks. [p. 278]

So we find the same devices invented over and over again, in just about every religion, and many nonreligious organizations as well. None of this is new today—as Lord Acton said more than a century ago, "All power tends to corrupt; absolute power corrupts absolutely"—but it was new once upon a time, when our ancestors were first exploring design revisions to our most potent institutions. [...]

3 THE GROWTH MARKET IN RELIGION

In [...] *One True God: Historical Consequences of Monotheism* (2001), Stark takes on the role of memetic engineer, analyzing the pros and cons of doctrine as if he were an advertising consultant. "What sorts of Gods have the greatest appeal?" (p. 2). Here he distinguishes two strategies: *God as essence* (such as Tillich's God as the Ground of All Being, entirely nonanthropomorphic, not in time and space, abstract) and *God as conscious supernatural being* (a God who listens to and answers prayers in real time, for instance). "There is no more profound religious difference than that between faiths involving divine beings and those limited to divine essences," he says, and the latter he judges to be hopeless, because "only divine beings *do* anything" (p. 10). Supernatural conscious beings are much better sellers because "the supernatural is the only plausible source of many benefits we greatly desire" (p. 12).

> People care about Gods because, if they exist, they are potential exchange partners possessed of immense resources. Furthermore, untold billions of people are certain that Gods do exist, precisely because they believe they have experienced long and satisfying exchange relations with them [p. 13]....Because Gods are conscious beings, they are potential exchange partners because all beings are assumed to want something for which they might be induced to give something valuable. [p. 15]

He adds that a responsive, fatherly God "makes an extremely attractive exchange partner who can be counted on to maximize human benefits" (p. 21), and he even proposes that a God without a counterbalancing Satan is an unstable concept—"*irrational* and *perverse*." Why? Because "one God of infinite scope must be responsible for *everything*, evil as well as good, and thus must be dangerously capricious, shifting intentions unpredictably and without reason" (p. 24). This is pretty much the same *raison d'être* that Jerry Siegel and Joe Shuster, the creators of *Superman*, appreciated when they invented kryptonite as something to counteract the Man of Steel: there is no drama possible—no defeats to overcome, no cliff-hangers—if your hero is too powerful! But, unlike the concept of kryptonite, these concepts of God and Satan have free-floating rationales, and are not the brainchildren of any particular authors:

> I do not mean to suggest that this portrait of the Gods is the product of conscious human "creation." No one sat down and decided, Let's believe in a supreme God, surround him/her with some subordinate beings, and postulate an inferior evil being on whom we can blame evil. Rather, this view tends to evolve over time because it is the most reasonable and satisfying conclusion from the available religious culture. [pp. 25–26]

Stark's footnote on this passage is not to be missed: "Nor am I prepared to deny that this evolution reflects progressive human discovery of the truth." Ah, that's the ticket! The story doesn't just get better; it *happens* to get closer to the truth. A lucky break? Maybe not. Wouldn't a really good God arrange things that way? Maybe, but the fact that dramatic considerations so conveniently dictate the details of the story does provide an explanation of why the details are what they are that rivals the traditional supposition that they are simply "the God's honest truth." [...]

NOW WHAT DO WE DO?

My description of the evolution of various features of religion [...] is definitely "just a theory"—or, rather, a family of proto-theories, in need of further development. In a nutshell, this is what it says: Religion evolved, but it doesn't have to be good for us in order to evolve. (Tobacco isn't good for us, but it survives just fine.) We don't all learn language because we think it's good for us; we all learn language because we cannot do otherwise (if we have normal nervous systems). In the case of religion, there is a lot more teaching and drill, a lot more deliberate social pressure, than there is in language learning. In this regard, religion is more like reading than talking. There are tremendous benefits to being able to read, and perhaps there are similar or greater benefits to being religious. But people may well love religion independently of any benefits it provides them. (I am delighted to learn that red wine in moderation is good for my health, since, *whether or not* it is good for me, I like it, and I want to go on drinking it. Religion could be like that.) It is not surprising that religion survives. It has been pruned and revised and edited for thousands of years, with millions of variants extinguished in the process, so it has plenty of features that appeal to people, and plenty of features that preserve the identity of its recipes for these very features, features that ward off or confound enemies and competitors, and secure allegiance. Only gradually have people come to have any appreciation of the reasons—the heretofore free-floating rationales—for these features. Religion is many things to many people. For some, the memes of religion are mutualists, providing undeniable benefits of sorts that cannot be found elsewhere. These people may well depend for their very lives on religion, the way we all depend on the bacteria in our guts that help us digest our food. Religion provides some people with a motivated organization for doing great things—working for social justice, education, political action, economic reform, and so forth. For others, the memes of religion are more toxic, exploiting less savory aspects of their psychology, playing on guilt, loneliness, the longing for self-esteem and importance. Only when we can frame a comprehensive view of the many aspects of religion can we formulate defensible policies for how to respond to religions in the future.

Some aspects of this theory sketch are pretty well established, but getting down to specifics and generating further testable hypotheses is work for the future. I wanted to give readers a good idea of what a testable theory would be like, what sorts of questions it would raise, and what sorts of explanatory principles it could invoke. My theory sketch may well be false in many regards, but if so, this will be shown by confirming some alternative theory of the same sort. In science, the tactic is to

put forward something that can be either fixed or refuted by something better. [...]

Since my proto-theory is not yet established and may prove to be wrong, it shouldn't be used yet to guide our policies. Having insisted at the outset that we need to do much more research so that we can make well-informed decisions, I would be contradicting myself if I now proceeded to prescribe courses of action on the basis of my initial foray. Recall, from chapter 3, the moral that Taubes drew in his history of the misguided activism that led us on the low-fat crusade: "It's a story of what can happen when the demands of public health policy—and the demands of the public for simple advice—run up against the confusing ambiguity of real science." There is pressure on us all to act decisively today, on the basis of the little we already (think we) know, but I am counseling patience. The current situation is scary—one religious fanaticism or another could produce a global catastrophe, after all—but we should resist rash "remedies" and other overreactions. It is possible, however, to discuss *options* today, and to think *hypothetically* of what the sound policies *would be* if something like my account of religion is correct. Such a consideration of possible policies can help motivate the further research, giving us pressing reasons for finding out which hypotheses are really true. [...]

So here is the only prescription I will make categorically and without reservation: Do more research. There is an alternative, and I am sure it is still hugely appealing to many people: Let's just close our eyes, trust to tradition, and wing it. Let's just *take it on faith* that religion is the key—or one of the keys—to our salvation. How can I quarrel with faith (for heaven's sake)? *Blind* faith? Please. Think. This is where we began. [...]

References

Boyer, Peter. *Religion Explained: The Evolutionary Origins of Religious Thought* (New York: Basic Books, 2001).

Bulbulia, Joseph. "Religious Costs as Adaptations that Signal Altruistic Intention," *Evolution and Cognition* 19 (2004): 19–42.

Burkert, Walter. *Creation of the Sacred: Tracks of Biology in Early Religions* (Cambridge, MA: Harvard University Press, 1996).

Darwin, Charles. *On the Origin of Species by Means of Natural Selection* (London, Murray, 1859).

Diamond, Jared. *Guns, Germs, and Steel: The Fates of Human Societies* (New York: Norton, 1997).

Stark, Rodney. *One True God: Historical Consequences of Monotheism* (Princeton: Princeton University Press, 2001).

Stark, Rodney and Roger Finke. *Acts of Faith: Explaining the Human Side of Religion* (Berkeley: University of California Press, 2000).

Study Questions

1. What are the reasons that Dennett thinks it is so important for science to study religion?

2. Which of the five hypotheses for the future of religion that Dennett describes do you think is most likely to be true? Why?

3. How plausible do you find Dennett's evolutionary explanation of religious belief? Why?

CHAPTER 2

Skepticism and the Analysis of Knowledge

James Beebe and Anand J. Vaidya

WHAT IS EPISTEMOLOGY?

Some of the most enduring questions of philosophy have been questions of *epistemology*—the philosophical study of knowledge and rationally justified belief. Epistemologists try to specify the requirements that a belief must satisfy in order to be justified or to count as knowledge. Epistemologists also investigate the extent of human knowledge. That is, they try to determine whether we can have genuine knowledge in certain domains via sense perception, reasoning, and the testimony of others. They also examine whether we can provide convincing responses to those (often called *skeptics*) who wish to challenge our claims to know. This unit presents works from the ancient world (second century CE), the modern period (beginning in the seventeenth century and continuing at least into the nineteenth), and the twentieth century that address different ways in which one might challenge the idea that we have genuine knowledge of reality, whether knowledge is justified true belief, and how it is that we should come to answer questions of epistemology.

Epistemologists have generally agreed that in order for a belief to count as knowledge, the belief must be held with a sufficiently strong degree of confidence, and it must also be true. They also agree that a belief must be *justified* or *warranted* to a sufficiently strong degree (e.g., by being supported by one's evidence). However, as we will explain later, providing an adequate explanation of this third requirement for knowledge has proven surprisingly difficult and there is no philosophical consensus on what the correct view is. According to this standard view of knowledge, one cannot know what is false, and one cannot obtain knowledge simply by having a true belief.

Justification and truth are distinct but importantly related matters. A belief is true just when it matches the facts, and a justification provides some reason for thinking that a belief matches the facts. Justification can be obtained from sound reasoning, observation, testimony, or introspection. If, for example, you awake to find that something has apparently chewed a hole in a sack of food in your kitchen, this may provide some reason for thinking that a mouse has been in your kitchen overnight. However, in the absence of any further evidence, your justification for believing that the culprit was a mouse rather than some other kind of animal may not be very strong. Perhaps it was a rat, a cat, or a rather large insect. If you also discover mouse droppings on the floor of your kitchen, you will then have stronger evidence for the presence of a mouse and your belief will be justified to a stronger degree. The rational justification of beliefs, then, comes in degrees. The degree of justification you possess for a given belief will be a function of the quantity and quality of the evidence or reasons you possess.

Epistemologists agree that a very small amount of evidence in favor of a true belief will not be sufficient to render that belief an instance of knowledge. Contemporary epistemologists also tend to agree that having a maximally strong or infallible justification is not necessary either. An infallible justification is one that guarantees the truth of that belief. It is impossible for you to possess this kind of justification and for your belief to be false. Thus, many contemporary thinkers endorse *fallibilism*: the view that one can have knowledge even when one's evidence does not guarantee the truth of what one believes.

Epistemologists throughout the history of philosophy have examined the question of whether it is possible to have infallible justification for one's beliefs and, if so, what the source of this kind of justification might be. If it were possible to have infallible justification for one's beliefs, one could enjoy the highest level of rational confidence in one's belief and one would also have a foolproof defense against those who might raise skeptical challenges against one's belief.

ANCIENT SKEPTICISM

The most influential ancient discussion of skepticism was *Outlines of Pyrrhonism* by Sextus Empiricus (c. 160–210 CE), a Greek physician and philosopher. Of the two great traditions of ancient skepticism, Academic and Pyrrhonist, only the latter called themselves "skeptics." The name "Pyrrhonism" is derived from Pyrrho of Elis (c. 365–270 BCE), who taught that suspending belief (as opposed to believing one way or the other) on matters that are uncertain could free one from a great deal of intellectual and emotional turmoil. Sextus describes the (Pyrrhonian) skeptic as someone who is still searching for the truth, as opposed to those he calls "Dogmatists," who believe they have already found the truth, and to the Academics, who believe that the truth cannot be discovered. Sextus insisted that the Academics were not genuine skeptics because firmly believing that the truth cannot be discovered involves having the same high degree of confidence that one knows what reality is like as the Dogmatists.

The Pyrrhonian skeptic proceeds by setting impressions, beliefs, or arguments against one another and showing how they often seem to cancel each other out. As you study philosophy, you may have the experience of thinking that, no matter how strong an argument in favor of one philosophical position may be, there will almost always be an equally strong argument in favor of the opposite position. This can make it quite difficult to decide which position to believe. The Pyrrhonian skeptic specializes in showing how this can be done for almost every fundamental topic of philosophical debate and argues that to spend one's time worrying about how to show that one side is really correct will only lead yourself and others into frustration. In such a case the Pyrrhonian advises you to not accept either side.

A statue appears one way to you in the bright morning sun and a different way to you at dusk. It appears one way to someone with good eyesight and a different way to someone with poor vision. One scholar argues that the statue is distinct from the block of stone out of which it was hewn, while another disagrees. The Pyrrhonian skeptic claims that those who suspend belief in the face of widespread and seemingly endless disagreement about the nature of things will have greater peace of mind than those who continue to strive to show that one theory about the underlying causes of things is superior to its rivals. Sextus contended that suspending belief on a wide variety of matters should not render life unlivable. He believed that it was permissible to accept propositions about how things appear and to let these appearances guide one's daily, practical life without endorsing any beliefs or theories about the underlying causes of these appearances.

Debates about the limits of human knowledge can be found in every period of the history of philosophy. On the one hand, it seems that we should agree with Socrates, the first statesman of philosophy, who claimed it is better to recognize that we don't have knowledge or wisdom in some domain than to go on thinking that we have such knowledge or wisdom when in fact we do not. The skeptic claims to be able to help us achieve this kind of "Socratic wisdom." On the other hand, as Aristotle once said, all humans by nature desire to know. We want to know and understand our world. The question of how it is possible to have genuine knowledge of the world in light of the many reasons for doubting our knowledge has been a perennial source of epistemological reflection.

THE METHOD OF CARTESIAN DOUBT

In the first part of his *Meditations on First Philosophy*, French philosopher and mathematician René Descartes (1596–1650) set out his method of doubt in an attempt to discover what, if anything, he fundamentally knows with certainty. The basic structure of his method of doubt can be given through a schematic argument, where P stands for some particular statement that one claims to know.

I know for certain that P is true, only if I cannot doubt that P is true.
I can doubt that P is true.
So, I do not know that P.

In the first meditation Descartes considers a variety of things he might know against the background of four distinct skeptical hypotheses. In general, the kinds of things that Descartes considers fall into two categories: the *a priori* and the *a posteriori*. A *priori* knowledge is knowledge that one has independent of sense experience. So, for example, when one reasons to the conclusion that 14 + 7 = 21, one's knowledge in that case is independent of sense experience and based on reason alone. On the other hand, *a posteriori* knowledge is knowledge that depends on sense experience. So, for example, when you come to know that there is a table in front of you by your visual and tactile experience, you come to have *a posteriori* knowledge. Descartes organizes his investigation of skepticism into three different strengths of skepticism.

The first kind of skepticism is based on sense deception, the fact that your senses on occasion deceive you about your external environment. For example, when one looks at an oar under water, the oar looks bent, although it is straight. This is a case in which our senses deceive us by presenting as true something that is not. Descartes wonders how it is that we can rule out that our senses are not deceiving us at any given time. If we cannot rule out that our senses are deceiving us—and it is difficult to see how we could do this "from the inside," as it were—we must accept that all of what we think we know based on sense experience is in fact not certain knowledge. We don't know that there is a table in front of us when we are looking at it because we cannot rule out that our senses are deceiving us. However, even if we cannot know the external world because knowledge of it depends on sense experience, the skepticism based on sense deception is not strong enough to undermine *a priori* knowledge, since it is knowledge that is *not* based on sense experience.

The second kind of skepticism Descartes considers is based upon dreaming. The central idea is that in a dream one is presented with a picture or image of something that feels exactly as it would feel if one were not dreaming. Suppose you are having a vivid dream in which you are running a marathon but you are not aware that you are dreaming. It will be the case that how things seem to you is indistinguishable from how things would actually seem in reality. Based upon this idea, Descartes argues that we can know facts about the external world, such as that we are running a marathon, only if we can rule out the possibility that we are dreaming. But since it seems that we cannot rule out this possibility, we may not know facts about the external world based upon sense experience. One important aspect of skepticism based on dreaming is that Descartes believes it is possible in our dreams to create objects that do not exist in reality at all, but that it is impossible for us to create in our dreams objects that have parts that we have not learned about from sense experience. For example, one can dream of a mermaid by putting the body of a woman on the body of a fish. What is represented is a creature that does not exist in reality. However, one cannot dream up or invent the body of a woman or the body of a fish. Dreams allow for recombination of ideas, but they do not allow for the construction of the basic units out of which things can be recombined. In this sense, Descartes acknowledges that we still are connected to an external world, because the contents of our dreams have to come from somewhere, even though at any given time we may not know anything about the contents of the external world if we are unable to rule out the possibility that we are dreaming. Finally, in a dream Descartes maintains that we still know *a priori* truths, since one can see that 2 + 2 must equal 4, regardless of whether one is dreaming.

A third kind of skepticism that Descartes considers is based on the notion of an evil demon or evil genius. The evil demon has the following important properties. It is able to control what you think, to put beliefs in your mind, and to control your mind in a totalizing way. Importantly, the evil demon has the ability to make you believe whatever he wants and to provide you with evidence that would make you think you actually know something. For example, an evil demon could make you believe that you are running a race and also make you feel as if you are running the race, even though you are doing nothing other than sitting in a chair. What is of central importance to skepticism based on the evil demon is that the evil demon has the ability to call into question one's knowledge of *a priori* truths. For we only know that 2 + 2 = 4 if we can rule out that an evil demon has not implanted in our mind the idea that 2 and 2 go together to make 4. And since we cannot rule out that an evil demon is deceiving us because if he were there would be no way for us to tell that we were being deceived, we do not even know any *a priori* truths. Skepticism based on the evil demon is the strongest kind of skepticism that Descartes considers in the first meditation.

BERKELEY'S IDEALISM

Irish bishop and philosopher George Berkeley (1685–1753) is famous for having defended the metaphysical position known as idealism. Berkeley's idealism maintains that the essence of things lies in their perception: to be is to be perceived. This position is in opposition to realism, the idea that there exists a mind-independent reality. An important component of Berkeley's idealism is that it also serves as an approach to responding to skepticism about the external world. The following line of reasoning captures the strategy. Skepticism about the external world can be understood as the claim that we have no grounds for believing that we know anything with certainty about the external world. One implication of this is that there is an external world that is independent of our minds, which is such that we cannot know anything about it. Berkeley's idealism challenges the idea that there is a mind-independent reality. If there is no mind-independent reality, and all of reality is mind dependent, then there is no way in which we can raise a doubt about whether or not we know a mind-independent reality.

Berkeley challenges realism along the following lines. There is a mind-independent reality only if it is possible for us to conceive of an object unconceived by anyone. Conceiving of an object is the mental equivalent of perceiving an object through vision. It is impossible to perceive an object unperceived by anyone since one would have to perceive it himself or herself. So, it is impossible to conceive of an object unconceived by anyone. So, there is no mind-independent reality. The argument has drawn the attention of great minds ever since it was produced.

MOORE'S COMMONSENSE RESPONSE TO SKEPTICISM

Common sense tells us that humans have hands, and that we know that we have hands. The skeptic tells us that it doesn't follow from the fact that we can see our hands that we know we have hands. The skeptic's reasons for saying this are that in order for us to know that we have hands, we must be able to rule out that we are dreaming or that our senses are deceiving us, and since we cannot do that, we don't know that we have hands. But common sense persists. We want to say the following: "While it might be true that we don't know many of the things we claim to know, such as the exact height of Mount Everest, it must be the case that an ordinary person when looking at his or her hands in an everyday normal situation knows that he or she has hands because he or she can see them, feel them, and control them by moving them." But the skeptic persists: "How do you know? Couldn't it be a dream?"

In a famous lecture titled "Proof of an External World" G. E. Moore gave a lecture in which he made some statements as part of a performance that he took to constitute a proof of an external world. Moore said:

> I can prove now, for instance, that two human hands exist. How? By holding up my two hands, and saying, as I make a certain gesture with the right hand, "Here is one hand," and adding, as I make a certain gesture with the left, "and here is another." And if, by doing this, I have proved ipso facto the existence of external things, you will all see that I can also do it now in a number of other ways: there is no need to multiply examples.
>
> But did I prove just now that two human hands were then in existence? I do want to insist that I did; that the proof which I gave was a perfectly rigorous one. And that it is perhaps impossible to give a better or more rigorous proof of anything whatever.

Moore claims that his performance of pointing to each of his hands by the opposite hand and saying, "here is one" and "here is another" constitutes a proof of external things. How does this statement fare against the skeptic? There are two things that need to be considered. First, is Moore's proof a successful proof of the existence of things external to us? Is it successful in the relevant sense of what is meant by "external" when the skeptic challenges our knowledge of the external world? Second, suppose that Moore's proof of the existence of an external world is successful. How does that challenge affect the epistemic skeptic that claims that one does not know that an external world exists, even if it does exist?

Philosophers have taken a host of positions on Moore's proof. Some have argued that his proof is unsuccessful as a proof of an external world. Others have thought that it is a successful proof of an external world, but that it does not answer the skeptic, since it is not a proof that one knows the external world. Yet others have thought that there is something absolutely ingenious in the idea that one can refute the skeptic by such a simple strategy.

GETTIER'S EPISTEMOLOGICAL CHALLENGE

A long-standing belief of Western philosophy that traces its roots back to Plato is the idea that knowledge is to be understood as justified true belief. To know that there is a table in front of you is to have a justified true belief that there is a table in front of you. The requirement of justification means that merely possessing true belief is insufficient for knowledge. So if you enter a strange, pitch-black room and simply guess that there is a table in front of you, that would not be enough for you to know it (even if the table is there). Knowledge requires more than a correct guess. The requirement of truth rules out justified beliefs that are, after all, false. Suppose you have good reason to believe a table is in front of you, but it is in fact an elaborately contrived illusion. Again, we would not say you have knowledge. American philosopher Edmund Gettier's (1927–) "Is Knowledge Justified True Belief" is considered to be one of the most important articles of twentieth-century epistemology. In this short piece Gettier challenges the classical conception of knowledge as justified true belief. He does so by providing intuitive cases in which a subject has a justified true belief but does not have knowledge. The idea is that if there are genuine cases of justified true belief without knowledge, then it cannot be the case that s knows that p if and only if s has a justified true belief that p. Something more must be required.

Consider the following case: Suppose that Jones believes his friend Smith owns a Ford because Smith always takes Jones to work in a Ford. Further suppose that Jones infers from this fact that one of his friends owns a Ford. Now suppose that in actuality Smith does not own a Ford; rather, he has just been renting one for the past two years during which Jones has known him. And further suppose that unbeknownst to Jones, one of his friends, Brown, who he has not seen in a long time, has just bought a Ford. Does Jones *know* that one of his friends owns a Ford?

The Gettier intuition is that Jones does not *know* that one of his friends owns a Ford. And this is maintained even though one of his friends, Brown, does own a Ford, and Jones actually has a justified true belief that one of his friends owns a Ford. The central idea supporting the Gettier intuition is that there are cases in which a person can have a justified belief in a statement, even though the justification for his or her belief does not come from the fact that makes the statement true.

RELIABILISM

While many epistemologists focus on finding the correct understanding of knowledge, there is also a considerable amount of attention that needs to be paid to other epistemic notions. Aside from knowledge, justification is the other concept in epistemology that has occupied the attention of many philosophers in the twentieth century. A traditional conception of justification holds that to have a justified belief on this conception is to have the capacity to engage in justifying a belief by offering a defense of it or an argument in favor of it, and to be further able to respond to objections to the defense. Conceiving of justification in this way requires that the agent be able to state reasons in favor of the belief and to coherently put them together in an argument.

In Goldman's "What Is Justified Belief?" he challenges this traditional conception of justification as involving the capacity to defend a belief by argument. Instead of assuming that a theory of justification must be an account that involves how an individual is able to defend a belief, he simply sets out to look for the set of conditions that make true the claim that S's belief at time t is justified. The requirement he imposes on a correct account is that it not be written in terms that are part of a theory of knowledge, since the theory is meant to explain the notion of justification.

In searching for a correct account of the truth conditions of "S's belief at time t is justified," Goldman argues against a number of accounts. Ultimately, Goldman articulates his own account, which is known as the *process reliabilism* account of justification. Roughly, this account maintains that a belief is justified if and only if it is the output of a reliable belief-forming process. An example of a reliable process is a properly functioning thermometer that is used in the environment for which it was built. Correspondingly, an example of an unreliable process would be a broken thermometer, which gives the correct temperature only 1 out of a 1,000 times. Goldman's account leaves it open whether a subject that is justified would know that he or she is justified. One may have a belief that is the output of a reliable belief-forming process even though one does not know that it is the output of a reliable belief-forming process.

EXPERIMENTAL EPISTEMOLOGY

In recent years experimental philosophers have begun to use the experimental methods of the cognitive sciences to shed light on debates within epistemology. Primarily, their contributions begin from the fact that most of the major movements and innovations of the last fifty years of contemporary epistemological debate have relied heavily upon intuitions elicited by key thought experiments. All of these uses of philosophical thought experiments are based on the assumption that the intuitions they elicit will be widely shared—indeed, that they *ought* to be shared by anyone who possesses the concepts of knowledge and justified belief and who has at least minimal capacities for reflection upon the correct application of those concepts. Recently, some work in experimental epistemology has put this simple assumption to the test, and the results have often been surprising.

As we saw earlier, Gettier famously introduced a class of cases in which subjects have justified true beliefs that do not appear to count as knowledge—at least in the eyes of professional epistemologists in the Western analytic tradition. Shaun Nichols, Stephen Stich, and Jonathan Weinberg, however, wanted to see how widespread this intuition was. So, they presented a Gettier case to participants from different cultural backgrounds. A report of their experiment is reprinted in this unit. Surprisingly, they found that, while most American college students of European ancestry (i.e., "westerners") gave the response that is widely viewed by Western epistemologists to be correct, many American college students of East Asian (i.e., Korean, Japanese, and Chinese) and South Asian (i.e., Indian, Pakistani, Bangladeshi) descent did not. Seventy-four percent of Western participants surveyed agreed that the protagonist in the story did not really know the fact in question, but 53 percent of East Asians and 61 percent of South Asians thought that he did.

Because of the importance in epistemology of thinking about skeptical challenges to our knowledge, Nichols, Stich, and Weinberg also presented participants with cases in which the possibility that an agent's belief is false is made vivid or salient to the reader but where this possibility is not something that the agent in question considers. Readers are also told that the possibility that the agent's belief is mistaken is merely a possibility—that is, it does not represent the actual world. A variety of epistemological theories predict that mentioning such a possibility should disincline participants to attribute knowledge to that agent. Contrary to this prediction, Nichols, Stich, and Weinberg found that South Asians appear to be much less likely than their Western counterparts to deny that the agents have knowledge in such cases.

When intuitive responses are found to diverge in cases where it had been previously assumed they would be unanimous, a challenge is posed to the evidential and argumentative force of these cases. If everyone who possessed the concept of knowledge agreed that the protagonists in Gettier cases lack knowledge, the cases could be persuasively used to impugn the "justified true belief" account of knowledge. But if there is significant disagreement, matters become more complicated. It could be that some respondents are simply confused or perhaps some participants (e.g., from one culture) are operating with one concept of knowledge, whereas other participants (e.g., from another culture) are operating with a different one. Some have suggested that in cases of disagreement, greater weight should be given to the intuitions of experts than to those of the philosophically untrained. Several experimental philosophers have suggested that the diversity and instability of epistemic intuitions point to a more radical conclusion, that is, that intuitions should not be used as evidence in philosophical theorizing at all.

Most epistemologists seem to believe (1) that whether a true belief counts as knowledge depends only upon epistemic factors such as evidence or reliability, and (2) that because the target of philosophical analyses of knowledge is the ordinary person's concept of knowledge, such analyses should be answerable to data about "what the ordinary person would say" in response to various epistemological thought experiments. However, work in experimental epistemology is beginning to show that the judgments ordinary people make about knowledge, justification, and evidence are quite variable, unstable, and possibly even irrational. While it may be possible to dismiss a small class of the surprising patterns of variation as due to performance errors or noise, if more and more experimental data is gathered that shows that ordinary people's knowledge attributions are influenced by a variety of nonepistemic factors such as culture, education, socioeconomic status, and the moral properties of actions, it will become increasingly difficult to endorse the conjunction of (1) and (2). Regardless of the fate of these two claims, to the degree that epistemologists engage with the ordinary person's notions of knowledge, evidence, and justified belief, they need to understand what those notions are—in all of their (perhaps messy) details. Experimental epistemology is currently attempting to provide us with this important kind of understanding.

Suggestions for Further Reading

Alexander, Joshua, and Jonathan M. Weinberg. "Analytic Epistemology and Experimental Philosophy." *Philosophy Compass* 2 (2007): 56.

Beebe, James, and Wesley Buckwalter. "The Epistemic Side-Effect Effect." *Mind & Language* 25 (2010): 474–498.

Bermudez, Jose. "Cartesian Skepticism: Arguments and Antecedents." In *The Oxford Handbook of Skepticism*, ed. John Greco. Oxford: Oxford University Press, 2008.

Campbell, John. "Berkeley's Puzzle." In *Conceivability and Possibility*, ed. Tamar Gendler and John Hawthorne, 127–145. Oxford: Oxford University Press, 2002.

Burnyeat, M., ed. *The Skeptical Tradition*. Berkeley: University of California Press, 1983.

Gallois, Andre. "Berkeley's Master Argument." *Philosophical Review* 83, no. 1 (1974): 55–69.

Goldman, Alvin, "Reliabilism." *The Stanford Encyclopedia of Philosophy* (Spring 2011 Edition), Edward N. Zalta (ed.). http://plato.stanford.edu/archives/spr2011/entries/reliabilism/ (accessed March 16, 2012).

Ichikawa, Jonathan. "Skepticism and the Imagination Model of Dreaming." *Philosophical Quarterly* 58, no. 232 (2009): 519–527.

Nagel, Jennifer. "Epistemic Intuitions." *Philosophy Compass* 2 (2007): 792–819.

Steup, Matthias, "The Analysis of Knowledge." *The Stanford Encyclopedia of Philosophy* (Fall 2008 Edition), Edward N. Zalta (ed.). http://plato.stanford.edu/archives/fall2008/entries/knowledge-analysis/ (accessed March 16, 2012).

Swain, Stacey, Joshua Alexander, and Jonathan M. Weinberg. "The Instability of Philosophical Intuitions: Running Hot and Cold on Truetemp." *Philosophy and Phenomenological Research* 76 (2008): 138–155.

Thorsrud, Harold. "Ancient Greek Skepticism." In *The Internet Encyclopedia of Philosophy,* ed. Jim Fieser and Bradley Dowden. http://www.iep.utm.edu/skepanci/ (accessed March 13, 2012).

Vogel, Jonathan. "Cartesian Skepticism and Inference to the Best Explanation." *Journal of Philosophy* 87, no. 11 (1990): 658–666.

Williams, Bernard. "Imagination and the Self." In *Problems of the Self*, ed. B. Williams, 26–45. Cambridge: Cambridge University Press, 1999.

Outlines of Pyrrhonism

2.1

SEXTUS EMPIRICUS

Sextus Empiricus's (c. 160–210 CE) *Outlines of Pyrrhonism* contains the most important discussion of skepticism from the ancient world. Sextus's works had little impact in the ancient world and indeed were virtually unknown in the Western world until they were rediscovered in the sixteenth century. After that time they had a considerable impact upon the thought of many leading philosophers in the early modern period, such as Michel de Montaigne, René Descartes, and David Hume.

Sextus describes the Pyrrhonian skeptic as someone who does not endorse any speculative explanation of the underlying causes or essences of the appearances that we encounter in our daily lives. In fact, the skeptic does not even endorse the view that such explanations can or cannot be found. When faced with deep and abiding disagreement about some philosophical matter, the ancient skeptic advises us to suspend belief or withhold judgment. Instead of thinking that we will find intellectual peace of mind when we have discovered and successfully defended the true explanation for reality, Sextus suggests that we will find greater inner tranquility when we opt out of the endless game of striving to show that one highly speculative view is superior to others.

BOOK I

Chapter I. Of the Main Difference between Philosophic Systems

The natural result of any investigation is that the investigators either discover the object of search or deny that it is discoverable and confess it to be inapprehensible or persist in their search. So, too, with regard to the objects investigated by philosophy, this is probably why some have claimed to have discovered the truth, others have asserted that it cannot be apprehended, while others again go on inquiring. Those who believe, they have discovered it are the "Dogmatists," specially so called—Aristotle, for example, and Epicurus and the Stoics and certain others; Cleitomachus and Carneades and other Academics treat it as inapprehensible: the Sceptics keep on searching. Hence it seems reasonable to hold that the main types of philosophy are three—the Dogmatic, the Academic, and the Sceptic. Of the other systems it will best become others to speak: our task at present is to describe in outline the Sceptic doctrines first premising that of none of our future statements do we positively affirm that the fact is exactly as we state it, but we simply record each fact, like a chronicler, as it appears to us at the moment.

Chapter II. Of the Arguments of Scepticism

Of the Sceptic philosophy one argument (or branch of exposition) is called "general," the other "special." In the general argument we set forth the distinctive features of Scepticism, stating its purport and principles, its logical methods, criterion, and end or aim; the "Tropes," also, or "Modes," which lead to suspension of

Sextus Empiricus, *Outlines of Pyrrhonism*, translated by R. G. Bury (London: W. Heinemann, 1933).

judgement, and in what sense we adopt the Sceptic formulae, and the distinction between Scepticism and the philosophies which stand next to it. In the special argument we state our objections regarding the several divisions of so-called philosophy. Let us, then, deal first with the general argument, beginning our description with the names given to the Sceptic School.

Chapter III. Of the Nomenclature of Scepticism

The Sceptic School, then, is also called "Zetetic" from its activity in investigation and inquiry, and "Ephectic" or Suspensive from the state of mind produced in the inquirer after his search, and "Aporetic" or Dubitative either from its habit of doubting and seeking, as some say, or from its indecision as regards assent and denial, and "Pyrrhonean" from the fact that Pyrrho appears to us to have applied himself to Scepticism more thoroughly and more conspicuously than his predecessors.

Chapter IV. What Scepticism Is

Scepticism is an ability, or mental attitude, which opposes appearances to judgements in any way whatsoever, with the result that, owing to the equipollence of the objects and reasons thus opposed, we are brought firstly to a state of mental suspense and next to a state of "unperturbedness" or quietude. Now we call it an "ability" not in any subtle sense, but simply in respect of its "being able." By "appearances" we now mean the objects of sense-perception, whence we contrast them with the objects of thought or "judgements." The phrase "in any way whatsoever" can be connected either with the word "ability," to make us take the word "ability," as we said, in its simple sense, or with the phrase "opposing appearances to judgements"; for inasmuch as we oppose these in a variety of ways—appearances to appearances, or judgements to judgements, or alternando appearances to judgements,—in order to ensure the inclusion of all these antitheses we employ the phrase "in any way whatsoever." Or, again, we join "in any way whatsoever" to "appearances and judgements" in

order that we may not have to inquire how the appearances appear or how the thought-objects are judged, but may take these terms in the simple sense. The phrase "opposed judgements" we do not employ in the sense of negations and affirmations only but simply as equivalent to "conflicting judgements." "Equipollence" we use of equality in respect of probability and improbability, to indicate that no one of the conflicting judgements takes precedence of any other as being more probable. "Suspense" is a state of mental rest owing to which we neither deny nor affirm anything. "Quietude" is an untroubled and tranquil condition of soul. And how quietude enters the soul along with suspension of judgement we shall explain in our chapter (XII) "Concerning the End."

Chapter V. Of the Sceptic

In the definition of the system there is also implicitly included that of the Pyrrhonean philosopher: he is the man who participates in this "ability."

Chapter VI. Of the Principles of Scepticism

The originating cause of Scepticism is, we say, the hope of attaining quietude. Men of talent, who were perturbed by the contradictions in things and in doubt as to which of the alternatives they ought to accept, were led on to inquire what is true in things and what false, hoping by the settlement of this question to attain quietude. The main basic principle of the Sceptic system is that of opposing to every proposition an equal proposition; for we believe that as a consequence of this we end by ceasing to dogmatize.

Chapter VII. Does the Sceptic Dogmatize?

When we say that the Sceptic refrains from dogmatizing we do not use the term "dogma," as some do, in the broader sense of "approval of a thing" (for the Sceptic gives assent to the feelings which are the necessary results of sense-impressions, and he would not, for example, say when feeling hot or cold "I believe that I am not hot or cold"); but we say that "he does not dogmatize" using "dogma" in the sense, which some give it, of "assent to one of the non-evident objects of scientific inquiry"; for the Pyrrhonean philosopher assents to nothing that is non-evident. Moreover, even in the act of enunciating the Sceptic formulae concerning things non-evident—such as the formula "No more (one thing than another)," or the formula "I determine nothing," or any of the others which we shall presently mention he does not dogmatize. For whereas the dogmatizer posits the things about which he is said to be dogmatizing as really existent, the Sceptic does not posit these formulae in any absolute sense; for he conceives that, just as the formula "All things are false" asserts the falsity of itself as well as of everything else, as does the formula "Nothing is true," so also the formula "No more" asserts that itself, like all the rest, is "No more (this than that)," and thus cancels itself along with the rest. And of the other formulae we say the same. If then, while the dogmatizer posits the matter of his dogma as substantial truth, the Sceptic enunciates his formulae so that they are virtually cancelled by themselves, he should not be said to dogmatize in his enunciation of them. And, most important of all, in his enunciation of these formulae he states what appears to himself and announces his own impression in an undogmatic way, without making any positive assertion regarding the external realities.

Chapter VIII. Has the Sceptic a Doctrinal Rule?

We follow the same lines in replying to the question "Has the Sceptic a doctrinal rule?" For if one defines a "doctrinal rule" as "adherence to a number of dogmas which are dependent both on one another and on appearances," and defines "dogma" as "assent to a nonevident proposition," then we shall say that he has not a doctrinal rule. But if one defines "doctrinal rule" as "procedure which, in accordance with appearance, follows a certain line of reasoning, that reasoning indicating how it is possible to seem to live rightly (the word 'rightly' being taken, not as referring to virtue only, but in a wider sense) and tending to enable one to suspend judgement,"

then we say that he has a doctrinal rule. For we follow a line of reasoning which, in accordance with appearances, points us to a life conformable to the customs of our country and its laws and institutions, and to our own instinctive feelings.

Chapter IX. Does the Sceptic Deal with Physics?

We make a similar reply also to the question "Should the Sceptic deal with physical problems?" For while, on the one hand, so far as regards making, firm and positive assertions about any of the matters dogmatically treated in physical theory, we do not deal with physics; yet, on the other hand, in respect of our mode of opposing to every proposition an equal proposition and of our theory of quietude we do treat of physics. This, too, is the way in which we approach the logical and ethical branches of so-called "philosophy."

Chapter X. Do the Sceptics Abolish Appearances?

Those who say that "the Sceptics abolish appearances," or phenomena, seem to me to be unacquainted with the statements of our School. For, as we said above, we do not overthrow the affective sense-impressions which induce our assent involuntarily; and these impressions are "the appearances." And when we question whether the underlying object is such as it appears, we grant the fact that it appears, and our doubt does not concern the appearance itself but the account given of that appearance,—and that is a different thing from questioning the appearance itself. For example, honey appears to us to be sweet (and this we grant, for we perceive sweetness through the senses), but whether it is also sweet in its essence is for us a matter of doubt, since this is not an appearance but a judgement regarding the appearance. And even if we do actually argue against the appearances, we do not propound such arguments with the intention of abolishing appearances, but by way of pointing out the rashness of the Dogmatists; for if reason is such a trickster as to all but snatch away the appearances from under our very eyes, surely we should view it with suspicion in the case of things non-evident so as not to display rashness by following it.

Chapter XI. Of the Criterion of Scepticism

That we adhere to appearances is plain from what we say about the Criterion of the Sceptic School. The word "Criterion" is used in two senses: in the one it means "the standard regulating belief in reality or unreality," (and this we shall discuss in our refutation); in the other it denotes the standard of action by conforming to which in the conduct of life we perform some actions and abstain from others; and it is of the latter that we are now speaking. The criterion, then, of the Sceptic School is, we say, the appearance, giving this name to what is virtually the sense-presentation. For since this lies in feeling and involuntary affection, it is not open to question. Consequently, no one, I suppose, disputes that the underlying object has this or that appearance; the point in dispute is whether the object is in reality such as it appears to be.

Adhering, then, to appearances we live in accordance with the normal rules of life, undogmatically, seeing that we cannot remain wholly inactive. And it would seem that this regulation of life is fourfold, and that one part of it lies in the guidance of Nature, another in the constraint of the passions, another in the tradition of laws and customs, another in the instruction of the arts. Nature's guidance is that by which we are naturally capable of sensation and thought; constraint of the passions is that whereby hunger drives us to food and thirst to drink; tradition of customs and laws, that whereby we regard piety in the conduct of life as good, but impiety as evil; instruction of the arts, that whereby we are not inactive in such arts as we adopt. But we make all these statements undogmatically.

Chapter XII. What Is the End of Scepticism?

Our next subject will be the end of the Sceptic system. Now an "end" is "that for which all actions or reasonings are undertaken, while it exists for the sake of none"; or, otherwise, "the ultimate object of appentency." We assert still that the Sceptic's End is quietude in respect of matters of opinion and moderate feeling in respect of things unavoidable. For the skeptic, having set out to philosophize with the object of passing judgment on the sense impressions and ascertaining which of them are true and which false, so as to attain quietude thereby, found himself involved in contradictions of equal weight, and being unable to decide between them suspended judgment; and as he was thus in suspense there followed, as it happened, the state of quietude in respect of matters of opinion. For the man who opines that anything is by nature good or bad is for ever being disquieted: when he is without the things which he deems good he believes himself to be tormented by things naturally bad and he pursues after the things which are, as he thinks, good; which when he has obtained he keeps falling into still more perturbations because of his irrational and immoderate elation, and in his dread of a change of fortune he uses every endeavor to avoid losing the things which he deems good. On the other hand, the man who determines nothing as to what is naturally good or bad neither shuns nor pursues anything eagerly; and, in consequence, he is unperturbed.

The Sceptic, in fact, had the same experience which is said to have befallen the painter Apelles. Once, they say, when he was painting a horse and wished to represent in the painting the horse's foam, he was so unsuccessful that he gave up the attempt and flung at the picture the sponge on which he used to wipe the paints off his brush, and the mark of the sponge produced the effect of a horse's foam. So, too, the Sceptics were in hopes of gaining quietude by means of a decision regarding the disparity of the objects of sense and of thought, and being unable to effect this they suspended judgment; and they found that quietude, as if by chance, followed upon their suspense, even as a shadow follows its substance.

We do not, however, suppose that the Sceptic is wholly untroubled; but we say that he is troubled by things unavoidable; for we grant that he is cold at times and thirsty, and suffers various affections of that kind. But even in these cases, whereas ordinary people are afflicted by two circumstances,—namely, by the affections themselves and, in no less a degree, by the belief that these conditions are evil by nature, —the Sceptic, by his rejection of the added belief in the natural badness of all these conditions, escapes here too with less discomfort. Hence we say that, while in regard to matters of opinion the Sceptic's End is quietude, in regard to things unavoidable it is "moderate affection." But some notable Sceptics have added the further definition "suspension of judgment in investigations."

Chapter XIII. Of the General Modes Leading to the Suspension of Judgement

Now that we have been saying that tranquillity follows on suspension of judgment, it will be our next task to explain how we arrive at this suspension. Speaking generally, one may say that it is the result of setting things in opposition. We oppose either appearances to appearances or objects of thought to objects of thought or alternando. For instance, we oppose appearances to appearances when we say "The same tower appears round from a distance, but square from close at hand"; and thoughts to thoughts, when in answer to him who argues the existence of providence from the order of the heavenly bodies we oppose the fact that often the good fare ill and the bad fare well, and draw from this the inference that providence does not exist. And thoughts we oppose to appearances, as when Anaxagoras countered the notion that snow is white with the argument,

"Snow is frozen water, and water is black; therefore snow also is black." With a different idea we oppose things present sometimes to things present, as in the foregoing examples, and sometimes to things past or future, as, for instance, when someone propounds to us a theory which we are unable to refute, we say to him in reply, "Just as, before the birth of the founder of the school to which you belong, the theory it holds was not as yet apparent as a sound theory, although it was really in existence, so likewise it is possible that the opposite theory to that which you now propound is already existent, though not yet apparent to us, so that we ought not as yet to yield assent to this theory which at the moment seems to be valid."

But in order that we may have a more exact understanding of these antitheses I will describe the modes by which suspension of judgment is brought about, but without making any positive assertion regarding either their number or their validity; for it is possible that they may be unsound or there may be more of them than I shall enumerate.

Study Questions

1. What is the distinction between the Dogmatist, the Academic, and the (Pyrrhonian) skeptic?
2. What is the ultimate end or goal of the skeptic's enterprise? How does this goal compare to the goals of others who pursue philosophy? Do you think the goal is something that we can or should try to achieve?
3. Do you think that we can ever know which philosophical positions are correct? Or do you agree with the skeptics who say that we should simply suspend judgment?

2.2   Meditation I: Concerning Those Things That Can Be Called into Doubt

     RENÉ DESCARTES

RENE DESCARTES (1591–1650) is considered the father of modern philosophy. He worked not only in philosophy but also in mathematics. He is also famous for having promoted a conception of matter that paved the way for mechanical explanations of physical phenomena in the seventeenth century.

He is most famous for his work *Meditations on First Philosophy*. In this work Descartes takes up issues concerning the extent and foundation of human knowledge, the essence of the human subject, proofs for the existence of God, the path for right discovery of the truth, and the foundation for the separation of mind and matter. This work set the agenda in philosophy for years to come and is still considered today to be one of the most important works of Western philosophy.

In Descartes' *First Meditation*, he presents his method of doubt and considers three distinct kinds of skepticism about knowledge of the external world and truths known by reason.

Several years have now passed since I first realized how numerous were the false opinions that in my youth I had taken to be true, and thus how doubtful were all those that I had subsequently built upon them. And thus I realized that once in my life I had to raze everything to the ground and begin again from the original foundations, if I wanted to establish anything firm and lasting in the sciences. But the task seemed enormous, and I was waiting until I reached a point in my life that was so timely that no more suitable time for undertaking these plans of action would come to pass. For this reason, I procrastinated for so long that I would henceforth be at fault, were I to waste the time that remains for carrying out the project by brooding over it. Accordingly, I have today suitably freed my mind of all cares, secured for myself a period of leisurely tranquillity, and am withdrawing into solitude. At last I will apply myself earnestly and unreservedly to this general demolition of my opinions.

Yet to bring this about I will not need to show that all my opinions are false, which is perhaps something I could never accomplish. But reason now persuades me that I should withhold my assent no less carefully from opinions that are not completely certain and indubitable than I would from those that are patently false. For this reason, it will suffice for the rejection of all of these opinions, if I find in each of them some reason for doubt. Nor therefore need I survey each opinion individually, a task that would be endless. Rather, because undermining the foundations will cause whatever has been built upon them to crumble of its own accord, I will attack straightaway those principles which supported everything I once believed.

René Descartes, *Meditations on First Philosophy*, fourth edition, translated by Donald Cress (Indianapolis, Ind.: Hacker, 1998).

Surely whatever I had admitted until now as most true I received either from the senses or through the senses. However, I have noticed that the senses are sometimes deceptive; and it is a mark of prudence never to place our complete trust in those who have deceived us even once.

But perhaps, even though the senses do sometimes deceive us when it is a question of very small and distant things, still there are many other matters concerning which one simply cannot doubt, even though they are derived from the very same senses: for example, that I am sitting here next to the fire, wearing my winter dressing gown, that I am holding this sheet of paper in my hands, and the like. But on what grounds could one deny that these hands and this entire body are mine? Unless perhaps I were to liken myself to the insane, whose brains are impaired by such an unrelenting vapor of black bile that they steadfastly insist that they are kings when they are utter paupers, or that they are arrayed in purple robes when they are naked, or that they have heads made of clay, or that they are gourds, or that they are made of glass. But such people are mad, and I would appear no less mad, were I to take their behavior as an example for myself.

This would all be well and good, were I not a man who is accustomed to sleeping at night, and to experiencing in my dreams the very same things, or now and then even less plausible ones, as these insane people do when they are awake. How often does my evening slumber persuade me of such ordinary things as these: that I am here, clothed in my dressing gown, seated next to the fireplace—when in fact I am lying undressed in bed! But right now my eyes are certainly wide awake when I gaze upon this sheet of paper. This head which I am shaking is not heavy with sleep. I extend this hand consciously and deliberately, and I feel it. Such things would not be so distinct for someone who is asleep. As if I did not recall having been deceived on other occasions even by similar thoughts in my dreams! As I consider these matters more carefully, I see so plainly that there are no definitive signs by which to distinguish being awake from being asleep. As a result,

I am becoming quite dizzy, and this dizziness nearly convinces me that I am asleep.

Let us assume then, for the sake of argument, that we are dreaming and that such particulars as these are not true: that we are opening our eyes, moving our head, and extending our hands. Perhaps we do not even have such hands, or any such body at all. Nevertheless, it surely must be admitted that the things seen during slumber are, as it were, like painted images, which could only have been produced in the likeness of true things, and that therefore at least these general things—eyes, head, hands, and the whole body— are not imaginary things, but are true and exist. For indeed when painters themselves wish to represent sirens and satyrs by means of especially bizarre forms, they surely cannot assign to them utterly new natures. Rather, they simply fuse together the members of various animals. Or if perhaps they concoct something so utterly novel that nothing like it has ever been seen before (and thus is something utterly fictitious and false), yet certainly at the very least the colors from which they fashion it ought to be true. And by the same token, although even these general things—eyes, head, hands and the like—could be imaginary, still one has to admit that at least certain other things that are even more simple and universal are true. It is from these components, as if from true colors, that all those images of things that are in our thought are fashioned, be they true or false.

This class of things appears to include corporeal nature in general, together with its extension; the shape of extended things; their quantity, that is, their size and number; as well as the place where they exist; the time through which they endure, and the like.

Thus it is not improper to conclude from this that physics, astronomy, medicine, and all the other disciplines that are dependent upon the consideration of composite things are doubtful, and that, on the other hand, arithmetic, geometry, and other such disciplines, which treat of nothing but the simplest and most general things and which are indifferent as to whether these things do or do not in fact exist, contain something certain and indubitable. For whether I am awake or asleep, two plus three make five, and a square does not have more than four sides. It does not seem possible that such obvious truths should be subject to the suspicion of being false.

Be that as it may, there is fixed in my mind a certain opinion of long standing, namely that there exists a God who is able to do anything and by whom I, such as I am, have been created. How do I know that he did not bring it about that there is no earth at all, no heavens, no extended thing, no shape, no size, no place, and yet bringing it about that all these things appear to me to exist precisely as they do now? Moreover, since I judge that others sometimes make mistakes in matters that they believe they know most perfectly, may I not, in like fashion, be deceived every time I add two and three or count the sides of a square, or perform an even simpler operation, if that can be imagined? But perhaps God has not willed that I be deceived in this way, for he is said to be supremely good. Nonetheless, if it were repugnant to his goodness to have created me such that I be deceived all the time, it would also seem foreign to that same goodness to permit me to be deceived even occasionally. But we cannot make this last assertion.

Perhaps there are some who would rather deny so powerful a God than believe that everything else is uncertain. Let us not oppose them; rather, let us grant that everything said here about God is fictitious. Now they suppose that I came to be what I am either by fate, or by chance, or by a connected chain of events, or by some other way. But because being deceived and being mistaken appear to be a certain imperfection, the less powerful they take the author of my origin to be, the more probable it will be that I am so imperfect that I am always deceived. I have nothing to say in response to these arguments. But eventually I am forced to admit that there is nothing among the things I once believed to be true which it is not permissible to doubt—and not out of frivolity or lack of forethought, but for valid and considered reasons. Thus I must be no less careful to withhold assent henceforth even from these

beliefs than I would from those that are patently false, if I wish to find anything certain.

But it is not enough simply to have realized these things; I must take steps to keep myself mindful of them. For long-standing opinions keep returning, and, almost against my will, they take advantage of my credulity, as if it were bound over to them by long use and the claims of intimacy. Nor will I ever get out of the habit of assenting to them and believing in them, so long as I take them to be exactly what they are, namely, in some respects doubtful, as has just now been shown, but nevertheless highly probable, so that it is much more consonant with reason to believe them than to deny them. Hence, it seems to me I would do well to deceive myself by turning my will in completely the opposite direction and pretend for a time that these opinions are wholly false and imaginary, until finally, as if with prejudices weighing down each side equally, no bad habit should turn my judgment any further from the correct perception of things. For indeed I know that meanwhile there is no danger or error in following this procedure, and that it is impossible for me to indulge in too much distrust, since I am now concentrating only on knowledge, not on action.

Accordingly, I will suppose not a supremely good God, the source of truth, but rather an evil genius, supremely powerful and clever, who has directed his entire effort at deceiving me. I will regard the heavens, the air, the earth, colors, shapes, sounds, and all external things as nothing but the bedeviling hoaxes of my dreams, with which he lays snares for my credulity. I will regard myself as not having hands, or eyes, or flesh, or blood, or any senses, but as nevertheless falsely believing that I possess all these things. I will remain resolute and steadfast in this meditation, and even if it is not within my power to know anything true, it certainly is within my power to take care resolutely to withhold my assent to what is false, lest this deceiver, however powerful, however clever he may be, have any effect on me. But this undertaking is arduous, and a certain laziness brings me back to my customary way of living. I am not unlike a prisoner who enjoyed an imaginary freedom during his sleep, but, when he later begins to suspect that he is dreaming, fears being awakened and nonchalantly conspires with these pleasant illusions. In just the same way, I fall back of my own accord into my old opinions, and dread being awakened, lest the toilsome wakefulness which follows upon a peaceful rest must be spent thenceforward not in the light but among the inextricable shadows of the difficulties now brought forward.

Study Questions

1. Explain Descartes' method of doubt.
2. Explain the difference between skepticism based on the fact that our senses deceive us on occasion and skepticism based on dreaming.
3. Of all the kinds of skeptical scenarios that Descartes considers, which one does he think is the strongest? Why?
4. Do you think Descartes' skepticism shows that we do not know anything about the external world? Why?

Principles of Human Knowledge

2.3

GEORGE BERKELEY

GEORGE BERKELEY (1685–1753) is considered to be one of the leading philosophers of the modern period of philosophy. He is famous for having contributed to psychological and philosophical theories of vision in his time. His two principal philosophical works are *Principles Concerning Human Knowledge* and *Three Dialogues Between Hylas and Philonous.*

In this selection Berkeley presents his famous master argument. This argument can be used as part of a foundation for responding to skepticism of the kind raised by Descartes. One component of skepticism about the external world is the claim that there is an external world that is independent of our experience. From this position the skeptic asks, how is it that we come to know anything about the external world? Berkeley's master argument challenges the idea that there is an external world that exists independently of our minds. His argument supports the idealist position that to exist is to be perceived.

9. Some there are who make a distinction betwixt *primary* and *secondary* qualities: by the former, they mean extension, figure, motion, rest, solidity or impenetrability and number: by the latter they denote all other sensible qualities, as colours, sounds, tastes, and so forth. The ideas we have of these they acknowledge not to be the resemblances of any thing existing without the mind or unperceived; but they will have our ideas of the primary qualities to be patterns or images of things which exist without the mind, in an unthinking substance which they call *matter*. By matter therefore we are to understand an inert, senseless substance, in which extension,

George Berkeley, *A Treatise Concerning the Principles of Human Knowledge*, edited by Jonathan Dancy (1998). By permission of Oxford University Press.

figure, and motion, do actually subsist. But it is evident from what we have already shewn, that extension, figure and motion are only ideas existing in the mind, and that an idea can be like nothing but another idea, and that consequently neither they nor their archetypes can exist in an unperceiving substance. Hence it is plain, that the very notion of what is called *matter* or *corporeal substance*, involves a contradiction in it.

10. They who assert that figure, motion, and the rest of the primary or original qualities do exist without the mind, in unthinking substances, do at the same time acknowledge that colours, sounds, heat, cold, and such like secondary qualities, do not, which they tell us are sensations existing in the mind alone, that depend on and are occasioned by the different size, texture and motion of the minute particles of matter. This they take for an undoubted truth, which they can demonstrate beyond all exception. Now if it be certain, that those original qualities are inseparably united with the other sensible qualities, and not, even in thought, capable of being abstracted from them, it plainly follows that they exist only in the mind. But I desire any one to reflect and try, whether he can by any abstraction of thought, conceive the extension and motion of a body, without all other sensible qualities. For my own part, I see evidently that it is not in my power to frame an idea of a body extended and moved, but I must withal give it some colour or other sensible quality which is acknowledged to exist only in the mind. In short, extension, figure, and motion, abstracted from all other qualities, are inconceivable. Where therefore the other sensible qualities are, there must these be also, to wit, in the mind and no where else.

11. Again, *great* and *small, swift* and *slow*, are allowed to exist no where without the mind, being entirely relative and changing as the frame or position of the organs of sense varies. The extension therefore which exists without the mind, is neither great nor small, the motion neither swift nor slow, that is, they are nothing at all. But say you, they are extension in general, and motion in general: thus we see how much the tenet of extended, moveable substances existing without the mind, depends on that strange doctrine of *abstract ideas*. And here I cannot but remark, how nearly the vague and indeterminate description of matter or corporeal substance, which the modern philosophers are run into by their own principles, resembles that antiquated and so much ridiculed notion of *materia prima*, to be met with in Aristotle and his followers. Without extension solidity cannot be conceived; since therefore it has been shewn that extension exists not in an unthinking substance, the same must also be true of solidity.

12. That number is entirely the creature of the mind, even though the other qualities be allowed to exist without, will be evident to whoever considers, that the same thing bears a different denomination of number, as the mind views it with different respects. Thus, the same extension is one or three or thirty six, according as the mind considers it with reference to a yard, a foot, or an inch. Number is so visibly relative, and dependent on men's understanding, that it is strange to think how any one should give it an absolute existence without the mind. We say one book, one page, one line; all these are equally units, though some contain several of the others. And in each instance it is plain, the unit relates to some particular combination of ideas arbitrarily put together by the mind.

13. Unity I know some will have to be a simple or uncompounded idea, accompanying all other ideas into the mind. That I have any such idea answering the word *unity*, I do not find; and if I had, methinks I could not miss finding it; on the contrary it should be the most familiar to my understanding, since it is said to accompany all other ideas, and to be perceived by all the ways of sensation and reflexion. To say no more, it is an *abstract idea*.

14. I shall farther add, that after the same manner, as modern philosophers prove certain sensible qualities to have no existence in matter, or without the mind, the same thing may be likewise proved of all other sensible qualities whatsoever. Thus, for instance, it is said that heat and cold

are affections only of the mind, and not at all patterns of real beings, existing in the corporeal substances which excite them, for that the same body which appears cold to one hand, seems warm to another. Now why may we not as well argue that figure and extension are not patterns or resemblances of qualities existing in matter, because to the same eye at different stations, or eyes of a different texture at the same station, they appear various, and cannot therefore be the images of any thing settled and determinate without the mind? Again, it is proved that sweetness is not really in the sapid thing, because the thing remaining unaltered the sweetness is changed into bitter, as in case of a fever or otherwise vitiated palate. Is it not as reasonable to say, that motion is not without the mind, since if the succession of ideas in the mind become swifter, the motion, it is acknowledged, shall appear slower without any alteration in any external object.

15. In short, let anyone consider those arguments, which are thought manifestly to prove that colours and tastes exist only in the mind, and he shall find they may with equal force, be brought to prove the same thing of extension, figure, and motion. Though it must be confessed this method of arguing doth not so much prove that there is no extension or colour in an outward object, as that we do not know by sense which is the true extension or colour of the object. But the arguments foregoing plainly shew it to be impossible that any colour or extension at all, or other sensible quality whatsoever, should exist in an unthinking subject without the mind, or in truth, that there should be any such thing as an outward object. [...]

21. Were it necessary to add any farther proof against the existence of matter, after what has been said, I could instance several of those errors and difficulties (not to mention impieties) which have sprung from that tenet. It has occasioned numberless controversies and disputes in philosophy, and not a few of far greater moment in religion. But I shall not enter into the detail of them in this place, as well because I think, arguments *a posteriori* are unnecessary for confirming

what has been, if I mistake not, sufficiently demonstrated *a priori*, as because I shall hereafter find occasion to say somewhat of them.

22. I am afraid I have given cause to think me needlessly prolix in handling this subject. For to what purpose is it to dilate on that which may be demonstrated with the utmost evidence in a line or two, to any one that is capable of the least reflexion? It is but looking into your own thoughts, and so trying whether you can conceive it possible for a sound, or figure, or motion, or colour, to exist without the mind, or unperceived. This easy trial may make you see, that what you contend for, is a downright contradiction. Insomuch that I am content to put the whole upon this issue; if you can but conceive it possible for one extended moveable substance, or in general, for any one idea or any thing like an idea, to exist otherwise than in a mind perceiving it, I shall readily give up the cause: And as for all that *compages* of external bodies which you contend for, I shall grant you its existence, though you cannot either give me any reason why you believe it exists, or assign any use to it when it is supposed to exist. I say, the bare possibility of your opinion's being true, shall pass for an argument that it is so.

23. But say you, surely there is nothing easier than to imagine trees, for instance, in a park, or books existing in a closet, and no body by to perceive them. I answer, you may so, there is no difficulty in it: but what is all this, I beseech you, more than framing in your mind certain ideas which you call *books* and *trees*, and at the same time omitting to frame the idea of any one that may perceive them? But do not you your self perceive or think of them all the while? This therefore is nothing to the purpose: it only shows you have the power of imagining or forming ideas in your mind; but it doth not shew that you can conceive it possible, the objects of your thought may exist without the mind: to make out this, it is necessary that you conceive them existing unconceived or unthought of, which is a manifest repugnancy. When we do our utmost to conceive the existence of external bodies, we are all

the while only contemplating our own ideas. But the mind taking no notice of itself, is deluded to think it can and doth conceive bodies existing unthought of or without the mind; though at the same time they are apprehended by or exist in it self. A little attention will discover to any one the truth and evidence of what is here said, and make it unnecessary to insist on any other proofs against the existence of material substance.

24. It is very obvious, upon the least inquiry into our own thoughts, to know whether it be possible for us to understand what is meant, by the *absolute existence of sensible objects in themselves, or without the mind*. To me it is evident those words mark out either a direct contradiction, or else nothing at all. And to convince others of this, I know no readier or fairer way, than to entreat they would calmly attend to their own thoughts: and if by this attention, the emptiness or repugnancy of those expressions does appear, surely nothing more is requisite for their conviction. It is on this therefore that I insist, to wit, that the absolute existence of unthinking things are words without a meaning, or which include a contradiction. This is what I repeat and inculcate, and earnestly recommend to the attentive thoughts of the reader. [...]

86. From the principles we have laid down, it follows, human knowledge may naturally be reduced to two heads, that of *ideas*, and that of *spirits*. Of each of these I shall treat in order. And first as to ideas or unthinking things, our knowledge of these hath been very much obscured and confounded, and we have been led into very dangerous errors, by supposing a twofold existence of the objects of sense, the one *intelligible*, or in the mind, the other *real* and without the mind: whereby unthinking things are thought to have a natural subsistence of their own, distinct from being perceived by spirits. This which, if I mistake not, hath been shewn to be a most groundless and absurd notion, is the very root of *scepticism*; for so long as men thought that real things subsisted without the mind, and that their knowledge was only so far forth *real* as it was conformable to

real things, it follows, they could not be certain that they had any real knowledge at all. For how can it be known, that the things which are perceived, are conformable to those which are not perceived, or exist without the mind?

87. Colour, figure, motion, extension and the like, considered only as so many *sensations* in the mind, are perfectly known, there being nothing in them which is not perceived. But if they are looked on as notes or images, referred to *things* or *archetypes* existing without the mind, then are we involved all in *scepticism*. We see only the appearances, and not the real qualities of things. What may be the extension, figure, or motion of any thing really and absolutely, or in it self, it is impossible for us to know, but only the proportion or the relation they bear to our senses. Things remaining the same, our ideas vary, and which of them, or even whether any of them at all represent the true quality really existing in the thing, it is out of our reach to determine. So that, for aught we know, all we see, hear, and feel, may be only phantom and vain chimera, and not at all agree with the real things, existing in *rerum natura*. All this scepticism follows, from our supposing a difference between *things* and *ideas*, and that the former have a subsistence without the mind, or unperceived. It were easy to dilate on this subject, and shew how the arguments urged by *sceptics* in all ages, depend on the supposition of external objects.

88. So long as we attribute a real existence to unthinking things, distinct from their being perceived, it is not only impossible for us to know with evidence the nature of any real unthinking being, but even that it exists. Hence it is, that we see philosophers distrust their senses, and doubt of the existence of heaven and earth, of every thing they see or feel, even of their own bodies. And after all their labour and struggle of thought, they are forced to own, we cannot attain to any self-evident or demonstrative knowledge of the existence of sensible things. But all this doubtfulness, which so bewilders and confounds the mind, and makes *philosophy* ridiculous in the eyes of the world, vanishes, if we annex a

meaning to our words, and do not amuse our selves with the terms *absolute, external, exist*, and such like, signifying we know not what. I can as well doubt of my own being, as of the being of those things which I actually perceive by sense: it being a manifest contradiction, that any sensible object should be immediately perceived by sight or touch, and at the same time have no existence in Nature, since the very existence of an unthinking being consists in *being perceived*.

89. Nothing seems of more importance, towards erecting a firm system of sound and real knowledge, which may be proof against the assaults of *scepticism*, than to lay the beginning in a distinct explication of what is meant by *thing, reality, existence*: for in vain shall we dispute concerning the real existence of things, or pretend to any knowledge thereof, so long as we have not fixed the meaning of those words. *Thing* or *being* is the most general name of all, it comprehends under it two kinds entirely distinct and heterogeneous, and which have nothing common but the name, to wit, *spirits* and *ideas*. The former are *active, indivisible substances*: the latter are *inert, fleeting, dependent beings*, which subsist not by themselves, but are supported by, or exist in minds or spiritual substances. We comprehend our own existence by inward feeling or reflexion, and that of other spirits by reason. We may be said to have some knowledge or notion of our own minds, of spirits and active beings, whereof in a strict sense we have not ideas. In like manner we know and have a notion of relations between things or ideas, which relations are distinct from the ideas or things related, inasmuch as the latter may be perceived by us without our perceiving the former. To me it seems that ideas, spirits and relations are all in their respective kinds, the object of human knowledge and subject of discourse: and that the term *idea* would be improperly extended to signify every thing we know or have any notion of.

90. Ideas imprinted on the senses are real things, or do really exist; this we do not deny, but we deny they can subsist without the minds which perceive them, or that they are resemblances of any archetypes existing without the mind: since the very being of a sensation or idea consists in being perceived, and an idea can be like nothing but an idea. Again, the things perceived by sense may be termed *external*, with regard to their origin, in that they are not generated from within, by the mind it self, but imprinted by a spirit distinct from that which perceives them. Sensible objects may likewise be said to be without the mind, in another sense, namely when they exist in some other mind. Thus when I shut my eyes, the things I saw may still exist, but it must be in another mind.

91. It were a mistake to think, that what is here said derogates in the least from the reality of things. It is acknowledged on the received principles, that extension, motion, and in a word all sensible qualities, have need of a support, as not being able to subsist by themselves. But the objects perceived by sense, are allowed to be nothing but combinations of those qualities, and consequently cannot subsist by themselves. Thus far it is agreed on all hands. So that in denying the things perceived by sense, an existence independent of a substance, or support wherein they may exist, we detract nothing from the received opinion of their *reality*, and are guilty of no innovation in that respect. All the difference is, that according to us the unthinking beings perceived by sense, have no existence distinct from being perceived, and cannot therefore exist in any other substance, than those unextended, indivisible substances, or *spirits*, which act, and think, and perceive them: whereas philosophers vulgarly hold, that the sensible qualities exist in an inert, extended, unperceiving substance, which they call *matter*, to which they attribute a natural subsistence, exterior to all thinking beings, or distinct from being perceived by any mind whatsoever, even the eternal mind of the Creator, wherein they suppose only ideas of the corporeal substances created by him: if indeed they allow them to be at all created.

92. For as we have shewn the doctrine of matter or corporeal substance, to have been the

main pillar and support of *scepticism*, so likewise upon the same foundation have been raised all the impious schemes of *atheism* and irreligion. Nay so great a difficulty hath it been thought, to conceive matter produced out of nothing, that the most celebrated among the ancient philosophers, even of these who maintained the being of a God, have thought matter to be uncreated and coeternal with him. How great a friend material substance hath been to *atheists* in all ages, were needless to relate. All their monstrous systems have so visible and necessary a dependence on it, that when this corner-stone is once removed, the whole fabric cannot choose but fall to the ground; insomuch that it is no longer worth while, to bestow a particular consideration on the absurdities of every wretched sect of *atheists*.

Study Questions

1. What does Berkeley think the defense of material substance rests on?
2. What is the master argument against the existence of material substance?
3. How is the human ability to perceive related to the human ability to conceive? Does Berkeley assume that they are the same? Does his argument rest on this idea?
4. Do you think giving up on the existence of a mind-independent reality is a good way to refute skepticism about the external world? Is the price of this strategy too high?

2.4   Proof of an External World

 G. E. MOORE

GEORGE EDWARD MOORE (1873–1958) is considered to be one of the founding fathers of analytic philosophy in the early part of the twentieth century. He taught at Cambridge University in the United Kingdom, along with Bertrand Russell, and he was a colleague and mentor of Ludwig Wittgenstein. He worked in ethics, metaphysics, and epistemology. His most famous work is *Principia Ethica*, one of the most important treatises on ethics in the twentieth century.

In this selection from "A Proof of the External World," Moore describes and implements a strategy for responding to skepticism by the use of commonsense arguments. Many philosophers in the twentieth century have found Moore's argument to be quite challenging. It attempts a simple proof of the external world by appealing to the fact that he has two hands.

The commonsense response seems to be inadequate as a response to skepticism while at the same time involving something extremely appealing.

G. E. Moore, "Proof of an External World," in E. Sosa, J. Kim, J. Fantl, and M. McGrath (eds.), *Epistemology: An Anthology, Second Edition* (Malden, MA: Blackwell, 2008).

It seems to me that, so far from its being true, as Kant declares to be his opinion, that there is only one possible proof of the existence of things outside of us, namely the one which he has given, I can now give a large number of different proofs, each of which is a perfectly rigorous proof; and that at many other times I have been in a position to give many others. I can prove now, for instance, that two human hands exist. How? By holding up my two hands, and saying, as I make a certain gesture with the right hand, "Here is one hand," and adding, as I make a certain gesture with the left, "and here is another." And if, by doing this, I have proved *ipso facto* the existence of external things, you will all see that I can also do it now in numbers of other ways: there is no need to multiply examples.

But did I prove just now that two human hands were then in existence? I do want to insist that I did; that the proof which I gave was a perfectly rigorous one; and that it is perhaps impossible to give a better or more rigorous proof of anything whatever. Of course, it would not have been a proof unless three conditions were satisfied; namely (1) unless the premiss which I adduced as proof of the conclusion was different from the conclusion I adduced it to prove; (2) unless the premiss which I adduced was something which I *knew* to be the case, and not merely something which I believed but which was by no means certain, or something which, though in fact true, I did not know to be so; and (3) unless the conclusion did really follow from the premiss. But all these three conditions were in fact satisfied by my proof. (1) The premiss which I adduced in proof was quite certainly different from the conclusion, for the conclusion was merely "Two human hands exist at this moment"; but the premiss was something far more specific than this—something which I expressed by showing you my hands, making certain gestures, and saying the words "Here is one hand, and here is another." It is quite obvious that the two were different, because it is quite obvious that the conclusion might have been true, even if the premiss had

been false. In asserting the premiss I was asserting much more than I was asserting in asserting the conclusion. (2) I certainly did at the moment *know* that which I expressed by the combination of certain gestures with saying the words "Here is one hand and here is another." I *knew* that there was one hand in the place indicated by combining a certain gesture with my first utterance of "here" and that there was another in the different place indicated by combining a certain gesture with my second utterance of "here." How absurd it would be to suggest that I did not know it, but only believed it, and that perhaps it was not the case! You might as well suggest that I do not know that I am now standing up and talking—that perhaps after all I'm not, and that it's not quite certain that I am! And finally (3) it is quite certain that the conclusion did follow from the premiss. This is as certain as it is that if there is one hand here and another here *now*, then it follows that there are two hands in existence *now*.

My proof, then, of the existence of things outside of us did satisfy three of the conditions necessary for a rigorous proof. Are there any other conditions necessary for a rigorous proof, such that perhaps it did not satisfy one of them? Perhaps there may be; I do not know; but I do want to emphasise that, so far as I can see, we all of us do constantly take proofs of this sort as absolutely conclusive proofs of certain conclusions—as finally settling certain questions, as to which we were previously in doubt. Suppose, for instance, it were a question whether there were as many as three misprints on a certain page in a certain book. A says there are, B is inclined to doubt it. How could A prove that he is right? Surely he *could* prove it by taking the book, turning to the page, and pointing to three separate places on it, saying "There's one misprint here, another here, and another here": surely that is a method by which it *might* be proved! Of course, A would not have proved, by doing this, that there were at least three misprints on the page in question, unless it was certain that there was a misprint in each of the places to which he pointed. But to say that he *might* prove it in this way, is to say that it *might* be certain that there was. And if such a thing as that could ever be certain, then assuredly it was certain just now that there was one hand in one of the two places I indicated and another in the other.

I did, then, just now, give a proof that there were *then* external objects; and obviously, if I did, I could *then* have given many other proofs of the same sort that there were external objects *then*, and could now give many proofs of the same sort that there are external objects *now*.

But, if what I am asked to do is to prove that external objects have existed *in the past*, then I can give many different proofs of this also, but proofs which are in important respects of a different *sort* from those just given. And I want to emphasise that, when Kant says it is a scandal not to be able to give a proof of the existence of external objects, a proof of their existence in the past would certainly *help* to remove the scandal of which he is speaking. He says that, if it occurs to anyone to question their existence, we ought to be able to confront him with a satisfactory proof. But by a person who questions their existence, he certainly means not merely a person who questions whether any exist at the moment of speaking, but a person who questions whether any have *ever* existed; and a proof that some have existed in the past would certainly therefore be relevant to *part* of what such a person is questioning. How then can I prove that there have been external objects in the past? Here is one proof. I can say: "I held up two hands above this desk not very long ago; therefore two hands existed not very long ago; therefore at least two external objects have existed at some time in the past, QED." This is a perfectly good proof, provided I *know* what is asserted in the premiss. But I *do* know that I held up two hands above this desk not very long ago. As a matter of fact, in this case you all know it too. There's no doubt whatever that I did. Therefore I have given a perfectly conclusive proof that external objects have existed in the past; and you will all see at once that, if this is a conclusive proof, I could

have given many others of the same sort, and could now give many others. But it is also quite obvious that this sort of proof differs in important respects from the sort of proof I gave just now that there were two hands existing *then*.

I have, then, given two conclusive proofs of the existence of external objects. The first was a proof that two human hands existed at the time when I gave the proof; the second was a proof that two human hands had existed at a time previous to that at which I gave the proof. These proofs were of a different sort in important respects. And I pointed out that I could have given, then, many other conclusive proofs of both sorts. It is also obvious that I could give many others of both sorts now. So that, if these are the sort of proof that is wanted, nothing is easier than to prove the existence of external objects.

But now I am perfectly well aware that, in spite of all that I have said, many philosophers will still feel that I have not given any satisfactory proof of the point in question. And I want briefly, in conclusion, to say something as to why this dissatisfaction with my proofs should be felt.

One reason why, is, I think, this. Some people understand "proof of an external world" as including a proof of things which I haven't attempted to prove and haven't proved. It is not quite easy to say *what* it is that they want proved—*what* it is that is such that unless they got a proof of it, they would not say that they had a proof of the existence of external things; but I can make an approach to explaining what they want by saying that if I had proved the propositions which I used as *premisses* in my two proofs, then they would perhaps admit that I had proved the existence of external things, but, in the absence of such a proof (which, of course, I have neither given nor attempted to give), they will say that I have not given what they mean by a proof of the existence of external things. In other words, they want a proof of what I assert *now* when I hold up my hands and say "Here's one hand and here's another"; and, in the other case, they want a proof of what I assert *now* when

I say "I did hold up two hands above this desk just now." Of course, what they really want is not merely a proof of these two propositions, but something like a general statement as to how *any* propositions of this sort may be proved. This, of course, I haven't given; and I do not believe it can be given: if this is what is meant by proof of the existence of external things, I do not believe that any proof of the existence of external things is possible. Of course, in some cases what might be called a proof of propositions which seem like these can be got. If one of you suspected that one of my hands was artificial he might be said to get a proof of my proposition "Here's one hand, and here's another," by coming up and examining the suspected hand close up, perhaps touching and pressing it, and so establishing that it really was a human hand. But I do not believe that any proof is possible in nearly all cases. How am I to prove now that "Here's one hand, and here's another"? I do not believe I can do it. In order to do it, I should need to prove for one thing, as Descartes pointed out, that I am not now dreaming. But how can I prove that I am not? I have, no doubt, conclusive reasons for asserting that I am not now dreaming; I have conclusive evidence that I am awake: but that is a very different thing from being able to prove it. I could not tell you what all my evidence is; and I should require to do this at least, in order to give you a proof.

But another reason why some people would feel dissatisfied with my proofs is, I think, not merely that they want a proof of something which I haven't proved, but that they think that, if I cannot give such extra proofs, then the proofs that I have given are not conclusive proofs at all. And this, I think, is a definite mistake. They would say: "If you cannot prove your premiss that here is one hand and here is another, then you do not know it. But you yourself have admitted that, if you did not

know it, then your proof was not conclusive. Therefore your proof was not, as you say it was, a conclusive proof." This view that, if I cannot prove such things as these, I do not know them, is, I think, the view that Kant was expressing in the sentence which I quoted at the beginning of this lecture, when he implies that so long as we have no proof of the existence of external things, their existence must be accepted merely on *faith*. He means to say, I think, that if I cannot prove that there is a hand here, I must accept it merely as a matter of faith—I cannot know it. Such a view, though it has been very common among philosophers, can, I think, be shown to be wrong—though shown only by the use of premisses which are not known to be true, unless we do know of the existence of external things. I can know things, which I cannot prove; and among things which I certainly did know, even if (as I think) I could not prove them, were the premisses of my two proofs. I should say, therefore, that those, if any, who are dissatisfied with these proofs merely on the ground that I did not know their premisses, have no good reason for their dissatisfaction.

Study Questions

1. What performance does Moore believe proves the existence of the external world?
2. What are the three conditions that Moore requires a proof of the external world to have?
3. What reasons does Moore give for thinking that others will find his proof inadequate?
4. Do you think that Moore's proof is an adequate proof of the external world? Why?
5. Do you think that Moore's proof, if successful, shows that we know that we have hands? Why?

2.5   Is Justified True Belief Knowledge?

 ## EDMUND GETTIER

EDMUND GETTIER (1927–) is Professor Emeritus of Philosophy at the University of Massachusetts at Amherst. His paper "Is Justified True Belief Knowledge?" is considered by many to be one of the most important papers in epistemology in the twentieth century. Although it is an extremely short paper, the ideas discussed in it have impacted not only debates about the analysis of knowledge but also debates about philosophical methodology.

The paper begins by stating a standard account of knowledge, called the tripartite account of knowledge, which can be traced back to Plato. The account maintains that a subject knows a proposition if and only if the subject has a justified true belief. Gettier goes on to show that under some fairly uncontroversial conditions there are cases in which a subject has a justified true belief, yet does not know. By drawing attention to these cases, Gettier set off a number of epistemologists thinking about what condition one could add to the justified true belief account of knowledge to avoid what came to be known as Gettier-style counterexamples.

Various attempts have been made in recent years to state necessary and sufficient conditions for someone's knowing a given proposition. The attempts have often been such that they can be stated in a form similar to the following[1]:

(a) S knows that P   *IFF*   (i) P is true,
(ii) S believes that P, and
(iii) S is justified in believing that P.

For example, Chisholm has held that the following gives the necessary and sufficient conditions for knowledge[2]:

(b) S knows that P   *IFF*   (i) S accepts P,
(ii) S has adequate evidence for P, and
(iii) P is true.

Ayer has stated the necessary and sufficient conditions for knowledge as follows[3]:

(c) S knows that P   *IFF*   (i) P is true,
(ii) S is sure that P is true, and
(iii) S has the right to be sure that P is true.

I shall argue that (a) is false in that the conditions stated therein do not constitute a *sufficient* condition for the truth of the proposition that S knows that P. The same argument will show that (b) and (c) fail if "has adequate evidence for" or "has the right to be sure that" is substituted for "is justified in believing that" throughout.

I shall begin by noting two points. First, in that sense of "justified" in which S's being justified in believing P is a necessary condition of S's knowing that P, it is possible for a person to

Gettier, Edmund, "Is Justified True Belief Knowledge?" *Analysis*, 23 (1963).

be justified in believing a proposition that is in fact false. Secondly, for any proposition P, if S is justified in believing P, and P entails Q, and S deduces Q from P and accepts Q as a result of this deduction, then S is justified in believing Q. Keeping these two points in mind, I shall now present two cases in which the conditions stated in (a) are true for some proposition, though it is at the same time false that the person in question knows that proposition.

CASE I

Suppose that Smith and Jones have applied for a certain job. And suppose that Smith has strong evidence for the following conjunctive proposition:

(d) Jones is the man who will get the job, and Jones has ten coins in his pocket.

Smith's evidence for (d) might be that the president of the company assured him that Jones would in the end be selected, and that he, Smith, had counted the coins in Jones's pocket ten minutes ago. Proposition (d) entails:

(e) The man who will get the job has ten coins in his pocket.

Let us suppose that Smith sees the entailment from (d) to (e), and accepts (e) on the grounds of (d), for which he has strong evidence. In this case, Smith is clearly justified in believing that (e) is true.

But imagine, further, that unknown to Smith, he himself, not Jones, will get the job. And, also, unknown to Smith, he himself has ten coins in his pocket. Proposition (e) is then true, though proposition (d), from which Smith inferred (e), is false. In our example, then, all of the following are true: (*i*) (e) is true, (*ii*) Smith believes that (e) is true, and (*iii*) Smith is justified in believing that (e) is true. But it is equally clear that Smith does not *know* that (e) is true; for (e) is true in virtue of the number of coins in Smith's pocket, while Smith does not know how many

coins are in Smith's pocket, and bases his belief in (e) on a count of the coins in Jones's pocket, whom he falsely believes to be the man who will get the job.

CASE II

Let us suppose that Smith has strong evidence for the following proposition:

(f) Jones owns a Ford.

Smith's evidence might be that Jones has at all times in the past within Smith's memory owned a car, and always a Ford, and that Jones has just offered Smith a ride while driving a Ford. Let us imagine, now, that Smith has another friend, Brown, of whose whereabouts he is totally ignorant. Smith selects three place-names quite at random, and constructs the following three propositions:

(g) Either Jones owns a Ford, or Brown is in Boston;
(h) Either Jones owns a Ford, or Brown is in Barcelona;
(i) Either Jones owns a Ford, or Brown is in Brest-Litovsk.

Each of these propositions is entailed by (f). Imagine that Smith realizes the entailment of each of these propositions he has constructed by (f), and proceeds to accept (g), (h), and (i) on the basis of (f). Smith has correctly inferred (g), (h), and (i) from a proposition for which he has strong evidence. Smith is therefore completely justified in believing each of these three propositions. Smith, of course, has no idea where Brown is.

But imagine now that two further conditions hold. First, Jones does *not* own a Ford, but is at present driving a rented car. And secondly, by the sheerest coincidence, and entirely unknown to Smith, the place mentioned in proposition (h) happens really to be the place where Brown is. If these two conditions hold then Smith does *not* know that (h) is true, even though (*i*) (h) *is* true, (*ii*) Smith does believe that (h) is true, and (*iii*) Smith is justified in believing that (h) is true.

These two examples show that definition (a) does not state a *sufficient* condition for someone's knowing a given proposition. The same cases, with appropriate changes, will suffice to show that neither definition (b) nor definition (c) do so either.

Notes

1. Plato seems to be considering some such definition at *Theaetetus* 201, and perhaps accepting one at *Meno* 98.
2. Roderick M. Chisholm, *Perceiving: a Philosophical Study*, Cornell University Press (Ithaca, New York, 1957), p. 16.

3. A. J. Ayer, *The Problem of Knowledge*, Macmillan (London, 1956), p. 34.

Study Questions

1. What is the traditional account of knowledge that Gettier sets out to challenge? What component of that traditional account does he challenge?
2. What are the assumptions about justification that Gettier assumes? Do you think they are acceptable?
3. Make up a Gettier-style counterexample of your own. State what features make it a Gettier-style counterexample.

2.6   What Is Justifiable Belief?

 ### ALVIN GOLDMAN

ALVIN GOLDMAN (1938–) is Board of Governors Professor of Philosophy at Rutgers University in New Jersey. He is a leading analytic epistemologist and philosopher of mind. He is well known for being an advocate of process reliabilism and for developing issues in social epistemology in a way that challenges how postmodernists and social constructionists have discussed it.

In the selection from Goldman, he argues that a number of analyses of justification fail intuitive requirements for being a good analysis. He then goes on to articulate the thesis that it is best to understand the idea of a person being justified by appeal to whether the belief the person forms comes from a reliable source, where a source is minimally said to be reliable when it is more often true than not. This view roughly maintains that a belief is justified if and only if it is the output of a reliable belief-forming process. Goldman goes on to consider a number of objections to his account. In responding to these objections he clarifies what is meant by the idea of a reliable process.

Alvin I. Goldman, "What is Justified Belief?" in E. Sosa, J. Kim, J. Fantl, and M. McGrath (eds.), *Epistemology: An Anthology, Second Edition* (Malden, MA: Blackwell, 2008).

The aim of this essay is to sketch a theory of justified belief. What I have in mind is an explanatory theory, one that explains in a general way why certain beliefs are counted as justified and others as unjustified. Unlike some traditional approaches, I do not try to prescribe standards for justification that differ from, or improve upon, our ordinary standards. I merely try to explicate the ordinary standards, which are, I believe, quite different from those of many classical, e.g., "Cartesian," accounts.

Many epistemologists have been interested in justification because of its presumed close relationship to knowledge. This relationship is intended to be preserved in the conception of justified belief presented here. In previous papers on knowledge, I have denied that justification is necessary for knowing, but there I had in mind "Cartesian" accounts of justification. On the account of justified belief suggested here, it is necessary for knowing, and closely related to it.

The term "justified," I presume, is an evaluative term, a term of appraisal. Any correct definition or synonym of it would also feature evaluative terms. I assume that such definitions or synonyms might be given, but I am not interested in them. I want a set of *substantive* conditions that specify when a belief is justified. Compare the moral term "right." This might be defined in other ethical terms or phrases, a task appropriate to meta-ethics. The task of normative ethics, by contrast, is to state substantive conditions for the rightness of actions. Normative ethics tries to specify non-ethical conditions that determine when an action is right. A familiar example is act-utilitarianism, which says an action is right if and only if it produces, or would produce, at least as much net happiness as any alternative open to the agent. These necessary and sufficient conditions clearly involve no ethical notions. Analogously, I want a theory of justified belief to specify in non-epistemic terms when a belief is justified. This is not the only kind of theory of justifiedness one might seek, but it is one important kind of theory and the kind sought here.

In order to avoid epistemic terms in our theory, we must know which terms are epistemic. Obviously, an exhaustive list cannot be given, but here are some examples: "justified," "warranted," "has (good) grounds," "has reason (to believe)," "knows that," "sees that," "apprehends that," "is probable" (in an epistemic or inductive sense), "shows that," "establishes that," and "ascertains that." By contrast, here are some sample non-epistemic expressions: "believes that," "is true," "causes," "it is necessary that," "implies," "is deducible from," and "is probable" (either in the frequency sense or the propensity sense). In general, (purely) doxastic, metaphysical, modal, semantic, or syntactic expressions are not epistemic.

There is another constraint I wish to place on a theory of justified belief, in addition to the constraint that it be couched in non-epistemic language. Since I seek an explanatory theory, i.e., one that clarifies the underlying source of justificational status, it is not enough for a theory to state "correct" necessary and sufficient conditions. Its conditions must also be appropriately deep or revelatory. Suppose, for example, that the following sufficient condition of justified belief is offered: "If S senses redly at t and S believes at t that he is sensing redly, then S's belief at t that he is sensing redly is justified." This is not the kind of principle I seek; for, even if it is correct, it leaves unexplained *why* a person who senses redly and believes that he does, believes this justifiably. Not every state is such that if one is in it and believes one is in it, this belief is justified. What is distinctive about the state of sensing redly, or "phenomenal" states in general? A theory of justified belief of the kind I seek must answer this question, and hence it must be couched at a suitably deep, general, or abstract level.

A few introductory words about my *explicandum* are appropriate at this juncture. It is often assumed that whenever a person has a justified belief, he knows that it is justified and knows what the justification is. It is further assumed that the person can state or explain what his justification is. On this view, a justification is an argument, defense, or set of reasons that can be given in support of a belief. Thus, one studies the nature of justified belief by considering what a person might *say* if asked to defend, or justify, his belief. I make none of these sorts of assumptions here. I leave it an open question whether, when a belief is justified, the believer *knows* it is justified. I also leave it an open question whether, when a belief is justified, the believer can *state* or *give* a justification for it. I do not even assume that when a belief is justified there is something "possessed" by the believer which can be called a "justification." I do assume that a justified belief gets its status of being justified from some processes or properties that make it justified. In short, there must be some justification-conferring processes or properties. But this does not imply that there must be an argument, or reason, or anything else, "possessed" at the time of belief by the believer.

A theory of justified belief will be a set of principles that specify truth-conditions for the schema ⌜S's belief in *p* at time *t* is justified⌝, i.e., conditions for the satisfaction of this schema in all possible cases. It will be convenient to formulate candidate theories in a recursive or inductive format, which would include (A) one or more base clauses, (B) a set of recursive clauses (possibly null), and (C) a closure clause. In such a format, it is permissible for the predicate "is a justified belief" to appear in recursive clauses. But neither this predicate, nor any other epistemic predicate, may appear in (the antecedent of) any base clause. [...]

In general, a strategy for defeating a noncausal principle of justifiedness is to find a case in which the principle's antecedent is satisfied but the belief is caused by some faulty belief-forming process. The faultiness of the belief-forming process will incline us, intuitively, to regard the belief as unjustified. Thus, correct principles

of justified belief must be principles that make causal requirements, where "cause" is construed broadly to include sustainers as well as initiators of belief (i.e., processes that determine, or help to overdetermine, a belief's continuing to be held). [...]

Granted that principles of justified belief must make reference to causes of belief, what kinds of causes confer justifiedness? We can gain insight into this problem by reviewing some faulty processes of belief-formation, i.e., processes whose belief-outputs would be classed as unjustified. Here are some examples: confused reasoning, wishful thinking, reliance on emotional attachment, mere hunch or guesswork, and hasty generalization. What do these faulty processes have in common? They share the feature of *unreliability*: they tend to produce *error* a large proportion of the time. By contrast, which species of belief-forming (or belief-sustaining) processes are intuitively justification-conferring? They include standard perceptual processes, remembering, good reasoning, and introspection. What these processes seem to have in common is *reliability*: the beliefs they produce are generally true. My positive proposal, then, is this. The justificational status of a belief is a function of the reliability of the process or processes that cause it, where (as a first approximation) reliability consists in the tendency of a process to produce beliefs that are true rather than false.

To test this thesis further, notice that justifiedness is not a purely categorical concept, although I treat it here as categorical in the interest of simplicity. We can and do regard certain beliefs as more justified than others. Furthermore, our intuitions of comparative justifiedness go along with our beliefs about the comparative reliability of the belief-causing processes.

Consider perceptual beliefs. Suppose Jones believes he has just seen a mountain-goat. Our assessment of the belief's justifiedness is determined by whether he caught a brief glimpse of the creature at a great distance, or whether he had a good look at the thing only 30 yards away. His belief in the latter sort of case is (*ceteris paribus*) more justified than in the former sort of case. And, if his belief is true, we are more prepared to say he *knows* in the latter case than in the former. The difference between the two cases seems to be this. Visual beliefs formed from brief and hasty scanning, or where the perceptual object is a long distance off, tend to be wrong more often than visual beliefs formed from detailed and leisurely scanning, or where the object is in reasonable proximity. In short, the visual processes in the former category are less reliable than those in the latter category. A similar point holds for memory beliefs. A belief that results from a hazy and indistinct memory impression is counted as less justified than a belief that arises from a distinct memory impression, and our inclination to classify those beliefs as "*knowledge*" varies in the same way. Again, the reason is associated with the comparative reliability of the processes. Hazy and indistinct memory impressions are generally less reliable indicators of what actually happened, so beliefs formed from such impressions are less likely to be true than beliefs formed from distinct impressions. Further, consider beliefs based on inference from observed samples. A belief about a population that is based on random sampling, or on instances that exhibit great variety, is intuitively more justified than a belief based on biased sampling, or on instances from a narrow sector of the population. Again, the degree of justifiedness seems to be a function of reliability. Inferences based on random or varied samples will tend to produce less error or inaccuracy than inferences based on non-random or non-varied samples.

Returning to a categorical concept of justifiedness, we might ask just *how* reliable a belief-forming process must be in order that its resultant beliefs be justified. A precise answer to this question should not be expected. Our conception of justification is *vague* in this respect. It does seem clear, however, that *perfect* reliability isn't required. Belief-forming processes that *sometimes* produce error still confer justi-

fication. It follows that there can be justified beliefs that are false.

I have characterized justification-conferring processes as ones that have a "tendency" to produce beliefs that are true rather than false. The term "tendency" could refer either to *actual* long-run frequency, or to a "propensity," i.e., outcomes that would occur in merely *possible* realizations of the process. Which of these is intended? Unfortunately, I think our ordinary conception of justifiedness is vague on this dimension too. For the most part, we simply assume that the "observed" frequency of truth versus error would be approximately replicated in the actual long-run, and also in relevant counterfactual situations, i.e., ones that are highly "realistic" or conform closely to the circumstances of the actual world. Since we ordinarily assume these frequencies to be roughly the same, we make no concerted effort to distinguish them. Since the purpose of my present theorizing is to capture our ordinary conception of justifiedness, and since our ordinary conception is vague on this matter, it is appropriate to leave the theory vague in the same respect.

We need to say more about the notion of a belief-forming "*process.*" Let us mean by a "process" a *functional operation* or procedure, i.e., something that generates a *mapping* from certain states—"inputs"—into other states— "outputs." The outputs in the present case are states of believing this or that proposition at a given moment. On this interpretation, a process is a *type* as opposed to a *token*. This is fully appropriate, since it is only types that have statistical properties such as producing truth 80 per cent of the time; and it is precisely such statistical properties that determine the reliability of a process. Of course, we also want to speak of a process as *causing* a belief, and it looks as if types are incapable of being causes. But when we say that a belief is caused by a given process, understood as a functional procedure, we may interpret this to mean that it is caused by the particular *inputs* to the process (and by the intervening events "through which" the functional procedure carries the inputs into the output) on the occasion in question.

What are some examples of belief-forming "processes" construed as functional operations? One example is reasoning processes, where the inputs include antecedent beliefs and entertained hypotheses. Another example is functional procedures whose inputs include desires, hopes, or emotional states of various sorts (together with antecedent beliefs). A third example is a memory process, which takes as input beliefs or experiences at an earlier time and generates as output beliefs at a later time. For example, a memory process might take as input a belief *at t_i* that Lincoln was born in 1809 and generate as output a belief *at t_n* that Lincoln was born in 1809. A fourth example is perceptual processes. Here it isn't clear whether inputs should include states of the environment, such as the distance of the stimulus from the cognizer, or only events within or on the surface of the organism, e.g., receptor stimulations. I shall return to this point in a moment.

A critical problem concerning our analysis is the degree of generality of the process-types in question. Input–output relations can be specified very broadly or very narrowly, and the degree of generality will partly determine the degree of reliability. A process-type might be selected so narrowly that only one instance of it ever occurs, and hence the type is either completely reliable or completely unreliable. (This assumes that reliability is a function of *actual* frequency only.) If such narrow process-types were selected, beliefs that are intuitively unjustified might be said to result from perfectly reliable processes, and beliefs that are intuitively justified might be said to result from perfectly unreliable processes.

It is clear that our ordinary thought about process-types slices them broadly, but I cannot at present give a precise explication of our intuitive principles. One plausible suggestion, though, is that the relevant processes are *content-neutral*. It might be argued, for example, that the process of *inferring p whenever the Pope asserts p* could

pose problems for our theory. If the Pope is infallible, this process will be perfectly reliable; yet we would not regard the belief-outputs of this process as justified. The content-neutral restriction would avert this difficulty. If relevant processes are required to admit as input beliefs (or other states) with *any* content, the aforementioned process will not count, for its input beliefs have a restricted propositional content, viz., "*the Pope asserts p.*"

In addition to the problem of "generality" or "abstractness" there is the previously mentioned problem of the "*extent*" of belief-forming processes. Clearly, the causal ancestry of beliefs often includes events outside the organism. Are such events to be included among the "inputs" of belief-forming processes? Or should we restrict the extent of belief-forming processes to "*cognitive*" events, i.e., events within the organism's nervous system? I shall choose the latter course, though with some hesitation. My general grounds for this decision are roughly as follows. Justifiedness seems to be a function of how a cognizer deals with his environmental input, i.e., with the goodness or badness of the operations that register and transform the stimulation that reaches him. ("Deal with," of course, does not mean *purposeful* action, nor is it restricted to *conscious* activity.) A justified belief is, roughly speaking, one that results from cognitive operations that are, generally speaking, good or successful. But "*cognitive*" operations are most plausibly construed as operations of the cognitive faculties, i.e., "information-processing" equipment *internal* to the organism.

With these points in mind, we may now advance the following base-clause principle for justified belief.

(5) If S's believing *p* at *t* results from a reliable cognitive belief-forming process (or set of processes), then S's belief in *p* at *t* is justified.

Since "reliable belief-forming process" has been defined in terms of such notions as belief, truth, statistical frequency, and the like, it is not an epistemic term. Hence, (5) is an admissible base clause.

It might seem as if (5) promises to be not only a successful base clause, but the only principle needed whatever, apart from a closure clause. In other words, it might seem as if it is a necessary as well as a sufficient condition of justifiedness that a belief be produced by reliable cognitive belief-forming processes. But this is not quite correct, given our provisional definition of "reliability."

Our provisional definition implies that a reasoning process is reliable only if it generally produces beliefs that are true, and similarly, that a memory process is reliable only if it generally yields beliefs that are true. But these requirements are too strong. A reasoning procedure cannot be expected to produce true belief if it is applied to false premises. And memory cannot be expected to yield a true belief if the original belief it attempts to retain is false. What we need for reasoning and memory, then, is a notion of "*conditional reliability*." A process is conditionally reliable when a sufficient proportion of its output-beliefs are true *given that its input-beliefs are true*.

With this point in mind, let us distinguish *belief-dependent* and *belief-independent* cognitive processes. The former are processes *some* of whose inputs are belief-states. The latter are processes *none* of whose inputs are belief-states. We may then replace principle (5) with the following two principles, the first a base-clause principle and the second a recursive-clause principle.

(6_A) If S's belief in *p* at *t* results ("immediately") from a belief-independent process that is (unconditionally) reliable, then S's belief in *p* at *t* is justified.

(6_B) If S's belief in *p* at *t* results ("immediately") from a belief-dependent process that is (at least) conditionally reliable, and if the beliefs (if any) on which this process operates in producing S's belief

in *p* at *t* are themselves justified, then S's belief in *p* at *t* is justified.

If we add to (6_A) and (6_B) the standard closure clause, we have a complete theory of justified belief. The theory says, in effect, that a belief is justified if and only if it is "*well-formed*," i.e., it has an ancestry of reliable and/or conditionally reliable cognitive operations. (Since a dated belief may be over-determined, it may have a number of distinct ancestral trees. These need not all be full of reliable or conditionally reliable processes. But at least one ancestral tree must have reliable or conditionally reliable processes throughout.)

The theory of justified belief proposed here, then, is an *Historical* or *Genetic* theory. It contrasts with the dominant approach to justified belief, an approach that generates what we may call (borrowing a phrase from Robert Nozick) "*Current Time-Slice*" theories. A Current Time-Slice theory makes the justificational status of a belief wholly a function of what is true of the cognizer *at the time* of belief. An Historical theory makes the justificational status of a belief depend on its prior history. Since my Historical theory emphasizes the reliability of the belief-generating processes, it may be called "*Historical Reliabilism*."

The most obvious examples of Current Time-Slice theories are "Cartesian" Foundationalist theories, which trace all justificational status (at least of contingent propositions) to current mental states. The usual varieties of Coherence theories, however, are equally Current Time-Slice views, since they too make the justificational status of a belief wholly a function of *current* states of affairs. For Coherence theories, however, these current states include all other beliefs of the cognizer, which would not be considered relevant by Cartesian Foundationalism. Have there been other Historical theories of justified belief? Among contemporary writers, Quine and Popper have Historical epistemologies, though the notion of "justification" is not their avowed *explicandum*. Among historical writers, it might seem that Locke and Hume had Genetic theories of sorts. But I think that their Genetic theories were only theories of ideas, not of knowledge or justification. Plato's theory of recollection, however, is a good example of a Genetic theory of knowing. And it might be argued that Hegel and Dewey had Genetic epistemologies (if Hegel can be said to have had a clear epistemology at all).

The theory articulated by (6_A) and (6_B) might be viewed as a kind of "Foundationalism" because of its recursive structure. I have no objection to this label, as long as one keeps in mind how different this "diachronic" form of Foundationalism is from Cartesian, or other "synchronic" varieties, of Foundationalism.

Current Time-Slice theories characteristically assume that the justificational status of a belief is something which the cognizer is able to know or determine at the time of belief. This is made explicit, for example, by Chisholm. The Historical theory I endorse makes no such assumption. There are many facts about a cognizer to which he lacks "privileged access," and I regard the justificational status of his beliefs as one of those things. This is not to say that a cognizer is necessarily ignorant, at any given moment, of the justificational status of his current beliefs. It is only to deny that he necessarily has, or can get, knowledge or true belief about this status. Just as a person can know without knowing that he knows, so he can have justified belief without knowing that it is justified (or believing justifiably that it is justified).

A characteristic case in which a belief is justified though the cognizer doesn't know that it's justified is where the original evidence for the belief has long since been forgotten. If the original evidence was compelling, the cognizer's original belief may have been justified, and this justificational status may have been preserved through memory. But since the cognizer no longer remembers how or why he came to believe, he may not know that the belief is justified. If

asked now to justify his belief, he may be at a loss. Still, the belief is justified, though the cognizer can't demonstrate or establish this.

The Historical theory of justified belief I advocate is connected in spirit with the causal theory of knowing I have presented elsewhere. I had this in mind when I remarked near the outset of the essay that my theory of justified belief makes justifiedness come out closely related to knowledge. Justified beliefs, like pieces of knowledge, have appropriate histories; but they may fail to be knowledge either because they are false or because they founder on some other requirement for knowing of the kind discussed in the post-Gettier knowledge-trade. [. . .]

Let us return now to the Historical theory. In the next section, I shall adduce reasons for strengthening it a bit. Before looking at these reasons, however, I wish to review two quite different objections to the theory.

First, a critic might argue that *some* justified beliefs do not derive their justificational status from their causal ancestry. In particular, it might be argued that beliefs about one's current phenomenal states and intuitive beliefs about elementary logical or conceptual relationships do not derive their justificational status in this way. I am not persuaded by either of these examples. Introspection, I believe, should be regarded as a form of retrospection. Thus, a justified belief that I am "now" in pain gets its justificational status from a relevant, though brief, causal history. The apprehension of logical or conceptual relationships is also a cognitive process that occupies time. The psychological process of "seeing" or "intuiting" a simple logical truth is very fast, and we cannot introspectively dissect it into constituent parts. Nonetheless, there are mental operations going on, just as there are mental operations that occur in *idiots savants*, who are unable to report the computational processes they in fact employ.

A second objection to Historical Reliabilism focuses on the reliability element rather than the causal or historical element. Since the theory is intended to cover all possible cases, it seems to imply that for any cognitive process C, if C is reliable in possible world W, then any belief in W that results from C is justified. But doesn't this permit easy counterexamples? Surely we can imagine a possible world in which wishful thinking is reliable. We can imagine a possible world where a benevolent demon so arranges things that beliefs formed by wishful thinking usually come true. This would make wishful thinking a reliable process in that possible world, but surely we don't want to regard beliefs that result from wishful thinking as justified.

There are several possible ways to respond to this case, and I am unsure which response is best, partly because my own intuitions (and those of other people I have consulted) are not entirely clear. One possibility is to say that in the possible world imagined, beliefs that result from wishful thinking *are* justified. In other words, we reject the claim that wishful thinking could never, intuitively, confer justifiedness.

However, for those who feel that wishful thinking couldn't confer justifiedness even in the world imagined, there are two ways out. First, it may be suggested that the proper criterion of justifiedness is the propensity of a process to generate beliefs that are true *in a non-manipulated environment*, i.e., an environment in which there is no purposeful arrangement of the world either to accord or conflict with the beliefs that are formed. In other words, the suitability of a belief-forming process is only a function of its success in "*natural*" situations, not situations of the sort involving benevolent or malevolent demons or any other such manipulative creatures. If we reformulate the theory to include this qualification, the counterexample in question will be averted.

Alternatively, we may reformulate our theory, or reinterpret it, as follows. Instead of construing the theory as saying that a belief in possible world W is justified if and only if it results from a cognitive process that is reliable in W, we may construe it as saying that a belief in possible world W is justified if and only if it results from a cognitive process that is reliable in *our world*. In short, our conception of justifiedness is derived as follows. We note certain cognitive processes in the actual world, and form beliefs about which of these are reliable. The ones we believe to be reliable are then regarded as justification-conferring processes. In reflecting on hypothetical beliefs, we deem them justified if and only if they result from processes already picked out as justification-conferring, or processes very similar to those. Since wishful thinking is not among these processes, a belief formed in a possible world W by wishful thinking would not be deemed justified, even if wishful thinking is reliable *in W*. I am not sure that this is a correct reconstruction of our intuitive conceptual scheme, but it would accommodate the benevolent demon case, at least if the proper thing to say in that case is that the wishful-thinking-caused beliefs are unjustified.

Even if we adopt this strategy, however, a problem still remains. Suppose that wishful thinking turns out to be reliable *in the actual world!* This might be because, unbeknownst to us at present, there is a benevolent demon who, lazy until now, will shortly start arranging things so that our wishes come true. The long-run performance of wishful thinking will be very good, and hence even the new construal of the theory will imply that beliefs resulting from wishful thinking (in *our* world) are justified. Yet this surely contravenes our intuitive judgment on the matter.

Perhaps the moral of the case is that the standard format of a "conceptual analysis" has its shortcomings. Let me depart from that format and try to give a better rendering of our aim and the theory that tries to achieve that aim. What we really want is an *explanation* of why we count, or would count, certain beliefs as justified and others as unjustified. Such an explanation must refer to our *beliefs* about reliability, not to the actual *facts*. The reason we *count* beliefs as justified is that they are formed by what we *believe* to be reliable belief-forming processes. Our beliefs about which belief-forming processes are reliable may be erroneous, but that does not affect the adequacy of the explanation. Since we *believe* that wishful thinking is an unreliable belief-forming process, we regard beliefs formed by wishful thinking as unjustified. What matters, then, is what we *believe* about wishful thinking, not what is *true* (in the long run) about wishful thinking. I am not sure how to express this point in the standard format of conceptual analysis, but it identifies an important point in understanding our theory.

Study Questions

1. What assumptions do traditional accounts of justification make?
2. Give an example of an account of justification that Goldman refutes. Explain how he refutes it.
3. What is Goldman's account of justification in terms of reliability? Explain one objection to it, and how Goldman responds.
4. Do you think it makes sense to say that a person can be justified in believing something even if he or she doesn't know that he or she is justified?

2.7   Meta-Skepticism: Meditations in Ethno-Epistemology

SHAUN NICHOLS, STEPHEN STICH, AND JONATHAN WEINBERG

In a cross-cultural study, SHAUN NICHOLS (University of Arizona), STEPHEN STICH (Rutgers University), and JONATHAN WEINBERG (University of Arizona) found significant variation in the intuitions of people from different cultures about a variety of thought experiments that have figured prominently in contemporary epistemological debate. Many other scholars have followed their lead in applying the methods of experimental psychology to the study of folk attributions of knowledge. While further research is required before we have a fully adequate picture of folk epistemological practice, the results of Nichols, Stich, and Weinberg and others should make epistemologists wary of drawing conclusions from their armchairs about what ordinary people think about knowledge.

Throughout the twentieth century, an enormous amount of intellectual fuel was spent debating the merits of a class of skeptical arguments which purport to show that knowledge of the external world is not possible. These arguments, whose origins can be traced back to Descartes, played an important role in the work of some of the leading philosophers of the twentieth century, including Russell, Moore and Wittgenstein, and they continue to engage

Shaun Nichols, Stephen Stich, and Jonathan M. Weinberg, "Meta-skepticism: Meditations in Ethno-epistemology." Reprinted by permission of the Publishers from "Meta-skepticism: Meditations in Ethno-epistemology," in *The Skeptics: Contemporary Essays*, ed. Steven Luper (Farnham: Ashgate, 2003). Copyright © 2003.

the interest of contemporary philosophers (for example Cohen 1999; DeRose 1995; Hill 1996; Klein 1981; Lewis 1996; McGinn 1993; Nozick 1981; Schiffer 1996; Unger 1975; Williams 1991). Typically, these arguments make use of one or more premises which the philosophers proposing them take to be intuitively obvious. Beyond an appeal to intuition, little or no defence is offered, and in many cases it is hard to see what else *could* be said in support of these premises. A number of authors have suggested that the intuitions undergirding these skeptical arguments are *universal*—shared by everyone (or almost everyone) who thinks reflectively about knowledge. In this chapter we will offer some evidence indicating that they are *far* from universal. Rather, the evidence suggests that many of the intuitions epistemologists invoke vary with the cultural background, socio-economic status and educational background of the person offering the intuition. And this, we will argue, is bad news for the skeptical arguments that rely on those intuitions. The evidence may also be bad news for skepticism itself—not because it shows that skepticism is *false*, but rather because, if we accept one prominent account of the link between epistemic intuitions and epistemic concepts, it indicates that skepticism may be much less *interesting* and much less *worrisome* than philosophers have taken it to be.

For the last two years, we have been conducting a series of experiments designed to test these hypotheses. In designing our experiments, we wanted our intuition probes—the cases that we would ask subjects to judge—to be similar to cases that have actually been used in the recent literature in epistemology. Would different groups show significantly different responses to standard epistemic thought experiments? The answer, it seems, is yes. While the results we have so far are preliminary, they are sufficient, we think, to suggest that there are substantial and systematic differences in the epistemic intuitions of people in different cultures and socio-economic groups. In Weinberg, Nichols and Stich (2001), we pre-sent a detailed account of our studies and results. For present purposes, it will suffice to sketch a few of the highlights.

The internalism/externalism debate has been central to analytic epistemology for decades. Internalism with respect to some epistemically evaluative property (for example knowledge) is the view that *only* factors within an agent's introspective grasp can be relevant to whether the agent's beliefs have that property. Other factors beyond the scope of introspection, such as the reliability of the psychological mechanisms that actually produced the belief, are epistemically external to the agent. In our experiments, we included a number of "Truetemp" cases inspired by Lehrer (2000), designed to explore whether externalist/internalist dimensions of our subjects' intuitions differed in subjects with different cultural backgrounds. Here is one of the questions we presented to our subjects:

> One day Charles is suddenly knocked out by a falling rock, and his brain becomes re-wired so that he is always absolutely right whenever he estimates the temperature where he is. Charles is completely unaware that his brain has been altered in this way. A few weeks later, this brain re-wiring leads him to believe that it is 71 degrees in his room. Apart from his estimation, he has no other reasons to think that it is 71 degrees. In fact, it is at that time 71 degrees in his room. Does Charles really know that it was 71 degrees in the room, or does he only believe it?

REALLY KNOWS   ONLY BELIEVES

In this intuition probe, Charles' belief is produced by a reliable mechanism, but it is stipulated that he is completely unaware of this reliability. This makes his reliability epistemically external. Therefore, to the extent that a subject population is unwilling to attribute knowledge in this case, we have evidence that suggests that the group's "folk epistemology" is internalist. Since the mechanism that leads to Charles' belief is not shared by other members of his community, Nisbett's work suggests that East Asians (EAs), with their strong commitment to social

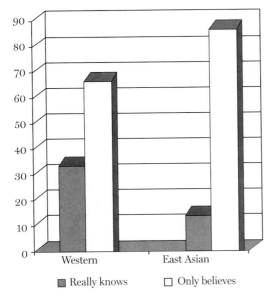

FIGURE 1 Individualistic Truetemp case.

harmony, might be less inclined than individualistic westerners (Ws) to count Charles' belief as knowledge. And, indeed, we found that while both EAs and Ws tended to deny knowledge, EA subjects were much more likely to deny knowledge than were Ws (Fisher Exact Test, p = .02). The results are shown in [Figure 1].

Another category of examples that has had a tremendous impact on analytic epistemology are "Gettier cases," in which a person has a true belief for which she has good evidence, though, as it happens, the evidence is false, or only accidentally true, or in some other way warrant-deprived. By their very construction, these cases are in many ways quite *similar* to unproblematic cases in which a person has good and true evidence for a true belief. Nisbett and his colleagues have shown that EAs are more inclined than Ws to make categorical judgements on the basis of similarity; Ws, on the other hand, are more disposed to focus on causation in describing the world and classifying things (Norenzayan *et al.* 1999; Watanabe 1998, 1999). In many Gettier cases, there is

a break in the causal link from the fact that makes the agent's belief true to her evidence for that belief. This suggests that EAs might be much less inclined than Ws to withhold the attribution of knowledge in Gettier cases. And, indeed, they are.

The intuition probe we used to explore cultural differences on Gettier cases was the following:

> Bob has a friend, Jill, who has driven a Buick for many years. Bob therefore thinks that Jill drives an American car. He is not aware, however, that her Buick has recently been stolen, and he is also not aware that Jill has replaced it with a Pontiac, which is a different kind of American car. Does Bob really know that Jill drives an American car, or does he only believe it?

REALLY KNOWS   ONLY BELIEVES

This probe produced a striking difference between the groups (Fisher Exact Test, p = .006). While a large majority of Ws give the standard answer in the philosophical literature, namely "Only believes," a majority of EAs have the *opposite* intuition—they said that Bob really knows. The results are shown in [Figure 2].

The data we've presented so far suggests that westerners and East Asians have significantly different epistemic intuitions. What about people in other cultures? We know of no experimental studies of cross-cultural differences in epistemic *practices* that are as rich and detailed as those of Nisbett and his colleagues. However, for some years Richard Shweder and his colleagues have been assembling evidence indicating that the thought processes of some groups of people on the Indian subcontinent are quite different from those of westerners (Shweder 1991). In some respects, the account of Indian thought that Shweder offers is rather similar to the account that Nisbett offers of East Asian thought—holism looms large in both accounts—though in other respects they are quite different. So one might suspect that

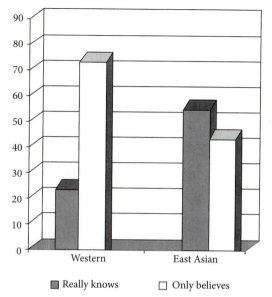

FIGURE 2 Gettier case: Western and East Asian.

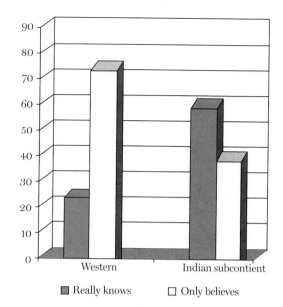

FIGURE 3 Gettier case: Western and Indian.

the epistemic intuitions of people from the Indian subcontinent (SCs) would be in some ways similar to those of EAs. And indeed they are. Like the EA subjects, SC subjects were much more likely than W subjects to attribute knowledge in a Gettier case (Fisher Exact Test, p = .002). The SC results on the Gettier case are shown in [Figure 3].

When we first analysed these data, we found them quite unsettling, since it seemed perfectly obvious to us that the people in Gettier cases *don't* have knowledge. But the results from our studies suggest that an important part of the explanation of our own clear intuitions about these cases is the fact that we were raised in a western culture. Nisbett was likewise surprised by his findings of cross-cultural differences in epistemic practices. In a recent review article, Nisbett and colleagues write:

> Almost two decades ago, Richard E. Nisbett wrote a book with Lee Ross entitled, modestly, *Human Inference* (Nisbett & Ross, 1980). Roy D'Andrade, a distinguished cognitive anthropologist, read

the book and told…Nisbett he thought it was a "good ethnography." The author was shocked and dismayed. But we now wholeheartedly agree with D'Andrade's contention about the limits of research conducted in a single culture. Psychologists who choose not to do cross-cultural psychology may have chosen to be ethnographers instead. (Nisbett *et al.* 2001: 307)

Our results suggest that philosophers who rely on their own intuitions about matters epistemic, and those of their colleagues, may have inadvertently made a similar choice. They too have chosen to be ethnographers; what they are doing is *ethno-epistemology*.

> It's clear that smoking cigarettes increases the likelihood of getting cancer. However, there is now a great deal of evidence that just using nicotine by itself without smoking (for instance, by taking a nicotine pill) does not increase the likelihood of getting cancer. Jim knows about this evidence and as a result, he believes that using nicotine does not increase the likelihood of getting cancer. It is possible that the tobacco companies dishonestly made

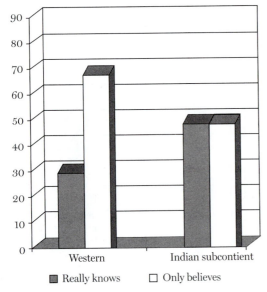

FIGURE 4 Zebra case: Western and Indian.

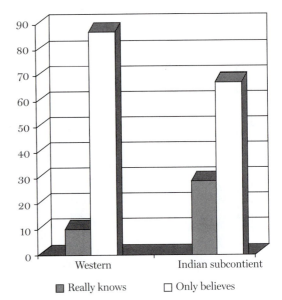

FIGURE 5 Conspiracy case: Western and Indian.

up and publicized this evidence that using nicotine does not increase the likelihood of cancer, and that the evidence is really false and misleading. Now, the tobacco companies did not actually make up this evidence, but Jim is not aware of this fact. Does Jim really know that using nicotine doesn't increase the likelihood of getting cancer, or does he only believe it?

REALLY KNOWS   ONLY BELIEVES

Mike is a young man visiting the zoo with his son, and when they come to the zebra cage, Mike points to the animal and says, "that's a zebra." Mike is right—it is a zebra. However, as the older people in his community know, there are lots of ways that people can be tricked into believing things that aren't true. Indeed, the older people in the community know that it's possible that zoo authorities could cleverly disguise mules to look just like zebras, and people viewing the animals would not be able to tell the difference. If the animal that Mike called a zebra had really been such a cleverly painted mule, Mike still would have thought that it was a zebra. Does Mike really

know that the animal is a zebra, or does he only believe that it is?

REALLY KNOWS   ONLY BELIEVES

Using this probe, we found a significant difference between western and subcontinental subjects (Fisher Exact Test, $p = .049$) [Figure 4]. One possible explanation of these data is that SCs, like low SES westerners, regard knowledge as less demanding than do high SES westerners. And in fact we found that SC subjects were also more likely than Ws to attribute knowledge in the conspiracy case (Fisher Exact Test, $p = .025$). The results are shown in [Figure 5]. SC and low SES subjects thus appear to be significantly less susceptible to skeptical intuitions, at least in these cases. These findings contrast sharply with our evidence on EAs. We did *not* find significant differences between EAs and high SES Ws on either the zebra case or the conspiracy case.

In Section 2, we proposed, as our third hypothesis, that epistemic intuitions might vary as a function of the number of philosophy courses one had taken. Though no data relevant to this third hypothesis was presented in our earlier paper on epistemic intuitions (Weinberg *et al.*, 2001) we have recently completed a study that provides some support for this hypothesis. In that study we presented subjects with a series of epistemic intuition probes, and we divided the subjects into two groups: subjects who had taken few philosophy courses (two or less) and subjects who had taken many philosophy courses (three or more). There were 48 students in the "low philosophy" group and 15 in the "high philosophy" group. One of the probes we presented was a brain-in-a-vat scenario. The probe reads as follows:

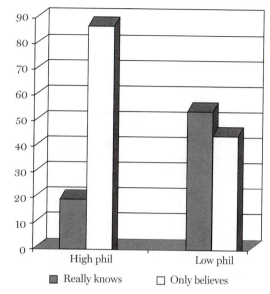

FIGURE 6 Brain in vat case.

George and Omar are roommates, and enjoy having late-night "philosophical" discussions. One such night Omar argues, "At some point in time, by, like, the year 2300, the medical and computer sciences will be able to simulate the real world very convincingly. They will be able to grow a brain without a body, and hook it up to a supercomputer in just the right way so that the brain has experiences exactly as if it were a real person walking around in a real world, talking to other people, and so on. And so the brain would believe it was a real person walking around in a real world, etc., except that it would be wrong—it's just stuck in a virtual world, with no actual legs to walk and with no other actual people to talk to. And here's the thing: how could you ever tell that it isn't really the year 2300 now, and that you're not really a virtual-reality brain? If you were a virtual-reality brain, after all, everything would look and feel exactly the same to you as it does now!"

George thinks for a minute, and then replies: "But, look, here are my legs." He points down to his legs. "If I were a virtual-reality brain, I wouldn't have any legs really—I'd only really be just a disembodied brain. But I know I have legs—just look at them!—so I must be a real person, and not a virtual-reality brain, because only real people have

real legs. So I'll continue to believe that I'm not a virtual-reality brain."

George and Omar are actually real humans in the actual real world today, and so neither of them are virtual-reality brains, which means that George's belief is true. But does George know that he is not a virtual-reality brain, or does he only believe it?

REALLY KNOWS   ONLY BELIEVES

We found a quite significant difference between low and high philosophy groups on this probe (Fisher Exact Test, p = .016). The evidence indicates that students with less philosophy are more likely to claim that the person knows he's not a brain in a vat. The results are presented in [Figure 6]. This suggests that the propensity for skeptical intuitions varies significantly as a function of exposure to philosophy. Indeed, so far this skeptical intuition case is the *only* probe on which we have found significant differences between students as a function of how many philosophy classes they have had.

5 SOME META-SKEPTICAL CONCLUSIONS

What conclusions can be drawn from these studies? The first and most obvious conclusion is that, though the empirical exploration of epistemic intuitions, and of philosophical intuitions more generally, is still in its infancy, the evidence currently available suggests that all three of our initial hypotheses may well be true. Epistemic intuitions, including skeptical intuitions, appear to vary systematically as a function of the cultural background, the socio-economic status and the number of philosophy courses taken by the person whose intuitions are being elicited. We want to emphasize that all the results we have reported should be regarded as quite preliminary. To make a suitably rich and compelling case for our hypotheses, it will be important to replicate and extend the findings we have reported. But our data thus far certainly lend support to the claim that there is a great deal of diversity in epistemic intuitions, and that a substantial part of that diversity is due to differences in cultural background, SES and philosophical training.

If that's right, and if, as we contended in Section 1, the defence of many of the premises used in arguments for skepticism comes to rest on an explicit or implicit appeal to intuition, then we can also conclude that the appeal of these skeptical arguments will be much more local than many philosophers suppose. For if people in different cultural and SES groups and people who have had little or no philosophical training do not share "*our*" intuitions (that is, the intuitions of the typical analytic philosopher who is white, western, high SES and has had *lots* of philosophical training) then they are unlikely to be as convinced or distressed as "*we*" are by arguments whose premises seem plausible only if one has the intuitions common in our very small cultural and intellectual tribe. *Pace* McGinn's "anthropological conjecture," skepticism is neither primitive nor inevitable. And *pace* Stroud there

is no reason to think that skepticism "appeals to something deep in our nature." Rather, it seems, its appeal is very much a product of our culture, our social status and our education!

We do not, of course, deny that some people (ourselves included!) find it very hard to loosen the grip of skeptical intuitions. Along with most high SES western philosophers, we find many skeptical intuitions to be obvious and compelling. However, we are inclined to think that the lesson to be drawn from our cross-cultural studies is that, however obvious they may seem, these intuitions are simply not to be trusted. If the epistemic intuitions of people in different groups disagree, they can't all be true. The fact that epistemic intuitions vary systematically with culture and SES indicates that these intuitions are caused (in part) by culturally local phenomena. And there is no reason to think that the culturally local phenomena that cause *our* intuitions track the truth any better than the culturally local phenomena that cause intuitions that differ from ours. Our predicament is in some ways analogous to the predicament of a person who is raised in a homogeneous and deeply religious culture and finds the truth of certain religious claims to be obvious or compelling. When such a person discovers that other people do not share his intuitions, he may well come to wonder why his intuitions are any more likely to be true than theirs. On second thought, our situation is a bit worse. The religious person might rest content with the thought that, for some reason or other God has chosen to cause his group to have religious intuitions that track the truth. Few philosophers will rest content with the parallel thought about their epistemic intuitions.

We are not, we should stress, defending a generalized skepticism that challenges the use of *all* intuitions in philosophy. Rather, our skepticism is focused on those intuitions that differ systematically from one social group to another. There is, of course, a sense in which the philosophical literature on skepticism also supports the conclusion that some of our epistemic intuitions are not to be trusted, since, as the quote from Cohen in Section 1 illustrates, much of that literature is devoted to showing that our epistemic intuitions appear to support a logically inconsistent set of propositions, and to arguing about which of these intuitions should be ignored. But our findings raise a quite different problem. For even if some individual or group had a completely consistent set of intuitions, the fact that these intuitions are determined, to a significant degree, by one's cultural, SES and educational background, and the fact that people in other groups have systematically different intuitions, raises the question of why the folks who have these consistent intuitions should trust any of them.

One way in which a philosopher might resist our contention that the systematic cultural variation in epistemic intuitions indicates that these intuitions are not to be trusted would be to argue that intuitive differences of the sort that we've reported are an indication that the people offering the intuitions *have different epistemic concepts*. In his recent book, *From Metaphysics to Ethics*, Frank Jackson clearly endorses the view that people whose epistemic intuitions differ on philosophically important cases should be counted as having different epistemic concepts.

> I have occasionally run across people who resolutely resist the Gettier cases. Sometimes it has seemed right to accuse them of confusion...but sometimes it is clear that they are not confused; what we then learn from the stand-off is simply that they use the word "knowledge" to cover different cases from most of us. In these cases it is, it seems to me, misguided to accuse them of error (unless they go on to say that their concept of knowledge is ours). (Jackson 1998: 32)

So for Jackson (unconfused) East Asians or Indians who insist that the people described in Gettier cases *do* have knowledge are not disagreeing with those of us who think they don't.

Rather, they are simply using the term "knowledge" to express a different concept. And, in all likelihood, an East Asian or Indian is *right* to insist that (as he uses the term) people in Gettier cases *do* have knowledge, just as, in all likelihood, we are right to insist that (as we use the term), they *don't*. Though Jackson focuses on the example of Gettier cases, we think it is clear that he would say much the same about people who react differently to the sorts of skeptical intuition probes discussed in Section 4. Those people, too, if they are not simply confused, should be viewed as having different epistemic concepts. Thus there is no real disagreement between people who react differently to skeptical intuition probes, and in all likelihood their intuitions are all true.

There is, of course, a substantial literature on concepts and concept individuation (see, for example, Margolis and Laurence 1999), and many of the leading contributors to that literature would strongly disagree with Jackson's claim that people who have different intuitions about Gettier cases have different concepts of knowledge (see, for example, Fodor 1998). We have no allegiance to any theory of concepts or to any account of concept individuation. But we think it is of considerable interest to simply *assume*, for argument's sake, that Jackson is right, and to ask what follows.

One important consequence of this assumption is that it undermines our attempt to argue from the results of our cross-cultural studies of epistemic intuitions to the conclusion that those intuitions are not to be trusted. Crucial to our argument was the claim that, since epistemic intuitions of people in different groups disagree, they can't all be true. But if Jackson is right about concepts, then our subjects are not really disagreeing at all; they are simply using the word "knowledge" (or "know") to express different concepts. So their intuitively supported claims about knowledge (or, to be more precise, about what *they* call "knowledge"), including those claims used in arguments for skepticism, *can* all be true, and as Jackson would have it, in all likelihood they *are*.

But while Jackson's account of concept individuation makes it easier to maintain that the premises of skeptical arguments are true, it makes it harder to see why the *conclusions* of those arguments are interesting or worrisome. To see the point, we need only note that, if Jackson is right about concepts and if we are right about the influence of culture, SES and philosophical training on epistemic intuitions, then it follows that the term "knowledge" is used to express *lots of concepts*. East Asians, Indians and high SES westerners all have different concepts; high and low SES westerners have different concepts; people who have studied lots of philosophy and people who have studied no philosophy have different concepts. And that, no doubt, is just the tip of the iceberg. Moreover, these concepts don't simply differ in *intension*, they differ in *extension*—they apply to different classes of actual and possible cases.

In the philosophical tradition, skepticism is taken to be worrisome because it denies that knowledge is possible, and that's bad because knowledge, it is assumed, is something very important. On Plato's view, "wisdom and knowledge are the highest of human things" (Plato 1892/1937: 352), and many people, both philosophers and ordinary folk, would agree. But obviously, if there are many concepts of knowledge, and if these concepts have different extensions, it can't be the case that *all* of them are the highest of human things. If Jackson is right about concepts, then the arguments for skepticism in the philosophical tradition pose a serious challenge to the possibility of having what high SES, white westerners with lots of philosophical training call "knowledge." But those arguments give us no reason to think that we can't have what other people—East Asians, Indians, low SES people, or scientists

who have never studied philosophy—would call "knowledge." And, of course, those skeptical arguments give us no reason at all to think that what high SES white western philosophers call "knowledge" is any better, or more important, or more desirable, or more useful than what these other folks call "knowledge," or that it is any closer to "the highest of human things." Without some reason to think that what white, western, high SES philosophers call "knowledge" is any more valuable, desirable or useful than any of the other commodities that other groups call "knowledge" it is hard to see why we should care if we can't have it.

Let us close with a brief review of the main themes of the chapter. Arguments for skepticism have occupied a central place in western philosophy. And it's easy to see why. Skeptical arguments threaten dramatic conclusions from premises that are intuitively compelling to many philosophers, including the three of us. A number of western philosophers maintain that the intuitions invoked in skeptical arguments have nothing to do with being western or a philosopher. Rather, these intuitions are regarded as intrinsic to human nature and cross-culturally universal. We've argued that our evidence poses a serious challenge to this universalist stance. Our data suggest that some of the most familiar skeptical intuitions are far from universal—they vary as a function of culture, SES and educational background. We find that this evidence generates a nagging sense that our own skeptical intuitions are parochial vestiges of our culture and education. Had we been raised in a different culture or SES group or had a different educational background, we would have been much less likely to find these intuitions compelling. This historical arbitrariness of our skeptical intuitions leads us to be skeptical that we can trust these intuitions to be true; for we see no reason to think that our cultural and intellectual tribe should be so privileged. One might, as we've noted, maintain that different cultural, SES and educational groups simply have different concepts of knowledge, and that on our concept of knowledge, the skeptical intuitions are true. Although this response is available, it saps the drama from the skeptical conclusion. It's not clear that skepticism would have held such a grip over the minds of epistemologists if the skeptic is reduced to the claim that the external world can't be "known," according to the concept of knowledge used by the relatively small cultural group to which we happen to belong. As one of us wrote some years ago, "The best first response to the skeptic who maintains that we cannot achieve certainty,...knowledge or what have you, is not to argue that we can. Rather, it is to ask, so what?" (Stich 1990: 26).

References

Burnyeat, M. 1982. "Idealism and Greek Philosophy: What Descartes Saw and Berkeley Missed." *Philosophical Review*, 91, 3–40.

Cohen, S. 1999. "Contextualism, Skepticism, and the Structure of Reasons." In J. Tomberlin (ed.) *Philosophical Perspectives*, 13. Cambridge, MA: Blackwell, 57–90.

DeRose, K. 1995. "Solving the Skeptical Problem." *Philosophical Review*, 104, 1–52.

DeRose, K. 1999. "Introduction: Responding to Skepticism." In K. DeRose & T. Warfield (eds.) *Skepticism: A Contemporary Reader*. New York: Oxford University Press.

Dretske, F. 1970. "Epistemic Operators." *Journal of Philosophy*, 67(24), 1007–1023.

Fodor, J. 1998. *Concepts: Where Cognitive Science Went Wrong*. Oxford: Oxford University Press.

Haidt, J., S. Koller & M. Dias 1993. "Affect, Culture and Morality." *Journal of Personality & Social Psychology*, 65, 4, 613–628.

Hill, C. 1996. "Process Reliabilism and Cartesian Skepticism." *Philosophy and Phenomenological Research*, 56, 567–581.

Jackson, F. 1998. *From Metaphysics to Ethics: A Defense of Conceptual Analysis*. Oxford: Clarendon Press.

Klein, P. 1981. *Certainty: A Refutation of Scepticism*. Minneapolis: University of Minnesota Press.

Lehrer, K. 1990. *Theory of Knowledge*. Boulder and London: Westview Press and Routledge.

Lewis, D. 1996. "Elusive Knowledge." *Australasian Journal of Philosophy*, 74, 549–567.

Margolis, E. and Laurence, S. 1999. *Concepts*. Cambridge, MA: MIT Press

McGinn, C. 1993. *Problems in Philosophy: The Limits of Inquiry*. Oxford: Blackwell.

Nagel, T. 1986. *The View from Nowhere*. Oxford: Oxford University Press.

Nisbett, R. and Ross, L. 1980. *Human Inference: Strategies and Shortcomings of Social Judgment*. Englewood Cliffs, NJ: Prentice-Hall.

Nisbett, R. E., K. Peng, I. Choi and A. Norenzayan. 2001. "Culture and Systems of Thought: Holistic Versus Analytic Cognition." *Psychological Review*, vol. 108, no. 2, p. 291–310.

Norenzayan, A., Nisbett, R. E., Smith, E. E., & Kim, B. J. 1999. *Rules vs. similarity as a basis for reasoning and judgment in East and West*. Ann Arbor: University of Michigan.

Nozick, R.1981. *Philosophical Explanations*. Cambridge, MA: Harvard University Press.

Pinker, S. 1997. *How the Mind Works*. New York: Norton.

Plato (1892/1937). *The Dialogues of Plato*, translated by B. Jowett. New York: Random House.

Schiffer, S. 1996. "Contextualist Solutions to Skepticism." *Proceedings of the Aristotelian Society*, 96, 317–333.

Shweder, R. 1991. *Thinking Through Cultures: Explorations in Cultural Psychology*. Cambridge. MA: Harvard University Press.

Stich, S. 1988. "Reflective Equilibrium, Analytic Epistemology and the Problem of Cognitive Diversity." *Synthese*, 74, 391–413.

Stich, S. 1990. *The Fragmentation of Reason: Preface to a Pragmatic Theory of Cognitive Evaluation*. Cambridge, MA: Bradford Books/ MIT Press.

Stroud, B. 1984. *The Significance of Philosophical Skepticism*. Oxford: Oxford University Press.

Unger, P. 1975. *Ignorance: A Case for Skepticism*. Oxford: Oxford University Press.

Watanabe, M. 1998. "Styles of reasoning in Japan and the United States: Logic of education in two cultures." Paper presented at the American Sociological Association Annual Meeting, San Francisco, August, 1998.

Watanabe, M. 1999. *Styles of reasoning in Japan and the United States: Logic of education in two cultures.* Unpublished Ph.D. thesis, Columbia University.

Weinberg, J., Nichols, S. and Stich, S. (2001). "Normativity & Epistemic Intuitions." *Philosophical Topics.*

Williams, M. 1996. *Unnatural Doubts.* Princeton: Princeton University Press.

Study Questions

1. What kind of variation between demographic groups did Nichols, Stich, and Weinberg find within the set of responses they obtained to some key epistemological thought experiments?

2. Explain how the results obtained by Nichols, Stich, and Weinberg seem to pose a challenge to the standard assumptions and methodology found in contemporary epistemology. How serious do you think this challenge is?

CHAPTER 3

Explanation and Causation

ALEXANDRA BRADNER

HOW DOES ECHOLOCATION WORK? WHY DO people cooperate? What makes silk so strong? How is it possible for sequences of random events to be correlated? Why is it so difficult to receive an A in this course?

The study of explanation is the study of questions, and the related study of understanding is the study of how we answer them. When we've solved a puzzle, hit upon an answer, or acquired a skill, a shift occurs: we "get it." But what exactly has changed? Philosophers of science, language, metaphysics, and epistemology have been trying to "get" explanation since the fourth century BCE, when Aristotle's *Posterior Analytics* and *Physics* offered an alternative to Plato's account of understanding in Book VI of the *Republic*. Where Plato recommends a particular form of conversation, called dialectic, as means to understanding concepts and their logical consequences, Aristotle suggests that we pay less attention to one another and closer attention to the external world. For Plato, understanding involves being able to articulate a true belief in a way that is acceptable to one's interlocutor. For Aristotle, understanding is being able to describe the most important aspects of a thing, to discern the thing's efficient cause, constitutive material, formal structure, and developmental trajectory. Plato thinks that understanding is something people can provide to one another, while Aristotle thinks understanding is something that comes from close observation of the world.

This chapter is organized around an Aristotelian insight about explanation: that we have many different intuitions about what it means to explain; and a Platonic insight about understanding: that doing philosophy

with one another increases our understanding. Although many philosophical discussions of explanation appear to be in conversation with one another, in that they
seem to employ the same terms and concepts, there is actually so much diversity in
this subfield that it is difficult to claim even a family resemblance among the various
debates and texts. In this unit, we will examine three classic philosophical texts and
two psychological texts with the aim of clarifying this array. Aristotle recognizes four
styles or modes of explanation, among which our contemporary concept of causation, *efficient causation*, is merely one. Hume and Lewis, on the other hand, focus
exclusively on efficient causation. Moreover, each of these philosophers investigates
the concept of causation for slightly different reasons: Aristotle's primary interest
is in building propositions we can accept from empirically discovered foundations;
Hume's primary interest is using what we know to amplify our knowledge further; and
Lewis's primary interest is analytic clarity. In Aristotelian terms, Aristotle is interested
in understanding; Hume, in demonstration; and Lewis, in definition.[1] To complicate
matters even more, psychologists and cognitive scientists have begun to explore causation and explanation with their own methods and tools. They are posing their own
research questions, triangulated through their own disciplines' interests, histories, and
canons. Early experimental psychologist Albert Michotte creates a new experimental
technique to suggest, contra Hume, that we can directly perceive causal connections,
while contemporary developmental psychologist Alison Gopnik, along with her interdisciplinary team of collaborators, develops a novel experimental apparatus to argue
for the *theory theory*, which suggests that children formulate theories about the causal
structure of the world according to the same rational process that enables scientists to
make sense of massive amounts of noisy data.

Our first author, Aristotle (384–322 BCE), wrote thoughtfully on a plurality of
philosophical subfields. But most significantly for our purposes, he was a naturalist.
For many years during his midlife, he traveled the coast of Asia Minor and islands of
Greece, observing diverse flora and fauna and carefully recording a quiet multitude of
parts, functions, and developmental trajectories. This diligent empirical work became,
literally, the foundation of his philosophical program. So it would not be anachronis-
tic to say that Aristotle was the first important empirical philosopher. His *a posteriori*
method and epistemic *foundationalism* was at the very heart of his response to the
writings of his teacher, Plato (429–347 BCE), whose dialogue *Meno* identified a very
serious epistemic problem: To understand something, for example, the concept of virtue, you might start by looking at examples of virtuous action. But, on reflection, this
strategy will not work, because in order to gather those examples, you must already
know what virtue is. It seems you must use the very concept you are trying to define
in order to define it. And this amounts to arguing in a circle. Plato reasons that the
only solution to this problem is to (somehow) come to know the concept *prior* to your
worldly search for examples.

From Aristotle's naturalistic perspective, the world is not quite so unarticulated—
so mushy, so uniform, so dizzying. After all, we manage to live here quite well. We
can come to know the things that matter to us through a very detailed process of
accretion. Bit by bit, we piece together our observations of specific individuals, their
parts, and their growth or generation until we can reasonably gather all of this local

data into more general sets or categories. We don't need to locate a transcendent organizing principle in order to structure or define a disparate collection of indiscrete pieces. Instead, there is in fact a way the world is, a way it is carved up into parts and pieces, and a way it ought to develop. The order is already here in the world, and we can come to know its form if we pay close attention.

The Aristotle selection in this chapter starts with the classic presentation in his *Physics* of the four causes—the material, efficient, formal, and final—which establishes the framework according to which causation, explanation, and understanding have been discussed ever since. But while this text is usually presented on its own, we have here placed it in the larger context of Aristotle's *Posterior Analytics*, his philosophy of science, and *Parts of Animals*, one portion of his extensive biology, without which the four causes are unnecessarily cryptic. The four causes are not really what we would call "causes" in our contemporary sense of the word. Aristotle's four causes are modes or styles of understanding. They identify four ways of connecting an individual to its more accidental attributes or parts. In coming to understand something, like a particular person, Socrates, we might investigate his material, of what he is made or composed. Socrates is composed of flesh and blood. But we might also investigate his efficient cause, that which is responsible for his very existence, that which brought him into existence. The efficient cause of Socrates is his parents. The last two modes of understanding are more difficult. Recall how Aristotle responds to Plato with the alternative suggestion that the world is *already* formed, organized, or knower ready. There is a way the world is, a way it develops, a trajectory or path it is on. The formal cause of Socrates is what distinguishes his otherwise indiscriminate lump of material from other indiscriminate lumps of material. This cause is the thing without which Socrates, quite literally, would not be Socrates. The last way to understand an individual is through its final cause. This mode of understanding asks us to consider where the individual is headed developmentally. Aristotle's universe is not static. As he observed in his travels, things are always changing, growing, and developing. And these changes are not random or spontaneous. Like a mathematical vector, directionality cannot be separated from magnitude; directionality is built in to the world. So an individual thing's final cause, conditioned by its formal cause, is the state where it would end up if it were to develop under its right, that is, under its natural or normal, conditions. The final cause of an acorn, for instance, is not to end up cracked into pieces on a sidewalk, but to blossom into a fully formed oak tree. So the final cause for Socrates is the fully formed version of himself, a Socrates who has flourished, which, for Aristotle, means a Socrates with health, wealth, true friends, and a supportive community, and, most of all, a Socrates fully engaged in his community and in possession of a highly developed sense of practical wisdom, which he calls upon to make appropriate—never extreme—choices.

The readings from Aristotle's *Parts of Animals* and *Posterior Analytics* help to deepen our understanding of the four causes. In *Posterior Analytics*, Aristotle explains why the four causes are important: they serve as *middle terms*. Middle terms are responsible for connecting attributes to the things. Aristotle thinks of knowledge as predication, and middle terms enable us to predicate. Thus, one can come to understand why a thing has a certain attribute by considering any of the following: the thing's material composition, its efficient cause, its form or nature, or its final stage or end. In many cases, Aristotle uses an animal's final cause to explain why the animal has a certain part. Why does a duck have webbed feet, for example? The final cause of a duck is to be a swimming bird. So, a duck has webbed feet in order to swim. The final cause connects the animal, the duck, with the part or attribute, the webbed feet. Note that we do not use the four causes to *demonstrate* that a duck has webbed feet. And we do not use the four causes to *define* the duck. The four causes do something different than demonstrate or define; they explain.

The influence of our second author, David Hume (1711–1776), cannot be underestimated. His *Treatise*, two *Enquiries*, and essays are works that made already thoughtful people think harder: Charles Darwin and Immanuel Kant were among Hume's many close readers. Within Hume's *Dialogues Concerning Natural Religion*, we find a brief statement of natural selection; and Kant, after reading Hume, spent the remainder of his career trying to find "transcendental" ways to draw connections that we cannot witness in our experience.

Hume learned from Descartes' first meditation, in his *Meditations on First Philosophy* (1641), that sense perception would always underdetermine our theories about the real world: our visual perception of the fire in front of us would never determine whether a real fire was the cause of that perception or whether a dream was the cause of that perception. Hume also embraced Descartes' suggestion in the second meditation that particular forms of certainty are possible: we seem to have incorrigible access to the contents of our own minds. We may not be certain there *is* a real fire there, but we are certain we *think* there is a fire there. For Hume, ideas are vivid if (and *only* if) they are copied from impressions. And he thinks of impressions quite literally: our mind is like a sheet of clay, and the parts of the world we can access directly, through our five senses, impress themselves onto our minds, as stamps would onto a pad, no inference or intentional process of connection required. It is the fact that these sense impressions are immediate, direct, and uncorrupted that accounts for their liveliness. We cannot be certain of any claims that are not directly anchored in or fully reducible to sense impressions—this is *classic empiricism*. But this epistemic investment in immediate sensation raises the puzzling question of how we might come to know the multitude of things we have *not* experienced.

Hume was simply too much of a naturalist to accept Descartes' hyperbolic solution to his hyperbolic doubts; that is, Hume could not accept the suggestion that God secures the representative connection between mind and world. George Berkeley's *A Treatise Concerning the Principles of Human Knowledge* (1710) had Hume convinced that only a *deus ex machina* could bridge the metaphysical gap between mental and material substance. Nevertheless, Descartes and his critics left Hume thinking about certainty and whether we could leverage our certainty about the contents of our own minds into broader knowledge claims. He was interested in whether there could be any ground whatsoever for the various kinds of outward connections we draw from our own ideas to what is spatiotemporally removed from those ideas. In short, Descartes' skepticism and Berkeley's idealism left Hume interested in the question of *amplification*, how we might "bootstrap" what we know through direct experience into claims about what we have not yet experienced.

The only way to genuinely build upon what we already know is to come to know some connection between what we already know and something else, something genuinely different.

(a) We might start with an idea of a shade of red—an idea generated from a visual impression—and amplify our knowledge by connecting that idea to its cause, an actual rose.

(b) Similarly, we might start with an idea of dark, foreboding clouds, again generated from a visual impression, and amplify our knowledge by connecting that idea to the prediction that it's going to rain in the future.

(c) Or we might start with an idea of several black-and-white penguins in our mind, one summarized from our many direct observations over the years and in many places, and amplify our knowledge by connecting that idea to the suggestion that Antarctica penguins (i.e., far-away penguins we have never experienced) are also black and white.

The reason that each of these connections seems to serve as an example of knowledge is because the connections do not seem random or contingent. They seem to involve a kind of necessity. But, if we focus on the idea that there is a necessary connection between each of the first things mentioned in (a) through (c) (in each case an idea) and each of the second things mentioned in (a) through (c) (variously, a presented object, a future event, and a group of far-away objects), Hume notices in section VII of the *Enquiry* that we don't have any direct experience or impression of such connections. As a result, such connections float freely, unanchored and equipollent with many other creatively hypothesized connections, perhaps those between sensations of red and claims about far-away penguins, or ideas of dark clouds and actual roses.

To make matters worse, Hume also presents his devastating problem of induction. He begins section IV by arguing that relations of ideas never tell us anything new.[2] Like a cow's four-part digestive system, when we relate ideas that are simply imperfect definitions of one another, we endlessly regurgitate what we already know. Matters of fact, like the fact that the sun will rise tomorrow, on the other hand, are worth knowing, for they do amplify our knowledge. Matters of fact synthesize or connect the idea of the sun with the idea of rising tomorrow. So how might we come to know more matters of fact? Aside from "the present testimony of our senses," we come to know matters of fact primarily though cause-effect reasoning. And this is a serious problem. We know we cannot *deduce* effects from causes because if the relationship between causes and effects were deductive, the opposite effect would be logically impossible, but it's not logically impossible. And we cannot *induce* effects from causes; we cannot collect our past experiences and use them to guarantee our predictions about what we have not experienced (what is temporally or spatially far away from us) without employing the very same form of reasoning we are trying to secure. Say, for example, that we want to justify our belief that the sun will rise tomorrow. It *seems* reasonable to say that our vast past experience of the sun's rising—the fact that we have experienced the sun's rising many, many times before—is relevant. But *why* is it reasonable to use past experience in this way? Hume argues that we can only employ past experience as a guide to the future if we assume that the future is going to be *like* the past, that is, if we assume that Nature is uniform, that the times and places we have not yet experienced contain *more of the same*: massive objects will still fall to the ground; cats will still hunt mice; and the sun will still rise. But on what basis can we assume *this*? *Why* is it *reasonable* to expect more of the same? We expect more of the same because we have *always* found Nature to be uniform: in the *past*, it turned out to be the case that the very recent past *was* the same as the distant past. In short, we have *past experience* of Nature's uniformity. But to assume without argument that this information is relevant is to assume what we were trying to prove in the first place. We are inquiring *as to whether* past experience is relevant to our beliefs about the future, so we cannot assume that past experience is relevant in order to demonstrate that it is. There is no non-question-begging way to justify the employment of cause-effect reasoning and, thus, no way to know matters of fact.

Inspired by Copernicus's suggestion that humanity is not the center of God's universe and Galileo's conclusion that the terrestrial and heavenly spheres are governed by the same secular laws of motion, philosophical Modernity became the quest to ground knowledge in scientific observation and testing, in sense perception, instead of in sacred texts and their divine interpreters. Hume ends this movement on a dark note by demonstrating (in several ways) that we cannot justify any attempt to amplify our knowledge beyond the ideas we have copied from our impressions—beyond our direct experience. We cannot know tomorrow, because we have no impressions of it yet. We cannot know Antarctica, because we're not there. And although we can experience the parts of the world that impress us, we cannot know these parts of the world, for we cannot ground the claim that the idea of red we have is the effect of a real rose.

Contemporary Anglo-American philosophers in the naturalist tradition haven't moved much beyond Hume's own "solution" to his problem in section V: Hume was prompted by his argument to give up on the traditional epistemological project of justification and focus instead on the science of mind, that is, on the noting, tracking, and recording of mental regularities and associations. We cannot *know* that the sun will rise tomorrow, but we all *expect* it to rise tomorrow. Our beliefs used to be the kinds of things that could be right or wrong, justified or unjustified. But, post-Hume, our beliefs are only associated or correlated with other things. It is simply unfounded or question begging to claim anything more for them. This might seem like a great loss. We now must reconceive our mental lives—the thoughtful decisions and theoretical positions that seem to define us—as the automated upshots of external conditioning. But contemporary Humean philosophers like Richard Rorty and Daniel Dennett have argued that this is merely the latest in a long series of disenchantments. Rather than a loss, this is an opportunity for more empirical and experimental philosophy, an opportunity to abandon the derivative and narrow project of philosophical reflection for the diverse and unpredictable nature of practical experience. *Empirical* philosophers are those who accept scientific data as an important constraint on philosophical theorizing. (In fact, many empirical philosophers follow Hume in refusing to recognize a distinction in kind between science and philosophy.) *Experimental* philosophers, as opposed to empirical philosophers, study how people shift their responses to classic philosophical thought experiments when different aspects of these thought experiments are altered. This chapter does not explore the experimental philosophy of explanation and causation. But the following Michotte and Gopnik readings are included here as examples of empirical philosophy.

Albert Michotte (1881–1965) is energized by Hume's skepticism. An esteemed Belgian experimental psychologist of action (rather than mere behavior or movement), he pursues the science of mind through laboratory experimentation, rather than philosophical reflection. But, unlike many early experimental psychologists, Michotte does not feel the need to restrict his theorizing only to those phenomena into which he can experimentally intervene. He hopes to use the scientific method to shed light on questions traditionally reserved for philosophical investigation.[3] Michotte turns to perception and causality in his sixties, when he takes up the Thomistic project of developing a philosophy of experience that is not single-mindedly focused on sense experience. He was not interested in mere physical response, as the behaviorists were, but in what he calls the "meaning" of the response: "[T]he act of giving could be performed in limitless ways, using quite different groups of muscles, and yet every observer would experience it as the same act of donation."[4] Michotte argues for two levels of psychic activity, sensation and higher level thought, but he claims that intellectual concepts are prefigured in perceptual categories. Thus, at the same time that he opposes behaviorism, he also challenges the "intellectualist" view of perception, the view that perception is an active process of logical inference or hypothesis making.[5] For Michotte, meaning is merely a direct sign or indication of what has been perceived. According to this view, meaning can be directly experienced.

How might one demonstrate this experimentally? In our selection from the *Perception of Causality*, Michotte introduces a new laboratory technique that enables him to make claims about the level of *perceptual meaning*, that is, the level beyond mere sensation at which people assign meanings to their sensations. In direct contrast to Hume, Michotte claims we *do* receive a direct impression of causality. By manipulating the time in which an object, B, moves after another object, A, has approached, Michotte alters whether participants describe what they observe as a case of collision, pushing, or noninteraction and, in so doing, suggests that there was something there, some causal impression, that he has taken away.[6] The theory of ampliation ("ampliation" meaning adding to what is already there, in this case there in the sensation) is soon introduced to explain the productive character of this causal impression. Michotte's method has been called "experimental phenomenology," for it studies subjective phenomena (and not mere sensation), but it accomplishes this by recording participants' responses in experimental situations, rather than through introspection.[7] Michotte was a phenomenologist who studied subjectivity from the outside.[8]

David Lewis (1941–2001) was a well-respected twentieth-century metaphysician who made important advances in the philosophy of modality (i.e., on questions of possibility, impossibility, necessity, and contingency). He starts his classic essay "Causation" with two notions of the concept from Hume—the *regularity* and *counterfactual* notions. The regularity notion states that causation is nothing but *constant conjunction*, in which similar objects are followed by similar objects. This is the predominant contemporary view. But there are many, many regularities, and it has been difficult to distinguish the regularities that pick up on what we might want to say are real causal connections from the regularities that do not. The counterfactual notion captures the richer intuition that a cause is "...something which makes a difference, and the difference it makes must be a difference from what would have happened without it."[9] A claim is *counter to the facts* if it did not, in fact, happen. It follows that a *counter-to-fact conditional* or *counterfactual* is a kind of statement that considers what would have been the case either if some fact that did not occur *had* in fact occurred or if some fact that did occur *had not* in fact occurred. Counterfactual claims often consider what would have been the case if some isolated event or factor were to have been added or removed.

Lewis starts by defining the *counterfactual dependence* of one *proposition* on another in terms of *possible worlds*. A "possible world" is simply a way everything might have been. So, where "A" is the antecedent and "C" is the consequent, the counterfactual "if A were the case, C would be the case" is true just in the case that we do find C in all of the similar-to-our-world possible worlds in which A is the case. Lewis does not analyze the "similarity" relation here, claiming, instead, that it is a primitive relation.[10] When we see that barometer readings routinely depend on the pressure, we are willing to invest in the claim that the instrument reading *depends* on the pressure. We take the covariation to be the product of this dependence. Similarly, when we see that C follows upon A in other possible worlds like ours, we are willing to invest in the claim that C *depends* on A, not just that C *regularly occurs* with A or that C is *associated* with A, but that C's following upon A is somehow meant to be. In order for C *not* to depend on A, we would have to significantly depart from reality.

Unlike Michotte, Lewis takes a very traditional philosophical approach to his subject matter—an analytic approach. He defines a concept in line with his own personal intuitions and then argues that his concept solves problems, in this case, the problems of epiphenomenal cause and preemption that its competitor, the regularity concept, cannot. Even if Lewis's concept can solve those problems (which is questionable, as many philosophers have generated compelling critical responses), we are left with the question of whether the ability to respond to challenges posed by other philosophers with competing intuitions is a sign of a concept's genuine reasonableness. Plato's shadow looms large here.

Alison Gopnik is a prolific experimental psychologist of causal learning, among many other subjects, at the University of California, Berkeley. In observing how young children play, more specifically, the way in which they come to master their toys through a messy process of trial and error, Gopnik has become an advocate for the theory theory, which claims that learning can be understood on the model of scientific theory formation. Just as scientists develop theories about the world and modify those theories in the face of new evidence, so even very young children do the same in trying to understand and explain the parts of the world into which they intervene. Her experimental work is directed at uncovering just how children's theories can be at once flexible, in their ability to incorporate new evidence, but also durable, in their ability to survive the initial temptation to bow to what turns out to be misleading evidence. Learning is a dynamic process, so any theory attributed to young learners would have to accommodate this intellectual drift.

Our selection is from Gopnik's recent "Learning from Doing: Intervention and Causal Inference in Children," written with former students Laura Schulz and Tamar Kushnir. In this paper, the authors work with the *interventionist theory of causation* developed by philosophers Jim Woodward, Christopher Hitchcock, and John Campbell, which opposes the *transmission* account of causation. Where the transmission account argues that causation must involve a spatiotemporally continuous process—the transmission of a "mark," like energy, for instance—the interventionist account argues that our understanding of causation need not invoke anything metaphysical: "X causes Y" means simply that "an intervention to change the value or probability distribution of X will change the value or probability distribution of Y."[11] Cause is understood in terms of possible interventions, rather than actual connections. Gopnik aims to show that young children use this theory to understand their interventions with the world. Where Michotte argued that we are able to glean the causal structure of the world directly, by perceiving causal connections, Gopnik suggests that we must actively theorize to grasp causal connections. But both psychologists help us to realize that philosophers would be ill served to develop the concepts of explanation, causation, and understanding on their own without the unpredictable and rich input that empirical work can offer.

So what is causation essentially? What is the one right way to define this concept? What are the necessary and sufficient conditions that a claim must fulfill to count as a cause? In the end, Lewis is the only one who is interested in understanding the answers to these kinds of questions. The rest of our theorists might be open to Aristotle's original intuition that there are many different styles, levels, and modes of explanation for the many different kinds of questions we would like to answer. Moreover, like Aristotle, these theorists believe that analytic discourse on its own is not powerful enough to generate understanding: empirical data can grip on even our most intractable philosophical mysteries. At the very least, science may serve its philosophical cousin as a less profligate voice.

Notes

1. Aristotle, *The Complete Works of Aristotle: The Revised Oxford Translation,* Vols. 1 and 2, ed. Jonathan Barnes (Princeton, NJ: Princeton University Press, 1971), *Posterior Analytics,* Book II: Parts 7, 8, and 10.
2. David Hume, *Enquiries,* ed. L. A. Selby-Bigge (Oxford: Clarendon, 2006), 163.
3. George Thinès, Alan Costall, and George Butterworth, eds., *Michotte's Experimental Phenomenology of Perception* (Cambridge: Cambridge University Press, 1987), 4.
4. Thines et al., *Michotte's Experimental Phenomenology,* 221. As quoted by Alan Costall, student of a Michotte translator.
5. Thinès et al., *Michotte's Experimental Phenomenology,* 2.
6. Thinès et al., *Michotte's Experimental Phenomenology,* 10.
7. Thinès et al., *Michotte's Experimental Phenomenology,* 15.
8. Thinès et al., *Michotte's Experimental Phenomenology,* 18.
9. David Lewis, "Causation," *Journal of Philosophy* 70, no. 17 (paper presented at the Seventieth Annual Meeting of the American Philosophical Association Eastern Division, October 11, 1973): 557.
10. Lewis, "Causation," 559. In subsequent works, he says more about this relation (which he calls "comparative overall similarity").
11. Laura Schulz, Tamar Kushnir, and Alison Gopnik, "Learning from Doing: Intervention and Causal Inference in Children," in *Causal Learning: Psychology, Philosophy, and Computation,* ed. Alison Gopnik and Laura Schulz (New York: Oxford University Press, 2007), 69.

Suggestions for Further Reading

Annas, Julia. "Aristotle on Inefficient Causes." *Philosophical Quarterly* 32, no. 129 (October 1, 1982): 311–326.

Aristotle. *Aristotle: On the Parts of Animals*, trans. James G. Lennox. New York: Oxford University Press, 2002.

Aristotle. *The Complete Works of Aristotle: The Revised Oxford Translation*. Vols. 1 and 2, ed. Jonathan Barnes. Princeton, NJ: Princeton University Press, 1971.

Baier, Annette. *A Progress of Sentiments: Reflections on Hume's Treatise*. Cambridge, MA: Harvard University Press, 1991.

Beauchamp, Tom L. *Hume and the Problem of Causation*. New York: Oxford University Press, 1981.

Carruthers, Peter, Stephen Stich, and Michael Siegal, eds. *The Cognitive Basis of Science*. Cambridge: Cambridge University Press, 2002.

Code, Alan. "The Priority of Final Causes over Efficient Causes in Aristotle's *Parts of Animals*." In *Aristotelische Biologie: Intentionen, Methoden, Ergebnisse*, ed. Wolfgang Kullmann and Sabine Föllinger, 127–143. Stuttgart: Franz Steiner Verlag, 1997.

Collins, John David, Edward J. Hall, and L. A. Paul. *Causation and Counterfactuals*. Cambridge, MA: MIT Press, 2004.

Falcon, Andrea. "Aristotle on Causality." In *Stanford Encyclopedia of Philosophy*. http://plato.stanford.edu/entries/aristotle-causality/ (accessed February 8, 2010).

Fogelin, Robert J. *Hume's Skepticism in the Treatise of Human Nature*. London: Routledge and Kegan Paul, 1985.

Friedman, Michael. "Causal Laws and the Foundations of Natural Science." In *The Cambridge Companion to Kant*, ed. Paul Guyer, 161–199. Cambridge: Cambridge University Press, 1992.

Garrett, Don. *Cognition and Commitment in Hume's Philosophy*. New York: Oxford University Press, 1997.

Gopnik, Alison, and Laura Schulz, eds. *Causal Learning: Psychology, Philosophy, and Computation*. Oxford: Oxford University Press, 2007.

Gotthelf, A., and J. G. Lennox eds. *Philosophical Issues in Aristotle's Biology*. Cambridge: Cambridge University Press, 1987.

Hankinson, R. J. *Cause and Explanation in Ancient Greek Thought*. Oxford: Clarendon, 1998.

Hart, H. L. A. *Causation in the Law*. 2nd ed. Oxford: Clarendon, 1985.

Horwich, Paul. *Asymmetries in Time: Problems in the Philosophy of Science*. Cambridge, MA: MIT Press, 1987.

Hume, David. *Enquiries Concerning Human Understanding and Concerning the Principles of Morals*. 3rd ed. Oxford: Oxford University Press, 1975.

Lennox, James. "Aristotle's Biology." In *Stanford Encyclopedia of Philosophy*. http://plato.stanford.edu/entries/aristotle-biology/ (accessed February 8, 2010).

Lennox, James G. *Aristotle's Philosophy of Biology: Studies in the Origins of Life Science* (Cambridge Studies in Philosophy and Biology). Cambridge: Cambridge University Press, 2001.

Lewis, David. "Postscripts to 'Causation.'" In *Philosophical Papers: Volume II*. Oxford: Oxford University Press, 1986.

Lewis, David. "Causation." *Journal of Philosophy* 70, no. 17 (October 11, 1973): 556–567.

Lombrozo, Tania. "Explanation and Categorization: How 'Why?' Informs 'What?'" *Cognition* 110, no. 2 (2009): 248–253.

Matthen, M. "The Four Causes in Aristotle's Embryology." In *Nature, Knowledge and Virtue: Essays in Memory of Joan Kung. Apeiron*, Special Issue 22.4, ed. Richard Kraut and Terry Penner, 159–180, Edmonton: Academic Printing and Publishing, 1989.

Menzies, Peter. "Counterfactual Theories of Causation." In *Stanford Encyclopedia of Philosophy*. http://plato.stanford.edu/entries/causation-counterfactual/ (accessed February 8, 2010).

McDermott, Michael. "Redundant Causation." *British Journal for the Philosophy of Science* 46, no. 4 (December 1, 1995): 523–544.

Michotte, Albert. *Michotte's Experimental Phenomenology of Perception*, ed. George Thinès, Alan Costall, and George Butterworth. Hillsdale: Erlbaum, 1990.

Michotte, Albert. *The Perception of Causality*. London: Methuen, 1963.

Moravcsik, Julius M. E. "Aristotle on Adequate Explanations." *Synthese: An International Journal for Epistemology, Methodology and Philosophy of Science* 28 (1974): 3–17.

Todd, Robert B. "The Four Causes: Aristotle's Exposition and the Ancients." *Journal of the History of Ideas* 37 (April 1, 1976): 319–322.

Sprague, Rosamund K. "The Four Causes: Aristotle's Exposition and Ours." *Monist* 52 (1968): 298–300.

Strawson, Galen. *The Secret Connexion: Causation, Realism, and David Hume*. Oxford: Clarendon, 1992.

Stroud, Barry. *Hume*. London: Routledge and Kegan Paul, 1995.

van Fraassen, Bas C. "A Re-examination of Aristotle's Philosophy of Science." *Dialogue: Canadian Philosophical Review* 19 (March 1, 1980): 20–45.

3.1   Physics, Posterior Analytics, Parts of Animals

  ARISTOTLE

ARISTOTLE (384–322 BCE) was born in Stagira, moved to Athens at seventeen to study with Plato, and eventually founded the Lyceum. Aristotle took a more earthly, naturalistic approach to philosophical questions than his teacher, choosing to constrain his theorizing with a series of naked-eye observations about the world, instead of a series of intense conversations with a master thinker. In the following selection from the *Physics*, we find the doctrine of the four causes, Aristotle's attempt to enumerate the most important styles or ways of understanding a thing. These four styles of understanding operate as "middle terms," in that they help us understand the respects in which a thing's attributes or properties are connected to that thing. (Not every property of a thing attaches to that thing in the same way.) In the selections from *Parts of Animals*, Aristotle uses his four causes to explain why organisms have the parts they do: why birds' ears do not have tissue flaps, why many animals have eyebrows, and why women have inferior parts. Notice how closely Aristotle studies these organisms. What kind of understanding is available to someone who makes such detailed discriminations, who divides the world so carefully into categories? What does Aristotle presuppose in looking for such natural "joints"?

PHYSICS

BOOK II

1. Of things that exist, some exist by nature, some from other causes. By nature the animals and their parts exist, and the plants and the simple bodies (earth, fire, air, water)—for we say that these and the like exist by nature.

All the things mentioned plainly differ from things which are *not* constituted by nature. For each of them has within itself a principle of motion and of stationariness (in respect of place, or of growth and decrease, or by way of alteration). On the other hand, a bed and a coat and anything else of that sort, *qua* receiving these designations—i.e. in so far as they are products of art—have no innate impulse to change. But in so far as they happen to be composed of stone or of earth or of a mixture of the two, they *do* have such an impulse, and just to that extent—which seems to indicate that nature is a principle or cause of being moved and of being at rest in that to which it belongs primarily, in virtue of itself and not accidentally.

I say "not accidentally," because (for instance) a man who is a doctor might himself be a cause of health to himself. Nevertheless it is not in so far as he is a patient that he possesses the art of medicine: it merely has happened that the same man is doctor and patient—and that is why these attributes are not always found together. So it is with all other artificial products. None of them has in itself the principle of its own production. But while in some cases (for instance houses and the other products of manual labour) that principle is in something else external to the thing, in others—those which may cause a change in themselves accidentally—it lies in the things themselves (but not in virtue of what they are).

Nature then is what has been stated. Things have a nature which have a principle of this kind. Each of them is a substance; for it is a subject, and nature is always in a subject.

The term "according to nature" is applied to all these things and also to the attributes which belong to them in virtue of what they are, for instance the property of fire to be carried upwards—which is not a nature nor has a nature but is by nature or according to nature.

What nature is, then, and the meaning of the terms "by nature" and "according to nature," has been stated. *That* nature exists, it would be absurd to try to prove; for it is obvious that there are many things of this kind, and to prove what is obvious by what is not is the mark of a man who is unable to distinguish what is self-evident from what is not. (This state of mind is clearly possible. A man blind from birth might reason about colours.) Presumably therefore such persons must be talking about words without any thought to correspond.

Some identify the nature or substance of a natural object with that immediate constituent of it which taken by itself is without arrangement, e.g. the wood is the nature of the bed, and the bronze the nature of the statue.

As an indication of this Antiphon points out that if you planted a bed and the rotting wood acquired the power of sending up a shoot, it would not be a bed that would come up, but *wood* which shows that the arrangement in accordance with the rules of the art is merely an accidental attribute, whereas the substance is the other, which, further, persists continuously through the process.

But if the material of each of these objects has itself the same relation to something else, say

bronze (or gold) to water, bones (or wood) to earth and so on, *that* (they say) would be their nature and substance. Consequently some assert earth, others fire or air or water or some or all of these, to be the nature of the things that are. For whatever any one of them supposed to have this character—whether one thing or more than one thing—this or these he declared to be the whole of substance, all else being its affections, states, or dispositions. Every such thing they held to be eternal (for it could not pass into anything else), but other things to come into being and cease to be times without number.

This then is one account of nature, namely that it is the primary underlying matter of things which have in themselves a principle of motion or change.

Another account is that nature is the shape or form which is specified in the definition of the thing.

For the word "nature" is applied to what is according to nature and the natural in the same way as "art" is applied to what is artistic or a work of art. We should not say in the latter case that there is anything artistic about a thing, if it is a bed only potentially, not yet having the form of a bed; nor should we call it a work of art. The same is true of natural compounds. What is potentially flesh or bone has not yet its own nature, and does not exist by nature, until it receives the form specified in the definition, which we name in defining what flesh or bone is. Thus on the second account of nature, it would be the shape or form (not separable except in statement) of things which have in themselves a principle of motion. (The combination of the two, e.g. man, is not nature but by nature.)

The form indeed is nature rather than the matter; for a thing is more properly said to be what it is when it exists in actuality than when it exists potentially. Again man is born from man but not bed from bed. That is why people say that the shape is not the nature of a bed, but the wood is—if the bed sprouted, not a bed but wood would come up. But even if the shape *is* art, then on the same principle the shape of man is his nature. For man is born from man.

Again, nature in the sense of a coming-to-be proceeds towards nature. For it is not like doctoring, which leads not to the art of doctoring but to health. Doctoring must start from the art, not lead to it. But it is not in this way that nature is related to nature. What grows *qua* growing grows from something into something. Into what then does it grow? Not into that from which it arose but into that to which it tends. The shape then is nature.

Shape and nature are used in two ways. For the privation too is in a way form. But whether in unqualified coming to be there is privation, i.e. a contrary, we must consider later.

2. [. . .] Since two sorts of thing are called nature, the form and the matter, we must investigate its objects as we would the essence of snubness, that is neither independently of matter nor in terms of matter only. Here too indeed one might raise a difficulty. Since there are two natures, with which is the student of nature concerned? Or should he investigate the combination of the two? But if the combination of the two, then also each severally. Does it belong then to the same or to different sciences to know each severally?

If we look at the ancients, natural science would seem to be concerned with the *matter*. (It was only very slightly that Empedocles and Democritus touched on form and essence.)

But if on the other hand art imitates nature, and it is the part of the same discipline to know the form and the matter up to a point (e.g. the doctor has a knowledge of health and also of bile and phlegm, in which health is realized and the builder both of the form of the house and of the matter, namely that it is bricks and beams, and so forth): if this is so, it would be the part of natural science also to know nature in both its senses.

Again, that for the sake of which, or the end, belongs to the same department of knowledge as the means. But the nature is the end or that for the sake of which. For if a thing undergoes a continuous change toward some end, that last stage is actually that for the sake of which. (That is why the poet was carried away into making an absurd statement when he said "he has the end for the sake of which he was born." For not every stage that is last claims to be an end, but only that which is best.)

For the arts make their material (some simply make it, others make it serviceable), and we use everything as if it was there for our sake. (We also are in a sense an end. "That for the sake of which" may be taken in two ways, as we said in our work *On Philosophy*.) The arts, therefore, which govern the matter and have knowledge are two, namely the art which uses the product and the art which directs the production of it. That is why the using art also is in a sense directive; but it differs in that it knows the form, whereas the art which is directive as being concerned with production knows the matter. For the helmsman knows and prescribes what sort of form a helm should have, the other from what wood it should be made and by means of what operations. In the products of art, however, we make the material with a view to the function, whereas in the products of nature the matter is there all along.

Again, matter is a relative thing—for different forms there is different matter.

How far then must the student of nature know the form or essence? Up to a point, perhaps, as the doctor must know sinew or the smith bronze (i.e. until he understands the purpose of each), and the student of nature is concerned only with things whose forms are separable indeed, but do not exist apart from matter. Man is begotten by man and by the sun as well. The mode of existence and essence of the separable it is the business of first philosophy to define.

3. Now that we have established these distinctions, we must proceed to consider causes, their character and number. Knowledge is the object of our inquiry, and men do not think they know a thing till they have grasped the "why" of it (which is to grasp its primary cause). So clearly we too must do this as regards both coming to be and passing away and every kind of natural

change, in order that, knowing their principles, we may try to refer to these principles each of our problems.

In one way, then, that out of which a thing comes to be and which persists, is called a cause, e.g. the bronze of the statue, the silver of the bowl, and the genera of which the bronze and the silver are species.

In another way, the form or the archetype, i.e. the definition of the essence, and its genera, are called causes (e.g. of the octave the relation of 2:1, and generally number), and the parts in the definition.

Again, the primary source of the change or rest; e.g. the man who deliberated is a cause, the father is cause of the child, and generally what makes of what is made and what changes of what is changed.

Again, in the sense of end or that for the sake of which a thing is done, e.g. health is the cause of walking about. ("Why is he walking about?" We say: "To be healthy," and, having said that, we think we have assigned the cause.) The same is true also of all the intermediate steps which are brought about through the action of something else as means towards the end, e.g. reduction of flesh, purging, drugs, or surgical instruments are means towards health. All these things are for the sake of the end, though they differ from one another in that some are activities, others instruments.

This then perhaps exhausts the number of ways in which the term "cause" is used.

As things are called causes in many ways, it follows that there are several causes of the same thing (not merely accidentally), e.g. both the art of the sculptor and the bronze are causes of the statue. These are causes of the statue *qua* statue, not in virtue of anything else that it may be—only not in the same way, the one being the material cause, the other the cause whence the motion comes. Some things cause each other reciprocally, e.g. hard work causes fitness and *vice versa*, but again not in the same way, but the one as end, the other as the principle of motion.

Further the same thing is the cause of contrary results. For that which by its presence brings about one result is sometimes blamed for bringing about the contrary by its absence. Thus we ascribe the wreck of a ship to the absence of the pilot whose presence was the cause of its safety.

All the causes now mentioned fall into four familiar divisions. The letters are the causes of syllables, the material of artificial products, fire and the like of bodies, the parts of the whole, and the premisses of the conclusion, in the sense of "that from which." Of these pairs the one set are causes in the sense of what underlies, e.g. the parts, the other set in the sense of essence—the whole and the combination and the form. But the seed and the doctor and the deliberator, and generally the maker, are all sources whence the change or stationariness originates, which the others are causes in the sense of the end or the good of the rest; for that for the sake of which tends to be what is best and the end of the things that lead up to it. (Whether we call it good or apparently good makes no difference.)

Such then is the number and nature of the kinds of cause.

Now the modes of causation are many, though when brought under heads they too can be reduced in number. For things are called causes in many ways and even within the same kind one may be prior to another: e.g. the doctor and the expert are causes of health, the relation 2:1 and number of the octave, and always what is inclusive to what is particular. Another mode of causation is the accidental and its genera, e.g. in one way Polyclitus, in another a sculptor is the cause of a statue, because being Polyclitus and a sculptor are accidentally conjoined. Also the classes in which the accidental attribute is included; thus a man could be said to be the cause of a statue or, generally, a living creature. An accidental attribute too may be more or less remote, e.g. suppose that a pale man or a musical man were said to be the cause of the statue.

All causes, both proper and accidental, may be spoken of either as potential or as actual; e.g.

the cause of a house being built is either a house-builder or a house-builder building.

Similar distinctions can be made in the things of which the causes are causes, e.g. of this statue or of a statue or of an image generally, of this bronze or of bronze or of material generally. So too with the accidental attributes. Again we may use a complex expression for either and say, e.g., neither "Polyclitus" nor a "sculptor" but "Polyclitus, the sculptor."

All these various uses, however, come to six in number, under each of which again the usage is twofold. It is either what is particular or a genus, or an accidental attribute or a genus of that, and these either as a complex or each by itself; and all either as actual or as potential. The difference is this much, that causes which are actually at work and particular exist and cease to exist simultaneously with their effect, e.g. this healing person with this being-healed person and that housebuilding man with that being-built house; but this is not always true of potential causes—the house and the housebuilder do not pass away simultaneously.

In investigating the cause of each thing it is always necessary to seek what is most precise (as also in other things): thus a man builds because he is a builder, and a builder builds in virtue of his art of building. This last cause then is prior; and so generally.

Further, generic effects should be assigned to generic causes, particular effects to particular causes, e.g. statue to sculptor, this statue to this sculptor; and powers are relative to possible effects, actually operating causes to things which are actually being effected.

This must suffice for our account of the number of causes and the modes of causation. [. . .]

8. We must explain then first why nature belongs to the class of causes which act for the sake of something; and then about the necessary and its place in nature, for all writers ascribe things to this cause, arguing that since the hot and the cold and the like are of such and such a kind, therefore certain things *necessarily* are and come to be—and if they mention any other cause

(one friendship and strife, another mind), it is only to touch on it, and then good-bye to it.

A difficulty presents itself: why should not nature work, not for the sake of something, nor because it is better so, but just as the sky rains, not in order to make the corn grow, but of necessity? (What is drawn up must cool, and what has been cooled must become water and descend, the result of this being that the corn grows.) Similarly if a man's crop is spoiled on the threshing-floor, the rain did not fall for the sake of this—in order that the crop might be spoiled—but that result just followed. Why then should it not be the same with the parts in nature, e.g. that our teeth should come up of necessity—the front teeth sharp, fitted for tearing, the molars broad and useful for grinding down the food—since they did not arise for this end, but it was merely a coincident result; and so with all other parts in which we suppose that there is purpose? Wherever then all the parts came about just what they would have been if they had come to be for an end, such things survived, being organized spontaneously in a fitting way; whereas those which grew otherwise perished and continue to perish, as Empedocles says his "man-faced oxprogeny" did.

Such are the arguments (and others of the kind) which may cause difficulty on this point. Yet it is impossible that this should be the true view. For teeth and all other natural things either invariably or for the most part come about in a given way; but of not one of the results of chance or spontaneity is this true. We do not ascribe to chance or mere coincidence the frequency of rain in winter, but frequent rain in summer we do; nor heat in summer but only if we have it in winter. If then, it is agreed that things are either the result of coincidence or for the sake of something, and these cannot be the result of coincidence or spontaneity, it follows that they must be for the sake of something; and that such things are all due to nature even the champions of the theory which is before us would agree. Therefore action for an end is present in things which come to be and are by nature.

Further, where there is an end, all the preceding steps are for the sake of that. [...] And since nature is twofold, the matter and the form, of which the latter is the end, and since all the rest is for the sake of the end, the form must be the cause in the sense of that for the sake of which.

Now mistakes occur even in the operations of art: the literate man makes a mistake in writing and the doctor pours out the wrong dose. Hence clearly mistakes are possible in the operations of nature also. If then in art there are cases in which what is rightly produced serves a purpose, and if where mistakes occur there was a purpose in what was attempted, only it was not attained, so must it be also in natural products, and monstrosities will be failures in the purposive effort. Thus in the original combinations the "ox-progeny," if they failed to reach a determinate end must have arisen through the corruption of some principle, as happens now when the seed is defective. [...]

Among the seeds anything must come to be at random. But the person who asserts this entirely does away with nature and what exists by nature. For those things are natural which, by a continuous movement originated from an internal principle, arrive at some end: the same end is not reached from every principle; nor any chance end, but always the tendency in each is towards the same end, if there is no impediment.

[...] When an event takes place always or for the most part, it is not accidental or by chance. In natural products the sequence is invariable, if there is no impediment.

It is absurd to suppose that purpose is not present because we do not observe the agent deliberating. Art does not deliberate. If the ship-building art were in the wood, it would produce the same results by nature. If, therefore, purpose is present in art, it is present also in nature. The best illustration is a doctor doctoring himself: nature is like that.

It is plain then that nature is a cause, a cause that operates for a purpose.

9. As regards what is of necessity, we must ask whether the necessity is hypothetical, or simple as well. The current view places what is of necessity in the process of production, just as if one were to suppose that the wall of a house necessarily comes to be because what is heavy is naturally carried downwards and what is light to the top, so that the stones and foundations take the lowest place, with earth above because it is lighter, and wood at the top of all as being the lightest. Whereas, though the wall does not come to be *without* these, it is not *due* to these, except as its material cause: it comes to be for the sake of sheltering and guarding certain things. Similarly in all other things which involve that for the sake of which: the product cannot come to be without things which have a necessary nature, but it is not due to these (except as its material); it comes to be for an end. For instance, why is a saw such as it is? To effect so-and-so and for the sake of so-and-so. This end, however, cannot be realized unless the saw is made of iron. It is, therefore, necessary for it to be of iron, if we are to have a saw and perform the operation of sawing. What is necessary then, is necessary on a hypothesis, not as an end. Necessity is in the matter, while that for the sake of which is in the definition. [...]

The necessary in nature, then, is plainly what we call by the name of matter, and the changes in it. Both causes must be stated by the student of nature, but especially the end; for that is the cause of the matter, not *vice versa;* and the end is that for the sake of which, and the principle starts from the definition or essence: as in artificial products, since a house is of such-and-such a kind, certain things must *necessarily* come to be or be there already, or since health is this, these things must necessarily come to be or be there already, so too if man is this, then these; if these, then those. Perhaps the necessary is present also in the definition. For if one defines the operation of sawing as being a certain kind of dividing, then this cannot come about unless the saw has teeth of a certain kind; and these cannot be unless it is of iron. For in the definition too there are some parts that stand as matter. [...]

POSTERIOR ANALYTICS

BOOK II

1. The things we seek are equal in number to those we understand. We seek four things: the fact, the reason why, if it is, what it is.

For when we seek whether it is this or this, putting it into a number (e.g. whether the sun is eclipsed or not), we seek the fact. Evidence for this: on finding that it is eclipsed we stop; and if from the start we know that it is eclipsed, we do not seek whether it is. When we know the fact we seek the reason why (e.g. knowing that it is eclipsed and that the earth moves, we seek the reason why it is eclipsed or why it moves).

Now while we seek these things in this way, we seek some things in another fashion—e.g. if a centaur or a god is or is not (I mean if one is or not *simpliciter* and not if one is white or not). And knowing that it is, we seek what it is (e.g. so what is a god? or what is a man?).

2. Now what we seek and what on finding we know are these and thus many. We seek, whenever we seek the fact or if it is *simpliciter*, whether there is or is not a middle term for it; and whenever we become aware of either the fact or if it is—either partially or *simpliciter*—and again seek the reason why or what it is, then we seek what the middle term is. (I mean by the fact that it is partially and *simpliciter*—partially: Is the moon eclipsed? or is it increasing? (for in such cases we seek if it is something or is not something); *simpliciter*: if the moon or night is or is not.) It results, therefore, that in all our searches we seek either if there is a middle term or what the middle term is.

For the middle term is the explanation, and in all cases that is sought. Is it eclipsed?—Is there some explanation or not? After that, aware that there is one, we seek what this is. For the explanation of a substance being not this or that but *simpliciter*, or of its being not *simpliciter* but one of the things which belong to it in itself or accidentally—that is the middle term. I mean by *simpliciter* the underlying subject (e.g. moon or earth or sun or triangle) and by one of the things eclipse, equality, inequality, whether it is in the middle or not.

For in all these cases it is evident that what it is and why it is are the same. What is an eclipse? Privation of light from the moon by the earth's screening. Why is there an eclipse? or Why is the moon eclipsed? Because the light leaves it when the earth screens it. What is a harmony? An arithmetical ratio between high and low. Why does the high harmonize with the low? Because an arithmetical ratio holds between the high and the low. Can the high and the low harmonize?— Is there an arithmetical ratio between them? Assuming that there is, what then is the ratio?

That the search is for the middle term is made clear by the cases in which the middle is perceptible. For if we have not perceived it, we seek, e.g. for the eclipse, if there is one or not. But if we were on the moon we would seek neither if it comes about nor why, but it would be clear at the same time. For from perceiving, it would come about that we knew the universal too. For perception tells us that it is now screening it (for it is clear that it is now eclipsed); and from this the universal would come about.

So, as we say, to know what it is is the same as to know why it is—and that either *simpliciter* and not one of the things that belong to it, or one of the things that belong to it, e.g. that it has two right angles, or that it is greater or less.

3. Now, that everything we seek is a search for a middle term is clear; let us now say how one proves what a thing is, and what is the fashion of the reduction, and what definition is and of what, first going through the puzzles about them. Let the start of what we are about to say be whatever is most appropriate to the neighbouring arguments.

A man might puzzle over whether one can know the same thing in the same respect by definition and by demonstration, or whether that is impossible.

For definition seems to be of what a thing is, and what a thing is is in every case universal and affirmative, but deductions are some of them negative and some not universal—e.g. those in the second figure are all negative and those in the third not universal.

Next, there is not definition even of all the affirmatives in the first figure—e.g. that every triangle has angles equal to two right angles. The argument for this is that to understand what is demonstrable is to have a demonstration; so that since there is demonstration of such things, clearly there will not also be definition of them—for someone might understand them in virtue of the definition without having the demonstration; for nothing prevents him from not having them together.

An induction, too, is sufficiently convincing; for we have never yet become aware of anything by giving a definition—neither of anything belonging in itself nor of any accidental.

Again, if definition is becoming familiar with some substance, it is evident that *such* things are not substances.

So it is clear that there is not definition of everything of which there is demonstration.

Well then, is there demonstration of everything of which there is definition, or not?

Well, one argument is the same in this case too. For of one thing, as one, there is one mode of understanding. Hence, if to understand what is demonstrable is to have a demonstration, something impossible will result; for anyone who has the definition without the demonstration will understand.

Again, the principles of demonstrations are definitions, and it has been proved earlier that there will not be demonstrations of these—either the principles will be demonstrable and there will be principles of the principles, and this will go on *ad infinitum*, or the primitives will be non-demonstrable definitions.

But if the objects of definition and demonstration are not all the same, are some of them the same? or is this impossible? For there is no demonstration of that of which there is definition.

For definition is of what a thing is and of substance; but all demonstrations evidently suppose and assume what a thing is—e.g. mathematical demonstrations assume what a unit is and what odd, and the others similarly.

Again, every demonstration proves something of something, i.e. that it is or is not; but in a definition one thing is not predicated of another—e.g. neither animal of two-footed nor this of animal, nor indeed figure of plane (for plane is not figure nor is figure plane).

Again, proving what a thing is and that it is are different. So the definition makes clear what it is, and the demonstration that this is or is not true of that. And of different things there are different demonstrations—unless they are related as a part to the whole (I mean by this that the isosceles has been proved to have two right angles if every triangle has been proved to be so; for one is a part and the other a whole). But these things—that it is and what it is—are not related to one another in this way; for neither is part of the other.

It is evident, therefore, that neither is there demonstration of everything of which there is definition, nor is there definition of everything of which there is demonstration, nor in general is it possible to have both of the same thing. Hence it is clear that definition and demonstration are neither identical nor the one included in the other; for then their underlying subjects would be similarly related. [...]

11. Since we think we understand when we know the explanation, and there are four types of explanation (one, what it is to be a thing; one, that if certain things hold it is necessary that this does; another, what initiated the change; and fourth, the aim), all these are proved through the middle term. [...]

And why did the Persian war come upon the Athenians? What is the explanation of the Athenians' being warred upon? Because they attacked Sardis with the Eretrians; for that initiated the change. War, *A*; being the first to attack, *B*; Athenians, *C*. Thus *B* belongs to *C* (being the first to attack to the Athenians), and *A* to *B* (for men make war on those who have first done them wrong). Therefore *A* belongs to *B* (being warred upon to those who first began), and this—*B*—to the Athenians (for they first began). Therefore here too the explanation, what initiated the change, is a middle term. [...]

14. In order to grasp problems, one should excerpt both the anatomies and the divisions; and in this way, laying down the genus common to all the subject-matter, one should excerpt (if e.g. animals are under consideration) whatever belongs to every animal; and having got this, again excerpt whatever follows every case of the first of the remaining terms (e.g. if it is bird, whatever follows every bird), and always excerpt in this way whatever follows the nearest term. For it is clear that we shall now be in a position to state the reason why what follows the items under the common genus belongs to them—e.g. why it belongs to man or to horse. Let *A* be animal, *B* what follows every animal, and *C*, *D*, *E* individual animals. Well, it is clear why *B* belongs to *D*; for it does so because of *A*. Similarly in the other cases too. and the same account will always hold for the others.

Now at present we argue in terms of the common names that have been handed down; but we must not only inquire in these cases, but also if anything else has been seen to belong in common, we must extract that and then inquire what it follows and what follows it—e.g. having a manyplies and not having upper incisors follow having horns; again, we should inquire what having horns follows. For it is clear why what we have mentioned will belong to them; for it will belong because they have horns.

Again, another way is excerpting in virtue of analogy; for you cannot get one identical thing which pounce and spine and bone should be called; but there will be things that follow them too, as though there were some single nature of this sort. [...]

19. Now as for deduction and demonstration, it is evident both what each is and how it

comes about—and at the same time this goes for demonstrative understanding too (for that is the same thing). But as for the principles—how they become familiar and what is the state that becomes familiar with them—that will be clear from what follows, when we have first set down the puzzles.

Now, we have said earlier that it is not possible to understand through demonstration if we are not aware of the primitive, immediate, principles. But as to knowledge of the immediates, one might puzzle both whether it is the same or not the same—whether there is understanding of each, or rather understanding of the one and some other kind of thing of the other—and also whether the states are not present in us but come about in us, or whether they are present in us but escape notice.

Well, if we have them, it is absurd; for it results that we have pieces of knowledge more precise than demonstration and yet this escapes notice. But if we get them without having them earlier, how might we become familiar with them and learn them from no pre-existing knowledge? For that is impossible, as we said in the case of demonstration too. It is evidently impossible, then, both for us to have them and for them to come about in us when we are ignorant and have no such state at all. Necessarily, therefore, we have some capacity, but do not have one of a type which will be more valuable than these in respect of precision.

And *this* evidently belongs to all animals; for they have a connate discriminatory capacity, which is called perception. And if perception is present in them, in some animals retention of the percept comes about, but in others it does not come about. Now for those in which it does not come about, there is no knowledge outside perceiving (either none at all, or none with regard to that of which there is no retention); but for some perceivers, it is possible to grasp it in their minds. And when many such things come about, then a difference comes about, so that some come to have an account from the retention of such things, and others do not.

So from perception there comes memory, as we call it, and from memory (when it occurs often in connection with the same thing), experience; for memories that are many in number from a single experience. And from experience, or from the whole universal that has come to rest in the soul (the one apart from the many, whatever is one and the same in all those things), there comes a principle of skill and of understanding—of skill if it deals with how things come about, of understanding if it deals with what is the case.

Thus the states neither belong in us in a determinate form, nor come about from other states that are more cognitive; but they come about from perception—as in a battle when a rout occurs, if one man makes a stand another does and then another, until a position of strength is reached. And the soul is such as to be capable of undergoing this.

What we have just said but not said clearly, let us say again: when one of the undifferentiated things makes a stand, there is a primitive universal in the mind (for though one perceives the particular, perception is of the universal—e.g. of man but not of Callias the man); again a stand is made in these, until what has no parts and is universal stands—e.g. *such and such* an animal stands, until animal does, and in this a stand is made in the same way. Thus it is clear that it is necessary for us to become familiar with the primitives by induction; for perception too instils the universal in this way.

Since of the intellectual states by which we grasp truth some are always true and some admit falsehood (e.g. opinion and reasoning—whereas understanding and comprehension are always true), and no kind other than comprehension is more precise than understanding, and the principles of demonstrations are more familiar, and all understanding involves an account—there will not be understanding of the principles; and since it is not possible for anything to be truer than understanding, except comprehension, there will be comprehension of the principles—both if we inquire from these facts and because

demonstration is not a principle of demonstration so that understanding is not a principle of understanding either—so if we have no other true kind apart from understanding, comprehension will be the principle of understanding. And the principle will be of the principle, and understanding as a whole will be similarly related to the whole object.

PARTS OF ANIMALS

BOOK I

[...] Ought the student of nature follow the plan adopted by the mathematicians in their astronomical demonstrations, and after considering the phenomena presented by animals, and their several parts, proceed subsequently to treat of the causes and the reason why; or ought he to follow some other method? Furthermore, the causes concerned in natural generation are, as we see, more than one. There is the cause for the sake of which, and the cause whence the beginning of motion comes. Now we must decide which of these two causes comes first, which second. Plainly, however, that cause is the first which we call that for the sake of which. For this is the account of the thing, and the account forms the starting-point, alike in the works of art and in works of nature. For the doctor and the builder define health or house, either by the intellect or by perception, and then proceed to give the accounts and the causes of each of the things they do and of why they should do it thus. Now in the works of nature the good and that for the sake of which is still more dominant than in works of art, nor is necessity a factor with the same significance in them all; though almost all writers try to refer their accounts to this, failing to distinguish the several ways in which necessity is spoken of. For there is absolute necessity, manifested in eternal phenomena; and there is hypothetical necessity, manifested in everything that is generated as in everything that is produced by art, be it a house or what it may. For if a house or other such final object is to be realized, it is necessary that first this and then that shall be produced and set in motion, and so on in continuous succession, until the end is reached, for the sake of which each prior thing is produced and exists. So also is it with the productions of nature. The mode of necessity, however, and the mode of demonstration are different in natural science from what they are in the theoretical sciences (we have spoken of this elsewhere). For in the latter the starting-point is that which is; in the former that which is to be. For since health, or a man, is of such and such a character, it is necessary for this or that to exist or be produced; it is not the case that, since this or that exists or has been produced, that of necessity exists or will exist. Nor is it possible to trace back the necessity of demonstrations of this sort to a starting-point, of which you can say that, since this exists, that exists. These however, again, are matters that have been dealt with in another treatise, where it was stated where necessity is present, where it is reciprocal and for what reason.

Another matter which must not be passed over without consideration is, whether the proper subject of our exposition is that with which the earlier writers concerned themselves, namely, the way each thing is naturally generated, or rather the way it *is*. For there is no small difference between these two views. The best course appears to be that we should follow the method already mentioned—begin with the phenomena presented by each group of animals, and, when this is done, proceed afterwards to state the causes of those phenomena—in the case of generation too. For in house building too, these things come about because the form of the house is such and such, rather than its being the case that the house is such and such because it comes about thus. For the generation is for the sake of the substance and not this for the sake of the generation. Empedo-

cles, then, was in error when he said that many of the characters presented by animals were merely the results of incidental occurrences during their development; for instance, that the backbone is as it is because it happened to be broken owing to the turning of the foetus in the womb. In so saying he overlooked the fact that propagation implies a creative seed endowed with certain powers. Secondly, he neglected another fact, namely, that the parent animal pre-exists, not only in account, but actually in time. For man is generated from man; and thus it is because the parent is such and such that the generation of the child is thus and so. The same statement holds good also for those which are apparently spontaneous, as also for the products of art. For the same result as is produced by art may occur spontaneously, e.g. health. Those things whose agent is pre-existent, such as the statuary's art, cannot possibly be produced spontaneously. Art indeed consists in the account of the product without its matter. So too with chance products; for they are produced in the same way as products of art.

The fittest mode, then, of treatment is to say, a man has such and such parts, because the essence of man is such and such, and because they are necessary conditions of his existence, or, if we cannot quite say this then the next thing to it, namely, that it is either quite impossible for a man to exist without them, or, at any rate, that it is good that they should be there. And this follows: because man is such and such the process of his development is necessarily such as it is; and therefore this part is formed first, that next; and after a like fashion should we explain the generation of all other works of nature.

Now that with which the ancient writers, who first philosophized about nature, busied themselves, was the material prinicple and the material cause. [. . .]

But if men and animals and their several parts are natural phenomena, then the natural philosopher must take into consideration flesh, bone, blood, and all the other homogeneous parts; not only these, but also the heterogeneous parts, such as face, hand, foot; and must examine how each of these comes to be what it is, and in virtue of what force. For it is not enough to say what are the stuffs out of which an animal is formed, to state, for instance, that it is made of fire or earth—if we were discussing a couch or the like, we should try to determine its form rather than its matter (e.g. bronze or wood), or if not, we should give the matter of the *whole*. For a couch is such and such a form embodied in this or that matter, or such and such a matter with this or that form; so that its shape and structure must be included in our description. For the formal nature is of greater importance than the material nature.

Does, then, configuration and colour constitute the essence of the various animals and of their several parts? For if so, what Democritus says will be correct. For such appears to have been his notion. At any rate he says that it is evident to every one what form it is that makes the man, seeing that he is recognizable by his shape and colour. And yet a dead body has exactly the same configuration as a living one; but for all that is not a man. So also no hand of bronze or wood or constituted in any but the appropriate way can possibly be a hand in more than name. For like a physician in a painting, or like a flute in a sculpture, it will be unable to perform its function. Precisely in the same way no part of a dead body, such I mean as its eye or its hand, is really an eye or a hand. What he says, then, is too simple—it is much the same as if a woodcarver were to insist that the hand he had cut out was really a hand. Yet the physiologists, when they give an account of the development and causes of the animal form, speak very much like such a craftsman. What are the forces by which the hand or the body was fashioned into its shape? The woodcarver will perhaps say, by the axe or the auger; the physiologist, by air and by earth. Of these two answers the woodcarver's is the better. For it is not enough for him to say that by the stroke of his tool this part was formed into a concavity, that into a flat surface; but he must state the reasons why he struck his blow in

such a way as to effect this, and for the sake of what he did so; namely, that the piece of wood should develop eventually into this or that shape. It is plain, then, that they are wrong, and that the true method is to state what the characters are that distinguish the animal—to explain what it is and what are its qualities—and to deal after the same fashion with its several parts; in fact, to proceed in exactly the same way as we should do, were we dealing with the form of a couch.

If now the form of the living being is the soul, or part of the soul, or something that without the soul cannot exist; as would seem to be the case, seeing at any rate that when the soul departs, what is left is no longer an animal, and that none of the parts remain what they were before, excepting in mere configuration, like the animals that in the fable are turned into stone; if, I say, this is so, then it will come within the province of the natural scientist to inform himself concerning the soul, and to treat of it, either in its entirety, or, at any rate, of that part of it which constitutes the essential character of an animal; and it will be his duty to say what a soul or this part of a soul is; and to discuss the attributes that attach to this essential character, especially as nature is spoken of—and is—twofold, as matter and as substance; nature as substance including both the motor cause and the final cause. Now it is in the latter of these two senses that either the whole soul or some part of it constitutes the nature of an animal; and inasmuch as it is the presence of the soul that enables matter to constitute the animal nature, much more than it is the presence of matter which so enables the soul, the inquirer into nature is bound to treat of the soul rather than of the matter. For though the wood of which they are made constitutes the couch and the tripod, it only does so because it is potentially such and such a form. [. . .]

Of the method itself the following is an example. In dealing with respiration we must show that it takes place for such or such a final object; and we must also show that this and that part of the process is necessitated by this and that other stage of it. By necessity we shall sometimes mean that the requisite antecedents must be there, if the final end is to be reached; and sometimes that things are thus and so by nature. [...]

12. In birds, [...] there are only the auditory passages. This is because their skin is hard and because they have feathers instead of hairs, so that they have not got the proper material for the formation of ears. Exactly the same is the case with such oviparous quadrupeds as are clad with scaly plates, and the same explanation applies to them. [...]

15. Both eyebrows and eyelashes exist for the protection of the eyes; the former that they may shelter them, like the eaves of a house, from any fluids that trickle down from the head; the latter to act like the palisades which are sometimes placed in front of enclosures, and keep out any objects which might otherwise get in. The brows are placed over the junction of two bones, which is the reason that in old age they often become so bushy as to require cutting. The lashes are set at the terminations of small blood-vessels. For the vessels come to an end where the skin itself terminates; and, in all places where these endings occur, the exudation of moisture of a corporeal character actually necessitates the growth of hairs, unless there be some operation of nature which interferes, by diverting the moisture to another purpose.

[...] In man the teeth are admirably constructed for their general office, the front ones being sharp, so as to cut the food into bits, and the molars broad and flat, so as to grind it to a pulp; while between these and separating them are the canines which, in accordance with the rule that the mean partakes of both extremes, share in the characters of those on either side, being broad in one part but sharp in another. [...]

The character [...] of these sharp teeth have been mainly determined by the requirements of speech. For the front teeth of man contribute in many ways to the formation of letter-sounds.

[...] Nature allots each weapon, offensive and defensive alike, to those animals alone that can use it; or, if not to them alone, to them in a more marked degree; and she allots it in its most perfect state to those that can use it best; and this whether it be a sting, or a spur, or horns, or tusks, or what it may of a like kind.

Thus as males are stronger and more choleric than females, it is in males that such parts as those just mentioned are found, either exclusively, as in some species, or more fully developed, as in others. For though females are of course provided with such parts as are necessary to them, the parts, for instance, which subserve nutrition, they have even these in an inferior degree, and the parts which answer no such necessary purpose they do not possess at all. This explains why stags have horns, while does have none; why the horns of cows are different from those of bulls, and, similarly, the horns of ewes from those of rams. It explains also why the females are often without spurs in species where the males are provided with them, and accounts for similar facts relating to all other such parts. [...]

Study Questions

1. Does any particular one of the four causes seem more explanatory than the others? Why?
2. What is the difference between demonstrating that an animal has a part and explaining why an animal has a part?
3. In *Posterior Analytics*, Book II, Parts 11 and 14, work out a few of Aristotle's examples. How does he use each of the four causes as a middle term to understand how attributes attach to things?
4. How might you connect what Aristotle says in *Posterior Analytics*, Book II, Part 19, to experimental philosophy? What role does intuition play in knowledge and understanding?

Enquiry Concerning Human Understanding   3.2

DAVID HUME

DAVID HUME (1711–1776) was a Scottish philosopher with special interests in epistemology, philosophy of mind, philosophy of religion, and moral philosophy. His work was clear, engaging, and provocative—so provocative, in fact, that he never held a university position and, instead, spent his later life working a series of midlevel political appointments while continuing to write. The selections here are from his *Enquiry Concerning Human Understanding* (1748), a sharply edited version of his much longer *Treatise of Human Nature* (1739–1740). In this work, Hume asks whether we can know anything beyond what we have directly experienced, whether we can amplify our knowledge. With his notorious argument against induction, he concludes that it is irrational to take epistemic leaps: there is no non-question-begging way to use past experience to justify our beliefs about what we have not yet experienced. Despite this, Hume fully expects human beings to continue to have expectations about far-away times and spaces. Past experience will continue to condition or prompt our beliefs about the future, even though past experience cannot justify these beliefs.

SECTION IV

Sceptical Doubts Concerning the Operations of the Understanding

Part I

ALL the objects of human reason or enquiry may naturally be divided into two kinds, to wit, *Relations of Ideas*, and *Matters of Fact*. Of the first kind are the sciences of Geometry, Algebra, and Arithmetic; and in short, every affirmation which is either intuitively or demonstratively certain. *That the square of the hypothenuse is equal to the square of the two sides*, is a proposition which expresses a relation between these figures. *That three times five is equal to the half of thirty*, expresses a relation between these numbers. Propositions of this kind are discoverable by the mere operation of thought, without dependence on what is anywhere existent in the universe. Though there never were a circle or triangle in nature, the truths demonstrated by Euclid would for ever retain their certainty and evidence.

Matters of fact, which are the second objects of human reason, are not ascertained in the same manner; nor is our evidence of their truth, however great, of a like nature with the foregoing. The contrary of every matter of fact is still possible; because it can never imply a contradiction, and is conceived by the mind with the same facility and distinctness, as if ever so conformable to reality. *That the sun will not rise to-morrow* is no less intelligible a proposition, and implies no more contradiction, than the affirmation, *that it will rise*. We should in vain, therefore, attempt to demonstrate its falsehood. Were it demonstratively false, it would imply a contradiction, and could never be distinctly conceived by the mind.

David Hume, *Enquiries Concerning Human Understanding and Concerning the Principles of Morals*, third edition (1975), edited by Selby-Bigge and Peter Harold Nidditch. By permission of Oxford University Press.

It may, therefore, be a subject worthy of curiosity, to enquire what is the nature of that evidence which assures us of any real existence and matter of fact, beyond the present testimony of our senses, or the records of our memory. [. . .]

All reasonings concerning matter of fact seem to be founded on the relation of *Cause and Effect*. By means of that relation alone we can go beyond the evidence of our memory and senses. If you were to ask a man, why he believes any matter of fact, which is absent; for instance, that his friend is in the country, or in France; he would give you a reason; and this reason would be some other fact; as a letter received from him, or the knowledge of his former resolutions and promises. A man finding a watch or any other machine in a desert island, would conclude that there had once been men in that island. All our reasonings concerning fact are of the same nature. And here it is constantly supposed that there is a connexion between the present fact and that which is inferred from it. Were there nothing to bind them together, the inference would be entirely precarious. The hearing of an articulate voice and rational discourse in the dark assures us of the presence of some person: Why? because these are the effects of the human make and fabric, and closely connected with it. If we anatomize all the other reasonings of this nature, we shall find that they are founded on the relation of cause and effect, and that this relation is either near or remote, direct or collateral. Heat and light are collateral effects of fire, and the one effect may justly be inferred from the other.

If we would satisfy ourselves, therefore, concerning the nature of that evidence, which assures us of matters of fact, we must enquire how we arrive at the knowledge of cause and effect.

I shall venture to affirm, as a general proposition, which admits of no exception, that the knowledge of this relation is not, in any instance, attained by reasonings *a priori*; but arises entirely from experience, when we find that any particular objects are constantly conjoined with each other. Let an object be presented to a man of ever so strong natural reason and abilities; if that object be entirely new to him, he will not be able, by the most accurate examination of its sensible qualities, to discover any of its causes or effects. Adam, though his rational faculties be supposed, at the very first, entirely perfect, could not have inferred from the fluidity and transparency of water that it would suffocate him, or from the light and warmth of fire that it would consume him. No object ever discovers, by the qualities which appear to the senses, either the causes which produced it, or the effects which will arise from it; nor can our reason, unassisted by experience, ever draw any inference concerning real existence and matter of fact.

This proposition, *that causes and effects are discoverable, not by reason but by experience*, will readily be admitted with regard to such objects, as we remember to have once been altogether unknown to us; since we must be conscious of the utter inability, which we then lay under, of foretelling what would arise from them. Present two smooth pieces of marble to a man who has no tincture of natural philosophy; he will never discover that they will adhere together in such a manner as to require great force to separate them in a direct line, while they make so small a resistance to a lateral pressure. Such events, as bear little analogy to the common course of nature, are also readily confessed to be known only by experience; nor does any man imagine that the explosion of gunpowder, or the attraction of a load-stone, could ever be discovered by arguments *a priori*. In like manner, when an effect is supposed to depend upon an intricate machinery or secret structure of parts, we make no difficulty in attributing all our knowledge of it to experience. Who will assert that he can give the ultimate reason, why milk or bread is proper nourishment for a man, not for a lion or a tiger?

But the same truth may not appear, at first sight, to have the same evidence with regard to events, which have become familiar to us from our first appearance in the world, which bear a close analogy to the whole course of nature, and which are supposed to depend on the simple qualities of objects, without any secret structure of parts. We are apt to imagine that we could discover these effects by the mere operation of our reason, without experience. We fancy, that were we brought on a sudden into this world, we could at first have inferred that one Billiard-ball would communicate motion to another upon impulse; and that we needed not to have waited for the event, in order to pronounce with certainty concerning it. Such is the influence of custom, that, where it is strongest, it not only covers our natural ignorance, but even conceals itself, and seems not to take place, merely because it is found in the highest degree.

But to convince us that all the laws of nature, and all the operations of bodies without exception, are known only by experience, the following reflections may, perhaps, suffice. Were any object presented to us, and were we required to pronounce concerning the effect, which will result from it, without consulting past observation; after what manner, I beseech you, must the mind proceed in this operation? It must invent or imagine some event, which it ascribes to the object as its effect; and it is plain that this invention must be entirely arbitrary. The mind can never possibly find the effect in the supposed cause, by the most accurate scrutiny and examination. For the effect is totally different from the cause, and consequently can never be discovered in it. Motion in the second Billiard-ball is a quite distinct event from motion in the first; nor is there anything in the one to suggest the smallest hint of the other. A stone or piece of metal raised into the air, and left without any support, immediately falls: but to consider the matter *a priori*, is there anything we discover in this situation which can beget the idea of a downward, rather than an upward, or any other motion, in the stone or metal?

And as the first imagination or invention of a particular effect, in all natural operations, is arbitrary, where we consult not experience; so must

we also esteem the supposed tie or connexion between the cause and effect, which binds them together, and renders it impossible that any other effect could result from the operation of that cause. When I see, for instance, a Billiard-ball moving in a straight line towards another; even suppose motion in the second ball should by accident be suggested to me, as the result of their contact or impulse; may I not conceive, that a hundred different events might as well follow from that cause? May not both these balls remain at absolute rest? May not the first ball return in a straight line, or leap off from the second in any line or direction? All these suppositions are consistent and conceivable. Why then should we give the preference to one, which is no more consistent or conceivable than the rest? All our reasonings *a priori* will never be able to show us any foundation for this preference.

In a word, then, every effect is a distinct event from its cause. It could not, therefore, be discovered in the cause, and the first invention or conception of it, *a priori*, must be entirely arbitrary. And even after it is suggested, the conjunction of it with the cause must appear equally arbitrary; since there are always many other effects, which, to reason, must seem fully as consistent and natural. In vain, therefore, should we pretend to determine any single event, or infer any cause or effect, without the assistance of observation and experience.

Hence we may discover the reason why no philosopher, who is rational and modest, has ever pretended to assign the ultimate cause of any natural operation, or to show distinctly the action of that power, which produces any single effect in the universe. It is confessed, that the utmost effort of human reason is to reduce the principles, productive of natural phenomena, to a greater simplicity, and to resolve the many particular effects into a few general causes, by means of reasonings from analogy, experience, and observation. But as to the causes of these general causes, we should in vain attempt their discovery; nor shall we ever be able to satisfy ourselves, by any particular explication of them. These ultimate springs and principles are totally shut up from human curiosity and enquiry. Elasticity, gravity, cohesion of parts, communication of motion by impulse; these are probably the ultimate causes and principles which we shall ever discover in nature; and we may esteem ourselves sufficiently happy, if, by accurate enquiry and reasoning, we can trace up the particular phenomena to, or near to, these general principles. The most perfect philosophy of the natural kind only staves off our ignorance a little longer: as perhaps the most perfect philosophy of the moral or metaphysical kind serves only to discover larger portions of it. Thus the observation of human blindness and weakness is the result of all philosophy, and meets us at every turn, in spite of our endeavours to elude or avoid it. [...]

Part II
But we have not yet attained any tolerable satisfaction with regard to the question first proposed. Each solution still gives rise to a new question as difficult as the foregoing, and leads us on to farther enquiries. When it is asked, *What is the nature of all our reasonings concerning matter of fact?* the proper answer seems to be, that they are founded on the relation of cause and effect. When again it is asked, *What is the foundation of all our reasonings and conclusions concerning that relation?* it may be replied in one word, Experience. But if we still carry on our sifting humour, and ask, *What is the foundation of all conclusions from experience?* this implies a new question, which may be of more difficult solution and explication. Philosophers, that give themselves airs of superior wisdom and sufficiency, have a hard task when they encounter persons of inquisitive dispositions, who push them from every corner to which they retreat, and who are sure at last to bring them to some dangerous dilemma. The best expedient to prevent this confusion, is to be modest in our pretensions; and even to discover the difficulty ourselves before it is objected to us.

By this means, we may make a kind of merit of our very ignorance.

I shall content myself, in this section, with an easy task, and shall pretend only to give a negative answer to the question here proposed. I say then, that, even after we have experience of the operations of cause and effect, our conclusions from that experience are *not* founded on reasoning, or any process of the understanding. This answer we must endeavour both to explain and to defend.

It must certainly be allowed, that nature has kept us at a great distance from all her secrets, and has afforded us only the knowledge of a few superficial qualities of objects; while she conceals from us those powers and principles on which the influence of these objects entirely depends. Our senses inform us of the colour, weight, and consistence of bread; but neither sense nor reason can ever inform us of those qualities which fit it for the nourishment and support of a human body. Sight or feeling conveys an idea of the actual motion of bodies; but as to that wonderful force or power, which would carry on a moving body for ever in a continued change of place, and which bodies never lose but by communicating it to others; of this we cannot form the most distant conception. But notwithstanding this ignorance of natural powers and principles, we always presume, when we see like sensible qualities, that they have like secret powers, and expect that effects, similar to those which we have experienced, will follow from them. If a body of like colour and consistence with that bread, which we have formerly eat, be presented to us, we make no scruple of repeating the experiment, and foresee, with certainty, like nourishment and support. Now this is a process of the mind or thought, of which I would willingly know the foundation. It is allowed on all hands that there is no known connexion between the sensible qualities and the secret powers; and consequently, that the mind is not led to form such a conclusion concerning their constant and regular conjunction, by anything which it knows of their nature. As to past *Experience*, it can be allowed to give *direct* and *certain* information of those precise objects only, and that precise period of time, which fell under its cognizance: but why this experience should be extended to future times, and to other objects, which for aught we know, may be only in appearance similar; this is the main question on which I would insist. The bread, which I formerly eat, nourished me; that is, a body of such sensible qualities was, at that time, endued with such secret powers: but does it follow, that other bread must also nourish me at another time, and that like sensible qualities must always be attended with like secret powers? The consequence seems nowise necessary. At least, it must be acknowledged that there is here a consequence drawn by the mind; that there is a certain step taken; a process of thought, and an inference, which wants to be explained. These two propositions are far from being the same, *I have found that such an object has always been attended with such an effect*, and *I foresee, that other objects, which are, in appearance, similar, will be attended with similar effects*. I shall allow, if you please, that the one proposition may justly be inferred from the other: I know, in fact, that it always is inferred. But if you insist that the inference is made by a chain of reasoning, I desire you to produce that reasoning. The connexion between these propositions is not intuitive. There is required a medium, which may enable the mind to draw such an inference, if indeed it be drawn by reasoning and argument. What that medium is, I must confess, passes my comprehension; and it is incumbent on those to produce it, who assert that it really exists, and is the origin of all our conclusions concerning matter of fact.

This negative argument must certainly, in process of time, become altogether convincing, if many penetrating and able philosophers shall turn their enquiries this way and no one be ever able to discover any connecting proposition or intermediate step, which supports the understanding in this conclusion. But as the question is yet new, every reader may not trust so far to his own penetration, as to conclude, because an

argument escapes his enquiry, that therefore it does not really exist. For this reason it may be requisite to venture upon a more difficult task; and enumerating all the branches of human knowledge, endeavour to show that none of them can afford such an argument.

All reasonings may be divided into two kinds, namely, demonstrative reasoning, or that concerning relations of ideas, and moral reasoning, or that concerning matter of fact and existence. That there are no demonstrative arguments in the case seems evident; since it implies no contradiction that the course of nature may change, and that an object, seemingly like those which we have experienced, may be attended with different or contrary effects. May I not clearly and distinctly conceive that a body, falling from the clouds, and which, in all other respects, resembles snow, has yet the taste of salt or feeling of fire? Is there any more intelligible proposition than to affirm, that all the trees will flourish in December and January, and decay in May and June? Now whatever is intelligible, and can be distinctly conceived, implies no contradiction, and can never be proved false by any demonstrative argument or abstract reasoning *à priori*.

If we be, therefore, engaged by arguments to put trust in past experience, and make it the standard of our future judgement, these arguments must be probable only, or such as regard matter of fact and real existence, according to the division above mentioned. But that there is no argument of this kind, must appear, if our explication of that species of reasoning be admitted as solid and satisfactory. We have said that all arguments concerning existence are founded on the relation of cause and effect; that our knowledge of that relation is derived entirely from experience; and that all our experimental conclusions proceed upon the supposition that the future will be conformable to the past. To endeavour, therefore, the proof of this last supposition by probable arguments, or arguments regarding existence, must be evidently going in a circle, and taking that for granted, which is the very point in question.

In reality, all arguments from experience are founded on the similarity which we discover among natural objects, and by which we are induced to expect effects similar to those which we have found to follow from such objects. And though none but a fool or madman will ever pretend to dispute the authority of experience, or to reject that great guide of human life, it may surely be allowed a philosopher to have so much curiosity at least as to examine the principle of human nature, which gives this mighty authority to experience, and makes us draw advantage from that similarity which nature has placed among different objects. From causes which appear *similar* we expect similar effects. This is the sum of all our experimental conclusions. Now it seems evident that, if this conclusion were formed by reason, it would be as perfect at first, and upon one instance, as after ever so long a course of experience. But the case is far otherwise. Nothing so like as eggs; yet no one, on account of this appearing similarity, expects the same taste and relish in all of them. It is only after a long course of uniform experiments in any kind, that we attain a firm reliance and security with regard to a particular event. Now where is that process of reasoning which, from one instance, draws a conclusion, so different from that which it infers from a hundred instances that are nowise different from that single one? This question I propose as much for the sake of information, as with an intention of raising difficulties. I cannot find, I cannot imagine any such reasoning. But I keep my mind still open to instruction, if any one will vouchsafe to bestow it on me.

Should it be said that, from a number of uniform experiments, we *infer* a connexion between the sensible qualities and the secret powers; this, I must confess, seems the same difficulty, couched in different terms. The question still recurs, on what process of argument this *inference* is founded? Where is the medium, the interposing ideas, which join propositions so very wide of each other? It is confessed that the colour, consistence, and other sensible qualities of bread appear not, of themselves, to have any connexion with the secret powers of nourishment and support. For otherwise we could infer these secret powers from the first appearance of these sensible qualities, without the aid of experience; contrary to the sentiment of all philosophers, and contrary to plain matter of fact. Here, then, is our natural state of ignorance with regard to the powers and influence of all objects. How is this remedied by experience? It only shows us a number of uniform effects, resulting from certain objects, and teaches us that those particular objects, at that particular time, were endowed with such powers and forces. When a new object, endowed with similar sensible qualities, is produced, we expect similar powers and forces, and look for a like effect. From a body of like colour and consistence with bread we expect like nourishment and support. But this surely is a step or progress of the mind, which wants to be explained. When a man says, *I have found, in all past instances, such sensible qualities conjoined with such secret powers*: And when he says, *Similar sensible qualities will always be conjoined with similar secret powers*, he is not guilty of a tautology, nor are these propositions in any respect the same. You say that the one proposition is an inference from the other. But you must confess that the inference is not intuitive; neither is it demonstrative: Of what nature is it, then? To say it is experimental, is begging the question. For all inferences from experience suppose, as their foundation, that the future will resemble the past, and that similar powers will be conjoined with similar sensible qualities. If there be any suspicion that the course of nature may change, and that the past may be no rule for the future, all experience becomes useless, and can give rise to no inference or conclusion. It is impossible, therefore, that any arguments from experience can prove this resemblance of the past to the future; since all these arguments are founded on the supposition of that resemblance. Let the course of things be allowed hitherto ever so regular; that alone, without some new argument or inference, proves not that, for the future, it will continue so. In vain do you pretend to have learned the nature of bodies from your past experience. Their secret nature, and consequently all their effects and influence, may change, without any change in their sensible qualities. This happens sometimes, and with regard to some objects: Why may it not happen always, and with regard to all objects? What logic, what process of argument secures you against this supposition? My practice, you say, refutes my doubts. But you mistake the purport of my question. As an agent, I am quite satisfied in the point; but as a philosopher, who has some share of curiosity, I will not say scepticism, I want to learn the foundation of this inference. No reading, no enquiry has yet been able to remove my difficulty, or give me satisfaction in a matter of such importance. Can I do better than propose the difficulty to the public, even though, perhaps, I have small hopes of obtaining a solution? We shall at least, by this means, be sensible of our ignorance, if we do not augment our knowledge. [. . .]

SECTION V

Sceptical Solution of These Doubts

Suppose a person, though endowed with the strongest faculties of reason and reflection, to be brought on a sudden into this world; he would, indeed, immediately observe a continual succession of objects, and one event following another; but he would not be able to discover anything farther. He would not, at first, by any reasoning, be able to reach the idea of cause and effect; since the particular powers, by which all natural operations are performed, never appear to the senses; nor is it reasonable to conclude, merely because one event, in one instance, precedes another, that therefore the one is the cause, the other the effect. Their conjunction may be

arbitrary and casual. There may be no reason to infer the existence of one from the appearance of the other. And in a word, such a person, without more experience, could never employ his conjecture or reasoning concerning any matter of fact, or be assured of anything beyond what was immediately present to his memory and senses.

Suppose, again, that he has acquired more experience, and has lived so long in the world as to have observed similar objects or events to be constantly conjoined together; what is the consequence of this experience? He immediately infers the existence of one object from the appearance of the other. Yet he has not, by all his experience, acquired any idea or knowledge of the secret power by which the one object produces the other; nor is it, by any process of reasoning, he is engaged to draw this inference. But still he finds himself determined to draw it: And though he should be convinced that his understanding has no part in the operation, he would nevertheless continue in the same course of thinking. There is some other principle which determines him to form such a conclusion.

This principle is Custom or Habit. For wherever the repetition of any particular act or operation produces a propensity to renew the same act or operation, without being impelled by any reasoning or process of the understanding, we always say, that this propensity is the effect of *Custom.* By employing that word, we pretend not to have given the ultimate reason of such a propensity. We only point out a principle of human nature, which is universally acknowledged, and which is well known by its effects. Perhaps we can push our enquiries no farther, or pretend to give the cause of this cause; but must rest contented with it as the ultimate principle, which we can assign, of all our conclusions from experience. It is sufficient satisfaction, that we can go so far, without repining at the narrowness of our faculties because they will carry us no farther. And it is certain we here advance a very intelligible proposition at least, if not a true one, when we assert that, after the constant conjunction of two objects—heat and flame, for instance, weight and solidity—we are determined by custom alone to expect the one from the appearance of the other. This hypothesis seems even the only one which explains the difficulty, why we draw from a thousand instances, an inference which we are not able to draw from one instance, that is, in no respect, different from them. Reason is incapable of any such variation. The conclusions which it draws from considering one circle are the same which it would form upon surveying all the circles in the universe. But no man, having seen only one body move after being impelled by another, could infer that every other body will move after a like impulse. All inferences from experience, therefore, are effects of custom, not of reasoning.[1]

Custom, then, is the great guide of human life. It is that principle alone which renders our experience useful to us, and makes us expect, for the future, a similar train of events with those which have appeared in the past. Without the influence of custom, we should be entirely ignorant of every matter of fact beyond what is immediately present to the memory and senses. We should never know how to adjust means to ends, or to employ our natural powers in the production of any effect. There would be an end at once of all action, as well as of the chief part of speculation. [. . .]

SECTION VII

Of the Idea of Necessary Connexion

Part I

[. . .] There are no ideas, which occur in metaphysics, more obscure and uncertain, than those of *power, force, energy* or *necessary connexion*, of which it is every moment necessary for us to treat in all our disquisitions. We shall, therefore, endeavour, in this section, to fix, if possible, the precise meaning of these terms, and thereby remove some part of that obscurity, which is so much complained of in this species of philosophy.

It seems a proposition, which will not admit of much dispute, that all our ideas are nothing but copies of our impressions, or, in other words, that it is impossible for us to *think* of any thing, which we have not antecedently *felt*, either by our external or internal senses. [. . .]

When we look about us towards external objects, and consider the operation of causes, we are never able, in a single instance, to discover any power or necessary connexion; any quality, which binds the effect to the cause, and renders the one an infallible consequence of the other. We only find, that the one does actually, in fact, follow the other. The impulse of one billiard-ball is attended with motion in the second. This is the whole that appears to the *outward* senses. The mind feels no sentiment or *inward* impression from this succession of objects: Consequently, there is not, in any single, particular instance of cause and effect, any thing which can suggest the idea of power or necessary connexion.

From the first appearance of an object, we never can conjecture what effect will result from it. But were the power or energy of any cause discoverable by the mind, we could foresee the effect, even without experience; and might, at first, pronounce with certainty concerning it, by the mere dint of thought and reasoning.

In reality, there is no part of matter, that does ever, by its sensible qualities, discover any power or energy, or give us ground to imagine, that it could produce any thing, or be followed by any other object, which we could denominate its effect. Solidity, extension, motion; these qualities are all complete in themselves, and never point out any other event which may result from them. The scenes of the universe are continually shifting, and one object follows another in an uninterrupted succession; but the power or force, which actuates the whole machine, is entirely concealed from us, and never discovers itself in any of the sensible qualities of body. We know, that, in fact, heat is a constant attendant of flame; but what is the connexion between them, we have no room so much as to conjecture or imagine. It is impossible, therefore, that the idea of power can be derived from the contemplation of bodies, in single instances of their operation; because no bodies ever discover any power, which can be the original of this idea.[2]

Since, therefore, external objects as they appear to the senses, give us no idea of power or necessary connexion, by their operation in particular instances, let us see, whether this idea be derived from reflection on the operations of our own minds, and be copied from any internal impression. It may be said, that we are every moment conscious of internal power; while we feel, that, by the simple command of our will, we can move the organs of our body, or direct the faculties of our mind. An act of volition produces motion in our limbs, or raises a new idea in our imagination. This influence of the will we know by consciousness. Hence we acquire the idea of power or energy; and are certain, that we ourselves and all other intelligent beings are possessed of power. This idea, then, is an idea of reflection, since it arises from reflecting on the operations of our own mind, and on the command which is exercised by will, both over the organs of the body and faculties of the soul.

We shall proceed to examine this pretension; and first with regard to the influence of volition over the organs of the body. This influence, we may observe, is a fact, which, like all other natural events, can be known only by experience, and can never be foreseen from any apparent energy or power in the cause, which connects it with the effect, and renders the one an infallible consequence of the other. The motion of our body follows upon the command of our will. Of this we are every moment conscious. But the means, by which this is effected; the energy, by which the will performs so extraordinary an operation; of this we are so far from being immediately conscious, that it must for ever escape our most diligent enquiry.

For *first*; is there any principle in all nature more mysterious than the union of soul with body; by which a supposed spiritual substance acquires such an influence over a material one, that the most refined thought is able to actuate the grossest matter? [...]

Secondly, We are not able to move all the organs of the body with a like authority; though we cannot assign any reason besides experience, for so remarkable a difference between one and the other. Why has the will an influence over the tongue and fingers, not over the heart or liver? This question would never embarrass us, were we conscious of a power in the former case, not in the latter. We should then perceive, independent of experience, why the authority of will over the organs of the body is circumscribed within such particular limits. Being in that case fully acquainted with the power or force, by which it operates, we should also know, why its influence reaches precisely to such boundaries, and no farther.

A man, suddenly struck with a palsy in the leg or arm, or who had newly lost those members, frequently endeavours, at first, to move them, and employ them in their usual offices. Here he is as much conscious of power to command such limbs, as a man in perfect health is conscious of power to actuate any member which remains in its natural state and condition. But consciousness never deceives. Consequently, neither in the one case nor in the other, are we ever conscious of any power. We learn the influence of our will from experience alone. And experience only teaches us, how one event constantly follows another; without instructing us in the secret connexion, which binds them together, and renders them inseparable.

Thirdly, We learn from anatomy, that the immediate object of power in voluntary motion, is not the member itself which is moved, but certain muscles, and nerves, and animal spirits, and, perhaps, something still more minute and more unknown, through which the motion is successively propagated, ere it reach the member itself whose motion is the immediate object of volition. Can there be a more certain proof, that the power, by which this whole operation is performed, so far from being directly and fully known by an inward sentiment or consciousness, is, to the last degree, mysterious and unintelligible? Here the mind wills a certain event: Immediately another event, unknown to ourselves, and totally different from the one intended, is produced: This event produces another, equally unknown: Till at last, through a long succession, the desired event is produced. But if the original power were felt, it must be known: Were it known, its effect must also be known; since all power is relative to its effect. And *vice versa*, if the effect be not known, the power cannot be known nor felt. How indeed can we be conscious of a power to move our limbs, when we have no such power; but only that to move certain animal spirits, which, though they produce at last the motion of our limbs, yet operate in such a manner as is wholly beyond our comprehension?

We may, therefore, conclude from the whole, I hope, without any temerity, though with assurance; that our idea of power is not copied from any sentiment or consciousness of power within ourselves, when we give rise to animal motion, or apply our limbs to their proper use and office. That their motion follows the command of the will is a matter of common experience, like other natural events: But the power or energy by which this is effected, like that in other natural events, is unknown and inconceivable.[3]

Shall we then assert, that we are conscious of a power or energy in our own minds, when, by an act or command of our will, we raise up a new idea, fix the mind to the contemplation of it, turn it on all sides, and at last dismiss it for some other idea, when we think that we have surveyed it with sufficient accuracy? I believe the same arguments will prove, that even this command of the will gives us no real idea of force or energy.

First, It must be allowed, that, when we know a power, we know that very circumstance in the cause, by which it is enabled to produce the effect: For these are supposed to be synonimous. We must, therefore, know both the cause and effect, and the relation between them. But do we pretend to be acquainted with the nature of the human soul and the nature of an idea, or the aptitude of the one to produce the other? This is a real creation; a production of something out of nothing: Which implies a power so great, that it may seem, at first sight, beyond the reach of any being, less than infinite. At least it must be owned, that such a power is not felt, nor known, nor even conceivable by the mind. We only feel the event, namely, the existence of an idea, consequent to a command of the will: But the manner, in which this operation is performed, the power by which it is produced, is entirely beyond our comprehension.

Secondly, The command of the mind over itself is limited, as well as its command over the body; and these limits are not known by reason, or any acquaintance with the nature of cause and effect, but only by experience and observation, as in all other natural events and in the operation of external objects. Our authority over our sentiments and passions is much weaker than that over our ideas; and even the latter authority is circumscribed within very narrow boundaries. Will any one pretend to assign the ultimate reason of these boundaries, or show why the power is deficient in one case, not in another.

Thirdly, This self-command is very different at different times. A man in health possesses more of it than one languishing with sickness. We are more master of our thoughts in the morning than in the evening: Fasting, than after a full meal. Can we give any reason for these variations, except experience? Where then is the power, of which we pretend to be conscious? Is there not here, either in a spiritual or material substance, or both, some secret mechanism or structure of parts, upon which the effect depends, and which, being entirely unknown to us, renders the power or energy of the will equally unknown and incomprehensible?

Volition is surely an act of the mind, with which we are sufficiently acquainted. Reflect upon it. Consider it on all sides. Do you find anything in it like this creative power, by which it raises from nothing a new idea, and with a kind of *Fiat*, imitates the omnipotence of its Maker, if I may be allowed so to speak, who called forth into existence all the various scenes of nature? So far from being conscious of this energy in the will, it requires as certain experience as that of which we are possessed, to convince us that such extraordinary effects do ever result from a simple act of volition.

The generality of mankind never find any difficulty in accounting for the more common and familiar operations of nature—such as the descent of heavy bodies, the growth of plants, the generation of animals, or the nourishment of bodies by food: But suppose that, in all these cases, they perceive the very force or energy of the cause, by which it is connected with its effect, and is for ever infallible in its operation. They acquire, by long habit, such a turn of mind, that, upon the appearance of the cause, they immediately expect with assurance its usual attendant, and hardly conceive it possible that any other event could result from it. It is only on the discovery of extraordinary phaenomena, such as earthquakes, pestilence, and prodigies of any kind, that they find themselves at a loss to assign a proper cause, and to explain the manner in which the effect is produced by it. It is usual for men, in such difficulties, to have recourse to some invisible intelligent principle as the immediate cause of that event which surprises them, and which, they think, cannot be accounted for from the common powers of nature. But philosophers, who carry their scrutiny a little farther, immediately perceive that, even in the most familiar events, the energy of the cause is as unintelligible as in the most unusual, and that we only learn by experience the frequent *Conjunction* of objects, without being ever able to comprehend anything like *Connexion* between them. [...]

Part II

Upon the whole, there appears not, throughout all nature, any one instance of connexion which is conceivable by us. All events seem entirely loose and separate. One event follows another; but we never can observe any tie between them. They seem *conjoined*, but never *connected*. And as we can have no idea of any thing which never appeared to our outward sense or inward sentiment, the necessary conclusion *seems* to be that we have no idea of connexion or power at all,

and that these words are absolutely without any meaning, when employed either in philosophical reasonings or common life.

But there still remains one method of avoiding this conclusion, and one source which we have not yet examined. When any natural object or event is presented, it is impossible for us, by any sagacity or penetration, to discover, or even conjecture, without experience, what event will result from it, or to carry our foresight beyond that object which is immediately present to the memory and senses. Even after one instance or experiment, where we have observed a particular event to follow upon another, we are not entitled to form a general rule, or foretell what will happen in like cases; it being justly esteemed an unpardonable temerity to judge of the whole course of nature from one single experiment, however accurate or certain. But when one particular species of event has always, in all instances, been conjoined with another, we make no longer any scruple of foretelling one upon the appearance of the other, and of employing that reasoning, which can alone assure us of any matter of fact or existence. We then call the one object, *Cause*; the other, *Effect*. We suppose that there is some connexion between them; some power in the one, by which it infallibly produces the other, and operates with the greatest certainty and strongest necessity.

It appears, then, that this idea of a necessary connexion among events arises from a number of similar instances which occur of the constant conjunction of these events; nor can that idea ever be suggested by any one of these instances, surveyed in all possible lights and positions. But there is nothing in a number of instances, different from every single instance, which is supposed to be exactly similar; except only, that after a repetition of similar instances, the mind is carried by habit, upon the appearance of one event, to expect its usual attendant, and to believe that it will exist. This connexion, therefore, which we *feel* in the mind, this customary transition of the imagination from one object to its usual attendant, is the sentiment or impression from which we form the idea of power or necessary connexion. Nothing farther is in the case. Contemplate the subject on all sides; you will never find any other origin of that idea. This is the sole difference between one instance, from which we can never receive the idea of connexion, and a number of similar instances, by which it is suggested. The first time a man saw the communication of motion by impulse, as by the shock of two billiard balls, he could not pronounce that the one event was *connected*: but only that it was *conjoined* with the other. After he has observed several instances of this nature, he then pronounces them to be *connected*. What alteration has happened to give rise to this new idea of *connexion*? Nothing but that he now *feels* these events to be *connected* in his imagination, and can readily foretell the existence of one from the appearance of the other. When we say, therefore, that one object is connected with another, we mean only that they have acquired a connexion in our thought, and give rise to this inference, by which they become proofs of each other's existence: A conclusion which is somewhat extraordinary, but which seems founded on sufficient evidence. Nor will its evidence be weakened by any general diffidence of the understanding, or sceptical suspicion concerning every conclusion which is new and extraordinary. No conclusions can be more agreeable to scepticism than such as make discoveries concerning the weakness and narrow limits of human reason and capacity.

[...] The only immediate utility of all sciences, is to teach us, how to control and regulate future events by their causes. Our thoughts and enquiries are, therefore, every moment, employed about this relation: Yet so imperfect are the ideas which we form concerning it, that it is impossible to give any just definition of cause, except what is drawn from something extraneous and foreign to it. Similar objects are always conjoined with similar. Of this we have experience. Suitably to this experience, therefore, we may define a cause to be *an object, followed by another, and where all the objects similar to the first are followed by objects similar to the second.* Or in other words *where, if*

the first object had not been, the second never had existed. The appearance of a cause always conveys the mind, by a customary transition, to the idea of the effect. Of this also we have experience. We may, therefore, suitably to this experience, form another definition of cause, and call it, *an object followed by another, and whose appearance always conveys the thought to that other.* But though both these definitions be drawn from circumstances foreign to the cause, we cannot remedy this inconvenience, or attain any more perfect definition, which may point out that circumstance in the cause, which gives it a connexion with its effect. We have no idea of this connexion, nor even any distinct notion what it is we desire to know, when we endeavour at a conception of it. We say, for instance, that the vibration of this string is the cause of this particular sound. But what do we mean by that affirmation? We either mean *that this vibration is followed by this sound, and that all similar vibrations have been followed by similar sounds:* Or, *that this vibration is followed by this sound, and that upon the appearance of one the mind anticipates the senses, and forms immediately an idea of the other.* We may consider the relation of cause and effect in either of these two lights; but beyond these, we have no idea of it.

Notes

1. Nothing is more usual than for writers, even, on *moral, political,* or *physical* subjects, to distinguish between *reason* and *experience,* and to suppose, that these species of argumentation are entirely different from each other. The former are taken for the mere result of our intellectual faculties, which, by considering *à priori* the nature of things, and examining the effects, that must follow from their operation, establish particular principles of science and philosophy. The latter are supposed to be derived entirely from sense and observation, by which we learn what has actually resulted from the operation of particular objects, and are thence able to infer, what will, for the future, result from them. Thus, for instance, the limitations and restraints of civil government, and a legal constitution, may be defended, either from *reason,* which reflecting on

the great frailty and corruption of human nature, teaches, that no man can safely be trusted with unlimited authority; or from *experience* and history, which inform us of the enormous abuses, that ambition, in every age and country, has been found to make of so imprudent a confidence.

[...] Though it be allowed, that reason may form very plausible conjectures with regard to the consequences of such a particular conduct in such particular circumstances; it is still supposed imperfect, without the assistance of experience, which is alone able to give stability and certainty to the maxims, derived from study and reflection.

But notwithstanding that this distinction be thus universally received, both in the active and speculative scenes of life, I shall not scruple to pronounce, that it is, at bottom, erroneous, at least, superficial.

If we examine those arguments, which, in any of the sciences above mentioned, are supposed to be the mere effects of reasoning and reflection, they will be found to terminate, at last, in some general principle or conclusion, for which we can assign no reason but observation and experience. The only difference between them and those maxims, which are vulgarly esteemed the result of pure experience, is, that the former cannot be established without some process of thought, and some reflection on what we have observed, in order to distinguish its circumstances, and trace its consequences: Whereas in the latter, the experienced event is exactly and fully similar to that which we infer as the result of any particular situation. [...] In both cases it is experience which is ultimately the foundation of our inference and conclusion.

There is no man so young and unexperienced, as not to have formed, from observation, many general and just maxims concerning human affairs and the conduct of life; but it must be confessed, that, when a man comes to put these in practice, he will be extremely liable to error, till time and farther experience both enlarge these maxims, and teach him their proper use and application. [...] The truth is, an unexperienced reasoner could be no reasoner at all, were he absolutely unexperienced; and when we assign that character to any one, we mean it only in a comparative sense, and suppose him possessed of experience, in a smaller and more imperfect degree.

2. Mr. Locke, in his chapter of power, says that, finding from experience, that there are several new productions in matter, and concluding that there must somewhere be a power capable of producing them, we arrive at last by this reasoning at the idea of power. But no reasoning can ever give us a new, original, simple idea; as this philosopher himself confesses. This, therefore, can never be the origin of that idea.

3. It may be pretended, that the resistance which we meet with in bodies, obliging us frequently to exert our force, and call up all our power, this gives us the idea of force and power. It is this *nisus*, or strong endeavour, of which we are conscious, that is the original impression from which this idea is copied. But, first, we attribute power to a vast number of objects, where we never can suppose this resistance or exertion of force to take place; to the Supreme Being, who never meets with any resistance; to the mind in its command over its ideas and limbs, in common thinking and motion, where the effect follows immediately upon the will, without any exertion or summoning up of force; to inanimate matter, which is not capable of this sentiment. *Secondly*, This sentiment of an endeavour to overcome resistance has no known connexion with any event: What follows it, we know by experience; but could not know it *à priori*. It must, however, be confessed, that the animal *nisus*, which we experience, though it can afford no accurate precise idea of power, enters very much into that vulgar, inaccurate idea, which is formed of it.

Study Questions

1. Are relations of ideas as useless as Hume suggests?
2. Can you clearly articulate Hume's argument against the ability to use induction to ground our beliefs about the future?
3. What is the difference between the argument in section IV and the one in section VII?
4. Many philosophers leave Hume's work feeling as if they have just experienced a great loss. Why would they think this? What has been lost? Do you agree? Has anything been gained?

3.3

3.3   The Perception of Causality

 ALBERT MICHOTTE

ALBERT MICHOTTE (1881–1965) was a Belgian experimental psychologist who taught at the University of Louven, where he earlier had studied biology and philosophy, ultimately writing a doctoral thesis on Herbert Spencer's *Principles of Ethics*. He was unsatisfied with behaviorism and its bare physical description of human action. But, at the same time, he was committed to the experimental method and its suspicion of hypothesized entities and forces that fail to have perceptual effects. *The Perception of Causality*, from which our selections are drawn, was originally published in 1946. In direct opposition to Hume's claim that we receive no direct impression of causal connections, Michotte designs a series of "launching" and "entraining" experiments to detect causal influence, to trace the genealogy of causal impression. As it turns out, the causal impressions we receive are neither conceptual acts of interpretation nor projected onto the world by us on the basis of past experience. By manipulating the time it takes a second object, B, to move after being approached by a first object, A, which then rests next to B, Michotte is able to make the causal impression disappear. He concludes that in seeing causation, observers see not simply a change of position, but action. Our selection closes with Michotte's theory of ampliation, which aims to explain the productive character of causal impression, the sense that there is more to causation than constant conjunction.

INTRODUCTION

The thesis which I put forward at the Yale conference was in direct disagreement with all theories of the traditional kind which we have just been considering, since I expressed the opinion that certain physical events give an immediate causal impression, and that one can "see" an object *act* on another object, *produce* in it certain changes, and *modify* it in one way or another.[1] I quoted various examples in this connexion, e.g. that of a hammer driving a nail into a plank, and that of a knife cutting a slice of bread. The question that arises is this: when we observe these operations, is our perception limited to the impression of two movements spatially and temporally

co-ordinated, such as the advance of the knife and the cutting of the bread? Or rather do we directly perceive the action as such—do we see the knife actually cut the bread? The answer does not seem to me to admit of any doubt. [...]

2. CAUSALITY AND ACTIVITY

[...] The next task is to give an account of our own research.

The first requirement was obviously to try to produce experimentally some typical causal impressions, and to determine by tests the conditions in which they occur. As might be expected, we began by examining the classic case of one

Albert Michotte, *The Perception of Causality* (London: Methuen, 1963).

object striking another. From our very first trials we were able to establish a fact which is important both theoretically and from the point of view of practical experimentation, viz. that the causal impression was not necessarily dependent on the use of "real," solid objects. It can be produced perfectly clearly by using objects which are simple coloured shapes without apparent thickness, or even images projected on a screen; and this is possible even when the observers know perfectly well what is going on. Our task was thus greatly simplified, and it became possible for us to carry out experiments of many different sorts. We were able to vary in a systematic way such things as the colour, size, and shape of the objects, the speed and direction of their movements, the amplitude of their paths, the temporal interval between the "action" and the "reaction," and so on.

Next we contrived to make the causal impression appear and disappear at will; and we were able to compare directly the cases where it occurs with those where it was absent. The study of these cases, as we shall find later, brings to light the operation of laws closely related to the Gestalt laws. It is thus possible to link causal impressions with other perceptual phenomena that are already known. We can also exclude categorically any attempt aimed at reducing this impression to a "projection" of our own power into things, or alternatively to a secondary "interpretation" based on past experience and acquired knowledge.

When we had disposed of these problems we were confronted with a second task, that of "understanding" the phenomenon, of making a theory about it, of seeking to find out why such and such conditions were necessary for its production, and why it possessed such and such properties. This constituted a counter-proof, such as would provide a definite demonstration of the original and primary character of the causal impression.

The method which we systematically used for this purpose was that of *genetic analysis*. This consisted essentially in simplifying in various ways the conditions which had been found necessary for producing the causal impression, and in comparing the resultant impressions with

those given by the original complete experiment. We could then see in what respects the two were different and in what respects they were similar, and were thus able, step by step, to trace the genesis of the causal impression. Moreover we could determine which among the many stimulus-conditions accounted for the presence of a character (that of productivity) which, considered in isolation, seemed at first sight to belong exclusively to the causal impression.

Briefly, the aim of this analysis was to reveal the genealogy of the causal impression, and if possible to re-discover by this means traces of more simple phenomena. These traces are so much modified in the causal impression that at first glance they may sometimes pass unrecognised.

The use of this kind of analysis in the psychology of perception is reminiscent of the method employed in all comparative sciences, e.g. comparative anatomy. Just as the latter succeeds in discovering the "significance" of rudimentary organs, and in connecting them with fully developed organs, by following the different stages of their evolution, so in the sphere of perception it is possible to follow the evolution of phenomena, and to recognise similarities of structure beneath the apparently very different forms which they may take. Just as this procedure enables us to "understand" a rudimentary organ, and to resolve the problem which it presents, so it will be possible by the same means to "understand" the characteristics of the causal impression. There is no need to call attention to the full implications of this method; its usefulness will be seen in the actual course of the exposition.

Although we had this twofold purpose, the experimental research did not itself fall into two distinct parts. The experiments for determining the conditions in which the causal impression appeared were usually also those which were helpful from the point of view of genetic analysis.

Our work is based on two fundamental experiments. Here is an account of them:

Exp. 1.[2] The observer sits at a distance of 1.50 metres from a screen, in which is cut a slit 150 mm. long and 5 mm. high. Immediately behind this screen is a uniform white background, on which stand out two squares of side 5 mm. One, a red square, is in the centre of the slit; the other, a black square, is 40 mm. to the left of the first. We shall call the black square "object A," and the red square "object B." The subject fixates object B. At a given moment object A sets off and moves towards B at a speed of about 30 cm. per sec. It stops at the moment when it comes into contact with B, while the latter then starts and moves away from A, either at the same speed or, preferably, at an appreciably lower one, e.g. 6 or 10 cm. per sec. Then it stops, after covering a distance of 2 cm. or more, according to the speed adopted.

A large number of the experiments quoted in this book will be described as modifications of the above. Unless there is an indication to the contrary, the speeds may be assumed to be equal.

The speeds mentioned in the various experiments are those which were actually used. They are not the only possible ones, however; and, except in the case of very slow movements, a divergence of a few cm. per sec. has little effect on the results obtained.

The result of this experiment is perfectly clear; the observers see object A bump into object B, and *send it off* (or "*launch*" it), *shove it forward, set it in motion, give it a push.* The impression is clear; it is the blow given by A which *makes B go,* which *produces* B's movement.

This experiment and the following one have been tried out on a large number of subjects (several hundreds) of all ages. All of them have given similar descriptions, with the exception of one or two, who, observing in an extremely analytical way, said that they saw two successive movements, simply co-ordinated in time. Moreover the same experiment has been tried hundreds of times on some subjects, and their impression of causality remained unaffected.[3]

Exp. 2. The conditions are the same as for the preceding experiment. The only difference consists in the fact that object A, after reaching object B, continues its course without changing its speed. From the time when they come into contact, object B

in its turn starts to move off at the same speed as object A. The two objects remain side by side during their common movement and form by their combination a bi-coloured rectangle, which covers a distance of 3 or 4 cm. before stopping.

Here we have the impression that object A *carries* object B *along* (or "entrains" it); that it *takes it with it,* that it *speeds it up in passing,* or again, if the speed and size of the objects are varied, that it *pushes it ahead.* The impression of causality is again clear; it is A which *makes B go forward,* which *produces* the change in B's position.

These are the two Type-experiments of causality; we shall call them respectively the *Launching Effect* and the *Entraining Effect.*[4]

In the case of these two experiments the production of movement is thus *directly experienced.* There is no question of an interpretation, nor of a "significance" superimposed on the impression of movement; in other words, what is actually "given" is not a mere representation or a symbol of causality. In the same way as stroboscopic movement is not, psychologically speaking, the "symbol" of a movement, but *is* a phenomenal movement, so the causality perceived here *is* a phenomenal causality.

Now obviously a movement seen at the cinema can "represent" the movement of a so-called "real" object; but it is a movement which represents another movement in the same way as a shape drawn on a canvas can represent the shape of a "real" object. Similarly, the causality sometimes perceived on the cinema screen may represent the causality exercised by one "real" object on another "real" object; but from a psychological point of view it is still one phenomenal causality representing another.

A slight modification of expts. 1 and 2 brings out particularly clearly the specific character of causality as we experience it. Let us suppose that we introduce an interval of a fifth of a second or more between the two phases of the experiment (i.e. between the time when object A joins object B, and the time when object B begins to move, whether or not it is accompanied by A), and let us then make a direct comparison between the two impressions received, first when there was an interval, and secondly when there was not.

The presence of the interval makes the causal impression disappear completely. A is seen to approach B, hit it, and stop beside it in such a way that they form one block, a bi-coloured rectangle. Then a new scene is presented independent of the preceding one; in exp. 1 B separates from A and moves away from it, and in exp. 2 the bi-coloured block simply begins to move as a block, as a "whole."

The result of this comparison is striking, and all observers agree in asserting that the impressions are radically different. In the one case we find two events intrinsically linked, with the first of them "producing" the second, and, in the other case, two events that are obviously separate, which arise successively, and which on their own give no impression of causality.

This last point needs to be emphasised, since, in theory, the two phases taken separately could quite well correspond to different causal influences. The approach of A towards B could give the impression that A is attracted by B; its stopping at the moment of contact could give the impression that B is an obstacle which prevents the movement of A from continuing; and the separation at the second stage could give the impression that B is repulsed by A, etc. Now in fact nothing like this happens. Not only is there no causal impression, but there is no tendency towards a causal "interpretation" in these cases.

On the other hand, the isolated phases do not instead constitute simple experiences of movement, of change of position. They present the remarkable characters of "approach" and "withdrawal" which we shall be studying later; and they also present a special character which we must call attention to at once, that of an undeniable *activity*.

This demands some explanation. The term "activity" is often used in books on psychology, but unfortunately in a rather different sense. It is therefore essential to make clear what is meant by it. In my use of this term there is no suggestion of a "liveliness" of movement, nor of an impression of agitation, nor of an impression of tension and excitement in the sense that has become familiar from Wundt's theory. When I speak of activity in connexion with the experiments which we have discussed, I mean to indicate that we see the object *act*, we see it *do something*. This is very different from the perception of a simple change of position, and even the most naïve observers frequently and unhesitatingly make a distinction between the two.

It is, of course, difficult to fix the lower limits of this impression, and one could discuss indefinitely the legitimacy of the application of the term "activity" to movement as such. This question, however, is irrelevant and of no special interest; for the essential facts are that observers spontaneously differentiate between the two cases, and that in addition activity is found to have differences in degree which are extremely marked. Whether there is, at the lower limit, a simple difference of degree or a qualitative difference is of minor importance.

In the present group of experiments and with the speeds which we have used—this is important—the impression is given that A "goes towards" B, that it *strikes it*, that it *hits it*, and that it unites with it, and again that B leaves A, that it *withdraws from it*, and sometimes that it *runs away* from it.[5]

In other cases, in particular when B stays still and A after reaching B returns to its starting-point, a different impression is given. If certain speed conditions are satisfied, it appears that A *strikes* B, or, when the movement recurs at fixed intervals, that A *hammers* or *pounds* B, and this constitutes a much more marked activity.

In the launching and entraining experiments the character of activity is still more marked; and it finally reaches its maximum in the case of live movements, such as creeping or swimming. We have produced these movements in a schematic form under controlled conditions, and the effect is astonishing.

Activity, then, is a phenomenal character *sui generis*. This is very interesting, since even if "internal" observation does not allow us to come to a definite conclusion on these points, it is obviously quite a different matter when there are "external" observations; in the latter case the experimental conditions can be modified in a systematic way, and can be repeated as many times as we please.

The question is also important from our special point of view, since activity and causality have often been confused by psychologists. To quote a particular example, it is this error which seems to be at the basis of Biran's theory, as we shall see at the end of this book. There are in fact two distinct "experiences," and these correspond on the perceptual plane to different stimulus-conditions. The conditions which give rise to the impression of activity are simpler than those of causality, and we come across them more often. Indeed they are produced each time there is an impression of causality. That is why all cases of causality are also cases of activity, while the converse is not true.

This distinction gives rise to certain difficulties which it is necessary to remove. It might seem that if one has the impression that an object is "doing something," causality must necessarily be involved. Such a view has something to recommend it, since even in the cases which I have quoted, and purely from the phenomenal point of view, it might justifiably be said that there is both a cause and an effect distinct from one another.

Thus in the impact example it seems quite clear that the coming into contact of these objects is an event distinct from the movement which brought them together, and results from it. Must we not, therefore, consider the movement of A towards B as the cause of the impact? Yet observers refuse to admit that in the case of the movement of A and its impact with B they have an impression of causality comparable in any way with that which the Launching Effect provides; and when they are asked whether there is a cause and an effect at that stage, and which

is the cause and which the effect, they seem at a loss. The movement of A does not *produce* the impact in the same sense as the impact produces the eventual movement of B.

The key to the enigma is given by the following considerations. It is true that by an analytical and abstract approach such as I have adopted above, it is possible, theoretically, to distinguish two successive events, the movement and the contact. But actually there are not *two events*; there is only one event which develops progressively. As we shall see later, the impact is not really limited to the coming into contact of the two objects; it constitutes a whole *process*, of which the movement and the contact are both constitutive parts. This process evolves. It begins with an approach which links the two objects from the start, and results in a union which becomes gradually closer. At its final stage, it ends in a complete fusion or welding together.[6] There is perhaps at this moment a rather abrupt qualitative change; but, in any case, this coming together is simply the limit, the ultimate phase of the progressive changes which lead to it. The whole is *one* gradual development.[7]

When observers say, for example, that A gives a "bash" to B, they certainly do not mean by this that it is the movement of A which gives the bash to B, for the word "bash" clearly includes the movement. Nor again do they mean that object A is itself the cause of the bash, which would amount to saying that it is the cause of its own movement. They simply mean, as one can easily see on reflexion, that object A executes the *operation of striking*.[8]

This action is peculiar to object A, and constitutes A's condition at that moment; A is the *sole executant* of the action. As far as object B is concerned, it takes no effective part in the process, and its rôle is limited to serving as a point of reference for object A. Thus the operation is closed and complete; it demands no consequence, and moreover it has none. As will be seen later, when we develop the theory of the causal impression in Chapters VIII, IX, and XIV, no consequence could possibly arise in these conditions; for if this is to happen, object B has to participate in the process as executant of one phase of the action.

This discussion of the distinction between phenomenal causality and activity was necessary in order to delimit the scope of this book. We shall not be concerned to any great extent with the question of activity, which has still to be studied, and which will be discussed on its own in a separate publication. [...]

AMPLIATION OF THE MOVEMENT

It is characteristic of all cases of launching that the causal impression involves the *separating* of the passive object from the active one with which it was previously united. This separating lasts either for a very short instant, as in launching-by-striking, or over a longer period, as in launching-by-expulsion.

It is characteristic of entraining and its derivatives that the causal impression in this case involves the *union* of the passive object with the active one, which afterwards shares with it kinematically the same "common fate."

In spite of the apparent dissimilarity between these two groups of phenomena, they can both be brought together under one and the same basic concept, that of ampliation of the movement. This can be defined in a very general way as follows: ampliation of the movement is a *process which consists in the dominant movement, that of the active object, appearing to extend itself on to the passive object, while remaining distinct from the change in position which the latter undergoes in its own right.* (We may assume that the "movement" of the active object and the "change in position" of the passive object can sometimes be seen as part of an overall "change in shape," and that the active object and the passive object can sometimes be one and the same object.)

This definition is necessarily very abstract, since it has to apply to all cases of perception of causality; but in spite of this it serves to establish a number of important conclusions.

First of all, we can deduce from it that the two main groups of causal impression which our observations have led us to distinguish are the only conceivable basic forms which ampliation of the movement can take.

The extension of the movement of the active object, which is the essence of ampliation, is dependent on the movement of the passive object being partially identified with the dominant movement, that of the active object. Now such an identification can take place in two ways only. Either the movements must be *successive* or they must be *simultaneous*. When they are *successive*—or, rather, when the displacement of the active object no longer plays any part in the causal impression after the impact—identification is possible only if the movement of the passive object appears to be the *continuation* or the *prolongation* of that of the active object.[9] This is what occurs in all cases of launching. When the movements are *simultaneous*—in other words when the displacement of the passive object and that of the active object continue together after the impact—identification is possible only if there is *fusion* of the movements because they are kinematically similar. This is what occurs in entraining, and also in propulsion and auto-locomotion. As we have seen, the last two are simply entrainings which are being continually renewed.

There are two sorts of extension—extension by prolongation and extension by fusion. *There are no other alternatives.* It follows that it is *impossible in principle* that there should be any types of causal impression other than launching and entraining. As far as this particular question is concerned, our enquiry is thus exhaustive.

Secondly, the concept of ampliation enables us to discover the basic reasons why the impression of causality cannot appear in the many *negative cases* mentioned and discussed during the book.

These were cases which seemed *a priori* as though they ought to favour a causal link; but in all cases some important feature of ampliation is missing.

Thus, since ampliation presupposes by definition that there is both a movement of the active object and a modification in the passive one, it is clear that there cannot be any causal impression in cases where one of the two objects is static. This excludes from the outset any possibility of impressions of attraction, repulsion, or active resistance (when a moving object approaches a motionless object, withdraws from it, or stops at the moment when it reaches it).[10] The same holds also of cases where an object strikes or hammers another and the latter undergoes no apparent change.

In addition, the change in the passive object must remain distinct from the movement of the active one. Thus there can be no question of any perception of causality where a single object performs successive movements of the same kind. These movements are found to merge completely and form a single movement whenever the interval between them is of the length required for the appearance of the causal impression. "Live" movement is the only example which we have met where two "movements" of a single object gave rise to ampliation; and this was made possible by the difference in kind between the movements—forward movement and change in shape.

It is obvious, however, that ampliation presupposes a certain degree of similarity between the movement of the active object and the change which takes place in the passive object; otherwise this change could not appear to be an "extension" of the active object's movement. This is why there is no causal impression when the displacements of the two objects occur in diametrically opposite directions, or even when there is a considerable difference of direction. Thus it is impossible in principle to produce an impression of active attraction by making one object (object A) move towards another (object B) at the moment when B is approaching A.[11]

Another feature of ampliation is that it covers only the time during which the extension of the movement is being established. The result is that in the case of the pure Transport Effect, which involves a static structural organisation, no causal impression occurs.

Again, ampliation presupposes that the movements are hierarchised, the dominant one being that of the motor object. This very fact excludes the possibility of any causal impression of braking. The speed of the object supposed to act as brake would clearly have to be less, at the moment of impact, than that of the other object. In that case the conditions of the experiment would be simply those of launching or entraining in flight; the more rapid movement would dominate the other on account of the hierarchy of speeds, and would necessarily play the part of "cause."

Lastly, to anticipate the discussion on qualitative causality in the next two chapters, we should note that the absence of any causal impression in the case of pure qualitative causality is what might be expected in view of the fact that in these cases no genuine ampliation is possible.

The theory of ampliation not only accounts for the absence of causal impressions in the negative cases; it also gives a basis for systematic construction of *paradoxical cases*. By this we mean experiments where the essential conditions for ampliation are fulfilled, but in such a way as to produce a causal impression which is at variance both with common sense and with our everyday knowledge of the laws of mechanics. Let us recall two typical examples of this; there are of course innumerable others.

The first example is that which occurs when object A is moving faster than object B and when both are travelling in the same direction; in this case a causal impression still occurs even though object B *slows down* after receiving the blow.[12]

The second example is that of launching experiments whose results show that the causal impression is more pronounced the slower the speed of object B in relation to that of object A.[13] The causal character is thus reinforced through the dominance of object A's movement becoming more emphasised, even though logically the efficacy of the cause ought to seem less rather than greater!

Negative and paradoxical cases clearly provide a crucial test for the theory of ampliation; and the result is confirmation at every point. A further advantage is that they provide a clear demonstration of the uselessness of any psychological theory which suggests that it is past experience which plays the crucial part in setting up causal links.

The most interesting part about the theory, however, still remains to be discussed. A particularly satisfying feature is that it enables us to understand the *productive character* of the causal impression. It is this character which has always been taken by unsophisticated thinkers to be the essential feature of causality, as Hume pointed out in the following passages:

> "Shou'd any one leave this instance, and pretend to define a cause by saying it is something productive of another, 'tis evident he wou'd say nothing. For what does he mean by *production*? Can he give any definition of it that will not be the same with that of causation? If he can; I desire it may be produc'd. If he cannot; here he runs in a circle, and gives a synonimous term instead of a definition."[14]

and

> "...observations I have already made, that the idea of production is the same with that of causation...."[15]

Here is a more recent passage to the same effect, taken from Durkheim:

> "The first thing which is involved in the notion of the causal relation is the idea of efficacy, of productive power, of active force. By cause we ordinarily mean something capable of producing a certain

change....Men have always thought of causality in dynamic terms."[16]

This productive character, however, involves a difficult problem, since if we follow the commonly accepted view and agree that empirical causality is merely the recurrence of regular sequences, the question arises as to where this special feature of "productivity" comes from.

It is difficult to see how Hume's introduction of the idea of "expectation" (i.e. the view that an event which regularly follows another event is therefore "expected" to occur) can account for this productivity, nor why the fact that we expect something should enable us to go beyond a purely temporal relation.[17] The widespread acceptance of Maine de Biran's theory can undoubtedly be explained by the fact that it seemed to provide a satisfactory solution to the problem.[18]

Now, however, the question arises in an altogether new form. The existence, in the world of "external" experience, of causal impressions, possessing a character *sui generis* of productivity, results in a recurrence of the same problem, and shows at the very least that the character of productivity need not necessarily be borrowed from "internal" experience. In that case we still need to discover how it arises.

The solution seems to me to present no difficulty. We need only take note of the following four points to be satisfied that ampliation of the movement involves a genuine production.

1. At the moment when ampliation occurs, there is the *appearance of a new event*, namely the change undergone by the passive object. This may be a simple displacement in space; it may be a forward movement, or it may be a change in shape.[19]

2. This new event appears *as a continuation of a previously existing event; it is the earlier event in an evolved form*. The essential feature of ampliation is that the movement (or change in shape) which previously belonged exclusively to the active object is *extended* on to the passive object.

3. The appearance of the new event does not involve the disappearance of the original one. The extension of the movement of the active object on to the passive one is something quite different from a total transformation of this movement, and quite different again from a mere substitution or division, since *the original movement continues to exist as such.* This is obvious in the case of entraining and its derivatives, but a similar situation is also found to occur in the launching cases, which are more puzzling. In these cases there is an apparent continuation of the movement of the motor object after the impact, and it is this which seems to bring about the displacement of the object moved, as was shown in Chapter VIII.

4. It follows that, at the moment when ampliation occurs, there is a *double existence,* that of the original event and that of the later one.

All these points can be summed up in one short sentence: the original process develops, and, without ceasing to be what it was before, "becomes also" something else, distinct from itself.

Now this sentence is surely an exact description of the process of reproduction, and is applicable quite literally to reproduction as it occurs in the organic world.

There, too, an evolution of the mother-organism results in a double existence which is associated at the start with a fundamental unity. A physiological duplication occurs which is similar, *mutatis mutandis,* to the phenomenal duplication. Moreover this duplication lasts from the moment when the new organism becomes distinct from the parent organism until it separates from it and has complete autonomy. This is exactly comparable to the way in which phenomenal duplication continues until the moment when the object moved passes beyond the limits of the radius of action.

The perception of causality is thus quite literally the perception of an act of production, or, to be more exact still, *an act of production immediately perceived*; it is not the perception of a simple "dependence" (whether or not clearly defined) as found in cases of weakened causality such as triggering.[20]

We are now in a position to understand why it is that in our experiments certain particular conditions were found necessary in order to give rise to a causal impression. They correspond to the different characteristics of reproduction. In particular the hierarchy of priority (priority in time and importance) is clearly necessary, since reproduction is impossible without it.

Again, since production is a phenomenal "given," the causal experience requires no further elaboration in order to acquire significance, but carries this significance already. The expressions which are used to describe this experience, far from investing it with a meaning or constituting an "interpretation" of it, are indeed simply a translation into conceptual terms of what, at the phenomenal level, *actually does occur.* The causal impression is indeed the *source* of this meaning; and as was pointed out in the Introduction, it is the causal impression which plays a large part in giving ordinary objects the meaning which they have for us.

When we consider this remarkable character of productivity possessed by the causal impression, and of the undoubted importance of the causal impression in connexion with human behaviour, we may be tempted to think of the phenomenon as having a unique position among the data of experience. There is no doubt, however, that such a view would be mistaken, and this is a point which requires emphasis.

In the first place, the causal impression shows obvious affinities with activity in other forms, so much so indeed that a careful study is needed to distinguish between them.

Secondly, the impression of production is made possible only by the occurrence of phenomenal duplication. It is because the physical movement of the passive object appears at the start in two forms that it can be seen as an "extension" of the motor object's movement. In launching and in ordinary entraining it is seen both as a change in position of the passive object and as the movement performed by the active object. In propulsion it is seen both as a forward movement of the passive object and as a merely partial aspect of the active object's change in shape. In auto-locomotion, where the unity is more pronounced, it is the total undivided operation which is seen both as a change in shape and as a forward movement. We pointed out at the time (Chapter VIII) the relationship between these duplications and the curious phenomenon of double representation, of which many further examples are coming to light in the field of static perceptions. Once again it seems that the causal impression is not an entirely isolated phenomenon, but can be linked up with other psychological facts.

Moreover, as has been made plain from the very beginning of this book, there can be no doubt as to where in general this impression belongs. The problem of the causal impression undoubtedly has its place among the whole group of psychological problems concerned with the way in which perceptions are structurally organised.

One final point remains to be examined. It is an important one, since it concerns the whole significance of the causal impression.

From time to time the following objection has been raised: "The result of your research is to show conclusively that the causal impression, a purely subjective creation, is an *illusion of causality*, to which we are subject when confronted with certain combinations of movements. This impression is nothing but a piece of deception, and gives us an erroneous picture of the physical world, since the *production* of the movement, or the *passage* of the movement from one body to another, cannot be recorded by any instrument."

This argument, although it does not affect the positive results of our research, seems a very compelling one, and it is desirable that we should pause for a moment so as to think out exactly the degree of "objectivity" belonging to the causal impression.[21]

As a preliminary, the first thing which we should remember is that a large number of perceptual phenomena do not correspond to the action of specific stimuli in the sense of being simply their psychological counterpart. The fact that they appear as they do is conditioned by certain *combinations* of stimuli which acquire their character both from the intrinsic properties of the individual stimuli and from their distribution in time and space. It is a well-known fact that these combinations often do not show any observable resemblance to the phenomena involved; and in particular the properties of structural organisation, such as integration, segregation, "belonging to," "dependence on," etc., are clearly strangers to the world of stimuli, which, as far as the visual sphere is concerned, is nothing more than a collection of light rays operating independently of one another. In short, the rôle of the stimuli is to supply an impulse which determines the response of the receiving organism, which then reacts in accordance with the endogenous laws of its own functioning in constructing the phenomenal world.

Yet, as Köhler has aptly pointed out, this phenomenal world is in general much nearer to the physical world of objects around us and reflects its properties much more faithfully than do the combinations of stimuli, although the latter are the only intermediaries linking one world with the other.[22]

It follows that the "objectivity" of an impression cannot be measured by its correspondence with this or that set of particular stimuli. Consequently the fact that in the case of physical impact no instrument can record the actual "production" of the movement in no way implies a lack of objectivity in the causal impression as such.

Moreover, the fact that it is possible to produce "illusions" of causality, as we have done in our experiments (where the two movements were produced independently of one another and there was no question of any "real" launchings or entrainings), is not at all peculiar to the causal impression. We all know that illusions can be produced in any field of perception. This must necessarily be so, since not only can different combinations of stimuli give rise to similar impressions, but also similar combinations of stimuli can have their origin in different physical conditions (as was the case in our experiments).

Fortunately, however, we are so made, and the world is so made, that *in normal conditions of everyday life* there is generally some degree of correspondence between our impressions and the things or physical events which give rise to them. When an object appears to us like a cube, it usually *is* a cube, and when an object appears to us to be moving, it usually *is* moving. "Illusions" are relatively rare, or at least they are not so important in practice as one might suppose, considering the ease with which they can be produced in laboratories. Moreover, the very fact that we can live and act in a way adapted to our environment shows that there is a very wide correspondence between the phenomenal world and the physical world.

Thus the fact that in general our perceptions have objective validity does not exclude the possibility of illusion, and the fact that in some conditions there occur illusions of causality certainly does not prove that our causal impressions in daily life are illusory.

It still remains, of course, to consider whether there is any sort of parallelism between these causal impressions and the physical events which normally give rise to them, e.g. the impact of one billiard ball on another.

A fundamental point needs to be stressed here. It would be quite wrong to try to discover the answer to our question by considering only the physical *movements* of these objects, for the causal impression is *something quite other than a mere perception of movements*. Thus, as was pointed out earlier (pp. 24 and 63), the impact itself is an event of a special character from the phenomenal point of view, having special properties. One such property is that of "force," which becomes accentuated as the difference between the speeds increases, and is sometimes

such that there is a tendency to refer to it as "*vis viva*" (p. 109). We should remember, too, that we see the impact drive away the projectile and thus perform a quantity of "work." Many examples of this kind could be given; we have met them continually during the course of this book. All of them are suggestive of concepts belonging to the field of *dynamics*; and it is clearly in this field that we should seek the answer to our problem.

As soon as we look at things in this way, the solution immediately becomes obvious. The impression of "force" clearly corresponds to the kinetic energy of the ball which is the motor object,[23] and the impression of "pushing away" corresponds to the *mechanical work done*, i.e. to the expenditure of kinetic energy in the displacement of the projectile.

Again, since the form that ampliation takes is that the "pushing away" is the *prolongation of the impact*, it follows that it is the movement of the motor object which seems to be bringing about the displacement of the projectile; and thus throughout the two phases of the operation the fundamental unity of the process is maintained. In other words there is a *conservation* of process. Is not "conservation of kinetic energy" here being genuinely transposed, in an appropriate form, to subjective experience?

Now conservation of process is a characteristic of the causal impression even when the speed of the projectile is less than that of the motor object (pp. 108 seq.). In the same way conservation of energy is said to take place even in cases where kinetic energy is lost after the impact, e.g. as a result of friction or lack of elasticity. It should be emphasised once again that this is obviously the case which most frequently occurs in nature and is also that which gives the clearest causal impression (p. 108).

Similar parallels are also to be found in a whole series of details.

Thus attention was drawn on p. 134 to the appearance of *inertia* of the projectile in cases of launching.

There is a further parallel in the fact that the causal impression is more pronounced when the difference between the speeds of the objects before the impact is more marked (see the experiments on launching-in-flight, pp. 69 seq.). This corresponds to the fact that the efficacy of the physical impact, measured in terms of the changes of speed which follow it, is greater, the greater the difference between the speeds at the moment of impact.

Again, when experiments were performed in which the speed of the projectile was greater than that of the motor object, the causal impression appeared only in cases where the ratios of the speeds were within a certain range. These limits were found to coincide in a remarkable way with those required by the laws of mechanics (note 8, pp. 111–12).

Finally, we saw that the causal impression is directly dependent on the relative direction of the paths followed by the two objects. When the path of the projectile is not in a direct line with that of the motor object, the impression is weakened, and it disappears completely when the paths of the objects are at right-angles to each other (pp. 101 seq.). Now it is well known that the same holds in mechanics; the work achieved by a force is zero when the point to which it is applied is moving at right-angles to the direction of this force.

In short, in spite of the many contradictions mentioned in the course of this book, there is an impressive amount of agreement between the laws of mechanics and the properties of the causal impression. The correspondence between them is indeed so extensive that anyone not very familiar with the procedure involved in framing the physical concepts of inertia, energy, conservation of energy, etc., might think that these concepts are simply derived from the data of immediate experience, and conversely that the "production" which characterises the causal impression should be regarded as something physical.

In view of all these considerations we may conclude that the perception of causality is as "objective" as all other perceptions. Just as in normal conditions of everyday life the impression of an object's movement usually corresponds with a physical movement and is "brought about" by it, so *the impression of launching (or of entraining) corresponds usually with the work of a mechanical force and is "brought about" by it.*[24] If we want to put this into everyday language, i.e. to describe the perception not in terms of its phenomenal content but in terms of the "physical object" apprehended, we can say that the causal impression is *the perception of the work of a mechanical force*, just as the impression of the movement of a car is the perception of its displacement in physical space.

In closing these chapters on the impression of mechanical causality, I cannot do better than quote here the conclusion reached by a discerning colleague of a philosophical turn of mind, who had been present at a series of demonstrations. "What it amounts to," he said, "is this. You start off with an illusion, and use it to prove that causal impressions are real and objective!" These words contain the full justification for the method followed in our research.

Notes

1. I prefer to use the phrase "causal impression" rather than "perception of causality" which is the title of this book. Although in my opinion they are equivalent, I think, perhaps, that the words "causal impression" which I shall use regularly in what follows, bring out more clearly the idea of an immediate datum, of something directly "lived" (cf. the German word "Erlebnis"). Thus "causal impression" could be exactly translated as "Verursachunserlebnis."

2. For ease of reference throughout the book, every experiment described has been given a number. As a result, even in the case of experiments differing only in details which seem unimportant at first sight, different numbers have been used.

3. It sometimes happens, however, that the causal impression does not appear at the first presentation of the experiment, especially when it is tried on "new" subjects who are not accustomed to

observing in the artificial conditions of the laboratory. Yet such subjects do not instead receive the impression of a clear co-ordination of two movements; they are all "mixed up" and do not realise what is going on at all, and their impression is chaotic and unorganised. Provided that the experiment is repeated a few times, however, a structuring in favour of causality will arise spontaneously.

This time-lag in perceptual organisation has no theoretical importance, for it clearly is due to the particular conditions of the experiment, its unusual nature, and especially perhaps to the small dimensions of the objects. (The latter has a great influence on structural organisation in cases of imperfect fixation, as will be seen later in Chapter III, exp. 7.) This time-lag can be eliminated completely by producing the experiment in a different way, e.g. by the projection method (cf. Chapter II), which allows us to use objects of considerable size. In these conditions the causal impression is forced upon us at the very start.

4. The term "effect" is, of course, used by physicists to indicate certain particular occurrences, such as the "Thomson Effect," etc. I shall be using it in the same sense. To guard against any possible misunderstanding we might say, using current psychological terms, that it indicates a phenomenal "given," which exists *sui generis*. Thus I shall speak of the "Withdrawal Effect," so as to distinguish the specific impression of "withdrawal" from the impression of simple movement which can quite well correspond to a withdrawal actually taking place in the visual field but where the objects are not seen in relationship to each other. (See Chapter IV, 2.)

5. In order to avoid all misunderstanding, it should be pointed out that the impression of activity is obviously linked with the perception of wholes. The moving and non-moving objects have to be integrated in one and the same "whole." This is, in fact, how we do see things if we observe naïvely. An "analytical" approach, on the other hand, which results in the isolation of the moving object, necessarily causes the character of activity to disappear, and substitutes an impression of simple movement.

6. See Chapter IV, 2.

7. The unity of the process is perhaps even more obvious in the opposite case, that of the separation of the objects; for it is clear that although their dissociation is distinct from the subsequent movement, it cannot possibly be considered as the cause of the latter, but only as the form taken by it in its first stages.

8. The phrase "give a bash" ("donner un coup") is ambiguous. It can imply, as in the present case, the exercise of an activity; but it can also denote a case of causality, as when the word "bash" is used to indicate a dent or other damage brought about by a blow. In this case a distinction can be clearly drawn between cause and effect.

9. The wording used in parenthesis is made necessary by some cases of launching-in-flight. See exp. 18, p. 71.

10. It will be remembered that in these conditions we sometimes receive the impression that the object "ought" to go farther; but this is quite a different matter from the impression of an active influence exerted by the motionless object.

11. In the case of repulsion the same would not hold, since the two movements would have the same direction. We must remember, however, that the conditions produced would be those of launching, triggering, or perhaps entraining, all at a distance; and these would be the impressions which would appear in this case. A specific impression of "repulsion" does not seem to exist; what takes place must presumably be a reasoned inference from the impressions mentioned above.

12. See p. 71.

13. This is true, of course, only as long as the difference between the speeds is not great enough to bring about complete segregation of the movements. See, pp. 108 seq. and p. 119.

14. D. HUME, *A Treatise of Human Nature*, part III, section ii.

15. D. HUME, ibid., section vi.

16. E. DURKHEIM, *The Elementary Forms of the Religious Life*, 1915, p. 363.

17. See Introduction, p. 8.

18. See Introduction, p. 11.

19. This is true even in cases in which object B was already moving before it separated from object A (or before it was entrained by object A). In this case there is the appearance of a new event, because of the "dividing off" which takes place at this moment (see p. 71).

20. All this of course applies in full only to the case of causality in the strict sense; in the case of immanent activity the reproductive aspect becomes reduced to the character of "vague productivity" mentioned earlier.

21. To avoid all misunderstanding I should perhaps make clear that when I speak of "objectivity" and "illusion" in this context, these words are not intended in any "ontological" sense, but refer only to what can be checked empirically.

22. W. KÖHLER, *Gestalt Psychology*, 1947, pp. 160 seq.

23. In this case the impression of "force" attends the motor object when it is *in action* and genuinely corresponds to kinetic energy. But this does not occur in the case of a simple impact where there is no change in the object struck. It would therefore be a mistake to link the impression of "force" with the concept of "power to do work," as was pointed out on p. 110.

24. The reason for this is clear. Normally it is only when such mechanical forces are operating that there is the requisite combination of physical *movements* for producing the causal impression; similarly it is a physical movement which normally provokes the successive stimulation of different points on the retina, and thus gives rise to an *impression* of movement.

Study Questions

1. Is Michotte primarily concerned with Hume's argument against inductive inference or his claims about the idea of necessary connection?

2. Did Michotte draw the right conclusions from his launching and entraining experiments? Are the empirical reports of hundreds of observers enough to counter Hume's philosophical argument? Why or why not? Can science speak to philosophy and vice versa?

3. How might "meaning" derive from perception (as opposed to theorizing), according to Michotte?

4. What exactly is "ampliation" and how does it account for the productive character of causation?

Causation

3.4

DAVID LEWIS

DAVID LEWIS (1941–2001) was an important twentieth-century Anglo-American philosopher particularly well known for his creative and persuasive work in analytic metaphysics. Intrigued but ultimately repelled by Hume's fixation on direct experience, Lewis's work considers what we might learn from the exploration of possible worlds, situations that could be and could have been the case. He has argued that whether or not something is possible can vary, as we should consider whether or not something is possible relative to particular circumstances. For example, it is at once possible that I might learn Chinese, because my vocal chords are in good repair, and impossible that I might learn Chinese, because I am so busy. In this selection, Lewis applies his interest in possibility to the concept of causation, which he analyzes in terms of counterfactual

David Lewis, "Causation," *The Journal of Philosophy*, 70, no. 17, (October 11, 1973). Reprinted by permission of the publication.

dependence. Instead of causes being the regular precursors of certain effects, as the regularity theory of causation claims, Lewis's counterfactual theory claims we can understand the concept of causation by entertaining possible worlds, that is, by thinking about whether particular effects follow upon particular causes in other possible worlds similar to ours.

HUME defined causation twice over. He wrote "we may define a cause to be *an object followed by another, and where all the objects, similar to the first, are followed by objects similar to the second. Or, in other words, where, if the first object had not been, the second never had existed.*"[1]

Descendants of Hume's first definition still dominate the philosophy of causation: a causal succession is supposed to be a succession that instantiates a regularity. To be sure, there have been improvements. Nowadays we try to distinguish the regularities that count—the "causal laws"—from mere accidental regularities of succession. We subsume causes and effects under regularities by means of descriptions they satisfy, not by over-all similarity. And we allow a cause to be only one indispensable part, not the whole, of the total situation that is followed by the effect in accordance with a law. In present-day regularity analyses, a cause is defined (roughly) as any member of any minimal set of actual conditions that are jointly sufficient, given the laws, for the existence of the effect. [. . .]

Much needs doing, and much has been done, to turn definitions like this one into defensible analyses. Many problems have been overcome. Others remain: in particular, regularity analyses tend to confuse causation itself with various other causal relations. If *c* belongs to a minimal set of conditions jointly sufficient for *e*, given the laws, then *c* may well be a genuine cause of *e*. But *c* might rather be an effect of *e*: one which could not, given the laws and some of the actual circumstances, have occurred otherwise than by being caused by *e*. Or *c* might be an epiphenomenon of the causal history of *e*: a more or less inefficacious effect of some genuine cause of *e*. Or *c* might be

a preempted potential cause of *e*: something that did not cause *e*, but that would have done so in the absence of whatever really did cause *e*.

It remains to be seen whether any regularity analysis can succeed in distinguishing genuine causes from effects, epiphenomena, and preempted potential causes—and whether it can succeed without falling victim to worse problems, without piling on the epicycles, and without departing from the fundamental idea that causation is instantiation of regularities. I have no proof that regularity analyses are beyond repair, nor any space to review the repairs that have been tried. Suffice it to say that the prospects look dark. I think it is time to give up and try something else.

A promising alternative is not far to seek. Hume's "other words"—that if the cause had not been, the effect never had existed—are no mere restatement of his first definition. They propose something altogether different: a counterfactual analysis of causation.

The proposal has not been well received. True, we do know that causation has something or other to do with counterfactuals. We think of a cause as something that makes a difference, and the difference it makes must be a difference from what would have happened without it. Had it been absent, its effects—some of them, at least, and usually all—would have been absent as well. Yet it is one thing to mention these platitudes now and again, and another thing to rest an analysis on them. That has not seemed worth while.[2] We have learned all too well that counterfactuals are ill understood, wherefore it did not seem that much understanding could be gained by using them to analyze causation or anything else. Pending a better understanding of counterfactuals, moreover, we had no way to fight seeming counterexamples to a counterfactual analysis.

But counterfactuals need not remain ill understood, I claim, unless we cling to false preconceptions about what it would be like to understand them. Must an adequate understanding make no reference to unactualized possibilities? Must it assign sharply determinate truth conditions? Must it connect counterfactuals rigidly to covering laws? Then none will be forthcoming. So much the worse for those standards of adequacy. Why not take counterfactuals at face value: as statements about possible alternatives to the actual situation, somewhat vaguely specified, in which the actual laws may or may not remain intact? There are now several such treatments of counterfactuals, differing only in details.[3] If they are right, then sound foundations have been laid for analyses that use counterfactuals.

In this paper, I shall state a counterfactual analysis, not very different from Hume's second definition, of some sorts of causation. Then I shall try to show how this analysis works to distinguish genuine causes from effects, epiphenomena, and preempted potential causes.

My discussion will be incomplete in at least four ways. Explicit preliminary settings-aside may prevent confusion.

1. I shall confine myself to causation among *events*, in the everyday sense of the word: flashes, battles, conversations, impacts, strolls, deaths, touchdowns, falls, kisses, and the like. Not that events are the only things that can cause or be caused; but I have no full list of the others, and no good umbrella-term to cover them all.

2. My analysis is meant to apply to causation in particular cases. It is not an analysis of causal generalizations. [. . .]

3. We sometimes single out one among all the causes of some event and call it "the" cause, as if there were no others. Or we single out a few as the "causes," calling the rest mere "causal factors" or "causal conditions." Or we speak of the "decisive" or "real" or "principal" cause. We may select the abnormal or extraordinary causes, or those under human control, or those we deem good or bad, or just those we want to talk about. I have nothing to say about these principles of invidious discrimination.[4] I am concerned with the prior question of what it is to be one of the causes (unselectively speaking). My analysis is meant to capture a broad and nondiscriminatory concept of causation.

4. I shall be content, for now, if I can give an analysis of causation that works properly under determinism. By determinism I do not mean any thesis of universal causation, or universal predictability-in-principle, but rather this: the prevailing laws of nature are such that there do not exist any two possible worlds which are exactly alike up to some time, which differ thereafter, and in which those laws are never violated. Perhaps by ignoring indeterminism I squander the most striking advantage of a counterfactual analysis over a regularity analysis: that it allows undetermined events to be caused.[5] I fear, however, that my present analysis cannot yet cope with all varieties of causation under indeterminism. The needed repair would take us too far into disputed questions about the foundations of probability.

COMPARATIVE SIMILARITY

To begin, I take as primitive a relation of *comparative over-all* similarity among possible worlds. We may say that one world is *closer to actuality* than another if the first resembles our actual world more than the second does, taking account of all the respects of similarity and difference and balancing them off one against another.

(More generally, an arbitrary world w can play the role of our actual world. In speaking of our actual world without knowing just which world is ours, I am in effect generalizing over all worlds. We really need a three-place relation: world w_1 is closer to world w than world w_2 is. I shall henceforth leave this generality tacit.)

I have not said just how to balance the respects of comparison against each other, so I have not said just what our relation of comparative similarity is to be. Not for nothing did I call it primitive. But I have said what *sort* of relation it is, and we are familiar with relations of that sort. We do make judgments of comparative over-all similarity— of people, for instance—by balancing off many respects of similarity and difference. Often our mutual expectations about the weighting factors are definite and accurate enough to permit communication. I shall have more to say later about the way the balance must go in particular cases to make my analysis work. But the vagueness of over-all similarity will not be entirely resolved. Nor should it be. The vagueness of similarity does infect causation, and no correct analysis can deny it.

The respects of similarity and difference that enter into the over-all similarity of worlds are many and varied. In particular, similarities in matters of particular fact trade off against similarities of law. The prevailing laws of nature are important to the character of a world; so similarities of law are weighty. Weighty, but not sacred. We should not take it for granted that a world that conforms perfectly to our actual laws is *ipso facto* closer to actuality than any world where those laws are violated in any way at all. It depends on the nature and extent of the violation, on the place of the violated laws in the total system of laws of nature, and on the countervailing similarities and differences in other respects. Likewise, similarities or differences of particular fact may be more or less weighty, depending on their nature and extent. Comprehensive and exact similarities of particular fact throughout large spatiotemporal regions seem to have special weight. It may be worth a small miracle to prolong or expand a region of perfect match.

Our relation of comparative similarity should meet two formal constraints. (1) It should be a weak ordering of the worlds: an ordering in which ties are permitted, but any two worlds are comparable. (2) Our actual world should be closest to actuality, resembling itself more than any other world resembles it. We do *not* impose the further constraint that for any set A of worlds there is a unique closest A-world, or even a set of A-worlds

tied for closest. Why not an infinite sequence of closer and closer A-worlds, but no closest?

COUNTERFACTUALS AND COUNTERFACTUAL DEPENDENCE

Given any two propositions A and C, we have their *counterfactual* $A \, \Box \!\rightarrow C$: the proposition that if A were true, then C would also be true. The operation $\Box \!\rightarrow$ is defined by a rule of truth, as follows. $A \, \Box \!\rightarrow C$ is true (at a world w) iff either (1) there are no possible A-worlds (in which case $A \, \Box \!\rightarrow C$ is *vacuous*), or (2) some A-world where C holds is closer (to w) than is any A-world where C does not hold. In other words, a counterfactual is nonvacuously true iff it takes less of a departure from actuality to make the consequent true along with the antecedent than it does to make the antecedent true without the consequent.

We did not assume that there must always be one or more closest A-worlds. But if there are, we can simplify: $A \, \Box \!\rightarrow C$ is nonvacuously true iff C holds at all the closest A-worlds.

We have not presupposed that A is false. If A is true, then our actual world is the closest A-world, so $A \, \Box \!\rightarrow C$ is true iff C is. Hence $A \, \Box \!\rightarrow C$ implies the material conditional $A \supset C$; and A and C jointly imply $A \, \Box \!\rightarrow C$.

Let $A_1, A_2, \ldots$ be a family of possible propositions, no two of which are compossible; let $C_1, C_2, \ldots$ be another such family (of equal size). Then if all the counterfactuals $A_1 \, \Box \!\rightarrow C_1, A_2 \, \Box \!\rightarrow C_2, \ldots$ between corresponding propositions in the two families are true, we shall say that the C's *depend counterfactually* on the A's. We can say it like this in ordinary language: whether C_1 or C_2 or … depends (counterfactually) on whether A_1 or A_2 or ….

Counterfactual dependence between large families of alternatives is characteristic of processes of measurement, perception, or control. Let $R_1, R_2, \ldots$ be propositions specifying the alternative readings of a certain barometer at a certain time. Let $P_1, P_2, \ldots$ specify the corresponding pressures of the surrounding air. Then, if the barometer is working properly to measure the pressure, the R's must depend counterfactually on the P's. As we say it: the reading depends on the pressure. Likewise, if I am seeing at a certain time, then my visual impressions must depend counterfactually, over a wide range of alternative possibilities, on the scene before my eyes. And if I am in control over what happens in some respect, then there must be a double counterfactual dependence, again over some fairly wide range of alternatives. The outcome depends on what I do, and that in turn depends on which outcome I want.[6]

CAUSAL DEPENDENCE AMONG EVENTS

If a family C_1, C_2,...depends counterfactually on a family A_1, A_2,...in the sense just explained, we will ordinarily be willing to speak also of causal dependence. We say, for instance, that the barometer reading depends causally on the pressure, that my visual impressions depend causally on the scene before my eyes, or that the outcome of something under my control depends causally on what I do. But there are exceptions. Let G_1, G_2,...be alternative possible laws of gravitation, differing in the value of some numerical constant. Let M_1, M_2,...be suitable alternative laws of planetary motion. Then the M's may depend counterfactually on the G's, but we would not call this dependence causal. Such exceptions as this, however, do not involve any sort of dependence among distinct particular events. The hope remains that causal dependence among events, at least, may be analyzed simply as counterfactual dependence.

We have spoken thus far of counterfactual dependence among propositions, not among events. Whatever particular events may be, presumably they are not propositions. But that is no problem, since they can at least be paired with propositions. To any possible event e, there corresponds the proposition $O(e)$ that holds at all and only those worlds where e occurs. This $O(e)$ is the proposition that e occurs.[7] (If no

two events occur at exactly the same worlds—if, that is, there are no absolutely necessary connections between distinct events—we may add that this correspondence of events and propositions is one to one.) Counterfactual dependence among events is simply counterfactual dependence among the corresponding propositions.

Let c_1, c_2,...and e_1, e_2,...be distinct possible events such that no two of the c's and no two of the e's are compossible. Then I say that the family e_1, e_2,...of events *depends causally* on the family c_1, c_2,...iff the family $O(e_1)$, $O(e_2)$,...of propositions depends counterfactually on the family $O(c_1)$, $O(c_2)$,....As we say it: whether e_1 or e_2 or...occurs depends on whether c_1 or c_2 or...occurs.

We can also define a relation of dependence among single events rather than families. Let c and e be two distinct possible particular events. Then e *depends causally* on c iff the family $O(e)$, $\sim O(e)$ depends counterfactually on the family $O(c)$, $\sim O(c)$. As we say it: whether e occurs or not depends on whether c occurs or not. The dependence consists in the truth of two counterfactuals: $O(c) \,\square\!\!\rightarrow O(e)$ and $\sim O(c) \,\square\!\!\rightarrow \sim O(e)$. There are two cases. If c and e do not actually occur, then the second counterfactual is automatically true because its antecedent and consequent are true: so e depends causally on c iff the first counterfactual holds. That is, iff e would have occurred if c had occurred. But if c and e are actual events, then it is the first counterfactual that is automatically true. Then e depends causally on c iff, if c had not been, e never had existed. I take Hume's second definition as my definition not of causation itself, but of causal dependence among actual events.

CAUSATION

Causal dependence among actual events implies causation. If c and e are two actual events such that e would not have occurred without c, then c is a cause of e. But I reject the converse. Causation must always be transitive; causal dependence may not be; so there can be causation without causal dependence. Let c, d, and e be three actual events such that d would not have occurred without c and e would not have occurred without d. Then c is a cause of e even if e would still have occurred (otherwise caused) without c.

We extend causal dependence to a transitive relation in the usual way. Let c, d, e, ... be a finite sequence of actual particular events such that d depends causally on c, e on d, and so on throughout. Then this sequence is a *causal chain*. Finally, one event is a *cause* of another iff there exists a causal chain leading from the first to the second. This completes my counterfactual analysis of causation. [...]

EFFECTS AND EPIPHENOMENA

I return now to the problems I raised against regularity analyses, hoping to show that my counterfactual analysis can overcome them.

The *problem of effects*, as it confronts a counterfactual analysis, is as follows. Suppose that c causes a subsequent event e, and that e does not also cause c. (I do not rule out closed causal loops a priori, but this case is not to be one.) Suppose further that, given the laws and some of the actual circumstances, c could not have failed to cause e. It seems to follow that if the effect e had not occurred, then its cause c would not have occurred. We have a spurious reverse causal dependence of c on e, contradicting our supposition that e did not cause c.

The *problem of epiphenomena*, for a counterfactual analysis, is similar. Suppose that e is an epiphenomenal effect of a genuine cause c of an effect f. That is, c causes first e and then f, but e does not cause f. Suppose further that, given the laws and some of the actual circumstances, c could not have failed to cause e; and that, given the laws and others of the circumstances, f could not have been caused otherwise than by c. It seems to follow that if the epiphenomenon e had not occurred, then its cause c would not have occurred and the further effect f of that same cause would not have occurred either. We have a

spurious causal dependence of f on e, contradicting our supposition that e did not cause f.

One might be tempted to solve the problem of effects by brute force: insert into the analysis a stipulation that a cause must always precede its effect (and perhaps a parallel stipulation for causal dependence). I reject this solution. (1) It is worthless against the closely related problem of epiphenomena, since the epiphenomenon e does precede its spurious effect f. (2) It rejects a priori certain legitimate physical hypotheses that posit backward or simultaneous causation. (3) It trivializes any theory that seeks to define the forward direction of time as the predominant direction of causation.

The proper solution to both problems, I think, is flatly to deny the counterfactuals that cause the trouble. If e had been absent, it is not that c would have been absent (and with it f, in the second case). Rather, c would have occurred just as it did but would have failed to cause e. It is less of a departure from actuality to get rid of e by holding c fixed and giving up some or other of the laws and circumstances in virtue of which c could not have failed to cause e, rather than to hold those laws and circumstances fixed and get rid of e by going back and abolishing its cause c. (In the second case, it would of course be pointless not to hold f fixed along with c.) The causal dependence of e on c is the same sort of irreversible counterfactual dependence that we have considered already.

To get rid of an actual event e with the least over-all departure from actuality, it will normally be best not to diverge at all from the actual course of events until just before the time of e. The longer we wait, the more we prolong the spatiotemporal region of perfect match between our actual world and the selected alternative. Why diverge sooner rather than later? Not to avoid violations of laws of nature. Under determinism *any* divergence, soon or late, requires some violation of the actual laws. If the laws were held sacred, there would be no way to get rid of e without changing all of the past; and nothing guarantees that the change could be kept negligible except in the recent past.

That would mean that if the present were ever so slightly different, then all of the past would have been different—which is absurd. So the laws are not sacred. Violation of laws is a matter of degree. Until we get up to the time immediately before e is to occur, there is no general reason why a later divergence to avert e should need a more severe violation than an earlier one. Perhaps there are special reasons in special cases—but then these may be cases of backward causal dependence.

Notes

1. *An Enquiry concerning Human Understanding*, Section VII.
2. One exception: Aardon Lyon, "Causality," *British Journal for Philosophy of Science*, XVIII, 1 (May 1967): 1–20.
3. See, for instance, Robert Stalnaker, "A Theory of Conditionals," in Nicholas Rescher, ed., *Studies in Logical Theory* (Oxford: Blackwell, 1968); and my *Counterfactuals* (Oxford: Blackwell, 1973).
4. Except that Morton G. White's discussion of causal selection, in *Foundations of Historical Knowledge* (New York: Harper & Row, 1965), pp. 105–181, would meet my needs, despite the fact that it is based on a regularity analysis.
5. That this ought to be allowed is argued in G. E. M. Anscombe, *Causality and Determination: An Inaugural Lecture* (Cambridge: University Press, 1971); and in Fred Dretske and Aaron Snyder, "Causal Irregularity," *Philosophy of Science*, XXXIX, 1 (March 1972): 69–71.
6. Analyses in terms of counterfactual dependence are found in two papers of Alvin I. Goldman: "Toward a Theory of Social Power," *Philosophical Studies*, XXIII (1972): 221–268; and "Discrimination and Perceptual Knowledge," presented at the 1972 Chapel Hill Colloquium.
7. Beware: if we refer to a particular event e by means of some description that e satisfies, then we must take care not to confuse $O(e)$, the proposition that e itself occurs, with the different proposition that some event or other occurs which satisfies the description. It is a contingent matter, in general, what events satisfy what descriptions. Let e be the death of Socrates—the death he actually died, to be distinguished from all the different deaths he might have died instead. Suppose that Socrates had fled, only to be eaten by a lion. Then e would not have occurred, and $O(e)$ would have been false; but a different event would have satisfied the description "the death of Socrates" that I used to refer to e. Or suppose that Socrates had lived and died just as he actually did, and afterwards was resurrected and killed again and resurrected again, and finally became immortal. Then no event would have satisfied the description. (Even if the temporary deaths are real deaths, neither of the two can be *the* death.) But e would have occurred, and $O(e)$ would have been true. Call a description of an event e *rigid* iff (1) nothing but e could possibly satisfy it, and (2) e could not possibly occur without satisfying it. I have claimed that even such common-place descriptions as "the death of Socrates" are nonrigid, and in fact I think that rigid descriptions of events are hard to find. That would be a problem for anyone who needed to associate with every possible event e a sentence $\phi(e)$ true at all and only those worlds where e occurs. But we need no such sentences—only propositions, which may or may not have expressions in our language.

Study Questions

1. What is the difference between the regularity theory of causation and the counterfactual theory?
2. Is Lewis's possible world concept reasonable?
3. Compare Lewis's method to Michotte's and then to Aristotle's. What are the differences between Lewis's method and Michotte's? Between Lewis's method and Aristotle's?

3.5   Learning from Doing

 LAURA SCHULZ, TAMAR KUSHNIR, AND ALISON GOPNIK

ALISON GOPNIK is a contemporary psychologist and Affiliate Philosopher at the University of California at Berkeley who studies children's learning and development. She is interested in how the study of early learning can offer some constraint on otherwise intractable philosophical questions and, conversely, how certain philosophical theories can help to illuminate how children learn. Her work is at the very forefront of empirical philosophy, which holds that philosophical arguments must not violate the claims of our most reliable scientific theories: if science tells us that something is likely the case, we may reject the philosophical theories that imply the opposite. In this edited version of "Learning from Doing: Intervention and Causal Inference in Children," written with students Laura Schulz and Tamar Kushnir, Gopnik argues that children operate with an interventionist theory of causation. On this view, there is no need to offer an ontological account of causal connection; we need not hypothesize about what is really happening metaphysically in order to understand causation. By playing around in the world, even very young children come to see that an intervention to change the value or probability distribution of one event will change the value or probability distribution of another. We learn to work with and manipulate things through play.

There is something fascinating about science. One gets such wholesale returns of conjecture out of such a trifling investment of fact.
—MARK TWAIN, 1883

Twain meant his comment as a witticism, of course, but there *is* something fascinating about science. From a few bones, scientists infer the existence of dinosaurs; from a few spectral lines, the composition of nebulae; and from a few fruit flies, the mechanisms of heredity. From a similarly trifling investment, some of us presume to conjecture even about the mechanisms of conjecture itself.

Why does science, at least some of the time, succeed? Why does it generate accurate predictions and effective interventions? With due respect for our accomplished colleagues, we believe it may be because getting wholesale returns out of minimal data is a commonplace feature of human cognition. Indeed, we believe the most fascinating thing about science may be its connection to human learning in general and in particular to the rapid, dramatic learning that takes place in early childhood. This view, the *theory theory*, suggests that starting in infancy, continuing through the life span, and canalized in scientific inquiry, many aspects of human learning can be best explained in terms of theory formation and theory change.

Theories have been described with respect to their structural, functional, and dynamic properties (Gopnik & Meltzoff, 1997). Thanks to

Laura Schulz, Tamar Kushnir, and Alison Gopnik, "Learning from Doing: Intervention and Causal Inference in Children," in *Causal Learning: Psychology, Philosophy, and Computation* (2007), edited by Alison Gopnik and Laura Schulz. By permission of Oxford University Press.

several decades of work in developmental psychology, we now know a great deal about the structural and functional aspects of children's theories. That is, in many domains, we know that children have abstract, coherent, causal representations of events, we know something about the content of those representations, and we know what types of inferences they support.

We know, for instance, that 6-month-olds' naïve physics includes principles of cohesion, continuity, and contact but not the details of support relations (Baillargeon, Kotovsky, & Needham, 1995; Spelke, Breinlinger, Macomber, & Jacobson, 1992; Spelke, Katz, Purcell, Ehrlich, & Breinlinger, 1994). We know that 4-year-olds' naïve biology supports inferences about growth, inheritance, and illness but not the adult concept of living thing or alive (Carey, 1985; Gelman & Wellman, 1991; Inagaki & Hatano, 1993; Kalish, 1996). We know that 2-year-olds' naïve psychology includes the concepts of intention and desire but not the concept of belief (Flavell, Green, & Flavell, 1995; Gopnik & Wellman, 1994; Perner, 1991). Moreover, we know that, across domains, children's naïve theories support coherent predictions, explanations, and even counterfactual claims (Harris, German, & Mills, 1996; Sobel, 2004; Wellman, Hickling, & Schult, 1997).

However, the theory theory is not just a theory about what children know or what children can do. It is, centrally, a claim about how children learn. In this respect, it is the dynamic rather than the structural and functional aspect of theories that is critical. If children's reasoning is like scientific theory formation, then children's naïve theories should be subject to confirmation, revision, and refutation, and children should be able to make inferences based on evidence from observation, experimentation, and combinations of the two.

Until recently, this dynamic feature of theories has been difficult to explain. If children's knowledge about the world takes the form of naïve theories—and if conceptual development in childhood is analogous to theory change in science—then we would expect the causal reasoning of even very young children to be very sophisticated. A causal "theory" (as distinct from, for instance, a causal module or a causal script) must support novel predictions and interventions, account for a wide range of data, enable inferences about the existence of unobserved and even unobservable causes, and change flexibly with evidence (Gopnik & Meltzoff, 1997). Moreover, theories have a complex relationship with evidence; they must be defeasible in the face of counterevidence, but they cannot be too defeasible. Because evidence is sometimes misleading and sometimes fails to be representative, the process of theory formation must be at once conservative and flexible.

In recent work, we have focused on causal learning as a fundamental dynamic mechanism underlying theory formation. In thinking about what causal knowledge is, we have been influenced by philosophical and computational work proposing an "interventionist" view of causation. [...] This view stands in contrast to many traditional ideas about causation in both adult and developmental psychology. However, we believe that an interventionist account of causation not only helps to elucidate tricky metaphysical questions in philosophy but also provides a particularly promising way to think about children's causal knowledge. [...]

Specifically, developmental researchers have largely accepted the idea that causal knowledge involves knowing that causes produce effects by transfer of information or energy through appropriate intervening mechanisms. In an influential monograph on children's causal reasoning, the psychologist Thomas Shultz wrote that children understand causation "primarily in terms of generative transmission" (1982, p. 48). Similarly, Schlottman writes that "mechanism is part of the very definition of a cause" (2001, p. 112), and Bullock et al. (1982, p. 211) conclude that the idea that "causes bring about their effects by transfer of causal impetus" is "central to the psychological definition of cause-effect relations."

Consistent with this causal mechanism or "generative transmission" approach, psychologists have suggested that even adults prefer information about plausible, domain-specific mechanisms of causal transmission to statistical and covariation information in making causal judgments (Ahn, Kalish, Medin, & Gelman, 1995). Some philosophers have also adopted a transmission perspective, arguing that causal interactions are characterized by spatiotemporally continuous processes involving the exchange of energy and momentum or the ability to transmit "a mark" (Dowe, 2000; Salmon, 1984, 1998).

However, although the generative transmission model of causation is arguably the dominant view of causal knowledge in the developmental literature, there are several respects in which this model critically fails to account for our causal intuitions. Many events that we believe are causally connected (e.g., losing track of time and being late for class; taxing cigarettes and reducing smoking) are not, at least in any obvious way, characterized by mechanisms of transmission. Second, as the philosopher Jim Woodward observes, there is no obvious reason why it should be of value to us to distinguish those events that transmit energy or information from those that do not (2003); those aspects of causality that make it of central importance to human cognition (prediction and control) do not seem to be captured by the concern with spatial and energy relations that characterize the transmission view. Furthermore, nothing in the generative transmission model distinguishes causally relevant from causally irrelevant features of transmission. Generative transmission models fail to explain why, for instance, the momentum transferred from a cue stick to a cue ball is causally relevant to the ball's movement, while the blue chalk mark, transmitted at the same time and in the same manner, is not. [...]

Critically, the tendency to equate causal understanding with an understanding of mechanisms of causal transmission may pose a particular problem for the theory theory. Research suggests that adults cannot generate a plausible account of causal mechanisms, even in domains in which they consider themselves highly knowledgeable (Rozenblit & Keil, 2002). Keil has suggested that we suffer from an "illusion of explanatory depth," and that our causal knowledge may amount to little more than "one or two connected causal beliefs" (2003). He has argued that "calling this causal knowledge folk 'science' seems almost a misnomer," and that "the rise of appeals to intuitive theories in many areas of cognitive science must cope with a powerful fact. People understand the workings of the world around them in far less detail than they think."

If having a theory is coextensive with having an account of causal mechanisms, then Keil's suggestion is troubling, particularly because an impoverished understanding of causal mechanisms is presumably even more characteristic of young children than adults. Perhaps children's causal reasoning is not particularly sophisticated after all.

However, the interventionist account explicit in recent philosophical work and implicit in computational models such as causal Bayes nets provides a quite different account of what it might mean to have causal knowledge. In the context of a causal model, the proposition that X causes Y ($X \rightarrow Y$) means, all else being equal, that an intervention to change the value or probability distribution of X will change the value or probability distribution of Y. That is, the causal arrows in the graphical models are defined, not with respect to their relevance to a domain, their spatiotemporal features, or their ability to transmit energy or force, but (mirroring the way causality is understood in science) in terms of possible interventions. These interventions need not actually be realized or even feasible, but they must be conceivable (see J. Woodward, 2003, for details). A causal relation then is defined not in terms of its physical instantiation but in terms of the real and counterfactual interventions it supports. A theory, in this view, represents a coherent and organized set of such relations rather than necessarily involving a set of beliefs about physical processes or mechanisms.

Both statisticians and philosophers have argued that this interventionist account captures precisely what it means for a variable to be a cause (see, e.g., Pearl, 2000, and J. Woodward, 2003). Learning algorithms based on these models support novel predictions, interventions, inferences about a range of causal structures, and inferences about unobserved causes. Arguably, then, knowledge of causal mechanisms and processes of transmission may not be of central importance for at least some of what we need theories to do....

Note that scientific theories, as well as naïve ones, often remain agnostic about processes of transmission while committing to hypothetical interventions. Newton developed his theory of gravitation without knowing any mechanism that might enable masses to attract one another; Darwin developed his theory of evolution without knowing any mechanism that might make variation in the species heritable. Thus, although we might say informally that Darwin posited natural and sexual selection as "mechanisms" for evolution, we do not mean that Darwin discovered spatiotemporally continuous processes by which energy or information is transferred. Rather, Darwin inferred that traits that enhance an organism's reproductive success will be more prevalent in the population; that is, changes to one set of variables will affect the outcome of other variables. Thus, scientific theories, like naïve ones, are not necessarily derived from, or committed to, particular causal mechanisms. Rather, in identifying the causal structure—the real and hypothetical interventions the variables support—theories help narrow the search space for the relevant physical processes.

Critically, we do not mean to suggest that substantive assumptions about spatiotemporal relations and domain-specific knowledge do not play a fundamental role in children's causal understanding. Indeed, one of the important challenges for cognitive science is to understand how knowledge about particular physical relations in the world is integrated with evidence about interventions and patterns of covariation. In what follows, we discuss some important interactions between children's substantive causal knowledge and formal learning mechanisms. Even more critically, we do not mean that children only learn causal relations from interventions. Children may infer causal relations in myriad ways, including from spatial relations, temporal relations, patterns of covariation and simply by being told. The claim rather is that certain patterns of interventions and outcomes indicate causal relationships, and when children infer that a relationship is causal, they commit to the idea that certain patterns of interventions and outcomes will hold.

One of the exciting features of the interventionist account of causation is that, together with theory theory, it generates an array of interesting and testable predictions about children's early learning. At a minimum, if children's causal knowledge takes the form of naïve theories and if causal knowledge is knowledge that supports interventions, then children should be able to (a) use patterns of evidence to create novel interventions; (b) do this for any of a variety of possible causal structures; (c) use evidence from interventions to infer the existence of unobserved causes; (d) distinguish evidence from observation and intervention in their inferences about causal structure; (e) effectively weigh new evidence from interventions against prior beliefs; and (f) distinguish good interventions from confounded ones.

In what follows, we walk through this alphabet of inferences. We discuss respects in which the causal Bayes net formalism provides a normative account of these components of theory formation, and we review evidence from our lab suggesting that young children are capable of this type of learning.

MAKING NOVEL INTERVENTIONS

In the absence of theories, you could safely navigate a lot of causal territory. Classical conditioning, trial-and-error learning, and hardwired causally significant representations (of the sort that make nestlings cower when hawks fly overhead, and arguably of the sort that is triggered by seeing one object strike and displace another; e.g., Michotte, 1962) are effective ways of tapping into real causal relations in the world. Each of these abilities lets us track regularities in the environment and predict some events from the occurrence of others. Some of these abilities even support effective interventions.

Like other animals, human beings seem to have innate, domain-specific causal knowledge (Spelke et al., 1992), the ability to detect statistical contingencies (Saffran, Aslin, & Newport, 1996), and the ability to learn from the immediate consequences of our own actions (Rovee-Collier, 1980; Watson & Ramey, 1987). Unlike other animals, however, we routinely use the contingencies and interventions we observe to design novel interventions. We routinely meet regularities with innovation.

Some of this inferential power may come from the way that human beings represent causal knowledge. Elsewhere (see Gopnik et al., 2004), we have suggested that causal Bayes net representations provide a causal map of events in the world. The analogy to a spatial map is helpful because it explains both some of the advantages of the causal Bayes net representation and some of the disadvantages of alternative ways of storing causal knowledge.

Some animals, like ants, seem to represent spatial relations egocentrically. Ants know where their nest is in relation to their own body movements, but if they are scooped up and displaced even slightly, they lose their way, even in familiar terrain (Sommer & Wehner, 2004). Other animals, like mice, construct spatial maps. Once mice have explored a territory, they can always take the shortest route to a goal, no matter where they are placed initially (Tolman, 1932). Such cognitive spatial maps reveal the underlying stability of geometric relations.

Causal relations can also be represented egocentrically in terms of the immediate outcome of one's own actions (e.g., as in operant learning). However, like an egocentric spatial representation, operant learning fails to represent the relationship of variables to one another. Operant learning restricts you to learning the immediate outcome of your own actions, and even these can only be learned by trial and error. However, if you represent causal events as they relate to one another, then—even if you are not part of the causal structure, or even if you own relationship to the event changes—the stability of the underlying causal structure is preserved. From such stability may come the ability to negotiate novelty.

Causal Bayes nets provide just such a coherent, nonegocentric representation of the causal relationship among events. In a literature rife with stories about cigarette smoking, stained fingers, and lung cancer; birth control pills, thrombosis, and strokes; and prisoners, sergeants, and firing squads, almost any concept can be illustrated with a macabre example. We work with preschoolers, however, so we make use of a more benign, indeed suburban, illustration (adapted from Pearl, 2000): Suppose you walk outside and see that the grass in your front yard is wet. You might guess that it has rained. Because you believe the weather is a common cause of the state of your front yard and your backyard, you will be able to infer that the grass in your backyard is most likely wet as well. You could represent this causal structure as the causal Bayes net in [Figure 1], in which each node is a binary variable taking either the value wet or dry.

In this causal structure, the state of the front yard and the state of the backyard are dependent in probability. Knowing something about the front yard will tell you (in probability) some-

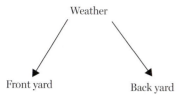

FIGURE 1 A causal Bayes net.

thing about the state of the backyard. That is, you can use knowledge of the causal graph and the known value of some variables in the system to predict the (otherwise unknown) value of other variables.

However, the critical thing about causal Bayes nets, indeed the thing that makes them causal, is that they can also support inferences about the effects of interventions. We discuss interventions in more detail in the following section, but roughly speaking, the arrow in the graph between the weather and the front yard encodes the proposition that, all else being equal, changing the state of the weather will change the state of the front yard. Importantly, the arrow retains this meaning even though (in the real world) we cannot actually intervene on the weather (short of global climate change, anyway). Knowing the causal graph lets you predict the outcome of interventions—whether or not you have ever seen them performed and indeed whether or not you could ever perform them. Thus, unlike hardwired representations or trial-by-error learning, causal graphs support genuinely novel inferences.

However, the absence of the arrow between the front yard and the backyard is also informative. Although the states of the yards are dependent in probability, there is no direct causal link between them; all else being equal, changing the one will not change the other. Causal graphs thus represent the distinction between predictions from observation (if the front yard is dry, then the backyard is probably dry as well) and predictions from intervention (wetting the front yard will not wet the backyard).

In a series of experiments, we looked at whether, consistent with the formalism, young children could use patterns of dependence and independence to make novel predictions and interventions (Gopnik, Sobel, Schulz, & Glymour, 2001; Schulz & Gopnik, 2004). We showed preschoolers, for instance, that three flowers were associated with a monkey puppet sneezing (see [Figure 2]). One flower (A) always made the monkey sneeze; the other flowers (B and C) only made the monkey sneeze when Flower A was also present.

Formally, A and the effect were unconditionally dependent; B, C, and the effect were independent conditional on A. Applied to this case (and assuming no unobserved common causes), a Bayes nets learning algorithm will construct the graph in [Figure 3]. The graph in [Figure 3] says that A causes the effect, and B and C do not. (It also says that there is an undetermined causal link between A, B, and C, represented by the circles and the ends of the edge connecting those variables. In fact, there is such a link, namely, the experimenter, who put all three flowers in the

FIGURE 2 Evidence about three flowers.

vase together.) This structure in turn generates predictions about interventions. In particular, it implies that an intervention on A will change the value of C, but an intervention on B or C will not have this effect.

Children were asked, "Can you make it so that Monkey won't sneeze?" Consistent with the prediction of the formalism, children screened off flowers B and C and removed only flower A from the vase. Control experiments established that the inference was caused by the pattern of conditional dependence and independence, not frequency information.

One might argue, however, that children have only a limited ability to make novel and appropriate inferences. Children might, for instance, be able to use patterns of dependence to differentiate equally plausible causal candidates within a domain (i.e., the causal power of one flower vs. another). However, innate or domain-specific knowledge might restrict the range of evidence children are willing to consider in the first place. Formal inference procedures might not be able to override or change children's prior beliefs.

However, if, consistent with the theory theory, children develop their causal understanding *from* patterns of evidence, then domain-specific judgments ought to be defeasible. Given appropriate evidence, children ought to be able to override prior knowledge and reason about truly novel events, including events that cross the boundaries of domains, and design truly novel interventions accordingly. To look at the extent to which children could flexibly use evidence and formal inferential procedures to make genuinely novel causal inferences, we pitted children's domain-specific knowledge against patterns of evidence.

We showed children, for instance, that three causes were associated with a machine turning on. Two of the causes were domain appropriate (buttons), and one was domain inappropriate (talking to the machine). Talking to the machine and the machine turning on were uncondition-ally dependent but conditional on talking; the buttons were independent of the effect. Thus, the structure was formally identical to the structure in [Figure 3]. We asked the children if they could turn off the machine. In a baseline condition, we provided children with no evidence and simply asked the children whether talking or pushing buttons was more likely to turn off the machine.

Consistent with past research showing that children's causal inferences respect domain boundaries, children in the baseline condition chose the domain-appropriate causes (the buttons) at ceiling. However, consistent with the predictions of the formalism, when asked to turn off the machine, 75% of the children ignored the buttons and said, "Machine, please stop." Children were able to use the pattern of conditional dependence and independence to create a new causal map and to generate an appropriate, but novel, causal intervention.

In this experiment, the relations between causes and effect were deterministic. Such definitive evidence might have made it particularly easy for children to override their prior knowledge. However, in another experiment (Kushnir, Gopnik, & Schaefer, 2005), we tested whether children's domain-specific preference for contact in physical causal relations could be overridden in light of probabilistic evidence that physical causes could act at a distance. We showed children a toy with a colored surface and told them, "Sometimes the toy lights up." Without further instruction, we gave children a block and asked them to make the toy light

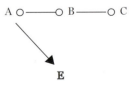

FIGURE 3 Graph representing inference that Flower A screens off B and C as a cause of E.

up. Of 16 children, 13 (81%) demonstrated a strong initial assumption of contact causality, touching the block to the surface of the toy (the other 3 did nothing). After their intervention, we showed children four pairs of blocks. In each pair, one block activated the toy one third of the time and always by contact. The other block activated the toy two thirds of the time and always at a distance (i.e., by being held 5–6 inches above the toy). At the end of the experiment, we asked children to make the toy light up again. A significant number of children revised their original intervention and activated the toy at a distance (McNemar's test, $p < .05$). Thus, children seem to be able to revise their domain-specific knowledge and create novel interventions, even when given only stochastic evidence for new causal relations.

If children's causal reasoning were constrained by innate representations or informationally encapsulated modules, then such flexibility and sensitivity to evidence would be surprising. However, it is less surprising from a theory theory perspective. The ability to overturn prior knowledge and learn something genuinely new is one of the chief virtues of scientific inquiry. It may also be one of the hallmarks of childhood. [...]

INFERRING THE EXISTENCE OF UNOBSERVED CAUSES

One of the critical respects in which science sometimes brings us genuinely new insight is by invoking unobserved causes to explain events. However, unobserved causes are not the exclusive provenance of scientific theories. Children's naïve physics relies on unobservable forces, children's naïve psychology on unobservable mental states, and children's concept of natural kinds on unobservable essences (e.g., Bullock et al., 1982). It is thus perhaps surprising that most psychological accounts of causal reasoning (Cheng, 1997; Shanks & Dickinson, 1987)

relegate unobserved causes to a background condition.

We already discussed respects in which the causal Bayes net formalism supports inferences about the unknown value of some variables from the known value of others. However, in some cases the formalism supports inferences about the existence of variables themselves. In particular, if the known values in the graph generate patterns of conditional dependence and independence that appear to violate the causal Markov assumption, then the formalism infers the existence of an unobserved cause.

In a series of experiments, participants (both adults and children) were introduced to a "stick-ball machine" (see [Figure 4]). The two stickballs could move up and down (either simultaneously or independently) without any visible intervention (because they could be manipulated from behind the machine). The experimenter could also visibly intervene on a stickball by pulling up on the stick. This might cause—or fail to cause—the other stickball to move.

We looked at whether, consistent with the causal Markov assumption, adults and kindergarteners could use interventions and the pattern of outcomes to infer the existence of an unobserved common cause. In these studies, participants saw that the movement of the two stickballs was correlated in probability. They then saw that an intervention on Stickball A (pulling on A) failed to move B, and that an intervention on B failed to move A. On comparison trials, participants were given evidence consistent with $A \rightarrow B$ (e.g., they saw that pulling on B failed to move A, but they did not see an intervention on A).

If the movements of A and B are probabilistically dependent but intervening to do A fails to increase the probability of B moving and intervening to do B fails to increase the probability of A moving, then the causal Markov assumption can be preserved only by inferring the existence of an unobserved common cause of A and B (i.e., that the true causal structure is $A \leftarrow U \rightarrow B$). This structure predicts the observed evidence: A and B are unconditionally dependent in probability, but an intervention on either A or B breaks the dependence.

Consistent with the formalism, both adults and children inferred the existence of an unobserved common cause when interventions on either stickball failed to correlate with the movement of the other. Adults drew the appropriate graph (A ← U → B); children inferred that "something else" (besides either of the stickballs) was making the stickballs move (Kushnir, Gopnik, Schulz, & Danks, 2003; Schaefer & Gopnik, 2003). Importantly, participants only postulated an unobserved common cause when no other graph was consistent with the observed pattern of dependencies. The causal Bayes net formalism thus provides a mechanism by which evidence about observed variables can lead to inferences about the existence of unobserved variables. Processes like these might help explain how both children and scientists bring new theoretical entities into the world.

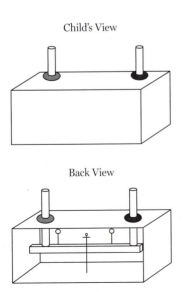

Child's View

Back View

FIGURE 4 The stickball machine.

DISTINGUISHING EVIDENCE FROM OBSERVATIONS AND INTERVENTIONS

At the core of the theory theory is the idea that children learn causal structure from evidence. There are two ways we can get (firsthand) evidence about an event: We can see the event happen, or we can make the event happen. Importantly, as we have implied in the previous sections, these two ways of getting data—seeing and doing—can lead to radically different conclusions, even when the evidence itself is otherwise identical. What you can learn depends not only on what you already know, but also on how you know it.

In the section on making novel interventions, we discussed a simple causal graph in which the weather was a common cause of the state of the front yard and the backyard (F ← W → B). We noted that, using this graph, you could predict the state of the backyard from the state of the front yard.

Suppose, however, that you buy a sprinkler for your front yard and set it to go off every morning at 6 a.m. Setting the sprinkler cuts the arrow between the weather and the front yard and breaks the dependence between the front yard and the backyard. The altered graph is shown in [Figure 5].

If the graph is as depicted in [Figure 5], then when you look outside and see that the grass in your front yard is wet, you will not be able to infer that the grass in your backyard is also wet. Evidence that was informative under observation is uninformative under this intervention.

One of the strengths of the causal Bayes net formalism is that it supports accurate inferences whether the evidence comes from observations, interventions, or combinations of the two. Because the causal graph under intervention is different from the graph under observation, the same evidence should lead to different inferences.

The theory theory implies that young children should be sophisticated causal reasoners. Are children also sensitive to the distinction between evidence from observations and evidence from

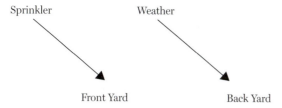

FIGURE 5 A causal Bayes net with a sprinkler.

interventions, and do they modify their inferences accordingly? Note that such sensitivity is not predicted by all models of causal reasoning. Accounts of causal reasoning that use the strength of the association between two variables as indicative of the probabilistic strength of the causal connection between them (see, e.g., Dickinson, Shanks, & Evenden, 1984; Shanks, 1985; Shanks & Dickinson, 1987; Wasserman, Elek, Chatlosh, & Baker, 1993) are indifferent to whether the association is caused by intervention or observation. Because of this, the predictions made by causal variants of the Rescorla-Wagner equation and the causal Bayes net formalism sometimes differ.

In a series of experiments (designed primarily to look at children's ability to distinguish common cause structures from causal chains), we looked at whether children's conclusions changed depending on whether they observed the relevant evidence with or without an intervention. Children were introduced to the stickball machine described in the section on inferring the existence of unobserved causes. Children were told the following: "Some stickballs are special. Special stickballs almost always make other stickballs move." Children were taught that one stickball might be special, both stickballs might be special, or neither stickball might be special.

In the test condition, children saw the stickballs move up and down simultaneously (without an intervention) three times. The experimenter then visibly intervened by pulling on the top of one stickball; the other stickball failed to move. In the control condition, the experimenter intervened

by pulling on one stickball, and both stickballs moved simultaneously three times. The experimenter then pulled on the stickball a fourth time, and the other stickball failed to move. At the end of the trials, the experimenter pointed to each stickball and asked, "Is this stickball special?"

In the test condition, there is a correlation between seeing stickball Y move and seeing stickball X move. However, intervening to move Y breaks the dependence. From a causal Bayes net perspective, this pattern of evidence is consistent with the graph X → Y but not with the graph Y → X. Children should say that X is special but deny that Y is special. In the control condition, intervening on Y and seeing X move are probabilistically dependent throughout. This is consistent with Y → X but not X → Y; children should say that Y is special, and X is not.

Note, however, that from an associative learning perspective, the strength of association between the stickballs is the same in both conditions. The movement of stickball Y is associated with the movement of stickball X every time but one. If children are reasoning associatively, then in both conditions they should say that Y is special.

The children (4.5-year-olds) distinguished between evidence from observations and interventions and reasoned not as predicted by associative learning models, but as predicted by the causal Bayes net formalism. That is, children were significantly more likely to affirm that X was special and deny that Y was special in the test condition than in the control condition and significantly more likely to affirm that Y was special and deny that X was special in the control condition than in the test (Gopnik et al., 2004; Schulz, 2001).

Similarly, in the unobserved cause studies discussed in the preceeding section, we reported that participants saw that intervening to move stickball X failed to move stickball Y, and intervening to move Y failed to move X. In control conditions, however, participants saw X move by itself and Y move by itself, but this time the stickballs moved without visible intervention—the experimenter simply pointed at X when it moved by itself and then pointed at Y while it moved by itself. Consistent with the predictions of the formalism, participants distinguished between the two conditions and only inferred the existence of an unobserved common cause of X and Y (X ← U → Y) in the intervention condition. (In the observation condition, they inferred the existence of two independent unobserved causes: U1 → X and U2 → Y.)

Pearl writes that, "Scientific activity, as we know it, consists of two basic components: Observations and interventions. The combination of the two is what we call a laboratory" (2000). Although making inferences about stick-ball machines may seem a far cry from scientific inquiry, the ability to distinguish evidence from observations and interventions is fundamental to both. Sensitivity to the different role played by these "basic components" may help support children's ability to learn the causal structure of events in the world....

DISTINGUISHING GOOD INTERVENTIONS FROM CONFOUNDED ONES

People who become exercised by the concept of child as scientist frequently point out what is indisputably the case: Children, unlike scientists, do not go around designing controlled experiments to test their theories. Moreover, when children do try to design experiments (i.e., because a teacher or a researcher asks them to), they perform poorly. Children tend to intervene on many variables at once, change interventions between conditions, and then draw all the wrong conclusions. Adults (and often scientists) do little better (Kuhn, 1989; Kuhn, Amsel, & O'Laughlin, 1988; Masnick & Klahr, 2003).

However, designing an experiment requires metacognition. To design an appropriate intervention, you have to know what makes an intervention appropriate. Learning from interventions does not require metacognition. You may have no idea what makes one intervention better than another and still be able to draw correct conclusions from the patterns of evidence that result.

In the previous sections, we provided evidence suggesting that when children are given good evidence, they draw normative causal conclusions. What happens, however, when children are given bad evidence? Are there conditions under which children realize that interventions are confounded? Does confounding change the types of inferences children make?

The conditional intervention principle defined an intervention to rule out instances of confounding: An intervention on X should be exogenous, should break all the arrows into X, and should not influence any other variable in the graph except through X. In the test condition of the gear toy experiment, we showed children evidence consistent with the conditional intervention principle, and children were able to learn the relationship of the gears to one another.

In the control condition, however, we concealed the state of the switch. Thus, just as in the test condition, children saw, for instance, that gear A spun when B was removed, but gear B failed to spin when gear A was removed. However, with the switch hidden, the children could not know whether B failed to spin because gear A was removed or because the experimenter failed to flip on the switch. That is, there was no way to know whether the intervention to remove gear A broke all the arrows into B or not. Although the movement of the gears was the same in both conditions, children in the control conditions responded at chance and—anecdotally—tried to look behind the machine to determine whether the switch was on or off.

In a different set of studies, we looked at children's sensitivity to probabilistic causes and the role played by their own interventions. In an observation condition, children saw an experimenter place a block on a toy three times in a row. The children saw that one block made the toy light up two of three times, and another block made the toy light up only one of three times. Children were told that each block had "special stuff" inside and were asked which block has more special stuff. The children distinguished the 2/3 probability from the 1/3 probability and said that the 2/3 block had more special stuff.

The intervention condition was identical except that children were allowed to intervene on the block on the third trial. For the 2/3 block, children saw the block light up the toy twice, but when they tried the block, it failed to light up. For the 1/3 block, children saw the block fail to light up the toy twice, but when they tried the block, the toy did light up. In this condition, children said that the 1/3 block had more special stuff. Children seemed to prefer making inferences based on their own interventions.

Critically, however, the children were also tested in a confounding control condition. In the control condition, children saw exactly the same evidence as in the test condition; however, this time when the child intervened, the experimenter simultaneously pushed a button "to make the toy light up." The child's "intervention" was thus no longer a real intervention—it did not break other arrows (like the experimenter pushing the button) into the effect. When the children's own interventions were confounded in this way, they did not express a preference for their own interventions; the children returned to judging the blocks on the basis of the probabilities (Kushnir, 2003; Kushnir & Gopnik, 2005).

These findings suggest that, although children may not be able to design controlled experiments, they do, at least in certain cases, recognize instances of confounding. Children seem to be sensitive to some of the fundamental features of experimental design and make different inferences when causal manipulations are consistent with the conditional intervention principle than when they are not.

Still, we might ask how, in the absence of controlled experiments, children are able to learn so much from interventions. We rely on experimental design heavily in science; how can children

learn so much in its absence? Why aren't children constantly running into confounded interventions and drawing inaccurate causal conclusions?

One possibility is that the very fact of being a child might serve children well. Children are notorious for being impulsive (they get into a lot of things) and perseverative (they get into the same things over and over again). Cast in a more positive light, children tend to intervene a lot, and they tend to replicate their interventions. Children's very immaturity and, in particular, the protracted development of their prefrontal cortex, which (in adults) seem to inhibit impulsivity (e.g., Casey, Giedd, & Thomas, 2000; Chao & Knight, 1998) and prevent perseveration (e.g., Goel & Grafman, 1995), may support causal learning.

How might immaturity and noise substitute for controlled experimental design? Note that to infer that X causes Y, you do not necessarily have to hold other causes of Y constant. You can also randomize other causes of Y. Children's tendency to intervene in many different contexts and their tendency to replicate their actions might be advantageous. Other causes of Y (whatever Y is) might exist, but children's own actions are unlikely always to coincide with those causes. Certainly, children may occasionally leap to the wrong causal conclusion from bad evidence. Wu and Cheng (1999), for instance, cite a childhood anecdote in which one of the authors dropped a vase at the same time that a power outage occurred and thus blamed herself for the blackout. However, such anecdotes are funny in part because they are rare. In general, children's own actions may be a trustworthy foundation for their causal inferences and naïve theories.

CONCLUSION

In many respects, the causal Bayes net formalism seems to provide a learning mechanism that captures the dynamic nature of theories—and in many respects, children's learning seems to be commensurate with the predictions made by the formalism. However, the causal Bayes net formalism may not tell the whole story. In particular, the formalism may not entirely satisfy Mark Twain. How we get such "wholesale returns of conjecture out of a trifling investment in fact" remains something of a mystery.

Causal Bayes net algorithms were developed for use in procedures like data mining, for which evidence is plentiful, but the causal relationships are obscure. Constraint-based search methods thus rely on the evidence of many trials or assume the available data are representative of a larger sample. Bayesian learning algorithms rely on either an abundance of data or an abundance of prior knowledge.

In our experiments, by contrast, evidence was scarce. Children made causal inferences from a minimal amount of data, often using only the evidence of a single trial. As Tenenbaum and Griffiths (2003) note, in "many cases...causal inference follow(s) from just one or a few observations, where there isn't even enough data to reliably infer correlation!"

Note, however, that the causal Bayes net formalism was also developed to infer causal structure from noisy, probabilistic data in contexts in which interventions were impossible (e.g., in epidemiological studies). By contrast, in all of our studies, children observed or performed interventions, and in most cases the evidence they saw was deterministic. Such contexts (when interventions are possible and determinism is assumed) may be plentiful in everyday life, and within such contexts, children may not need the full apparatus of the causal Bayes net learning algorithms. Children may be able to represent structure as a causal Bayes net and may use some of the same principles about the relationship between evidence and structure without requiring the full power of the learning algorithms. [...] Thus, the causal Bayes net formalism may be "too big" for what children need to accomplish.

Alternatively, causal Bayes nets formalism may be "too small." The algorithms may miss a level of abstraction (what Tenenbaum & Niyogi, 2003, [...] call a *causal grammar*) that encompasses higher-order causal laws that are assumed but never explicitly presented to the children (i.e., that blocks activate detectors, and detectors do not activate blocks). Children may be successful at learning causal relationships from a few observations (in our lab and in the world) because they are already bringing a rich theoretical structure to bear on the inferential tasks. Thus, the causal Bayes net algorithms may allow children to learn structure from minimal data only when they are embedded within higher-order causal theories (see Tenenbaum & Griffiths, 2003; Tenenbaum & Niyogi, 2003). [...]

Critically, however, this account may only move the problem of causal inference back a step. Knowledge of higher-order causal laws might support children's ability to learn particular causal relations. However, somehow children must also learn the higher-order causal laws—and it seems tempting to assume that children infer higher-order causal laws from particular causal relations. One of the challenges for future research is to determine whether such circles can be benign rather than vicious. In principle, children might be able to bootstrap an abstract causal grammar from clear evidence for particular causal relationships and then use the higher-order theory to handle more complex or ambiguous evidence for particular causal relations.

However, even if (as we expect) the causal Bayes net formalism does not end up being "just right," it more than any other current computational account suggests a learning mechanism that does justice to much of the breadth and depth of children's naïve theories. In supporting novel predictions, novel interventions, structure learning, inferences about unobserved causes, distinctions between observations and interventions, and the criteria for a good intervention, the causal Bayes net formalism captures much that is critical about a theory. Our hope is that children's ability to engage in theory formation and theory change might similarly set the standard for future computational accounts of learning.

If you are persuaded by little else by this chapter, we hope we have at least convinced you of the value of interdisciplinary work. Research in computer science, artificial intelligence, and philosophy has suggested some of the fundamental assumptions that might underlie the development of children's naïve theories. Work in developmental psychology has demonstrated that young children are able to learn the causal structure of events with remarkable speed and accuracy. We hope that investigators in all these areas will continue to find causal learning, in both children and science, fascinating for years to come.

References

Ahn, W., Kalish, C. W., Medin, D. L., & Gelman, S. A. (1995). The role of covariation versus mechanism information in causal attribution. *Cognition, 57*, 299–352.

Baillargeon, R., Kotovsky, L., & Needham, A. (1995). The acquisition of physical knowledge in infancy. In D. Sperber & D. Premack (Eds.), *Causal cognition: A multidisciplinary debate. Symposia of the Fyssen Foundation; Fyssen Symposium, 6th January 1993, Pavillon Henri IV, St-Germain-en-Laye, France* (pp. 79–115). New York: Clarendon Press/Oxford University Press.

Bullock, M., Gelman, R., & Baillargeon, R. (1982). The development of causal reasoning. In W. J. Friedman (Ed.), *The developmental psychology of time* (pp. 209–254). New York: Academic Press.

Carey, S. (1985). *Conceptual change in childhood.* Cambridge, MA: MIT Press/Bradford Books.

Casey, B. J., Giedd, J. N., & Thomas, K. M. (2000). Structural and functional brain development and its relation to cognitive development. *Biological Psychology, 54*, 241–257.

Chao, L. L., & Knight, R. T. (1998). Contribution of human prefrontal cortex to delay performance. *Journal of Cognitive Neuroscience, 10*, 167–177.

Cheng, P. W. (1997). From covariation to causation: A causal power theory. *Psychological Review, 104*, 367–405.

Dickinson, A., Shanks, D. R., & Evendon, J. (1984). Judgment of act-outcome contingency: The role of selective attribution. *Quarterly Journal of Experimental Psychology, 36*, 29–50.

Dowe, P. (2000). *Physical causation.* New York: Cambridge University Press.

Flavell, J. H., Green, F. L., & Flavell, E. R. (1995). Young children's knowledge about thinking. *Monographs of the Society for Research in Child Development, 60*, v-96.

Gelman, S. A., & Wellman, H. M. (1991). Insides and essence: Early understandings of the non-obvious. *Cognition, 38*, 213–244.

Goel, V., & Grafman, J. (1995). Are the frontal lobes implicated in "planning" functions? Interpreting data from the Tower of Hanoi. *Neuropsychologia, 33*, 623–642.

Gopnik, A., Glymour, C., Sobel, D. M., Schulz, L., Kushnir, T., & Danks, D. (2004). A theory of causal learning in children: Causal maps and Bayes nets. *Psychological Review, 111*, 1–31.

Gopnik, A., & Meltzoff, A. N. (1997). *Words, thoughts and theories.* Cambridge, MA: MIT Press.

Gopnik, A., Sobel, D. M., Schulz, L. E., & Glymour, C. (2001). Causal learning mechanisms in very young children: 2-, 3-, and 4-year-olds infer causal relations from patterns of variation and covariation. *Developmental Psychology, 37*, 620–629.

Gopnik, A., & Wellman, H. M. (1994). The theory theory. In S. A. Gelman & L. A. Hirschfeld (Eds.), *Mapping the mind: Domain specificity in cognition and culture; based on a conference entitled "Cultural Knowledge and Domain Specificity," held in Ann Arbor, Michigan, October 13–16, 1990* (pp. 257–293). New York: Cambridge University Press.

Harris, P. L., German, T., & Mills, P. (1996). Children's use of counterfactual thinking in causal reasoning. *Cognition, 61*, 233–259.

Inagaki, K., & Hatano, G. (1993). Young children's understanding of the mind body distinction. *Child Development, 64*, 1534–1549.

Kalish, C. (1996). Causes and symptoms in preschoolers' conceptions of illness. *Child Development, 67*, 1647–1670.

Keil, F. C. (2003). Folkscience: Coarse interpretations of a complex reality. *Trends in Cognitive Sciences, 18*, 663–692.

Kuhn, D. (1989). Children and adults as intuitive scientists. *Psychological Review, 96*, 674–689.

Kuhn, D., Amsel, E. & O'Laughlin, M. (1988). *The development of scientific thinking skills.* Orlando, FL: Academic Press.

Kushnir, T. (2003, April). *Seeing versus doing: The effect of direct intervention on preschooler's understanding of probabilistic causes.* Poster presented at the biennial meeting of the Society for Research in Child Development, Tampa, FL.

Kushnir, T., & Gopnik, A. (2005). Children infer causal strength from probabilities and interventions. *Psychological Science, 16(9)*, 678–683.

Kushnir, T., Gopnik, A., & Schaefer, C. (2005, April). *Children infer hidden causes from probabilistic evidence.* Paper presented at the biennial meeting of the Society for Research in Child Development, Atlanta, GA.

Kushnir, T., Gopnik, A., Schulz, L., & Danks, D. (2003). Inferring hidden causes. In R. Alterman & D. Kirsh (Eds.), *Proceedings of the 25th Annual Meeting of the Cognitive Science Society.* Boston, pp. 699–703.

Masnick, A. M., & Klahr, D. (2003). Error matters: An initial exploration of elementary school children's understanding of experimental error. *Journal of Cognition & Development, 4*, 67–98.

Michotte, A. (1962). *The perception of causality.* New York: Basic Books. (Original work published 1946).

Pearl, J. (2000). *Causality.* New York: Oxford University Press.

Perner, J. (1991). *Understanding the representational mind.* Cambridge, MA: MIT Press.

Rovee-Collier, C. (1980). Reactivation of infant memory *Science, 208*, 1159–1161.

Rosenblit, L. R., & Keil, F. C. (2002). The misunderstood limits of folk science: an illusion of explanatory depth. *Cognitive Science, 26*, 521–562.

Saffran, J. R., Aslin, R. N., & Newport, E. L. (1996). Statistical learning by 8-month-old infants. *Science, 274*, 1926–1928.

Salmon, W. (1984). *Scientific explanation and the causal structure of the world.* Princeton, NJ: Princeton University Press.

Salmon, W. (1998). *Causality and explanation.* Oxford, England: Oxford University Press.

Schaefer, C., & Gopnik, A. (2003, April). *Causal reasoning in young children: The role of unobserved variables.* Paper presented at the biennial meeting of the Society for Research in Child Development, Tampa, FL.

Schlottman, A. (2001). Perception versus knowledge of cause and effect in children: When seeing is believing. *Current Directions in Psychological Science, 10*, 111–115.

Schulz, L. E., (2001, December). *Spinning wheels and bossy ones: Children, causal structure and the calculus of intervention.* Paper presented at the Causal Inference in Humans and Machines Workshop of the Neural Information Processing Systems annual meeting, Vancouver, BC.

Schulz, L., & Gopnik, A. (2004). Causal learning across domains. *Developmental Psychology, 40*, 162–176.

Shanks, D. R. (1985). Forward and backward blocking in human contingency judgment. *Quarterly Journal of Experimental Psychology: Comparative and Physiological Psychology, 37*, 1–21.

Shanks, D. R., & Dickinson, A. (1987). Associative accounts of causality judgment. In G. H. Bower (Ed.), *The psychology of learning and motivation: Advances in research and theory* (Vol. 21, pp. 229–261). San Diego, CA: Academic Press.

Shultz, T. R. (1982). Rules of causal attribution. *Monographs of the Society for Research in Child Development, 47*, 1–51.

Sobel, D. M. (2004). Emploring the coherence of young children's explanatory abilities: Evidence from generating counter factuals. *British Journal of Developmental Psychology, 22*, 37–58.

Sommer, S., & Wehner, R. (2004). The ant's estimation of distance travelled: Experiments with desert ants, *Cataglyphis fortis. Journal of Comparative Physiology A, Neuroethology Sensory Neural Behavioral Physiology, 190*, 1–6.

Spelke, E. S., Breinlinger, K., Macomber, J., & Jacobson, K. (1992). Origins of knowledge. *Psychological Review, 99*, 605–632.

Spelke, E. S., Katz, G., Purcell, S. E., Ehrlich, S. M., & Breinlinger, K. (1994). Early knowledge of object motion: Continuity and inertia. *Cognition, 51*, 131–176.

Tenenbaum, J. B., & Griffiths, T. L., (2003). Theory-based causal inference. In S. Becker, S. Thrun, & K. Obemayer (Eds.), *Advances in neural information processing systems 15*. Cambridge, MA: MIT Press (pp. 35–42).

Tenenbaum, J., & Niyogi, S. (2003). Learning causal laws. In R. Alterman & D. Kirsh (Eds.), *Proceedings of the 25th Annual Conference of the Cognitive Science Society.* Boston, pp. 1152–1157.

Tolman, E. C. (1932). *Purposive behavior in animals and men.* New York: Century.

Waldmann, M. R. (2000). Competition among causes but not effects in predictive and diagnostic learning. *Journal of Experimental Psychology: Learning, Memory, and Cognition, 26,* 53–76.

Waldmann, M. R. (2001). Predictive versus diagnostic causal learning: Evidence from an overshadowing paradigm. *Psychonomic Bulletin and Review, 8,* 600–608.

Waldmann, M. R., & Hagmayer, Y. (2005). Seeing versus doing: Two modes of accessing causal knowledge. *Journal of Experimental Psychology: Learning, Memory, and Cognition, 31,* 216–227.

Wasserman, E. A., Elek, S. M, Chatlosh, D. L., & Baker, A. G. (1993). Rating causal relations: Role of probability in judgments of response-outcome contingency. *Journal of Experimental Psychology: Learning, Memory, and Cognition, 19,* 174–188.

Watson, J. S., & Ramey, C. T. (1987). Reactions to response-contingent stimulation in early infancy. In J. Oates, & S. Sheldon (Eds.), *Cognitive development in infancy; cognitive development in infancy; portions of this paper were initially reported at the biennial meeting of the Society for Research in Child Development. Santa Monica, CA, 1969* (pp. 77–85). Hillsdale, NJ: Erlbaum.

Wellman, H. M., Hickling, A. K., & Schult, C. A. (1997). Young children's psychological, physical, and biological explanations. *New Directions for Child Development, 75,* 7–25.

Woodward, A. L. (1998). Infants selectively encode the goal object of an actor's reach. *Cognition, 69,* 1–34.

Woodward, A. L., Phillips, A. T., & Spelke, E. S. (1993). Infants' expectations about the motion of animate versus inanimate objects. In *Proceedings of the 15th annual meeting of the Cognitive Science Society* (pp. 1087–1091). Hillsdale, NJ: Erlbaum.

Woodward, J. (2003). *Making things happen: A theory of causal explanation.* New York: Oxford University Press.

Wu, M., & Cheng, P. W. (1999). Why causation need not follow from statistical association: Boundary conditions for the evaluation of generative and preventive causal powers. *Psychological Science, 10,* 92–97.

Study Questions

1. What is the theory theory? Is it reasonable?
2. What is the difference between evidence from observation and evidence from intervention? Why does the causal Bayes net formalism do a better job than other theories at maintaining this distinction? Is this a distinction worth maintaining? Don't we observe our interventions?
3. If we want to understand the concept of explanation, why might it help to study how children learn? Why might focusing on children be wrongheaded?
4. What would Hume think about Gopnik's approach? About Michotte's?

Part II

Mind and Self

CHAPTER 4

Mental States

MARK PHELAN AND ERIC MANDELBAUM

INTRODUCTION

ONE MIGHT THINK THAT MAN IS a rational animal, as Aristotle (supposedly) did. Or one might prefer Oscar Wilde's formulation instead: "One is tempted to define man as a rational animal who always loses his temper when he is called upon to act in accordance with the dictates of reason" (Wilde 2007, 80). Either interpretation presupposes that people believe that things are a certain way, desire that they be some way or other, and sometimes intend to change the world to fit with their desires. To attribute *rationality* to people requires attributing *mentality* to people. It is these mental states, seeing that p, desiring that q, believing that r, intending that x, feeling that y, that are the focus of this section.

We will be specifically interested in three questions. The first is the question of whether mental states exist or not (call this the *ontological* question, for ontology is the study of what exists). There are multiple views one could hold: one could think that mental states exist just like chairs, tables, and electrons exist; one could think that mental states exist, but only in a loose sense—they exist in the same way that the average family exists (with its 1.86 children); or one could think that mental states just do not exist at all, like werewolves, unicorns, and honest politicians. Assuming that mental states exist, the second question concerns itself with what mental states are (call this the *identity* question, for it essentially inquires as to the identity of mental states). Assuming mental states exist at all, are they a wholly separate type of entity from the physical? Are mental states properties that naturally emerge from certain configurations of physical states of the brain? Are mental states functional entities, ones that are what they are only in virtue of a certain role they play, like a mousetrap or a doorknob? The third is the question of how we know about the existence of mental states (call this the *epistemological* question, for epistemology is the study of knowledge). Do we know they exist because our best theories of human behavior—either philosophical, scientific, or commonsensical—require that they exist? Or do we know about their existence in some other way?

The importance of these questions stretches beyond the philosophy of mind; these are basic philosophical questions of how humans fit into the overall structure of the world. Is the mind, as physicalism holds, just made out of the same physical parts as other objects in the universe, like paper, rocks, scissors, and spiral nebulae? Or, as dualism suggests, is the mind such that it truly differs from all other extant substances? If the mind is special, then this implies that things with minds are, in a sense, special, too. Like the search for extraterrestrial intelligence, either answer we end up with will be a bit jarring but will also help us understand our place in the world a little better.

DESCARTES AND DUALISM

In his *Meditations on First Philosophy*, René Descartes argues in favor of the view that the mind is neither identical nor reducible to the body. Descartes' position on the mind is a variety of *substance dualism*; it holds that mental substances are a fundamentally different kind of thing than physical substances. Descartes arrives at this position through nonempirical, or *a priori*, reflection (reflection from the armchair, as it were). As he mentions at the beginning of *Meditations on First Philosophy* (p. 84, this volume), Descartes embraces a methodological approach to philosophy according to which we start reasoning from what we cannot doubt. When it comes to considering the mind's relation to the physical body, this methodological approach recommends that we reason according to the following rule:

> …anything we experience as being in us, and which we see can also exist in wholly inanimate bodies, must be attributed only to our body. On the other hand, anything in us which we cannot conceive in any way as capable of belonging to a body must be attributed to our soul. (p. 207, this volume)

Descartes' argument for dualism relies on a connection between what we can conceive and what is possible. The argument adopts the principle that if we can conceive of X without conceiving of Y, then it must be the case that X is not identical to Y. Descartes goes on to argue that, since he can conceive of a body without a mind (e.g., a dead body) and a mind without a body (e.g., God, or an immortal disembodied soul), the body and mind must be distinct.

Whatever the theoretical strengths of substance dualism, Paul Bloom's short piece contends that it is an *intuitive* position. Bloom contends that we are natural-born dualists. In this and other work (e.g., Bloom 2004), Bloom argues for an innate, dedicated mental mechanism whose function is to detect others' mental states. The presence of such a mechanism is supposed to account for the ease with which people can explain one another's behavior. Human behavior is much more complicated than the behavior, for example, of cars, yet almost everyone is adept at explaining the behavior of people by positing beliefs, desires, and other mental states, whereas explaining the behavior of cars is an acquired skill, one contained in a far smaller percentage of the population. What's more, children develop this ability to explain the behavior of others naturally, without any real instruction or even learning. Additionally, the small subgroup of people that have profound trouble explaining the behavior of others, people with autism, appear to have a developmental disorder. Based on this evidence, Bloom concludes that humans are mind readers from an early age; and he posits that when children learn about death, an intuitive dualism follows from this universal tendency to think in terms of mental states. Among other evidence in favor of natural-born dualism, Bloom refers to an experiment by Jesse Bering and David Bjorklund (2004). In these studies, preschool children are presented with a puppet show, in which Brown Mouse is having a terrible day. He's lost, sick, thirsty, and very sleepy. And things get even worse for Brown Mouse, because he's soon eaten by Mr. Alligator! After seeing the play, children are asked a series of questions. Though they tend to recognize that Brown Mouse won't ever need to go to the bathroom again and that his brain no longer works, they still think that he's hungry and that he wants to go home. In other words, kids tend to say that Brown Mouse's mental states persist, even when his biological processes cease. This is evidence that the belief in an immortal, disembodied mind is natural. As Bloom (2004) writes:

> Young children do not know that they will one day die. But once they learn about the inevitable destruction of their body, the notion of an afterlife comes naturally. This is the most important consequence of seeing the world as Descartes did. (p. 208)

Regardless of its intuitive appeal and the philosophical arguments in favor of it, substance dualism is a startlingly bold hypothesis. It puts the mind outside of the physical world altogether. Descartes, however, did not intend to put the mind outside of the *causal* world altogether. Descartes thought the mind and the brain interact with one another. According to his view, neural activity leads to thought and feeling in our nonphysical minds; and the immateriality of a feeling is no bar on its influencing our behavior. Thus, Descartes' form of dualism is also a type of *interactionist dualism* (in addition to being a variety of substance dualism). The interactionist thinks that although the mind and body are separate, they can interact in causal ways. Since Descartes embraces the conjunction of substance dualism and interactionist dualism, we will refer to the conjunction of these two theses as *Cartesian dualism.*

In a lengthy correspondence with Descartes (several letters of which are reprinted in this volume), Princess Elisabeth of Bohemia raised an important challenge to Cartesian dualism. As she noted, it is quite difficult to see how the mind can interact with the body if the mind is necessarily a nonphysical thing. Causation seems to only hold between physical entities; in other words, causation only holds in the world of the physical. If the physical is a closed causal system, then how can a nonphysical entity, like the mind, interact with a physical entity? Causation seems to need some form of contact or, at least, some relationship over a distance (like gravitational pull), but how can a nonextended entity either make contact with or even stand at any distance removed from a physical thing? As Cottingham et al. (1985) note, Descartes' reply to this question is as follows:

> ...that the body causes the soul to have feelings and passions, and the soul causes the body to move, through an inexplicable "union" between the soul and body—did not satisfy the princess. Nor was she satisfied when Descartes sought to answer her questions with vague moralizing and practical advice for the control of the passions. (325)

Descartes eventually obliged Elisabeth's request that he "define the passions, in order to know them better" (p. 207, this volume). Relying on his previous ground-breaking anatomical research involving experimenting via vivisection to investigate muscular movement, among other empirical undertakings, Descartes wrote his final treatise, *The Passions of the Soul*, as a response to Elisabeth. Descartes surmised that the mind and the body must interact somewhere, and he concluded that the pineal gland was the most reasonable seat of the mind/body interactions. Anatomically, this was a reasonable guess given the limited understanding of neuroanatomy at the time, for the pineal gland is centrally located between the two hemispheres of the brain. Thus, it seems that the pineal gland might be the type of juncture that could affect the entire brain. However, this somewhat clever solution does not speak to the conceptual question that Elisabeth raised: How is it possible for a nonphysical entity to causally affect a physical one? If the physical world is a causally closed system, then how can a fundamentally nonphysical entity affect the physical world in any way?

Phelan et al. raise a further challenge for Cartesian dualism. One of the greatest promises of Cartesian dualism is purported to be the possibility that the nonphysical mind is protected from the ravages of the physical body. However, cases of brain damage indicate that physical injuries to the brain cause serious harm to the mind. Cartesian dualism needs to be able to explain why the nonphysical mind seems to be damaged by physical damage to the brain, for this seems to suggest that ravages to the physical body do indeed cause ravages to the mind.

Because of the interaction problem, the challenge of brain damage, and other problems, Cartesian dualism is rejected by most contemporary philosophers.

THE ELIMINATION OF THE MENTAL

If our intuitive theory of mind, Cartesian dualism, is fraught with so many conceptual problems, why not just abandon it, like other intuitive but conceptually problematic belief systems? The fact that an explanation comes naturally to us does not serve as justification for the explanation. For example, before receiving some rudimentary training in physics, people think that balls that are ejected from curved tubes will follow curved trajectories. This natural explanation of the path of the ball is part of our basic "folk physics." But such folk judgments are often the product of mental processes that rely on heuristics, or fast and imprecise rules, for dealing with a world in which numerous physical variables make timely and accurate physical predictions difficult to come by. The fact that folk explanations are overwhelmingly of a heuristic and ultimately false nature gives us some reason to reject them, or so claims the *eliminativist* Paul

Churchland. Like Bloom, Churchland claims that people employ an intuitive psychological theory—or *folk psychology*—that underlies their explanations of the behavior of others. However, Churchland goes on to claim that folk psychology is so badly mistaken that the very concepts it uses—belief, desire, intention—do not correspond to real entities in the world. Churchland likens folk psychology to failed physical and biological theories of yore like phlogiston theory and vitalism. Churchland argues that folk psychology is a stagnant theory, one that has not evolved in any meaningful way in eons. According to Churchland, folk psychology also fails to explain a wide array of data that should be in its explanatory purview. Churchland also charges folk psychology with being unable to integrate itself with what he sees as the emerging synthesis among various previously distinct disciplines. As the prototypical eliminative materialist, Churchland holds that not only is dualism false but also that beliefs, desires, and intentions do not exist.[1]

ELIMINATIVISM'S RELIANCE ON ARGUMENTS FROM REFERENCE

What motivated Churchland to argue for the elimination of beliefs, desires, and intentions is the idea that folk psychological terms such as *belief* and *desire* don't actually refer to anything. If none of the terms used in a particular branch of science actually picks out any real things, then we have a good reason for getting rid of that science. Suppose, for example, that there were no such things as electrons, protons, or any of the fundamental posits of physics. In that case, we would have a pretty good reason for concluding that our science of physics was deeply mistaken and in need of rejection or fundamental reconceptualization. But, as Mallon et al. argue in their included piece, determining whether or not a scientific term actually refers to anything in the world is a nontrivial matter, and, importantly, it presupposes some theory of what it is for a scientific concept to refer to an object in the world.

Mallon et al. identify this argument for eliminativism as an *argument from reference*. In an argument from reference, a theorist first adopts a particular theory of how terms refer. Churchland and other eliminativists, for example, assume that concepts refer to whatever satisfies the description people typically associate with that term. Next, the theorist who is using an argument from reference goes on to show that, if the adopted theory of reference is correct, the terms of whatever scientific or philosophical theory they are discussing have some specific property. Churchland and other eliminativists, for instance, contend that if our terms refer descriptively, then the terms used in our folk psychological explanations fail to refer to anything, because nothing in the world satisfies the descriptions people associate with beliefs, desires, and so on. Finally, the proponent of an argument from reference goes on to draw some philosophically significant conclusion. For example, Churchland and other eliminativists conclude that folk psychological theories must be rejected because their terms (belief, desire, etc.) fail to map onto the actual world.

Arguments from reference, such as Churchland's argument for the elimination of mental states, only work if the particular theory of reference they invoke is the correct theory of reference. But how do we determine if a particular theory of reference is correct? As Mallon et al. point out, "the correct theory of reference...is commonly thought to be constrained by our intuitions about...reference...in actual and fictional cases" (p. 223, this volume). This method of settling on *the* correct theory of reference seems to assume that intuitions about actual and fictional cases will be more or less universally shared. However, as Mallon et al. conclude from a review of some recent experimental work, there is good reason to conclude that there may be cross-cultural and individual differences between people's intuitions about important fictional cases. If so, our intuitions fail to show that one theory of reference is *the* correct one, and Churchland's conclusion, among the conclusions that assume a particular theory of reference, fail to follow.

FODOR, FUNCTIONALISM, AND THE PERSISTENCE OF THE ATTITUDES

Mallon et al. try to undercut eliminativism by going negative: they argue that a crucial premise in the eliminativist argument, the premise relying on a theory of reference, is unsupportable. However, one can also try to stave off eliminativism by offering a positive account of what mental states are. *Functionalism* attempts to offer such an account.

Between such stark positions as dualism and eliminativism lies functionalism. The functionalist thinks that states such as believing, hoping, wanting, doubting, and so on, are functional states—that is, states that function in a certain way and are identified by their functions. For the functionalist, what makes something a belief is not that it has a certain structure (e.g., it does not matter that psychological states are composed out of neurological states); rather, what matters for the identity of a psychological state is that it serves a certain role in one's psychological economy. The functionalist points out that psychological states are like lots of other things that we identify based on what they do. What makes something a mousetrap, for example, is that it serves a certain function, that is, trapping mice. Be it a snap trap or glue trap, it's the role it plays in our homes that is important. What is not important to identifying a mousetrap is the specific materials out of which it is built; a mousetrap can be built out of wood, metal, plastic, and so on. Likewise, the functionalist holds that what makes something, for example, a belief, is that it serves a certain role in a mental economy.

Jerry Fodor attempts to secure the ontological footing of psychological states in just this way. For Fodor, as things stand in our world, psychological states happen to always be instantiated by neurological states; that is, every given instance of a psychological state is also an instance of a neurological state. However, Fodor thinks that different kinds of psychological states, such as beliefs, are not just identical to different kinds of neurological states. To put it crudely, there isn't a belief neuron, nor is believing always achieved by some particular part of the brain. Instead, a mental state like "believes" is realized by lots of different neurological states (and could even, in principle, be realized by nonneurological [e.g., silicon] robot CPU states). Again, what is ultimately important is the role a state plays, not what it is made of.

On the picture just sketched, the functionalist arrives at a middle position between the extremities of embracing a dualism and eliminating psychological states altogether.

Since most functionalists think that the things that happen to play the psychological state role are all, as a matter of fact, neurological states, most functionalists don't need to posit any nonphysical realm of the mind, as Descartes did. On the other hand, because psychological states are not just neurological states, one can still talk about them in terms of their distinctively psychological roles.

Of course, one might still ask the functionalist, why posit psychological states at all? It is this question that Fodor's paper takes up. Fodor is a full-fledged psychological realist: he thinks psychological states are mental representations that have real causal powers, just as tables, chairs, and protons do. Taking beliefs, desires, and the like to have real causal powers allows us to explain vast amounts of human behavior. Fodor argues that our theory of mind works so well that it is easy to overlook its innumerable successes. Just by uttering certain words, we can predict disparate people's behavior despite numerous individual differences (and these predictions can be quite complicated, traversing a vast amount of time and space). Fodor takes such predictive accuracy as a strong reason for believing in the existence of mental states. After all, how could we account for such predictive accuracy if mental states, the entities we use in such predictions, were actually nonexistent? And note that, in other areas of science when we use a certain entity for prediction and explanation, we assume that entity really exists. When we speak of gravitational fields causing smaller celestial bodies to be attracted to larger celestial bodies, we take it that such a gravitational field actually exists. Part of our reason for believing in its existence is that by positing such a phenomenon, we can explain our observations. Our understanding and predicting of behavior involves positing mental states, so Fodor thinks we have good reason to allow such states into our ontology, as we would in any other investigative inquiry.

REAL PATTERNS AND INTERPRETIVE STANCES

Just as the functionalist takes a more moderate ontological stance than the dualist and eliminative materialist, Dennett seeks to take an even more concessive position. Dennett is an *interpretationist*. As opposed to the functional realism of someone like Fodor, Dennett proposes that mental states are not necessarily inner, causal states of people. Whereas the functionalist thinks that beliefs and desires give us a mechanistic explanation of behavior, the interpretationist only goes so far as to claim that intentional states are tools we use in predicting behavior. For the interpretationist, beliefs and desires are like centers of gravity and the average American family. The average American family needn't exist (and in fact couldn't exist if it has only 1.86 children), but it could still be quite useful to use in predicting certain facts. For example, were someone to offer you $100 to predict how many children are in the randomly chosen Jones family, it would be reasonable to use your knowledge of the average American family, as well as your knowledge that there are no 86% children, to generate a guess of 2. Although such a concept is useful, that does not imply that it refers to an existing entity.

Dennett describes explaining people's behavior in terms of *intentional states* (another term for mental states such as beliefs and desires) as taking the "intentional stance" (Dennett, 1987) toward a person (or object, for that matter). Taking the intentional stance involves predicting behavior by positing beliefs and desires that it is rational for the person (or object) in question to have. For Dennett, there is no further fact of the matter about what beliefs the person actually has; rather, we assign beliefs against an assumption of rationality. Hence, the interpretationist does not take belief ascription to be a merely descriptive endeavor like most scientific observations are. For a typical example of scientific observation, consider how in comparative psychology experimenters often use experimental paradigms where they observe how long, for example, a rhesus macaque monkey looks directly at a stimulus. Coding how long the monkeys looked in a certain direction is, when all goes well, merely a descriptive endeavor. Since, for Dennett, belief ascription does not follow this strictly descriptive route, belief ascription does not seem properly scientific. Dennett concludes that, contra Churchland, beliefs exist but not necessarily in the "industrial strength" way of Fodor. Instead, Dennett thinks that they describe certain patterns of behavior. Beliefs do not necessarily carve the world at its joints, but they are helpful in picking real patterns that emerge from neural activity. In sum, Dennett is a materialist who wants to stave off eliminativism and Fodor's industrial-strength realism by embracing beliefs as an abstract description of a pattern of underlying neural activity.

FOLK PSYCHOLOGY AS A FULL-BLOODED THEORY

One recurring theme of this discussion has been that people use their ascriptions of mental states to predict other people's behavior to some greater or lesser extent. But there are other questions we might ask about the process of mental state ascription. For instance, many contemporary philosophers and cognitive scientists have asked what the specific psychological mechanisms are that allow us to attribute mental states to others. *Theory theory* provides one answer to this question. It is the position that people understand other people's minds on the basis of an unconscious, tacit theory about how people's minds work. In particular, the theory theory of Gopnik and Wellman claims that children gain an understanding of others' minds by using a tacit theory. The theory theory theorist sees the child as a little scientist, gathering evidence, testing hypotheses, and revising his theories of the mind accordingly.

Gopnik and Wellman's argument in favor of theory theory has two main moves. First, they analyze what it takes for something to count as a theory, and then they marshal evidence from developmental psychology to support their contentions. They claim that theories posit abstract entities to interpret, predict, and explain certain phenomena. These entities should cohere in a lawful way with one another and with the observed phenomena. Theories aren't just static bodies of entities in lawful correlation with one another; instead, theories are dynamic entities, entities that change as new evidence comes in. For example, when a theory's hypotheses are disproven, they are replaced by better, more confirmed hypotheses.

After delineating some characteristics of theories, Gopnik and Wellman delve into the developmental data to show that the child's theory of mind undergoes certain transitions. For example, Gopnik and Wellman claim that the two-year-old only posits desires and perceptions. However, the three-year-old countenances a greater number of mental states such as pretending, knowing, and dreaming. Yet the three-year-old still has trouble with belief, particularly false belief. The three-year-old does not have a robust understanding of how someone can misrepresent some state of affairs. By the time the three-year-old matures to a five-year-old, his or her theories too have matured. The five-year-old understands representations and misrepresentations and can, in particular, make sense of false belief. In this way, Gopnik and Wellman interpret the child as holding a theory that gains theoretical depth and explanatory power as the child develops. Between two and five years old, the child's theory gains more abstract entities and the child understands the relations between such entities and the relations between the entities and the world better as time goes on.

THE PERSON AS SCIENTIST, THE PERSON AS MORALIST

Joshua Knobe also addresses the topic of how we use mental states to explain one another's behavior. Knobe's paper takes aim at a Gopnik and Wellman–style theory theory. Gopnik and Wellman suggest that the way children learn about others' minds is akin to the way that scientists develop theoretical frameworks. In opposition, Knobe contends that people's everyday reasoning is unlike scientific reasoning in that everyday reasoning is suffused with moral considerations. Contra Gopnik and Wellman, Knobe has developed the view that "there is literally a non-conscious process whereby moral judgments influence intuitions about intentional action which then serve as input to the mechanisms underlying intuitions about [other people's mental states]" (2007, 98). (In the included selection, Knobe reviews some of the evidence supporting this claim.) This has the result that the attribution and use of mental states for the purposes of explaining action itself rests in part on moral considerations. Knobe concludes that when we explain one another's behaviors, we are not merely tough-minded scientists, as Gopnik and Wellman's theory suggests. When we want to account for our attributions of mental states, we must also recognize that the theory that drives those attributions is driven in part by moral considerations.

Note

1. We focus on beliefs, desires, and intentions—or *propositional attitudes*—as opposed to mental states in general, because Churchland believes that sensations needn't necessarily be eliminated. Churchland thinks sensations will be identified with brain states and ultimately reduced to them, whereas he thinks we need to eliminate all the propositional attitudes from our ontology.

References

Bloom, P. *Descartes' Baby: How the Science of Child Development Explains What Makes Us Human.* New York: Basic Books, 2004.

Cottingham, J., R. Stoothoff, and D. Murdoch. *The Philosophical Writings of Descartes.* Cambridge: Cambridge University Press, 1985.

Dennett, D. "True Believers." In *The Intentional Stance.* Cambridge, MA: MIT Press, 1987.

Descartes, R. *The Passions of the Soul* I XXXI. In *The Philosophical Works of Descartes.* Vol. 1, trans. and ed. E. Haldane and G. Ross. Cambridge: Cambridge University Press, 1969.

Knobe, J. "Reason Explanation in Folk Psychology." *Midwest Studies in Philosophy* 31, no. 1 (2007): 90–106.

Wilde, O. *The Critic as Artist (Upon the Importance of Doing Nothing and Discussing Everything)*. New York: Mondial, 2007.

Suggestions for Further Reading

Alexander, J., R. Mallon, and J. M. Weinberg. "Accentuate the Negative." *Review of Philosophy and Psychology* 1, no. 2 (2010): 297–314.

Aydede, M., and G. Guzeldere. "Cognitive Architecture, Concepts, and Introspection: An Information-Theoretic Solution to the Problem of Phenomenal Consciousness." *Nous* 39, no. 2 (2005): 197–255.

Baron-Cohen, S. *Mindblindness: An Essay on Autism and Theory of Mind*. Cambridge, MA: MIT Press/Bradford Books, 1995.

Bealer, G. "Self-Consciousness." *Philosophical Review* 106, no. 1 (1997): 69–117.

Bering, J., and D. Bjorklund. "The Natural Emergence of Afterlife Reasoning as a Developmental Regularity." *Developmental Psychology* 40 (2004): 217–233.

Chalmers, D. *The Conscious Mind*. Oxford: Oxford University Press, 1996.

Chalmers, David J. "Phenomenal Concepts and the Knowledge Argument." In *There's Something About Mary: Essays on Phenomenal Consciousness and Frank Jackson's Knowledge Argument*, ed. P. Ludlow, Y. Nagasawa, and D. Stoljar. Cambridge, MA: MIT Press, 2004.

Dennett, D. "The Unimagined Preposterousness of Zombies." *Journal of Consciousness Studies* 2, no. 4 (1995): 322–326.

Dennett, Daniel C. "What Robomary Knows." In *Phenomenal Concepts and Phenomenal Knowledge: New Essays on Consciousness and Physicalism*, ed. T. Alter and S. Walter. New York: Oxford University Press, 2006.

Descartes, R. *Meditations on First Philosophy*. Englewood Cliffs, NJ: Prentice Hall, 1960.

Fodor, J. "Special Sciences (or: The Disunity of Science as a Working Hypothesis)." *Synthese* 28 (1974): 77–115.

Jackson, F. "Epiphenomenal Qualia." *Philosophical Quarterly* 32 (1982): 127–136.

Jackson, F. "What Mary Didn't Know." *Journal of Philosophy* 83 (1986): 291–295.

Knobe, J., and S. Nichols, eds. *Experimental Philosophy*. New York: Oxford University Press, 2008.

Knobe, J., and J. Prinz. "Intuitions about Consciousness: Experimental Studies." *Phenomenology and the Cognitive Sciences* 7, no. 1 (2008): 67–83.

Kripke, S. *Naming and Necessity*. Oxford: Blackwell, 1980.

Levine, J. "Materialism and Qualia: The Explanatory Gap." *Pacific Philosophical Quarterly* 64 (1983): 354–361.

Lewis, D. "What Experience Teaches." In *Mind and Cognition*, ed. W. Lycan. Oxford: Wiley-Blackwell, 1990.

Lycan, W. G. "Kripke and the Materialists." *Journal of Philosophy* 71 (1974): 677–689.

Lycan, W. G. "Perspectival Representation and the Knowledge Argument." In *Consciousness: New Philosophical Perspectives*, ed. Q. Smith and A. Jokic. New York: Oxford University Press, 2003.

Machery, E., R. Mallon, S. Nichols, and S. P. Stich. "Semantics, Cross-cultural Style." *Cognition* 92, no. 3 (2004): B1–B12.

Nichols, S., and S. Stich. *Mindreading: An Integrated Account of Pretence, Self-Awareness and Understanding Other Minds*. Oxford: Oxford University Press, 2003.

Prinz, J. "Level-Headed Mysterianism and Artificial Experience." *Journal of Consciousness Studies* 10, no. 4–5 (2003): 111–132.

How Can Souls Move Bodies?   4.1

RENÉ DESCARTES AND PRINCESS ELISABETH OF BOHEMIA

PRINCESS ELISABETH OF BOHEMIA (1618–1680) was the exiled Protestant princess of the Palatinate, a region in southwest Germany. She spent much of her life in The Hague, where her family held court in absentia. Studious and inquisitive, Elisabeth excelled at art, languages, literature, and culture. Her siblings gave her the nickname "La Grecque," or the Greek. Refusing an offer of marriage from the Catholic King Wladislav of Poland during the Catholic-Protestant hostilities of the Thirty Years' War, Elisabeth joined the Lutheran convent at Hertford in Germany in 1660, becoming abbess several years later.

RENÉ DESCARTES (1596–1650) was a member of the French gentry class educated at the Jesuit College of La Fleche and the University of Poitiers. As a young soldier in the Netherlands, Descartes made foundational contributions to geometry. Descartes went on to make important contributions to physics, optics, and anatomy. His philosophical works, especially *Meditations on First Philosophy*, make him one of the most important philosophers of all time.

According to Cartesian dualism, the position defended by Descartes in his *Meditations on First Philosophy*, the mental and the physical are fundamentally different substances that, nonetheless, causally interact with one another. In the excerpted correspondence, Princess Elisabeth of Bohemia challenges Descartes to explain how a physical body can interact with a nonphysical mind. This enduring challenge for Cartesian dualism has come to be known as the interaction problem. After several letters clarifying the issue, Descartes suggests that a rational explanation for how body and mind interact may not be available, but that we can clearly sense that the two *do* interact. For example, who could doubt that physical sensations—or "passions"—lead us to entertain certain ideas in our minds? Elisabeth is not satisfied with this response and urges Descartes to "define the passions, in order to know them better" (p. 207). As later correspondence suggests, Elisabeth's request led Descartes to write *The Passions of the Soul*, his final response to the interaction problem, excerpts of which conclude this selection.

L. Shapiro, "Correspondence Between Princess Elisabeth of Bohemia and René Descartes" and "The Philosophical Writings of Descartes," Cottingham, J., Stoothoff, R., Murdoch, D., from *The Passions of the Soul.*

CORRESPONDENCE BETWEEN PRINCESS ELISABETH OF BOHEMIA AND RENÉ DESCARTES

ELISABETH TO DESCARTES, MAY 6, 1643

[...] I ask you please to tell me how the soul of a human being (it being only a thinking substance) can determine the bodily spirits,[1] in order to bring about voluntary actions. For it seems that all determination of movement happens through the impulsion of the thing moved, by the manner in which it is pushed by that which moves it, or else by the particular qualities and shape of the surface of the latter. Physical contact is required for the first two conditions, extension for the third. You entirely exclude the one [extension] from the notion you have of the soul, and the other [physical contact] appears to me incompatible with an immaterial thing. [...]

DESCARTES TO ELISABETH, MAY 21, 1643

I can say with truth that the question your Highness proposes seems to me that which, in view of my published writings, one can most rightly ask me. For there are two things about the human soul on which all the knowledge we can have of its nature depends: one of which is that it thinks, and the other is that, being united to the body, it can act on and be acted upon by it. I have said almost nothing about the latter, and have concentrated solely on making the first better understood, as my principal aim was to prove the distinction between the soul and the body. Only the first was able to serve this aim, and the other would have been harmful to it. But, as your Highness sees so clearly that one cannot conceal anything from her, I will try here to explain the manner in which I conceive of the union of the soul with the body and how the soul has the power [*force*] to move it.

First, I consider that there are in us certain primitive notions that are like originals on the pattern of which we form all our other knowledge. There are only very few of these notions; for, after the most general—those of being, number, and duration, etc.—which apply to all that we can conceive, we have, for the body in particular, only the notion of extension, from which follow the notions of shape and movement; and for the soul alone, we have only that of thought, in which are included the perceptions of the understanding and the inclinations of the will; and finally, for the soul and the body together, we have only that of their union, on which depends that of the power the soul has to move the body and the body to act on the soul, in causing its sensations and passions.

I consider also that all human knowledge [*science*] consists only in distinguishing well these notions, and in attributing each of them only to those things to which it pertains. For, when we want to explain some difficulty by means of a notion which does not pertain to it, we cannot fail to be mistaken; just as we are mistaken when we want to explain one of these notions by another; for being primitive, each of them can be understood only through itself. Although the use of the senses has given us notions of extension, of shapes, and of movements that are much more familiar than the others, the principal cause of our errors lies in our ordinarily wanting to use these notions to explain those things to which they do not pertain. For instance, when we want to use the imagination to conceive the nature of the soul, or better, when one wants to conceive the way in which the soul moves the body, by appealing to the way one body is moved by another body.

That is why, since, in the *Meditations* which your Highness deigned to read, I was trying to make conceivable the notions which pertain to the soul alone, distinguishing them from those which pertain to the body alone, the first thing that I ought to explain subsequently is the manner of conceiving those which pertain to the union of the soul with the body, without those which pertain to the body alone, or to the soul alone. To which it seems to me that what I wrote at the end of my response to the sixth objections can be useful; for we cannot look for these simple notions elsewhere than in our soul, which has them all in itself by its nature, but which does not always distinguish one from the others well enough, or even attribute them to the objects to which it ought to attribute them.

Thus, I believe that we have heretofore confused the notion of the power with which the soul acts on the body with the power with which one body acts on another; and that we have attributed the one and the other not to the soul, for we did not yet know it, but to diverse qualities of bodies, such as heaviness, heat, and others, which we have imagined to be real, that is to say, to have an existence distinct from that of body, and by consequence, to be substances, even though we have named them qualities. In order to understand them, sometimes we have used those notions that are in us for knowing body, and sometimes those which are there for knowing the soul, depending on whether what we were attributing to them was material or immaterial. For example, in supposing that heaviness is a real quality, of which we have no other knowledge but that it has the power to move a body in which it is toward the center of the earth, we have no difficulty in conceiving how it moves the body, nor how it is joined to it; and we do not think that this happens through a real contact of one surface against another, for we experience in ourselves that we have a specific notion for conceiving that; and I think that we use this notion badly, in applying it to heaviness, which, as I hope to demonstrate in my Physics, is nothing really distinct from body. But I do think that it was given to us for conceiving the way in which the soul moves the body. [...]

ELISABETH TO DESCARTES, JUNE 10, 1643

[...] Now the interests of my house, which I must not neglect, now some conversations and social obligations which I cannot avoid, beat down so heavily on this weak mind with annoyance or boredom, that it is rendered useless for anything else at all for a long time afterward: this will serve, I hope, as an excuse for my stupidity in being unable to comprehend, by appeal to the idea you once had of heaviness, the idea through which we must judge how the soul (nonextended and immaterial) can move the body; nor why this power [*puissance*] to carry the body toward the center of the earth, which you earlier falsely attributed to a body as a quality, should sooner persuade us that a body can be pushed by some immaterial thing, than the demonstration of a contrary truth (which you promise in your physics) should confirm us in the opinion of its impossibility. In particular, since this idea (unable to pretend to the same perfection and objective reality as that of God) can be feigned due to the ignorance of that which truly moves these bodies toward the center, and since no material cause presents itself to the senses, one would then attribute this power to its contrary, an immaterial cause. But I nevertheless have never been able to conceive of such an immaterial thing as anything other than a negation of matter which cannot have any communication with it.

I admit that it would be easier for me to concede matter and extension to the soul than to concede the capacity to move a body and to be moved by it to an immaterial thing. For, if the first is achieved through *information*, it would be necessary that the spirits, which cause the movements, were intelligent, a capacity you accord to nothing corporeal. And even though, in your *Metaphysical Meditations*, you show the possibility of the second, it is altogether very difficult to understand that a soul, as you have described it, after having had the faculty and the custom of reasoning well, can lose all of this by some vapors, and that, being able to subsist without the body, and having nothing in common with it, the soul is still so governed by it.

But after all, since you have undertaken to instruct me, I entertain these sentiments only as friends which I do not intend to keep, assuring myself that you will explicate the nature of an immaterial substance and the manner of its actions and passions in the body, just as well as you have all the other things that you have wanted to teach. [. . .]

DESCARTES TO ELISABETH, JUNE 28, 1643

[. . .] I notice a great difference between these three sorts of notions. The soul is conceived only by the pure understanding [*l'entendement*]; the body, that is to say, extension, shapes, and motions, can also be known by the understanding alone, but is much better known by the understanding aided by the imagination; and finally, those things which pertain to the union of the soul and the body are known only obscurely by the understanding alone, or even by the understanding aided by the imagination; but they are known very clearly by the senses. From which it follows that those who never philosophize and who use only their senses do not doubt in the least that the soul moves the body and that the body acts on the soul. But they consider the one and the other as one single thing, that is to say, they conceive of their union. For to conceive of the union between two things is to conceive of them as one single thing. Metaphysical thoughts which exercise the pure understanding serve to render the notion of the soul familiar. The study of mathematics, which exercises principally the imagination in its consideration of shapes and movements, accustoms us to form very distinct notions of body. And lastly, it is in using only life and ordinary conversations and in abstaining from meditating and studying those things which exercise the imagination that we learn to conceive the union of the soul and the body. [. . .]

But [. . .] it does not seem to me that the human mind is capable of conceiving very distinctly, and at the same time, the distinction between the soul and the body and their union, since to do so it is necessary to conceive them as one single thing and at the same time to conceive them as two, which is contradictory. On this matter (supposing your Highness still had the reasons which prove the distinction of the soul and body at the forefront of her mind and not wanting to ask her to remove them from there in order to represent to herself the notion of the union that each always experiences within himself without philosophizing, in knowing that he is a single person who has together a body and a thought, which are of such a nature that this thought can move the body and sense what happens to it), I availed myself in my previous letter of a comparison between heaviness and those other qualities which we commonly imagine to be united to some bodies just as thought is united to our own, and I was not worried that this comparison hangs on qualities that are not real, even though we imagine them so, since I believed that your Highness was already entirely persuaded that the soul is a substance distinct from body.

But since your Highness notices that it is easier to attribute matter and extension to the soul than to attribute to it the capacity to move a body and to be moved by one without having matter, I beg her to feel free to attribute this matter and this extension to the soul, for to do so is to do nothing but conceive it as united with the body. After having well conceived this and having experienced it within herself, it will be easy for her to consider that the matter that she has attributed to this thought is not the thought itself, and that the extension of this matter is of another nature than the extension of this thought, in that the first is determined to a certain place, from which it excludes all other extended bodies, and this is not the case with the second. In this way your Highness will not neglect to return easily to the knowledge of the distinction between the soul and the body, even though she has conceived their union.

Finally, though I believe it is very necessary to have understood well once in one's life the principles of metaphysics, since it is these that give us knowledge of God and of our soul, I also believe that it would be very harmful to occupy one's understanding often in meditating on them. For in doing so, it could not attend so well to the functions of the imagination and the senses. The best is to content oneself in retaining in one's memory and in one's belief the conclusions that one has at one time drawn from such meditation, and then to employ the rest of the time one has for study in those thoughts where the understanding acts with imagination or the senses. [. . .]

ELISABETH TO DESCARTES, SEPTEMBER 13, 1645

If my conscience were to rest satisfied with the pretexts you offer for my ignorance, as if they were remedies for it, I would be greatly indebted to it, and would be exempted from repenting having so poorly employed the time I have enjoyed the use of reason, which I have had longer than others of my age, since my birth and fortune have forced me to exercise my judgment earlier than most, in order to lead a life that is very trying and free of the prosperity that could prevent me from thinking of myself and also free of the subjection that would have obliged me to rely on the prudence of a governess.

All the same, neither this prosperity nor the flatteries which accompany it are, I believe, absolutely capable of removing the strength of mind of well-born minds and of preventing them from receiving any change of fortune as a philosopher. [. . .]

I would [. . .] like to see you define the passions, in order to know them better.[2] For those who call the passions perturbations of the mind would persuade me that the force of the passions consists only in overwhelming and subjecting reason to them, if experience did not show me that there are passions that do carry us to reasonable actions. But I assure myself that you will shed more light on this subject, when you explicate how the force of the passions renders them even more useful when they are subject to reason. [. . .]

Notes

1. "Bodily" or "animal spirits" refer to tiny *physical* particles thought by medieval physicians to be the intermediary between a physical body and a nonphysical mind. Descartes expounds on the notion later in this selection, in excerpts from *The Passions of the Soul.*—Eds.
2. This demand on Elisabeth's part can reasonably be seen as leading Descartes to write *The Passions of the Soul.* As subsequent letters reveal, Descartes responds by beginning to draft what will become that work. It was first published, in French, in 1649.

THE PASSIONS OF THE SOUL

2. To understand the passions of the soul we must distinguish its functions from those of the body

Next I note that we are not aware of any subject which acts more directly upon our soul than the body to which it is joined. Consequently we should recognize that what is a passion in the soul is usually an action in the body. Hence there is no better way of coming to know about passions than by examining the difference between the soul and the body in order to learn to which of the two we should attribute each of the functions present in us.

3. The rule we must follow in order to do this

We shall not find this very difficult if we bear in mind that anything we experience as being in us, and which we see can also exist in wholly inanimate bodies, must be attributed only to our body. On the other hand, anything in us which we cannot conceive in any way as capable of belonging to a body must be attributed to our soul.

4. The heat and the movement of the limbs proceed from the body, and thoughts from the soul

Thus, because we have no conception of the body as thinking in any way at all, we have reason to believe that every kind of thought present in us belongs to the soul. And since we do not doubt that there are inanimate bodies which can move in as many different ways as our bodies, if not more, and which have as much heat or more (as experience shows in the case of a flame, which has in itself much

more heat and movement than any of our limbs),
we must believe that all the heat and all the movements present in us, in so far as they do not depend
on thought, belong solely to the body. [. . .]

10. *How the animal spirits are produced in the brain*

What is, however, more worthy of consideration here is that all the most lively and finest parts
of the blood, which have been rarefied by the
heat in the heart, constantly enter the cavities of
the brain in large numbers. What makes them go
there rather than elsewhere is that all the blood
leaving the heart through the great artery follows
a direct route towards this place, and since not all
this blood can enter there because the passages
are too narrow, only the most active and finest
parts pass into it while the rest spread out into
the other regions of the body. Now these very
fine parts of the blood make up the animal spirits.
For them to do this the only change they need to
undergo in the brain is to be separated from the
other less fine parts of the blood. For what I am
calling "spirits" here are merely bodies: they have
no property other than that of being extremely
small bodies which move very quickly, like the
jets of flame that come from a torch. They never
stop in any place, and as some of them enter the
brain's cavities, others leave it through the pores
in its substance. These pores conduct them into
the nerves, and then to the muscles. In this way
the animal spirits move the body in all the various
ways it can be moved. [. . .]

16. *How all the limbs can be moved by the objects of the senses and by the spirits without the help of the soul*

Finally it must be observed that the mechanism of our body is so composed that all the
changes occurring in the movement of the spirits may cause them to open some pores in the
brain more than others. Conversely, when one
of the pores is opened somewhat more or less
than usual by an action of the sensory nerves,
this brings about a change in the movement of
the spirits and directs them to the muscles which
serve to move the body in the way it is usually
moved on the occasion of such an action. Thus

every movement we make without any contribution from our will—as often happens when
we breathe, walk, eat and, indeed, when we
perform any action which is common to us and
the beasts—depends solely on the arrangement
of our limbs and on the route which the spirits, produced by the heat of the heart, follow
naturally in the brain, nerves and muscles. This
occurs in the same way as the movement of a
watch is produced merely by the strength of its
spring and the configuration of its wheels.

17. *The functions of the soul*

Having thus considered all the functions
belonging solely to the body, it is easy to recognize
that there is nothing in us which we must attribute to our soul except our thoughts. These are of
two principal kinds, some being actions of the soul
and others its passions. Those I call its actions are
all our volitions, for we experience them as pro-
ceeding directly from our soul and as seeming to
depend on it alone. On the other hand, the various perceptions or modes of knowledge present
in us may be called its passions, in a general sense,
for it is often not our soul which makes them such
as they are, and the soul always receives them from
the things that are represented by them. [. . .]

31. *There is a little gland in the brain where the soul exercises its functions more particularly than in the other parts of the body*

We need to recognize also that although the
soul is joined to the whole body, nevertheless
there is a certain part of the body where it exercises its functions more particularly than in all the
others. It is commonly held that this part is the
brain, or perhaps the heart—the brain because
the sense organs are related to it, and the heart
because we feel the passions as if they were in it.
But on carefully examining the matter I think I
have clearly established that the part of the body
in which the soul directly exercises its functions
is not the heart at all, or the whole of the brain. It
is rather the innermost part of the brain, which is
a certain very small gland situated in the middle
of the brain's substance and suspended above the
passage through which the spirits in the brain's
anterior cavities communicate with those in its

posterior cavities. The slightest movements on the part of this gland may alter very greatly the course of these spirits, and conversely any change, however slight, taking place in the course of the spirits may do much to change the movements of the gland.

32. *How we know that this gland is the principal seat of the soul*

Apart from this gland, there cannot be any other place in the whole body where the soul directly exercises its functions. I am convinced of this by the observation that all the other parts of our brain are double, as also are all the organs of our external senses—eyes, hands, ears and so on. But in so far as we have only one simple thought about a given object at any one time, there must necessarily be some place where the two images coming through the two eyes, or the two impressions coming from a single object through the double organs of any other sense, can come together in a single image

or impression before reaching the soul, so that they do not present to it two objects instead of one. We can easily understand that these images or other impressions are unified in this gland by means of the spirits which fill the cavities of the brain. But they cannot exist united in this way in any other place in the body except as a result of their being united in this gland.

Study Questions

1. Explain Elisabeth's fundamental challenge for Descartes' account of the mind-body relation.
2. What is the example of heaviness in Descartes' first letter supposed to show?
3. What is Descartes' principle for determining whether a property should be attributed to the body or the mind?
4. According to Descartes, how does the body interact with the mind?

The Duel between Body and Soul 4.2

PAUL BLOOM

PAUL BLOOM (1963–) is Professor of Psychology and Cognitive Science at Yale University. His research focuses on the development and nature of our commonsense understanding of ourselves and other people. Aside from his work on how we understand the relation between bodies and minds, Bloom has investigated the nature of moral reasoning, emotions (such as disgust and pleasure), and our understanding of fiction and art. Recently, he has argued that our sense of pleasure is importantly related to our understanding of objects as encompassing a hidden essence. In this short piece from the *New York Times*, Bloom alludes to some of the arguments and evidence from his 2004 book, *Descartes' Baby*, which leads Bloom to conclude that we are natural-born dualists. In his most recent book, *The Science of Pleasure: Why We Like What We Like*, Bloom contends that our propensity to experience pleasure in something is importantly connected to our assessments of its essential nature.

New Haven—What people think about many of the big issues that will be discussed in the next two months—like gay marriage, stem-cell research and the role of religion in public life—is intimately related to their views on human nature. And while there may be differences between Republicans and Democrats, one fundamental assumption is accepted by almost everyone. This would be reassuring—if science didn't tell us that this assumption is mistaken.

People see bodies and souls as separate; we are common-sense dualists. The President's Council on Bioethics expressed this belief system with considerable eloquence in its December 2003 report "Being Human": "We have both corporeal and noncorporeal aspects. We are embodied spirits and inspirited bodies (or, if you will, embodied minds and minded bodies)."

Our dualism makes it possible for us to appreciate stories where people are liberated from their bodies. In the movie "13 Going on 30," a teenager wakes up as Jennifer Garner, just as a 12-year-old was once transformed into Tom Hanks in "Big." Characters can trade bodies, as in "Freaky Friday," or battle for control of a single body, as when Steve Martin and Lily Tomlin fight it out in "All of Me."

Body-hopping is not a Hollywood invention. Franz Kafka tells of a man who wakes up one morning as a gigantic insect. Homer, writing hundreds of years before the birth of Christ, describes how the companions of Odysseus were transformed into pigs—but their minds were unchanged, and so they wept. Children easily understand stories in which the frog becomes a prince or a villain takes control of a superhero's body.

In fact, most people think that a far more radical transformation actually takes place; they believe that the soul can survive the complete destruction of the body. The soul's eventual fate varies; most Americans believe it ascends to heaven or descends into hell, while people from other cultures believe that it enters a parallel spirit world, or occupies some other body, human or animal.

Our dualist perspective also frames how we think about the issues that are most central to our lives. It is no accident that a bioethics committee is talking about spirits. When people wonder about the moral status of animals or fetuses or stem cells, for instance, they often ask: Does it have a soul? If the answer is yes, then it is a precious individual, deserving of compassion and care.

In the case of abortion, our common-sense dualism can support either side of the issue. We use phrases like "my body" and "my brain," describing our bodies and body parts as if they were possessions. Some people insist that all of us—including pregnant women—own our bodies, and therefore can use them as we wish. To others, the organism residing inside a pregnant body has a soul of its own, possibly from the moment of conception, and would thereby have its own rights.

Admittedly, not everyone explicitly endorses dualism; some people wouldn't be caught dead talking about souls or spirits. But common-sense dualism still frames how we think about such issues. That's why people often appeal to science to answer the question "When does life begin?" in the hopes that an objective answer will settle the abortion debate once and for all. But the question is not really about life in any biological sense. It is instead asking about the magical moment at which a cluster of cells becomes more than a mere physical thing. It is a question about the soul.

And it is not a question that scientists could ever answer. The qualities of mental life that we associate with souls are purely corporeal; they emerge from biochemical processes in the brain. This is starkly demonstrated in cases in which damage to the brain wipes out capacities as central to our humanity as memory, self-control and decision-making.

One implication of this scientific view of mental life is that it takes the important moral questions away from the scientists. As the Harvard psychologist Steven Pinker points out, the qualities that we are most interested in from a moral standpoint—consciousness and the capacity to experience pain—result from brain processes that emerge gradually in both development and evolution. There is no moment at which a soulless body becomes an ensouled one, and so scientific research cannot provide objective answers to the questions that matter the most to us.

Some scholars are confident that people will come to accept this scientific view. In the domain of bodies, after all, most of us accept that common sense is wrong. We concede that apparently solid objects are actually mostly empty space, and consist of tiny particles and fields of energy. Perhaps the same sort of reconciliation will happen in the domain of souls, and it will come to be broadly recognized that dualism, though intuitively appealing, is factually mistaken.

I am less optimistic. I once asked my 6-year-old son, Max, about the brain, and he said that it is very important and involved in a lot of thinking—but it is not the source of dreaming or feeling sad, or loving his brother. Max said that's what he does, though he admitted that his brain might help him out. Studies from developmental psychology suggest that young children do not see their brain as the source of conscious experience and will. They see it instead as a tool we use for certain mental operations. It is a cognitive prosthesis, added to the soul to increase its computing power.

This understanding might not be so different from that of many adults. People are often surprised to find out that certain parts of the brain are shown to be active—they "light up"—in a brain scanner when subjects think about religion, sex or race. This surprise reveals the tacit assumption that the brain is involved in some aspects of mental life but not others. Even experts, when describing such results, slip into dualistic language: "I think about sex and this activates such-as-so part of my brain"—as if there are two separate things going on, first the thought and then the brain activity.

It gets worse. The conclusion that our souls are flesh is profoundly troubling to many, as it clashes with the notion that the soul survives the death of the body. It is a much harder pill to swallow than evolution, then, and might be impossible to reconcile with many religious views. Pope John Paul II was clear about this, conceding our bodies may have evolved, but that theories which "consider the spirit as emerging from the forces of living matter, or as a mere epiphenomenon of this matter, are incompatible with the truth about man."

This clash is not going to be easily resolved. The great conflict between science and religion in the last century was over evolutionary biology. In this century, it will be over psychology, and the stakes are nothing less than our souls.

Study Questions

1. In what ways does our dualistic perspective frame our understanding of the world?
2. Why is Bloom not very optimistic that people will come to accept the scientific view that the qualities of mental life emerge from the biochemical processes in the brain?

4.3   Brain Damage, Mind Damage, and Dualism

MARK PHELAN, ERIC MANDELBAUM, AND SHAUN NICHOLS

MARK PHELAN (1976–) is an Assistant Professor of Philosophy at Lawrence University of Wisconsin. Previously, he was a Postdoctoral Researcher in the Philosophy and Cognitive Science Departments at Yale University. His work focuses on interactions between linguistic pragmatic phenomena and cognitive processing. His papers focus on such topics as figurative language, intentional action, group minds, the nature of evidence, and experimental research on pragmatic processing. Eric Mandelbaum (1981–) is a Mind/Brain/Behavior Postdoctoral Fellow at Harvard University. His contribution to this essay was supported by an Oxford Martin Research Fellowship at the University of Oxford. His work focuses on cognitive architecture, belief acquisition, belief storage, implicit racism, and unconscious inference. Shaun Nichols (1964–) is a Professor of Philosophy at the University of Arizona and a leading experimental philosopher. In this selection the authors argue that brain damage poses a fatal objection to Cartesian dualism over and above the interaction problem for dualism.

Living is a rather good thing. Living longer is (generally) better. Asked if they would rather keep living after today, most people would agree that they would. However, there might come a point when living doesn't seem like such a wonderful thing. If you find yourself at age 110 bedridden, incapable of controlling basic bodily functions, and in constant agony, living may not look so good anymore. From this we can suppose that, if what came with immortality were the agonizing ravages of our physical bodies, we might not want immortality. If living in agony isn't good, then living in agony forever would be infinitely worse.

But perhaps the most important thing about a person—the mind—is protected from the inevitable decay of the biological organism. According to a family of influential philosophical views—a family we'll characterize with the label "dualism"—the mind is an immaterial soul that can continue existing after biological death.[1] In the European philosophical tradition, dualism is most prominently associated with René Descartes, who argued that the mind is an immaterial substance that communicates with the physical brain. As a result, he maintained that "the decay of the body does not imply the destruction of the mind." And this, he thought, "afford[s] to men the hope of a future life." For, "while the body can very easily perish," Descartes writes, "the mind is immortal by its nature" (Descartes 1641/1984, 10). Although this venerable philosophical view of the mind may seem abstract and detached from everyday life, it resonates with what most people think, according to the psychologist Paul Bloom. Bloom writes: "most people…believe that the soul can survive the complete destruction of the body" (p. 210, this volume). By contrast, other prominent philosophical theories of the mind make it difficult to see how this is possible. Physicalist accounts of the mind, accounts that equate mental states to neurological states of the brain, identify the mind with a decaying organism, and

M. Phelan, E. Mandelbaum, and S. Nichols, "Brain Damage, Mind Damage, and Dualism."

thus seem to preclude the continued existence of a mind after (biological) death.

While dualism appears to provide for the possibility of the immortality of the mind,[2] it faces the problem of *interaction*—if the mind is an immaterial substance, how can it causally interact with physical bodies (Elisabeth, p. 204, this volume)? Some philosophers are optimistic that dualism can address the interaction problem (see, e.g., Lycan 2010). Although it is intuitively puzzling how an immaterial soul can push around physical objects, one reply is to acknowledge that there are lots of puzzling phenomena in the world, especially when it comes to what causes what. For present purposes, we want to set aside the interaction objection itself. The effects of brain damage, we will argue, pose an acute explanatory challenge over and above the interaction problem.

Let's explore the problem of brain damage by considering the famous case of Clive Wearing (CW). CW lived a normal life for almost 50 years, when he contracted a form of viral encephalitis. The virus not only caused "anterograde amnesia," a disability where one can no longer form new memories, but it also caused a fairly severe form of "retrograde amnesia," a disability where one cannot recall events and facts from before the onset of the neurological trauma. Brain scans on CW show that the areas associated with memory (e.g., the hippocampus) were largely destroyed. Having both deficits, CW's case covers two clear types of amnesia: an inability to recall events and facts prior to a traumatic incident and an inability to form new memories after a traumatic incident.[3]

According to dualism, the mind and the brain are distinct substances, with the mind existing wholly outside the physical world. Yet the effects of brain damage are quite difficult to explain if the mind is on an entirely separate plane from the body, for brain damage seems to have drastic effects on mental states like memory. So, if the mind is a nonphysical soul, not susceptible to the "corruption of the body," then how could brain damage—a physical process—damage the mind?

Following the scientists who work on patients like CW, we have said that CW's case involves the dramatic loss of specific memories of the past as well as critical mental capacities for forming memories. Moreover, we have followed the scientists in suggesting that the damage to the mind was caused by brain damage. But the dualist might maintain that this is all a mistake. While it might appear that CW has mind damage, the dualist may insist that this is not really the case, instead alleging that his mind remains completely undamaged. For the dualist to defend this view, though, she needs to provide some explanation for the *appearance* of mental damage. Dualism's most promising strategy for explaining the apparent mental damage rests on the idea of a brain-mind interface.[4] Suppose the brain is (in part) a kind of modem or information router, one that sends physical inputs from the body to the immaterial mind and receives transmissions from the mind, transforming them into electrochemical responses that the body can use.[5] If the brain and the mind normally communicate with one another, then some failure to send information in one direction or the other may explain the behavior of a brain-damaged patient like CW. This strategy, if defensible, would preserve the possibility that the mind is not damaged by brain damage, in keeping with dualism.

Let's clarify the specifics of this strategy by focusing on CW's retrograde amnesia. CW, like most amnesiacs, has selective amnesia. For example, he can remember that he has children, but he cannot remember their childhood; he can remember how to play piano, but he cannot remember any past episodes of playing the piano; he can remember that he is married, but he can no longer remember getting married. How can the dualist explain these phenomena? If there has been no mental damage, then why can't CW retrieve his memories?

To preserve the integrity of the nonphysical soul, the dualist might say that the problem is restricted to the communication between the (undamaged) mind and the damaged brain. However, it isn't enough for the dualist simply to say, "It's a communication problem." Since we are, for the moment at least, granting that interaction between the immaterial mind and the physical body is possible, we are willing to grant that such communication is possible. But we are now comparing the merits of the physicalist explanation of these deficits to the merits of a dualist account. Since the physicalist supposes that the mind is, at the very least, affected by the brain, the physicalist can point to connections between the brain damage and the corresponding mental deficits. Such an explanation can give a fairly detailed account of how such damage occurs, and such an account would be explanatorily superior to the dualist merely saying, "It's a communication problem." So, for the dualist, more needs to be said about the nature of the problem. There are two obvious options available. One possibility is that while the mind is perfectly fine, the brain garbles input that comes to it from the mind (see the "dualist distorted input view" on Figure 1). The other possibility is that the brain produces the wrong output sent to the mind (see the "dualist distorted out-

put view" on Figure 1). Let's consider each of these explanations in turn.

Let's begin with the distorted input view by focusing on a specific example. When asked, "Do you remember your wedding?" CW claims that he does not. The dualist might maintain that CW has the memories of his wedding stored in his immaterial mind, but the neurological damage causes his response to come out wrong: instead of saying, "It was in a beautiful setting, with lots of friends there to celebrate with us...," he just says, "I don't remember." But this dualist response leaves one wanting: why would the brain damage only selectively affect some of CW's responses? Compare: if he is asked whether he is married, he will respond affirmatively. So, in order for the dualist response to be viable, it must explain the selective effects, in particular, why CW's answer "comes out wrong" in some cases but not others; otherwise, such a response

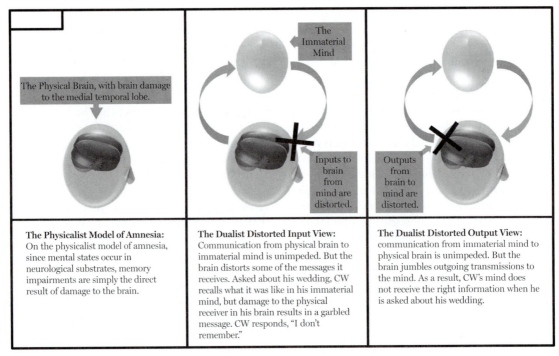

The Physicalist Model of Amnesia:
On the physicalist model of amnesia, since mental states occur in neurological substrates, memory impairments are simply the direct result of damage to the brain.

The Dualist Distorted Input View:
Communication from physical brain to immaterial mind is unimpeded. But the brain distorts some of the messages it receives. Asked about his wedding, CW recalls what it was like in his immaterial mind, but damage to the physical receiver in his brain results in a garbled message. CW responds, "I don't remember."

The Dualist Distorted Output View:
communication from immaterial mind to physical brain is unimpeded. But the brain jumbles outgoing transmissions to the mind. As a result, CW's mind does not receive the right information when he is asked about his wedding.

FIGURE 1

lacks sufficient explanatory detail to compete with the physicalist explanation. Perhaps, instead, the dualist will respond by saying that the mind does not send out the correct memory; instead, it just sends out instructions to say, "I don't remember." But again, why should the soul send out these instructions only selectively? And, anyway, why send out instructions to say *that*?

Perhaps it is better for the dualist to explain CW's problems by looking at things from the other direction, by supposing these are problems with the outgoing line, not the incoming one (see the "dualist distorted output view" on Figure 1). On this take, the dualist would respond that because the line is down, the signals from the brain can't get through to the mind to allow the formation of new memories; in other words, the anterograde amnesiac brain can't send the signals out to the mind to get stored in memory. When someone asks CW, "Do you remember your wedding?" the sounds get transmitted into his ears, but when his brain-modem sends the signals to his mind, it just comes out as jumbled garbage. Hence, his mind does not receive the right information in order to form the question. However, this dualist response makes it puzzling why CW answers, "I don't remember." If you asked someone on the street how to get to the Eiffel Tower, a reasonable response would be, "I don't know" (assuming she didn't know). If, on the other hand, all she heard was mumbled garbage, a reasonable response would be, "Come again?" But CW never responds by saying, "I didn't hear you" or "I don't understand the question"; rather, he seems to perfectly understand the question and just cannot answer it, for he can't ascertain the requisite knowledge required to answer it.

So, neither the distorted input view nor the distorted output view provides a very satisfying explanation of *the mere appearance* of mind damage resulting from a damaged brain.[6] Perhaps the dualist has no option but to countenance *actual damage to the mind* stemming from physical damage to the brain. This raises further explanatory burdens for dualism, to be sure. But, more important for the present context, it also seems to defeat dualism's promise to maintain our minds in the face of biological decay. If the dualist explains CW's responses as most scientists do, in terms of actual mind damage (i.e., the dramatic loss of specific memories of the past along with critical mental capacities for forming new memories), then the dualist admits that the death of the brain can deprive whatever soul lives on of past memories of its human life, as well as the capacity to store new experiences of the afterlife.[7] This means the immortal soul will lose the love we feel when we recall when our children were young, the pride in our past accomplishments, the happiness we experience when we remember times spent with our dear friends.... If the dualist has to embrace mind damage, then she must accept that the joy of remembrances of such past events dies with our physical body. And one might ask what good eternal life is for a soul that loses that.

Notes

1. This is to paint with a very broad brush. There are many different types of dualism that one might hold. In this essay, we focus on what is called "substance dualism," according to which the mind consists in an altogether different type of substance than the body, the mind being a mental substance and the body being a physical one. More specifically, we focus on a substance dualism that allows for causal interaction between the physical and mental substances. "Property dualism" is a much weaker position than substance dualism. The property dualist thinks that there is just one type of substance in this world, physical substance, but two ultimate types of properties: physical and mental properties. The mental properties are analyzed as basic and fundamental properties that somehow emerge from the brain. We focus on substance dualism because, unlike property dualism, substance dualism (at least in its traditional form) maintains that the death of the brain wouldn't cause the death of the mind.

2. The issue of immortality is complicated by questions about what makes a person the same across time.

For instance, on some views, the persistence of the soul would not necessarily mean the persistence of the self. For this article, we set aside those additional complications (but see Chapter 7 on the self).

3. For further discussion of CW see Sacks' (2007) *New Yorker* article.

4. Indeed, Descartes himself had an elaborate theory about how the mind and the brain communicated with one another (see Reading 4.1, this volume).

5. Of course, had one not granted a solution to the interaction problem, the problem would arise here, too, if one wondered how physical signals can affect a nonphysical mind (and how a nonphysical mind can send a physical signal).

6. The dualist might attempt other explanations. For instance, the dualist might reply that the brain isn't a single modem, but is instead a slew of modems communicating with the mind for different purposes, and this is what explains CW's pattern of behavior. But it's not clear that this response is adequate. Suppose we were to ask the dualist, how many modems does the brain have exactly? As we mentioned earlier, CW seems to be both unable to recall events and facts from prior to his illness and unable to form new memories after his illness, but there are people who have just one kind of deficit or the other. So, the dualist would have to posit two different modems to account for these two separable problems. And it seems that the dualist can't stop here. Numerous other kinds of brain damage would seem to require other modems: some traumas render people unable to identify tools; some cause people to fail to identify animals; some cause people to be unable to recognize who people are from seeing their face.... Should we assume there is a modem for each type of deficit? We started by assuming that maybe the brain is the modem for the mind and now we are asked to suppose that the brain contains multitudes of modems. Perhaps the most important challenge for the *multiple modem* line of response is to articulate some underlying principle that would justify positing a modem at any point. It would be *un*principled for the dualist just to posit another modem every time there is some datum his theory didn't predict. Alternatively, the dualist might avoid unprincipled multiplication of modems by pointing to neural complexity. Like a computer, the brain has complex, interrelated processes. Though your laptop has just one Wi-Fi card installed, various patterns of local damage to different internal processes can render it unable to connect to the Internet in distinctive ways. Maybe the dualist would suggest something similar is going on in various cases of brain damage. But this response still faces the challenge of explaining the *specific pattern* of CW's deficits. Assume, as this response suggests, that localized damage renders CW's brain unable to transmit questions about past events to his immaterial mind. That still leaves it a mystery why CW responds, "I don't remember," to a question his mind never received. These two examples show how difficult it is for the dualist to articulate an account of the mind-brain relation that explains actual patterns of behavior that follow brain damage.

7. One might also think that our memories are what underwrite our personal identity (Parfit 1984). Thus, it may not even make sense to say that it would be *your* soul that survived death.

References

Bloom, P. "The Duel Between Body and Soul." *New York Times*, September 10, 2004. Reprinted in this volume.

Descartes. R. *Meditations on First Philosophy*, trans. John Cottingham, Robert Stoothoff, and Dugald Murdoch. In *The Philosophical Writings of Descartes*. Cambridge: Cambridge University Press, 1641/1984.

Lycan, W. "Giving Dualism Its Due." *Australasian Journal of Philosophy* 87, no. 4 (2010): 551–563.

Parfit, D. *Reasons and Person*. Oxford: Oxford University Press, 1984.

Sacks, O. "The Abyss: Music and Amnesia." *New Yorker*, September 24, 2007. http://www.new yorker.com/reporting/2007/09/24/070924fa_fact_sacks?currentPage=all (accessed December 1, 2010).

Study Questions

1. Why is the brain damage objection a different objection from the interaction objection?
2. Why might the dualist distorted input view be seen as unappealing?
3. Why might the dualist distorted output view be seen as unappealing?

Eliminative Materialism and the Propositional Attitudes

4.4

PAUL CHURCHLAND

PAUL CHURCHLAND (1942–) recently retired from the Vaultz Chair of Philosophy at the University of California, San Diego. He is a member of San Diego's Institute for Neural Computation. Churchland has published on the philosophy of mind, philosophy of science, and perception. His book, *Matter and Consciousness,* remains a popular introductory text to the philosophy of mind more than twenty years after its initial publication. Among his most famous doctrines is the one defended in this selection: that the propositional attitudes should be eliminated from our ontology. Churchland has also argued that perception is, contra Fodor, not modular but is constantly being affected even at its lowest levels by our cognition.

Eliminative materialism is the thesis that our common-sense conception of psychological phenomena constitutes a radically false theory, a theory so fundamentally defective that both the principles and the ontology of that theory will eventually be displaced, rather than smoothly reduced, by completed neuroscience. Our mutual understanding and even our introspection may then be reconstituted within the conceptual framework of completed neuroscience, a theory we may expect to be more powerful by far than the common-sense psychology it displaces, and more substantially integrated within physical science generally. My purpose in this paper is to explore these projections, especially as they bear on (1) the principal elements of common-sense psychology: the propositional attitudes (beliefs, desires, etc.), and (2) the conception of rationality in which these elements figure.

This focus represents a change in the fortunes of materialism. Twenty years ago, emotions, qualia, and "raw feels" were held to be the principal stumbling blocks for the materialist program.

With these barriers dissolving,[1] the locus of opposition has shifted. Now it is the realm of the intentional, the realm of the propositional attitude, that is most commonly held up as being both irreducible to and ineliminable in favor of anything from within a materialist framework. Whether and why this is so, we must examine.

Such an examination will make little sense, however, unless it is first appreciated that the relevant network of common-sense concepts does indeed constitute an empirical theory, with all the functions, virtues, *and perils* entailed by that status. I shall therefore begin with a brief sketch of this view and a summary rehearsal of its rationale. The resistance it encounters still surprises me. After all, common sense has yielded up many theories. Recall the view that space has a preferred direction in which all things fall; that weight is an intrinsic feature of a body; that a force-free moving object will promptly return to rest; that the sphere of the heavens turns daily; and so on. These examples are clear, perhaps, but people seem willing to concede a theoretical component within common sense only

Paul Churchland, "Eliminative Materialism and the Propositional Attitudes," *The Journal of Philosophy*, 78, no. 2, (1981). Reprinted by permission of the publication.

if (1) the theory and the common sense involved are safely located in antiquity, and (2) the relevant theory is now so clearly false that its speculative nature is inescapable. Theories are indeed easier to discern under these circumstances. But the vision of hindsight is always 20/20. Let us aspire to some foresight for a change. […]

WHY FOLK PSYCHOLOGY MIGHT (REALLY) BE FALSE

Given that folk psychology is an empirical theory, it is at least an abstract possibility that its principles are radically false and that its ontology is an illusion. With the exception of eliminative materialism, however, none of the major positions takes this possibility seriously. None of them doubts the basic integrity or truth of folk psychology (hereafter, "FP"), and all of them anticipate a future in which its laws and categories are conserved. This conservatism is not without some foundation. After all, FP does enjoy a substantial amount of explanatory and predictive success. And what better grounds than this for confidence in the integrity of its categories?

What better grounds indeed? Even so, the presumption in FP's favor is spurious, born of innocence and tunnel vision. A more searching examination reveals a different picture. First, we must reckon not only with FP's successes, but with its explanatory failures, and with their extent and seriousness. Second, we must consider the long-term history of FP, its growth, fertility, and current promise of future development. And third, we must consider what sorts of theories are *likely* to be true of the etiology of our behavior, given what else we have learned about ourselves in recent history. That is, we must evaluate FP with regard to its coherence and continuity with fertile and well-established theories in adjacent and overlapping domains—with evolutionary theory, biology, and neuroscience, for example—because active coherence with the rest of what we presume to know is perhaps the final measure of any hypothesis.

A serious inventory of this sort reveals a very troubled situation, one which would evoke open skepticism in the case of any theory less familiar and dear to us. Let me sketch some relevant detail. When one centers one's attention not on what FP can explain, but on what it cannot explain or fails even to address, one discovers that there is a very great deal. As examples of central and important mental phenomena that remain largely or wholly mysterious within the framework of FP, consider the nature and dynamics of mental illness, the faculty of creative imagination, or the ground of intelligence differences between individuals. Consider our utter ignorance of the nature and psychological functions of sleep, that curious state in which a third of one's life is spent. Reflect on the common ability to catch an outfield fly ball on the run, or hit a moving car with a snowball. Consider the internal construction of a 3-D visual image from subtle differences in the 2-D array of stimulations in our respective retinas. Consider the rich variety of perceptual illusions, visual and otherwise. Or consider the miracle of memory, with its lightning capacity for relevant retrieval. On these and many other mental phenomena, FP sheds negligible light.

One particularly outstanding mystery is the nature of the learning process itself, especially where it involves large-scale conceptual change, and especially as it appears in its pre-linguistic or entirely nonlinguistic form (as in infants and animals), which is by far the most common form in nature. FP is faced with special difficulties here, since its conception of learning as the manipulation and storage of propositional attitudes founders on the fact that how to formulate, manipulate, and store a rich fabric of propositional attitudes is itself something that is learned, and is only one among many acquired cognitive skills. FP would thus appear constitutionally incapable of even addressing this most basic of mysteries.[2]

Failures on such a large scale do not (yet) show that FP is a false theory, but they do move that prospect well into the range of real possibility, and they do show decisively that FP is *at best* a highly superficial theory, a partial and unpenetrating gloss on a deeper and more complex reality. Having reached this opinion, we may be forgiven for exploring the possibility that FP provides a positively misleading sketch of our internal kinematics and dynamics, one whose success is owed more to selective application and forced interpretation on our part than to genuine theoretical insight on FP's part.

A look at the history of FP does little to allay such fears, once raised. The story is one of retreat, infertility, and decadence. The presumed domain of FP used to be much larger than it is now. In primitive cultures, the behavior of most of the elements of nature were understood in intentional terms. The wind could know anger, the moon jealousy, the river generosity, the sea fury, and so forth. These were not metaphors. Sacrifices were made and auguries undertaken to placate or divine the changing passions of the gods. Despite its sterility, this animistic approach to nature has dominated our history, and it is only in the last two or three thousand years that we have restricted FP's literal application to the domain of the higher animals.

Even in this preferred domain, however, both the content and the success of FP have not advanced sensibly in two or three thousand years. The FP of the Greeks is essentially the FP we use today, and we are negligibly better at explaining human behavior in its terms than was Sophocles. This is a very long period of stagnation and infertility for any theory to display, especially when faced with such an enormous backlog of anomalies and mysteries in its own explanatory domain. Perfect theories, perhaps, have no need to evolve. But FP is profoundly imperfect. Its failure to develop its resources and extend its range of success is therefore darkly curious, and one must query the integrity of its basic categories. To use Imre Lakatos' terms, FP is a stagnant or degenerating research program, and has been for millennia.

Explanatory success to date is of course not the only dimension in which a theory can display virtue or promise. A troubled or stagnant theory may merit patience and solicitude on other grounds; for example, on grounds that it is the only theory or theoretical approach that fits well with other theories about adjacent subject matters, or the only one that promises to reduce to or be explained by some established background theory whose domain encompasses the domain of the theory at issue. In sum, it may rate credence because it holds promise of theoretical integration. How does FP rate in this dimension?

It is just here, perhaps, that FP fares poorest of all. If we approach *homo sapiens* from the perspective of natural history and the physical sciences, we can tell a coherent story of his constitution, development, and behavioral capacities which encompasses particle physics, atomic and molecular theory, organic chemistry, evolutionary theory, biology, physiology, and materialistic neuroscience. That story, though still radically incomplete, is already extremely powerful, outperforming FP at many points even in its own domain. And it is deliberately and self-consciously coherent with the rest of our developing world picture. In short, the greatest theoretical synthesis in the history of the human race is currently in our hands, and parts of it already provide searching descriptions and explanations of human sensory input, neural activity, and motor control.

But FP is no part of this growing synthesis. Its intentional categories stand magnificently alone, without visible prospect of reduction to that larger corpus. A successful reduction cannot be ruled out, in my view, but FP's explanatory impotence and long stagnation inspire little faith that its categories will find themselves neatly reflected in the framework of neuroscience. On the contrary, one is reminded of how alchemy must have looked as elemental chemistry was taking form, how Aristotelean cosmology must have looked as classical mechanics was being articulated, or how the vitalist conception of life must have looked as organic chemistry marched forward.

In sketching a fair summary of this situation, we must make a special effort to abstract from the fact that FP is a central part of our current *lebenswelt*, and serves as the principal vehicle of our interpersonal commerce. For these facts provide FP with a conceptual inertia that goes far beyond its purely theoretical virtues. Restricting ourselves to this latter dimension, what we must say is that FP suffers explanatory failures on an epic scale, that it has been stagnant for at least twenty-five centuries, and that its categories appear (so far) to be incommensurable with or orthogonal to the categories of the background physical science whose long-term claim to explain human behavior seems undeniable. Any theory that meets this description must be allowed a serious candidate for outright elimination.

We can of course insist on no stronger conclusion at this stage. Nor is it my concern to do so. We are here exploring a possibility, and the facts demand no more, and no less, than it be taken seriously. The distinguishing feature of the eliminative materialist is that he takes it very seriously indeed.

Notes

1. See Paul Feyerabend, "Materialism and the Mind-Body Problem," *Review of Metaphysics*, xvii.1, 65 (September 1963): 49–66; Richard Rorty, "Mind-Body Identity, Privacy, and Categories," *ibid.*, xix.1, 73 (September 1965): 24–54; and my *Scientific Realism and the Plasticity of Mind* (New York: Cambridge, 1979).

2. A possible response here is to insist that the cognitive activity of animals and infants is linguaformal in its elements, structures, and processing right from birth. J. A. Fodor, in *The Language of Thought* (New York: Crowell 1975), has erected a positive theory of thought on the assumption that the innate forms of cognitive activity have precisely the form here denied. For a critique of Fodor's view, see Patricia Churchland, "Fodor on Language Learning," *Synthese*, xxxviii, 1 (May 1978): 149–159.

Study Questions

1. If the propositional attitudes don't exist, then why do they explain behavior so well?
2. Assume that Churchland is right about the propositional attitudes playing no explanatory role in, for example, visual perception. Would that fact be a reason for eliminating the attitudes?
3. Churchland believes that the modern synthesis is bringing different disciplines together, causing a consilience of different interests. If this is the case, then why do we see a proliferation, not reduction, of different departments across university campuses?

4.5   Against Arguments from Reference

 RON MALLON, EDOUARD MACHERY, SHAUN NICHOLS, AND STEPHEN STICH

RON MALLON (1971–) is an Associate Professor of Philosophy at Washington University–St. Louis. His research is in social philosophy, philosophy of cognitive psychology, and moral psychology. During his time visiting the University of Hong Kong, Mallon was crucial in carrying out the first cross-cultural experimental investigation of philosophical theories of reference. He has also made significant experimental contributions

R. Mallon, E. Machery, S. Nichols, and S. Stich (2009). "Against Arguments from Reference," in D. Chalmers, R. Manley, and R. Wasserman (eds.), *Metametaphysics* (2009). By permission of Oxford University Press.

on the topics of moral psychology and philosophical methodology. Edouard Machery (1975–) is an Associate Professor of the History and Philosophy of Science at the University of Pittsburgh. His research focuses on concepts, cognition, and reference and how each of these is influenced by evolution and culture. Machery has authored or coauthored seminal works of experimental philosophy on topics such as reference, the folk understanding of consciousness, and moral psychology. Shaun Nichols (1964–) is a Professor of Philosophy at the University of Arizona. Nichols' experimental work has focused on topics such as free will, intentional agency, and moral responsibility, among others. He has also published extensively on the imagination, the emotions, and moral judgments. He has a forthcoming book on free will. Stephen Stich (1943–) is Board of Governors Professor of Philosophy and Cognitive Science at Rutgers University and Honorary Professor of Philosophy at the University of Sheffield. Prior to joining the Rutgers faculty in 1989, he taught at the University of Michigan, the University of Maryland, and the University of California, San Diego. His publications include 6 books, a dozen anthologies, and over 150 articles. He was one of the founders of the experimental philosophy movement, and his former students—including Shaun Nichols, Jonathan Weinberg, Ron Mallon, and Edouard Machery—are now among the leaders in the field. In the included excerpts, the authors argue from specific experimental findings that an important class of philosophical arguments—arguments from reference—are subject to a devastating problem.

ARGUMENTS FROM REFERENCE

Arguments from reference are common in projects throughout philosophy. These arguments can be analyzed into three stages. In the first, philosophers implicitly or explicitly adopt a substantive theory of the reference of a term t (or of a class of terms T, such as theoretical terms).[1] In the second stage, they claim that the reference of t or of members of T has some specific properties. For instance, in some arguments from reference, philosophers argue that the reference relation obtains or fails to obtain—that is, that t refers or fails to refer. Or, in other arguments from reference, they argue that the reference of t has changed. Finally, a philosophically significant conclusion is drawn. These conclusions include metaphysical conclusions—conclusions to the effect that the referent of t exists or does not exist (e.g. Stich 1983; Zack 1993)—and epistemological conclusions—conclusions about the nature of our knowledge about the referent of t (e.g. Boyd 1983, 1988; Kitcher 1993).

Where can we find such arguments from reference? Everywhere in philosophy, it would seem. We begin by reviewing how arguments from reference play a key role in the philosophy of mind, then we suggest they play a similarly important role in other areas including the philosophy of science, social theory, and metaethics.

The Philosophy of Mind: The Debate over Eliminative Materialism

Eliminativists in the philosophy of mind (Churchland 1981; Stich 1983) defend the surprising claim that the propositional attitudes like beliefs and desires that figure in the explanations of behavior offered by folk psychology literally do not exist. Eliminativists argue that these propositional attitudes are posits of a folk theory of mind that is spectacularly false in light of the emerging sciences of the mind and brain. They conclude that the posits of this theory—beliefs and desires—don't exist.

Consider how this argument fits the three steps of the arguments from reference.

(Step 1) Assumption of a substantive theory of reference.

Eliminativists propose that mental state terms like "belief" and "desire" are defined by their role in a folk theory, namely the folk theory of mind. They assume that if these terms have referents, they must be entities that satisfy (or come close to satisfying) the relevant definitions. That is, eliminativists assume some version of a descriptivist theory of reference for mental state terms like "belief" and "desire." While such theories may take a variety of forms, they typically agree on the following points:

D1. Competent speakers associate a description with a term *t*. This description specifies a set of properties.

D2. An object is the referent of *t* if and only if it uniquely or best satisfies the description associated with it.

In the absence of an entity that satisfies the description (or at least comes close), the term is empty.

(Step 2) Claim about reference.

Eliminativists claim that the emerging scientific facts suggest that nothing satisfies the descriptions folk psychology associates with "belief" and "desire." Thus, "belief" and "desire" do not refer.

(Step 3) Philosophically significant conclusion.

Eliminativists conclude that, since "belief" and "desire" do not refer, beliefs and desires do not exist.

How does this eliminativist argument fare? As William Lycan (1988) has pointed out, the eliminativist conclusion follows from the falsity of folk psychology only on the assumption of some descriptivist theory of reference (in step 1).[2] But descriptivist theories of reference

have been sharply contested by causal-historical theories of reference, such as those defended by Kripke (1972/1980) and Putnam (1975). Like descriptivist theories, causal-historical theories of reference may take a variety of forms. However, they typically agree on the following points:

C1. A term *t* is introduced into a linguistic community for the purpose of referring to a particular thing (e.g. a person or a property). The term continues to refer to that thing as long as its uses are linked to the thing via an appropriate causal chain of successive users: every user of the term acquired it from another user, who acquired it in turn from someone else, and so on, back to the first user who introduced the term.

C2. Speakers may associate descriptions with terms. But after the term is introduced, the associated description does not play any role in the fixation of the referent. The referent may entirely fail to satisfy the description.

If, like Lycan, one adopts some causal-historical theory of reference, the eliminativist conclusion does not follow. Here is how Lycan makes the point:

> I am entirely willing to give up fairly large chunks of our commonsensical or platitudinous theory of belief or desire (or of almost anything else) and decide that we were just wrong about a lot of things, without drawing the inference that we are no longer talking about belief or desire. To put the matter crudely, I incline away from Lewis's Carnapian and/or Rylean cluster theory of reference of theoretical terms, and toward Putnam's (1975) causal-historical theory. (Lycan 1988, 31–32)

So, by assuming a different theory of reference than the eliminativist, Lycan draws the opposite conclusion, viz. that beliefs and desires *do* exist.

Of course the simple descriptivist and causal-historical theories we sketch here do not exhaust options for specifying a substantive theory of reference. But the moral we want to draw is quite general: depending on the substantive theory of reference one assumes about a term or a class of terms, one can draw different metaphysical conclusions. [...]

SEMANTICS, CROSS-CULTURAL STYLE

Finding the Correct Theory of Reference: The Method of Cases

The arguments sketched in the previous section all hinge on what the correct theory of reference is. But how do we know which theory of reference is correct? Unfortunately, philosophers of language have rarely addressed this methodological issue explicitly. However, it is clear from the arguments for and against specific theories of reference that the correct theory of reference for a term (or for a class of terms such as proper names) is commonly thought to be constrained by our intuitions about the reference of this term (or about the reference of the members of a given class of terms) in actual and fictional cases. For instance, according to Evans (1973), people have the intuition that nowadays the proper name "Madagascar" refers to the large island near the south of Africa, even when they learn that the term was historically used to refer to a region on the mainland of Africa.

We propose that to find the correct theory of reference, philosophers of language are committed to using what is sometimes called "the method of cases":

The method of cases: The correct theory of reference for a class of terms *T* is the theory which is best supported by the intuitions competent users of *T* have about the reference of members of *T* across actual and possible cases.

The method of cases has played a crucial role in the challenge posed to traditional descriptivist theories of reference by the causal-historical theories championed by Kripke and others. Indeed,

Kripke's masterstroke was to propose a number of cases that elicited widely shared intuitions that were inconsistent with traditional descriptivist theories (Kripke 1972/1980).[3]

It will be useful to briefly review one of Kripke's most widely discussed cases involving the reference of proper names. In this case ("the Gödel case"), Kripke imagines a scenario in which a name is widely associated with a description that is false of the original bearer of that name *a*, but true of some other person, *b*. Because descriptivist theories of reference hold that a term refers to the thing that (uniquely or best) satisfies the description associated with the term, a descriptivist theory of reference would seem to hold that the name in Kripke's example refers to *b*, the satisfier of the description. But, Kripke maintains, this is just wrong.

> Suppose that Gödel was not in fact the author of [Gödel's] theorem. A man called "Schmidt"...actually did the work in question. His friend Gödel somehow got hold of the manuscript and it was thereafter attributed to Gödel. On the [descriptivist] view...when our ordinary man uses the name "Gödel," he really means to refer to Schmidt, because Schmidt is the unique person satisfying the description "the man who discovered the incompleteness of arithmetic."...But it seems we are not. We simply are not. (Kripke 1972/1980, 83–84)

In contrast, a causal-historical theory of the reference of proper names is consistent with the intuition that the name continues to refer to its original bearer *a*, because *a* is the person causally-historically linked with contemporary uses of the name. Many contemporary descriptivists allow that these intuitions have falsified traditional forms of descriptivism and try to accommodate these intuitions within more sophisticated descriptivist theories (Evans 1973; Jackson 1998b).

A plausible justification for the method of cases might be the assumption that language users have an implicit theory of reference that produces intuitions about reference. The project for reference theorists can then be conceived by analogy with the Chomskyan project in linguistics. Philosophers of language use people's intuitions about reference to reconstruct the implicit theory that is part of each speaker's cognitive endowment (Segal 2001).

Despite agreement on the method of cases and agreement on many of the intuitions about the cases used in the philosophical literature, a consensus on the correct theory of reference remains elusive.[4] As this paper goes to press, intuitions about cases continue to underdetermine the selection of a correct theory of reference. However, our argument is based not on the diversity of theories that may be constructed around the same set of intuitions, but on the possibility of variation in the intuitions themselves.

Philosophers interested in reference are well aware that intuitions might differ for different classes of terms (e.g. natural kind terms, names, artifact terms, etc.). For instance, cases involving natural kind terms might elicit causal-historical intuitions, while cases involving artifact terms might elicit descriptivist intuitions (e.g. Schwartz 1978, 1980). Because intuitions might differ for different classes of terms, philosophers interested in reference are willing to allow different accounts of reference for different classes of terms (e.g. Devitt and Sterelny 1999). However, as we have previously noted (Machery et al. 2004), the possibility of diverse intuitions about the same cases, for instance about Kripke's Gödel case, plays little role in the contemporary search for a theory of reference. Indeed, contemporary participants in semantic debates seem to assume that the relevant intuitions about cases are more or less universal, and that exceptions can be explained away. As to why we should believe this, little is said. Just what happens to the search for a theory of reference (and the arguments that depend on it) if this assumption is mistaken, is a subject we turn to below. First, however, we consider a fledgling empirical program that casts doubt on this

assumption, suggesting systematic diversity in intuitions about reference.

Cultural Variation in Intuitions about Reference

Recent work in cultural psychology and empirical philosophy has suggested the existence of real and systematic differences in philosophical intuitions. In an important series of experiments, Richard Nisbett and colleagues found large and systematic differences between people in East Asian cultures and people in Western cultures on a number of basic cognitive processes including perception, attention and memory. This burgeoning research program has also discovered group differences in describing, predicting and explaining events, in categorization of objects and in belief revision in the face of new arguments and evidence (for review, see Nisbett et al. 2001; Nisbett 2003; Nisbett and Miyamoto 2005). These findings suggest a dramatic role for culture in shaping human cognition. Inspired by this research program, Weinberg et al. (2001) decided to explore cultural differences in intuitions about cases drawn from philosophical epistemology. These cases were designed to elicit intuitions about the appropriate application of the concept of knowledge, and Weinberg et al. found that there are indeed systematic cross-cultural differences in epistemic intuitions.

The success of Nisbett's research program and Weinberg et al.'s results suggested that other philosophical intuitions, including intuitions about reference, might also admit of systematic cultural differences. In an earlier paper (Machery et al. 2004), we set out to explore this possibility. We began by noting that existing cross-cultural work suggests that East-Asians' categorization judgments depend heavily on similarity while Westerners are more inclined to focus on causation in classification (Watanabe 1998, 1999; Norenzayan et al. 1999), and we hypothesized that this emphasis on causation might make Westerners more likely to rely on causation in linking terms with their referents, favoring the sort of intuitions that Kripke used in support of his causal-historical theory. In fact, this is just what we found.

We constructed a set of vignettes suggested by Kripke's Gödel case, discussed above (Kripke 1972/1980, 93–92). The vignettes were presented in English to American and Chinese subjects.[5] One of the vignettes was closely modeled on Kripke's own Gödel case (see Machery et al. 2004 for more details on the experiment):

Suppose that John has learned in college that Gödel is the man who proved an important mathematical theorem, called the incompleteness of arithmetic. John is quite good at mathematics and he can give an accurate statement of the incompleteness theorem, which he attributes to Gödel as the discoverer. But this is the only thing that he has heard about Gödel. Now suppose that Gödel was not the author of this theorem. A man called "Schmidt," whose body was found in Vienna under mysterious circumstances many years ago, actually did the work in question. His friend Gödel somehow got hold of the manuscript and claimed credit for the work, which was thereafter attributed to Gödel. Thus he has been known as the man who proved the incompleteness of arithmetic. Most people who have heard the name "Gödel" are like John; the claim that Gödel discovered the incompleteness theorem is the only thing they have ever heard about Gödel. When John uses the name "Gödel," is he talking about:

(A) the person who really discovered the incompleteness of arithmetic?
or
(B) the person who got hold of the manuscript and claimed credit for the work?

In two separate studies using four different vignettes, we found that Americans were more likely than Chinese to give causal-historical responses. Thus, we found that probes modeled on Kripke's Gödel case (including one that used Kripke's own words) elicit culturally variable intuitions. As we had predicted, Chinese participants tended to have descriptivist intuitions, while Americans tended to have Kripkean intuitions.

It is important to note that we found significant intra-cultural differences as well. While for each vignette a majority of Americans gave causal-historical responses, in each case a sizable minority of the population (as high as 45% in one case) gave descriptivist responses. Similarly for the Chinese population, for each vignette, a majority of Chinese participants gave descriptivist responses, but in each case a sizable minority (in some cases over 30%) gave causal-historical responses. […]

METAPHYSICS WITHOUT ARGUMENTS FROM REFERENCE

Arguments from reference are a basic philosophical currency, used to establish philosophically significant conclusions in a variety of areas. But if we are right, arguments from reference have to be rejected, given the plausible (but, by no means, conclusively established) assumption that the intuitions many take to be important in finding the correct theory of reference are themselves diverse. The three ways we have considered of accommodating the diversity in intuitions about reference in order to build a theory of reference undermine these arguments from reference.

(i) If philosophers give up on substantive theories of reference, then, obviously, they ought to give up on arguments from reference, since arguments from reference begin with a substantive theory of reference.

(ii) If philosophers endorse a theory of reference because it gives support to their metaphysical commitments, then they do not need arguments from reference. And as long as concrete proposals concerning the justification of theories of reference on the basis of something other than the method of cases have not been put forward, we will remain skeptical of this response to the variation in intuitions about reference.

(iii) If philosophers endorse referential pluralism, then they must justify the assumption that intuitions about reference provide evidence about reference, although variation in these intuitions do not map onto variation in languages or dialects. Supposing this can be done, philosophers must accommodate a relativization of the conclusion of the arguments from reference to intuition groups that may cross cut languages, cultural groups, and so forth. This might be a way to accommodate the variation in intuitions about reference provided that we know which intuition group a person belongs to. However, we do not know. Without this knowledge referential pluralism leads to the absurd view that we do not know when people agree, when they disagree and when they speak at cross-purposes.

So philosophers must choose. They can abandon arguments from reference. Or they can hold on to the hope that, despite evidence to the contrary, variation in intuitions about reference does not really exist. One of these is clearly a safer bet.

Notes

1. We use the term "substantive" to rule out deflationary accounts of reference such as those suggested by Field (1986, 1994) and Horwich (1990).
2. In this article, we take for granted that if "belief" and "desire" refer descriptively and if the folk theory of mind is massively erroneous, then beliefs and desires do not exist. However, it is worth noting that this inference has been contested. Bishop and Stich (1998) have argued that one needs an additional premise to get from the claim that "belief" does not refer to the desired conclusion that beliefs do not exist. Moreover, they claim that it is not clear how any of the premises that might fill the gap could be defended. We argue that even if Bishop and Stich's (1998) challenge were met, arguments from reference *still* wouldn't work.
3. In his reply to Kripke, Evans (1973) also relies on intuitions about the reference of proper names, such as "Madagascar." Putnam (1973, 1975) relies on intuitions about the reference of natural kind terms such as "gold." See also Schwartz (1978, 1980) and Devitt (1981).
4. Recanati 1993; Abbott 1997, 1999, 2002; Jackson 1998a, b; Devitt and Sterelny 1999; Geurts 1997, 2002; Garcia-Carpintero 2000; Segal 2001; Soames 2002; Reimer 2002, 2004; Jeshion 2004.
5. The Chinese subjects were students at the University of Hong Kong where the language of instruction is English; all participants were fluent speakers of English.

References

Abbott, B. (1997). A note on the nature of "water." *Mind*, 106: 311–319.

Abbott, B. (1999). Water = H$_2$O. *Mind*, 108: 145–148.

Abbott, B. (2002). Definiteness and proper names: Some bad news for the description theory. *Journal of Semantics*, 19: 191–201.

Adams, R. M. (1979). Divine command ethics modified again. *Journal of Religious Ethics*, 7(1): 66–79.

Andreasen, R. O. (1998). A new perspective on the race debate. *British Journal for the Philosophy of Science*, 49: 199–225.

Andreasen, R. O. (2000). Race: Biological reality or social construct? *Philosophy of Science*, 67: S653–S666.

Appiah, K. A. (1995). The Uncompleted Argument: Du Bois and the Illusion of Race. In L. A. Bell and D. Blumenfeld (eds.), *Overcoming Racism and Sexism*. Lanham, MD: Rowman and Littlefield, 59–78.

Appiah, K. A. (1996). Race, culture, identity: Misunderstood connections. In K. A. Appiah and A. Gutmann (eds.), *Color Conscious: The Political Morality of Race*. Princeton, NJ: Princeton University Press, 30–105.

Bezuidenhout, A., & Reimer, M., eds. (2004). *Descriptions and Beyond*. Oxford: Oxford University Press.

Bishop, M., & Stich, S. P. (1998). The flight to reference, or how not to make progress in the philosophy of science. *Philosophy of Science*, 65: 33–49.

Bishop, M., & Trout, J. D. (2005). *Epistemology and the Psychology of Human Judgment*. Oxford: Oxford University Press.

Boyd, R. (1983). On the current status of the issue of scientific realism. *Erkenntnis*, 19: 45–90.

Boyd, R. (1988). How to be a moral realist. In G. Sayre-McCord (ed.), *Essays on Moral Realism*. Ithaca: Cornell University Press.

Boyd, R. (2002). Scientific Realism. *The Stanford Encyclopedia of Philosophy (Summer 2002 Edition)*, Edward N. Zalta (ed.), URL: http://plato.stanford.edu/archives/sum2002/entries/scientific-realism/.

Boyd, R. (2003a). Finite beings, finite goods: The semantics, metaphysics and ethics of naturalist consequentialism, part I. *Philosophy and Phenomenological Research*, 66: 505–553.

Boyd, R. (2003b). Finite beings, finite goods: The semantics, metaphysics and ethics of naturalist consequentialism, part II. *Philosophy and Phenomenological Research*, 67: 24–47.

Churchland, P. M. (1981). Eliminative materialism and the propositional attitudes. *Journal of Philosophy*, 78: 67–90.

Dennett, D. (1996). Cow-sharks, Magnets, and Swampman. *Mind & Language*, 11(1): 76–77.

Devitt, M. (1981). *Designation*. New York: Columbia University Press.

Devitt, M., & Sterelny, K. (1999). *Language and Reality: An Introduction to the Philosophy of Language* (2nd ed.). Cambridge, MA: MIT Press.

Donnellan, K. (1966). Reference and Definite Descriptions. *Philosophical Review*, 75: 281–304.

Evans, G. (1973). The causal theory of names. *Supplementary Proceedings of the Aristotelian Society*, 47: 187–208.

Feyerabend, P. K. (1962). Explanation, reduction and empiricism. In H. Feigl and G. Maxwell (eds.), *Minnesota Studies in the Philosophy of Science, vol. 3: Scientific Explanation, Space, and Time*. Minneapolis: University of Minnesota Press, 28–97.

Field, H. (1986). The deflationary concept of truth. In G. MacDonald and C. Wright (eds.), *Fact, Science, and Value*. Oxford: Blackwell, 55–117.

Field, H. (1994). Deflationist views of meaning and content. *Mind*, 103: 249–285.

Fodor, J. (1987). *Psychosemantics: The Problem of Meaning in the Philosophy of Mind*. Cambridge, MA: MIT Press.

Garcia-Carpintero. M. (2002). A presuppositional account of reference-fixing. *Journal of Philosophy*, 97(3): 109–147.

Geurts, B. (1997). Good news about the description theory of names. *Journal of Semantics*, 14: 319–348.

Geurts, B. (2002). Bad news for anyone? A reply to Abbott. *Journal of Semantics*, 19: 203–207.

Glasgow, J. (2003). On the new biology of race. *Journal of Philosophy*, 100: 456–474.

Horwich, P. (1990). *Truth*. Oxford: Blackwell.

Jackson, F. (1998a). *From Metaphysics to Ethics: A Defense of Conceptual Analysis*. Oxford: Oxford University Press.

Jackson, F. (1998b). Reference and description revisited. In J. Tomberlin (ed.), *Language, Mind, and Ontology (12). Philosophical Perspectives*. Oxford: Blackwell, 201–218.

Jeshion, R. (2004). Descriptive descriptive names. In A. Bezuidenhout and M. Reimer, (eds.), 2004.

Kitcher, P. (1993). *The Advancement of Science*. Oxford: Oxford University Press.

Kitcher, P. (1999). Race, ethnicity, biology, culture. In Leonard Harris (ed.), *Racism*. New York: Humanity Books, 87–120.

Kripke, S. (1972/1980). *Naming and Necessity*. Cambridge, MA: Harvard University Press.

Kripke, S. (1977). Speaker's reference and semantic reference. In P. A. French, T. E. Uehling, Jr., and H. K. Wettstein (eds.), *Midwest Studies in Philosophy vol. II: Studies in the Philosophy of Language*. Morris, MN: University of Minnesota, 255–276.

Kuhn, T. S. (1970). *The Structure of Scientific Revolutions*, 2nd ed. Chicago: University of Chicago Press.

Lasersohn, P. (2005). Context dependence, disagreement, and predicates of personal taste. *Linguistics and Philosophy*, 28: 643–686.

Laurence, S., & Margolis, E. (2003). Concepts and conceptual analysis. *Philosophy and Phenomenological Research*, 67: 253–282.

Lewis, D. (1970). How to define theoretical terms. *Journal of Philosophy*, 67: 427–446.

Lycan, W. (1988). *Judgement and Justification*. Cambridge: Cambridge University Press.

Machery, E., Mallon, R., Nichols, S., & Stich, S. (2004). Semantics cross-cultural style. *Cognition*, 92: B1–B12.

MacFarlane J. (2004). Epistemic modalities and relative truth. URL: http://socrates.berkeley.edu/_jmacf/epistmod.pdf.

Mallon, R. (2006). Race: Normative, not metaphysical or semantic. *Ethics*, 116 (3): 525–551.

Mallon, R. (2007). Arguments from reference and the worry about dependence. *Midwest Studies in Philosophy*, 31(1): 160–183.

Mills, C. (1998). *Blackness Visible: Essays on Philosophy and Race*. Ithaca, NY: Cornell University Press.

Nisbett, R. E. (2003). *The Geography of Thought: How Asians and Westerners Think Differently…and Why*. New York: Free Press.

Nisbett, R. E., & Miyamoto, Y. (2005). The influence of culture: Holistic versus analytic perception. *Trends in Cognitive Sciences*, 9(10): 467–473.

Nisbett, R. E., Peng, K., Choi, I., & Norenzayan, A. (2001). Culture and systems of thought: Holistic vs. analytic cognition. *Psychological Review*, 108: 291–310.

Norenzayan, A., Smith, E., & Kim, B. (2002). Cultural preferences for formal versus intuitive reasoning. *Cognitive Science*, 26: 653–684.

Papineau, D. (1996). Doubtful intuitions. *Mind & Language*, 11(1): 130–132.

Putnam, H. (1973). Explanation and reference. In G. Pearce and P. Maynard (eds.), *Conceptual Change*. Dordrecht: Reidel.

Putnam, H. (1975). The meaning of "meaning." In H. Putnam (ed.), *Mind, Language and Reality*. Cambridge: Cambridge University Press.

Recanati, F. (1993). *Direct Reference*. Oxford: Basil Blackwell.

Reimer, M. (2002). Ordinary proper names. In G. Preyer and G. Peter (eds.), *On Logical Form and Language*. Oxford: Oxford University Press.

Reimer, M. (2004). Descriptive names. In A. Bezuidenhout and M. Reimer (eds.), 2004.

Schwartz, S. P. (1978). Putnam on artifacts. *Philosophical Review*, 87: 566–574.

Schwartz, S. P. (1980). Natural kind terms. *Cognition*, 7: 301–315.

Segal, G. (2001). Two theories of names. *Mind & Language*, 16(5): 547–563.

Soames, S. (2002). *Beyond Necessity: The Unfinished Semantic Agenda of Naming and Necessity*. New York: Oxford University Press.

Stich, S. P. (1983). *From Folk Psychology to Cognitive Science*. Cambridge, MA: MIT Press.

Stich, S. P. (1996). *Deconstructing the Mind*. Oxford: Oxford University Press.

Taylor, P. (2000). Appiah's uncompleted argument: DuBois and the reality of race. *Social Theory and Practice*, 26(1): 103–128.

Watanabe, M. (1998). Styles of reasoning in Japan and the United States: Logic of education in two cultures. Paper presented at the American Sociological Association annual meeting, San Francisco, CA.

Watanabe, M. (1999). Styles of reasoning in Japan and the United States: Logic of education in two cultures. Unpublished PhD thesis, Columbia University, New York.

Weinberg, J., Nichols, S., & Stich, S. (2001). Normativity and Epistemic Intuitions. *Philosophical Topics*, 29, (1&2): 429–459.

Zack, N. (1993). *Race and Mixed Race*. Philadelphia: Temple University Press.

Zack, N. (2002). *Philosophy of Science and Race*. New York: Routledge.

Study Questions

1. What is an argument from reference?
2. How does philosophical practice suggest we support a theory of reference?
3. Why are intuitions about reference insufficient to support any particular theory of reference?

The Persistence of the Attitudes 4.6

JERRY FODOR

JERRY FODOR (1935–) is the State of New Jersey Professor of Philosophy at Rutgers University. He has spent his career working in the philosophy of mind, the philosophy of psychology, and the philosophy of science. Before moving to Rutgers he was a Professor of Philosophy and Psychology at MIT. While at MIT he was colleagues with and influenced by Noam Chomsky. Just as Chomsky argued that our capacity to create language is theoretically infinite (in that we can create an arbitrarily long sentence that had never been previously created), so compositional, so too Fodor argued that thought is also theoretically unbounded, so compositional. He has also famously argued that the special sciences (like psychology, economics, geology, and so on) are autonomous, meaning not smoothly reducible to physics; that the mind is "modular," meaning there are autonomous, fast, encapsulated mental processes (e.g., vision, language comprehension) that are not under our person-level control; and that all of our concepts are innate. In this selection Fodor argues that the folk psychological posits of belief and desire are real, respectable entities worthy of the investigation of psychology and cognitive science more generally.

A Midsummer Night's Dream, act 3, scene 2.
Enter Demetrius and Hermia.

Dem.   O, why rebuke you him that loves
      you so?
    Lay breath so bitter on your bitter foe.

Herm. Now I but chide, but I should use
      thee worse;
    For thou, I fear, hast given me cause
      to curse.
    If thou hast slain Lysander in his sleep,
    Being o'er shoes in blood, plunge in
      the deep,
    And kill me too.
    The sun was not so true unto the day
    As he to me: would he have stol'n away
    From sleeping Hermia? I'll believe as
      soon

This whole earth may be bor'd; and
    that the moon
May through the centre creep, and so
    displease
Her brother's noontide with the antip-
    odes.
It cannot be but thou hast murder'd
    him;
So should a murderer look; so dead,
    so grim.

Very nice. And also very *plausible*; a convincing (though informal) piece of implicit, nondemonstrative, theoretical inference.

Here, leaving out a lot of lemmas, is how the inference must have gone: Hermia has reason to believe herself beloved of Lysander. (Lysander has told her that he loves her—repeatedly and in elegant iambics—and inferences from how people say they feel to how they do feel are reliable, ceteris paribus.) But if Lysander does indeed love Hermia, then, a fortiori, Lysander wishes Hermia well. But if Lysander wishes Hermia well, then Lysander does not voluntarily desert Hermia at night in a darkling wood. (There may be lions. "There is not a more fearful wild-fowl than your lion living.") But Hermia was, in fact, so deserted by Lysander. Therefore not voluntarily. Therefore *in*voluntarily. Therefore it is plausible that Lysander has come to harm. At whose hands? Plausibly at Demetrius's hands. For Demetrius is Lysander's rival for the love of Hermia, and the presumption is that rivals in love do *not* wish one another well. Specifically, Hermia believes that Demetrius believes that a live Lysander is an impediment to the success of his (Demetrius's) wooing of her (Hermia). Moreover, Hermia believes (correctly) that if x wants that P, and x believes that not-P unless Q, and x believes that x can bring it about that Q, then (ceteris paribus) x tries to bring it about that Q. Moreover, Hermia believes (again correctly) that, by and large, people succeed in bringing about what they try to bring about. *So:* Knowing and believing all this, Hermia infers that perhaps Demetrius has killed Lysander. And we, the audience, who know what Hermia knows and believes and who share, more or less, her views about the psychology of lovers and rivals, understand how she has come to draw this inference. We sympathize.

In fact, Hermia has it all wrong. Demetrius is innocent and Lysander lives. The intricate theory that connects beliefs, desires, and actions—the implicit theory that Hermia relies on to make sense of what Lysander did and what Demetrius may have done; and that *we* rely on to make sense of Hermia's inferring what she does; and that Shakespeare relies on to predict and manipulate our sympathies (*"deconstruction" my foot*, by the way)—this theory makes no provision for nocturnal interventions by mischievous fairies.

Unbeknownst to Hermia, a peripatetic sprite has sprung the ceteris paribus clause and made her plausible inference go awry. "Reason and love keep little company together now-a-days: the more the pity that some honest neighbours will not make them friends."

Granting, however, that the theory fails from time to time—and not just when fairies intervene—I nevertheless want to emphasize *(1) how often it goes right, (2) how deep it is, and (3) how much we do depend upon it.* Commonsense belief/desire psychology has recently come under a lot of philosophical pressure, and it's possible to doubt whether it can be saved in face of the sorts of problems that its critics have raised. There is, however, a prior question: whether it's worth the effort of trying to save it. That's the issue I propose to start with.

HOW OFTEN IT WORKS

Hermia got it wrong; her lover was less constant than she had supposed. Applications of commonsense psychology mediate our relations with one another, and when its predictions fail these relations break down. The resulting disarray is likely to happen in public and to be highly noticeable.

Herm.   Since night you lov'd me; yet since
            night you left me;
            Why, then, you left me,—O, the gods
            forbid!—
            In earnest, shall I say?
Lys.   Ay, by my life;
            And never did desire to see thee more.
            Therefore be out of hope....

This sort of thing makes excellent theater; the *successes* of commonsense psychology, by contrast, are ubiquitous and—for that very reason—practically invisible.

Commonsense psychology works so well it disappears. It's like those mythical Rolls Royce cars whose engines are sealed when they leave the factory; only it's better because it isn't mythical. Someone I don't know phones me at my office in New York from—as it might be—Arizona. "Would you like to lecture here next Tuesday?" are the words that he utters. "Yes, thank you. I'll be at your airport on the 3 p.m. flight" are the words that I reply. That's *all* that happens, but it's more than enough; the rest of the burden of predicting behavior—of bridging the gap between utterances and actions—is routinely taken up by theory. And the theory works so well that several days later (or weeks later, or months later, or years later; you can vary the example to taste) and several thousand miles away, there I am at the airport, and there he is to meet me. Or if I *don't* turn up, it's less likely that the theory has failed than that something went wrong with the airline. It's not possible to say, in quantitative terms, just how successfully commonsense psychology allows us to coordinate our behaviors. But I have the impression that we manage pretty well with one another; often rather better than we cope with less complex machines.

The point—to repeat—is that the theory from which we get this extraordinary predictive power is just good old commonsense belief/desire psychology. That's what tells us, for example, how to infer people's intentions from the sounds they make (if someone utters the form of words "I'll be at your airport on the 3 p.m. flight" then, ceteris paribus, he intends to be at your airport on the 3 p.m. flight) and how to infer people's behavior from their intentions (if someone intends to be at your airport on the 3 p.m. flight, then, ceteris paribus, he will produce behavior of a sort which will eventuate in his arriving at that place at that time, barring mechanical failures and acts of God). And all this works not just with people whose psychology you know intimately: your closest friends, say, or the spouse of your bosom. It works with *absolute strangers*; people you wouldn't know if you bumped into them. And it works not just in laboratory conditions—where you can control the interacting variables—but also, indeed preeminently, in field conditions where all you know about the sources of variance is what commonsense psychology tells you about them. Remarkable. If we could do that well with predicting the weather, no one would ever get his feet wet; and yet the etiology of the weather must surely be child's play compared with the causes of behavior.

Yes, but what about all those ceteris paribuses? I commence to digress:

Philosophers sometimes argue that the appearance of predictive adequacy that accrues to the generalizations of commonsense psychology is spurious. For, they say, as soon as you try to make these generalizations explicit, you see that they have to be hedged about with ceteris paribus clauses; hedged about in ways that make them *trivially* incapable of disconfirmation. "False or vacuous" is the charge.

Consider the defeasibility of "if someone utters the form of words 'I'll be at your airport on the 3 p.m. flight,' then he intends to be at your airport on the 3 p.m. flight." This generalization does *not* hold if, for example, the speaker is lying; or if the speaker is using the utterance as an example (of a false sentence, say); or if he is a monolingual speaker of Urdu who happens to have uttered the sentence by accident; or if the speaker is talking in his sleep; or . . . whatever. You can, of course, defend the generalization in the usual way; you can say that "*all else being equal*, if someone utters the form of words 'I'll be at your airport on the 3 p.m. flight.' then he intends to be at your airport on the 3 p.m. flight." But perhaps this last means nothing more than: "if someone says that he intends to be there, then he does intend to be there—unless he doesn't." That, of course, is predictively adequate for sure; nothing that happens will disconfirm it; nothing that happens could.

A lot of philosophers seem to be moved by this sort of argument; yet, even at first blush, it would be surprising if it were any good. After all, we do use commonsense psychological generalizations to predict one another's behavior; and the predictions do—very often—come out true.

But how could that be so if the generalizations that we base the predictions on are *empty*?

I'm inclined to think that what is alleged about the implicit reliance of commonsense psychology on uncashed ceteris paribus clauses is in fact a perfectly general property of the *explicit* generalizations in *all* the special sciences; in all empirical explanatory schemes, that is to say, other than basic physics. Consider the following modest truth of geology: A meandering river erodes its outside bank. "False or vacuous"; so a philosopher might argue. "Take it straight—as a strictly universal generalization—and it is surely false. Think of the case where the weather changes and the river freezes; or the world comes to an end; or somebody builds a dam; or somebody builds a concrete wall on the outside bank; or the rains stop and the river dries up...or whatever. You can, of course, defend the generalization in the usual way—by appending a ceteris paribus clause: 'All else being equal, a meandering river erodes its outside bank.' But perhaps this last means nothing more than: 'A meandering river erodes its outside bank—unless it doesn't.' That, of course, is predictively adequate for sure. Nothing that happens will disconfirm it; nothing that happens could."

Patently, something has gone wrong. For "All else being equal, a meandering river erodes its outside bank" is neither false nor vacuous, and it doesn't mean "A meandering river erodes its outside bank—unless it doesn't." It is, I expect, a long story how the generalizations of the special sciences manage to be both hedged and informative (or, if you like, how they manage to support counterfactuals even though they have exceptions). Telling that story is part of making clear why we have special sciences at all; why we don't just have basic physics (see Fodor, *SS*). It is also part of making clear how idealization works in science. For surely "Ceteris paribus, a meandering river erodes its outside bank" means something like "A meandering river erodes its outside bank in any nomologically possible world where the operative idealizations of geology are

satisfied." That this is, in general, stronger than "*P* in any world where not not-*P*" is certain. So if, as it would appear, commonsense psychology relies upon its ceteris paribus clauses, so too does geology.

There is, then, a face similarity between the way implicit generalizations work in commonsense psychology and the way explicit generalizations work in the special sciences. But maybe this similarity is *merely* superficial. Donald Davidson is famous for having argued that the generalizations of real science, unlike those that underlie commonsense belief/desire explanations, are "perfectible." In the real, but not the intentional, sciences we can (in principle, anyhow) get rid of the ceteris paribus clauses by actually enumerating the conditions under which the generalizations are supposed to hold.

By this criterion, however, the only real science is basic physics. For it simply isn't true that we can, even in principle, specify the conditions under which—say—geological generalizations hold *so long as we stick to the vocabulary of geology*. Or, to put it less in the formal mode, the causes of exceptions to geological generalizations are, quite typically, not themselves *geological* events. Try it and see: "A meandering river erodes its outer banks unless, for example, the weather changes and the river dries up." But "weather" isn't a term in *geology*; nor are "the world comes to an end," "somebody builds a dam," and indefinitely many other descriptors required to specify the sorts of things that can go wrong. All you can say that's any use is: If the generalization failed to hold, then the operative idealizations must somehow have failed to be satisfied. But so, too, in commonsense psychology: If he didn't turn up when he intended to, then something must have gone wrong.

Exceptions to the generalizations of a special science are typically *inexplicable* from the point of view of (that is, in the vocabulary of) that science. That's one of the things that makes it a *special* science. But, of course, it may nevertheless be perfectly possible to explain the exceptions *in the vocabulary of some other science.* In the most familiar case, you go "down" one or more levels and use the vocabulary of a more "basic" science. (The current failed to run through the circuit because the terminals were oxidized; he no longer recognizes familiar objects because of a cerebral accident. And so forth.) The availability of this strategy is one of the things that the hierarchical arrangement of our sciences buys for us. Anyhow, to put the point succinctly, the same pattern that holds for the special sciences seems to hold for commonsense psychology as well. On the one hand, its ceteris paribus clauses are ineliminable from the point of view of its proprietary conceptual resources. But, on the other hand, we have—so far at least—no reason to doubt that they can be discharged in the vocabulary of some lower-level science (neurology, say, or biochemistry; at worst, physics).

If the world is describable as a closed causal system at all, it is so only in the vocabulary of our most basic science. From this nothing follows that a psychologist (or a geologist) needs to worry about.

I cease to digress. The moral so far is that the predictive adequacy of commonsense psychology is beyond rational dispute; nor is there any reason to suppose that it's obtained by cheating. If you want to know where my physical body will be next Thursday, mechanics—our best science of middle-sized objects after all, and reputed to be pretty good in its field—is *no use to you at all.* Far the best way to find out (usually, in practice, the *only* way to find out) is: *ask me!* [...]

ITS INDISPENSABILITY

We have, in practice, no alternative to the vocabulary of commonsense psychological explanation; we have no other way of describing our behaviors and their causes if we want our behaviors and their causes to be subsumed by any counterfactual-supporting generalizations that we know about. This is, again, hard to see because it's so close.

For example, a few paragraphs back, I spoke of the commonsense psychological generalization *people generally do what they say that they will do* as bridging the gap between an exchange of utterances ("Will you come and lecture...," "I'll be at your airport on Thursday...") and the consequent behaviors of the speakers (my arriving at the airport, his being there to meet me). But this understates the case for the indispensability of commonsense psychology, since without it we can't even describe the utterances as forms of words (to say nothing of describing the ensuing behaviors as kinds of acts). *Word* is a *psychological* category. (It is, indeed, *irreducibly* psychological, so far as anybody knows; there are, for example, no acoustic properties that all and only tokens of the same word type must share. In fact, surprisingly, there are no acoustic properties that all and only *fully intelligible* tokens of the same word type must share. Which is why our best technology is currently unable to build a typewriter that you can dictate to.)

As things now stand—to spell it out—we have *no* vocabulary for specifying event types that meets the following four conditions:

1. My behavior in uttering "I'll be there on Thursday..." counts as an event of type T_i.
2. My arriving there on Thursday counts as an event of Type T_j.
3. "Events of type T_j are consequent upon events of type T_i" is even roughly true and counterfactual supporting.
4. Categories T_i and T_j are other than irreducibly psychological.

For the only known taxonomies that meet conditions 1–3 acknowledge such event types as uttering the *form of words* "I'll be there on Thursday," or *saying that* one will be there on Thursday, or *performing the act* of meeting someone at the airport; so they fail condition 4.

Philosophers and psychologists used to dream of an alternative conceptual apparatus, one in which the commonsense inventory of types of *behavior* is replaced by an inventory of types of *movements*; the counterfactual-supporting generalizations of psychology would then exhibit the contingency of these movements upon environmental and/or organic variables. That behavior is indeed contingent upon environmental and organic variables is, I suppose, not to be denied; yet the generalizations were not forthcoming. Why? There's a standard answer: It's because behavior consists of actions, and actions cross-classify movements. The generalization is that the burnt child avoids the fire; but what movement constitutes avoidance depends on where the child is, where the fire is...and so, drearily, forth. If you want to know what generalizations subsume a behavioral event, you have to know what *action type* it belongs to; knowing what *motion type* it belongs to usually doesn't buy anything. I take all that to be Gospel.

Yet it is generally assumed that this situation *must* be remediable, at least in principle. After all, the generalizations of a completed physics would presumably subsume every motion of every thing, hence the motions of organisms *inter alia*. So, if we wait long enough, we will after all have counterfactual-supporting generalizations that subsume the motions of organisms *under that description*. Presumably, God has them already.

This is, however, a little misleading. For, the (putative) generalizations of the (putative) completed physics would apply to the motions of organisms qua motions, but not qua organismic. Physics presumably has as little use for the categories of macrobiology as it does for the categories of commonsense psychology; it dissolves the beha*ver* as well as the beha*vior*. What's left is atoms in the void. The subsumption of the motions of organisms—and of everything else—by the counterfactual-supporting general-izations of physics does not therefore guarantee that there is any science whose ontology recognizes organisms and their motions. That is: The subsumption of the motions of organisms—and of everything else—by the laws of physics does not guarantee that there are any laws about the motions of organisms qua motions of organisms. So far as anybody knows—barring, perhaps, a little bit of the psychology of classical reflexes—there are no such laws; and there is no metaphysical reason to expect any.

Anyhow, this is all poppycock. Even if psychology were dispensable *in principle*, that would be no argument for dispensing with it. (Perhaps geology is dispensable in principle; every river is a physical object after all. Would that be a reason for supposing that rivers aren't a natural kind? Or that "meandering rivers erode their outside banks" is untrue?) What's relevant to whether commonsense psychology is worth defending is its dispensability *in fact*. And here the situation is absolutely clear. We have no idea of how to explain ourselves to ourselves except in a vocabulary which is *saturated* with belief/desire psychology. One is tempted to transcendental argument: What Kant said to Hume about physical objects holds, mutatis mutandis, for the propositional attitudes; we can't give them up *because we don't know how to*.

Study Questions

1. How can one be a physicalist and believe in mental states without believing that mental states reduce to neurological states?
2. How can we be justified in positing mental states if we cannot observe them?
3. On Fodor's view, how do mental states affect the physical?

Real Patterns   **4.7**

DANIEL DENNETT

DANIEL DENNETT (1942–) is the Austin B. Fletcher Professor of Philosophy and co-director of the Center for Cognitive Studies at Tufts University. Dennett's work originally focused on topics in the philosophy of mind, particularly consciousness and the ontology of intentional states. In his work on consciousness, developed primarily in his book *Consciousness Explained*, Dennett criticized the idea of a "Cartesian theater," the metaphor that the images of the mind are "played" out on a screen for the mind to apprehend. Dennett has also argued that intentional states are just instruments we use to predict other people's behavior and do not describe the actual workings of the brain, which is the thesis Dennett argues for in the given selection in this section. In his later career Dennett broadened his focus to include writing on free will, the philosophy of biology, and the philosophy of religion, where he has defended atheism.

Are there really beliefs? Or are we learning (from neuroscience and psychology, presumably) that, strictly speaking, beliefs are figments of our imagination, items in a superseded ontology? Philosophers generally regard such ontological questions as admitting just two possible answers: either beliefs exist or they do not. There is no such state as quasi existence; there are no stable doctrines of semirealism. Beliefs must either be vindicated along with the viruses or banished along with the banshees. A bracing conviction prevails, then, to the effect that when it comes to beliefs (and other mental items) one must be either a realist or an eliminative materialist.

I. REALISM ABOUT BELIEFS

This conviction prevails in spite of my best efforts over the years to undermine it with various analogies: are *voices* in your ontology?[1] Are *centers of gravity* in your ontology?[2]

It is amusing to note that my analogizing beliefs to centers of gravity has been attacked from both sides of the ontological dichotomy, by philosophers who think it is simply obvious that centers of gravity are useful fictions, and by philosophers who think it is simply obvious that centers of gravity are perfectly real:

The trouble with these supposed parallels…is that they are all strictly speaking *false*, although they are no doubt useful simplifications for many purposes. It is false, for example, that the gravitational attraction between the Earth and the Moon involves two point masses; but it is a good enough first approximation for many calculations. However, this is not at all what Dennett really wants to say about intentional states. For he insists that to adopt the intentional stance and interpret an agent as acting on certain beliefs and desires is to discern a pattern in his actions which is genuinely there (a pattern which is missed if we instead adopt a scientific stance): Dennett certainly does not hold that the role of intentional ascriptions is merely to give us a useful

D. Dennett, "Real Patterns," *The Journal of Philosophy*, 88, no. 1 (1991). Reprinted by permission of the publication.

approximation to a truth that can be more accurately expressed in non-intentional terms.[3]

Compare this with Fred Dretske's[4] equally confident assertion of realism:

> I am a realist about centers of gravity....The earth obviously exerts a gravitational attraction on *all* parts of the moon—not just its center of gravity. The *resultant* force, a vector sum, acts through a point, but this is something quite different. One should be very clear about what centers of gravity are *before* deciding whether to be literal about them, *before* deciding whether or not to be a center-of-gravity realist (*ibid.*, p. 511).

Dretske's advice is well-taken. What are centers of gravity? They are mathematical points—abstract objects or what Hans Reichenbach called *abstracta*—definable in terms of physical forces and other properties. The question of whether abstract objects are real—the question of whether or not "one should be a realist about them"—can take two different paths, which we might call the metaphysical and the scientific. The metaphysical path simply concerns the reality or existence of abstract objects generally, and does not distinguish them in terms of their scientific utility. Consider, for instance, the *center of population* of the United States. I define this as the mathematical point at the intersection of the two lines such that there are as many inhabitants north as south of the latitude, and as many inhabitants east as west of the longitude. This point is (or can be) just as precisely defined as the center of gravity or center of mass of an object. (Since these median strips might turn out to be wide, take the midline of each strip as the line; count as inhabitants all those within the territorial waters and up to twenty miles in altitude—orbiting astronauts do not count—and take each inhabitant's navel to be the determining point, etc.) I do not know the center of population's current geographic location, but I am quite sure it is west of where it was ten years ago. It jiggles around constantly, as people move about, taking rides on planes, trains, and automobiles, etc. I doubt that this abstract object is of any value at all

in any scientific theory, but just in case it is, here is an even more trivial abstract object: Dennett's lost sock center: the point defined as the center of the smallest sphere that can be inscribed around all the socks I have ever lost in my life.

These abstract objects have the same metaphysical status as centers of gravity. Is Dretske a realist about them all? Should we be? I do not intend to pursue this question, for I suspect that Dretske is—and we should be—more interested in the scientific path to realism: centers of gravity are real because they are (somehow) *good* abstract objects. They deserve to be taken seriously, learned about, used. If we go so far as to distinguish them as *real* (contrasting them, perhaps, with those abstract objects which are *bogus*), that is because we think they serve in perspicuous representations of real forces, "natural" properties, and the like. This path brings us closer, in any case, to the issues running in the debates about the reality of beliefs.

I have claimed that beliefs are best considered to be abstract objects rather like centers of gravity. Smith considers centers of gravity to be useful fictions while Dretske considers them to be useful (and hence?) real abstractions, and each takes his view to constitute a criticism of my position. The optimistic assessment of these opposite criticisms is that they cancel each other out; my analogy must have hit the nail on the head. The pessimistic assessment is that more needs to be said to convince philosophers that a mild and intermediate sort of realism is a positively attractive position, and not just the desperate dodge of ontological responsibility it has sometimes been taken to be. I have just such a case to present, a generalization and extension of my earlier attempts, via the concept of a *pattern*. My aim on this occasion is not so much to prove that my intermediate doctrine about the reality of psychological states is right, but just that it is quite possibly right, because a parallel doctrine is demonstrably right about some simpler cases.

We use folk psychology—interpretation of each other as believers, wanters, intenders, and the like—to predict what people will do next. Prediction is not the only thing we care about, of course. Folk psychology helps us understand and empathize with others, organize our memories, interpret our emotions, and flavor our vision in a thousand ways, but at the heart of all these is the enormous predictive leverage of folk psychology. Without its predictive power, we could have no interpersonal projects or relations at all; human activity would be just so much Brownian motion; we would be baffling ciphers to each other and to ourselves—we could not even conceptualize our own flailings. In what follows, I shall concentrate always on folk-psychological prediction, not because I make the mistake of ignoring all the other interests we have in people aside from making bets on what they will do next, but because I claim that our power to *interpret* the actions of others depends on our power—seldom explicitly exercised—to predict them.[5]

Where utter patternlessness or randomness prevails, nothing is predictable. The success of folk-psychological prediction, like the success of any prediction, depends on there being some order or pattern in the world to exploit. Exactly where in the world does this pattern exist? What is the pattern a pattern *of*?[6] Some have thought, with Fodor, that the pattern of belief must in the end be a pattern of structures in the brain, formulae written in the language of thought. Where else could it be? Gibsonians might say the pattern is "in the light"—and Quinians (such as Donald Davidson and I) could almost agree: the pattern is discernible in agents' (observable) behavior when we subject it to "radical interpretation" (Davidson) "from the intentional stance" (Dennett).

When are the elements of a pattern real and not merely apparent? Answering this question will help us resolve the misconceptions that have led to the proliferation of "ontological positions" about beliefs, the different grades or kinds of realism. I shall concentrate on five salient exemplars arrayed in the space of possibilities: Fodor's industrial-strength Realism (he writes it with a capital "R"); Davidson's regular strength realism; my

mild realism; Richard Rorty's milder-than-mild irrealism, according to which the pattern is *only* in the eyes of the beholders, and Paul Churchland's eliminative materialism, which denies the reality of beliefs altogether.

In what follows, I shall assume that these disagreements all take place within an arena of common acceptance of what Arthur Fine[7] calls NOA, the natural ontological attitude. That is, I take the interest in these disagreements to lie not in differences of opinion about the ultimate metaphysical status of physical things or abstract things (e.g., electrons or centers of gravity), but in differences of opinion about whether beliefs and other mental states are, shall we say, *as real as* electrons or centers of gravity. I want to show that mild realism is the doctrine that makes the most sense when what we are talking about is real patterns, such as the real patterns discernible from the intentional stance.[8]

In order to make clear the attractions and difficulties of these different positions about patterns, I shall apply them first to a much simpler, more readily visualized, and uncontroversial sort of pattern.

II. THE REALITY OF PATTERNS

Consider the six objects in [Figure 1] (which I shall call *frames*):

We can understand a frame to be a finite subset of data, a window on an indefinitely larger world

FIGURE 1

of further data. In one sense *A–F* all display different patterns; if you look closely you will see that no two frames are exactly alike ("atom-for-atom replicas," if you like). In another sense, *A–F* all display the same pattern; they were all made by the same basic process, a printing of ten rows of ninety dots, ten black dots followed by ten white dots, etc. The overall effect is to create five equally spaced black squares or bars in the window. I take it that this pattern, which I shall dub *bar code*, is a real pattern if anything is. But some random (actually pseudo-random) "noise" has been allowed to interfere with the actual printing. The noise ratio is as follows:

A: 25%	*B*: 10%
C: 25%	*D*: 1%
E: 33%	*F*: 50%

It is impossible to see that *F* is not purely (pseudo-) random noise; you will just have to take my word for it that it was actually generated by the same program that generated the other five patterns; all I changed was the noise ratio.

Now, what does it mean to say that a pattern in one of these frames is real, or that it is really there? Given our privileged information about how these frames were generated, we may be tempted to say that there is a single pattern in all six cases—even in *F*, where it is "indiscernible." But I propose that the self-contradictory air of "indiscernible pattern" should be taken seriously. We may be able to make some extended, or metaphorical, sense of the idea of indiscernible patterns (or invisible pictures or silent symphonies), but in the root case a pattern is "by definition" a candidate for pattern *recognition*. (It is this loose but unbreakable link to observers or perspectives, of course, that makes "pattern" an attractive term to someone perched between instrumentalism and industrial-strength realism.)

Fortunately, there is a standard way of making these intuitions about the discernibility-in-principle of patterns precise. Consider the task of transmitting information about one of the frames from one place to another. How many

bits of information will it take to transmit each frame? The least efficient method is simply to send the "bit map," which identifies each dot *seriatim* ("dot one is black, dot two is white, dot three is white,..."). For a black-and-white frame of 900 dots (or pixels, as they are called), the transmission requires 900 bits. Sending the bit map is in effect verbatim quotation, accurate but inefficient. Its most important virtue is that it is equally capable of transmitting any pattern or any particular instance of utter patternlessness.

Gregory Chaitin's[9] valuable definition of mathematical randomness invokes this idea. A series (of dots or numbers or whatever) is random if and only if the information required to describe (transmit) the series accurately is *incompressible:* nothing shorter than the verbatim bit map will preserve the series. Then a series is not random—has a pattern—if and only if there is some more efficient way of describing it.[10] Frame *D*, for instance, can be described as "ten rows of ninety: ten black followed by ten white, etc., *with the following exceptions:* dots 57, 88,...." This expression, suitably encoded, is much shorter than 900 bits long. The comparable expressions for the other frames will be proportionally longer, since they will have to mention, verbatim, more exceptions, and the degeneracy of the "pattern" in *F* is revealed by the fact that its description in this system will be no improvement over the bit map—in fact, it will tend on average to be trivially longer, since it takes some bits to describe the pattern that is then obliterated by all the exceptions.

Of course, there are bound to be other ways of describing the evident patterns in these frames, and some will be more efficient than others—in the precise sense of being systematically specifiable in fewer bits.[11] Any such description, if an improvement over the bit map, is the description of a real pattern in the data.[12]

Consider bar code, the particular pattern seen in *A–E*, and almost perfectly instantiated in *D*. *That* pattern is quite readily discernible to the naked human eye in these presentations of the data, because of the particular pattern-recognition machinery hard-wired in our visual systems—edge detectors, luminance detectors, and the like. But the very same data (the very same streams of bits) presented in some other format might well yield no hint of pattern to us, especially in the cases where bar code is contaminated by salt and pepper, as in frames *A* through *C*. For instance, if we broke the 900-bit series of frame *B* into 4-bit chunks, and then translated each of these into hexadecimal notation, one would be hard pressed indeed to tell the resulting series of hexadecimal digits from a random series, since the hexadecimal chunking would be seriously out of phase with the decimal pattern—and hence the "noise" would not "stand out" as noise. There are myriad ways of displaying any 900-bit series of data points, and not many of them would inspire us to concoct an efficient description of the series. Other creatures with different sense organs, or different interests, might readily perceive patterns that were imperceptible to us. The patterns would be *there* all along, but just invisible to *us*.

The idiosyncracy of perceivers' capacities to discern patterns is striking. Visual patterns with axes of vertical symmetry stick out like sore thumbs for us, but if one simply rotates the frame a few degrees, the symmetry is often utterly beyond noticing. And the "perspectives" from which patterns are "perceptible" are not restricted to variations on presentation to the sense modalities. Differences in knowledge yield striking differences in the capacity to pick up patterns. Expert chess players can instantly perceive (and subsequently recall with high accuracy) the total board position in a real game, but are much worse at recall if the same chess pieces are randomly placed on the board, even though to a novice both boards are equally hard to recall.[13] This should not surprise anyone who considers that an expert speaker of English would have much less difficulty perceiving and recalling

The frightened cat struggled to get loose.

than

Te ser.ioghehnde t srugfcalde go tgtt ohle

which contains the same pieces, now somewhat disordered. Expert chess players, unlike novices, not only know how to *play* chess; they know how to *read* chess—how to see the patterns at a glance.

A pattern exists in some data—is real—if *there is* a description of the data that is more efficient than the bit map, whether or not anyone can concoct it. Compression algorithms, as general-purpose pattern describers, are efficient ways of transmitting exact copies of frames, such as *A–F*, from one place to another, but our interests often favor a somewhat different goal: transmitting *inexact* copies that nevertheless preserve "the" pattern that is important to us. For some purposes, we need not list the exceptions to bar code, but only transmit the information that the pattern is bar code with *n*% noise. Following this strategy, frames *A* and *C*, though discernibly different under careful inspection, count as *the same pattern*, since what matters to us is that the pattern is bar code with 25% noise, and we do not care which particular noise occurs, only that it occurs.

Sometimes we are interested in not just ignoring the noise, but eliminating it, improving the pattern in transmission. Copy-editing is a good example. Consider the likely effect thes santince wull hive hod on tha cupy adutor whu preparis thas monescrupt fur prunteng. *My* interest in this particular instance is that the "noise" be transmitted, not removed, though I actually do not care exactly *which* noise is there.

Here then are three different attitudes we take at various times toward patterns. Sometimes we care about exact description or reproduction of detail, at whatever cost. From this perspective, a real pattern in frame *A* is *bar code with the following exceptions: 7, 8, 11,....* At other times we care about the noise, but not where in particular it occurs. From this perspective, a real pattern in frame *A* is *bar code with 25% noise*. And some-times, we simply tolerate or ignore the noise. From this perspective, a real pattern in frame *A* is simply: *bar code*. But is bar code really there in frame *A*? I am tempted to respond: Look! You can see it with your own eyes. But there is some-thing more constructive to say as well.

When two individuals confront the same data, they may perceive different patterns in them, but since we can have varied interests and perspec-tives, these differences do not all count as dis-agreements. Or in any event they should not. If Jones sees pattern α (with n% noise) and Brown sees pattern β (with m% noise) there may be no ground for determining that one of them is right and the other wrong. Suppose they are both using their patterns to bet on the next datum in the series. Jones bets according to the "pure" pattern α, but budgets for n% errors when he looks for odds. Brown does likewise, using pat-tern β. If both patterns are real, they will both get rich. That is to say, so long as they use their expectation of deviations from the "ideal" to temper their odds policy, they will do better than chance—perhaps very much better.

Now suppose they compare notes. Suppose that α is a simple, easy-to-calculate pattern, but with a high noise rate—for instance, suppose α is bar code as it appears in frame *E*. And suppose that Brown has found some periodicity or pro-gression in the "random" noise that Jones just tolerates, so that β is a much more complicated description of pattern-superimposed-on-pattern. This permits Brown to do better than chance, we may suppose, at predicting when the "noise" will come. As a result, Brown budgets for a lower error rate—say only 5%. "What you call noise, Jones, is actually pattern," Brown might say. "Of course there is still *some* noise in my pattern, but my pattern is better—more real—than yours! Yours is actually just a mere appearance." Jones might well reply that it is all a matter of taste; he notes how hard Brown has to work to calcu-late predictions, and points to the fact that he is getting just as rich (or maybe richer) by using a

simpler, sloppier system and making more bets at good odds than Brown can muster. "My pattern is perfectly real—look how rich I'm getting. If it were an illusion, I'd be broke."

This crass way of putting things—in terms of betting and getting rich—is simply a vivid way of drawing attention to a real, and far from crass, trade-off that is ubiquitous in nature, and hence in folk psychology. Would we prefer an extremely compact pattern description with a high noise ratio or a less compact pattern description with a lower noise ratio? Our decision may depend on how swiftly and reliably we can discern the simple pattern, how dangerous errors are, how much of our resources we can afford to allocate to detec-tion and calculation. These "design decisions" are typically not left to us to make by individual and deliberate choices; they are incorporated into the design of our sense organs by genetic evolu-tion, and into our culture by cultural evolution. The product of this design evolution process is what Wilfrid Sellars[14] calls our *manifest image*, and it is composed of folk physics, folk psychol-ogy, and the other pattern-making perspectives we have on the buzzing blooming confusion that bombards us with data. The ontology gen-erated by the manifest image has thus a deeply pragmatic source.[15]

Do these same pragmatic considerations apply to the scientific image, widely regarded as the final arbiter of ontology? Science is supposed to carve nature at the joints—at its *real* joints, of course. Is it permissible in science to adopt a carving system so simple that it makes sense to tolerate occasional misdivisions and consequent mispre-dictions? It happens all the time. The ubiquitous practice of using idealized models is exactly a matter of trading off reliability and accuracy of prediction against computational tractability. A particularly elegant and handy oversimplifica-tion may under some circumstances be irresist-ible. The use of Newtonian rather than Einstein-ian mechanics in most mundane scientific and engineering calculations is an obvious example. A tractable oversimplification may be attractive even in the face of a high error rate; considering inherited traits to be carried by single genes "for" those traits is an example; considering agents in the marketplace to be perfectly rational self-aggrandizers with perfect information is another.

III. PATTERNS IN LIFE

The time has come to export these observations about patterns and reality to the controversial arena of belief attribution. The largish leap we must make is nicely expedited by pausing at a stepping-stone example midway between the world of the dot frames and the world of folk psychology: John Horton Conway's Game of Life. In my opinion, every philosophy student should be held responsible for an intimate acquaintance with the Game of Life. It should be considered an essential tool in every thought-experimenter's kit, a prodigiously versatile generator of philosophically important examples and thought experiments of admirable clarity and vividness. In *The Intentional Stance*, I briefly exploited it to make a point about the costs and benefits of risky prediction from the intentional stance,[16] but I have since learned that I presumed too much familiarity with the underlying ideas. Here, then, is a somewhat expanded basic introduction to Life.[17]

Life is played on a two-dimensional grid, such as a checkerboard or a computer screen; it is not a game one plays to win; if it is a game at all, it is solitaire. The grid divides space into square cells, and each cell is either ON or OFF at each moment. Each cell has eight neighbors: the four adjacent cells north, south, east, and west, and the four diagonals: northeast, southeast, southwest, and northwest. Time in the Life world is also discrete, not continuous; it advances in ticks, and the state of the world changes between each tick according to the following rule:

> Each cell, in order to determine what to do in the next instant, counts how many of its eight neighbors is ON at the present instant. If the answer is exactly two, the cell stays in its present state (ON or OFF) in the next instant. If the answer is exactly three, the cell is ON in the next instant whatever its current state. Under all other conditions the cell is OFF.

The entire physics of the Life world is captured in that single, unexceptioned law. [While this is the fundamental law of the "physics" of the Life world, it helps at first to conceive this curious physics in biological terms: think of cells going ON as births, cells going OFF as deaths, and succeeding instants as generations. Either overcrowding (more than three inhabited neighbors) or isolation (less than two inhabited neighbors) leads to death.] By the scrupulous application of this single law, one can predict with perfect accuracy the next instant of any configuration of ON and OFF cells, and the instant after that, and so forth. In other words, the Life world is a toy world that perfectly instantiates Laplace's vision of determinism: given the state description of this world at an instant, we finite observers can perfectly predict the future instants by the simple application of our one law of physics. Or, in my terms, when we adopt the physical stance toward a configuration in the Life world, our powers of prediction are perfect: there is no noise, no uncertainty, no probability less than one. Moreover, it follows from the two-dimensionality of the Life world that nothing is hidden from view. There is no backstage; there are no hidden variables; the unfolding of the physics of objects in the Life world is directly and completely visible.

There are computer simulations of the Life world in which one can set up configurations on the screen and then watch them evolve according to the single rule. In the best simulations, one can change the scale of both time and space, alternating between close-up and bird's-eye view. A nice touch added to some color versions is that ON cells (often just called pixels) are color-coded by their age; they are born blue, let us say, and then change color each generation, moving through green to yellow to orange to red to brown to black and then staying black unless they die. This permits one to see at a glance how old certain patterns are, which cells are co-generational, where the birth action is, and so forth.[18]

One soon discovers that some simple configurations are more interesting than others. In addition to those configurations which never change—the "still lifes" such as four pixels in a square—and those which evaporate entirely—such as any long diagonal line segment, whose two tail pixels die of isolation each instant until the line disappears entirely—there are configurations with all manner of periodicity. Three pixels in a line make a simple flasher, which becomes three pixels in a column in the next instant, and reverts to three in a line in the next, ad infinitum, unless some other configuration encroaches. Encroachment is what makes Life interesting: among the periodic configurations are some that swim, amoeba-like, across the plane. The simplest is the *glider*, the five-pixel configuration shown taking a single stroke to the southeast in [Figure 2]. Then there are the eaters, the puffer trains, and space rakes, and a host of other aptly named denizens of the Life world that emerge in the ontology of a new level, analogous to what I have called the design level. This level has its own language, a transparent foreshortening of the tedious descriptions one could give at the physical level. For instance:

> An eater can eat a glider in four generations. Whatever is being consumed, the basic process is the same. A bridge forms between the eater and its prey. In the next generation, the bridge region dies from overpopulation, taking a bite out of both eater and prey. The eater

then repairs itself. The prey usually cannot. If the remainder of the prey dies out as with the glider, the prey is consumed (*ibid.*, p. 38).

Note that there has been a distinct ontological shift as we move between levels; whereas at the physical level there is no motion, and the only individuals, cells, are defined by their fixed spatial location, at this design level we have the motion of persisting objects; it is one and the same glider that has moved southeast in [Figure 2], changing shape as it moves, and there is one less glider in the world after the eater has eaten it in [Figure 3]. (Here is a warming-up exercise for what is to follow: should we say that there is *real* motion in the Life world, or only *apparent* motion? The flashing pixels on the computer screen are a paradigm case, after all, of what a psychologist would call apparent motion. Are there *really* gliders that move, or are there just patterns of cell state that move? And if we opt for the latter, should we say at least that these moving patterns are real?)

Notice, too, that at this level one proposes generalizations that require "usually" or "provided nothing encroaches" clauses. Stray bits of debris from earlier events can "break" or "kill" one of the objects in the ontology at this level; their *salience as real things* is considerable, but not guaranteed. To say that their salience is considerable is to say that one can, with some small risk, ascend to this design level, adopt its ontology, and proceed to predict—sketchily and riskily—the behavior of larger configurations or systems of configurations, without bothering to compute the physical level. For instance, one can set oneself the task of designing some interesting supersystem out of the "parts" that the design level makes available. Surely the most impressive triumph of this design activity in the Life world is the proof that a working model of a universal Turing machine can in principle be constructed in the Life plane! Von Neumann had already shown that in principle a two-dimensional universal Turing machine could be constructed out of cellular automata, so it was "just" a matter of

Glider

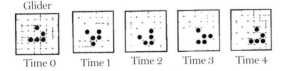

Time 0   Time 1   Time 2   Time 3   Time 4

FIGURE 2 (from Poundstone, *op. cit.*).

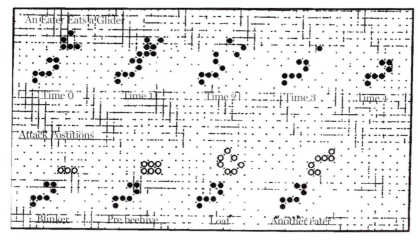

FIGURE 3 (from Poundstone, *op. cit.*).

"engineering" to show how, in principle, it could be constructed out of the simpler cellular automata defined in the Life world. Glider streams can provide the tape, for instance, and the tape reader can be some huge assembly of eaters, gliders, and other bits and pieces. What does this huge Turing machine look like? Poundstone calculates that the whole construction, a self-reproducing machine incorporating a universal Turing machine, would be on the order of 10^{13} pixels.

> Displaying a 10^{13}-pixel pattern would require a video screen about 3 million pixels across at least. Assume the pixels are 1 millimeter square (which is very high resolution by the standards of home computers). Then the screen would have to be 3 kilometers (about two miles) across. It would have an area about six times that of Monaco.
>
> Perspective would shrink the pixels of a self-reproducing pattern to invisibility. If you got far enough away from the screen so that the entire pattern was comfortably in view, the pixels (and even the gliders, eaters and guns) would be too tiny to make out. A self-reproducing pattern would be a hazy glow, like a galaxy (*ibid.*, pp. 227–8).

Now, since the universal Turing machine can compute any computable function, it can play chess—simply by mimicking the program of any chess-playing computer you like. Suppose, then, that such an entity occupies the Life plane, playing chess against itself. Looking at the configuration of dots that accomplishes this marvel would almost certainly be unilluminating to anyone who had no clue that a configuration with such powers could exist. But from the perspective of one who had the hypothesis that this huge array of black dots was a chess-playing computer, enormously efficient ways of predicting the future of that configuration are made available. As a first step one can shift from an ontology of gliders and eaters to an ontology of symbols and machine states, and, adopting this higher design stance toward the configuration, predict its future *as* a Turing machine. As a second and still more efficient step, one can shift to an ontology of chessboard positions, possible chess moves, and the grounds for evaluating them; then, adopting the intentional stance toward the configuration, one can predict its future *as* a chess player performing intentional actions—making chess moves and trying to achieve checkmate. Once one has fixed on an interpretation scheme, permitting one to say which configurations of pixels count as which symbols (either, at the Turing machine level, the symbols "0" or "1," say, or at the intentional level, "*QxBch*" and the other symbols for chess moves), one can use the interpretation scheme to predict, for instance, that the next configuration to emerge from the galaxy will be such-and-such a glider stream (the symbols for "*RxQ*," say). There is risk involved in either case, because the chess program being run on the Turing machine may be far from perfectly rational, and, at a different level, debris may wander onto the scene and "break" the Turing machine configuration before it finishes the game.

In other words, real but (potentially) noisy patterns abound in such a configuration of the Life world, there for the picking up if only we are lucky or clever enough to hit on the right perspective. They are not *visual* patterns but, one might say, *intellectual* patterns. Squinting or twisting the page is not apt to help, while posing fanciful interpretations (or what W. V. Quine would call "analytical hypotheses") may uncover a goldmine. The opportunity confronting the observer of such a Life world is analogous to the opportunity confronting the cryptographer staring at a new patch of cipher text, or the opportunity confronting the Martian, peering through a telescope at the Superbowl Game. If the Martian hits on the intentional stance—or folk psychology—as the right level to look for pattern, shapes will readily emerge through the noise.

IV. THE REALITY OF INTENTIONAL PATTERNS

The scale of compression when one adopts the intentional stance toward the two-dimensional chess-playing computer galaxy is stupendous: it is the difference between figuring out in your head what white's most likely (best) move is versus calculating the state of a few trillion pixels through a few hundred thousand generations. But the scale of the savings is really no greater in the Life world than in our own. Predicting that someone will duck if you throw a brick at

him is easy from the folk-psychological stance; it is and will always be intractable if you have to trace the photons from brick to eyeball, the neurotransmitters from optic nerve to motor nerve, and so forth.

For such vast computational leverage one might be prepared to pay quite a steep price in errors, but in fact one belief that is shared by all of the representatives on the spectrum I am discussing is that "folk psychology" provides a description system that permits highly reliable prediction of human (and much nonhuman) behavior.[19] They differ in the explanations they offer of this predictive prowess, and the implications they see in it about "realism."

For Fodor, an industrial-strength Realist, beliefs and their kin would not be real unless the pattern dimly discernible from the perspective of folk psychology could also be discerned (more clearly, with less noise) as a pattern of structures in the brain. The pattern would have to be discernible from the different perspective provided by a properly tuned *syntactoscope* aimed at the purely formal (non-semantic) features of Mentalese terms written in the brain. For Fodor, the pattern seen through the noise by everyday folk psychologists would tell us nothing about reality, unless it, and the noise, had the following sort of explanation: what we discern from the perspective of folk psychology is the net effect of two processes: an ulterior, hidden process wherein the pattern exists quite pure, overlaid, and partially obscured by various intervening sources of noise: performance errors, observation errors, and other more or less random obstructions. He might add that the interior belief-producing process was in this respect *just* like the process responsible for the creation of frames *A–F*. If you were permitted to peer behind the scenes at the program I devised to create the frames, you would see, clear as a bell, the perfect bar-code periodicity, with the noise thrown on afterward like so much salt and pepper.

This is often the explanation for the look of a data set in science, and Fodor may think that it is either the only explanation that can ever be given, or at any rate the only one that makes any sense of the success of folk psychology. But the rest of us disagree. As G. E. M. Anscombe[20] put it in her pioneering exploration of intentional explanation, "if Aristotle's account [of reasoning using the practical syllogism] were supposed to describe actual mental processes, it would in general be quite absurd. The interest of the account is that it describes an order which is there whenever actions are done with intentions..." (*ibid.*, p. 80).

But how *could* the order be there, so visible amidst the noise, if it were not the direct outline of a concrete orderly process in the background? Well, it *could* be there thanks to the statistical effect of very many concrete minutiae producing, as if by a hidden hand, an approximation of the "ideal" order. Philosophers have tended to ignore a variety of regularity intermediate between the regularities of planets and other objects "obeying" the laws of physics and the regularities of rule-following (that is, rule-*consulting*) systems.[21] These intermediate regularities are those which are preserved under selection pressure: the regularities dictated by principles of good design and hence homed in on by self-designing systems. That is, a "rule of thought" may be much more than a mere regularity; it may be a *wise* rule, a rule one would design a system by if one were a system designer, and hence a rule one would expect self-designing systems to "discover" in the course of settling into their patterns of activity. Such rules no more need be explicitly represented than do the principles of aerodynamics that are honored in the design of birds' wings.[22]

The contrast between these different sorts of pattern-generation processes can be illustrated. The frames in [Figure 1] were created by a hard-edged process (ten black, ten white, ten black, ...) obscured by noise, while the frames in [Figure 4] were created by a process almost the reverse of that: the top frame shows a pattern created by a normal distribution of black dots around means at $x = 10, 30, 50, 70,$ and 90 (rather like

Mach bands or interference fringes); the middle and bottom frames were created by successive applications of a very simple contrast enhancer applied to the top frame: a vertical slit "window" three pixels high is thrown randomly onto the frame; the pixels in the window vote, and majority rules. This gradually removes the salt from the pepper and the pepper from the salt, creating "artifact" edges such as those discernible in the bottom frame. The effect would be more striking at a finer pixel scale, where the black merges imperceptibly through grays to white but I chose to keep the scale at the ten-pixel period of bar code. I do not mean to suggest that it is impossible to tell the patterns in [Figure 4] from the patterns in [Figure 1]. Of course it is possible; for one thing, the process that produced the frames in [Figure 1] will almost always show edges at exactly 10, 20, 30, ... and almost never at 9, 11, 19, 21, ... while there is a higher probability of these "displaced" edges being created by the process of [Figure 4] (as a close inspection of [Figure 4] reveals). Fine tuning could of course reduce these probabilities, but that is not my point. My point is that *even if* the evidence is substantial that the discernible pattern is produced by one process rather than another, it can be rational to ignore those differences and use the simplest pattern description (e.g., *bar code*) as one's way of organizing the data.

Fodor and others have claimed that an interior language of thought is the best explanation of the hard edges visible in "propositional attitude psychology." Churchland and I have offered an alternative explanation of these edges, an explanation for which the process that produced the frames in [Figure 4] is a fine visual metaphor. The process that produces the data of folk psychology, we claim, is one in which the multidimensional complexities of the underlying processes are projected *through linguistic behavior*, which creates an appearance of definiteness and precision, thanks to the discreteness of words.[23] As Churchland[24] puts it, a person's declarative utterance is a "one-dimensional *projection*—

FIGURE 4

through the compound lens of Wernicke's and Broca's areas onto the idiosyncratic surface of the speaker's language—a one-dimensional projection of a four- or five-dimensional 'solid' that is an element in his true kinematic state" (*ibid.*, p. 85).

Fodor's industrial-strength Realism takes beliefs to be things in the head—just like cells and blood vessels and viruses. Davidson and I both like Churchland's alternative idea of propositional-attitude statements as indirect "measurements" of a reality diffused in the behavioral dispositions of the brain (and body).[25] We think beliefs are quite real enough to call real just so long as belief talk measures these complex behavior-disposing organs as predictively as it does. What do we disagree about? As John Haugeland[26] has pointed out, Davidson is more of a realist than I am, and I have recently tracked down the source of this disagreement to a difference of opinion we have about the status of Quine's principle of indeterminacy of translation, which we both accept.

For Davidson, the principle is not the shocker it is often taken to be; in fact, it is well-nigh trivial—the two different translation manuals between which no fact of the matter decides are like two different scales for measuring temperature.

We know there is no contradiction between the temperature of the air being 32° fahrenheit and 0° celsius; there is nothing in this "relativism" to show that the properties being measured are not "real." Curiously, though, this conclusion has repeatedly been drawn.... Yet in the light of the considerations put forward here, this comes to no more than the recognition that more than one set of one person's utterances might be equally successful in capturing the contents of someone else's thoughts or speech. Just as numbers can capture all the empirically significant relations among weights or temperatures in infinitely many ways, so one person's utterances can capture all the significant features of another person's thoughts and speech in different ways. This fact does not challenge the "reality" of the attitudes or meanings thus reported.[27]

On Davidson's view, no substantive disagreements emerge from a comparison of the two description schemes, and so they can quite properly be viewed as competing descriptions of the same reality.

I think this is a flawed analogy. A better one is provided by the example of "rival" descriptions of patterns-with-noise. Consider two rival intentional interpretations of a single individual; they agree on the general shape of this individual's collection of beliefs (and desires, etc), but because of their different idealizations of the pattern, they do not agree point-for-point. Recalling a famous analogy of Quine's[28] and extending it beyond radical translation to radical interpretation (as Davidson and I both wish to do), we get the image in [Figure 5].

To the left we see Brown's intentional interpretation of Ella; to the right, Jones's interpretation. Since these are intentional interpretations, the pixels or data points represent beliefs and so forth, not (for instance) bits of bodily motion or organs or cells or atoms, and since these are rival intentional interpretations of a single individual, the patterns discerned are not statistical averages (e.g., "Democrats tend to favor welfare programs") but personal cognitive idiosyncrasies (e.g., "She thinks she should get her queen out early"). Some of the patterns may indeed be simple observed periodicities (e.g., "Ella wants

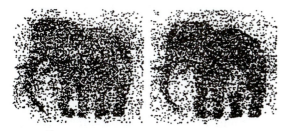

FIGURE 5

to talk about football on Mondays") but we are to understand the pattern to be what Anscombe called the "order which is there" in the rational coherence of a person's set of beliefs, desires, and intentions.

Notice that here the disagreements can be substantial—at least before the fact: when Brown and Jones make a series of predictive bets, they will not always make the same bet. They may *often* disagree on what, according to their chosen pattern, will happen next. To take a dramatic case, Brown may predict that Ella will decide to kill herself; Jones may disagree. This is not a trivial disagreement of prediction, and in principle this momentous difference may emerge in spite of the overall consonance of the two interpretations.

Suppose, then, that Brown and Jones make a series of predictions of Ella's behavior, based on their rival interpretations. Consider the different categories that compose their track records. First, there are the occasions where they agree and are right. Both systems look good from the vantage point of these successes. Second, there are the occasions where they agree and are wrong. Both chalk it up to noise, take their budgeted loss and move on to the next case. But there will also be the occasions where they disagree, where their systems make different predictions, and in these cases sometimes (but not always) one will win and the other lose. (In the real world, predictions are not always from among binary alternatives, so in many cases they will disagree and both be wrong.) When one wins and the other loses, it will look to the myopic observer as if one "theory" has scored

a serious point against the other, but when one recognizes the possibility that both may chalk up such victories, and that there may be no pattern in the victories which permits either one to improve his theory by making adjustments, one sees that local triumphs may be insufficient to provide any ground in reality for declaring one account a closer approximation of the truth.

Now, some might think this situation is *always* unstable; eventually one interpretation is bound to ramify better to new cases, or be deducible from some larger scheme covering other data, etc. That might be true in many cases, but—and this, I think, is the central point of Quine's indeterminacy thesis—it need not be true in all. *If* the strategy of intentional-stance description is, as Quine says, a "dramatic idiom" in which there is ineliminable use of idealization, and if Fodor's industrial-strength Realism is thus not the correct explanation of the reliable "visibility" of the pattern, such radical indeterminacy is a genuine and stable possibility.

This indeterminacy will be most striking in such cases as the imagined disagreement over Ella's suicidal mindset. If Ella does kill herself, is Brown shown to have clearly had the better intentional interpretation? Not necessarily. When Jones chalks up his scheme's failure in this instance to a bit of noise, this is no more ad hoc or unprincipled than the occasions when Brown was wrong about whether Ella would order the steak not the lobster, and chalked those misses up to noise. This is not at all to say that an interpretation can never be shown to be just wrong; there is plenty of leverage within the principles of intentional interpretation to refute particular hypotheses—for instance, by forcing their defense down the path of Pickwickian explosion ("You see, she didn't believe the gun was loaded because she thought that those bullet-shaped things were chocolates wrapped in foil, which was just a fantasy that occurred to her because...."). It *is* to say that there could be two interpretation schemes that were reliable and compact predictors over the long run, but that nevertheless disagreed on crucial cases.

It might seem that in a case as momentous as Ella's intention to kill herself, a closer examination of the details just prior to the fatal moment (if not at an earlier stage) would have to provide additional support for Brown's interpretation at the expense of Jones's interpretation. After all, there would be at least a few seconds—or a few hundred milliseconds—during which Ella's decision to pull the trigger got implemented, and during that brief period, at least, the evidence would swing sharply in favor of Brown's interpretation. That is no doubt true, and it is *perhaps* true that had one gone into enough detail earlier, all this last-second detail could have been predicted—but to have gone into *those* details earlier would have been to drop down from the intentional stance to the design or physical stances. From the intentional stance, these determining considerations would have been invisible to both Brown and Jones, who were both prepared to smear over such details as noise in the interests of more practical prediction. Both interpreters concede that they will make false predictions, and moreover, that when they make false predictions there are apt to be harbingers of misprediction in the moments during which the *dénouement* unfolds. Such a brief swing does not constitute refutation of the interpretation, any more than the upcoming misprediction of behavior does.

How, then, does this make me less of a realist than Davidson? I see that there could be two different systems of belief attribution to an individual which differed *substantially* in what they attributed—even in yielding substantially different predictions of the individual's future behavior—and yet where no deeper fact of the matter could establish that one was a description of the individual's *real* beliefs and the other not. In other words, there could be two different, but equally real, patterns discernible in the noisy world. The rival theorists would not even agree on which parts of the world were pattern and which were noise, and yet nothing deeper would settle the issue.[29] The choice of a pattern would indeed be up to the observer, a matter to be decided on idiosyncratic

pragmatic grounds. I myself do not see any feature of Davidson's position that would be a serious obstacle to his shifting analogies and agreeing with me. But then he would want to grant that indeterminacy is not such a trivial matter after all.[30]

What then is Rorty's view on these issues? Rorty wants to deny that any brand of "realism" could *explain* the (apparent?) success of the intentional stance. But since we have already joined Fine and set aside the "metaphysical" problem of realism, Rorty's reminding us of this only postpones the issue. Even someone who has transcended the scheme/content distinction and has seen the futility of correspondence theories of truth must accept the fact that *within* the natural ontological attitude we sometimes explain success by correspondence: one does better navigating off the coast of Maine when one uses an up-to-date nautical chart than one does when one uses a road map of Kansas. Why? Because the former accurately represents the hazards, markers, depths, and coastlines of the Maine coast, and the latter does not. Now why does one do better navigating the shoals of interpersonal relations using folk psychology than using astrology? Rorty might hold that the predictive "success" we folk-psychology players relish is itself an artifact, a mutual agreement engendered by the egging-on or consensual support we who play this game provide each other. He would grant that the game has no rivals in popularity, due—in the opinion of the players—to the power it gives them to understand and anticipate the animate world. But he would refuse to endorse this opinion. How, then, would he distinguish this popularity from the popularity among a smaller coterie of astrology?[31] It is undeniable that astrology provides its adherents with a highly articulated system of patterns that they *think* they see in the events of the world. The difference, however, is that no one has ever been able to get rich by betting on the patterns, but only by selling the patterns to others.

Rorty would have to claim that this is not a significant difference; the rest of us, however, find abundant evidence that our allegiance to folk psychology as a predictive tool can be defended in coldly objective terms. We agree that there is a real pattern being described by the terms of folk psychology. What divides the rest of us is the nature of the pattern, and the ontological implications of that nature.

Let us finally consider Churchland's eliminative materialism from this vantage point. As already pointed out, he is second to none in his appreciation of the power, to date, of the intentional stance as a strategy of prediction. Why does he think that it is nevertheless doomed to the trash heap? Because he anticipates that neuroscience will eventually—perhaps even soon—discover a pattern that is so clearly superior to the noisy pattern of folk psychology that everyone will readily abandon the former for the latter (except, perhaps, in the rough-and-tumble of daily life). This might happen, I suppose. But Churchland here is only playing a hunch, a hunch that should not be seen to gain plausibility from reflections on the irresistible forward march of science. For it is not enough for Churchland to suppose that in principle, neuroscientific levels of description will explain more of the variance, predict more of the "noise" that bedevils higher levels. This is, of course, bound to be true in the limit—if we descend all the way to the neurophysiological "bit map." But as we have seen, the trade-off between ease of use and immunity from error for such a cumbersome system may make it profoundly unattractive.[32] If the "pattern" is scarcely an improvement over the bit map, talk of eliminative materialism will fall on deaf ears—just as it does when radical eliminativists urge us to abandon our ontological commitments to tables and chairs. A truly general-purpose, robust system of pattern description more valuable than the intentional stance is not an impossibility, but anyone who wants to bet on it might care to talk to me about the odds they will take.

What does all this show? Not that Fodor's industrial-strength Realism must be false, and not that Churchland's eliminative materialism must be false, but just that both views are gratuitously

strong forms of materialism—presumptive theses way out in front of the empirical support they require. Rorty's view errs in the opposite direction, ignoring the impressive empirical track record that distinguishes the intentional stance from the astrological stance. Davidson's intermediate position, like mine, ties reality to the brute existence of pattern, but Davidson has overlooked the possibility of two or more *conflicting* patterns being superimposed on the same data—a more radical indeterminacy of translation than he had supposed possible. Now, once again, is the view I am defending here a sort of instrumentalism or a sort of realism? I think that the view itself is clearer than either of the labels, so I shall leave that question to anyone who still finds illumination in them.

Notes

1. *Content and Consciousness* (Boston: Routledge & Kegan Paul, 1969), ch. 1.
2. "Three Kinds of Intentional Psychology," in R. Healey, ed., *Reduction, Time and Reality* (New York: Cambridge, 1981); and *The Intentional Stance* (Cambridge: MIT, 1987).
3. Peter Smith, "Wit and Chutzpah," review of *The Intentional Stance* and Jerry A. Fodor's *Psychosemantics, Times Higher Education Supplement* (August 7, 1988), p. 22.
4. "The Stance Stance," commentary on *The Intentional Stance*, in *Behavioral and Brain Sciences*, XI (1988): 511–2.
5. R. A. Sharpe, in "Dennett's Journey Towards Panpsychism," *Inquiry*, XXXII (1989): 233–240, takes me to task on this point, using examples from Proust to drive home the point that "Proust draws our attention to possible lives and these possible lives are various. But in none of them is prediction of paramount importance" (240). I agree. I also agree that what makes people interesting (in novels and in real life) is precisely their unpredictability. But that unpredictability is only interesting against the backdrop of routine predictability on which all interpretation depends. As I note in *The Intentional Stance* (p. 79) in response to a similar objection of Fodor's, the same is true of chess: the game is interesting only because of the unpredictability of one's opponent, but that is to say: the

intentional stance can usually eliminate *only* ninety percent of the legal moves.

6. Norton Nelkin, "Patterns," *Mind and Language* 9.1 (1994): 56–87.

7. *The Shaky Game: Einstein Realism and the Quantum Theory* (Chicago: University Press, 1986); see esp. p. 153n, and his comments there on Rorty, which I take to be consonant with mine here.

8. See *The Intentional Stance*, pp. 38–42, "Real patterns, deeper facts, and empty questions."

9. "Randomness and Mathematical Proof," *Scientific American*, CCXXXII (1975): 47–52.

10. More precisely: "A series of numbers is random if the smallest algorithm capable of specifying it to a computer has about the same number of bits of information as the series itself" (Chaitin, p. 48). This is what explains the fact that the "random number generator" built into most computers is not really properly named, since it is some function describable in a few bits (a little subroutine that is called for some output whenever a program requires a "random" number or series). If I send you the description of the pseudo-random number generator on my computer, you can use it to generate exactly the same infinite series of random-seeming digits.

11. Such schemes for efficient description, called compression algorithms, are widely used in computer graphics for saving storage space. They break the screen into uniformly colored regions, for instance, and specify region boundaries (rather like the "paint by numbers" line drawings sold in craft shops). The more complicated the picture on the screen, the longer the compressed description will be; in the worst case (a picture of confetti randomly sprinkled over the screen) the compression algorithm will be stumped, and can do no better than a verbatim bit map.

12. What about the "system" of pattern description that simply baptizes frames with proper names (*A* through *F*, in this case) and tells the receiver which frame is up by simply sending "*F*"? This looks much shorter than the bit map until we consider that such a description must be part of an entirely general system. How many proper names will we need to name all possible 900-dot frames? Trivially, the 900-bit binary number, 11111111.... To send the "worst-case" proper name will take exactly as many bits as sending the bit map. This confirms our intuition that proper names are maximally inefficient ways of couching generalizations ("Alf is tall and Bill is tall and . . .").

13. A. D. de Groot, *Thought and Choice in Chess* (The Hague: Mouton, 1965).

14. *Science, Perception and Reality* (Boston: Routledge & Kegan Paul, 1963).

15. In "Randomness and Perceived Randomness in Evolutionary Biology," *Synthese*, XLIII (1980): 287–329, William Wimsatt offers a nice example (296): while the insectivorous bird tracks individual insects, the anteater just averages over the ant-infested area; one might say that, while the bird's manifest image quantifies over insects, "ant" is a mass term for anteaters. See the discussion of this and related examples in my *Elbow Room* (Cambridge: MIT, 1984), pp. 108–110.

16. *The Intentional Stance*, pp. 37–9.

17. Martin Gardner introduced the Game of Life to a wide audience in two columns in *Scientific American* in October, 1970, and February, 1971. William Poundstone, *The Recursive Universe: Cosmic Complexity and the Limits of Scientific Knowledge* (New York: Morrow, 1985), is an excellent exploration of the game and its philosophical implications.

18. Poundstone, *op. cit.*, provides simple BASIC and IBM-PC assembly language simulations you can copy for your own home computer, and describes some of the interesting variations.

19. To see that the opposite poles share this view, see Fodor, *Psychosemantics* (Cambridge: MIT, 1987), ch. 1, "Introduction: the Persistence of the Attitudes"; and Paul Churchland, *Scientific Realism and the Plasticity of Mind* (New York: Cambridge, 1979), esp. p. 100: "For the P-theory [folk psychology] is in fact a marvelous intellectual achievement. It gives its possessor an explicit and systematic insight into the behaviour, verbal and otherwise, of some of the most complex agents in the environment, and its overall prowess in that respect remains unsurpassed by anything else our considerable theoretical efforts have produced."

20. *Intention* (New York: Blackwell, 1957).

21. A notable early exception is Sellars, who discussed the importance of just this sort of regularity in "Some Reflections on Language Games," *Philosophy of Science*, XXI (1954): 204–228. See especially the subsection of this classic paper, entitled "Pattern Governed and Rule Obeying Behavior," reprinted in Sellars's *Science, Perception and Reality*, pp. 324–7.

22. Several interpreters of a draft of this article have supposed that the conclusion I am urging here is that beliefs (or their contents) are *epiphenomena* having no causal powers, but this is a misinterpretation traceable to a simplistic notion of causation. If one finds a predictive pattern of the sort just described one has *ipso facto* discovered a causal power—a difference in the world that makes a subsequent difference testable by standard empirical methods of variable manipulation. Consider the crowd-drawing power of a sign reading "Free Lunch" placed in the window of a restaurant, and compare its power in a restaurant in New York to its power in a restaurant in Tokyo. The intentional level is obviously the right level at which to predict and explain such causal powers; the sign more reliably produces a particular belief in one population of perceivers than in the other, and variations in the color of typography of the sign are not as predictive of variations in crowd-drawing power as are variations in (perceivable) meaning. The fact that the regularities on which these successful predictions are based are efficiently capturable (only) in intentional terms and are not derived from "covering laws" does not show that the regularities are not "causal"; it just shows that philosophers have often relied on pinched notions of causality derived from exclusive attention to a few examples drawn from physics and chemistry. Smith has pointed out to me that here I am echoing Aristotle's claim that his predecessors had ignored final causes.

23. See my discussion of the distinction between beliefs and (linguistically infected) *opinions*, in *Brainstorms* (Montgomery, VT: Bradford, 1978), ch. 16, and in "The Illusions of Realism," in *The Intentional Stance*, pp. 110–6.

24. "Eliminative Materialism and the Propositional Attitudes," this JOURNAL, LXXVIII, 2 (February 1981): 67–90, esp. p. 85.

25. Churchland introduces the idea in *Scientific Realism and the Plasticity of Mind*, pp. 100–7. My adoption of the idea was in "Beyond Belief," in A. Woodfield, ed., *Thought and Object* (New York: Oxford, 1982), repr. as ch. 5 of *The Intentional Stance*. Davidson's guarded approval is expressed in "What is Present to the Mind?" read at the Sociedad Filosófica Ibero Americana meeting in Buenos Aires, 1989.

26. See the discussion of Haugeland's views in the last chapter of *The Intentional Stance*,

"Mid-Term Examination: Compare and Contrast," pp. 348–9.

27. Davidson, "What is Present to the Mind?" (ms.), p. 10.

28. "Different persons growing up in the same language are like different bushes trimmed and trained to take the shape of identical elephants. The anatomical details of twigs and branches will fulfill the elephantine form differently from bush to bush, but the overall outward results are the same." *Word and Object* (Cambridge: MIT, 1960), p. 8.

29. Cf. "The Abilities of Men and Machines," in *Brainstorms*, where I discuss two people who agree exactly on the future behavior of some artifact, but impose different Turing-machine interpretations of it. On both interpretations, the machine occasionally "makes errors" but the two interpreters disagree about which cases are the errors. (They disagree about which features of the object's behavior count as signal and which as noise.) Which Turing machine is it really? This question has no answer.

30. Andrej Zabludowski seems to me to have overlooked this version of indeterminacy in "On Quine's Indeterminacy Doctrine," *Philosophical Review*, XCVIII (1989): 35–64.

31. Cf. my comparison of "the astrological stance" to the intentional stance, *The Intentional Stance*, p. 16.

32. As I have put it, physical-stance predictions trump design-stance predictions, which trump intentional-stance predictions—but one pays for the power with a loss of portability and a (usually unbearable) computational cost.

Study Questions

1. What does it mean for mental states to have an intermediate existence? What does this intermediate existence consist of?

2. If we ascribe beliefs and desires to an inanimate object and thereby fruitfully predict that object's behavior, does that mean that the inanimate object has beliefs?

3. If beliefs exist because it's useful for us to posit them, does that then imply that souls exist if it's useful for us to posit them? Why or why not?

4.8   Why the Child's Theory of Mind Really Is a Theory

 ## ALISON GOPNIK AND HENRY M. WELLMAN

ALISON GOPNIK (1955–) is a Professor in the Psychology Department at the University of California, Berkeley, and Henry Wellman (1948–) is the Harold Stevenson Collegiate Professor of Psychology at the University of Michigan. Both have been leading proponents of "theory theory." Gopnik is the author of the *Philosophical Baby: What Children's Minds Tell Us about Truth, Love and the Meaning of Life*. Wellman is the author of the book *The Child's Theory of Mind*. Both Gopnik and Wellman have published extensively on topics in developmental psychology. In this selection Gopnik and Wellman argue that children hold a tacit theory of how other people's minds work and apply the theory to observations just as scientists do with scientific theories.

How do children (and indeed adults) understand the mind? In this paper we contrast two accounts. One is the view that the child's early understanding of mind is an implicit theory analogous to scientific theories, and changes in that understanding may be understood as theory changes. The second is the view that the child need not really understand the mind, in the sense of having some set of beliefs about it. She bypasses conceptual understanding by operating a working model of the mind and reading its output. Fortunately, the child has such a model easily available, as all humans do, namely her own mind. The child's task is to learn how to apply this model to predict and explain others' mental states and actions. This is accomplished by running simulations on her working model, that is observing the output of her own mind, given certain inputs, and then applying the results to others.

The first position has a certain prominence; research on children's understanding of mind has come to be called "children's theory of mind." This position is linked to certain philosophers of mind such as Churchland (1984)

and Stich (1983) who characterize ordinary understanding of mind, our mentalistic folk psychology, as a theory. It is also part of a recent tendency to describe cognitive development as analogous to theory change in science (Carey, 1985, 1988; Karmiloff-Smith & Inhelder, 1975; Wellman & Gelman, 1988; Keil, 1989; Gopnik, 1984, 1988). The second position, in a somewhat different form, has a venerable philosophical tradition, going back to Descartes. This is the tradition of emphasizing the special importance of the first-person case in understanding the mind. More recently Gordon and Goldman have advocated a "simulation theory" of mind (ST), and this position has been taken up in the developmental literature by Harris (1991, this issue) and Johnson (1988).

We do not believe that this is a dispute that can be settled on conceptual or *a priori* grounds. Rather it is a contest between two empirically testable hypotheses about the nature of "folk psychology." We believe that the child's understanding of mind is helpfully construed as a theory, and that changes in understanding may be thought

A. Gopnik and H. Wellman, "Why the Child's Theory of Mind Really Is a Theory," *Mind and Language*, 7 (John Wiley & Sons, Inc.: March 1, 1992). Reprinted with permission of the publisher.

of as theory changes. But we believe this because such an account provides the best explanation for the currently available developmental evidence.

In spite of the prominence of the "theory theory" (TT), the exact nature of such folk psychological theories has rarely been spelt out in much detail, and in fact, this is often raised as an objection to this view. What exactly are the theoretical entities and laws that are involved in this theory? How is it constructed from the available evidence? We will first attempt to provide some of this detailed exposition. When the full story is told, we believe, a theory theory of early developments is compelling indeed. Second, we will argue that a contrasting simulation account fails to fit the data in key places and fails more generally to provide as comprehensive a view of development.

1. THE THEORY THEORY

The question of what distinguishes a theory from other types of conceptual schemas is, of course, an enormous and difficult one. Nevertheless, it seems to us that there are characteristic features of both theories and theory change that can be outlined in very broad and simplified terms.

Theoretical constructs are abstract entities postulated, or recruited from elsewhere, to provide a separate causal-explanatory level of analysis that accounts for evidential phenomena. Gravity is not itself two bodies moving in relation to one another, it is postulated to explain such phenomena. Such theoretical constructs are typically phrased in a vocabulary that is quite different from the evidential vocabulary. For example, Kepler's theory of the planets includes ideas about elliptical orbits that are notoriously not visible when we look at the stars' motions in the sky. Theories in biology postulate unseen entities, like viruses and bacteria, with distinctive properties some of which are implicated in transmission of disease. Theoretical constructs need not be definitively unobservable, but they must appeal to a set of entities removed from, and

underlying, the evidential phenomena themselves. They are designed to explain (not merely type and generalize) those empirical phenomena. So, one characteristic of theories is their abstractness. They postulate entities and analyses that explain the data but are not simply restatements of the data.[1]

Theoretical constructs do not work independently, they work together in systems characterized by laws or structure. A second characteristic of theories is their coherence. The theoretical entities and terms postulated by a theory are closely, "lawfully," interrelated with one another.

The coherence and abstractness of theories together give them a characteristic explanatory force.[2] These features of theories also give them a very characteristic sort of predictiveness. To put it crudely, we can map a bit of evidence on to one part of the theory, grind through the intratheoretic relations, come out at a very different place in the theory and then map back from that part of the theory to some new piece of evidence. In this way, the set of abstract entities encompass a wide range of events, events that might not even seem comparable at the evidential level of description. A theory not only makes predictions, it makes predictions about a wide variety of evidence, including evidence that played no role in the theory's initial construction. Kepler's account allows one to predict the behavior of new celestial objects, moons for example, which were quite unknown at the time the theory was formulated. Theories in biology allow us to predict that antibiotics will inhibit many bacterial infections, including some, like scarlet fever, that present none of the symptoms of an infected wound, or some, like Legionnaire's disease, that were unknown when the theory was formulated. They also allow us to predict that such drugs will be useless against viral infections, even when the symptoms of the viral infection are identical to those of a bacterial one.

Some of these predictions will be correct, they will accurately predict future events described at the evidential level, and will do so in ways that no mere empirical generalization could capture. Others will be incorrect. Since theories go beyond the evidence, and since theories are never completely right, some of their predictions will be falsified. In still other cases the theory will make no prediction at all. In fact, the theory may in some circumstances have less predictive power than a large set of empirical observations. This is because explanatory depth and force do not simply equate with predictive accuracy. We can make predictions about events without explaining them: Kepler's theory still leaves many of Tycho Brahe's observations unexplained. The differences in cases of theoretical prediction are two-fold. First, a few theoretical entities and laws can lead to a wide variety of unexpected predictions. Second, in the case of a theory, prediction is intimately tied to explanation.

An additional characteristic of theories, related to this central function of explanation, is that they produce interpretations of evidence, not simply descriptions of evidence and generalizations about it. Indeed theories influence which pieces of evidence we consider salient or important. In modern medicine, for example similar sets of symptoms do not necessarily yield the same disease diagnosis. An empirical typology of similar symptoms is overriden by deeper more theoretic biological explanations. The interpretive effects of theories may be stronger still, it is notoriously true that theoretical preconceptions may lead a scientist to dismiss some kinds of evidence as simply noise, or the result of methodological failures. Nor is this simply prejudice. On the contrary, deciding which evidence to ignore is crucial to the effective conduct of a scientific research program.

All these characteristics of theories ought also to apply to children's understanding of mind, if such understandings are theories of mind. That is, such theories should involve appeal to abstract unobservable entities, with coherent relations among them. Theories should invoke characteristic explanations phrased in terms of these abstract entities and laws. They should also lead

to characteristic patterns of predictions, including extensions to new types of evidence and false predictions, not just to more empirically accurate prediction. Finally, theories should lead to distinctive interpretations of evidence, a child with one theory should interpret even fundamental facts and experiences differently than a child with a different theory.

So far we have been talking mostly about the static features of theories, the features that might distinguish them from other cognitive structures such as typologies or schemas. But a most important thing about theories is their defeasibility. Theories are open to defeat via evidence and because of this theories change. In fact, a tenet of modern epistemology is that any aspect of a theory, even the most central ones, may change. The dynamic features of theories, the processes involved in theory formation and change, are equally characteristic and perhaps even more important from a developmental point of view.

While any very precise specification, any algorithm, for theory change may elude us, there are certainly substantive things to be said about how it typically takes place. There are characteristic intermediate processes involved in the transition from one theory to another. One particularly critical factor is the accumulation of counter-evidence to the theory. The initial reaction, as it were, of a theory to counter-evidence may be a kind of denial. The interpretive mechanisms of the theory may treat the counter-evidence as noise, mess, not worth attending to. At a slightly later stage the theory may develop *ad hoc* auxiliary hypotheses designed to account specifically for such counter-evidence. Auxiliary hypotheses may also be helpful because they phrase the counter-evidence in the accepted vocabulary of the earlier theory. Such auxiliary hypotheses, however, often appear, over time, to undermine the coherence that is one of a theory's strengths. The theory gets ugly and messy instead of being beautiful and simple.

A final step requires the availability or formulation of some alternative model to the original theory. A theory may limp along for some time under the weight of its auxiliary hypotheses if no alternative way of making progress is available. But the fertility of the alternative idea itself may not be recognized immediately. Initially it may only be applied to the problematic cases. We may see only later on that the new idea also provides an explanation for the evidence that was explained by the earlier theory.

The development of the heliocentric theory of the planets provides some good examples of these processes. Auxiliary hypotheses involving more and more complex arrangements of epicycles were initially invoked to deal with counter-evidence. Later heliocentrism was introduced by Copernicus. It is worth noting though that Copernicus' theory fails to apply the central heliocentric idea very widely. In many respects Copernicus' account is more like the Ptolemaic ones, than, say, Tycho Brahe's account. It includes epicycles, for example. Brahe's account acknowledges many of the flaws of the Ptolemaic ones, and uses the idea of heliocentrism to deal with them (other planets revolve around the sun which revolves around the earth). But Brahe fails to accept the central idea that the earth itself goes round the sun. Only with Kepler is there a really coherent heliocentric account that deals both with the anomalies and with the earlier data itself.

We propose that these same dynamic features should be apparent in children's transition from one theory to a later one, and specifically from one view of the mind to another. Children should ignore certain kinds of counter-evidence initially, then account for them by auxiliary hypotheses, then use the new theoretical idea in limited contexts, and only finally reorganize their knowledge so that new theoretical entities play a central role.

2. THE CHILD'S THEORIES OF MIND

We propose that there is a change from one mentalistic psychological theory to another somewhere between $2\frac{1}{2}$ and around 4. The change is not a simple all-or-none one, but rather involves a more gradual transition from one view of the mind to another. Indeed this change manifests the telltale intermediate processes that are characteristic of theory change. Two-year-olds have an early theory that is incorrect in that it does not posit the existence of mental representational states, prototypically beliefs. In 3-year-olds there is an intermediate phase where children demonstrate an understanding of the existence of representational states, at times, but only as auxiliary hypotheses. That is children in this phase can acknowledge that representational states of mind exist, if forced to do so in certain ways, but this realization is peripheral to their central explanatory theory. In a third phase, beginning around 4, children reorganize their central explanatory theory, it becomes properly a belief-desire psychology. Children begin to realize that what the actor thinks—his or her representation of the world rather than the world itself—inevitably determines actions.

2.1 The 2-year-old Theory

The 2-year-old is clearly a mentalist and not a behaviorist. Indeed, it seems unlikely to us that there is ever a time when normal children are behaviorists. Even in infancy, children seem to have some notions, however vague, of internal states as evidenced in early primary intersubjectivity (Trevarthen & Hubley, 1978) and imitation (Meltzoff & Moore, 1977; Meltzoff & Gopnik, 1993) and later, more clearly, in social referencing and joint attention behaviors (*e.g.* Wellman, 1993). It seems plausible that mentalism is the starting state of psychological knowledge. But such primary mentalism, whenever it first appears, does not include all the sorts of mental states that we as adults recognize. More specifically, even at two years psychological knowledge seems to be structured largely in terms of two types of internal states, desires, on the one hand and perceptions, on the other. However, this knowledge excludes any understanding of representation.

Desire and perception alone provide examples of the two basic categories of explanatory entities in folk psychology—the two types of theoretical constructs that Searle calls "world-to-mind" and "mind-to-world" states (Searle, 1983). An understanding of desire encompasses an early knowledge that what's in the mind can change what's in the world. An understanding of perception, on the other hand, encompasses an early knowledge that what's in the mind depends on what's in the world. Moreover, both desire and perception, as theoretical constructs, work to explain action but may also be divorced from any particular actions that an agent may perform.

Importantly, however, desire and perception can be, and at first are, understood in nonrepresentational terms. Desires at first are conceived simply as drives towards objects (Wellman & Woolley, 1990). Perceptions are at first understood simply as awareness of objects (Flavell, 1988). In neither case need the child conceive of a complex propositional or representational relationship between these mental states and the world. Instead, these very young children seem to treat desire and perception as fairly simple causal links between the mind and the world. Given that an agent desires an object, the agent will act to obtain it. Given that an object is within a viewer's line of sight, the viewer will see it. These causal constructs are simple, but they have considerable predictive power. In particular, together they allow the first form of "the practical syllogism": "If an agent desires X, and sees it exists, he will do things to get it." Even that form of the practical syllogism is a powerful inferential folk psychological law. It allows children to infer for example, that if John wants a cookie and sees one in the cookie jar, he will go there for it. If he doesn't want it, or doesn't see it, he won't.

2.2 The 3-year-old Theory

By three, children begin to show signs of a more elaborate mental ontology. Given the difficulties of testing children younger than three, the earliest emergence of this aspect of the theory is difficult to document. While 2-year-olds' successes on desire and perception tasks are striking, their failures on other tasks are more difficult to interpret. However, natural language can provide us with one avenue for exploring these abilities. Before three, children make extensive and appropriate use of terms for desire and perception (Bretherton & Beeghly, 1982). More cognitive mental terms (think, know, remember, make-believe, dream) only begin to emerge at around the third birthday (Shatz, Wellman & Silber, 1983).

There is further evidence that at three children begin to have a more general notion of belief and also of such representational but "not real" mental states as pretenses, dreams, and images (e.g. Wellman & Estes, 1986). When these concepts first appear, however, they have an interesting character, framed by the child's larger theory which is still a desire-perception theory. This manifests itself in two ways. First, understanding of belief appears to be initially modelled on a non-representational understanding, that is modelled on an earlier understanding of desire and especially perception. Second, even when the notion of belief, as a representation, appears it first plays little if any role in the child's explanations of behavior. In these respects the child's first conception of belief seems to be a conceptual construction based on reworking earlier theoretical constructs. Moreover, even the more advanced representational notion initially functions like an auxiliary hypothesis rather than a central theoretical construct.

To elaborate, 3-year-olds' first understanding of belief seems like their earlier understanding of perception in that it shares something of that construct's nonrepresentational character. Specifically, belief does not at first easily encompass a sense of misrepresentation. On this view, belief, like perception and desire, involves rather direct causal links between objects and believers. This view has variously been called a "copy theory" (Wellman, 1990), a "Gibsonian theory" (Astington & Gopnik, 1991a) a "situation theory" (Perner, 1991), or a "cognitive connection" (Flavell, 1988) theory of belief. The similar idea in all these accounts is that belief contents directly reflect the world. The introduction of a notion of belief promises an important additional complexity to the child's theory of mind. Initially however, the notion seems to be quite strongly embedded in the nonrepresentational desire-perception framework of the earlier theory.

At times, however, at least as the fourth year progresses, 3-year-olds are able to recognize the existence of beliefs that clearly misrepresent. They can explain already completed, ineffective actions as indicating a false belief by the actor and can at times even acknowledge the presence of mistaken, wrong beliefs (*e.g.* Siegal & Beattie, 1991; Moses, 1990). However, these same children do not often construe actions as stemming from false beliefs. When predicting action they typically, consistently, resistantly act as if the actor's desire along with the objective facts determine action, ignoring a role for false belief in influencing action (*e.g.* Gopnik & Astington, 1988; Perner, Leekham & Wimmer, 1987; Wellman & Bartsch, 1988). Similarly, when asked the contents of person's belief, they consistently, resistantly cite the facts (*e.g.* Perner *et al.*, 1987; Moses & Flavell, 1990). In short, when predicting action and when diagnosing belief contents, 3-year-olds evidence largely a nonrepresentational desire-perception understanding.

What about "non-real" mental states, such as pretenses, dreams, and images? There is evidence that children actually have such fictional mental states as young as 18 months (*e.g.* Leslie, 1987). Evidence that they understand such states, however, is much less clear. By the third birthday, however, children have some conceptual knowledge of these aspects of mental life (*e.g.* Wellman & Estes, 1986; Harris, Brown, Marriot, Whittall & Harmer, 1991). Moreover, they may distinguish such imaginary or hypothetical states from the states of desire and perception. However, these states appear to play

little role in children's explanation of ordinary behavior. More significantly, these states have little causal connection to objects (that, in fact, is what is distinctive about them). While children see desires as states that modify the world, and perceptions as states that are modified by the world, pretenses, images and dreams, on their view, bear no causal relation to the world at all. It is possible that postulating these states, which are representational but divorced from reality, also plays a role in the eventual development of the full representational theory.

In summary, mental representations exist for 3-year-olds, but only as a relatively isolated auxiliary hypothesis necessary to explain certain (to them) peripheral mental phenomena—the odd infrequent misrepresentation and explanatorily impotent fictional representations.

2.3 The 5-year-old View

By four or five, children, at least in our culture, have developed a quite different view of the mind, one that we have called a "representational model of mind" (Forguson & Gopnik, 1988). On this view almost all psychological functioning is mediated by representations. Desires, perceptions, beliefs, pretenses and images all involve the same fundamental structure, a structure sometimes described in terms of propositional attitudes and propositional contents. These mental states all involve representations of reality, rather than realities themselves. In philosophical terms, the child's view of the mind becomes fully "intentional." To use Dretske's terminology perceiving becomes perceiving that, and desiring becomes desiring that, we might even add, that believing becomes believing that (Dretske, 1981). This new view provides a kind of Copernican, or better Keplerian, revolution in the child's view of the mind. In addition to distinguishing different types of mental states with different relations to a real world of objects, the child sees that all mental life partakes of the same representational character. Many characteristics of all mental states, such as their diversity, and their tendency to change, can be explained by the properties of representations. This newly unified view not only provides new predictions, explanations and interpretations; it also provides a new view of the very evidence that was accounted for earlier by the desire-perception theory.

3. THE CHILD'S THEORY AS THEORY

What evidence do we have for thinking that these understandings are theoretical in the sense that we have been outlining so far? The following: The child's understanding involves general constructs about the mind that go beyond the focal evidential phenomena. These constructs feature importantly in explanation. They allow children to make predictions about behavior in a wide variety of circumstances, including predictions about behavior they have never actually experienced and incorrect predictions. Finally, they lead to distinctive interpretations of evidence.

3.1 Explanations

Children's explanations of actions show a characteristic theory-like pattern. In open-ended explanation tasks (Bartsch & Wellman, 1989; Wellman & Banerjee, 1991) children are simply presented an action or reaction ("Jane is looking for her kitty under the piano") and asked to explain it ("Why is she doing that?"). There are many mental states that might be associated with such situations. Yet 3- and 4-year-old children's answers to such open-ended questions are organized around beliefs and desires just as adults' are ("she wants the kitty"; "she thinks it's under the piano"). Moreover, there is a shift in explanatory type between two and five. Two-year-olds' explanations almost always mention desires, but not beliefs. Asked why the girl looks for her doll under the bed they will talk about the fact that she wants the doll, but not the fact that she believes the doll is there. Three-year-olds invoke beliefs and desires, and some threes

and most 4- and 5-year-olds consistently refer to the representational character of these states, explaining failure in terms of falsity. These same trends can be seen in the explanations children give in their spontaneous speech (Bartsch & Wellman, 1990).

3.2 Predictions

Consider the desire-perception theory. Even that early theory allows children to make a variety of predictions about actions and perceptions, both their own and others. For example, they should be able to predict that desires may differ, and that, given a desire, an actor will try to fulfil that desire. They should know that desires may not be fulfilled. They should predict that fulfilled desires will lead to happiness, while unfulfilled desires will lead to sadness (Wellman & Woolley, 1990). And there is evidence that, in fact, all these kinds of predictions are made by very young children (e.g. Wellman & Woolley, 1990; Yuill, 1984; Astington & Gopnik, 1991b). Similarly, a child with the desire-perception theory should be able to predict the perceptions of others in a wide variety of circumstances, including those in which the perceptions are different from their own. Such very early activities as shared attention and social referencing behaviors already indicate some capacity to understand the perception of others (Wellman, 1993). Other aspects of this understanding quickly develop. By 2½ these Level-1 understandings, as Flavell calls them, are firmly and reliably in place (Flavell, 1988). At this age children can reliably predict when an agent will or will not see (and hear and touch) an object (e.g. Flavell, Everett, Croft & Flavell, 1981). They can also predict how seeing an object will lead to later actions. However, they are unable to make predictions about representational aspects of perception, what Flavell calls Level-2 understanding. They fail to predict, for example, that an object that is clearly seen by both parties can look one way to one viewer and another way to another.

These predictions may seem so transparent to adults that we think of them not as predictions at all but simply as empirical facts. A little reflection, however, should make us realize that the notion of desire or perception used by these very young children is theoretically broad and powerful. Children can use the notion of desire appropriately and make the correct predictions when the desired objects are objects, or events, or states of affairs. They can attribute desires to themselves and others even when they do not act to fulfill the desires and when the desires are not in fact fulfilled. Similarly, children seem to make accurate predictions about perception across a wide range of events, involving factors as different as screens, blindfolds, and visual angles, and do so across different perceptual modalities. Again, they may do so even when the perceptions do not lead to any immediate observable actions. Moreover, given novel and unfamiliar information about an agent's desires and perceptions, children will make quite accurate predictions about the agent's actions.

More significantly, however, these children also make incorrect predictions in cases where the desire-perception theory breaks down. Both desires and perceptions, on the 2-year-old view, involve simple non-representational causal links between the world and the mind. Even the early non-representational notions of belief have this quality. This theory cannot handle cases of misrepresentation. Presented with such cases it makes the wrong predictions. The theory also cannot handle other problems that require an understanding of the complexity of the representational relations between mind and world. For example, the theory breaks down when one must consider the fact that the same belief may come from different sources, or that there may be different degrees of certainty of beliefs.

The most well-known instance of such an incorrect prediction is, of course, the false-belief error in 3-year-olds (Wimmer & Perner, 1983; Perner *et al.*, 1987). The focus on false belief tasks may, however, be somewhat unfortunate since it has promoted a mind-set in which any ability to perform "correctly" on a false-belief task is taken as evidence that the child has a representational theory of the mind. As we will see, there are cases in which 3-year-olds indicate some understanding of false belief. However, to begin with it is worth pointing out the much greater ubiquity and generality of the incorrect false-belief predictions. Three-year-olds make erroneous predictions, not only in the "classic" tasks, but also in many other cases involving beliefs about location, identity, number and properties. They make incorrect predictions for "real" others, for puppets, for children, and for hypothetical story characters. Incorrect predictions are made when the question is phrased in terms of what the other thinks, what the other will say and what the other will do, and across a wide range of syntactic frames. They are made by North American (Gopnik & Astington, 1988), British (Perner *et al.*, 1987), and Austrian (Wimmer & Perner, 1983) children, and recently by Baka children of the Cameroons (Avis & Harris, 1991).

Moreover, and more significantly from the point of view of the theory theory, these incorrect belief predictions are mirrored in 3-year-olds' performance on a wide range of other tasks. A brief inventory would include (a) appearance-reality tasks, which themselves have proved robust across many variations of culture, question and material (Flavell, Green & Flavell, 1986), (b) questions about the sources of belief (Gopnik & Graf, 1988) and the understanding of subjective probability (Moore, Pure & Furrow, 1990), and (c) the understanding of pictorial representational systems (Zaitchek, 1990). In some of these tasks the desire-perception theory makes incorrect predictions, and children consistently give the same wrong answer. In others, it makes no predictions at all and the children respond at random. On any information-processing account these tasks would require quite different kinds of competences. Moreover, the standard methodology of these studies has included control tasks, involving similar or identical information-processing demands, which children seem entirely capable of answering. Nor do any dimensions of familiarity, at least in any simple terms, seem to underlie the difference between tasks at which children succeed and fail.

3.3 Interpretations

In these cases children are clearly using belief and desire to make predictions—one of the central functions of theoretical constructs. In addition to the explanatory and predictive effects, children also show strong interpretive effects. Suppose we present the child with counter-evidence to the theory? If the child is simply reporting her empirical experience we might expect that she will report that evidence correctly. In fact, however, children consistently misreport and misinterpret evidence when it conflicts with their theoretical preconceptions. Flavell and his colleagues have some provocative but simple demonstrations of evidential misinterpretation (Flavell, Flavell, Green & Moses, 1990). A child sees a blue cup, agrees that it is blue and not white, and sees the cup hidden behind a screen. At this point another adult comes into the room, and she says "I cannot see the cup. Hmm, I think it is white." Then the child is asked what color he thinks the cup is and what color the adult thinks it is. To be correct the child need only report the adult's actual words, but 3-year-olds err by attributing to the character a true belief. Even if corrected, "well actually she really thinks it's white," 3-year olds continue to insist the adult has a factually correct belief: "She thinks it's blue." Moreover, as we will see, three-year-old children consistently misreport their own immediately past mental states.

3.4 Transitional Phenomena

In developmental psychology we are often better at describing the states at two points in development than at describing changes from one state to another. Nevertheless, recent evidence suggests that during the period from three to four many children are in a state of transition between the two theories, similar, say to the fifty years between the publication of *De Revolutionibus* and Kepler's discovery of elliptical orbits. This is rather bad luck for developmentalists since this period has been the focus of much of our investigation. But it also means that we may have some intriguing evidence about the mechanisms that lead from one theory to another.

We have already seen in our discussion of interpretation how children with the earlier theory begin by simply denying the existence of the counter-evidence. Johnny and I really did think and act as if there were pencils in the box when we first saw it. We have also seen that at around three children develop a first non-representational account of belief, which extends their original desire-perception psychology. We can also ask where the first signs of an understanding of misrepresentation, the centerpiece of the 5-year-old theory, begin to appear. Recall that we suggested, in the scientific case, that in a transitional period the crucial idea of the new theory may appear as an auxiliary hypothesis couched in the vocabulary of the original theory, or be used in order to deal with particularly salient types of counter-evidence, but may not be widely applied. There is evidence for both these phenomena in the period from three to four. Children seem to us to initially develop the idea of misrepresentation in familiar contexts like those of desire and perception, without extending the idea more generally. They also initially apply the idea only when they are forced to by counter-evidence.

There is evidence that by placing the misrepresentation questions in the context of the earlier theory we can begin to see (or perhaps, in fact, induce) glimmerings of the later theory. Desire and perception may be construed either non-representationally, or representationally. In fact, in the adult theory, desire and perception are as representational as belief. What we want and see (by and large) is not the thing itself but the thing as represented. Understanding some aspects of desire and perception requires this sort of representational understanding. When we are satiated with something we no longer desire it, but the object itself has not changed. When different types of people have different tastes or values, their desires differ but the objects of desire remain the same (Flavell *et al.*, 1990). There is evidence that these representational aspects of desire are understood earlier than equivalently representational aspects of belief (Gopnik & Slaughter, 1991). However, 3-year-old children still do not perform as well on these tasks as they do on simple nonrepresentational desire tasks. Similarly, while non-representational aspects of perception are understood by 2½, representational ones, what Flavell calls level-2 perspective-taking, are only understood later (Flavell *et al.*, 1981; Flavell *et al.*, 1986; Masangkay, McCluskey, McIntyre, Sims-Knight, Vaughn & Flavell, 1974). However, there is evidence that these aspects of perception are understood before corresponding aspects of belief. Both in Flavell's earlier studies and in a recent study we conducted (Gopnik & Slaughter, 1992), children were better at misrepresentation tasks involving perception than they were at similar appearance-reality and false-belief tasks.

We have suggested that for the 2-year-old the central theoretical constructs are non-representational desires and perceptions while for the 5-year-old they are representational beliefs. Three-year-old precursors seem to include both non-representational accounts of belief and representational accounts of desire and perception. This is reminiscent of the way that Copernicus and Tycho Brahe mix epicycles and heliocentrism.

There is also evidence that early signs of an understanding of misrepresentation may come when children are forced to consider counter-evidence to their theory. In particular, Bartsch and Wellman (1989) found, as others had, that 3-year-old children continued to make incorrect false-belief predictions even given counter-evidence. However, if children were asked to explain the counter-evidence, at least some of them began to talk about misrepresentation as a way of doing so. Making the counter-evidence

particularly salient seemed to help to induce the application of the theory in this transitional age group. Similarly, in a recent study, Mitchell and Lacohee (1991) found that children in a representational change task who selected an explicit physical token of their earlier belief (a picture of what they thought was in the box) were better able to avoid later misrepresentation of that belief. That is, these children seemed to recognize the contradiction between the action they had just performed (picking a picture of candies) which was well within the scope of their memory, and their theoretical prediction about their past belief. Some evidence from natural language may also be relevant. Before age three (or slightly earlier) we simply do not find genuine references to belief. At about three, however, we begin to see such references, and also to see beginnings of contrastive uses of belief terms (Bartsch & Wellman, 1990). These uses may occur in contexts in which some particularly salient piece of counter-evidence to the earlier theory takes place. During the following year, however, the use of these terms increases drastically.

In short, children seem to first understand both belief and representation as small extensions of the original non-representational desire-perception theory, essentially as auxiliary hypotheses. This stage appears to be an intermediate one between a fully non-representational and a fully representational theory of mental states.

Do 3-year-olds really understand false belief then? Did Copernicus really understand planetary movement? The answer in both cases is that the question is a bad one. One of the strengths of the theory theory is that it makes such questions otiose. "Understanding" false belief, or developing an idea of representation, involves the development of a coherent, widely applicable theory. It may be possible to have some elements of that theory, or to apply them in some cases, without operating with the full predictive power of the theory, particularly in a transitional state.

We argue therefore, that the transition from 2½ to 5 shows all the signs of being a theory change. While initially the theory protects itself from counter-evidence, the force of such counter-evidence eventually begins to push the theory in the direction of change. The first signs of the theory shift may emerge when counter-evidence is made particularly salient. Moreover, the theory initially deals with such counter-evidence by making relatively small adjustments to concepts that are already well-entrenched, such as desire and perception. Finally, by 4 or 5 the new theory has more completely taken over from the old. The predictions are widely and readily applicable to a range of cases.

4. SIMULATION THEORY

In the theory theory, to predict someone's behavior we have recourse to theoretical constructs such as beliefs and desires. Explaining someone's behavior involves more than empirical generalization (X has always done this in similar situations in the past). It involves appeal to constructs at a very different level of vocabulary—X wants Y and believes Z. A distinction between a phenomenal description and a theoretical explanation is crucial.

On the simulation theory, however, the child's (and adult's) understanding of mind is more closely linked to the phenomenal than to the theoretical. Understanding states of mind involves empirically discovering the states or results of a model. Consider again an understanding of the planets. An appeal to theoretical notions such as heavenly bodies revolving around one another can be contrasted to use of a planetarium-model to predict the star's appearance. (Here we want to be careful to focus on a user of a planetarium who has no deeper understanding of its workings and not focus on the planetarium's creator, for example, who presumably understood something theoretical about planetary motion in order to build a successful device.) The user need only see, empirically, that the planetarium's behavior mimics the stars, then the user can make

predictions by "running" the planetarium rather than waiting for the actual events. And the user can achieve a sort of explanation, explanation-by-demonstration, as well. Let's say the user experiences a real eclipse for the first time, noting that in the middle of the day it very uncharacteristically gets dark, although there are no clouds in sight. "Why?" he asks himself. Is this a breakdown in all his empirical generalizations about the system; is it to be expected again; what happened? By running the planetarium under appropriate conditions the user can "see" the phenomenon again, see that it occurs regularly, in the model; see that it is a natural although infrequent empirical fact. If asked by someone else "What was that (eclipse)?" or "Why did that happen?" the user can explain-by-demonstrating: "Look, it (the eclipse) was one of these (demonstrate the model's state). It happens when the other stars are like this."

The simulation theory contends that our prediction and explanation of mental phenomena is like that of the planetarium user. The child (or adult) doesn't need and doesn't appeal to a theory of mind, a conceptual understanding of mental states, to predict behavior or understand others. Instead she simply runs a perfect working model of a mind, her own mind. By considering the output of her own mind she can predict the mental states and resultant behaviors of others. And to explain curious or unexpected actions she can run her model, find a suitable simulated demonstration of the phenomena, and then explain it as "look, it's one of these."

Consider, for example, the classic false-belief task. The child sees a candy box, finds out that it is full of pencils, and then is asked what another person will think is inside it. Simulation theorists contend that the child need not have anything like a theoretical construct of belief (or desire) to solve this task. She simply has access to her own first-hand mental system and uses that. When asked what the character "thinks," she need not understand beliefs as something like a representational construct, she simply simulates the experience and reports her own specific resulting state—"Oh, I (she) thinks there is candy in the box." The earlier failure to solve this task, on this view, reflects a failure of simulation, rather than a failure of knowledge. It is not that the younger child fails to understand beliefs as states of misrepresentation, as we described it earlier, it is just that the younger child makes an egocentric simulation, projecting her own current mental states onto the other, rather than adjusting the simulation to the other's particular condition.

The simulation view has a number of telling empirical consequences; we will focus on two. The first concerns the centrality of your own mind in any understanding of the minds of others. To answer questions about others, according to ST, you must conduct a simulation on a model, and that model is your own mind. On the simulation view, therefore, the outputs of your own mental system are particularly central to all discourse about the mind. Moreover, these outputs must be easily and transparently accessible. This must be true in order for the simulation account to work at all in the case of other people. A presupposition of the account is that it is possible to read off and report the output of your own mental states, and to use them in explanation, prediction and inference. Moreover, access to your own states requires no inference or interpretation, no conceptual intermediaries, no theorizing; you simply read them off. A consequence of this view is that one cannot erroneously misinterpret, or misconceive, one's own mental state. You could of course run a bad simulation, in the sense that you entered the wrong inputs. But given those inputs, the output must be accurate. It must accurately reflect what your mind would actually do in that situation, because it IS what your mind actually does in that situation.

On the theory view, in contrast, erroneous self-interpretations are not only possible, they are to be expected. One typical characteristic of theories, after all, is that they allow and often even force interpretation of the evidence. If the theoretical prediction and evidence are in conflict it is often the evidence rather than the theory which is reinterpreted. Equally, on the theory theory psychological constructs, such as beliefs and desires, are generically applicable to the self or to others. If you possess a faulty conception of some mental state, say belief, then you will incorrectly attribute that mental state to others, and you should make parallel incorrect attributions to yourself. In short on the Simulation Theory false interpretations of your own mental states should not occur. On the Theory Theory such false interpretations should occur whenever your theoretical constructs are faulty.

A second empirical consequence, related to this first one, concerns how development should proceed. For both TT and ST we can predict that there will be development: children should first be good at predicting/explaining "easy" states and then later "hard" ones. But the notions of easy and hard should differ dramatically between these two theories. For ST the critical difference should be between states that are difficult or easy to simulate. Presumably, the metric for such ease and difficulty must be intimately related to the similarity of the states to the child's own states. In this sense the simulation theory is in another long and honorable tradition, the tradition of "perspective-taking" views in development. Several of the simulation theorists in this Special Issue for example presume that young children's errors are "egocentric." That is, the child's early errors consist of not correctly adjusting their simulation to the other person's condition. Note that on this theory there is no reason to expect that different mental states should be easier or harder to attribute to others. Take beliefs and desires. Both beliefs and desires are equally available to the child as states of her own mind. At a young age we could predict that reading off one's own beliefs and desires should be equally easy, and attributing conflicting beliefs and desires to someone else should be equally difficult.

In contrast, for the theory theory the critical metric concerns states that are easy or difficult to conceive of. Earlier we described what we take to be a succession of changes in the child's conceptions of mental states, as the child develops and replaces a succession of theories. Especially important is a difference between an early non-representational understanding of mind and a later more representational understanding. Early on children have a relatively adequate understanding of non-representational desire-perception states. Later they develop an understanding of the representational state of belief, specifically, and a representational understanding of mind more generally (including a representational understanding of certain aspects of perception and desire). Theoretical conceptions of the sort we have described are equally applicable to the self and others. If a theory has formulated a particular theoretical construct, such as the concept of false representations, it should in principle be able to use this concept equally to explain the child's own behavior and the behavior of others. If the theory does not include this construct, it should not be so applicable to either the self or others. In short, for the theory theory it will not be so important whether the mental states to be reasoned about are those of self or other. What is important is the relevant conceptions of mental states that the child must bring to bear. Thus, we find different developmental predictions from the two theories.

We want to describe several empirical findings based on these two main issues that tell against the simulation account. (1) Three-year-old children make false attributions to themselves, that exactly parallel their false attributions to others. (2) Three-year-old children make correct non-egocentric attributions to themselves and others for some mental states. (3) Children refer to only some mental states in their explanations, and refer to different mental states at different stages of their development. (4) Children's understanding of other psychological phenomena changes in parallel with their understanding of false belief. Understanding these phenomena does not require simulation, but it does require a representational theory of the mind.

The first set of findings concern children's ability to understand and report their own mental states. For example, children not only fail to understand that other's beliefs can misrepresent; they also fail to understand that their own beliefs can. In our original experiment (Gopnik & Astington, 1988) we used an analog of the "false-belief" task. We presented children with a variety of deceptive objects, such as the candy box full of pencils, and allowed them to discover the true nature of the objects. We then asked the children the standard false-belief question, "What will Nicky (another child) think is inside the box?" But we also asked children about their own false beliefs about the box: "When you first saw the box, before we opened it, what did you think was inside it?" The pattern of results for self and for other was very similar. 3-year-olds tend to say that Nicky will think what is true. But they also report that they themselves thought what was true, that they had originally thought there were pencils in the box. Children's ability to answer the false-belief question about their own belief was significantly correlated to their ability to answer the question about the others' belief, even with age controlled, a result recently replicated by Moore *et al.* (1990). Children who could not answer the question about the other, also could not answer it about themselves.

The children also received an additional control task. They saw a closed container (a toy house) with one object inside it, then the house was opened, the object was removed and a different object was placed inside. Children were asked "When you first saw the house, before we opened it, what was inside it?" This question had the same form as the belief question. However, it asked about the past physical state of the house rather than asking about a past mental state. Children were only included in the experiment if they answered this question correctly, and so demonstrated that they could understand that the question referred to the past and could remember the past state of affairs. Several different syntactic forms of the question were asked to further ensure that the problem was not a linguistic one. Recently, this experiment has been replicated, with additional controls, by Wimmer and Hartl (1991).

In more recent experiments we have investigated whether children could understand changes in mental states other than belief (Gopnik & Slaughter, 1991). A crucial comparison is to desires and perceptions. In three different tasks we presented children with situations in which their desires were satiated and so changed. For example, initially the child desired one of two short books. That one was read to him and the child said he now desired the other book. The test question was just like the one for past beliefs: "When you first saw the books, before we read one, which one did you want?" In these tasks 3-year-old children were considerably better at reporting past now-changed desires than past now-changed beliefs. Similarly, we presented children with situations in which their perception was changed. Children saw an object on one side of a screen and they were then moved to the other side of the screen where they saw a different object. We asked "When you first sat on the chair, before we moved over here, what did you see on the table?" Children were completely able to report their past perceptions.

These experiments concern the child's report of their own mental states, beliefs, desires and perceptions. From a simulation point of view, why do the children make errors when they are simply reading off their own mental states? And why do they make errors for one state but not the other? Perhaps the trouble is that the questions require not a report of current mental states, but a memory of past states. Two things need to be kept in mind in considering this objection. First, the span of time we are talking about is very brief, at the most one or two minutes and often much shorter. At least for adults such experiences are well within the immediate introspective span. If I were to report the output of my mental system in such a situation, I would report the change in my belief that comes with the new discovery, with

all its attendant phenomenological vividness and detail. The very psychological experience of the change in belief depends on the fact that I continue to remember the previous belief. A simulation account must presuppose some ability to report immediately past states (after all any state will be past by the time it is reported).

Second, and perhaps more crucially, is the difference between belief and other states such as desire and perception. The data suggest that even these young children can report some mental states that are just immediately past. The poor performance for beliefs therefore cannot be simply a problem of poor memory or lost access. This finding presents a paradox for simulation accounts. If reporting these immediately past states requires simulation, then 3-year-olds are perfectly good simulators of their past desires and perceptions: why not beliefs? If reporting past states does not require simulation, because these states are just read off, then why do the 3-year-olds have so much trouble reporting past beliefs?

In essence, children find some sorts of mental state attributions to be difficult and some to be easy. But the difference between the easy and hard attributions is not clearly related to the distinction between self and other, as expected from ST. The distinction is related to the ability to conceive of and interpret some types of mental states and not others, for self and for other. From a theory point of view this makes sense. Even your own mental states come in several conceptual varieties, such as beliefs, desires, and perceptions, and you could be correct at reporting one variety and erroneous at another depending on your conceptual understanding of that state.

A second difficulty concerns whether children are at first generally egocentric about the mind and then overcome this by learning they must adjust their simulations for others. In Gordon's terms, is there evidence for a stage of early "total projection"? The developmental data do not fit this general mold; there is evidence for non-egocentric understanding quite early for some states. We have already described one such task, the early "level-1" perspective-taking task, in which children can predict that the other child will not see what they see themselves. Similarly quite young children can predict that someone else will have a desire different from their own (Wellman & Woolley, 1990). One issue for simulation theory therefore must be to explain why children who can obviously "adjust their simulations" for some states do not do so for others, say beliefs. Indeed, even for belief itself, the data do not suggest that children's main difficulty involves misattributing their own beliefs to others. Instead, it involves a failure to understand that beliefs can misrepresent.

This is only one example of many results that suggest that young children's errors at understanding the mind are not properly termed "egocentric." Even very young children are quite able to attribute to others mental states different from their own. Instead, they err by sometimes misunderstanding what certain mental states are really like.

A third empirical problem is that the simulation theory has difficulty explaining the structure of the explanations that children offer. It is commonplace to say that the child's theory is not, of course, an explicit theory but rather an implicit one, which may have to be inferred from behavior rather than being openly stated. However, in examining children's natural language and particularly their explanations for aberrant actions, we can see many explicit explanatory appeals to beliefs and desires and relations between them. One example comes from open-ended explanation tasks. In these (Wellman & Bartsch, 1989; Wellman & Banerjee, 1991) children are simply presented an action or reaction ("Jane is looking for her kitty under the piano") and asked to explain it ("Why is she doing that?"). Consider a task in which the child is asked to explain why Jane is looking for the kitty. In such an actual situation the child herself would be and should be experiencing many mental states—a fear that the kitten is lost, a creak in her back from bending

down, a sensation that it is dark and not very visible under the piano, a fear the kitty will scratch, a belief the kitty is under there, a desire to find the kitty, a fantasy the kitty is a small tiger, and more. Yet children's answers to such open-ended questions are organized predominantly around beliefs and desires just as adults' are. On a simulation account why would the child answer with beliefs and desires more than fears and fantasies, pains and sensations or any of a vast number of experientially available mental states? On a simulation account there is no principled reason for the child to organize mental experiences into beliefs and desires and report those appropriately. Other empirical categories seem more compelling for categorizing and reporting first-hand mental experience (*e.g.* pains and sensations). On a theory-theory account, in contrast, there is a good reason why such explanations predominantly appeal to beliefs and desires. These are the theoretical constructs that structure the child's understanding of mental states.

More important is the shift in explanatory type between two and five, to which we have already referred. Two-year-olds' explanations almost always mention desires, but never beliefs. Asked why the girl looks for her doll under the bed they will talk about the fact that she wants the doll, but not the fact that she believes the doll is there. Three-year-olds invoke beliefs and desires, and some threes and most 4- and 5-year-olds consistently refer to the representational character of these states, explaining failure in terms of falsity. These same trends can be seen in the explanations children give in their spontaneous speech (Bartsch & Wellman, 1990).

From a ST point of view, the child's own mind, even at the very youngest ages, is a device that itself contains states like beliefs as well as desires. The child's model outputs both beliefs and desires. Why should children's explanations and predictions first privilege desires over beliefs? There is no reason to expect this if the child is simply running simulations and reporting their outcomes. From TT there is a good reason why children's explanations and predictions at first ignore beliefs and especially false beliefs or misrepresentations. Young children have yet to come to a theoretical conception of belief as an explanatory psychological construct.

A fourth difficulty involves the predictive scope of the simulation theory *versus* the theory theory. The simulation theory provides a good account of one particular type of deficit, perspective-taking difficulties, when they occur (although as mentioned earlier ST seems to mischaracterize the nature and the developmental progression of egocentric errors). However, ST fails to account for other related difficulties. For example, we (Gopnik & Graf, 1988) investigated children's ability to identify the sources of their beliefs, elaborating on a question first posed by Wimmer, Hogrefe and Perner (1988). As noted in Goldman's and Stich and Nichols' papers, there was originally some evidence suggesting that children had difficulty understanding how perceptual access leads to knowledge. More recently, however, other studies have suggested that children can indeed understand that people who see an object will know about it, while those who do not see the object will not. However, there still appear to be important limits on children's understanding of sources. For example, O'Neill, Flavell and Astington (1992) found that three-year-old children could not differentiate which source a particular piece of information might come from. They claimed for example that someone who had simply felt an object would know its color, or someone who had seen an object would know its weight.

In our experiments, we tested children's understanding of the sources of their own beliefs. Children found out about objects that were placed in a drawer in one of three ways, either they saw the objects, they were told about them, or they figured them out from a simple clue. Then we asked "What's in the drawer?" and all the children answered correctly. Immediately after this question we asked about the source of the child's knowledge "How do you know there's an x in the drawer? Did you see it, did I tell you about it, or did you figure it out from a clue?" Again three-year-olds made frequent errors on this task. While they knew what the objects were, they could not say how they knew. They might say, for example, that we had told them about an object when they had actually seen it. Their performance was at better than chance levels, but was still significantly worse than the performance of four-year-olds, who were near ceiling. In a follow-up experiment (O'Neill & Gopnik, 1991) we added a condition with different and simpler source contrasts (tell, see and feel) and presented children with only two alternative possibilities at a time. We also included a control task which ensured that the children understood the meaning of "tell," "see" and "feel." Despite these simplifications of the task, the performance of the three-year-olds was similar to their performance in the original experiment. These experiments provide another striking example of the child's failure to accurately report his own mental states when they conflict with his theoretical preconceptions, and of the parallels between attributions to the self and to others.

Similarly, there is evidence for deficits in children's understanding of subjective probability. Moore *et al.* (1990) found that three-year-olds were unable to determine that a person who knew about an object was a more reliable source of information than one who merely guessed or thought. Similarly, three-year-olds, in contrast to four-year-olds, showed no preference for getting information from someone who was certain they knew what was in a box rather than someone who expressed uncertainty about their knowledge. These children seemed to divide cognitive states into full knowledge or total ignorance, they did not appreciate that belief could admit of degrees.

We believe that understanding sources and subjective probability is difficult for young children because these notions involve an understanding of the causal structure of the representational system. These aspects of the mind are not particularly different for the child and the other. However, they do require a complex causal account of the origins of beliefs. This account is at the heart of the causal-explanatory framework that eventually allows children to fully understand the representational character of the mind. These tasks should be difficult if children have not yet worked out a representational theory of mind, as we suggest, and thus should be related in development to false-belief errors. ST offers no explanation for their appearance or their relation to false-belief errors. Understanding sources and subjective probability does not seem to require complex simulation abilities, especially not when the child's own states are being reported.

In sum, the developmental pattern of children's errors and accuracies is not consistent with the view that the outputs of your own mind are simply and directly accessible, and that these outputs are attributed to others through a process of simulation. If such an account were correct, children's errors should differ between self and other in some clear fashion over development. Instead the errors divide between certain theoretical construals of inner mental states, such as beliefs *versus* desires, for both the self and the other. The child's understanding of mind is filtered through a coherent conceptual understanding of the mind; a theory. The theory organizes their interpretation of the phenomena of mental life and provides a causal-explanatory understanding of how the world informs the mind and mind guides behavior.

5. PRECOCITY AND THEORY FORMATION

We would like to end by considering an argument that Gordon, Goldman, and Stich and Nichols share. This is the claim that children's folk psychological abilities are intellectually precocious. Children could not develop an elaborate psychological theory in a mere three or four

years. Gordon and Goldman use this as an argument for simulation; children need not develop a theory of the mind, they only need to develop a mind, and run simulations on it. Stich and Nichols reply that this is an indication that important aspects of the theory are innate. We think the assumptions behind both of these arguments are ill-founded. In particular they rest on the idea that we have some *a priori* way of measuring the temporal course of conceptual change, of saying what is slow or fast or easy or difficult.

Even in the case of scientific theory change, this seems a dubious claim. How long does it take to make a theory? If we measure change sociologically it may, of course, take years or even centuries. But how long does an individual theory change take? How long did Kepler take to formulate the heliocentric theory? How long does it take a current-day student immersed in a culture that has assimilated heliocentrism to appreciate and internalize it? Days, weeks, months?

Claiming that three or four years is insufficient time for substantial theory development seems even more dubious when we consider the general cognitive achievements of young children. Developing a theory of mind is indeed an impressive achievement, but it may seem less unique if one considers parallel developments in a variety of domains. While there may be innate abilities that play a role in these achievements, there is much evidence that a great deal of abstract and complex knowledge is also learned in this period. For example, no matter how powerful the universal constraints on grammar may be, there is still an enormous amount of language-specific structure that varies sharply from one language to another. Young children quickly master these language-specific principles as well as manifesting mastery of universals (Slobin, 1981; Maratsos, 1983). More relevantly to the present case, children acquire large amounts of physical knowledge in this period. While some aspects of children's "folk physics" are innately given, others, such as their appreciation of gravity and support, appear to be learned in months or weeks, even during infancy itself (Spelke, 1991). By four or five children also seem to have an initial understanding of biological kinds. They recognize, for example, that membership in such a kind depends on an animal's internal state, and even on its reproductive potential (Gelman & Coley, 1992).

These achievements are certainly impressive. But as we consider them it is well to remember the general intensity of the child's cognitive life. Naturalistic language data, for example, suggest that the three-year-old child may be working on the theory of mind virtually all his waking hours. And quite possibly many of his sleeping ones as well. Who knows what adults could accomplish in three years of similarly concentrated intellectual labor?

It is certainly true that there are some innately given kinds of psychological knowledge. However, it seems to us that these are most likely to be "starting state" theories, initial conceptions of the mind that are themselves subject to radical revision in the face of evidence. They do not function as constraints on the final possibilities, in the way that, say, a Chomskyan account would propose. Moreover, it seems very unlikely that we can determine, *a priori*, which aspects of psychological knowledge are likely to be innate and which are likely to be learned. Children, for example, seem to start out as mentalists, though they must learn to be representationalists.

The evidence of developmental psychology, and indeed the evidence of common observation, suggests that young children have learning capacities (and we would claim theory formation abilities) far in excess of anything we might imagine in our daily cognitively stodgy experience as adults. Indeed we would say, not that children are little scientists but that scientists are big, and relatively slow, children. The historical progress of science is based on cognitive abilities that are first seen in very young children.

We might end by telling an evolutionary just-so story to this effect. The long immaturity of human children is a notable and distinctive feature of human beings. It seems plausible that the cognitive plasticity that is also characteristic of human beings is related to this immaturity. Human beings, unlike other species, have unique cognitive capacities to adjust their behavior to what they find out about the world. A long period of protected immaturity, the story might go, plus powerful theory-formation abilities, enable children to learn about the specific cultural and physical features of their world. These capacities typically go into abeyance once ordinary adults have learned most of what they need to know. Still, their continued existence makes specialized scientific investigation possible. Science, on this view, might be a sort of spandrel, parasitic on cognitive development itself. Young children may not only really be theorizers, they may well be better ones than we are.

Notes

1. It is important to be as clear as possible about the way in which we take theoretical constructs to be abstract, unobservable, and postulated. We mean abstract in the sense of "thought of apart from" observable particularities, we do not mean abstruse or merely ideal. By unobservable we mean not obviously a part of the evidential phenomena to-be-explained; not that theoretical entities are necessarily incapable of being observed in any fashion whatsoever. Thus, we could postulate that genes control inherited features such as eye color and height, in order to provide a theoretical account, and still fully expect that genes are observable in some fashion. It is simply that genes are not directly evident in, observable in, the phenomena of eye color and height themselves. Similarly, postulated does not mean conjured out of thin air, it means recruited for explanatory purposes from outside the evidential phenomena themselves. Thus (natural) selection can be postulated to account for the origin of species but at the same time selection can be fully concrete and observable, in the realm of human animal breeding for example. It is the recruitment of selection to account for natural speciation that is postulational, selection itself is not a mere postulated entity.

2. On the theory theory, the ages of development are not crucial. In fact we would expect to find, as indeed we do, wide variation in the ages at which succes-

sive theories develop. We would expect to find similar sequences of development, however. We will use ages as a rough way of referring to successive theories.

References

Astington, J. W. and Gopnik, A. 1991a: Developing Understanding of Desire and Intention. In A. Whiten (eds.), *Natural Theories of Mind*. Oxford: Basil Blackwell, 39–50.

Astington, J. W. and Gopnik, A. 1991b: Theoretical Explanations of Children's Understanding of the Mind. *British Journal of Developmental Psychology*, 9, 7–31.

Avis, J. and Harris, P. L. 1991: Belief-desire Reasoning Among Baka Children. *Child Development*, 62, 460–67.

Bartsch, K. and Wellman, H. M. 1989: Young Children's Attribution of Action to Beliefs and Desires. *Child Development*, 60, 946–64.

Bartsch, K. and Wellman, H. M. 1990: Everyday Talk About Beliefs and Desires: Evidence of Children's Developing Theory of Mind. Paper presented at the meeting of the Piaget Society, Philadelphia, PA.

Bretherton, I. and Beeghly, M. 1982: Talking About Internal States: The Acquisition of an Explicit Theory of Mind. *Developmental Psychology*, 18, 906–921.

Carey, S. 1985: *Conceptual Change in Childhood*. Cambridge, MA.: MIT Press.

Carey, S. 1988: Conceptual Differences Between Children and Adults. *Mind and Language*, 3, 167–181.

Churchland, P. M. 1984: *Matter and Consciousness*. Cambridge, MA.: MIT Press.

Dretske, F. 1981: *Knowledge and the Flow of Information*. Cambridge, MA.: MIT Press.

Estes, D., Wellman, H. M. and Woolley, J. D. 1989: Children's Understanding of Mental Phenomena. In H. Reese (ed.), *Advances in Child Development and Behavior*. New York: Academic Press, 41–87.

Flavell, J. H., Everett, B. A., Croft, K. and Flavell, E. R. 1981: Young Children's Knowledge About Visual Perception: Further Evidence for the Level 1–Level 2 Distinction. *Developmental Psychology*, 17, 99–103.

Flavell, J. H., Green, F. L. and Flavell, E. R. 1986: Development of Knowledge About the Appearance-Reality Distinction. *Monographs of the Society for Research in Child Development*, 51 (Serial No. 212).

Flavell, J. H., Flavell, E. R. and Green, F. L. 1987: Young Children's Knowledge About Apparent-Real and Pretend-real Distinctions. *Developmental Psychology*, 23, 816–22.

Flavell, J. H. 1988: The Development of Children's Knowledge About the Mind: From Cognitive Connections to Mental Representations. In J. Astington, P. Harris and D. Olson (eds.), *Developing Theories of Mind*. New York: Cambridge University Press, 244–67.

Flavell, J. H., Flavell, E. R., Green, F. L. and Moses, L. J. 1990: Young Children's Understanding of Fact Beliefs versus Value Beliefs. *Child Development*, 61, 915–28.

Forguson, L. and Gopnik, A. 1988: The Ontogeny of Common Sense. In J. Astington, P. Harris and D. Olson (eds.), *Developing Theories of Mind*. New York: Cambridge University Press, 226–43.

Gelman, S. A. and Coley, J. D. 1992: Language and Categorization: The Acquisition of Natural Kind Terms. In S. A. Gelman and J. P. Byrnes (eds.), *Perspectives on Languages and Thought*. Cambridge: Cambridge University Press.

Gopnik, A. 1984: Conceptual and Semantic Change in Scientists and Children: Why There Are No Semantic Universals. *Linguistics*, 20, 163–79.

Gopnik, A. 1988: Conceptual and Semantic Development as Theory Change. *Mind and Language*, 3, 197–217.

Gopnik, A. and Astington, J. W. 1988: Children's Understanding of Representational Change and its Relation to the Understanding of False Belief and the Appearance–Reality Distinction. *Child Development*, 59, 26–37.

Gopnik, A. and Graf, P. 1988: Knowing How You Know: Young Children's Ability to Identify and Remember the Sources of Their Beliefs. *Child Development*, 59, 1366–71.

Gopnik, A. and Slaughter, V. 1991: Young Children's Understanding of Changes in Their Mental States. *Child Development*, 62, 98–110.

Gopnik, A. and Slaughter, V. 1992: Children's Understanding of Perception and Belief. Unpublished manuscript.

Harris, P. L. 1991: The Work of the Imagination. In A. Whiten (ed.), *Natural Theories of Mind*. Oxford: Basil Blackwell, 283–304.

Harris, P. L., Brown, E., Marriot, C., Whittal, S. and Harmer, S. 1991: Monsters, Ghosts and Witches: Testing the Limits of the Fantasy-reality Distinction in Young Children. *British Journal of Developmental Psychology*, 9, 105–123.

Johnson, C. N. 1988: Theory of Mind and the Structure of Conscious Experience. In J. Astington, P. Harris and D. Olson (eds.), *Developing Theories of Mind*. New York: Cambridge University Press, 47–63.

Karmiloff-Smith, A. and Inhelder, B. 1975: If You Want to Get Ahead, Get a Theory. *Cognition*, 3, 195–212.

Keil, F. C. 1989: *Concepts, Kinds, and Cognitive Development*. Cambridge, MA.: MIT Press.

Leslie, A. M. 1987: Pretense and Representation: The Origins of "Theory of Mind." *Psychological Review*, 94, 412–26.

Masangkay, Z. S., McCluskey, K. A., McIntyre, C. W., Sims-Knight, J., Vaughn, B. E. and Flavell, J. H. 1974: The Early Development of Inferences About the Visual Percepts of Others. *Child Development*, 45, 357–66.

Meltzoff, A. N. and Gopnik, A. 1993: The Role of Imitation in Understanding Persons and Developing Theories of Mind. In S. Baron-Cohen and H. Tager-Flusberg (eds.), *The Theory of Mind Deficit in Autism*. New York: Cambridge University Press.

Meltzoff, A. N. and Moore, M. K. 1977: Imitation of Facial and Manual Gestures by Human Neonates. *Science*, 198, 75–8.

Mitchell, P. and Lacohee, H. 1991: Children's Early Understanding of False Belief. *Cognition*.

Moore, C., Pure, K. and Furrow, P. 1990: Children's Understanding of the Modal Expression of Certainty and Uncertainty and its Relation to the Development of a Representational Theory of Mind. *Child Development*, 61, 722–30.

Moses, L. J. 1990: Young Children's Understanding of Intention and Belief. Unpublished Ph.D. dissertation, Stanford University.

Moses, L. J. and Flavell, J. H. 1990: Inferring False Beliefs from Actions and Reactions. *Child Development*, 61, 929–45.

O'Neill, D. K., Astington, J. W. and Flavell, J. H. 1992: Young Children's Understanding of the Role that Sensory Experiences Play in Knowledge Acquisition. *Child Development*.

O'Neill, D. K. and Gopnik, A. 1991: Young Children's Ability to Identify the Sources of Their Beliefs. *Developmental Psychology*, 27, 390–99.

Perner, J., Leekam, S. R. and Wimmer, H. 1987: Three-year-olds' Difficulty with False Belief. *British Journal of Developmental Psychology*, 5, 125–37.

Perner, J. 1991: *Understanding the Representational Mind*. Cambridge, MA.: MIT Press.

Searle, J. R. 1983: *Intentionality*. New York: Cambridge University Press.

Shatz, M., Wellman, H. M. and Silber, S. 1983: The Acquisition of Mental Verbs: A Systematic Investigation of First References to Mental State. *Cognition*, 14, 301–321.

Siegal, M. and Beattie, K. 1991: Where to Look First for Children's Understanding of False Beliefs. *Cognition*, 38, 1–12.

Slobin, D. I. 1981: The Origin of Grammatical Encoding of Events. In W. Deutsch (ed.), *The Child's Construction of Language*. New York: Academic Press.

Spelke, E. S. 1991: Physical Knowledge in Infancy. In S. C. and R. Gelman (eds.), *The Epigenesis of Mind: Essays on Biology and Cognition*. Hillsdale NJ.: Lawrence Erlbaum Associates, 133–69.

Stich, S. 1983: *From Folk Psychology to Cognitive Science*. Cambridge, MA.: MIT Press.

Trevarthen, C. and Hubley, P. 1978: Secondary Intersubjectivity: Confidence, Confiders, and Acts of Meaning in the First Year of Life. In A. Lock (ed.), *Before Speech: The Beginning of Interpersonal Communication*. New York: Academic Press.

Wellman, H. W. 1993: Early Understanding of Mind: The Normal Case. In S. Baron-Cohen, H. Tager-Flusberg, Cohen and Volkman (eds.), *Understanding Other Minds: Perspectives From Autism*. Oxford: Oxford University Press.

Wellman, H. M. and Estes, D. 1986: Early Understanding of Mental Entities: A Reexamination of Childhood Realism. *Child Development*, 57, 910–23.

Wellman, H. M. and Bartsch, K. 1988: Young Children's Reasoning About Beliefs. *Cognition*, 30, 239–77.

Wellman, H. M. and Gelman, S. 1988: Children's Understanding of the Nonobvious. In R. J. Sternberg (ed.), *Advances in the psychology of intelligence Volume 4*. Hillsdale, NJ.: Lawrence Erlbaum Associates.

Wellman, H. M. 1990: *The Child's Theory of Mind*. Cambridge MA.: MIT Press.

Wellman, H. M. and Woolley, J. D. 1990: From Simple Desires to Ordinary Beliefs: The Early Development of Everyday Psychology. *Cognition*, 35, 245–75.

Wellman, H. M. and Banerjee, M. 1991: Mind and Emotion: Children's Understanding of the Emotional Consequences of Beliefs and Desires. *British Journal of Developmental Psychology*, 9, 191–224.

Wellman, H. M. and Gelman, S. A. 1992: Cognitive Development: Foundational Theories of Core Domains. *Annual Review of Psychology*.

Wimmer, H. and Perner, J. 1983: Beliefs About Beliefs: Representation and Constraining Function of Wrong Beliefs in Young Children's Understanding of Deception. *Cognition*, 13, 103–128.

Wimmer, H., Hogrefe, J. and Perner, J. 1988: Children's Understanding of Informational Access as Source of Knowledge. *Child Development*, 59, 386–96.

Wimmer, H. and Hartl, M. 1991: Against the Cartesian View on Mind: Young Children's Difficulty with Own False Beliefs. *British Journal of Developmental Psychology*, 9, 125–38.

Yuill, N. 1984: Young Children's Coordination of Motive and Outcome in Judgments of Satisfaction and Morality. *British Journal of Developmental Psychology*, 2, 73–81.

Zaitchek, D. 1990: When Representations Conflict With Reality: The Preschooler's Problem with False Beliefs and "False" Photographs. *Cognition*, 35, 41–68.

Study Questions

1. Why wouldn't something count as a theory for Gopnik and Wellman if it just described evidence and generalization?
2. Can a child be said to have the concept of belief if he or she does not understand misbelieving?
3. According to Gopnik and Wellman, a theory must be capable of revision. Yet many religious theories of the creation of the world seem unrevisable—does this make them something less than a theory?

4.9   Person as Scientist, Person as Moralist

 JOSHUA KNOBE

JOSHUA KNOBE (1974–) is an Assistant Professor of Philosophy at Yale University and a founding figure in the experimental philosophy movement. Much of his work focuses on the analysis of the fundamental concepts at work in moral judgment. In particular, he has been concerned with the interrelations between moral questions and questions about intention, causation, and free will. His work on these issues has been published in *Journal of Philosophy*, *Noûs*, *Analysis*, and *Philosophical Studies*. He edited the anthology *Experimental Philosophy* with Shaun Nichols. Popular presentations of

J. Knobe, "Person as Scientist, Person as Moralist," *Behavioral and Brain Sciences* 33, no. 4, copyright © 2010. Reprinted with the permission of Cambridge University Press.

his research have appeared in the *New York Times*, the *BBC*, *Scientific American*, *Slate*, and *Chronicle of Higher Education*. In this paper, Knobe contends that a large class of our explanations of the actions of others is influenced by moral considerations.

Consider the way research is conducted in a typical modern university. There are departments for theology, drama, philosophy…and then there are departments specifically devoted to the practice of *science*. Faculty members in these science departments generally have quite specific responsibilities. They are not supposed to make use of all the various methods and approaches one finds in other parts of the university. They are supposed to focus on observation, experimentation, the construction of explanatory theories.

Now consider the way the human mind ordinarily makes sense of the world. One plausible view would be that the human mind works something like a modern university. There are psychological processes devoted to religion (the mind's theology department), to aesthetics (the mind's art department), to morality (the mind's philosophy department)…and then there are processes specifically devoted to questions that have a roughly "scientific" character. These processes work quite differently from the ones we use in thinking about, say, moral or aesthetic questions. They proceed using more or less the same sorts of methods we find in university science departments.

This metaphor is a powerful one, and it has shaped research programs in many different areas of cognitive science. Take the study of *folk psychology*. Ordinary people have a capacity to ascribe mental states (beliefs, desires, etc.), and researchers have sometimes suggested that people acquire this capacity in much the same way that scientists develop theoretical frameworks (e.g., Gopnik & Wellman 1992). Or take *causal cognition*. Ordinary people have an ability to determine whether one event caused another, and it has been suggested that they do so by looking at the same sorts of statistical information scientists normally consult (e.g., Kelley 1967). Numerous other fields have taken a similar path. In each case, the basic strategy is to look at the methods used by professional research scientists and then to hypothesize that people actually use similar methods in their ordinary understanding. This strategy has clearly led to many important advances.

Yet, in recent years, a series of experimental results have begun pointing in a rather different direction. These results indicate that people's ordinary understanding does not proceed using the same methods one finds in the sciences. Instead, it appears that people's intuitions in both folk psychology and causal cognition can be affected by *moral* judgments. That is, people's judgments about whether a given action truly is morally good or bad can actually affect their intuitions about what that action caused and what mental states the agent had. […]

3.1. Intentional Action

Perhaps the most highly studied of these effects is the impact of people's moral judgments on their use of the concept of *intentional action*. This is the concept people use to distinguish between behaviors that are performed intentionally (e.g., hammering in a nail) and those that are performed unintentionally (e.g., accidentally bringing the hammer down on one's own thumb). It might at first appear that people's use of this distinction depends entirely on certain facts about the role of the agent's mental states in his or her behavior, but experimental studies consistently indicate that something more complex is actually at work here. It seems that people's moral judgments can somehow influence their intuitions about whether a behavior is intentional or unintentional.

To demonstrate the existence of this effect, we can construct pairs of cases that are exactly the same in almost every respect but differ in their moral status. For a simple example, consider the following vignette:

> The vice-president of a company went to the chairman of the board and said, "We are thinking of starting a new program. It will help us increase profits, but it will also harm the environment."
>
> The chairman of the board answered, "I don't care at all about harming the environment. I just want to make as much profit as I can. Let's start the new program."
>
> They started the new program. Sure enough, the environment was harmed.

Faced with this vignette, most subjects say that the chairman *intentionally* harmed the environment. One might initially suppose that this intuition relies only on certain facts about the chairman's own mental states (e.g., that he specifically knew his behavior would result in environmental harm). But the data suggest that something more is going on here. For people's intuitions change radically when one alters the moral status of the chairman's behavior by simply replacing the word "harm" with "help":

> The vice-president of a company went to the chairman of the board and said, "We are thinking of starting a new program. It will help us increase profits, and it will also help the environment."
>
> The chairman of the board answered, "I don't care at all about helping the environment. I just want to make as much profit as I can. Let's start the new program."
>
> They started the new program. Sure enough, the environment was helped.

Faced with this second version of the story, most subjects actually say that the chairman *unintentionally* helped the environment. Yet it seems that the only major difference between the two vignettes lies in the moral status of the chairman's behavior. So it appears that people's moral judgments are somehow impacting their intuitions about intentional action.

Of course, it would be unwise to draw any strong conclusions from the results of just one experiment, but this basic effect has been replicated and extended in numerous further studies. To begin with, subsequent experiments have further explored the harm and help cases to see what exactly about them leads to the difference in people's intuitions. These experiments suggest that moral judgments truly are playing a key role, since participants who start out with different moral judgments about the act of harming the environment end up arriving at different intuitions about whether the chairman acted intentionally (Tannenbaum et al. 2009). But the effect is not limited to vignettes involving environmental harm; it emerges when researchers use different cases (Cushman & Mele 2008; Knobe 2003a) and even when they turn to cases with quite different structures that do not involve side-effects in any way (Knobe 2003b; Nadelhoffer 2005). Nor does the effect appear to be limited to any one particular population: It emerges when the whole study is translated into Hindi and conducted on Hindi-speakers (Knobe & Burra 2006) and even when it is simplified and given to 4-year-old children (Leslie et al. 2006a). At this point, there is really a great deal of evidence for the claim that people's moral judgments are somehow impacting their intuitions about intentional action.

Still, as long as all of the studies are concerned only with intuitions about intentional action specifically, it seems that our argument will suffer from a fatal weakness. For someone might say: "Surely, we have very strong reason to suppose that the concept of intentional action works in more or less the same way as the other concepts people normally use to understand human action. But we have good theories of many of these other concepts—the concepts of deciding, wanting, causing, and so forth—and these other theories do not assign any role to moral considerations. So the best bet is that moral considerations do not play any role in the concept of intentional action either."

In my view, this is actually quite a powerful argument. Even if we have strong evidence for a certain view about the concept of intentional action specifically, it might well make sense to abandon this view in light of theories we hold about various other, seemingly similar concepts.

3.2. Further Mental States

As it happens, though, the impact of moral considerations does not appear to be limited to people's use of the word "intentionally." The very same effect also arises for numerous other expressions: "intention," "deciding," "desire," "in favor of," "advocating," and so forth.

To get a grip on this phenomenon, it may be helpful to look in more detail at the actual procedure involved in conducting these studies. In one common experimental design, subjects are randomly assigned to receive either the story about harming the environment or the story about helping the environment and then, depending on the case, are asked about the degree to which they agree or disagree with one of the following sentences:

(1)

a. The chairman of the board harmed the environment intentionally.

○   ○   ○   ○   ○   ○   ○

definitely   unsure   definitely
disagree   agree

b. The chairman of the board helped the environment intentionally.

○   ○   ○   ○   ○   ○   ○

definitely   unsure   definitely
disagree   agree

When the study is conducted in this way, one finds that subjects show moderate agreement with the claim that the chairman harmed intentionally and moderate disagreement with the claim that he helped intentionally (Knobe 2004a). The difference between the ratings in these two conditions provides evidence that people's moral intuitions are affecting their intuitions about intentional action.

It appears, however, that this effect is not limited to the concept of intentional action

specifically. For example, suppose we eliminate the word "intentionally" and instead use the word "decided." The two sentences then become:

(2) a. The chairman decided to harm the environment.

b. The chairman decided to help the environment.

Faced with these revised sentences, subjects show more or less the same pattern of intuitions. They tend to agree with the claim that the agent decided to harm, and they tend to disagree with the claim that the agent decided to help (Pettit & Knobe 2009).

Now suppose we make the case a little bit more complex. Suppose we do not use the adverb "intentionally" but instead use the verb "intend." So the sentences come out as:

(3) a. The chairman intended to harm the environment.

b. The chairman intended to help the environment.

One then finds a rather surprising result. People's responses in both conditions are shifted over quite far toward the "disagree" side. In fact, people's intuitions end up being shifted over so far that they do not, on the whole, agree in either of the two conditions (Shepard 2009; cf. Cushman 2010; Knobe 2004b; McCann 2005). Nonetheless, the basic pattern of the responses remains the same. Even though people's responses don't go all the way over to the "agree" side of the scale in either condition, they are still *more* inclined to agree in the harm case than they are in the help case.

Once one conceptualizes the issue in this way, it becomes possible to find an impact of moral considerations in numerous other domains. Take people's application of the concept *in favor*. Now consider a case in which an agent says:

I know that this new procedure will [bring about some outcome]. But that is not what we should be concerned about. The new procedure will increase profits, and that should be our goal.

Will people say in such a case that the agent is "in favor" of bringing about the outcome?

Here again, it seems that moral judgments play a role. People disagree with the claim that the agent is "in favor" when the outcome is morally good, whereas they stand at just about the midpoint between agreement and disagreement when the outcome is morally bad (Pettit & Knobe 2009). And similar effects have been observed for people's use of many other concepts: *desiring, intending, choosing*, and so forth (Pettit & Knobe 2009; Tannenbaum et al. 2009).

Overall, these results suggest that the effect obtained for intuitions about intentional action is just one example of a far broader phenomenon. The effect does not appear to be limited to the concept *intentionally*, nor even to closely related concepts such as *intention* and *intending*. Rather, it seems that we are tapping into a much more general tendency, whereby moral judgments impact the application of a whole range of different concepts used to pick out mental states and processes.[...]

3.4. Causation

All of the phenomena we have been discussing thus far may appear to be quite tightly related, and one might therefore suspect that the effect of morality would disappear as soon as one turns to other, rather different cases. That, however, seems not to be the case. Indeed, the very same effect arises in people's intuitions about *causation* (Alicke 2000; Cushman 2010; Hitchcock & Knobe 2009; Knobe, forthcoming; Knobe & Fraser 2008; Solan & Darley 2001).

For a simple example here, consider the following vignette:

> The receptionist in the philosophy department keeps her desk stocked with pens. The administrative assistants are allowed to take pens, but faculty members are supposed to buy their own.
>
> The administrative assistants typically do take the pens. Unfortunately, so do the faculty

members. The receptionist repeatedly e-mailed them reminders that only administrators are allowed to take the pens.

> On Monday morning, one of the administrative assistants encounters Professor Smith walking past the receptionist's desk. Both take pens. Later that day, the receptionist needs to take an important message ... but she has a problem. There are no pens left on her desk.

Faced with this vignette, most subjects say that the professor did cause the problem but that the administrative assistant did not cause the problem (Knobe & Fraser 2008). Yet, when we examine the case from a purely scientific standpoint, it seems that the professor's action and the administrative assistant's action bear precisely the same relation to the problem that eventually arose. The main difference between these two causal factors is just that the professor is doing something wrong (violating the departmental rule) while the administrative assistant is doing exactly what she is supposed to (acting in accordance with the rules of the department). So it appears that people's judgment that the professor is doing something wrong is somehow affecting their intuitions about whether or not the professor *caused* the events that followed.

Now, looking just at this one case, one might be tempted to suppose that the effect is not at all a matter of moral judgment but simply reflects people's intuitive sense that the professor's action is more "unusual" or "strange" than the administrative assistant's. But subsequent studies strongly suggest that there is something more afoot here. People continue to show the same basic effect even when they are informed that the administrative assistants *never* take pens whereas the professors always do (Roxborough & Cumby 2009), and there is a statistically significant effect whereby pro-life subjects are more inclined than pro-choice subjects to regard the act of seeking an abortion as a cause of subsequent outcomes (Cushman et al. 2008). All in all, the evidence seems strongly to suggest that people's moral judgments are actually impacting their causal intuitions.

3.5. Doing and Allowing

People ordinarily distinguish between actually breaking something and merely allowing it to break, between actually raising something and merely allowing it to rise, between actually killing someone and merely allowing someone to die. This distinction has come to be known as the distinction between *doing* and *allowing*.

To explore the relationship between people's intuitions about doing and allowing and their moral judgments, we used more or less the same methodology employed in these earlier studies (Cushman et al. 2008). Subjects were randomly assigned to receive different vignettes. Subjects in one condition received a vignette in which the agent performs an action that appears to be morally permissible:

> Dr. Bennett is an emergency-room physician. An unconscious homeless man is brought in, and his identity is unknown. His organ systems have shut down and a nurse has hooked him up to a respirator. Without the respirator he would die. With the respirator and some attention from Dr. Bennett he would live for a week or two, but he would never regain consciousness and could not live longer than two weeks.
>
> Dr. Bennett thinks to himself, "This poor man deserves to die with dignity. He shouldn't spend his last days hooked up to such a horrible machine. The best thing to do would be to disconnect him from the machine."
>
> For just that reason, Dr. Bennett disconnects the homeless man from the respirator, and the man quickly dies.

These subjects were then asked whether it would be more appropriate to say that the doctor *ended* the homeless man's life or that he *allowed* the homeless man's life to end.

Meanwhile, subjects in the other condition were given a vignette that was almost exactly the same, except that the doctor's internal monologue takes a somewhat different turn:

> ...Dr. Bennett thinks to himself, "This bum deserves to die. He shouldn't sit here soaking up my valuable time and resources. The best thing to do would be to disconnect him from the machine."

These subjects were asked the same question: whether it would be more appropriate to say that the doctor ended the man's life or allowed it to end.

Notice that the doctor performs exactly the same behavior in these two vignettes, and in both vignettes, he performs this behavior in the hopes that it will bring about the man's death. The only difference between the cases lies in the moral character of the doctor's reasons for hoping that the man will die. Yet this moral difference led to a striking difference in people's intuitions about *doing* versus *allowing*. Subjects who received the first vignette tended to say that the doctor "allowed" the man's life to end, whereas subjects who received the second vignette tended to say that the doctor "ended" the man's life. (Moreover, even within the first vignette, there was a correlation whereby subjects who thought that euthanasia was generally morally wrong were less inclined to classify the act as an "allowing.") Overall, then, the results of the study suggest that people's moral judgments are influencing their intuitions here as well.

It would, of course, be foolhardy to draw any very general conclusions from this one study, but the very same effect has also been observed in other studies using quite different methodologies (Cushman et al. 2008), and there is now at least some good provisional evidence in support of the view that people's intuitions about doing and allowing can actually be influenced by their moral judgments.

3.6. Additional Effects

Here we have discussed just a smattering of different ways in which people's moral judgments can impact their intuitions about apparently non-moral questions. But our review has been far from exhaustive: there are also studies showing that moral judgments can affect intuitions about *knowledge* (Beebe & Buckwalter, 2010), *happiness* (Nyholm 2009), *valuing* (Knobe & Roedder 2009), *act individuation* (Ulatowski 2009), *freedom* (Phillips & Knobe 2009), and *naturalness* (Martin 2009). Given that all of these studies were conducted just in the past few years, it seems highly probable that a number of additional effects along the same basic lines will emerge in the years to come.[. . .]

6. CONCLUSION

This target article began with a metaphor. The suggestion was that people's ordinary way of making sense of the world might be similar, at least in certain respects, to the way research is conducted in a typical modern university. Just as a university would have specific departments devoted especially to the sciences, our minds might include certain specific psychological processes devoted especially to constructing a roughly "scientific" kind of understanding.

If one thinks of the matter in this way, one immediately arrives at a certain picture of the role of moral judgments in people's understanding as a whole. In a university, there might be faculty members in the philosophy department who were hired specifically to work on moral questions, but researchers in the sciences typically leave such questions to one side. So maybe the mind works in much the same way. We might have certain psychological processes devoted to making moral judgments, but there would be other processes that focus on developing a purely "scientific" understanding of what is going on in a situation and remain neutral on all questions of morality.

I have argued that this picture is deeply mistaken. The evidence simply does not suggest that there is a clear division whereby certain psychological processes are devoted to moral questions and others are devoted to purely scientific questions. Instead, it appears that everything is jumbled together. Even the processes that look most "scientific" actually take moral considerations into account. It seems that we are moralizing creatures through and through.

References

Alicke, M. (2000) Culpable control and the psychology of blame. *Psychological Bulletin* 126:556–74.

Beebe, J. R. & Buckwalter, W. (2010) The epistemic side-effect effect. *Mind and Language*.

Cushman, F. (2010) Judgments of morality, causation and intention: Assessing the connections. Unpublished manuscript, Harvard University.

Cushman, F., Knobe, J. & Sinnott-Armstrong, W. (2008) Moral appraisals affect doing/allowing judgments. *Cognition* 108:353–80.

Cushman, F. & Mele, A. (2008) Intentional action: Two-and-a-half folk concepts? In: *Experimental philosophy*, ed. J. Knobe & S. Nichols, pp. 171–88. Oxford University Press.

Gopnik, A. & Wellman, H. M. (1992) Why the child's theory of mind really is a theory. *Mind and Language* 7:145–71.

Hitchcock, C. & Knobe, J. (2009) Cause and norm. *Journal of Philosophy* 106(11):587–612.

Kelley, H. H. (1967) Attribution theory in social psychology. In: *Nebraska Symposium on Motivation*, ed. D. Levine, pp. 192–238. University of Nebraska Press.

Knobe, J. (2003a) Intentional action and side effects in ordinary language. *Analysis* 63:190–93.

Knobe, J. (2003b) Intentional action in folk psychology: An experimental investigation. *Philosophical Psychology* 16:309–24.

Knobe, J. (2004a) Folk psychology and folk morality: Response to critics. *Journal of Theoretical and Philosophical Psychology* 24(2):270–79.

Knobe, J. (2004b) Intention, intentional action and moral considerations. *Analysis* 64:181–87.

Knobe, J. (forthcoming) Action tree and moral judgment. *Topics in Cognitive Science*.

Knobe, J. & Burra, A. (2006) Intention and intentional action: A cross-cultural study. *Journal of Culture and Cognition* 6:113–32.

Knobe, J. & Fraser, B. (2008) Causal judgment and moral judgment: Two experiments. In: *Moral psychology, vol. 2: The cognitive science of morality: Intuition and diversity*, ed. W. Sinnott-Armstrong, pp. 441–8. MIT Press.

Knobe, J. & Roedder, E. (2009) The ordinary concept of valuing. *Philosophical Issues* 19(1):131–47.

Leslie, A. M., Knobe, J. & Cohen, A. (2006a) Acting intentionally and the side-effect effect: Theory of mind and moral judgment. *Psychological Science* 17:421–07.

Martin, K. (2009) An experimental approach to the normativity of "natural." Paper presented at the Annual Meeting of the South Carolina Society for Philosophy, Rock Hill, South Carolina, February 27–28, 2009.

McCann, H. (2005) Intentional action and intending: Recent empirical studies. *Philosophical Psychology* 18:737–48.

Nadelhoffer, T. (2005) Skill, luck, control, and folk ascriptions of intentional action. *Philosophical Psychology* 18:343–54.

Nyholm, S. (2009) Moral judgments and happiness. Unpublished manuscript, University of Michigan.

Pettit, D. & Knobe, J. (2009) The pervasive impact of moral judgment. *Mind and Language* 24:586–604.

Phillips, J. & Knobe, J. (2009) Moral judgments and intuitions about freedom. *Psychological Inquiry* 20:30–36.

Roxborough, C. & Cumby, J. (2009) Folk psychological concepts: Causation. *Philosophical Psychology* 22:205–13.

Shepard, J. (2009) The side-effect effect in Knobe's environment case and the Simple View of intentionality. Unpublished manuscript, Georgia State University.

Solan, L. & Darley, J. (2001) Causation, contribution, and legal liability: An empirical study. *Law and Contemporary Problems* 64:265–98.

Tannenbaum, D., Ditto, P. & Pizarro, D. (2009) Different moral values produce different judgments of intentional action. Unpublished manuscript, University of California, Irvine.

Ulatowski, J. (2009) Action under a description. Unpublished manuscript, University of Wyoming.

Study Questions

1. What are reason explanations?
2. What evidence does Knobe think suggests that reason explanations are only possible for actions we perform on purpose?
3. Why does Knobe think reason explanations are subject to moral considerations?

CHAPTER 5

Consciousness

EMILY ESCH AND JOSHUA WEISBERG

INTRODUCTION

Consciousness is both utterly familiar and deeply puzzling. As conscious creatures, we are intimately familiar with consciousness, yet explanations of its nature and purpose have eluded philosophers and scientists for centuries. Consciousness is philosophically puzzling because of the apparent gap between how consciousness seems to us subjectively, "from the inside," and the way things are explained in physical theory. As the nineteenth-century biologist Thomas Huxley memorably explains, "How it is that anything so remarkable as a state of consciousness comes about as a result of irritating nervous tissue, is just as unaccountable as the appearance of the Djin, when Aladdin rubbed his lamp."[1]

Adding to the confusion, there appears to be no room for error in our first-person access to our conscious states. Our conscious states make up how things seem to us, and could we really be wrong about how things *seem* to us? Our special epistemic access leads to some strong *metaphysical* claims about consciousness. According to philosophers known as *physicalists*, all things, conscious minds included, are ultimately physical in nature. This view has been successful in explaining the nonmental world.[2] But given the special nature of the conscious mind as it's revealed in subjective reflection, it seems that the conscious mind cannot be physical (or cannot be *merely* physical—see later). Consciousness seems to have features that no physical theory could explain. Take, for example, what contemporary philosophers call *qualia*. Qualia are the seemingly indescribable qualities of sensation—the redness of a red experience, the painfulness of an experience of stubbing one's toe. Qualia can appear to be distinct from any physical process or property, as illustrated by the following thought experiment. Can you imagine that all physical matter stays the same but some of the qualia change, for instance, that objects that once looked green now look red? If it is really possible for the physical facts about color to remain the same but for the appearances of the colors to change, then it might be that qualia really aren't physical features of the conscious mind.

Traditional debates over consciousness are dominated by arguments about epistemology and metaphysics—arguments turning on how we know about consciousness, and what consciousness (and physical matter) could or could not be. More recent debates over consciousness, however, tend to focus in the first instance on the *concept* of consciousness. It may be that we conceive of consciousness as some philosophers do, as a unified, indivisible substance. But perhaps this isn't the only way to conceive of consciousness, and it may not be the best way to do so. The concept "consciousness" might pick out a range of different things, and our philosophical conclusions may depend on which concept we use. It may be that scientists or laypeople use a very different concept of consciousness, one that does not lead to surprising philosophical conclusions. Thus, disentangling the various uses of the concept "consciousness" is an important first step in addressing the purported philosophical puzzle of conscious experience.

EPISTEMIC AND METAPHYSICAL DEBATES ABOUT CONSCIOUSNESS

Theories of consciousness can be divided into two broad metaphysical categories: dualist and physicalist. Dualists claim that there is a radical difference between conscious mental states and physical states; physicalists claim that in some fundamental sense conscious mental states *are* physical states. Both dualists and physicalists bear the responsibility of explaining how the mental and the physical are related. It seems to be an obvious commonsensical fact that mental states affect physical states and vice versa. For example, my desire for a drink (conscious mental state) causes me to walk (physical state) to the fridge, and the paper cut on my finger (physical state) causes pain (conscious mental state). For physicalists, arguably, this explanatory burden is easier. Physicalists might explain the relationship as one of identity, in which the mental states are just brain states. For physicalists, the main challenge is explaining how it is possible that our subjective experiences can ultimately be nothing over and above brain processes. Many people share the intuition, expressed by Huxley at the beginning of this introduction, that it is utterly mysterious how consciousness could arise from brain matter.

The readings in this unit begin with a selection by René Descartes, who argues that mental substances are essentially thinking things and physical substances are essentially extended things. On this view, called substance dualism, thinking things aren't extended; that is, they do not take up space. Descartes supports substance dualism with the following argument. We know from reflection that the conscious mind is essentially unified and indivisible. But physical matter, by its nature, is always divisible.

Since a thing cannot be both essentially unified and essentially divisible, the conscious mind cannot be physical.[3] Like many arguments on this topic, the key premise is supported by the special epistemic access we seem to have to our own conscious minds.

The substance dualist faces a serious problem: how to explain the apparent fact that the mind and the body interact. For largely anatomical reasons, Descartes believed that the two substances interacted through the pineal gland. But despite offering empirical evidence for the location of the interaction, Descartes failed to provide any philosophical conception of how this interaction could work. We have no good model for understanding how a nonspatial mental state can interact with anything; our model of how one thing causes another is rooted in the physical.

In addition to the idea that consciousness is immaterial, Descartes was committed to the epistemic claim that we are aware of all of our thoughts. In other words, Descartes believed that there are no unconscious mental states.[4] This commitment, now known as the *transparency thesis*, was subsequently endorsed by many later philosophers but has recently been severely undermined by empirical research. Another feature central to Descartes' view of consciousness is the role of reflection. According to Descartes, each of our thoughts includes the first-person perspective.[5] That is, our thoughts automatically involve reference to the self. Call this the *reflection thesis*. Descartes' commitment to the reflection thesis is made apparent in Descartes most famous argument, the *cogito ergo sum*, better known as the claim "I am thinking, therefore I exist." This argument arises out of Descartes' attempt to avoid the skeptical conclusions that ended the "First Meditation." There, Descartes had presented a thought experiment in which an evil demon is fooling the narrator into believing all kinds of false things, including the existence of an external world. There is one category of beliefs, however, that Descartes argues the evil demon cannot trick us into believing falsely: the belief that I am thinking (or experiencing or imagining) when I am not thinking (or experiencing or imagining). Since every thought includes the "I," each time I have a thought, I can know that I currently exist.

A very different understanding of consciousness is found in Gottfried Leibniz's *Monadology*. Leibniz disagrees with Descartes' claims that there are two fundamental kinds of substances, that we are always aware of our mental states, and that all mental states include the first-person perspective. But Leibniz also denies physicalism. In a famous thought experiment, he explains why consciousness cannot be physical:

> Suppose that there be a machine, the structure of which produces thinking, feeling, and perceiving; imagine this machine enlarged but preserving the same proportions, so that you could enter it as if it were a mill. This being supposed, you might visit its inside; but what would you observe there? Nothing but parts which push and move each other, and never anything that could explain perception.[6]

Leibniz seems to be claiming that no matter how complicated the inner workings of the machine, there would never be anything there that would explain consciousness. He denies, that is, a view that has gained popularity in recent times, the view that consciousness might arise out of the organization of many smaller parts. Leibniz's mill analogy illustrates what has come to be known as the *explanatory gap*. The explanatory gap is the gap between our understanding of the physical brain processes and our understanding of the nature of consciousness. We currently have no way of conceiving how the underlying brain processes can explain many of the qualitative features of consciousness. The gap here is epistemic, in that it involves a limit in our current understanding, but it is frequently used to argue for metaphysical conclusions.

Leibniz, for example, uses the existence of such a gap to argue that explaining consciousness requires the supposition of simple substances that bring in consciousness at a more fundamental level. These simple substances he calls "monads" and they are the fundamental constituents of reality. All monads are characterized as perceiving, by which Leibniz means that they represent external objects. Some of them not only perceive but also are aware of the fact that they are perceiving. This kind of awareness Leibniz calls *apperception*. In this way, Leibniz builds his theory of consciousness from basic representational states, a version of a view that has become popular with contemporary philosophers. Leibniz believes that humans have both bare perceptions and apperceptions; in other words, sometimes we are aware of our mental states and sometimes we are not, a denial of both the transparency thesis and the reflection thesis. Leibniz explains the appearance of interaction among the monads, including the monad that makes up an individual's mind and the monads that make up her body, with a doctrine called *pre-established harmony*. Each monad, Leibniz believes, could only affect itself, but the actions of each monad are coordinated by God with the actions of all the other monads in the universe, so it appears that they are interacting.

A third position, epiphenomenalism, agrees with Leibniz that the commonsense belief that mental states cause behavior is false. Epiphenomenalists believe that mental states arise from brain processes, but that these mental states cannot affect the body.[7] Unlike the interactionism of Descartes, epiphenomenalists claim that the causation works in only one direction—from body to mind. For example, bodily injury causes one to feel pain, but the pain itself doesn't cause any behavior. One of the first advocates of this theory was the biologist Thomas Huxley. He explains the relationship between consciousness and the body like this:

> The consciousness of brutes would appear to be related to the mechanism of their body simply as a collateral product of its working, and to be as completely without any power of modifying that working as the steam-whistle which accompanies the work of a locomotive engine is without influence upon its machinery. Their volition, if they have any, is an emotion indicative of physical changes, not a cause of such changes.[8]

Huxley extends this line of reasoning to humans. The conscious state he uses as an example—the feeling of choosing to do one thing over another—accompanies the underlying physical changes but is not the cause of the choosing. Humans are, Huxley claims, "conscious automata."[9]

A more contemporary defense of epiphenomenalism is found in the selection by Frank Jackson. Jackson's defense of epiphenomenalism is motivated by his arguments against physicalism. Jackson argues that there are certain sensations, like the smell of a rose or the hurtfulness of pain, that cannot be explained in purely physical terms. These features of our experience, qualia, resist explanation by science. Jackson makes his argument by using a powerful thought experiment. He imagines a scenario in which a woman, Mary, grows up in a black-and-white room without ever being exposed to color. Though she never sees any colors, Mary is taught all the physical information about color and color perception. Jackson argues that when Mary leaves her black-and-white room for the first time and experiences the colored world, she learns something new. This is a problem for the physicalist because she is committed to the view that everything is physical. The fact that Mary learns something new shows, Jackson claims, that physicalism cannot be true, because Mary already knew all the physical facts. In the final section of his paper, Jackson tries to dispel some of the worries traditionally associated with epiphenomenalism. Unlike Huxley, Jackson doesn't think that all conscious mental states are causally inert. Instead, he defends the weaker claim that only certain properties of mental states, namely, qualia, are causally inert.

While Jackson's thought experiment has garnered much attention since its original publication, few philosophers have been willing to accept epiphenomenalism. The main problem with epiphenomenalism is that it runs counter to some deeply held intuitions. By claiming that conscious mental states (or the conscious properties of our mental states) are causally inert, the epiphenomenalist is committed to the position that, for example, the hurtfulness of pain doesn't itself cause its victim to cry, scream, limp, and so forth. In addition to running counter to our intuition that the hurtfulness of pain is at least partially responsible for our behavior, epiphenomenalism also faces empirical challenges. It is difficult to see, for example, how causally inefficacious conscious states are compatible with contemporary evolutionary theory. If conscious mental states have no effect on behavior, then it is unclear how they came about or were preserved.

"THE" CONCEPT OF CONSCIOUSNESS

A major trend in philosophy, from the turn of the twentieth century onward, is a focus on the concepts used in thinking about philosophical problems. Perhaps if we can get our concepts straight, many of the seemingly intractable debates of traditional philosophy will become tractable. Or maybe the debates will be exposed as mere confusions brought on by misusing ordinary concepts. Failing to specify which concept is being used in a philosophical discussion can lead to confusion and faulty reasoning. And being precise about our concepts helps us to get straight what is at issue in these debates. Unfortunately, philosophers disagree about which concept is the right one to use in thinking about consciousness. Some modern-day dualists claim that physicalists ignore the crucial concept picking out qualia. Physicalists counter that the dualists' way of carving up the conceptual cake creates apparent philosophical problems where there are none. And both sides appeal to our "everyday" concept of consciousness, each holding that their side is on the side of ordinary thinking. This allows them to paint their opponents as radical revisionists, running roughshod over commonsense intuition. And this, in turn, raises the question of just what the folk concept of consciousness might be. In this section, we'll first spell out the philosophical concept of consciousness most central to current debates. Then we'll discuss new work that attempts to discover, by empirical methods, just what concept ordinary people use when they consider consciousness. We'll also discuss an interesting neurological syndrome—blindsight—and explain how it may be used to clarify these conceptual questions.

The philosophical concept of consciousness most at issue in the contemporary readings in this chapter is what Ned Block has termed "phenomenal consciousness."[10]

Phenomenal consciousness refers to the consciousness of experiences, states that there is something it is like for the subject to be in. Prime examples of phenomenally conscious states are conscious perceptions, like the visual experience of a red apple, and conscious pains, like the awful sensation of a paper cut. A state is phenomenally conscious because it consciously "feels" the way it does. Phenomenally conscious states are thus defined in terms of the qualia mentioned earlier. Further, Block holds that phenomenal consciousness cannot be explained without remainder in causal, functional, or representational terms. Whether Block is correct about this last claim is a key point of contention in recent debates about consciousness. It is phenomenal consciousness, for example, that leads to what David Chalmers terms the "hard problem" of consciousness (see later). Some philosophers, among them Patricia Churchland, are doubtful that phenomenal consciousness exists in the pure sense intended by Block and Chalmers. This new conceptual debate mirrors the historical concerns mentioned earlier. If there is a special concept of consciousness defined in terms of qualia, then it is hard to see how any explanation of consciousness in physical terms could be complete. There will always be an "explanatory gap" between consciousness and the physical. And because of this epistemic gap, we have reason to doubt that consciousness is ultimately physical. If there really is phenomenal consciousness, physicalism might be in trouble.

Chalmers's embrace of a distinct phenomenal concept of consciousness is central to his argument that explaining consciousness poses a special "hard problem" for science. Echoing Leibniz, he contends that even if we knew all about the way the brain functions during conscious experience, and even if we were to learn all the physical facts, right down to the quantum level, about such an event, we'd still not know *why* such physical processes are conscious. Phenomenally conscious experience, Chalmers contends, cannot be explained in terms of the structure or function of brains—conceivably, the very same structures and functional processes could occur in the absence of consciousness. Chalmers concludes that consciousness is an additional *fundamental* feature of the universe, like electromagnetism or mass, inexplicable in any other terms. But that does not mean, according to Chalmers, that we can't develop a theory of how consciousness connects with physical matter. It is possible we'll discover fundamental laws linking experience and physical phenomena like neural activity. Consciousness will not be explained in terms of other, more basic things, but it will be lawfully connected to the physical world of natural science. To explain electromagnetism, new entities and laws were introduced into science; the same will occur with an explanation of consciousness, according to Chalmers.[11] Still, it is an error for philosophers and scientists to approach the problem of consciousness with the same set of tools they use to explain the physical features of reality. No matter how much we learn about how the physical brain works, we still will not have an explanation of why some of our brain states are phenomenally conscious.

Patricia Churchland strongly disagrees with Chalmers's pessimism about the possibility of explaining phenomenally conscious experience. First, she questions the grounds for Chalmers's claim that there is a special hard problem of consciousness. She points out that many of the problems labeled as "easy" by Chalmers pose great difficulties in neuroscience. How, exactly, are we supposed to tell the difference between difficult but "easy" problems and "real," hard problems? She contends that Chalmers's claim amounts to nothing but an extended "argument from ignorance": we don't know how to explain phenomenal consciousness now; therefore, phenomenal consciousness is inexplicable. But this form of argument is fallacious. Many times in the past, people had thought they'd reached the end of what could be said about a particular puzzle, only to find that new thinking and new discoveries delivered a solution. The mere fact of our current ignorance says little about the possibility of a future explanation. Churchland supports her contention by citing, among other examples, the claims made by "vitalists" in biology about the possibility of explaining life. Vitalists thought that "mechanism"—the idea that biological processes are just mechanistic, biochemical processes—could not explain what it is for an organism to be alive. But advances in mechanistic biochemistry eventually showed how mechanism could explain the very processes vitalists worried about. Prior to those advances, it may have seemed inconceivable to vitalists that all there was to life was complex biochemical processes. But that was because they were ignorant of the relevant science. The situation is the same, Churchland contends, with Chalmers and consciousness. His "hard problem" is just the usual problem faced by scientists in explaining difficult and complex phenomena. It does not mark off a special philosophical gap, despite how things may seem at present. In other words, normal physical brain processes may well explain everything that needs explaining about consciousness. Despite our current ignorance, we shouldn't be "hornswoggled" by Chalmers's alleged hard problem.

The next selection, on blindsight, provides an example of how advances in neuroscience might inform our understanding of consciousness. Blindsight occurs in some subjects when there is damage to the main visual areas of the brain but some residual visual functioning remains. Extensively studied by neuroscientist Larry Weiskrantz, blindsight subjects show the following surprising dissociation.[12] Despite reporting that they can see nothing in affected regions of their visual field, they can correctly guess at well above chance about the presence, orientation, movement, and other features of stimuli presented in their "blind fields." Neuroscientist Martha Farah provides a nice empirical summary of the brain regions and processes involved in blindsight, and she offers a sample of neuroscientific explanations of the syndrome.

Blindsight is among the many empirical results undermining Descartes' "transparency thesis," which claims that there are no unconscious mental states. Blindsight subjects visually perceive their targets (this allows them to guess above chance), but there is nothing it's like for them to perceive in this way—their visual perceptions are not conscious. Blindsight also provides a way to clarify the concepts of phenomenal consciousness. It seems that visual information is still in some sense accessible to blindsight subjects—they can, when prompted to guess, correctly determine many of the properties of stimuli in front of them. But there is nothing it's like for them to consciously see the stimuli. Thus, it *may* be that blindsight is an example of seeing, in some functional sense, without phenomenal consciousness. Phenomenal consciousness, on this idea, is whatever is missing from the "seeing" in blindsight. The function of seeing—detecting what's in front of our eyes—still occurs in blindsight, but the "feel" of seeing—the qualia—seems to be lacking. Thus, qualia can be separated from the functional processes of the brain. They appear to be independent of function. However, those philosophers who deny that phenomenal consciousness is independent of brain function note that the "seeing" in blindsight is greatly attenuated: subjects must be prompted to guess at what's in their blind field and cannot access many of the features accessible in normal vision. So perhaps what we have here is a case of attenuated brain function and because of this, a lack of phenomenal consciousness. So brain function and phenomenal consciousness may not come apart after all. This prompts the introduction of "super blindsight," presented in philosopher Michael Tye's contribution to this chapter. Perhaps some imagined blindsighter could learn to cue herself about what is in her blind field. She might even become so adept at doing so that she behaves just like people with normal vision—all the functional processes might be the same. But it's still plausible that something is missing, even in super blindsight. The missing elements, according to Chalmers and his allies, is phenomenal consciousness. Even if such a case is impossible, it does help to clarify what is meant by phenomenal consciousness. But the existence of blindsight also helps to strengthen Churchland's point. Blindsight is an unexpected discovery about the nature of visual awareness arising from new knowledge of the brain. It has the potential at least to alter how we think about consciousness. Just imagine what another hundred (or thousand!) years of detailed empirical study of the brain might uncover. Can we really be so confident that we won't find that phenomenal consciousness is just a physical feature of the brain after all?

But there remain questions about the status of philosophers' claims about the proper concept of consciousness. Perhaps their definitions are prompted by prior philosophical assumptions. If one already thinks consciousness can't be explained in physical terms, it will seem intuitively plausible that there is a concept of consciousness picking out consciousness in just that way. But this might simply be a theoretical bias, one that can be dismissed by those lacking such intuitions. To avoid such an objection to the very idea of phenomenal consciousness, philosophers like Chalmers contend that phenomenal consciousness as they spell it out captures at least some of what ordinary people mean by consciousness. If that is the case, then the concept can't be so lightly dismissed. One of the things a theory of consciousness ought to do, surely, is explain our pretheoretic concepts and intuitions about the phenomenon. The question then becomes, do the folk really possess a concept of *phenomenal* consciousness? This is the issue addressed in Justin Sytsma's contribution. Sytsma reviews a number of recent experimental philosophy studies of the commonsense conception of consciousness. Experimental philosophy employs empirical means in addressing philosophical questions. One way of doing so is to survey nonphilosophers about their intuitions concerning possible scenarios. Based on the results of these surveys, it's possible to reconstruct the underlying concepts best explaining the survey results. According to Sytsma, recent work plausibly points against the claim that the ordinary people fully subscribe to the philosophical concept of phenomenal consciousness. Notably, test subjects were willing to a significant degree to attribute perceptual states like seeing red or smelling bananas to robots, something that is allegedly ruled out by the philosophical concept of phenomenal consciousness as it's understood by Block and Chalmers. Robots can be *completely* characterized in functional, physical terms, so phenomenal consciousness should not be ascribed to them if phenomenal consciousness is conceived of as independent of brain function. But nonphilosophers are willing to ascribe conscious perceptual states to robots nonetheless. Sytsma further details studies showing that the folk concept of consciousness tracks the *valence* of mental states (whether they are pleasant or unpleasant, for example), and that drives subjects' willingness or unwillingness to ascribe certain mental states to robots. This may suggest that there's still a substantial "hard problem," that of explaining valence. But Sytsma argues that valence seems fully amenable to explanation in functional-physical terms, so this new "hard" problem does not arise.

This concludes our brief introduction to the chapter on consciousness. Historically, the debate has been driven by substantial epistemological and metaphysical assumptions about our access to consciousness and its nature, as well as about the nature of physical reality. More recent debate focuses on the concept of consciousness. There is no question that explaining consciousness is extremely difficult, no matter who is correct here. But it is reasonable to ask how philosophers are initially thinking about what needs to be explained. Accepting a distinct concept of phenomenal consciousness may heighten the sense of mystery involved in consciousness. And this may seem appropriate given the unique access we have to our conscious states. But it also may put up an illegitimate conceptual barrier to a physical explanation of consciousness.

Notes

1. Thomas Huxley, *Lessons in Elementary Physiology*, 2nd ed. (New York: McMillan, 1866), 210.
2. Except God, perhaps. See Unit 2.
3. Cf. René Descartes, *Meditations on First Philosophy*, ed. John Cottingham (New York: Cambridge University Press, 1996), 59.
4. Descartes' use of the term *thoughts* is very broad; it included products of the imagination, sense experiences, doubting, willing, and reasoning.
5. This claim comes in weaker and stronger versions; it's not clear which version Descartes held.
6. Gottfried Leibniz, *Monadology and Other Philosophical Essays*, trans. and ed. Paul Schrecker and Anne Martin Schrecker (New York: Bobbs-Merrill, 1965), 150.
7. It's a further issue whether they might have other causal effects. Some versions of epiphenomenalism claim that they do; others claim that they are completely causally inert.
8. Thomas Huxley, "On the Hypothesis That Animals Are Automata, and Its History," in *Collected Essays*, Vol. 1 (New York: Appleton, 1896), 240.
9. Ibid., 244.
10. Ned Block, "On Confusion on a Function of Consciousness," *Behavioral and Brain Sciences* 18 (1995): 227–247, reprinted in *The Nature of Consciousness: Philosophical Debates*, ed. Ned Block, Owen Flanagan, and Güven Güzeldere (Cambridge, MA: MIT Press, 1997), 380–382.
11. Cf. David Chalmers, "Facing Up to the Problem of Consciousness," *Journal of Consciousness Studies* 2, no. 3 (1995): 200–219.
12. Larry Weiskrantz, *Consciousness Lost and Found: A Neuropsychological Exploration* (Oxford: Oxford University Press, 1997).

References

Block, Ned. "On Confusion on a Function of Consciousness." *Behavioral and Brain Sciences* 18 (1995), reprinted in *The Nature of Consciousness: Philosophical Debates*, ed. Ned Block, Owen Flanagan, and Güven Güzeldere, 375–416. Cambridge, MA: MIT Press, 1997.

Descartes, René. *Meditations on First Philosophy*, ed. John Cottingham. New York: Cambridge University Press, 1996.

Huxley, Thomas. *Lessons in Elementary Physiology.* 2nd ed. New York: McMillan, 1866.

Huxley, Thomas. *Collected Essays.* Vol. 1. New York: Appleton, 1896.

Leibniz, Gottfried. *Monadology and Other Philosophical Essays,* trans. and ed. Paul Schrecker and Anne Martin Schrecker. New York: Bobbs-Merrill, 1965.

Lichtenberg, Georg. *Aphorisms,* trans. R. J. Hollingdale. London: Penguin, 1990.

Kriegel, Uriah. "Consciousness and Self-Consciousness." *The Monist* 87, no. 2 (2004): 182–205.

Metzinger, Thomas. "Phenomenal Transparency and Cognitive Self-Reference." *Phenomenology and the Cognitive Sciences* 2, no. 4 (2004): 353–393.

Rosenthal, David M. "A Theory of Consciousness." In *The Nature of Consciousness: Philosophical Debates,* ed. Ned Block, Owen Flanagan, and Güven Güzeldere, 729–753. Cambridge, MA: MIT Press, 1997.

Weiskrantz, Larry. *Consciousness Lost and Found: A Neuropsychological Exploration.* Oxford: Oxford University Press, 1997.

Suggestions for Further Reading

Arico, Adam. "Folk Psychology, Consciousness, & Context Effects." *Review of Philosophy and Psychology,* no. 1 (2010): 371–393.

Baars, Bernard. *A Cognitive Theory of Consciousness.* Cambridge: Cambridge University Press, 1988.

Bayne, Timothy. "The Unity of Consciousness and the Split-Brain Syndrome." *Journal of Philosophy* 105, no. 6 (2008): 277–300.

Carruthers, Peter. *Phenomenal Consciousness: A Naturalistic Theory.* Cambridge: Cambridge University Press, 2000.

Chalmers, David J. *The Conscious Mind: In Search of a Fundamental Theory.* Oxford and New York: Oxford University Press, 1996.

Dennett, Daniel C. *Consciousness Explained.* Boston: Little Brown, 1991.

Dretske, Fred. *Naturalizing the Mind.* Cambridge, MA: MIT Press, 1995.

Knobe, Josh, and Jesse Prinz. "Intuitions about Consciousness: Experimental Studies." *Phenomenology and the Cognitive Sciences* 7, no. 1 (2008): 67–85.

Levine, Joseph. *Purple Haze: The Puzzle of Consciousness.* Oxford and New York: Oxford University Press, 2001.

Lewis, David. "Should a Materialist Believe in Qualia?" *Australasian Journal of Philosophy* 73 (1995): 140–144.

Ludlow, Peter, Yujin Nagasawa, and Daniel Stoljar, eds. *There's Something about Mary: Essays on Phenomenal Consciousness and Frank Jackson's Knowledge Argument.* Cambridge, MA: MIT Press, 2004.

Lycan, William G. *Consciousness and Experience.* Cambridge, MA: MIT Press/Bradford Books, 1996.

Nagel, Thomas. "What Is It Like to Be a Bat?" *Philosophical Review* 83, no. 4 (1974): 435–450.

Papineau, David. *Thinking About Consciousness.* Oxford: Clarendon, 2002.

Perry, John. *Knowledge, Possibility and Consciousness.* Cambridge, MA: MIT Press, 2001.

Rosenthal, David M. *Consciousness and Mind.* Oxford: Clarendon, 2005.

Siewert, Charles. *The Significance of Consciousness.* Princeton: Princeton University Press, 1998.

Sytsma, Justin, and Edouard Machery. "How to Study Folk Intuitions about Phenomenal Consciousness." *Philosophical Psychology* 22, no. 1 (2009): 21–35.

Tye, Michael. *Ten Problems of Consciousness.* Cambridge, MA: MIT Press, 1995.

5.1   Meditations on First Philosophy

     ## RENÉ DESCARTES

RENÉ DESCARTES (1596–1650) was a French philosopher and considered by many to be the "father of modern philosophy." During his lifetime, he received the support of two royal figures, Elisabeth, the Princess of Bohemia, and Christina, the Queen of Sweden. Queen Christina brought Descartes to her court to establish an academy and teach her philosophy. He failed to survive the first winter and died of pneumonia. Many attribute his death to the queen's demand for philosophical instruction in the early morning hours; Descartes was in the habit of working in bed until noon. In addition to his philosophical work, Descartes produced groundbreaking work in mathematics. Influenced by the mechanical view of nature popular at the time, he developed a theory of matter that was compatible with mechanistic principles. This selection includes excerpts from the sixth of six "Meditations" in Descartes' most famous work *Meditations on First Philosophy*.

[...] FIRST, I KNOW THAT EVERYTHING WHICH I clearly and distinctly understand is capable of being created by God so as to correspond exactly with my understanding of it. Hence the fact that I can clearly and distinctly understand one thing apart from another is enough to make me certain that the two things are distinct, since they are capable of being separated, at least by God. The question of what kind of power is required to bring about such a separation does not affect the judgement that the two things are distinct. Thus, simply by knowing that I exist and seeing at the same time that absolutely nothing else belongs to my nature or essence except that I am a thinking thing, I can infer correctly that my essence consists solely in the fact that I am a thinking thing. It is true that I may have (or,

to anticipate, that I certainly have) a body that is very closely joined to me. But nevertheless, on the one hand I have a clear and distinct idea of myself, in so far as I am simply a thinking, non-extended thing; and on the other hand I have a distinct idea of body, in so far as this is simply an extended, non-thinking thing. And accordingly, it is certain that I am really distinct from my body, and can exist without it. [...]

The first observation I make at this point is that there is a great difference between the mind and the body, inasmuch as the body is by its very nature always divisible, while the mind is utterly indivisible. For when I consider the mind, or myself in so far as I am merely a thinking thing, I am unable to distinguish any parts within myself; I understand myself to be something quite single

René Descartes, "Sixth Meditation," in *Descartes: Meditations on First Philosophy*, translated and edited by John Cottingham (New York: Cambridge University Press).

and complete. Although the whole mind seems to be united to the whole body, I recognize that if a foot or arm or any other part of the body is cut off, nothing has thereby been taken away from the mind. As for the faculties of willing, of understanding, of sensory perception and so on, these cannot be termed parts of the mind, since it is one and the same mind that wills, and understands and has sensory perceptions. By contrast, there is no corporeal or extended thing that I can think of which in my thought I cannot easily divide into parts; and this very fact makes me understand that it is divisible. This one argument would be enough to show me that the mind is completely different from the body, even if I did not already know as much from other considerations. [. . .]

Study Questions

1. Why does Descartes dismiss the notion that he is a reasonable animal? Is this a good reason?

2. How does Descartes characterize the body? Why does he think that he is not his body? Is he right?

3. The wax argument at the end of the Meditation is supposed to demonstrate that we know the nature of minds better than we know the nature of bodies. Do you think this is a good argument? Do you agree with Descartes that we know the nature of minds better than we know the nature of bodies?

The Monadology   5.2

GOTTFRIED LEIBNIZ

GOTTFRIED LEIBNIZ (1646–1716) was a German philosopher and mathematician. In mathematics, he shares with Isaac Newton the discovery of the differential and integral calculus. In philosophy, Leibniz wrote on a variety of topics including metaphysics, logic, epistemology, ethics, and philosophy of religion. The following reading is the beginning of one of his better known works, *Monadology*. In this short book, Leibniz argues against both the materialist and the Cartesian dualist and presents his own metaphysical view which is based on the idea of simple substances he calls "monads" (and sometimes "entelechies"). The selection here includes an often quoted passage in which Leibniz argues that materialism must be false because it is inconceivable that the organization of moving parts could explain phenomenal consciousness. This clears the way for a presentation of his positive account of the workings of minds, which rests on two main functions, perception and appetition. Perception is the ability to represent and appetition is the tendency to change our perceptions. Unlike Descartes, Leibniz believes that nonhuman animals have minds governed by the same principles as human minds.

Gottfried Leibniz, *Monadology and Other Philosophical Essays*, translated and edited by Paul Schrecker and Anne Martin Schrecker (New York: Bobbs-Merrill Co., 1965).

1. THE OBJECT OF THIS DISCOURSE, the *monad*, is nothing else than a simple substance, which enters into the composites; *simple* meaning, which has no parts.

2. And there must be simple substances, since there are composites; for the composite is nothing else than an accumulation or aggregate of the simples.

3. But where there are no parts, neither extension, nor figure, nor divisibility is possible. Thus, these monads are the veritable atoms of nature, and, in one word, the elements of all things.

4. Hence no dissolution is to be feared for them, and a simple substance cannot perish naturally in any conceivable manner.

5. For the same reason, no simple substance can come into being naturally, since it cannot be formed by composition.

6. Thus it may be maintained that monads cannot begin or end otherwise than instantaneously, that is, they can begin only by creation, and end only by annihilation; while what is complete begins and ends through and in its parts.

7. It is impossible also to explain how a monad can be altered, that is, internally changed, by any other creature. For there is nothing in it which might be transposed, nor can there be conceived in it any internal movement which could be excited, directed, or diminished. In composites this is possible, since the parts can interchange place. The monads have no windows through which anything could come in or go out.

8. Nevertheless, the monads must have some qualities, otherwise they would not even be beings. And if the simple substances did not differ through their qualities, there would be no means at all of perceiving any change in things. For what is in the composites can come only from the ingredient simples. So the monads, if they were without qualities, would be indistinguishable the one from the other, since they do not differ in quantity either. The plenum being presupposed, no space, consequently, could ever receive through movement anything but the equivalent of what has been in it, and one state of things would be indiscernible from another.

9. Each monad must even be different from every other. For in nature there are never two beings which are perfectly like one another, and between which it would not be possible to find an internal difference, that is, a difference founded on an intrinsic denomination.

10. I take it also for granted that all created beings, consequently the created monads as well, are subject to change, and that this change is even continual in each one.

11. In consequence of what has been said, the natural changes of the monads must result from an *internal principle*, since no external cause could influence their interior.

12. But besides the principle of change, there must be a *particular trait of what is changing*, which produces, so to speak, the specification and variety of the simple substances.

13. This particular must comprehend a multiplicity in the unity, that is, in the simple. For since all natural change proceeds by degrees, something changes and something remains. Consequently, there must be in the simple substance a plurality of affections and relations, though it has no parts.

14. The passing state which comprehends and represents a multiplicity in the unity or simple substance is nothing but what is called *perception*; it must be clearly distinguished from apperception or consciousness, as will become clear later on. On this point the Cartesian doctrine has been very defective, since it has entirely neglected those perceptions which are not apperceived; the same failure to distinguish has made the Cartesians believe that only spirits are monads, and that there are neither animal souls nor other entelechies. Therefore, they, like the unlearned, have confused a long swoon with death, strictly speaking, and yielded to the scholastic prejudice that there are entirely separated souls. The same error has even confirmed unsound minds in the opinion that souls are mortal.

15. The action of the internal principle which produces change, that is, the passage from one perception to another, may be called *appetition*. It is true that appetition may not always entirely attain the whole perception toward which it

tends, but it always obtains something and arrives at new perceptions.

16. We ourselves experience a multiplicity in the simple substance, when we observe that the least thought which we apperceive in ourselves comprehends a variety in its object. Thus, all those who recognize that the soul is a simple substance must recognize this multiplicity in the monad. Pierre Bayle should not have found a difficulty in this theory, as he indeed did in the article "Rorarius" of his *Dictionary*.

17. Moreover, it must be avowed that *perception* and what depends upon it *cannot possibly be explained by mechanical reasons*, that is, by figure and movement. Suppose that there be a machine, the structure of which produces thinking, feeling, and perceiving; imagine this machine enlarged but preserving the same proportions, so that you could enter it as if it were a mill. This being supposed, you might visit its inside; but what would you observe there? Nothing but parts which push and move each other, and never anything that could explain perception. This explanation must therefore be sought in the simple substance, not in the composite, that is, in the machine. However, there is nothing else to be found in the simple substance but perceptions and their changes. In this alone can consist all the *internal actions* of simple substances.

18. The name *entelechies* would fit all the simple substances or created monads. For they have in themselves a certain perfection (ἔχουσι τὸ ἐντελές) [*echousi to enteles*], and they are endowed with a self-sufficiency (αὐτάρκεια) [*autarkeia*] which makes them the sources of their own actions and, so to speak, incorporeal automata.

19. If we want to call *soul* all that has perception and appetition, in the general sense explained above, we might give the name soul to all simple substances or created monads. But since sensation is something more than a simple perception, I agree that the general name monad or entelechy may suffice for those simple substances which have nothing but perception and appetition; the name souls may then be reserved for those having perception that is more distinct and is accompanied by memory.

20. Indeed, we experience in ourselves a state in which we remember nothing and have no distinct perception at all, e.g., when we faint or are overcome by a deep and dreamless sleep. In this state the soul is not noticeably different from a simple monad. However, since this state does not last, the soul being able to pull itself out of it, the soul is more than a simple monad.

21. Besides, it does not follow at all that in such a state the simple substance entirely lacks perception. For the reasons propounded a while ago, this lack is not possible; for the monad cannot perish, nor can it subsist without some affection, which is nothing but its perception. But when there is a great multitude of minute perceptions lacking distinctness, one becomes dizzy: for example, when you turn around several consecutive times, you get a vertigo which may make you faint and leave you without any distinct perception. Death may throw animals into such a state for a time.

22. The present state of a simple substance is the natural result of its precedent state, so much so that the present is pregnant with the future.

23. Therefore, since on awakening from such a swoon, you apperceive your perceptions, it follows that you must have had some perceptions immediately before, though you did not apperceive them. For a perception cannot come naturally except from another perception, just as movement cannot come naturally except from another movement.

24. Hence it is evident that if in our perceptions there were nothing distinct nor anything, so to speak, in relief and of a more marked taste, we would always be in a swoon. And that is the state of the mere naked monads.

25. We see indeed that nature has given distinct perceptions to the animals, for care has been taken to provide them with organs which collect several light rays or several air waves, to unite them and thereby give them greater effect. Something similar occurs in scent, taste, and touch, and perhaps in many other senses unknown to us. I shall explain soon how what occurs in the soul represents what occurs in the sense organs.

26. Memory provides the souls with a sort of *consistency* which imitates reason but has to be distinguished from it. For we see that animals, perceiving something which impresses them and of which they have previously had a resembling perception, are brought by the representation of their memory to expect what has been associated with this perception in the past and are moved to feelings similar to those they had then. If you show a stick to a dog, for instance, it remembers the pain caused by it and howls or runs away.

27. The vividness of the imagination which strikes and moves animals comes from either the strength or the frequency of preceding perceptions. For often one strong impression produces at once the effect of a long *habit* or of many reiterated impressions of minor strength.

28. Men act like animals in so far as the succession of their perceptions is brought about by the principle of memory. In this they resemble medical empiricists whose practice is not backed by theory. In fact, we are mere empiricists in three quarters of all our actions. If you expect, for instance, that the sun will rise tomorrow because up to now it has always happened, you act as an empiricist. The astronomer alone judges by reason.

29. Knowledge of necessary and eternal truths, however, distinguishes us from mere animals and grants us *reason* and the sciences, elevating us to the knowledge of ourselves and of God. This possession is what is called our reasonable soul or *spirit*. […]

Study Questions

1. List the properties of a monad.
2. Explain why Leibniz thinks that perception can never be understood on mechanical grounds. Do you agree?
3. Leibniz claims that in three-quarters of our acts, humans are just like other animals acting out of "practice rather than theory." What does Leibniz mean? Do you agree?

5.3   On the Hypothesis That Animals Are Automata, and Its History

T. H. HUXLEY

THOMAS HENRY HUXLEY (1825–1895) was an English biologist who is famous for his defense of Charles Darwin's theory of evolution. Huxley, known as "Darwin's bulldog," participated in a famously spirited discussion of evolution with the Anglican bishop Samuel Wilberforce and was a tireless promoter of Darwin's theory. He was deeply involved in promoting scientific literacy among nonscientists. His own research was primarily in anatomy and vertebrate paleontology. Unsatisfied with merely collecting and classifying fossils, Huxley investigated the evolutionary relationships that held among them. In this short selection, Huxley is arguing against the view, made famous by Descartes, that animals are mere machines with no conscious mental life. In arguing for the idea that nonhuman animals are conscious just as humans are conscious, Huxley introduces a theory that became known as "epiphenomenalism," which states that the conscious mental states are a by-product of the brain, with no ability to effect changes in the body.

Thomas H. Huxley, "On the Hypothesis that Animals Are Automata, and Its History," in *Nature Publishing Group* (New York: D. Appleton, 1874). Reprinted by permission from Macmillan Publishers Ltd: *Nature Publishing Group*, 1875.

[…] BUT THOUGH WE MAY SEE REASON to disagree with Descartes' hypothesis that brutes are unconscious machines, it does not follow that he was wrong in regarding them as automata. They may be more or less conscious, sensitive, automata; and the view that they are such conscious machines is that which is implicitly, or explicitly, adopted by most persons. When we speak of the actions of the lower animals being guided by instinct and not by reason, what we really mean is that, though they feel as we do, yet their actions are the results of their physical organisation. We believe, in short, that they are machines, one part of which (the nervous system) not only sets the rest in motion, and co-ordinates its movements in relation with changes in surrounding bodies, but is provided with special apparatus, the function of which is the calling into existence of those states of consciousness which are termed sensations, emotions, and ideas. I believe that this generally accepted view is the best expression of the facts at present known.

It is experimentally demonstrable—any one who cares to run a pin into himself may perform a sufficient demonstration of the fact—that a mode of motion of the nervous system is the immediate antecedent of a state of consciousness. All but the adherents of "Occasionalism," or of the doctrine of "Pre-established Harmony" (if any such now exist), must admit that we have as much reason for regarding the mode of motion of the nervous system as the cause of the state of consciousness, as we have for regarding any event as the cause of another. How the one phenomenon causes the other we know, as much or as little, as in any other case of causation; but we have as much right to believe that the sensation is an effect of the molecular change, as we have to believe that motion is an effect of impact; and there is as much propriety in saying that the brain evolves sensation, as there is in saying that an iron rod, when hammered, evolves heat.

As I have endeavoured to show, we are justified in supposing that something analogous to what happens in ourselves takes place in the brutes, and that the affections of their sensory nerves give rise to molecular changes in the brain, which again give rise to, or evolve, the corresponding states of consciousness. Nor can there be any reasonable doubt that the emotions of brutes, and such ideas as they possess, are similarly dependent upon molecular brain changes. Each sensory impression leaves behind a record in the structure of the brain—an "ideagenous" molecule, so to speak, which is competent, under certain conditions, to reproduce, in a fainter condition, the state of consciousness which corresponds with that sensory impression; and it is these "ideagenous molecules" which are the physical basis of memory.

It may be assumed, then, that molecular changes in the brain are the causes of all the states of consciousness of brutes. Is there any evidence that these states of consciousness may, conversely, cause those molecular changes which give rise to muscular motion? I see no such evidence. The frog walks, hops, swims, and goes through his gymnastic performances quite as well without consciousness, and consequently without volition, as with it; and, if a frog, in his natural state, possesses anything corresponding with what we call volition, there is no reason to think that it is anything but a concomitant of the molecular changes in the brain which form part of the series involved in the production of motion.

The consciousness of brutes would appear to be related to the mechanism of their body simply as a collateral product of its working, and to be as completely without any power of modifying that working as the steam-whistle which accompanies the work of a locomotive engine is without influence upon its machinery. Their volition, if they have any, is an emotion indicative of physical changes, not a cause of such changes. […]

It is quite true that, to the best of my judgment, the argumentation which applies to brutes holds equally good of men; and, therefore, that all states of consciousness in us, as in them, are immediately caused by molecular changes of the brain-substance. It seems to me that in men, as in brutes, there is no proof that any state of consciousness is the cause of change in the motion of the matter of the organism. If these positions are well based, it follows that our mental conditions are simply the symbols in consciousness of the changes which takes place automatically in the organism; and that, to take an extreme illustration, the feeling we call volition is not the cause of a voluntary act, but the symbol of that state of the brain which is the immediate cause of that act. We are conscious automata, endowed with free will in the only intelligible sense of that much-abused term—inasmuch as in many respects we are able to do as we like—but none the less parts of the great series of causes and effects which, in unbroken continuity, composes that which is, and has been, and shall be—the sum of existence. [. . .]

Study Questions

1. Huxley draws an analogy between the steam whistle of a train and conscious states. Explain the point of this analogy.
2. Huxley claims that conscious states are a mere by-product of the brain without any ability to affect the body. What are the implications of this view?
3. Huxley seems to think that the conscious life of humans and the conscious life of non-human animals is more or less the same. Do you agree?

5.4   Epiphenomenal Qualia

FRANK JACKSON

FRANK JACKSON (1943–) is an Australian philosopher who teaches at Australia National University and Princeton University. Jackson's work has been influential in philosophy of mind, metaphysics, meta-ethics, epistemology, and methodology. In this reading, Jackson presents "the knowledge argument," which introduces what became a famous thought experiment. Jackson imagines a scenario in which a woman, Mary, grows up in a black-and-white room without ever being exposed to color. Though she never sees any colors, Mary is taught all the physical facts about color and color perception. Jackson argues that when Mary leaves her black-and-white room for the first time and experiences the colored world, she learns something new. This shows, Jackson claims, that physicalism cannot be true. The thought experiment caught the attention of the public, becoming a central element in David Lodge's novel *Thinks...*, and was part of a British television series called *Brainspotting*.

It is undeniable that the physical, chemical and biological sciences have provided a great deal of information about the world we live in and about ourselves. I will use the label "physical information" for this kind of information, and also for information that automatically comes along with it. For example, if a medical scientist tells me enough about the processes that go on in my nervous system, and about how they relate to happenings in the world around me, to what has happened in the past and is likely to happen in the future, to what happens to other similar and

Frank Jackson, "Epiphenomenal Qualia," *The Philosophical Quarterly*, 32 (1982).

dissimilar organisms, and the like, he or she tells me—if I am clever enough to fit it together appropriately—about what is often called the functional role of those states in me (and in organisms in general in similar cases). This information, and its kin, I also label "physical."

I do not mean these sketchy remarks to constitute a definition of "physical information," and of the correlative notions of physical property, process, and so on, but to indicate what I have in mind here. It is well known that there are problems with giving a precise definition of these notions, and so of the thesis of Physicalism that all (correct) information is physical information.[1] But—unlike some—I take the question of definition to cut across the central problems I want to discuss in this paper.

I am what is sometimes known as a "qualia freak." I think that there are certain features of the bodily sensations especially, but also of certain perceptual experiences, which no amount of purely physical information includes. Tell me everything physical there is to tell about what is going on in a living brain, the kind of states, their functional role, their relation to what goes on at other times and in other brains, and so on and so forth, and be I as clever as can be in fitting it all together, you won't have told me about the hurtfulness of pains, the itchiness of itches, pangs of jealousy, or about the characteristic experience of tasting a lemon, smelling a rose, hearing a loud noise or seeing the sky.

There are many qualia freaks, and some of them say that their rejection of Physicalism is an unargued intuition.[2] I think that they are being unfair to themselves. They have the following argument. Nothing you could tell of a physical sort captures the smell of a rose, for instance. Therefore, Physicalism is false. By our lights this is a perfectly good argument. It is obviously not to the point to question its validity, and the premise is intuitively obviously true both to them and to me.

I must, however, admit that it is weak from a polemical point of view. There are, unfortunately

for us, many who do not find the premise intuitively obvious. The task then is to present an argument whose premises are obvious to all, or at least to as many as possible. This I try to do in §I with what I will call "the Knowledge argument." In §II I contrast the Knowledge argument with the Modal argument and in §III with the "What is it like to be" argument. In §IV I tackle the question of the causal role of qualia. The major factor in stopping people from admitting qualia is the belief that they would have to be given a causal role with respect to the physical world and especially the brain,[3] and it is hard to do this without sounding like someone who believes in fairies. I seek in §IV to turn this objection by arguing that the view that qualia are epiphenomenal is a perfectly possible one.

I. THE KNOWLEDGE ARGUMENT FOR QUALIA

People vary considerably in their ability to discriminate colours. Suppose that in an experiment to catalogue this variation Fred is discovered. Fred has better colour vision than anyone else on record; he makes every discrimination that anyone has ever made, and moreover he makes one that we cannot even begin to make. Show him a batch of ripe tomatoes and he sorts them into two roughly equal groups and does so with complete consistency. That is, if you blindfold him, shuffle the tomatoes up, and then remove the blindfold and ask him to sort them out again, he sorts them into exactly the same two groups.

We ask Fred how he does it. He explains that all ripe tomatoes do not look the same colour to him, and in fact that this is true of a great many objects that we classify together as red. He sees two colours where we see one, and he has in consequence developed for his own use two words "red$_1$" and "red$_2$" to mark the difference. Perhaps he tells us that he has often tried to teach the difference between red$_1$ and red$_2$ to his friends but has got nowhere and has concluded that the rest of the world is red$_1$-red$_2$ colour-blind—or perhaps he has had partial success with his children, it doesn't matter. In any case he explains to us that it would be quite wrong to think that because "red" appears in both "red$_1$" and "red$_2$" that the two colours are shades of the one colour. He only uses the common term "red" to fit more easily into our restricted usage. To him red$_1$ and red$_2$ are as different from each other and all the other colours as yellow is from blue. And his discriminatory behaviour bears this out: he sorts red$_1$ from red$_2$ tomatoes with the greatest of ease in a wide variety of viewing circumstances. Moreover, an investigation of the physiological basis of Fred's exceptional ability reveals that Fred's optical system is able to separate out two groups of wavelengths in the red spectrum as sharply as we are able to sort out yellow from blue.[4]

I think that we should admit that Fred can see, really see, at least one more colour than we can; red$_1$ is a different colour from red$_2$. We are to Fred as a totally red-green colour-blind person is to us. H. G. Wells' story "The Country of the Blind" is about a sighted person in a totally blind community.[5] This person never manages to convince them that he can see, that he has an extra sense. They ridicule this sense as quite inconceivable, and treat his capacity to avoid falling into ditches, to win fights and so on as precisely that capacity and nothing more. We would be making their mistake if we refused to allow that Fred can see one more colour than we can.

What kind of experience does Fred have when he sees red$_1$ and red$_2$? What is the new colour or colours like? We would dearly like to know but do not; and it seems that no amount of physical information about Fred's brain and optical system tells us. We find out perhaps that Fred's cones respond differentially to certain light waves in the red section of the spectrum that make no difference to ours (or perhaps he has an extra cone) and that this leads in Fred to a wider range of those brain states responsible for visual discriminatory behaviour. But none of this

tells us what we really want to know about his colour experience. There is something about it we don't know. But we know, we may suppose, everything about Fred's body, his behaviour and dispositions to behaviour and about his internal physiology, and everything about his history and relation to others that can be given in physical accounts of persons. We have all the physical information. Therefore, knowing all this is *not* knowing everything about Fred. It follows that Physicalism leaves something out.

To reinforce this conclusion, imagine that as a result of our investigations into the internal workings of Fred we find out how to make everyone's physiology like Fred's in the relevant respects; or perhaps Fred donates his body to science and on his death we are able to transplant his optical system into someone else—again the fine detail doesn't matter. The important point is that such a happening would create enormous interest. People would say, "At last we will know what it is like to see the extra colour, at last we will know how Fred has differed from us in the way he has struggled to tell us about for so long." Then it cannot be that we knew all along all about Fred. But *ex hypothesi* we did know all along everything about Fred that features in the physicalist scheme; hence the physicalist scheme leaves something out.

Put it this way. *After* the operation, we will know *more* about Fred and especially about his colour experiences. But beforehand we had all the physical information we could desire about his body and brain, and indeed everything that has ever featured in physicalist accounts of mind and consciousness. Hence there is more to know than all that. Hence Physicalism is incomplete.

Fred and the new colour(s) are of course essentially rhetorical devices. The same point can be made with normal people and familiar colours. Mary is a brilliant scientist who is, for whatever reason, forced to investigate the world from a black and white room *via* a black and white television monitor. She specialises in the neurophysiology of vision and acquires, let us suppose, all the physical information there is to obtain about what goes on when we see ripe tomatoes, or the sky, and use terms like "red," "blue", and so on. She discovers, for example, just which wave-length combinations from the sky stimulate the retina, and exactly how this produces *via* the central nervous system the contraction of the vocal chords and expulsion of air from the lungs that results in the uttering of the sentence "The sky is blue." (It can hardly be denied that it is in principle possible to obtain all this physical information from black and white television, otherwise the Open University would *of necessity* need to use colour television.)

What will happen when Mary is released from her black and white room or is given a colour television monitor? Will she *learn* anything or not? It seems just obvious that she will learn something about the world and our visual experience of it. But then it is inescapable that her previous knowledge was incomplete. But she had *all* the physical information. *Ergo* there is more to have than that, and Physicalism is false.

Clearly the same style of Knowledge argument could be deployed for taste, hearing, the bodily sensations and generally speaking for the various mental states which are said to have (as it is variously put) raw feels, phenomenal features or qualia. The conclusion in each case is that the qualia are left out of the physicalist story. And the polemical strength of the Knowledge argument is that it is so hard to deny the central claim that one can have all the physical information without having all the information there is to have. [...]

II. THE BOGEY OF EPIPHENOMENALISM

Is there any really *good* reason for refusing to countenance the idea that qualia are causally impotent with respect to the physical world? I will argue for the answer no, but in doing this I will say nothing about two views associated with the classical epiphenomenalist position. The first is that mental *states* are inefficacious with respect to the physical world. All I will be concerned to defend is that it is possible to hold that certain *properties* of certain mental states, namely those I've called qualia, are such that their possession or absence makes no difference to the physical world. The second is that the mental is *totally* causally inefficacious. For all I will say it may be that you have to hold that the instantiation of *qualia* makes a difference to *other mental states* though not to anything physical. Indeed general considerations to do with how you could come to be aware of the instantiation of qualia suggest such a position.[6]

Three reasons are standardly given for holding that a quale like the hurtfulness of a pain must be causally efficacious in the physical world, and so, for instance, that its instantiation must sometimes make a difference to what happens in the brain. None, I will argue, has any real force. (I am much indebted to Alec Hyslop and John Lucas for convincing me of this.)

(i) It is supposed to be just obvious that the hurtfulness of pain is partly responsible for the subject seeking to avoid pain, saying "It hurts" and so on. But, to reverse Hume, anything can fail to cause anything. No matter how often *B* follows *A*, and no matter how initially obvious the causality of the connection seems, the hypothesis that *A* causes *B* can be overturned by an over-arching theory which shows the two as distinct effects of a common underlying causal process.

To the untutored the image on the screen of Lee Marvin's fist moving from left to right immediately followed by the image of John Wayne's head moving in the same general direction looks as causal as anything.[7] And of course throughout countless Westerns images similar to the first are followed by images similar to the second. All this counts for precisely nothing when we know the over-arching theory concerning how the relevant images are both effects of an underlying causal process involving the projector and the film. The epiphenomenalist can say exactly the same about the connection between, for example, hurtfulness and behaviour. It is simply a consequence of the fact that certain happenings in the brain cause both.

(ii) The second objection relates to Darwin's Theory of Evolution. According to natural selection the traits that evolve over time are those conducive to physical survival. We may assume that qualia evolved over time—we have them, the earliest forms of life do not—and so we should expect qualia to be conducive to survival. The objection is that they could hardly help us to survive if they do nothing to the physical world.

The appeal of this argument is undeniable, but there is a good reply to it. Polar bears have particularly thick, warm coats. The Theory of Evolution explains this (we suppose) by pointing out that having a thick, warm coat is conducive to survival in the Arctic. But having a thick coat goes along with having a heavy coat, and having a heavy coat is *not* conducive to survival. It slows the animal down.

Does this mean that we have refuted Darwin because we have found an evolved trait—having a heavy coat—which is not conducive to survival? Clearly not. Having a heavy coat is an unavoidable concomitant of having a warm coat (in the context, modern insulation was not available), and the advantages for survival of having a warm coat outweighed the disadvantages of having a heavy one. The point is that all we can extract from Darwin's theory is that we should expect any evolved characteristic to be *either* conducive to survival *or* a by-product of one that is so conducive. The epiphenomenalist holds that qualia fall into the latter category. They are a by-product of certain brain processes that are highly conducive to survival.

(iii) The third objection is based on a point about how we come to know about other minds. We know about other minds by knowing about other behaviour, at least in part. The nature of the inference is a matter of some controversy, but it is not a matter of controversy that it proceeds

from behaviour. That is why we think that stones do not feel and dogs do feel. But, runs the objection, how can a person's behaviour provide any reason for believing he has qualia like mine, or indeed any qualia at all, unless this behaviour can be regarded as the *outcome* of the qualia. Man Friday's footprint was evidence of Man Friday because footprints are causal outcomes of feet attached to people. And an epiphenomenalist cannot regard behaviour, or indeed anything physical, as an outcome of qualia.

But consider my reading in *The Times* that Spurs won. This provides excellent evidence that *The Telegraph* has also reported that Spurs won, despite the fact that (I trust) *The Telegraph* does not get the results from *The Times*. They each send their own reporters to the game. *The Telegraph's* report is in no sense an outcome of *The Times*, but the latter provides good evidence for the former nevertheless.

The reasoning involved can be reconstructed thus. I read in *The Times* that Spurs won. This gives me reason to think that Spurs won because I know that Spurs' winning is the most likely candidate to be what caused the report in *The Times*. But I also know that Spurs' winning would have had many effects, including almost certainly a report in *The Telegraph*.

I am arguing from one effect back to its cause and out again to another effect. The fact that neither effect causes the other is irrelevant. Now the epiphenomenalist allows that qualia are effects of what goes on in the brain. Qualia cause nothing physical but are caused by something physical. Hence the epiphenomenalist can argue from the behaviour of others to the qualia of others by arguing from the behaviour of others back to its causes in the brains of others and out again to their qualia.

You may well feel for one reason or another that this is a more dubious chain of reasoning than its model in the case of newspaper reports. You are right. The problem of other minds is a major philosophical problem, the problem of other newspaper reports is not. But there is no special problem of Epiphenomenalism as opposed to, say, Interactionism here.

There is a very understandable response to the three replies I have just made. "All right, there is no knockdown refutation of the existence of epiphenomenal qualia. But the fact remains that they are an excrescence. They *do* nothing, they *explain* nothing, they serve merely to soothe the intuitions of dualists, and it is left a total mystery how they fit into the world view of science. In short we do not and cannot understand the how and why of them."

This is perfectly true; but is no objection to qualia, for it rests on an overly optimistic view of the human animal, and its powers. We are the products of Evolution. We understand and sense what we need to understand and sense in order to survive. Epiphenomenal qualia are totally irrelevant to survival. At no stage of our evolution did natural selection favour those who could make sense of how they are caused and the laws governing them, or in fact why they exist at all. And that is why we can't.

It is not sufficiently appreciated that Physicalism is an extremely optimistic view of our powers. If it is true, we have, in very broad outline admittedly, a grasp of our place in the scheme of things. Certain matters of sheer complexity defeat us—there are an awful lot of neurons—but in principle we have it all. But consider the antecedent probability that everything in the Universe be of a kind that is relevant in some way or other to the survival of *homo sapiens*. It is very low surely. But then one must admit that it is very likely that there is a part of the whole scheme of things, maybe a big part, which no amount of evolution will ever bring us near to knowledge about or understanding. For the simple reason that such knowledge and understanding is irrelevant to survival.

Physicalists typically emphasise that we are a part of nature on their view, which is fair enough. But if we are a part of nature, we are as nature has left us after however many years of evolution it is, and each step in that evolutionary progres-

sion has been a matter of chance constrained just by the need to preserve or increase survival value. The wonder is that we understand as much as we do, and there is no wonder that there should be matters which fall quite outside our comprehension. Perhaps exactly how epiphenomenal qualia fit into the scheme of things is one such.

This may seem an unduly pessimistic view of our capacity to articulate a truly comprehensive picture of our world and our place in it. But suppose we discovered living on the bottom of the deepest oceans a sort of sea slug which manifested intelligence. Perhaps survival in the conditions required rational powers. Despite their intelligence, these sea slugs have only a very restricted conception of the world by comparison with ours, the explanation for this being the nature of their immediate environment. Nevertheless they have developed sciences which work surprisingly well in these restricted terms. They also have philosophers, called slugists. Some call themselves tough-minded slugists, others confess to being soft-minded slugists.

The tough-minded slugists hold that the restricted terms (or ones pretty like them which may be introduced as their sciences progress) suffice in principle to describe everything without remainder. These tough-minded slugists admit in moments of weakness to a feeling that their theory leaves something out. They resist this feeling and their opponents, the soft-minded slugists, by pointing out—absolutely correctly—that no slugist has ever succeeded in spelling out how this mysterious residue fits into the highly successful view that their sciences have and are developing of how their world works.

Our sea slugs don't exist, but they might. And there might also exist super beings which stand to us as we stand to the sea slugs. We cannot adopt the perspective of these super beings, because we are not them, but the possibility of such a perspective is, I think, an antidote to excessive optimism.[8]

Notes

1. See, e.g., D. H. Mellor, "Materialism and Phenomenal Qualities," *Aristotelian Society Supp. Vol.* 47 (1973), 107–19; and J. W. Cornman, *Materialism and Sensations* (New Haven and London, 1971).

2. Particularly in discussion, but see, e.g., Keith Campbell, *Metaphysics* (Belmont, 1976), p. 67.

3. See, e.g., D. C. Dennett, "Current Issues in the Philosophy of Mind," *American Philosophical Quarterly*, 15 (1978), 249–61.

4. Put this, and similar simplifications below, in terms of Land's theory if you prefer. See, e.g., Edwin H. Land, "Experiments in Color Vision," *Scientific American*, 200 (5 May 1959), 84–99.

5. H. G. Wells, *The Country of the Blind and Other Stories* (London, n.d.).

6. See my review of K. Campbell, *Body and Mind*, in *Australasian Journal of Philosophy*, 50 (1972), 77–80.

7. Cf. Jean Piaget, "The Child's Conception of Physical Causality," reprinted in *The Essential Piaget* (London, 1977).

8. I am indebted to Robert Pargetter for a number of comments and, despite his dissent, to §IV of Paul E. Meehl. "The Compleat Autocerebroscopist" in *Mind, Matter, and Method,* ed. Paul Feyerabend and Grover Maxwell (Minneapolis, 1966).

Study Questions

1. Using the super-scientist Mary thought experiment, present the premises and conclusions of the knowledge argument. Is the argument compelling? Why or why not?

2. Jackson points out that the knowledge argument is different from Thomas Nagel's argument that we could never know what it is like to be a bat. How do these two arguments differ?

3. If, as the knowledge argument concludes, qualitative states are not physical, then they can't be the cause of our actions. Is this a problem for the knowledge argument? Why or why not?

5.5   The Puzzle of Conscious Experience

DAVID CHALMERS

DAVID CHALMERS (1966–) is Distinguished Professor of Philosophy and Director of the Centre for Consciousness at the Australian National University, and Visiting Professor of Philosophy at NYU. He has written extensively on consciousness, including the books *The Conscious Mind: In Search of a Fundamental Theory* (1996) and *The Character of Consciousness* (2010). He has also made important contributions in philosophy of mind, philosophy of language, epistemology, and metaphysics. He is one of the founders of the Association for the Scientific Study of Consciousness and one of the main organizers of the biennial "Towards a Science of Consciousness" conference held in Tucson, Arizona. His selection argues that explaining consciousness poses a special "hard problem" for science.

CONSCIOUS EXPERIENCE IS AT ONCE THE most familiar thing in the world and the most mysterious. There is nothing we know about more directly than consciousness, but it is extraordinarily hard to reconcile it with everything else we know. Why does it exist? What does it do? How could it possibly arise from neural processes in the brain? These questions are among the most intriguing in all of science.

From an objective viewpoint, the brain is relatively comprehensible. When you look at this page, there is a whir of processing: photons strike your retina, electrical signals are passed up your optic nerve and between different areas of your brain, and eventually you might respond with a smile, a perplexed frown or a remark. But there is also a subjective aspect. When you look at the page, you are conscious of it, directly experiencing the images and words as part of your private, mental life. You have vivid impressions of colored flowers and vibrant sky. At the same time, you may be feeling some emotions and forming some thoughts. Together such experiences make up consciousness: the subjective, inner life of the mind.

For many years, consciousness was shunned by researchers studying the brain and the mind. The prevailing view was that science, which depends on objectivity, could not accommodate something as subjective as consciousness. The behaviorist movement in psychology, dominant earlier in this century, concentrated on external behavior and disallowed any talk of internal mental processes. Later, the rise of cognitive science focused attention on processes inside the head. Still, consciousness remained off-limits, fit only for late-night discussion over drinks.

Over the past several years, however, an increasing number of neuroscientists, psychologists and philosophers have been rejecting the idea that consciousness cannot be studied and are attempting to delve into its secrets. As might be expected of a field so new, there is a tangle of diverse and conflicting theories, often using basic concepts in incompatible ways. To help unsnarl the tangle, philosophical reasoning is vital.

The myriad views within the field range from reductionist theories, according to which consciousness can be explained by the standard methods of neuroscience and psychology, to the position of the so-called mysterians, who say we will never understand consciousness at all. I believe that on close analysis both of these views can be seen to be mistaken and that the truth lies somewhere in the middle.

Against reductionism I will argue that the tools of neuroscience cannot provide a full account of conscious experience, although they have much to offer. Against mysterianism I will hold that consciousness might be explained by a new kind of theory. The full details of such a theory are still out of reach, but careful reasoning and some educated inferences can reveal something of its general nature. For example, it will probably involve new fundamental laws, and the concept of information may play a central role. These faint glimmerings suggest that a theory of consciousness may have startling consequences for our view of the universe and of ourselves.

THE HARD PROBLEM

Researchers use the word "consciousness" in many different ways. To clarify the issues, we first have to separate the problems that are often clustered together under the name. For this purpose, I find it useful to distinguish between the "easy problems" and the "hard problem" of consciousness. The easy problems are by no means trivial—they are actually as challenging as most in psychology and biology—but it is with the hard problem that the central mystery lies.

The easy problems of consciousness include the following: How can a human subject discriminate sensory stimuli and react to them appropriately? How does the brain integrate information from many different sources and use this information to control behavior? How is it that subjects can verbalize their internal states? Although all these questions are associated with consciousness, they all concern the objective mechanisms of the cognitive system. Consequently, we have every reason to expect that continued work in cognitive psychology and neuroscience will answer them.

The hard problem, in contrast, is the question of how physical processes in the brain give rise to subjective experience. This puzzle involves the inner aspect of thought and perception: the way things feel for the subject. When we see, for example, we experience visual sensations, such as that of vivid blue. Or think of the ineffable sound of a distant oboe, the agony of an intense pain, the sparkle of happiness or the meditative quality of a moment lost in thought. All are part of what I am calling consciousness. It is these phenomena that pose the real mystery of the mind.

To illustrate the distinction, consider a thought experiment devised by the Australian philosopher Frank Jackson. Suppose that Mary, a neuroscientist in the 23rd century, is the world's leading expert on the brain processes responsible for color vision. But Mary has lived her whole life in a black-and-white room and has never seen any other colors. She knows everything there is to know about physical processes in the brain—its biology, structure and function. This understanding enables her to grasp everything there is to know about the easy problems: how the brain discriminates stimuli, integrates information and produces verbal reports. From her knowledge of color vision, she knows the way color names correspond with wavelengths on the light spectrum. But there is still something crucial about color vision that Mary does not know: what it is like to experience a color such as red. It follows that there are facts about conscious experience that cannot be deduced from physical facts about the functioning of the brain.

Indeed, nobody knows why these physical processes are accompanied by conscious experience at all. Why is it that when our brains process light of a certain wavelength, we have an experience of deep purple? Why do we have any experience at all? Could not an unconscious automaton have performed the same tasks just as well? These are questions that we would like a theory of consciousness to answer.

I am not denying that consciousness arises from the brain. We know, for example, that the subjective experience of vision is closely linked to processes in the visual cortex. It is the link itself that perplexes, however. Remarkably, subjective experience seems to emerge from a physical process. But we have no idea how or why this is.

IS NEUROSCIENCE ENOUGH?

Given the flurry of recent work on consciousness in neuroscience and psychology, one might think this mystery is starting to be cleared up. On closer examination, however, it turns out that almost all the current work addresses only the easy problems of consciousness. The confidence of the reductionist view comes from the progress on the easy problems, but none of this makes any difference where the hard problem is concerned.

Consider the hypothesis put forward by neurobiologists Francis Crick of the Salk Institute for Biological Studies in San Diego and Christof Koch of the California Institute of Technology. They suggest that consciousness may arise from certain oscillations in the cerebral cortex, which become synchronized as neurons fire 40 times per second. Crick and Koch believe the phenomenon might explain how different attributes of a single perceived object (its color and shape, for example), which are processed in different parts of the brain, are merged into a coherent whole. In this theory, two pieces of information become bound together precisely when they are represented by synchronized neural firings.

The hypothesis could conceivably elucidate one of the easy problems about how information is integrated in the brain. But why should synchronized oscillations give rise to a visual experience, no matter how much integration is taking place? This question involves the hard problem, about which the theory has nothing to offer. Indeed, Crick and Koch are agnostic about whether the hard problem can be solved by science at all. [...]

The same kind of critique could be applied to almost all the recent work on consciousness. In his 1991 book *Consciousness Explained*, philosopher Daniel C. Dennett laid out a sophisticated theory of how numerous independent processes in the brain combine to produce a coherent response to a perceived event. The theory might do much to explain how we produce verbal reports on our internal states, but it tells us very little about why there should be a subjective experience behind these reports. Like other reductionist theories, Dennett's is a theory of the easy problems.

The critical common trait among these easy problems is that they all concern how a cognitive or behavioral function is performed. All are ultimately questions about how the brain carries out some task—how it discriminates stimuli, integrates information, produces reports and so on. Once neurobiology specifies appropriate neural mechanisms, showing how the functions are performed, the easy problems are solved.

The hard problem of consciousness, in contrast, goes beyond problems about how functions are performed. Even if every behavioral and cognitive function related to consciousness were explained, there would still remain a further mystery: Why is the performance of these functions accompanied by conscious experience? It is this additional conundrum that makes the hard problem hard.

THE EXPLANATORY GAP

Some have suggested that to solve the hard problem, we need to bring in new tools of physical explanation: nonlinear dynamics, say, or new discoveries in neuroscience, or quantum mechanics. But these ideas suffer from exactly the same difficulty. Consider a proposal from Stuart R. Hameroff of the University of

Arizona and Roger Penrose of the University of Oxford. They hold that consciousness arises from quantum-physical processes taking place in microtubules, which are protein structures inside neurons. It is possible (if not likely) that such a hypothesis will lead to an explanation of how the brain makes decisions or even how it proves mathematical theorems, as Hameroff and Penrose suggest. But even if it does, the theory is silent about how these processes might give rise to conscious experience. Indeed, the same problem arises with any theory of consciousness based only on physical processing.

The trouble is that physical theories are best suited to explaining why systems have a certain physical structure and how they perform various functions. Most problems in science have this form; to explain life, for example, we need to describe how a physical system can reproduce, adapt and metabolize. But consciousness is a different sort of problem entirely, as it goes beyond the explanation of structure and function.

Of course, neuroscience is not irrelevant to the study of consciousness. For one, it may be able to reveal the nature of the neural correlate of consciousness—the brain processes most directly associated with conscious experience. It may even give a detailed correspondence between specific processes in the brain and related components of experience. But until we know why these processes give rise to conscious experience at all, we will not have crossed what philosopher Joseph Levine has called the explanatory gap between physical processes and consciousness. Making that leap will demand a new kind of theory.

A TRUE THEORY OF EVERYTHING

In searching for an alternative, a key observation is that not all entities in science are explained in terms of more basic entities. In physics, for example, space-time, mass and charge (among other things) are regarded as fundamental features of the world, as they are not reducible to anything simpler. Despite this irreducibility, detailed and useful theories relate these entities to one another in terms of fundamental laws. Together these features and laws explain a great variety of complex and subtle phenomena.

It is widely believed that physics provides a complete catalogue of the universe's fundamental features and laws. As physicist Steven Weinberg puts it in his 1992 book *Dreams of a Final Theory*, the goal of physics is a "theory of everything" from which all there is to know about the universe can be derived. But Weinberg concedes that there is a problem with consciousness. Despite the power of physical theory, the existence of consciousness does not seem to be derivable from physical laws. He defends physics by arguing that it might eventually explain what he calls the objective correlates of consciousness (that is, the neural correlates), but of course to do this is not to explain consciousness itself. If the existence of consciousness cannot be derived from physical laws, a theory of physics is not a true theory of everything. So a final theory must contain an additional fundamental component.

Toward this end, I propose that conscious experience be considered a fundamental feature, irreducible to anything more basic. The idea may seem strange at first, but consistency seems to demand it. In the 19th century it turned out that electromagnetic phenomena could not be explained in terms of previously known principles. As a consequence, scientists introduced electromagnetic charge as a new fundamental entity and studied the associated fundamental laws. Similar reasoning should apply to consciousness. If existing fundamental theories cannot encompass it, then something new is required.

Where there is a fundamental property, there are fundamental laws. In this case, the laws must relate experience to elements of physical theory. These laws will almost certainly not interfere with those of the physical world; it seems that the latter form a closed system in their own right. Rather the laws will serve as a bridge, specifying how experience depends on underlying physical processes. It is this bridge that will cross the explanatory gap.

Thus, a complete theory will have two components: physical laws, telling us about the behavior of physical systems from the infinitesimal to the cosmological, and what we might call psychophysical laws, telling us how some of those systems are associated with conscious experience. These two components will constitute a true theory of everything.

SEARCHING FOR A THEORY

Supposing for the moment that they exist, how might we uncover such psychophysical laws? The greatest hindrance in this pursuit will be a lack of data. As I have described it, consciousness is subjective, so there is no direct way to monitor it in others. But this difficulty is an obstacle, not a dead end. For a start, each one of us has access to our own experiences, a rich trove that can be used to formulate theories. We can also plausibly rely on indirect information, such as subjects' descriptions of their experiences. Philosophical arguments and thought experiments also have a role to play. Such methods have limitations, but they give us more than enough to get started.

These theories will not be conclusively testable, so they will inevitably be more speculative than those of more conventional scientific disciplines. Nevertheless, there is no reason they should not be strongly constrained to account accurately for our own first-person experiences, as well as the evidence from subjects' reports. If we find a theory that fits the data better than any other theory of equal simplicity, we will have good reason to accept it. Right now we do not have even a single theory that fits the data, so worries about testability are premature.

We might start by looking for high-level bridging laws, connecting physical processes to experience at an everyday level. The basic contour of such a law might be gleaned from the observation that when we are conscious of something, we are generally able to act on it and speak about it—which are objective, physical functions. Conversely, when some information is directly available for action and speech, it is generally conscious. Thus, consciousness correlates well with what we might call "awareness": the process by which information in the brain is made globally available to motor processes such as speech and bodily action.

The notion may seem trivial. But as defined here, awareness is objective and physical, whereas consciousness is not. Some refinements to the definition of awareness are needed, in order to extend the concept to animals and infants, which cannot speak. But at least in familiar cases, it is possible to see the rough outlines of a psychophysical law: where there is awareness, there is consciousness, and vice versa.

To take this line of reasoning a step further, consider the structure present in the conscious experience. The experience of a field of vision, for example, is a constantly changing mosaic of colors, shapes and patterns and as such has a detailed geometric structure. The fact that we can describe this structure, reach out in the direction of many of its components and perform other actions that depend on it suggests that the structure corresponds directly to that of the information made available in the brain through the neural processes of awareness.

Similarly, our experiences of color have an intrinsic three-dimensional structure that is mirrored in the structure of information processes in the brain's visual cortex. This structure is illustrated in the color wheels and charts used by artists. Colors are arranged in a systematic pattern—red to green on one axis, blue to yellow on another, and black to white on a third. Colors that are close to one another on a color wheel are experienced as similar. [...] It is extremely likely that they also correspond to similar perceptual representations in the brain, as part of a system of complex three-dimensional coding among neurons that is not yet fully understood. We can recast the underlying concept as a principle of structural coherence: the structure of conscious experience is mirrored by the structure of information in awareness, and vice versa.

Another candidate for a psychophysical law is a principle of organizational invariance. It holds that physical systems with the same abstract organization will give rise to the same kind of conscious experience, no matter what they are made of. For example, if the precise interactions between our neurons could be duplicated with silicon chips, the same conscious experience would arise. The idea is somewhat controversial, but I believe it is strongly supported by thought experiments describing the gradual replacement of neurons by silicon chips. [...] The remarkable implication is that consciousness might someday be achieved in machines.

INFORMATION: PHYSICAL AND EXPERIENTIAL

The ultimate goal of a theory of consciousness is a simple and elegant set of fundamental laws, analogous to the fundamental laws of physics. The principles described above are unlikely to be fundamental, however. Rather they seem to be high-level psychophysical laws, analogous to macroscopic principles in physics such as those of thermodynamics or kinematics. What might the underlying fundamental laws be? No one knows, but I don't mind speculating.

I suggest that the primary psychophysical laws may centrally involve the concept of information. The abstract notion of information, as put forward in the 1940s by Claude E. Shannon of the Massachusetts Institute of Technology, is that of a set of separate states with a basic structure of similarities and differences between them. We can think of a 10-bit binary code as an information state, for example. Such information states can be embodied in the physical world. This happens whenever they correspond to physical states (voltages, say); the differences between them can be transmitted along some pathway, such as a telephone line.

We can also find information embodied in conscious experience. The pattern of color patches in a visual field, for example, can be seen as analogous to that of the pixels covering a display screen. Intriguingly, it turns out that we find the same information states embedded in conscious experience and in underlying physical processes in the brain. The three-dimensional encoding of color spaces, for example, suggests that the information state in a color experience corresponds directly to an information state in the brain. We might even regard the two states as distinct aspects of a single information state, which is simultaneously embodied in both physical processing and conscious experience.

A natural hypothesis ensues. Perhaps information, or at least some information, has two basic aspects: a physical one and an experiential one. This hypothesis has the status of a fundamental principle that might underlie the relation between physical processes and experience. Wherever we find conscious experience, it exists as one aspect of an information state, the other aspect of which is embedded in a physical process in the brain. This proposal needs to be fleshed out to make a satisfying theory. But it fits nicely with the principles mentioned earlier—systems with the same organization will embody the same information, for example— and it could explain numerous features of our conscious experience.

The idea is at least compatible with several others, such as physicist John A. Wheeler's suggestion that information is fundamental to the physics of the universe. The laws of physics might ultimately be cast in informational terms, in which case we would have a satisfying congruence between the constructs in both physical and psychophysical laws. It may even be that a theory of physics and a theory of consciousness could

eventually be consolidated into a single grander theory of information.

A potential problem is posed by the ubiquity of information. Even a thermostat embodies some information, for example, but is it conscious? There are at least two possible responses. First, we could constrain the fundamental laws so that only some information has an experiential aspect, perhaps depending on how it is physically processed. Second, we might bite the bullet and allow that all information has an experiential aspect—where there is complex information processing, there is complex experience, and where there is simple information processing, there is simple experience. If this is so, then even a thermostat might have experiences, although they would be much simpler than even a basic color experience, and there would certainly be no accompanying emotions or thoughts. This seems odd at first, but if experience is truly fundamental, we might expect it to be widespread. In any case, the choice between these alternatives should depend on which can be integrated into the most powerful theory.

Of course, such ideas may be all wrong. On the other hand, they might evolve into a more powerful proposal that predicts the precise structure of our conscious experience from physical processes in our brains. If this project succeeds, we will have good reason to accept the theory. If it fails, other avenues will be pursued, and alternative fundamental theories may be developed. In this way, we may one day resolve the greatest mystery of the mind.

Study Questions

1. What is the "hard problem" of consciousness?
2. Why does Chalmers think neuroscience can't explain conscious experience?
3. What does Chalmers mean when he says that consciousness may be a fundamental feature of reality?

The Hornswoggle Problem   5.6

PATRICIA CHURCHLAND

PATRICIA CHURCHLAND (1943–) recently retired as a Professor of Philosophy from the University of California, San Diego. She is at the vanguard of philosophers attempting to address questions in the philosophy of mind with insights from neuroscience. This research program is spelled out in her 1986 book *Neurophilosophy: Toward a Unified Science of the Mind-Brain*, as well as in her 2002 *Brain-Wise: Studies in Neurophilosophy*, and numerous articles. She was the recipient of a MacArthur Foundation "genius grant" in 1991. Her selection challenges Chalmers's claim that there is a special hard problem of consciousness.

I. INTRODUCTION

Conceptualizing a problem so we can ask the right questions and design revealing experiments is crucial to discovering a satisfactory solution to the problem. Asking where animal spirits are concocted, for example, turns out not to be the right question to ask about the heart. When Harvey asked instead, "how much blood does the heart pump in an hour?", he conceptualized the problem of heart function very differently. The reconceptualization was pivotal in coming to understand that the heart is really a pump for circulating blood; there are no animal spirits to concoct. My strategy here, therefore, is to take the label, "The Hard Problem" in a constructive spirit—as an attempt to provide a useful conceptualization concerning the very nature of consciousness that could help steer us in the direction of a solution. My remarks will focus mainly on whether in fact anything positive is to be gained from the "Hard Problem" char-

acterization, or whether that conceptualization is counterproductive. I cannot hope to do full justice to the task in short compass, especially as the contemporary characterization of the problem of consciousness as *the* intractable problem has a rather large literature surrounding it. The watershed articulation of consciousness as "the most difficult problem" is Thomas Nagel's classic paper "What is it like to be a bat?" (1974). In his opening remarks, Nagel comes straight to the point: "Consciousness is what makes the mind-body problem really intractable." Delineating a contrast between the problem of consciousness and all other mind-body problems, Nagel asserts: "While an account of the physical basis of mind must explain many things, this [conscious experience] appears to be the most difficult." Following Nagel's lead, many other philosophers, including Frank Jackson, Saul Kripke, Colin McGinn, John Searle, and most recently, David Chalmers, have extended and developed Nagel's basic idea that consciousness is not trac-

Patricia Churchland, "The Hornswoggle Problem," *Journal of Consciousness Studies*, 3, No. 5–6. Reprinted with permission from Churchland, P. (1996), "The Hornswoggle Problem," *Journal of Consciousness Studies*, 3 (5-6), pp. 402–8.

table neuroscientifically. Although I agree that consciousness is, certainly, a difficult problem, difficulty *per se* does not distinguish it from oodles of other neuroscientific problems. Such as how the brains of homeotherms keep a constant internal temperature despite varying external conditions. Such as the brain basis for schizophrenia and autism. Such as why we dream and sleep. Supposedly, something sets consciousness apart from all other macro-function brain riddles such that it stands alone as **The Hard Problem**. As I have tried to probe precisely what that is, I find my reservations multiplying.

II. CARVING UP THE PROBLEM SPACE

The-Hard-Problem label invites us to adopt a principled empirical division between consciousness (The Hard Problem) and problems on the "Easy" (or perhaps hard but not Hard?) side of the ledger. The latter presumably encompass problems such as the nature of short-term memory, long-term memory, autobiographical memory, the nature of representation, the nature of sensory motor integration, top-down effects in perception—not to mention such capacities as attention, depth perception, intelligent eye movement, skill acquisition, planning, decision-making, and so forth. On the other side of the ledger, all on its own, stands consciousness—a uniquely Hard Problem. My lead-off reservation arises from this question: what is the rationale for drawing the division exactly there? Dividing off consciousness from all of the so-called "easy problems" listed above implies that we could understand all those phenomena and still not know what it was for. . . . what? The "qualia-light" to go on?? Is that an insightful conceptualization? What exactly is the evidence that we could explain all the "Easy" phenomena and still not understand the neural mechanisms for consciousness? (Call this the "left-out" hypothesis.) That someone can imagine the possibility is not

evidence for the real possibility. It is only evidence that somebody or other believes it to be a possibility. That, on its own, is not especially interesting. Imaginary evidence, needless to say, is not as interesting as real evidence, and what needs to be produced is some real evidence.

The left-out hypothesis—that consciousness would still be a mystery, even if we could explain all the Easy problems—is dubious on another count: it begs the question against those theories that are exploring the possibility that functions such as attention and short-term memory are crucial elements in the consciousness. (See especially Crick 1994, P. M. Churchland 1995.) The rationale sustaining this approach stems from observations such as: that awake persons can be unaware of stimuli to which they are not paying attention, but can become aware of those stimuli when attention shifts. There is a vast psychological literature, and a nontrivial neuroscientific literature, on this topic. Some of it powerfully suggests that attention and awareness are pretty closely connected. The approach might of course be wrong, for it is an empirical conjecture. But if it is wrong, it is wrong because of the facts, not because of an arm-chair definition. The trouble with the Hard-Problem characterization is that on the strength of a proprietary definition, it rejects them as wrong. I do find that unappealing, since the nature of consciousness is an empirical problem, not a problem that can be untangled by semantic gerrymandering.

What drives the left-out hypothesis? Essentially, a thought-experiment, which roughly goes as follows: we can conceive of a person, like us in all the aforementioned Easy-to-explain capacities (attention, short-term memory etc.), but lacking qualia. This person would be exactly like us, save that he would be a Zombie—an anaqualiac, one might say. Since the scenario is conceivable, it is possible, and since it is possible, then whatever consciousness is, it is explanatorily independent of those activities. (Something akin to this was argued by Saul Kripke in the 1970's.)

I take this argument to be a demonstration of the feebleness of thought-experiments. Saying something is possible does not thereby guarantee it is a possibility, so how do we know the anaqualiac idea is really possible? To insist that it must be is simply to beg the question at issue. As Francis Crick has observed, it might be like saying that one can imagine a possible world where gasses do not get hot, even though their constituent molecules are moving at high velocity. As an argument against the empirical identification of temperature with mean molecular KE, the thermodynamic thought-experiment is feebleness itself.

Is the problem on the "Hard" side of the ledger sufficiently well-defined to sustain the division as a fundamental empirical principle? Although it is easy enough to agree about the presence of qualia in certain prototypical cases, such as the pain felt after a brick has fallen on a bare foot, or the blueness of the sky on a sunny summer afternoon, things are less clear-cut once we move beyond the favored prototypes. Some of our perceptual capacities are rather subtle, as, for example, positional sense is often claimed to be. Some philosophers, e.g. Elizabeth Anscombe, have actually opined that we can know the position of our limbs without any "limb-position" qualia. As for me, I am inclined to say I do have qualitative experiences of where my limbs are—it feels different to have my fingers clenched than unclenched, even when they are not visible. The disagreement itself, however, betokens the lack of consensus once cases are at some remove from the central prototypes.

Vestibular system qualia are yet another non prototypical case. Is there something "vestibular-y" it feels like to have my head moving? To know which way is up? Whatever the answer here, at least the answer is not glaringly obvious. Do eye movements have eye-movement qualia? Some maybe do, and some maybe do not. Are there "introspective qualia," or is introspection just paying attention to perceptual qualia and talking to yourself? Ditto, plus or minus a bit, for self-awareness. Thoughts are also a bit problematic in the qualia department. Some of my thoughts seem to me to be a bit like talking to myself and hence like auditory imagery but some just come out of my mouth as I am talking to someone or affect decisions without ever surfacing as a bit of inner dialogue. None of this is to deny the pizzazz of qualia in the prototypical cases. Rather, the point is just that prototypical cases give us only a starting point for further investigation, and nothing like a full characterization of the class to which they belong.

My suspicion with respect to The Hard Problem strategy is that it seems to take the class of conscious experiences to be much better defined than it is. The point is, if you are careful to restrict your focus to the prototypical cases, you can easily be hornswoggled into assuming the class is well-defined. As soon as you broaden your horizons, troublesome questions about fuzzy boundaries, about the connections between attention, short-term memory and awareness, are present in full, what-do-we-do-with-that glory.

Are the Easy Problems known to be easier than The Hard Problem? Is the Hard/Easy division grounded in fact? To begin with, it is important to acknowledge that for none of the so-called "easy" problems, do we have an understanding of their solution. (See the partial list on p. 310) It is just false that we have anything approximating a comprehensive theory of sensori-motor control or attention or short-term memory or long-term memory. Consider one example. A signature is recognizably the same whether signed with the dominant or non-dominant hand, with the foot, with the mouth or with the pen strapped to the shoulder. How is "my signature" represented in the nervous system? How can completely different muscle sets be invoked to do the task, even when the skill was not acquired using those muscles? We do not understand the general nature of motor representation.

Notice that it is not merely that we are lacking details, albeit important details. The fact is, we are lacking important conceptual/theoretical ideas about how the nervous system performs fundamental functions—such as time management, such as motor control, such as learning, such as information retrieval. We do not understand the role of back projections, or the degree to which processing is organized hierarchically. These are genuine puzzles, and it is unwise to "molehill" them in order to "mountain" up the problem of consciousness. Although quite a lot is known at the cellular level, the fact remains that how real neural networks work and how their output properties depend on cellular properties still abounds with nontrivial mysteries. Naturally I do not wish to minimize the progress that has been made in neuroscience, but it is prudent to have a cautious assessment of what we really do not yet understand.

Carving the explanatory space of mind-brain phenomena along the Hard and the Easy line, as Chalmers proposes, poses the danger of inventing an explanatory chasm where there really exists just a broad field of ignorance. It reminds me of the division, deep to medieval physicists, between sublunary physics (motion of things below the level of the moon) and superlunary physics (motion of things above the level of the moon). The conviction was that sublunary physics was tractable, and is essentially based on Aristotelian physics. Heavy things fall because they have gravity, and fall to their Natural Place, namely the earth, which is the center of the universe. Things like smoke have levity, and consequently they rise, up being their Natural Place. Everything in the sublunary realm has a Natural Place, and that is the key to explaining the behavior of sublunary objects. Superlunary events, by contrast, we can neither explain nor understand, but in any case, they have neither the gravity nor levity typical of sublunary things.

This old division was not without merit, and it did entail that events such as planetary motion and meteors were considered unexplainable in terrestrial terms, but probably were Divinely governed. Although I do not know that Chalmers' Easy/Hard distinction will prove ultimately

as misdirected as the Sublunary/Superlunary distinction, neither do I know it is any more sound. What I do suspect, however, is that it is much too early in the science of nervous systems to command much credence.

One danger inherent in embracing the distinction as a principled empirical distinction is that it provokes the intuition that only a real humdinger of a solution will suit The Hard Problem. Thus the idea seems to go as follows: the answer, if it comes at all, is going to have to come from somewhere Really Deep—like quantum mechanics, or—Wow—perhaps it requires a whole new physics. As the lone enigma, consciousness surely cannot be just a matter of a complex dynamical system doing its thing. Yes, there are emergent properties from nervous systems such as co-ordinated movement as when an owl catches a mouse, but consciousness must be an emergent property like unto no other. After all, it is The Hard Problem! Consequently, it will require a very deep, very radical solution. That much is evident sheerly from the hardness of The Hard Problem.

I confess I cannot actually see that. I do not know anything like enough to see how to solve either the problem of sensori-motor control or the problem of consciousness. I certainly cannot see enough to know what one problem will, and the other will not, require a Humdinger solution.

III. USING IGNORANCE AS A PREMISE

In general, what substantive conclusions can be drawn when science has not advanced very far on a problem? Not much. One of the basic skills we teach our philosophy students is how to recognize and diagnose the range of nonformal fallacies that can undermine an ostensibly appealing argument: what it is to beg the question, what a non sequitur is, and so on. A prominent item in the fallacy roster is *argumentum ad ignorantiam*—argument from ignorance. The canonical version of this fallacy uses ignorance as the key premise from which a substantive conclusion is drawn. The canonical version looks like this: We really do not understand much about a phenomenon P. (Science is largely ignorant about the nature of P.)

Therefore: we do know that:

(1) P can never be explained

or

(2) Nothing science could ever discover would deepen our understanding of P.

or

(3) P can never be explained in terms of properties of kind S.

In its canonical version, the argument is obviously a fallacy: none of the tendered conclusions follow, not even a little bit. Surrounded with rhetorical flourish, much brow furrowing and hand-wringing, however, versions of this argument can hornswoggle the unwary. From the fact that we do not know something, nothing very interesting follows—we just don't know. Nevertheless, the temptation to suspect that our ignorance is telling us something positive, something deep, something metaphysical or even radical, is ever-present. Perhaps we like to put our ignorance in a positive light, supposing that but for the *Profundity* of the phenomenon, we would have knowledge. But there are many reasons for not knowing, and the specialness of the phenomenon is, quite regularly, not the real reason. I am currently ignorant of what caused an unusual rapping noise in the woods last night. Can I conclude it must be something special, something unimaginable, something…alien…other-worldly? Evidently not. For all I can tell now, it might merely have been a raccoon gnawing on the compost bin. Lack of evidence for something is just that: lack of evidence. It is not positive evidence for something else, let alone something of a humdinger-ish sort. That conclusion is not very glamorous perhaps, but when ignorance is a premise, that is about all you can grind out of it.

Now if neuroscience had progressed as far on the problems of brain function as molecular biology has progressed on transmission of hereditary traits, then of course we would be in a different position. But it has not. The only thing you can conclude from the fact that attention is mysterious, or sensorimotor integration is mysterious, or that consciousness is mysterious, is that we do not understand the mechanisms.

Moreover, the mysteriousness of a problem is not a fact about the problem, it is not a metaphysical feature of the universe—it is an epistemological fact about us. It is about where we are in current science, it is about what we can and cannot understand, it is about what, given the rest of our understanding, we can and cannot imagine. It is not a property of the problem itself. It is sometimes assumed that there can be a valid transition from "we cannot now explain" to "we can never explain," so long as we have the help of a subsidiary premise, namely, "I cannot imagine how we could ever explain…." But it does not help, and this transition remains a straight-up application of argument from ignorance. Adding "I cannot imagine explaining P" merely adds a psychological fact about the speaker, from which again, nothing significant follows about the nature of the phenomenon in question. Whether we can or cannot imagine a phenomenon being explained in a certain way is a psychological fact about us, not an objective fact about the nature of the phenomenon itself. To repeat, it is an epistemological fact—about what, given our current knowledge, we can and cannot understand. It is not a metaphysical fact about the nature of the reality of the universe.

Typical of vitalists generally, my high school biology teacher argued for vitalism thus: I cannot imagine how you could get living things out of dead molecules. Out of bits of proteins, fats, sugars—how could life itself emerge? He thought it was obvious from the sheer mysteriousness of the matter that it could have no solution in biology or chemistry. He assumed he could tell that it would require a Humdinger solution. Typical of lone survivors, a passenger of a crashed plane will say: I cannot imagine how I alone could have survived the crash, when all other passengers died instantly. Therefore God must have plucked me from the jaws of death.

Given that neuroscience is still very much in its early stages, it is actually not a very interesting fact that someone or other cannot imagine a certain kind of explanation of some brain phenomenon. Aristotle could not imagine how a complex organism could come from a fertilized egg. That of course was a fact about Aristotle, not a fact about embryogenesis. Given the early days of science (500 BC), it is no surprise that he could not imagine what it took many scientists hundreds of years to discover. I cannot imagine how ravens can solve a multistep problem in one trial, or how temporal integration is achieved, or how thermoregulation is managed. But this is a (not very interesting) psychological fact about me. One could, of course, use various rhetorical devices to make it seem like an interesting fact about me, perhaps by emphasizing that it is a really really hard problem, but if we are going to be sensible about this, it is clear that my inability to imagine how thermoregulation works is *au fond*, pretty boring. The "I-cannot-imagine" gambit suffers in another way. Being able to imagine an explanation for P is a highly open-ended and under-specified business. Given the poverty of delimiting conditions of the operation, you can pretty much rig the conclusion to go whichever way your heart desires. Logically, however, that flexibility is the kiss of death.

Suppose someone claims that she can imagine the mechanisms for sensorimotor integration in the human brain but cannot imagine the mechanisms for consciousness. What exactly does this difference amount to? Can she imagine the former in detail? No, because the details are not known. What is it, precisely, that she can imagine? Suppose she answers that in a very general way she imagines that sensory neurons interact with interneurons that interact with motor neu-

rons, and via these interactions, sensorimotor integration is achieved. Now if that is all "being able to imagine" takes, one might as well say one can imagine the mechanisms underlying consciousness. Thus: "The interneurons do it." The point is this: if you want to contrast being able to imagine brain mechanisms for attention, short-term memory, planning etc., with being unable to imagine mechanisms for consciousness, you have to do more that say you can imagine neurons doing one but cannot imagine neurons doing the other. Otherwise one simply begs the question.

To fill out the point, consider several telling examples from the history of science. Before the turn of the twentieth century, people thought that the problem of the precession of the perihelion of Mercury was essentially trivial. It was annoying, but ultimately, it would sort itself out as more data came in. With the advantage of hindsight, we can see that assessing this as an easy problem was quite wrong—it took the Einsteinian revolution in physics to solve the problem of the precession of the perihelion of Mercury. By contrast, a really hard problem was thought to be the composition of the stars. How could a sample ever be obtained? With the advent of spectral analysis, that turned out to be a readily solvable problem. When heated, the elements turn out to have a kind of fingerprint, easily seen when light emitted from a source is passed through a prism.

Consider now a biological example. Before 1953, many people believed, on rather good grounds actually, that in order to address the copying problem (transmission of traits from parents to offspring), you would first have to solve the problem of how proteins fold. The former was deemed a much harder problem than the latter, and many scientists believed it was foolhardy to attack the copying problem directly. As we all know now, the basic answer to the copying problem lay in the base-pairing of DNA, and it was solved first. Humbling it is to realize that the problem of protein folding (secondary and tertiary) is still not solved. That, given the lot we now know, does seem to be a hard problem.

What is the point of these stories? They reinforce the message of the argument from ignorance: from the vantage point of ignorance, it is often very difficult to tell which problem is harder, which will fall first, what problem will turn out to be more tractable than some other. Consequently our judgments about relative difficulty or ultimate tractability should be appropriately qualified and tentative. Guesswork has a useful place, of course, but let's distinguish between blind guesswork and educated guesswork, and between guesswork and confirmed fact. The philosophical lesson I learned from my biology teacher is this: when not much is known about a topic, don't take terribly seriously someone else's heartfelt conviction about what problems are scientifically tractable. Learn the science, do the science, and see what happens.

References

Churchland, Paul M. (1995). *The engine of reason; the seat of the soul.* Cambridge, MA: MIT Press.
Crick, Francis (1994). *The Astonishing Hypothesis.* New York: Scribner and sons.
Jackson, Frank (1982). "Epiphenomenal qualia." *Philosophical Quarterly.* Vol. 32.
Nagel, Thomas (1974). "What is it like to be a bat?" *Philosophical Review.* Vol. 83.

Study Questions

1. What does Churchland mean when she claims that Chalmers's argument for the hard problem of consciousness is just an argument from ignorance?
2. Why does Churchland bring up "vitalism" in arguing against Chalmers?
3. Why does Churchland think there's no good way to tell the difference between the "easy" problems in neuroscience and Chalmers's "hard" problem?

Visual Perception and Visual Awareness after Brain Damage: A Tutorial

5.7a

MARTHA J. FARAH

MARTHA J. FARAH (1955–) is Walter H. Annenberg Professor in Natural Sciences and the director of the Center for Neuroscience and Society at the University of Pennsylvania. She is a leading researcher in cognitive neuroscience and is author of *Visual Agnosia* (1990) and *The Cognitive Neuroscience of Vision* (2000), among many other publications. Farah's selection provides an empirical description of "blindsight" and sketches several possible neuroscientific explanations for the phenomenon.

Martha J. Farah, "Visual Perception and Visual Awareness After Brain Damage: A Tutorial Overview," in *The Nature of Consciousness: Philosophical Debates*, N. Block, O. Flanagan, and G. Guzeldere (Cambridge, MA: The MIT Press). Umilta, Carlo, and Morris Moscovitch, eds., *Attention and Performance XV: Conscious and NonConscious Information Processing*, excerpts from Farah essay, "Visual Perception and Visual Awareness After Brain Damage: A Tutorial Overview," pages 37–75, © 1994 Massachusetts Institute of Technology, by permission of The MIT Press

BLINDSIGHT

Blindsight refers to the preserved visual abilities of patients with damage to primary visual cortex, for stimuli presented in regions of the visual field formerly represented by the damaged cortex. The first documentation of this phenomenon was made by Poppel, Held, and Frost (1973), who found that patients with large scotomata could move their eyes to the location of a light flash presented in the scotomatous region of their visual field. Although the eye movements were not highly accurate, they were better than would be expected by chance and were not accompanied by any conscious visual experience according to patients' reports.

Representative Findings

Shortly after this initial report, Weiskrantz and his colleagues undertook extensive and rigorous investigations of what they termed "blindsight" (Weiskrantz, Sanders, and Marshall 1974; Weiskrantz 1986). They were able to demonstrate a much greater degree of preserved visual function in some of their subjects than in the initial series. Case D.B., in particular, was the subject of many investigations in which the abilities to point to stimulus locations, to detect movement, to discriminate the orientation of lines and gratings, and to discriminate shapes such as X's and O's were found to be remarkably preserved. [Figure 1] shows the results of an early study of localization by pointing in this patient. Over subsequent years, a number of different patients with blindsight have been studied in different laboratories (Weiskrantz 1990). The pattern of preserved and impaired abilities has been found to vary considerably from case to case. Detection and localization of light and detection of motion are invariably preserved to some degree. In addition, many patients can discriminate orientation, shape, direction of movement, and flicker. Color vision mechanisms appear to be preserved in some cases, as indicated by Stoerig and Cowey's (1990) findings [Figure 2]. Normal subjects show a characteristic profile of spectral sensitivity, that

is, different intensity thresholds for detection of light of different wavelengths. Although subjects with blindsight showed overall higher thresholds for above-chance detection, their spectral sensitivity functions had the same shape, indicating preserved functioning of opponent-process color mechanisms, despite no conscious awareness of color (or even light) perception.

An interesting new source of data on blindsight comes from the use of indirect measures of the subject's visual information processing capabilities in the blind field. Marzi et al. (1986) showed that subjects with blindsight, like normal subjects, respond more quickly in a simple reaction time task when there are two stimuli instead of one and that this is true even when the second stimulus falls in the blind field. Rafal et al. (1990) studied the effects of a second stimulus in the blind field on the speed with which hemianopic subjects could make a saccade to a stimulus in their normal field. With their task, a second stimulus was found to inhibit the saccade. Like the facilitation of manual reaction time found by Marzi et al., this inhibition shows that the stimulus was perceived, in that it influenced performance. Significantly, Rafal et al. found this effect only when the second stimulus was presented to the temporal half of the retina, that is, to the half of the retina that projects to the superior colliculus. The projections from the retina to the cortical visual system are symmetrical, with equal connectivity between each hemiretina and the lateral geniculate nucleus (LGN).

AWARENESS OF PERCEPTION

Just as the particular set of visual abilities and level of performance vary from patient to patient, so does the nature of patients' subjective report. Some subjects claim to be guessing on the basis of no subjective sense whatsoever. These include the subjects whose highly systematic data are shown in [Figures 1 and 2]. In other studies, patients report some "feeling" that guides their responses, but the feeling is not described as specifically visual in nature. For example, patients will state that

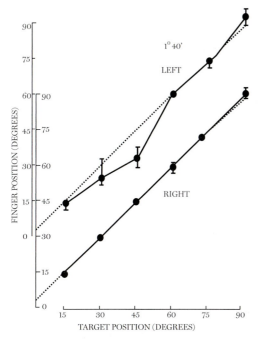

FIGURE 1 Average finger-reaching responses to targets at different positions in left (blind) and right visual field for case D.B. Bars show range of responses. From Weiskrantz et al. (1974).

they felt the onset of a stimulus or felt it to be in a certain location. Shape discriminations between circles and crosses are made on the basis of "jagged" versus "smooth" feelings, which are nevertheless not subjectively visual. Some subjects may occasionally report specifically visual sensations, such as "dark shadows," particularly for very intense or salient stimuli. In his 1986 book, Weiskrantz includes descriptions of the subjective reports of his subjects, as well as the objective data collected from them in a variety of studies.

EXPLANATIONS OF BLINDSIGHT

The mechanism of blindsight has been a controversial topic. Some researchers have argued that the phenomenon is mediated, directly or indirectly, by residual functioning of primary visual cortex and should therefore be considered an

artifact. Even for researchers who reject the artifact explanation, the mechanism of blindsight has not been settled decisively, and there remain at least two different types of account.

Campion, Latto, and Smith (1983) presented the most comprehensive and influential critique of blindsight, alleging that it is no different from normal vision in being mediated by primary visual cortex, either indirectly, by light from the scotomatous region of the visual field reflecting off other surfaces into regions of the visual field represented by intact primary visual cortex, or directly, by residual functioning of lesioned areas of primary visual cortex. The latter idea is an example of a quality of representation account. They supported their arguments with experiments involving both hemianopic subjects, whose blindsight performance was correlated with conscious awareness, and normal subjects, presenting stimuli to the natural blind spot and assessing the degree to which scattered light was sufficient for various visual judgments. More recently, Fendrich, Wessinger, and Gazzaniga (1992) showed that what appeared to be a small island of functional primary visual cortex in one subject could support above-chance detection and even shape discrimination, despite the subject's belief that he was guessing in these tasks. The hypothesis of primary visual cortex mediation of blindsight meets several difficulties in accounting for the totality of the empirical data now available on blindsight. For example, it is difficult to see how scattered light would enable case D.B. to perceive black figures on a bright background or how this account could explain the qualitative differences in his performance within his natural blind spot and his acquired blind region. Unlike Fendrich et al.'s subject, the blindsight performance of most subjects is not sharply limited to a small patch of the blind field. Residual functioning of spared cortex is clearly not a possibility for hemidecorticate subjects, and yet they too show a wide range of blindsight abilities. Finally, recall the results of Rafal et al. (1990) on inhibition of saccades by stimuli presented to the blind field. This result has the important property of demonstrating subcortical mediation of blindsight by a posi-

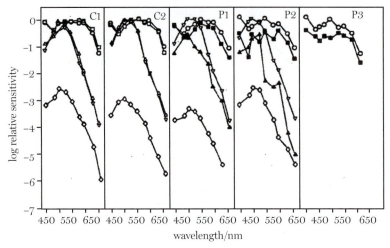

FIGURE 2 Relative spectral sensitivity of normal subjects (C) and patients with blindsight (P). From Stoerig and Cowey (1990).

tive finding, nasal-temporal asymmetries, rather than by the negation of possibilities for primary visual cortex involvement. Although it is possible that some of the abilities classified in some patients as blindsight do derive from spared striate cortex, the available data seem to suggest that additional mechanisms play an important role too.

Other than spared primary visual cortex, what other neural systems might mediate the preserved abilities in blindsight? Initially, the answer was thought to be the so-called subcortical visual system, which consists of projections from the retina to the superior collicus, and on to the pulvinar and cortical visual areas. This is an instance of a privileged role account, in that both cortical and subcortical visual systems are hypothesized to mediate various types of visual information processing but the mediation of visual awareness is taken to be the privileged role of the cortical visual system. Although it might at first seem puzzling that both visual systems mediate vision but only one mediates awareness thereof, the puzzle may be more apparent than real. There is, after all, much neural information processing that operates outside the realm of conscious awareness—for example, body temperature regulation. According to the hypothesis of subcortical mediation of

blindsight, at least some of the neural information processing of visual representations also operates without conscious awareness. Perhaps the reason this seems strange at first, and in fact engendered such extreme skepticism in some quarters, is that we use the phrase "visual perception" in two ways: to process representations of visual stimuli within our nervous systems and to become aware of visually transduced stimuli. According to the subcortical mediation hypothesis, both visual systems mediate visual perception in the first sense, whereas only the cortical visual system mediates visual perception in the second sense.

There is evidence in favor of the subcortical mediation hypothesis for at least some blindsight abilities. The close functional similarities between the known specializations of the subcortical visual system and many of the preserved abilities in blindsight, such as detection and localization of onsets and moving stimuli (Schiller and Koerner 1971), constitute one source of evidence. In addition, the nasal-temporal asymmetries found in Rafal et al.'s (1990) study are indicative of collicular mediation.

Recently, however, Cowey and Stoerig (1989) have suggested that the so-called cortical visual system, which projects from the retina to cortex by way of the LGN, may also contribute to blindsight. They marshaled evidence, from their own experiments and other research, of a population of cells in the LGN that project directly to extrastriate visual cortex and could therefore bring stimulus information into such areas as V4 and MT in the absence of primary visual cortex. This type of mechanism fits most naturally with the quality of representation hypotheses. According to this account, many of the same visual association areas are engaged in blindsight as in normal vision. What distinguishes normal vision and visual performance without awareness is that in the latter, only a subset of the normal inputs arrives in extrastriate visual cortex. The remaining inputs are both fewer in number and lacking whatever type of processing is normally accomplished in primary visual cortex. Consciousness of the functioning of extrastriate visual areas may occur only when these areas are operating on more complete and more fully processed visual representations. Evidence for this hypothesis is still preliminary. Although the anatomical connections between the LGN and the extrastriate visual areas have been shown to exist, their functional significance in blindsight has not been fully established. A systematic comparison between the blindsight abilities of patients with circumscribed striate lesions and with hemidecortication (which removes extrastriate visual areas as well) should reveal the functional role of the LGN-to-extrastriate projections in blindsight.

In sum, although some dissociations between visual performance and subjective awareness may be mediated by spared primary visual cortex, it seems fairly clear that the range of abilities documented in blindsight does not result from degraded normal vision (where "normal" means relying on primary visual cortex). It is also clearly not a single homogeneous phenomenon. At the level of preserved visual abilities, subjective experience, and neural mechanisms, there is apparently much variation from subject to subject. An important research goal in this area would be to establish correspondences among these three levels of individual difference as a means of characterizing

the functional and experiential roles of different components of the visual system. In the meantime, we can discern two main types of mechanism that may account for the dissociations between visual abilities and conscious awareness in blindsight: subcortical visual mechanisms and direct projections from the LGN to extrastriate areas.

References

Campion, J., Latto, R., and Smith, Y. M. (1983). Is blindsight an effect of scattered light, spared cortex, and near-threshold vision? *Behavioral and Brain Sciences, 3*, 423–447.

Cowey, A., and Stoerig, P. (1989). Projection patterns of surviving neurons in the dorsal lateral geniculate nucleus following discrete lesions of striate cortex: Implications for residual vision. *Experimental Brain Research, 75*, 631–638.

Fendrich, R., Wessinger, C. M., and Gazzaniga, M. S. (1992). Residual vision in a scotoma: Implications for blindsight. *Science, 258*, 1489–1491.

Marzi, C. A., Tassinari, C., Aglioti, S., and Lutzemberger, L. (1986). Spatial summation across the vertical meridian in hemianopics: A test of blindsight. *Neuropsychologia, 24*, 749–758.

Poppel, E., Held, R., and Frost, D. (1973). Residual visual functions after brain wounds involving the central visual pathways in man. *Nature, 243*, 2295–2296.

Rafal, R., Smith, J., Krantz, J., Cohen, A., and Brennan, C. (1990). Extrageniculate vision in hemianopic humans: Saccade inhibition by signals in the blind field. *Science, 250*, 118–121.

Schiller, P. H., and Koerner, F. (1971). Discharge characteristics of single units in superior collicus of the alert rhesus monkey. *Journal of Neurophysiology, 36*, 920–936.

Stoerig, P., and Cowey, A. (1990). Wavelength sensitivity in blindsight. *Nature, 342*, 916–918.

Weiskrantz, L. (1986). *Blindsight: A case study and implications.* Oxford: Oxford University Press.

Weiskrantz, L. (1990). Outlooks for blindsight: Explicit methodologies for implicit processes. *Proceedings of the Royal Society of London, B239*, 247–278.

Weiskrantz, L., Sanders, M. D., and Marshall, J. (1974). Visual capacity in the hemianopic visual field following a restricted occipital ablation. *Brain, 97*, 709–728.

5.7b   Ten Problems of Consciousness

MICHAEL TYE

MICHAEL TYE is a Professor of Philosophy at the University of Texas at Austin. He is author of *Ten Problems of Consciousness* (1995) and several other important books on consciousness and the philosophy of mind. Tye's selection extends the idea of blindsight to "super blindsight," in order to make clear the challenge facing any explanation of consciousness.

THE PROBLEM OF SUPER BLINDSIGHT

There is a condition known as blindsight that has been extensively studied in the last decade in psychology. People with blindsight have large blind areas or scotoma in their visual fields, due to brain damage in the postgeniculate region (typically the occipital cortex), and yet, under certain circumstances, they can issue accurate statements with respect to the contents of those areas (see Weiskrantz 1986). For example, blindsight subjects can make accurate guesses with respect to such things as presence, position, orientation, and movement of visual stimuli. They can also guess correctly as to whether an *X* is present or an *O*. Some blindsight patients can even make accurate color judgments about the blind field. Additionally, when a pattern is flashed into the blind region, it typically attracts the eye toward it just as with normally sighted subjects.

It appears, then, that, given appropriate instructions, blindsight subjects can function in a way that is significantly like normally sighted subjects with regard to the blind areas in their visual fields, without there being anything experiential or phenomenally conscious going on. There is, however, one immediate, obvious observable difference between blindsight subjects and the rest of us: they do not spontaneously issue any public reports about the contents of their blind fields. In each case, they respond only when they are forced to choose between certain alternative possibilities. Moreover, they do not believe what they say.

Imagine now a person with blindsight who has been trained to will herself to respond, to guess what is in her blind field without being directed to guess, and who, through time, comes to believe the reports she issues with respect to a range of stimuli in her blind field. Imagine too that these reports are the same as those you and I would produce when confronted with the same stimuli. Call this "super blindsight." [. . .]

As far as I know, there are no actual super-blindsight subjects. But there could be. Their possibility raises some interesting and puzzling questions. What exactly is the difference between a super-blindsight subject's believing that there are such and such stimuli present and a normally sighted subject's experiencing that they are present? Is it just that the latter undergoes a state with a much richer *content* than the former, so that the difference resides in the fact that what is experienced has a wealth of detail to it that is missing in what is believed? More generally, how is the case of super blindsight to be treated by philosophical theories of phenomenal consciousness?

Reference

Weiskrantz, L. (1986). *Blindsight: A case study and implications.* Oxford: Oxford University Press.

Study Questions

1. What is blindsight, and how do scientists test for it?
2. What are some of the leading scientific explanations for blindsight?
3. What is "super blindsight," and why does it pose a problem for explaining consciousness?

Folk Psychology and Phenomenal Consciousness   5.8

JUSTIN SYTSMA

JUSTIN SYTSMA (1974–) is an Assistant Professor in the Department of Philosophy and the Humanities at the East Tennessee State University, and he received his Ph.D. from the University of Pittsburgh. His research focuses on the philosophy of psychology and the philosophy of mind. He has made important contributions to experimental philosophy and is at work on an experimental philosophy textbook. He has a beard to make himself look older. Sytsma's selection reviews a number of experimental studies of the folk concept of consciousness, and it argues that the folk may not possess the philosopher's concept of phenomenal consciousness.

Over the course of the last several decades a great deal of progress has been made on the question of how people understand a variety of psychological phenomena. This work on folk theory of mind, or *folk psychology*, is typically involved in explaining how we are able to predict agentive behavior by ascribing and reasoning about mental states like beliefs and desires. In particular, folk psychology is thought to be involved in our judgments that certain objects are agents and our interpretation of their movements as intentional actions (Malle; Gopnik and Meltzoff; Wellman; Perner).

There is also a range of mental states, however, that have been extremely important in the philosophical discussions of the mind since at least the time of Descartes, but that have attracted little attention from psychologists working on folk psychology. These are states such as feeling pain, seeing red, hearing a C#—in brief the states that are thought to be *phenomenally conscious*, in philosophers' jargon. While researchers have had relatively little to say with regard to folk psychological judgments about these mental states, this has changed in recent years with a spate of exciting new work being done by experimental philosophers and psychologists (Gray, Gray, and Wegner; Knobe and Prinz; Sytsma and Machery "How to Study," "Two Conceptions"; Sytsma "Dennett's Theory"; Arico; Arico, Fiala,

Justin Sytsma, "Folk Psychology and Phenomenal Consciousness," *Philosophy Compass*, 5, no. 8 (John Wiley & Sons, Inc.: August 1, 2010). Reprinted with permission of the publisher.

Goldberg, and Nichols; Huebner; Huebner, Bruno, and Sarkissian).

Following Joshua Knobe and Jesse Prinz, much of this literature has focused on the question of whether the folk have, perhaps implicitly, something like the philosophical concept of phenomenal consciousness. I (now) think that this is unfortunate for several reasons. First, to answer this question requires having a clear understanding of the philosophical concept, but philosophers are not always clear on the point and it is arguable that there are in fact many different concepts at play. Second, an adequate answer to this question requires a metric for comparing the similarity of concepts, which might depend on the theory of concepts that one endorses. Finally, the literature most clearly deals with a prior question that can be answered without giving a full articulation of the philosophical concept of phenomenal consciousness or how a folk concept might be similar to it. The prior question is whether or not the folk classify mental states as philosophers do: Do the folk treat mental states as dividing into two basic kinds (those that philosophers take to be phenomenally conscious and those that they do not), tending to treat mental states of each kind similarly?

Focusing on the question of how the folk classify the mental states that philosophers take to be phenomenally conscious, we do not need to give a full account of the concept of phenomenal consciousness. Rather, it will suffice to note which mental states philosophers classify as being phenomenally conscious. Philosophers of mind typically hold that there is "something it is like" (Nagel) to be in a diverse range of mental states. These mental states are thought to be phenomenally conscious in virtue of having distinctive phenomenal qualities and uncontroversial examples include *perceptual states* (seeing red, hearing a C#) and *bodily sensations* (feeling pain, nausea); further, *felt emotions* and *felt moods* (happiness, depression) are often added to this list (Levin; Tye). Phenomenally conscious

mental states are generally contrasted with states like beliefs and desires that are thought to be non-phenomenal.

In this article, I will examine recent empirical research on how ordinary people understand the mental states that philosophers take to be phenomenally conscious.[1] In particular, I will consider two questions: Are the ascriptions that the folk make with regard to phenomenally conscious mental states involved in their judgments about whether an action is morally right or wrong? And, do the folk classify mental states as philosophers do, treating them as dividing into two basic kinds—mental states that are phenomenally conscious and mental states that are not phenomenally conscious?

I will survey recent work on these two questions, respectively, in Sections 1 and 2. Overall, this research suggests an affirmative answer to the first question, at least for some of the relevant mental states, but a tentative negative answer to the second question. Specifically, work by Justin Sytsma and Edouard Machery ("Two Conceptions") indicates that the folk do not tend to classify mental states as philosophers do. They go on to suggest that the fundamental division for the folk instead centers on whether or not a mental state is thought to have a valence. This *valence hypothesis* is explored in Section 3, and I suggest that it is compatible with the research linking the folk classification of mental states to moral cognition. Finally, in Section 4, I consider further directions that research on the folk understanding of mental states that philosophers classify as phenomenally conscious is taking.

1. PHENOMENAL CONSCIOUSNESS AND MORAL PATIENCY

Heather Gray, Kurt Gray, and Daniel Wegner present evidence that people distinguish between two broad aspects of having a mind. They gave participants 78 pair-wise comparisons of 13 characters (including a 7-week-old fetus, adult man, frog, a dead woman, and the robot Kismet) for one of 24 mental capacities and personal judgments. For example, one comparison solicited the participants' judgments about whether a 5-year-old girl is more or less likely to be able to feel pain than a wild chimpanzee. Gray et al. found a clear divide between those capacities that they grouped under what they termed the "Experience dimension" (including hunger, fear, pain, pleasure, rage) and those grouped under the "Agency dimension" (including self-control, morality, memory, emotion recognition). The possession of the different Experience capacities were correlated with each other across agents, as were the different Agency capacities, while the possession of these mental capacities were poorly correlated across the two groupings. Thus, while a 5-month-old human infant scored low on Agency and high on Experience, God scored high on Agency and low on Experience. (See Arico et al., however, for an empirically supported argument that agency cues are nonetheless used in making judgments about experiential mental states.)

Gray et al. also found that moral judgments about the characters related to their two dimensions of mind perception. Specifically, they found that Agency is tied to *moral agency* (whether or not an entity is capable of morally right or wrong action), while Experience is tied to *moral patiency* (whether or not an entity can have morally right or wrong action done to it). Their participants held that some agents are open to moral blame, but not moral harm, while other agents are open to moral harm, but not moral blame.

Gray et al.'s results indicate that the folk treat a range of experiential states as being similar—tending to ascribe them to the same entities—and that the ascription of such states correlate with their judgments about moral patiency. But, how should we understand Gray et al.'s Experience dimension? The choice of terminology is suggestive of the philosophical concept of phenomenal consciousness, which is often dis-

cussed in terms of *conscious experience* (or just *experience* for short). Nonetheless, Gray et al.'s Experience dimension only includes examples of some of the types of mental states that philosophers take to be phenomenally conscious. Thus, it does not include any examples of perceptual states (does not include seeing red or hearing a C#, for example). As such, this study does not tell us whether the folk tend to classify mental states as philosophers do, nor does it tell us whether folk ascriptions of mental states that philosophers take to be phenomenally conscious are correlated with their judgments about moral patiency (as opposed to some subset of those states).

As discussed in the following section, Knobe and Prinz present empirical evidence suggesting that the folk do in fact classify mental states as philosophers do. They take this to show that the folk have the philosophical concept of phenomenal consciousness. Knobe and Prinz then use this evidence to argue that folk psychology is not solely geared toward the explanation and prediction of behavior. They hold that whether or not ascriptions of phenomenally conscious mental states might facilitate behavioral explanation or prediction, they play a clear role in people's moral judgments. They tested this in their fifth of five studies. In this study, participants were asked to give a free-response answer indicating why they think that a person who has a job working with fish might be interested in ascribing either *memory* or *feeling* to the fish. The answers were then independently coded as calling on either "prediction, explanation or control" or "moral judgments." Knobe and Prinz found that 100% of the responses for memory called on the former (while only 9% called on moral judgment); in contrast, all of the responses for feeling called on moral judgment (while none called on prediction, explanation or control). They conclude that "it seems that ascriptions of phenomenal consciousness are best understood in terms of their role in facilitating moral judgment" (82).

2. CLASSIFYING PHENOMENALLY CONSCIOUS MENTAL STATES

Despite the links drawn between moral cognition and ascriptions of phenomenally conscious mental states by Knobe and Prinz, it is important to reiterate that there are two distinct questions to be asked: First, are judgments about (at least some of) the mental states that philosophers take to be phenomenally conscious involved in ascriptions of moral patiency? Second, do the folk classify mental states as philosophers do? While the above work indicates that folk judgments about some of the mental states that philosophers take to be phenomenally conscious are involved in moral cognition, the evidence is less clear with regard to the question of whether the folk classify mental states in a way that corresponds with the philosophical concept of phenomenal consciousness.

In addition to giving a positive answer to the first question, Knobe and Prinz also gave a positive answer to the second question. Most importantly, in the second of their five studies, they asked participants to indicate how natural sounding a range of ten sentences ascribing mental states to a group agent (Acme Corporation) were. They found that participants rated the five sentences that ascribed mental states that philosophers typically take to be phenomenally conscious as less natural sounding than the five sentences that ascribed mental states that philosophers do not typically take to be phenomenally conscious.[2] The results are shown in [Figure 1].

Knobe and Prinz interpret this body of evidence as showing that (i) the folk distinguish between phenomenally conscious mental states and mental states that are not phenomenally conscious and (ii) that in contrast to the latter mental states, the ascription of phenomenally conscious mental states does not merely depend on the functional properties of the ascribee's states.

This conclusion has attracted the attention of critics, however (Arico; Sytsma and Machery "How to Study"). Notably, Sytsma and Machery target the conclusion that the folk specifically distinguish between mental states that are

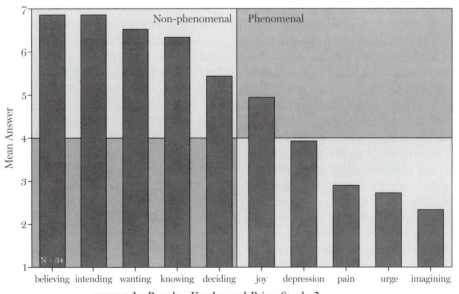

FIGURE 1: Results, Knobe and Prinz Study 2.

phenomenally conscious and mental states that are not phenomenally conscious. They contend that there is a natural alternative to Knobe and Prinz's explanation of their data, noting that corporations and individual humans differ in some significant behavioral and functional ways. Unlike an individual, Acme Corporation is distributed; while it is comprised, in part, of individual human bodies, it does not have its own body with which to bodily express joy or disgust, for example. As such, when people deny that Acme Corporation can experience great joy, it is unclear whether they focus on the supposed phenomenality of this state as opposed to the striking functional and behavioral differences between corporations and humans. For this reason, Sytsma and Machery charge that Knobe and Prinz's empirical work is ultimately inconclusive about whether or not the folk have the philosophical concept of phenomenal consciousness.

In fact, in a subsequent article Sytsma and Machery ("Two Conceptions") found that the folk do not classify mental states as philosophers do. They began by noting that phenomenal consciousness is a technical term in philosophy of mind. As discussed in the introduction, the definitions of the key terms in this area are often contentious, but the standard line is that there is something it is like to be in phenomenally conscious mental states. Sytsma and Machery show that these states are standardly said to have phenomenal qualities, or *qualia*, in virtue of which they are phenomenally conscious. For example, Peter Caruthers notes that "many philosophers use the term 'qualia' liberally, to refer to those properties of mental states (whatever they may be) in virtue of which the states in question are phenomenally conscious" (15). Sytsma and Machery then illustrate that uncontroversial examples of phenomenally conscious mental states include perceptual states (such as seeing red) and bodily sensations (such as feeling pain).

Sytsma and Machery argue that if the folk have the philosophical concept of phenomenal consciousness, then they should tend to clas-

sify mental states as philosophers do, treating paradigmatic examples of phenomenally conscious mental states similarly. Specifically, both philosophers and non-philosophers should deny that an entity that is presumably too simple to be phenomenally conscious can either see red or feel pain. Sytsma and Machery reasoned that if it is correct that the folk classify mental states as philosophers do, then we would expect both groups to treat perceptual states like seeing red analogously to bodily sensations like feeling pain, tending to deny both to a simple non-humanoid robot. The first of their three studies tested this hypothesis. This online study was open to both philosophers and non-philosophers, with participants being given a description of an agent (either an undergraduate student or a simple robot) performing behaviorally analogous tasks that were designed to elicit judgments that the undergraduate had undergone a phenomenally conscious mental state. In each of the scenarios either the undergraduate or the robot was instructed to manipulate one of three boxes distinguished by color. In two of the four scenarios, that manipulation was successful and the participants were asked whether the agent "saw red," answering on a 7-point scale anchored at 1 with "clearly no," at 4 with "not sure," and at 7 with "clearly yes." In the other two scenarios, the agent was electrically shocked and participants were asked whether the agent "felt pain," answering on the same scale.

Dividing the participants into two groups on the basis of their philosophical training, Sytsma and Machery found that the responses of philosophers were consistent with the hypothesis, while the responses of non-philosophers were not. They found that the philosophers surveyed treated the perceptual experience and the bodily sensation analogously, refusing to ascribe either state to the robot and ascribing both states to the undergraduate. In sharp contrast to philosophers, however, non-philosophers did not treat these states analogously: While non-philosophers were willing to ascribe both the perceptual state of seeing red and the bodily sensation of feeling pain to the undergraduate, they diverged from philosophers in ascribing seeing red to the robot. Like philosophers, the non-philosophers surveyed were not willing to ascribe feeling pain to the robot. The results are shown graphically in [Figure 2].

In contrast to the prediction derived from Knobe and Prinz's claim that the folk have the philosophical concept of phenomenal consciousness, Sytsma and Machery's results suggest that there is a divergence between how philosophers and the folk classify mental states. On average, the folk (but not philosophers) were willing to ascribe the perceptual state of seeing red to a simple robot. As such, their results offer some preliminary evidence that in contrast to philoso-

phers, the folk do not tend to treat the mental states tested as being of the same type, i.e. as both being phenomenally conscious.

Sytsma and Machery discuss a number of objections that have been raised against the conclusion they draw from their first study. Most prominently, it has been argued that non-philosophers do take mental states like seeing red and feeling pain to be phenomenally conscious, but that they simply do not make use of those judgments in this study. Specifically, it has been suggested that non-philosophers distinguish between two senses of the term "see"—one that only requires that the agent make the relevant discriminations between perceptual stimuli and one that requires that the agent be in the relevant phenomenally conscious mental state; the

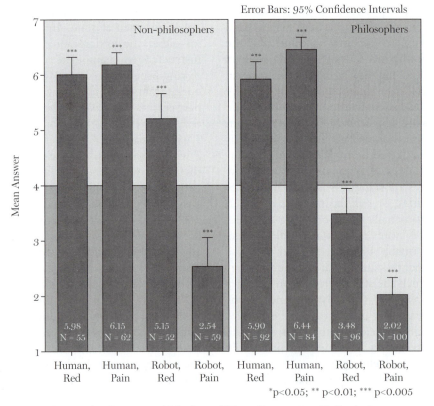

FIGURE 2: Results, Sytsma and Machery ("Two Conceptions") Study 1.

critic then argues that the non-philosophers in Sytsma and Machery's study read the test question in the first sense when they affirmed that the robot "sees red." This argument was suggested by Bryce Huebner and forcefully put forward by Eric Schwitzgebel in his commentary on Sytsma and Machery's paper at the 2008 *Society for Philosophy and Psychology* meeting.

Sytsma ("Dennett's Theory") has responded to this objection further, presenting evidence that the folk by and large hold a naïve view of colors, treating the colors that we are acquainted with in ordinary perception as mind-independent qualities of external objects. This view of colors is not straightforwardly compatible with dividing "seeing" into the two senses suggested above: The relevant discriminations are with regard to the colors that we are acquainted with and these colors are not taken to be mental. More surprisingly, Sytsma presents evidence suggesting that the folk also by and large hold a naïve view of pains.

Accepting for the sake of discussion that the folk do not classify mental states as philosophers do, how do they classify mental states? Sytsma and Machery investigate this question in two follow-up studies. Their results suggest that the folk classify mental states in terms of whether or not they are thought to have a valence.

3. FOLK ASCRIPTIONS AND VALENCE

Sytsma and Machery's second and third studies used the same methodology as their first—comparing a simple robot to a normal human—to explore the responses of non-philosophers for the mental states of feeling anger and smelling a range of olfactory stimuli. In their second study they found that while participants treated feeling anger analogously to feeling pain (denying both of the robot), they were split on the attribution of smelling banana to the robot (the mean response was not significantly different from a neutral response).

Sytsma and Machery hypothesized that the folk's willingness to ascribe mental states to a simple robot was sensitive to whether or not they associated a valence with that state; that is, whether or not they thought it was essential to being in the state is that it be either liked or disliked, or have an "hedonic value" (Robbins and Jack). This hypothesis is nicely congruent with recent work by Nick Haslam and colleagues showing that people in Australia, China, and Italy found that in comparison to humans, robots "are most deficient in emotion and desire" (254).

In contrast to externally directed states like seeing a red box that are plausibly thought to lack valence, internally directed states like feeling pain are plausibly thought to critically involve a negative valence. States like smelling banana, however, both involve perceptual discriminations of external stimuli and are plausibly thought to involve a positive valence that is not critical to the perceptual discriminations. Sytsma and Machery hypothesized that the folk were divided in their judgments about whether the robot smelled banana because while they hold that the robot is capable of perceiving the scent of banana, they also hold that it is incapable of liking that scent. They then predicted that the folk would be willing to ascribe olfactory perceptual states to the robot that they did not associate with either a positive or a negative valence.

Sytsma and Machery's third study tested this prediction by comparing participants' responses for three olfactory stimuli—a familiar stimulus that participants were likely to think is pleasant to smell (banana), a familiar stimulus that participants were likely to think is unpleasant to smell (vomit), and a stimulus that participants were unlikely to be familiar with and therefore unlikely to think of as either pleasant or unpleasant to smell (isoamyl acetate). They found that while the mean responses for banana and vomit were not significantly different from the neutral response, participants readily ascribed the state of smelling isoamyl acetate to the robot.

One potential objection to Sytsma and Machery's third study is that the folk did not treat the olfactory perceptual states differently because they made different judgments about whether these states had a valence, but treated them differently because one of the stimuli was thought to be more relevant to the robot's interests. Thus, it might be that participants were more likely to say that the robot smelled isoamyl acetate than banana because detecting chemicals is more relevant to the robot's interests than detecting pieces of fruit.[3] If this hypothesis is correct, then Sytsma and Machery's third study does not provide evidence in favor of the valence hypothesis, suggesting that an alternative explanation might be needed of why the folk treat perceptual states like seeing red differently from bodily sensations like feeling pain (both of which are plausibly relevant to the robot's interests).

Nonetheless, setting this objection aside for the sake of discussion, Sytsma and Machery argue that rather than classify mental states in terms of whether or not they are thought to be phenomenally conscious, the folk instead classify them in terms of whether or not they thought it was essential to being in the state that it have a valence. While this conclusion might seem to contradict the studies reviewed in Section 1, it is in fact quite compatible with the finding that folk ascriptions of some mental states are relevant to their moral cognition. In effect, Sytsma and Machery reinterpret Gray et al.'s results, noting that their Experience dimension does not include examples of one of the most paradigmatic types of phenomenally conscious mental states: It includes no perceptual experiences such as seeing red or smelling banana. It is therefore possible that judgments of moral patiency are most directly linked to judgments that an agent is capable of having mental states that are thought to have a valence and not specifically to the agent being capable of having phenomenally conscious mental states. Thus, the fifth study conducted by Knobe and Prinz compares remembering with feeling. While remembering where to find food in a lake is not clearly suggestive of valence, this is not the case for feeling. In fact, it is reasonable to assume that in asking why a fisherman might want to know about whether fish are capable of feeling, there is an implication that the state of interest is pain (which is clearly associated with valence).

Sytsma and Machery conclude that if their hypothesis is correct, then it potentially has significant philosophical implications. Most notably, their findings cast doubt on a common justification given for the reality of the "hard problem of consciousness" (Chalmers, *The Conscious Mind*). While philosophers like David Chalmers often justify the claim that there is a real problem, here, by arguing that phenomenal consciousness is undeniable because it is "the most central and manifest aspect of our mental lives" ("Facing Up" 207), Sytsma and Machery's results suggest that phenomenal consciousness might not be so central and manifest. If their account of how the folk classify mental states is correct, then this suggests that the folk do not find it to be obvious that mental states like seeing red and feeling pain have something central in common (namely that they are phenomenally conscious), despite their first-person experience with such mental states.

An obvious response to Sytsma and Machery's argument is that just because the folk do not classify mental states as philosophers do, this does not imply that a hard problem does not arise with regard to some of the mental states that philosophers take to be phenomenally conscious. In particular, it might be argued that a new hard problem emerges for those states that people are unwilling to ascribe to the simple robot—that is, mental states that they think have a valence.

The core of the hard problem of consciousness is that certain mental states seem to resist functional explanation. As David Chalmers expresses the point ("Facing Up" 203): "Even when we have explained the performance of all the cognitive and behavioral functions in the vicinity of experience—perceptual discrimination, categorization, internal access, verbal report—there may still remain a further unanswered question: *Why is the performance of these functions accompanied by experience?*" This core of the hard problem could be maintained while restricting the range of "experiences" that are thought to pose a problem. Thus, it might be argued that mental states that have a valence are not fully open to functional or neuroscientific explanation and that this is indicated by the folk's unwillingness to ascribe these mental states to the robot. If the folk conception of mental states with valence is such that even after the relevant performances have been explained there seems to remain an outstanding question of why those performances are accompanied by valence, then Chalmers's argument could be re-run. Currently, however, it is not clear that the folk do (or should) conceive of valence in a way that resists functional explanation or that might generate a *hard problem of valence*.

Sytsma ("Phenomenological Obviousness") argues that Sytsma and Machery's results have a related implication for some scientific work, putting pressure on scientists interested in explaining phenomenal consciousness. The argument is that the existence of phenomenal consciousness is often taken to be obvious to a subject just in undergoing the relevant mental states. But, it is not clear that phenomenal consciousness is obvious to the folk despite their undergoing states like seeing red and feeling pain. As such, Sytsma argues that these researchers owe us an alternative justification for their claims that the supposed scientific phenomenon of phenomenal consciousness actually exists.

Whether or not Sytsma and Machery's theory of how the folk classify mental states is correct, and whether or not it has significant philosophical and scientific implications if it is, are questions that continue to be pursued.

4. FURTHER DIRECTIONS

The research reviewed above has made significant progress toward understanding how the folk classify mental states and the role of these classifications in judgments about moral patiency. This work suggests that while folk ascriptions of some mental states that philosophers take to be phenomenally conscious are involved in the judgments that the folk make about moral patiency, the way that they classify mental states might not coincide closely with the philosophical distinction between mental states that are phenomenally conscious and mental states that are not phenomenally conscious. Nonetheless, there is still much more work to be done in this area. In this section I discuss a few further directions that this work is taking.

As we saw above, Sytsma and Machery ("Two Conceptions") present preliminary evidence that how the folk classify mental states is linked to judgments about valence. Currently, however, their findings only relate to a small sub-set of those states that philosophers take to be phenomenally conscious and only involve comparisons to one type of non-human agent (a simple robot). Further, there are potential objections to the studies supporting their theory. Additional research is under way to replicate and extend these results, investigating whether they generalize to other mental states and to a wider range of agents.

It is also important to investigate what cues drive folk ascriptions of the mental states that philosophers classify as phenomenally conscious. Work on this topic has been pioneered by Bryce Huebner and by Adam Arico, Brian Fiala, Robert Goldberg, and Shaun Nichols. Huebner has conducted two experiments comparing ascriptions of belief, pain, and happiness to four agents: a normal human, a cyborg with a human brain but a robot body, a cyborg with a human body but a robot brain, and a robot. Across the experiments he found that there was no significant difference in the participants' willingness to ascribe beliefs to each of the four agents. In contrast, Huebner found that they were significantly less likely to ascribe feeling pain to the two agents with robotic bodies than to the two with human bodies. For the case of happiness, however, participants were significantly more likely to ascribe the emotion to the human than to any of the other three agents. This suggests that information about both type of body and type of brain are important to folk ascriptions of some mental states (feeling happiness), that information about type of body is most important to ascriptions of some mental states (feeling pain), and that neither is especially important to ascriptions of some mental states (belief). Further, based on these results, Huebner argues that judgments about emotions play a central role in determining what degree of moral concern an agent deserves.

Arico et al. have investigated the role of simple agency cues (facial features, motion trajectories, contingent interaction) in ascriptions of different mental states. They ran a reaction time study in which participants performed a property-attribution task. They were presented with a sequence of object/attribution pairs and asked to indicate whether the object was capable of having the attribute. The attributes of interest involved three mental states that are typically associated with valence—feeling anger, feeling happy, and feeling pain. Objects were drawn from categories including insects, plants, vehicles, and natural moving objects (such as clouds). Arico et al. found that participants were significantly more likely to ascribe the three mental states noted above to insects than to any of the items lacking simple agency cues. Further, in denying that insects were capable of having these mental states, participants were significantly slower than when denying those states to vehicles or natural moving objects. Interestingly, the same pattern held for plants, with participants showing no significant difference in reaction times between plants and insects. Arico et al. suggest that this might indicate the importance of judgments that an entity is living for ascriptions of mental states that philosophers take to be phenomenally conscious.

5. CONCLUSION

In investigating folk psychology, cognitive and developmental psychologists have primarily investigated how people understand mental states like beliefs and desires that philosophers typically classify as non-phenomenal. This has changed in recent years with a number of intriguing studies looking at the folk understanding of phenomenally consciousness mental states being performed by experimental philosophers and psychologists. I have surveyed this literature, focusing on two questions: (1) Are folk ascriptions of mental states that philosophers take to be phenomenal related to folk judgments about moral patiency? (2) Do the folk classify mental states as philosophers do, treating them as dividing into two basic kinds (phenomenal and non-phenomenal mental states)? The current evidence suggests a restricted positive answer to the first question and a tentative negative answer to the second question. The empirical studies surveyed indicate that folk ascriptions of at least some of the mental states that philosophers classify as phenomenally conscious are related to their judgments about moral patiency and tentatively suggest that the folk do not classify mental states as philosophers do, tending to treat some paradigmatic examples of phenomenally conscious mental states dissimilarly.

Notes

1. I will not consider other interesting work on how people understand terms like "consciousness" more generally (see, for example, De Brigard; Wilkes).
2. The five non-phenomenal sentences are: Acme Corp. believes that its profit margin will soon increase; Acme Corp. intends to release a new product this January; Acme Corp. wants to change its corporate image; Acme Corp. knows that it can never compete with GenCorp in the pharmaceuticals market; Acme Corp. has just decided to adopt a new marketing plan. The five phenomenal sentences are: Acme Corp. is now

experiencing great joy; Acme Corp. is getting depressed; Acme Corp. is feeling excruciating pain; Acme Corp. is experiencing a sudden urge to pursue internet advertising; Acme Corp. is now vividly imagining a purple square.

3. I wish to thank an anonymous reviewer for *Philosophy Compass* for raising this objection.

Works Cited

Arico, A. "Folk Psychology, Consciousness, and Context Effects." *Review of Philosophy and Psychology* (forthcoming).

Arico, A., B. Fiala, R. Goldberg, and S. Nichols. "The Folk Psychology of Consciousness." *Mind & Language* 26 (2011): 327–52.

Carruthers, P. *Phenomenal consciousness: A naturalistic theory.* Cambridge: Cambridge University Press, 2000.

Chalmers, D. "Facing Up to the Problem of Consciousness." *Journal of Consciousness Studies* 2 (1995): 200–19.

———. *The Conscious Mind.* Oxford: Oxford University Press, 1996.

De Brigard, F. "Attention, Consciousness, and Commonsense." *Journal of Consciousness Studies* (2010).

Gopnik, A. and A. N. Metlzoff. *Words, thoughts, and theories.* Cambridge: MIT Press, 1997.

Gray, H., K. Gray, and D. Wegner. "Dimensions of Mind Perception." *Science* 619 (2007): 315.

Haslam, N., Y. Kashima, S. Loughnan, J. Shi, and C. Suitner. "Subhuman, Inhuman, and Superhuman: Contrasting Humans with Nonhumans in Three Cultures." *Social Cognition* 26 (2008): 248–258.

Huebner, B. "Commonsense concepts of phenomenal consciousness: Does anyone care about functional zombies?" *Phenomenology and the Cognitive Sciences* (2010).

Huebner, B., M. Bruno, and H. Sarkissian. "What Does the Nation of China Think About Phenomenal States?" *Review of Philosophy and Psychology* (2010).

Knobe, J. and J. Prinz. "Intuitions about consciousness: Experimental studies." *Phenomenology and the Cognitive Sciences* 7 (2008): 67–85.

Levin, J. "Qualia." *Routledge Encyclopedia of Philosophy.* Ed. E. Craig. 1998. London: Routledge.

4 July, 2007 <http://www.rep.routledge.com/article/V029>.

Malle, B. "Folk theory of mind: Conceptual foundations of human social cognition." *The new unconscious.* Eds. R. Hassin, J. Uleman, and J. Bargh. New York: Oxford University Press, 2005. 225–255.

Nagel, T. "What is it like to be a bat?" *The Philosophical Review* 83 (1974): 435–450.

Perner, J. *Understanding the representational mind.* Cambridge: MIT Press, 1991.

Robbins, P. and A. Jack. "The Phenomenal Stance." *Philosophical Studies* 127 (2006): 59–85.

Sytsma, J. "Phenomenological Obviousness and the New Science of Consciousness." *Philosophy of Science* 76 (2009): 958–969.

———. "Dennett's Theory of the Folk Theory of Consciousness." *Journal of Consciousness Studies* (2010).

Sytsma, J. and E. Machery. "How to Study Folk Intuitions about Phenomenal Consciousness." *Philosophical Psychology* 22 (2009): 21–35.

———. "Two Conceptions of Subjective Experience." *Philosophical Studies* (2010).

Tye, M. "Qualia." *Routledge Encyclopedia of Philosophy.* Ed. E. Zalta. 2003. London: Routledge. 4 July, 2007 <http://plato.stanford.edu/entries/qualia/>.

Wellman, H. *The child's theory of mind.* Cambridge: MIT Press, 1990.

Wilkes, K. "———, Yishi, Duh, Um and Consciousness." *Consciousness in Contemporary Science.* Eds. A. Marcel and E. Bisiach. 1988. Oxford: Oxford University Press.

Study Questions

1. What methods do the experimental philosophers use to discover the "folk concept" of consciousness?

2. Why do some of the results Sytsma reports challenge the claim that the folk have a concept of phenomenal consciousness?

3. What does Sytsma mean by "valence," and why does he think it provides a better explanation of the results of the experiments?

CHAPTER 6

Free Will and Moral Responsibility

STEPHEN G. MORRIS AND CHRIS WEIGEL

EVEN THOUGH THE SUBJECT OF *FREE will* is among the oldest and most hotly debated issues in all of philosophy, pinning down exactly what "free will" means is no easy task. Perhaps most fundamentally, free will is generally considered to be a metaphysical property that is required for moral responsibility. As one contemporary philosopher, Galen Strawson, puts it, "It is a matter of historical fact that concern about moral responsibility has been the main motor...of discussion of the issue of free will"[1] Beyond this, free will is also widely considered to be a prerequisite for praise and blame, as well as for personal dignity. To say that one exercised free will over an action means, minimally, that the person exhibited an important kind of control over the action in question. This notion of control is usually cashed out partly in terms of an individual's ability to make an informed choice or to choose a particular action from among alternatives. A big question here has to do with what it means to say that one can choose from among alternatives. Though most philosophers agree that acting of one's own free will requires that one have the ability to do otherwise than what one actually did, philosophers frequently disagree about what it means to say that "one could have done otherwise." In two of the essays appearing in this section—those by Nielsen and Chisholm—we get conflicting views about how participants in the free will debate should understand the ability to do otherwise.

A different, yet not entirely unrelated, aspect of control involves the idea that one is able to make choices and pursue actions without being under undue constraint. One of the more contentious topics among contemporary philosophers in the free will debate relates to the question of what counts as the kind of constraint that prevents free will. The vast majority of people (in industrialized Western cultures at least) who have some basic understanding of what "free will" means are quick to assert that they sometimes possess it. Nonetheless, the fact that philosophers continue to disagree (after thousands of years of debate no less) about what free will requires and whether anyone has it is a testament to the significant difficulties—both conceptual and empirical—that challenge the commonplace view that human beings are capable of exercising free will.

To understand the ways that philosophers continue to disagree, consider three standard positions. The first position is *libertarianism* (free will libertarianism, not political libertarianism). The libertarian holds that we have free will, and that this entails that *causal determinism* is false. According to causal determinism, every state of the universe is completely caused by prior states. An influential statement of causal determinism comes from the French mathematician and philosopher Pierre Laplace, who in 1814 speculated as follows:

> We may regard the present state of the universe as the effect of its past and the cause of its future. An intellect which at a certain moment would know all forces that set nature in motion, and all positions of all items of which nature is composed, if this intellect were also vast enough to submit these data to analysis, it would embrace in a single formula the movements of the greatest bodies of the universe and those of the tiniest atom; for such an intellect nothing would be uncertain and the future just like the past would be present before its eyes.[2]

The libertarian is faced with the question of how free actions arise, since the libertarian rejects the idea that they are causally determined, and since it seems that free actions cannot be uncaused or be a product of chance. Within libertarianism, there is much debate about the right answer to the question of how free actions arise. The selection in this chapter that represents libertarianism, Chisholm's "Human Freedom and the Self," argues that free actions are caused, but not deterministically or even probabilistically as other events are presumably caused. Rather, free actions are caused by the *agent*. This means that there are two kinds of causation: *event causation* and *agent causation*. Chisholm's essay tries to make sense of agent causation by showing it is not *ad hoc* or incoherent.

A second position that one might take regarding free will is *hard determinism*. The hard determinist holds that causal determinism is true and that this entails that free will does not exist. Though the number of philosophers subscribing to hard determinism has steadily declined in recent years—due in no small part to the decrease in popularity of causal determinism that has coincided with the rise of quantum physics—a position similar to hard determinism has been rigorously defended by some contemporary philosophers: free will *skepticism*. The skeptic says that free will doesn't exist regardless of whether or not causal determinism is true. Say you decide to steal a shirt. The skeptic reasons that if that action was caused by the initial state of the universe plus the laws of nature—in other words, if it was causally determined—then you didn't act freely. On the other hand, the skeptic believes that any action that is not causally determined is essentially random. Since the skeptic asserts that free actions cannot be random, it follows that any actions that are not causally determined cannot be free. Since free will is generally taken to be a necessary condition for moral responsibility, and since skeptics reject the possibility of free will for human beings, skeptics seem committed to the view that people cannot be morally responsible. In "The Impossibility of Moral Responsibility," Galen Strawson presents a challenge to anyone who thinks that human moral responsibility is possible. Moral responsibility, he argues, requires something that is impossible for human beings, namely, that something be the cause of itself. Since self-causation for finite beings is impossible, so is human moral responsibility.

These positions—libertarianism, skepticism, and hard determinism—all have something in common. They all assume that free will and causal determinism are incompatible. *Incompatibilism* says that if free will exists, causal determinism cannot be true, and if causal determinism is true, free will cannot exist. *Compatibilism* contrasts with libertarianism, skepticism, and hard determinism by rejecting the view that free will is incompatible with causal determinism. Instead, the compatibilist says that free will can exist even if causal determinism is true. In his article, "The Compatibility of Freedom and Determinism," Nielsen presents compatibilism in its classical version. Nielsen examines the meaning of the term *freedom* and argues that it contrasts not with "exemption from causal law," but rather with "compulsion" or "coercion." Sometimes our actions are compelled or coerced; sometimes they are not. The former actions are unfree and the latter actions can be free even if they all are causally determined.

Compatibilists in the latter part of the twentieth century and beyond have been unsatisfied with resting the distinction between free and unfree actions on the notion of compulsion and coercion. These more recent compatibilist views have preserved the central insight of compatibilism—the view that we can have free will even if causal determinism is true—while giving a more nuanced understanding of what free will requires. Harry Frankfurt's theory, presented in "Freedom of the Will and the Concept of a Person," relies on the insight that there is a difference between acting freely and having freedom of the will. For Frankfurt, we have many desires and fulfill many of them as well. When we do so, we act freely. But fulfilling these desires cannot be sufficient for having freedom of the will. Instead, Frankfurt notes, we have attitudes about our desires: some of our desires are desirable, while others are not. When we are able to have the desires we want to have, and to make those desirable desires move us to action, we have freedom of the will.

It is safe to say that there has never been more activity from philosophers writing on the subject of free will than at present. In recent years numerous philosophers have spent a great deal of effort developing ways to strengthen the arguments supporting each of the three primary positions in the free will debate (compatibilism, libertarianism, and skepticism). Despite these efforts, however, the free will debate is locked in a stalemate that shows little sign of diminishing anytime soon. Simply put, philosophers have found little to no success in their efforts to persuade those in opposite camps to change their positions. Compatibilists have worked hard to dispel the worry that determinism compromises the kind of control over one's actions that many take to be necessary for free will. Unfortunately, they have not persuaded libertarians and skeptics. Libertarians have worked hard to provide an account of how indeterminism can contribute in an intelligible way to the capacity for free will. Unfortunately, they have not persuaded compatibilists and skeptics. And the skeptics' arguments against free will have found little traction with libertarians and compatibilists, who find that such arguments are insufficient to justify a position that they find highly counterintuitive.

It is important here to recognize the important role that *intuitions* play in perpetuating the disagreements surrounding free will. All of the complex philosophical argumentation aside, the position on free will that one takes ultimately boils down to one's intuitions—or gut feelings—about whether or not certain types of agents have free will. Compatibilists and incompatibilists, to take one example, seem to have different gut reactions to cases involving determined agents. If questions about free will boil down to how one *feels* about particular cases, one might suppose that there are no hard facts about free will—only individual opinions. While this is certainly a possibility, participants in the free will debate typically operate under the assumption that there *are* facts about free will. Given the centrality of intuitions to the free will debate, one can generally view the efforts of those who argue for one or another of the positions on free will as attempts to make their own view seem intuitive to the opposition. This has typically been carried out by constructing increasingly complex sets of conditions for free will that human agents supposedly either can or cannot meet (depending on whether a philosopher is taking a pro–free will or anti–free will stance) and by devising similarly complex hypothetical cases meant to fire up whichever intuitions would lead one's opponents to find one's own position intuitive. In light of the stalemates that have resulted from this kind of approach to persuade opponents, philosophers in the free will debate have often employed a different strategy to justify their views. Since most philosophers agree that the target of the discussion about free will is our commonsense (or "folk") understanding of free will and moral responsibility, some have argued that their positions are correct on the grounds that they cohere best with folk intuitions. Experimental philosophy can be seen as an extension of this type of approach to the free will debate. Rather than just making intuitive claims about what the folk believe, however, experimental philosophers studying free will set out to scientifically test folk intuitions about free will and moral responsibility. These studies can speak directly to theoretical claims. For example, Woolfolk, Doris, and Darley (2006) wonder whether a central claim of Frankfurt's is true, the claim that freedom of the will requires that we have the will we want to have.[3] They give evidence that folk notions of freedom are sympathetic to that claim by showing that we attribute more moral responsibility to actors who embrace their actions than to actors who act reluctantly. Experimental philosophers also explore the psychological processes that are behind people's judgments about free will and moral responsibility, providing insight about the role of things like affect and abstraction in thinking about free will and moral responsibility.

In "Surveying Freedom: Folk Intuitions about Free Will and Moral Responsibility," Nahmias, Morris, Nadelhoffer, and Turner agree that a successful free will theory should match up with folk intuitions. They agree that, all things being equal, a theory that fits well with commonsense attitudes has more in its favor than one that does not. Nahmias et al. set out to test what views the folk actually have about free will and related concepts like moral responsibility. By employing the experimental approach to the question of what folk intuitions about free will are like, Nahmias and his colleagues believe that they can provide their conclusions with the kind of empirical backing that their predecessors' conclusions were lacking. As they point out in their essay, most philosophers (some compatibilists included) have traditionally believed that the folk tend to be incompatibilists about free will. After carrying out a series of surveys, however, Nahmias et al. collected data yielding the somewhat surprising result that the folk tended to give strongly compatibilist responses to survey questions about free will and moral responsibility. These results led them to conclude that the folk are not incompatibilists regarding free will and determinism. Instead of being the final word on this very old debate, however, Nahmias et al. have been a force in sparking other debates about what exactly folk intuitions are.[4]

While using surveys to better understand people's intuitions about free will and moral responsibility has been a frequent tactic employed by experimental philosophers, there is a very different kind of experimental work that bears on issues of free will. This research has to do with the science of human decision making and the roles that conscious awareness and unconscious brain processes play in producing our decisions and actions. Within this line of research, philosophers have given the most attention to a series of experiments conducted by the psychologist Benjamin Libet.

Libet aimed to better understand the origins of our behavior by measuring the temporal relationships between a subject's action along with the subject's awareness of making a decision to act and the onset of a subject's brain activity that is associated with the action in question. Libet asked people to move their finger some time in the near future and he measured electrical activity in their brains while they did this. What Libet found in his experiments was that the brain activity, also known as the "readiness potential," that seems to be in some sense the initiating cause of the action occurs well before the subject becomes consciously aware of deciding to perform the action.[5] This result—which has been reproduced in several subsequent studies—has led many to conclude that the brain activity that initiates actions occurs *prior* to any conscious decision to act. In "A selection from *The Illusion of Conscious Will*," psychologist Daniel Wegner discusses Libet's experiments in some detail and provides his take of what some of the implications are. According to Wegner, Libet's experiments establish that first the readiness potential occurs, then we consciously will our finger to move, and then we move our finger. The important point for Wegner is that the conscious willing occurs *after* the onset of the readiness potential.

Earlier it was suggested that even philosophers seem unable to agree about what "free will" means. Even so, it is fair to say that there are certain core properties of the concept that they virtually all agree on. Among these is the view that having acted of one's own free will requires that one exerted *control* over the action in question. Though the question of what exactly constitutes control is a contentious one, we can say, at the very least, that control over an action requires that the action is in some way the result of a *conscious decision*. But in light of Libet's experiments, some have concluded that conscious decision making plays little or no role in producing our actions. This view is apparently shared by Wegner, who says the following at the conclusion of *The Illusion of Conscious Will*:

> The fact is, it seems to us that we each have conscious will. It seems we have selves. It seems we have minds. It seems we are agents. It seems we cause what we do....[I]t is sobering and ultimately accurate to call all this an illusion....(pp. 341–342)

If Wegner is correct, this would have profound effects on the way we view ourselves and our capacity to act of our own free will. The implications for free will would seem pretty straightforward—no conscious will equals no free will. But is Wegner correct? The philosopher Alfred Mele has been among the most vocal opponents of the interpretations of Libet's work offered by both Wegner and Libet himself. In "A selection from *Free Will and Luck*," Mele argues that even if Libet is correct in believing that unconscious brain activity is the initial cause of our actions, there is still room left open for consciousness to play an important role in bringing our intentional actions about. If Mele is correct, Libet's research may not pose the problem for free will that many have supposed. As it stands, however, the threat to free will presented by empirical research like that of Libet's continues to elicit discussion and concern among philosophers. Settling on what conclusions about free will should be drawn from the empirical work of Libet and others is one of the main tasks facing philosophers today.

Notes

1. Galen Strawson. "The Impossibility of Moral Responsibility," *Philosophical Studies*, 75, no. 1–2 (1994): 5–24.
2. Pierre Simon Laplace, *A Philosophical Essay on Probabilities*, trans. from the 6th French ed. by Frederick Wilson Truscott and Frederick Lincoln Emory (New York: Dover, 1841/1951), 4.
3. See Robert Woolfolk, John Doris, and John Darley, "Identification, Situational Constraint, and Social Cognition: Studies in the Attribution of Moral Responsibility," *Cognition* 100 (2006): 283–301.
4. See, for example, Shaun Nichols and Joshua Knobe, "Moral Responsibility and Determinism: The Cognitive Science of Folk Intuitions," *Nous* 41, no. 4 (2008): 663–685.
5. For a more in-depth discussion of Libet's experiments, see B. Libet, C. A. Gleason, E. W. Wright, and D. K. Pearl, "Time of Conscious Intention to Act in Relation to Onset of Cerebral Activity (Readiness-Potential): The Unconscious Initiation of a Freely Voluntary Act," *Brain* 106 (1983): 623–642; Benjamin Libet, "Unconscious Cerebral Initiative and the Role of Conscious Will in Voluntary Action," *Behavioral and Brain Sciences* 8 (1985): 529–566; and Benjamin Libet, *Neurophysiology of Consciousness* (Boston: Birkhauser, 1993).

References

Chisholm, Roderick. "Human Freedom and the Self." In *Free Will*, ed. Gary Watson, 24–35. Oxford: Oxford University Press, 1964/1982.

Frankfurt, Harry. "Freedom of the Will and the Concept of a Person." *Journal of Philosophy* 68, no. 1 (1971): 5–20.

Kornhuber, H., and L. Deecke. "Hirnpotentialänderungen bei Willkürbewegungen und passiven Bewegungen des Menschen: Bereitschaftspotential und reafferente Potentiale." *Pflügers Archiv fur Gesamte Psychologie* 284 (1965): 1–17.

Laplace, Pierre Simon. *A Philosophical Essay on Probabilities*, trans. from the 6th French ed. by Frederick Wilson Truscott and Frederick Lincoln Emory, 4. New York: Dover, 1841/1951.

Libet, B., C. A. Gleason, E. W. Wright, and D. K. Pearl. "Time of Conscious Intention to Act in Relation to Onset of Cerebral Activity (Readiness-Potential): The Unconscious Initiation of a Freely Voluntary Act." *Brain* 106 (1983): 623–642.

Libet, Benjamin. "Unconscious Cerebral Initiative and the Role of Conscious Will in Voluntary Action." *Behavioral and Brain Sciences* 8 (1985): 529–566.

Libet, Benjamin. *Neurophysiology of Consciousness.* Boston: Birkhauser, 1993.

Nahmias, E., S. Morris, T. Nadelhoffer, and J. Turner. "Surveying Freedom: Folk Intuitions about Free Will and Moral Responsibility." *Philosophical Psychology* 18, no. 5 (2005): 561–584.

Nichols, Shaun, and Joshua Knobe. "Moral Responsibility and Determinism: The Cognitive Science of Folk Intuitions." *Nous* 41, no. 4 (2008): 663–685.

Nielsen, Kai. "The Compatibility of Freedom and Determinism." In *Free Will,* ed. Robert Kane, 34–46. Malden, MA: Blackwell, 1971/2002.

Strawson, Galen. "The Impossibility of Moral Responsibility." *Philosophical Studies* 75, no. 1–2 (1994): 5–24.

Wegner, Daniel. *The Illusion of Conscious Will.* Cambridge, MA: MIT Press, 2002.

Woolfolk, Robert, John Doris, and John Darley. "Identification, Situational Constraint, and Social Cognition: Studies in the Attribution of Moral Responsibility." *Cognition* 100 (2006): 283–230.

Suggestions for Further Reading

Clarke, Randolph. "Toward a Credible Agent-Causal Account of Free Will." *Nous* 27 (1993): 191–203.

Dennett, Daniel. *Freedom Evolves.* New York: Viking, 2003.

Faraci, David, and David Shoemaker. "Insanity, Deep Selves, and Moral Responsibility: The Case of JoJo." *Review of Philosophy and Psychology* 1 (2010): 319–332.

Fischer, J. M., R. Kane, D. Pereboom, and M. Vargas, eds. *Four Views on Free Will.* Malden, MA: Blackwell, 2007.

Frankfurt, Harry. "Alternate Possibilities and Moral Responsibility." *Journal of Philosophy* 66 (1969): 829–839.

Kane, Robert. "Two Kinds of Incompatibilism." *Philosophy and Phenomenological Research* 50 (1989): 219–254.

Kane, Robert. *A Contemporary Introduction to Free Will.* Oxford: Oxford University Press, 2005.

Kane, Robert, ed. *The Oxford Handbook of Free Will.* Oxford: Oxford University Press, 2005.

Mele, Alfred. *Free Will and Luck.* Oxford: Oxford University Press, 2006.

Mele, Alfred. *Effective Intentions: The Power of Conscious Will.* Oxford: Oxford University Press, 2009.

Nahmias, E. "When Consciousness Matters: A Critical Review of Daniel Wegner's *The Illusion of Conscious Will.*" *Philosophical Psychology* 15, no. 4 (2002): 527–542.

Nahmias, E., S. Morris, T. Nadelhoffer, and J. Turner. "Is Incompatibilism Intuitive?" *Philosophy and Phenomenological Research* 73 (2006): 28–53.

Nahmias, Eddy, and Dylan Murray. 2010. "Experimental Philosophy on Free Will: An Error Theory for Incompatibilist Intuitions." In *New Waves in Philosophy of Action,* ed. J. Aguilar, A. Buckareff, and K. Frankish. New York: Palgrave-Macmillan, 189–216.

O'Connor, Timothy, ed. *Agents, Causes and Events: Essays on Indeterminism and Free Will.* Oxford: Oxford University Press, 1995.

Sie, Maureen, and Arno Wouters. "The BCN Challenge to Compatibilist Free Will and Personal Responsibility." *Neuroethics* 3 (2010): 121–133.

Vargas, Manuel. "Revisionism." In *Four Views on Free Will,* ed. J. Fischer, R. Kane, D. Pereboom, and M. Vargas, 126–165. Malden, MA: Blackwell, 2007.

Watson, Gary, ed. *Free Will.* Oxford: Oxford University Press, 2003.

Wegner, Daniel. *The Illusion of Conscious Will.* Cambridge, MA: MIT Press, 2002.

Woolfolk, Robert, John Doris, and John Darley. "Identification, Situational Constraint, and Social Cognition: Studies in the Attribution of Moral Responsibility." *Cognition* 100 (2006): 283–301.

Pereboom, Derk. *Living Without Free Will*. Cambridge: Cambridge University Press, 2006.

Strawson, Peter. *Freedom and Resentment and Other Essays*. London: Methuen, 1974.

van Inwagen, Peter. *An Essay on Free Will*. Oxford: Clarendon, 1983.

6.1 The Compatibility of Freedom and Determinism

KAI NIELSEN

KAI NIELSEN (1926–) is Professor Emeritus of Philosophy at the University of Calgary. Nielsen specializes in ethics and social and political philosophy, and writes extensively about the philosophy of religion. In this selection, Nielsen presents a version of classical compatibilism, a view that has great historical importance (defenders have included Thomas Hobbes, David Hume, John Stuart Mill, G. E. Moore, and A. J. Ayer). His driving question is, "Is determinism compatible with our central beliefs concerning the freedom of conduct and moral responsibility?" He argues that the opposite of freedom is not exemption from the laws of nature; rather, the opposite of freedom is coercion or compulsion. In addition to being free from compulsion, Nielsen puts forth two additional conditions that, taken together, constitute a sufficient condition for acting of one's own free will. These other conditions are acting voluntarily in a sense that distinguishes one's action from that of a kleptomaniac and having the ability to do otherwise than one did had one chosen to do so. Since Nielsen maintains that all three conditions can be met in a deterministic world, it is incorrect to think that determinism precludes free will.

1. [. . .]WHAT I NOW WISH TO CONSIDER is what I take to be the most significant question we can ask about determinism and human conduct: Is determinism compatible with our central beliefs concerning the freedom of conduct and moral responsibility? It was because they thought that such beliefs were plainly incompatible that Dostoevsky and James were so nagged by determinism. With such philosophers as Thomas Hobbes, David Hume, John Stuart Mill, Moritz Schlick, and A. J. Ayer—all staunch defenders of the compatibility thesis—there is a vast shift not only in argument but also in attitude. There is no *Angst* over the ubiquitousness of causal laws. There is no feeling that life would be meaningless and man would be a prisoner of his past if determinism were true. Holbach is wrong. Even if determinism is true, freedom is not an illusion. The belief that it is an illusion is a philosophical confusion resting on a failure to pay sufficiently close attention either to the actual role of our concept of freedom in our lives or to the actual nature of determinism. It is such a twin failure that generates the conflicts we have been investigating.

The crucial point to note initially is that Mill and Schlick, as much as Holbach and Darrow, are thoroughgoing determinists. But they are determinists who do not believe that freedom and determinism are incompatible. James dismissed this position contemptuously with the label "soft determinism." For him "soft determinism" had an emotive force similar to" soft on Communism." But while a summer bachelor is no bachelor at all, a soft determinist is just as much a determinist as a hard determinist. I shall continue to use the label "soft determinism"—although I shall not use it in any derogatory sense—to refer to the view that maintains that

Kai Nielsen, "The Compatibility of Freedom and Determinism," in *Reason and Practice* (New York, New York: Harper & Row, 1971).

determinism and human freedom are logically compatible. (Sometimes in the literature they are called "compatibilists.") A view such as Holbach's or Darrow's, which Schlick says rests on "a whole series of confusions," I shall call "hard determinism." (Sometimes in the literature "hard determinists" are called "incompatibilists," for they believe freedom and determinism are incompatible.) But both hard and soft determinists agree that every event or state, including every human action or attitude, has a cause; that is, for anything whatsoever there are sufficient conditions for its occurrence.

The at least *prima facie* surprising thing is that these soft determinists still believe in the freedom of conduct and believe that human beings are—at least sometimes, anyway—responsible moral agents capable of acting in specific situations in ways other than those in which they in fact acted. Let us see how the soft determinist argument unfolds.

2. Morality, soft determinists argue, has or should have no interest in the determinism/indeterminism controversy. Morality is indeed vitally interested in the freedom of conduct, for it only makes sense to say that men ought to do one thing rather than another on the assumption that sometimes they can do other than what they in fact do. If no man can do other than what he does in fact do, then all talk of what men ought to do or what is right and wrong is indeed senseless. But to be interested in the freedom of conduct, as morality properly is, is not at all to be interested in some mysterious and no doubt illusory "freedom of the will." "Freedom" has its opposite, "compulsion" or "coercion." A man is free if he does not act under compulsion. He is free when he is able to do what he wants to do or when his acts and actions are in accordance with his own choices and decisions, and when what he wants to do or what he chooses is not determined by some person, force, or some disposition, such as kleptomania, which has gained ascendency over him. He is, by contrast, unfree to the extent that he is unable to achieve what he wants to achieve

and to act in accordance with choices based on his own rational deliberation because of either outside influence or psychological malaise. "Freedom" does not mean some scarcely intelligible state of affairs, "exemption or partial exemption from causal law" or "breach of causal continuity." To be free is to have the ability and opportunity to do what one wants to do and to act in accordance with one's own rational deliberations, without constraint and compulsion. It is something which, of course, admits of degrees.

Mill, Schlick, and Ayer argue that an anthropomorphic view of our language tricks us into thinking that man cannot be free if determinism is true. People tend to think that if determinism is true, events are in the power of other events and a person's acts or actions cannot alter the course of events. What will happen in the future is already fixed by immutable causal laws. But such views rest on unrealistic anthropomorphic thinking. They are scarcely a part of a tough-minded deterministic world perspective.

Similar anthropomorphic transformations are made with "necessity" and the little word "cause." And this, too, leads to needless befuddlement by causing us to misunderstand the actual workings of our language. It is, for example, terribly easy for the unwary to confuse causal and logical necessitation. But there is a very considerable difference in the meaning of "must" in "If you cut off his head, he must die" and "If it is a square, it must have four sides." In the latter case—an example of logical necessitation—"having four sides" follows by virtue of the meaning of the term "square." The "must" refers to this logical relationship. In the former case, it holds in virtue of something in the world. People also infer mistakenly that the event or effect is somehow contained in the cause. But this mystification is hardly intelligible.

There is also, as Schlick points out, a persistent confusion between laws of nature and legal laws. The word "law" has very different meanings in such cases. Legal laws *prescribe* a certain course of action. Many of them are intended to constrain or coerce you into acting in a certain way.

But laws of nature are not prescriptions to act in a certain way. They do not constrain you; rather, they are statements of regularities, of *de facto* invariable sequences that are parts of the world. In talking of such natural laws we often bring in an uncritical use of "force," as if the earth were being pushed and pulled around by the sun. Putting the matter this way makes one feel as if one is always being compelled or constrained, when in reality one is not. Without the anthropomorphic embellishment, it becomes evident that a determinist commits himself, when he asserts that *A* causes *B*, to the view that *whenever* an event or act of type *A* occurs, an event or act of type *B* will occur. The part about compulsion or constraint is metaphorical. It is because of the metaphor, and not because of the fact, that we come to think that there is an antithesis between causality and freedom. It is the *manner* here and not the *matter* that causes the trouble.

Demythologized and correctly conceived, causal necessity as applied to human actions is, Mill argues, simply this: Given the motives that are present to an individual's mind, and given the character and disposition of the individual, the manner in which he will act can be "unerringly inferred." That is to say, if we knew the person thoroughly, and knew all the inducements acting upon him, we could predict or retrodict his conduct with as much certainty as we can predict any physical event. This, Mill argues, is a bit of common sense and is in reality not in conflict with our operative concept of human freedom, for even if we say that all human acts are in principle predictable, this is not to say that people are acting under compulsion or constraint, for to say that their actions are predictable is not to say or even to give one to understand that they are being manipulated by anything or anybody. Being under some sort of compulsion or constraint is what limits our freedom.

3. […] A kleptomaniac cannot correctly be said to be a free agent, in respect to his stealing, because even if he does go through what appears

to be deliberations about whether to steal or not to steal, such deliberations are irrelevant to his actual behavior in the respect of whether he will or will not steal. Whatever he resolved to do, he would steal all the same.

This case is important because it clearly shows the difference between the man—the kleptomaniac—who is not free with respect to his stealing and an ordinary thief who is. The ordinary thief goes through a process of deciding whether or not to steal, and his decision decisively effects his behavior. If he actually resolved to refrain from stealing, he could carry out his resolution. But this is not so with the kleptomaniac. Thus, this observable difference between the ordinary thief and the kleptomaniac, quite independently of the issue of determinism, enables us to ascertain that the former is freer than the latter....

4. Yet, in spite of these evident contrasts, we are still haunted, when we are in the grip of a philosophical perplexity about freedom and determinism, by the question, or muddle felt as a question: Do not all causes equally necessitate? Is it not arbitrary "to say that a person is free when he is necessitated in one fashion but not when he is necessitated in another"?

Soft determinists reply that if "necessitate" merely means "cause," then of course "All causes equally necessitate" is equivalent to "All causes equally cause"—and that is hardly news. But "All causes equally constrain or compel" is not true. If one event is the cause of another, we are stating that the event said to be the effect would not have occurred if it had not been for the occurrence of the event said to be the cause. But this states nothing about compulsion or constraint. There is indeed an invariable concomitance between the two classes of events; but there is no compulsion in any but a metaphorical sense. Such invariable concomitance gives a necessary but not sufficient condition for causation. It is difficult and perhaps even impossible to say what constitutes a sufficient condition. But given the frequent situations in which we speak of one thing causing another without asserting or implying a compulsion or constraint, they plainly are not further necessary conditions. (When I watch a wren in the park my behavior has causes sufficient for its occurrence, but I was neither compelled, constrained, nor forced to watch the wren.) Whatever more we need beyond invariable concomitance for causation, compulsion isn't one of the elements.

Even in a deterministic world we can do other than what we in fact do, since all "cans" are constitutionally iffy. That is to say, they are all hypothetical. This dark saying needs explanation. Consider what we actually mean by saying, "I could have done otherwise." It means, soft determinists argue, "I should have acted otherwise if I had chosen" or "I would have done otherwise if I had wanted to." And "I can do X" means "If I want to I shall do X" or "If I choose to do X I will do X."

In general soft determinists argue, we say a man is free rather than unfree when the following conditions hold:

1. He could have done otherwise if he had chosen to.
2. His actions are voluntary in the sense that the kleptomaniac's stealing is not.
3. Nobody compelled him to choose as he did.

Now it should be noted that these conditions are frequently fulfilled or satisfied. Thus, "freedom" has a definite contrast and application. Basically it contrasts with constraint. Since this is so, we can say when it is true or probably true to assert that a man is free, and when it is false or probably false to say that he is free. Given the truth of this, it is evident that a man can act as a free and responsible moral agent even though his actions are determined. If we are not talking about some obscure notion of "free will" but about what Schlick calls the "freedom of conduct," freedom is after all compatible with determinism.

Study Questions

1. What is the difference between *Freedom of Conduct* and *Freedom of the Will* for Nielsen?
2. Do you agree with Nielsen that there is a significant difference between determinism and constraint?
3. How does Nielsen account for the difference between the kleptomaniac and the ordinary thief? Assuming that determinism is true, do you agree with Nielsen that it is appropriate to hold the thief accountable but not the kleptomaniac?

Human Freedom and the Self   6.2

RODERICK CHISHOLM

RODERICK CHISHOLM (1916–1999) spent most of his career in the Philosophy Department at Brown University. He has published in most major areas of philosophy. In this selection, Chisholm presents a version of libertarianism. Chisholm sees that free will conflicts both with causal determinism and with indeterminism. In other words, he thinks that free actions are not caused by events that are not in the agent's power, but they also are not the product of chance. Chisholm therefore says that when an agent

Roderick Chisholm, "Human Freedom and the Self," © Lindley Lecture, University of Kansas, 1964.

is responsible, there is an event that is caused by the agent, not by any other event. A common critique of agent causal views is that they are unable to adequately explain why a purportedly free act happened. When pressed to explain the difference between event A happening without a prior cause and event A happening as a result of an agent cause, Chisholm acknowledges that the explanation that he would offer—namely, that only in the latter case did the agent cause it to happen—would not satisfy his opponent. Nonetheless, he maintains that since ordinary event (or transeunt) causation is equally mysterious, agent causation is no less problematic than the ordinary notion of causation between events.

1. THE METAPHYSICAL PROBLEM OF HUMAN freedom might be summarized in the following way: Human beings are responsible agents; but this fact appears to conflict with a deterministic view of human action (the view that every event that is involved in an act is caused by some other event); and it *also* appears to conflict with an indeterministic view of human action (the view that the act, or some event that is essential to the act, is not caused at all). To solve the problem, I believe, we must make somewhat far-reaching assumptions about the self or agent—about the man who performs the act.

Perhaps it is needless to remark that, in all likelihood, it is impossible to say anything significant about this ancient problem that has not been said before.[1]

2. Let us consider some deed, or misdeed, that may be attributed to a responsible agent: one man, say, shot another. If the man *was* responsible for what he did, then, I would urge, what was to happen at the time of the shooting was something that was entirely up to the man himself. There was a moment at which it was true, both that he could have fired the shot and also that he could have refrained from firing it. And if this is so, then even though he did fire it, he could have done something else instead. (He didn't find himself firing the shot "against his will," as we say.) I think we can say, more generally, then, that if a man is responsible for a certain event or a certain state of affairs (in our example, the shooting of another man), then

that event or state of affairs was brought about by some act of his, and the act was something that was in his power either to perform or not to perform.

But now if the act which he *did* perform was an act that was also in his power *not* to perform, then it could not have been caused or determined by any event that was not itself within his power either to bring about or not to bring about. For example, if what we say he did was really something that was brought about by a second man, one who forced his hand upon the trigger, say, or who, by means of hypnosis, compelled him to perform the act, then since the act was caused by the *second* man it was nothing that was within the power of the *first* man to prevent. And precisely the same thing is true, I think, if instead of referring to a second man who compelled the first one, we speak instead of the *desires* and *beliefs* which the first man happens to have had. For if what we say he did was really something that was brought about by his own beliefs and desires, if these beliefs and desires in the particular situation in which he happened to have found himself caused him to do just what it was that we say he did do, then, since *they* caused it, *he* was unable to do anything other than just what it was that he did do. It makes no difference whether the cause of the deed was internal or external; if the cause was some state or event for which the man himself was not responsible, then he was not responsible for what we have been mistakenly calling his act. If a flood caused the poorly constructed dam to break, then, given the flood and the constitution of the dam, the break, we may say, *had* to occur and nothing could have happened in its place. And if the flood of desire caused the weak-willed man to give in, then he, too, had to do just what it was that he did do and he was no more responsible than was the dam for the results that followed. It is true, of course, that if the man is responsible for the beliefs and desires that he happens to have, then he may also be responsible for the things they lead him to do. But the question now becomes: *is* he responsible for the beliefs and desires he happens to have? If he is, then there was a time when they were within his power either to acquire or not to acquire, and we are left, therefore, with our general point.

One may object: But surely if there were such a thing as a man who is really *good*, then he would be responsible for things that he would do; yet, he would be unable to do anything other than just what it is that he does do, since, being good, he will always choose to do what is best. The answer, I think, is suggested by a comment that Thomas Reid makes upon an ancient author. The author had said of Cato, "He was good because he could not be otherwise," and Reid observes: "This is saying, if understood literally and strictly, is not the praise of Cato, but of his constitution, which was no more the work of Cato than his existence."[2] If Cato was himself responsible for the good things that he did, then Cato, as Reid suggests, was such that, although he had the power to do what was not good, he exercised his power only for that which was good.

All of this, if it is true, may give a certain amount of comfort to those who are tender-minded. But we should remind them that it also conflicts with a familiar view about the nature of God—with the view that St. Thomas Aquinas expresses by saying that "every movement both of the will and of nature proceeds from God as the Prime Mover."[3] If the act of the sinner *did* proceed from God as the Prime Mover, then God was in the position of the second agent we

just discussed—the man who forced the trigger finger, or the hypnotist—and the sinner, so-called, was *not* responsible for what he did. (This may be a bold assertion, in view of the history of western theology, but I must say that I have never encountered a single good reason for denying it.)

There is one standard objection to all of this and we should consider it briefly.

3. The objection takes the form of a stratagem—one designed to show that determinism (and divine providence) is consistent with human responsibility. The stratagem is one that was used by Jonathan Edwards and by many philosophers in the present century, most notably, G. E. Moore.[4]

One proceeds as follows: The expression

(a) He could have done otherwise,

it is argued, means no more nor less than

(b) If he had chosen to do otherwise, then he would have done otherwise.

(In place of "chosen," one might say "tried," "set out," "decided," "undertaken," or "willed.") The truth of statement (b) it is then pointed out, is consistent with determinism (and with divine providence); for even if all of the man's actions were causally determined, the man could still be such that, *if* he had chosen otherwise, then he would have done otherwise. What the murderers saw, let us suppose, along with his beliefs and desires, *caused* him to fire the shot; yet he was such that *if*, just then, he had chosen or decided *not* to fire the shot, then he would not have fired it. All of this is certainly possible. Similarly, we could say, of the dam, that the flood caused it to break and also that the dam was such that, *if* there had been no flood or any similar pressure, then the dam would have remained intact. And therefore, the argument proceeds, if (b) is consistent with determinism, and if (a) and (b) say the same thing, then (a) is also consistent with determinism; hence we can say that the agent *could* have done otherwise even though he was caused to do what he did do; and therefore determinism and moral responsibility are compatible.

Is the argument sound? The conclusion follows from the premises, but the catch, I think, lies in the first premises—the one saying that statement (a) tells us no more nor less than what statement (b) tells us. For (b), it would seem, could be true while (a) is false. That is to say, our man might be such that, if he had chosen to do otherwise, then he would have done otherwise, and yet *also* such that he could not have done otherwise. Suppose, after all, that our murderer could not have *chosen*, or could not have *decided*, to do otherwise. Then the fact that he happens also to be a man such that, if he had chosen not to shoot he would not have shot, would make no difference. For if he could *not* have chosen *not* to shoot, then he could not have done anything other than just what it was that he did do. In a word: from our statement (b) above ("If he had chosen to do otherwise, then he would have done otherwise"), we cannot make an inference to (a) above ("He could have done otherwise") unless we can *also* assert:

(c) He could have chosen to do otherwise.

And therefore, if we must reject this third statement (c), then, even though we may be justified in asserting (b), we are not justified in asserting (a). If the man could not have chosen to do otherwise, then he would not have done otherwise—*even if* he was such that, if he *had* chosen to do otherwise, then he would have done otherwise.

The stratagem in question, then, seems to me not to work, and I would say, therefore, that the ascription of responsibility conflicts with a deterministic view of action.

4. Perhaps there is less need to argue that the ascription of responsibility also conflicts with an indeterministic view of action—with the view that the act, or some event that is essential to the act, is not caused at all. If the act—the firing of the shot—was not caused at all, if it was fortuitous or capricious, happening so to speak out of the blue, then, presumably, no one—and nothing—was responsible for the act. Our conception of action, therefore, should be neither deterministic nor indeterministic. Is there any other possibility?

5. We must not say that every event involved in the act is caused by some other event; and we must not say that the act is something that is not caused at all. The possibility that remains, therefore, is this: We should say that at least one of the events that are involved in the act is caused, not by any other events, but by something else instead. And this something else can only be the agent—the man. If there is an event that is caused, not by other events, but by the man, then there are some events involved in the act that are not caused by other events. But if the event in question is caused by the man then it *is* caused and we are not committed to saying that there is something involved in the act that is not caused at all.

But this, of course, is a large consequence, implying something of considerable importance about the nature of the agent or the man.

6. If we consider only inanimate natural objects, we may say that causation, if it occurs, is a relation between *events* or *states of affairs*. The dam's breaking was an event that was caused by a set of other events—the dam being weak, the flood being strong, and so on. But if a man is responsible for a particular deed, then, if what I have said is rue, there is some event, or set of events, that is caused, *not* by other events or states of affairs, but by the agent, whatever he may be.

I shall borrow a pair of medieval terms, using them, perhaps, in a way that is slightly different from that for which they were originally intended. I shall say that when one event or state of affairs (or set of events or states of affairs) causes some other event or state of affairs, then we have an instance of *transeunt* causation. And I shall say that when an *agent*, as distinguished from an event, causes an event or state of affairs, then we have an instance of *immanent* causation.

The nature of what is intended by the expression "immanent causation" may be illustrated by this sentence from Aristotle's *Physics*: "Thus, a staff moves a stone, and is moved by a hand, which is moved by a man." (VII, 5, 256a, 6–8) If the man was responsible, then we have in this illustration a number of instances of causation—most of them transeunt but at least one of them immanent. What the staff did to the stone was an instance of transeunt causation, and thus we may describe it as a relation between events: "the motion of the staff caused the motion of the stone." And similarly for what the hand did to the staff: "the motion of the hand caused the motion of the staff." And, as we know from physiology, there are still other events which caused the motion of the hand. Hence we need not introduce the agent at this particular point, as Aristotle does—we *need* not, though we *may*. We *may* say that the hand was moved by the man, but we may *also* say that the motion of the hand was caused by the motion of certain muscles; and we may say that the motion of the muscles was caused by certain events that took place within the brain. But some event, and presumably one of those that took place within the brain, was caused by the agent and not by any other events.

There are, of course, objections to this way of putting the matter; I shall consider the two that seem to me to be most important.

7. One may object, firstly: "If the *man* does anything, then, as Aristotle's remark suggests, what he does is to move the *hand*. But he certainly does not *do* anything to his brain—he may not even know that he *has* a brain. And if he doesn't do anything to the brain, and if the motion of the hand was caused by something that happened within the brain, then there is no point in appealing to 'immanent causation' as being something incompatible with 'transeunt causation'—for the whole thing, after all, is a matter of causal relations among events or states of affairs."

The answer to this objection, I think, is this: It is true that the agent does not *do* anything with his brain, or to his brain, in the sense in which he *does* something with his hand and does

something to the staff. But from this it does not follow that the agent was not the immanent cause of something that happened within his brain.

We should not a useful distinction that has been proposed by Professor A. I. Melden—namely, the distinction between "making something A happen" and "doing A."[5] If I reach for the staff and pick it up, then one of the things that I *do* is just that—reach for the staff and pick it up. And if it is something that I do, then there is a very clear sense in which it may be said to be something that I know that I do. If you ask me, "Are you doing something, or trying to do something, with the staff?", I will have no difficulty in finding an answer. But in doing something with the staff, I also make various things happen which are not in this same sense things that I do: I will make various air-particles move; I will free a number of blades of grass from the pressure that had been upon them; and I may cause a shadow to move from one place to another. If these are merely things that I make happen, as distinguished from things that I do, then I may know nothing whatever about them; I may not have the slightest idea that, in moving the staff, I am bringing about any such thing as the motion of air-particles, shadows, and blades of grass.

We may say, in answer to the first objection, therefore, that it is true that our agent does nothing to his brain or with his brain; but from this it does not follow that the agent is not the immanent cause of some event within his brain; for the brain event may be something which, like the motion of the air-particles, he made happen in picking up the staff. The only difference between the two cases is this: in each case, he made something happen when he picked up the staff; but in the one case—the motion of the air-particles or of the shadows—it was the motion of the staff that caused the event to happen; and in the other case—the event that took place in the brain—it was this event that caused the motion of the staff.

The point is, in a word, that whenever a man does something A, then (by "immanent causation") he makes a certain cerebral event happen, and this cerebral event (by "transeunt causation") makes A happen.

8. The second objection is more difficult and concerns the very concept of "immanent causation," or causation by an agent, as this concept is to be interpreted here. The concept is subject to a difficulty which has long been associated with that of the prime mover unmoved. We have said that there must be some event A, presumably some cerebral event, which is caused not by any other event, but by the agent. Since A was not caused by any other event, then the agent himself cannot be said to have undergone any change or produced any other event (such as "an act of will" or the like) which brought A about. But if, when the agent made A happen, there was no event involved other than A itself, no event which could be described as *making* A happen, what did the agent's causation consist of? What, for example, is the difference between A's just happening, and the agent's *causing* A to happen? We cannot attribute the difference to any event that took place within the agent. And so far as the event A itself is concerned, there would seem to be a discernible difference. Thus Aristotle said that the activity of the prime mover is nothing in addition to the motion that it produces, and Suarez said that "the action is in reality nothing but the effect as it flows from the agent."[6] Must we conclude, then, that there is no more to the man's action in causing event A than there is to the event A's happening by itself? Here we would seem to have a distinction without a difference—in which case we have failed to find a *via media* between a deterministic and an indeterministic view of action.

The only answer, I think, can be this: that the difference between the man's causing A, on the one hand, and the event A just happening, on the other, lies in the fact that, in the first case but not the second, the event A *was* caused and was caused by the man. There was a brain event A; the agent did, in fact, cause the brain event; but there was nothing that he did to cause it.

This answer may not entirely satisfy and it will be likely to provoke the following question:

"But what are you really *adding* to the assertion that A happened when you utter the words 'The agent *caused* A to happen'?" As soon as we have put the question this way, we see, I think, that whatever difficulty we may have encountered is one that may be traced to the concept of causation generally—whether "immanent" or "transeunt." The problem, in other words, is not a problem that is peculiar to our conception of human action. It is a problem that must be faced by anyone who makes use of the concept of causation at all; and therefore, I would say, it is a problem for everyone but the complete indeterminist.

For the problem, as we put it, referring just to "immanent causation," or causation by an agent, was this: "What is the difference between saying, of an event A, that A just happened and saying that someone caused A to happen?" The analogous problem, which holds for "transeunt causation," or causation by an event, is this: "What is the difference between saying, of two events A and B, that B happened and then A happened and saying that B's happening was the *cause* of A's happening?" And the only answer that one can give is this—that in the one case the agent was the cause of A's happening and in the other case event B was the cause of A's happening. The nature of transeunt causation is no more clear than is that of immanent causation.

9. But we may plausibly say—and there is a respectable philosophical tradition to which we may appeal—that the notion of immanent causation, or causation by an agent, is in fact more clear than that of transeunt causation, or causation by an event, and that it is only by understanding our own causal efficacy, as agents, that we can grasp the concept of *cause* at all. Hume may be said to have shown that we do not derive the concept of *cause* from what we perceive of external things. How, then, do we derive it? The most plausible suggestion, it seems to me, is that of Reid, once again: namely that "the conception of an efficient cause may very probably be derived from the experience we have had...of our own power to produce certain effects."[7] If we did not understand the concept of immanent causation, we would not understand that of transeunt causation.

10. It may have been noted that I have avoided the term "free will" in all of this. For even if there is such a faculty as "the will," which somehow sets our acts agoing, the question of freedom, as John Locke said, is not the question "*whether the will be free*"; it is the question "*whether a man be free.*"[8] For if there is a "will," as a moving faculty, the question is whether the man is free to will to do these things that he does will to do—and also whether he is free *not* to will any of those things that he does will to do, and, again, whether he is free to will any of those things that he does not will to do. Jonathan Edwards tried to restrict himself to the question—"Is the man free to do what it is that he wills?"—but the answer to this question will not tell us whether the man is responsible for what it is that he *does* will to do. Using still another pair of medieval terms, we may say that the metaphysical problem of freedom does not concern the *actus imperatus*; it does not concern the question whether we are free to accomplish whatever it is that we will or set out to do; it concerns the *actus elicitus*, the question whether we are free to will or to set out to do those things that we do will or set out to do.

11. If we are responsible, and if what I have been trying to say is true, then we have a prerogative which some would attribute only to God: each of us, when we act, is a prime mover unmoved. In doing what we do, we cause certain events to happen, and nothing—or no one—causes us to cause those events to happen.

12. If we are thus prime movers unmoved and if our actions, or those for which we are responsible, are not causally determined, then they are not causally determined by our *desires*. And this means that the relation between what we want or what we desire, on the one hand, and what it is that we do, on the other, is not as simple as most philosophers would have it.

We may distinguish between what we might call the "Hobbist approach" and what we might call the "Kantian approach" to this question. The Hobbist approach is the one that is generally accepted at the present time, but the Kantian approach, I believe, is the one that is true. According to Hobbism, if we *know*, of some man, what his beliefs and desires happen to be and how strong they are, if we know what he feels certain of, what he desires more than anything else, and if we know the state of his body and what stimuli he is being subjected to, then we may *deduce*, logically, just what it is that he will do—or, more accurately, just what it is that he will try, set out, or undertake to do. Thus Professor Melden has said that "the connection between wanting and doing is logical."[9] But according to the Kantian approach to our problem, and this is the one that I would take, there is no such logical connection between wanting and doing, nor need there even be a causal connection. No set of statements about a man's desires, beliefs, and stimulus situation at any time implies any statement telling us what the man will try, set out, or undertake to do at that time. As Reid put it, though we may "reason from men's motives to their actions and, in many cases, with great probability," we can never do so "with absolute certainty."[10]

This means that, in one very strict sense of the terms, there can be no science of man. If we think of science as a matter of finding out what laws happen to hold, and if the statement of a law tells us what kinds of events are caused by what other kinds of events, then there will be human actions which we cannot explain by subsuming them under any laws. We cannot say, "It is causally necessary that, given such and such desires and beliefs, and being subject to such and such stimuli, the agent will do so and so." For at times the agent, if he chooses, may rise above his desires and do something else instead....

Notes

1. The general position to be presented here is suggested in the following writings, among others: Aristotle, *Eudaimonian Ethics*, bk. Ii, ch. 6; *Nichomachean Ethics*, bk. iii, chs. 1–5; Thomas Reid,

Essays on the Active Powers of Man; C. A. Campbell, "Is 'Free Will' a Pseudo-Problem?" *Mind* (1951), 441–65; Roderick M. Chisholm, "Responsibility and Avoidability," and Richard Taylor, "Determination and the Theory of Agency," in *Determinism and Freedom in the Age of Modern Science*, ed. Sidney Hook (New York, 1958).

2. Thomas Reid, *Essays on the Active Powers of Man*, essay iv, ch. 4 (*Works*, 600).
3. *Summa Theologica*. First Part of the Second Part, qu. Vi ("On the Voluntary and Involuntary").
4. Jonathan Edwards, *Freedom of the Will* (New Haven, 1957); G. E. Moore, *Ethics* (Home University Library, 1912), ch. 6.
5. A. I. Melden, *Free Action* (London, 1961), especially ch. 3. Mr. Melden's own views, however, are quite the contrary of those that are proposed here.
6. Aristotle, *Physics*, bk. Iii, ch. 3; Suarez, *Disputationes Metaphysicae*, Disputation 18, s. 10.
7. Reid, *Works*, 524.
8. *Essay Concerning Human Understanding*, bk. ii, ch. 21.
9. Melden, 166.
10. Reid, *Works*, 608, 612.

Study Questions

1. How does the libertarian account of free will differ from that of the compatibilist? What are some advantages and disadvantages of each account?
2. How does Chisholm's understanding of *the ability to do otherwise* differ from his compatibilist opponents? Whose understanding do you think is most relevant in terms of exercising free will?
3. Do you think that Chisholm's account of free actions in terms of being caused by the agent himself or herself constitutes an adequate explanation for how free will is possible for human beings?

6.3   The Impossibility of Moral Responsibility

GALEN STRAWSON

GALEN STRAWSON (1952–) is Professor of Philosophy at the University of Reading. He writes extensively on free will, consciousness, and the self. In this selection, Strawson is concerned with whether human beings can possess the kind of ultimate responsibility over our actions that many of us consider ourselves to have. It is the kind of responsibility that grounds belief in, for instance, the retributivist justification for punishing criminals and the notion of divine retribution in the afterlife. Strawson argues that such genuine moral responsibility does not exist. This is because genuine moral responsibility requires that we be responsible not only for how we act but also for how we are. Since no one chooses his or her heredity or environment—or to put it another way, since no one is the cause of oneself—it follows that no one is truly responsible. Though Strawson's goal in this essay is ostensibly to undermine the notion that human beings can be morally responsible, it should be noted that he employs the same type of argumentation elsewhere to reject the possibility of free will for human beings.

Galen Strawson, "The Impossibility of Moral Responsibility," *Philosophical Studies*, 75. With kind permission from Springer Science + Business Media: Philosophical Studies, The Impossibility of Moral Responsibility, 75, 1994, Galen Strawson.

1. THERE IS AN ARGUMENT, WHICH I will call the Basic Argument which appears to prove that we cannot be truly or ultimately morally responsible for our actions. According to the Basic Argument it makes no difference whether determinism is true or false. We cannot be truly or ultimately morally responsible for our actions in either case.

The Basic Argument has various expressions in the literature of free will, and its central idea can be quickly conveyed. (1) Nothing can be *causa sui*—nothing can be the cause of itself. (2) In order to be truly morally responsible for one's actions one would have to be *causa sui*, at least in certain crucial mental respects. (3) Therefore nothing can be truly morally responsible.

In this paper I want to reconsider the Basic Argument, in the hope that anyone who thinks that we can be truly or ultimately morally responsible for our actions will be prepared to say exactly what is wrong with it. I think that the point that it has to make is obvious, and that it has been underrated in recent discussion of free will—perhaps because it admits of no answer. I suspect that it is obvious in such a way that insisting on it too much is likely to make it seem less obvious than it is, given the innate contra-suggestibility of human beings in general and philosophers in particular. But I am not worried about making it seem less obvious than it is so long as it gets adequate attention. As far as its validity is concerned, it can look after itself.

A more cumbersome statement of the Basic Argument goes as follows.[1]

1) Interested in free action, we are particularly interested in actions that are performed for a reason (as opposed to "reflex" actions or mindlessly habitual actions).

2) When one acts for a reason, what one does is a function of how one is, mentally speaking. (It is also a function, of one's height, one's strength, one's place and time, and so on. But the mental factors are crucial when moral responsibility is in question.)

3) So if one is to be truly responsible for how one acts, one must be truly responsible for how one is, mentally speaking—at least in certain respects.

4) But to be truly responsible for how one is, mentally speaking, in certain respects, one must have brought it about that one is the way one is, mentally speaking, in certain respects. And it is not merely that one must have caused oneself to be the way one is, mentally speaking. One must have consciously and explicitly chosen to be the way one is, mentally speaking, in certain respects, and one must have succeeded in bringing it about that one is that way.

5) But one cannot really be said to choose, in a conscious, reasoned, fashion, to be the way one is mentally speaking, in any respect at all, unless one already exists, mentally speaking, already equipped with some principles of choice, P1—preferences, values, pro-attitudes, ideals—in the light of which one chooses how to be.

6) But then to be truly responsible, on account of having chosen to be the way one is, mentally speaking, in certain respects, one must be truly responsible for one's having the principles of choice P1 in the light of which one chose how to be.

7) But for this to be so one must have chosen P1, in a reasoned, conscious, intentional fashion.

8) But for this, i.e. 7, to be so one must already have had some principles of choice P2, in the light of which one chose P1.

9) And so on. Here we are setting out on a regress that we cannot stop. True self-determination is impossible because it requires the actual completion of an infinite series of choices of principles of choice.[2]

10) So true moral responsibility is impossible, because it requires true self-determination, as noted in (3).

This may seem contrived, but essentially the same argument can be given in a more natural form. (1) It is undeniable that one is the way one is, initially, as a result of heredity and early experience, and it is undeniable that these are things for which one cannot be held to be in any way responsible (morally or otherwise). (2) One cannot at any later stage of life hope to accede to true moral responsibility for the way one is by trying to change the way one already is as a result of heredity and previous experience. For (3) both the particular way in which one is moved to try to change oneself, and the degree of one's success in one's attempt at change, will be determined by how one already is as a result of heredity and previous experience. And (4) any further changes that one can bring about only after one has brought about certain initial changes will in turn be determined, via the initial changes, by heredity and previous experience. (5) This may not be the whole story, for it may be that some changes in the way one is are traceable not to heredity and experience but to the influence of indeterministic or random factors. But it is absurd to suppose that indeterministic or random factors, for which one is ex hypothesi in no way responsible, can in themselves contribute in any way to one's being truly morally responsible for how one is.

The claim, then, is not that people cannot change the way they are. They can, in certain respects (which tend to be exaggerated by North Americans and underestimated, perhaps, by Europeans). The claim is only that people cannot be supposed to change themselves in such a way as to be or become truly or ultimately morally responsible for the way they are, and hence for their actions.

2. I have encountered two main reactions to the Basic Argument. On the one hand it convinces almost all the students with whom I have discussed the topic of free will and moral responsibility.[3] On the other hand it often tends to be dismissed, in contemporary discussion of free will and moral responsibility, as wrong, or irrelevant, or fatuous, or too rapid, or an expression of metaphysical megalomania.

I think that the Basic Argument is certainly valid in showing that we cannot be morally responsible in the way that many suppose. And I think that it is the natural light, not fear, that has convinced the students I have taught that this is so. That is why it seems worthwhile to restate the argument in a slightly different—simpler and looser—version, and to ask again what is wrong with it.

Some may say that there is nothing wrong with it, but that it is not very interesting, and not very central to the free will debate. I doubt whether any non-philosopher or beginner in philosophy would agree with this view. If one wants to think about free will and moral responsibility, consideration of some version of the Basic Argument is an overwhelmingly natural place to start. It certainly has to be considered at some point in a full discussion of free will and moral responsibility, even if the point it has to make is obvious. Belief in the kind of absolute moral responsibility that it shows to be impossible has for a long time been central to the Western religious, moral, and cultural tradition, even if it is now slightly on the wane (a disputable view). It is a matter of historical fact that concern about moral responsibility has been the main motor—indeed the *ratio essendi*—of discussion of the issue of free will. The only way in which one might hope to show (1) that the Basic Argument was not central to the free will debate would be to show (2) that the issue of moral responsibility was not central to the free will debate. There are, obviously, ways of taking the word "free" in which (2) can be maintained. But (2) is clearly false none the less.[4]

In saying that the notion of moral responsibility criticized by the Basic Argument is central to the Western tradition, I am not suggesting that it is some artificial and local Judaeo-Christian-Kantian construct that is found nowhere else in the history of the peoples of the world, although even if it were that would hardly diminish its interest and importance for us. It is natural to suppose that Aristotle also subscribed to it,[5] and it is significant that anthropologists have suggested that most human societies can be classified either as "guilt cultures" or as "shame cultures." It is true that neither of these two fundamental moral emotions necessarily presupposes a conception of oneself as truly morally responsible for what one has done. But the fact that both are widespread does at least suggest that a conception of moral responsibility similar to our own is a natural part of the human moral-conceptual repertoire.

In fact the notion of moral responsibility connects more tightly with the notion of guilt than with the notion of shame. In many cultures shame can attach to one because of what some member of one's family—or government—has done, and not because of anything one has done oneself; and in such cases the feeling of shame need not (although it may) involve some obscure, irrational feeling that one is somehow responsible for the behaviour of one's family or government. The case of guilt is less clear. There is no doubt that people can feel guilty (or can believe that they feel guilty) about things for which they are not responsible, let alone morally responsible. But it is much less obvious that they can do this without any sense or belief that they are in fact responsible.

3. Such complications are typical of moral psychology, and they show that it is important to try to be precise about what sort of responsibility is under discussion. What sort of "true" moral responsibility is being said to be both impossible and widely believed in?

An old story is very helpful in clarifying this question. This is the story of heaven and hell. As I understand it, true moral responsibility is responsibility of such a kind that, if we have it, then it *makes sense*, at least, to suppose that it could be just to punish some of us with (eternal) torment in hell and reward others with (eternal) bliss in heaven. The stress on the words "makes sense" is important, for one certainly does not have to believe in any version of the story of heaven and hell in order to understand the notion of true

moral responsibility that it is being used to illustrate. Nor does one have to believe in any version of the story of heaven and hell in order to believe in the existence of true moral responsibility. On the contrary: many atheists have believed in the existence of true moral responsibility. The story of heaven and hell is useful simply because it illustrates, in a peculiarly vivid way, the *kind* of absolute or ultimate accountability or responsibility that many have supposed themselves to have, and that many do still suppose themselves to have. It very clearly expresses its scope and force.

But one does not have to refer to religious faith in order to describe the sorts of everyday situation that are perhaps primarily influential in giving rise to our belief in true responsibility. Suppose you set off for a shop on the evening of a national holiday, intending to buy a cake with your last ten pound note. On the steps of the shop someone is shaking an Oxfam tin. You stop, and it seems completely clear to you that it is entirely up to you what you do next. That is, it seems to you that you are truly, radically free to choose, in such a way that you will be ultimately morally responsible for whatever you do choose. Even if you believe that determinism is true, and that you will in five minutes time be able to look back and say that what you did was determined, this does not seem to undermine your sense of the absoluteness and inescapability of your freedom, and of your moral responsibility for your choice. The same seems to be true even if you accept the validity of the Basic Argument stated in section I, which concludes that one cannot be in any way ultimately responsible for the way one is and decides. In both cases, it remains true that as one stands there, one's freedom and true moral responsibility seem obvious and absolute to one.

Large and small, morally significant or morally neutral, such situations of choice occur regularly in human life. I think they lie at the heart of the experience of freedom and moral responsibility. They are the fundamental source of our inability to give up belief in true or ultimate moral responsibility. There are further questions to be asked about why human beings experience these situations of choice as they do. It is an interesting question whether any cognitively sophisticated, rational, self-conscious agent must experience situations of choice in this way.[6] But they are the experiential rock on which the belief in true moral responsibility is founded.

4. I will restate the Basic Argument. First, though, I will give some examples of people who have accepted that some sort of true or ultimate responsibility for the way one is is a necessary condition of true or ultimate moral responsibility for the way one acts, and who, certain that they are truly morally responsible for the way they act, have believed the condition to be fulfilled.[7]

E.H. Carr held that "normal adult human beings are morally responsible for their own personality." Jean-Paul Sartre talked of "the choice that each man makes of his personality," and held that "man is responsible for what he is." In a later interview he judged that his earlier assertions about freedom were incautious; but he still held that "in the end one is always responsible for what is made of one" in some absolute sense. Kant described the position very clearly when he claimed that "man *himself* must make or have made himself into whatever, in a moral sense, whether good or evil, he is to become. Either condition must be an effect of his free choice; for otherwise he could not be held responsible for it and could therefore be *morally* neither good nor evil." Since he was committed to belief in radical moral responsibility, Kant held that such self-creation does indeed take place, and wrote accordingly of "man's character, which he himself creates" and of "knowledge of oneself as a person who ... is his own originator." John Patten, the current British Minister for Education, a Catholic apparently preoccupied by the idea of sin, has claimed that "it is ... self-evident that as we grow up each individual chooses whether to be good or bad." It seems clear enough that he sees such choice as sufficient to give us true moral responsibility of the heaven-and-hell variety.[8]

The rest of us are not usually so reflective, but it seems that we do tend, in some vague and unexamined fashion, to think of ourselves as responsible for—answerable for—how we are. The point is quite a delicate one, for we do not ordinarily suppose that we have gone through some sort of active process of self-determination at some particular past time. Nevertheless it seems accurate to say that we do unreflectively experience ourselves, in many respects, rather as we might experience ourselves if we did believe that we had engaged in some such activity of self-determination.

Sometimes a part of one's character—a desire or tendency—may strike one as foreign or alien. But it can do this only against a background of character traits that are not experienced as foreign, but are rather "identified" with (it is a necessary truth that it is only relative to such a background that a character trait can stand out as alien). Some feel tormented by impulses that they experience as alien, but in many a sense of general identification with their character predominates, and this identification seems to carry within itself an implicit sense that one is, generally, somehow in control of and answerable for how one is (even, perhaps, for aspects of one's character that one does not like). Here, then, I suggest that we find, semi-dormant in common thought, an implicit recognition of the idea that true moral responsibility for what one does somehow involves responsibility for how one is. Ordinary thought is ready to move this way under pressure.

There is, however, another powerful tendency in ordinary thought to think that one can be truly morally responsible even if one's character is ultimately wholly non-self-determined—simply because one is fully self-consciously aware of oneself as an agent facing choices. I will return to this point later on.

5. Let me now restate the Basic Argument in very loose—as it were conversational—terms. New forms of words allow for new forms of objection, but they may be helpful none the less.

(1) You do what you do, in any situation in which you find yourself, because of the way you are.

So,

(2) To be truly morally responsible for what you do you must be truly responsible for the way you are—at least in certain crucial mental respects.

Or:

(1) What you intentionally do, given the circumstances in which you (believe you) find yourself, flows necessarily from how you are.

Hence

(2) you have to get to have some responsibility for how you are in order to get to have some responsibility for what you intentionally do, given the circumstances in which you (believe you) find yourself.

Comment. Once again the qualification about "certain mental respects" is one I will take for granted. Obviously one is not responsible for one's sex, one's basic body pattern, one's height, and so on. But if one were not responsible for anything about oneself, how one could be responsible for what one did, given the truth of (1) This is the fundamental question, and it seems clear that if one is going to be responsible for any aspect of oneself, it had better be some aspect of one's mental nature.

I take it that (1) is incontrovertible, and that it is (2) that must be resisted. For if (1) and (2) are conceded the case seems lost, because the full argument runs as follows.

(1) You do what you do because of the way you are.

So

(2) To be truly morally responsible for what you do you must be truly responsible for

the way are—at least in certain crucial mental respects.

But,

(3) You cannot be truly responsible for the way you are, so you cannot be truly responsible for what you do.

Why can't you be truly responsible for the way you are? Because

(4) To be truly responsible for the way you are, you must have intentionally brought it about that you are the way you are, and this is impossible.

Why is it impossible? Well, suppose it is not. Suppose that

(5) You have somehow intentionally brought it about that you are the way you now are, and that you have brought this about in such a way that you can now be said to be truly responsible for being the way you are now.

For this to be true

(6) You must already have had a certain nature N in the light of which you intentionally brought it about that you are as you now are.

But then

(7) For it to be true you and you alone are truly responsible for how you now are, you must be truly responsible for having had the nature N in the light of which you intentionally brought it about that you are the way you now are.

So

(8) You must have intentionally brought it about that you had that nature N, in which case you must have existed already with a prior nature in the light of which you intentionally brought it about that you had the nature N in the light of

which you intentionally brought it about that you are the way you now are....

Here one is setting off on the regress. Nothing can be *causa sui* in the required way. Even if such causal "aseity" is allowed to belong unintelligibly to God, it cannot plausibly be supposed to be possessed by ordinary finite human beings. "The *causa sui* is the best self-contradiction that has been conceived so far," as Nietzsche remarked in 1886:

> it is a sort of rape and perversion of logic. But the extravagant pride of man has managed to entangle itself profoundly and frightfully with just this nonsense. The desire for "freedom of the will" in the superlative metaphysical sense, which still holds sway, unfortunately, in the minds of the half-educated; the desire to bear the entire and ultimate responsibility for one's actions oneself, and to absolve God, the world, ancestors, chance, and society involves nothing less than to be precisely this *causa sui* and, with more than Baron Munchhausen's audacity, to pull oneself up into existence by the hair, out of the swamps of nothingness.... (*Beyond Good and Evil*, § 21)

The rephrased argument is essentially exactly the same as before, although the first two steps are now more simply stated. It may seem pointless to repeat it, but the questions remain. Can the Basic Argument simply be dismissed? Is it really of no importance in the discussion of free will and moral responsibility? (No and No) Shouldn't any serious defense of free will and moral responsibility thoroughly acknowledge the respect in which the Basic Argument is valid before going on to try to give its own positive account of the nature of free will and moral responsibility? Doesn't the argument go to the heart of things if the heart of the free will debate is a concern about whether we can be truly morally responsible in the absolute way that we ordinarily suppose? (Yes and Yes)

We are what we are, and we cannot be thought to have made ourselves *in such a way* that we can be held to be free in our actions *in such a way* that we can be held to be morally responsible for

our actions *in such a way* that any punishment or reward for our actions is ultimately just or fair. Punishments and rewards may seem deeply appropriate or intrinsically "fitting" to us in spite of this argument, and many of the various institutions of punishment and reward in human society appear to be practically indispensable in both their legal and non-legal forms. But if one takes the notion of justice that is central to our intellectual and cultural tradition seriously, then the evident consequence of the Basic Argument is that there is a fundamental sense in which no punishment or reward is ever ultimately just. It is exactly as just to punish or reward people for their actions as it is to punish or reward them for the (natural) colour of their hair or the (natural) shape of their faces. The point seems obvious, and yet it contradicts a fundamental part of our natural self-conception, and there are elements in human thought that move very deeply against it. When it comes to questions of responsibility, we tend to feel that we are somehow responsible for the way we are. Even more importantly, perhaps, we tend to feel that our explicit self-conscious awareness of ourselves as agents who are able to deliberate about what to do, in situations of choice, suffices to constitute us as morally responsible free agents in the strongest sense, whatever the conclusion of the Basic Argument....

7. There is nothing new in the somewhat incantatory argument of this paper. It restates certain points that may be in need of restatement. "Everything has been said before," said Andre Gide, echoing La Bruyere, "but since nobody listens we have to keep going back and beginning all over again." This is an exaggeration, but it may not be a gross exaggeration, so far as general observations about the human condition are concerned.

The present claim, in any case, is simply this: time would be saved, and a great deal of readily available clarity would be introduced into the discussion of the nature of moral responsibility, if the simple point that is established by the Basic Argument were more generally acknowledged and clearly stated. Nietzsche thought that thoroughgoing acknowledgement of the point was long overdue, and his belief that there might be moral advantages in such an acknowledgement may deserve further consideration.[9]

Notes

1. Adapted from G. Strawson, 1986, pp. 28–30.
2. That is, the infinite series must have a beginning and an end, which is impossible.
3. Two have rejected it in fifteen years. Both had religious commitments, and argued, on general and radical sceptical grounds, that we can know almost nothing, and cannot therefore know that true moral responsibility is not possible in some way that we do not understand.
4. It is notable that both Robert Kane (1989) and Alfred Mele (1995), in two of the best recent incompatibilist discussions of free will and autonomy, have relatively little to say about moral responsibility.
5. Cf. *Nichomachean Ethics* III. 5.
6. Cf. MacKay (1960), and the discussion of the "Genuine Incompatibilist Determinist" in G. Strawson (1986, pp. 281–6).
7. I suspect that they have started out from their subjective certainty that they have true moral responsibility. They have then been led by reflection to the realization that they cannot really have such moral responsibility if they are not in some crucial way responsible for being the way they are. They have accordingly concluded that they are indeed responsible for being the way they are.
8. Carr in *What Is History?*, p. 89; Sartre in *Being and Nothingness, Existentialism and Humanism,* p. 29, and in the *New Left Review* 1969 (quoted in Wiggins, 1975); Kant in *Religion within the Limits of Reason Alone,* p. 40, *The Critique of Practical Reason,* p. 101 (Ak. V. 98), and in *Opus Postumum,* p. 213; Patten in *The Spectator,* January 1992.

    These quotations raise many questions which I will not consider. It is often hard, for example, to be sure what Sartre is saying. But the occurrence of the quoted phrases is significant on any plausible interpretation of his views. As for Kant, it may be thought to be odd that he says what he does, in so far as he grounds the possibility of our freedom in our possession of an unknowable, non-temporal noumenal nature. It is, however, plausible to suppose that he thinks that radical or ultimate self-determination must take place even in the noumenal realm, in some unintelligibly non-temporal manner, if there is to be true moral responsibility.

9. Cf. R. Schacht (1983) pp. 304–9. The idea that there might be moral advantages in the clear headed admission that true or ultimate moral responsibility is impossible has recently been developed in another way by Saul Smilansky (1994).

References

Aristotle, 1953. *Nichomachean Ethics,* trans. J. A. K. Thomson, Allen and Unwin, London.

Campen, C.A., 1957. "Has the Self 'Free Will'?," in C.A. Campbell, *On Selfhood and Godhood,* Allen and Unwin, London.

Carr, E.H., 1961. *What Is History?,* Macmillan, London.

Kane, R., 1989. "Two Kinds of Incompatibilism," *Philosophy and Phenomenological Research* 50, pp. 219–254.

Kant, I., 1956. *Critique of Practical Reason,* trans. L. W. Beck, Bobbs-Merrill, Indianapolis.

Kant, I., 1960. *Religion within the Limits of Reason Alone,* trans. T. M. Greene and H. H. Hudson, Harper and Row, New York.

Kant, I., 1993. *Opus postumum,* trans. E. Ffirster and M. Rosen, Cambridge University Press, Cambridge.

MacKay, D.M., 1960. "On the Logical Indeterminacy of Free Choice," *Mind* 69, pp. 31–40.

Mele, A., 1995. *Autonomous Agents: From Self-Control to Autonomy,* Oxford University Press, New York.

Nietzsche, F. 1966. *Beyond Good and Evil,* trans. Walter Kaufmann, Random House, New York.

Novalis, 1802. *Heinrich von Ofterdingen.*

Sartre, J.P., 1969. *Being and Nothingness,* trans. Hazel E. Barnes, Methuen, London.

Sartre, I.-P., 1989. *Existentialism and Humanism,* trans. Philip Mairet, Methuen, London.

Schacht, R., 1983. *Nietzsche,* Routledge and Kegan Paul, London.

Smilansky, S., 1994. "The Ethical Advantages of Hard Determinism," *Philosophy and Phenomenological Research.*

Strawson, G., 1986. *Freedom and Belief,* Clarendon Press, Oxford.

Van Inwagen, P., 1989. "When Is the Will Free?," *Philosophical Perspectives* 3, pp. 399–422.

Wiggins, D., 1975. "Towards a Reasonable Libertarianism," in T. Honderich, ed., *Essays on Freedom of Action,* Routledge, London.

Study Questions

1. Strawson has argued that free will and moral responsibility are impossible for human beings whether or not determinism is true.

What do you think is the best objection to Strawson?

2. Do you think that the type of responsibility that concerns Strawson—the "ultimate" type of moral responsibility that grounds retributivism—is really what is driving the free will debate among philosophers?

3. Do you think that human society could prosper without the belief that humans can be truly morally responsible in Strawson's sense?

6.4   Freedom of the Will and the Concept of a Person

HARRY G. FRANKFURT

HARRY FRANKFURT (1929–) is Professor Emeritus of Philosophy at Princeton University. He has published widely on free will and moral responsibility and is perhaps best known for his argument that freedom does not require the ability to do otherwise, and for his ideas contained in this selection. Here, he argues that freedom of the will is compatible with causal determinism. It arises not just when we do what we will: otherwise, we would have to say that rabbits have free will, which doesn't show why freedom of the will is important for being a person. Rather, having freedom of the will arises when we have the will that we want to have.

WHAT PHILOSOPHERS HAVE LATELY COME TO accept as analysis of the concept of a person is not actually analysis of *that* concept at all. [. . .] It might have been expected that no problem would be of more central and persistent concern to philosophers than that of understanding what we ourselves essentially are. Yet this problem is so generally neglected that it has been possible to make off with its very name almost without being noticed and, evidently, without evoking any widespread feeling of loss.

There is a sense in which the word "person" is merely the singular form of "people" and in which both terms connote no more than membership in a certain biological species. In those senses of the word which are of greater philosophical interest, however, the criteria for being a person do not serve primarily to distinguish the members of our own species from the members of other species. Rather, they are designed to capture those attributes which are the subject of our most humane concern with ourselves and

Harry G. Frankfurt, "Freedom of the Will and the Concept of a Person," *Journal of Philosophy*, Volume LXVIII, no. 1 (January 14, 1971). Reprinted by permission of the publisher (Taylor & Francis Ltd, http://www.tandfonline.com).

the source of what we regard as most important and most problematical in our lives. Now these attributes would be of equal significance to us even if they were not in fact peculiar and common to the members of our own species. What interests us most in the human condition would not interest us less if it were also a feature of the condition of other creatures as well.

[...] It is my view that one essential difference between persons and other creatures is to be found in the structure of a person's will. Human beings are not alone in having desires and motives, or in making choices. They share these things with the members of certain other species, some of whom even appear to engage in deliberation and to make decisions based upon prior thought. It seems to be peculiarly characteristic of humans, however, that they are able to form what I shall call "second-order desires" or "desires of the second order."

Besides wanting and choosing and being moved *to do* this or that, men may also want to have (or not to have) certain desires and motives. They are capable of wanting to be different, in their preferences and purposes, from what they are. Many animals appear to have the capacity for what I shall call "first-order desires" or "desires of the first order," which are simply desires to do or not to do one thing or another. No animal other than man, however, appears to have the capacity for reflective self-evaluation that is manifested in the formation of second-order desires.

I.

[...] Consider first those statements of the form "*A* wants to *X*" which identify first-order desires—that is, statements in which the term "to *X*" refers to an action. A statement of this kind does not, by itself, indicate the relative strength of *A*'s desire to *X*. It does not make it clear whether this desire is at all likely to play a decisive role in what *A* actually does or tries to do. For it may correctly be said that *A* wants to *X* even when his desire

to *X* is only one among his desires and when it is far from being paramount among them. Thus, it may be true that *A* wants to *X* when he strongly prefers to do something else instead; and it may be true that he wants to *X* despite the fact that, when he acts, it is not the desire to *X* that motivates him to do what he does. On the other hand, someone who states that *A* wants to *X* may mean to convey that it is this desire that is motivating or moving *A* to do what he is actually doing or that *A* will in fact be moved by this desire (unless he changes his mind) when he acts.

It is only when it is used in the second of these ways that, given the special usage of "will" that I propose to adopt, the statement identifies *A*'s will. To identify an agent's will is either to identify the desire (or desires) by which he is motivated in some action he performs or to identify the desire (or desires) by which he will or would be motivated when or if he acts. An agent's will, then, is identical with one or more of his first-order desires. But the notion of the will, as I am employing it, is not coextensive with the notion of first-order desires. It is not the notion of something that merely inclines an agent in some degree to act in a certain way. Rather, it is the notion of an *effective* desire—one that moves (or will or would move) a person all the way to action. Thus the notion of the will is not coextensive with the notion of what an agent intends to do. For even though someone may have a settled intention to do *X*, he may nonetheless do something else instead of doing *X* because, despite his intention, his desire to do *X* proves to be weaker or less effective than some conflicting desire.

Now consider those statements of the form "*A* wants to *X*" which identify second-order desires—that is, statements in which the term "to *X*" refers to a desire of the first order. There are also two kinds of situation in which it may be true that *A* wants to want to *X*. In the first place, it might be true of *A* that he wants to have a desire to *X* despite the fact that he has a univocal desire, altogether free of conflict and ambivalence, to refrain from *X*-ing. Someone might want to have a certain desire, in other words, but univocally want that desire to be unsatisfied.

Suppose that a physician engaged in psychotherapy with narcotics addicts believes that his ability to help his patients would be enhanced if he understood better what it is like for them to desire the drug to which they are addicted. Suppose that he is led in this way to want to have a desire for the drug. If it is a genuine desire that he wants, then what he wants is not merely to feel the sensations that addicts characteristically feel when they are gripped by their desires for the drug. What the physician wants, insofar as he wants to have a desire, is to be inclined or moved to some extent to take the drug.

It is entirely possible, however, that, although he wants to be moved by a desire to take the drug, he does not want this desire to be effective. He may not want it to move him all the way to action. He need not be interested in finding out what it is like to take the drug. And insofar as he now wants only to *want* to take it, and not to *take* it, there is nothing in what he now wants that would be satisfied by the drug itself. He may now have, in fact, an altogether univocal desire *not* to take the drug; and he may prudently arrange to make it impossible for him to satisfy the desire he would have if his desire to want to take the drug should in time be satisfied.

It would thus be incorrect to infer, from the fact that the physician now wants to desire to take the drug, that he already does desire to take it. His second-order desire to be moved to take the drug does not entail that he has a first-order desire to take it. If the drug were now to be administered to him, this might satisfy no desire that is implicit in his desire to want to take it. While he wants to want to take the drug, he may have *no* desire to take it; it may be that *all* he wants is to taste the desire for it. That is, his desire to have a certain desire that he does not have may not be a desire that his will should be at all different than it is.

Someone who wants only in this truncated way to want to X stands at the margin of preciosity, and the fact that he wants to want to X is not pertinent to the identification of his will. There is, however, a second kind of situation that may be described by "A wants to want to X"; and when the statement is used to describe a situation of this second kind, then it does pertain to what A wants his will to be. In such cases the statement means that A wants the desire to X to be the desire that moves him effectively to act. It is not merely that he wants the desire to X to be among the desires by which, to one degree or another, he is moved or inclined to act. He wants this desire to be effective—that is, to provide the motive in what he actually does. Now when the statement that A wants to want to X is used in this way, it does entail that A already has a desire to X. It could not be true both that A wants the desire to X to move him into action and that he does not want to X. It is only if he does want to X that he can coherently want the desire to X not merely to be one of his desires but, more decisively, to be his will.

Suppose a man wants to be motivated in what he does by the desire to concentrate on his work. It is necessarily true, if this supposition is correct, that he already wants to concentrate on his work. This desire is now among his desires. But the question of whether or not his second-order desire is fulfilled does not turn merely on whether the desire he wants is one of his desires. It turns on whether this desire is, as he wants it to be, his effective desire or will. If, when the chips are down, it is his desire to concentrate on his work that moves him to do what he does, then what he wants at that time is indeed (in the relevant sense) what he wants to want. If it is some other desire that actually moves him to act when he acts, on the other hand, then what he wants at that time is not (in the relevant sense) what he wants to want. This will be so despite the fact that the desire to concentrate on his work continues to be among his desires.

II.

Someone has a desire of the second order either when he wants simply to have a certain desire or when he wants a certain desire to be his will. In situations of the latter kind, I shall call his second-order desires "second-order volitions" or "volitions of the second order." Now it is having second-order volitions, and not having second-order desires generally, that I regard as essential to being a person. It is logically possible, however unlikely, that there should be an agent with second-order desires but with no volitions of the second order. Such a creature, in my view, would not be a person. I shall use the term "wanton" to refer to agents who have first-order desires but who are not persons because, whether or not they have desires of the second order, they have no second-order volitions.

The essential characteristic of a wanton is that he does not care about his will. His desires move him to do certain things, without its being true of him either that he wants to be moved by those desires or that he prefers to be moved by other desires. The class of wantons includes all nonhuman animals that have desires and all very young children. Perhaps it also includes some adult human beings as well. In any case, adult humans may be more or less wanton; they may act wantonly, in response to first-order desires concerning which they have no volitions of the second order, more or less frequently.

The fact that a wanton has no second-order volitions does not mean that each of his first-order desires is translated heedlessly and at once into action. He may have no opportunity to act in accordance with some of his desires. Moreover, the translation of his desires into action may be delayed or precluded either by conflicting desires of the first order or by the intervention of deliberation. For a wanton may possess and employ rational faculties of a high order. Nothing in the concept of a wanton implies that he cannot reason or that he cannot deliberate concerning how to do what he wants to do. What distinguishes the rational wanton from other rational agents is that he is not concerned with the desirability of his desires themselves. He ignores the question of what his will is to be. Not only does he pursue whatever course of action he is most strongly

inclined to pursue, but he does not care which of his inclinations is the strongest.

Thus a rational creature, who reflects upon the suitability to his desires of one course of action or another, may nonetheless be a wanton. In maintaining that the essence of being a person lies not in reason but in will, I am far from suggesting that a creature without reason may be a person. For it is only in virtue of his rational capacities that a person is capable of becoming critically aware of his own will and of forming volitions of the second order. The structure of a person's will presupposes, accordingly, that he is a rational being.

The distinction between a person and a wanton may be illustrated by the difference between two narcotics addicts. Let us suppose that the physiological condition accounting for the addiction is the same in both men, and that both succumb inevitably to their periodic desires for the drug to which they are addicted. One of the addicts hates his addiction and always struggles desperately, although to no avail, against its thrust. He tries everything that he thinks might enable him to overcome his desires for the drug. But these desires are too powerful for him to withstand, and invariably, in the end, they conquer him. He is an unwilling addict, helplessly violated by his own desires.

The unwilling addict has conflicting first-order desires: he wants to take the drug and also wants to refrain from taking it. In addition to these first-order desires, however, he has a volition of the second order. He is not neutral with regard to the conflict between his desire to take the drug and his desire to refrain from taking it. It is the latter desire, and not the former, that he wants to constitute his will; it is the latter desire, rather than the former, that he wants to be effective and to provide the purpose that he will seek to realize in what he actually does.

The other addict is a wanton. His actions reflect the economy of his first-order desires, without his being concerned whether the desires that move him to act are desires by which he wants to be moved to act. If he encounters problems in obtaining the drug or in administering it to himself, his responses to his urges to take it may involve deliberation. But it never occurs to him to consider whether he wants the relations among his desires to result in his having the will he has. The wanton addict may be an animal, and thus incapable of being concerned about his will. In any event he is, in respect of his wanton lack of concern, no different from an animal.

The second of these addicts may suffer a first-order conflict similar to the first-order conflict suffered by the first. Whether he is human or not, the wanton may (perhaps due to conditioning) both want to take the drug and want to refrain from taking it. Unlike the unwilling addict, however, he does not prefer that one of his conflicting desires should be paramount over the other; he does not prefer that one first-order desire rather than the other should constitute his will. It would be misleading to say that he is neutral as to the conflict between his desires, since this would suggest that he regards them as equally acceptable. Since he has no identity apart from his first-order desires, it is true neither that he prefers one to the other nor that he prefers not to take sides.

It makes a difference to the unwilling addict, who is a person, which of his conflicting first-order desires wins out. Both desires are his, to be sure; and whether he finally takes the drug or finally succeeds in refraining from taking it, he acts to satisfy what is in a literal sense his own desire. In either case he does something he himself wants to do, and he does it not because of some external influence whose aim happens to coincide with his own but because of his desire to do it. The unwilling addict identifies himself, however, through the formation of a second-order volition, with one rather than with the other of his conflicting first-order desires. He makes one of them more truly his own and, in so doing, he withdraws himself from the other. It is in virtue of this identification and withdrawal, accomplished through the formation of

a second-order volition, that the unwilling addict may meaningfully make the analytically puzzling statements that the force moving him to take the drug is a force other than his own, and that it is not of his own free will but rather against his will that this force moves him to take it.

The wanton addict cannot or does not care which of his conflicting first-order desires wins out. His lack of concern is not due to his inability to find a convincing basis for preference. It is due either to his lack of the capacity for reflection or to his mindless indifference to the enterprise of evaluating his own desires and motives. There is only one issue in the struggle to which his first-order conflict may lead: whether the one or the other of his conflicting desires is the stronger. Since he is moved by both desires, he will not be altogether satisfied by what he does no matter which of them is effective. But it makes no difference *to him* whether his craving or his aversion gets the upper hand. He has no stake in the conflict between them and so, unlike the unwilling addict, he can neither win nor lose the struggle in which he is engaged. When a *person* acts, the desire by which he is moved is either the will he wants or a will he wants to be without. When a *wanton* acts, it is neither.

III.

There is a very close relationship between the capacity for forming second-order volitions and another capacity that is essential to persons—one that has often been considered a distinguishing mark of the human condition. It is only because a person has volitions of the second order that he is capable both of enjoying and of lacking freedom of the will. The concept of a person is not only, then, the concept of a type of entity that has both first-order desires and volitions of the second order. It can also be construed as the concept of a type of entity for whom the freedom of its will may be a problem. This concept excludes all wantons, both infrahuman and human, since they fail to satisfy an essential condition for the enjoyment of freedom of the will. And it excludes those suprahuman beings, if any, whose wills are necessarily free.

Just what kind of freedom is the freedom of the will? This question calls for an identification of the special area of human experience to which the concept of freedom of the will, as distinct from the concepts of other sorts of freedom, is particularly germane. In dealing with it, my aim will be primarily to locate the problem with which a person is most immediately concerned when he is concerned with the freedom of his will.

According to one familiar philosophical tradition, being free is fundamentally a matter of doing what one wants to do. Now the notion of an agent who does what he wants to do is by no means an altogether clear one: both the doing and the wanting, and the appropriate relation between them as well, require elucidation. But although its focus needs to be sharpened and its formulation refined, I believe that this notion does capture at least part of what is implicit in the idea of an agent who *acts* freely. It misses entirely, however, the peculiar content of the quite different idea of an agent whose *will* is free.

We do not suppose that animals enjoy freedom of the will, although we recognize that an animal may be free to run in whatever direction it wants. Thus, having the freedom to do what one wants to do is not a sufficient condition of having a free will. It is not a necessary condition either. For to deprive someone of his freedom of action is not necessarily to undermine the freedom of his will. When an agent is aware that there are certain things he is not free to do, this doubtless affects his desires and limits the range of choices he can make. But suppose that someone, without being aware of it, has in fact lost or been deprived of his freedom of action. Even though he is no longer free to do what he wants to do, his will may remain as free as it was before. Despite the fact that he is not free to translate his desires into actions or to act according to the determinations of his will, he may still form those desires and make those determinations as freely as if his freedom of action had not been impaired.

When we ask whether a person's will is free we are not asking whether he is in a position to translate his first-order desires into actions. That is the question of whether he is free to do as he pleases. The question of the freedom of his will does not concern the relation between what he does and what he wants to do. Rather, it concerns his desires themselves. But what question about them is it?

It seems to me both natural and useful to construe the question of whether a person's will is free in close analogy to the question of whether an agent enjoys freedom of action. Now freedom of action is (roughly, at least) the freedom to do what one wants to do. Analogously, then, the statement that a person enjoys freedom of the will means (also roughly) that he is free to want what he wants to want. More precisely, it means that he is free to will what he wants to will, or to have the will he wants. Just as the question about the freedom of an agent's action has to do with whether it is the action he wants to perform, so the question about the freedom of his will has to do with whether it is the will he wants to have.

It is in securing the conformity of his will to his second-order volitions, then, that a person exercises freedom of the will. And it is in the discrepancy between his will and his second-order volitions, or in his awareness that their coincidence is not his own doing but only a happy chance, that a person who does not have this freedom feels its lack. The unwilling addict's will is not free. This is shown by the fact that it is not the will he wants. It is also true, though in a different way, that the will of the wanton addict is not free. The wanton addict neither has the will he wants nor has a will that differs from the will he wants. Since he has no volitions of the second order, the freedom of his will cannot be a problem for him. He lacks it, so to speak, by default.

People are generally far more complicated than my sketchy account of the structure of a person's will may suggest. There is as much opportunity for ambivalence, conflict, and self-deception with regard to desires of the second order, for example, as there is with regard to first-order desires. If there is an unresolved conflict among someone's second-order desires, then he is in danger of having no second-order volition; for unless this conflict is resolved, he has no preference concerning which of his first-order desires is to be his will. This condition, if it is so severe that it prevents him from identifying himself in a sufficiently decisive way with *any* of his conflicting first-order desires, destroys him as a person. For it either tends to paralyze his will and to keep him from acting at all, or it tends to remove him from his will so that his will operates without his participation. In both cases he becomes, like the unwilling addict though in a different way, a helpless bystander to the forces that move him.

Another complexity is that a person may have, especially if his second-order desires are in conflict, desires and volitions of a higher order than the second. There is no theoretical limit to the length of the series of desires of higher and higher orders; nothing except common sense and, perhaps, a saving fatigue prevents an individual from obsessively refusing to identify himself with any of his desires until he forms a desire of the next higher order. The tendency to generate such a series of acts of forming desires, which would be a case of humanization run wild, also leads toward the destruction of a person.

It is possible, however, to terminate such a series of acts without cutting it off arbitrarily. When a person identifies himself *decisively* with one of his first-order desires, this commitment "resounds" throughout the potentially endless array of higher orders. Consider a person who, without reservation or conflict, wants to be motivated by the desire to concentrate on his work. The fact that his second-order volition to be moved by this desire is a decisive one means that there is no room for questions concerning the pertinence of desires or volitions of higher

orders. Suppose the person is asked whether he wants to want to want to concentrate on his work. He can properly insist that this question concerning a third-order desire does not arise. It would be a mistake to claim that, because he has not considered whether he wants the second-order volition he has formed, he is indifferent to the question of whether it is with this volition or with some other that he wants his will to accord. The decisiveness of the commitment he has made means that he has decided that no further question about his second-order volition, at any higher order, remains to be asked. It is relatively unimportant whether we explain this by saying that this commitment implicitly generates an endless series of confirming desires of higher orders, or by saying that the commitment is tantamount to a dissolution of the pointedness of all questions concerning higher orders of desire.

Examples such as the one concerning the unwilling addict may suggest that volitions of the second order, or of higher orders, must be formed deliberately and that a person characteristically struggles to ensure that they are satisfied. But the conformity of a person's will to his higher-order volitions may be far more thoughtless and spontaneous than this. Some people are naturally moved by kindness when they want to be kind, and by nastiness when they want to be nasty, without any explicit forethought and without any need for energetic self-control. Others are moved by nastiness when they want to be kind and by kindness when they intend to be nasty, equally without forethought and without active resistance to these violations of their higher-order desires. The enjoyment of freedom comes easily to some. Others must struggle to achieve it.

IV.

My theory concerning the freedom of the will accounts easily for our disinclination to allow that this freedom is enjoyed by the members of any species inferior to our own. It also satisfies another condition that must be met by any such theory, by making it apparent why the freedom of the will should be regarded as desirable. The enjoyment of a free will means the satisfaction of certain desires—desires of the second or of higher orders—whereas its absence means their frustration. The satisfactions at stake are those which accrue to a person of whom it may be said that his will is his own. The corresponding frustrations are those suffered by a person of whom it may be said that he is estranged from himself, or that he finds himself a helpless or a passive bystander to the forces that move him. A person who is free to do what he wants to do may yet not be in a position to have the will he wants. Suppose, however, that he enjoys both freedom of action and freedom of the will. Then he is not only free to do what he wants to do; he is also free to want what he wants to want. It seems to me that he has, in that case, all the freedom it is possible to desire or to conceive. There are other good things in life, and he may not possess some of them. But there is nothing in the way of freedom that he lacks.

It is far from clear that certain other theories of the freedom of the will meet these elementary but essential conditions: that it be understandable why we desire this freedom and why we refuse to ascribe it to animals. Consider, for example, Roderick Chisholm's quaint version of the doctrine that human freedom entails an absence of causal determination.[1] Whenever a person performs a free action, according to Chisholm, it's a miracle. The motion of a person's hand, when the person moves it, is the outcome of a series of physical causes; but some event in this series, "and presumably one of those that took place within the brain, was caused by the agent and not by any other events" (18). A free agent has, therefore, "a prerogative which some would attribute only to God: each of us, when we act, is a prime mover unmoved" (23).

This account fails to provide any basis for doubting that animals of subhuman species enjoy the freedom it defines. Chisholm says nothing that makes it seem less likely that a rabbit performs a miracle when it moves its leg than that a man does so when he moves his hand. But why, in any case, should anyone *care* whether he can interrupt the natural order of causes in the way Chisholm describes? Chisholm offers no reason for believing that there is a discernible difference between the experience of man who miraculously initiates a series of causes when he moves his hand and a man who moves his hand without any such breach of the normal causal sequence. There appears to be no concrete basis for preferring to be involved in the one state of affairs rather than in the other.

It is generally supposed that, in addition to satisfying the two conditions I have mentioned, a satisfactory theory of the freedom of the will necessarily provides an analysis of one of the conditions of moral responsibility. The most common recent approach to the problem of understanding the freedom of the will has been, indeed, to inquire what is entailed by the assumption that someone is morally responsible for what he has done. In my view, however, the relation between moral responsibility and the freedom of the will has been very widely misunderstood. It is not true that a person is morally responsible for what he has done only if his will was free when he did it. He may be morally responsible for having done it even though his will was not free at all.

A person's will is free only if he is free to have the will he wants. This means that, with regard to any of his first-order desires, he is free either to make that desire his will or to make some other first-order desire his will instead. Whatever his will, then, the will of the person whose will is free could have been otherwise; he could have done otherwise than to constitute his will as he did. It is a vexed question just how "he could have done otherwise" is to be understood in contexts such as this one. But although this question is important to the theory of freedom, it has no bearing on the theory of moral responsibility. For the assumption that a person is morally responsible for what he has done does not entail that the person was in a position to have whatever will he wanted.

This assumption *does* entail that the person did what he did freely, or that he did it of his own free will. It is a mistake, however, to believe that someone acts freely only when he is free to do whatever he wants or that he acts of his own free will only if his will is free. Suppose that a person has done what he wanted to do, that he did it because he wanted to do it, and that the will by which he was moved when he did it was his will because it was the will he wanted. Then he did it freely and of his own free will. Even supposing that he could have done otherwise, he would not have done otherwise; and even supposing that he could have had a different will, he would not have wanted his will to differ from what it was. Moreover, since the will that moved him when he acted was his will because he wanted it to be, he cannot claim that his will was forced upon him or that he was a passive bystander to its constitution. Under these conditions, it is quite irrelevant to the evaluation of his moral responsibility to inquire whether the alternatives that he opted against were actually available to him.

In illustration, consider a third kind of addict. Suppose that his addiction has the same physiological basis and the same irresistible thrust as the addictions of the unwilling and wanton addicts, but that he is altogether delighted with his condition. He is a willing addict, who would not have things any other way. If the grip of his addiction should somehow weaken, he would do whatever he could to reinstate it; if his desire for the drug should begin to fade, he would take steps to renew its intensity.

The willing addict's will is not free, for his desire to take the drug will be effective regardless of whether or not he wants this desire to constitute his will. But when he takes the drug, he takes it freely and of his own free will. I am inclined to understand his situation as involving the overdetermination of his first-order desire to take the drug. This desire is his effective desire because he is physiologically addicted. But it is his effective desire also because he wants it to be.

His will is outside his control, but, by his second-order desire that his desire for the drug should be effective, he has made this will his own. Given that it is therefore not only because of his addiction that his desire for the drug is effective, he may be morally responsible for taking the drug.

My conception of the freedom of the will appears to be neutral with regard to the problem of determinism. It seems conceivable that it should be causally determined that a person is free to want what he wants to want. If this is conceivable, then it might be causally determined that a person enjoys free will. There is no more than an innocuous appearance of paradox in the proposition that it is determined, ineluctably and by forces beyond their control, that certain people have free wills and that others do not. There is no incoherence in the proposition that some agency other than a person's own is responsible (even *morally* responsible) for the fact that he enjoys or fails to enjoy freedom of the will. It is possible that a person should be morally responsible for what he does of his own free will and that some other person should also be morally responsible for his having done it.

On the other hand, it seems conceivable that it should come about by chance that a person is free to have the will he wants. If this is conceivable, then it might be a matter of chance that certain people enjoy freedom of the will and that certain others do not. Perhaps it is also conceivable, as a number of philosophers believe, for states of affairs to come about in a way other than by chance or as the outcome of a sequence of natural causes. If it is indeed conceivable for the relevant states of affairs to come about in some third way, then it is also possible that a person should in that third way come to enjoy the freedom of the will.

Note

1. "Freedom and Action," in K. Lehrer, ed., *Freedom and Determinism* (New York: Random House, 1966), pp. 11–44.

Study Questions

1. How does Frankfurt distinguish between choosing freely and having freedom of the will? Do you agree that there is a difference?

2. Frankfurt ties freedom of the will to second-order volitions. What are these? He also addresses the worry that we could have third, fourth, or fifth (and so on) desires that conflict with these second-order volitions. What does he say in response to this worry? Is his response convincing?

3. What, according to Frankfurt, is a wanton? Do you think any existing human beings are wantons, or are wantons just theoretical possibilities?

Surveying Freedom: Folk Intuitions about Free Will and Moral Responsibility   6.5

EDDY NAHMIAS, STEPHEN MORRIS, THOMAS NADELHOFFER, AND JASON TURNER

EDDY NAHMIAS (1969-) is an Associate Professor in the Philosophy Department and Neuroscience Institute at Georgia State University. His research is centered on questions of human agency; he is currently working on a book entitled *Rediscovering Free Will*. The paper excerpted here represents collaboration with Stephen Morris (1970-), Assistant Professor of Philosophy at the College of Staten Island (CUNY); Thomas Nadelhoffer, Assistant Professor of Philosophy at Dickinson College; and Jason Turner (1978–), Assistant Professor of Philosophy at the University of Leeds. The paper argues that the philosophical debate about free will is tied to the ordinary concept. Many philosophers claim that the folk intuitively hold that free will conflicts with causal determinism. The paper presents experiments that suggest that this is not the case. After discussing their conclusions, Nahmias and his colleagues provide alternative ways to account for their data and make recommendations for pursuing similar empirical work in the future. Their highly influential findings have motivated research programs that explore folk intuitions about free will and moral responsibility, as well as the philosophical import of those intuitions.

1. INTRODUCTION: MOTIVATING THE PROJECT OF TESTING FOLK INTUITIONS

...Philosophers disagree about the proper role that folk concepts, common sense, and prephilosophical intuitions should play in shaping our philosophical ideas and theories. Whereas some have dismissively viewed the beliefs and intuitions of non-philosophers with either suspicion or scorn, others have attempted to refute speculative philosophical theories—

E. Nahmias, S. Morris, T. Nadelhoffer, and J. Turner, "Surveying Freedom: Folk Intuitions about Free Will and Moral Responsibility," *Philosophical Psychology*, 18.

such as skepticism or idealism—by appealing to what they take to be our commonsense intuitions. Such intuitions play a conspicuous role in the free will debate, where philosophers often motivate their position by claiming that it is commonsensical, fits with ordinary intuitions, accounts for our practices of attributing moral responsibility, and captures a conception of freedom we value. However, few philosophers have tried to ascertain what these commonsense intuitions actually are. More often than not, philosophers are content to place their own intuitions into the mouths of the folk in a way that supports their own position—neglecting to verify whether their intuitions agree with what the majority of non-philosophers actually think.

This paper represents a preliminary attempt to correct for this oversight. In this section we describe our project and the motivation for it. We then discuss two studies we performed to test folk intuitions about free will, moral responsibility, and the ability to do otherwise (section 2). We then consider some of the difficulties facing this kind of empirical research and discuss how such research might impact the philosophical debates about free will (section 3). We hope our research will spark further interest in the examination of ordinary people's intuitions about free will and related concepts and in developing methods to study such intuitions.

We suggest that the best way to arrive at a sound—and empirically accurate, rather than merely speculative—understanding of folk intuitions is to conduct surveys of non-philosophers in an effort to generate the much needed data. [...] Our project can thus be viewed as part of a gathering storm of "experimental philosophy"—recent attempts to empirically test the claims philosophers make about folk intuitions in epistemology, ethics, and action theory. In this paper, we expand the scope of this novel, and we believe illuminating, approach to philosophy by applying it to the free will debate. [...] There is substantial disagreement among philosophers about what ordinary people's intuitions are, as

we'll illustrate shortly. This disagreement likely stems from the philosophers' own divergent intuitions. We suspect that this conflict indicates that philosophers' intuitions have been corrupted by their theories, making it uncertain whether their own case is "typical" and all the more necessary to survey the intuitions of pre-theoretical folk.

While compatibilists believe we can have free will and be morally responsible even if causal determinism is true, incompatibilists maintain that the existence of free will entails the falsity of causal determinism. Libertarians are incompatibilists who think we have free will; skeptics are incompatibilists who think we don't. To say that these parties find themselves in a stalemate would be an understatement. One indication of how intractable the debate has become—and how entrenched the respective parties are—is the fact that so many philosophers claim that their own position has the most intuitive appeal and best fits our ordinary conception of free will and our practices of responsibility attribution.

We find, on the one hand, incompatibilists who suggest that their view is commonsensical and that compatibilism is counter-intuitive [...] By making these sorts of claims, incompatibilists are presumably trying to situate the burden of proof on compatibilists—demanding that they explain how compatibilist theories of free will could satisfy our ordinary notions—while at the same time motivating the metaphysically demanding libertarian theories that some incompatibilists defend (e.g., agent causation) and that other incompatibilists (skeptics) attack as impossible or implausible.

On the other hand, compatibilists also appeal to commonsense intuitions, suggesting that the folk do not demand the libertarian conception of free will, which requires an ability to do otherwise purportedly incompatible with determinism. [...] Frankfurt-style cases (Frankfurt, 1969) are designed to bring to light the intuition that the freedom necessary for moral responsibility does not require the ability to do otherwise and hence is compatible with determinism.[1] Susan

Wolf (1990) motivates her compatibilist "Reason View" in part by claiming that it "seems to accord with and account for the whole set of our intuitions about responsibility" (p. 89). [...]

Obviously, to the extent that incompatibilists and compatibilists claim that their own respective positions best accord with and account for our prephilosophical intuitions, they cannot both be right. Moreover, they can't really claim to know if they are right, since no one has systematically tested to see what people's prephilosophical intuitions are. [...] It is therefore important to determine the content of these intuitions. However, finding an adequate method for testing such intuitions is no easy task. Here we discuss our own attempts to collect data on folk intuitions about free will and moral responsibility, some difficulties facing this sort of research, and suggestions for further research. We also examine the question of what role such data about folk intuitions should play in the philosophical debate.

In our attempts to get at folk intuitions, we employed thought-experiment scenarios to see how ordinary people respond to different compatibilist and incompatibilist hypotheses. This data is important because any adequate philosophical analysis of free will should be, as Alfred Mele (2001) suggests, "anchored by commonsense judgments" about particular cases—after all, if a philosophical analysis of free will runs entirely afoul of what the majority of non-philosophers say, this analysis "runs the risk of having nothing more than a philosophical fiction as its subject matter" (p. 27). In this respect we also agree with Jackson (1998) that the fundamental issue in the free will debate should be "whether free action according to our ordinary conception, or something suitably close to our ordinary conception, exists and is compatible with determinism" and that to identify our ordinary conception we must "appeal to what seems to us most obvious and central about free action...as revealed by our intuitions about possible cases" (p. 31).

Consider, for instance, the aforementioned claims that the majority of nonphilosophers have incompatibilist intuitions. On the surface, this is a straightforward empirical claim that entails certain predictions about how people would respond to various thought experiments. So, for example, if it were true that most nonphilosophers do share the incompatibilists' intuitions, then we should expect that if they were given a thought experiment involving an (otherwise ordinary) agent in a deterministic scenario, a majority of them would not attribute free will and moral responsibility to the agent. Conversely, those compatibilists who claim that the folk share their intuitions should predict that a majority of people would attribute free will and moral responsibility to such an agent. Yet, until a concerted effort is made to probe folk intuitions and judgments via systematic psychological experiments, the truth of these sorts of empirical claims goes unchecked.

We are not, however, suggesting that discovering what folk intuitions really are would resolve the free will problem. There are various responses either side could make if it turned out their view did not fit with ordinary intuitions, some of which we'll discuss below. Nonetheless, if a philosophical theory does turn out to be privileged by the endorsement of the folk, that would seem to position the burden of proof on the shoulders of those who argue contrary to folk intuitions. If it turns out that a significant majority of people make judgments that support either compatibilist or incompatibilist views, that would at least give "squatters' rights" to whichever position has such support. At least, this seems to be the idea expressed by those incompatibilists and compatibilists quoted above who claim to have commonsense intuition on their side. [...]

In our view, the best way to identify whether people have the intuition that determinism conflicts with free will is to survey laypersons who have not studied—and hence have not been influenced by—the relevant philosophical arguments about free will. Such people should be presented with scenarios portraying determinism and then

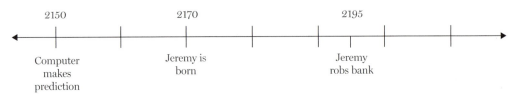

FIGURE 1 Jeremy Case 1: Bank Robbing Scenario.

asked whether they believe an agent acts in such a scenario of his or her own free will and is morally responsible. Negative responses would indicate the intuition that determinism conflicts with free will and responsibility; positive responses would indicate that people do not have this incompatibilist intuition. By collecting such data we hope to shed light on ordinary concepts and intuitions in a way that will be useful to all of the parties in the free will debate. However, as we will discuss in section 3, surveying intuitions about free will and determinism poses some particularly difficult problems. And while we have attempted to address some of these problems, we nevertheless view our studies as preliminary and exploratory and hope they will generate interest in further research. [...]

2. STUDIES ON FOLK INTUITIONS

To find out what the freedom-relevant intuitions of the folk really are we performed a number of empirical studies. These studies test the incompatibilist prediction that most people will judge that agents in a deterministic scenario do not act of their own free will and are not morally responsible for their actions.[2]

2.1. Study 1: Jeremy Cases

In some initial surveys we found that people do not understand the concept "determinism" in the technical way philosophers use it. Rather, they tend to define "determinism" in contrast with free will. This result alone, we suggest, does not bolster the incompatibilist position. It does

not suggest that people consider "determinism," as defined in (one of) the technical ways philosophers define it, to be incompatible with free will or moral responsibility. Rather, it seems that many people think "determinism" means the opposite of free will, as suggested by the phrase "the problem of free will and determinism."[3]

So, in order to test whether folk judgments support incompatibilist intuitions, we developed thought experiments describing deterministic scenarios, roughly in the philosophical sense of the concept, without begging any questions by using the term "determinism" or describing determinism as involving constraint, fatalism, or reductionism. The first survey we ran uses a Laplacean notion of determinism.[4] Participants read the following scenario in [Figure 1] (including the timeline) and answered two questions about it (then, on the back of the questionnaire, they responded to a manipulation check, were invited to explain their answer, and offered some demographic information).

> Scenario: Imagine that in the next century we discover all the laws of nature, and we build a supercomputer which can deduce from these laws of nature and from the current state of everything in the world exactly what will be happening in the world at any future time. It can look at everything about the way the world is and predict everything about how it will be with 100% accuracy. Suppose that such a supercomputer existed, and it looks at the state of the universe at a certain time on March 25, 2150 AD, 20 years before Jeremy Hall is born. The computer then deduces from this information and the laws of nature that Jeremy will definitely

rob Fidelity Bank at 6:00 pm on January 26, 2195. As always, the supercomputer's prediction is correct; Jeremy robs Fidelity Bank at 6:00 pm on January 26, 2195.

For this study (and those discussed below), participants were undergraduates who had not studied the free will problem. [...] The results indicate that a significant majority of participants (76%) judged that Jeremy robs the bank of his own free will.

We wondered whether some people were inclined to judge that Jeremy acts freely because he performs a blameworthy action. Perhaps their emotional response primed them to hold him responsible for robbing the bank, and this—combined with a tacit belief that responsible actions must be performed of one's own free will—led some participants to answer in the way they did, masking the effect of the determinism in this case (i.e., case 1, "negative action"). To test for this possibility, we ran two more sets of surveys with identical wording except that in one case (case 2, "positive action") Jeremy performs the praiseworthy act of saving a child from a burning building, and in another (case 3, "neutral action") he goes jogging.[5]

However, in both these cases participants' responses closely tracked those from the blameworthy case: 68% said Jeremy saves the child of his own free will, and 79% said he goes jogging of his own free will. Hence, the moral status of an action, and any emotional responses it evokes, appeared to have no significant effect on judgments of free will. The majority of participants judged that Jeremy acts of his own free will in this deterministic scenario regardless of the type of action involved (see [Figure 2]).

In order to test directly whether people judge that an agent is morally responsible for his actions in a deterministic scenario, we asked participants (in case 4): "Do you think that, when Jeremy robs the bank, he is morally blameworthy for it?" and (in case 5): "Do you think that, when Jeremy saves the child, he is morally praiseworthy

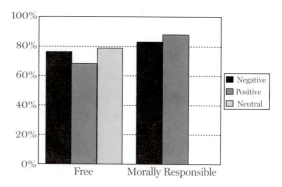

FIGURE 2 Judgments of Free Will and Moral Responsibility. Percentage of participants who judged Jeremy acted of his own free will when he robbed a bank (negative), saved a child (positive), and went jogging (neutral), as compared with percentage of participants who judged Jeremy morally responsible when he robbed a bank (negative) and saved a child (positive).

for it?" Results from these participants closely tracked those offered by participants who had responded to questions about free will (though a slightly higher proportion of participants judged that Jeremy is morally responsible than had those who judged that he acts of his own free will): 83% judged he was blameworthy in the negative case and 88% judged he was praiseworthy in the positive case....

...This consistency accords well with philosophers' claims that judgments about free will are closely related to judgments about moral responsibility.

Finally, we examined whether people's judgments of an agent's ability to choose otherwise in a deterministic scenario would track judgments about his free will and moral responsibility, since philosophers disagree both about whether determinism conflicts with people's ordinary conception of the ability to do (or choose) otherwise and also about whether free will and moral responsibility require the ability to do otherwise. In these cases, participants were asked—again, imagining the scenarios were actual—whether or not Jeremy could have chosen not to rob the bank (case 6), whether he could have chosen not to save the child (case 7), or whether he could have chosen not to go jogging (case 8).

In the blameworthy variation, participants' judgments of Jeremy's ability to choose otherwise (ACO) did in fact track the judgments of free will and responsibility we collected, with 67% responding that Jeremy could have chosen not to rob the bank. However, in the praiseworthy case, judgments of ACO were significantly different from judgments of his free will and responsibility: Whereas a large majority of participants had judged that Jeremy is free and responsible for saving the child, a majority (62%) answered "no" to the question: "Do you think he could have chosen not to save the child?" Finally, in the morally neutral case, judgments of ACO were also significantly different from judgments of free will—again, whereas a large majority had judged that Jeremy goes jogging of his own free will, a majority (57%) answered "no" to the question: "Do you think he could have chosen not to go jogging?" (See [Figure 3].)

We offer two related interpretations of these interesting results. First, the results may suggest that some folk have Frankfurtian intuitions (see note 5). That is, they think, as suggested by Frankfurt (1969), that an agent's action may be free and responsible without the agent's having the ability to do otherwise—though this trend did not appear with the blameworthy actions.[6] So perhaps these intuitions are more pronounced regarding agents who perform praiseworthy (or morally neutral) actions. This would support Wolf's (1980) asymmetry thesis—roughly, that we tend to judge an agent to be blameworthy only if we believe he could do otherwise, but we are willing to judge an agent to be praiseworthy even if we believe he could not do otherwise.[7] In any case, it appears that judgments of free will and responsibility can diverge from judgments about the ability to do otherwise.

The main finding in Study 1 is that most people do not judge determinism—at least as described in this scenario—to be incompatible

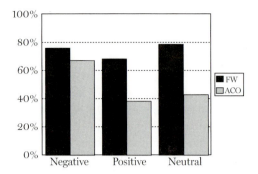

FIGURE 3 Comparison of Free Will and ACO Judgments. Comparison of percentage of participants who judged that Jeremy acted of his own free will (FW) to those who judged that he could have chosen otherwise (ACO) in robbing a bank (negative), saving a child (positive), and going jogging (neutral).

with an agent's acting of his own free will or with his being morally responsible for his actions.[8] Repeatedly, we found that the number of participants making judgments inconsistent with incompatibilist intuitions is two to three times greater than the number making judgments indicative of incompatibilist intuitions.[9]

2.2. Study 2: Fred and Barney Cases

One might object that in the Jeremy cases, by trying to avoid a question-begging description of determinism, we did not make the deterministic nature of the scenario salient enough to the participants.[10] Perhaps they were more focused on the fact that Jeremy's actions were predicted by the supercomputer than the fact that the prediction was made based on deterministic laws. (If so, it would still be an important result that most people do not judge such predictability to conflict with free will and responsibility.[11]) To explore this possibility, we developed another scenario that, we believe, presents determinism in a different and more salient way in that it points out that the agents' behavior is sufficiently caused by factors beyond their control (i.e., genes and upbringing):

Scenario. Imagine there is a world where the beliefs and values of every person are caused completely by the combination of one's genes and one's environment. For instance, one day in this world, two identical twins, named Fred and Barney, are born to a mother who puts them up for adoption. Fred is adopted by the Jerksons and Barney is adopted by the Kindersons. In Fred's case, his genes and his upbringing by the selfish Jerkson family have caused him to value money above all else and to believe it is OK to acquire money however you can. In Barney's case, his (identical) genes and his upbringing by the kindly Kinderson family have caused him to value honesty above all else and to believe one should always respect others' property. Both Fred and Barney are intelligent individuals who are capable of deliberating about what they do.

One day Fred and Barney each happen to find a wallet containing $1000 and the identification of the owner (neither man knows the owner). Each man is sure there is nobody else around. After deliberation, Fred Jerkson, because of his beliefs and values, keeps the money. After deliberation, Barney Kinderson, because of his beliefs and values, returns the wallet to its owner.

Given that, in this world, one's genes and environment completely cause one's beliefs and values, it is true that if Fred had been adopted by the Kindersons, he would have had the beliefs and values that would have caused him to return the wallet; and if Barney had been adopted by the Jerksons, he would have had the beliefs and values that would have caused him to keep the wallet.

Despite this seemingly potent description of complete causation by genes and environment, a significant majority of participants (76%) judged both that Fred kept the wallet of his own free will and Barney returned it of his own free will (case 9).[12] This response pattern was very similar to the pattern of participants' judgments about free will in the Jeremy cases, suggesting that this scenario probed similar intuitions about the relationship between deterministic causation and free will. We also tested whether participants judge that Fred is "morally blameworthy for keeping the wallet" and that Barney is "morally

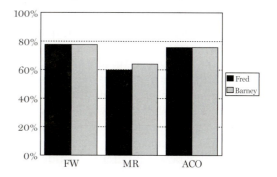

FIGURE 4 Judgments of Free Will, Moral Responsibility and ACO. Percentage of subjects who judged that Fred and Barney acted of their own free will (FW), were morally responsible for their actions (MR), and could have chosen otherwise (ACO).

praiseworthy for returning the wallet" (case 10). For most participants (94%) these judgments were consistent, and the response patterns were not significantly different from the judgments we collected about free will: 60% judged that Fred is blameworthy and 64% judged that Barney is praiseworthy.[13] Finally, we tested whether participants judge that Fred and Barney could do otherwise than they did (case 11). Again, results closely tracked judgments of freedom and responsibility, with 76% of participants responding that both Fred and Barney could have done otherwise.[14] (See [Figure 4].)

2.3. Discussion

We suggest that—in the absence of further studies contradicting our results or alternative explanations of them—these studies suggest that ordinary people's pre-theoretical intuitions about free will and responsibility do not support incompatibilism. It appears to be false—or certainly too hasty—to claim that "most ordinary persons...believe there is some kind of conflict between freedom and determinism" (Kane, 1999, p. 218), and that "We come to the table, nearly all of us, as pretheoretic incompatibilists" (Ekstrom, 2002, p. 310). Rather, when pretheoretic participants considered an agent (Jeremy) whose action is unerringly predicted based on the state of the universe before his birth and the laws of nature, a significant majority judged that the agent acts of his own free will and is morally responsible for the action, and this tendency shows up when the action in question is morally negative, positive, or neutral. Hence, most participants did not recognize an incompatibility between determinism described in these terms and free will or moral responsibility. Furthermore, when participants considered agents (Fred and Barney) whose beliefs, values, and actions are completely caused by their genes and upbringing, a significant majority judged that these agents act of their own free will and are morally responsible for their actions. Hence, most participants did not recognize an incompatibility between determinism described in these terms and free will or moral responsibility. Judgments about the ability of agents in a deterministic scenario to do or choose otherwise were more complex and, given their important role in the philosophical debates, clearly demand more research.[15]

Notice that, by claiming that most people do not express incompatibilist intuitions in these cases, we are not endorsing the stronger claim that the folk do have compatibilist intuitions. To be sure, compatibilists should take comfort from results suggesting that their opponents do not have the support of pre-theoretical intuitions on their side. Our results, however, were not unanimous—we consistently found a non-negligible minority of participants offering incompatibilist judgments. Such results may support the idea that individuals have conflicting intuitions about free will or moral responsibility. Or they may indicate that intuitions vary significantly between different individuals who themselves have consistent intuitions.[16]

Nonetheless, we think that our results place the burden of proof on the shoulders of incompatibilists. Incompatibilists are especially apt to cite folk intuitions in support of their view, in

part because their conception of free will is more metaphysically demanding and therefore requires extra intuitive support to offset the strength of their claims.[17] Put simply: if our ordinary intuitions do not demand indeterminism, then why should our theories? If incompatibilists claim that compatibilism is a "wretched subterfuge," a radical revision of commonsense beliefs, then we recommend that some empirical evidence should be offered to back up this claim.

3. OBJECTIONS, REPLIES, AND PHILOSOPHICAL IMPLICATIONS

Our studies falsified the prediction that most lay persons will express incompatibilist intuitions by judging that agents in a deterministic scenario lack free will and moral responsibility. Again, however, we view these results as preliminary, not conclusive, and hence as motivation for further research on folk intuitions about freedom and responsibility and for further consideration of the role such intuitions should play in the free will debate. One shortcoming of our studies is that they were limited to a college student population. They should be replicated using participants with more diverse educational backgrounds and socio-economic statuses. Ideally, they would also be replicated with participants from other cultures to test whether there are important differences among various cultures' conceptions of free will and moral responsibility. [...][18]

A potential problem more specific to our studies is that the presence of determinism might not have been salient enough in the scenarios. We have already explained why we think it would be problematic to use the word "determinism" to test whether ordinary people have incompatibilist intuitions. But if the description of determinism is overly watered down, then people may simply fail to notice its presence and therefore botch the (supposed) inference to the conclusion that agents in the scenario are not free and responsible. We agree that the more salient determinism is in the scenarios, the more significant the results would be (see Black & Tweedale, 2002). Amping up determinism, however, is not as easy as it might seem. [...]

Attempts to make determinism more salient without teaching participants technical notions run the risk of adding new factors that may themselves mask whatever effects determinism has on people's judgments with more obvious threats to free will. For instance, determinism would be very salient if we changed the Jeremy scenario so that his action was caused by a brilliant neuroscientist who manipulated the initial conditions of Jeremy's life in a way that she knew would inevitably lead to his specific action. Here, the deterministic causation is clear—but so is the presence of a "covert controller." If participants then judged that Jeremy did not act freely or was not morally responsible for his act, we would not be able to determine whether it was because their intuitions about free will and moral responsibility are responding to the determinism in the scenario or to the presence of an active manipulator.[19] It would also beg the question to describe determinism as entailing that the agent could not do otherwise, since some compatibilists disagree with incompatibilists about whether the ordinary conception of "can" relevant to freedom and responsibility is inconsistent with determinism. [...]

With that being said, if one is able to find a way to increase the salience of determinism without masking it with a different free-will threat, we welcome the attempt. If turning up the volume on the "determinism knob" of the scenarios does cause participants to withdraw their judgments of free will and moral responsibility (and if this is clearly not a result of masking determinism), then we would withdraw our current interpretation of the data. If a more clearly deterministic case does not result in more judgments of unfree and unresponsible, though, our interpretation is strengthened. In any case, the claim that people will withdraw judgments of freedom when determinism is made more

salient is an empirical claim. Philosophers are well positioned to develop the relevant thought experiments to test this claim. But how people will respond to such scenarios cannot be settled from our philosophical La-Z-Boys. This response generalizes to any empirical or methodological objections to our studies. We are not closing the door on the question of whether the folk have incompatibilist intuitions; on the contrary, we are opening the door to further research exploring such questions. [...]

We hope this paper will motivate philosophers in the free will debate to do two things. First, we think philosophers should be more explicit about how they think their theories of free will and moral responsibility align with—and diverge from—people's actual intuitions and practices. And second, to the extent that they claim their theories do align closely with these intuitions and practices, they should be more explicit and careful about their reasons for believing such alignment exists. We are not suggesting that philosophers should make a practice of surveying the folk about every question of interest. They can at least, however, perform the following thought experiment: "How would I determine whether the folk would agree with this particular claim about free will and moral responsibility? If it turned out they did agree, what evidential value would that have for the claim? If, on the other hand, it turned out they did not agree, what problems would that raise for the claim, and how might I respond to them? And if it simply does not matter whether or not prephilosophical people would agree with the claim, why is that?" Considering questions like these will help ensure that, as we continue to argue about free will, our arguments will be about more than just a philosophical fiction.

Notes

1. Frankfurt cases aim to pump the intuition that an agent can be responsible for an action even if he could not do otherwise: for instance, if there were a neuroscientist ready to manipulate the agent to

do A if he were not going to do it on his own, then the agent could not do otherwise than A, but if the agent did A on his own without the neuroscientist intervening, it seems the agent is nonetheless responsible for A-ing.

2. We should note that two of the four authors are compatibilists and two are incompatibilists. Every effort was made not to prejudice the data through misleading experimental design, and the diversity of opinions within the team was beneficial to this end (though frustrating at times!). We also sent our surveys to a dozen or so philosophers with various views in the free will debate and received no responses suggesting that the surveys were in any significant sense misleading or problematic.

3. Examples of participants' definitions of "determinism" include: "Being unable to choose," "That people have a set fate," and "The lack of free will." Many others thought it meant "determined," as in "resolute." Fischer (1994, p. 152) predicted that the phrase "causal determinism" may seem threatening to people but that this alone would not indicate they have incompatibilist intuitions.

4. Laplace defines "determinism" in terms of an intelligent being such that if it had complete knowledge of the laws of nature and the current state of the universe, it could know all past events and predict all future events. Van Inwagen's (1983) technical definition of "determinism" is related: a proposition describing the complete state of the universe at one time and the laws of nature logically entails a proposition describing the complete state of the universe at any other time. Laplacean determinism entails van Inwagen determinism, but the converse is not true.

5. For all of these cases we used different sets of participants to avoid any order or interference effects due to participants' attempting to keep their judgments consistent across different cases—i.e., any given participant read just one survey and answered just one experimental question.

6. To test this interpretation, it would be better to have the same participants making judgments about both the ability to do otherwise and free will (or moral responsibility). See Woolfolk et al. (forthcoming) for empirical results suggesting that ordinary people have Frankfurtian intuitions.

7. We suspect that it is particularly difficult to probe intuitions about modal concepts such as the ability

to do otherwise (see note 35). See Turner and Nahmias (2006).

8. Participants' explanations of their answers suggest that some of them even had fledgling compatibilist theories in mind. For instance, some suggested that Jeremy acts freely because no outside forces compel him, because he controls his actions or consciously decides to do them, or because the prediction is based on what he decides to do. (Similarly, some of the minority who judged that Jeremy is unfree offered fledgling incompatibilist arguments.)

9. We should add that in numerous pilot studies as we fine-tuned descriptions of the scenarios, experimental questions, and manipulation checks, we were surprised by the consistency of the results: in almost every set of surveys, 70–85% of participants judged that Jeremy acts of his own free will or that he is morally responsible for his action.

10. We should note that we tried several variations of the wording of the Jeremy case, including one that said, "The computer then deduces from this information and the laws of nature that it is physically impossible for Jeremy to do anything other than to rob Fidelity Bank [save the child, etc.]" and results showed the same trends. [. . .] For further discussion of this concern about the salience of determinism, see section 3.

11. We wonder whether some participants, having reconciled themselves to the problem of God's foreknowledge and free will, were less inclined to see the supercomputer's foreknowledge as a threat to free will. We obtained information about participants' self-reported religiosity, but we have not yet correlated this information with the results.

12. Methods for study 2 were the same as study 1 except that participants answered two experimental questions (one about Fred and one about Barney). Fewer participants judged that the scenario was impossible and fewer missed the manipulation check (three participants who answered differently for Fred and Barney were not included in the analysis of results).

13. Comparison tests show no significant differences between the response pattern of participants in case 9 and the pattern of blameworthy judgments in case 10, or in the response patterns of

participants in case 9 and the pattern of praise-worthy judgments in case 10. Interestingly, a smaller majority of participants in these cases judged that the agents were morally responsible than those judging Jeremy to be morally responsible (in cases 4 and 5).

14. Comparisons between the response patterns of participants in case 8 and those in case 11 were not significantly different. Because we asked the same participants about both Fred's and Barney's ability to do otherwise, and all participants made consistent judgments, we were unable to confirm the interesting results from study 1 suggesting that such judgments vary depending on whether the action is blameworthy or praiseworthy/neutral.

15. As we suggested above, in some cases the pattern of responses suggests to us that people may have Frankfurtian intuitions whereby they are willing to assign blame despite believing the agent could not do otherwise. In other cases, the responses suggest people may be employing a conditional conception of the ability to do otherwise, such that the agents could do otherwise despite their actions being determined.

16. This would suggest an interesting explanation (perhaps found in the work of William James and Ludwig Wittgenstein) for the long-standing free will stalemate. After decades of argument, compatibilists and incompatibilists tend to retain conflicting intuitions about crucial disputes in the debate; perhaps they end up where they do in part because they start off where they do—as ordinary folk with different intuitions about the concept of free will and its relationship to determinism.

17. Libertarian theories require, at a minimum, indeterministic causation—in just the right place (Kane, 1999)—and often also an ontologically distinct type of causation, agent causation, that demands either substance dualism or emergent causation (O'Connor, 2000). Furthermore, in general, claims about the incompatibility of any two concepts require more evidence to establish than claims about their compatibility, in part because concepts that are not obviously incompatible should be assumed to be compatible barring an argument to the contrary. (See Lycan, 2003; Nahmias et al., 2006.)

18. See Weinburg et al. (2001) and Nichols et al. (2003) for experimental work on epistemological intuitions suggesting that these intuitions vary among people with different educational backgrounds and between people from American and Asian cultures.

19. We ran pilot studies suggesting this. Scenarios describing an agent who was neutrally manipulated to deliberate and act in a certain way elicited almost unanimous judgments that he was neither free nor responsible. When combined with the results from studies 1 and 2, this suggests to us that people do not have the intuition, sometimes advanced by incompatibilists, that determinism is no different than such covert manipulation (see Pereboom, 2001), though further tests of this question would be useful.

References

Black, S., & Tweedale, J. (2002). Responsibility and alternative possibilities: The use and abuse of examples. *The Journal of Ethics*, 6, 281–303.

Fischer, J. M. (1994). *The metaphysics of free will.* Cambridge, MA: Blackwell.

Frankfurt, H. (1969). Alternate possibilities and moral responsibility. *Journal of Philosophy*, 66, 5–20.

Jackson, F. (1998). *From metaphysics to ethics: A defense of conceptual analysis.* New York: Oxford University Press.

Kane, R. (1999). Responsibility, luck, and chance: Reflections on free will and indeterminism. *Journal of Philosophy*, 96, 217–240.

Lycan, W. (2003). Free will and the burden of proof. In A. O'Hear (Ed.), *Minds and persons: Royal Institute of Philosophy supplement* (pp. 107–122). Cambridge, England: Cambridge University Press.

Mele, A. (2001). *Acting intentionally: Probing folk notions.* In B. Malle, L. Moses & D. Baldwin (Eds.), *Intentions and intentionality: Foundations of social cognition* (pp. 27–43). Cambridge, MA: MIT Press.

Nahmias, E., Morris, S., Nadelhoffer, T., & Turner, J. (2006). Is incompatibilism intuitive? *Philosophy and Phenomenological Research*, 73, 28–53.

Nichols, S., Stich, S., & Weinburg, J. (2003). Metaskepticism: Meditations in ethno-epistemology. In S. Luper (Ed.),

The skeptics (pp. 227–247). Burlington, VT: Ashgate.

O'Connor, T. (2000). *Persons and causes: The metaphysics of free will.* New York: Oxford University Press.

Turner, J., & Nahmias, E. (2006). Are the folk agent-causationists? A response to Shaun Nichols' "The folk psychology of free will." *Mind and Language*, 21, 597–609.

van Inwagen, P. (1983). *An essay on free will.* Oxford, England: Oxford University Press.

Weinburg, J., Nichols, S., & Stich, S. (2001). Normativity and epistemic intuitions. *Philosophical Topics*, 29, 429–460.

Wolf, S. (1980). Asymmetrical freedom. *Journal of Philosophy*, 77, 157–166.

Wolf, S. (1990). *Freedom within reason.* New York: Oxford University Press.

Woolfolk, R., Doris, J., & Darley, J. (forthcoming). The intuitive scientist as moral

cognizer: Constraint, identification, and responsibility.

Study Questions

1. Why do Nahmias and his colleagues believe that surveying the folk can help inform the free will debate? What are some advantages of their approach? What are some disadvantages?

2. What do you think is the best way for the incompatibilist to challenge the conclusion by Nahmias et al. that the folk do not have incompatibilist intuitions?

3. Suppose that the position that folk intuitions, on the whole, are not incompatibilist becomes the consensus view among philosophers. How big of a problem do you think this would be for incompatibilists?

6.6   The Illusion of Conscious Will

 ### DANIEL WEGNER

DANIEL M. WEGNER (1948–) works in the Psychology Department at Harvard University as the John Lindsley Professor in Memory of William James. He publishes widely in many areas, including conscious will, mind perception, and action identification. In this selection, Wegner examines the work of Benjamin Libet. Libet asked people to lift their finger some time in the near future. He found that people exhibit brain activity that arguably causes the movement, but this brain activity occurs before the subjects are aware of their conscious decision to move. This seems to show that we don't have free will, since the event that initiates the movement begins before the person is aware of making a decision to move. Wegner examines the implications of this research for the question of whether we have free will, sparking important discussions about whether free will is possible. This research, and Wegner's widely discussed interpretation of it, has been very influential in contemporary discussions of free will.

Daniel M. Wegner, *The Illusion of Conscious Will*, pp. 50–54 (Cambridge: Bradford Books, 2002) © 2002 Massachusetts Institute of Technology, by permission of The MIT Press.

AT SOME ARBITRARY TIME IN THE next few seconds, please move your right index finger. That's correct, please perform a consciously willed action. Now, here's an interesting question: What was your brain up to at the time? In an elaborate experiment, Kornhuber and Deecke (1965) arranged to measure this event in a number of people by assessing the electrical potentials on the scalp just before and after such voluntary finger movements. Continuous recordings were made of electrical potentials at several scalp electrodes while the experimenter waited for the subject to lift that finger. The actual point when the finger moved was measured precisely by electromyography (EMG, a sensor to detect muscle movement), and this was repeated for as many as 1,000 movements per experiment with each subject. Then, using the movement onset as a reference point, the average scalp electrical potentials could be graphed for the time period surrounding all those voluntary actions.

ET voila—the spark of will! Brain electrical activity was found to start increasing about 0.8 seconds before the voluntary finger movement. Kornhuber and Deecke dubbed this activity the *readiness potential* (RP). [. . .]

When exactly in this sequence does the person experience *conscious* will? Benjamin Libet and colleagues (1983; Libet 1985; 1993) had the bright idea of asking people just this question and invented a way to time their answers. [. . .] Participants in these studies were also asked to move a finger spontaneously while wearing EMG electrodes on the finger and scalp EEG electrodes for RP measurement. And as in the prior studies the participants were asked to move the finger at will. [. . .] In this case, however, the participant was also seated before a visible clock. On the circular screen of an oscilloscope, a spot of light revolved in a clockwise path around the circumference of the screen, starting at the twelve o'clock position and revolving each 2.65 seconds—quite a bit faster than the second hand of a real clock. A circular scale with illuminated lines marked units around the edge, each of which corresponded to 107 milliseconds of real time. The participant's task was simply to report for each finger movement where the dot was on the clock when he experienced *"conscious awareness of 'wanting' to perform* a given self-initiated movement" (Libet et al. 1983, 627). [. . .]

The results were truly noteworthy, although in some sense this is exactly what you would have to expect: The conscious willing of finger movement occurred at a significant interval *after* the onset of the RP but also at a significant interval *before* the actual finger movement (and also at a significant interval before the awareness of movement). [. . .] These findings suggest that the brain starts doing something first (we don't know just what that is). Then the person becomes conscious of wanting to do the action. This would be where the conscious will kicks in, at least, in the sense that the person first becomes conscious of trying to act. Then, and still a bit *prior* to the movement, the person reports becoming aware of the finger actually moving. Finally, the finger moves. [. . .]

The conclusion suggested by the research is that the experience of conscious will kicks in at some point *after* the brain has already started preparing for the action. Libet sums up these observations by saying that "the initiation of the voluntary act appears to be an unconscious cerebral process. Clearly, free will or free choice or whether *to act now* could not be the initiating agent, contrary to one widely held view. This is of course also contrary to each individual's own introspective feeling that he/she consciously initiates such voluntary acts." [. . .]

References

Kornhuber, H. H., and L. Deecke. 1965. Hirn-potentialandeerungen bei Wilkurbewegungen und passive Bewegungen des Menschen: Bereitschaftspotential und reafferente Potentiale. *Pflugers Archiv fur Gesamte Psychologie* 284: 1–17.

Libet, B., C. A. Gleason, E. W. Wright, and D. K. Pearl. 1983. Time of conscious intention to act in relation to onset of cerebral activity (readiness-potential): The unconscious initiation of a freely voluntary act. *Brain* 106: 623–642.

Libet, B. 1985. Unconscious cerebral initiative and the role of conscious will in voluntary action. *The Behavioral and Brain Sciences* 8: 529–566.

Libet, B. 1992. The neural time-factor in perception, volition, and free will. *Revue de Metaphysique et de Morale* 97: 255–272.

Libet, B. 1993. *Neurophysiology of consciousness.* Boston: Birkhauser.

Study Questions

1. What is the "readiness potential"? Do you think it is accurate to say that the readiness

potential causes the finger to move? Why or why not?

2. Is it possible, as Wegner suggests, that your free will does not in fact cause you to initiate the movement of your finger?

3. If people came to accept that this research establishes that we do not have free will, do you think that they would cease to act morally? What implication does your answer have for the free will debate?

6.7   Free Will and Luck

ALFRED R. MELE

ALFRED R. MELE (1951–) is the William H. and Lucyle T. Werkmeister Professor of Philosophy at Florida State University. He has written several books and published numerous articles on topics including free will, the philosophy of action, and mental causation. In this selection, Mele considers what lessons we should draw from Libet's work on human decision making. While Libet's experiments give support to the claim that the initial causes of our intentional actions are rooted in unconscious brain processes, Mele challenges the notion that this fact—if true—suggests that consciousness has no important role to play in bringing about our actions. In arguing that Libet's experiments leave open the possibility that conscious decision making plays a significant causal role in what we do, Mele believes that he can head off the claim that Libet's work suggests that human beings do not possess free will.

[THE WORK OF BENJAMIN LIBET] HAS attracted a great deal of attention in a variety of fields, including philosophy. Psychologists Patrick Haggard, Chris Newman, and Elena Magno (1999, p. 291) describe an article by Libet and colleagues (Libet, Gleason et al. 1983) as "one of the most philosophically challenging papers in modern scientific psychology." A

striking thesis of that 1983 article is that "the brain...'decides' to initiate or, at the least, prepare to initiate [certain actions] at a time before there is any reportable subjective awareness that such a decision has taken place" (p. 640; also see Libet 1985, p. 536). In a recent article, Libet pointedly asserts: "If the 'act now' process is initiated unconsciously, then conscious free

Alfred R. Mele, *Free Will and Luck* (2008). By permission of Oxford University Press.

will is not doing it" (2001, p. 62; also see 2004, p. 136).

Elsewhere, I have used some of Libet's results to shed light on some philosophical questions about self-control and akrasia (Mele 1997; 2003, ch. 8). What I found useful were the data, not Libet's interpretation of them. To use his data without misleading my readers, I found it necessary to criticize a certain central element of *Libet's* interpretation of them that is directly relevant to the thesis I quoted from Libet, Gleason et al. 1983. [. . .] Part of the problem is that Libet and his colleagues ignore a directly relevant conceptual distinction between deciding and intending, on the one hand, and motivational states like wanting, on the other. [. . .]

Because Libet uses such terms as "intention," "decision," "wanting," "wish," and "urge" interchangeably, some conceptual preliminaries are in order in interpreting his work. I start with a distinction between wanting and intending. [. . .]

Wanting to do something is distinguishable from intending to do it: One can want (or desire, or have an urge) to A without being at all settled on A-ing. Yesterday, I wanted to meet a friend at a 7:00 movie and I wanted to join another friend at a 7:00 lecture. I knew that I could do either but not both. I needed to make up my mind about what to do. In forming an intention to go to the movie, I made up my mind to do that. [. . .]

It should also be noted that some of our decisions and intentions are for the nonimmediate future and others are not. I might decide on Tuesday to attend a meeting on Friday, and I might decide now to phone my father now. The intention formed in the former decision is aimed at action three days in the future. (Of course, if I need to prepare for the meeting—or need to write a note on my calendar to remind myself of it—the intention may motivate relevant overt conduct sooner than that.) The intention I form when I decide to phone my father now is about what to do now. I call intentions and decisions

of these kinds, respectively, *distal* and *proximal* intentions and decisions (Mele 1992, pp. 143–44, 158). Proximal decisions and intentions also include decisions and intentions to continue doing something that one is doing and decisions and intentions to start A-ing (e.g., start climbing a hill) straightaway. [. . .]

At what point, if any, does a specific intention to flex arise in Libet's subjects? Again, Libet, Gleason et al. write: "the brain . . . 'decides' to initiate or . . . prepare to initiate the act . . . before there is any reportable subjective awareness that such a decision has taken place" (1983, p. 640). [. . .]

In a recent article, Libet writes that "it is only the final 'act now' process that produces the voluntary *act*. That 'act now' process begins in the brain about 550 msec before the act, and it begins unconsciously" (2001, p. 61). "There is," he says, "an unconscious gap of about 400 msec between the onset of the cerebral process and when the person becomes consciously aware of his/her decision or wish or intention to act." (Incidentally, a page later, he identifies what the agent becomes aware of as "the intention/wish/urge to act" [p. 62].) Libet adds: "If the 'act now' process is initiated unconsciously, then conscious free will is not doing it." [. . .]

One might say that "the 'act now' process" in Libet's spontaneous subjects begins with the formation or acquisition of a proximal intention to flex, much closer to the onset of muscle motion than −550 ms, or that it begins earlier, with the beginning of a process that issues in the intention. I will not argue about that. Suppose we say that "the 'act now' process" begins with the unconscious emergence of a (roughly) proximal urge to (prepare to) flex—or with a pretty reliable relatively proximal causal contributor to such an urge—at about −550 ms and that the urge plays a significant role in producing a proximal intention to flex many milliseconds later. We can then agree with Libet that, given that the "process is initiated unconsciously, . . . conscious free will is not doing it"—that is, is not initiating "the 'act now' process." But who would have thought that conscious free will has the job of producing urges (or causal contributors to urges)? In the philosophical literature, free will's primary locus of operation is typically identified as deciding (or choosing), and for all Libet has shown, his subjects make their decisions (or choices) consciously.

Libet asks (2001, p. 62), "How would the 'conscious self' initiate a voluntary act if, factually, the process to 'act now' is initiated unconsciously?" In this paragraph, I offer an answer. One significant piece of background is that an "'act now' process" that is initiated unconsciously may be aborted by the agent; that apparently is what happens in instances of spontaneous vetoing, if "'act now' processes" start when Libet says they do. Now, processes have parts, and the various parts of a process may have more and less proximal initiators. A process that is initiated by an unconscious urge* may have a subsequent part that is directly initiated by the conscious formation or acquisition of an intention. "The 'conscious self'"—which need not be understood as something mysterious—might more proximally initiate a voluntary act that is less proximally initiated by an unconscious urge*. (Readers who, like me, prefer to use "self" only as an affix may prefer to say that the acquisition or formation of a relevant proximal intention, which intention is consciously acquired or formed, might more proximally initiate an intentional action that is less proximally initiated by an unconscious urge*.)

Recall that Libet himself says that "conscious volitional control may operate...to select and control ['the volitional process'], either by permitting or triggering the final motor outcome of the unconsciously initiated process or by vetoing the progression to actual motor activation" (1985, p. 529). "Triggering" is a kind of initiating. In "triggering the final motor outcome,"

the acquisition of a proximal [conscious] intention would be initiating an action in a more direct way than does the urge* that initiated a process that issued in the intention. According to one view of things, when proximal action-desires help to initiate overt actions, they do so by helping to produce pertinent proximal intentions, the formation or acquisition of which directly initiates actions (Mele 1992, pp. 71–77, 143–44, 168–70, 176–77, 190–91). What Libet says about triggering here coheres with this.

References

Haggard, Patrick, C. Newman, and E. Magno. 1999. "On the Perceived Time of Voluntary Actions." *British Journal of Psychology* 90: 291–303.

Libet, Benjamin. 1985. "Unconscious Cerebral Initiative and the Role of Conscious Will in Voluntary Action." *Behavioral and Brain Sciences* 8: 529–66.

———. 2001. "Consciousness, Free Action and the Brain." *Journal of Consciousness Studies* 8: 59–65.

———. 2004. *Mind Time*. Cambridge, MA: Harvard University Press.

Libet, Benjamin, C. Gleason, E. Wright, and D. Pearl. 1983. "Time of Unconscious Intention to Act in Relation to Onset of Cerebral Activity (Readiness-Potential)." *Brain* 106: 623–42.

Mele, Alfred. 1992. *Springs of Action*. New York: Oxford University Press.

———. 1997. "Strength of Motivation and Being in Control: Learning from Libet." *American Philosophical Quarterly* 34: 319–33.

———. 2003. *Motivation and Agency*. New York: Oxford University Press.

Study Questions

1. Why does Mele think that *wanting* to do something is different from *intending* to do something?

[Note: Mele distinguishes between urges and urges*. "Urges*" is a broader term; it includes (1) urges to flex, (2) urges to prepare to flex, (3) brain events that cause urges to flex, (4) brain events that cause urges to prepare to flex, (5) imaginings of flexing very soon.—Eds.]

2. What is the difference between *proximal* and *distal* intentions, according to Mele?

3. Assuming that Libet is correct in thinking that the initial process that causes our actions is an unconscious one, in what way does Mele believe that our conscious decision making can influence our actions?

CHAPTER 7

Persons and the Self

Emily Esch

THE CONCEPT OF THE SELF IS notoriously slippery.[1] There are at least four characteristics of the concept that are central to both the ordinary notion and philosophical concerns: agency, personality, higher level awareness, and unity. Selves are agents, in the sense that selves initiate and perform actions. Because selves are agents, we hold selves responsible, both ethically and practically, for the actions they perform. Personality traits are also part of the ordinary conception of selves. People assign themselves certain personality traits and not others, and, more important, they identify with these traits. The particular cluster of personality traits possessed by a self is often used to explain what makes individuals unique. Unlike other animals, humans are aware of themselves as selves. Our ability to be aware of our mental states and actions, both past and present, makes it possible for us, in a way that it isn't for other animals, to form a concept of the self.

Most important for this chapter, selves explain the unity of a human person. Selves explain how people are connected to their past and future. Bodies change, mental states change, but people tend to believe that in some sense of the word they are the *same* people now that they were in the past and will be in the future. The connection between past, present, and future selves is called *diachronic unity*. A different sort of unity—*synchronic unity*—is also explained by appeal to selves. This is the sense we have that all the various experiences that occur at a time are occurring to the same subject. Think for a moment of your current experiences; if you are like most people, you are simultaneously having experiences of seeing the page, hearing background noise, feeling warm or cold, and thinking about what to do after you've finished the reading. These various experiences are unified in a single subject—you.

The selections in this chapter focus on unity and in particular on diachronic unity, which is central to what philosophers call "the problem of *personal identity*." As was just mentioned, many people have the intuition that there is some sense in which they are the same person now as they were in the past and will be in the future. The problem of personal identity is explaining how this can be possible, given the fact that people are constantly undergoing physical and psychological changes. The problem of personal identity can be understood as a subset of a more general problem of identity. The more general problem of identity is well illustrated by the thought experiment known as "the ship of Theseus." The seventeenth-century English philosopher Thomas Hobbes, reworking an ancient thought experiment, asks us to imagine a ship whose planks are removed and replaced one by one. The planks that are removed are eventually made into an exact replica of the original ship. The question raised by this thought experiment is, which ship is the original ship? As Hobbes points out, the answer cannot be both.

> For if, for example, that ship of Theseus, concerning the difference whereof made by continual reparation in taking out the old planks and putting in the new, the sophisters of Athens were wont to dispute, were, after all the planks were changed, the same numerical ship it was at the beginning; and if some man had kept the old planks as they were taken out, and by putting them afterwards together in the same order, had again made a ship of them, this, without doubt, had also been the same numerical ship with that which was in the beginning; and so there would have been two ships numerically the same, which is absurd.[2]

This thought experiment introduces the concept of *numerical identity*. Numerical identity is the relation that each object bears to itself that makes it one and the same thing. Numerical identity is a one-to-one relation; this is why Hobbes claims that it is "absurd" that two distinct ships are numerically identical to the original ship. Given the definition of numerical identity, this is impossible: two things cannot simultaneously be one and the same thing. But, of course, there is a sense in which these two ships are the same; after all, the rebuilt ship is a replica of the sailing ship, and as such it shares all the same properties. Philosophers call this *qualitative identity*: two things are qualitatively identical if and only if they share all the same properties.

Different answers can be given to the question, which ship is numerically identical to the original ship? What answer you give will depend on what properties you think are essential to something being the same ship. If, for example, you believe that the stuff the ship is made of is most important, then you will identify the rebuilt ship as the original ship, since it is constructed of the original material. If, on the other hand, you think that what is most important is the functioning of the ship, you will choose the sailing ship, since it has continued to perform its function as a ship throughout the replacement of its planks. In coming up with your answer, you will be distinguishing the *essential properties* from the merely accidental ones.

Essential properties are those properties that, if lost, will cause the thing that had them to cease to exist. *Accidental properties* are those properties that a thing can lose without ceasing to exist. This is easier to understand through examples. Having four legs is an accidental property of being a dog. If Fido loses a leg, he will still remain a dog and he still remains the same individual dog. However, being a member of the species *canis lupus familiaris* is an essential property of being a dog and of being Fido. If Fido were to be magically turned into an egg, he would no longer exist.

With this terminology in place, we can return to the problem of personal identity. As in the ship of Theseus thought experiment, when we ask whether a person is the same person now as she was ten years ago, we are asking whether she is numerically identical, not qualitatively identical, to the person she was ten years ago. This should be made more obvious when we think about how many of our qualities, both mental and physical, have changed over time. This is why there is a problem—many, if not most, of our properties change over time, so it seems that these properties can't be the foundation for our belief that people are the same over time. One way to begin to approach the problem is to ask, what properties are essential to an individual person and what properties are merely accidental? If there are essential properties of an individual, then it seems that possession of these properties ensures numerical identity. For example, someone who believes that the only essential property of a person is her soul will also believe that if a person at one time has the same soul as a person at another time, then that means that it's the same (numerically identical) person, despite any bodily or psychological changes.

In his influential book *Meditations on First Philosophy*, published in 1641, Descartes explains what he believes makes up the core of the self: "But what then am I? A thing that thinks. What is that? A thing that doubts, understands, affirms, denies, is willing, is unwilling, and also imagines and has sensory perceptions."[3] Descartes makes two important claims in this passage. First, he draws a distinction between the thing that does the thinking and the thoughts themselves. Second, Descartes identifies himself as the thing that does the thinking. This view, now known as the *Ego Theory*, provides an answer to the problem of diachronic unity. Since the individual is not identical to her thoughts but to the thing that has these thoughts, the Ego Theorist can explain how a person persists through time. This thing that thinks is a simple, constant presence throughout one's life and as such can serve to unify the individual through constant changes. The thoughts and experiences change, but the subject of these mental states never does. Descartes' account of the self is still popular today. Here is the British philosopher Galen Strawson, explaining his own view and arguing that it is the ordinary one: "[The ordinary, human sense of the self] is the sense that people have of themselves as being, specifically, a mental presence; a mental someone; a single mental thing that is a conscious subject of experience."[4]

In the first reading in this chapter, John Locke provides us with an alternative to the Ego Theory of personal identity. While discussion about the nature of the self has been around since the ancient Greek philosophers, John Locke is usually credited with formulating the problem of personal identity as a problem of providing conditions under which a person remains numerically identical despite undergoing changes. He embeds his discussion of personal identity in a general discussion of identity. Locke carefully distinguishes the identity conditions of masses of matter from the identity conditions of living things. As he says, "[A] Colt grown up to a Horse, sometimes fat, sometimes lean, is all the while the same Horse."[5] What is essential to continued existence in the case of a living being is not that the different stages are composed of the same bits of material, but that the parts of the being are organized in such a way that the being "partakes in one Common Life."[6] In other words, the actual material that composes a living being is an accidental property, not an essential one.

Locke discusses three possible candidates for explaining personal identity—*human*, *substance*, and *person*—and dismisses the first two.[7] Locke explains that when we think of people as *humans*, we are thinking of them as living beings just like other animals. He believes that the same identity conditions that hold for animals are the conditions that mark the continued existence of the same human. This, however, is not suitable as an explanation for personal identity, according to Locke, because we can conceive of cases where two people switch bodies. In these switching cases, Locke argues, the person goes with her mental states. Thus, it seems that personal identity cannot be linked to having the same functioning body.

As Locke notes, we also might explain a person's continued existence as the existence of the same soul, or immaterial substance. In his criticism of this position, Locke seems to have in mind a view like Descartes', which, as we've seen, distinguishes the thing that has the thoughts from the thoughts themselves. Because this thinking thing is simple and changeless, it seems like a good candidate for explaining what stays the same in a person over time. However, Locke points out that this very feature, the soul's lack of distinguishing characteristics, is what makes it unsuitable as an account of personal identity. For without any distinguishing characteristics, souls can be switched from one body to the next without anybody noticing the difference. But if we cannot recognize a difference between having one soul or another, then having the same soul cannot be the thing that makes us the same over time.

Having dispensed with the concepts of *human* and *substance* as providing good criteria for establishing personal identity, Locke turns to the concept of a person. This, he thinks, is the key to understanding personal identity. For Locke, a person is defined as a thinking, intelligent being that can think of itself as the same thinking thing in various times and places. These features Locke calls consciousness, and he believes that it is being of the same consciousness that makes one the same person. Consciousness, on this account, is distinct from both bodies and souls. It is possible for the same consciousness to inhabit different bodies, just as it is possible for the same consciousness to be passed from one thinking substance to another. According to Locke, what makes you the same person is that you have the same consciousness.

Locke's account of personal identity was challenged by a Scottish philosopher of the eighteenth century, Thomas Reid. Reid's own view is a version of the Ego Theory:

> My personal identity, therefore, implies the continued existence of that indivisible thing which I call myself. Whatever this self may be, it is something which thinks, and deliberates, and resolves, and acts, and suffers. I am not thought, I am not action, I am not feeling; I am something that thinks, and acts, and suffers. My thoughts, and actions, and feelings, change every moment; they have no continued, but a successive existence; but that *self* or *I*, to which they belong, is permanent, and has the same relation to all the succeeding thoughts, actions, and feelings, which I call mine.[8]

In addition to providing a famous counterexample to Locke's account, known as the Brave Officer case, Reid levels three main arguments against Locke in the reading selected for this chapter. First, Reid rightly notes that Locke conflates memory and consciousness. Locke frequently claims that the crucial component underlying personal identity is whether or not the person remembers her earlier actions. If someone can remember an episode from earlier in her past, then she is the same as the person who performed the action. But, as Reid points out, the concepts of memory and consciousness are distinct; in Reid's words, they are two different "faculties." Second, Reid argues that Locke conflates what makes us the same person with what makes us know that we are the same person. To state this in a different way, Reid accuses Locke of using an epistemological argument (an argument about knowledge of the self) for a metaphysical claim (a claim about what the self is). Reid accepts that the way a person *knows* whether or not he is identical to an earlier person is by remembering performing the action, but this does not imply that personal identity *consists* in the memories. A person's evidence for believing that she is identical to the young girl who got a pony for Christmas is the fact that she can remember the episode, but what makes her the same person, Reid claims, is that she has the same permanent and indivisible self. Finally, Reid argues that both memory and consciousness are poor candidates for explaining our personal identity, since they are constantly changing. We need, Reid argues, something unchanging to explain how a person can undergo change yet remain the same.

The third selection, by Reid's contemporary, the philosopher David Hume, defends a Lockean-style view against the Ego Theory. Like Locke, Hume is an *empiricist*, and believes all knowledge is based in sense experience. Hume thinks that all legitimate concepts (which Hume called *ideas*) could be traced back to their original source, which he called an impression. We can understand these impressions to be sensations that come from the external world. So, for example, the concept *red* is formed from our experiences of the impressions we get from red things. One of the jobs of the philosopher is tracing back our concepts to the original impressions. If it turns out that there is no original impression, then, Hume believed, that was reason to abandon the concept.

This is important for Hume's account of personal identity, because his account is motivated by the fact that Hume could never find an impression of a simple, single ego. Instead of an ego, Hume finds only the mental states (perceptions, beliefs, memories, etc.) themselves. In a famous passage, Hume says:

> There are some philosophers, who imagine we are every moment intimately conscious of what we call our SELF; that we feel its existence and its continuance in existence; and are certain, beyond the evidence of a demonstration, both of its perfect identity and simplicity....For my part, when I enter most intimately into what I call *myself*, I always stumble on some particular perception or other of heat or cold, light or shade, love or hatred, pain or pleasure. I never can catch *myself* at any time without a perception, and never can observe any thing but the perception.[9]

The fact that he never perceives a self, but only various mental states, leads Hume to propose what has come to be known as the Bundle Theory of personal identity. According to the *Bundle Theory*, there is no single self underlying all our mental states. Rather, selves are long trains of mental states that are connected by a variety of causal relations.

Some doubt whether this should count as personal identity at all, and Hume's view is sometimes called a "no-self" view. A version of Hume's Bundle Theory has been recently defended by Derek Parfit. Parfit claims that the first Bundle Theorist was Buddha, who claimed:

A sentient being does exist, you think, O Mara? You are misled by a false conception. This bundle of elements is void of Self, In it there is no sentient being. Just as a set of wooden parts Receives the name of carriage, So do we give to elements The name of fancied being.[10]

Like Hume, Buddha appears to be claiming that questions about what to call the self are grammatical questions, not metaphysical ones. Parfit concurs, but he acknowledges that most people either explicitly or implicitly believe in the Ego Theory.[11] In the fourth reading in this section, Parfit presents a series of clever thought experiments designed to show that belief in the Ego Theory is incoherent. Personal identity, according to Parfit, is determined by whether two people are psychologically continuous (sharing memories, desires, and other psychological states) with each other; if two people are psychologically continuous, then they count as the same person. An implication of this view is that personal identity no longer consists of numerical identity, since it is logically possible that two people are psychologically continuous with an original person. (Imagine a case in which a person undergoes fission, amoeba-like, to become two qualitatively identical people.)

Parfit claims that the Bundle Theory is difficult for people to accept, but that we have both rational and empirical grounds for accepting it. He uses the existence of a class of patients who have undergone surgery to sever the corpus callosum, the bundle of nerves that connect the two hemispheres, to empirically argue for the Bundle Theory.[12,13] Surprisingly, these patients function extraordinarily well in ordinary conditions. But problems do show up under certain conditions. In order to understand the behavior of these split-brain patients, two biological facts are important. First, the left hemisphere controls the right side of the body and the right hemisphere controls the left side. Second, the left hemisphere is associated with language; the right hemisphere is typically nonverbal. Researchers noticed that when patients held common items (which were blocked from view) in their left hand, they couldn't name the items. However, if asked to point to a picture of the item, the patients had no trouble. Similarly, if a subject held an item in her right hand (but blocked from view), she could easily name the object, but she would be unable to point to the correct image with her left hand. Parfit argues that the behavior of the split-brain patients provides compelling evidence against the Ego Theory, since it seems that these patients have at least two distinct streams of consciousness during the experiments. If this interpretation is correct, then it seems to support the belief that there is no single subject underlying all of our experiences, even in those whose corpus callosum remains intact.

The final reading in this section takes the possibility that there is more than one self to another level. In "The First Person Plural," the psychologist Paul Bloom focuses his attention on David Hume's analogy of the self as a republic, with the various members fighting for attention and control. In the selection in this volume, Hume states, "I cannot compare the soul more properly to any thing than to a republic or commonwealth, in which the several members are united by the reciprocal ties of government and subordination." Most philosophers have interpreted Hume as drawing an analogy between mental states and the members of a republic. Bloom, however, uses the analogy to illustrate the idea that each person consists of multiple selves:

[The view I'm interested in] is conservative in that it accepts that brains give rise to selves that last over time, plan for the future, and so on. But it is radical in that it gives up the idea that there is just one self per head. The idea is that instead, within each brain, different selves are continually popping in and out of existence. They have different desires, and they fight for control—bargaining with, deceiving, and plotting against one another.[14]

Bloom marshals a variety of fascinating phenomena to illustrate his account. He points out that some schizophrenics engage with what they take to be external selves and that many children develop imaginary friends. He claims that our enjoyment of fiction, like novels or movies, depends on our ability to become another person, if only briefly. He describes the case of a weak-willed dieter as a struggle between the self that wants to be slim and the self that wants a piece of chocolate cake. He describes several instances of the process of *self-binding* in which our long-term selves try to thwart the desires of our short-term selves (e.g., by calling ahead to a hotel and asking them to remove the items from the minibar).

Many philosophers would likely reject Bloom's case for the existence of multiple selves. As mentioned earlier, a common interpretation of Hume's metaphor is that within each person there are competing interests that cannot both be satisfied—you want to go to the party tonight, but you also want to do well on your morning exam. These internal conflicts are the source of much of our great art and literature, and philosophers have been writing about these conflicts as long as they have been doing philosophy. The idea that we are composed of many selves is metaphorically appealing, but there may be good conceptual reasons for reserving the concept *self* for the kinds of things that exhibit the four features (agency, personality, higher order awareness, and unity) mentioned at the beginning of the chapter. The types of examples that Bloom provides lack all or most of these features.

The Ego Theory and the Bundle Theory take very different positions on the nature of the self, but both are serious attempts to explain the diachronic unity that ordinary people feel over the course of their lives. Bloom, while acknowledging that people possess this feeling of being a single subject over time, dismisses the idea as an illusion created by a brain shaped by evolutionary forces. This view, that persons are composed of multiple selves competing among one another for dominance, is becoming more popular as we learn more about the brain and human behavior.[15] Each of the four features identified as central to our traditional understanding of the self is vulnerable to new empirical evidence, and it might turn out that our old ideas about the self need to be radically revised. But it is also possible that some form of the traditional concept survives. As Bloom himself notes, our social structures and personal relationships depend on our belief in the continuity of persons: marriages, contracts, friendships, and legal systems are all based on the assumption that people remain the same over time.

Notes

1. The fragmentation of the literature has spurred at least one philosopher to argue for abandoning the concept. See Eric Olson, "There Is No Problem of the Self," *Journal of Consciousness Studies* 5, no. 5–6 (1998): 645–657. For a discussion of the various uses of "self" by psychologists, see Mark Leary and June Price Tangney, *Handbook of Self and Identity* (New York: Guilford, 2005).

2. Thomas Hobbes, *The English Works of Thomas Hobbes of Malmesbury,* Vol. 1 (Boston: Elibron Classics, 2005), 136–137.

3. René Descartes, *Meditations on First Philosophy,* ed. John Cottingham (New York: Cambridge University Press, 1996), 19.

4. Galen Strawson, "The Self," *Journal of Consciousness Studies,* 4, no. 5–6 (1997): 405–428.

5. John Locke, *An Essay Concerning Human Understanding,* ed. P. H. Nidditch (Oxford: Clarendon, 1975), 330.

6. Ibid., 331.

7. Following the conventions of his time, Locke uses the word *man* in place of *human.*

8. Thomas Reid, *Essays on the Intellectual Powers of Man,* ed. Derek Brookes (University Park, PA: Penn State University Press, 2002), 264.

9. David Hume, *A Treatise of Human Nature,* ed. David Fate Norton and Mary J. Norton (New York: Oxford University Press, 2002), 164–165.

10. Quoted in Derek Parfit, "Divided Minds and the Nature of Person," in *Mindwaves,* ed. Colin Blakemore and Susan Greenfield (New York: Basil Blackwell, 1987), 21.

11. Parfit is addressing a western audience; it is likely that our beliefs about the self are at least in part culturally constructed. See Stephen Heine, "Self as a Cultural Product," *Journal of Personality* 69, no. 6 (2001): 881–906 for an overview of the literature comparing Western and Eastern conceptions of the self.

12. The early work on split-brain patients was done by Roger Sperry and Michael Gazzaniga; Sperry eventually received a Nobel Prize in Medicine for this research. See Michael Gazzaniga, "The Split Brain Revisited," *Scientific American* 279, no. 1 (1998): 35–39 for a more recent discussion.

13. Parfit wasn't the first philosopher to use the split-brain cases for this purpose. A similar argument is made by Thomas Nagel in "Brain Bisection and the Unity of Consciousness," *Synthese: An International Journal for Epistemology, Methodology and Philosophy of Science* 22, no. 1 (1971): 396–413.

14. Paul Bloom, "The First Person Plural," *The Atlantic,* November 2008, 90–98.

15. See V. S. Ramachandran and Sandra Blakeslee, *Phantoms in the Brain* (New York: Quill, 1999); Keith Stanovich, *The Robot's Rebellion* (Chicago: University of Chicago Press, 2004); and Nicholas Humphrey and Daniel C. Dennett, "Speaking for Our Selves: An Assessment of Multiple Personality Disorder," *Raritan* 9, no. 1 (1989): 68–98.

References

Bloom, Paul. "First Person Plural." *The Atlantic.* November 2008. Pp. 90–98.

Descartes, René. *Meditations on a First Philosophy,* ed. John Cottingham. New York: Cambridge University Press, 1996.

Gazzaniga, Michael. "The Split Brain Revisited." *Scientific American* 279, no. 1 (1998): 35–39.

Heine, Stephen. "Self as a Cultural Product." *Journal of Personality* 69, no. 6 (2001): 881–906.

Hobbes, Thomas. *The English Works of Thomas Hobbes of Malmesbury.* Vol. 1. Boston: Elibron Classics, 2005.

Hume, David. *Treatise of Human Nature,* ed. David F. Norton and Mary J. Norton. New York: Oxford University Press, 2002.

Humphrey, Nicholas, and Daniel C. Dennett. "Speaking for Our Selves: An Assessment of Multiple Personality Disorder." *Raritan* 9, no. 1 (1989): 68–98.

Leary, Mark R., and June Price Tangney. *Handbook of Self and Identity*. New York: Guilford, 2005.

Locke, John. *An Essay Concerning Human Understanding*, ed. P. H. Nidditch. Oxford: Clarendon, 1975.

Nagel, Thomas. "Brain Bisection and the Unity of Consciousness." *Synthese: An International Journal for Epistemology, Methodology and Philosophy of Science* 22, no. 1 (1971): 396–413.

Olson, Eric. "There Is No Problem of the Self." *Journal of Consciousness Studies* 5, no. 5–6 (1998): 645–657.

Parfit, Derek. "Divided Minds and the Nature of Persons." In *Mindwaves*, ed. Colin Blakemore and Susan Greenfield, 19–25. New York: Basil Blackwell, 1987.

Ramachandran, V. S., and Sandra Blakeslee. *Phantoms in the Brain*. New York: Quill, 1999.

Reid, Thomas. *Essays on the Intellectual Powers of Man: A Critical Edition*, ed. Derek R. Brookes. University Park, PA: Penn State University Press, 2002.

Stanovich, Keith. *The Robot's Rebellion*. Chicago: University of Chicago Press, 2004.

Strawson, Galen. "The Self." *Journal of Consciousness Studies* 4, no. 5–6 (1997): 405–428.

Suggestions for Further Reading

Baker, Lynne Rudder. "When Does a Person Begin?" *Social Philosophy and Policy* 22, no. 2 (2005): 25–48.

Bargh, John, and Tanya Chartrand. "The Unbearable Automaticity of Being." *American Psychologist* 54, no. 7 (1999): 462–479.

Bruner, Jerome. "Life as Narrative." *Social Research* 71, no. 3 (2004): 691–710.

Dennett, Daniel. "The Self as a Centre of Narrative Gravity." In *Self and Consciousness: Multiple Perspectives,* ed. F. Kessel, P. Cole, and D. Johnson. Hillsdale, NJ: Erlbaum, 1992.

Doris, John. "Skepticism about Persons." *Philosophical Issues* 19, no. 1 (2009): 57–91.

Frankfurt, Harry. "Freedom of the Will and the Concept of a Person." *Journal of Philosophy* 68, no. 1 (1971): 5–20.

Gendler, Tamar Szabó. "Exceptional Persons: On the Limits of Imaginary Cases." *Journal of Consciousness Studies* 5, no. 5–6 (1998): 592–610.

Nichols, Shaun, and Michael Bruno. "Intuitions about Personal Identity: An Empirical Study." *Philosophical Psychology* 23, no. 3 (2010): 293–312.

Parfit, Derek. *Reasons and Persons*. Oxford: Clarendon, 1984.

Schechtman, Marya. *The Constitution of Selves*. Ithaca, NY: Cornell University Press, 1996.

Shoemaker, Sydney. "Persons, Animals and Identity." *Synthese: An International Journal for Epistemology, Methodology and Philosophy of Science* 162, no. 3 (2008): 313–324.

Williams, Bernard. "The Self and the Future." *Philosophical Review* 79, no. 2 (1970): 161–180.

An Essay Concerning Human Understanding 7.1

JOHN LOCKE

JOHN LOCKE (1632–1704) was one of the most important English philosophers of the modern period. While most famous for his work in political philosophy, especially his development of the social contract theory, Locke was also interested in epistemology, metaphysics, and philosophy of mind. Locke was one of the first empiricists, claiming that the mind is a tabula rasa, or blank slate, and that all knowledge is constructed out of sense experience. Locke is also credited as the first philosopher to inquire into the nature of personal identity, and many of his original thought experiments are still discussed today. In this selection, Locke draws a distinction among the concepts of *person*, *man*, and *substance*. Neither being the same man nor being the same substance is sufficient for being the same person. Rather, Locke argues that personal identity consists in having the same consciousness, which he understands as a thinking, intelligent being who can know itself as the same self at different times and places. This allows for the possibility that the same person can inhabit multiple bodies.

1. WHEREIN IDENTITY CONSISTS

ANOTHER occasion the mind often takes of comparing, is the very being of things, when, considering ANYTHING AS EXISTING AT ANY DETERMINED TIME AND PLACE, we compare it with ITSELF EXISTING AT ANOTHER TIME, and thereon form the ideas of IDENTITY and DIVERSITY. When we see anything to be in any place in any instant of time, we are sure (be it what it will) that it is that very thing, and not another which at that same time exists in another place, how like and undistinguishable soever it may be in all other respects: and in this consists IDENTITY, when the ideas it is attributed to vary not at all from what they were that moment wherein we consider their former existence, and to which we compare the present. For we never finding, nor conceiving it possible, that two things of the same kind should exist in the same place at the same time, we rightly conclude, that, whatever exists anywhere at any time, excludes all of the same kind, and is there itself alone. When therefore we demand whether anything be the SAME or no, it refers always to something that existed such a time in such a place, which it was certain, at that instant, was the same with itself, and no other. From whence it follows, that one thing cannot have two beginnings of existence, nor two things one beginning; it being impossible for two things of the same kind to be or exist in the same instant, in the very same place; or one and the same thing in different places. That, therefore, that had one beginning, is the same thing; and that which had a different beginning in time and place from that, is not the same, but diverse. That which has made the difficulty about this relation has been the little care and attention used in having precise notions of the things to which it is attributed. [. . .]

John Locke, *An Essay Concerning Human Understanding*, Book II, "Of Identity and Diversity," edited by Pauline Phemister (2008). By permission of Oxford University Press.

3. IDENTITY OF MODES AND RELATIONS

All other things being but modes or relations ultimately terminated in substances, the identity and diversity of each particular existence of them too will be by the same way determined: only as to things whose existence is in succession, such as are the actions of finite beings, v. g. MOTION and THOUGHT, both which consist in a continued train of succession, concerning THEIR diversity there can be no question: because each perishing the moment it begins, they cannot exist in different times, or in different places, as permanent beings can at different times exist in distant places; and therefore no motion or thought, considered as at different times, can be the same, each part thereof having a different beginning of existence.

4. PRINCIPIUM INDIVIDUATIONIS

From what has been said, it is easy to discover what is so much inquired after, the PRINCIPIUM INDIVIDUATIONIS; and that, it is plain, is existence itself; which determines a being of any sort to a particular time and place, incommunicable to two beings of the same kind. This, though it seems easier to conceive in simple substances or modes; yet, when reflected on, is not more difficult in compound ones, if care be taken to what it is applied: v.g. let us suppose an atom, i.e. a continued body under one immutable superficies, existing in a determined time and place; it is evident, that, considered in any instant of its existence, it is in that instant the same with itself. For, being at that instant what it is, and nothing else, it is the same, and so must continue as long as its existence is continued; for so long it will be the same, and no other. In like manner, if two or more atoms be joined together into the same mass, every one of those atoms will be the same, by the foregoing rule: and whilst they exist united together, the mass, consisting of the same atoms, must be the same mass, or the same body, let the

parts be ever so differently jumbled. But if one of these atoms be taken away, or one new one added, it is no longer the same mass or the same body. In the state of living creatures, their identity depends not on a mass of the same particles, but on something else. For in them the variation of great parcels of matter alters not the identity: an oak growing from a plant to a great tree, and then lopped, is still the same oak; and a colt grown up to a horse, sometimes fat, sometimes lean, is all the while the same horse: though, in both these cases, there may be a manifest change of the parts; so that truly they are not either of them the same masses of matter, though they be truly one of them the same oak, and the other the same horse. The reason whereof is, that, in these two cases—a MASS OF MATTER and a LIVING BODY—identity is not applied to the same thing.

5. IDENTITY OF VEGETABLES

We must therefore consider wherein an oak differs from a mass of matter, and that seems to me to be in this, that the one is only the cohesion of particles of matter any how united, the other such a disposition of them as constitutes the parts of an oak; and such an organization of those parts as is fit to receive and distribute nourishment, so as to continue and frame the wood, bark, and leaves, &c., of an oak, in which consists the vegetable life. That being then one plant which has such an organization of parts in one coherent body, partaking of one common life, it continues to be the same plant as long as it partakes of the same life, though that life be communicated to new particles of matter vitally united to the living plant, in a like continued organization conformable to that sort of plants. For this organization, being at any one instant in any one collection of matter, is in that particular concrete distinguished from all other, and IS that individual life, which existing constantly from that moment both forwards and backwards, in the same continuity of insensibly succeeding parts united to the living body of the plant, it has that identity which makes the same plant, and all the parts of it, parts of the same plant, during all the time that they exist united in that continued organization, which is fit to convey that common life to all the parts so united.

6. IDENTITY OF ANIMALS

The case is not so much different in BRUTES but that any one may hence see what makes an animal and continues it the same. Something we have like this in machines, and may serve to illustrate it. For example, what is a watch? It is plain it is nothing but a fit organization or construction of parts to a certain end, which, when a sufficient force is added to it, it is capable to attain. If we would suppose this machine one continued body, all whose organized parts were repaired, increased, or diminished by a constant addition or separation of insensible parts, with one common life, we should have something very much like the body of an animal; with this difference, That, in an animal the fitness of the organization, and the motion wherein life consists, begin together, the motion coming from within; but in machines the force coming sensibly from without, is often away when the organ is in order, and well fitted to receive it.

7. THE IDENTITY OF MAN

This also shows wherein the identity of the same MAN consists; viz. in nothing but a participation of the same continued life, by constantly fleeting particles of matter, in succession vitally united to the same organized body. He that shall place the identity of man in anything else, but, like that of other animals, in one fitly organized body, taken in any one instant, and from thence continued, under one organization of life, in several successively fleeting particles of matter united to it, will find it hard to make an embryo, one of

years, mad and sober, the SAME MAN, by any supposition, that will not make it possible for Seth, Ismael, Socrates, Pilate, St. Austin, and Caesar Borgia, to be the same man. For if the identity of SOUL ALONE makes the same MAN; and there be nothing in the nature of matter why the same individual spirit may not be united to different bodies, it will be possible that those men, living in distant ages, and of different tempers, may have been the same man: which way of speaking must be from a very strange use of the word man, applied to an idea out of which body and shape are excluded. And that way of speaking would agree yet worse with the notions of those philosophers who allow of transmigration, and are of opinion that the souls of men may, for their miscarriages, be detruded into the bodies of beasts, as fit habitations, with organs suited to the satisfaction of their brutal inclinations. But yet I think nobody, could he be sure that the SOUL of Heliogabalus were in one of his hogs, would yet say that hog were a MAN or Heliogabalus. [. . .]

9. SAME MAN

An animal is a living organized body; and consequently the same animal, as we have observed, is the same continued LIFE communicated to different particles of matter, as they happen successively to be united to that organized living body. And whatever is talked of other definitions, ingenious observation puts it past doubt, that the idea in our minds, of which the sound man in our mouths is the sign, is nothing else but of an animal of such a certain form. Since I think I may be confident, that, whoever should see a creature of his own shape or make, though it had no more reason all its life than a cat or a parrot, would call him still a MAN; or whoever should hear a cat or a parrot discourse, reason, and philosophize, would call or think it nothing but a CAT or a PARROT; and say, the one was a dull irrational man, and the other a very intelligent rational parrot.

10. SAME MAN

For I presume it is not the idea of a thinking or rational being alone that makes the IDEA OF A MAN in most people's sense: but of a body, so and so shaped, joined to it; and if that be the idea of a man, the same successive body not shifted all at once, must, as well as the same immaterial spirit, go to the making of the same man.

11. PERSONAL IDENTITY

This being premised, to find wherein personal identity consists, we must consider what PERSON stands for;—which, I think, is a thinking intelligent being, that has reason and reflection, and can consider itself as itself, the same thinking thing, in different times and places; which it does only by that consciousness which is inseparable from thinking, and, as it seems to me, essential to it: it being impossible for any one to perceive without PERCEIVING that he does perceive. When we see, hear, smell, taste, feel, meditate, or will anything, we know that we do so. Thus it is always as to our present sensations and perceptions: and by this every one is to himself that which he calls SELF:—it not being considered, in this case, whether the same self be continued in the same or divers substances. For, since consciousness always accompanies thinking, and it is that which makes every one to be what he calls self, and thereby distinguishes himself from all other thinking things, in this alone consists personal identity, i.e. the sameness of a rational being: and as far as this consciousness can be extended backwards to any past action or thought, so far reaches the identity of that person; it is the same self now it was then; and it is by the same self with this present one that now reflects on it, that that action was done.

12. CONSCIOUSNESS MAKES PERSONAL IDENTITY

But it is further inquired, whether it be the same identical substance. This few would think they had reason to doubt of, if these perceptions, with their consciousness, always remained present in the mind, whereby the same thinking thing would be always consciously present, and, as would be thought, evidently the same to itself. But that which seems to make the difficulty is this, that this consciousness being interrupted always by forgetfulness, there being no moment of our lives wherein we have the whole train of all our past actions before our eyes in one view, but even the best memories losing the sight of one part whilst they are viewing another; and we sometimes, and that the greatest part of our lives, not reflecting on our past selves, being intent on our present thoughts, and in sound sleep having no thoughts at all, or at least none with that consciousness which remarks our waking thoughts,—I say, in all these cases, our consciousness being interrupted, and we losing the sight of our past selves, doubts are raised whether we are the same thinking thing, i.e. the same SUBSTANCE or no. Which, however reasonable or unreasonable, concerns not PERSONAL identity at all. The question being what makes the same person; and not whether it be the same identical substance, which always thinks in the same person, which, in this case, matters not at all: different substances, by the same consciousness (where they do partake in it) being united into one person, as well as different bodies by the same life are united into one animal, whose identity is preserved in that change of substances by the unity of one continued life. For, it being the same consciousness that makes a man be himself to himself, personal identity depends on that only, whether it be annexed solely to one individual substance, or can be continued in a succession of several substances. For as far as any intelligent being CAN repeat the idea of any past action with the same consciousness it had of it at first, and with the same consciousness it has of any present action; so far it is the same personal self. For it is by the consciousness it has of its present thoughts and actions, that it is SELF TO ITSELF now, and so will be the same self, as far as the same consciousness can extend to actions past or to come; and would be by distance of time, or change of substance, no more two persons, than a man be two men by wearing other clothes to-day than he did yesterday, with a long or a short sleep between: the same consciousness uniting those distant actions into the same person, whatever substances contributed to their production.

13. PERSONAL IDENTITY IN CHANGE OF SUBSTANCE

That this is so, we have some kind of evidence in our very bodies, all whose particles, whilst vitally united to this same thinking conscious self, so that WE FEEL when they are touched, and are affected by, and conscious of good or harm that happens to them, are a part of ourselves; i.e. of our thinking conscious self. Thus, the limbs of his body are to every one a part of himself; he sympathizes and is concerned for them. Cut off a hand, and thereby separate it from that consciousness he had of its heat, cold, and other affections, and it is then no longer a part of that which is himself, any more than the remotest part of matter. Thus, we see the SUBSTANCE whereof personal self consisted at one time may be varied at another, without the change of personal identity; there being no question about the same person, though the limbs which but now were a part of it, be cut off.

14. PERSONALITY IN CHANGE OF SUBSTANCE

But the question is, Whether if the same substance which thinks be changed, it can be the same person; or, remaining the same, it can be different persons?

And to this I answer: First, This can be no question at all to those who place thought in a purely material animal constitution, void of an immaterial substance. For, whether their supposition be true or no, it is plain they conceive personal identity preserved in something else than identity of substance; as animal identity is preserved in identity of life, and not of substance. And therefore those who place thinking in an immaterial substance only, before they can come to deal with these men, must show why personal identity cannot be preserved in the change of immaterial substances, or variety of particular immaterial substances, as well as animal identity is preserved in the change of material substances, or variety of particular bodies: unless they will say, it is one immaterial spirit that makes the same life in brutes, as it is one immaterial spirit that makes the same person in men; which the Cartesians at least will not admit, for fear of making brutes thinking things too.

15. WHETHER IN CHANGE OF THINKING SUBSTANCES THERE CAN BE ONE PERSON

But next, as to the first part of the question, Whether, if the same thinking substance (supposing immaterial substances only to think) be changed, it can be the same person? I answer, that cannot be resolved but by those who know there can what kind of substances they are that do think; and whether the consciousness of past actions can be transferred from one thinking substance to another. I grant were the same consciousness the same individual action it could not: but it being a present representation of a past action, why it may not be possible, that that may be represented to the mind to have been which really never was, will remain to be shown. And therefore how far the consciousness of past actions is annexed to any individual agent, so that another cannot possibly have it, will be hard for us to determine, till we know what kind of action it is that cannot be done without a reflex act of perception accompanying it, and how performed by thinking substances, who cannot think without being conscious of it. But that which we call the same consciousness, not being the same individual act, why one intellectual substance may not have represented to it, as done by itself, what IT never did, and was perhaps done by some other agent—why, I say, such a representation may not possibly be without reality of matter of fact, as well as several representations in dreams are, which yet whilst dreaming we take for true—will be difficult to conclude from the nature of things. And that it never is so, will by us, till we have clearer views of the nature of thinking substances, be best resolved into the goodness of God; who, as far as the happiness or misery of any of his sensible creatures is concerned in it, will not, by a fatal error of theirs, transfer from one to another that consciousness which draws reward or punishment with it. How far this may be an argument against those who would place thinking in a system of fleeting animal spirits, I leave to be considered. But yet, to return to the question before us, it must be allowed, that, if the same consciousness (which, as has been shown, is quite a different thing from the same numerical figure or motion in body) can be transferred from one thinking substance to another, it will be possible that two thinking substances may make but one person. For the same consciousness being preserved, whether in the same or different substances, the personal identity is preserved.

16. WHETHER, THE SAME IMMATERIAL SUBSTANCE REMAINING, THERE CAN BE TWO PERSONS

As to the second part of the question, Whether the same immaterial substance remaining, there may be two distinct persons; which question seems to me to be built on this,—Whether the same immaterial being, being conscious of the action of its past duration, may be wholly stripped of all the consciousness of its past existence, and lose it beyond the power of ever retrieving it again: and so as it were beginning a new account from a new period, have a con-

sciousness that CANNOT reach beyond this new state. All those who hold pre-existence are evidently of this mind; since they allow the soul to have no remaining consciousness of what it did in that pre-existent state, either wholly separate from body, or informing any other body; and if they should not, it is plain experience would be against them. So that personal identity, reaching no further than consciousness reaches, a pre-existent spirit not having continued so many ages in a state of silence, must needs make different persons. Suppose a Christian Platonist or a Pythagorean should, upon God's having ended all his works of creation the seventh day, think his soul hath existed ever since; and should imagine it has revolved in several human bodies; as I once met with one, who was persuaded his had been the SOUL of Socrates (how reasonably I will not dispute; this I know, that in the post he filled, which was no inconsiderable one, he passed for a very rational man, and the press has shown that he wanted not parts or learning;)— would any one say, that he, being not conscious of any of Socrates's actions or thoughts, could be the same PERSON with Socrates? Let any one reflect upon himself, and conclude that he has in himself an immaterial spirit, which is that which thinks in him, and, in the constant change of his body keeps him the same: and is that which he calls HIMSELF: let him also suppose it to be the same soul that was in Nestor or Thersites, at the siege of Troy, (for souls being, as far as we know anything of them, in their nature indifferent to any parcel of matter, the supposition has no apparent absurdity in it,) which it may have been, as well as it is now the soul of any other man: but he now having no consciousness of any of the actions either of Nestor or Thersites, does or can he conceive himself the same person with either of them? Can he be concerned in either of their actions? attribute them to himself, or think them his own more than the actions of any other men that ever existed? So that this consciousness, not reaching to any of the actions of either of those men, he is no more one SELF with either of them than of the soul of immaterial spirit that now informs him had been created, and began to exist, when it began to inform his present body; though it were never so true, that the same SPIRIT that informed Nestor's or Thersites' body were numerically the same that now informs his. For this would no more make him the same person with Nestor, than if some of the particles of smaller that were once a part of Nestor were now a part of this man the same immaterial substance, without the same consciousness, no more making the same person, by being united to any body, than the same particle of matter, without consciousness, united to any body, makes the same person. But let him once find himself conscious of any of the actions of Nestor, he then finds himself the same person with Nestor.

17. THE BODY, AS WELL AS THE SOUL, GOES TO THE MAKING OF A MAN

And thus may we be able, without any difficulty, to conceive the same person at the resurrection, though in a body not exactly in make or parts the same which he had here,—the same consciousness going along with the soul that inhabits it. But yet the soul alone, in the change of bodies, would scarce to any one but to him that makes the soul the man, be enough to make the same man. For should the soul of a prince, carrying with it the consciousness of the prince's past life, enter and inform the body of a cobbler, as soon as deserted by his own soul, every one sees he would be the same PERSON with the prince, accountable only for the prince's actions: but who would say it was the same MAN? The body too goes to the making the man, and would, I guess, to everybody determine the man in this case, wherein the soul, with all its princely thoughts about it, would not make another man: but he would be the same cobbler to every one besides himself. I know that, in the ordinary way of speaking, the same person, and

the same man, stand for one and the same thing. And indeed every one will always have a liberty to speak as he pleases, and to apply what articulate sounds to what ideas he thinks fit, and change them as often as he pleases. But yet, when we will inquire what makes the same SPIRIT, MAN, or PERSON, we must fix the ideas of spirit, man, or person in our minds; and having resolved with ourselves what we mean by them, it will not be hard to determine, in either of them, or the like, when it is the same, and when not.

18. CONSCIOUSNESS ALONE UNITES ACTIONS INTO THE SAME PERSON

But though the same immaterial substance or soul does not alone, wherever it be, and in whatsoever state, make the same MAN; yet it is plain, consciousness, as far as ever it can be extended— should it be to ages past—unites existences and actions very remote in time into the same PERSON, as well as it does the existences and actions of the immediately preceding moment: so that whatever has the consciousness of present and past actions, is the same person to whom they both belong. Had I the same consciousness that I saw the ark and Noah's flood, as that I saw an overflowing of the Thames last winter, or as that I write now, I could no more doubt that I who write this now, that saw the Thames overflowed last winter, and that viewed the flood at the general deluge, was the same SELF,—place that self in what SUBSTANCE you please—than that I who write this am the same MYSELF now whilst I write (whether I consist of all the same substance material or immaterial, or no) that I was yesterday. For as to this point of being the same self, it matters not whether this present self be made up of the same or other substances—I being as much concerned, and as justly accountable for any action that was done a thousand years since, appropriated to me now by this self-consciousness, as I am for what I did the last moment.

19. SELF DEPENDS ON CONSCIOUSNESS, NOT ON SUBSTANCE

SELF is that conscious thinking thing,—whatever substance made up of, (whether spiritual or material, simple or compounded, it matters not)—which is sensible or conscious of pleasure and pain, capable of happiness or misery, and so is concerned for itself, as far as that consciousness extends. Thus every one finds that, whilst comprehended under that consciousness, the little finger is as much a part of himself as what is most so. Upon separation of this little finger, should this consciousness go along with the little finger, and leave the rest of the body, it is evident the little finger would be the person, the same person; and self then would have nothing to do with the rest of the body. As in this case it is the consciousness that goes along with the substance, when one part is separate from another, which makes the same person, and constitutes this inseparable self: so it is in reference to substances remote in time. That with which the consciousness of this present thinking thing CAN join itself, makes the same person, and is one self with it, and with nothing else; and so attributes to itself, and owns all the actions of that thing, as its own, as far as that consciousness reaches, and no further; as every one who reflects will perceive.

20. PERSONS, NOT SUBSTANCES, THE OBJECTS OF REWARD AND PUNISHMENT.

In this personal identity is founded all the right and justice of reward and punishment; happiness and misery being that for which every one is concerned for HIMSELF, and not mattering what becomes of any SUBSTANCE, not joined to, or affected with that consciousness. For, as it is evident in the instance I gave but now, if the consciousness went along with the little finger when it was cut off, that would be the same self which was concerned for the whole body yesterday, as making part of itself, whose actions then it cannot but admit as its own now. Though, if the same body should still live, and immediately from the separation of the little finger have its own peculiar consciousness, whereof the little finger knew nothing, it would not at all be concerned for it, as a part of itself, or could own any of its actions, or have any of them imputed to him.

21. WHICH SHOWS WHEREIN PERSONAL IDENTITY CONSISTS

This may show us wherein personal identity consists: not in the identity of substance, but, as I have said, in the identity of consciousness, wherein if Socrates and the present mayor of Queenborough agree, they are the same person: if the same Socrates waking and sleeping do not partake of the same consciousness, Socrates waking and sleeping is not the same person. And to punish Socrates waking for what sleeping Socrates thought, and waking Socrates was never conscious of, would be no more of right, than to punish one twin for what his brother-twin did, whereof he knew nothing, because their outsides were so like, that they could not be distinguished; for such twins have been seen.

Study Questions

1. Locke claims that much confusion can be avoided if the concepts of *person*, *man*, and *substance* are kept separate. Explain the differences and why Locke rejects being the same man and being the same substance as candidates for being the same person.

2. Locke claims that we can make sense of the idea of the consciousness of a prince being placed in the body of a cobbler. In such a case, Locke claims, the prince would be a different man, but the same person. Do you agree?

3. One implication of Locke's account is that if a person cannot remember performing an act, she is not responsible for it (see section 20). Explain how this follows from Locke's account of personal identity. Is it a good implication or a bad one?

Essays on the Intellectual Powers of Man   7.2

THOMAS REID

THOMAS REID (1710–1796), a Scottish philosopher, was a founder of the "commonsense" school of philosophy. The commonsense school argued that there are a number of common principles that we are justified in believing without providing evidence of their truth and that these common principles provide an epistemological foundation for science and ordinary reasoning. In addition to his work on common sense, Reid is well known for his work on the epistemology of sensation, his agent-causation account of free will, and his acute criticisms of Locke, Berkeley, and Hume. Below is one of Reid's most famous objections to Locke's theory of personal identity, known as the Brave Officer paradox, in which a general remembers stealing a flag as a soldier, when stealing the flag the soldier remembers being flogged as a boy, but the general has no memory of being flogged. Reid points out that this thought experiment demonstrates a troubling consequence of Locke's account, which holds that the boy is identical to the soldier, the soldier is identical to the general, but the boy is not identical to the general. In addition to violating many people's intuitions, this violates the law of transitivity, which states that if $a = b$ and $b = c$, then $a = c$.

OF IDENTITY

The conviction which every man has of his identity, as far back as his memory reaches, needs no aid of philosophy to strengthen it; and no philosophy can weaken it, without first producing some degree of insanity.

The philosopher, however, may very properly consider this conviction as a phenomenon of human nature worthy of his attention. If he can discover its cause, an addition is made to his stock of knowledge; if not, it must be held as a part of our original constitution, or an effect of that constitution produced in a manner unknown to us.

We may observe, first of all, that this conviction is indispensably necessary to all exercise of reason. The operations of reason, whether in action or in speculation, are made up of successive parts. The antecedent are the foundation

Thomas Reid, "Of Mr. Locke's Account of our Personal Identity," *Essays on the Intellectual Powers of Man: A Critical Edition*, edited by Derek R. Brookes (University Park, PA: Penn State University Press, 2002/1785).

of the consequent, and, without the conviction that the antecedent have been seen or done by me, I could have no reason to proceed to the consequent, in any speculation, or in any active project whatever.

There can be no memory of what is past without the conviction that we existed at the time remembered. There may be good arguments to convince me that I existed before the earliest thing I can remember; but to suppose that my memory reaches a moment farther back than my belief and conviction of my existence, is a contradiction.

The moment a man loses this conviction, as if he had drunk the water of Lethe, past things are done away; and, in his own belief, he then begins to exist. Whatever was thought, or said, or done, or suffered before that period, may belong to some other person; but he can never impute it to himself, or take any subsequent step that supposes it to be his doing.

From this it is evident that we must have the conviction of our own continued existence and identity, as soon as we are capable of thinking or doing anything, on account of what we have thought, or done, or suffered before; that is, as soon as we are reasonable creatures.

That we may form as distinct a notion as we are able of this phenomenon of the human mind, it is proper to consider what is meant by identity in general, what by our own personal identity, and how we are led into that invincible belief and conviction which every man has of his own personal identity, as far as his memory reaches.

Identity in general I take to be a relation between a thing which is known to exist at one time, and a thing which is known to have existed at another time. If you ask whether they are one and the same, or two different things, every man of common sense understands the meaning of your question perfectly. Whence we may infer with certainty, that every man of common sense has a clear and distinct notion of identity.

If you ask a definition of identity, I confess I can give none; it is too simple a notion to admit of logical definition: I can say it is a relation, but I cannot find words to express the specific difference between this and other relations, though I am in no danger of confounding it with any other. I can say that diversity is a contrary relation, and that similitude and dissimilitude are another couple of contrary relations, which every man easily distinguishes in his conception from identity and diversity.

I see evidently that identity supposes an uninterrupted continuance of existence. That which has ceased to exist cannot be the same with that which afterwards begins to exist; for this would be to suppose a being to exist after it ceased to exist, and to have had existence before it was produced, which are manifest contradictions. Continued uninterrupted existence is therefore necessarily implied in identity.

Hence we may infer, that identity cannot, in its proper sense, be applied to our pains, our pleasures, our thought, or any operation of our minds. The pain felt this day is not the same individual pain which I felt yesterday, though they may be *similar* in kind and degree, and have the same cause. The same may be said of every feeling, and of every operation of mind. They are all successive in their nature, like time itself, no two moments of which can be the same moment.

It is otherwise with the parts of absolute space. They always are, and were, and will be the same. So far, I think, we proceed upon clear ground in fixing the notion of identity in general.

It is perhaps more difficult to ascertain with precision the meaning of personality; but it is not necessary in the present subject: it is sufficient for our purpose to observe, that all mankind place their personality in something that cannot be divided or consist of parts.

A part of a person is a manifest absurdity. When a man loses his estate, his health, his strength, he is still the same person, and has lost nothing of his personality. If he has a leg or an arm cut off, he is the same person he was before. The amputated member is no part of his person, otherwise it would have a right to a part of his estate, and be liable for a part of his engagements. It would be entitled to a share of his merit and demerit, which is manifestly absurd. A person is something indivisible, and is what Leibniz calls a *monad*.

My personal identity, therefore, implies the continued existence of that indivisible thing which I call *myself*. Whatever this self may be, it is something which thinks, and deliberates, and resolves, and acts, and suffers. I am not thought, I am not action, I am not feeling; I am something that thinks, and acts, and suffers. My thoughts, and actions, and feelings, change every moment: they have no continued, but a successive, existence; but that *self*, or *I*, to which they belong, is permanent, and has the same relation to all the succeeding thoughts, actions, and feelings which I call mine.

Such are the notions that I have of my personal identity. But perhaps it may be said, this may all be fancy without reality. How do you know—what evidence have you—that there is such a permanent self which has a claim to all the thoughts, actions, and feelings which you call yours?

To this I answer, that the proper evidence I have of all this is remembrance, I remember that twenty years ago I conversed with such a person; I remember several things that passed in that conversation: my memory testifies, not only that this was done, but that it was done by me who now remember it. If it was done by me, I must have existed at that time, and continued to exist from that time to the present: if the identical person whom I call myself had not a part in that conversation, my memory is fallacious; it gives a distinct and positive testimony of what is not true. Every man in his senses believes what he distinctly remembers, and every thing he remembers convinces him that he existed at the time remembered.

Although memory gives the most irresistible evidence of my being the identical person that did such a thing, at such a time, I may have other good evidence of things which befell me, and which I do not remember: I know who bare me, and suckled me, but I do not remember these events.

It may here be observed (though the observation would have been unnecessary, if some great philosophers had not contradicted it), that it is not my remembering any action of mine that makes me to be the person who did it. This remembrance makes me to know assuredly that I did it; but I might have done it, though I did not remember it. That relation to me, which is expressed by saying that I did it, would be the same, though I had not the least remembrance of it. To say that my remembering that I did such a thing, or, as some choose to express it, my being conscious that I did it, makes me to have done it, appears to me as great an absurdity as it would be to say, that my belief that the world was created made it to be created.

When we pass judgment on the identity of other persons than ourselves, we proceed upon other grounds, and determine from a variety of circumstances, which sometimes produce the firmest assurance, and sometimes leave room for doubt. The identity of persons has often furnished matter of serious litigation before tribunals of justice. But no man of a sound mind ever doubted of his own identity, as far as he distinctly remembered.

The identity of a person is a perfect identity: wherever it is real, it admits of no degrees; and it is impossible that a person should be in part the same, and in part different; because a person is a *monad*, and is not divisible into parts. The evidence of identity in other persons than ourselves does indeed admit of all degrees, from what we account certainty, to the least degree of probability. But still it is true, that the same person is perfectly the same, and cannot be so in part, or in some degree only.

For this cause, I have first considered personal identity, as that which is perfect in its kind, and the natural measure of that which is imperfect.

We probably at first derive our notion of identity from that natural conviction which every man has from the dawn of reason of his own identity and continued existence. The operations of our minds are all successive, and have no continued existence. But the thinking being has a continued existence, and we have an invincible belief, that it remains the same when all its thoughts and operations change.

Our judgments of the identity of objects of sense seem to be formed much upon the same grounds as our judgments of the identity of other persons than ourselves.

Wherever we observe great similarity, we are apt to presume identity, if no reason appears to the contrary. Two objects ever so like, when they are perceived at the same time, cannot be the same; but if they are presented to our senses at different times, we are apt to think them the same, merely from their similarity.

Whether this be a natural prejudice, or from whatever cause it proceeds, it certainly appears in children from infancy; and when we grow up, it is confirmed in most instances by experience: for we rarely find two individuals of the same species that are not distinguishable by obvious differences.

A man challenges a thief whom he finds in possession of his horse or his watch, only on similarity. When the watchmaker swears that he sold this watch to such a person, his testimony is grounded on similarity. The testimony of witnesses to the identity of a person is commonly grounded on no other evidence.

Thus it appears, that the evidence we have of our own identity, as far back as we remember, is totally of a different kind from the evidence we have of the identity of other persons, or of objects of sense. The first is grounded on memory, and gives undoubted certainty. The last is grounded on similarity, and on other circumstances, which in many cases are not so decisive as to leave no room for doubt.

It may likewise be observed, that the identity of objects of sense is never perfect. All bodies, as they consist of innumerable parts that may be disjoined from them by a great variety of causes, are subject to continual changes of their

substance, increasing, diminishing, changing insensibly. When such alterations are gradual, because language could not afford a different name for every different state of such a changeable being, it retains the same name, and is considered as the same thing. Thus we say of an old regiment, that it did such a thing a century ago, though there now is not a man alive who then belonged to it. We say a tree is the same in the seed-bed and in the forest. A ship of war, which has successively changed her anchors, her tackle, her sails, her masts, her planks, and her timbers, while she keeps the same name, is the same.

The identity, therefore, which we ascribe to bodies, whether natural or artificial, is not perfect identity; it is rather something which, for the convenience of speech, we call identity. It admits of a great change of the subject, providing the change be gradual; sometimes, even of a total change. And the changes which in common language are made consistent with identity differ from those that are thought to destroy it, not in kind, but in number and degree. It has no fixed nature when applied to bodies; and questions about the identity of a body are very often questions about words. But identity, when applied to persons, has no ambiguity, and admits not of degrees, or of more and less. It is the foundation of all rights and obligations, and of all accountableness; and the notion of it is fixed and precise.

OF MR. LOCKE'S ACCOUNT OF OUR PERSONAL IDENTITY

In a long chapter upon Identity and Diversity, Mr. Locke has made many ingenious and just observations, and some which I think cannot be defended. I shall only take notice of the account he gives of our own personal identity. His doctrine upon this subject has been censured by Bishop Butler, in a short essay subjoined to his *Analogy*, with whose sentiments I perfectly agree.

Identity, as was observed (Chap. 4 of this Essay), supposes the continued existence of the being of which it is affirmed, and therefore can be applied only to things which have a continued existence. While any being continues to exist, it is the same being; but two beings which have a different beginning or a different ending of their existence cannot possibly be the same. To this, I think, Mr. Locke agrees.

He observes, very justly, that, to know what is meant by the same person, we must consider what the word *person* stands for; and he defines a person to be an intelligent being, endowed with reason and with consciousness, which last he thinks inseparable from thought.

From this definition of a person, it must necessarily follow, that, while the intelligent being continues to exist and to be intelligent, it must be the same person. To say that the intelligent being is the person, and yet that the person ceases to exist while the intelligent being continues, or that the person continues while the intelligent being ceases to exist, is to my apprehension a manifest contradiction.

One would think that the definition of a person should perfectly ascertain the nature of personal identity, or wherein it consists, though it might still be a question how we come to know and be assured of our personal identity.

Mr. Locke tells us, however, "that personal identity, that is, the sameness of a rational being, consists in consciousness alone, and, as far as this consciousness can be extended backwards to any past action or thought, so far reaches the identity of that person. So that whatever has the consciousness of present and past actions is the same person to whom they belong."

This doctrine has some strange consequences, which the author was aware of. Such as, that if the same consciousness can be transferred from one intelligent being to another, which he thinks we cannot show to be impossible, *then two or twenty intelligent beings may be the same person*. And if the intelligent being may lose the consciousness of the actions done by him, which surely is possible, then he is not the person that did those actions; so that *one intelligent being may be two*

or twenty different persons, if he shall so often lose the consciousness of this former actions.

There is another consequence of this doctrine, which follows no less necessarily, though Mr. Locke probably did not see it. It is, *that a man may be, and at the same time not be, the person that did a particular action.*

Suppose a brave officer to have been flogged when a boy at school for robbing an orchard, to have taken a standard from the enemy in his first campaign, and to have been made a general in advanced life; suppose, also, which must be admitted to be possible, that, when he took the standard, he was conscious of his having been flogged at school, and that, when made a general, he was conscious of his taking the standard, but had absolutely lost the consciousness of his flogging.

These things being supposed, it follows, from Mr. Locke's doctrine, that he who was flogged at school is the same person who took the standard, and that he who took the standard is the same person who was made a general. Whence it follows, if there be any truth in logic, that the general is the same person with him who was flogged at school. But the general's consciousness does not reach so far back as his flogging; therefore, according to Mr. Locke's doctrine, he is not the person who was flogged. Therefore the general is, and at the same time is not, the same person with him who was flogged at school.

Leaving the consequences of this doctrine to those who have leisure to trace them, we may observe, with regard to the doctrine itself,

First, that Mr. Locke attributes to consciousness the conviction we have of our past actions, as if a man may now be conscious of what he did twenty years ago. It is impossible to understand the meaning of this, unless by consciousness he meant memory, the only faculty by which we have an immediate knowledge of our past actions.

Sometimes, in popular discourse, a man says he is conscious that he did such a thing, meaning that he distinctly remembers that he did it. It is unnecessary, in common discourse, to fix accurately the limits between consciousness and memory. This was formerly shown to be the case with regard to sense and memory: and therefore distinct remembrance is sometimes called sense, sometimes consciousness, without any inconvenience.

But this ought to be avoided in philosophy, otherwise we confound the different powers of the mind, and ascribe to one what really belongs to another. If a man can be conscious of what he did twenty years or twenty minutes ago, there is no use for memory, nor ought we to allow that there is any such faculty. The faculties of consciousness and memory are chiefly distinguished by this, that the first is an immediate knowledge of the present, the second an immediate knowledge of the past.

When, therefore, Mr. Locke's notion of personal identity is properly expressed, it is, that personal identity consists in distinct remembrance: for, even in the popular sense, to say that I am conscious of a part action means nothing else than that I distinctly remember that I did it.

Secondly, it may be observed, that, in this doctrine, not only is consciousness confounded with memory, but, which is still more strange, personal identity is confounded with the evidence which we have of our personal identity.

It is very true, that my remembrance that I did such a thing is the evidence I have that I am the identical person who did it. And this, I am apt to think, Mr. Locke meant. But to say that my remembrance that I did such a thing, or my consciousness, makes me the person who did it, is, in my apprehension, an absurdity too gross to be entertained by any man who attends to the meaning of it; for it is to attribute to memory or consciousness a strange magical power of producing its object, though that object must have existed before the memory or consciousness which produced it.

Consciousness is the testimony of one faculty; memory is the testimony of another faculty; and to say that the testimony is the cause of the thing testified, this surely is absurd, if any thing be, and could not have been said by Mr. Locke, if he had not confounded the testimony with the thing testified.

When a horse that was stolen is found and claimed by the owner, the only evidence he can have, or that a judge or witnesses can have, that this is the very identical horse which was his property, is similitude. But would it not be ridiculous from this to infer that the identity of a horse consists in similitude only? The only evidence I have that I am the identical person who did such actions is, that I remember distinctly I did them; or, as Mr. Locke expresses it, I am conscious I did them. To infer from this, that personal identity consists in consciousness, is an argument which, if it had any force, would prove the identity of a stolen horse to consist solely in similitude.

Thirdly, is it not strange that the sameness or identity of a person should consist in a thing which is continually changing, and is not any two minutes the same?

Our consciousness, our memory, and every operation of the mind, are still flowing like the water of a river, or like time itself. The consciousness I have this moment can no more be the same consciousness I had last moment, than this moment can be the last moment. Identity can only be affirmed of things which have a continued existence. Consciousness, and every kind of thought, are transient and momentary, and have no continued existence; and, therefore, if personal identity consisted in consciousness, it would certainly follow, that no man is the same person any two moments of his life; and as the right and justice of reward and punishment are founded on personal identity, no man could be responsible for his actions.

But though I take this to be the unavoidable consequence of Mr. Locke's doctrine concerning personal identity, and though some persons may have liked the doctrine the better on this account, I am far from imputing any thing of this kind to Mr. Locke. He was too good a man not to have rejected with abhorrence a doctrine which he believed to draw this consequence after it.

Fourthly, there are many expressions used by Mr. Locke, in speaking of personal identity, which to me are altogether unintelligible, unless we suppose that he confounded that sameness or identity which we ascribed to an individual with the identity which, in common discourse, is often ascribed to many individuals of the same species.

When we say that pain and pleasure, consciousness and memory, are the same in all men, this sameness can only mean similarity, or sameness of kind. That the pain of one man can be the same individual pain with that of another man is no less impossible, than that one man should be another man: the pain felt by me yesterday can no more be the pain I feel to-day, than yesterday can be this day; and the same thing may be said of every passion and of every operation of the mind. The same kind or species of operation may be in different men, or in the same man at different times; but it is impossible that the same individual operation should be in different men, or in the same man at different times.

When Mr. Locke, therefore, speaks of "the same consciousness being continued through a succession of different substances"; when he speaks of "repeating the idea of a past action, with the same consciousness we had of it at the first," and of "the same consciousness extending to actions past and to come"; these expressions are to me unintelligible, unless he means not the same individual consciousness, but a consciousness that is similar, or of the same kind.

If our personal identity consists in consciousness, as this consciousness cannot be the same individually any two moments, but only of the same kind, it would follow, that we are not for any two moments the same individual persons, but the same kind of persons.

As our consciousness sometimes ceases to exist, as in sound sleep, our personal identity must cease with it. Mr. Locke allows, that the same thing cannot have two beginnings of existence, so that our identity would be irrecoverably gone every time we ceased to think, if it was but for a moment.

Study Questions

1. Explain the thought experiment of the boy, the officer, and the general. Why does Reid think this demonstrates a problem for Locke's account?
2. Reid claims that Locke conflates the faculties of consciousness and memory. What, precisely, is Reid's complaint? Is Reid correct that this is a problem with Locke's account?
3. Reid claims that consciousness is a bad candidate for explaining the continued existence of an individual person because consciousness is constantly changing. Is he right? What else might our continued existence depend on?

7.3   Treatise of Human Nature

    DAVID HUME

DAVID HUME (1711–1776) was a Scottish philosopher, historian, and economist whose work was influential in many different spheres. Hume turned his skeptical eye toward a variety of topics—including causation, perceptual knowledge, the intelligent design argument, morality, and personal identity—and many of his positions have been adopted by contemporary philosophers, including his accounts of causation, morality, and personal identity. The following selection is taken from his most influential philosophical work, *A Treatise of Human Nature*, published before Hume turned thirty. Hume argues that when he turns his mind on itself, he never finds any evidence of a simple, enduring self; all he perceives are the mental states themselves (beliefs, memories, perceptions, experiences, emotions). He then provides an account for the common belief that there exists a self by explaining how the psychological workings of our mind give rise to the illusion that there is such an enduring self. He concludes that the interesting philosophical questions about personal identity cannot be answered, but instead should be taken as grammatical issues.

SECT. VI. OF PERSONAL IDENTITY

There are some philosophers who imagine we are every moment intimately conscious of what we call our SELF; that we feel its existence and its continuance in existence; and are certain, beyond the evidence of a demonstration, both of its perfect identity and simplicity. The strongest sensation, the most violent passion, say they, instead of distracting us from this view, only fix it the more intensely, and make us consider their influence on self either by their pain or pleasure. To attempt a farther proof of this were to weaken its evidence; since no proof can be derived from any fact, of which we are so intimately conscious; nor is there any thing, of which we can be certain, if we doubt of this.

Unluckily all these positive assertions are contrary to that very experience, which is pleaded for them, nor have we any idea of self, after the manner it is here explained. For from what impression coued this idea be derived? This question it is impossible to answer without a manifest contradiction and absurdity; and yet it is a question, which must necessarily be answered, if we would have the idea of self pass for clear and intelligible. It must be some one impression, that gives rise to every real idea. But self or person is not any one impression, but that to which our several impressions and ideas are supposed to have a reference. If any impression gives rise to the idea of self, that impression must continue invariably the same, through the whole course of our lives; since self is supposed to exist after that manner. But there is no impression constant and invariable. Pain and pleasure, grief and joy, passions and sensations succeed each other, and never all exist at the same time. It cannot, therefore, be from any of these impressions, or from any other, that the

David Hume, *A Treatise of Human Nature* (2000), edited by David F. Norton and Mary J. Norton. By permission of Oxford University Press.

idea of self is derived; and consequently there is no such idea.

But farther, what must become of all our particular perceptions upon this hypothesis? All these are different, and distinguishable, and separable from each other, and may be separately considered, and may exist separately, and have no need of any thing to support their existence. After what manner, therefore, do they belong to self; and how are they connected with it? For my part, when I enter most intimately into what I call myself, I always stumble on some particular perception or other, of heat or cold, light or shade, love or hatred, pain or pleasure. I never can catch myself at any time without a perception, and never can observe any thing but the perception. When my perceptions are removed for any time, as by sound sleep; so long am I insensible of myself, and may truly be said not to exist. And were all my perceptions removed by death, and coued I neither think, nor feel, nor see, nor love, nor hate after the dissolution of my body, I should be entirely annihilated, nor do I conceive what is farther requisite to make me a perfect non-entity. If any one, upon serious and unprejudiced reflection thinks he has a different notion of himself, I must confess I call reason no longer with him. All I can allow him is, that he may be in the right as well as I, and that we are essentially different in this particular. He may, perhaps, perceive something simple and continued, which he calls himself; though I am certain there is no such principle in me.

But setting aside some metaphysicians of this kind, I may venture to affirm of the rest of mankind, that they are nothing but a bundle or collection of different perceptions, which succeed each other with an inconceivable rapidity, and are in a perpetual flux and movement. Our eyes cannot turn in their sockets without varying our perceptions. Our thought is still more variable than our sight; and all our other senses and faculties contribute to this change; nor is there any single power of the soul, which remains unalterably the same, perhaps for one moment. The mind is a kind of theatre, where several perceptions successively make their appearance; pass, re-pass, glide away, and mingle in an infinite variety of postures and situations. There is properly no simplicity in it at one time, nor identity in different; whatever natural propension we may have to imagine that simplicity and identity. The comparison of the theatre must not mislead us. They are the successive perceptions only, that constitute the mind; nor have we the most distant notion of the place, where these scenes are represented, or of the materials, of which it is composed.

What then gives us so great a propension to ascribe an identity to these successive perceptions, and to suppose ourselves possest of an invariable and uninterrupted existence through the whole course of our lives? In order to answer this question, we must distinguish betwixt personal identity, as it regards our thought or imagination, and as it regards our passions or the concern we take in ourselves. The first is our present subject; and to explain it perfectly we must take the matter pretty deep, and account for that identity, which we attribute to plants and animals; there being a great analogy betwixt it, and the identity of a self or person.

We have a distinct idea of an object, that remains invariable and uninterrupted through a supposed variation of time; and this idea we call that of identity or sameness. We have also a distinct idea of several different objects existing in succession, and connected together by a close relation; and this to an accurate view affords as perfect a notion of diversity, as if there was no manner of relation among the objects. But though these two ideas of identity, and a succession of related objects be in themselves perfectly distinct, and even contrary, yet it is certain, that in our common way of thinking they are generally confounded with each other. That action of the imagination, by which we consider the uninterrupted and invariable object, and that by which we reflect on the succession of related objects, are almost the same to the feeling, nor is there much more effort of thought required in the latter case than in the former. The relation facilitates the transition of the mind from one object to another, and renders its passage as smooth as if it contemplated one continued object. This resemblance is the cause of the confusion and mistake, and makes us substitute the notion of identity, instead of that of related objects. However at one instant we may consider the related succession as variable or interrupted, we are sure the next to ascribe to it a perfect identity, and regard it as enviable and uninterrupted. Our propensity to this mistake is so great from the resemblance above-mentioned, that we fall into it before we are aware; and though we incessantly correct ourselves by reflection, and return to a more accurate method of thinking, yet we cannot long sustain our philosophy, or take off this biass from the imagination. Our last resource is to yield to it, and boldly assert that these different related objects are in effect the same, however interrupted and variable. In order to justify to ourselves this absurdity, we often feign some new and unintelligible principle, that connects the objects together, and prevents their interruption or variation. Thus we feign the continued existence of the perceptions of our senses, to remove the interruption: and run into the notion of a soul, and self, and substance, to disguise the variation. But we may farther observe, that where we do not give rise to such a fiction, our propension to confound identity with relation is so great, that we are apt to imagine something unknown and mysterious, connecting the parts, beside their relation; and this I take to be the case with regard to the identity we ascribe to plants and vegetables. And even when this does not take place, we still feel a propensity to confound these ideas, though we are not able fully to satisfy ourselves in that particular, nor find any thing invariable and uninterrupted to justify our notion of identity.

Thus the controversy concerning identity is not merely a dispute of words. For when we attribute identity, in an improper sense, to variable or interrupted objects, our mistake is not confined to the expression, but is commonly attended with a fiction, either of something invariable and uninterrupted, or of something mysterious and inexplicable, or at least with a propensity to such fictions. What will suffice to prove this hypothesis to the satisfaction of every fair enquirer, is to shew from daily experience and observation, that the objects, which are variable or interrupted, and yet are supposed to continue the same, are such only as consist of a succession of parts, connected together by resemblance, contiguity, or causation. For as such a succession answers evidently to our notion of diversity, it can only be by mistake we ascribe to it an identity; and as the relation of parts, which leads us into this mistake, is really nothing but a quality, which produces an association of ideas, and an easy transition of the imagination from one to another, it can only be from the resemblance, which this act of the mind bears to that, by which we contemplate one continued object, that the error arises. Our chief business, then, must be to prove, that all objects, to which we ascribe identity, without observing their invariableness and uninterruptedness, are such as consist of a succession of related objects.

In order to this, suppose any mass of matter, of which the parts are contiguous and connected, to be placed before us; it is plain we must attribute a perfect identity to this mass, provided all the parts continue uninterruptedly and invariably the same, whatever motion or change of place we may observe either in the whole or in any of the parts. But supposing some very small or inconsiderable part to be added to the mass, or subtracted from it; though this absolutely destroys the identity of the whole, strictly speaking; yet as we seldom think so accurately, we scruple not to pronounce a mass of matter the same, where we find so trivial an alteration. The passage of the thought from the object before the change to the object after it, is so smooth and easy, that we scarce perceive the transition, and are apt to imagine, that it is nothing but a continued survey of the same object.

There is a very remarkable circumstance, that attends this experiment; which is, that though the change of any considerable part in a mass of matter destroys the identity of the whole, yet we must measure the greatness of the part, not absolutely, but by its proportion to the whole. The addition or diminution of a mountain would not be sufficient to produce a diversity in a planet: though the change of a very few inches would be able to destroy the identity of some bodies. It will be impossible to account for this, but by reflecting that objects operate upon the mind, and break or interrupt the continuity of its actions not according to their real greatness, but according to their proportion to each other: And therefore, since this interruption makes an object cease to appear the same, it must be the uninterrupted progress of the thought, which constitutes the imperfect identity.

This may be confirmed by another phenomenon. A change in any considerable part of a body destroys its identity; but it is remarkable, that where the change is produced gradually and insensibly we are less apt to ascribe to it the same effect. The reason can plainly be no other, than that the mind, in following the successive changes of the body, feels an easy passage from the surveying its condition in one moment to the viewing of it in another, and at no particular time perceives any interruption in its actions. From which continued perception, it ascribes a continued existence and identity to the object.

But whatever precaution we may use in introducing the changes gradually, and making them proportionable to the whole, it is certain, that where the changes are at last observed to become considerable, we make a scruple of ascribing identity to such different objects. There is, however, another artifice, by which we may induce the imagination to advance a step farther; and that is, by producing a reference of the parts to each other, and a combination to some common end or purpose. A ship, of which a considerable part has been changed by frequent reparations, is still considered as the same; nor does the difference of the materials hinder us from ascribing an identity to it. The common end, in which the parts conspire, is the same under all their variations, and affords an easy transition of the imagination from one situation of the body to another.

But this is still more remarkable, when we add a sympathy of parts to their common end, and suppose that they bear to each other, the reciprocal relation of cause and effect in all their actions and operations. This is the case with all animals and vegetables; where not only the several parts have a reference to some general purpose, but also a mutual dependence on, and connexion with each other. The effect of so strong a relation is, that though every one must allow, that in a very few years both vegetables and animals endure a total change, yet we still attribute identity to them, while their form, size, and substance are entirely altered. An oak, that grows from a small plant to a large tree, is still the same oak; though there be not one particle of matter, or figure of its parts the same. An infant becomes a man, and is sometimes fat, sometimes lean, without any change in his identity.

We may also consider the two following phænomena, which are remarkable in their kind. The first is, that though we commonly be able to distinguish pretty exactly betwixt numerical and specific identity, yet it sometimes happens, that we confound them, and in our thinking and reasoning employ the one for the other. Thus a man, who hears a noise, that is frequently interrupted and renewed, says, it is still the same noise; though it is evident the sounds have only a specific identity or resemblance, and there is nothing numerically the same, but the cause, which produced them. In like manner it may be said without breach of the propriety of language, that such a church, which was formerly of brick, fell to ruin, and that the parish rebuilt the same church of free-stone, and according to modern architecture. Here neither the form nor materials are the same, nor is there any thing common to the two objects, but their relation to the inhabitants of the parish; and yet this alone is sufficient to make us denominate them the same. But we must observe, that in these cases the first object is in a manner annihilated before the second comes into existence; by which means, we are never presented in any one point of time with the idea of difference and multiplicity: and for that reason are less scrupulous in calling them the same.

Secondly, We may remark, that though in a succession of related objects, it be in a manner requisite, that the change of parts be not sudden nor entire, in order to preserve the identity, yet where the objects are in their nature changeable and inconstant, we admit of a more sudden transition, than would otherwise be consistent with that relation. Thus as the nature of a river consists in the motion and change of parts; though in less than four and twenty hours these be totally altered; this hinders not the river from continuing the same during several ages. What is natural and essential to any thing is, in a manner, expected; and what is expected makes less impression, and appears of less moment, than what is unusual and extraordinary. A considerable change of the former kind seems really less to the imagination, than the most trivial alteration of the latter; and by breaking less the continuity of the thought, has less influence in destroying the identity.

We now proceed to explain the nature of personal identity, which has become so great a question in philosophy, especially of late years in England, where all the abstruser sciences are studied with a peculiar ardour and application. And here it is evident, the same method of reasoning must be continued which has so successfully explained the identity of plants, and animals, and ships, and houses, and of all the compounded and changeable productions either of art or nature. The identity, which we ascribe to the mind of man, is only a fictitious one, and of a like kind with that which we ascribe to vegetables and animal bodies. It cannot, therefore, have a different origin, but must proceed from a like operation of the imagination upon like objects.

But lest this argument should not convince the reader; though in my opinion perfectly decisive; let him weigh the following reasoning, which is still closer and more immediate. It is evident, that the identity, which we attribute to the human mind, however perfect we may imagine it to be, is not able to run the several different perceptions into one, and make them lose their characters of distinction and difference, which are essential to them. It is still true, that every distinct perception, which enters into the composition of the mind, is a distinct existence, and is different, and distinguishable, and separable from every other perception, either contemporary or successive. But, as, notwithstanding this distinction and separability, we suppose the whole train of perceptions to be united by identity, a question naturally arises concerning this relation of identity; whether it be something that really binds our several perceptions together, or only associates their ideas in the imagination. That is, in other words, whether in pronouncing concerning the identity of a person, we observe some real bond among his perceptions, or only feel one among the ideas we form of them. This question we might easily decide, if we would recollect what has been already proud at large, that the understanding never observes any real connexion among objects, and that even the union of cause and effect, when strictly examined, resolves itself into a customary association of ideas. For from thence it evidently follows, that identity is nothing really belonging to these different perceptions, and uniting them together; but is merely a quality, which we attribute to them, because of the union of their ideas in the imagination, when we reflect upon them. Now the only qualities, which can give ideas an union in the imagination, are these three relations above-mentioned. These are the uniting principles in the ideal world, and without them every distinct object is separable by the mind, and may be separately considered, and appears not to have any more connexion with any other object, than if disjoined by the greatest difference and remoteness. It is, therefore, on some of these three relations of resemblance, contiguity and causation, that identity depends; and as the very essence of these relations consists in their producing an easy transition of ideas; it follows, that our notions of personal identity, proceed entirely from the smooth and uninterrupted progress of the thought along a train of connected ideas, according to the principles above-explained.

The only question, therefore, which remains, is, by what relations this uninterrupted progress of our thought is produced, when we consider the successive existence of a mind or thinking person. And here it is evident we must confine ourselves to resemblance and causation, and must drop contiguity, which has little or no influence in the present case.

To begin with resemblance; suppose we coued see clearly into the breast of another, and observe that succession of perceptions, which constitutes his mind or thinking principle, and suppose that he always preserves the memory of a considerable part of past perceptions; it is evident that nothing coued more contribute to the bestowing a relation on this succession amidst all its variations. For what is the memory but a faculty, by which we raise up the images of past perceptions? And as an image necessarily resembles its object, must not. The frequent placing of these resembling perceptions in the chain of thought, convey the imagination more easily from one link to another, and make the whole seem like the continuance of one object? In this particular, then, the memory not only discovers the identity, but also contributes to its production, by producing the relation of resemblance among the perceptions. The case is the same whether we consider ourselves or others.

As to causation; we may observe, that the true idea of the human mind, is to consider it as a system of different perceptions or different existences, which are linked together by the relation of cause and effect, and mutually produce, destroy, influence, and modify each other. Our impressions give rise to their correspondent ideas; and these ideas in their turn produce other impressions. One thought chaces another, and draws after it a third, by which it is expelled in its turn. In this respect, I cannot compare the soul more properly to any thing than to a republic or commonwealth, in which the several members are united by the reciprocal ties of government and subordination, and give rise to other persons, who propagate the same republic in the incessant changes of its parts. And as the same individual republic may not only change its members, but also its laws and constitutions; in like manner the same person may vary his character and disposition, as well as his impressions and ideas, without losing his identity. Whatever changes he endures, his several parts are still connected by the relation of causation. And in this view our identity with regard to the passions serves to corroborate that with regard to the imagination, by the making our distant perceptions influence each other, and by giving us a present concern for our past or future pains or pleasures.

As a memory alone acquaints us with the continuance and extent of this succession of perceptions, it is to be considered, upon that account chiefly, as the source of personal identity. Had we no memory, we never should have any notion of causation, nor consequently of that chain of causes and effects, which constitute our self or person. But having once acquired this notion of causation from the memory, we can extend the same chain of causes, and consequently the identity of our persons beyond our memory, and can comprehend times, and circumstances, and actions, which we have entirely forgot, but suppose in general to have existed. For how few of our past actions are there, of which we have any memory? Who can tell me, for instance, what were his thoughts and actions on the 1st of January 1715, the 11th of March 1719, and the 3rd of August 1733? Or will he affirm, because he has entirely forgot the incidents of these days, that the present self is not the same person with the self of that time; and by that means overturn all the most established notions of personal identity? In this view, therefore, memory does not so much produce as discover personal identity, by shewing us the relation of cause and effect among our different perceptions. It will be incumbent on those, who affirm that memory produces entirely our personal identity, to give a reason why we can thus extend our identity beyond our memory.

The whole of this doctrine leads us to a conclusion, which is of great importance in the present affair, viz. that all the nice and subtile questions concerning personal identity can never possibly be decided, and are to be regarded rather as gramatical than as philosophical difficulties. Identity depends on the relations of ideas; and these relations produce identity, by means of that easy transition they occasion. But as the relations, and the easiness of the transition may diminish by insensible degrees, we have no just standard, by which we can decide any dispute concerning the time, when they acquire or lose a title to the name of identity. All the disputes concerning the identity of connected objects are merely verbal, except so far as the relation of parts gives rise to some fiction or imaginary principle of union, as we have already observed.

What I have said concerning the first origin and uncertainty of our notion of identity, as applied to the human mind, may be extended with little or no variation to that of simplicity. An object, whose different co-existent parts are bound together by a close relation, operates upon the imagination after much the same manner as one perfectly simple and indivisible and requires not a much greater stretch of thought in order to its conception. From this similarity of operation we attribute a simplicity to it, and

feign a principle of union as the support of this simplicity, and the center of all the different parts and qualities of the object.

Thus we have finished our examination of the several systems of philosophy, both of the intellectual and natural world; and in our miscellaneous way of reasoning have been led into several topics; which will either illustrate and confirm some preceding part of this discourse, or prepare the way for our following opinions. It is now time to return to a more close examination of our subject, and to proceed in the accurate anatomy of human nature, having fully explained the nature of our judgment and understandings.

Study Questions

1. Hume argues that when he introspects he never finds anything but perceptions; that is, he never finds a stable consistent thing that might be called the self. Do you agree with Hume? Do you think that lack of introspective access to a self demonstrates that there is no self?

2. Hume draws an analogy between the soul and a republic, in which none of the various members of the republic or even its laws are necessary for the continued existence of the republic. Explain the ways in which the soul is like a republic and the ways in which the soul is different from a republic. Overall, do you believe that this analogy is apt?

3. Hume claims that memory "produces" rather than "discovers" personal identity. Explain what you think this means. How does it compare to Locke's account?

Divided Minds and the Nature of Persons   7.4

DEREK PARFIT

DEREK PARFIT (1942–) is an English philosopher and Emeritus Fellow of All Souls College, Oxford, where he taught for many years. His primary research interests are in personal identity, rationality, and ethics. His influential book *Reasons and Persons* (1984) explored the connections between these topics. He returned to these issues in his two-volume magnus opus *On What Matters* (2011). In the following selection, Parfit uses the empirical example of split-brain patients to argue for a Bundle Theory of personal identity. The Bundle Theory states that persons are long series of causally connected mental states, such as beliefs, memories, and experiences. Parfit contrasts the Bundle Theory with the Ego Theory, which claims that persons consist in the permanent existence of a single subject of experience.

It was the split-brain cases which drew me into philosophy. Our knowledge of these cases depends on the results of various psychological tests, as described by Donald MacKay. These tests made use of two facts. We control each of our arms, and see what is in each half of our visual fields, with only one of our hemispheres. When someone's hemispheres have been disconnected, psychologists can thus present to this person two different written questions in the two halves of his visual field, and can receive two different answers written by this person's two hands.

Here is a simplified imaginary version of the kind of evidence that such tests provide. One of these people looks fixedly at the centre of a wide screen, whose left half is red and right half is blue. On each half in a darker shade are the words, "How many colours can you see?" With both hands the person writes, "Only one." The words are now changed to read, "Which is the only colour that you can see?" With one of his hands the person writes "Red" with the other he writes "Blue."

If this is how such a person responds, I would conclude that he is having two visual sensations—that he does, as he claims, see both red and blue. But in seeing each colour he is not aware of seeing the other. He has two streams of consciousness, in each of which he can see only one colour. In one stream he sees red, and at the same time, in his other stream, he sees blue. More generally, he could be having at the same time two series of thoughts and sensations, in having each of which he is unaware of having the other.

This conclusion has been questioned. It has been claimed by some that there are not *two* streams of consciousness, on the ground that the sub-dominant hemisphere is a part of the brain whose functioning involves no consciousness. If this were true, these cases would lose most of their interest. I believe that it is not true, chiefly because, if a person's dominant hemisphere is destroyed, this person is able to react in the way in which, in the split-brain cases, the sub-dominant hemisphere reacts, and we do not believe that such a person is just an automaton, without

Derek Parfit, "Divided Minds and the Nature of Persons," in C. Blakemore and S. Greenfield (eds.), *Mindwaves* (New York: Basil Blackwell, 1987). Reprinted with permission of John Wiley & Sons Ltd.

consciousness. The sub-dominant hemisphere is, of course, much less developed in certain ways, typically having the linguistic abilities of a three-year-old. But three-year-olds are conscious. This supports the view that, in split-brain cases, there *are* two streams of consciousness.

Another view is that, in these cases, there are two persons involved, sharing the same body. Like Professor MacKay, I believe that we should reject this view. My reason for believing this is, however, different. Professor MacKay denies that there are two persons involved because he believes that there is only one person involved. I believe that, in a sense, the number of persons involved is none.

THE EGO THEORY AND THE BUNDLE THEORY

To explain this sense I must, for a while, turn away from the split-brain cases. There are two theories about what persons are, and what is involved in a person's continued existence over time. On the *Ego Theory*, a person's continued existence cannot be explained except as the continued existence of a particular *Ego*, or *subject of experiences*. An Ego Theorist claims that, if we ask what unifies someone's consciousness at any time—what makes it true, for example, that I can now both see what I am typing and hear the wind outside my window—the answer is that these are both experiences which are being had by me, this person, at this time. Similarly, what explains the unity of a person's whole life is the fact that all of the experiences in this life are had by the same person, or subject of experiences. In its best-known form, the *Cartesian view*, each person is a persisting purely mental thing—a soul, or spiritual substance.

The rival view is the *Bundle Theory*. Like most styles in art—Gothic, baroque, rococo, etc.—this theory owes its name to its critics. But the name is good enough. According to the Bundle Theory, we can't explain either the unity of consciousness at any time, or the unity of a whole life, by referring to a person. Instead we must claim that there are long series of different mental states and events—thoughts, sensations, and the like—each series being what we call one life. Each series is unified by various kinds of causal relation, such as the relations that hold between experiences and later memories of them. Each series is thus like a bundle tied up with string.

In a sense, a Bundle Theorist denies the existence of persons. An outright denial is of course absurd. As Reid protested in the eighteenth century, "I am not thought, I am not action, I am not feeling; I am something which thinks and acts and feels." I am not a series of events, but a person. A Bundle Theorist admits this fact, but claims it to be only a fact about our grammar, or our language. There are persons or subjects in this language-dependent way. If, however, persons are believed to be more than this—to be separately existing things, distinct from our brains and bodies, and the various kinds of mental states and events—the Bundle Theorist denies that there are such things.

The first Bundle Theorist was Buddha, who taught "anatta," or the *No Self view*. Buddhists concede that selves or persons have "nominal existence," by which they mean that persons are merely combinations of other elements. Only what exists by itself, as a separate element, has instead what Buddhists call "actual existence." Here are some quotations from Buddhist texts:

> At the beginning of their conversation the king politely asks the monk his name, and receives the following reply: "Sir, I am known as 'Nagasena'; my fellows in the religious life address me as 'Nagasena.' Although my parents gave me the name...it is just an appellation, a form of speech, a description, a conventional usage. 'Nagasena' is only a name, for no person is found here."

> A sentient being does exist, you think, O Mara? You are misled by a false conception. This bundle of elements is void of Self, In it there is no sentient being. Just as a set of wooden parts

Receives the name of carriage, So do we give to elements The name of fancied being.

Buddha has spoken thus: "O Brethren, actions do exist, and also their consequences, but the person that acts does not. There is no one to cast away this set of elements, and no one to assume a new set of them. There exists no Individual, it is only a conventional name given to a set of elements."[1]

Buddha's claims are strikingly similar to the claims advanced by several Western writers. Since these writers knew nothing of Buddha, the similarity of these claims suggests that they are not merely part of one cultural tradition, in one period. They may be, as I believe they are, true.

WHAT WE BELIEVE OURSELVES TO BE

Given the advances in psychology and neurophysiology, the Bundle Theory may now seem to be obviously true. It may seem uninteresting to deny that there are separately existing Egos, which are distinct from brains and bodies and the various kinds of mental states and events. But this is not the only issue. We may be convinced that the Ego Theory is false, or even senseless. Most of us, however, even if we are not aware of this, also have certain beliefs about what is involved in our continued existence over time. And these beliefs would only be justified if something like the Ego Theory was true. Most of us therefore have false beliefs about what persons are, and about ourselves.

These beliefs are best revealed when we consider certain imaginary cases, often drawn from science fiction. One such case is *teletransportation*. Suppose that you enter a cubicle in which, when you press a button, a scanner records the states of all of the cells in your brain and body, destroying both while doing so. This information is then transmitted at the speed of light to some other planet, where a replicator produces a perfect organic copy of you. Since the brain of your Replica is exactly like yours, it will seem

to remember living your life up to the moment when you pressed the button, its character will be just like yours, and it will be in every other way psychologically continuous with you. This psychological continuity will not have its normal cause, the continued existence of your brain, since the causal chain will run through the transmission by radio of your "blueprint."

Several writers claim that, if you chose to be teletransported, believing this to be the fastest way of travelling, you would be making a terrible mistake. This would not be a way of travelling, but a way of dying. It may not, they concede, be quite as bad as ordinary death. It might be some consolation to you that, after your death, you will have this Replica, which can finish the book that you are writing, act as parent to your children, and so on. But, they insist, this Replica won't be you. It will merely be someone else, who is exactly like you. This is why this prospect is nearly as bad as ordinary death.

Imagine next a whole range of cases, in each of which, in a single operation, a different proportion of the cells in your brain and body would be replaced with exact duplicates. At the near end of this range, only 1 or 2 per cent would be replaced; in the middle, 40 or 60 per cent; near the far end, 98 or 99 per cent. At the far end of this range is pure teletransportation, the case in which all of your cells would be "replaced."

When you imagine that some proportion of your cells will be replaced with exact duplicates, it is natural to have the following beliefs. First, if you ask, "Will I survive? Will the resulting person be me?", there must be an answer to this question. Either you will survive, or you are about to die. Second, the answer to this question must be either a simple "Yes" or a simple "No." The person who wakes up either will or will not be you. There cannot be a third answer, such as that the person waking up will be half you. You can imagine yourself later being half-conscious. But if the resulting person will be fully conscious, he cannot be half you. To state these beliefs together: to the question, "Will the resulting person be me?", there must always *be* an answer, which must be all-or-nothing.

There seem good grounds for believing that, in the case of teletransportation, your Replica would not be you. In a slight variant of this case, your Replica might be created while you were still alive, so that you could talk to one another. This seems to show that, if 100 per cent of your cells were replaced, the result would merely be a Replica of you. At the other end of my range of cases, where only 1 per cent would be replaced, the resulting person clearly *would* be you. It therefore seems that, in the cases in between, the resulting person must be either you, or merely a Replica. It seems that one of these must be true, and that it makes a great difference which is true.

HOW WE ARE NOT WHAT WE BELIEVE

If these beliefs were correct, there must be some critical percentage, somewhere in this range of cases, up to which the resulting person would be you, and beyond which he would merely be your Replica. Perhaps, for example, it would be you who would wake up if the proportion of cells replaced were 49 per cent, but if just a few more cells were also replaced, this would make all the difference, causing it to be someone else who would wake up.

That there must be some such critical percentage follows from our natural beliefs. But this conclusion is most implausible. How could a few cells make such a difference? Moreover, if there is such a critical percentage, no one could ever discover where it came. Since in all these cases the resulting person would believe that he was you, there could never be any evidence about where, in this range of cases, he would suddenly cease to be you.

On the Bundle Theory, we should reject these natural beliefs. Since you, the person, are not a separately existing entity, we can know exactly what would happen without answering the question of what will happen to you. Moreover, in the cases in the middle of my range, it is an empty ques-

tion whether the resulting person would be you, or would merely be someone else who is exactly like you. These are not here two different possibilities, one of which must be true. These are merely two different descriptions of the very same course of events. If 50 per cent of your cells were replaced with exact duplicates, we could call the resulting person you, or we could call him merely your Replica. But since these are not here different possibilities, this is a mere choice of words.

As Buddha claimed, the Bundle Theory is hard to believe. It is hard to accept that it could be an empty question whether one is about to die, or will instead live for many years.

What we are being asked to accept may be made clearer with this analogy. Suppose that a certain club exists for some time, holding regular meetings. The meetings then cease. Some years later, several people form a club with the same name, and the same rules. We can ask, "Did these people revive the very same club? Or did they merely start up another club which is exactly similar?" Given certain further details, this would be another empty question. We could know just what happened without answering this question. Suppose that someone said: "But there must be an answer. The club meeting later must either be, or not be, the very same club." This would show that this person didn't understand the nature of clubs.

In the same way, if we have any worries about my imagined cases, we don't understand the nature of persons. In each of my cases, you would know that the resulting person would be both psychologically and physically exactly like you, and that he would have some particular proportion of the cells in your brain and body—90 per cent, or 10 per cent, or, in the case of teletransportation, 0 per cent. Knowing this, you know everything. How could it be a real question what would happen to you, unless you are a separately existing Ego, distinct from a brain and body, and the various kinds of mental state and event? If there are no such Egos, there is nothing else to ask a real question about.

Accepting the Bundle Theory is not only hard; it may also affect our emotions. As Buddha claimed, it may undermine our concern about our own futures. This effect can be suggested by redescribing this change of view. Suppose that you are about to be destroyed, but will later have a Replica on Mars. You would naturally believe that this prospect is about as bad as ordinary death, since your Replica won't be you. On the Bundle Theory, the fact that your Replica won't be you just consists in the fact that, though it will be fully psychologically continuous with you, this continuity won't have its normal cause. But when you object to teletransportation you are not objecting merely to the abnormality of this cause. You are objecting that this cause won't get *you* to Mars. You fear that the abnormal cause will fail to produce a further and all-important fact, which is different from the fact that your Replica will be psychologically continuous with you. You do not merely want there to be psychological continuity between you and some future person. You want to *be* this future person. On the Bundle Theory, there is no such special further fact. What you fear will not happen, in this imagined case, *never* happens. You want the person on Mars to be you in a specially intimate way in which no future person will ever be you. This means that, judged from the standpoint of your natural beliefs, even ordinary survival is about as bad as teletransportation. *Ordinary survival is about as bad as being destroyed and having a Replica.*

HOW THE SPLIT-BRAIN CASES SUPPORT THE BUNDLE THEORY

The truth of the Bundle Theory seems to me, in the widest sense, as much a scientific as a philosophical conclusion. I can imagine kinds of evidence which would have justified believing in the existence of separately existing Egos, and believing that the continued existence of these Egos is what explains the continuity of each mental life. But there is in fact very little evidence in favour of this Ego Theory, and much for the alternative Bundle Theory.

Some of this evidence is provided by the split-brain cases. On the Ego Theory, to explain what unifies our experiences at any one time, we should simply claim that these are all experiences which are being had by the same person. Bundle Theorists reject this explanation. This disagreement is hard to resolve in ordinary cases. But consider the simplified split-brain case that I described. We show to my imagined patient a placard whose left half is blue and right half is red. In one of this person's two streams of consciousness, he is aware of seeing only blue, while at the same time, in his other stream, he is aware of seeing only red. Each of these two visual experiences is combined with other experiences, like that of being aware of moving one of his hands. What unifies the experiences, at any time, in each of this person's two streams of consciousness? What unifies his awareness of seeing only red with his awareness of moving one hand? The answer cannot be that these experiences are being had by the same person. This answer cannot explain the unity of each of this person's two streams of consciousness, since it ignores the disunity between these streams. This person is now having all of the experiences in both of his two streams. If this fact was what unified these experiences, this would make the two streams one.

These cases do not, I have claimed, involve two people sharing a single body. Since there is only one person involved, who has two streams of consciousness, the Ego Theorist's explanation would have to take the following form. He would have to distinguish between persons and subjects of experiences, and claim that, in split-brain cases, there are *two* of the latter. What unifies the experiences in one of the person's two streams would have to be the fact that these experiences are all being had by the same subject of experiences. What unifies the experiences in this person's other stream would have to be the fact that they are being had by another subject of experiences. When this explanation takes this form, it becomes much less plausible. While we could assume that "subject of experiences," or "Ego," simply meant "person" it was easy to believe that there are subjects of experiences. But if there can be subjects of experiences that are not persons, and if in the life of a split-brain patient there are at any time two different subjects of experiences—two different Egos—why should we believe that there really are such things? This does not amount to a refutation. But it seems to me a strong argument against the Ego Theory.

As a Bundle Theorist, I believe that these two Egos are idle cogs. There is another explanation of the unity of consciousness, both in ordinary cases and in split-brain cases. It is simply a fact that ordinary people are, at any time, aware of having several different experiences. This awareness of several different experiences can be helpfully compared with one's awareness, in short-term memory, of several different experiences. Just as there can be a single memory of just having had several experiences, such as hearing a bell strike three times, there can be a single state of awareness both of hearing the fourth striking of this bell, and of seeing, at the same time, ravens flying past the bell-tower.

Unlike the Ego Theorist's explanation, this explanation can easily be extended to cover split-brain cases. In such cases there is, at any time, not one state of awareness of several different experiences, but two such states. In the case I described, there is one state of awareness of both seeing only red and of moving one hand, and there is another state of awareness of both seeing only blue and moving the other hand. In claiming that there are two such states of awareness, we are not postulating the existence of unfamiliar entities, two separately existing Egos which are not the same as the single person whom the case involves. This explanation appeals to a pair of mental states which would have to be described anyway in a full description of this case.

I have suggested how the split-brain cases provide one argument for one view about the nature of persons. I should mention another such argument, provided by an imagined extension of these cases, first discussed at length by David Wiggins.[2]

In this imagined case a person's brain is divided, and the two halves are transplanted into a pair of different bodies. The two resulting people live quite separate lives. This imagined case shows that personal identity is not what matters. If I was about to divide, I should conclude that neither of the resulting people will be me. I will have ceased to exist. But this way of ceasing to exist is about as good—or as bad—as ordinary survival.

Some of the features of Wiggins's imagined case are likely to remain technically impossible. But the case cannot be dismissed, since its most striking feature, the division of one stream of consciousness into separate streams, has already happened. This is a second way in which the actual split-brain cases have great theoretical importance. They challenge some of our deepest assumptions about ourselves.[3]

Notes

1. For the sources of these and similar quotations, see my *Reasons and Persons* (1984) pp. 502–3, 532. Oxford: Oxford Univ. Press.
2. At the end of his *Identity and Spatio-temporal Continuity* (1967) Oxford: Blackwell.
3. I discuss these assumptions further in part 3 of my *Reasons and Persons*.

Study Questions

1. Explain the differences between the Ego Theory and the Bundle Theory. Which theory more closely resembles your own view?
2. Parfit assumes that many people will refuse to enter the teletransporter. Do you agree? Explain why or why not you would feel comfortable entering the machine.
3. Parfit says that his belief in the Bundle Theory is a scientific as well as a philosophical conclusion. What do you think is the difference between scientific and philosophical conclusions? Do you agree with Parfit that the scientific evidence supports the Bundle Theory?

First Person Plural

7.5

PAUL BLOOM

PAUL BLOOM (1963–) is a Professor of Psychology at Yale University and coeditor of *Behavioral and Brain Sciences*, one of the most influential interdisciplinary journals in cognitive science. He is the author of *Descartes' Baby* (2004), which explores the idea that humans have a natural tendency to divide the world into bodies and souls. His most recent book, *How Pleasure Works* (2010), investigates the cognitive and social components of our pleasure-seeking behavior. In the selection below, excerpted from a longer article in the magazine *The Atlantic*, Bloom argues that there is no single self with which we can identify ourselves. Basing his argument on a wide range of empirical evidence, Bloom concludes that we should give up the traditional view that there is a single self that connects our past and future and embrace the Whitmanesque idea that we all "contain multitudes."

Imagine a long, terrible dental procedure. You are rigid in the chair, hands clenched, soaked with sweat—and then the dentist leans over and says, "We're done now. You can go home. But if you want, I'd be happy to top you off with a few minutes of mild pain."

There is a good argument for saying "Yes. Please do."

The psychologist and recent Nobel laureate Daniel Kahneman conducted a series of studies on the memory of painful events, such as colonoscopies. He discovered that when we think back on these events, we are influenced by the intensity of the endings, and so we have a more positive memory of an experience that ends with mild pain than of one that ends with extreme pain, even if the mild pain is added to the same amount of extreme pain. At the moment the dentist makes his offer, you would, of course, want to say no—but later on, you would be better off if you had said yes, because your overall memory of the event wouldn't be as unpleasant.

Such contradictions arise all the time. If you ask people which makes them happier, work or vacation, they will remind you that they work for money and spend the money on vacations. But if you give them a beeper that goes off at random times, and ask them to record their activity and mood each time they hear a beep, you'll likely find that they are happier at work. Work is often engaging and social; vacations are often boring and stressful. Similarly, if you ask people about their greatest happiness in life, more than a third mention their children or grandchildren, but when they use a diary to record their happiness, it turns out that taking care of the kids is a downer—parenting ranks just a bit higher than housework, and falls below sex, socializing with friends, watching TV, praying, eating, and cooking.

The question "What makes people happy?" has been around forever, but there is a new approach to the science of pleasure, one that draws on recent work in psychology, philosophy, economics, neuroscience, and emerging fields such as neuroeconomics. This work has led to new ways—every-

Paul Bloom, "First Person Plural," *The Atlantic* (November, 2008).

thing from beepers and diaries to brain scans—to explore the emotional value of different experiences, and has given us some surprising insights about the conditions that result in satisfaction.

But what's more exciting, I think, is the emergence of a different perspective on happiness itself. We used to think that the hard part of the question "How can I be happy?" had to do with nailing down the definition of *happy*. But it may have more to do with the definition of *I*. Many researchers now believe, to varying degrees, that each of us is a community of competing selves, with the happiness of one often causing the misery of another. This theory might explain certain puzzles of everyday life, such as why addictions and compulsions are so hard to shake off, and why we insist on spending so much of our lives in worlds—like TV shows and novels and virtual-reality experiences—that don't actually exist. And it provides a useful framework for thinking about the increasingly popular position that people would be better off if governments and businesses helped them inhibit certain gut feelings and emotional reactions.

Like any organ, the brain consists of large parts (such as the hippocampus and the cortex) that are made up of small parts (such as "maps" in the visual cortex), which themselves are made up of smaller parts, until you get to neurons, billions of them, whose orchestrated firing is the stuff of thought. The neurons are made up of parts like axons and dendrites, which are made up of smaller parts like terminal buttons and receptor sites, which are made up of molecules, and so on.

This hierarchical structure makes possible the research programs of psychology and neuroscience. The idea is that interesting properties of the whole (intelligence, decision-making, emotions, moral sensibility) can be understood in terms of the interaction of components that themselves lack these properties. This is how computers work; there is every reason to believe that this is how we work, too.

But there is no consensus about the broader implications of this scientific approach. Some scholars argue that although the brain might contain neural subsystems, or modules, specialized for tasks like recognizing faces and understanding language, it also contains a part that constitutes a person, a self: the chief executive of all the subsystems. As the philosopher Jerry Fodor once put it, "If, in short, there is a community of computers living in my head, there had also better be somebody who is in charge; and, *by God, it had better be me.*"

More-radical scholars insist that an inherent clash exists between science and our long-held conceptions about consciousness and moral agency: if you accept that our brains are a myriad of smaller components, you must reject such notions as character, praise, blame, and free will. Perhaps the very notion that there are such things as *selves*—individuals who persist over time—needs to be rejected as well.

The view I'm interested in falls between these extremes. It is conservative in that it accepts that brains give rise to selves that last over time, plan for the future, and so on. But it is radical in that it gives up the idea that there is just one self per head. The idea is that instead, within each brain, different selves are continually popping in and out of existence. They have different desires, and they fight for control—bargaining with, deceiving, and plotting against one another.

The notion of different selves within a single person is not new. It can be found in Plato, and it was nicely articulated by the 18th-century Scottish philosopher David Hume, who wrote, "I cannot compare the soul more properly to any thing than to a republic or commonwealth, in which the several members are united by the reciprocal ties of government and subordination." Walt Whitman gave us a pithier version: "I am large, I contain multitudes."

The economist Thomas Schelling, another Nobel laureate, illustrates the concept with a simple story:

As a boy I saw a movie about Admiral Byrd's Antarctic expedition and was impressed that as a boy he had gone outdoors in shirtsleeves to toughen himself against the cold. I resolved to go to bed at night with one blanket too few. That decision to go to bed minus one blanket was made by a warm boy; another boy awoke cold in the night, too cold to retrieve the blanket...and resolving to restore it tomorrow. The next bedtime it was the warm boy again, dreaming of Antarctica, who got to make the decision, and he always did it again.

Examples abound in our own lives. Late at night, when deciding not to bother setting up the coffee machine for the next morning, I sometimes think of the man who will wake up as a different person, and wonder, *What did he ever do for me?* When I get up and there's no coffee ready, I curse the lazy bastard who shirked his duties the night before.

But anyone tempted by this theory has to admit just how wrong it feels, how poorly it fits with most of our experience. In the main, we do think of ourselves as singular individuals who persist over time. If I were to learn that I was going to be tortured tomorrow morning, my reaction would be terror, not sympathy for the poor guy who will be living in my body then. If I do something terrible now, I will later feel guilt and shame, not anger at some other person.

It could hardly be otherwise. Our brains have evolved to protect our bodies and guide them to reproduce, hence our minds must be sensitive to maintaining the needs of the continuing body— my children today will be my children tomorrow; if you wronged me yesterday, I should be wary of you today. Society and human relationships would be impossible without this form of continuity. Anyone who could convince himself that the person who will wake up in his bed tomorrow is *really* someone different would lack the capacity for sustained self-interest; he would feel no long-term guilt, love, shame, or pride.

The multiplicity of selves becomes more intuitive as the time span increases. Social psychologists have found certain differences in how we think of ourselves versus how we think of other people—for instance, we tend to attribute our own bad behavior to unfortunate circumstances, and the bad behavior of others to their nature. But these biases diminish when we think of *distant* past selves or *distant* future selves; we see such selves the way we see other people. Although it might be hard to think about the person who will occupy your body tomorrow morning as someone other than you, it is not hard at all to think that way about the person who will occupy your body 20 years from now. This may be one reason why many young people are indifferent about saving for retirement; they feel as if they would be giving up their money to an elderly stranger.

Life would be swell if all the selves inhabiting a single mind worked as a team, pulling together for a common goal. But they clash, and sometimes this gives rise to what we call addictions and compulsions.

This is not the traditional view of human frailty. The human condition has long been seen as a battle of good versus evil, reason versus emotion, will versus appetite, superego versus id. The iconic image, from a million movies and cartoons, is of a person with an angel over one shoulder and the devil over the other.

The alternative view keeps the angel and the devil, but casts aside the person in between. The competing selves are not over your shoulder, but inside your head: the angel and the devil, the self who wants to be slim and the one who wants to eat the cake, all exist within one person. Drawing on the research of the psychiatrist George Ainslie, we can make sense of the interaction of these selves by plotting their relative strengths over time, starting with one (the cake eater) being weaker than the other (the dieter). For most of the day, the dieter hums along at his regular power (a 5 on a scale of 1 to 10, say), motivated by the long-term goal of weight loss, and is stronger than the cake eater (a 2). Your consciousness tracks whichever self is winning, so *you* are deciding not to eat the cake. But as you get closer and closer to the cake, the power of the cake eater rises (3...4...), the lines cross, the cake eater takes over (6), and that becomes the conscious *you*; at this point, you decide to eat the cake. It's as if a baton is passed from one self to another.

Sometimes one self can predict that it will later be dominated by another self, and it can act to block the crossing—an act known as self-binding, which Thomas Schelling and the philosopher Jon Elster have explored in detail. Self-binding means that the dominant self schemes against the person it might potentially become—the 5 acts to keep the 2 from becoming a 6. Ulysses wanted to hear the song of the sirens, but he knew it would compel him to walk off the boat and into the sea. So he had his sailors tie him to the mast. Dieters buy food in small portions so they won't overeat later on; smokers trying to quit tell their friends never to give them cigarettes, no matter how much they may later beg. In her book on gluttony, Francine Prose tells of women who phone hotels where they are going to stay to demand a room with an empty minibar. An alarm clock now for sale rolls away as it sounds the alarm; to shut it off, you have to get up out of bed and find the damn thing.

You might also triumph over your future self by feeding it incomplete or incorrect information. If you're afraid of panicking in a certain situation, you might deny yourself relevant knowledge—you don't look down when you're on the tightrope; you don't check your stocks if you're afraid you'll sell at the first sign of a downturn. Chronically late? Set your watch ahead. Prone to jealousy? Avoid conversations with your spouse about which of your friends is the sexiest.

Working with the psychologists Frank Keil, of Yale University, and Katherine Choe, now at Goucher College, I recently studied young children's understanding of self-binding, by showing them short movies of people engaged in self-binding and other behaviors and asking them to explain what was going on. The children, aged 4 to 7, easily grasped that someone might put a video game on a high shelf so that another person couldn't get it. But self-binding confused them: they were mystified when people put away

the game so that they themselves couldn't get hold of it.

But even though young children don't understand self-binding, they are capable of doing it. In a classic study from the 1970s, psychologists offered children a marshmallow and told them they could either have it right away, or get more if they waited for a few minutes. As you would expect, waiting proved difficult (and performance on this task is a good predictor, much later on, of such things as SAT scores and drug problems), but some children managed it by self-binding—averting their eyes or covering the marshmallow so as to subvert their temptation-prone self for the greater pleasure of the long-term self.

Even pigeons can self-bind. Ainslie conducted an experiment in which he placed pigeons in front of a glowing red key. If they pecked it immediately, they got a small reward right away, but if they waited until the key went dark, they got a larger one. They almost always went for the quick reward—really, it's hard for a pigeon to restrain itself. But there was a wrinkle: the key glowed green for several seconds before turning red. Pecking the key while it was green would prevent it from turning red and providing the option of the small, quick reward. Some of the pigeons learned to use the green key to help themselves hold out for the big reward, just as a person might put temptation out of reach.

For adult humans, though, the problem is that the self you are trying to bind has resources of its own. Fighting your Bad Self is serious business; whole sections of bookstores are devoted to it. We bribe and threaten and cajole, just as if we were dealing with an addicted friend. Vague commitments like "I promise to drink only on special occasions" often fail, because the Bad Self can weasel out of them, rationalizing that it's *always* a special occasion. Bright-line rules like "I will never play video games again" are also vulnerable, because the Bad Self can argue that these are unreasonable—and, worse, once you slip, it can argue that the plan is unworkable. For every argument made by the dieting self—"This diet is really working" or "I really need to lose weight"—the cake eater can respond with another—"This will never work" or "I'm too vain" or "You only live once." Your long-term self reads voraciously about the benefits of regular exercise and healthy eating; the cake eater prefers articles showing that obesity isn't really such a problem. It's not that the flesh is weak; sometimes the flesh is pretty damn smart.

It used to be simpler. According to the traditional view, a single, long-term-planning self—a *you*—battles against passions, compulsions, impulses, and addictions. We have no problem choosing, as individuals or as a society, who should win, because only one interest is at stake—one person is at war with his or her desires. And while knowing the right thing to do can be terribly difficult, the decision is still based on the rational thoughts of a rational being.

Seeing things this way means we are often mistaken about what makes us happy. Consider again what happens when we have children. Pretty much no matter how you test it, children make us less happy. The evidence isn't just from diary studies; surveys of marital satisfaction show that couples tend to start off happy, get less happy when they have kids, and become happy again only once the kids leave the house. As the psychologist Daniel Gilbert puts it, "Despite what we read in the popular press, the only known symptom of 'empty-nest syndrome' is increased smiling." So why do people believe that children give them so much pleasure? Gilbert sees it as an illusion, a failure of affective forecasting. Society's needs are served when people believe that having children is a good thing, so we are deluged with images and stories about how wonderful kids are. We think they make us happy, though they actually don't.

The theory of multiple selves offers a different perspective. If struggles over happiness involve clashes between distinct internal selves, we can no longer be so sure that our conflicting judgments over time reflect irrationality or error.

There is no inconsistency between someone's anxiously hiking through the Amazon wishing she were home in a warm bath and, weeks later, feeling good about being the sort of adventurous soul who goes into the rain forest. In an important sense, the person in the Amazon is not the same person as the one back home safely recalling the experience, just as the person who honestly believes that his children are the great joy in his life might not be the same person who finds them terribly annoying when he's actually with them.

Even if each of us is a community, all the members shouldn't get equal say. Some members are best thought of as small-minded children—and we don't give 6-year-olds the right to vote. Just as in society, the adults within us have the right—indeed, the obligation—to rein in the children. In fact, talk of "children" versus "adults" within an individual isn't only a metaphor; one reason to favor the longer-term self is that it really is older and more experienced. We typically spend more of our lives not wanting to snort coke, smoke, or overeat than we spend wanting to do these things; this means that the long-term self has more time to reflect. It is less selfish; it talks to other people, reads books, and so on. And it tries to control the short-term selves. It joins Alcoholics Anonymous, buys the runaway clock, and sees the therapist. As Jon Elster observes, the long-term, sober self is a truer self, because it tries to bind the short-term, drunk self. The long-term, sober self is the adult.

So what's not to like? There is a real appeal to anything that makes self-binding easier. As I write this article, I'm using a program that disables my network connections for a selected amount of time and does not allow me to switch them back on, thereby forcing me to actually write instead of checking my e-mail or reading blogs. A harsher (and more expensive) method, advised by the author of a self-help book, is to remove your Internet cable and FedEx it to yourself—guaranteeing a day without online distractions. One can also chemically boost the long-term self through drugs such as Adderall, which improves concentration and focus. The journalist Joshua Foer describes how it enabled him to write for hour-long chunks, far longer than he was usually capable of: "The part of my brain that makes me curious about whether I have new e-mails in my inbox apparently shut down."

It's more controversial, of course, when someone else does the binding. I wouldn't be very happy if my department chair forced me to take Adderall, or if the government fined me for being overweight and not trying to slim down (as Alabama is planning to do to some state employees). But some "other-binding" already exists—think of the mandatory waiting periods for getting a divorce or buying a gun. You are not prevented from eventually taking these actions, but you are forced to think them over, giving the contemplative self the chance to override the impulsive self. And since governments and businesses are constantly asking people to make choices (about precisely such things as whether to be an organ donor), they inevitably have to provide a default option. If decisions have to be made, why not structure them to be in individuals' and society's best interests?

The main problem with all of this is that the long-term self is not always right. Sometimes the short-term self should not be bound. Of course, most addictions are well worth getting rid of. When a mother becomes addicted to cocaine, the pleasure from the drug seems to hijack the neural system that would otherwise be devoted to bonding with her baby. It obviously makes sense here to bind the drug user, the short-term self. On the other hand, from a neural and psychological standpoint, a mother's love for her baby can also be seen as an addiction. But here binding would be strange and immoral; this addiction is a good one. Someone who becomes morbidly obese needs to do more self-binding, but an obsessive dieter might need to do less. We think one way about someone who gives up Internet porn to spend time building houses for the poor, and another way

entirely about someone who successfully thwarts his short-term desire to play with his children so that he can devote more energy to making his second million. The long-term, contemplative self should not always win.

This is particularly true when it comes to morality. Many cruel acts are perpetrated by people who can't or don't control their short-term impulses or who act in certain ways—such as getting drunk—that lead to a dampening of the contemplative self. But evil acts are also committed by smart people who adopt carefully thought-out belief systems that allow them to ignore their more morally astute gut feelings. Many slave owners were rational men who used their intelligence to defend slavery, arguing that the institution was in the best interests of those who were enslaved, and that it was grounded in scripture: Africans were the descendants of Ham, condemned by God to be "servants unto servants." Terrorist acts such as suicide bombings are not typically carried out in an emotional frenzy; they are the consequences of deeply held belief systems and long-term deliberative planning. One of the grimmest examples of rationality gone bad can be found in the psychiatrist Robert Jay Lifton's discussion of Nazi doctors. These men acted purposefully for years to distance themselves from their emotions, creating what Lifton describes as an "Auschwitz self" that enabled them to prevent any normal, unschooled human kindness from interfering with their jobs.

I wouldn't want to live next door to someone whose behavior was dominated by his short-term selves, and I wouldn't want to be such a person, either. But there is also something wrong with people who go too far in the other direction. We benefit, intellectually and personally, from the interplay between different selves, from the balance between long-term contemplation and short-term impulse. We should be wary about tipping the scales too far. The community of selves shouldn't be a democracy, but it shouldn't be a dictatorship, either.

Study Questions

1. Bloom claims that the hard part of answering the question "How can I be happy?" lies not in understanding what *happiness* means, but rather understanding what *I* means. Explain this claim. Do you agree?

2. Bloom finds his own view that a person consists of a multiplicity of selves is similar to David Hume's account of the self. How are the two accounts alike? How are they different?

3. The idea that a person is a community of many selves seems to be in conflict with people's personal experience of being a self. From the inside, it feels as if there is only a single self having experiences and making decisions. Does this demonstrate that Bloom's account must be wrong? Why or why not?

Part III

Value Theory

CHAPTER 8

Meta-Ethics

TAMLER SOMMERS

WHAT IS META-ETHICS?

Ethical inquiry in philosophy has traditionally divided into two categories: *normative ethics* and *meta-ethics*. Normative ethics seeks to arrive at judgments about how we ought to live, what we ought to do, and whether a particular kind of act is morally permissible or impermissible. Questions in normative ethics include:

- Is the abortion of a six-month-old fetus permissible?
- Is female circumcision a violation of fundamental human rights?
- Is it wrong to torture a prisoner if he or she has information about a major terrorist attack?
- What virtues are necessary to live a good and moral life?

Meta-ethical inquiry, by contrast, does not seek to arrive at moral judgments or determine right from wrong and how we ought to live. The task of meta-ethics is to examine the *status* of these normative judgments and questions—to determine what they mean and whether they can be objective or universally true. Here are some examples of meta-ethical questions:

- Can moral claims like "abortion is wrong" be objectively true? What, if anything, could make "abortion is wrong" or "abortion is permissible" true?
- Are there any such things as universal human rights?
- What do we mean when we say "torture is always wrong"?
- Are there objective standards that allow us to call one life better than another?

The selections in this unit address the central issues in meta-ethics and reflect the leading positions that philosophers have adopted. For the remainder of this introductory reading, I will discuss these issues and positions and then suggest some ways that empirical investigation can help to move the debates in meta-ethics forward.

TWO CENTRAL QUESTIONS IN META-ETHICS

The first question concerns whether there are such things as moral facts. Let us call this "the objectivity question." A recent well-publicized example can illustrate how this question is often addressed in the popular press. In April 2007, NFL star quarterback Michael Vick was convicted for operating "Bad Newz Kennels," an illegal dog-fighting ring. The trial revealed that Vick had been hosting dog fights for several years and, with other members of the ring, had electrocuted dogs who had lost or not fought well. Public sentiment for the most part was severe. Many columnists argued that Vick should be banned for life from the NFL. A small portion of the sentiment, however, expressed some sympathy for Vick. In the inner-city environment where Vick grew up, dog fighting is not regarded as immoral. As a young child, Vick was not surrounded by the same values as the people who were so harshly condemning him today. Furthermore, Vick's crime seemed to getting undue attention because he was rich and black. In a column for *The New Republic*, the novelist (and writer for *The Wire*) George Pelecanos acknowledges that race played a part in the public reaction, but laments the use of the phrase "it's the culture" to lessen the severity of the offense. Pelecanos concludes:

> Let's be clear: Dogfighting itself should not be debated with regard to race, nor should it be reduced to ridiculous and illogical argument. Training dogs to fight is wrong. Murdering dogs is wrong. The issue is not complex. There is no other side.[1]

Pelecanos is making a strong normative judgment here to be sure: dog fighting is wrong. But he appears to be making a meta-ethical judgment as well. Culture does not determine the rightness or wrongness of dog fighting. The wrongness of dog fighting is a *fact*, no matter who you are or where you live. By implying that there are moral truths that are independent of our culture or environment, Pelecanos is taking a stand on the objectivity question.

Many people are attracted to the idea that there are universal moral truths. But there's a problem. As Herodotus observed almost 2,500 years ago (Reading 8.1), there are deep cross-cultural differences about moral values, and people tend to think the values of their own culture are the correct ones. How can we account for the existence of this moral diversity? One possibility is that there are universal moral truths out there in the world, but some people have not yet discovered them. After all, there are cultures who believe that the earth is flat, but this does not cause us to claim that there is no universal truth about the shape of the earth. Philosophers and others (like Pelecanos) who endorse this picture of morality are known as *moral realists*. Another possibility is that moral principles are more like rules in a country club, rules of etiquette, or personal codes of conduct: they only apply in a specific context and cannot be evaluated outside of it. According to this view, there are no universally true moral judgments or principles; moral beliefs can only be true for particular cultures or individuals if they can be true at all. Philosophers defending this account are referred to as *moral antirealists* or *irrealists*. As you'll see, antirealism comes in a number of different varieties. But the objectivity question in meta-ethics boils down to which of these positions—realism or antirealism—is more plausible.

A related but independent question in meta-ethics concerns the *meaning* of moral claims, whether or not they purport to be true or objective. To understand this question, it is helpful to examine some nonmoral examples. Consider two groups of statements:

Group 1
The earth is more than 6,000 years old.
Pi is the ratio of the circumference of a circle to its diameter.
John McCain was elected president of the United States in 2008.

Group 2
Blueberries are delicious.
Halle Berry is more beautiful than Jessica Alba.
Dogs are much better pets than cats.

What distinguishes the first group from the second? The statements in the first group are meant to be objective. The truth or falsity of these claims is not dependent on the beliefs or attitudes of the speaker. The first two statements are true and the third is false, whether you believe them or not. Philosophers refer to statements of this sort as *truth apt* or capable of being true or false.

In the second group, by contrast, the statements do not seem to make any claim to objectivity. Although the surface grammar is similar, the statements in this group are expressions of the attitudes and preferences of the speaker. They are not the kind of statements that are meant to express universal truths. They do not seem to be *truth apt*. We might have heated debates about the virtues of dogs versus cats or the hotness of our favorite movie stars, but in the end we seem to recognize that there is no objective fact of the matter. Indeed, we have expressions that reflect this, such as "beauty is in the eye of the beholder" and "it's a matter of taste."

The question of meaning in meta-ethics may be expressed like this: are moral claims more like the statements in group 1 or more like the statements in group 2? Do moral claims purport to be objective? Are they *truth apt*? Or are they more like subjective expressions of preferences, attitudes, and desires (however passionate)? Philosophers who believe moral statements are truth apt are known as *cognitivists*; philosophers who deny this are referred to as *noncognitivists*.

LEADING META-ETHICAL POSITIONS

Broadly speaking, the leading positions in meta-ethics can be grouped according to their answers to the two big meta-ethical questions discussed earlier:

	Objective Moral Values?	**Moral Statements Truth Apt?**
Error Theory/ Moral Skepticism	No	Yes
Moral Realism	Yes	Yes
Emotivism/ Noncognitivism	No	No

With this in mind, let us examine each of these positions in more detail.

Moral Skepticism/Error Theory

As J. L. Mackie (Reading 8.4) describes it, moral skepticism is the view that "there are no objective moral values." But Mackie's position provides an answer to the question of meaning as well. According to Mackie, moral claims do make a claim to objectivity; they are truth apt. However, since objective values do not exist, moral claims are never true. This is why Mackie refers to his position as an *error theory*. Whenever we make a moral claim, we are appealing to the existence of something that does not exist. For Mackie, moral discourse resembles something like "witch discourse" at a time when people believed in witches. People would make both general claims about witches (e.g. "Witches have the power to cause illnesses and disease") and particular claims (e.g., "Suzy Gardner is a witch"). The speakers meant for these statements to be statements of fact. The claims purported to be true, but they were never true. Even when there was disagreement—for example, "Suzy Gardner is definitely *not* a witch"—both speakers were making errors insofar as they believed the property "being a witch" applied to *some* people (if not to Suzy Gardner). According to Mackie, people who make claims like "dog fighting is morally wrong" are similarly misguided—they presume the existence of a nonexistent property, objective wrongness.

One common misconception about moral skeptics is that they reject the whole idea of behaving in accordance with conventional morality. This is a mistake. Moral skeptics may consistently embrace the usefulness of current moral practices and attitudes. They may be repulsed by conventionally immoral actions and do their best to resist committing them. They may even embrace the illusion of objectivity that (they believe) pervades moral discourse. A moral skeptic might be thrilled that people make the mistake of believing in the objective wrongness of dog fighting, because the mistaken belief prevents a practice the skeptic abhors. Moral skepticism entails only that the belief in moral objectivity—useful or not—*is* an illusion.

For Mackie, an essential part of the meaning of moral judgments is that they are "objectively prescriptive"—that is, they *bind* us to perform (or refraining to perform) certain actions. "We want our moral judgments to be authoritative for other agents," Mackie writes, "as well as for ourselves" (p. 458). This is what makes Mackie a cognitivist. If moral judgments were merely meant to be expressions of attitudes, then they would lack this feature of objective prescriptivity.

This feature of objective prescriptivity also leads Mackie to reject realism. In Reading 8.4—excerpted from his book *Ethics: Inventing Right and Wrong*—Mackie develops two famous arguments against moral realism: the *argument from queerness* and the *argument from relativity*. Although they are presented independently, they are best seen as working together to form an inference to the best explanation argument for denying objective moral values.

Starting with the argument from queerness, Mackie observes that objective values, if they existed, would be "entities and qualities of a very strange sort, utterly different from anything else in the universe" (p. 458). Correspondingly, if one could identify these values, it would have to be through some strange "faculty of moral perception or intuition" that is completely different from the ways we identify other things in the world. The queerness of objective values resides largely in the authority they would have over our behavior. What other entities are there in the world that exist unseen and exert some kind of force that binds us to behave in a certain way? What a bizarre notion. Extraordinary claims require extraordinary evidence, and so we should reject our belief in objective values unless we find extraordinary evidence for their existence.

Let us now turn to the argument from relativity, which offers an *inference to the best explanation*, one that appeals to the significant variation of moral codes across cultures. Mackie recognizes that moral disagreement in itself does not support skepticism, since there is disagreement in many areas of inquiry that we believe to have objectively correct answers. But according to Mackie, "the argument from relativity has some force because the actual variations in moral codes are more readily explained by the hypothesis that they reflect ways of life than by the hypothesis that they express perceptions, most of them seriously inadequate and badly distorted, of objective values" (p. 454).[2] As stated, this argument is incomplete because Mackie has not yet told us *why* the "ways of life" explanation is more plausible than the "distorted perceptions of objective values" explanation. We see an answer when we combine this argument with the argument from queerness. The purely naturalistic "ways of life" hypothesis is more *parsimonious*; it does not require us to affirm the existence of something so strange and unlike anything else.[3]

Even when the arguments are combined, however, there is still one premise that needs further support. Mackie has given no evidence that there is a plausible naturalistic explanation for the moral disagreement (or moral agreement for that matter). That matter can only be settled empirically.[4] See "How Empirical Inquiry Can Help," below, for more discussion on this point.

Moral Realism

Moral realists, like error theorists, are cognitivists—they believe that moral judgments involve a claim to objectivity. (That said, not all moral realists regard moral claims as objectively prescriptive or categorically binding in the way that Mackie does.) But unlike the skeptic, moral realists assert that there are indeed moral facts that make some of these judgments true. Realist theories have two primary aims. First, they seek to provide an account of moral truth that captures at least most of what we mean and what we want when it comes to morality. Second, they try to show that the account is plausible, consistent with our more general understanding of the world at large. How realists try to accomplish the latter aim varies, depending in large part on their other metaphysical commitments. Theists, for example, may not feel compelled to show how objective values could exist without a supernatural entity. These realists develop accounts of moral facts that do not require God, Platonic forms, or other nonnatural entities and forces.

One argument for moral realism is presented in Reading 8.5 by Michael Smith. Smith first seeks to provide an analysis of rightness that captures the "platitudes" of morality. Three essential features of moral facts according to Smith are that they are objective, that they provide *reasons* for agents to act in a certain way, and that they *motivate* agents to act in this way. According to Smith, a successful realist theory must have an answer to the question "why be moral" posed so forcefully by Glaucon and Adeimantus in Plato's *Republic* (Reading 8.2). Smith arrives at this definition of moral rightness: *an act is morally right for us just in case it is the act we would want to do if we were fully rational.*[5] To illustrate, imagine that you find a lost wallet and are wondering whether to return it. On Smith's account, it is morally right to return the wallet if, under conditions of ideal rationality, we would all want to return it in those circumstances. This definition of moral rightness clearly provides us with reasons to act morally. And the account links morality with motivation since moral rightness is defined in terms of the desires of our perfectly rational counterparts.

But are there moral facts as Smith defines them? Like many realists, Smith argues for the plausibility of his account by responding to relevant skeptical challenges. To Mackie's argument from queerness, Smith replies that there is nothing strange or non-natural about trying to determine what a fully rational version of ourselves would want to do. Although the concept of a fully rational person is an idealization, the attempt to better approximate them is perfectly consistent with a broadly naturalistic understanding of human cognition and behavior. The challenge of moral disagreement is more problematic for Smith, however, because of his assumptions about the convergence of desires of fully rational people.[6] Entrenched moral disagreement across cultures might indicate that people have fundamentally different desires. And if there is no single thing that all fully rational people would want to do in a situation, then there is no moral fact about what we ought to do in that situation.

In response to this challenge, Smith first cautions us not to underestimate the amount of moral *agreement* on issues that were once controversial. Furthermore, according to Smith, disagreement on these issues was "removed via a process of moral argument." The resolution of controversies concerning, for example, slavery and women's rights is for Smith a sign of moral progress. "The empirical fact that moral argument tends to elicit the agreement of our fellows," Smith writes, "gives us reason to believe that there will be convergence in our desires under conditions of full rationality" (p. 461). Finally, Smith argues that much of the moral disagreement that remains can be traced to irrationality on one side or the other (or both). Often what seems like a moral disagreement boils down to a disagreement over the relevant nonmoral facts. (See James Rachels's critique of cultural relativism, Reading 8.6, for a more detailed elaboration of this point.) Other moral disagreements can be traced to religious commitments that the followers have no good reason to hold. Disagreement of this sort, Smith claims, "casts no doubt on the possibility of an agreement if were to engage in free and rational debate" (p. 461). Each of these responses, it should be clear, depends on crucial empirical assumptions that are open to challenge.[7] One considerable virtue of Smith's analysis is its precision, which helps to illuminate the central points of dispute between the realist and antirealist, pointing the way for progress on this 2,000-year-old debate.

Noncognitivism

Noncognitivism in contemporary meta-ethics emerged as a part of the logical positivist movement in the early part of the twentieth century. The central concern of logical positivists was to distinguish meaningful statements from nonmeaningful ones. Employing their infamous verification principle, they sought to lay waste to entire debates in metaphysics and theology. For a claim to be meaningful, they argued, it must either be tautological (e.g., mathematical statements or logical inferences) or be subject to verification through empirical investigation. According to the positivists, a claim like "there is a God," which meets neither of these criteria, is "literal nonsense."

Positivists like A. J. Ayer (Reading 8.3) were happy to condemn theological and other highly metaphysical debates as meaningless. Moral claims, however, presented a bit of a problem. On the one hand, moral statements do not appear to meet either of the criteria laid out in the verification principle. But they do not seem to be meaningless either. Ayer's solution was to argue that moral statements are not propositions at all but rather expressions of feelings of disapproval which can neither be true nor false. For Ayer, a claim like "breaking promises is wrong" does not purport to be factual; rather, it is equivalent to saying in a very disapproving tone: "breaking promises!" (The early noncognitivist theories were often referred to as the "boo-yay theory of morality." "Breaking promises is wrong" turns out to mean "Boo breaking promises!") A more specific claim like "Bill was wrong to break that promise to his daughter" is equivalent to "Bill broke that promise to his daughter!" Part of that statement is truth apt (whether Bill did indeed break the promise), but the moral part—the wrongness—is not.

The central challenge for noncognitivism is to explain why moral judgments at the very least *seem* to be factual in nature. Recall Pelecanos's remarks about Michael Vick's offense: "Training dogs to fight is wrong. Murdering dogs is wrong. The issue is not complex. There is no other side." On the surface, at least, Pelecanos does not appear to be merely expressing his disapproval of dog fighting. On the contrary, he seems to be explicitly rejecting this emotivist reading of his moral judgment. Assuming Pelecanos's perspective is typical, we might wonder why we should take noncognitivism seriously. But noncognitivism has its advantages as well. For one thing, it does not attribute widespread error to moral discourse. And unlike many forms of moral realism, noncognitivism does not have to account for the existence of moral properties that bind all agents to action, no matter what their particular motivations or desires. In this way, noncognitivism has a "best of both worlds" quality, unburdened by the most problematic elements of error theory and moral realism.

One common objection to noncognitivism focuses again on the prevalence of moral disagreement and debate. If moral claims are simply expressions of emotions and attitudes, the objection goes, how could such disagreement exist? We do not have elaborate debates about whether blueberries are delicious precisely because we recognize that ultimately, our claims are expressions of taste and preference. On moral questions, however, we do engage in such debates and are frustrated when we fail to persuade our opponents to share our views. Doesn't this suggest that when we make moral claims we believe we are *right*?

Interestingly, Ayer's reply to the challenge of disagreement resembles the replies of realists like Rachels and Smith. Ayer argues that upon closer examination, moral disputes commonly turn out to be disputes over nonmoral facts rather than values.

Debates about factory farming, for example, often boil down to disagreements over how much suffering the animals experience—*not* over the moral permissibility of causing that degree of suffering. The dependence of moral judgments on disputed beliefs about relevant nonmoral facts creates the *appearance* of disagreement about moral values when in fact there is none. The difference between Ayer's view and Smith's concerns how they regard the *outcome* of these disagreements. According to Ayer, once the nonmoral facts are agreed upon and our opponents are still unpersuaded, we abandon the attempt to persuade them. We say they have a "distorted or undeveloped moral sense; which signifies merely that he employs a different set of values from our own" (p. 452). Realists like Smith and Rachels believe that agreement about nonmoral facts and further rational argument will ultimately resolve moral disputes, precisely because there is a right answer to the moral questions as well as the nonmoral ones.

HOW EMPIRICAL INQUIRY CAN HELP

The last section outlined the three major positions in contemporary meta-ethics: realism, skepticism, and noncognitivism. Within these categories, there is a multiplicity of theories, different from one another in important ways. The selections in this unit provide a representative sample of each position, but we cannot do full justice to their complexity in this volume. I conclude this unit introduction with some remarks on how experimental philosophy, and empirical investigation in general, may bear on the central issues in meta-ethics.

First, empirical inquiry can shed light on the nature and extent of moral diversity. No one denies that there is widespread variation in moral values and attitudes across cultures. The debate focuses on the nature of the disagreement, whether or not it is intractable or fundamental. The majority of realist theories operate under the assumption that disagreement about moral values would largely dissolve under conditions of greater rationality. The prospects for such a convergence of moral attitudes and judgments are in large part an empirical question. Recall Smith's claims that much of the entrenched disagreement that exists today can be traced to the irrationality of one of the disputants. In Reading 8.7, Doris and Stich present some preliminary evidence that challenges this claim. Appealing to research in psychology on honor cultures in the American South, the authors argue that disagreements over when violence is justified is rooted in core differences in the value systems of honor and nonhonor cultures. In these disagreements, both parties seem to agree on the relevant nonfacts, and so it is difficult to see "how charges of abnormality or irrationality can be made without one side begging the question against the other" (p. 484).[8] When presented with specific examples of deep disagreement, it is incumbent on the realist to show precisely how one of the sides is being irrational. Otherwise, their optimism will seem ungrounded. For their part, moral skeptics must also offer a plausible empirical explanation for the strength and depth of our moral convictions and for moral phenomena in general—one that of course does not require the existence of moral facts.[9] There are a lot of promissory notes on both sides currently and close attention to the relevant empirical literature can help to move beyond them.

Another subject of empirical inquiry concerns the nature of moral motivation and the question: why be moral? Even assuming there is such a thing as objective moral truth, there remains the problem of the amoralist. In Reading 8.2, Plato gives an illustration of this problem with his famous thought experiment "The Ring of Gyges." Give a just person a ring that will make him invisible (and thus immune to all the negative consequences that normally come from acting immorally), and his actions will be indistinguishable from those of a thoroughly unjust and immoral person—he will steal, murder, and sleep with anyone to gain power and serve his own interests. These unscrupulous ring-bearers *recognize* moral principles. They just see no reason to comply with them. The question, then, is whether we have any reason to be moral when we can get away with being immoral.

This challenge has led some philosophers to assert that moral theories, in addition to determining right and wrong action, must also provide an answer to the question: why be moral? Many realists (like Smith) and error theorists (like Mackie) endorse an *internalist* view of moral belief. On this view, if you believe that a certain act is wrong, then you recognize that you have reason to refrain from performing it and are motivated accordingly.[10] (By definition, then, the ring-bearers who see no reason to act morally do not *truly* believe they have moral obligations.) These reason-giving and motivational requirements are important for the realist since they seem to give morality its practical force. They are important for error theorists as well because they constitute a large part of the alleged "queerness" of objective moral values.

But are these requirements an essential part of the concept of morality? Once again, empirical investigation can help to shed light on this question. Doris and Stich describe a number of experiments that appear to undermine internalist claims. First, they appeal to some preliminary survey work by Shaun Nichols on the subject of psychopaths. A large majority of respondents in Nichols's studies replied that psychopaths are capable of understanding that hurting people is morally wrong but at the same time do not care about hurting others for their own gain. These results challenge Smith's claim that morality has a motivational platitude. Doris and Stich go on to describe research in neuroscience and clinical psychology indicating that psychopaths do not appear to suffer from rational impairments. If psychopaths are able to distinguish right from wrong, do not feel compelled at all to act morally, and suffer no clear defect in rationality, then Smith's internalist form of moral realism looks unsustainable. Smith and other internalist realists have ways of responding, but it appears they must engage the empirical literature to do so.

Finally, empirical inquiry can shed light on what I have termed "the question of meaning," which is at the center of the debate between realists, relativists, and non-cognitivists. Realists and skeptics alike assume that ordinary people are *intuitive moral realists*: they believe that objective moral values are out there in the world. Realists use this assumption to shift the burden of proof to the antirealist. Since objectivism is so intuitive, they argue, we need an overwhelming amount of evidence and argument to reject it. Skeptics like Mackie are even more dependent on the truth of this assumption. Without a widespread belief in moral objectivity, there would be no error in his error theory. In our final selection (Reading 8.8), Jennifer Cole Wright and Hagop Sarkissian summarize some recent work in experimental philosophy that challenges the assumption that people are intuitive realists. The results seem to be welcome news for moral relativists and noncognitivists. The most common complaint about these positions is that they fail to capture our intuitive conception of what morality *is*. Of course, many of the studies are preliminary, and it is too early to come to any confident meta-ethical conclusions. But this research makes important contributions to the debate over the meaning of moral claims and identifies new ways for the debate to progress.

Notes

1. George Pelecanos, "Dogfighting's Poisonous Politics," *New Republic*, September 1, 2007.
2. See Loeb (1998), Doris and Stich (2005) (Reading 8.7), and Doris and Plakias (2008) for excellent discussions of Mackie's argument from relativity.
3. The argument gains further plausibility when combined with Gilbert Harman's claim that moral facts do not explain our moral observations. See Harman (1977) for further elaboration of this argument and Dreier and Copp (2005) for a nice overview of how all of these arguments can work together to support moral antirealism.
4. Joyce (2006) attempts to provide an evolutionary account of our moral sense in support of Mackie's error theory. See Allhoff (2009) for a critical response.
5. There is another requirement as well: that the act be of the "appropriate substantive kind"; it is the kind of act we associate with morality, as opposed to morally neutral acts such as choose beer over wine.
6. The majority of moral realists make similar assumptions about the convergence of judgments or desires under conditions of more ideal rationality. On this point, see Doris and Plakias (2008).
7. See Loeb (1998), Doris and Stich (2005) (Reading 8.7), and Doris and Plakias (2008) for an excellent discussion of how empirical consideration bears on this debate. See also my interview with Stephen Stich in Sommers (2009b).
8. See also Sommers (2009a) for further descriptions of variation in honor and nonhonor cultures.
9. Again, see Joyce (2006) for one such attempt.
10. "Reason internalists" may accept the reason criterion but reject the motivation criterion.

References and Suggestions for Further Reading

Allhoff, F. "The Evolution of the Moral Sentiments and the Metaphysics of Morals." *Ethical Theory and Moral Practice* 12, no. 1 (2009): 97–114.

Ayer, A. J. *Language, Truth and Logic*. Dover, 1952.

Bloom, A. D. *The Republic of Plato*. New York: Basic Books, 1991.

Copp, D. *The Oxford Handbook of Ethical Theory*. New York: Oxford University Press, 2006.

Doris, J., and S. Stich. "As a Matter of Fact: Empirical Perspectives on Ethics." In *The Oxford Handbook of Contemporary Philosophy*, 114–152. New York: Oxford University Press, 2005.

Doris, J. M., and A. Plakias. "How to Argue about Disagreement: Evaluative Diversity and Moral Realism." In *Moral Psychology*. Vol. 2, ed. W. Sinnott-Armstrong. Cambridge, MA: MIT Press, 2008.

Dreier, J., and D. Copp. "Moral Relativism and Moral Nihilism." *The Oxford Handbook of Ethical Theory*, 240–265. New York: Oxford University Press, 2005.

Gibbard, A. *Wise Choices, Apt Feelings: A Theory of Normative Judgment.* Cambridge, MA: Harvard University Press, 1992.

Harman, G. *The Nature of Morality: An Introduction to Ethics.* New York: Oxford University Press, 1977.

Herodotus, A. De Sélincourt, and A. R. Burn. *Herodotus: The Histories.* Baltimore: Penguin, 1954.

Joyce, R. *The Evolution of Morality.* Cambridge, MA: MIT Press, 2006.

Loeb, D. "Moral Realism and the Argument from Disagreement." *Philosophical Studies* 90, no. 3 (1998): 281–303.

Mackie, J. L. *Ethics: Inventing Right and Wrong.* London: Harmondsworth, 1977.

Nichols, Shaun. *Sentimental Rules: On the Natural Foundations of Moral Judgment.* Oxford, New York: Oxford University Press, 2004.

Nisbett, R. E., and D. Cohen. *Culture of Honor: The Psychology of Violence in the South.* Boulder, CO: Westview, 1996.

Prinz, J. J. *The Emotional Construction of Morals.* New York: Oxford University Press, 2007.

Rachels, J., and S. Rachels. *The Elements of Moral Philosophy.* New York: McGraw-Hill, 1993.

Smith, M. A. *The Moral Problem.* Oxford: Wiley-Blackwell, 1994.

Sommers, T. "The Two Faces of Revenge: Moral Responsibility and the Culture of Honor." *Biology and Philosophy* 24, no. 1 (2009a): 35–50.

Sommers, T. *A Very Bad Wizard: Morality Behind the Curtain.* San Francisco: McSweeney's, 2009b.

Sturgeon, N. "Ethical Naturalism." In *The Oxford Handbook of Ethical Theory,* 91–122. New York: Oxford University Press, 2006.

8.1   Culture Is King

 HERODOTUS

HERODOTUS (484–425 BCE) is considered the first historian of Western civilization, and he traveled widely to gather information about the Persian wars. In the course of his travels, Herodotus observed the diversity of customs and values of the peoples. In this excerpt from *The Histories*, Herodotus chronicles the differences in beliefs about how to treat one's dead, as well as the horror that each culture feels about the customs of the other.

If anyone, no matter who, were given the opportunity of choosing from amongst all the nations in the world the set of beliefs which he thought best, he would inevitably, after careful consideration of their relative merits, choose that of his own country. Everyone without exception believes his own native customs, and the religion he was brought up in, to be the best; and that being so, it is unlikely that anyone but a madman would mock at such things. There is abundant evidence that this is the universal feeling about the ancient customs of one's country. One might recall, in particular, an anecdote of Darius. When he was king of Persia, he summoned the Greeks who happened to be present at his court, and asked them what they would take to eat the dead bodies of their fathers. They replied that they would not do it for any money in the world. Later, in the presence of the Greeks, and through an interpreter, so that they could understand what was said, he asked some Indians, of the tribe called Callatiae, who do in fact eat their parents' dead bodies, what they would take to burn them. They uttered a cry of horror and forbade him to mention such a dreadful thing. One can see by this what custom can do, and Pindar, in my opinion, was right when he called it "king of all."

Study Questions

1. Is Herodotus making a purely descriptive point in these passages, or is he expressing a meta-ethical position as well?
2. Can these differences be explained away as a product of irrationality on one side or the other?

Why Be Moral?   8.2

PLATO

PLATO'S (428–347 BCE) remarkable body of work has set the agenda for much of Western philosophy to this day. The vast majority of his writings are dialogues with Socrates as the central character. In his masterpiece *The Republic*, Plato aims to defend the claim that behaving justly is good for its own sake, not just for the consequences just behavior usually brings about. This excerpt from Book II lays out a famous challenge to this view. Glaucon and Adeimantus (Plato's brothers in real life) argue that people are just only because they fear the consequences of behaving otherwise. In support of this view, Glaucon presents two thought experiments in which unjust behavior is rewarded rather than punished. Under such circumstances, Glaucon argues, no one will think twice about acting unjustly to acquire power and riches.

Now, when I had said this, I thought I was freed from argument. But after all, as it seems, it was only a prelude. For Glaucon is always most courageous in everything, and so now he wouldn't accept Thrasymachus' giving up but said, "Socrates, do you want to seem to have persuaded us, or truly to persuade us, that it is in every way better to be just than unjust?"

"I would choose to persuade you truly," I said, "if it were up to me."

"Well, then," he said, "you're not doing what you want. Tell me, is there in your opinion a kind of good that we would choose to have not because we desire its consequences, but because we delight in it for its own sake—such as enjoyment and all the pleasures which are harmless and leave no after effects other than the enjoyment in having them?"

"In my opinion, at least," I said, "there is a good of this kind."

"And what about this? Is there a kind we like both for its own sake and for what comes out of it, such as thinking and seeing and being healthy? Surely we delight in such things on both accounts."

"Yes," I said.

"And do you see a third form of good, which includes gymnastic exercise, medical treatment when sick as well as the practice of medicine, and the rest of the activities from which money is made? We would say that they are drudgery but beneficial to us; and we would not choose to have them for themselves but for the sake of the wages and whatever else comes out of them."

"Yes, there is also this third," I said, "but what of it?"

"In which of them," he said, "would you include justice?"

"I, for my part, suppose," I said, "that it belongs in the finest kind, which the man who is going to be blessed should like both for itself and for what comes out of it."

"Well, that's not the opinion of the many," he said, "rather it seems to belong to the form of drudgery, which should be practiced for the sake of wages and the reputation that comes from

Plato, *The Republic of Plato: Basic Books*, translated by Allan Bloom (Perseus Books Group, 1991). Reprinted with permission of the publisher.

opinion; but all by itself it should be fled from as something hard."

"I know this is the popular opinion," I said, "and a while ago justice, taken as being such, was blamed by Thrasymachus while injustice was praised. But I, as it seems, am a poor learner."

"Come, now," he said, "hear me too, and see if you still have the same opinion. For it looks to me as though Thrasymachus, like a snake, has been charmed more quickly than he should have been; yet to my way of thinking there was still no proof about either. For I desire to hear what each is and what power it has all alone by itself when it is in the soul—dismissing its wages and its consequences. So I shall do it this way, if you too consent: I'll restore Thrasymachus' argument, and first I'll tell what kind of thing they say justice is and where it came from; second, that all those who practice it do so unwillingly, as necessary but not good; third, that it is fitting that they do so, for the life of the unjust man is, after all, far better than that of the just man, as they say. For, Socrates, though that's not at all my own opinion, I am at a loss: I've been talked deaf by Thrasymachus and countless others, while the argument on behalf of justice—that it is better than injustice—I've yet to hear from anyone as I want it. I want to hear it extolled all by itself, and I suppose I would be most likely to learn that from you. That's the reason why I'll speak in vehement praise of the unjust life, and in speaking I'll point out to you how I want to hear you, in your turn, blame injustice and praise justice. See if what I'm saying is what you want."

"Most of all," I said. "What would an intelligent man enjoy talking and hearing about more again and again?"

"What you say is quite fine," he said. "Now listen to what I said I was going to tell first— what justice is and where it came from.

"They say that doing injustice is naturally good, and suffering injustice bad, but that the bad in suffering injustice far exceeds the good in doing it; so that, when they do injustice to one another and suffer it and taste of both, it seems

profitable—to those who are not able to escape the one and choose the other—to set down a compact among themselves neither to do injustice nor to suffer it. And from there they began to set down their own laws and compacts and to name what the law commands lawful and just. And this, then, is the genesis and being of justice; it is a mean between what is best—doing injustice without paying the penalty—and what is worst—suffering injustice without being able to avenge oneself. The just is in the middle between these two, cared for not because it is good but because it is honored due to a want of vigor in doing injustice. The man who is able to do it and is truly a man would never set down a compact with anyone not to do injustice and not to suffer it. He'd be mad. Now the nature of justice is this and of this sort, and it naturally grows out of these sorts of things. So the argument goes.

"That even those who practice it do so unwillingly, from an incapacity to do injustice, we would best perceive if we should in thought do something like this: give each, the just man and the unjust, license to do whatever he wants, while we follow and watch where his desire will lead each. We would catch the just man red-handed going the same way as the unjust man out of a desire to get the better; this is what any nature naturally pursues as good, while it is law which by force perverts it to honor equality. The license of which I speak would best be realized if they should come into possession of the sort of power that it is said the ancestor of Gyges, the Lydian, once got. They say he was a shepherd toiling in the service of the man who was then ruling Lydia. There came to pass a great thunderstorm and an earthquake; the earth cracked and a chasm opened at the place where he was pasturing. He saw it, wondered at it, and went down. He saw, along with other quite wonderful things about which they tell tales, a hollow bronze horse. It had windows; peeping in, he saw there was a corpse inside that looked larger than human size. It had nothing on except a gold ring on its hand; he slipped it off and went out. When there was the usual gathering of the shepherds to make the monthly report to the king about the flocks, he too came, wearing the ring. Now, while he was sitting with the others, he chanced to turn the collet of the ring to himself, toward the inside of his hand; when he did this, he became invisible to those sitting by him, and they discussed him as though he were away. He wondered at this, and, fingering the ring again, he twisted the collet toward the outside; when he had twisted it, he became visible. Thinking this over, he tested whether the ring had this power, and that was exactly his result: when he turned the collet inward, he became invisible, when outward, visible. Aware of this, he immediately contrived to be one of the messengers to the king. When he arrived, he committed adultery with the king's wife and, along with her, set upon the king and killed him. And so he took over the rule.

"Now if there were two such rings, and the just man would put one on, and the unjust man the other, no one, as it would seem, would be so adamant as to stick by justice and bring himself to keep away from what belongs to others and not lay hold of it, although he had license to take what he wanted from the market without fear, and to go into houses and have intercourse with whomever he wanted, and to slay or release from bonds whomever he wanted, and to do other things as an equal to a god among humans. And in so doing, one would act no differently from the other, but both would go the same way. And yet, someone could say that this is a great proof that no one is willingly just but only when compelled to be so. Men do not take it to be a good for them in private, since wherever each supposes he can do injustice, he does it. Indeed, all men suppose injustice is far more to their private profit than justice. And what they suppose is true, as the man who makes this kind of an argument will say, since if a man were to get hold of such license and were never willing to do any injustice and didn't lay his hands

on what belongs to others, he would seem most wretched to those who were aware of it, and most foolish too, although they would praise him to each others' faces, deceiving each other for fear of suffering injustice. So much for that.

"As to the judgment itself about the life of these two of whom we are speaking, we'll be able to make it correctly if we set the most just man and the most unjust in opposition; if we do not, we won't be able to do so. What, then, is this opposition? It is as follows: we shall take away nothing from the injustice of the unjust man nor from the justice of the just man, but we shall take each as perfect in his own pursuit. So, first, let the unjust man act like the clever craftsmen. An outstanding pilot or doctor is aware of the difference between what is impossible in his art and what is possible, and he attempts the one, and lets the other go; and if, after all, he should still trip up in any way, he is competent to set himself aright. Similarly, let the unjust man also attempt unjust deeds correctly, and get away with them, if he is going to be extremely unjust. The man who is caught must be considered a poor chap. For the extreme of injustice is to seem to be just when one is not. So the perfectly unjust man must be given the most perfect injustice, and nothing must be taken away; he must be allowed to do the greatest injustices while having provided himself with the greatest reputation for justice. And if, after all, he should trip up in anything, he has the power to set himself aright; if any of his unjust deeds should come to light, he is capable both of speaking persuasively and of using force, to the extent that force is needed, since he is courageous and strong and since he has provided for friends and money. Now, let us set him down as such, and put beside him in the argument the just man in his turn, a man simple and noble, who, according to Aeschylus, does not wish to seem, but rather to be, good. The seeming must be taken away. For if he should seem just, there would be honors and gifts for him for seeming to be such. Then it wouldn't be plain whether he is such for the sake of the just or for the sake of the gifts and honors. So he must be stripped of everything except justice, and his situation must be made the opposite of the first man's. Doing no injustice, let him have the greatest reputation for injustice, so that his justice may be put to the test to see if it is softened by bad reputation and its consequences. Let him go unchanged till death, seeming throughout life to be unjust although he is just, so that when each has come to the extreme—the one of justice, the other of injustice—they can be judged as to which of the two is happier."

"My, my," I said, "my dear Glaucon, how vigorously you polish up each of the two men—just like a statue—for their judgment."

"As much as I can," he said. "With two such men it's no longer hard, I suppose, to complete the speech by a description of the kind of life that awaits each. It must be told, then. And if it's somewhat rustically told, don't suppose that it is I who speak, Socrates, but rather those who praise injustice ahead of justice. They'll say that the just man who has such a disposition will be whipped; he'll be racked; he'll be bound; he'll have both his eyes burned out; and, at the end, when he has undergone every sort of evil, he'll be crucified and know that one shouldn't wish to be, but to seem to be, just. After all, Aeschylus' saying applies far more correctly to the unjust man. For really, they will say, it is the unjust man, because he pursues a thing dependent on truth and does not live in the light of opinion, who does not wish to seem unjust but to be unjust,

> Reaping a deep furrow in his mind
> From which trusty plans bear fruit.

First, he rules in the city because he seems to be just. Then he takes in marriage from whatever station he wants and gives in marriage to whomever he wants; he contracts and has partnerships with whomever he wants, and, besides benefiting himself in all this, he gains because he has no qualms about doing injustice. So then, when he enters contests, both private and public, he wins and gets the better of his enemies. In getting the better, he is wealthy and does good to friends and harm to enemies. To the gods he makes sacrifices and sets up votive offerings, adequate and magnificent, and cares for the gods and those human beings he wants to care for far better than the just man. So, in all likelihood, it is also more appropriate for him to be dearer to the gods than is the just man. Thus, they say, Socrates, with gods and with humans, a better life is provided for the unjust man than for the just man."

When Glaucon had said this, I had it in mind to say something to it, but his brother Adeimantus said in his turn, "You surely don't believe, Socrates, that the argument has been adequately stated?"

"Why not?" I said.

"What most needed to be said has not been said," he said.

"Then," I said, "as the saying goes, 'let a man stand by his brother.' So, you too, if he leaves out anything, come to his defense. And yet, what he said was already enough to bring me to my knees and make it impossible to help out justice."

And he said, "Nonsense. But still hear this too. We must also go through the arguments opposed to those of which he spoke, those that praise justice and blame injustice, so that what Glaucon in my opinion wants will be clearer. No doubt, fathers say to their sons and exhort them, as do all those who have care of anyone, that one must be just. However, they don't praise justice by itself but the good reputations that come from it; they exhort their charges to be just so that, as a result of the opinion, ruling offices and marriages will come to the one who seems to be just, and all the other things that Glaucon a moment ago attributed to the just man as a result of his having a good reputation. And these men tell even more of the things resulting from the opinions. For by throwing in good reputation with the gods, they can tell of an inexhaustible store of goods that they say gods give to the holy. And in this way they join both the noble Hesiod and Homer. The former says that for the just the gods make the oaks

Bear acorns on high, and bees in the
middle,
And the fleecy sheep heavily laden with
wool

and many other very good things connected
with these. And the other has pretty much the
same to tell, as when he says,

As for some blameless king who in fear
of the gods
Upholds justice, the black earth bears
Barley and wheat, the trees are laden
with fruit,
The sheep bring forth without fail, and
the sea provides fish.

And Musaeus and his son give the just even
headier goods than these from the gods. In their
speech they lead them into Hades and lay them
down on couches; crowning them, they prepare a
symposium of the holy, and they then make them
go through the rest of time drunk, in the belief
that the finest wage of virtue is an eternal drunk.
Others extend the wages from the gods yet further than these. For they say that a holy and oath-
keeping man leaves his children's children and a
whole tribe behind him. So in these and like ways
they extol justice. And, in turn, they bury the
unholy and unjust in mud in Hades and compel
them to carry water in a sieve; and they bring
them into bad reputation while they are still alive.
Thus, those penalties that Glaucon described as
the lot of the just men who are reputed to be
unjust, these people say are the lot of the unjust.
But they have nothing else to say. This then is the
praise and blame attached to each.

"Furthermore, Socrates, consider still another
form of speeches about justice and injustice, spoken in prose and by poets. With one tongue they
all chant that moderation and justice are fair,
but hard and full of drudgery, while intemper-
ance and injustice are sweet and easy to acquire,
and shameful only by opinion and law. They say
that the unjust is for the most part more profitable than the just; and both in public and in
private, they are ready and willing to call happy

and to honor bad men who have wealth or some
other power and to dishonor and overlook those
who happen in some way to be weak or poor,
although they agree they are better than the others. But the most wonderful of all these speeches
are those they give about gods and virtue. They
say that the gods, after all, allot misfortune and a
bad life to many good men too, and an opposite
fate to opposite men. Beggar priests and diviners
go to the doors of the rich man and persuade him
that the gods have provided them with a power
based on sacrifices and incantations. If he himself,
or his ancestors, has committed some injustice,
they can heal it with pleasures and feasts; and if
he wishes to ruin some enemies at small expense,
he will injure just and unjust alike with certain
evocations and spells. They, as they say, persuade
the gods to serve them. And they bring the poets
forward as witnesses to all these arguments about
vice, and they present it as easy, saying that,

Vice in abundance is easy to choose,
The road is smooth and it lies very near,
While the gods have set sweat before
virtue,
And it is a long road, rough and steep.

And they use Homer as a witness to the perversion of the gods by human beings because he
too said:

The very gods can be moved by prayer
too.
With sacrifices and gentle vows and
The odor of burnt and drink offerings,
human beings turn them aside with
their prayers,
When someone has transgressed and
made a mistake.

And they present a babble of books by Musaeus
and Orpheus, offspring of the Moon and the
Muses, as they say, according to whose prescriptions they busy themselves about their sacrifices.
They persuade not only private persons, but cities as well, that through sacrifices and pleasurable games there are, after all, deliverances and
purifications from unjust deeds for those still

living. And there are also rites for those who are dead. These, which they call initiations, deliver us from the evils in the other place; while, for those who did not sacrifice, terrible things are waiting.

"My dear Socrates," he said, "with all these things being said—of this sort and in this quantity—about virtue and vice and how human beings and gods honor them, what do we suppose they do to the souls of the young men who hear them? I mean those who have good natures and have the capacity, as it were, to fly to all the things that are said and gather from them what sort of man one should be and what way one must follow to go through life best. In all likelihood he would say to himself, after Pindar, will I 'with justice or with crooked deceits scale the higher wall' where I can fortify myself all around and live out my life? For the things said indicate that there is no advantage in my being just, if I don't also seem to be, while the labors and penalties involved are evident. But if I'm unjust, but have provided myself with a reputation for justice, a divine life is promised. Therefore, since as the wise make plain to me, 'the seeming overpowers even the truth' and is the master of happiness, one must surely turn wholly to it. As facade and exterior I must draw a shadow painting of virtue all around me, while behind it I must trail the wily and subtle fox of the most wise Archilochus. 'But,' says someone, 'it's not always easy to do bad and get away with it unnoticed.' 'Nothing great is easy,' we'll say. 'But at all events, if we are going to be happy we must go where the tracks of the arguments lead. For, as to getting away with it, we'll organize secret societies and clubs; and there are teachers of persuasion who offer the wisdom of the public assembly and the court. On this basis, in some things we'll persuade and in others use force; thus we'll get the better and not pay the penalty.' 'But it surely isn't possible to get away from the gods or overpower them.' 'But, if there are no gods, or if they have no care for human things, why should we care at all about getting away? And if there are gods and they care, we know of them or have heard of them from nowhere else than the laws and the poets who have given genealogies; and these are the very sources of our being told that they are such as to be persuaded and perverted by sacrifices, soothing vows, and votive offerings. Either both things must be believed or neither. If they are to be believed, injustice must be done and sacrifice offered from the unjust acquisitions. For if we are just, we won't be punished by the gods. That is all. And we'll refuse the gains of injustice. But if we are unjust, we shall gain and get off unpunished as well, by persuading the gods with prayers when we transgress and make mistakes.' 'But in Hades we'll pay the penalty for our injustices here, either we ourselves or our children's children.' 'But, my dear,' will say the man who calculates, 'the initiations and the delivering gods have great power, as say the greatest cities and those children of gods who have become poets and spokesmen of the gods and reveal that this is the case.'

"Then, by what further argument could we choose justice before the greatest injustice? For, if we possess it with a counterfeited seemly exterior, we'll fare as we are minded with gods and human beings both while we are living and when we are dead, so goes the speech of both the many and the eminent. After all that has been said, by what device, Socrates, will a man who has some power—of soul, money, body or family—be made willing to honor justice and not laugh when he hears it praised? So, consequently, if someone can show that what we have said is false and if he has adequate knowledge that justice is best, he undoubtedly has great sympathy for the unjust and is not angry with them; he knows that except for someone who from a divine nature cannot stand doing injustice or who has gained knowledge and keeps away from injustice, no one else is willingly just; but because of a lack of courage, or old age, or some other weakness, men blame injustice because they are unable to do it. And that this is so is plain. For the first man of this kind to come to power is the first to do injustice to the best of his ability. And there is no other cause of all this than that which gave rise to this whole argument of his and mine with you, Socrates. We said, 'You surprising man, of all you who claim to be praisers of justice—beginning with the heroes at the beginning (those who have left speeches) up to the human beings of the present—there is not one who has ever blamed injustice or praised justice other than for the reputations, honors, and gifts that come from them. But as to what each itself does with its own power when it is in the soul of a man who possesses it and is not noticed by gods and men, no one has ever, in poetry or prose, adequately developed the argument that the one is the greatest of evils a soul can have in it, and justice the greatest good. For if all of you had spoken in this way from the beginning and persuaded us, from youth onwards, we would not keep guard over each other for fear injustice be done, but each would be his own best guard, afraid that in doing injustice he would dwell with the greatest evil. [...]"

Study Questions

1. Even if Glaucon is right about the behavior of the ring-wearers, does that prove that justice is not an intrinsic good?
2. Does Socrates accept too great a burden in the second thought experiment by conceding that the just man must be happier than the unjust man?
3. What meta-ethical views are consistent with Glaucon and Adeimantus's argument?
4. What empirical assumptions is Glaucon making in his argument?

Emotivism   8.3

A. J. AYER

A. J. AYER (1910–1989) was the Wykeham Professor of Logic at Oxford and a leading figure in the logical positivism movement of the early twentieth century. In this excerpt from his book *Language, Truth, and Logic*—first published in 1936 when Ayer was twenty-five—Ayer presents his noncognitivist analysis of moral statements. Ayer argues that moral judgments are best understood as expressions of emotion rather than statements of fact. A judgment such as "stealing money is wrong," according to Ayer, does not purport to be objectively true. Rather, it is the speaker's way of expressing disapproval about the act of stealing.

[...] Considering the use which we have made of the principle that a synthetic proposition is significant only if it is empirically verifiable, it is clear that the acceptance of an "absolutist" theory of ethics would undermine the whole of our main argument. And as we have already rejected the "naturalistic" theories which are commonly supposed to provide the only alternative to "absolutism" in ethics, we seem to have reached a difficult position. We shall meet the difficulty

A. J. Ayer, *Language, Truth and Logic* (Dover Publications, Inc., 1952). Reprinted with permission of the publisher.

by showing that the correct treatment of ethical statements is afforded by a third theory, which is wholly compatible with our radical empiricism.

We begin by admitting that the fundamental ethical concepts are unanalysable, inasmuch as there is no criterion by which one can test the validity of the judgements in which they occur. So far we are in agreement with the absolutists. But, unlike the absolutists, we are able to give an explanation of this fact about ethical concepts. We say that the reason why they are unanalysable is that they are mere pseudo-concepts. The presence of an ethical symbol in a proposition adds nothing to its factual content. Thus if I say to someone, "You acted wrongly in stealing that money," I am not stating anything more than if I had simply said, "You stole that money." In adding that this action is wrong I am not making any further statement about it. I am simply evincing my moral disapproval of it. It is as if I had said, "You stole that money," in a peculiar tone of horror, or written it with the addition of some special exclamation marks. The tone, or the exclamation marks, adds nothing to the literal meaning of the sentence. It merely serves to show that the expression of it is attended by certain feelings in the speaker.

If now I generalise my previous statement and say, "Stealing money is wrong," I produce a sentence which has no factual meaning—that is, expresses no proposition which can be either true or false. It is as if I had written "Stealing money!!"—where the shape and thickness of the exclamation marks show, by a suitable convention, that a special sort of moral disapproval is the feeling which is being expressed. It is clear that there is nothing said here which can be true or false. Another man may disagree with me about the wrongness of stealing, in the sense that he may not have the same feelings about stealing as I have, and he may quarrel with me on account of my moral sentiments. But he cannot, strictly speaking, contradict me. For in saying that a certain type of action is right or wrong, I am not making any factual statement, not even

a statement about my own state of mind: I am merely expressing certain moral sentiments. And the man who is ostensibly contradicting me is merely expressing his moral sentiments. So that there is plainly no sense in asking which of us is in the right. For neither of us is asserting a genuine proposition.

What we have just been saying about the symbol "wrong" applies to all normative ethical symbols. Sometimes they occur in sentences which record ordinary empirical facts besides expressing ethical feeling about those facts: sometimes they occur in sentences which simply express ethical feeling about a certain type of action, or situation, without making any statement of fact. But in every case in which one would commonly be said to be making an ethical judgement, the function of the relevant ethical word is purely "emotive." It is used to express feeling about certain objects, but not to make any assertion about them.

It is worth mentioning that ethical terms do not serve only to express feeling. They are calculated also to arouse feeling, and so to stimulate action. Indeed some of them are used in such a way as to give the sentences in which they occur the effect of commands. Thus the sentence "It is your duty to tell the truth" may be regarded both as the expression of a certain sort of ethical feeling about truthfulness and as the expression of the command "Tell the truth." The sentence "You ought to tell the truth" also involves the command "Tell the truth," but here the tone of the command is less emphatic. In the sentence "It is good to tell the truth" the command has become little more than a suggestion. And thus the "meaning" of the word "good," in its ethical usage, is differentiated from that of the word "duty" or the word "ought." In fact we may define the meaning of the various ethical words in terms both of the different feelings they are ordinarily taken to express, and also the different responses which they are calculated to provoke.

We can now see why it is impossible to find a criterion for determining the validity of ethical judgements. It is not because they have an "abso-lute" validity which is mysteriously independent of ordinary sense-experience, but because they have no objective validity whatsoever. If a sentence makes no statement at all, there is obviously no sense in asking whether what it says is true or false. And we have seen that sentences which simply express moral judgements do not say anything. They are pure expressions of feeling and as such do not come under the category of truth and falsehood. They are unverifiable for the same reason as a cry of pain or a word of command is unverifiable—because they do not express genuine propositions.

Thus, although our theory of ethics might fairly be said to be radically subjectivist, it differs in a very important respect from the orthodox subjectivist theory. For the orthodox subjectivist does not deny, as we do, that the sentences of a moralizer express genuine propositions. All he denies is that they express propositions of a unique nonempirical character. His own view is that they express propositions about the speaker's feelings. If this were so, ethical judgements clearly would be capable of being true or false. They would be true if the speaker had the relevant feelings, and false if he had not. And this is a matter which is, in principle, empirically verifiable. Furthermore they could be significantly contradicted. For if I say, "Tolerance is a virtue," and someone answers, "You don't approve of it," he would, on the ordinary subjectivist theory, be contradicting me. On our theory, he would not be contradicting me, because, in saying that tolerance was a virtue, I should not be making any statement about my own feelings or about anything else. I should simply be evincing my feelings, which is not at all the same thing as saying that I have them.

The distinction between the expression of feeling and the assertion of feeling is complicated by the fact that the assertion that one has a certain feeling often accompanies the expression of that feeling, and is then, indeed, a factor in the expression of that feeling. Thus I may simultaneously express boredom and say that I am bored, and in that case my utterance of the words, "I am bored," is one of the circumstances which make it true to say that I am expressing or evincing boredom. But I can express boredom without actually saying that I am bored. I can express it by my tone and gestures, while making a statement about something wholly unconnected with it, or by an ejaculation, or without uttering any words at all. So that even if the assertion that one has a certain feeling always involves the expression of that feeling, the expression of a feeling assuredly does not always involve the assertion that one has it. And this is the important point to grasp in considering the distinction between our theory and the ordinary subjectivist theory. For whereas the subjectivist holds that ethical statements actually assert the existence of certain feelings, we hold that ethical statements are expressions and excitants of feeling which do not necessarily involve any assertions.

We have already remarked that the main objective to the ordinary subjectivist theory is that the validity of ethical judgements is not determined by the nature of their author's feelings. And this is an objection which our theory escapes. For it does not imply that the existence of any feelings is a necessary and sufficient condition of the validity of an ethical judgement. It implies, on the contrary, that ethical judgements have no validity.

There is, however, a celebrated argument against subjectivist theories which our theory does not escape. It has been pointed out by Moore that if ethical statements were simply statements about the speaker's feelings, it would be impossible to argue about questions of value. To take a typical example: if a man said that thrift was a virtue, and another replied that it was a vice, they would not, on this theory, be disputing with one another. One would be saying that he approved of thrift, and the other that *he* didn't; and there is no reason why both these statements should not be true. Now Moore held it to be obvious that we do dispute about questions of value, and accordingly concluded that the particular form of subjectivism which he was discussing was false.

It is plain that the conclusion that it is impossible to dispute about questions of value follows from our theory also. For as we hold that such sentences as "Thrift is a virtue" and "Thrift is a vice" do not express propositions at all, we clearly cannot hold that they express incompatible propositions. We must therefore admit that if Moore's argument really refutes the ordinary subjectivist theory, it also refutes ours. But, in fact, we deny that it does refute even the ordinary subjectivist theory. For we hold that one really never does dispute about questions of value.

This may seem, at first sight, to be a very paradoxical assertion. For we certainly do engage in disputes which are ordinarily regarded as disputes about questions of value. But, in all such cases, we find, if we consider the matter closely, that the dispute is not really about a question of value, but about a question of fact. When someone disagrees with us about the moral value of a certain action or type of action, we do admittedly resort to argument in order to win him over to our way of thinking. But we do not attempt to show by our arguments that he has the "wrong" ethical feeling towards a situation whose nature he has correctly apprehended. What we attempt to show is that he is mistaken about the facts of the case. We argue that he has misconceived the agent's motive; or that he has misjudged the effects of the action, or its probable effects in view of the agent's knowledge; or that he has failed to take into account the special circumstances in which the agent was placed. Or else we employ more general arguments about the effects which actions of a certain type tend to produce, or the qualities which are usually manifested in their performance. We do this in the hope that we have only to get our opponent to agree with us about the nature of the empirical facts for him to adopt the same moral attitude towards them as we do. And as the people with whom we argue have generally received the same moral education as ourselves, and live in the same social order, our expectation is usually justified. But if our opponent happens to have undergone a different process of moral "conditioning" from ourselves, so that, even when he acknowledges all the facts, he still disagrees with us about the moral value of the actions under discussion, then we abandon the attempt to convince him by argument. We say that it is impossible to argue with him because he has a distorted or undeveloped moral sense; which signifies merely that he employs a different set of values from our own. We feel that our own system of values is superior, and therefore speak in such derogatory terms of his. But we cannot bring forward any arguments to show that our system is superior. For our judgement that it is so is itself a judgement of value, and accordingly outside the scope of argument. It is because argument fails us when we come to deal with pure questions of value, as distinct from questions of fact, that we finally resort to mere abuse.

In short, we find that argument is possible on moral questions only if some system of values is presupposed. If our opponent concurs with us in expressing moral disapproval of all actions of a given type t, then we may get him to condemn a particular action A, by bringing forward arguments to show that A is of type t. For the question whether A does or does not belong to that type is a plain question of fact. Given that a man has certain moral principles, we argue that he must, in order to be consistent, react morally to certain things in a certain way. What we do not and cannot argue about is the validity of these moral principles. We merely praise or condemn them in the light of our own feelings.

If anyone doubts the accuracy of this account of moral disputes, let him try to construct even an imaginary argument on a question of value which does not reduce itself to an argument about a question of logic or about an empirical matter of fact. I am confident that he will not succeed in producing a single example. And if that is the case, he must allow that its involving the impossibility of purely ethical arguments is not, as Moore thought, a ground of objection to our theory, but rather a point in favour of it.

Having upheld our theory against the only criticism which appeared to threaten it, we may now use it to define the nature of all ethical enquiries. We find that ethical philosophy consists simply in saying that ethical concepts are pseudo-concepts and therefore unanalysable. The further task of describing the different feelings that the different ethical terms are used to express, and the different reactions that they customarily provoke, is a task for the psychologist. There cannot be such a thing as ethical science, if by ethical science one means the elaboration of a "true" system of morals. For we have seen that, as ethical judgements are mere expressions of feeling, there can be no way of determining the validity of any ethical system, and, indeed, no sense in asking whether any such system is true. All that one may legitimately enquire in this connection is, What are the moral habits of a given person or group of people, and what causes them to have precisely those habits and feelings? And this enquiry falls wholly within the scope of the existing social sciences.

Study Questions

1. How does Ayer interpret the claim "you were wrong to steal that money"?
2. Why is the existence of moral disagreement a problem for emotivists and noncognitivists? How plausible is Ayer's response to Moore on this issue? Could empirical investigation help to settle their dispute?
3. Does Ayer give any arguments against moral skepticism or error theory in this section? If so, what are they? If not, why should we accept noncognitivism over error theory?

Error Theory   8.4

J. L. MACKIE

J. L. MACKIE (1917–1981) was an Australian philosopher and a naturalist in the tradition of David Hume. Mackie's 1977 book *Ethics* is a defense of moral skepticism, the view that there are no objective values although moral discourse presumes that there are. In this excerpt, Mackie presents two famous arguments for this position—the *argument from relativity* and the *argument from queerness*. Together they form an inference to the best explanation argument against the existence of objective values.

MORAL SCEPTICISM

There are no objective values. This is a bald statement of the thesis of this chapter, but before arguing for it I shall try to clarify and restrict it in ways that may meet some objections and prevent some misunderstanding.

The claim that values are not objective, are not part of the fabric of the world, is meant to include not only moral goodness, which might be most naturally equated with moral value, but also other things that could be more loosely called moral values or disvalues—rightness and wrongness, duty, obligation, an action's being rotten and contemptible, and so on. It also includes non-moral values, notably aesthetic ones, beauty and various kinds of artistic merit. I shall not discuss these explicitly, but clearly much the same considerations apply to aesthetic and to moral values, and there would be at least some initial implausibility in a view that gave the one a different status from the other.

The claim to objectivity, however ingrained in our language and thought, is not self-validating. It can and should be questioned. But the denial of objective values will have to be put forward not as the result of an analytic approach, but as an "error theory," a theory that although most people in making moral judgements implicitly claim, among other things, to be pointing to something objectively prescriptive, these claims are all false. It is this that makes the name "moral scepticism" appropriate.

But since this is an error theory, since it goes against assumptions ingrained in our thought and built into some of the ways in which language is used, since it conflicts with what is sometimes called common sense, it needs very solid support. It is not something we can accept lightly or casually and then quietly pass on. If we are to adopt this view, we must argue explicitly for it. Traditionally it has been supported by arguments of two main kinds, which I shall call the argument from relativity and the argument from queerness.

THE ARGUMENT FROM RELATIVITY

The argument from relativity has as its premiss the well-known variation in moral codes from one society to another and from one period to another, and also the differences in moral beliefs between different groups and classes within a complex community. Such variation is in itself merely a truth of descriptive morality, a fact of anthropology which entails neither first order nor second order ethical views. Yet it may indirectly support second order subjectivism: radical differences between first order moral judgements make it difficult to treat those judgements as apprehensions of objective truths. But it is not the mere occurrence of disagreements that tells against the objectivity of values. Disagreement on questions in history or biology or cosmology does not show that there are no objective issues in these fields for investigators to disagree about. But such scientific disagreement results from speculative inferences or explanatory hypotheses based on inadequate evidence, and it is hardly plausible to interpret moral disagreement in the same way. Disagreement about moral codes seems to reflect people's adherence to and participation in different ways of life. The causal connection seems to be mainly that way round: it is that people approve of monogamy because they participate in a monogamous way of life rather than that they participate in a monogamous way of life because they approve of monogamy. Of course, the standards may be an idealization of the way of life from which they arise: the monogamy in which people participate may be less complete, less rigid, than that of which it leads them to approve. This is not to say that moral judgements are purely conventional. Of course there have been and are moral heretics and moral reformers, people who have turned against the established rules and practices of their own communities for moral reasons, and often for moral reasons that we would endorse. But this can usually be understood as the extension, in ways which, though new and unconventional, seemed to them to be required for consistency, of rules to which they already adhered as arising out of an existing way of life. In short, the argument from relativity has some force simply because the actual variations in the moral codes are more readily explained by the hypothesis that they reflect ways of life than by the hypothesis that they express perceptions, most of them seriously inadequate and badly distorted, of objective values.

But there is a well-known counter to this argument from relativity, namely to say that the items for which objective validity is in the first place to be claimed are not specific moral rules or codes but very general basic principles which are recognized at least implicitly to some extent in all society—such principles as provide the foundations of what Sidgwick has called different methods of ethics: the principle of universalizability, perhaps, or the rule that one ought to conform to the specific rules of any way of life in which one takes part, from which one profits, and on which one relies, or some utilitarian principle of doing what tends, or seems likely, to promote the general happiness. It is easy to show that such general principles, married with differing concrete circumstances, different existing social patterns or different preferences, will beget different specific moral rules; and there is some plausibility in the claim that the specific rules thus generated will vary from community to community or from group to group in close agreement with the actual variations in accepted codes.

The argument from relativity can be only partly countered in this way. To take this line the moral objectivist has to say that it is only in these principles that the objective moral character attaches immediately to its descriptively specified ground or subject: other moral judgements are objectively valid or true, but only derivatively and contingently—if things had been otherwise, quite different sorts of actions would have been right. And despite the prominence in recent philosophical ethics of universalization, utilitarian principles, and the like, these are very far from constituting the whole of what is actually affirmed as basic in ordinary moral thought. Much of this is concerned rather with what Hare calls "ideals" or, less kindly, "fanaticism." That is, people judge that some things are good or right, and others are bad or wrong, not

because—or at any rate not only because—they exemplify some general principle for which widespread implicit acceptance could be claimed, but because something about those things arouses certain responses immediately in them, though they would arouse radically and irresolvably different responses in others. "Moral sense" or "intuition" is an initially more plausible description of what supplies many of our basic moral judgements than "reason." With regard to all these starting points of moral thinking the argument from relativity remains in full force.

THE ARGUMENT FROM QUEERNESS

Even more important, however, and certainly more generally applicable, is the argument from queerness. This has two parts, one metaphysical, the other epistemological. If there were objective values, then they would be entities or qualities or relations of a very strange sort, utterly different from anything else in the universe. Correspondingly, if we were aware of them, it would have to be by some special faculty of moral perception or intuition, utterly different from our ordinary ways of knowing everything else. These points were recognized by Moore when he spoke of non-natural qualities, and by the intuitionists in their talk about a "faculty of moral intuition." Intuitionism has long been out of favour, and it is indeed easy to point out its implausibilities. What is not so often stressed, but is more important, is that the central thesis of intuitionism is one to which any objectivist view of values is in the end committed: intuitionism merely makes unpalatably plain what other forms of objectivism wrap up. Of course the suggestion that moral judgements are made or moral problems solved by just sitting down and having an ethical intuition is a travesty of actual moral thinking. But, however complex the real process, it will require (if it is to yield authoritatively prescriptive conclusions) some input of this distinctive sort, either premisses or forms of argument or both. When we ask the awkward question, how we can be aware of this authoritative prescriptivity, of the truth of these distinctively ethical premisses or of the cogency of this distinctively ethical pattern of reasoning, none of our ordinary accounts of sensory perception or introspection or the framing and confirming of explanatory hypotheses or inference or logical construction or conceptual analysis, or any combination of these, will provide a satisfactory answer; "a special sort of intuition" is a lame answer, but it is the one to which the clear-headed objectivist is compelled to resort.

Indeed, the best move for the moral objectivist is not to evade this issue, but to look for companions in guilt. For example, Richard Price argues that it is not moral knowledge alone that such an empiricism as those of Locke and Hume is unable to account for, but also our knowledge and even our ideas of essence, number, identity, diversity, solidity, inertia, substance, the necessary existence and infinite extension of time and space, necessity and possibility in general, power, and causation. If the understanding, which Price defines as the faculty within us that discerns truth, is also a source of new simple ideas of so many other sorts, may it not also be a power of immediately perceiving right and wrong, which yet are real characters of actions?

This is an important counter to the argument from queerness. The only adequate reply to it would be to show how, on empiricist foundations, we can construct an account of the ideas and beliefs and knowledge that we have of all these matters. I cannot even begin to do that here, though I have undertaken some parts of the task elsewhere. I can only state my belief that satisfactory accounts of most of these can be given in empirical terms. If some supposed metaphysical necessities or essences resist such treatment, then they too should be included, along with objective values, among the targets of the argument from queerness.

This queerness does not consist simply in the fact that ethical statements are "unverifiable." Although logical positivism with its verifiability theory of descriptive meaning gave an impetus to non-cognitive accounts of ethics, it is not only logical positivists but also empiricists of a much more liberal sort who should find objective values hard to accommodate. Indeed, I would not only reject the verifiability principle but also deny the conclusion commonly drawn from it, that moral judgements lack descriptive meaning. The assertion that there are objective values or intrinsically prescriptive entities or features of some kind, which ordinary moral judgements presuppose, is, I hold, not meaningless but false.

Plato's Forms give a dramatic picture of what objective values would have to be. The Form of the Good is such that knowledge of it provides the knower with both a direction and an overriding motive; something's being good both tells the person who knows this to pursue it and makes him pursue it. An objective good would be sought by anyone who was acquainted with it, not because of any contingent fact that this person, or every person, is so constituted that he desires this end, but just because the end has to-be-pursuedness somehow built into it. Similarly, if there were objective principles of right and wrong, any wrong (possible) course of action would have not-to-be-doneness somehow built into it. Or we should have something like Clarke's necessary relations of fitness between situations and actions, so that a situation would have a demand for such-and-such an action somehow built into it.

The need for an argument of this sort can be brought out by reflection on Hume's argument that "reason"—in which at this stage he includes all sorts of knowing as well as reasoning—can never be an "influencing motive of the will." Someone might object that Hume has argued unfairly from the lack of influencing power (not contingent upon desires) in ordinary objects of knowledge and ordinary reasoning, and might maintain that values differ from natural objects precisely in their power, when known, automatically to influence the will. To this Hume could, and would need to, reply that this objection involves the postulating of value-entities or value-features of quite a different order from anything else with which we are acquainted, and of a corresponding faculty with which to detect them. That is, he would have to supplement his explicit argument with what I have called the argument from queerness.

Another way of bringing out this queerness is to ask, about anything that is supposed to have some objective moral quality, how this is linked with its natural features. What is the connection between the natural fact that an action is a piece of deliberate cruelty—say, causing pain just for fun—and the moral fact that it is wrong? It cannot be an entailment, a logical or semantic necessity. Yet it is not merely that the two features occur together. The wrongness must somehow be "consequential" or "supervenient"; it is wrong because it is a piece of deliberate cruelty. But just what *in the world* is signified by this "because"? And how do we know the relation that it signifies, if this is something more than such actions being socially condemned, and condemned by us too, perhaps through our having absorbed attitudes from our social environment? It is not even sufficient to postulate a faculty which "sees" the wrongness: something must be postulated which can see at once the natural features that constitute the cruelty, and the wrongness, and the mysterious consequential link between the two. Alternatively, the intuition required might be the perception that wrongness is a higher order property belonging to certain natural properties; but what is this belonging of properties to other properties, and how can we discern it? How much simpler and more comprehensible the situation would be if we could replace the moral quality with some sort of subjective response which could be causally related to the detection of the natural features on which the supposed quality is said to be consequential.

It may be thought that the argument from queerness is given an unfair start if we thus relate it to what are admittedly among the wilder products of philosophical fancy—Platonic Forms, non-natural qualities, self-evident relations of fitness, faculties of intuition, and the like. Is it equally forceful if applied to the terms in which everyday moral judgements are more likely to be expressed—though still, as has been argued in the original work, with a claim to objectivity—"you must do this," "you can't do that," "obligation," "unjust," "rotten," "disgraceful," "mean," or talk about good reasons for or against possible actions? Admittedly not; but that is because the objective prescriptivity, the element a claim for whose authoritativeness is embedded in ordinary moral thought and language, is not yet isolated in these forms of speech, but is presented along with relations to desires and feelings, reasoning about the means to desired ends, interpersonal demands, the injustice which consists in the violation of what are in the context the accepted standards of merit, the psychological constituents of meanness, and so on. There is nothing queer about any of these, and under cover of them the claim for moral authority may pass unnoticed. But if I am right in arguing that it is ordinarily there, and is therefore very likely to be incorporated almost automatically in philosophical accounts of ethics which systematize our ordinary thought even in such apparently innocent terms as these, it needs to be examined, and for this purpose it needs to be isolated and exposed as it is by the less cautious philosophical reconstructions.

PATTERNS OF OBJECTIFICATION

Considerations of these kinds suggest that it is in the end less paradoxical to reject than to retain the common-sense belief in the objectivity of moral values, provided that we can explain how this belief, if it is false, has become established and is so resistant to criticisms. This proviso is not difficult to satisfy.

On a subjectivist view, the supposedly objective values will be based in fact upon attitudes which the person has who takes himself to be recognizing and responding to those values. If we admit what Hume calls the mind's "propensity to spread itself on external objects," we can understand the supposed objectivity of moral qualities as arising from what we can call the projection or objectification of moral attitudes. This would be analogous to what is called the "pathetic fallacy," the tendency to read our feelings into their objects. If a fungus, say, fills us with disgust, we may be inclined to ascribe to the fungus itself a non-natural quality of foulness. But in moral contexts there is more than this propensity at work. Moral attitudes themselves are at least partly social in origin: socially established—and socially necessary—patterns of behaviour put pressure on individuals, and each individual tends to internalize these pressures and to join in requiring these patterns of behaviour of himself and of others. The attitudes that are objectified into moral values have indeed an external source, though not the one assigned to them by the belief in their absolute authority. Moreover, there are motives that would support objectification. We need morality to regulate interpersonal relations, to control some of the ways in which people behave towards one another, often in opposition to contrary inclinations. We therefore want our moral judgements to be authoritative for other agents as well as for ourselves: objective validity would give them the authority required. Aesthetic values are logically in the same position as moral ones; much the same metaphysical and epistemological considerations apply to them. But aesthetic values are less strongly objectified than moral ones; their subjective status, and an "error theory" with regard to such claims to objectivity as are incorporated in aesthetic judgements, will be more readily accepted, just because the motives for their objectification are less compelling.

But it would be misleading to think of the objectification of moral values as primarily the projection of feelings, as in the pathetic fallacy. More important are wants and demands. As Hobbes says, "whatsoever is the object of any man's Appetite or Desire, that is it, which he for his part calleth *Good*"; and certainly both the adjective "good" and the noun "goods" are used in non-moral contexts of things because they are such as to satisfy desires. We get the notion of something's being objectively good, or having intrinsic value, by reversing the direction of dependence here, by making the desire depend upon the goodness, instead of the goodness on the desire. And this is aided by the fact that the desired thing will indeed have features that make it desired, that enable it to arouse a desire or that make it such as to satisfy some desire that is already there. It is fairly easy to confuse the way in which a thing's desirability is indeed objective with its having in our sense objective value. The fact that the word "good" serves as one of our main moral terms is a trace of this pattern of objectification.

Study Questions

1. Why does Mackie think objective moral values would have to be so queer? What features of objective values, according to Mackie, makes them unlike other properties or entities?
2. Mackie is aware that the mere fact of disagreement does not undermine the objectivity of the disputed issues. How does Mackie distinguish moral disagreement from scientific disagreement, an area that does admit of objective treatment?
3. Mackie and Ayer agree that there are no objective moral values. Which of the two antirealist positions do you find more plausible and why?

The Moral Problem 8.5

MICHAEL SMITH

MICHAEL SMITH (1954–) IS McCosh Professor of Philosophy at Princeton University. In this excerpt from his 1994 book *The Moral Problem*, Smith aims to provide an account of moral rightness that can be objective and have motivational force. An act is morally right, according to Smith, just in case it is the act that we would all want to do *if we were fully rational*. After presenting his analysis, Smith defends the existence of moral facts against the objections of Philippa Foot, Gilbert Harman, and J. L. Mackie.

THE SOLUTION TO THE MORAL PROBLEM

We now have a solution to the moral problem at hand. That is, we can now explain why the following three propositions:

1. Moral judgements of the form "It is right that I Φ" express a subject's beliefs about an objective matter of fact, a fact about what it is right for her to do.
2. If someone judges that it is right that she Φs then, *ceteris paribus*, she is motivated to Φ.
3. An agent is motivated to act in a certain way just in case she has an appropriate desire and a means-end belief, where belief and desire are, in Hume's terms, distinct existences.

are both consistent and true. Let me briefly explain why.

If our concept of rightness is the concept of what we would desire ourselves to do if we were fully rational, where this is a desire for something of the appropriate substantive kind, then it does indeed follow that our moral judgements are expressions of our beliefs about an objective matter of fact. For our moral judgements are expressions of our beliefs about what we have normative reason to do, where such reasons are

in turn categorical requirements of rationality. (1) is thus true. Moreover, as we have seen, such beliefs do indeed connect with motivation in the manner of (2). And, again as we have seen, their doing so does not in any way compomise the claim that motivation is to be explained in Humean terms: that is, in terms of belief and desire, where belief and desire are distinct existences. (3) too is thus true. So far so good. But does the analysis allow us not only to solve the moral problem, but to do so in a way that allows us to square morality with a broader naturalism? It seems to me that it does.

The analysis tells us that the rightness of acts in certain circumstances C—using our earlier terminology, let's call this the "evaluated possible world"—is the feature that we would want acts to have in C if we were fully rational, where these wants have the appropriate content—and, again, using our earlier terminology, let's call this world, the world in which we are fully rational, the "evaluating possible world." Now though, for reasons already given, this does not itself constitute a naturalistic definition of rightness—though it is merely a non-reductive, summary style analysis (chapter 5)—it does provide us with the materials to construct a two-stage argument of the following kind.

Michael Smith, *The Moral Problem* (Wiley-Blackwell, 1994).

Conceptual claim:	Rightness in circumstances C is the feature we would want acts to have in C if we were fully rational, where these wants have the appropriate content
Substantive claim:	Fness is the feature we would want acts to have in C if we were fully rational, and Fness is a feature of the appropriate kind
Conclusion:	Rightness in C is Fness

And this argument is, in turn, broadly naturalistic in two respects. First, it is naturalistic in so far as the features that we would want our acts to have under conditions of full rationality, the features that we would want acts to instantiate in the evaluated possible world, are themselves all natural features whenever the evaluated world is itself naturalistic. Our non-reductive, summary style definition of rightness, in conjunction with a substantive claim of the kind described, thus allows us to identify rightness with a natural feature of acts in naturalistic worlds like the actual world: for example, in this case, with Fness.

And second, even though the analysis is not itself naturalistic—even though it defines rightness in terms of full rationality where this may not itself be definable in naturalistic terms— fully rational creatures in the evaluating possible world are themselves naturalistically realized. For a fully rational creature is simply someone with a certain psychology and, as you will recall, a natural feature is simply a feature that figures in one of the natural or social sciences, *including psychology* (chapter 2). Of course, the psychology of a fully rational creature is an idealized psychology, but such an idealization requires nothing non-natural for its realization. Thus, if we wanted to, we could construct non-reductive analyses of the key normative concepts we use to characterize the normative features of such

an idealized creature's psychology—the unity, the coherence, and the like, of its desires—and then use these analyses to construct two-stage arguments, much like that just given, in order to identify these normative features of a fully rational creature's psychology with natural features of its psychology (for an analogy, see note 9 to chapter 2). Coherence and unity, though not naturalistically definable are therefore themselves just natural features of a psychology. The evaluating possible world is therefore naturalistic in the relevant respect as well.

The analysis of rightness provided thus makes the legitimacy of moral talk depend ultimately upon the possibility of identifying moral features, like rightness, with natural features of acts. Absent such identifications, we would have to conclude that moral features are simply not instantiated at all; that moral talk is, much as Mackie thought, based on an error of presupposition. But can we say more? Can we say whether moral talk is or is not legitimate?

ARE THERE ANY MORAL FACTS?

The substantive claim in the two-stage argument described above tells us that moral talk is legitimate just in case a certain condition is met. My handing back a wallet I found in the street in such and such circumstances is right, for example, only if, under conditions of full rationality, we would all want that if we find a wallet in the street in such and such circumstances, then we hand it back. Of course, if this is indeed true, then it is an *a priori* truth. The fact that we would have such a desire under conditions of full rationality will be a consequence of the theory that systematically justifies our desires, and this task of theory construction is itself a relatively *a priori* enterprise; it is a task that requires reflection and conversation, not empirical investigation. However that does not mean that it is an *obvious* truth. For it might not only take a good deal of reflection and conversation for any individual to discover this to be true, it might also take time and effort to convince anyone else. And of course, even after all of that time and effort, it might turn out that we are wrong. What we thought was an *a priori* truth might have been no truth at all. In deciding whether or not moral talk is legitimate, then, it seems to me that we have no alternative but to admit that we are venturing an opinion on something about which we can have no cast-iron guarantee.

However, for all that, it seems to me that we should none the less have some confidence in the legitimacy of moral talk. For, in short, the empirical fact that moral argument tends to elicit the agreement of our fellows gives us reason to believe that there will be a convergence in our desires under conditions of full rationality. For the best explanation of that tendency is our convergence upon a set of extremely unobvious *a priori* moral truths. And the truth of these unobvious *a priori* moral truths requires, in turn, a convergence in the desires that fully rational creatures would have.

Now this argument is likely to meet with some resistance. After all, isn't there currently much entrenched moral disagreement? And don't such disagreements constitute profound obstacles to a convergence in our desires in fact emerging? This is true, but it does not count against the force of the argument. Indeed, once we remember the following three points, such disagreements can be seen to add to the force of the argument.

First, we must remember that alongside such entrenched disagreements as we in fact find we also find massive areas of entrenched agreement. As I see it, this is the real significance of the fact that we have and use the so-called "thick" moral concepts, concepts that at once both describe some naturalistic state of affairs and positively or negatively evaluate it: concepts like courage, brutality, honesty, duplicity, loyalty, meanness, kindness, treachery, and the like (Williams, 1985: 129). For what the prevalence of such concepts suggests is that there is in fact considerable agreement about what is right and

wrong: acts of brutality, duplicity, meanness and treachery are wrong, at least other things being equal, whereas acts of courage, honesty, loyalty, and kindness are right, again, other things being equal. What the prevalence of such concepts suggests is therefore that moral agreement is in fact *so* extensive that our language has developed in such a way as to build an evaluative component into certain naturalistically descriptive concepts.

Second, when we look at current areas of entrenched disagreement, we must remember that in the past similarly entrenched disagreements were removed *inter alia* via a process of moral argument. I am thinking in particular of the historical, and in some places still current, debates over slavery, worker's rights, women's rights, democracy and the like. We must not forget that there has been considerable moral progress, and that what moral progress consists in is the removal of entrenched disagreements of just the kind that we currently face.

And third and finally, we must remember that where entrenched disagreements currently seem utterly intractable we can often explain why this is the case in ways that make them seem less threatening to the idea of a convergence in the opinions of fully rational creatures. For example, one or the other parties to the disagreement all too often forms their moral beliefs in response to the directives of a religious authority rather than as the result of the exercise of their own free thought in concert with their fellows. But beliefs formed exclusively in this way have dubious rational credentials. They require that we privilege one group's opinions about what is to be done—those of the religious authority—over another's—those of the followers—for no good reason. The fact that disagreement persists for this sort of reason thus casts no doubt on the possibility of an agreement if we were to engage in free and rational debate.

In light of these points it seems to me that, notwithstanding such disagreements as there are and will perhaps remain, we should therefore in fact be quite optimistic about the possibility of an agreement about what is right and wrong being reached under more idealized conditions of reflection and discussion. We might eventually come to be pessimistic, of course. Our epistemic situation might deteriorate, widespread disagreements might emerge, disagreements that seem both unresolvable and inexplicable. And if that were to happen, then we might well quite justifiably come to think that Mackie was right after all, that there are no moral facts, though there would still be room for doubt. The point is simply that this *is not* our current epistemic situation. [. . .]

Foot's and Harman's Objection

Foot's main objection to rationalism is that we can give no content to the idea that the immoral person is irrational.

> Attempts have sometimes been made to show that some kind of irrationality is involved in ignoring the "should" of morality: in saying "Immoral—so what?" as one says "Not *comme il faut*—so what?" But as far as I can see these have rested on some illegitimate assumption, as, for instance, of thinking that the amoral man who agrees that some piece of conduct is immoral but takes no notice of that, is inconsistently disregarding a rule of conduct that he has accepted; or again of thinking it inconsistent to desire that others will not do to one what one proposes to do to them. The fact is that the man who rejects morality because he sees no reason to obey its rules can be convicted of villainy but not inconsistency. (1972: 161)

Foot's objection here is, in effect, that there is no way of rationally criticizing the desires of those who reject morality, so the rationalist who claims that there is must be making some "illicit assumption."

Gilbert Harman objects to rationalism—or, as he calls it, "absolutism"—in a similar vein.

> [T]here are people, such as the successful criminal, who do not observe the alleged requirement not to harm or injure others and this is not due to inattention, failure to consider or appreciate certain arguments, ignorance of relevant evidence, errors in reasoning, irrationality, unreasonableness, or weakness of will . . .
>
> The absolutist might argue that the criminal must be irrational or at least unreasonable. Seeing that a proposed course of action will probably cause serious injury to some outsider, the criminal does not treat this as a reason not to undertake that course of action. This must be irrational or unreasonable, because such a consideration simply is such a reason and indeed is an obvious reason, a basic reason, not one that has to be derived in some complex way through arcane reasoning. But then it must be irrational or at least unreasonable for the criminal not to care sufficiently about others, since the criminal's lack of concern for others is what is responsible for the criminal's not taking the likelihood of harm to an outsider to be a reason against a proposed course of action . . .
>
> The relativist's reply to such an argument is that, on any plausible characterization of reasonableness and unreasonableness (or rationality and irrationality) as notions that can be part of the scientific conception of the world, the absolutist's claim is just false. Someone can be completely rational without feeling concern and respect for outsiders. (1985: 39–40)

In effect, then, both Harman and Foot challenge the rationalist to explain an uncontroversial sense in which the successful criminal is being irrational. Contrary to both, however, it seems to me easy to meet this challenge.

The successful criminal must begin his deliberations from some evaluative premise or other. Let's imagine that he begins from the premise that he has a normative reason to gain wealth no matter what the cost to others. Now, given this premise we can certainly imagine that he is not inconsistent, that he does not disregard a rule of conduct that he has himself already accepted, that he is not inattentive, that he does not suffer from weakness of will and so on and so forth . . . But all that that shows is that the flaw in his reasoning lies in the premise from which he begins: that he has a normative reason to gain wealth no matter what the cost to others. For, as we have seen, this is equivalent to the claim that fully rational creatures would want that, if they find themselves in the circumstances of the successful criminal, then they gain wealth no matter what the cost to others. And the successful criminal's opinion notwithstanding, it seems quite evident that we have no reason to believe that this is true. Fully rational creatures would want no such thing.

Note what I have not said. I have not said that the fact that we all disagree with the successful criminal entails that he is wrong. Perhaps we are all mistaken about what fully rational creatures would want. But the mere fact that it is logically possible that we are wrong gives us no more reason to endorse the opinions of the successful criminal and doubt our own convictions than the mere fact that it is logically possible that we are wrong when we think that the sun will rise tomorrow gives us reason to endorse the opinions of the prophets of doom.

Harman tells us that the fact that the successful criminal does not observe the moral requirement not to harm others cannot be traced to a "failure to consider or appreciate certain arguments." But it seems to me that that should now seem quite wrong. After all, the successful criminal thinks that he has a normative reason to gain wealth no matter what the cost to others, and he sticks with this opinion despite the fact that virtually everyone disagrees with him. Moreover, he does so without good reason. For he can give no account of why his own opinion about what fully rational creatures would want should be privileged over the opinion of others; he can give no account of why his opinion should be right, others' opinions should be wrong. He can give no such account because he rejects the very idea that the folk possess between them a stock of wisdom about such matters against which each person's opinions should be tested. And yet, ultimately, this is the only court of appeal there is for claims about what we have

normative reason to do. The successful criminal thus seems to me to suffer from the all too common vice of *intellectual arrogance*. He therefore does indeed suffer from a "failure to consider or appreciate certain arguments," for he doesn't feel the force of arguments that come from *others* at all. [. . .]

Mackie's Objections

John Mackie tells us that

> . . . Kant himself thought that moral judgements are categorical imperatives . . . So far as ethics is concerned, my thesis that there are no objective values is specifically the denial that any such categorically imperative element is objectively valid. (1977: 29)

Mackie's two famous objections to the claim that there exist objective values are thus directed quite specifically against the rationalist.

Consider his first argument.

> If there were objective values, then they would be entities or qualities or relations of a very strange sort, utterly different from anything else in the universe. Correspondingly, if we were aware of them, it would have to be by some special faculty of moral perception or intuition, utterly different from ordinary ways of knowing everything else. (1977: 38)

But can Mackie really lay a charge of strangeness against rightness, at least as that feature of acts has been analysed here? It seems not.

To say that performing an act of a certain sort in certain circumstances is right is, I have argued, to say *inter alia* that there is a normative reason to perform it. And this, in turn, is simply to say that fully rational creatures would desire that such an act be performed in such circumstances, where such a desire is of the appropriate substantive kind. On this account, moral features like rightness thus simply are not "entities or qualities or relations of a very strange sort"; no "special faculty or moral perception of intuition" is required in order to gain knowledge of them. All that is required is the ability to think about what a more rational person would want. And this, in turn, just requires the ability to engage in an attempt to find a systematic and unified justification of the various desires that we have; to engage in a process of reflective equilibrium. The charge of strangeness is thus entirely misplaced.

Consider now Mackie's second argument. The idea here is that

> ...radical differences between first order moral judgements make it difficult to treat those judgements as apprehensions of objective truths. But it is not the mere occurrence of disagreements that tells against the objectivity of values. Disagreement on questions in history or biology or cosmology does not show that there are no objective issues in these fields for investigators to disagree about. But such scientific disagreement results from speculative inferences or explanatory hypotheses based on inadequate evidence, and it is hardly plausible to interpret moral disagreement in the same way. Disagreement about moral codes seems to reflect people's adherence to and participation in different ways of life. (1977: 36)

Mackie thus agrees that the availability of a rational procedure for resolving moral disagreement would render the "mere occurrence" of moral disagreements harmless, from the rationalist's point of view. But he suggests that the idea that there exists such a procedure is "hardly plausible." His actual arguments for this claim are, however, hardly convincing.

Mackie tells us that moral disagreement cannot plausibly be interpreted as resulting from "speculative inferences or explanatory hypotheses based on inadequate evidence." But, in many ways, this is just false. For, as we have seen, when we construct moral theories we are trying to find out what we have normative reason to do, and when we try to find out what we have normative reason to do we are trying to find out what fully rational creatures would want, and when we try to find out what fully rational creatures would want we embark on a procedure of justification of our various desires that is very similar indeed to the enterprise of theory construction in science in response to observational evidence. Both are simply applications of the idea of reflective equilibrium.

Of course, perhaps Mackie is saying that this attempt to provide our desires with a systematic justification is doomed to failure; that no such justification will be forthcoming; that there is no *single* thing that fully rational creatures would all want us to do in the various circumstances in which we find ourselves. Perhaps that is the real point of his argument from relativity. But if so then the reply is again simple enough. For though it is certainly logically possible that no systematic justification of our desires is forthcoming, in light of the remarks we made in the previous section about the power of moral argument to elicit agreement, it seems more reasonable to think that such a justification is forthcoming.

This is not to deny, of course, that the real test of Mackie's argument from relativity lies in the ultimate outcome of debate in normative ethics. The real question is whether we will, by engaging in such debate, come up with answers to moral questions that secure the free agreement of those who participate. If we do not, then our confidence that such agreement is to be had may be undermined, and quite rightly so. But that gives us no reason for scepticism *now*. We must give the arguments and see what their outcome is.

References

Foot, Philippa. 1972. "Morality as a System of Hypothetical Imperatives," reprinted in Foot (1978), pp. 157–173.

———. 1978. *Virtues and Vices*. Berkeley, CA: University of California Press.

Harman, Gilbert. 1977. *The Nature of Morality*. Oxford: Oxford University Press.

Mackie, John. 1977. *Ethics: Inventing Right and Wrong*. London: Penguin.

Williams, Bernard. 1985. *Ethics and the Limits of Philosophy*. Cambridge, MA: Harvard University Press.

1. How effectively does Smith respond to the challenge of moral disagreement? What empirical assumptions does he make in his response?
2. Why is Harman's "successful criminal" such a problem for Smith? How plausible is

Smith's claim that the criminal's irrationality stems from his intellectual arrogance?

3. Smith claims that his analysis of moral facts is "broadly naturalistic." Do you agree? If so, has Smith successfully responded to Mackie's argument from queerness? Why or why not?

The Challenge of Cultural Relativism   8.6

JAMES RACHELS

JAMES RACHELS (1941–2003) was a moral philosopher at the University of Alabama, best known for his work on euthanasia, animal welfare, and meta-ethics. He also authored the best-selling ethics textbook *The Elements of Moral Philosophy*. In this excerpt from the book, Rachels attempts to respond to the challenge of moral disagreement across cultures. Rachels argues that differences about moral values are more superficial than they seem and are often due to disagreement over empirical rather than ethical issues. Furthermore, according to Rachels, there are core ethical principles that all cultures seem to share.

> Morality differs in every society, and is a convenient term for socially approved habits.
>
> —RUTH BENEDICT, *Patterns of Culture* (1934)

2.1. HOW DIFFERENT CULTURES HAVE DIFFERENT MORAL CODES

Darius, a king of ancient Persia, was intrigued by the variety of cultures he encountered in his travels. He had found, for example, that the Callatians (a tribe of Indians) customarily ate the bodies of their dead fathers. The Greeks, of course, did not do that—the Greeks practiced cremation and regarded the funeral pyre as the natural and

fitting way to dispose of the dead. Darius thought that a sophisticated understanding of the world must include an appreciation of such differences between cultures. One day, to teach this lesson, he summoned some Greeks who happened to be present at his court and asked them what they would take to eat the bodies of their dead fathers. They were shocked, as Darius knew they would be, and replied that no amount of money could persuade them to do such a thing. Then Darius called in some Callatians, and while the Greeks listened asked them what they would take to burn their dead fathers' bodies. The Callatians were horrified and told Darius not even to mention such a dreadful thing.

J. Rachels, *The Elements of Moral Philosophy*, third edition (McGraw Hill College Publications, 1999).

This story [...] illustrates a recurring theme in the literature of social science: Different cultures have different moral codes. What is thought right within one group may be utterly abhorrent to the members of another group, and vice versa. [...]

It is easy to give additional examples of the same kind. Consider the Eskimos. [...]

Eskimo customs turned out to be very different from our own. The men often had more than one wife, and they would share their wives with guests, lending them for the night as a sign of hospitality. Moreover, within a community, a dominant male might demand and get regular sexual access to other men's wives. The women, however, were free to break these arrangements simply by leaving their husbands and taking up with new partners—free, that is, so long as their former husbands chose not to make trouble. [...]

The Eskimos also seemed to have less regard for human life. Infanticide, for example, was common. Knud Rasmussen, one of the most famous early explorers, reported that he met one woman who had borne 20 children but had killed 10 of them at birth. Female babies, he found, were especially liable to be destroyed, and this was permitted simply at the parents' discretion, with no social stigma attached to it. Old people also, when they became too feeble to contribute to the family, were left out in the snow to die [...]

To the general public, these were disturbing revelations. Our own way of living seems so natural and right that for many of us it is hard to conceive of others living so differently. And when we do hear of such things, we tend immediately to categorize those other peoples as "backward" or "primitive." But to anthropologists and sociologists, there was nothing particularly surprising about the Eskimos. Since the time of Herodotus, enlightened observers have been accustomed to the idea that conceptions of right and wrong differ from culture to culture. If we assume that our ideas of right and

wrong will be shared by all peoples at all times, we are merely naive.

2.2. CULTURAL RELATIVISM

To many thinkers, this observation—"Different cultures have different moral codes"—has seemed to be the key to understanding morality. The idea of universal truth in ethics, they say, is a myth. The customs of different societies are all that exist. These customs cannot be said to be "correct" or "incorrect," for that implies we have an independent standard of right and wrong by which they may be judged. But there is no such independent standard; every standard is culture-bound. The great pioneering sociologist William Graham Sumner, writing in 1906, put the point like this:

> The "right" way is the way which the ancestors used and which has been handed down. The tradition is its own warrant. It is not held subject to verification by experience. The notion of right is in the folkways. It is not outside of them, of independent origin, and brought to test them. In the folkways, whatever is, is right. This is because they are traditional, and therefore contain in themselves the authority of the ancestral ghosts. When we come to the folkways we are at the end of our analysis.

This line of thought has probably persuaded more people to be skeptical about ethics than any other single thing. Cultural Relativism, as it has been called, challenges our ordinary belief in the objectivity and universality of moral truth. It says, in effect, that there is no such thing as universal truth in ethics; there are only the various cultural codes, and nothing more. Moreover, our own code has no special status; it is merely one among many.

As we shall see, this basic idea is really a compound of several different thoughts. It is important to separate the various elements of the theory because, on analysis, some parts turn out to be correct, while others seem to be mistaken. As a beginning, we may distinguish the following claims, all of which have been made by cultural relativists:

1. Different societies have different moral codes.
2. There is no objective standard that can be used to judge one societal code better than another.
3. The moral code of our own society has no special status; it is merely one among many.
4. There is no "universal truth" in ethics; that is, there are no moral truths that hold for all peoples at all times.
5. The moral code of a society determines what is right within that society; that is, if the moral code of a society says that a certain action is right, then that action *is* right, at least within that society.
6. It is mere arrogance for us to try to judge the conduct of other peoples. We should adopt an attitude of tolerance toward the practices of other cultures.

Although it may seem that these six propositions go naturally together, they are independent of one another, in the sense that some of them might be false even if others are true. In what follows, we will try to identify what is correct in Cultural Relativism, but we will also be concerned to expose what is mistaken about it.

2.3. THE CULTURAL DIFFERENCES ARGUMENT

Cultural Relativism is a theory about the nature of morality. At first blush it seems quite plausible. However, like all such theories, it may be evaluated by subjecting it to rational analysis; and when we analyze Cultural Relativism we find that it is not so plausible as it first appears to be.

The first thing we need to notice is that at the heart of Cultural Relativism there is a certain *form of argument*. The strategy used by cultural relativists is to argue from facts about the differences between cultural outlooks to a conclusion about the status of morality. Thus we are invited to accept this reasoning:

(1) The Greeks believed it was wrong to eat the dead, whereas the Callatians believed it was right to eat the dead.

(2) Therefore, eating the dead is neither objectively right nor objectively wrong. It is merely a matter of opinion, which varies from culture to culture.

Or, alternatively:

(1) The Eskimos see nothing wrong with infanticide, whereas Americans believe infanticide is immoral.

(2) Therefore, infanticide is neither objectively right nor objectively wrong. It is merely a matter of opinion, which varies from culture to culture.

Clearly, these arguments are variations of one fundamental idea. They are both special cases of a more general argument, which says:

(1) Different cultures have different moral codes.

(2) Therefore, there is no objective "truth" in morality. Right and wrong are only matters of opinion, and opinions vary from culture to culture.

We may call this the Cultural Differences Argument. To many people, it is persuasive. But from a logical point of view, is it sound?

It is not sound. The trouble is that the conclusion does not follow from the premise—that is, even if the premise is true, the conclusion still might be false. The premise concerns what people *believe*: In some societies, people believe one thing; in other societies, people believe differently. The conclusion, however, concerns *what really is the case*. The trouble is that this sort of conclusion does not follow logically from this sort of premise.

Consider again the example of the Greeks and Callatians. The Greeks believed it was wrong to eat the dead; the Callatians believed it was right. Does it follow, *from the mere fact that they disagreed*, that there is no objective truth in the matter? No, it does not follow; for it could be that the practice was objectively right (or wrong) and that one or the other of them was simply mistaken.

To make the point clearer, consider a different matter. In some societies, people believe the earth is flat. In other societies, such as our own, people believe the earth is (roughly) spherical. Does it follow, *from the mere fact that people disagree*, that there is no "objective truth" in geography? Of course not; we would never draw such a conclusion because we realize that, in their beliefs about the world, the members of some societies might simply be wrong. There is no reason to think that if the world is round everyone must know it. Similarly, there is no reason to think that if there is moral truth everyone must know it. The fundamental mistake in the Cultural Differences Argument is that it attempts to derive a substantive conclusion about a subject from the mere fact that people disagree about it.[...]

2.4. THE CONSEQUENCES OF TAKING CULTURAL RELATIVISM SERIOUSLY

Even if the Cultural Differences Argument is invalid, Cultural Relativism might still be true. What would it be like if it were true?

In the passage quoted above, William Graham Sumner summarizes the essence of Cultural Relativism. He says that there is no measure of right and wrong other than the standards of one's society: "The notion of right is in the folkways. It is not outside of them, of independent origin, and brought to test them. In the folkways, whatever is, is right."

Suppose we took this seriously. What would be some of the consequences?

1. *We could no longer say that the customs of other societies are morally inferior to our own.* This, of course, is one of the main points stressed by Cultural Relativism. We would have to stop condemning other societies merely because they are "different." So long as we concentrate on certain examples, such as the funerary practices of the Greeks and Callatians, this may seem to be a sophisticated, enlightened attitude.

However, we would also be stopped from criticizing other, less benign practices. Suppose a society waged war on its neighbors for the purpose of taking slaves. Or suppose a society was violently anti-Semitic and its leaders set out to destroy the Jews. Cultural Relativism would preclude us from saying that either of these practices was wrong. We would not even be able to say that a society tolerant of Jews is *better* than the anti-Semitic society, for that would imply some sort of transcultural standard of comparison. The failure to condemn *these* practices does not seem enlightened; on the contrary, slavery and anti-Semitism seem wrong wherever they occur. Nevertheless, if we took Cultural Relativism seriously, we would have to regard these social practices as also immune from criticism.

2. *We could decide whether actions are right or wrong just by consulting the standards of our society.* Cultural Relativism suggests a simple test for determining what is right and what is wrong: All one need do is ask whether the action is in accordance with the code of one's society. Suppose in 1975 a resident of South Africa was wondering whether his country's policy of *apartheid*—a rigidly racist system—was morally correct. All he has to do is ask whether this policy conformed to his society's moral code. If it did, there would have been nothing to worry about, at least from a moral point of view.

This implication of Cultural Relativism is disturbing because few of us think that our society's code is perfect; we can think of ways it might be improved. Yet Cultural Relativism would not only forbid us from criticizing the codes of other societies; it would stop us from criticizing our own. After all, if right and wrong are relative to culture, this must be true for our own culture just as much as for other cultures.

3. *The idea of moral progress is called into doubt.* [...]

Our idea of social *reform* will also have to be reconsidered. Reformers such as Martin Luther King, Jr., have sought to change their societies for the better. Within the constraints imposed by Cultural Relativism, there is one way this might be done. If a society is not living up to its own ideals, the reformer may be regarded as acting for the best: The ideals of the society are the standard by which we judge his or her proposals as worthwhile. But the "reformer" may not challenge the ideals themselves, for those ideals are by definition correct. According to Cultural Relativism, then, the idea of social reform makes sense only in this limited way.

These three consequences of Cultural Relativism have led many thinkers to reject it as implausible on its face. It does make sense, they say, to condemn some practices, such as slavery and anti-Semitism, wherever they occur. It makes sense to think that our own society has made some moral progress, while admitting that it is still imperfect and in need of reform. Because Cultural Relativism says that these judgments make no sense, the argument goes, it cannot be right.

2.5. WHY THERE IS LESS DISAGREEMENT THAN IT SEEMS

The original impetus for Cultural Relativism comes from the observation that cultures differ dramatically in their views of right and wrong. But just how much do they differ? It is true that there are differences. However, it is easy to overestimate the extent of those differences. Often, when we examine what seems to be a dramatic difference, we find that the cultures do not differ nearly as much as it appears. [...]

[...] Many factors work together to produce the customs of a society. The society's values are only one of them. Other matters, such as the religious and factual beliefs held by its members, and the physical circumstances in which they must live, are also important. We cannot conclude, then, merely because customs differ, that there is a disagreement about *values*. The difference in customs may be attributable to some other aspect of social life. Thus there may be less disagreement about values than there appears to be.

Consider again the Eskimos, who often kill perfectly normal infants, especially girls. We do not approve of such things; a parent who killed a baby in our society would be locked up. Thus there appears to be a great difference in the values of our two cultures. But suppose we ask why the Eskimos do this. The explanation is not that they have less affection for their children or less respect for human life. An Eskimo family will always protect its babies if conditions permit. But they live in a harsh environment, where food is in short supply. A fundamental postulate of Eskimo thought is: "Life is hard, and the margin of safety small." A family may want to nourish its babies but be unable to do so.

As in many "primitive" societies, Eskimo mothers will nurse their infants over a much longer period of time than mothers in our culture. The child will take nourishment from its mother's breast for four years, perhaps even longer. So even in the best of times there are limits to the number of infants that one mother can sustain. Moreover, the Eskimos are a nomadic people—unable to farm, they must move about in search of food. Infants must be carried, and a mother can carry only one baby in her parka as she travels and goes about her outdoor work. Other family members help whenever they can.

Infant girls are more readily disposed of because, first, in this society the males are the primary food providers—they are the hunters, according to the traditional division of labor—and it is obviously important to maintain a sufficient number of food providers. But there is an important second reason as well. Because the hunters suffer a high casualty rate, the adult men who die prematurely far outnumber the women who die early. Thus if male and female infants survived in equal numbers, the female adult population would greatly outnumber the male adult population. Examining the available statistics, one writer concluded that "were it not for female infanticide...there would be approximately one-and-a-half times as many females in the average Eskimo local group as there are food-producing males."

So among the Eskimos, infanticide does not signal a fundamentally different attitude toward children. Instead, it is a recognition that drastic measures are sometimes needed to ensure the family's survival. Even then, however, killing the baby is not the first option considered. Adoption is common; childless couples are especially happy to take a more fertile couple's "surplus." Killing is only the last resort. I emphasize this in order to show that the raw data of the anthropologists can be misleading; it can make the differences in values between cultures appear greater than they are. The Eskimos' values are not all that different from our values. It is only that life forces upon them choices that we do not have to make.

2.6. HOW ALL CULTURES HAVE SOME VALUES IN COMMON

It should not be surprising that, despite appearances, the Eskimos are protective of their children. How could it be otherwise? How could a group survive that did *not* value its young? It is easy to see that, in fact, all cultural groups must protect their infants:

(1)   Human infants are helpless and cannot survive if they are not given extensive care for a period of years.

(2)   Therefore, if a group did not care for its young, the young would not survive, and the older members of the group

would not be replaced. After a while the group would die out.

(3)   Therefore, any cultural group that continues to exist must care for its young. Infants that are not cared for must be the exception rather than the rule.

Similar reasoning shows that other values must be more or less universal. Imagine what it would be like for a society to place no value at all on truth telling. When one person spoke to another, there would be no presumption at all that he was telling the truth for he could just as easily be speaking falsely. Within that society, there would be no reason to pay attention to what anyone says. (I ask you what time it is, and you say "Four o'clock." But there is no presumption that you are speaking truly; you could just as easily have said the first thing that came into your head. So I have no reason to pay attention to your answer; in fact, there was no point in my asking you in the first place.) Communication would then be extremely difficult, if not impossible. And because complex societies cannot exist without communication among their members, society would become impossible. It follows that in any complex society there must be a presumption in favor of truthfulness. There may of course be exceptions to this rule: There may be situations in which it is thought to be permissible to lie. Nevertheless, these will be exceptions to a rule that *is* in force in the society.

Here is one further example of the same type. Could a society exist in which there was no prohibition on murder? What would this be like? Suppose people were free to kill other people at will, and no one thought there was anything wrong with it. In such a "society," no one could feel secure. Everyone would have to be constantly on guard. People who wanted to survive would have to avoid other people as much as possible. This would inevitably result in individuals trying to become as self-sufficient as possible—after all, associating with others would be dangerous. Society on any large scale would collapse. Of course, people might band together in smaller groups with others that they *could* trust not to harm them. But notice what this means: They would be forming smaller societies that did acknowledge a rule against murder. The prohibition of murder, then, is a necessary feature of all societies.

There is a general theoretical point here, namely, that *there are some moral rules that all societies will have in common, because those rules are necessary for society to exist.* The rules against lying and murder are two examples. And in fact, we do find these rules in force in all viable cultures. Cultures may differ in what they regard as legitimate exceptions to the rules, but this disagreement exists against a background of agreement on the larger issues. Therefore, it is a mistake to overestimate the amount of difference between cultures. Not every moral rule can vary from society to society.

2.7. JUDGING A CULTURAL PRACTICE TO BE UNDESIRABLE

In 1996, a 17-year-old girl named Fauziya Kassindja arrived at Newark International Airport and asked for asylum. She had fled her native country of Togo, a small west African nation, to escape what people there call "excision."

Excision is a permanently disfiguring procedure that is sometimes called "female circumcision," although it bears little resemblance to the Jewish ritual. More commonly, at least in Western newspapers, it is referred to as "genital mutilation." According to the World Health Organization, the practice is widespread in 26 African nations, and two million girls each year are "excised." In some instances, excision is part of an elaborate tribal ritual, performed in small traditional villages, and girls look forward to it because it signals their acceptance into the adult world. In other instances, the practice is carried out by families living in cities on young women who desperately resist. [...]

Fauziya was imprisoned for two years while the authorities decided what to do with her. She was finally granted asylum, but not before she became the center of a controversy about how foreigners should regard the cultural practices of other peoples. A series of articles in the *New York Times* encouraged the idea that excision is a barbaric practice that should be condemned. Other observers were reluctant to be so judgmental—live and let live, they said; after all, our practices probably seem just as strange to them.

Suppose we are inclined to say that excision is bad. Would we merely be applying the standards of our own culture? If Cultural Relativism is correct, that is all we can do, for there is no culture-neutral moral standard to which we may appeal. Is that true?

Is There a Culture-Neutral Standard of Right and Wrong?

There is, of course, a lot that can be said against the practice of excision. Excision is painful and it results in the permanent loss of sexual pleasure. Its short-term effects include hemorrhage, tetanus, and septicemia. Sometimes the woman dies. Long-term effects include chronic infection, scars that hinder walking, and continuing pain.

Why, then, has it become a widespread social practice? It is not easy to say. Excision has no obvious social benefits. Unlike Eskimo infanticide, it is not necessary for the group's survival. Nor is it a matter of religion. Excision is practiced by groups with various religions, including Islam and Christianity, neither of which commend it.

Nevertheless, a number of reasons are given in its defense. Women who are incapable of sexual pleasure are said to be less likely to be promiscuous; thus there will be fewer unwanted pregnancies in unmarried women. Moreover, wives for whom sex is only a duty are less likely to be unfaithful to their husbands; and because they will not be thinking about sex, they will be more attentive to the needs of their husbands and children. Husbands, for their part, are said to enjoy sex more with wives who have been excised.

(The women's own lack of enjoyment is said to be unimportant.) Men will not want unexcised women, as they are unclean and immature. And above all, it has been done since antiquity, and we may not change the ancient ways.

It would be easy, and perhaps a bit arrogant, to ridicule these arguments. But we may notice an important feature of this whole line of reasoning: it attempts to justify excision by showing that excision is beneficial—men, women, and their families are all said to be better off when women are excised. Thus we might approach this reasoning, and excision itself, by asking which is true: Is excision, on the whole, helpful or harmful?

Here, then, is the standard that might most reasonably be used in thinking about excision: We may ask *whether the practice promotes or hinders the welfare of the people whose lives are affected by it.* And, as a corollary, we may ask if there is an alternative set of social arrangements that would do a better job of promoting their welfare. If so, we may conclude that the existing practice is deficient.

But this looks like just the sort of independent moral standard that Cultural Relativism says cannot exist. It is a single standard that may be brought to bear in judging the practices of any culture, at any time, including our own. Of course, people will not usually see this principle as being "brought in from the outside" to judge them, because, like the rules against lying and homicide, the welfare of its members is a value internal to all viable cultures.

Why Thoughtful People May Nevertheless Be Reluctant to Criticize Other Cultures.
Although they are personally horrified by excision, many thoughtful people are reluctant to say it is wrong, for at least three reasons.

First, there is an understandable nervousness about "interfering in the social customs of other peoples." Europeans and their cultural descendents in America have a shabby history of destroying native cultures in the name of Christianity and Enlightenment, not to mention

self-interest. Recoiling from this record, some people refuse to make any negative judgments about other cultures, especially cultures that resemble those that have been wronged in the past. We should notice, however, that there is a difference between (a) judging a cultural practice to be morally deficient and (b) thinking that we should announce the fact, conduct a campaign, apply diplomatic pressure, or send in the army to do something about it. The first is just a matter of trying to see the world clearly, from a moral point of view. The second is another matter altogether. Sometimes it may be right to "do something about it," but often it will not be.

People also feel, rightly enough, that they should be tolerant of other cultures. Tolerance is, no doubt, a virtue—a tolerant person is willing to live in peaceful cooperation with those who see things differently. But there is nothing in the nature of tolerance that requires you to say that all beliefs, all religions, and all social practices are equally admirable. On the contrary, if you did not think that some were better than others, there would be nothing for you to tolerate.

Finally, people may be reluctant to judge because they do not want to express contempt for the society being criticized. But again, this is misguided: To condemn a particular practice is not to say that the culture is on the whole contemptible or that it is generally inferior to any other culture, including one's own. It could have many admirable features. In fact, we should expect this to be true of most human societies—they are mixes of good and bad practices. Excision happens to be one of the bad ones.

2.8. WHAT CAN BE LEARNED FROM CULTURAL RELATIVISM

At the outset, I said that we were going to identify both what is right and what is wrong in Cultural Relativism. Thus far I have mentioned only its mistakes: I have said that it rests on an invalid argument, that it has consequences that make it implausible on its face, and that the extent of moral disagreement is far less than it implies. This all adds up to a pretty thorough repudiation of the theory. Nevertheless, it is still a very appealing idea, and the reader may have the feeling that all this is a little unfair. The theory must have something going for it, or else why has it been so influential? In fact, I think there is something right about Cultural Relativism, and now I want to say what that is. There are two lessons we should learn from the theory, even if we ultimately reject it.

1. Cultural Relativism warns us, quite rightly, about the danger of assuming that all our preferences are based on some absolute rational standard. They are not. Many (but not all) of our practices are merely peculiar to our society, and it is easy to lose sight of that fact. In reminding us of it, the theory does a service. [...]

2. The second lesson has to do with keeping an open mind. In the course of growing up, each of us has acquired some strong feelings: We have learned to think of some types of conduct as acceptable, and others we have learned to reject. Occasionally, we may find those feelings challenged. We may encounter someone who claims that our feelings are mistaken. For example, we may have been taught that homosexuality is immoral, and we may feel quite uncomfortable around gay people and see them as alien and "different." Now someone suggests that this may be a mere prejudice; that there is nothing evil about homosexuality; that gay people are just people, like anyone else, who happen, through no choice of their own, to be attracted to others of the same sex. But because we feel so strongly about the matter, we may find it hard to take this seriously. Even after we listen to the arguments, we may still have the unshakable feeling that homosexuals must, somehow, be an unsavory lot.

Cultural Relativism, by stressing that our moral views can reflect the prejudices of our society, provides an antidote for this kind of dogmatism.

When he tells the story of the Greeks and Callatians, Herodotus adds:

> For if anyone, no matter who, were given the opportunity of choosing from amongst all the nations of the world the set of beliefs which he thought best, he would inevitably, after careful consideration of their relative merits, choose that of his own country. Everyone without exception believes his own native customs, and the religion he was brought up in, to be the best.

Realizing this can result in our having more open minds. We can come to understand that our feelings are not necessarily perceptions of the truth—they may be nothing more than the result of cultural conditioning. Thus when we hear it suggested that some element of our social code is *not* really the best, and we find ourselves instinctively resisting the suggestion, we might stop and remember this. Then we may be more open to discovering the truth, whatever that might be. [...]

Study Questions

1. Which of the six claims made by cultural relativists does Rachels think are acceptable claims? Which does he think are mistaken? Why?
2. Rachels identifies what he calls the "Cultural Differences Argument" for cultural relativism. Do you agree with Rachels that this is the best formulation of the argument for cultural relativism?
3. What argument does Rachels give (Section 2.5) for there being less moral disagreement between cultures than cultural relativists would have us believe? Do you agree? Why or why not?
4. What argument does Rachels give (Section 2.5) for there being a core of shared values across cultures? Do you agree? Why or why not?

8.7   Empirical Approaches to Meta-Ethics

 ## JOHN DORIS AND STEPHEN STICH

JOHN DORIS (1963–) IS PROFESSOR OF Philosophy at Washington University, St. Louis. Stephen Stich (1943–) is Board of Governors Professor at Rutgers University. In this article, the authors identify a number of ways in which empirical investigation can shed light on meta-ethical issues. Stich and Doris describe research that appears to undermine assumptions made by Michael Smith about both the conceptual and psychological possibility of the amoralist. In addition, the authors point to research in psychology and anthropology on moral disagreement that poses new challenges to realists like Rachels and Smith.

Too many moral philosophers and commentators on moral philosophy...have been content to invent their psychology or anthropology from scratch....

—S. DARWALL, A. GIBBARD, AND
P. RAILTON (EDS.),
Moral Discourse and Practice

1. INTRODUCTION

Regarding the assessment of Darwall and colleagues, we couldn't agree more: Far too many moral philosophers have been content to *invent* the psychology or anthropology on which their theories depend, advancing or disputing empirical claims with little concern for empirical evidence. [...] This empirical complacency has impeded progress in ethical theory and discouraged investigators in the biological, behavioural, and social sciences from undertaking philosophically informed research on ethical issues. [...]

The most obvious, and most compelling, motivation for our perspective is simply this: It is not possible to step far into the ethics literature without stubbing one's toe on empiri-

cal claims. The thought that moral philosophy can proceed unencumbered by facts seems to us an unlikely one: There are just too many places where answers to important ethical questions require—and have very often presupposed—answers to empirical questions.

A small but growing number of philosophers, ourselves included, have become convinced that answers to these empirical questions should be informed by systematic empirical research. [...] Science has produced much experimental and theoretical work that appears importantly relevant to ongoing debates in ethical theory, and some moral philosophers have lately begun to pursue empirical investigations. To explore the issues fully requires far more space than is available here; we must content ourselves with developing a few rather programmatic examples of how an empirically sensitive philosophical ethics might proceed.

Our point is not that reference to empirical literatures can be expected, by itself, to resolve debates in moral theory. Rather, we hope to convince the reader that these literatures are often deeply relevant to important debates, and it is therefore intellectually irresponsible to ignore them. Sometimes empirical findings seem to contradict what particular disputing parties assert or presuppose, while in other cases, they appear to reconfigure the philosophical topography, revealing that certain lines of argument must traverse empirically difficult terrain. Often, philosophers who follow these challenging routes will be forced to make additional empirical conjectures, and these conjectures, in their turn, must be subject to empirical scrutiny. The upshot, we conclude, is that an intellectually responsible philosophical ethics is one that continuously engages the relevant empirical literature. [...]

3. MORAL MOTIVATION

Suppose a person believes that she ought to do something: donate blood to the Red Cross, say, or send a significant contribution to an international relief agency. Does it follow that she will be moved actually to act on this belief? Ethical theorists use internalism to mark an important cluster of answers to this question, answers maintaining that the motivation to act on a moral judgement is a necessary or intrinsic concomitant of the judgement itself, or that the relevant motivation is inevitably generated by the very same mental faculty that produces the judgement.[1] One familiar version of internalism is broadly Kantian, emphasizing the role of rationality in ethics. As Deigh (1999: 289) characterizes the position, "reason is both the pilot and the engine of moral agency. It not only guides one toward actions in conformity with one's duty, but it also produces the desire to do one's duty and can invest that desire with enough strength to overrule conflicting impulses of appetite and passion." A notorious difficulty for internalism is suggested by Hume's (1975: 282–4) "sensible knave," a person who recognizes that the unjust and dishonest acts he contemplates are wrong, but is completely unmoved by this realization. More recent writers (e.g. Nichols 2002) have suggested that the sensible knave (or, as

philosophers often call him, "the amoralist") is more than a philosophical fiction, since clinical psychologists and other mental heath professionals have for some time noted the existence of sociopaths or psychopaths, who appear to *know* the difference between right and wrong but quite generally lack motivation to *do* what is right. If this understanding of the psychopath's moral psychology is accurate, internalism looks to be suffering empirical embarrassment.[2]

Internalists have adopted two quite different responses to this challenge, one conceptual and the other empirical. The first relies on conceptual analysis to argue that a person couldn't really believe that an act is wrong if he has no motivation to avoid performing it. For example, Michael Smith claims it is "a conceptual truth that agents who make moral judgements are motivated accordingly, at least absent weakness of the will and the like" (Smith 1994: 66). Philosophers who adopt this strategy recognize that imaginary knaves and real psychopaths may *say* that something is "morally required" or "morally wrong" and that they may be expressing a judgement that they sincerely accept. But if psychopaths are not motivated in the appropriate way, their words do not mean what non-psychopaths mean by these words and the concepts they express with these words are not the ordinary moral concepts that non-psychopaths use. Therefore psychopaths "do not *really* make moral judgements at all" (Smith 1994: 67).

This strategy only works if ordinary moral concepts require that people who *really* make moral judgements have the appropriate sort of motivation. But there is considerable disagreement in cognitive science about whether and how concepts are structured, and about how we are to determine when something is built into or entailed by a concept (Margolis and Laurence 1999). Indeed, one widely discussed approach maintains that concepts have no semantically relevant internal structure to be analysed—thus there are no conceptual entailments (Fodor 1998). Obviously, internalists who appeal to conceptual analysis must reject this account, and in so doing they must take a stand in the broadly empirical debate about the nature of concepts. [...]

In the interests of developing a non-partisan analysis, Nichols (2002) has been running a series of experiments in which philosophically unsophisticated undergraduates are presented with questions like these:

> John is a psychopathic criminal. He is an adult of normal intelligence, but he has no emotional reaction to hurting other people. John has hurt, and indeed killed, other people when he has wanted to steal their money. He says that he knows that hurting others is wrong, but that he just doesn't care if he does things that are wrong. Does John really understand that hurting others is morally wrong?

> Bill is a mathematician. He is an adult of normal intelligence, but he has no emotional reaction to hurting other people. Nonetheless, Bill never hurts other people simply because he thinks that it is irrational to hurt others. He thinks that any rational person would be like him and not hurt other people. Does Bill really understand that hurting others is morally wrong? (Nichols 2004; 74)

Nichols's preliminary results are exactly the opposite of what Smith would have one expect. An overwhelming majority of subjects maintained that John, the psychopath, did understand that hurting others is morally wrong, while a slight majority maintained that Bill, the rational mathematician, did not. The implication seems to be that the subjects' concept of moral judgement does not typically include a "motivational platitude." These results do not, of course, constitute a decisive refutation of Smith's conceptual analysis, since Smith can reply that responses like those Nichols reports would not be part of the maximally consistent set of platitudes that people would endorse after due reflection. But this too is an empirical claim; if Smith is to offer a compelling defence of it he should—with our enthusiastic encouragement—adduce some systematic empirical evidence.

A second internalist strategy for dealing with the problem posed by the amoralist is empirical: even if amoralists are conceptually possible, the internalist may insist, their existence is psychologically impossible. As a matter of psychological fact, this argument goes, people's moral judgements are accompanied by the appropriate sort of motivation.[3] A Kantian elaboration of this idea, on which we will focus, maintains that people's moral judgements are accompanied by the appropriate sort of motivation *unless their rational faculties are impaired.* (We'll shortly see that much turns on the fate of the italicized clause.) Recent papers by Roskies (2003) and Nichols (2002) set out important challenges to this strategy.

Roskies' argument relies on Damasio and colleagues' work with patients suffering injuries to the ventromedial (VM) cortex (Damasio *et al.* 1990; Saver and Damasio 1991; Bechara *et al.* 2000). On a wide range of standard psychological tests, including tests for intelligence and reasoning abilities, these patients appear quite normal. They also do as well as normal subjects on Kohlberg's tests of *moral* reasoning, and when presented with hypothetical situations they offer moral judgements that concur with those of normal subjects. However, these patients appear to have great difficulty inacting in accordance with those judgements. As a result, although they often led exemplary lives prior to their injury, their post-trauma social lives are a shambles. They disregard social conventions, make disastrous business and personal decisions, and often engage in anti-social behaviour. Accordingly, Damasio and his colleagues describe the VM patients' condition as "acquired sociopathy" (Saver and Damasio 1991).

Roskies maintains that VM patients do not act on their moral judgements because they suffer a *motivational* deficit. Moreover, the evidence indicates that these individuals do not have a *general* difficulty in acting on evaluative judgements; rather, Roskies (2003, 10) maintains, action with respect to moral and social evaluation is differentially impaired. In addition to the behavioural evidence, this interpretation is supported by the anomalous pattern of skin-conductance responses (SCRs) that VM patients display.[4] Normal individuals produce an SCR when presented with emotionally charged or value-laden stimuli, while VM patients typically do not produce SCRs in response to such stimuli. SCRs are not entirely lacking in VM patients, however. SCRs are produced when VM patients are surprised or startled, for example, demonstrating that the physiological basis for these responses is intact. In addition, their presence is reliably correlated with cases in which patients' actions are consistent with their judgements about what to do, and their absence is reliably correlated with cases in which patients fail to act in accordance with their judgements. Thus, Roskies contends, the SCR is a reliable indicator of motivation. So the fact that VM patients, unlike normal subjects, do not exhibit SCRs in response to morally charged stimuli suggests that their failure to act in morally charged situations results from a motivational deficit.

On the face of it, acquired sociopathy confounds internalists maintaining that the moral judgements of rational people are, as a matter of psychological fact, always accompanied by appropriate motivation.[5] Testing indicates that the general reasoning abilities of these patients are not impaired, and even their moral reasoning seems to be quite normal. So none of the empirical evidence suggests the presence of a cognitive disability. An internalist might insist that these post-injury judgements are not *genuine* instances of moral judgements because VM patients no longer know the standard meaning of the moral words they use. But unless it is supported by an appeal to a conceptual analysis of the sort we criticized earlier, this is a rather implausible move; as Roskies notes, all tests of VM patients indicate that their language, their declarative knowledge structures, and their cognitive functioning are intact. There are, of course, many questions about acquired sociopathy that remain unanswered and much work is yet to be done. However these questions get answered, the literature on VM patients is one that moral philosophers embroiled in the internalism debate would be ill advised to ignore; once again, the outcome of a debate in ethical theory looks to be contingent on empirical issues.

The same point holds for other work on antisocial behaviour. Drawing on Blair's (1995) studies of psychopathic murderers imprisoned in Great Britain, Nichols (2002) has recently argued that the phenomenon of psychopathy poses a deep and complex challenge for internalism. Again, the general difficulty is that psychopaths seem to be living instantiations of Hume's sensible knave: although they appear to be rational and can be quite intelligent, psychopaths are manipulative, remorseless, and devoid of other-regarding concern. While psychopaths sometimes acknowledge that their treatment of other people is wrong, they are quite indifferent about the harm that they have caused; they seem to have no motivation to avoid hurting others (R. D. Hare 1993).

Blair's (1995) evidence complicates this familiar story. He found that psychopaths exhibit surprising deficits on various tasks where subjects are presented with descriptions of "moral" transgressions like a child hitting another child and "conventional" transgressions like a child leaving the classroom without the teacher's permission. From early childhood, normal children distinguish moral from conventional transgressions on a number of dimensions: they view moral transgressions as more serious, they explain why the acts are wrong by appeal to different factors (harm and fairness for moral transgressions, social acceptability for conventional transgressions), and they understand conventional transgressions, unlike moral transgressions, to be dependent on authority (Turiel *et al.* 1987; Nucci 1986). For example, presented with a hypothetical case where a teacher says there is no rule about leaving the classroom without permission, children think it is OK to leave without permission. But presented with a hypothetical where a teacher says there is no rule against hitting other children, children do not judge that hitting is acceptable. Blair has shown that while autistic children, children with Down syndrome, and a control group of incarcerated non-psychopath murderers have relatively little trouble in drawing the moral–conventional distinction and classifying cases along these lines, incarcerated psychopaths are unable to do so.

This inability might be evidence for the hypothesis that psychopaths have a reasoning deficit, and therefore do not pose a problem for internalists who maintain that a properly functioning reasoning faculty reliably generates some motivation to do what one believes one ought to do. But, as Nichols (2002) has pointed out, the issue cannot be so easily resolved, because psychopaths have also been shown to have *affective* responses that are quite different from those of normal subjects. When shown distressing stimuli (like slides of people with dreadful injuries) and threatening stimuli (like slides of an angry man wielding a weapon), normal subjects exhibit much the same suite of physiological responses. Psychopaths, by contrast, exhibit normal physiological responses to threatening stimuli, but abnormally low physiological responses to distressing stimuli (Blair *et al.* 1997). Thus, Nichols argues, it may well be that the psychopath's deficit is not an abnormal reasoning system, but an abnormal affect system, and it is these affective abnormalities, rather than any rational disabilities, that are implicated in psychopaths' failure to draw the moral–conventional distinction.[6] If his interpretation is correct, it looks as though the existence of psychopaths does undermine the Kantian internalist's empirical generalization: contra the Kantian, there exists a substantial class of individuals *without rational disabilities* who are not motivated by their moral judgements.

We are sympathetic to Nichols's account, but as in the case of VM patients, the internalist is free to insist that a fuller understanding of psychopathy will reveal that the syndrome does indeed involve rational disabilities. Resolving

this debate will require conceptual work on how to draw the boundary between reason and affect, and on what counts as an abnormality in each of these domains. But it will also require much more empirical work aimed at understanding exactly how psychopaths and non-psychopaths differ. The internalist—or at least the Kantian internalist—who wishes to diffuse the difficulty posed by psychopathy must proffer an empirically tenable account of the psychopath's cognitive architecture that locates the posited rational disability. We doubt that such an account is forthcoming. But—to instantiate once more our take-home message—our present point is that if internalists are to develop such an account, they must engage the empirical literature.

4. MORAL DISAGREEMENT

Numerous contemporary philosophers, including Brandt (1959), Harman (1977: 125–36), Railton (1986*a,b*), and Lewis (1989), have proposed dispositional theories of moral rightness or non-moral good, which "make matters of value depend on the affective dispositions of agents" (see Darwall *et al.* 1997: 28–9).[7] The various versions differ in detail,[8] but a rendering by Brandt is particularly instructive. According to Brandt (1959: 241–70), ethical justification is a process whereby initial judgements about particular cases and general moral principles are revised by testing these judgements against the attitudes, feelings, or emotions that would emerge under appropriately idealized circumstances. Of special importance on Brandt's (1959: 249–51, 261–4) view are what he calls "qualified attitudes"—the attitudes people would have if they were, *inter alia*, (1) impartial, (2) fully informed about and vividly aware of the relevant facts, and (3) free from any "abnormal" states of mind, like insanity, fatigue, or depression.[9]

As Brandt (1959: 281–4) noted, much depends on whether all people would have the same attitudes in ideal circumstances—i.e. on whether their attitudes would *converge* in ideal circumstances. If they would, then certain moral judgements—those where the idealized convergence obtains—are justified for all people, and others—those where such convergence fails to obtain—are not so justified. But if people's attitudes generally fail to converge under idealized circumstances, qualified attitude theory apparently lapses into a version of relativism, since any given moral judgement may comport with the qualified attitudes of one person, and thus be justified for him, while an incompatible judgement may comport with the attitudes of another person, and thus be justified for her.[10]

Brandt, who was a pioneer in the effort to integrate ethical theory and the social sciences, looked primarily to anthropology to help determine whether moral attitudes can be expected to converge under idealized circumstances. It is of course well known that anthropology includes a substantial body of work, such as the classic studies of Westermarck (1906) and Sumner (1934), detailing the radically divergent moral outlooks found in cultures around the world. But as Brandt (1959: 283–4) recognized, typical ethnographies do not support confident inferences about the convergence of attitudes under *ideal* conditions, in large measure because they often give limited guidance regarding how much of the moral disagreement can be traced to disagreement about factual matters that are not moral in nature, such as those having to do with religious or cosmological views.

With this sort of difficulty in mind, Brandt (1954) undertook his own anthropological study of Hopi peoples in the American southwest, and found issues for which there appeared to be serious moral disagreement between typical Hopi and white American attitudes that could not plausibly be attributed to differences in belief about non-moral facts. A notable example is the Hopi attitude towards causing animals to suffer, an attitude that might be expected to disturb many non-Hopis: "[Hopi c]hildren sometimes catch birds and make 'pets' of them. They may be tied to a string, to be taken out and 'played' with. This play is rough, and birds seldom survive long. [According to one informant:] 'Sometimes they get tired and die. Nobody objects to this'" (Brandt 1954: 213).

Brandt (1959: 103) made a concerted effort to determine whether this difference in moral outlook could be traced to disagreement about non-moral facts, but he could find no plausible explanation of this kind; his Hopi informants didn't believe that animals lack the capacity to feel pain, for example, nor did they believe that animals are rewarded for martyrdom in the afterlife. According to Brandt (1954: 245), the Hopi do not regard animals as unconscious or insensitive; indeed, they apparently regard animals as "closer to the human species than does the average white man." The best explanation of the divergent moral judgements, Brandt (1954: 245) concluded, is a "basic difference of attitude." Accordingly, although he cautions that the uncertainties of ethnography make confident conclusions on this point difficult, Brandt (1959: 284) argues that accounts of moral justification like his qualified attitude theory *do* end in relativism, since "groups do sometimes make divergent appraisals when they have identical beliefs about the objects."

[. . .] As we see it, the problem is not only that moral disagreement often persists, but also that for important instances of moral disagreement—such as the treatment of animals—it is obscure what sort of considerations, be they methodological or substantive, *could* settle the issues (see Sturgeon 1988: 229). Indeed, moral disagreement might be plausibly expected to continue even when the disputants are in methodological agreement concerning the appropriate standards for moral argument. One way of putting the point is to say that application of the same method may, for different individuals or cultures, yield divergent moral judgements that are equally acceptable by the lights of the method, even in reflective conditions that the method countenances as ideal.[11] [. . .]

In contemporary ethical theory, an impressive group of philosophers are 'moral realists' (see Railton, 1986*a*,*b*; Boyd 1988; Sturgeon 1988; Brink 1989; M. Smith 1994). [...]

Realists may argue that, in contrast to the impression one gets from the anthropological literature, there already exists substantial moral convergence. But while moral realists have often taken pretty optimistic positions on the extent of actual moral agreement (e.g. Sturgeon 1988: 229; M. Smith 1994: 188), there is no denying that there is an abundance of persistent moral disagreement. That is, on many moral issues— think of abortion and capital punishment—there is a striking failure of convergence even after protracted argument. The relativist has a ready explanation for this phenomenon: moral judgement is not objective [...], and moral argument cannot be expected to accomplish what Smith [1994] and other realists think it can.[12] Conversely, the realist's task is to *explain away* failures of convergence; she must provide an explanation of the phenomena consistent with it being the case that moral judgement is objective and moral argument is rationally resolvable. For our purposes, what needs to be emphasized is that the relative merits of these competing explanations cannot be fairly determined without close discussion of actual cases. Indeed, as acute commentators with both realist (Sturgeon 1988: 230) and anti-realist (Loeb 1998: 284) sympathies have noted, the argument from disagreement cannot be evaluated by a priori philosophical means alone; what's needed, as Loeb observes, is "a great deal of further empirical research into the circumstances and beliefs of various cultures."

Brandt (1959: 101–2) lamented that the anthropological literature of his day did not always provide as much information on the exact contours and origins of moral attitudes and beliefs as philosophers wondering about the prospects for convergence might like. However, social psychology and cognitive science have recently produced research which promises to further discussion; the closing decades of the twentieth century witnessed an explosion of "cultural psychology" investigating the cognitive and emotional processes of different cultures (Shweder and Bourne 1982; Markus and Kitayama 1991; Ellsworth 1994; Nisbett and Cohen 1996; Nisbett 1998; Kitayama and Markus 1999). A representative finding is that East Asians are more sensitive than Westerners to the field or context as opposed to the object or actor in their explanations of physical and social phenomena, a difference that may be reflected in their habits of ethical judgement. Here we will focus on some cultural differences found rather closer to home, differences discovered by Nisbett and his colleagues while investigating regional patterns of violence in the American North and South. We argue that these findings support Brandt's pessimistic conclusions regarding the possibility of convergence in moral judgement.

The Nisbett group's research can be seen as applying the tools of cognitive social psychology to the "culture of honour," a phenomenon that anthropologists have documented in a variety of groups around the world. Although such peoples differ in many respects, they manifest important commonalties:

> A key aspect of the culture of honor is the importance placed on the insult and the necessity to respond to it. An insult implies that the target is weak enough to be bullied. Since a reputation for strength is of the essence in the culture of honor, the individual who insults someone must be forced to retract; if the instigator refuses, he must be punished—with violence or even death. (Nisbett and Cohen 1996: 5)

According to Nisbett and Cohen (1996: 5–9), an important factor in the genesis of southern honour culture was the presence of a herding economy. Apparently, honour cultures are particularly likely to develop where resources are liable to theft, and where the state's coercive apparatus cannot be relied upon to prevent or punish thievery. These conditions often occur in relatively remote areas where herding is the main viable form of agriculture; the "portability" of herd animals makes them prone to theft. In areas where farming rather than herding is the principal form of subsistence, cooperation among neighbours is more important, stronger government infrastructures are more common, and resources—like decidedly unportable farmland—are harder to steal. In such agrarian social economies, cultures of honour tend not to develop. The American South was originally settled primarily by peoples from remote areas of Britain. Since their homelands were generally unsuitable for farming, these peoples have historically been herders; when they emigrated from Britain to the South, they initially sought out remote regions suitable for herding, and in such regions, the culture of honour flourished.

In the contemporary South police and other government services are widely available and herding has all but disappeared as a way of life, but certain sorts of violence continue to be more common than they are in the North. Nisbett and Cohen (1996) maintain that patterns of violence in the South, as well as attitudes towards violence, insults, and affronts to honour, are best explained by the hypothesis that a culture of honour persists among contemporary white non-Hispanic southerners. In support of this hypothesis, they offer a compelling array of evidence, including:

- demographic data indicating that (1) among southern whites, homicides rates are higher in regions more suited to herding than agriculture, and (2) white males in the South are much more likely than white males in other regions to be involved in homicides resulting from arguments, although they are *not* more likely to be involved in homicides that occur in the course of a robbery or other felony (Nisbett and Cohen 1996, ch. 2);
- survey data indicating that white southerners are more likely than northerners to believe that violence would be "extremely

justified" in response to a variety of affronts, and that if a man failed to respond violently, he was "not much of a man" (Nisbett and Cohen 1996, ch. 3);
- legal scholarship indicating that southern states "give citizens more freedom to use violence in defending themselves, their homes, and their property" than do northern states (Nisbett and Cohen 1996: 63).

Two experimental studies—one in the field, the other in the laboratory—are especially striking.

In the field study (Nisbett and Cohen 1996: 73–5), letters of inquiry were sent to hundreds of employers around the United States. The letters purported to be from a hard-working 27-year-old Michigan man who had a single blemish on his otherwise solid record. In one version, the "applicant" revealed that he had been convicted for manslaughter. The applicant explained that he had been in a fight with a man who confronted him in a bar and told onlookers that "he and my fiancée were sleeping together. He laughed at me to my face and asked me to step outside if I was man enough." According to the letter, the applicant's nemesis was killed in the ensuing fray. In the other version of the letter, the applicant revealed that he had been convicted of motor vehicle theft, perpetrated at a time when he needed money for his family. Nisbett and his colleagues assessed 112 letters of response, and found that southern employers were significantly more likely to be cooperative and sympathetic in response to the manslaughter letter than were northern employers, while no regional differences were found in responses to the theft letter. One southern employer responded to the manslaughter letter as follows (Nisbett and Cohen 1996: 75):

> As for your problems of the past, anyone could probably be in the situation you were in. It was just an unfortunate incident that shouldn't be held against you. Your honesty shows that you are sincere....I wish you the best of luck for

your future. You have a positive attitude and a willingness to work. These are qualities that businesses look for in employees. Once you are settled, if you are near here, please stop in and see us.

No letters from northern employers were comparably sympathetic.

In the laboratory study (Nisbett and Cohen 1996: 45–8) subjects—white males from both northern and southern states attending the University of Michigan—were told that saliva samples would be collected to measure blood sugar as they performed various tasks. After an initial sample was collected, the unsuspecting subject walked down a narrow corridor where an experimental confederate was pretending to work on some filing. Feigning annoyance at the interruption, the confederate bumped the subject and called him an "asshole." A few minutes after the incident, saliva samples were collected and analysed to determine the level of cortisol—a hormone associated with high levels of stress, anxiety and arousal, and testosterone—a hormone associated

with aggression and dominance behaviour. As [Figure 1] indicates, southern subjects showed dramatic increases in cortisol and testosterone levels, while northerners exhibited much smaller changes.

The two studies just described suggest that southerners respond more strongly to insult than northerners, and take a more sympathetic view of others who do so, manifesting just the sort of attitudes that are supposed to typify honour cultures. We think that the data assembled by Nisbett and his colleagues make a persuasive case that a culture of honour persists in the American South. Apparently, this culture affects people's judgements, attitudes, emotions, behaviour, and even their physiological responses. Additionally, there is evidence that child-rearing practices play a significant role in passing the culture of honour on from one generation to the next, and also that relatively permissive laws regarding gun-ownership, self-defence, and corporal punishment in the schools both reflect and reinforce southern honour culture (Nisbett and Cohen

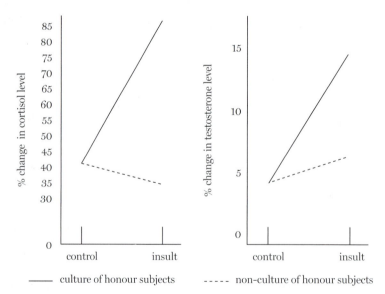

FIGURE 1 The results of an experiment by Nisbett and Cohen in which levels of cortisol and testosterone increased much more substantially in culture of honour subjects who were insulted by a confederate.

1996: 60–3, 67–9). In short, it seems to us that the culture of honour is deeply entrenched in contemporary southern culture, despite the fact that many of the material and economic conditions giving rise to it no longer widely obtain.[13]

We believe that the North–South cultural differences adduced by Nisbett and colleagues support Brandt's conclusion that moral attitudes will often fail to converge, even under ideal conditions. The data should be especially troubling for the realist, for despite the differences that we have been recounting, contemporary northern and southern Americans might be expected to have rather more in common—from circumstance to language to belief to ideology—than do, say, Yanomamö and Parisians. So if there is little ground for expecting convergence under ideal conditions in the case at hand, there is probably little ground in a good many others. To develop our argument a bit further, let us revisit the idealization conditions mentioned at the beginning of this section: impartiality, full factual information, and normality.

Impartiality. One strategy favoured by moral realists concerned to explain away moral disagreement is to say that such disagreement stems from the distorting effects of individual interest (see Sturgeon 1988: 229–30); perhaps persistent disagreement doesn't so much betray deep features of moral argument and judgement as it does the doggedness with which individuals pursue their perceived advantage. For instance, seemingly moral disputes over the distribution of wealth may be due to perceptions—perhaps mostly inchoate—of individual and class interests rather than to principled disagreement about justice; persisting moral disagreement in such circumstances fails the impartiality condition, and is therefore untroubling to the moral realist.

But it is rather implausible to suggest that North–South disagreements over when violence is justified will fail the impartiality condition. There is no reason to think that southerners would be unwilling to universalize their judgements across relevantly similar individuals in relevantly similar circumstances, as indeed Nisbett and Cohen's "letter study" suggests. One can advocate a violent honour code without going in for special pleading.[14] We do not intend to denigrate southern values; our point is that while there may be good reasons for criticizing the honour-bound southerner, it is not obvious that the reason can be failure of impartiality, if impartiality is (roughly) to be understood along the lines of a willingness to universalize one's moral judgements.

Full and vivid awareness of relevant non-moral facts. Moral realists have argued that moral disagreements very often derive from disagreement about non-moral issues. According to Boyd (1988: 213; cf. Brink 1989: 202–3; Sturgeon 1988: 229), "careful philosophical examination will reveal...that agreement on nonmoral issues would eliminate almost all disagreement about the sorts of moral issues which arise in ordinary moral practice." Is this a plausible conjecture for the data we have just considered? We find it hard to imagine what agreement on non-moral facts could do the trick, for we can readily imagine that northerners and southerners might be in full agreement on the relevant non-moral facts in the cases described. Members of both groups would presumably agree that the job applicant was cuckolded, for example, or that calling someone an "asshole" is an insult. We think it much more plausible to suppose that the disagreement resides in differing and deeply entrenched evaluative attitudes regarding appropriate responses to cuckolding, challenge, and insult. [. . .]

It is of course possible that full and vivid awareness of the non-moral facts might motivate the sort of change in southern attitudes envisaged by the (at least the northern) moral realist; were southerners to become vividly aware that their culture of honour was implicated in violence, they might be moved to change their moral outlook. (We take this way of putting the example to be the most natural one, but nothing philosophical turns on it. If you like, substitute the possibility of bloody-minded northerners endorsing honour values after exposure to the facts.) On the other hand, southerners might insist that the values of honour should be nurtured even at the cost of promoting violence; the motto "Death before dishonour," after all, has a long and honourable history. The burden of argument, we think, lies with the realist who asserts—culture and history notwithstanding—that southerners would change their mind if vividly aware of the pertinent facts.

Freedom from abnormality. Realists may contend that much moral disagreement may result from failures of rationality on the part of discussants (Brink 1989: 199–200). Obviously, disagreement stemming from cognitive impairments is no embarrassment for moral realism; at the limit, that a disagreement persists when some or all disputing parties are quite insane shows nothing deep about morality. But it doesn't seem plausible that southerners' more lenient attitudes towards certain forms of violence are readily attributed to widespread cognitive disability. Of course, this is an empirical issue, and we don't know of any evidence suggesting that southerners suffer some cognitive impairment that prevents them from understanding demographic and attitudinal factors in the genesis of violence, or any other matter of fact. What is needed to press home a charge of irrationality is evidence of cognitive impairment independent of the attitudinal differences, and further evidence that this impairment is implicated in adherence to the disputed values in the face of the (putatively) undisputed non-moral facts. In this instance, as in many others, we have difficulty seeing how charges of abnormality or irrationality can be made without one side begging the question against the other.

We are inclined to think that Nisbett and colleagues' work represents a potent counter-example to any theory maintaining that rational argument tends to convergence on important moral issues; the evidence suggests that the North–South differences in attitudes towards violence and honour might well persist even under the sort of ideal conditions we have considered. Admittedly, our conclusions must be tentative. On the philosophical side, we have not considered every plausible strategy for "explaining away" moral disagreement and grounding expectations of convergence.[15] On the empirical side, we have reported on but a few studies, and those we do consider here, like any empirical work, might be criticized on either conceptual or methodological grounds.[16] Finally, we should make clear what we are *not* claiming; we do not take our conclusions here—even if fairly earned—to be a "refutation" of moral realism, in as much as there may be versions of moral realism that do not require convergence. Rather, we hope to have given an idea of the empirical work philosophers must encounter if they are to make defensible conjectures regarding moral disagreement. Our theme recurs: Responsible treatment of the empirical issues requires reference to empirical science, whatever the science is ultimately taken to show.

Notes

1. A stipulation: We refer to views in the neighbourhood of what Darwall (1983: 54) calls "judgement internalism," the thesis that it is "a necessary condition of a genuine instance of a certain sort of judgment that the person making the judgment be disposed to act in a way appropriate to it." Space limitations force us to ignore myriad complications; for more detailed discussion, see Svavarsdóttir (1999).

2. There is august precedent for supposing that the internalism debate has empirical elements. In his classic discussion, Frankena (1976: 73) observed that progress here requires reference to "the psychology of human motivation"—"The battle, if war there be, cannot be contained; its field is the whole human world." We hope that Frankena would have appreciated our way of joining the fight.

3. We prescind from questions as to whether the motivation need be overriding, although we suspect formulations not requiring overridingness are more plausible.

4. SCR is a measure of physiological arousal, which is also sometimes called galvanic skin response, or GSR.

5. Roskies herself does not offer acquired sociopathy as a counter-example to the Kantian version of empirical internalism, but we believe the evidence *is* in tension with the Kantian view we describe.

6. Here Nichols offers support for the "sentimentalist" tradition, which maintains that emotions (or "sentiments") play a central role in moral judgement. For a helpful treatment of sentimentalism, see D'Arms and Jacobson (2000).

7. These views reflect a venerable tradition linking moral judgement to the affective states that people would have under idealized conditions; it extends back to Hutcheson (1738), Hume (1975, 1978), and Adam Smith 1759.

8. A particularly important difference concerns the envisaged link between moral claims and affective reactions. Firth (1952: 317–45) and Lewis (1989) see the link as a matter of meaning, Railton (1986*b*) as a synthetic identity, and Brandt (1959: 241–70) both as a matter of justification and, more tentatively, as a matter of meaning.

9. Brandt was a prolific and self-critical thinker, and the 1959 statement may not represent his mature views, but it well illustrates how empirical issues can impact a familiar approach to ethical theory. For a helpful survey of Brandt's career, sec Rosati (2000).

10. On some readings, qualified attitude theories may end up a version of *scepticism* if attitudes don't converge under ideal circumstances. Suppose a theory holds "an action is morally right (or morally wrong) iff all people in ideal conditions would judge that action is morally right (or morally wrong)." Then if convergence fails to obtain in ideal conditions, this theory entails that there are no morally right (or morally wrong) actions.

11. This way of putting the argument is at once uncontentious and contentious. It is uncontentious because it does not entail a radical methodological relativism of the sort, say, that insists there is nothing to choose between consulting an astrologer and the method of reflective equilibrium as an approach to moral inquiry (see Brandt 1959: 274–5). But precisely because of this, the empirical conjecture that moral judgements will not converge is highly contentious, since a background of methodological agreement would appear to make it more likely that moral argument could end in substantive moral agreement.

12. See Williams (1985: 136): "In a scientific inquiry there should ideally be convergence on an answer, where the best explanation of the convergence involves the idea that the answer represents how things are; in the area of the ethical, at least at high level of generality, there is no such coherent hope."

13. The last clause is important, since realists (e.g. Brink 1989: 200) sometimes argue that apparent moral disagreement may result from cultures applying similar moral values to different economic conditions (e.g. differences in attitudes towards the sick and elderly between poor and rich cultures). But this explanation seems of dubious relevance to the described differences between contemporary northerners and southerners, who are plausibly interpreted as applying different values to similar economic conditions.

14. The legal scholarship that Nisbett and Cohen (1996: 57–78) review makes it clear that southern legislatures are often willing to enact laws reflecting the culture of honour view of the circumstances under which violence is justified, which suggests there is at least some support among southerners for the idea that honour values should be universalizable.

15. In addition to the expedients we have considered, realists may plausibly appeal to, *inter alia*, requirements for internal coherence and the different "levels" of moral thought (theoretical versus popular, abstract versus concrete, general versus particular) at which moral disagreement may or may not be manifested. Brink (1989: 197–210) and Loeb (1998) offer valuable discussions with considerably more detail than we offer here, Brink manifesting realist sympathies and Loeb tending towards anti-realism.

16. We think Nisbett and Cohen will fare pretty well under such scrutiny. See Tetlock's (1999) favourable review.

References

Bechara, A., Damasio, H., and Damasio, A. R. 2000. "Emotion, Decision Making and the Orbitofrontal Cortex." *Cerebral Cortex*, 10: 295–307.

Blair, R. J. 1995. "A Cognitive Developmental Approach to Morality: Investigating the Psychopath." *Cognition*, 57, 1–29.

Blair, R. J., Jones, L., Clark, F. and Smith, M. 1997. "The Psychopathic Individual: A Lack of Responsiveness to Distress Cues?" *Psychophysiology*, 34, 192–198.

Boyd, R. N. 1988. "How to Be A Moral Realist." In G. Sayre-McCord (ed.), *Essays on Moral Realism*. Ithaca and London: Cornell University Press.

Brandt, R. B. 1954. *Hopi Ethics: A Theoretical Analysis*. Chicago: The University of Chicago Press.

Brandt, R. B. 1959. *Ethical Theory: The Problems of Normative and Critical Ethics*. Englewood Cliffs, NJ: Prentice-Hall.

Brink, D. O. 1989. *Moral Realism and the Foundations of Ethics*. Cambridge: Cambridge University Press.

Damasio, A. R., Tranel, D., and Damasio, H. 1990. Individuals With Sociopathic Behavior Caused by Frontal Damage Fail to Respond Autonomically to Social Stimuli. *Behavioral Brain Research*, 41: 81–94.

D'Arms, J., and Jacobson, D. 2000. "Sentiment and Value." *Ethics* 110: 722–748.

Darwall, S. L. 1983. *Impartial Reason*. Ithaca, N.Y.: Cornell University Press.

Darwall, S., Gibbard, A. and Railton, P. (eds.). 1997. *Moral Discourse and Practice: Some Philosophical Approaches*. New York and Oxford: Oxford University Press.

Deigh, J. 1999. Ethics. In R. Audi (ed.), *The Cambridge Dictionary of Philosophy*. Cambridge: Cambridge University Press, 284–289.

Ellsworth, P. C. 1994. "Sense, Culture, and Sensibility." In H. Markus and S. Kitayama (eds.), *Emotion and Culture: Empirical Studies in Mutual Influence*. Washington: American Psychological Association.

Firth, R. 1952. "Ethical Absolutism and the Ideal Observer Theory." *Philosophy and Phenomenological Research* 12: 317–345.

Fodor, J. 1998. *Concepts: Where Cognitive Science Went Wrong*. Oxford: Oxford University Press.

Frankena, W. K. 1976. "Obligation and Motivation in Recent Moral Philosophy." In K. E. Goodpaster (ed.), *Perspectives on Morality: Essays of William K. Frankena*. Notre Dame: University of Notre Dame Press.

Hare, R. D. 1993 *Without Conscience: the disturbing world of the psychopaths among us*, New York: Pocket Books.

Harman, G. 1977. *The Nature of Morality*. New York: Oxford University Press.

Hume, D. 1975. *Enquiries Concerning Human Understanding and Concerning the Principles of Morals*, 3rd ed. Oxford: Oxford University Press. Originally published 1777.

Hume, D. 1978. *A Treatise of Human Nature* (2nd edn.). Oxford: Oxford University Press. Originally published, 1740.

Hutcheson, F. 1738. *An Enquiry into the Origin of Our Ideas of Beauty and Virtue, in Two Treatises*. London: D. Midwinter.

Kitayama, S., and Markus, H. R. 1999. "*Yin* and *Yang* of the Japanese Self: The Cultural Psychology of Personality Coherence." In D. Cervone and Y. Shoda (eds.) *The Coherence of Personality: Social-Cognitive Bases of Consistency, Variability, and Organization*. New York and London: The Guilford Press.

Lewis, D. 1989. "Dispositional Theories of Value." *Proceedings of the Aristotelian Society* 63 (supp): 113–37.

Loeb, D. 1998. "Moral Realism and the Argument from Disagreement." *Philosophical Studies* 90: 281–303.

Margolis, E. and Laurence, S. 1999. *Concepts*. Cambridge, MA: MIT Press.

Markus, H. R., and Kitayama, S. 1991. "Culture and the Self: Implications for Cognition, Emotion, and Motivation." *Psychological Review* 98: 224–253.

Nichols, S. 2002. "How Psychopaths Threaten Moral Rationalism, or Is It Irrational to be Amoral?" *The Monist*, 85, 285–304.

Nisbett, R. E. 1998. "Essence and Accident." In J. M. Darley and J. Cooper (eds.), *Attribution and Social Interaction: The Legacy of Edward E. Jones*. Washington, DC: American Psychological Association.

Nisbett, R. E., and Cohen, D. 1996. *Culture of Honor: The Psychology of Violence in the South*. Boulder, CO: Westview Press.

Nucci, L. 1986. "Children's Conceptions of Morality, Social Conventions and Religious Prescription." In C. Harding, (ed.), *Moral Dilemmas: Philosophical and Psychological Reconsiderations of the Development of Moral Reasoning.* Chicago: Precedent Press.

Railton, P. 1986a. "Facts and Values." *Philosophical Topics* 14: 5–31.

Railton, P. 1986b. "Moral Realism." *Philosophical Review* 95: 163–207.

Rosati, C. S. 2000. "Brandt's Notion of Therapeutic Agency." *Ethics* 110: 780–811.

Roskies, A. (2003). "Are ethical judgments intrinsically motivational? Lessons from 'acquired sociopathy.'"

Saver, J. L. and Damasio, A. R. 1991. "Preserved access and processing of social knowledge in a patient with acquired sociopathy due to ventromedial frontal damage." *Neuropsychologia*, 29:1241–1249.

Shweder, R. A., and Bourne, E. J. 1982. "Does the Concept of the Person Vary Cross-Culturally?" In A. J. Marsella and G. M. White (eds.), *Cultural Conceptions of Mental Health and Therapy.* Boston, MA: D. Reidel Publishing Company.

Smith, A. 2002. *The Theory of Moral Sentiments.* New York: Cambridge University Press. Originally published 1759.

Smith, M. 1994. *The Moral Problem.* Oxford: Blackwell.

Sturgeon, N. L. 1988. "Moral Explanations." In G. Sayre-McCord (ed.), *Essays on Moral Realism.* Ithaca and London: Cornell University Press.

Sumner, W. G. 1934. *Folkways.* Boston: Ginn and Company.

Tetlock, P. E. 1999. "Review of *Culture of Honor: The Psychology of Violence in the South.*" *Political Psychology* 20: 211–13.

Turiel, E., Killen, M., & Helwig, C. 1987. "Morality: Its Structure, Functions, and Vagaries," in J. Kagan & S. Lamb (eds.) *The Emergence of Morality in Young Children.* Chicago: University of Chicago Press, 155–244.

Westermark, E. 1906. *Origin and Development of the Moral Ideas,* 2 vols. New York: MacMillan.

Williams, B. A. O. 1985. *Ethics and the Limits of Philosophy.* Cambridge, MA: Harvard University Press.

Study Questions

1. According to the authors, why is empirical research important for (how can it contribute to) our philosophical accounts of ethics? Do you agree? Why or why not?

2. Page 476 presents Nichols' empirical evidence against the internalist claim that the amoralist is *conceptually* impossible. Please explain specifically how the research findings undermine this view. Do you agree that this evidence undermines the claim? Why or why not?

3. Pages 476–477 present Roskies' argument against the internalist claim that the amoralist is *psychologically* impossible. Explain specifically how the research findings undermine this view. Do you agree that this evidence undermines the claim? Why or why not?

4. What does Brandt mean when he argues that even under ideal circumstances "groups do sometimes make divergent appraisals when they have identical beliefs about the objects"? What evidence does he give for this conclusion? Why would Brandt's claim undermine the arguments of Smith and Rachels?

8.8   Folk Meta-Ethical Commitments

 JENNIFER COLE WRIGHT AND HAGOP SARKISSIAN

The various essays in this chapter have represented attempts by philosophers to explain the nature and status of morality as a human practice. In undertaking this project, philosophers have typically assumed that people's ordinary folk understanding of morality involves a belief in objective moral truths. This latter question about how ordinary individuals themselves think of the moral domain is one that has been explored in recent years by researchers in the social sciences. In this article, Jen Wright (1969–), Assistant Professor of Psychology at College of Charleston, and Hagop Sarkissian (1974–), Assistant Professor of Philosophy at City University of New York–Baruch College, review this research and suggest how it bears on the philosophical project of meta-ethics.

INTRODUCTION

In this section of the book, we've been looking at various attempts that people have made to come to an accurate understanding of the nature and status of morality. This involves asking questions like: Are moral rules universal or culturally bound? Do moral judgments come from rational or emotional faculties? Can moral claims be true or false? Regardless of their particular theories, the philosophers examined in this section have taken one position or another on the phenomenon of morality—that is, the way we normally use moral discourse, evaluate moral problems, and think of the moral domain as compared to other domains.

Perhaps the most obvious example of a philosopher taking a definite stance on normal moral practice is J. L. Mackie, who makes broad claims about it as part of his "error theory" of morality (see Reading 8.4). Mackie famously claims that ordinary moral discourse purports to refer to objective moral properties that exist apart from any particular human opinion or perspective, and that are not dependent upon any person's or group's particular desires, preferences, or values

(Mackie 1977, 33). However, Mackie argues that there is no good reason to believe that such properties—along with their purported power to provide universal reasons for action to all—actually exist, as they would be unlike any other properties in the world. Mackie thus supports an error theory about ordinary moral practice—meaning that our ordinary moral judgments (judgments that make objective moral claims) are false.

There are at least two different ways that Mackie's theory could be wrong. First, it could turn out that there really *are* such things as moral properties. If such properties existed (even if not in precisely the way that Mackie characterizes them), then the folk would obviously *not* be in error in presupposing them as part of their ordinary moral discourse. Indeed, many philosophers who have found Mackie's arguments unconvincing have been motivated to describe precisely how such real moral properties might exist.

Another way that Mackie could be wrong is if the folk don't actually assume (or tacitly embrace) any objective moral properties in their ordinary discourse. In other words, if the folk reject moral objectivism, then it seems (once again) that they

Jennifer Cole Wright and Hagop Sarkissian, "Folk Meta-Ethical Commitments." Reprinted with permission from Jennifer Cole Wright.

couldn't be committing any real "error" about the nature of morality. In this final reading, we will pursue this latter question of whether or not the folk really *are* (as Mackie and many others have assumed) moral objectivists.

OBJECTIVISM AND RELATIVISM

What does it mean for someone to be a moral objectivist? Roughly speaking, objectivism holds that the moral domain, like the scientific domain, is grounded in universal and fundamental *facts* that exist (largely) independently of people's beliefs, preferences, attitudes, norms, or conventions. For example, actions such as consciously discriminating against someone because of his or her gender or race would be morally wrong not because people simply prefer not to discriminate, because they have strong negative emotional responses against discriminating, or even because as a society they have come to agree that discriminating is wrong. Rather, there are certain features of discrimination itself (e.g., cruelty and unfairness) that "ground" its wrongness—and would do so even if people generally felt ambivalent or deemed such behavior to be perfectly acceptable.[1] This means that in most cases where there is disagreement about whether a particular action (e.g., racial/gender discrimination) is morally unacceptable, if two individuals hold opposite opinions, then at least one of them must be mistaken (Railton 1986; Shafer-Landau 2003; Smith 1994).

There are many meta-ethical theories that reject objectivism in some way. Here, we will contrast objectivism with one of its primary rival theories: relativism.[2] Relativism holds that the moral domain—much like other normative domains (e.g., social/conventional)—is ultimately grounded in the beliefs, preferences, attitudes, habits, norms, and/or conventions of people (whether individuals or groups). This means that moral claims can only be assessed relative to a particular moral framework, or a particular set of moral values; in cases of moral disagreement, different moral claims could both be right if asserted from different moral frameworks (Dreier 1990; Harman 1975; Pinillos 2010; Prinz 2007; Wong 1984, 2006).

As we mentioned a moment ago, regardless of which meta-ethical position philosophers defend, they typically assume that people are naturally moral objectivists. Michael Smith, for example, wrote that most people

> seem to think moral questions have correct answers; that the correct answers are made correct by objective moral facts; that moral facts are wholly determined by circumstances and that, by engaging in moral conversation and argument, we can discover what these objective moral facts determined by the circumstances are. (Smith 1994, 6)

And Mackie (1977, 35) similarly argued that "objectivity...is ingrained in our language and thought," that "most people in making moral judgments implicitly claim, among other things, to be pointing to something objectively prescriptive" (which led to his claim that people's moral claims are generally false). In short, the claim that ordinary people are moral objectivists enjoys a surprising degree of support among moral philosophers, even those with disparate theoretical commitments (e.g., Blackburn 1984; Brink 1989; Mackie 1977; Shafer-Landau 2003; Smith 1994). But are all these philosophers correct—*are* people moral objectivists? The answer to this seems important, as many philosophers take it to be part of their job description to explain how ordinary folk objectivism fits into a broader theory about the nature and status of morality. Luckily, whether folk are moral objectivists is an empirical question—one that can be pursued using scientific methods. So, what does the research tell us?

PEOPLE AS OBJECTIVISTS? SUPPORTING EVIDENCE

There is an extensive body of empirical research that supports (if sometimes only indirectly) this philosophical assumption. People of all ages—whether children, adolescents, or adults—all have significantly stronger negative reactions toward people with dissimilar beliefs, values, and practices when they involve moral issues than when they involve other types of issues (Skitka, Bauman, and Sargis 2005; Skitka and Mullen 2002; Wainryb et al. 1998, 2001, 2004; Wright, Cullum, and Schwab 2008). For example, Wainryb et al. (2004; see also Wainryb and Ford, 1998) found that five-, seven-, and nine-year-olds were more intolerant toward dissimilar moral beliefs (e.g., whether or not hitting another child is okay) than other types of beliefs, such as taste/preference (e.g., whether or not chocolate ice cream is yucky), beliefs about the world (e.g., whether or not rain is wet), and more ambiguous beliefs (e.g., whether or not a dog is not playing with a toy because he is tired). Similarly, children, adolescents, and adults were more tolerant of beliefs that differed from their own when they were based on nonmoral "informational" assumptions than when they were based on moral differences. Specifically, children and adults reported it to be more acceptable for someone to believe that boys should be given more privileges than girls when this belief was allegedly based on the "informational" assumption that boys are generally smarter and more responsible than girls than on the moral assumption that boys should be treated nicer than girls (Wainryb et al. 1998; see also Wainryb 1993; Wainryb et al. 2001).

When asked to rate how supportive they were of four different types of diversity (*demographic*, *politico-moral*, *socio-sexual*, and *personal activities*), adults were by far the least supportive of politico-moral diversity, especially when it was encountered in an intimate context (Haidt et al. 2003; see also Rosenberg 2001). Similarly, the strength of a person's moral conviction (i.e., how morally important the issue was believed to be) predicted a variety of interpersonal outcomes including intolerance for different opinions and unwillingness to interact with dissimilar others, as well as the tendency to view them in an unfavorable light (Skitka et al. 2005; Skitka and Houston 2001; Skitka and Mullen, 2002). And adults

were also found to be the least willing to interact with, help, sit next to, and share resources with someone with dissimilar beliefs when that person differed from them with respect to his or her moral beliefs (Wright et al. 2008).

In general, people of all ages treat moral wrongs as more serious, less permissible, less response dependent, more severely punishable, and more universally generalizable than social/conventional wrongs (Turiel 1983, 1998; also Davidson et al. 1983; Goodwin and Darley 2008; Nichols 2004; Nichols and Folds-Bennett 2003; Nucci 1981; Smetana 1981, 1983; Smetana and Braeges 1990). And, perhaps most tellingly, they tend to view moral transgressions as wrong even in the absence of rules and/or in the presence of social sanctions (Smetana 1981, 1983; Stoddart and Turiel 1985; Turiel 1983).

PEOPLE AS OBJECTIVISTS? CONFLICTING EVIDENCE

Taken together, these studies strongly support the assumption that people are moral objectivists. After all, attributing to folk a belief in moral objectivity would seem the most straightforward way to explain the results. Yet more recent research has sought to explore people's meta-ethical commitments more directly, and the results paint a more complicated picture. For example, when asked specific questions about morality's grounding, Nichols (2004) found that even though many people gave objectivist responses (i.e., stating that if two people disagreed about a moral claim, one of them had to be wrong), a significant portion (Study 1: 42.5 percent; Study 3: 25.6 percent) of them did not, stating instead that there was no objective fact of the matter and that, even in the presence of disagreement, all parties could be right.

Goodwin and Darley (2008, 2010) found that while people, on average, tended to give more objective groundings to moral transgressions than they did to other transgressions (such as conventional or broadly aesthetic), they were nonetheless internally inconsistent with this objectivity. That is, when presented with a selection of moral transgressions, they gave objective groundings to only *some* of them (e.g., opening gunfire in a crowd, conscious discrimination, robbery, and cheating on an exam) while giving clearly relative groundings to other issues—issues that would seem, in at least some cases, to be highly charged and divisive (e.g., donating money to charity, abortion, assisted suicide, and stem cell research).

Beebe and Sakris (2010) found a similarly interesting variation in people's meta-ethical commitments—only this time driven by age. In their study, the young adults (seventeen to twenty-nine years) that they interviewed were significantly more likely to provide a relative grounding for a given set of moral issues than either a younger age group (fourteen to sixteen years) or an older age group (thirty to seventy-seven years), the oldest age group giving the strongest objective grounding of the three.

It is standard procedure in studies such as these for the experimenters *themselves* to classify the transgressions or disagreements they present as being "moral" in nature while others merely conventional (aesthetic, etc.). This leaves room to doubt whether the people who participated in the studies actually agreed with the experimenters and viewed the issues as "moral" as well. Recent studies on moral conviction and tolerance (Cullum and Wright 2010; Wright 2010; Wright et al. 2008) found that people of all ages disagree (both within and between age groups) about what qualifies as a moral issue. So, it could be that the reason why people gave relativist groundings for some of the moral transgressions they were presented with by Goodwin and Darley (2008, 2010) and Beebe and Sakris (2010) was that they did not actually consider them to be *moral* transgressions. In other words, people might actually be objectivists about morality, but simply disagree about whether particular transgressions or disagreements are moral in nature.

To test this, Wright et al. (in press) gave people the opportunity to identify which transgressions they viewed as moral and then measured their meta-ethical commitments for those issues specifically. Though the sorts of issues people identified as moral differed somewhat from Goodwin and Darley's (2008) original list (e.g., people did not view donating money to charity as a moral issue), nonetheless, people displayed the same sort of variation when grounding their self-identified moral issues. While people reported some of the moral issues they identified (e.g., discrimination and robbery) as being objectively grounded, at the same time they refused to ground others (e.g., abortion and assisted suicide) in the same way. Such results suggest that people's meta-ethical commitments do indeed vary: not only are some people more objectivist about morality than others but also people are more objectivist about *some* parts of morality than others.

Sarkissian et al. (2011) provide additional support against the view that people are consistently moral objectivists. In a series of studies, they asked people to consider other people's judgments about two different behaviors—first, a father killing his child because he finds him unattractive, and second, a man who tests the sharpness of a newly purchased knife by randomly stabbing a passerby on the street. People were told that one of their fellow classmates had judged these behaviors to be morally wrong, while another thought it was not morally wrong. When asked whether both these individuals could be correct in their judgments, people responded in predictably objectivist ways. That is, they denied that both individuals could be correct. But when one of the disagreeing individuals was depicted as being from a different cultural group—either a Mamilon (an Amazonian tribesman whose tribe had remained isolated from modern society) or a Pentar (an extraterrestrial being whose primary goal in life was to create pentagrams)—people began to give more relativist responses. That is, they were much less likely to say that someone had to be mistaken when one of the moral judgments came from a Mamilon, and even less so when it came from a Pentar. And this was true even when the study was altered in a variety of ways—for example, by telling people that the father killing his child was an American, and the stabber a fellow student. So, even when the person engaging in the behavior was from the same culture, people still accepted that someone from a different culture could view the behavior differently than they did and not be wrong.

META-ETHICAL PLURALISM?

While there is clear empirical evidence for moral objectivism in the "folk," there is also clear evidence for relativism. What the evidence suggests is that whether people express a relative or an objective meta-ethical commitment depends on many factors—for example, their age, the specific issue they are considering, and where a potential source of disagreement is coming from.

Does this mean that Mackie's error theory is at least partially correct—that at least *some* of the time people are making moral claims that refer to objective moral properties? Perhaps. But before we conclude that this is the case, it might be worth looking more closely at the circumstances under which people gave objectivist responses. For example, Sarkissian et al. (2011) found that people's responses looked objectivist when the sources of disagreement were both located within the same culture. But arguably, even a die-hard relativist (of the cultural variety) would acknowledge the fact that when two people from within a culture disagree about the moral status of an action, both of them can't be correct. After all, being members of the same culture, both people occupy the same moral framework or "vantage point" from which the moral status of the action is determined. Arguably, then, people's meta-ethical commitments could have been more consistently relativist than it first appeared.

In a similar vein, Goodwin and Darley (2010) hypothesized that one reason for people's apparent internal variation in their meta-ethical commitments (providing objectivist groundings for some issues and relativist groundings for others) could be that they were simply conflating *objectivity* with *perceived consensus*. That is, perhaps people were more likely to give a relative grounding for those issues whose rightness/wrongness they perceived as being contentious and up for debate. In support of this hypothesis, they found a very strong across-items correlation between objectivity and perceived consensus (r = .84).[3] And, if we consider the issues for which people have provided strong relativist groundings (i.e., abortion, assisted suicide, and stem cell research), these *do* appear to be issues that—unlike conscious racial discrimination or robbing a bank—people are currently debating about, often quite publicly.

If this is correct, then it may be that even when people are making objectivist claims, they are not (as Mackie believed) making reference to objective moral properties that exist independently from people's beliefs, values, and practices. Rather, they are making reference to the fact that certain issues (though not others) are generally viewed and treated similarly by people, even across cultural lines. In other words, they may be making reference to certain beliefs and values that they believe (perhaps mistakenly) unite people together—beliefs and values that many human beings share. This is still a relativist position, only one that considers it possible (at least in some instances) to have a moral vantage point that encompasses all of humanity.

A question remains: why have so many philosophers assumed that the folk are moral objectivists? Here, we end with some speculative thoughts. It's likely the case that ordinary folk are seldom asked to think of individuals or cultures very different from themselves when deliberating about moral issues. Instead, they usually think about moral issues within their own communities and discuss them with other individuals not very different from themselves. If this is the normal context for moral deliberation, it might make sense to think that moral issues generally admit of only one correct answer—that we will not find multiple correct answers to a single moral question.

IMPLICATIONS FOR META-ETHICS

Philosophers are undoubtedly correct in their commitment to make sense of ordinary moral practice. Morality is a distinctively human institution, and one cannot go about trying to understand it without taking actual moral practice into account. But it may turn out that there is simply no answer to the general question: are the folk objectivists about morality? It could be that folk are objectivists about some issues rather than others, or that some folk are objectivists and others are not. So perhaps philosophers should approach their task in a different way: rather than trying to make sense of folk objectivism, they could try to make sense of a practice where people's views are pluralistic, complex, and not entirely self-consistent. The research we've surveyed in this section would be very useful in making headway in this new task.

Notes

1. The story of how "wrongness" gets instantiated, whether there are moral facts or only nonmoral facts, and so on, varies between philosophers, and here we remain entirely neutral between views.
2. The word "relativism" is used in different ways in different disciplines. We are using it here to describe any view according to which moral claims can only be assessed relative to a particular culture or system of values (e.g., Harman 1975; Wong 1996, 2006).
3. Wright et al. (in press) also found a correlation between objectivity and perceived consensus, though not as strong ($r = .36$, $p < .001$).

References

Beebe, J., and D. Sakris. "Moral Objectivism across the Lifespan." Talk given at the *MERG Conference*, New York City, May 2010.

Blackburn, Simon. *Spreading the Word: Groundings in the Philosophy of Language.* New York: Oxford University Press, 1984.

Brink, David O. *Moral Realism and the Foundations of Ethics.* New York: Cambridge University Press, 1989.

Cullum, J., and J. C. Wright. *The Structural Differences between Moral vs. Non-Moral Beliefs.* Unpublished manuscript. 2010.

Davidson, P., E. Turiel, and A. Black. "The Effect of Stimulus Familiarity on the Use of Criteria and Justifications in Children's Social Reasoning." *British Journal of Developmental Psychology* 1, no. 1 (1983): 49–65.

Dreier, James. "Internalism and Speaker Relativism." *Ethics* 101, no. 1 (1990): 6–26.

Goodwin, G., and J. Darley. "The Psychology of Meta-Ethics: Exploring Objectivism." *Cognition* 106 (2008): 1339–1366.

Goodwin, G. P., and J. M. Darley. "The Perceived Objectivity of Ethical Beliefs: Psychological Findings and Implications for Public Policy." *Review of Philosophy and Psychology* 1 (2010): 1–28.

Haidt, J., E. Rosenberg, and H. Hom. "Differentiating Diversities: Moral Diversity Is Not Like Other Kinds." *Journal of Applied Social Psychology* 33 (2003): 1–36.

Harman, Gilbert. "Moral Relativism Defended." *Philosophical Review*, 84, no. 1 (1975): 3–22.

Nichols, S. "After Objectivity: An Empirical Study of Moral Judgment." *Philosophical Psychology* 17, no. 1 (2004): 5–28.

Nichols, S., and T. Folds-Bennett. "Are Children Moral Objectivists? Children's Judgments about Moral and Response-Dependent Properties." *Cognition* 90 (2003): B23–B32.

Nucci, L. "Conceptions of Personal Issues: A Domain Distinct from Moral or Societal Concepts." *Child Development* 52 (1981): 114–121.

Mackie, J. L. *Ethics: Inventing Right and Wrong.* New York: Penguin, 1977.

Pinillos, N. Ángel. *Knowledge and Moral Relativism.* Unpublished manuscript. Arizona State University, 2010.

Prinz, Jesse. *The Emotional Construction of Morals.* New York: Oxford University Press, 2007.

Railton, Peter. "Moral Realism." *The Philosophical Review*, 95, no. 2 (1986): 163–207.

Rosenberg, E. *Attitudes Towards Diversity.* Unpublished distinguished majors thesis, University of Virginia, 2001.

Sarkissian, H., J. Park, D. Tien, J. C. Wright, and J. Knobe. "Folk Moral Relativism." *Mind & Language.* Volume 26, Issue 4, 482–505, September 2011.

Shafer-Landau, Russ. *Moral Realism: A Defence.* New York: Oxford University Press, 2003.

Skitka, L. J., C. W. Bauman, and E. G. Sargis. "Moral Conviction: Another Contributor to Attitude Strength or Something More?" *Journal of Personality and Social Psychology* 88 (2005): 895–917.

Skitka, L. J., and D. A. Houston. "When Due Process Is of No Consequence: Moral Mandates and Presumed Defendant Guilt or Innocence." *Social Justice Research* 14 (2001): 305–326.

Skitka, L. J., and E. Mullen. "The Dark Side of Moral Conviction." *Analyses of Social Issues and Public Policy* 7 (2002): 35–41.

Smetana, J. G. "Preschool Children's Conceptions of Moral and Social Rules." *Child Development* 52 (1981): 1333–1336.

Smetana, J. G. "Social-Cognitive Development: Domain Distinctions and Coordinations." *Developmental Review* 3 (1983): 131–147.

Smetana, J. G., and J. Braeges. "The Development of Toddlers' Moral and Conventional Judgments." *Merrill-Palmer Quarterly* 36, no. 3 (1990): 329–346.

Smith, Michael. *The Moral Problem.* Oxford: Blackwell, 1994.

Stoddart, T., and E. Turiel. "Children's Concepts of Cross-Gender Activities." *Child Development* 56, no. 5 (1985): 1241–1253.

Turiel, E. *The Development of Social Knowledge: Morality and Conventions.* New York: Cambridge University Press, 1983.

Turiel, E. "The Development of Morality." In *Handbook of Child Psychology: Vol. 3, Social, Emotional, and Personality Development.* 5th ed., ed. N. Eisenberg, 701–778. New York: Wiley, 1998.

Wainryb, C. "The Application of Moral Judgments to Other Cultures: Relativism and Universality." *Child Development* 64 (1993): 924–933.

Wainryb, C., and S. Ford. "Young Children's Evaluations of Acts Based on Beliefs Different from Their Own." *Merrill-Palmer Quarterly* 44 (1998): 484–503.

Wainryb, C., L. Shaw, M. Langley, K. Cottam, and R. Lewis. "Children's Thinking about Diversity of Belief in the Early School Years: Judgments of Relativism, Tolerance, and Disagreeing Persons." *Child Development* 75, no. 3 (2004): 687–703.

Wainryb, C., L. Shaw, M. Laupa, and K. Smith. "Children's, Adolescents', and Young Adults' Thinking about Different Types of Disagreements." *Developmental Psychology* 37 (2001): 373–386.

Wainryb, C., L. Shaw, and C. Maianu. "Tolerance and Intolerance: Children's and Adolescents' Judgments of Dissenting Beliefs, Speech, Persons, and Conduct." *Child Development* 69, no. 6 (1998): 1541.

Wong, David B. *Moral Relativity.* Berkeley: University of California Press, 1984.

Wong, David B. "Pluralistic Relativism." *Midwest Studies in Philosophy* 20 (1996): 378–399.

Wong, David B. *Natural Moralities: A Defence of Pluralistic Relativism.* New York: Oxford University Press, 2006.

Wright, J.C. (in press). Children's and adolescents' tolerance for divergent beliefs: Exploring the cognitive and affective dimensions of moral conviction in our youth. *British Journal of Developmental Psychology.*

Wright, J. C., J. Cullum, and N. Schwab. "The Cognitive and Affective Dimensions of Moral Conviction: Implications for Tolerance and Interpersonal Behaviors." *Personality and Social Psychology Bulletin* 34, no. 11 (2008): 1461–1476.

Wright, J. C., P. T. Grandjean, and C. McWhite. "The Meta-Ethical Grounding of Our Moral Beliefs: Objectivism Revisited." *Philosophical Psychology.* 2012.

Study Questions

1. What is the difference between moral objectivism and relativism?

2. What do most philosophers assume is true about ordinary moral discourse? Reflecting on your own experiences, do you agree with this assumption? Why or why not?

3. What evidence do the authors provide in support of the view that people are moral objectivists? Do you think it is strong evidence? Why or why not?

4. What evidence do the authors provide against the view that people are moral objectivists? Do you think it is strong evidence? Why or why not?

CHAPTER 9

Normative Ethics

KEVIN TIMPE

ETHICS IS THE BRANCH OF PHILOSOPHY that deals with how we ought to live, where the "ought" is taken to have moral or normative—rather than merely pragmatic—force. Ethics is customarily broken down into three further areas: meta-ethics, normative ethics, and applied ethics. Meta-ethics, the subject of Chapter 8, focuses on the meaning of moral language and questions about the nature of moral claims. In contrast, normative ethics focuses on the content of morality. Different normative ethical theories attempt to answer the questions "How ought one live and act, morally speaking?" and "What are our moral obligations?" So normative ethics seeks to discover the general principles that underlie moral practice, and different theories in normative ethics will supply different principles. Finally, applied ethics attempts to take the results of normative ethical reflection and apply them to specific domains of human life and action, as indicated by the names of its various subfields: medical ethics, business ethics, computer ethics, engineering ethics, sexual ethics, and so on. The readings in this section focus almost exclusively on the normative aspects of ethics, though at times meta-ethical issues also arise.

Acting morally will often be easier if one first knows what the demands of morality are. Knowing the moral thing to do on a given occasion requires knowledge of two different things.[1] First, one must know the general moral rules or principles that govern behavior in the occasion at hand. Second, one must also know contingent nonmoral facts about the occasion so that one knows how to properly apply those general moral rules. To introduce an example to which I will return later, suppose that one is out shopping

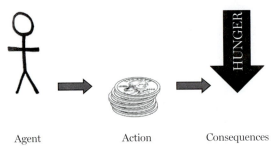

FIGURE 9.1 Elements of normative theories

and passes—as I used to often when I lived in southern California—a person holding a cardboard sign that reads "Hungry, food or money please. God Bless." What should one do? The answer will depend both on the general moral rules or principles and on contingent facts about the situation. In order to know if a particular act of feeding a person is morally good, one would need to know both a necessary moral truth (for instance, that all acts of feeding the hungry are morally good) and a contingent nonmoral truth (for instance, that this person is hungry).[2] It is the first of these two kinds of knowledge that different normative theories aim to provide; as we shall see in the first three readings, there is considerable disagreement about the fundamental moral principles. We now turn to leading theories about the nature of these necessary moral principles.

There is a plethora of competing normative ethical theories. For present purposes, we shall restrict our focus to three of the historically most influential views. To situate these views with respect to one another, it may be helpful to consider three elements that are involved in a moral action: the agent, the action done, and the consequences of that action. So, let us suppose that the person asking for money really is hungry and will use the money that you give to her, if you do so, to buy needed nourishment. Furthermore, suppose that you have money to spare, and thus will not be made worse off to any significant degree by giving her the money. Let us also assume that your giving her the money is the morally right thing to do. But one can give differing accounts of *why* it is the morally right thing to do. These three elements are shown in Figure 9.1.

Each of the three leading families of normative ethics views—virtue theory, deontology, and consequentialism—focuses primarily on one of these three disparate elements. This is not to say that the other two elements do not matter; but it is a helpful heuristic tool to begin understanding the difference between the three families of views by seeing which of the three elements is primary in explaining the morality of the action. Whereas virtue theory focuses primarily on the agent, deontology focuses primarily on the action, and consequentialism focuses primarily—not surprisingly, given the name—on the consequences.

Let us begin with *virtue ethics*. This approach to normative ethics has a distinguished philosophical pedigree, going back to Plato's *Republic* and Aristotle's *Nicomachean Ethics*.[3] Despite some fundamental disagreements about the nature of virtue, both Plato and Aristotle thought that the morally good life is one that exemplifies various forms of *aretē* (ἀρετή), which is translated as either "excellence" or, via the Latin *virtus*, "virtue." As mentioned earlier, virtue ethics focuses on moral *agents* rather than their actions or the consequences of those actions. According to virtue ethicists, having the *virtues* makes agents objectively better off; that is, it is good for the agent to be virtuous. This accords with the etymology of the term insofar as the virtuous agent will be the excellent agent, morally speaking. To see why this is, one must first see what the goal or end is at which ethics aims.

According to Aristotle, the virtue ethicist we'll focus on in this chapter, all actions are teleological in nature; that is, they aim at accomplishing a *telos* or goal: "Every art and every inquiry, and similarly every action and pursuit, is thought to aim at some good; and for this reason the good has rightly been declared to be that at which all things aim."[4] Since ethics is the normative discipline that governs human actions, one must then ask what the *telos* or goal of our actions is. Like Plato before him, Aristotle thinks it uncontroversial that the highest goal of human actions is happiness: "For practically every person individually and for everyone in common there is a goal that all aim at in whatever they choose and avoid; and this, to speak in summary form, is happiness and its parts."[5] What is controversial, he thinks, is what the nature of happiness consists in. While neither Plato nor Aristotle think that happiness can be reduced to virtue alone, they both think that popular accounts of happiness that understand it primarily as desire satisfaction or wealth are critically incomplete. *Eudaimonia*, to use the Greek term that is translated as happiness, has a different connotation than does the standard use of happiness in English. Aristotle thinks that *eudaimonia* is not simply a subjective psychological state characterized by positive feelings or affections. It is, rather, an objective state of "living and doing well."[6] To live well one must be virtuous, even if other goods—such as friends, health, and some degree of wealth—are also needed.

> Since happiness is an activity of the soul in accordance with perfect virtue, we must consider the nature of virtue; for perhaps we shall thus see better the nature of happiness.[7]

Aristotle distinguishes two kinds of virtue: intellectual virtues and moral virtues. Intellectual virtues, such as prudence and wisdom, are achieved through instruction and teaching. But the moral virtues, or excellences of character, can only be acquired by habituation. (Here, Aristotle makes the etymological link between moral virtue, ἠθική, and habit, ἔθος.) We become just by doing just actions; we become brave by doing brave deeds.

Aristotle's phrase for a moral virtue is *ēthikē aretē*, literally "virtue of character." These excellences of character are dispositions to act and feel in certain ways, which make a person good and thus capable of achieving happiness understood as *eudaimonia*. Aristotle thought a moral disposition was virtuous when it was in proper proportion, which he described as a mean between two extremes:

> We must, however, not only describe virtue as a state of character, but also say what sort of state it is.... Virtue, then is a state of character concerned with choice, lying in a mean,

> i.e., the mean relative to us, this being determined by a rational principle, and by that principle by which the man of practical wisdom would determine it. Now it is a mean between two vices, that which depends on excess and that which depends on defect; and again it is a mean because the vices respectively fall short of or exceed what is right in both passions and actions, while virtue both finds and chooses that which is intermediate.[8]

Most virtues are a mean between two vices, one of excess and one of deficiency. For example, courage is the disposition to feel the proper amount of fear called for by a particular situation. The vice of foolhardiness is being disposed to feel too little fear, while the vice of cowardliness is the disposition to feel too much fear. Furthermore, insofar as the excellences of character include a person's emotions and feelings, and not just her actions, there is a distinction between acting virtuously and doing a virtuous action. Merely doing the right action is not sufficient to have the moral excellences. One must also be the right sort of individual or have the right sort of character. This is why, for Aristotle, ethics is primarily about the quality of the agent, and not primarily about the action or its consequences.

While versions of the other two approaches often do incorporate the virtues (both Kant and Mill, to be discussed later, relate the moral life to virtues in parts of their writings), what is distinctive of virtue ethics is that it holds that virtue is the most basic or foundational element of morality. In contrast, Mill, for example, thinks the virtues are important for morality insofar as the possession of the virtues increases utility (more about what this is shortly). And Kant thinks that we have an obligation to develop the virtues insofar as we would want all rational agents to do so as well.

The second general family of views is *deontology*. Etymologically derived from the Greek root *déon*, which means that "which is binding" or one's "duty," deontological approaches to ethics hold that morality is based on universal laws that are binding on all moral agents. The most famous deontological view, and the one that we'll focus on in this chapter, is that by Immanuel Kant. Kant labels that foundational universal binding moral law the *categorical imperative*, and he thinks that it is knowable by all rational agents. Kant expresses the categorical imperative in a number of ways which he takes to be coextensive, if not identical. The first of these is as follows:

> Act only in accordance with that maxim through which you can at the same time will that it should become a universal law.[9]

While the basic idea here is fairly intuitive, what he means by a categorical imperative requires some unpacking. First, by imperative, Kant means a kind of command. In this case, Kant thinks that the command is given by reason itself. Kant then goes on to differentiate two different kinds of commands: hypothetical and categorical. A hypothetical imperative is an imperative that commands what you should do, but only if (hypothetically, if you will) you want to achieve a certain end. For example, if you will to attend medical school, you must take the MCAT exam. In contrast, a categorical imperative is one that obligates all rational agents, and not just those with a particular end. An example here is "do not lie." Kant thinks that all moral agents have the obligation not to lie, and we can see why by looking at the categorical imperative.

The first step, according to Kant, in evaluating the morality of an action is to formulate the *maxim* behind the action. Maxims have the following form:

In circumstance *C*, I will to do action *A* in order to bring about end *E*.

Kant thinks that every intentional action has a maxim supporting it, even if that maxim is not consciously formulated by the agent. The second step in evaluating an action is to try and universalize it so that all moral agents would follow it. One then needs to ask the following two questions about the universalized maxim:

(i) Is it possible for this maxim to be universalized; that is, could all rational agents act according to this maxim?

(ii) Would I want this maxim to be universalized; that is, would I will to live in a world where all rational agents would act according to this maxim?

If, in response to (i), the maxim cannot be universalized, then the action in question is morally impermissible and one has a duty not to perform it. If, on the other hand, the maxim could be universalized but one wouldn't want it to be, per question (ii), then one also has a duty to not perform the action under consideration.

As mentioned previously, Kant formulates the categorical imperative in a number of different ways. Another formulation is as follows:

So act that you use humanity, whether in your own person or in the person of any other, always at the same time as an end, never merely as a means.[10]

The reason that Kant thinks this way of putting the categorical imperative is identical with the previous is as follows. First, note that Kant is *not* saying that we can never use other rational agents as means. Rather, he's saying that we should never treat others *merely* as means. For if we treated others merely as means, then we must be willing, per the first formulation of the categorical imperative, for others to treat us merely as means to their own ends. Insofar as we ourselves want to be treated with respect and not merely as means to an end, we should not treat others in that manner.

So for Kant, only those actions that satisfy the categorical imperative are morally good, and it is one's duty to perform those actions. But it is not just enough to do the morally right action. As seen earlier, Kant thinks that the maxim one is adopting, and thus the end that one is attempting to achieve, is also crucial. He thinks that one must act not only "*in accord with* duty" but also "*from* duty." That is, one must be doing the action in question because it is the morally right thing to do, and not for some other reason. For example, if I only refrain from lying to my wife because I'm afraid of getting caught, then Kant would say I'm acting in accord with duty but not from duty. Instead, the reason I should refrain from lying to my wife is that one has a duty not to lie. As Kant puts it, "in the case of what it is to be morally good it is not enough that it *conform* with the moral law, but it must also be done *for the sake of the law*."[11] So, in saying that deontological views focus primarily on the action, this should be understood, in the case of Kant at least, to include the intention behind that action.

The third general family of views is *consequentialism*. Like the other two strands of normative ethics, there is a significant degree of diversity within consequentialism. Most generally, however, consequentialism holds that of all the actions available to an agent at a given time, the morally right action to perform is the one that would produce the best overall consequences. (If there is no single best action because a number of available actions would produce equally good consequences, then any of those actions would be morally right for the agent to perform at that time.)

While versions of consequentialism can be found earlier in philosophy, it became particularly popular in the eighteenth century when a particular form of consequentialism called *utilitarianism* burst onto the scene with the publication of Jeremy Bentham's *An Introduction to the Principles of Morals and Legislation*. In the first chapter of this work, titled "On the Principle of Utility," Bentham begins by making the connection between morality, on the one hand, and pleasure and pain on the other:

> The principle of utility is the foundation of the present work: it will be proper therefore at the outset to give an explicit and determinate account of what is meant by it. By the principle of utility is meant that principle which approves or disapproves of every action whatsoever, according to the tendency which it appears to have to augment or diminish the happiness of the party whose interest is in question: or, what is the same thing in other words, to promote or to oppose that happiness. . . . By utility is meant that property in any object, whereby it tends to produce benefit, advantage, pleasure, good, or happiness, (all this in the present case come to the same thing) or (what comes again to the same thing) to prevent the happening of mischief, pain, evil, or unhappiness to the party whose interest is considered.[12]

According to Bentham, then, it is the pleasure or pain caused by our actions that is the relevant consequence that matters for morality. One implication of this is that there are no intrinsically good or bad actions, as proponents of both virtue ethics and deontology hold. A second implication is that we cannot privilege our own happiness, as there is no difference between a unit of my own pleasure and another's.

The principle of utility is, for Bentham, a self-evident first principle from which the rest of ethics can be deduced as a logical consequence. How so? That is, how can we use this principle to tell us whether we should perform a particular action or not? How do we go about measuring the utility that our actions would cause? Bentham lists seven factors to consider in evaluating a pleasure or pain:

1. Its *intensity*.
2. Its *duration*.
3. Its *certainty* or *uncertainty*.
4. Its *propinquity* or *remoteness* [in time] . . .
5. Its *fecundity*, or the chance it has of being followed by sensations of the *same* kind. . . .
6. Its *purity*, or the chance it has of *not* being followed by sensations of the *opposite* kind. . . .
7. Its *extent*; that is, the number of persons to whom it *extends*; or (in other words) who are affected by it.[13]

Using these seven factors for any particular act, the hedonic calculus will tell us the quantity of pleasure and pain each potential action would cause. The action that brings about the greatest quantity is the morally right and obligatory action to perform.

A friend of Bentham's, James Mill, was so impressed with Bentham's ideas on ethics and other topics that he "carefully educated and prepared [his eldest son] to become the transmitter and torch bearer of Benthamite Utilitarianism."[14] That son,

John Stuart Mill, would become a leading philosophical and political reformer in the nineteenth century in England. Like Bentham, Mill thought that the principle of utility was the foundational principle of all morality, which alone grounds all of ethics. However, Mill also thought there was something crucially lacking in Bentham's account of ethics, with the result that his account of utilitarianism was incomplete, a fault Mill tried to correct in his own form of utilitarianism. In addition to the myriad factors regarding pains and pleasures that Bentham noted, Mill thought there were qualitatively different pleasures:

> It is quite compatible with the principle of utility to recognise the fact, that some kinds of pleasure are more desirable and more valuable than others. It would be absurd that while, in estimating all other things, quality is considered as well as quantity, the estimation of pleasures should be supposed to depend on quantity alone.[15]

It is also common to interpret Bentham as an *act utilitarian*, where the hedonic calculus is performed on each individual action (e.g., would this particular act of lying bring about better consequences than not lying?). Though this is controversial, many scholars think that Mill was instead a *rule utilitarian*, where the hedonic calculus is performed on moral rules (e.g., does lying in general bring about better consequences than not lying?) and then individual actions are evaluated by those rules. Many subsequent utilitarians have seen Mill's broadening of Bentham's approach to be vital.

In recent years, a number of scholars have sought to bring empirical work to bear on normative ethics. One leading motivation behind this new approach is what Owen Flanagan has called "psychological realism": "roughly, the idea that ethical reflection should be predicated on a moral psychology bearing a recognizable resemblance to actual human psychologies."[16] In Reading 9.4, John Doris uses a plethora of data from psychology to argue that virtue ethics rests on a faulty conception of the virtues. As Doris puts it in a more recent book on the same theme:

> Like many others, I find the lore of virtue deeply compelling, yet I cannot help noticing that much of this lore rests on psychological theory that is some 2,500 years old. A theory is not bad simply because it is old, but in this case developments of more recent vintage suggest that the old ideas are in trouble. In particular, modern experimental psychology has discovered that circumstance has surprisingly more to do with how people behave than traditional images of character and virtue allow.[17]

According to Doris and other such scholars, most individuals overestimate the role of dispositional factors such as moral character in explaining an individual's behavior and underestimate the role the situation plays in explaining an agent's behavior. Another critic of traditional virtue ethics, Gilbert Harman, expresses this idea as follows:

> In trying to characterize and explain a distinctive action, ordinary thinking tends to hypothesize a corresponding distinctive characteristic of the agent and tends to overlook the relevant details of the agent's perceived situation.... Ordinary attributions of character traits to people are often deeply misguided and it may even be the case that there...[are] no ordinary traits of the sort people think there are.[18]

Philosophers such as Doris and Harman have used this work in the social sciences to develop an alternative approach to moral character, commonly known as "situationism," which can be summarized in the following claims:

1. **Nonrobustness Claim**: moral character traits are not robust—that is, they are not consistent across a wide spectrum of trait-relevant situations. Whatever moral character traits an individual has are situation specific.
2. **Consistency Claim**: while a person's moral character traits are relatively stable over time, this should be understood as consistency of situation-specific traits, rather than robust traits.
3. **Fragmentation Claim**: a person's moral character traits do not have the evaluative integrity suggested by the Integrity Claim. There may be considerable disunity in a person's moral character among her situation-specific character traits.

Thus, situationism provides a very different way of understanding moral character than does virtue ethics. According to situationists, the empirical evidence favors their view of moral character over views like Aristotle's.

Other scholars are bringing empirical work to bear on normative ethics in other directions. Joshua Greene, among others, has argued that we can learn important lessons about ethics not just via social psychology, but from the natural sciences as well:

> Whereas I am sceptical of attempts to derive moral principles from scientific facts, I agree with the proponents of naturalized ethics that scientific facts can have profound moral implications, and that moral philosophers have paid too little attention to relevant work in the natural sciences.[19]

As mentioned in the introduction to this volume, much of philosophy traditionally appeals to intuitions about particular cases or thought experiments, and ethics is no different. A classical thought experiment used to differentiate deontological and consequentialist judgments is "the trolley problem."

> **The Trolley Problem:** An out-of-control trolley is running down a section of track. In its path are five workers who are unaware of the trolley and, if nothing is done, will be killed by it. Between the trolley and the five workers is a switch that would divert the trolley onto another section of track, saving the five workers. However, on this second section of track is a single worker who will be killed by the trolley if the switch is flipped. You are standing next to the switch. Should you flip it or do nothing?[20]

The following permutation of the trolley problem, often referred to as "the footbridge case," can be used to differentiate deontological and consequentialist reasoning:

> **Footbridge:** You are standing on a footbridge over the trolley track. You can see a trolley hurtling down the track, out of control. You turn around to see where the trolley is headed, and there are five workmen on the track where it exits from under the footbridge. What to do? Being an expert on trolleys, you know of one certain way to stop an out-of-control trolley: Drop a really heavy weight in its path. But where to find one? It just so happens that standing next to you on the footbridge is a fat man, a really fat man. He is leaning over the railing, watching the trolley; all you have to do is to give him a little shove, and over the railing he will go, onto the track in the path of the trolley. Would it be permissible for you to do this?[21]

Consequentialists typically answer this question regarding the fat man case in the affirmative, insofar as one dead person involves better consequences than five dead people.

Deontologists, on the other hand, typically answer the question in the negative, insofar as pushing the fat man over the railing to stop the trolley would involve using him merely as a means to an end, namely, saving the five workers.

By putting people in functional magnetic resonance imaging (fMRI) machines and giving them traditional thought experiments such as the trolley problem and the footbridge case, Greene has provided evidence that moral judgments are the products of at least two different neural systems in the brain, those associated with higher cognitive function such as executive control and those associated with emotion-related processes.

> Deontological judgments tend to be driven by emotional responses, and…deontological philosophy, rather than being grounded in moral *reasoning*, is to a large extent an exercise in moral *rationalization*. This is in contrast to consequentialism, which…arises from rather different psychological processes, ones that are more "cognitive," and more likely to involve genuine moral reasoning.[22]

Furthermore, in his studies, even those people who were willing to push the fat man off the footbridge took longer to respond than did those who decided not to. This suggests that these individuals had the same initial emotional reaction against doing so, but that they reasoned themselves out of it. Beyond these descriptive conclusions, Greene also suggests that we can draw some normative implications from the empirical evidence. For once we know that deontological judgments are largely, if not entirely, the result of emotional responses to particular cases, then we have reason, Greene thinks, for discounting the force of those judgments in favor of more rational consequentialist ones. Neuroscience, he thinks, can help us make ethical headway.

Notes

1. In what follows, I intend the terms "moral" and "ethical," as well as their cognates, to be synonymous, although they are sometimes taken to have different meanings.
2. See, for instance, the discussion in Richard Swinburne, "God Makes the Difference to Morality," in *The Psychology of Character and Virtue*, ed. Craig Steven Titus (Washington, DC: Catholic University Press of America, 2009), 121–124.
3. Plato, *Republic*, 2nd ed., trans. G. M. A. Grube (Indianapolis: Hackett, 1992), and Aristotle, *Nicomachean Ethics*, trans. David Ross (Oxford: Oxford University Press, 1925).
4. Aristotle, *Nicomachean Ethics*, I.1.
5. Aristotle, *Rhetoric*, trans. George A. Kennedy (Oxford: Oxford University Press, 2006), 1360b4–7.
6. Aristotle, *Nicomachean Ethics*, I.4.
7. Ibid., I.13.
8. Ibid., II.6.
9. Immanuel Kant, "Groundwork for the Metaphysics of Morals," in *Practical Philosophy*, trans. and ed. Mary J. Gregor (Cambridge: Cambridge University Press, 1996), 30.
10. Ibid., 80.
11. Ibid., 45.
12. Jeremy Bentham, "An Introduction to the Principles of Morals and Legislation," in *Utilitarianism and On Liberty*, ed. Mary Warnock (Malden, MA: Blackwell, 2003), 18.

13. Ibid., 41f.
14. Wendy Donner, "Mill's Utilitarianism," in *The Cambridge Companion to Mill*, ed. John Skorupski (Cambridge: Cambridge University Press, 1998), 255.
15. John Stuart Mill, "Utilitarianism," in *Utilitarianism and On Liberty*, ed. Mary Warnock (Malden, MA: Blackwell, 2003), 187.
16. John Doris, *Lack of Character: Personality and Moral Behavior* (Cambridge: Cambridge University Press, 2002), 112. Doris here is building off earlier work by Owen Flanagan, *Varieties of Moral Personality* (Cambridge, MA: Harvard University Press, 1991), 32.
17. John Doris, *Lack of Character: Personality and Moral Behavior* (Cambridge: Cambridge University Press, 2002), ix.
18. Gilbert Harman, "Moral Psychology Meets Social Psychology: Virtue Ethics and the Fundamental Attribution Error," *Proceedings of the Aristotelian Society* 99 (1999): 315f.
19. Joshua Greene, (2003) "From Neural 'Is' to Moral 'Ought': What Are the Implications of Neuroscientific Moral Psychology?" *Nature Reviews Neuroscience 4*, 847.
20. The trolley problem is first introduced by Philippa Foot, "The Problem of Abortion and the Doctrine of the Double Effect," in *Virtues and Vices* (Oxford: Basil Blackwell, 1978), 23; it has subsequently been the subject of countless articles. See, for instance, Margary Bedford Naylor, "The Moral of the Trolley Problems," *Philosophy and Phenomenological Research* 48 (1988): 711–722.
21. Judith Jarvis Thomson, *Rights, Restitution, and Risk* (Cambridge, MA: Harvard University Press, 1986), 109.
22. Joshua Greene, "The Secret Joke of Kant's Soul," in *Moral Psychology, Vol. 3: The Neuroscience of Morality: Emotion, Disease, and Development*, ed. Walter Sinnott-Armstrong (Cambridge, MA: MIT Press, 2007), 36.

References

Aristotle. *Nicomachean Ethics*, trans. David Ross. Oxford: Oxford University Press, 1925.

Aristotle. *On Rhetoric*, trans. George A. Kennedy. Oxford: Oxford University Press, 2006.

Donner, Wendy. "Mill's Utilitarianism." In *The Cambridge Companion to Mill,* ed. John Skorupski. Cambridge: Cambridge University Press, 1998.

Doris, John. *Lack of Character: Personality and Moral Behavior*. Cambridge: Cambridge University Press, 2002.

Flanagan, Owen. *Varieties of Moral Personality*. Cambridge, MA: Harvard University Press, 1991.

Foot, Philippa. "The Problem of Abortion and the Doctrine of the Double Effect." In *Virtues and Vices*. Oxford: Basil Blackwell, 1978.

Harman, Gilbert. "Moral Psychology Meets Social Psychology: Virtue Ethics and the Fundamental Attribution Error." *Proceedings of the Aristotelian Society* 99 (1999): 315–331.

Greene, Joshua. "The Secret Joke of Kant's Soul." In *Moral Psychology, Vol. 3: The Neuroscience of Morality: Emotion, Disease, and Development,* ed. Walter Sinnott-Armstrong. Cambridge, MA: MIT Press, 2007.

Kant, Immanuel. "Groundwork for the Metaphysics of Morals." In *Practical Philosophy*, trans. and ed. Mary J. Gregor. Cambridge: Cambridge University Press, 1996.

Naylor, Margary Bedford. "The Moral of the Trolley Problems." *Philosophy and Phenomenological Research* 48 (1988): 711–722.

Plato. *Republic*. 2nd ed., trans. G. M. A. Grube. Indianapolis: Hackett, 1992.

Swinburne, Richard. "God Makes the Difference to Morality." In *The Psychology of Character and Virtue*, ed. Craig Steven Titus. Washington, DC: Catholic University of America Press, 2009.

Thomson, Judith Jarvis. *Rights, Restitution, and Risk*. Cambridge, MA: Harvard University Press, 1986.

Warnock, Mary, ed. *Utilitarianism and On Liberty*. Malden, MA: Blackwell, 2003.

Suggestions for Further Reading

Adams, Robert Merrihew. *A Theory of Virtue: Excellence in Being for the Good*. Oxford: Oxford University Press, 2006.

Appah, Kwame. *Experiments in Ethics*. Cambridge, MA: Harvard University Press, 2010.

Berker, Selim. "The Normative Insignificance of Neuroscience." *Philosophy and Public Affairs*, 37, no. 4 (2009): 293–329.

Blackburn, Simon. *Ethics: A Very Short Introduction*. Oxford: Oxford University Press, 2009.

Crisp, Roger, and Michael Slote, eds. *Virtue Ethics*. Oxford: Oxford University Press, 1997.

Harman, Gilbert. *The Nature of Morality*. Oxford: Oxford University Press, 1977.

Kahane, Guy, and Nicholas Shackel. "Do Abnormal Responses Show Utilitarian Bias?" *Nature* 452, no. 7185 (March 2008): E5.

Kamtekar, Rachana. "Situationism and Virtue Ethics on the Content of Our Character." *Ethics* 114 (2004): 548–491.

MacKinnon, Barbara. *Ethics: Theory and Contemporary Issues*. 6th ed. Belmont, CA: Wadsworth Publishing, 2008.

Peterson, Thomas, and Jesper Ryberg, eds. *Normative Ethics: 5 Questions*. Copenhagen, Denmark: Automatic Press, 2007.

Ross, W. D. *The Right and the Good*. 2nd ed., ed. Philip Stratton-Lake. Oxford: Oxford University Press, 2003.

Singer, Peter, ed. *A Companion to Ethics*. Oxford: Blackwell, 1991.

Tiberius, Valerie. *The Reflective Life: Living Wisely With Our Limits*. New York: Oxford University Press, 2010.

9.1   Nicomachean Ethics

 ARISTOTLE

ARISTOTLE (384–322 BCE) was an ancient Greek philosopher, a student of Plato's at the Academy, and the tutor of Alexander the Great. He wrote on a wide range of topics, including ethics, politics, rhetoric, metaphysics, biology, and meteorology. Aristotle gives one of the classical presentations of virtue ethics in his *Nicomachean Ethics*, part of which is produced here. He begins by arguing that the final end, or ultimate goal, that all human action aims at is happiness—*eudaimonia*—which is desired for its own sake. By happiness, Aristotle means not just having positive psychological states, but an objective state of "living and doing well." Crucial to living and doing well are the virtues, which are perfections of the soul. Becoming virtuous, for Aristotle, involves both learning and developing our moral characters via training, a process referred to as habituation. At the heart of Aristotle's understanding of moral virtue is the doctrine of the mean, according to which a virtue is in between two vices. The virtues are rationally informed dispositions to act, think, or feel in ways that are appropriate.

BOOK I

1. Every art and every inquiry, and similarly every action and pursuit, is thought to aim at some good; and for this reason the good has rightly been declared to be that at which all things aim. But a certain difference is found among ends; some are activities, others are products apart from the activities that produce them. Where there are ends apart from the actions, it is the nature of the products to be better than the activities. Now, as there are many actions, arts, and sciences, their ends also are many; the end of the medical art is health, that of shipbuilding a vessel, that of strategy victory, that of economics wealth. But where such arts fall under a single capacity—as bridle-making and the other arts concerned with the equipment of horses fall under the art of riding, and this and every military action under strategy, in the same way other arts fall under yet

others—in all of these the ends of the master arts are to be preferred to all the subordinate ends; for it is for the sake of the former that the latter are pursued. It makes no difference whether the activities themselves are the ends of the actions, or something else apart from the activities, as in the case of the sciences just mentioned.

2. If, then, there is some end of the things we do, which we desire for its own sake (everything else being desired for the sake of this), and if we do not choose everything for the sake of something else (for at that rate the process would go on to infinity, so that our desire would be empty and vain), clearly this must be the good and the chief good. Will not the knowledge of it, then, have a great influence on life? Shall we not, like archers who have a mark to aim at, be more likely to hit upon what is right? If so, we must try, in outline at least, to determine what it is, and of which of the sciences or capacities it is

Aristotle, *Nicomachean Ethics*, Book 1, translated by David Ross (1980). By permission of Oxford University Press.

the object. It would seem to belong to the most authoritative art and that which is most truly the master art. And politics appears to be of this nature; [...] For even if the end is the same for a single man and for a state, that of the state seems at all events something greater and more complete whether to attain or to preserve; though it is worth while to attain the end merely for one man, it is finer and more godlike to attain it for a nation or for city-states. These, then, are the ends at which our inquiry aims, since it is political science, in one sense of that term. [...]

7. Let us again return to the good we are seeking, and ask what it can be. It seems different in different actions and arts; it is different in medicine, in strategy, and in the other arts likewise. What then is the good of each? Surely that for whose sake everything else is done. In medicine this is health, in strategy victory, in architecture a house, in any other sphere something else, and in every action and pursuit the end; for it is for the sake of this that all men do whatever else they do. Therefore, if there is an end for all that we do, this will be the good achievable by action, and if there are more than one, these will be the goods achievable by action.

So the argument has by a different course reached the same point; but we must try to state this even more clearly. Since there are evidently more than one end, and we choose some of these (e.g. wealth, flutes, and in general instruments) for the sake of something else, clearly not all ends are final ends; but the chief good is evidently something final. Therefore, if there is only one final end, this will be what we are seeking, and if there are more than one, the most final of these will be what we are seeking. Now we call that which is in itself worthy of pursuit more final than that which is worthy of pursuit for the sake of something else, and that which is never desirable for the sake of something else more final than the things that are desirable both in themselves and for the sake of that other thing, and therefore we call final without qualification that which is always desirable in itself and never for the sake of something else.

Now such a thing happiness, above all else, is held to be; for this we choose always for itself and never for the sake of something else, but honour, pleasure, reason, and every virtue we choose indeed for themselves (for if nothing resulted from them we should still choose each of them), but we choose them also for the sake of happiness, judging that through them we shall be happy. Happiness, on the other hand, no one chooses for the sake of these, nor, in general, for anything other than itself.

From the point of view of self-sufficiency the same result seems to follow; for the final good is thought to be self-sufficient. [...] The self-sufficient we now define as that which when isolated makes life desirable and lacking in nothing; and such we think happiness to be; and further we think it most desirable of all things, not a thing counted as one good thing among others—if it were so counted it would clearly be made more desirable by the addition of even the least of goods; for that which is added becomes an excess of goods, and of goods the greater is always more desirable. Happiness, then, is something final and self-sufficient, and is the end of action. [...]

13. Since happiness is an activity of soul in accordance with perfect virtue, we must consider the nature of virtue; for perhaps we shall thus see better the nature of happiness. The true student of politics, too, is thought to have studied virtue above all things; for he wishes to make his fellow citizens good and obedient to the laws. As an example of this we have the lawgivers of the Cretans and the Spartans, and any others of the kind that there may have been. And if this inquiry belongs to political science, clearly the pursuit of it will be in accordance with our original plan. But clearly the virtue we must study is human virtue; for the good we were seeking was human good and the happiness human happiness. By human virtue we mean not that of the body but that of the soul; and happiness also we call an activity of soul. But if this is so, clearly the student of politics must know somehow the facts about the soul, as the man who is to heal the

eyes must know about the whole body also; and all the more since political science is more prized and better than medical; but even among doctors the best educated spend much labour on acquiring knowledge of the body. The student of politics, then, must study the soul, and must study it with these objects in view, and do so just to the extent which is sufficient for the questions we are discussing; for further precision would perhaps involve more labour than our purposes require.

Some things are said about it, adequately enough, even in the discussions outside our school, and we must use these; e.g. that one element in the soul is irrational and one has a rational principle. [...]

Of the irrational element one division seems to be widely distributed, and vegetative in its nature, I mean that which causes nutrition and growth; for it is this kind of power of the soul that one must assign to all nurslings and to embryos, and this same power to full-grown creatures; this is more reasonable than to assign some different power to them. Now the excellence of this seems to be common to all species and not specifically human; [...] however; let us leave the nutritive faculty alone, since it has by its nature no share in human excellence.

There seems to be also another irrational element in the soul—one which in a sense, however, shares in a rational principle. For we praise the rational principle of the continent man and of the incontinent, and the part of their soul that has such a principle, since it urges them aright and towards the best objects; but there is found in them also another natural element beside the rational principle, which fights against and resists that principle. For exactly as paralysed limbs, when we intend to move them to the right, turn on the contrary to the left, so is it with the soul; the impulses of incontinent people move in contrary directions. But while in the body we see that which moves astray, in the soul we do not. No doubt, however, we must none the less suppose that in the soul too there is something beside the rational principle, resisting and opposing it. In

what sense it is distinct from the other elements does not concern us. Now even this seems to have a share in a rational principle, as we said; at any rate in the continent man it obeys the rational principle—and presumably in the temperate and brave man it is still more obedient; for in him it speaks, on all matters, with the same voice as the rational principle.

Therefore the irrational element also appears to be twofold. For the vegetative element in no way shares in a rational principle, but the appetitive and in general the desiring element in a sense shares in it, in so far as it listens to and obeys it; this is the sense in which we speak of "taking account" of one's father or one's friends, not that in which we speak of "accounting" for a mathematical property. That the irrational element is in some sense persuaded by a rational principle is indicated also by the giving of advice and by all reproof and exhortation. And if this element also must be said to have a rational principle, that which has a rational principle (as well as that which has not) will be twofold, one subdivision having it in the strict sense and in itself, and the other having a tendency to obey as one does one's father.

Virtue too is distinguished into kinds in accordance with this difference; for we say that some of the virtues are intellectual and others moral, philosophic wisdom and understanding and practical wisdom being intellectual, liberality and temperance moral. For in speaking about a man's character we do not say that he is wise or has understanding, but that he is good-tempered or temperate; yet we praise the wise man also with respect to his state of mind; and of states of mind we call those which merit praise virtues.

BOOK II

1. VIRTUE, then, being of two kinds, intellectual and moral, intellectual virtue in the main owes both its birth and its growth to teaching (for which reason it requires experience and time),

while moral virtue comes about as a result of habit, whence also its name (ἠθική) is one that is formed by a slight variation from the word ἔθος (habit). From this it is also plain that none of the moral virtues arises in us by nature; for nothing that exists by nature can form a habit contrary to its nature. For instance the stone which by nature moves downwards cannot be habituated to move upwards, not even if one tries to train it by throwing it up ten thousand times; nor can fire be habituated to move downwards, nor can anything else that by nature behaves in one way be trained to behave in another. Neither by nature, then, nor contrary to nature do the virtues arise in us; rather we are adapted by nature to receive them, and are made perfect by habit.

Again, of all the things that come to us by nature we first acquire the potentiality and later exhibit the activity (this is plain in the case of the senses; for it was not by often seeing or often hearing that we got these senses, but on the contrary we had them before we used them, and did not come to have them by using them); but the virtues we get by first exercising them, as also happens in the case of the arts as well. For the things we have to learn before we can do them, we learn by doing them, e.g. men become builders by building and lyre-players by playing the lyre; so too we become just by doing just acts, temperate by doing temperate acts, brave by doing brave acts.

This is confirmed by what happens in states; for legislators make the citizens good by forming habits in them, and this is the wish of every legislator, and those who do not effect it miss their mark, and it is in this that a good constitution differs from a bad one.

Again, it is from the same causes and by the same means that every virtue is both produced and destroyed, and similarly every art; for it is from playing the lyre that both good and bad lyre-players are produced. And the corresponding statement is true of builders and of all the rest; men will be good or bad builders as a result of building well or badly. For if this were not so,

there would have been no need of a teacher, but all men would have been born good or bad at their craft. This, then, is the case with the virtues also; by doing the acts that we do in our transactions with other men we become just or unjust, and by doing the acts that we do in the presence of danger, and by being habituated to feel fear or confidence, we become brave or cowardly. The same is true of appetites and feelings of anger; some men become temperate and good-tempered, others self-indulgent and irascible, by behaving in one way or the other in the appropriate circumstances. Thus, in one word, states of character arise out of like activities. This is why the activities we exhibit must be of a certain kind; it is because the states of character correspond to the differences between these. It makes no small difference, then, whether we form habits of one kind or of another from our very youth; it makes a very great difference, or rather *all* the difference.

2. Since, then, the present inquiry does not aim at theoretical knowledge like the others (for we are inquiring not in order to know what virtue is, but in order to become good, since otherwise our inquiry would have been of no use), we must examine the nature of actions, namely how we ought to do them; for these determine also the nature of the states of character that are produced, as we have said. Now, that we must act according to the right rule is a common principle and must be assumed—it will be discussed later, i.e. both what the right rule is, and how it is related to the other virtues. [. . .]

First, then, let us consider this, that it is the nature of such things to be destroyed by defect and excess, as we see in the case of strength and of health (for to gain light on things imperceptible we must use the evidence of sensible things); exercise either excessive or defective destroys the strength, and similarly drink or food which is above or below a certain amount destroys the health, while that which is proportionate both produces and increases and preserves it. So too is it, then, in the case of temperance and courage and the other virtues. For the man who flies from and fears everything and does not stand his ground against anything becomes a coward, and the man who fears nothing at all but goes to meet every danger becomes rash; and similarly the man who indulges in every pleasure and abstains from none becomes self-indulgent, while the man who shuns every pleasure, as boors do, becomes in a way insensible; temperance and courage, then, are destroyed by excess and defect, and preserved by the mean.

But not only are the sources and causes of their origination and growth the same as those of their destruction, but also the sphere of their actualization will be the same; for this is also true of the things which are more evident to sense, e.g. of strength; it is produced by taking much food and undergoing much exertion, and it is the strong man that will be most able to do these things. So too is it with the virtues; by abstaining from pleasures we become temperate, and it is when we have become so that we are most able to abstain from them; and similarly too in the case of courage; for by being habituated to despise things that are fearful and to stand our ground against them we become brave, and it is when we have become so that we shall be most able to stand our ground against them.

3. We must take as a sign of states of character the pleasure or pain that supervenes upon acts; for the man who abstains from bodily pleasures and delights in this very fact is temperate, while the man who is annoyed at it is self-indulgent, and he who stands his ground against things that are terrible and delights in this or at least is not pained is brave, while the man who is pained is a coward. For moral excellence is concerned with pleasures and pains; it is on account of the pleasure that we do bad things, and on account of the pain that we abstain from noble ones. Hence we ought to have been brought up in a particular way from our very youth, as Plato says, so as both to delight in and to be pained by the things that we ought; this is the right education. [. . .]

Again, as we said but lately, every state of soul has a nature relative to and concerned with the kind of things by which it tends to be made worse or better; but it is by reason of pleasures and pains that men become bad, by pursuing and avoiding these—either the pleasures and pains they ought not or when they ought not or as they ought not, or by going wrong in one of the other similar ways that may be distinguished. Hence men even define the virtues as certain states of impassivity and rest; not well, however, because they speak absolutely, and do not say "as one ought" and "as one ought not" and "when one ought or ought not," and the other things that may be added. We assume, then, that this kind of excellence tends to do what is best with regard to pleasures and pains, and vice does the contrary.

The following facts also may show us that virtue and vice are concerned with these same things. There being three objects of choice and three of avoidance, the noble, the advantageous, the pleasant, and their contraries, the base, the injurious, the painful, about all of these the good man tends to go right and the bad man to go wrong, and especially about pleasure; for this is common to the animals, and also it accompanies all objects of choice; for even the noble and the advantageous appear pleasant.

Again, it has grown up with us all from our infancy; this is why it is difficult to rub off this passion, engrained as it is in our life. And we measure even our actions, some of us more and others less, by the rule of pleasure and pain. For this reason, then, our whole inquiry must be about these; for to feel delight and pain rightly or wrongly has no small effect on our actions. [. . .]

That virtue, then, is concerned with pleasures and pains, and that by the acts from which it arises it is both increased and, if they are done differently, destroyed, and that the acts from which it arose are those in which it actualizes itself—let this be taken as said.

4. The question might be asked, what we mean by saying that we must become just by doing just acts, and temperate by doing temperate acts; for if men do just and temperate acts, they are already just and temperate, exactly as, if they do what is in accordance with the laws of grammar and of music, they are grammarians and musicians.

Or is this not true even of the arts? [...]

The case of the arts and that of the virtues are not similar; for the products of the arts have their goodness in themselves, so that it is enough that they should have a certain character, but if the acts that are in accordance with the virtues have themselves a certain character it does not follow that they are done justly or temperately. The agent also must be in a certain condition when he does them; in the first place he must have knowledge, secondly he must choose the acts, and choose them for their own sakes, and thirdly his action must proceed from a firm and unchangeable character. These are not reckoned in as conditions of the possession of the arts, except the bare knowledge; but as a condition of the possession of the virtues knowledge has little or no weight, while the other conditions count not for a little but for everything, i.e. the very conditions which result from often doing just and temperate acts.

Actions, then, are called just and temperate when they are such as the just or the temperate man would do; but it is not the man who does these that is just and temperate, but the man who also does them *as* just and temperate men do them. It is well said, then, that it is by doing just acts that the just man is produced, and by doing temperate acts the temperate man; without doing these no one would have even a prospect of becoming good.

But most people do not do these, but take refuge in theory and think they are being philosophers and will become good in this way, behaving somewhat like patients who listen attentively to their doctors, but do none of the things they are ordered to do. As the latter will not be made well in body by such a course of treatment, the former will not be made well in soul by such a course of philosophy.

5. Next we must consider what virtue is. Since things that are found in the soul are of three kinds—passions, faculties, states of character—virtue must be one of these. By passions I mean appetite, anger, fear, confidence, envy, joy, friendly feeling, hatred, longing, emulation, pity, and in general the feelings that are accompanied by pleasure or pain; by faculties the things in virtue of which we are said to be capable of feeling these, e.g. of becoming angry or being pained or feeling pity; by states of character the things in virtue of which we stand well or badly with reference to the passions, e.g. with reference to anger we stand badly if we feel it violently or too weakly, and well if we feel it moderately; and similarly with reference to the other passions.

Now neither the virtues nor the vices are *passions*, because we are not called good or bad on the ground of our passions, but are so called on the ground of our virtues and our vices, and because we are neither praised nor blamed for our passions (for the man who feels fear or anger is not praised, nor is the man who simply feels anger blamed, but the man who feels it in a certain way), but for our virtues and our vices we *are* praised or blamed.

Again, we feel anger and fear without choice, but the virtues are modes of choice or involve choice. Further, in respect of the passions we are said to be moved, but in respect of the virtues and the vices we are said not to be moved but to be disposed in a particular way.

For these reasons also they are not *faculties*; for we are neither called good or bad, nor praised or blamed, for the simple capacity of feeling the passions; again, we have the faculties by nature, but we are not made good or bad by nature; we have spoken of this before.

If, then, the virtues are neither passions nor faculties, all that remains is that they should be *states of character*. [...]

6. We must, however, not only describe virtue as a state of character, but also say what sort of state it is. We may remark, then, that every virtue or excellence both brings into good condition the thing of which it is the excellence and makes the work of that thing be done well; e.g. the excellence of the eye makes both the eye and its work good; for it is by the excellence of the eye that we see well. Similarly the excellence of the horse makes a horse both good in itself and good at running and at carrying its rider and at awaiting the attack of the enemy. Therefore, if this is true in every case, the virtue of man also will be the state of character which makes a man good and which makes him do his own work well.

How this is to happen we have stated already, but it will be made plain also by the following consideration of the specific nature of virtue. In everything that is continuous and divisible it is possible to take more, less, or an equal amount, and that either in terms of the thing itself or relatively to us; and the equal is an intermediate between excess and defect. By the intermediate in the object I mean that which is equidistant from each of the extremes, which is one and the same for all men; by the intermediate relatively to us that which is neither too much nor too little—and this is not one, nor the same for all. For instance, if ten is many and two is few, six is the intermediate, taken in terms of the object; for it exceeds and is exceeded by an equal amount; this is intermediate according to arithmetical proportion. But the intermediate relatively to us is not to be taken so; if ten pounds are too much for a particular person to eat and two too little, it does not follow that the trainer will order six pounds; for this also is perhaps too much for the person who is to take it, or too little—too little for Milo [a famous athlete of the day—Eds.], too much for the beginner in athletic exercises. The same is true of running and wrestling. Thus a master of any art avoids excess and defect, but seeks the intermediate and chooses this—the intermediate not in the object but relatively to us.

If it is thus, then, that every art does its work well—by looking to the intermediate and judging its works by this standard (so that we often say of good works of art that it is not possible either to take away or to add anything, implying

that excess and defect destroy the goodness of works of art, while the mean preserves it; and good artists, as we say, look to this in their work), and if, further, virtue is more exact and better than any art, as nature also is, then virtue must have the quality of aiming at the intermediate. I mean moral virtue; for it is this that is concerned with passions and actions, and in these there is excess, defect, and the intermediate. For instance, both fear and confidence and appetite and anger and pity and in general pleasure and pain may be felt both too much and too little, and in both cases not well; but to feel them at the right times, with reference to the right objects, towards the right people, with the right motive, and in the right way, is what is both intermediate and best, and this is characteristic of virtue. Similarly with regard to actions also there is excess, defect, and the intermediate. Now virtue is concerned with passions and actions, in which excess is a form of failure, and so is defect, while the intermediate is praised and is a form of success; and being praised and being successful are both characteristics of virtue. Therefore virtue is a kind of mean, since, as we have seen, it aims at what is intermediate.

Again, it is possible to fail in many ways (for evil belongs to the class of the unlimited, as the Pythagoreans conjectured, and good to that of the limited), while to succeed is possible only in one way (for which reason also one is easy and the other difficult—to miss the mark easy, to hit it difficult); for these reasons also, then, excess and defect are characteristic of vice, and the mean of virtue;

For men are good in but one way, but bad in many.

Virtue, then, is a state of character concerned with choice, lying in a mean, i.e. the mean relative to us, this being determined by a rational principle, and by that principle by which the man of practical wisdom would determine it. Now it is a mean between two vices, that which depends on excess and that which depends on defect; and again it is a mean because the vices respectively fall short of or exceed what is right in both passions and actions, while virtue both finds and chooses that which is intermediate. Hence in respect of what it is, i.e. the definition which states its essence, virtue is a mean, with regard to what is best and right an extreme.

But not every action nor every passion admits of a mean; for some have names that already imply badness, e.g. spite, shamelessness, envy, and in the case of actions adultery, theft, murder; for all of these and such like things imply by their names that they are themselves bad, and not the excesses or deficiencies of them. It is not possible, then, ever to be right with regard to them; one must always be wrong. Nor does goodness or badness with regard to such things depend on committing adultery with the right woman, at the right time, and in the right way, but simply to do any of them is to go wrong. It would be equally absurd, then, to expect that in unjust, cowardly, and voluptuous action there should be a mean, an excess, and a deficiency; for at that rate there would be a mean of excess and of deficiency, an excess of excess, and a deficiency of deficiency. But as there is no excess and deficiency of temperance and courage because what is intermediate is in a sense an extreme, so too of the actions we have mentioned there is no mean nor any excess and deficiency, but however they are done they are wrong; for in general there is neither a mean of excess and deficiency, nor excess and deficiency of a mean.

7. We must, however, not only make this general statement, but also apply it to the individual facts. For among statements about conduct those which are general apply more widely, but those which are particular are more true, since conduct has to do with individual cases, and our statements must harmonize with the facts in these cases. We may take these cases from our table. With regard to feelings of fear and confidence courage is the mean; of the people who exceed, he who exceeds in fearlessness has no name (many of the states have no name), while the man who exceeds in confidence is rash, and he who exceeds in fear and falls short in confidence is a coward. With regard to pleasures and pains— not all of them, and not so much with regard to the pains—the mean is temperance, the excess self-indulgence. Persons deficient with regard to the pleasures are not often found; hence such persons also have received no name. But let us call them "insensible."

With regard to giving and taking of money the mean is liberality, the excess and the defect prodigality and meanness. In these actions people exceed and fall short in contrary ways; the prodigal exceeds in spending and falls short in taking, while the mean man exceeds in taking and falls short in spending. (At present we are giving a mere outline or summary, and are satisfied with this; later these states will be more exactly determined.) With regard to money there are also other dispositions—a mean, magnificence (for the magnificent man differs from the liberal man; the former deals with large sums, the latter with small ones), an excess, tastelessness and vulgarity, and a deficiency, niggardliness; these differ from the states opposed to liberality, and the mode of their difference will be stated later.

With regard to honour and dishonour the mean is proper pride, the excess is known as a sort of "empty vanity," and the deficiency is undue humility; and as we said liberality was related to magnificence, differing from it by dealing with small sums, so there is a state similarly related to proper pride, being concerned with small honours while that is concerned with great. For it is possible to desire honour as one ought, and more than one ought, and less, and the man who exceeds in his desires is called ambitious, the man who falls short unambitious, while the intermediate person has no name. The dispositions also are nameless, except that that of the ambitious man is called ambition. Hence the people who are at the extremes lay claim to the middle place; and we ourselves sometimes call the intermediate person ambitious and sometimes unambitious, and sometimes praise the ambitious man and sometimes the unambitious. The reason of our doing this will be stated in what follows; but now let us speak of the remaining states according to the method which has been indicated.

With regard to anger also there is an excess, a deficiency, and a mean. Although they can scarcely be said to have names, yet since we call the intermediate person good-tempered let us call the mean good temper; of the persons at the extremes let the one who exceeds be called irascible, and his vice irascibility, and the man who falls short an unirascible sort of person, and the deficiency unirascibility. [...]

There are also means in the passions and concerned with the passions; since shame is not a virtue, and yet praise is extended to the modest man. For even in these matters one man is said to be intermediate, and another to exceed, as for instance the bashful man who is ashamed of everything; while he who falls short or is not ashamed of anything at all is shameless, and the intermediate person is modest. Righteous indignation is a mean between envy and spite, and these states are concerned with the pain and pleasure that are felt at the fortunes of our neighbours; the man who is characterized by righteous indignation is pained at undeserved good fortune, the envious man, going beyond him, is pained at all good fortune, and the spiteful man falls so far short of being pained that he even rejoices. But these states there will be an opportunity of describing elsewhere; with regard to justice, since it has not one simple meaning, we shall, after describing the other states, distinguish its two kinds and say how each of them is a mean; and similarly we shall treat also of the rational virtues.

8. There are three kinds of disposition, then, two of them vices, involving excess and deficiency respectively, and one a virtue, viz. the mean, and all are in a sense opposed to all; for the extreme states are contrary both to the intermediate state and to each other, and the intermediate to the extremes; as the equal is greater relatively to the less, less relatively to the greater, so the middle states are excessive relatively to the deficiencies, deficient relatively to the excesses, both in passions and in actions. For the brave man appears rash relatively to the coward, and cowardly relatively to the rash man; and similarly the temperate man appears self-indulgent relatively to the insensible man, insensible relatively to the self-indulgent, and the liberal man prodigal relatively to the mean man, mean relatively to the prodigal. Hence also the people at the extremes push the intermediate man each over to the other, and the brave man is called rash by the coward, cowardly by the rash man, and correspondingly in the other cases.

These states being thus opposed to one another, the greatest contrariety is that of the extremes to each other, rather than to the intermediate; for these are further from each other than from the intermediate, as the great is further from the small and the small from the great than both are from the equal. Again, to the intermediate some extremes show a certain likeness, as that of rashness to courage and that of prodigality to liberality; but the extremes show the greatest unlikeness to each other; now contraries are defined as the things that are furthest from each other, so that things that are further apart are more contrary.

To the mean in some cases the deficiency, in some the excess, is more opposed; e.g. it is not rashness, which is an excess, but cowardice, which is a deficiency, that is more opposed to courage, and not insensibility, which is a deficiency, but self-indulgence, which is an excess, that is more opposed to temperance. This happens from two reasons, one being drawn from the thing itself; for because one extreme is nearer and liker to the intermediate, we oppose not this but rather its contrary to the intermediate. E.g., since rashness is thought liker and nearer to courage, and cowardice more unlike, we oppose rather the latter to courage; for things that are further from the intermediate are thought more contrary to it. This, then, is one cause, drawn from the thing itself; another is drawn from ourselves; for the things to which we ourselves more naturally tend seem more contrary to the intermediate. For instance, we ourselves tend more naturally to pleasures, and hence are more easily carried away towards self-indulgence than towards propriety. We describe as contrary to the mean, then, rather the directions in which we more often go to great lengths; and therefore self-indulgence, which is an excess, is the more contrary to temperance.

9. That moral virtue is a mean, then, and in what sense it is so, and that it is a mean between two vices, the one involving excess, the other deficiency, and that it is such because its character is to aim at what is intermediate in passions and in actions, has been sufficiently stated. Hence also it is no easy task to be good. For in everything it is no easy task to find the middle, e.g. to find the middle of a circle is not for everyone but for him who knows; so, too, anyone can get angry—that is easy—or give or spend money; but to do this to the right person, to the right extent, at the right time, with the right motive, and in the right way, *that* is not for everyone, nor is it easy; wherefore goodness is both rare and laudable and noble. [...]

But we must consider the things towards which we ourselves also are easily carried away; for some of us tend to one thing, some to another; and this will be recognizable from the pleasure and the pain we feel. We must drag ourselves away to the contrary extreme; for we shall get into the intermediate state by drawing well away from error, as people do in straightening sticks that are bent.

Now in everything the pleasant or pleasure is most to be guarded against; for we do not judge it impartially. We ought, then, to feel towards pleasure as the elders of the people felt towards Helen, and in all circumstances repeat their saying; for if we dismiss pleasure thus we are less likely to go astray. It is by doing this, then, (to sum the matter up) that we shall best be able to hit the mean.

But this is no doubt difficult, and especially in individual cases; for it is not easy to determine both how and with whom and on what provocation and how long one should be angry; for we too sometimes praise those who fall short and call them good-tempered, but sometimes we praise those who get angry and call them manly. The man, however, who deviates little from goodness is not blamed, whether he do so in the direction of the more or of the less, but only the man who deviates more widely; for *he* does not fail to be noticed. But up to what point and to what extent a man must deviate before he becomes blameworthy it is not easy to determine by reasoning, any more than anything else that is perceived by the senses; such things depend on particular facts, and the decision rests with perception. So much, then, is plain, that the intermediate state is in all things to be praised, but that we must incline sometimes towards the excess, sometimes towards the deficiency; for so shall we most easily hit the mean and what is right.

Study Questions

1. Can you think of counterexamples to the claim that virtues are means between two extremes?
2. Aristotle thought *eudaimonia* ("living and doing well") was more important than happiness understood as positive psychological states. Do you agree?
3. Do you think Aristotle is correct that vicious individuals cannot be happy?

9.2   Groundwork of the Metaphysics of Morals

IMMANUEL KANT

IMMANUEL KANT (1724–1804) is the central figure in modern philosophy, having made important contributions to metaphysics, political philosophy, and aesthetics. With respect to ethics, Kant aimed to show that all moral obligation is based on a principle that could be shown *a priori* via reason. He called this principle the categorical imperative. One acts immorally, and irrationally, when one acts in a way that violates the categorical imperative. In this reading, Kant begins with the claim that the will is the only thing that is good unconditionally; all other goods can be misused. A will is good when it is wholly determined by moral demands or, as he often refers to this, by what morality requires of us. What morality requires of us is our duty, and the content of that duty is found in satisfying the categorical imperative. Though Kant expresses the categorical imperative in a number of ways, he took those different formulations to be coextensive, if not identical.

It is impossible to think of anything at all in the world, or indeed even beyond it, that could be considered good without limitation except a good will. Understanding, wit, judgment and the like, whatever such *talents* of mind may be called, or courage, resolution, and perseverance in one's plans, as qualities of *temperament*, are undoubtedly good and desirable for many purposes, but they can also be extremely evil and harmful if the will which is to make use of these gifts of nature, and whose distinctive constitution is therefore called *character*, is not good. It is the same with *gifts of fortune*. Power, riches, honor, even health and that complete well-being and satisfaction with one's condition called *happiness*, produce boldness and thereby often arrogance as well unless a good will is present which corrects the influence of these on the mind and, in so doing, also corrects the whole principle of action and brings it into conformity with universal ends—not to mention that an impartial rational spectator can take no delight in seeing the uninterrupted prosperity of a being graced with no feature of a pure and good will, so that a good will seems to constitute the indispensable condition even of worthiness to be happy.

Some qualities are even conducive to this good will itself and can make its work much easier; despite this, however, they have no inner unconditional worth but always presuppose a good will, which limits the esteem one otherwise rightly has for them and does not permit their being taken as absolutely good. Moderation in affects and passions, self-control, and calm reflection are not only good for all sorts of purposes but even seem to constitute a part of the *inner* worth of a person; but they lack much that would be required to declare them good without limitation (however unconditionally they were praised by the ancients); for, without the basic principles of a good will they can become extremely evil, and the coolness of a scoundrel makes him not only far more dangerous but also immediately more abominable in our eyes than we would have taken him to be without it.

A good will is not good because of what it effects or accomplishes, because of its fitness to attain some proposed end, but only because of its volition, that is, it is good in itself and, regarded for itself, is to be valued incomparably higher than all that could merely be brought about by it in favor of some inclination and indeed, if you will, of the sum of all inclinations. Even if, by a special disfavor of fortune or by the niggardly provision of a stepmotherly nature, this will should wholly lack the capacity to carry out its purpose—if with its greatest efforts it should yet achieve nothing and only the good will were left (not, of course, as a mere wish but as the summoning of all means insofar as they are in our control)—then, like a jewel, it would still shine by itself, as something that has its full worth in itself. Usefulness or fruitlessness can neither add anything to this worth nor take anything away from it. [...]

We have, then, to explicate the concept of a will that is to be esteemed in itself and that is good apart from any further purpose, as it already dwells in natural sound understanding and needs not so much to be taught as only to be clarified—this concept that always takes first place in estimating the total worth of our actions and constitutes the condition of all the rest. In order to do so, we shall set before ourselves the concept of duty, which contains that of a good will though under certain subjective limitations and hindrances, which, however, far from concealing it and making it unrecognizable, rather bring it out by contrast and make it shine forth all the more brightly.

I here pass over all actions that are already recognized as contrary to duty, even though they may be useful for this or that purpose; for in their case the question whether they might have been done *from duty* never arises, since they even conflict with it. I also set aside actions that are really in conformity with duty but to which human beings have *no inclination* immediately and which they still perform because they are impelled to do so through another inclination. For in this case it is easy to distinguish whether an action in conformity with duty is done *from duty* or from a self-seeking purpose. It is much more difficult to note this distinction when an action conforms with duty and the subject has, besides, an *immediate* inclination to it. For example, it certainly conforms with duty that a shopkeeper not overcharge an inexperienced customer, and where there is a good deal of trade a prudent merchant does not overcharge but keeps a fixed general price for everyone, so that a child can buy from him as well as everyone else. People are thus served *honestly*; but this is not nearly enough for us to believe that the merchant acted in this way from duty and basic principles of honesty; his advantage required it; it cannot be assumed here that he had, besides, an immediate inclination toward his customers, so as from love, as it were, to give no one preference over another in the matter of price. Thus the action was done neither from duty nor from immediate inclination but merely for purposes of self-interest.

On the other hand, to preserve one's life is a duty, and besides everyone has an immediate inclination to do so. But on this account the often anxious care that most people take of it still has no inner worth and their maxim has no moral content. They look after their lives *in conformity with duty* but not *from duty*. On the other hand, if adversity and hopeless grief have quite taken away the taste for life; if an unfortunate man, strong of soul and more indignant about his fate than despondent or dejected, wishes for death and yet preserves his life without loving it, not from inclination or fear but from duty, then his maxim has moral content. [...]

The second proposition[1] is this: an action from duty has its moral worth *not in the purpose* to be attained by it but in the maxim in accordance with which it is decided upon, and therefore does not depend upon the realization of the object of the action but merely upon the *principle of volition* in accordance with which the action is done without regard for any object of the faculty of desire. That the purposes we may have for our actions, and their effects as ends and incentives of the will, can give actions no unconditional and moral worth is clear from what has gone before. In what, then, can this worth lie, if it is not to be in the will in relation to the hoped for effect of the action? It can lie nowhere else *than in the principle of the will* without regard for the ends that can be brought about by such an action. [...]

The third proposition, which is a consequence of the two preceding, I would express as follows: *duty is the necessity of an action from respect for law*. For an object as the effect of my proposed action I can indeed have *inclination* but *never respect*, just because it is merely an effect and not an activity of a will. In the same way I cannot have respect for inclination as such, whether it is mine or that of another; I can at most in the first case approve it and in the second sometimes even love it, that is, regard it as favorable to my own advantage. Only what is connected with my will merely as ground and never as effect, what does not serve my inclination but outweighs it or at least excludes it altogether from calculations in making a choice—hence the mere law for itself—can be an object of respect and so a command. Now, an action from duty is to put aside entirely the influence of inclination and with it every object of the will; hence there is left for the will nothing that could determine it except objectively the *law* and subjectively *pure respect* for this practical law, and so the maxim[2] of complying with such a law even if it infringes upon all my inclinations. [...]

But what kind of law can that be, the representation of which must determine the will, even without regard for the effect expected from it, in order for the will to be called good absolutely and without limitation? Since I have deprived the will of every impulse that could arise for it from obeying some law, nothing is left but the conformity of actions as such with universal law, which alone is to serve the will as its principle, that is, *I ought never to act except in such a way that I could also will that my maxim should become a universal law*. Here mere conformity to law as such, without having as its basis some law determined for certain actions, is what serves the will as its principle, and must so serve it, if duty is not to be everywhere an empty delusion and a chimerical concept. [...]

From what has been said it is clear that all moral concepts have their seat and origin completely a priori in reason, and indeed in the most common reason just as in reason that is speculative in the highest degree; that they cannot be abstracted from any empirical and therefore merely contingent cognitions; that just in this purity of their origin lies their dignity, so that they can serve us as supreme practical principles; that in adding anything empirical to them one subtracts just that much from their genuine influence and from the unlimited worth of actions; that it is not only a requirement of the greatest necessity for theoretical purposes, when it is a matter merely of speculation, but also of the greatest practical importance to draw its concepts and laws from pure reason, to set them forth pure and unmixed, and indeed to determine the extent of this entire practical or pure rational cognition, that is, to determine the entire faculty of pure practical reason; and in so doing, it is of the greatest practical importance not to make its principles dependent upon the special nature of human reason—as speculative philosophy permits and even at times finds necessary—but instead, just because moral laws are to hold for every rational being as such, to derive them from the universal concept of a rational being as such, and in this way to set forth completely the whole of morals, which needs anthropology for its *application* to human beings, at first independently of this as pure philosophy, that is, as metaphysics (as can well be done in this kind of quite separated cognitions), [for we are] well aware that, unless we are in possession of this, it would be—I will not say futile to determine precisely for speculative appraisal the moral element of duty in all that conforms with duty, but—impossible to base morals on their genuine principles even for common and practical use, especially that of moral instruction, and thereby to bring about pure moral dispositions and engraft them onto people's minds for the highest good in the world. [...]

Everything in nature works in accordance with laws. Only a rational being has the capacity to act *in accordance with the representation* of laws, that is, in accordance with principles, or has a *will*. Since *reason* is required for the derivation of actions from laws, the will is nothing other than practical reason. If reason infallibly determines the will, the actions of such a being that are cognized as objectively necessary are also subjectively necessary, that is, the will is a capacity to choose *only that* which reason independently of inclination cognizes as practically necessary, that is, as good. However, if reason solely by itself does not adequately determine the will; if the will is exposed also to subjective conditions (certain incentives) that are not always in accord with the objective ones; in a word, if the will is not *in itself* completely in conformity with reason (as is actually the case with human beings), then actions that are cognized as objectively necessary are subjectively contingent, and the determination of such a will in conformity with objective laws is *necessitation*: that is to say, the relation of objective laws to a will that is not thoroughly good is represented as the determination of the will of a rational being through grounds of reason, indeed, but grounds to which this will is not by its nature necessarily obedient.

The representation of an objective principle, insofar as it is necessitating for a will, is called a command (of reason), and the formula of the command is called an **imperative**.

All imperatives are expressed by an *ought* and indicate by this the relation of an objective law of reason to a will that by its subjective constitution is not necessarily determined by it (a necessitation). They say that to do or to omit something would be good, but they say it to a will that does not always do something just

because it is represented to it that it would be good to do that thing. Practical good, however, is that which determines the will by means of representations of reason, hence not by subjective causes but objectively, that is, from grounds that are valid for every rational being as such. It is distinguished from the *agreeable*, as that which influences the will only by means of feeling from merely subjective causes, which hold only for the senses of this or that one, and not as a principle of reason, which holds for everyone. [...]

Now, all imperatives command either *hypothetically* or *categorically*. The former represent the practical necessity of a possible action as a means to achieving something else that one wills (or that it is at least possible for one to will). The categorical imperative would be that which represented an action as objectively necessary of itself, without reference to another end.

Since every practical law represents a possible action as good and thus as necessary for a subject practically determinable by reason, all imperatives are formulae for the determination of action that is necessary in accordance with the principle of a will which is good in some way. Now, if the action would be good merely as a means *to something else* the imperative is *hypothetical*; if the action is represented as *in itself* good, hence as necessary in a will in itself conforming to reason, as its principle, *then it is categorical*. [...]

Hence the hypothetical imperative says only that the action is good for some *possible* or *actual* purpose. [...]

Finally there is one imperative that, without being based upon and having as its condition any other purpose to be attained by certain conduct, commands this conduct immediately. This imperative is **categorical**. It has to do not with the matter of the action and what is to result from it, but with the form and the principle from which the action itself follows; and the essentially good in the action consists in the disposition, let the result be what it may. This imperative may be called the imperative **of morality**. [...]

We shall thus have to investigate entirely a priori the possibility of a *categorical* imperative, since we do not here have the advantage of its reality being given in experience, so that the possibility would be necessary not to establish it but merely to explain it. In the meantime, however, we can see this much: that the categorical imperative alone has the tenor of a practical law; all the others can indeed be called *principles* of the will but not laws, since what it is necessary to do merely for achieving a discretionary purpose can be regarded as in itself contingent and we can always be released from the precept if we give up the purpose; on the contrary, the unconditional command leaves the will no discretion with respect to the opposite, so that it alone brings with it that necessity which we require of a law.

Second, in the case of this categorical imperative or law of morality the ground of the difficulty (of insight into its possibility) is also very great. It is an a priori synthetic practical proposition; and since it is so difficult to see the possibility of this kind of proposition in theoretical cognition, it can be readily gathered that the difficulty will be no less in practical cognition.

In this task we want first to inquire whether the mere concept of a categorical imperative may not also provide its formula containing the proposition which alone can be a categorical imperative. For, how such an absolute command is possible, even if we know its tenor, will still require special and difficult toil, which, however, we postpone to the last section.

When I think of a *hypothetical* imperative in general I do not know beforehand what it will contain; I do not know this until I am given the condition. But when I think of a *categorical* imperative I know at once what it contains. For, since the imperative contains, beyond the law, only the necessity that the maxim be in conformity with this law, while the law contains no condition to which it would be limited, nothing is left with which the maxim of action is to conform but the universality of a law as such;

and this conformity alone is what the imperative properly represents as necessary.

There is, therefore, only a single categorical imperative and it is this: *act only in accordance with that maxim through which you can at the same time will that it become a universal law*.

Now, if all imperatives of duty can be derived from this single imperative as from their principle, then, even though we leave it undecided whether what is called duty is not as such an empty concept, we shall at least be able to show what we think by it and what the concept wants to say.

Since the universality of law in accordance with which effects take place constitutes what is properly called *nature* in the most general sense (as regards its form)—that is, the existence of things insofar as it is determined in accordance with universal laws—the universal imperative of duty can also go as follows: *act as if the maxim of your action were to become by your will a* **universal law of nature**.

We shall now enumerate a few duties in accordance with the usual division of them into duties to ourselves and to other human beings and into perfect and imperfect duties.

1) Someone feels sick of life because of a series of troubles that has grown to the point of despair, but is still so far in possession of his reason that he can ask himself whether it would not be contrary to his duty to himself to take his own life. Now he inquires whether the maxim of his action could indeed become a universal law of nature. His maxim, however, is: from self-love I make it my principle to shorten my life when its longer duration threatens more troubles than it promises agreeableness. The only further question is whether this principle of self-love could become a universal law of nature. It is then seen at once that a nature whose law it would be to destroy life itself by means of the same feeling whose destination is to impel toward the furtherance of life would contradict itself and would therefore not subsist as nature; thus that maxim could not possibly be a law of

nature and, accordingly, altogether opposes the supreme principle of all duty.

2) Another finds himself urged by need to borrow money. He well knows that he will not be able to repay it but sees also that nothing will be lent him unless he promises firmly to repay it within a determinate time. He would like to make such a promise, but he still has enough conscience to ask himself: is it not forbidden and contrary to duty to help oneself out of need in such a way? Supposing that he still decided to do so, his maxim of action would go as follows: when I believe myself to be in need of money I shall borrow money and promise to repay it, even though I know that this will never happen. Now this principle of self-love or personal advantage is perhaps quite consistent with my whole future welfare, but the question now is whether it is right. I therefore turn the demand of self-love into a universal law and put the question as follows: how would it be if my maxim became a universal law? I then see at once that it could never hold as a universal law of nature and be consistent with itself, but must necessarily contradict itself. For, the universality of a law that everyone, when he believes himself to be in need, could promise whatever he pleases with the intention of not keeping it would make the promise and the end one might have in it itself impossible, since no one would believe what was promised him but would laugh at all such expressions as vain pretenses.

3) A third finds in himself a talent that by means of some cultivation could make him a human being useful for all sorts of purposes. However, he finds himself in comfortable circumstances and prefers to give himself up to pleasure than to trouble himself with enlarging and improving his fortunate natural predispositions. But he still asks himself whether his maxim of neglecting his natural gifts, besides being consistent with his propensity to amusement, is also consistent with what one calls duty. He now sees that a nature could indeed always subsist with such a universal law, although (as with the South Sea Islanders)

the human being should let his talents rust and be concerned with devoting his life merely to idleness, amusement, procreation—in a word, to enjoyment; only he cannot possibly will that this become a universal law or be put in us as such by means of natural instinct. For, as a rational being he necessarily wills that all the capacities in him be developed, since they serve him and are given to him for all sorts of possible purposes.

Yet a *fourth*, for whom things are going well while he sees that others (whom he could very well help) have to contend with great hardships, thinks: what is it to me? let each be as happy as heaven wills or as he can make himself; I shall take nothing from him nor even envy him; only I do not care to contribute anything to his welfare or to his assistance in need! Now, if such a way of thinking were to become a universal law the human race could admittedly very well subsist, no doubt even better than when everyone prates about sympathy and benevolence and even exerts himself to practice them occasionally, but on the other hand also cheats where he can, sells the right of human beings or otherwise infringes upon it. But although it is possible that a universal law of nature could very well subsist in accordance with such a maxim, it is still impossible to **will** that such a principle hold everywhere as a law of nature. For, a will that decided this would conflict with itself, since many cases could occur in which one would need the love and sympathy of others and in which, by such a law of nature arisen from his own will, he would rob himself of all hope of the assistance he wishes for himself.

These are a few of the many actual duties, or at least of what we take to be such, whose derivation from the one principle cited above is clear. We must *be able to will* that a maxim of our action become a universal law: this is the canon of moral appraisal of action in general. Some actions are so constituted that their maxim cannot even be *thought* without contradiction as a universal law of nature, far less could one *will* that it *should* become such. In the case of others that inner impossibility is indeed not to be found, but it is still impossible to *will* that their maxim be raised to the universality of a law of nature because such a will would contradict itself. It is easy to see that the first is opposed to strict or narrower (unremitting) duty, the second only to wide (meritorious) duty; and so all duties, as far as the kind of obligation (not the object of their action) is concerned, have by these examples been set out completely in their dependence upon the one principle.

If we now attend to ourselves in any transgression of a duty, we find that we do not really will that our maxim should become a universal law, since that is impossible for us, but that the opposite of our maxim should instead remain a universal law, only we take the liberty of making an *exception* to it for ourselves (or just for this once) to the advantage of our inclination. Consequently, if we weighed all cases from one and the same point of view, namely that of reason, we would find a contradiction in our own will, namely that a certain principle be objectively necessary as a universal law and yet subjectively not hold universally but allow exceptions. [. . .]

The will is thought as a capacity to determine itself to acting in conformity with the *representation of certain laws*. And such a capacity can be found only in rational beings. Now, what serves the will as the objective ground of its self-determination is an end, and this, if it is given by reason alone, must hold equally for all rational beings. What, on the other hand, contains merely the ground of the possibility of an action the effect of which is an end is called a *means*. The subjective ground of desire is an *incentive;* the objective ground of volition is a *motive;* hence the distinction between subjective ends, which rest on incentives, and objective ends, which depend on motives, which hold for every rational being. Practical principles are *formal* if they abstract from all subjective ends, whereas they are *material* if they have put these, and consequently certain incentives, at their basis. The ends that a rational being proposes at his discretion as *effects* of his actions (material ends) are

all only relative; for only their mere relation to a specially constituted faculty of desire on the part of the subject gives them their worth, which can therefore furnish no universal principles, no principles valid and necessary for all rational beings and also for every volition, that is, no practical laws. Hence all these relative ends are only the ground of hypothetical imperatives.

But suppose there were something the *existence of which in itself* has an absolute worth, something which as *an end in itself* could be a ground of determinate laws; then in it, and in it alone, would lie the ground of a possible categorical imperative, that is, of a practical law.

Now I say that the human being and in general every rational being *exists* as an end in itself, *not merely as a means* to be used by this or that will at its discretion; instead he must in all his actions, whether directed to himself or also to other rational beings, always be regarded *at the same time as an end*. All objects of the inclinations have only a conditional worth; for, if there were not inclinations and the needs based on them, their object would be without worth. But the inclinations themselves, as sources of needs, are so far from having an absolute worth, so as to make one wish to have them, that it must instead be the universal wish of every rational being to be altogether free from them. Thus the worth of any object *to be acquired* by our action is always conditional. Beings the existence of which rests not on our will but on nature, if they are beings without reason, still have only a relative worth, as means, and are therefore called *things*, whereas rational beings are called *persons* because their nature already marks them out as an end in itself, that is, as something that may not be used merely as a means, and hence so far limits all choice (and is an object of respect). These, therefore, are not merely subjective ends, the existence of which as an effect of our action has a worth *for us*, but rather *objective ends*, that is, beings the existence of which is in itself an end, and indeed one such that no other end, to which they would serve *merely* as means, can be put in its place, since without it nothing of *absolute worth* would be found anywhere; but if all worth were conditional and therefore contingent, then no supreme practical principle for reason could be found anywhere.

If, then, there is to be a supreme practical principle and, with respect to the human will, a categorical imperative, it must be one such that, from the representation of what is necessarily an end for everyone because it is an *end in itself*, it constitutes an *objective* principle of the will and thus can serve as a universal practical law. The ground of this principle is: *rational nature exists as an end in itself*. The human being necessarily represents his own existence in this way; so far it is thus a *subjective* principle of human actions. But every other rational being also represents his existence in this way consequent on just the same rational ground that also holds for me; thus it is at the same time an *objective* principle from which, as a supreme practical ground, it must be possible to derive all laws of the will. The practical imperative will therefore be the following: *So act that you use humanity, whether*

in your own person or in the person of any other, always at the same time as an end, never merely as a means. We shall see whether this can be carried out.

Notes

1. Though not explicit, the first proposition of morality is that an action must be done from duty in order to have moral—Eds.
2. A *maxim* is the subjective principle of volition.

Study Questions

1. Do you think that Kant's claim that "it is impossible to think of anything at all in the world...that could be considered good without limitation except a good will" is correct? Why or why not?
2. To what degree do you think that two formulations of the categorical imperative given in this reading are the same?
3. Kant connects moral worth with rationality. Do you think we have any moral obligations to nonrational animals?

Utilitarianism   9.3

JOHN STUART MILL

JOHN STUART MILL (1806–1873) was a British philosopher, economist, political theorist, and advocate for women's rights. His philosophical thought was influenced greatly by John Locke, David Hume, and—especially in terms of ethics—Jeremy Bentham. Mill is a paradigmatic example of a consequentialist approach to ethics; he argues that the moral worth of every action is to be judged solely in terms of the consequences of those actions. Furthermore, the primary consequences he thinks matter are the securing of pleasure and the avoidance of pain. Unlike Bentham before him, however, he differentiates between qualitatively different kinds of pleasures.

John Stuart Mill, *Utilitarianism*, edited by Mary Warnock (Malden, MA: Blackwell, 2003).

GENERAL REMARKS

1. There are few circumstances among those which make up the present condition of human knowledge, more unlike what might have been expected, or more significant of the backward state in which speculation on the most important subjects still lingers, than the little progress which has been made in the decision of the controversy respecting the criterion of right and wrong. From the dawn of philosophy, the question concerning the *summum bonum*, or, what is the same thing, concerning the foundation of morality, has been accounted the main problem in speculative thought, has occupied the most gifted intellects, and divided them into sects and schools, carrying on a vigorous warfare against one another. And after more than two thousand years the same discussions continue, philosophers are still ranged under the same contending banners, and neither thinkers nor mankind at large seem nearer to being unanimous on the subject, than when the youth Socrates listened to the old Protagoras, and asserted (if Plato's dialogue be grounded on a real conversation) the theory of utilitarianism against the popular morality of the so-called sophist. [...]

It would, however, be easy to show that whatever steadiness or consistency these moral beliefs have attained, has been mainly due to the tacit influence of a standard not recognised. Although the non-existence of an acknowledged first principle has made ethics not so much a guide as a consecration of men's actual sentiments, still, as men's sentiments, both of favour and of aversion, are greatly influenced by what they suppose to be the effects of things upon their happiness, the principle of utility, or as Bentham latterly called it, the greatest happiness principle, has had a large share in forming the moral doctrines even of those who most scornfully reject its authority. Nor is there any school of thought which refuses to admit that the influence of actions on happiness is a most material and even predominant consideration in many of the details of morals, however unwilling to acknowledge it as the fundamental principle of morality, and the source of moral obligation. [...]

5. On the present occasion, I shall, without further discussion of the other theories, attempt to contribute something towards the understanding and appreciation of the Utilitarian or Happiness theory, and towards such proof as it is susceptible of. It is evident that this cannot be proof in the ordinary and popular meaning of the term. Questions of ultimate ends are not amenable to direct proof. Whatever can be proved to be good, must be so by being shown to be a means to something admitted to be good without proof. The medical art is proved to be good, by its conducing to health; but how is it possible to prove that health is good? The art of music is good, for the reason, among others, that it produces pleasure; but what proof is it possible to give that pleasure is good? If, then, it is asserted that there is a comprehensive formula, including all things which are in themselves good, and that what ever else is good, is not so as an end, but as a mean, the formula may be accepted or rejected, but is not a subject of what is commonly understood by proof. We are not, however, to infer that its acceptance or rejection must depend on blind impulse, or arbitrary choice. There is a larger meaning of the word proof, in which this question is as amenable to it as any other of the disputed questions of philosophy. The subject is within the cognizance of the rational faculty; and neither does that faculty deal with it solely in the way of intuition. Considerations may be presented capable of determining the intellect either to give or withhold its assent to the doctrine; and this is equivalent to proof. [...]

WHAT UTILITARIANISM IS

1. A passing remark is all that needs be given to the ignorant blunder of supposing that those who stand up for utility as the test of right and wrong, use the term in that restricted and merely colloquial sense in which utility is opposed to pleasure. [...] Those who know anything about the matter are aware that every writer, from Epicurus to Bentham, who maintained the theory of utility, meant by it, not something to be contradistinguished from pleasure, but pleasure itself, together with exemption from pain; and instead of opposing the useful to the agreeable or the ornamental, have always declared that the useful means these, among other things. Yet the common herd, including the herd of writers, not only in newspapers and periodicals, but in books of weight and pretension, are perpetually falling into this shallow mistake. [...]

2. The creed which accepts as the foundation of morals, Utility, or the Greatest Happiness Principle, holds that actions are right in proportion as they tend to promote happiness, wrong as they tend to produce the reverse of happiness. By happiness is intended pleasure, and the absence of pain; by unhappiness, pain, and the privation of pleasure. To give a clear view of the moral standard set up by the theory, much more requires to be said; in particular, what things it includes in the ideas of pain and pleasure; and to what extent this is left an open question. But these supplementary explanations do not affect the theory of life on which this theory of morality is grounded—namely, that pleasure, and freedom from pain, are the only things desirable as ends; and that all desirable things (which are as numerous in the utilitarian as in any other scheme) are desirable either for the pleasure inherent in themselves, or as means to the promotion of pleasure and the prevention of pain.

3. Now, such a theory of life excites in many minds, and among them in some of the most estimable in feeling and purpose, inveterate dislike. To suppose that life has (as they express it) no higher end than pleasure—no better and nobler object of desire and pursuit—they designate as utterly mean and grovelling; as a doctrine worthy only of swine, to whom the followers of Epicurus were, at a very early period, contemptuously likened; and modern holders of the doctrine are occasionally made the subject of equally polite comparisons by its German, French and English assailants.

4. When thus attacked, the Epicureans have always answered, that it is not they, but their accusers, who represent human nature in a degrading light; since the accusation supposes human beings to be capable of no pleasures except those of which swine are capable. If this supposition were true, the charge could not be gainsaid, but would then be no longer an imputation; for if the sources of pleasure were precisely the same to human beings and to swine, the rule of life which is good enough for the one would be good enough for the other. The comparison of the Epicurean life to that of beasts is felt as degrading, precisely because a beast's pleasures do not satisfy a human being's conceptions of happiness. Human beings have faculties more elevated than the animal appetites, and when once made conscious of them, do not regard anything as happiness which does not include their gratification. I do not, indeed, consider the Epicureans to have been by any means faultless in drawing out their scheme of consequences from the utilitarian principle. To do this in any sufficient manner, many Stoic, as well as Christian elements require to be included. But there is no known Epicurean theory of life which does not assign to the pleasures of the intellect, of the feelings and imagination, and of the moral sentiments, a much higher value as pleasures than to those of mere sensation. It must be admitted, however, that utilitarian writers in general have placed the superiority of mental over bodily pleasures chiefly in the greater permanency, safety, uncostliness, &c., of the former—that is, in their circumstantial advantages rather than in their intrinsic nature. And on all these points utilitarians have fully proved their case; but they might have taken the other, and, as it may be called, higher ground, with entire consistency. It is quite compatible with the principle of utility to recognize the fact, that some *kinds* of pleasure are more desirable and more valuable than others. It would be absurd that while, in estimating all other things, quality is considered as well as quantity, the estimation of pleasures should be supposed to depend on quantity alone.

5. If I am asked, what I mean by difference of quality in pleasures, or what makes one pleasure more valuable than another, merely as a pleasure, except its being greater in amount, there is but one possible answer. Of two pleasures, if there be one to which all or almost all who have experience of both give a decided preference, irrespective of any feeling of moral obligation to prefer it, that is the more desirable pleasure. If one of the two is, by those who are competently acquainted with both, placed so far above the other that they prefer it, even though knowing it to be attended with a greater amount of discontent, and would not resign it for any quantity of the other pleasure which their nature is capable of, we are justified in ascribing to the preferred enjoyment a superiority in quality, so far outweighing quantity as to render it, in comparison, of small account.

6. Now it is an unquestionable fact that those who are equally acquainted with, and equally capable of appreciating and enjoying, both, do give a most marked preference to the manner of existence which employs their higher faculties. Few human creatures would consent to be changed into any of the lower animals, for a promise of the fullest allowance of a beast's pleasures; no intelligent human being would consent to be a fool, no instructed person would be an ignoramus, no person of feeling and conscience would be selfish and base, even though they should be persuaded that the fool, the dunce, or the rascal is better satisfied with his lot than they are with theirs. [...]

Whoever supposes that this preference takes place at a sacrifice of happiness—that the superior being, in anything like equal circumstances, is not happier than the inferior—confounds the two very different ideas, of happiness, and content. It is indisputable that the being whose capacities of enjoyment are low, has the greatest chance of having them fully satisfied; and a highly endowed being will always feel that any happiness which he can look for, as the world is constituted, is imperfect. But he can learn to bear its imperfections, if they are at all bearable; and they will not make him envy the being who is indeed unconscious of the imperfections, but only because he feels not at all the good which those imperfections qualify. It is better to be a human being dissatisfied than a pig satisfied; better to be Socrates dissatisfied than a fool satisfied. And if the fool, or the pig, is of a different opinion, it is because they only know their own side of the question. The other party to the comparison knows both sides.

7. It may be objected, that many who are capable of the higher pleasures, occasionally, under the influence of temptation, postpone them to the lower. But this is quite compatible with a full appreciation of the intrinsic superiority of the higher. Men often, from infirmity of character, make their election for the nearer good, though they know it to be the less valuable; and this no less when the choice is between two bodily pleasures, than when it is between bodily and mental. They pursue sensual indulgences to the injury of health, though perfectly aware that health is the greater good. [...]

8. From this verdict of the only competent judges, I apprehend there can be no appeal. On a question which is the best worth having of two pleasures, or which of two modes of existence is the most grateful to the feelings, apart from its moral attributes and from its consequences, the judgment of those who are qualified by knowledge of both, or, if they differ, that of the majority among them, must be admitted as final. And there needs be the less hesitation to accept this judgment respecting the quality of pleasures, since there is no other tribunal to be referred to even on the question of quantity. What means are there of determining which is the acutest of two pains, or the intensest of two pleasurable sensations, except the general suffrage of those who are familiar with both? Neither pains nor pleasures are homogeneous, and pain is always heterogeneous with pleasure. What is there to decide whether a particular pleasure is worth purchasing at the cost of a particular pain, except the feelings and judgment of the experienced? When, therefore, those feelings and judgment declare the pleasures derived from the higher faculties to be preferable *in kind*, apart from the question of intensity, to those of which the animal nature, disjoined from the higher faculties, is susceptible, they are entitled on this subject to the same regard.

9. I have dwelt on this point, as being a necessary part of a perfectly just conception of Utility or Happiness, considered as the directive rule of human conduct. But it is by no means an indispensable condition to the acceptance of the utilitarian standard; for that standard is not the agent's own greatest happiness, but the greatest amount of happiness altogether; and if it may possibly be doubted whether a noble character is always the happier for its nobleness, there can be no doubt that it makes other people happier, and that the world in general is immensely a gainer by it. Utilitarianism, therefore, could only attain its end by the general cultivation of nobleness of character, even if each individual were only benefited by the nobleness of others, and his own, so far as happiness is concerned, were a sheer deduction from the benefit. But the bare enunciation of such an absurdity as this last, renders refutation superfluous.

10. According to the Greatest Happiness Principle, as above explained, the ultimate end, with reference to and for the sake of which all other things are desirable (whether we are considering our own good or that of other people), is an existence exempt as far as possible from pain, and as rich as possible in enjoyments, both in point of quantity and quality; the test of quality, and the rule for measuring it against quantity, being the preference felt by those who, in their opportunities of experience, to which must be added their habits of self-consciousness and self-observation, are best furnished with the means of comparison. This, being, according to the utilitarian opinion, the end of human action, is necessarily also the standard of morality; which may accordingly be defined, the rules and precepts for human conduct, by the observance of which an existence such as has been described might be, to the greatest extent possible, secured to all mankind; and not to them only, but, so far as the nature of things admits, to the whole sentient creation.

11. Against this doctrine, however, arises another class of objectors, who say that happiness, in any form, cannot be the rational purpose of human life and action; because, in the first place, it is unattainable: and they contemptuously ask, What right hast thou to be happy? [...] Next they say, that men can do *without* happiness; that all noble human beings have felt this, and could not have become noble but by learning the lesson of Entsagen, or renunciation; which lesson, thoroughly learnt and submitted to, they affirm to be the beginning and necessary condition of all virtue.

12. The first of these objections would go to the root of the matter were it well founded; for if no happiness is to be had at all by human beings, the attainment of it cannot be the end of morality, or of any rational conduct. Though, even in that case, something might still be said for the utilitarian theory; since utility includes not solely the pursuit of happiness, but the prevention or mitigation of unhappiness; and if the former aim be chimerical, there will be all the greater scope and more imperative need for the latter, so long at least as mankind think fit to live, and do not take refuge in the simultaneous act of suicide recommended under certain conditions by Novalis. When, however, it is thus positively

asserted to be impossible that human life should be happy, the assertion, if not something like a verbal quibble, is at least an exaggeration. If by happiness be meant a continuity of highly pleasurable excitement, it is evident enough that this is impossible. A state of exalted pleasure lasts only moments, or in some cases, and with some intermissions, hours or days, and is the occasional brilliant flash of enjoyment, not its permanent and steady flame. Of this the philosophers who have taught that happiness is the end of life were as fully aware as those who taunt them. The happiness which they meant was not a life of rapture; but moments of such, in an existence made up of few and transitory pains, many and various pleasures, with a decided predominance of the active over the passive, and having as the foundation of the whole, not to expect more from life than it is capable of bestowing. A life thus composed, to those who have been fortunate enough to obtain it, has always appeared worthy of the name of happiness. And such an existence is even now the lot of many, during some considerable portion of their lives. The present wretched education, and wretched social arrangements, are the only real hindrance to its being attainable by almost all. […]

15. And this leads to the true estimation of what is said by the objectors concerning the possibility, and the obligation, of learning to do without happiness. Unquestionably it is possible to do without happiness; it is done involuntarily by nineteen twentieths of mankind, even in those parts of our present world which are least deep in barbarism; and it often has to be done voluntarily by the hero or the martyr, for the sake of something which he prizes more than his individual happiness. But this something, what is it, unless the happiness of others, or some of the requisites of happiness? It is noble to be capable of resigning entirely one's own portion of happiness, or chances of it: but, after all, this self-sacrifice must be for some end; it is not its own end; and if we are told that its end is not happiness, but virtue, which is better than happiness, I ask, would the

sacrifice be made if the hero or martyr did not believe that it would earn for others immunity from similar sacrifices? Would it be made, if he thought that his renunciation of happiness for himself would produce no fruit for any of his fellow creatures, but to make their lot like his, and place them also in the condition of persons who have renounced happiness? All honour to those who can abnegate for themselves the personal enjoyment of life, when by such renunciation they contribute worthily to increase the amount of happiness in the world; but he who does it, or professes to do it, for any other purpose, is no more deserving of admiration than the ascetic mounted on his pillar. He may be an inspiriting proof of what men *can* do, but assuredly not an example of what they *should*.

16. Though it is only in a very imperfect state of the world's arrangements that any one can best serve the happiness of others by the absolute sacrifice of his own, yet so long as the world is in that imperfect state, I fully acknowledge that the readiness to make such a sacrifice is the highest virtue which can be found in man. I will add, that in this condition of the world, paradoxical as the assertion may be, the conscious ability to do without happiness gives the best prospect of realizing such happiness as is attainable. For nothing except that consciousness can raise a person above the chances of life, by making him feel that, let fate and fortune do their worst, they have not power to subdue him: which, once felt, frees him from excess of anxiety concerning the evils of life, and enables him, like many a Stoic in the worst times of the Roman Empire, to cultivate in tranquillity the sources of satisfaction accessible to him, without concerning himself about the uncertainty of their duration, any more than about their inevitable end.

17. Meanwhile, let utilitarians never cease to claim the morality of self-devotion as a possession which belongs by as good a right to them, as either to the Stoic or to the Transcendentalist. The utilitarian morality does recognize in human beings the power of sacrificing their own greatest

good for the good of others. It only refuses to admit that the sacrifice is itself a good. A sacrifice which does not increase, or tend to increase, the sum total of happiness, it considers as wasted. The only self-renunciation which it applauds, is devotion to the happiness, or to some of the means of happiness, of others; either of mankind collectively, or of individuals within the limits imposed by the collective interests of mankind.

18. I must again repeat, what the assailants of utilitarianism seldom have the justice to acknowledge, that the happiness which forms the utilitarian standard of what is right in conduct, is not the agent's own happiness, but that of all concerned. As between his own happiness and that of others, utilitarianism requires him to be as strictly impartial as a disinterested and benevolent spectator. In the golden rule of Jesus of Nazareth, we read the complete spirit of the ethics of utility. To do as one would be done by, and to love one's neighbour as oneself, constitute the ideal perfection of utilitarian morality. As the means of making the nearest approach to this ideal, utility would enjoin, first, that laws and social arrangements should place the happiness, or (as speaking practically it may be called) the interest, of every individual, as nearly as possible in harmony with the interest of the whole; and secondly, that education and opinion, which have so vast a power over human character, should so use that power as to establish in the mind of every individual an indissoluble association between his own happiness and the good of the whole; especially between his own happiness and the practice of such modes of conduct, negative and positive, as regard for the universal happiness prescribes: so that not only he may be unable to conceive the possibility of happiness to himself, consistently with conduct opposed to the general good, but also that a direct impulse to promote the general good may be in every individual one of the habitual motives of action, and the sentiments connected therewith may fill a large and prominent place in every human being's sentient existence. [...]

19. The objectors to utilitarianism cannot always be charged with representing it in a discreditable light. On the contrary, those among them who entertain anything like a just idea of its disinterested character, sometimes find fault with its standard as being too high for humanity. They say it is exacting too much to require that people shall always act from the inducement of promoting the general interests of society. But this is to mistake the very meaning of a standard of morals, and to confound the rule of action with the motive of it. It is the business of ethics to tell us what are our duties, or by what test we may know them; but no system of ethics requires that the sole motive of all we do shall be a feeling of duty; on the contrary, ninety-nine hundredths of all our actions are done from other motives, and rightly so done, if the rule of duty does not condemn them. It is the more unjust to utilitarianism that this particular misapprehension should be made a ground of objection to it, inasmuch as utilitarian moralists have gone beyond almost all others in affirming that the motive has nothing to do with the morality of the action, though much with the worth of the agent. He who saves a fellow creature from drowning does what is morally right, whether his motive be duty, or the hope of being paid for his trouble: he who betrays the friend that trusts him, is guilty of a crime, even if his object be to serve another friend to whom he is under greater obligations. But to speak only of actions done from the motive of duty, and in direct obedience to principle: it is a misapprehension of the utilitarian mode of thought, to conceive it as implying that people should fix their minds upon so wide a generality as the world, or society at large. The great majority of good actions are intended, not for the benefit of the world, but for that of individuals, of which the good of the world is made up; and the thoughts of the most virtuous man need not on these occasions travel beyond the particular persons concerned, except so far as is necessary to assure himself that in benefiting them he is not violating the rights—that is,

the legitimate and authorized expectations—of any one else. The multiplication of happiness is, according to the utilitarian ethics, the object of virtue: the occasions on which any person (except one in a thousand) has it in his power to do this on an extended scale, in other words, to be a public benefactor, are but exceptional; and on these occasions alone is he called on to consider public utility; in every other case, private utility, the interest or happiness of some few persons, is all he has to attend to. Those alone the influence of whose actions extends to society in general, need concern themselves habitually about so large an object. [...]

20. The same considerations dispose of another reproach against the doctrine of utility, founded on a still grosser misconception of the purpose of a standard of morality, and of the very meaning of the words right and wrong. It is often affirmed that utilitarianism renders men cold and unsympathizing; that it chills their moral feelings towards individuals; that it makes them regard only the dry and hard consideration of the consequences of actions, not taking into their moral estimate the qualities from which those actions emanate. If the assertion means that they do not allow their judgment respecting the rightness or wrongness of an action to be influenced by their opinion of the qualities of the person who does it, this is a complaint not against utilitarianism, but against having any standard of morality at all; for certainly no known ethical standard decides an action to be good or bad because it is done by a good or a bad man, still less because done by an amiable, a brave, or a benevolent man, or the contrary. These considerations are relevant, not to the estimation of actions, but of persons; and there is nothing in the utilitarian theory inconsistent with the fact that there are other things which interest us in persons besides the rightness and wrongness of their actions. The Stoics, indeed, with the paradoxical misuse of language which was part of their system, and by which they strove to raise themselves above all concern about anything but virtue, were fond of saying that he who has that has everything; that he, and only he, is rich, is beautiful, is a king. But no claim of this description is made for the virtuous man by the utilitarian doctrine. Utilitarians are quite aware that there are other desirable possessions and qualities besides virtue, and are perfectly willing to allow to all of them their full worth. They are also aware that a right action does not necessarily indicate a virtuous character, and that actions which are blameable often proceed from qualities entitled to praise. When this is apparent in any particular case, it modifies their estimation, not certainly of the act, but of the agent. I grant that they are, notwithstanding, of opinion, that in the long run the best proof of a good character is good actions; and resolutely refuse to consider any mental disposition as good, of which the predominant tendency is to produce bad conduct. This makes them unpopular with many people; but it is an unpopularity which they must share with every one who regards the distinction between right and wrong in a serious light; and the reproach is not one which a conscientious utilitarian need be anxious to repel. [...]

22. It may not be superfluous to notice a few more of the common misapprehensions of utilitarian ethics, even those which are so obvious and gross that it might appear impossible for any person of candour and intelligence to fall into them: since persons, even of considerable mental endowments, often give themselves so little trouble to understand the bearings of any opinion against which they entertain a prejudice, and men are in general so little conscious of this voluntary ignorance as a defect, that the vulgarest misunderstandings of ethical doctrines are continually met with in the deliberate writings of persons of the greatest pretensions both to high principle and to philosophy. We not uncommonly hear the doctrine of utility inveighed against as a *godless* doctrine. If it be necessary to say anything at all against so mere an assumption, we may say that the question depends upon what idea we have formed of the moral character of the Deity. If it be a true belief that God desires, above all things, the happiness of his creatures, and that this was his purpose in their creation, utility is not only not a godless doctrine, but more profoundly religious than any other. If it be meant that utilitarianism does not recognize the revealed will of God as the supreme law of morals, I answer, that an utilitarian who believes in the perfect goodness and wisdom of God, necessarily believes that whatever God has thought fit to reveal on the subject of morals, must fulfil the requirements of utility in a supreme degree. But others besides utilitarians have been of opinion that the Christian revelation was intended, and is fitted, to inform the hearts and minds of mankind with a spirit which should enable them to find for themselves what is right, and incline them to do it when found, rather than to tell them, except in a very general way, what it is: and that we need a doctrine of ethics, carefully followed out, to *interpret* to us the will of God. Whether this opinion is correct or not, it is superfluous here to discuss; since whatever aid religion, either natural or revealed, can afford to ethical investigation, is as open to the utilitarian moralist as to any other. He can use it as the testimony of God to the usefulness or hurtfulness of any given course of action, by as good a right as others can use it for the indication of a transcendental law, having no connexion with usefulness or with happiness. [...]

24. Again, defenders of utility often find themselves called upon to reply to such objections as this—that there is not time, previous to action, for calculating and weighing the effects of any line of conduct on the general happiness. This is exactly as if any one were to say that it is impossible to guide our conduct by Christianity, because there is not time, on every occasion on which anything has to be done, to read through the Old and New Testaments. The answer to the objection is, that there has been ample time, namely, the whole past duration of the human species. During all that time mankind have been learning by experience the tendencies of actions; on which experience all the prudence, as well as all the morality of life, is dependent. People talk as if the commencement of this course of experience had hitherto been put off, and as if, at the moment when some man feels tempted to meddle with the property or life of another, he had to begin considering for the first time whether murder and theft are injurious to human happiness. Even then I do not think that he would find the question very puzzling; but, at all events, the matter is now done to his hand. [...]

But to consider the rules of morality as improvable, is one thing; to pass over the intermediate generalizations entirely, and endeavour to test each individual action directly by the first principle, is another. It is a strange notion that the acknowledgment of a first principle is inconsistent with the admission of secondary ones. To inform a traveller respecting the place of his ultimate destination, is not to forbid the use of landmarks and direction-posts on the way. The proposition that happiness is the end and aim of morality, does not mean that no road ought to be laid down to that goal, or that persons going thither should not be advised to take one direction rather than another. Men really ought to leave off talking a kind of nonsense on this subject, which they would neither talk nor listen to on other matters of practical concernment. Nobody argues that the art of navigation is not founded on astronomy, because sailors cannot wait to calculate the Nautical Almanack. Being rational creatures, they go to sea with it ready calculated; and all rational creatures go out upon the sea of life with their minds made up on the common questions of right and wrong, as well as on many of the far more difficult questions of wise and foolish. And this, as long as foresight is a human quality, it is to be presumed they will continue to do. Whatever we adopt as the fundamental principle of morality, we require subordinate principles to apply it by: the impossibility of doing without them, being common to all systems, can afford no argument against any one in particular: but gravely to argue as if no such secondary principles could be had, and as if mankind had remained till now, and always must remain, without drawing any general conclusions from the experience of human life, is as high a pitch, I think, as absurdity has ever reached in philosophical controversy. […]

Study Questions

1. Mill thinks the only way to adjudicate which of two pleasures is "higher" is to appeal to the experience of individuals who have experienced both. What are potential problems with this approach?
2. To what degree do you think that Mill's utilitarian view captures our ordinary moral thinking?
3. According to Mill, it can be morally permissible (indeed, even morally obligatory) to harm an individual person to secure benefits to others. Do you think this is correct, or do individuals have inherent moral rights?

9.4   Persons, Situations, and Virtue Ethics

 ### JOHN DORIS

JOHN DORIS (1963–) is a Professor in the Philosophy and Philosophy-Neuroscience-Psychology programs at Washington University in Saint Louis. He helped found the Moral Psychology Research Group, which fosters collaborative interdisciplinary research on moral reasoning, character, moral emotion, positive psychology, moral rules, the neural correlates of ethical judgment, and the attribution of moral responsibility. His research is located at the intersection of psychology, cognitive science, and philosophical ethics. His book *Lack of Character* (2002), which quickly became a classic of the situationist critique of virtue ethics, argues that reflection on experimental social psychology raises significant problems for traditional conceptions of moral character. Doris's current research involves both theoretical and empirical research on moral responsibility, evaluative diversity, psychopathology, and the self.

I. CHARACTEROLOGICAL PSYCHOLOGY, EMPIRICAL INADEQUACY

Imagine a person making a call in a suburban shopping plaza. As the caller leaves the phone booth, along comes Alice, who drops a folder full of papers that scatter in the caller's path. Will the caller stop and help before the only copy of Alice's magnum opus is trampled by the bargain-hungry throngs? Perhaps it depends on the person: Jeff, an entrepreneur incessantly scheming about fattening his real estate holdings, probably won't, while Nina, a political activist who takes in stray cats, probably will. Nina is the compassionate type; Jeff isn't. In these circumstances we expect their true colors to show. But this may be a mistake, as an experiment conducted by Isen and Levin (1972) shows. There, the paper-dropper was an experimental confederate. For one group of callers, a dime was planted in the phone's coin return slot; for the other, the slot was empty. Here are the results (after Isen and Levin 1972: 387):

	Helped	Did not help
Dime	14	2
No dime	1	24

If greedy Jeff finds the dime, he'll likely help; if caring Nina doesn't, she very likely won't. This finding exemplifies a 70-year "situationist" experimental tradition in social and personality psychology, a tradition which has repeatedly demonstrated that the behavioral reliability expected on standard theoretical constructions of personality is not revealed in the systematic observation of behavior. I will suggest that situationist research has revisionary implications for ethical thought, particularly for the neo-Aristotelian ethical theory prominent in moral philosophy for the past quarter century. For such a claim to be fairly earned, we would have to examine decades of research and debate in social and personality psychology, a project I undertake elsewhere.[1] Here, my ambitions are modest: I hope only to produce the beginnings of a suspicion that Aristotelian moral psychology may be more problematic than philosophers engaged in the ethics and character debate have thought.

In this section, I argue that Aristotelian approaches to ethics, in so far as they presuppose certain distinctive commitments in descriptive psychology, may be subject to damaging empirical criticisms. But I first need to say something about my empirically motivated methodology, because there has been considerable skepticism regarding the relevance of empirical considerations to ethical theorizing. This much skepticism is certainly reasonable: to show that an ethical theory is *descriptively* inadequate is not to show that it is *normatively* inadequate, so even if my empirical critique problematizes Aristotelian descriptive psychology, the prospects for Aristotelian normative theory remain undecided. My reasons for caution here are not claims regarding the "theoretical autonomy" of ethical reflection or putatively clear distinctions between theoretical and practical reason; such claims are the subject of substantial controversy, and justly so. But I am quite willing to allow that ethical inquiry is methodologically "discontinuous" with descriptive or scientific endeavors[...]; "ethics," as Stevenson (1963: 13) said, "must not be psychology." Results in descriptive psychology, taken by themselves, cannot be decisive factors in evaluating normative claims.[2] Accordingly, after considering empirical difficulties facing Aristotelian descriptive psychology and sketching what I contend is a more empirically adequate situationist alternative, in sections two and three I consider how the competing moral psychologies fare on normative grounds. If I am right, the approach to moral psychology suggested by situationism enjoys certain advantages over Aristotelianism as a foundation for normative thought. Moreover, while motivating this claim inevitably requires more than empirical assessment of the alternatives, it will emerge that the advantages of situationism as a grounding for normative reflection are, in substantial measure, a result of its more empirically adequate descriptive psychology. Ethics is not simply psychology, but in this instance there are interesting and important connections between the two endeavors. To begin, then, I must give a sense of the issues on the descriptive side.

We believe the person of good character is not easily swayed by circumstance, and we have a rich normative vocabulary reflecting this ideal: "steady," "dependable," "steadfast," "unwavering," "unflinching." Conversely, when a person's behavior disappoints, we are equipped with terms of abuse to mark what we take to be lack of character: "weak," "fickle," "disloyal," "unfaithful," "irresolute." Apparently, character is expected to have regular behavioral manifestations: we believe that the person of good character will behave appropriately, even in situations with substantial pressures to moral failure, and we are similarly confident that we would be foolish to rely on the person of bad character. This interpretative strategy presupposes that the attribution of a character trait allows us to predict an individual's behavior in novel circumstances; we may not have previously observed Jim's behavior on a foundering ship, but if we know he is courageous, we know that he will perform his office properly should such a situation arise.[3] Unfortunately, experimental evidence of the sort just mentioned suggests that this approach, however commonplace it may be, is inadequate to the facts of actual behavior: trait attribution is often surprisingly inefficacious in predicting behavior in particular novel situations, because differing behavioral outcomes often seem a function of situational variation more than individual disposition. To put things crudely, people typically lack character. But while characterological moral psychology is problematic from the perspective of empirical psychology, it enjoys an impeccable philosophical provenance—it is a faithful rendering of certain features of Aristotle's, and neo-Aristotelian, ethical thought.

For Aristotle, good character is "firm and unchangeable" [...], the virtues are *hexeis* [...], and a *hexis* is a disposition that is "permanent and hard to change" [...]. Virtues are supposed to have reliable behavioral manifestations: although good people may suffer misfortunes that impede the activity of virtue, they will never (*oudepote*) behave viciously [...]. In addition, Aristotle thinks that virtue is typified by the performance of right actions in the most difficult and demanding circumstances [...]; the practically wise *phronimos* will follow the appropriate course of action *whatever* circumstance he is in [...]. In sum, we can say that Aristotelian virtues are *robust*, or substantially resistant to contrary situational pressures, in their behavioral manifestations.

Aristotelians also tend to maintain some version of an *evaluative consistency* thesis, maintaining that in a given personality the occurrence of a trait with a particular evaluative valence is probabilistically related to the occurrence of other traits with similar evaluative valences.[4] For example, the expectation is that a generous person is more likely compassionate than callous; a compassionate and generous person is evaluatively consistent, while a callous and generous person is not. Then for the Aristotelian, good character is supposed to be an integrated association of robust traits.

What would count as evidence supporting the attribution of Aristotelian traits and personality structures? I submit that the evidence we require is observed *behavioral reliability*—behavior consistent with a trait or grouping of related traits across a range of relevant eliciting situations that may vary widely in their particulars. That is, we are justified in inferring the existence of an Aristotelian personality structure when a person's behavior reliably conforms to the patterns expected on postulation of that structure. In the psychological lexicon, we can say that trait attribution requires substantial *cross-situational consistency* in behavior (e.g., Mischel 1968; Ross and Nisbett 1991). If I am right about the experimental data, systematic observation typically reveals failures of cross-situational consistency; behavior is very often surprisingly unreliable. We have good reason to consider an alternative, more empirically adequate, conception of moral personality.

Situationist social psychology suggests such an alternative. Situationism's three central theses concern behavioral variation, the nature of traits, and trait organization in personality structure:

(i) Behavioral variation across a population owes more to situational differences than dispositional differences among persons. Individual dispositional differences are not as strongly behaviorally individuating as we might have supposed; to a surprising extent we are safest predicting, for a particular situation, that a person will behave pretty much as most others would.[5]

(ii) Empirical evidence problematizes the attribution of robust traits.[6] Whatever behavioral reliability we do observe may be readily short-circuited by situational variation: in a run of trait-relevant situations with diverse features, an individual to whom we have attributed a given trait will often behave inconsistently with regard to the behavior expected on attribution of that trait. Note that this is not to deny the possibility of temporal stability in behavior; the situationist acknowledges that individuals may exhibit behavioral regularity over time across a run of substantially similar situations (Ross and Nisbett 1991: 101; Wright and Mischel 1987: 1161–2; Shoda, Mischel, and Wright 1994: 681–3).

(iii) Personality structure is not typically evaluatively consistent. For a given person, the dispositions operative in one situation may have a very different evaluative status than those manifested in another situation—evaluatively inconsistent dispositions may "cohabitate" in a single personality.[7]

This situationist conception of personality is not an unrepentant skepticism about personological determinants of behavior such as that associated with Skinnerian behaviorism; although the situationist rejects the notion of robust traits effecting cross-situationally consistent behavior, she allows the possibility of temporally stable, situation-particular, "local" traits that may reflect dispositional differences among persons. These local traits may be extremely fine-grained: a person might be reliably helpful in iterated trials of the same situation (such as when she finds a dime in a mall phone booth and someone drops a pile of papers in her path), and reliably unhelpful in other, often surprisingly similar, circumstances (say when confronted with the same dropped papers when her search for change is disappointed). The difficulty for the Aristotelian is that local traits are not likely to produce the patterns of behavior expected on broad trait categories like "compassionate" or "courageous"; even seemingly insignificant variations in situation may "tap" different dispositions, effecting inconsistent behavior. We might say that systematically observed behavior, rather

than suggesting evaluatively consistent personality structures, suggests instead *fragmented* personality structures—evaluatively inconsistent associations of large numbers of local traits. Thus, virtue-theoretic conceptions of moral personality, such as Geach's (1977) inventory of seven cardinal virtues, or Aristotle's somewhat less parsimonious inventory of twelve virtues of character and eight intellectual virtues, will seem too roughly hewn in light of the many and various moral dispositions people actually possess.

But we are not forced to choose between overly parsimonious characterological accounts and "fragmented" constructions of personality so theoretically unwieldy as to be useless in the explanation and prediction of behavior; situationism allows that a suitably fine-grained inventory of local traits may provide an account of personality that is both empirically adequate and theoretically useful. Were we in possession of a reasonably complete inventory of an individual's local traits, we would know quite a bit about how we could expect that individual to behave, although the expected behavior would not be consistent with regard to broad trait categories. Further, there is no empirical reason to deny that some individuals may possess constellations of local traits that are more or less conducive to success in their particular life circumstances; a person may possess an association of traits, albeit an evaluatively fragmented one, that better serves her in the life she has chosen, or fallen into.

It is important to notice that situationism is not embarrassed by the considerable behavioral regularity we do observe: because the preponderance of our life circumstances may involve a relatively structured range of situations, behavioral patterns are not, for the most part, haphazard (see Mischel 1968: 281). Still, we have reason to doubt that behavioral regularity is as substantial as casual observation—which even when directed at our intimates may occur on occasions limited in both number and diversity—may suggest. Every person, in the course of his or her life, exhibits a multitude of behaviors; since social observation is usually piecemeal and unsystematic, we should be hesitant to take our limited sampling of behaviors as evidence for confident interpretations of personality. At bottom, the question is whether the behavioral regularity we observe is to be primarily explained by reference to robust dispositional structures or situational regularity. The situationist insists that the striking variability of behavior with situational variation favors the latter hypothesis.

To summarize: According to the first situationist thesis, behavioral variation among individuals often owes more to distinct circumstances than distinct personalities; the difference between the person who behaves honestly and the one who fails to do so, for example, may be more a function of situation than character. Moreover, behavior may vary quite radically when compared with that expected on the postulation of a given trait. We have little assurance that a person to whom we attributed a trait will consistently behave in a trait-relevant fashion across a run of trait-relevant situations with variable pressures to such behavior; the putatively "honest" person may very well not consistently display honest behavior across a diversity of situations where honesty is appropriate.[8] This is just what we would expect on the second situationist thesis, which rejects notions of robust traits. Finally, as the third thesis suggests, expectations of evaluative consistency are likely to be disappointed. Behavioral evidence suggests that personality is comprised of evaluatively fragmented trait-associations rather than evaluatively integrated ones: e.g., for a given person, a local disposition to honesty will often be found together with local dispositions to dishonesty.

Some care is required, because the salience of situationist criticism depends on how characterological psychology is interpreted. Personality and social psychologists (e. g., Brody 1988: 31; Pervin 1994: 108) standardly treat personality traits as dispositions productive of behavior, and philosophers have typically understood virtues

along the same lines. As Hardie (1980: 107) reads Aristotle, a virtue is a "dispositional property" defined in terms of "hypothetical statements mentioning the conditions of [its] manifestations." On this *dispositionalist* account, to attribute a virtue is to (implicitly) assert a subjunctive conditional: if a person possesses a virtue, she will exhibit virtue-relevant behavior in a given virtue-relevant eliciting condition with some markedly above chance probability p. Just as with dispositional interpretations of properties in other areas, we want more of a story than the conditional provides, lest our account seem uninformative or trivial, but whatever further story we tell, the conditional does reflect the behavioral reliability that is a central characteristic of virtue. For my purposes the problem is that, even if we add the probabilistic qualification, the conditional is too strong: trait attribution does not ground confident predictions of particular behaviors (with probabilities markedly above chance, or approaching certainty), especially in situations where the behavior is outside the population norm for that situation.[9] If dispositionalism is committed to confident predictions of particular behaviors, it is subject to empirical difficulty. [...]

At this juncture, the Aristotelian may charge that my arguments have missed the mark: she can allow that situationist research problematizes notions of personality in psychology, together with certain philosophical and lay conceptions of character, and still deny that it makes trouble for her conception of virtue. The psychology literature I rely on concerns personality traits generically construed, with relatively little self-conscious attention to traits we might be tempted to count as virtues, and I have apparently taken the liberty of relating results from that literature to the particular case of the virtues. Like many other writers on ethics, I believe a dispositional analysis applies to virtues as well as other traits. But I have neglected to discuss one important regard in which virtues are not "generic" traits; it may be argued that the virtues are extremely rare, not widely instantiated, traits.[10] If so, the Aristotelian can argue as follows: the situationist research may show that the ordinary person's character is not as sturdy as we might hope, but it cannot rule out the possibility that there is some small percentage of people who are truly virtuous.[11] The fact that many people failed morally in the observed situations tells us little about the adequacy of Aristotelian descriptive psychology, since such disappointing demographics are exactly what the virtue theorist would expect. Indeed, a virtue-based approach can explain the situationist data: it is precisely because so few people are truly virtuous that we see the results that we do. On this reading, the Aristotelian's empirical claims are modest enough to be unembarrassed by the data; the account is only committed to the existence of a few exemplary individuals, by reference to which we guide our conduct. For example, Blum's (1994: 94–6) virtue ethic does not require commitments regarding the general realizability of virtue: "it is given to very few to be moral exemplars," he says, regardless of "how conscientiously one sets oneself to become anything like the moral paragons one admires." Blum's (1994: 95–6) claim is not that many of us, or even any of us, can successfully emulate Aristotelian ideals of character, but rather that reflecting on these ideals can help us become people who are, and do, better: through reflection on moral exemplars, we may improve our own character and conduct. If the practical efficacy of emulation is not undercut by the extreme difficulty of the object of emulation being fully realized, emulation is not problematized by situationism.

This argument deserves to be taken seriously, but it is worth noting that such "empirically modest" accounts may deprive Aristotelianism of a substantial measure of its traditional appeal. Aristotelians have typically emphasized moral development and education (Aristotle 1984: e.g., 1099b29–32; 1103b21–31; McDowell: 1979: 333); the ideal of virtue, it is tempting to think, is a sort of model for the condition actual persons (with the right sort of nurturing) might achieve, or at least closely approximate. Recent philosophical writing on moral development and character (e.g., McDowell 1996, Herman 1996) is naturally read as emphasizing the sort of character agents may inculcate, rather than the advantages of reflection on a rarefied ideal. Moreover, it has commonly been held that virtues are to be appealed to in the explanation of behavior (e.g., Brandt 1988: 64); MacIntyre (1984: 199) goes so far as to argue that virtue theory is a necessary element in behavioral science. Perhaps these claims are compatible with an empirically modest moral psychology; perhaps developmental and explanatory appeals to virtue are meant to be of extremely limited empirical applicability. But it seems to me that such assertions are not typically qualified in ways that suggest empirical caution. Indeed, we may wonder if an empirically modest reading of Aristotelianism can account for its recent popularity, a popularity that appears to owe much to the promise of an engaging and lifelike moral psychology. So if we push the "argument from rarity" too far, it becomes uncertain what the distinctive attractions of Aristotelianism are supposed to be. But again, as I said at the outset, an empirically compelling moral psychology is not the only *desideratum* for ethical theory. So I must join the question directly: to what extent does reflection on a few extraordinary individuals facilitate ethically desirable behavior?[12] Or more broadly: what exactly are the practical advantages enjoyed by ideals of virtue? [...]

III. CHARACTER AND DELIBERATION

If I am right, situationism suggests a certain redirection of our ethical attention. Rather than striving to develop characters that will determine our behavior in ways significantly independent of circumstance, we should invest more of our energies in attending to the features of our environment that impact behavioral out-comes. It may seem as though, in accepting this emphasis, we would be abdicating our status as persons—autonomous agents who can, in some deep sense, chart the courses of our own lives. While this way of putting the concern is over-stated, I agree that my approach requires revi-sion of heuristics that may be deeply entrenched in our self-conceptions, in so far as these con-ceptions have Aristotelian characterological underpinnings. But evaluation of ethical theo-ries, like any problem in theory choice, involves determining the most attractive combination of costs and benefits; no theory, least of all in ethics, comes for free. In concluding, I'll try to show that the discomfort we experience in embracing a situationist moral psychology may be at least partly ameliorated by the promise of substantial advantages in the practice of deliberation.

Reflection on situationism has an obvious benefit in deliberation: it may serve to remind us that, for people like us, the world is a mor-ally dangerous place. In an attitude study related to his obedience experiments, Milgram (1974: 27–31) asked respondents to predict the max-imum intensity shock they would deliver were the subjects "required" to punish the confed-erate "victim" with incrementally increasing shocks: the mean prediction was around 150 volts (level 10), and no subject said they would go beyond 300 volts (level 20). When these subjects were asked to predict the behavior of others, they predicted that at most 1 or 2% of subjects would deliver the maximum shock of 450 volts (level 30). In fact, for a standard per-mutation of the experiment (version 5; Milgram 1974: 56–61), the mean maximum shock was 360 (level 24), and 65% continued to the high-est possible shock of 450 volts (level 30). The usual expectation seems to be that behavior is much more situation-independent than it actu-ally is; apparently, we tend to see character traits as substantially robust, with typical dispositions to moral decency serving as guarantors against destructive behavior even in circumstances like the Milgram experiment where the situational pressures to moral failure are relatively intense. Milgram's study indicates that perception and reality are markedly discrepant in this regard.[13] The consequence of this discrepancy, I contend, is an increased probability of moral failure; many times our confidence in character is precisely what puts us at risk in morally dangerous situa-tions.[14] Far from being practically indispensable, characterological discourse is a heuristic we may often have very good reason to dispense with in our deliberations.

Take a prosaic example. Imagine that a col-league with whom you have had a long flirtation invites you for dinner, offering enticement of sumptuous food and fine wine, with the excuse that you are temporarily orphaned while your spouse is out of town. Let's assume the obvious way to read this text is the right one, and assume further that you regard the infidelity that may result as a morally undesirable outcome. If you are like one of Milgram's respondents, you might think that there is little cause for concern; you are, after all, a morally upright person, and a spot of claret never did anyone a bit of harm. On the other hand, if you take the lessons of situation-ism to heart, you avoid dinner like the plague, because you know that you may not be able to predict your behavior in a problematic situation on the basis of your antecedent values. You do not doubt that you sincerely value fidelity; you simply doubt your ability to act in conformity with this value once the candles are lit and the wine begins to flow.[15] Relying on character once in the situation is a mistake, you agree; the way to achieve the ethically desirable result is to recog-nize that situational pressures may all too easily overwhelm character, and avoid the dangerous situation. I don't think it wild speculation to claim that this is a better strategy than donning your most fetching clothes and dropping by for a "harmless" evening, secure in the knowledge of your righteousness.

The way to get things right more often, I suggest, is by attending to the determinative features of situations. We should try, so far as we are able, to avoid "near occasions for sin"—morally dangerous circumstances. At the same time, we should seek near occasions for happier behaviors—situations conducive to ethically desirable conduct. This means that the determinants of moral success or failure may emerge earlier in an activity than we might think. In our example, the difficulty to be addressed lies less in an exercise of will after dinner than in deciding to engage the situation in the first place, a decision that may occur in a lower pressure, relatively "cool" context where even exquisitely situation-sensitive creatures such as ourselves may be able to act in accordance with their values. For instance, it may be easier to "do the right thing" over the phone than it would be in the moral "hot zone" of an intimate encounter. Then condemnation for ethical failure might very often be directed, not at a particular failure of the will in action, but at a certain culpable naiveté, or insufficiently careful attention to situations. The implication of this is that our duties may be surprisingly complex, involving not simply obligations to particular actions, but a sort of "cognitive responsibility" to attend, in our deliberations, to the determinative features of situations. If it is true that this cognitive responsibility may frequently be exercised in "cooler" decision contexts, this approach might effect a considerable reliability in ethical behavior.

Unfortunately, I doubt our optimism here should be unbounded. Those with knowledge of the Milgram paradigm, for example, are relatively unlikely to be obedient dupes in highly similar situations, but this knowledge may be difficult to apply in different circumstances. Further, many morally dangerous features of situations will have a degree of subtlety that will make them difficult to unmask, however we try; they may seem as innocuous as not finding change in the coin return, or running a few minutes late for an appointment. In short, we may often be in "Milgram situations" without being so aware—at a seminar, or in a meeting. So my approach

cannot offer guarantees. But it can, I submit, focus our ethical attention where it may do the most good: deliberation contexts where reflection on our values may be most likely to make a difference.

The virtue theorist may now object that she and I are simply talking about different things. The examples I have given concern the *description* of herself under which the agent deliberates and acts, while virtue theory concerns the *ideal* the agent deliberates and acts according to. The virtue theorist may grant that a situationist account of personality is often the most effective descriptive psychology for guiding our deliberations, since it will increase our sensitivity to moral risk. But the question remains as to what regulative ideal should guide our conduct, and the virtue theorist might charge that I have said nothing that should cause us to reject the ideal of virtue in this role. There is the possibility, as we have seen Blum suggest [. . .], that the agent is best served by attempting to emulate an exemplar—perhaps looking to such ideals is the most effective way to facilitate ethically desirable conduct. It is crucial to see that this has the look of an empirical claim concerning the ways in which actual persons interact with ideals; whatever the empirical commitments of the background moral psychology, on this approach our choice of normative theories is impacted by empirical considerations regarding the influence of ideals on conduct. [. . .]

What I take myself to have shown, so far, is that situationist moral psychology may help ground desirable habits of ethical deliberation. Indeed, we have seen that situationist moral psychology may figure prominently even in virtue-based deliberation. I have also shown, by reflecting on Milgram's experiments and an example of my own, that characterological moral thought may have substantial pitfalls, in so far as it may foster a dangerous neglect of situational influences. Still, there may be situations where characterological reflection, properly understood, is the best approach to ethical deliberation. But this is a claim in need of an argument, especially given the attractions of the situationist approach. [...]

In closing, let me review the dialectic: Aristotelian virtue ethics, when construed as invoking a generally applicable descriptive psychology, may appear more attractive than competitors such as Kantianism and consequentialism, in that characterological moral psychology might allow a more compelling account of moral development and agency. But understood this way, character-based approaches are subject to damaging empirical criticism. If, on the other hand, virtue theory is reformed as a normative theory concerned with regulative ideals more than empirically-constrained psychology, the empirical critique is disarmed, but virtue theory no longer has the selling point of a compelling descriptive psychology. At this juncture the virtue theorist must offer argument to the effect that her favored regulative ideals (however, exactly, they are to be construed), are better suited to effecting morally desirable conduct than alternatives offered by her competitors. I have argued that characterological ideals are not obviously indispensable in some central areas of normative practice, and also noted some attractions of the situationist alternative. This does not suggest that virtue theory is no longer in the running; but it does suggest that it is not, without further argument, out in front of the pack.

Notes

1. In my *Lack of Character: Personality and Moral Behavior* (2002, Cambridge University Press), I offer more detailed discussion of the relevant psychology and a more involved treatment of its normative implications. Flanagan (1991) provided the first sustained account of situationism in philosophy; although our conclusions differ, my discussion is indebted to his.

2. However, it may be that conclusions in descriptive psychology will be one factor we consider when attempting to bring our ethical judgments into

Rawlsian reflective equilibrium (see Rawls 1971: 20–1, 432). [...]

3. There are quantities of empirical work suggesting that this strategy is both widespread and problematic. For a useful review of psychological research demonstrating overconfident behavioral prediction based on trait attribution, see Gilbert and Malone (1995). The example is from Conrad's (1957/1900) *Lord Jim*; there Conrad is preoccupied with Jim's unexpected failure to behave courageously when his ship is endangered.

4. See Flanagan (1991: 283–90). Aristotle (1984: 1144b30–1145a2) apparently maintains a reciprocity thesis: because of their common origin in practical reason, possession of one particular virtue entails possession of all the virtues (for explication of Aristotle's argument, see Irwin 1988: 67–71). Some contemporary followers of Aristotle maintain a unity thesis; McDowell claims that the virtues are not independent capacities, but different manifestations of a "single complex sensitivity" (1979: 333; cf. Murdoch 1970: 57–8). [...]

5. See Ross and Nisbett (1991: 113). This allows us to see that eschewing characterological psychology does not make behavioral prediction impossible—among other things, behavior will to some extent vary reliably with the situation.

6. Note that (i) and (ii) are distinct. A disposition, such as a disposition to display aversive behavior when in excruciating pain, may be robust without being strongly individuating. Conversely, a person may exhibit strongly individuating behavior without possessing robust traits, if his circumstances are sufficiently atypical. Thus, a lack of individuation alone does not imply a lack of robustness, nor does a lack of robustness alone imply a lack of individuation.

7. Many observers of the Holocaust have noted the "paradoxical" levels of inconsistency exhibited by genocidal killers; brutality can coexist all too comfortably, it seems, with compassion (Levi 1989: 56; Lifton 1986, e.g., 337; Todorov 1996: 141). The virtuous no less than the vicious exemplify this paradox; in this age of unstinting biography, we repeatedly find that moral heroes as well as moral monsters exhibit gross inconsistencies in moral personality (Flanagan 1991: 6–12).

8. Some of the genocidal Nazi doctors at Auschwitz behaved decently, and even admirably, before the death camp; prior to his appointment at Auschwitz, the war criminal Wirths surreptitiously treated Jews after it had become illegal to do so (Lifton 1986: 386). Note that such "transformation" was not necessarily a function of situational factors that are readily construed as coercive; Lifton (1986: 198) maintains that it was possible for Auschwitz doctors to avoid perpetrating atrocities "without repercussions."

9. Predictions by laypersons appear substantially overconfident in this regard. In one study, Kunda and Nisbett (1986: 210–11) found that subjects' estimated probability that an individual they rated as more honest than another in one situation would retain the same ranking in the next observed situation was typically around .8. This probability reflects an estimated correlation of approximately .81, while the relevant empirical study found the correlation to be .23, which translates into a probability of under .6, not highly above chance. Shweder (1977: 642) found that subjects estimated that a given individual performing "extrovert" behaviors in two different situations would correlate at .92, again far outstripping the correlation of .08 found in empirical work.

10. In some regards, Aristotle may be skeptical about the general realizability of virtue: he claims that the continent person is able to act according to his resolutions more, and the incontinent person less, than most people (1984: 1152a30). Presumably, the genuinely virtuous temperate person would be rarer still. On the other hand, Aristotle expects that virtue is possible for most people, if they are not hopelessly deficient in the capacities required for the appropriate study (1984: 1099b 18–19).

11. This is something I can easily grant: it would be a surprising empirical argument indeed that ruled out the bare *possibility* of a particular psychology being realized. Of course, there may be a limited percentage of individuals observation would reveal to be relatively "pure types," but the evidence suggests that this is not the usual case.

12. My use of "ethically desirable behavior" is not meant to beg questions in normative ethics; I assume only that there is a substantial range of cases on which a variety of ethical perspectives can agree. For example, the Kantian, consequentialist, and Aristotelian may agree that it would have been ethically desirable for Nazis to disobey genocidal orders, even if their accounts of why this is so differ.

13. This is also suggested by Zimbardo's (1973: 53–6) "prison experiment": some "guards" in his simulated penitentiary rapidly descended into barbaric behavior despite their initial confidence that they were not the sort of person who would do such things.

14. As Zimbardo (1974:566) suggested in his comments on Milgram's (1974) book, "the reason we can be so readily manipulated is precisely because we maintain an illusion of personal invulnerability and personal control."

15. Situationism does not deny that people may consistently avow values; the difficulty is that there is reason to doubt that values, even if consistently embraced, will effect consistent behavioral patterns. Failures of behavior to conform with avowed values and self-conceptions are well-documented in psychology (Mischel 1968: 25; Ross and Nisbett 1991: 98–9); for a compelling demonstration of this sort of phenomenon, see McClelland (1985: 818–20).

References

Aristotle. 1984. *The Complete Works of Aristotle, Oxford Revised Translation*. Edited by J. Barnes. Princeton: Princeton University Press.

Blum, L. A. 1994. *Moral Perception and Particularity*. Cambridge: Cambridge University Press.

Brandt, R. B. 1988. "The Structure of Virtue." *Midwest Studies in Philosophy* 13.

Brody, N. 1988. *Personality: In Search of Individuality*. New York: Academic.

Conrad, J. 1957. *Lord Jim*. Harmondsworth: Penguin Books. Originally published 1900.

Dummett, M. 1976. "What is a Theory of Meaning? (II)." In G. Evans and J. McDowell (eds.), *Truth and Meaning*. Oxford: Oxford University Press.

Flanagan, O. 1991. *Varieties of Moral Personality*. Cambridge, MA.: Harvard University Press.

Geach, P. T. 1977. *The Virtues*. Cambridge: Cambridge University Press.

Gilbert, D. T., and Malone, P. S. 1995. "The Correspondence Bias." *Psychological Bulletin* 117.

Hardie, W. F. R. 1980. *Aristotle's Ethical Theory* (2nd edn.). Oxford: Oxford University Press.

Herman, B. 1996. "Making Room for Character." In S. Engstrom and J. Whiting (eds.), *Aristotle, Kant, and the Stoics: Rethinking Happiness and Duty*. Cambridge: Cambridge University Press.

Irwin, T. H. 1988. "Disunity in the Aristotelian Virtues." *Oxford Studies in Ancient Philosophy: Supplementary Volume*, 1988.

Isen, A. M. and Levin, H. 1972. "Effect of Feeling Good on Helping: Cookies and Kindness." *Journal of Personality and Social Psychology* 21.

Kunda, Z., and Nisbett, R. N. 1986. "The Psychometrics of Everyday Life." *Cognitive Psychology* 18.

Levi, P. 1989. *The Drowned and the Saved*. Translation by R. Rosenthal, New York: Vintage Books.

Lifton, R. J. 1986. *The Nazi Doctors*. New York: Basic Books.

MacIntyre, A. 1984. *After Virtue* (2nd. edn.). Notre Dame: University of Notre Dame Press.

McClelland, D. C. 1985. "How Motives, Skills, and Values Determine What People Do." *American Psychologist* 40.

McDowell, J. 1979. "Virtue and Reason." *Monist* 62.

McDowell, J. 1996. "Deliberation and Moral Development in Aristotle's Ethics." In S. Engstrom and J. Whiting (eds.), *Aristotle, Kant, and the Stoics: Rethinking Happiness and Duty*. Cambridge: Cambridge University Press.

Milgram, S. 1974. *Obedience to Authority*. New York: Harper and Row.

Mischel, W. 1968. *Personality and Assessment*. New York: John J. Wiley and Sons.

Murdoch, I. 1970. *The Sovereignty of Good*. London: Routledge and Kegan Paul.

Pervin, L. A. 1994. "A Critical Analysis of Current Trait Theory." *Psychological Inquiry* 5.

Rawls, J. 1971. *A Theory of Justice*. Cambridge, MA: Harvard University Press.

Ross, L., and Nisbett, R. E. 1991. *The Person and the Situation*. Philadelphia: Temple University Press.

Shoda, Y., Mischel, W., and Wright, J. C. 1994. "Intraindividual Stability in the Organization and Patterning of Behavior: Incorporating Psychological Situations Into the Idiographic Analysis of Personality." *Journal of Personality and Social Psychology* 67.

Shweder, R. A. 1977. "Likeness and Likelihood in Everyday Thought: Magical Thinking in Judgments about Personality." *Current Anthropology* 18.

Stevenson, C.L. 1963. "The Emotive Meaning of Ethical Terms." In C. L. Stevenson, *Facts and Values*. New Haven: Yale University Press. Originally published, 1937.

Todorov, T. 1996. *Facing the Extreme: Moral Life in the Concentration Camps*. New York: Metropolitan Books.

Wright, J. C., and Mischel, W. 1987. "A Conditional Approach to Dispositional Constructs: The Local Predictability of Social Behavior." *Journal of Personality and Social Psychology* 53.

Zimbardo, P. 1973. "The Mind is a Formidable Jailer: A Pirandellian Prison." *The New York Times Magazine*, April 8, 1973.

Zimbardo, P. 1974. "On 'Obedience to Authority.'" *American Psychologist* 29.

Study Questions

1. What plausible answer is there as to why 65 percent of individuals would, in the Milgram shock experiment, deliver the maximum shock when, according to their own reports, they thought doing so resulted in the serious harm or even death of the "victim"?

2. To what degree do you think the experimental data Doris cites calls into question a traditional understanding of virtue, such as that presented and defended by Aristotle?

3. To what degree should moral theory be informed by psychology and other related empirical disciplines?

From Neural "Is" to Moral "Ought"   9.5

JOSHUA D. GREENE

JOSHUA D. GREENE (1974–) is a philosopher, experimental psychologist, and neuroscientist. He is an Assistant Professor in the Department of Psychology and the Director of the Moral Cognition Laboratory at Harvard University. He received his A.B. in Philosophy from Harvard University in 1997 and his Ph.D. in Philosophy from Princeton University in 2002. From 2002 to 2006, he trained as a postdoctoral fellow at Princeton's Department of Psychology and Center for the Study of Brain, Mind, and Behavior. His primary research interest is the psychological and neuroscientific study of moral judgment, focusing on the interplay between automatic emotional responses and controlled cognitive processes in moral decision making. His broader interests cluster around the intersection of philosophy, psychology, and neuroscience. His research has been supported by the National Science Foundation, the National Institutes of Health, and the MacArthur Foundation. He is currently writing a book about the philosophical implications of our emerging scientific understanding of morality.

Many moral philosophers boast a well-cultivated indifference to research in moral psychology. This is regrettable, but not entirely groundless.[1] Philosophers have long recognized that facts concerning how people actually think or act do not imply facts about how people ought to think or act, at least not in any straightforward way. This principle is summarized by the Humean[2] dictum that one can't derive an "ought" from an "is." In a similar vein, moral philosophers since Moore[3] have taken pains to avoid the "naturalistic fallacy," the mistake of identifying that which is natural with that which is right or good (or, more broadly, the mistake of identifying moral properties with natural properties). Prominent among those accused by Moore of committing this fallacy was Herbert Spencer, the father of "social Darwinism," who aimed to ground moral and political philosophy in evolutionary principles.

Spencer coined the phrase "survival of the fittest," giving Darwin's purely biological notion of fitness a socio-moral twist: for the good of the species, the government ought not to interfere with nature's tendency to let the strong dominate the weak.

Spencerian social Darwinism is long gone, but the idea that principles of natural science might provide a foundation for normative ethics has won renewed favour in recent years. Some friends of "naturalized ethics" argue, contra Hume and Moore, that the doctrine of the naturalistic fallacy is itself a fallacy, and that facts about right and wrong are, in principle at least, as amenable to scientific discovery as any others. Most of the arguments in favour of ethics as continuous with natural science have been rather abstract, with no attempt to support particular moral theories on the basis of particular scientific

Joshua Greene, "From Neural 'Is' to Moral 'Ought': What are the Moral Implications of Neuroscientific Moral Psychology?" *Nature Reviews Neuroscience* 4 (2003). Reprinted with permission of the publication.

research. Casebeer's neuroscientific defense of Aristotelian virtue theory (this issue) is a notable exception in this regard.[4]

A critical survey of recent attempts to naturalize ethics is beyond the scope of this article. Instead I will simply state that I am sceptical of naturalized ethics for the usual Humean and Moorean reasons. Contemporary proponents of naturalized ethics are aware of these objections, but in my opinion their theories do not adequately meet them. Casebeer, for example, examines recent work in neuroscientific moral psychology and finds that actual moral decision-making looks more like what Aristotle recommends and less like what Kant and Mill recommend. From this he concludes that the available neuroscientific evidence counts against the moral theories of Kant and Mill, and in favour of Aristotle's. This strikes me as a *non sequitur*. How do we go from. "This is how we think" to "This is how we ought to think"? Kant argued that our actions should exhibit a kind of universalizability that is grounded in respect for other people as autonomous rational agents. Mill argued that we should act so as to produce the greatest sum of happiness. So long as people are capable of taking Kant's or Mill's advice, how does it follow from neuroscientific data—indeed, how could it follow from such data—that people ought to ignore Kant's and Mill's recommendations in favour of Aristotle's? In other words, how does it follow from the proposition that Aristotelian moral thought is more natural than Kant's or Mill's that Aristotle's is better?

Whereas I am sceptical of attempts to derive moral principles from scientific facts, I agree with the proponents of naturalized ethics that scientific facts can have profound moral implications, and that moral philosophers have paid too little attention to relevant work in the natural sciences. My understanding of the relationship between science and normative ethics is, however, different from that of naturalized ethicists. Casebeer and others view science and normative ethics as continuous and are therefore interested in normative

moral theories that resemble or are "consilient" with theories of moral psychology. Their aim is to find theories of right and wrong that in some sense match natural human practice. By contrast, I view science as offering a "behind the scenes" look at human morality. Just as a well-researched biography can, depending on what it reveals, boost or deflate one's esteem for its subject, the scientific investigation of human morality can help us to understand human moral nature, and in so doing change our opinion of it.

NEUROSCIENCE AND NORMATIVE ETHICS

There is a growing consensus that moral judgements are based largely on intuition—"gut feelings" about what is right or wrong in particular cases.[5] Sometimes these intuitions conflict, both within and between individuals. Are all moral intuitions equally worthy of our allegiance, or are some more reliable than others? Our answers to this question will probably be affected by an improved understanding of where our intuitions come from, both in terms of their proximate psychological/neural bases and their evolutionary histories.

Consider the following moral dilemma (adapted from Unger[6]). You are driving along a country road when you hear a plea for help coming from some roadside bushes. You pull over and encounter a man whose legs are covered with blood. The man explains that he has had an accident while hiking and asks you to take him to a nearby hospital. Your initial inclination is to help this man, who will probably lose his leg if he does not get to the hospital soon. However, if you give this man a lift, his blood will ruin the leather upholstery of your car. Is it appropriate for you to leave this man by the side of the road in order to preserve your leather upholstery [. . .]?

Most people say that it would be seriously wrong to abandon this man out of concern for one's car seats. Now consider a different case (also adapted from Unger[6]), which nearly all of us have faced. You are at home one day when the mail arrives. You receive a letter from a reputable international aid organization. The letter asks you to make a donation of two hundred dollars to their organization. The letter explains that a two-hundred-dollar donation will allow this organization to provide needed medical attention to some poor people in another part of the world. Is it appropriate for you to not make a donation to this organization in order to save money [. . .]?

Most people say that it would not be wrong to refrain from making a donation in this case. And yet this case and the previous one are similar. In both cases, one has the option to give someone much needed medical attention at a relatively modest financial cost. And yet, the person who fails to help in the first case is a moral monster, whereas the person who fails to help in the second case is morally unexceptional. Why is there this difference?

About thirty years ago, the utilitarian philosopher Singer argued that there is no real moral difference between cases such as these two, and that we in the affluent world ought to be giving far more than we do to help the world's most unfortunate people.[7] (Singer currently gives about 20% of his annual income to charity.) Many people, when confronted with this issue, assume or insist that there must be "some good reason" for why it is alright to ignore the severe needs of unfortunate people in far off countries, but deeply wrong to ignore the needs of someone like the unfortunate hiker in the first story. (Indeed, you might be coming up with reasons of your own right now.)

Maybe there is "some good reason" for why it is okay to spend money on sushi and power windows while millions who could be saved die of hunger and treatable illnesses. But maybe this pair of moral intuitions has nothing to do with "some good reason" and everything to do with the way our brains happen to be built.

To explore this and related issues, my colleagues and I conducted a brain imaging study in which participants responded to the above moral dilemmas as well as many others.[8] The dilemma with the bleeding hiker is a "personal" moral dilemma, in which the moral violation in question occurs in an "upclose-and-personal" manner. The donation dilemma is an "impersonal" moral dilemma, in which the moral violation in question does not have this feature. To make a long story short, we found that judgements in response to "personal" moral dilemmas, compared with "impersonal" ones, involved greater activity in brain areas that are associated with emotion and social cognition. Why should this be?

An evolutionary perspective is useful here. Over the last four decades, it has become clear that natural selection can favour altruistic instincts under the right conditions, and many believe that this is how human altruism came to be. If that is right, then our altruistic instincts will reflect the environment in which they evolved rather than our present environment. With this in mind, consider that our ancestors did not evolve in an environment in which total strangers on opposite sides of the world could save each others' lives by making relatively modest material sacrifices. Consider also that our ancestors did evolve in an environment in which individuals standing face-to-face could save each others' lives, sometimes only through considerable personal sacrifice. Given all of this, it makes sense that we would have evolved altruistic instincts that direct us to help others in dire need, but mostly when the ones in need are presented in an "up-close-and-personal" way.

What does this mean for ethics? Again, we are tempted to assume that there must be "some good reason" why it is monstrous to ignore the needs of someone like the bleeding hiker, but perfectly acceptable to spend our money on unnecessary luxuries while millions starve and die of preventable diseases. Maybe there is "some good reason" for this pair of attitudes, but the evolutionary account given above suggests otherwise: we ignore the plight of the world's poorest people not because we implicitly appreciate the nuanced structure of moral obligation, but because, the way our brains are wired up, needy people who are "up close and personal" push our emotional buttons, whereas those who are out of sight languish out of mind.

This is just a hypothesis. I do not wish to pretend that this case is closed or, more generally, that science has all the moral answers. Nor do I believe that normative ethics is on its way to becoming a branch of the natural sciences, with the "is" of science and the "ought" of morality gradually melding together. Instead, I think that we can respect the distinction between how things are and how things ought to be while acknowledging, as the preceding discussion illustrates, that scientific facts have the potential to influence our moral thinking in a deep way.

NEUROSCIENCE AND META-ETHICS

Philosophers routinely distinguish between ethics and "meta-ethics." Ethics concerns particular moral issues (such as our obligations to the poor) and theories that attempt to resolve such issues (such as utilitarianism or Aristotelian virtue ethics). Meta-ethics, by contrast, is concerned with more foundational issues, with the status of ethics as a whole. What do we mean when we say something like "Capital punishment is wrong"? Are we stating a putative fact, or merely expressing an opinion? According to "moral realism" there are genuine moral facts, whereas moral anti-realists or moral subjectivists maintain that there are no such facts. Although this debate is unlikely to be resolved any time soon, I believe that neuroscience and related disciplines have the potential to shed light on these matters by helping us to understand our common-sense conceptions of morality.

I begin with the assumption (lamentably, not well tested) that many people, probably most people, are moral realists. That is, they believe that some things really are right or wrong, independent of what any particular person or group thinks about it. For example, if you were to turn the corner and find a group of wayward youths torturing a stray cat, you might say to yourself something like, "That's wrong!", and in saying this you would mean not merely that you are opposed to such behaviour, or that some group to which you belong is opposed to it, but rather that such behaviour is wrong in and of itself, regardless of what anyone happens to think about it. In other words, you take it that there is a wrongness inherent in such acts that you can perceive, but that exists independently of your moral beliefs and values or those of any particular culture.

This realist conception of morality contrasts with familiar anti-realist conceptions of beauty and other experiential qualities. When gazing upon a dazzling sunset, we might feel as if we are experiencing a beauty that is inherent in the evening sky, but many people acknowledge that such beauty, rather than being in the sky, is ultimately "in the eye of the beholder." Likewise for matters of sexual attraction. You find your favourite movie star sexy, but take no such interest in baboons. Baboons, on the other hand, probably find each other very sexy and take very little interest in the likes of Tom Cruise and Nicole Kidman. Who is right, us or the baboons? Many of us would plausibly insist that there is simply no fact of the matter. Although sexiness might seem to be a mind-independent property of certain individuals, it is ultimately in the eye (that is, the mind) of the beholder.

The big meta-ethical question, then, might be posed as follows: are the moral truths to which we subscribe really full-blown truths, mind-independent facts about the nature of moral reality, or are they, like sexiness, in the mind of the beholder? One way to try to answer this question is to examine what is in the minds of the relevant beholders. Understanding how we make moral judgements might help us to determine whether our judgements are perceptions of external truths or projections of internal attitudes. More specifically, we might ask whether the appearance of moral truth can be explained in a way that does not require the reality of moral truth.

As noted above, recent evidence from neuroscience and neighbouring disciplines indicates that moral judgement is often an intuitive, emotional matter. Although many moral judgements are difficult, much moral judgement is accomplished in an intuitive, effortless way. An interesting feature of many intuitive, effortless cognitive processes is that they are accompanied by a perceptual phenomenology. For example, humans can effortlessly determine whether a given face is male or female without any knowledge of how such judgements are made. When you look at someone, you have no experience of working out whether that person is male or female. You just see that person's maleness or femaleness. By contrast, you do not look at a star in the sky and see that it is receding. One can imagine creatures that automatically process spectroscopic redshifts, but as humans we do not. All of this makes sense from an evolutionary point of view. We have evolved mechanisms for making quick, emotion-based social judgements, for "seeing" rightness and wrongness, because our intensely social lives favour such capacities, but there was little selective pressure on our ancestors to know about the movements of distant stars.

We have here the beginnings of a debunking explanation of moral realism: we believe in moral realism because moral experience has a perceptual phenomenology, and moral experience has a perceptual phenomenology because natural selection has outfitted us with mechanisms for making intuitive, emotion-based moral judgements, much as it has outfitted us with mechanisms for making intuitive, emotion-based judgements about who among us are the most suitable mates. Therefore, we can understand our inclination towards moral realism not as an insight into the nature of moral truth, but as a by-product of the efficient cognitive processes

we use to make moral decisions. According to this view, moral realism is akin to naive realism about sexiness, like making the understandable mistake of thinking that Tom Cruise is objectively sexier than his baboon counterparts. (Note that according to this view moral judgement is importantly different from gender perception. Both involve efficient cognitive processes that give rise to a perceptual phenomenology, but in the case of gender perception the phenomenology is veridical: there really are mind-independent facts about who is male or female.)

Admittedly, this argument requires more elaboration and support, and some philosophers might object to the way I have framed the issue surrounding moral realism. Others might wonder how one can speak on behalf of moral anti-realism after sketching an argument in favour of increasing aid to the poor. (Brief reply: giving up on moral realism does not mean giving up on moral values. It is one thing to care about the plight of the poor, and another to think that one's caring is objectively correct.) However, the point of this brief sketch is not to make a conclusive scientific case against moral realism, but simply to explain how neuroscientific evidence, and scientific evidence more broadly, have the potential to influence the way we understand morality. [...]

Understanding where our moral instincts come from and how they work can, I argue, lead us to doubt that our moral convictions stem from perceptions of moral truth rather than projections of moral attitudes. Some might worry that this conclusion, if true, would be very unfortunate. First, it is important to bear in mind that a conclusion's being unfortunate does not make it false. Second, this conclusion might not be unfortunate at all. A world full of people who regard their moral convictions as reflections of personal values rather than reflections of "the objective moral truth" might be a happier and more peaceful place than the world we currently inhabit.

The maturation of human morality will, in many ways, resemble the maturation of an individual person. As we come to understand ourselves better—who we are, and why we are the way we are—we will inevitably change ourselves in the process. Some of our beliefs and values will survive this process of self-discovery and reflection, whereas others will not. The course of our moral maturation will not be entirely predictable, but I am confident that the scientific study of human nature will have an increasingly important role in nature's grand experiment with moral animals.

Notes

1. Doris, J. M. & Stich, S. P. in *The Oxford Handbook of Contemporary Analytic Philosophy* (eds Jackson, F. & Smith, M.) (Oxford Univ. Press, New York, 2003).

2. Hume, D. *A Treatise of Human Nature* (eds Selby-Bigge. L. A. & Nidditch, P. H.) (Clarendon, Oxford, 1739/1978).

3. Moore, G. E. *Principia Ethica* (Cambridge University Press, Cambridge, 1903/1959).

4. Casebeer, W. D. Moral cognition and its neural constituents, *Nature Rev. Neurosci*, **4**, 841–847 (2003).

5. Haidt, J. The emotional dog and its rational tail: a social intuitionist approach to moral judgment. *Psychol. Rev.* **108**, 814–834 (2001).

6. Unger, P. *Living High and Letting Die: Our Illusion of Innocence* (Oxford Univ. Press, New York, 1996).

7. Singer, P. Famine, affluence, and morality. *Philos. Public Affairs* **1**, 229–243 (1972).

8. Greene, J. D., Sommerville, R. B., Nystrom, L. E., Darley, J. M. & Cohen, J. D. An fMRI investigation of emotional engagement in moral judgment. *Science* **293**, 2105–2108 (2001).

Study Questions

1. Do you see a morally relevant difference between the hiking accident case and the giving to charity case? If so, what is it?

2. What, if any, do you think are the normative implications of the scientific studies about how we reason mentioned by Greene?

3. Do you think that moral judgments are based solely on intuition? If so, does this call into question their truth?

CHAPTER 10: EPILOGUE

Philosophical Methodology

Anand J. Vaidya and Michael Shaffer

ORIGINS OF CONCEPTUAL ANALYSIS

Philosophy is perhaps the oldest academic discipline, and it is interesting that, arguably, philosophy has retained one of its core methods from its organized beginnings in the work of Plato during the period from the fifth to the fourth century BCE up to today. This method is known as *conceptual analysis,* and it is tied to the idea that we possess the ability to reliably determine the meanings of words or concepts by reflecting on the proper use of the word or concept. What is most important about this method is that it is supposed to be practicable from "the armchair" without needing to know any of what goes on in the laboratory or on the street. In other words, it makes philosophical knowledge an *a priori* rather than an *a posteriori* matter.

Plato is responsible for having first articulated this view of philosophy, and Plato's *Meno* illustrates it very well. Superficially, *Meno* is about the concept of virtue and whether virtue can be taught, but once we go beyond the surface reading it is clear that *Meno* is also a demonstration of how we could come to know anything. Plato believes that knowledge of the truth about something is acquired by a process involving the proposing of a definition of the thing and the use of intuitions about the thing to determine the correctness of such definitions. For Plato, such correct definitions (or *conceptual analyses*) are specifications of *forms*.

Forms are the abstract, perfect objects that individual instances of the form have in common. For example, the form of an apple is a perfect and abstract archetype of appleness, whereas individual apples that we encounter (and eat!) in our everyday lives are concrete and imperfect instantiations of the form of apple.

On Plato's view, such perfect forms exist independently of physical reality, and in a later part of *Meno* (not excerpted here) and in another dialogue called *Phaedo*, Plato suggests the infamous view that *we already know truths about the forms even though we are not aware of this fact in ordinary circumstances.* Plato held that our souls existed prior to our being born, and they became directly acquainted with the forms prior to being embodied. We forget these things at birth, and so it turns out that all inquiry is really a matter of recollecting knowledge that is already in us. This view is known as *the doctrine of anamnesis.* Such a doctrine explains how the *a priori* or "armchair" process of inquiry exhibited in *Meno* could give rise to genuine knowledge: it does so by evoking what we already implicitly know.

Meno provides us with a paradigmatic example of the method of conceptual analysis. In this regard, *Meno* is an exceptionally important historical work since the method it employs has become one of the orthodox methods of philosophical inquiry. The most crucial aspects of the process of conceptual analysis demonstrated in *Meno* are the following ones: First, the analysis of a concept takes the form of a proposed definition. These definitions of concepts take the form of sets of simple necessary and sufficient conditions. For example, one proposed analysis of knowledge is that something is known if and only if it is a justified, true belief. Second, the adequacy of any proposed definition can be tested against actual and/or imagined cases. Third, the testing of a proposed analysis proceeds by eliciting spontaneous judgments or "intuitions" (which for Plato, but not for contemporary philosophers, are a manifestation of our memory). This, then, is one of the points of *Meno:* the introduction and endorsing of a particular method of philosophical inquiry.

The justification of this method as first introduced by Plato looks importantly dependent on the Platonic concept of intuition as manifesting recollection of the forms by our immortal souls. Nowadays, this Platonic commitment is not essential to standard philosophical methodology though the basic structure of the method itself has endured. In order, then, to get a better grasp of the standard philosophical method as it is understood today, we can usefully turn our attention to the work of René Descartes.

In his *Meditations on First Philosophy* Descartes wants to determine what, if anything, he knows with absolute certainty. He then finds himself in a deeply troubling situation. At first it appears to Descartes both that he cannot be certain of any of his sensory ideas and that he cannot be certain of any of his nonsensory ideas, since it seems possible that he could be the object of the deceptions of an evil being who possesses powers equivalent to that of God. What Descartes then discovers is that there is in fact a small set of ideas that cannot be doubted even in this extreme case of deception, initial appearances to the contrary. These ideas are necessarily true, conceptual in nature, and known *a priori*. For Descartes it is these truths that supposedly can be known directly by intuition and independent of any sensory experience. They are implicitly in us, ready to be accessed by exercising the faculty of intuition.

In Descartes we see a somewhat more contemporary version of Plato's theory, but Descartes' view of intuition is importantly different from that of Plato. In his *Rules for the Direction of the Mind*, Descartes explains that:

> By intuition I understand neither the fleeting testimony of the senses nor the deceptive judgment of the imagination with its false constructions, but a conception of a pure and attentive mind, so easy and so distinct, that no doubt at all remains about what we understand. Or, what comes to the same thing, intuition is the indubitable conception of a pure and attentive mind arising from the light of reason alone; it is more certain even than deduction, because it is simpler, even though, as we noted above, people cannot err in deduction either. Thus everyone can intuit with his mind that he exists, that he is thinking, that a triangle is bounded by only three lines, a sphere by a single surface, and the like.

So, Descartes believes that intuition is a reliable and infallible nonsensory mental faculty for determining conceptual truths, not by recalling the forms, but by apprehending these truths directly via "the light of reason alone." In this view there is no longer any tie to the doctrine of anamnesis.

Contemporary philosophers who practice conceptual analysis have, in turn, amended Descartes' theory of intuition. For while some philosophers have maintained much of Plato's account of philosophical method, as well as Descartes' abandonment of the doctrine of anamnesis, many contemporary philosophers believe that intuition is a reliable but *fallible* nonsensory mental faculty for determining conceptual truths, wherever they originate. That is, crucially, they believe that such intuitions can sometimes be wrong. Despite the modifications it has undergone, this modern conception of philosophical methodology is one of Plato's greatest legacies.

CONCEPTS AND FAMILY RESEMBLANCES

One of the most important critiques of this traditional method of conceptual analysis comes from Ludwig Wittgenstein's *Philosophical Investigations*. Wittgenstein's critique of conceptual analysis begins with the assumption that the conceptual analysis of a concept requires that *if C is a concept, then there exists a set of necessary and sufficient conditions for falling under C.*

But, as Wittgenstein points out, this seems to be false. Consider the concept *game*. If we look at chess and basketball, we might say that what it is for something to be an instance of *game* is for there to be a winner and a loser, since in each of these games there is a winner and a loser. However, if we look at the game ring-around-the-rosy, as Wittgenstein presents it, then we would discover that there are some games with no winner and loser. Furthermore, if we look at the game of playing house, then again we would say that there is no winner or loser. For Wittgenstein, these considerations suggest that games are similar to one another like members of a family. Some games share some features, and others have others, but there is no simple set of necessary and sufficient conditions that all games share.

In general, there are two readings of Wittgenstein's comments on family resemblance relations. On the one hand, there are those that believe that the examples are intended to apply to all concepts such that it is true that there are no concepts that have a set of simple necessary and sufficient conditions. On this reading, we treat both the concept *game* and the concept *being an even number* the same. On the other hand, there are those that believe that the examples are intended only to refute the claim that *all* concepts have simple necessary and sufficient conditions. On this reading, the concept *game* is an example of a concept that does not fit the traditional model advocated by Plato. This reading leaves open the idea that some concepts, such as the concept of being an even number, have simple necessary and sufficient conditions, while others do not.

PLATO'S METHOD MEETS COGNITIVE SCIENCE

We have already seen that not all philosophers accept that conceptual analysis of the sort Plato practiced is the correct way to address philosophical problems. This is most apparent in the case of philosophers who subscribe to naturalism about philosophy. W. V. O. Quine's work embodies the most famous example of this sort of view. Quine criticized the idea that anything could be known independent of experience and regarded *all* statements, including philosophical claims, as subject to revision in light of empirical evidence. For Quine, all knowledge is continuous with scientific knowledge.

Quine, then, is the key figure behind the development of naturalism from the later 1930s through the 1990s. Quine's naturalism is a general approach to the study of knowledge that in particular rejects the idea that there is any *a priori* knowledge. He believes that traditional philosophical methodology should be reconstructed so as to take account of empirical science and that the problems of philosophy can be resolved *a posteriori*, using the experimental methods of the sciences that are the best methods for inquiry. But Quine himself never proceeded to practice philosophy in the experimental manner that he advocated.

More recently, Stephen Stich has championed a form of the Quinean view in response to the contemporary defenders of the standard philosophical method, but in a much more overtly *experimental* manner. This can be seen clearly because Stich has explicitly endorsed the following Quinean view of philosophical methodology:

> The idea that philosophy could be kept apart from the sciences would have been dismissed out of hand by the great philosophers of the 17th and 18th centuries. But many contemporary philosophers believe that they can practice their craft without knowing what is going on in the natural and social sciences. If facts are needed, they rely on their "intuition," or they simply invent them. The results of philosophy done this way are typically sterile and often silly. There are no proprietary philosophical questions that are worth answering, nor is there any productive philosophical method that does not engage the sciences. But there are lots of deeply important (and fascinating and frustrating) questions about minds, morals, language, culture and more. To make progress on them we need to use anything that science can tell us, and any method that works.

Stich's negative reaction to *a priori* approaches to philosophy stems in particular from his critical response to the use of intuition. What Stich recognized in the 1980s was that the use of intuitions in conceptual analysis has a curious and troubling feature.

Specifically, if a group of cognitive agents thought in a manner that was different from us and had very different intuitions than ours about what counts as the correct application of a concept, then using this method of philosophy would justify quite different accounts of things like *knowledge, virtue,* or *freedom of the will* to them. This, in turn, suggests that such reliance on intuitions can in principle be used to justify *any* principle so long as a group has the requisite intuitions.

Perhaps the right thing to do is to insist that *our intuitions* are the right ones. Our intuitions (but not theirs) track the truth. But Stich could see no principled reason to suppose that any one group's intuitions track truth any better than those of another group. If so, then there is no principled reason to accept one result rather than another. That is, we have no reason to prefer an analysis supported by one group's intuitions over some alternate analysis supported by another group's intuitions.

The existence of groups with different intuitions looked to Stich like a problematic possibility, but it might have remained *only a possibility*. Perhaps there really were in fact no such disagreements about intuitions. Stich himself initially adopted this view. But then Stich became aware of cross-cultural investigations by psychologists like Richard Nisbett and Jonathan Haidt. Specifically, Nisbett and other psychologists had been studying real cognitive differences between people in different actual cultures, specifically differences between some Asian and Western cultures. Haidt and his colleagues were conducting other studies concerning differences in moral judgments between members of different social classes. The results of these studies suggested to Stich that his theoretical speculation about the relativistic aspect of intuition-based methods in philosophy might be *more* than mere speculation.

Stich and some of his colleagues then proceeded to conduct experiments to see if members of different groups actually had different intuitions about what knowledge is, and what they found is that actually different cultural groups have actually different intuitions about such cases! These disagreements in intuitions seem to show that intuition is not a reliable source of knowledge, and by now a large number of experimental studies have been conducted showing such variations in intuitions regarding a wide variety of topics in philosophy. Such results have led Stich to conclude that the continuing use of Plato's method of philosophical inquiry is just a big mistake! This is a radical and controversial conclusion to be sure, and one that most philosophers disagree with. Nonetheless, assessing the results of this experimental philosophical challenge is a crucial task, for it seems to cast doubt on a 2,500-year-old strand of philosophical investigation. It also suggests something further: that whether we take up Stich's challenge or oppose it, the methods of the empirical sciences might be crucial to the investigation of philosophical problems.

EXPERIMENTAL PHILOSOPHY AND PHILOSOPHICAL INTUITION

Ernest Sosa is a leading contemporary epistemologist who has contributed to the current debate over philosophical methodology. In "Experimental Philosophy and Philosophical Intuition," he recounts his theory of intuition and responds to the challenge to the use of intuition in philosophy through a reinterpretation of intuitive disagreement.

Sosa argues for a specific conception of what intuitions are. This *competence-based account* maintains that to *intuit that* P is to be attracted to assent to P simply through thinking about P. For example, to intuit that 2 + 2 = 4 is to be attracted to assent to the truth of that arithmetical fact simply through thinking about "2," "4," "=," and "+." Sosa further maintains that an intuition is *rational* if and only if the intuition derives from a "competence" and the content of the intuition is either implicitly or explicitly "modal"—that is, it involves a judgment about what is possible, or what is necessary.

Using the *competence-based* account of intuition, Sosa maintains that intuitions in philosophy are rational intuitions. For example, the Gettier intuition (see Chapter 2) is a rational philosophical intuition because it is an attraction to assent to the claim that,

> In a case relevantly like those Gettier described], the subject has a justified true belief *p*, but not knowledge that *p*.

And this attraction arises from a competence in the theory of knowledge.

Given Stich's challenge to philosophical appeals to intuition, Sosa offers a response. Answering Stich involves reconciling the fact that groups of people may have contradictory philosophical intuitions, with the claim that intuitions are a source of justification for beliefs about philosophical matters. How can we come to know the nature of knowledge, free will, or morality by appeal to intuition if there is widespread disagreement about whether a certain hypothetical case is a case of knowledge, freedom, or morally permissible action?

Sosa answers this question by highlighting that one cannot infer from the fact that there is a *verbal* disagreement over a philosophical issue, such as the nature of knowledge, that there is a *substantial* disagreement in intuition. The response gains ground by pointing out that one way in which two subjects can disagree verbally, but not substantially, is if either of them fails to understand the question asked or interprets the question differently, or if one of them fails to be sufficiently attentive.

References

Descartes, R. "*Rules for the Direction of Mind* (1618-1628)." In *Philosophical Essays and Correspondence*, ed. Roger Ariew, 2–27. Indianapolis: Hackett, 2000.

Quine, W. V. O. *From a Logical Point of View*. Cambridge, MA: Harvard University Press, 1953.

Stich, S. "Stephen Stich." http://www.pyke-eye.com/view/phil_II_23.html (accessed March 15, 2012).

Suggestions for Further Reading

Bealer, George. "A Priori Knowledge and the Scope of Philosophy." *Philosophical Studies* 81 (1996): 121–142.

DePaul, Michael R., and William Ramsey, eds. *Rethinking Intuition: The Psychology of Intuition and Its Role in Philosophical Inquiry*. Lanham, MD: Rowman and Littlefield, 1998.

Descartes, René. *Meditations on First Philosophy.* In *Philosophical Essays and Correspondence,* ed. Roger Ariew, 97–141. Indianapolis: Hackett, 2000.

Kauppinen, Antti. "The Rise and Fall of Experimental Philosophy." *Philosophical Explorations* 10, no. 2 (2007): 95–118.

Kornblith, Hilary, ed. *Naturalizing Epistemology.* 2nd ed. Cambridge, MA: MIT Press, 1994.

Ludwig, Kirk. "The Epistemology of Thought Experiments: First Person versus Third Person Approaches." *Midwest Studies in Philosophy* 31 (2007): 128–159.

Nagel, Jennifer. "Epistemic Intuitions." *Philosophy Compass* 2, no. 6 (2007): 792–819.

Plato. *Phaedo,* trans. David Gallop. Oxford: Oxford University Press, 2009.

Plato. *Theatetus,* trans. Robin Waterfield. London: Penguin, 1987.

Quine, Willard Van Orman. "Epistemology Naturalized." In *Naturalizing Epistemology.* 2nd ed., ed. Hilary Kornblith, 15–32. Cambridge, MA: MIT Press, 1994.

Quine, Willard Van Orman, and Joseph Ullian. *The Web of Belief.* New York: Random House, 1970.

Rosch, Eleanor, and Carolyn Mervis. "Family Resemblances: Studies in the Internal Structure of Categories." In *Rethinking Intuition,* ed. William Ramsey and Michael DePaul, 17–44. Lanham, MD: Rowman and Littlefield, 1998.

Vaidya, Anand. "Philosophical Methodology: The Current Debate." *Philosophical Psychology* 23, no. 3 (2010): 391–417.

Weinberg, Jonathan. "How to Challenge Intuitions Empirically without Risking Skepticism." *Midwest Studies in Philosophy* 31 (2007): 318–343.

10.1   Meno

    PLATO

PLATO (c. 427–347 BCE) is one of the forefathers of philosophy along with his teacher Socrates and his student Aristotle. He is perhaps, the single most important figure in the development of philosophy as we know it. He founded the Academy (the first university) in Athens and had wide-ranging interests in all areas of philosophy, mathematics, and politics.

The selection is from the dialogue *Meno.* This dialogue takes the form of a discussion between Socrates and his younger friend Meno. The surface topic of the dialogue is the nature of virtue and whether it can be taught, but the real significance of the dialogue is that it offers an account of the nature of inquiry in general. In *Meno,* Plato defends the view that all knowledge can be acquired *a priori* using the method of conceptual analysis. Such inquiry leads us to a recollection of what our immortal souls know from previously inhabiting the realm of eternal and divine forms. Here we find what is one of the first presentations of a philosophical method that has been a central component of philosophy for almost 2,500 years.

MENO: Can you tell me, Socrates—is virtue something that can be taught? Or does it come by practice? Or is it neither teaching nor practice that gives it to a man but natural aptitude or something else?

SOCRATES: Well, Meno, in the old days the Thessalians had a great reputation among the Greeks for their wealth and their horsemanship. Now it seems they are philosophers as well—especially the men of Larissa, where your friend Aristippus comes from. It is Gorgias who has done it. He went to that city and captured the hearts of the foremost of the Aleuadae for his wisdom—among them your own admirer Aristippus—not to speak of other leading Thessalians. In particular he got you into the habit of answering any question you might be asked, with the confidence and dignity appropriate to those who know the answers, just as he himself invites questions of every kind from anyone in the Greek world who wishes to ask, and never fails to answer them. But here at Athens, my dear Meno, it is just the reverse. There is a dearth of wisdom, and it looks as if it had migrated from our part of the country to yours. At any rate if you put your question to any of our people, they will all alike laugh and say, You must think I am singularly fortunate, to know whether virtue can be taught or how it is acquired. The fact is that far from knowing whether it can be taught, I have no idea what virtue itself is.

That is my own case. I share the poverty of my fellow countrymen in this respect, and confess to my shame that I have no knowledge about virtue at all. And how

Plato, "Meno," translated by W. K. C. Gutherie, in the *Collected Dialogues of Plato* (Princeton, NJ: Princeton University Press, 1961).

can I know a property of something when I don't even know what it is? Do you suppose that somebody entirely ignorant who Meno is could say whether he is handsome and rich and wellborn or the reverse? Is that possible, do you think?

MENO: No. But is this true about yourself, Socrates, that you don't even know what virtue is? Is this the report that we are to take home about you?

SOCRATES: Not only that, you may say also that, to the best of my belief. I have never yet met anyone who did know.

MENO: What! Didn't you meet Gorgias when he was here?

SOCRATES: Yes.

MENO: And you still didn't think he knew?

SOCRATES: I'm a forgetful sort of person, and I can't say just now what I thought at the time. Probably he did know, and I expect you know what he used to say about it. So remind me what it was, or tell me yourself if you will. No doubt you agree with him.

MENO: Yes, I do.

SOCRATES: Then let's leave him out of it, since after all he isn't here. What do you yourself say virtue is? I do ask you in all earnestness not to refuse me, but to speak out. I shall be only too happy to be proved wrong if you and Gorgias turn out to know this, although I said I had never met anyone who did.

MENO: But there is no difficulty about it. First of all, if it is manly virtue you are after, it is easy to see that the virtue of a man consists in managing the city's affairs capably, and so that he will help his friends and injure his foes while taking care to come to no harm himself. Or if you want a woman's virtue, that is easily described. She must be a good housewife, careful with her stores and obedient to her husband. Then there is another virtue for a child, male or female, and another for an old man, free or slave as you like, and a great many more kinds

of virtue, so that no one need be at a loss to say what it is. For every act and every time of life, with reference to each separate function, there is a virtue for each one of us, and similarly, I should say, a vice.

SOCRATES: I seem to be in luck. I wanted one virtue and I find that you have a whole swarm of virtues to offer. But seriously, to carry on this metaphor of the swarm, suppose I asked you what a bee is, what is its essential nature, and you replied that bees were of many different kinds. What would you say if I went on to ask. And is it in being bees that they are many and various and different from one another? Or would you agree that it is not in this respect that they differ, but in something else, some other quality like size or beauty?

MENO: I should say that in so far as they are bees, they don't differ from one another at all.

SOCRATES: Suppose I then continued, Well, this is just what I want you to tell me. What is that character in respect of which they don't differ at all, but are all the same? I presume you would have something to say?

MENO: I should.

SOCRATES: Then do the same with the virtues. Even if they are many and various, yet at least they all have some common character which makes them virtues. That is what ought to be kept in view by anyone who answers the question, What is virtue? Do you follow me?

MENO: I think I do, but I don't yet really grasp the question as I should wish.

SOCRATES: Well, does this apply in your mind only to virtue, that there is a different one for a man and a woman and the rest? Is it the same with health and size and strength, or has health the same character everywhere, if it is health, whether it be in a man or any other creature?

MENO: I agree that health is the same in a man or in a woman.

SOCRATES: And what about size and strength? If a woman is strong, will it be the same thing, the same strength, that makes her strong? My meaning is that in its character as strength, it is no different, whether it be in a man or in a woman. Or do you think it is?

MENO: No.

SOCRATES: And will virtue differ, in its character as virtue, whether it be in a child or an old man, a woman or a man?

MENO: I somehow feel that this is not on the same level as the other cases.

SOCRATES: Well then, didn't you say that a man's virtue lay in directing the city well, and a woman's in directing her household well?

MENO: Yes.

SOCRATES: And is it possible to direct anything well—city or household or anything else—if not temperately and justly?

MENO: Certainly not.

SOCRATES: And that means with temperance and justice?

MENO: Of course.

SOCRATES: Then both man and woman need the same qualities, justice and temperance, if they are going to be good.

MENO: It looks like it.

SOCRATES: And what about your child and old man? Could they be good if they were incontinent and unjust?

MENO: Of course not.

SOCRATES: They must be temperate and just?

MENO: Yes.

SOCRATES: So everyone is good in the same way, since they become good by possessing the same qualities.

MENO: So it seems.

SOCRATES: And if they did not share the same virtue, they would not be good in the same way.

MENO: No.

SOCRATES: Seeing then that they all have the same virtue, try to remember and tell me what Gorgias and you, who share his opinion, say it is.

MENO: It must be simply the capacity to govern men, if you are looking for one quality to cover all the instances.

SOCRATES: Indeed I am. But does this virtue apply to a child or a slave? Should a slave be capable of governing his master, and if he does, is he still a slave?

MENO: I hardly think so.

SOCRATES: It certainly doesn't sound likely. And here is another point. You speak of "capacity to govern." Shall we not add, "justly but not otherwise"?

MENO: I think we should, for justice is virtue.

SOCRATES: Virtue, do you say, or *a* virtue?

MENO: What do you mean?

SOCRATES: Something quite general. Take roundness, for instance. I should say that it is a shape, not simply that it is shape, my reason being that there are other shapes as well.

MENO: I see your point, and I agree that there are other virtues besides justice.

SOCRATES: Tell me what they are. Just as I could name other shapes if you told me to, in the same way mention some other virtues.

MENO: In my opinion then courage is a virtue and temperance and wisdom and dignity and many other things.

SOCRATES: This puts us back where we were. In a different way we have discovered a number of virtues when we were looking for one only. This single virtue, which permeates each of them, we cannot find.

MENO: No, I cannot yet grasp it as you want, a single virtue covering them all, as I do in other instances.

SOCRATES: I'm not surprised, but I shall do my best to get us a bit further if I can. You understand, I expect, that the question applies to everything. If someone took the example I mentioned just now, and asked you, "What is shape?" and you replied that roundness is shape, and he then asked you as I did, "Do you mean it is shape or *a* shape?" you would reply of course that it is *a* shape.

MENO: Certainly.

SOCRATES: Your reason being that there are other shapes as well.

MENO: Yes.

SOCRATES: And if he went on to ask you what they were, you would tell him.

MENO: Yes.

SOCRATES: And the same with color—if he asked you what it is, and on your replying, "White," took you up with, "Is white color or *a* color?" you would say that it is *a* color, because there are other colors as well.

MENO: I should.

SOCRATES: And if he asked you to, you would mention other colors which are just as much colors as white is.

MENO: Yes.

SOCRATES: Suppose then he pursued the question as I did, and objected, "We always arrive at a plurality, but that is not the kind of answer I want. Seeing that you call these many particulars by one and the same name, and say that every one of them is a shape, even though they are the contrary of each other, tell me what this is which embraces round as well as straight, and what you mean by shape when you say that straightness is a shape as much as roundness. You do say that?"

MENO: Yes.

SOCRATES: "And in saying it, do you mean that roundness is no more round than straight, and straightness no more straight than round?"

MENO: Of course not.

SOCRATES: "Yet you do say that roundness is no more a shape than straightness, and the other way about."

MENO: Quite true.

SOCRATES: "Then what is this thing which is called 'shape'? Try to tell me." If when asked this question either about shape or color you said, "But I don't understand what you want, or what you mean," your questioner would perhaps be surprised and say, "Don't you see that I am looking for what is the same in all of them?" Would you even so be unable to reply, if the question was, "What is it that is common to roundness and straightness and the other things which you call shapes?" Do your best to answer, as practice for the question about virtue.

MENO: No, you do it, Socrates.

SOCRATES: Do you want me to give in to you?

MENO: Yes.

SOCRATES: And will you in your turn give me an answer about virtue?

MENO: I will.

SOCRATES: In that case I must do my best. It's in a good cause.

MENO: Certainly.

SOCRATES: Well now, let's try to tell you what shape is. See if you accept this definition. Let us define it as the only thing which always accompanies color. Does that satisfy you, or do you want it in some other way? I should be content if your definition of virtue were on similar lines.

MENO: But that's a naïve sort of definition, Socrates.

SOCRATES: How?

MENO: Shape, if I understand what you say, is what always accompanies color. Well and good—but if somebody says that he doesn't know what color is, but is no better off with it than he is with shape, what sort of answer have you given him, do you think?

SOCRATES: A true one, and if my questioner were one of the clever, disputatious, and quarrelsome kind, I should say to him, "You have heard my answer. If it is wrong, it is for you to take up the argument and refute it." However, when friendly people, like you and me, want to converse with each other, one's reply must be milder and more conducive to discussion. By that I mean that it must not only be true, but must employ terms with which the questioner admits he is familiar. So I will try to answer you like that. Tell me, therefore, whether you recognize the term "end"; I mean limit or boundary—all these words I use in the same sense. Prodicus might perhaps quarrel with us, but I assume you speak of something being bounded or coming to an end. That is all I mean, nothing subtle.

MENO: I admit the notion, and believe I understand your meaning.

SOCRATES: And again, you recognize "surface" and "solid," as they are used in geometry?

MENO: Yes.

SOCRATES: Then with these you should by this time understand my definition of shape. To cover all its instances, I say that shape is that in which a solid terminates, or more briefly, it is the limit of a solid.

MENO: And how do you define color?

SOCRATES: What a shameless fellow you are, Meno. You keep bothering an old man to answer, but refuse to exercise your memory and tell me what was Gorgias' definition of virtue.

MENO: I will, Socrates, as soon as you tell me this.

SOCRATES: Anyone talking to you could tell blindfold that you are a handsome man and still have your admirers.

MENO: Why so?

SOCRATES: Because you are forever laying down the law as spoiled boys do, who act the tyrant as long as their youth lasts. No doubt you have discovered that I can never resist good looks. Well, I will give in and let you have your answer.

MENO: Do by all means.

SOCRATES: Would you like an answer à la Gorgias, such as you would most readily follow?

MENO: Of course I should.

SOCRATES: You and he believe in Empedocles' theory of effluences, do you not?

MENO: Wholeheartedly.

SOCRATES: And passages to which and through which the effluences make their way?

MENO: Yes.

SOCRATES: Some of the effluences fit into some of the passages, whereas others are too coarse or too fine.

MENO: That is right.

SOCRATES: Now you recognize the term "sight"?

MENO: Yes.

SOCRATES: From these notions, then, "grasp what I would tell" as Pindar says. Color is an effluence from shapes commensurate with sight and perceptible by it.

MENO: That seems to me an excellent answer.

SOCRATES: No doubt it is the sort you are used to. And you probably see that it provides a way to define sound and smell and many similar things.

MENO: So it does.

SOCRATES: Yes, it's a high-sounding answer, so you like it better than the one on shape.

MENO: I do.

SOCRATES: Nevertheless, son of Alexidemus, I am convinced that the other is better, and I believe you would agree with me if you had not, as you told me yesterday, to leave before the Mysteries, but could stay and be initiated.

MENO: I would stay, Socrates, if you gave me more answers like this.

SOCRATES: You may be sure I shan't be lacking in keenness to do so, both for your sake and mine, but I'm afraid I may not be able to do it often. However, now it is your turn to do as you promised, and try to tell me the general nature of virtue. Stop making many out of one, as the humorists say when somebody breaks a plate. Just leave virtue whole and sound and tell me what it is, as in the examples I have given you.

MENO: It seems to me then, Socrates, that virtue is, in the words of the poet, "to rejoice in the fine and have power," and I define it as desiring fine things and being able to acquire them.

SOCRATES: When you speak of a man desiring fine things, do you mean it is good things he desires?

MENO: Certainly.

SOCRATES: Then do you think some men desire evil and others good? Doesn't everyone, in your opinion, desire good things?

MENO: No.

SOCRATES: And would you say that the others suppose evils to be good, or do they still desire them although they recognize them as evil?

MENO: Both, I should say.

SOCRATES: What? Do you really think that anyone who recognizes evils for what they are, nevertheless desires them?

MENO: Yes.

SOCRATES: Desires in what way? To possess them?

MENO: Of course.

SOCRATES: In the belief that evil things bring advantage to their possessor, or harm?

MENO: Some in the first belief, but some also in the second.

SOCRATES: And do you believe that those who suppose evil things bring advantage understand that they are evil?

MENO: No, that I can't really believe.

SOCRATES: Isn't it clear then that this class, who don't recognize evils for what they are, don't desire evil but what they think is good, though in fact it is evil; those who through ignorance mistake bad things for good obviously desire the good?

MENO: For them I suppose that is true.

SOCRATES: Now as for those whom you speak of as desiring evils in the belief that they do harm to their possessor, these presumably know that they will be injured by them?

MENO: They must.

SOCRATES: And don't they believe that whoever is injured is, in so far as he is injured, unhappy?

MENO: That too they must believe.

SOCRATES: And unfortunate?

MENO: Yes.

SOCRATES: Well, does anybody want to be unhappy and unfortunate?

MENO: I suppose not.

SOCRATES: Then if not, nobody desires what is evil, for what else is unhappiness but desiring evil things and getting them?

MENO: It looks as if you are right, Socrates, and nobody desires what is evil.

SOCRATES: Now you have just said that virtue consists in a wish for good things plus the power to acquire them. In this definition the wish is common to everyone, and in that respect no one is better than his neighbor.

MENO: So it appears.

SOCRATES: So if one man is better than another, it must evidently be in respect of the power, and virtue, according to your account, is the power of acquiring good things.

MENO: Yes, my opinion is exactly as you now express it.

SOCRATES: Let us see whether you have hit the truth this time. You may well be right. The power of acquiring good things, you say, is virtue?

MENO: Yes.

SOCRATES: And by good do you mean such things as health and wealth?

MENO: I include the gaining both of gold and silver and of high and honorable office in the state.

SOCRATES: Are these the only classes of goods that you recognize?

MENO: Yes, I mean everything of that sort.

SOCRATES: Right. In the definition of Meno, hereditary guest-friend of the Great King, the acquisition of gold and silver is virtue. Do you add "just and righteous" to the word "acquisition," or doesn't it make any difference to you? Do you call it virtue all the same even if they are unjustly acquired?

MENO: Certainly not.

SOCRATES: Vice then?

MENO: Most certainly.

SOCRATES: So it seems that justice or temperance or piety, or some other part of virtue, must attach to the acquisition. Otherwise, although it is a means to good things, it will not be virtue.

MENO: No, how could you have virtue without these?

SOCRATES: In fact lack of gold and silver, if it results from failure to acquire it—either for oneself or another—in circumstances which would have made its acquisition unjust, is itself virtue.

MENO: It would seem so.

SOCRATES: Then to have such goods is no more virtue than to lack them. Rather we may say that whatever is accompanied by justice is virtue, whatever is without qualities of that sort is vice.

MENO: I agree that your conclusion seems inescapable.

SOCRATES: But a few minutes ago we called each of these—justice, temperance, and the rest—a part of virtue?

MENO: Yes, we did.

SOCRATES: So it seems you are making a fool of me.

MENO: How so, Socrates?

SOCRATES: I have just asked you not to break virtue up into fragments, and given you models of the type of answer I wanted, but taking no notice of this you tell me that virtue consists in the acquisition of good things with justice, and justice, you agree, is a part of virtue.

MENO: True.

SOCRATES: So it follows from your own statements that to act with a part of virtue is virtue, if you call justice and all the rest parts of virtue. The point I want to make is that whereas I asked you to give me an account of virtue as a whole, far from telling me what it is itself you say that every action is virtue which exhibits a part of virtue, as if you had already told me what the whole is, so that I should recognize it even if you chop it up into bits. It seems to me that we must put the same old question to you, my dear Meno—the question. What is virtue?—if every act becomes virtue when combined with a part of virtue. That is, after all, what it means to say that every act performed with justice is virtue. Don't you agree that the same question needs to be put? Does anyone know what a part of virtue is, without knowing the whole?

MENO: I suppose not.

SOCRATES: No, and if you remember, when I replied to you about shape just now, I believe we rejected the type of answer that employs terms which are still in question and not yet agreed upon.

MENO: We did, and rightly.

SOCRATES: Then please do the same. While the nature of virtue as a whole is still under question, don't suppose that you can explain it to anyone in terms of its parts, or by any similar type of explanation. Understand rather that the same question remains to be answered: you say this and that about virtue, but what *is* it? Does this seem nonsense to you?

MENO: No, to me it seems right enough.

SOCRATES: Then go back to the beginning and answer my question. What do you and your friend say that virtue is?

MENO: Socrates, even before I met you they told me that in plain truth you are a perplexed man yourself and reduce others to perplexity. At this moment I feel you are exercising magic and witchcraft upon me and positively laying me under your spell until I am just a mass of helplessness. If I may be flippant, I think that not only in outward appearance but in other respects as well you are exactly like the flat sting ray that one meets in the sea. Whenever anyone comes into contact with it, it numbs him, and that is the sort of thing that you seem to be doing to me now. My mind and my lips are literally numb, and I have nothing to reply to you. Yet I have spoken about virtue hundreds of times, held forth often on the subject in front of large audiences, and very well too, or so I thought. Now I can't even say what it is. In my opinion you are well advised not to leave Athens and live abroad. If you behaved like this as a foreigner in another country, you would most likely be arrested as a wizard.

SOCRATES: You're a real rascal, Meno. You nearly took me in.

MENO: Just what do you mean?

SOCRATES: I see why you used a simile about me.

MENO: Why do you think?

SOCRATES: To be compared to something in return. All good-looking people, I know perfectly well, enjoy a game of comparisons. They get the best of it, for naturally handsome folk provoke handsome similes. But I'm not going to oblige you. As for myself, if the sting ray paralyzes others only through being paralyzed itself, then the comparison is just, but not otherwise. It isn't that, knowing the answers myself, I perplex other people. The truth is rather that I infect them also with the perplexity I feel myself. So with virtue now. I don't know what it is. You may have known before you came into contact with me, but now you look as if you don't. Nevertheless I am ready to carry out, together with you, a joint investigation and inquiry into what it is.

Study Questions

1. What is a form?
2. Propose a conceptual analysis for each of the following concepts: (1) *even number*, (2) *triangle*, (3) *and*, (4) *just*. Can you think of any cases in which you are inclined to apply the concept but that are not covered by your analysis? Can you think of other cases to which your analysis applies but that you are not inclined to treat as instances of the concept?
3. What is Plato's view of the standard method of philosophy? Are there any good reasons for accepting it? Are there any disciplines that it makes (at least some) sense of?
4. What, on Plato's view, justifies his account of inquiry? Is it compatible with what current science tells us about human beings? Do modernized versions of Plato's account of inquiry suffer from any similar problems?

10.2   Philosophical Investigations

 LUDWIG WITTGENSTEIN

LUDWIG WITTGENSTEIN (1889–1951) is one of the most influential philosophers of the twentieth century. Wittgenstein was born in Vienna, Austria. He studied aeronautical engineering at Manchester University in the United Kingdom, which led him to mathematics and philosophy. He studied philosophy with Bertrand Russell and G. E. Moore at Cambridge. His work is generally divided into three phases: early, middle, and late. In the early phase of his career he served in the Austrian Military in World War I. He was taken captive in a German military camp in 1917. During his time there he prepared the notes for his first major work *Tractatus Logico-Philosophicus,* in which he claimed to have solved all the problems of philosophy by a careful analysis of logic, language, and their relation to the world. In his late period, roughly 1930 to his death, he prepared his ideas for his next major work, *Philosophical Investigations,* in which he explored ideas about ordinary language, psychology, mathematics, and philosophical methodology.

The selection we have chosen for this chapter on philosophical methodology is a short piece from Wittgenstein's *Investigations,* sections 65–71. In these sections, Wittgenstein reflects on the attempt to get at the definition of a general term, such as "game," which has many diverse instances, such as chess and basketball. In his reflection, term he proposes the idea that in some cases it seems like the instances that fall under a general term do not share any set of properties in common. Rather, they are related by what Wittgenstein calls "family resemblances."

65. Here we come up against the great question that lies behind all these considerations.—For someone might object against me: "You make things easy for yourself! You talk about all sorts of language-games, but have nowhere said what is essential to a language-game, and so to language: what is common to all these activities, and makes them into language or parts of language. So you let yourself off the very part of the investigation that once gave you the most headache, the part about the *general form of the proposition* and of language."

And this is true.—Instead of pointing out something common to all that we call language,

I'm saying that these phenomena have no one thing in common in virtue of which we use the same word for all—but there are many different kinds of *affinity* between them. And on account of this affinity, or these affinities, we call them all "languages." I'll try to explain this.

66. Consider, for example, the activities that we call "games." I mean board-games, card-games, ball-games, athletic games, and so on. What is common to them all?—Don't say: "They *must* have something in common, or they would not be called 'games'"—but *look and see* whether there is anything common to all.—For

Ludwig Wittgenstein, *Philosophical Investigations,* third edition, translated by G. E. M Anscombe (Basil Blackwell & Mott Ltd., 1958).

if you look at them, you won't see something that is common to *all*, but similarities, affinities, and a whole series of them at that. To repeat: don't think, but look!—Look, for example, at board-games, with their various affinities. Now pass to card-games; here you find many correspondences with the first group, but many common |32| features drop out, and others appear. When we pass next to ball-games, much that is common is retained, but much is lost.—Are they all "*entertaining*"? Compare chess with noughts and crosses. Or is there always winning and losing, or competition between players? Think of patience. In ball-games, there is winning and losing; but when a child throws his ball at the wall and catches it again, this feature has disappeared. Look at the parts played by skill and luck, and at the difference between skill in chess and skill in tennis. Think now of singing and dancing games; here we have the element of entertainment, but how many other characteristic features have disappeared! And we can go through the many, many other groups of games in the same way, can see how similarities crop up and disappear.

And the upshot of these considerations is: we see a complicated network of similarities overlapping and criss-crossing: similarities in the large and in the small.

67. I can think of no better expression to characterize these similarities than "family resemblances"; for the various resemblances between members of a family—build, features, colour of eyes, gait, temperament, and so on and so forth—overlap and criss-cross in the same way.—And I shall say: "games" form a family.

And likewise the kinds of number, for example, form a family. Why do we call something a "number"? Well, perhaps because it has a—direct—affinity with several things that have hitherto been called "number"; and this can be said to give it an indirect affinity with other things that we also call "numbers." And we extend our concept of number, as in spinning a thread we twist fibre on fibre. And the strength of the thread resides not in the fact that some one fibre runs through its whole length, but in the overlapping of many fibres.

But if someone wanted to say, "So there is something common to all these constructions—namely, the disjunction of all their common properties"—I'd reply: Now you are only playing with a word. One might as well say, "There is a Something that runs through the whole thread—namely, the continuous overlapping of these fibres."

68. "Right; so in your view the concept of number is explained as the logical sum of those individual interrelated concepts: cardinal numbers, rational numbers, real numbers, and so forth; and in the same way, the concept of a game as the logical sum of corresponding subconcepts."—This need not be so. For I *can* give the concept of number rigid boundaries |33| in this way, that is, use the word "number" for a rigidly bounded concept; but I can also use it so that the extension of the concept is *not* closed by a boundary. And this is how we do use the word "game." For how is the concept of a game bounded? What still counts as a game, and what no longer does? Can you say where the boundaries are? No. You can *draw* some, for there aren't any drawn yet. (But this never bothered you before when you used the word "game.")

"But then the use of the word is unregulated—the 'game' we play with it is unregulated."—It is not everywhere bounded by rules; but no more are there any rules for how high one may throw the ball in tennis, or how hard, yet tennis is a game for all that, and has rules too.

69. How would we explain to someone what a game is? I think that we'd describe *games* to him, and we might add to the description: "This *and similar things* are called 'games.'" And do we know any more ourselves? Is it just that we can't tell others exactly what a game is?—But this is not ignorance. We don't know the boundaries because none have been drawn. To repeat, we can draw a boundary—for a special purpose. Does it take this to make the concept usable? Not at all! Except perhaps for that special

purpose. No more than it took the definition: 1 pace = 75 cm to make the measure of length "one pace" usable. And if you want to say "But still, before that it wasn't an exact measure of length," then I reply: all right, so it was an inexact one.—Though you still owe me a definition of exactness.

70. "But if the concept 'game' is without boundaries in this way, you don't really know what you mean by a 'game.'"—When I give the description "The ground was quite covered with plants," do you want to say that I don't know what I'm talking about until I can give a definition of a plant?

An explanation of what I meant would be, say, a drawing and the words "The ground looked roughly like this." Perhaps I even say: "It looked *exactly* like this."—Then were just *these* blades of grass and *these* leaves there, arranged just like this? No, that is not what it means. And I wouldn't accept any picture as the exact one in *this* sense. |34|

71. One can say that the concept of a game is a concept with blurred edges.—"But is a blurred concept a *concept* at all?"—Is a photograph that is not sharp a picture of a person at all? Is it even always an advantage to replace a picture that is not sharp by one that is? Isn't one that isn't sharp often just what we need?

Frege compares a concept to a region, and says that a region without clear boundaries can't be called a region at all. This presumably means that we can't do anything with it.—But is it senseless to say "Stay roughly here"? Imagine that I were standing with someone in a city square and said that. As I say it, I do not bother drawing any boundary, but just make a pointing gesture—as if I were indicating a particular spot. And this is just how one might explain what a game is. One gives examples and intends them to be taken in a particular way.—I do not mean by this expression, however, that he is supposed to see in those examples that common feature which I—for some reason—was unable to formulate, but that he is now to employ those examples in a particular way. Here giving examples is not an *indirect* way of explaining—in default of a better one. For any general explanation may be misunderstood too. *This*, after all, is how we play the game. (I mean the language-game with the word "game.")

Study Questions

1. Give an example of two games that have something in common; then give an example of something that is a game that does not share that commonality.
2. What does Wittgenstein mean by the notion of "family resemblances"?
3. How might one use Wittgenstein's notion of "family resemblances" to criticize the project of conceptual analysis as portrayed by Plato?

Plato's Method Meets Cognitive Science 10.3

STEPHEN P. STICH

STEPHEN STICH (1943–) is Board of Governors Professor of Philosophy at Rutgers University in New Jersey, where he has been on the faculty since 1989. He received his Ph.D. in philosophy from Princeton University in 1968. He is an Honorary Professor of Philosophy at the University of Sheffield and has held a wide variety of distinguished positions including being a Fellow of the Center for Advanced Study in the Behavioral Sciences. He has taught at the University of California, San Diego; the University of Maryland; and the University of Michigan, among other places. His areas of interest include cognitive science, the theory of rationality, and experimental philosophy.

The selection we have chosen for this chapter on philosophical methodology is a piece that offers an autobiographical account of Stich's realization that intuition-based, philosophical methodology is deeply problematic. In this selection he recalls his initial realization that appeals to intuition might vary across cultural groups and then relates how this realization was turned from mere conjecture into a real problem under the influence of the work of some experimental psychologists. Here Stich presents the basic experimental critique of intuition as unreliable based on the variability of intuitions across groups.

Normative questions—particularly questions about what we should believe and how we should behave—have always been high on the agenda for philosophers, and over the centuries there has been no shortage of answers proposed. But this abundance of answers raises yet another fundamental philosophical question: How should we *evaluate* the proposed answers; how can we determine whether an answer to a normative question is a good one? The best known and most widely used method for evaluating answers to normative questions can be traced all the way back to Plato. Recently, however, cognitive scientists interested in cross cultural differences have reported findings that pose a serious challenge to this venerable philosophical method. Indeed, in light of these new findings some philosophers—I am one of them—have come to think that after 2400 years it may be time for philosophy to stop relying on Plato's method. In the pages that follow I'll sketch the path that led me to this conclusion.

To introduce the method, let's begin with an example of its use by one of its most brilliant practitioners, Plato himself. Here is a famous passage from *The Republic* in which Socrates recounts using the method in a conversation about the nature of justice.

> Well said, Cephalus, I replied: but as concerning justice, what is it?—to speak the truth and to pay your debts—no more than this? And even to this are there not exceptions? Suppose a friend when in his right mind has deposited arms with me and he asks for them when he is not in his right

Stephen Stich, "Plato's Method Meets Cognitive Science," *Free Inquiry* 21 © 2001 by the Council for Secular Humanism. This article originally appeared in *Free Inquiry* magazine, spring 2001.

mind, ought I to given them back to him? No one would say that I ought or that I should be right in doing so, any more than they would say that I ought always to speak the truth to one who is in his condition.

You are quite right, he replied.

But then, I said, speaking the truth and paying your debts is not a correct definition of justice.

Quite correct, Socrates.[1]

The central idea of Plato's method, clearly on display here, is to test normative claims against people's spontaneous judgments about real and hypothetical cases. Contemporary philosophers often call these spontaneous judgments "intuitions." If the normative claim and people's intuitions agree, the claim is vindicated. But if, as in Socrates' dialogue with Cephalus, a normative principle conflicts with people's intuitions, then something has to give. Sometimes we may hold on to the normative claim and ignore a recalcitrant intuition. But if a normative principle conflicts with lots of intuitions or, as in the example from *The Republic*, if it conflicts with an intuition that we would be very reluctant to give up, then Plato's method requires that we reject the principle and try to come up with another one.

Though philosophers have been using this method for over two millennia, it is far from clear why we should trust it. Why should we think that a normative principle that has been sanctioned by the method is likely to be a good one? Indeed, why do principles that cohere with our intuitions have any special status at all? Plato, of course, had an answer to this question. It was part of his famous theory of *anamnesis* or recollection. Though scholars would give a much more nuanced account, the basic idea is that before we were born our souls had an opportunity to gain knowledge of the Forms which determine the true nature of knowledge, justice, piety—and everything else. When the soul enters the body the whole business is so traumatic that the soul forgets what it knew about the Forms. Fortunately, the knowledge is not totally lost. It still

guides our judgments about cases like the one that Socrates poses for Cephalus, and by using Plato's method with diligence we can succeed in recovering explicit knowledge of the Forms.

It's certainly an ingenious story, though even in Plato's time few people accepted it, and it would be hard to find a contemporary philosopher who takes the stuff about the soul's prior encounter with the Forms at all seriously. But useable methods are not exactly thick on the ground in philosophy, so while Plato's account of why his method works has been roundly rejected, the method itself most definitely has not. Consider, for example, the following enormously influential passage in which Nelson Goodman, one of the great analytic philosophers of the last half of the 20th century, offers a wonderfully lucid account of the method that he and others in the analytic tradition have long been using.

How do we justify a *de*duction? Plainly by showing that it conforms to the general rules of deductive inference.... Analogously, the basic task in justifying an inductive inference is to show that it conforms to the general rules of *in*duction.

Yet, of course, the rules themselves must eventually be justified. The validity of a deduction depends not upon conformity to any purely arbitrary rules we may contrive, but upon conformity to valid rules.... But how is the validity of rules to be determined?... Principles of deductive inference are justified by their conformity with accepted deductive practice. Their validity depends upon accordance with the particular deductive inferences that we actually make and sanction. If a rule yields inacceptable inferences, we drop it as invalid. Justification of general rules thus derives from judgments rejecting or accepting particular deductive inferences.

This looks flagrantly circular. I have said that deductive inferences are justified by their conformity to valid general rules, and that general rules are justified by their conformity to valid inferences. But this circle is a virtuous one. The point is that rules and particular inferences alike are justified by being brought into agreement with each other.

A rule is amended if it yields an inference we are unwilling to accept; an inference is rejected if it violates a rule we are unwilling to amend. The process of justification is the delicate one of making mutual adjustments between rules and accepted inferences; and in the agreement achieved lies the only justification needed for either.[2]

In *A Theory of Justice*, one of the most influential philosophical books of the last fifty years, John Rawls advocates much the same method for justifying principles in the moral domain. Rawls also introduced a new name for the method; he called it *the method of reflective equilibrium.*

But what about our concern over the justification of the method? What do contemporary philosophers have on offer to replace Plato's myth about the prenatal adventures of the soul? Goodman, it seems, thinks that passing the reflective equilibrium test is (as philosophers sometimes say) *constitutive* of justification or validity for normative principles. Passing the reflective equilibrium test is what it *is* for a principle to be justified. There is no need to tell tales about dimly remembered encounters with the Forms. In the agreement between principles and intuitions, Goodman maintains, lies the only justification that is needed for either.

I first encountered Goodman's account of the reflective equilibrium method when, as an undergraduate at the University of Pennsylvania in the early 1960s, I had the great good fortune to take a class with Goodman. It all seemed overwhelmingly plausible to me at that time and for many years after. During those years, I had some very good company, since the method was ubiquitous in post World War II Anglo-American philosophy. But then, about 15 years ago, I began to have some doubts. In my initial attempts to articulate those doubts I did what philosophers so often do—I described a hypothetical case: Suppose we were to encounter cognitive agents—Martians, perhaps, or members of an exotic tribe—who reasoned and formed beliefs very differently from the way we do. Suppose further that these exotic folks also have very different intuitions about rea-

soning, and that when the method of reflective equilibrium is used with their intuitions it turns out that their way of reasoning is justified, though when the method is used with our intuitions, it turns out that our very different way of reasoning is justified. Surely, I argued, something has gone very wrong here, since it seems that the method of reflective equilibrium can justify *any* way of going about the business of reasoning, no matter how bizarre, so long as the folks who use the method have the intuitions to match. We could, of course, avoid the problem by insisting that in employing the method we must use *our* intuitions, not theirs. But it is (to put it mildly) less than obvious how this move could be defended. Since we don't believe that our intuitions have been shaped by a prenatal glimpse at the Forms, why should we privilege our intuitions over those of some other group?

Though I thought this was a rather clever objection to the method of reflective equilibrium, others were unconvinced. And they had an interesting argument: We rely on *our* intuitions in philosophy for much the same reason that we rely on our intuitions in mathematics. They are the only game in town—the only *real* intuitions that anyone has. Why should we worry about what might be justified by the intuitions of imaginary Martians, they asked, when there are no such Martians? That's a good question, and one to which, until recently, I had no good answer.

About three years ago, however, I happened to run across my old friend, the psychologist Richard Nisbett, and he began to tell me about some enormously exciting experiments that he has been doing. For decades, scholars have been claiming that people in East Asian cultures have very different "mentalities" from people in Western cultures. The Chinese, scholars have claimed, and others influenced by Chinese culture, perceive and think about the world around them in very different ways from people in Western cultures, and these differences are reflected in the way they describe and explain events and in the beliefs and theories they accept. Nisbett and his colleagues had begun to explore whether these claims about differences in mentalities could be experimentally verified, and—to my amazement and to the amazement of most cognitive scientists as well—they discovered that many of them could. There is a growing body of evidence indicating large and systematic differences between East Asians and Westerners on a long list of cognitive processes including attention, memory and perception. The two groups also differ in the way they go about describing, predicting and explaining events, in the way they categorize objects and in the way they revise beliefs in the face of new arguments and evidence.[3] This work suddenly made it very plausible that the first part of my hypothetical case is more than just a philosophical fantasy. There really are people whose reasoning and belief forming strategies are very different from ours. Indeed, there are over a billion of them!

But what about the second part of my thought experiment, the part that focused on intuitions? Nisbett hadn't looked for cross cultural differences in intuitions, but when I mentioned the possibility to him, he thought it was worth a try. So, in collaboration with Shaun Nichols and Jonathan Weinberg, I decided to run a few experiments designed to explore whether in addition to the differences that Nisbett found between Asian and Western processes of acquiring knowledge, there might also be differences between Asian and Western intuitions about what knowledge *is*.

One of the oldest and most durable doctrines in epistemology is an account of knowledge that was first proposed by Plato in a dialog called the *Theaetetus*. To count as an instance of knowledge, on this view, a belief must be true, and the believer must have some justification for believing it. Neither lucky guesses nor false beliefs count as knowledge. This analysis of knowledge as *justified true belief* was the received view from Plato's time until 1963, when Edmund Gettier published a number of hypothetical cases in which people had justified true beliefs, though what made the beliefs true was not causally related to what made

the beliefs justified. Here is an example of the sort of case that Gettier proposed.

> Bob has a friend, Jill, who has driven a Buick for many years. Bob therefore thinks that Jill drives an American car. He is not aware, however, that her Buick has recently been stolen, and he is also not aware that Jill has replaced it with a Pontiac, which is a different kind of American car. Does Bob really know that Jill drives an American car, or does he only believe it?

Cases like this have had a vast impact on philosophers. Just about every epistemologist has the strong intuition that Bob does not really have knowledge in "Gettier cases," and those intuitions have led the overwhelming majority of philosophers to conclude that Plato's *justified true belief* account of knowledge is mistaken or incomplete.

But Nichols, Weinberg and I had a hunch. Gettier cases are typically very similar to unproblematic cases in which the fact that makes the belief true *is* causally involved in the justification of the belief. And Nisbett's group has shown that East Asians are more inclined than Westerners to make judgments on the basis of similarity. Westerners, on the other hand, are more disposed to focus on causation in describing the world and classifying things. So, we speculated, perhaps East Asians might be somewhat less inclined than Westerners to withhold the attribution of knowledge in Gettier cases. The results of an experiment designed to test this speculation were nothing short of startling. As expected a substantial majority of Western subjects (74%) claim that Bob *only believes* that Jill drives an American car, but a majority of East Asian subjects (57%) claim that Bob *really knows*! With South Asian subjects, the difference is even more remarkable. Sixty one percent of our Indian, Pakistani and Bangladeshi subjects report that Bob *really knows*. The "Gettier intuitions" that led to the rejection of the Platonic account of knowledge are, it appears, *very* culturally local.

Encouraged by these findings, we embarked on a much more ambitious project designed to test a variety of philosophical "intuition probes" on a variety of different groups. So far we've found a total of six intuition probes—all modeled on hypothetical cases that have been widely discussed by epistemologists—on which different groups have significantly different intuitions. In some cases the differences are between people with different cultural backgrounds, while in other cases they are between people of different socio-economic status (SES). High SES Americans and low SES Americans have different epistemic intuitions! Moreover, in many cases these differences are quite dramatic. So why haven't philosophers noticed them? Well, since years of education is a major factor in determining SES, *all* philosophy professors are high SES, and the overwhelming majority of us are white and of Western European ancestry.

What conclusions should we draw from these studies? Perhaps the first thing to say is that it is early days yet. All six of the intuition probes on which we've found significant group differences ask subjects to say whether the case counts as knowledge or mere belief. It would be fascinating to know whether there are also cultural and SES differences when subjects are asked to judge what a person *should believe* or whether a belief is *justified*, and we are currently collecting data using these intuition probes. Further down the road, we'd like to look at moral intuitions to see if they exhibit the same cultural diversity that we're finding in epistemic intuitions.[4] If we continue to find the sorts of systematic cultural differences in philosophical intuitions that our first studies have uncovered, the conclusion I'd be inclined to draw is that *Plato's method should be rejected as a strategy for answering normative questions*, since it will yield wildly different results depending on whose intuitions we use. Another option would be to go relativistic and conclude

that the epistemic and moral norms appropriate for the rich are different from those appropriate for the poor, and that the norms appropriate for white people are different from those appropriate for people of color. But even if one is inclined to relativism in matters normative—and I am—this strikes me as relativism gone mad. Surely a much more reasonable conclusion is that philosophy's 2400 year long infatuation with Plato's method has been a terrible mistake.[5]

Notes

1. *The Dialogues of Plato*, translated by B. Jowett. I, 131, p. 595. New York: Random House.
2. *Fact, Fiction and Forecast*, pp. 66–67. Indianapolis: Bobbs-Merrill (1965).
3. R. Nisbett, K. Peng, I. Choi, & A. Norenzayan, "Culture and systems of thought: holistic vs. analytic cognition," *Psychological Review*, 2001.
4. There is already some very impressive evidence indicating that people in different SES groups have different moral intuitions. See J. Haidt, S. Koller & M. Dias. "Affect, Culture and Morality," *J. of Personality & Social Psychology*, 65, 4, 613–628, 1993.
5. I'd like to thank Shaun Nichols for his helpful feedback on an earlier draft of this article.

Study Questions

1. Why does Stich believe that intuitions can't be relied upon to solve philosophical problems?
2. How could we resolve conflicts in intuitions held by different cultural groups? How do these possible resolutions illuminate the challenge posed by experimental philosophy?
3. What would philosophical inquiry look like if Stich's critique is correct? How would this be different from an intuition-based method of philosophy? Would this be philosophy?

10.4   Experimental Philosophy and Philosophical Intuition

ERNEST SOSA

ERNEST SOSA (1940–) is Board of Governors Professor of Philosophy at Rutgers University in New Jersey. He was born in Cuba and received his Ph.D. in philosophy from the University of Pittsburgh in 1964. He taught at Brown University until 2007, upon which he took up his current post at Rutgers University. Although a wide-ranging philosopher who has made valuable contributions to a number of areas of philosophy, he is most recognized for his work in epistemology.

The selection we have chosen for this chapter on philosophical methodology is a piece that serves as a response to an objection to the appeal to intuition offered by Stich. Some traditional philosophy appeals to intuitions about hypothetical cases in order to form justified beliefs about the answers to philosophical questions, such as the nature of knowledge, free will, or morally permissible action. Stich and other experimental philosophers have argued that the appeal to intuition is problematic because in some cases people from different cultures do not share the same intuition. In this piece Sosa presents a theory of intuition called the *competence-based* account. He then responds to the experimental philosophers' challenge by distinguishing between merely verbal disagreements and substantive disagreements.

Our topic is experimental philosophy AS a naturalistic movement and its bearing on the value of intuitions in philosophy. I explore first how the movement might bear on philosophy more generally and how it might amount to something novel and promising. Then I turn to one accomplishment repeatedly claimed for it already: namely, the discrediting of armchair intuitions as used in philosophy.[1]

Experimental philosophy bears on traditional philosophy in at least two ways. It puts in question what is or is not believed *intuitively* by people generally. And it challenges the *truth* of beliefs that *are* generally held, ones traditionally important in philosophy. Each challenge is based on certain experimental results.

How might such experimental results bear on philosophical issues? Here's an example. Traditional skepticism relies crucially on the idea that for all we can really tell, life is but a dream. Whether one enjoys waking life or an extended dream, one has the very same stream of consciousness regardless, so how can one possibly tell the difference? This depends on a conception of dreams as something like hallucinations, however, and we might discover that dreams are not quite like that. Perhaps to dream is much more like imagining than like hallucinating. If

Ernest Sosa, "Experimental Philosophy and Philosophical Intuition," in J. Knobe & S. Nichols (eds.), *Experimental Philosophy* (2008). By permission of Oxford University Press.

so, how might this bear on the traditional skeptical problematic?

Even if it *is* part of common sense that in dreams we have conscious experiences intrinsically just like those of waking life, an experimentally based approach might show that common sense is just wrong, in a way that bears crucially on a perennial problematic of philosophy, that of radical skepticism.

Mining the sciences is not in itself novel, of course. Philosophers have been doing that for a very long time, with striking results. Just think of how twentieth-century physics bears on the philosophy of space and time, or split-brain phenomena on issues of personal identity, to take just two examples. Perhaps the novelty is rather that experimental philosophers do not so much *borrow* from the scientists as that they *become* scientists. This they do by designing and running experiments aimed to throw light on philosophically interesting issues. And if philosophers are ill equipped to probe the brain in the ways of neuroscientists, it is easy enough to broaden the movement's self-conception to include interdisciplinary work, provided neuroscientists care enough about such issues with philosophical import, as no doubt some already do. Indeed, many experimental philosophers would already define the movement in this interdisciplinary way.

In any case, most of the actual work so far done in experimental philosophy has involved social psychology. Some of the best-known work has involved surveys designed to probe, and to question, people's intuitions on various philosophical issues. So the novelty might involve the methodologically self-conscious pursuit of such an approach. This anyhow is the side of experimental philosophy that I will be discussing. If the movement is to substantiate a claim to novel results of striking interest to philosophy, this work on intuitions, and other work similarly dependent on surveys, would seem to be particularly important.[2]

My defense against experimentalist objections to armchair intuitions is anchored in the fact that verbal disagreement need not be substantive.

This defense will be developed presently, but first: How should we conceive of intuitions?

It is often claimed that analytic philosophy appeals to armchair intuitions in the service of "conceptual analysis." But this is deplorably misleading. The use of intuitions in philosophy should not be tied exclusively to conceptual analysis. Consider some main subjects of prominent debate: utilitarian versus deontological theories in ethics, for example, or Rawls's theory of justice in social and political philosophy, or the externalism/internalism debate in epistemology; and many others could be cited to similar effect. These are not controversies about the conceptual analysis of some concept. They seem moreover to be disputes about something more objective than just a description or analysis of our individual or shared concepts of the relevant phenomena. Yet they have been properly conducted in terms of hypothetical examples and intuitions about these examples. The questions involved are about rightness or justice or epistemic justification. Some such questions concern an ethical or epistemic subject matter, and not just our corresponding concepts.

There can be such a subject matter, beyond our concepts of it, moreover, even if rightness, justice, and epistemic justification are not *natural kinds*. Nor need they be socially constructed kinds, either. Indeed, we can regard philosophical controversies as objective without ever going into the ontological status of the entities involved, if any. Mostly we can conduct our controversies, for example, just in terms of where the *truth* lies with regard to them, leaving aside questions of objectual ontology.

Prima facie there is a role for intuition in simple arithmetic and geometry, moreover, but *not only* there. Just consider how extensively we rely on intuition. Take, for example, any two sufficiently different shapes that you perceive on a surface, say the shapes of any two words. If they are words in a foreign language, you may not even have a good *recognitional* grasp, a good concept of any of those shapes. Still you may know perfectly well that they are different. And what you know is not just that the actual *tokens* are different: you also know that any word token *so* shaped *would* be differently shaped from any *thus* shaped (as you demonstrate the two shapes in turn). Or take any shape and any color, or any shape and any sound. And so on, and so forth. Why deny ourselves a similar intuitive access to the simple facts involved in our hypothetical philosophical examples? That we enjoy such access would seem to be the default position, absent some specific objection.

I apply virtue epistemology to the specific case of a priori knowledge, and more specifically to foundational a priori knowledge, to *intuitive* justification and knowledge. Traditionally such intuitions have been understood in accordance with two prominent models: (a) the perceptual, eye-of-the-mind model, and (b) the Cartesian introspective model. Each of these models is subject to fatal objections, however, which prepares the way for my proposed competence-based account.

On my proposal, to intuit that p is to be attracted to assent simply through entertaining that representational content. The intuition is *rational* if and only if it derives from a *competence* and the content is explicitly or implicitly modal (i.e., attributes necessity or possibility). This first approximation is then defended against the two main published lines of attack on intuitions: the calibration objection and the cultural divergence objection.[3]

One might quite properly wonder why we should restrict ourselves to modal propositions. And there is no very deep reason. It's just that this seems the proper domain for philosophical uses of intuition. True, contingent intuitions might also derive from a competence. For example, there is a "taking experience at face value" competence, whose resulting intuitions would be *of the form* "if things appear thus and so, then they *are* thus and so." These I would call "empirical" intuitions, however, to be distinguished from the "rational" intuitions involved in abstract, a priori, armchair thought of the kind we do in philosophy.

It might be objected that the proposed account is *too externalist*. But two sources of such worry need to be distinguished. One is the *access* worry, the other the *control* worry, and the two are largely independent. These raise large and fascinating issues of internalism versus externalism. Here I can only gesture, inadequately, at my preferred stance.

First, regarding access, we cannot well insist on armchair access to the justifying power of our sources, since their justifying power depends crucially on their reliability, and this is not knowable from the armchair for our competences generally. (This is not to deny that a source's justifying power is boosted, reaching a special level, when we *do* have access to its reliability; or at least that, when the source operates in combination with such awareness, we attain a higher, reflective level for the resulting beliefs.)

Second, regarding control, we cannot well insist on *total* control. We must depend on favorable circumstances in all sorts of ways, and these are often relevantly beyond our control. We must depend on a kind of epistemic luck.

If we insist that true knowledge requires *armchair* access to the reliability of our competences or *total* control regardless of our situation, the outcome is extreme skepticism, which I do not regard as a *reductio* exactly, though I do think it limits the interest of the notions of *absolute* knowledge thus induced.

When we rely on intuitions in philosophy, then, in my view we manifest a competence that enables us to get it right on a certain subject matter, by basing our beliefs on the sheer understanding of their contents. How might survey results create a problem for us? Suppose a subgroup clashes with another on some supposed truth, and suppose they all ostensibly affirm as they do based on the sheer understanding of the content affirmed. We then have a prima facie problem. Suppose half of them affirm <p> while half deny it, with everyone basing their respective attitudes on the sheer understanding of the representational content <p>. Obviously, half of them are getting it right, and half wrong. Of those who get it right, now, how plausible can it be that their beliefs constitute or derive from rational intuition, from an attraction to assent that manifests a real competence?

Not that it is logically incoherent to maintain exactly that. But how plausible can it be, absent some theory of error that will explain why so many are going wrong when we are getting it right? Unless we can cite something different in the conditions or in the constitution of the misled, doubt will surely cloud the claim to competence by those who ex hypothesi are getting it right.

If there is a large disagreement in color judgments within a certain population, how can we sustain the claim to competence by those whose excellent color vision guides them systematically to the truth? Presumably we need to explain the error of the others by appeal to some defect in their lighting conditions or in their color vision, something wrong with their rods and cones or the like. Even if we reject the perceptual model of intuition, so long as we still appeal to competence, we need something analogous to the error theory that protects our color vision from the disagreement of the color blind and of those misled by bad light. We need an error theory that attributes the error of those who disagree with us to bad constitution (blindness) or to bad situation (bad light).

That would seem to be so, moreover, regardless of whether the subject matter is fully objective (as, perhaps, with shape perception), or quasi-objective and reaction-dependent (as, perhaps, with color perception, or with socially constructed phenomena).

So there will definitely be a prima facie problem for the appeal to intuitions in philosophy if surveys show that there is extensive enough disagreement on the subject matter supposedly open to intuitive access.

The bearing of these surveys on traditional philosophical issues is questionable, however, because the experimental results really concern in the first instance only people's responses to certain words. But verbal disagreement *need* not reveal any substantive, real disagreement, if ambiguity and context might account for the verbal divergence. If today I say, "Mary went to the bank yesterday," and tomorrow you say, "Mary did not go to the bank yesterday," we need not disagree, given ambiguity and contextual variation. The experimentalists have not yet done enough to show that they have crossed the gaps created by such potential differences in meaning and context, so as to show that supposedly commonsense intuitive belief is really not as widely shared as philosophers have assumed it to be. Nor has it been shown beyond reasonable doubt that there really are philosophically important disagreements rooted in cultural or socioeconomic differences (or so I have argued elsewhere in some detail) (see Bishop & Murphy, 2007).

Within the movement itself, one finds a growing recognition that the supposed "intuitive disagreements" may be only verbal. Thus, a recent paper by Shaun Nichols and Joseph Ulatowski contains the following proposal:

> Our hypothesis is that "intentional" exhibits interpretive diversity, i.e., it admits of different interpretations. Part of the population, when given…[certain] sorts of cases, interpret "intentional" one way; and part of the population interpret it in another way. On one interpretation both cases are intentional and on the other interpretation, neither is. In linguistics and philosophy of language, there are several ways that a term can admit of different interpretations: the term might be ambiguous, polysemous, or exhibit certain forms of semantic underspecification. We mean for the interpretive diversity hypothesis to be neutral about which form of interpretive diversity holds for "intentional."[4]

To the extent that experimental philosophy adopts this way of accounting for diversity of verbal intuitive responses, it will avoid substantive clashes in favor of merely verbal disagreement. But once such disagreements are seen to be verbal, the supposed problem for philosophical intuition evaporates.

The defense of philosophical intuition by appeal to "merely verbal disagreement" may be rejected because the implied failures of communication would threaten to make intuition reports useless for joint philosophical theorizing. Although this point is sometimes pressed, I can see no real threat in it. The appeal to divergence of interpretation is a *defensive* move, made against those who claim that there *is* serious disagreement in supposed intuitions. It is only against such a claim of disagreement that we must appeal to verbal divergence. But any such claim need be taken seriously only when adequately backed by evidence. And this is surely a matter to be taken up case by case. Among possible sources of such attention-demanding evidence, two stand out. First, the evidence might be gathered empirically, through surveys. Second, the evidence might be internal to our field, owed to dialectic with fellow philosophers, where we seem to disagree persistently, for example, on what to think about various hypothetical cases. One attractive option, once we have reached that stage, having exhausted other options, would be to consider whether we may be "interpreting" our terms somewhat differently.

Consider a further case study of how an apparent clash of intuitions can turn out to be only verbal. We turn to a recent paper by Shaun Nichols and Joshua Knobe about the bearing of intuitions on the problematic of free will and determinism (Nichols & Knobe 2007). In their view intuitions relevant to this problematic are heavily influenced by affect. Here is a brief description of the study, its results, and the morals drawn.

First the distinction between a fully determinist universe D and an indeterminist universe I is presented to experimental subjects, 90% of whom report that our own universe is more like I than like D.

Now for the shocking results: When subjects are asked the abstract question whether agents in D are fully morally responsible, 86% say that they are not: no agent can be fully morally responsible for doing what he is fully determined to do. However, when a dastardly deed is attributed with a wealth of detail to a particular agent in D, and those same subjects are asked whether that agent is then fully morally responsible, 72% report that in their view he is!

Nichols and Knobe consider various ways to account for this amazing divergence. In the end, they find it most plausible to think that some performance error is responsible. Affect, they suggest, degrades intellectual performance in general, whether the relevant competence be memory, perception, inference, etc.

Of course, that explanation will leave intuition affected as lightly as are perception, memory, and inference, unless some further relevant difference can be specified.

In any case, there is an alternative explanation that will cast no affect-involving doubt on the intuitions in play. This other possibility came to mind on reading their paper and was soon confirmed in the article on moral responsibility in the Stanford Encyclopedia of Philosophy, where we are told that at least two different senses of "moral responsibility" have emerged: the attributability sense, and the accountability sense.

On the attributability view, to say that S is responsible for action A is to say that A is attributable to S as his own doing, and, we are told in the article, as an action that reveals something about S's character.

On the accountability view, to say that S is responsible for action A is to say that S is properly *held* accountable or responsible for A, in such a way that various good (or bad) things may be visited upon S *for* doing A.

So, here again, quite possibly the striking divergence reported above is explicable mainly if not entirely through verbal divergence.

Indeed, we may plausibly go beyond the explanation suggested in the Stanford Encyclopedia, by suggesting that in common parlance "accountability" need *not* be tied to manifestation of character. Those attracted to "agent causation," including philosophers such as Thomas Reid and Roderick Chisholm, would not make that linkage. So, there is a notion of attributability-responsibility that is inherently incompatibilist in requiring only that the agent have caused his action, free of antecedent determinants, *free even of determination by his or her character.*

If so, we may then find different "interpretations" at work in the verbal disagreement between the affect-affected intuiters (who react to the specific description of the dastardly deed) and the cold theoretical intuiters (who respond to the abstract question of whether any agent can be responsible in D). Of course, it remains to be seen why the one concept is more readily engaged by the affect elicited with the specific case, and the other more readily by cold reasoning about the abstract issue. But pessimism about explaining this would seem premature.

Let us turn next to a further line of experiment-based objection against philosophical intuition, which appears in a recent paper by Stacey Swain, Joshua Alexander, and Jonathan M. Weinberg, as follows:

> We found that intuitions in response to…[Keith Lehrer's Truetemp Case] vary according to whether, and what, other thought experiments are considered first. Our results show that: (1) willingness to attribute knowledge in the Truetemp Case increases after being presented with a clear case of nonknowledge, and (2) willingness to attribute knowledge in the Truetemp Case decreases after being presented with a clear case of knowledge. We contend that this instability undermines the supposed evidential status of these intuitions. (Swain, Alexander, & Weinberg, 2008)

Well, maybe, to *some* extent. But surely the effects of priming, framing, and other such contextual factors will affect the epistemic status of intuition in general, only in the sort of way that they affect the epistemic status of perceptual observation in general. One would think that the ways of preserving the epistemic importance of perception in the face of such effects on perceptual

judgments would be analogously available for the preservation of the epistemic importance of intuition in the face of such effects on intuitive judgments. The upshot is that we have to be *careful* in how we use intuition, not that intuition is useless. It is of course helpful to be shown how intuition can go astray in unfavorable conditions, just as perception can go similarly astray. But the important question is untouched: Can intuition enjoy relative to philosophy an evidential status analogous to that enjoyed by perception relative to empirical science?

We turn, finally, to a recent line of attack on philosophical intuition, one also in line with the experimental philosophy movement.[5] According to a recent book by Michael Bishop and J. D. Trout, epistemology should look beyond its navel and adopt the more worthy project of developing prescriptions that will have some use in the real world. By contrast, the methods of "Standard Analytic Epistemology" (SAE) "are suited to the task of providing an account of the considered epistemic judgments of (mostly) well-off Westerners with Ph.D.'s in Philosophy" (Bishop & Trout, 2005).

Normative disciplines concerned with prescription and evaluation have a theoretical side and a more applied side. The latter we might call "casuistry" *in a broad sense.* We are familiar with the casuistry of advice columnists, priests, parents, therapists, and friends, tailored to specific individual cases, and we also know the more general, policy-oriented casuistry of applied ethics, a large and thriving sub-discipline. Insofar as there is such a thing as applied epistemology, I suppose it is to be found largely, though not exclusively, in the similarly large and active field of critical reasoning.

It may be objected that even if intuition is defensible abstractly as a possible source of normative knowledge, its role in epistemic casuistry will be small by comparison with our knowledge of the relevant scientific facts about our intellectual equipment and its social and physical setting, about its reliability, and about the reliability of various information-gathering methods.

That may or may not be so. I find it difficult to assess such size of role, especially since the prospects for epistemic casuistry are so unclear, and I mean epistemic casuistry *as a discipline*, with generally applicable rules. Of course, we know a lot about reliable methods, for example, about how to determine a huge variety of facts through the use of a corresponding variety of instruments. And we also know how to use library sources, which newspapers to trust, which statistical methods are reliable, et cetera. But there really is no discernible unified discipline there. Such casuistry would encompass all the manuals for all the various instruments and how to read all the various gauges, for one thing. And it would also include the variegated practical lore on how to tell what's what and on what basis: the lore of navigation, jungle guidance, farming tips, and so on and so forth. That is all of course extremely useful, but it is no part of the traditional problematic of epistemology. Nor is there any reason to replace either of epistemic casuistry or traditional epistemology with the other. Each has its own time and place.

Traditional epistemology enjoys the coherence provided by its unified set of central questions concerning the nature, conditions, and extent of knowledge and justification. Some may regard such questions with distaste. But philistinism is not to be feared by a discipline that has attracted unexcelled minds over the course of millennia, and in cultures as diverse as those of Buddhist India and classical Greece, and many others.

In any case, even if the role of intuition in epistemic casuistry is small, I fail to see an objection here. Our question has been whether intuition can be understood clearly and defended adequately as a source of foundational a priori justification. Once that is accomplished, our task is completed, especially if intuition's role in epistemic casuistry is *indispensable*, no matter how large or small.

Nevertheless, Bishop and Trout press their case against the theoretical side of SAE, as follows:

> As we have…argued, when it comes to epistemic judgments, the theories of SAE define what we "*do* do" not what we "*must* or *ought* to do." They…merely tell us how we *do* make epistemic judgments (and by "we," we mean the tiny fraction of the world's population who has studied SAE)….
>
> The proponent of SAE is replacing normative questions about how to evaluate reason and belief with descriptive questions about how proponents of SAE evaluate reason and belief. (Bishop & Trout, 2005, p. 110)

But this misconstrues the way intuition is supposed to function in epistemology and in philosophy more generally, which is by analogy with the way observation is supposed to function in empirical science.

Empirical theories are required to accord well enough with the deliverances of scientific observation. Does empirical inquiry merely tell us how we *do* make empirical observations? (And by "we" I mean only the tiny fraction of the world's population who has studied empirical science.) Is the proponent of empirical science replacing questions about the tides, the circulation of the blood, the movements of the planets, and so on, with questions about how proponents of empirical science make certain observations?

That implied parody is supposed to bring out the misconstrual that I find in Bishop and Trout. Intuitions are supposed to function like observations. The data for empirical science include not *just* claims *about* the observations of some few specialists. The set of empirical data includes also claims about the subject matter of the specialists' fields of study, about truths concerning the natural phenomena under study. Similarly, philosophical data would include not *just* claims *about* the intuitions shared by some few specialists. Also prominently included would be claims about the subject matter of the philosophers' fields of study, including evaluative or normative truths of epistemology, for example.

Perhaps there is some crucial difference between natural phenomena and evaluative phenomena that rules out any such analogy. Perhaps there are no normative truths, for example, by contrast with the evident availability of empirical truths. But if this is the real issue, then we need to consider whether in principle there could or could not be the truths that there seem intuitively, commonsensically, to be. And how could we possibly approach such a question except philosophically, through the sort of reflection plus dialectic that depends crucially on philosophical intuition?

Even if it turns out that there *is* such a fundamental semantic divergence between empirical and normative subject matter, finally, a relevant analogy between observation and intuition might *still* survive such semantic divergence. This too would need to be debated philosophically. Progress on such issues of metaphilosophy depends thus on progress *within* philosophy.

Notes

1. This essay was originally a paper presented in the "Experimental Philosophy" symposium at the 2006 Pacific Division meetings of the APA.
2. Of course, even if just doing interdisciplinary work with scientists is not surprisingly distinctive or novel, it is still a time-honored tradition, which contemporary experimental philosophy might admirably extend.
3. I argue for this approach more fully in earlier papers (Beyer & Burri, 2007; DePaul & Ramsey, 1998; Greenough & Lynch, 2006). And I return to it in Sosa (2007).
4. "Intuitions and Individual Differences: the Knobe Effect Revisited," available at http://www.rci.rutgers.edu/~stich/Experimental_Philosophy_Seminar/experimental_philosophy_seminar_readings.htm.
5. Of course, not every advocate of "experimental philosophy" would endorse everything in the loose conglomerate that falls under that flexible title. Furthermore, there is a recent strain of experimental philosophy with a more positive view of intuitions. Proponents of this strain use experimental evidence to reach a better understanding of those intuitions and of their underlying competence(s). Compare,

for examples, the following: Knobe, 2006; Nahmias, Morris, Nadelhoffer, & Turner, 2006; Nichols, 2002 (my thanks here to Joshua Knobe).

References

Beyer, C., & Burri, A. (2007). Intuitions: Their nature and epistemic efficacy. *Grazer Philosophische Studien. Philosophical Knowledge—Its Possibility and Scope* [Special issue].

Bishop, M., & Murphy, D. (eds.) (2007). A defense of intuitions. In *Stich and his critics*. Oxford: Blackwell Publishers. Available at http://homepage.mac.com/ernestsosa/Menu2.html.

Bishop, M. A., & Trout, J. D. (2005). *Epistemology and the psychology of human judgment* (p. 107). New York: Oxford University Press.

DePaul, M., & Ramsey, W. (eds.) (1998). Minimal intuition. In *Rethinking intuition*. New Jersey: Rowman & Littlefield.

Greenough, P., & Lynch, M. (eds.) (2006). Intuitions and truth. In *Truth and realism*. New York: Oxford University Press.

Knobe, J. (2006). The concept of intentional action: A case study in the uses of folk psychology. *Philosophical Studies.*

Nahmias, E., Morris, S., Nadelhoffer, T., & Turner, J. (2006). Is incompatibilism intuitive? *Philosophy and Phenomenological Research,* pp. 28–53.

Nichols, S. (2002). Norms with feeling: Towards a psychological account of moral judgment. *Cognition, 84,* 221–236.

Nichols, S., & Knobe, J. (2007). Moral responsibility and determinism: The cognitive science of folk intuitions. *Noûs.*

Sosa, E. (2007). *A virtue epistemology: Apt belief and reflective knowledge*, Vol. 1. New York: Oxford University Press.

Swain, S., Alexander, J., & Weinberg, J. M. (2008). The instability of philosophical intuitions: Running hot and cold on Truetemp. *Philosophy and Phenomenological Research,* Vol. 76(1), pp. 138–155. Available at http://www.indiana.edu/~eel/.

Study Questions

1. Explain Sosa's competence-based account of intuition. Are philosophical intuitions rational intuitions or empirical intuitions?

2. How does disagreement between two subjects about a hypothetical case pose a potential problem for the use of intuition in philosophy?

3. How does Sosa's distinction between verbal and substantive disagreement offer a response to the problem posed by disagreement?

4. Make a list of the ways in which intuition and perception are similar and different. Given your list, do you think that intuition is a source of justification for beliefs just like perception is a source of justification for beliefs? Explain your answer.

Glossary

a posteriori   A piece of knowledge is said to be known *a posteriori* if and only if the justification for the belief is dependent on sense experience. A typical instance of *a posteriori* knowledge is the knowledge one has of the statement that there is a table in front of him or her. In addition, *a posteriori* knowledge is characterized as knowledge that cannot be known in any other way.

a priori   A piece of knowledge is said to be known *a priori* if and only if the justification for the belief is independent of sense experience. A typical instance of *a priori* knowledge is the knowledge one has of the statement 2 + 2 = 4. In addition, *a priori* knowledge is often characterized as knowledge that *can* be known independent of sense experience, even if in a particular instance it is known on the basis of sense experience. For example, one could come to know that 2 + 2 = 4 by using a calculator, even though it could be known simply by reasoning.

accidental property   This is a property which if lost does not affect the identity of the thing which has it. For example, being rectangular is an accidental property of many books. Compare to *essential property*.

agent causation   Agent causation is the libertarian view holding that free human actions are unique in that unlike other events in the universe, they are not caused by other events. Rather, they are caused by the agent himself or herself. While some agent causal proponents have offered further analysis of this type of causation, others find it unnecessary, if not impossible, to do so.

ampliation   Ampliation means adding to (or "amplifying") what is already there. Michotte believed that our minds add an impression of causal connectedness to certain sorts of connected sensations.

apperception   Apperception is reflective awareness of one's mental states. This is in contrast with our conscious awareness of external objects (i.e., perception).

appetition   Appetition is a term used by Leibniz to refer to an internal principle which motivates and guides the changes from perception to perception.

begging the question   Begging the question is when you assume the very claim you are trying to prove or when you use the very strategy of proof that you are trying to secure. Here is an example: I know I should believe God exists and is great, because I read so in a sacred text. And I know that I should trust that text, because God wrote it and God is great.

Bundle Theory   This is a theory of personal identity that says that persons consist of a series of different mental states which is unified by various causal relations. These relations are like the string one might use to tie together a bundle. The Bundle Theory denies that there is a single subject of experiences. Sometimes called the Humean Bundle Theory, because it was advocated by David Hume.

Cartesian dualism   Cartesian dualism is the view articulated by the philosopher René Descartes, according to which both substance dualism and interactionist dualism are true. According to this view, the mental and the physical are fundamentally different substances that causally interact to guide the body.

categorical imperative   For Kant, the categorical imperative is the foundational moral principle which holds that "Act only in accordance with that maxim through which you can at the same time will that it should become a universal law." Another version states that "so act that you use humanity, whether in your own person or in the person of any other, always at the same time as an end, never merely as a means."

causal Bayes net formalism   This is the formula that Alison Gopnik and her collaborators use to capture the concept of causation. As a Bayesian formalism, its virtue is its ability to reveal how changes in certain variables are likely to affect other variables.

classical model of concepts   The classical model of concepts maintains that all concepts have simple necessary and sufficient conditions for membership. The model is stated as follows: x falls under concept C if and only if x has properties $P_1 \ldots P_n$.

cogito ergo sum   This is Latin for "I think, therefore I exist." This was used by René Descartes to argue that one cannot be fooled into thinking she exists when she doesn't, since thinking requires a thinker.

cognitive science   Cognitive science is the science of the mind. A currently developing field of science encompassing insights from several older disciplines, including computer science, linguistics, neuroscience, philosophy, and psychology.

compatibilism   This is the view that free will and moral responsibility is possible even if determinism should turn out to be true.

conceptual analysis   Conceptual analysis is the process of proposing sets of necessary and sufficient conditions as definitions of some concept.

conceptual truth   Conceptual truths are necessary truths concerning concepts.

consequentialism   Consequentialism is the family of views in normative ethics which have in common the claim that the moral assessment of actions is fundamentally a matter of the balance of good consequences over bad consequences that would be produced by that action.

cosmological arguments   Cosmological arguments are a family of *a posteriori* arguments for the existence of God which include a premise about a general feature of the world, such as that a contingent universe exists or that things change, and argues that the best explanation for that feature is the existence of God.

de jure objections   These are objections to religious belief which claim not that such beliefs are false, but rather that they are unwarranted or rationally unjustified or otherwise rationally unacceptable.

de facto objections   These are objections to religious belief which focus on the purported falsity of such beliefs.

deontology   Deontological views in ethics hold that certain actions are intrinsically right or wrong, regardless of the good or bad consequences that they may generate. The most influential form of deontology is developed by Immanuel Kant, who grounds duty in the satisfaction of the categorical imperative.

design arguments   Design arguments are a family of *a posteriori* arguments (i.e., arguments that incorporate sense data in at least one premise) for the existence of God which begin by identifying some particular or specific property of the universe, such as the apparent fine-tuning of the laws of nature for life, and conclude that God's existence is the best explanation for the feature in question. Design arguments are also sometimes called teleological arguments for the existence of God.

determinism/causal determinism   This is the view that every event or state of affairs necessarily follows from previous events and the laws of nature. So according to determinism, all events (including human actions) are theoretically predictable with 100 percent accuracy. The issue of what impact the truth of determinism would have on free will is the central issue of contention between compatibilists and incompatibilists.

diachronic unity   This is the unity that a thing exhibits over time. In the case of personal identity, it is the idea that persons remain the same over time.

doctrine of anamnesis   Plato's doctrine of anamnesis maintains that coming to know is just the remembering of truths about the forms forgotten at birth. On Plato's view, we can remember these truths because our souls are nonmaterial and preexisted our current lives. When not attached to a body, these souls inhabited the realm of the forms where they became directly acquainted with the forms.

dualism   Dualism is any of a group of views holding that there are important relations between two fundamental kinds of phenomena, the mental and the physical. Varieties include:

> **interactionist dualism**   The doctrine that there is causal interaction between mental and physical phenomena.

> **substance dualism**   The view that there are two fundamentally basic types of substance in the world: mental and physical substance. Neither substance is more fundamental than the other substance.

ego theory   This is a theory of personal identity that claims an individual's continued existence is dependent upon the continued existence of an ego or subject of experiences. According to this theory, a person's life is unified over time by the fact that the same subject is present from beginning to end. It is sometimes called the Cartesian Ego Theory, because it was advocated by René Descartes.

eliminative materialism   This is the theory that mental states will not be reduced to physical states, but instead will be completely eliminated from our fundamental ontological picture.

empiricism   Empiricism is a doctrine that experience is the only source of knowledge. Empiricism should be compared with rationalism, which is the doctrine that reason alone can be a source of knowledge.

entelechy   In Aristotelian philosophy, entelechy is a being that has been fully actualized. In Leibniz's system, it is a simple substance that is the basic constituent of the universe, synonymous with the term *monad*.

epiphenomenalism   Epiphenomenalism holds that the mental and physical are separate and that mental events do not cause physical events. A substance or property dualist who held that the mind never causally interacts with the brain would be an epiphenomenalist.

epiphenomenon   An epiphenomenon is a thing which is the by-product of another process and which has no causal powers to affect the process itself. For example, the steam-whistle which results from the mechanism of a locomotive is an epiphenomenon. Some philosophers have claimed that mental states are epiphenomena; they are mere by-products of brain processes with no causal powers to influence behavior.

epistemology   This is the philosophical study of knowledge and justified belief. The central questions of epistemology are the following: What can we know? What is the nature of knowledge? What is it to be justified in believing something? Does knowledge derive only from sense experience?

essential property   This is a property that is necessary for the continued existence of an object. For example, the shape of a ring is an essential property of being a ring. If the ring is melted down, it is no longer a ring. Compare to *accidental property*.

eudaimonia   Often translated as "happiness," *eudaimonia* is perhaps better understood as "living and doing well" or "flourishing." According to Aristotle, *eudaimonia* is an activity of the soul in accordance with virtue. It is also the proper end of all human actions. While virtue is essential to *eudaimonia*, happiness also requires other goods that may be outside the direct control of the agent (e.g., health, good fortune).

event causation/transeunt causation   This is a relation between two events or states of affairs, wherein one brings about the other. It is the ordinary concept of causation, the concept that arises in scientific discourse. It is the concept in use in the phrase "freezing the pipes will cause them to burst." It is the kind of causation that proponents of agent causation believe cannot account for a free action.

evil, evidential problem of   The evidential problem of evil is a family of arguments which aim to show that the existence of evil gives us reason or evidence to believe that an omnipotent, omniscient, omnibenevolent God does not exist. Evidential versions of the problem of evil are thus weaker than the logical problem of evil.

evil, logical problem of   The logical problem of evil is an argument which aims to show a logical inconsistency between the existence of evil and the existence of an omnipotent, omniscient, omnibenevolent God. Insofar as evil exists, this argument would, if sound, prove that an omnipotent, omniscient, omnibenevolent God does not exist.

experimental philosophy   Experimental philosophy is a philosophical movement in which people attend to the results of, and even perform, experiments to help address philosophical questions.

explanatory gap   This is the apparent lack of explanatory connection between consciousness and scientific theory.

Proponents of the explanatory gap claim that no matter how much we learn in scientific terms, we will never fully understand consciousness.

fallibilism   This is the view that one can have knowledge even when one's evidence does not guarantee the truth of what one believes. Evidence that simply makes one's belief highly probable (but not certain) can be enough for knowledge.

fallible faculty   A faculty is fallible just in case it is subject to error. So vision is a fallible faculty because we can misperceive things using vision.

family resemblance model of concepts   The family resemblance model of concepts maintains that some (if not all) concepts do not have simple necessary and sufficient conditions. It maintains, for example, that *x* and *y* can both fall under a concept C even though *x* and *y* do not share all of the same properties relevant to falling under C.

final cause   Final cause is that for the sake of which something exists; its purpose; its most fully actualized state of being. Final cause is one of Aristotle's four causes. It can serve as a middle term to connect parts of animals with the animals themselves, to connect attributes with things.

formal cause   Formal cause is that without which an entity would not be itself or distinguishable from other entities; its essence; its constituting structure; the thing responsible for the entity's trajectory of development. Formal cause is one of Aristotle's four causes. It can serve as a middle term to connect parts of animals with the animals themselves, to connect attributes with things.

the forms   Plato's forms are nonmaterial, perfect, divine, and eternal specification of every possible type of thing that can exist.

functionalism   Functionalism is the view that mental states like belief and desire are functional entities, identified and individuated by their functional properties, such as their typical causes and effects. The functionalist is generally a physicalist, though strictly speaking needn't be.

Gettier-style counterexample   A Gettier-style counterexample is a counterexample to the claim that a justified true belief is an instance of knowledge. The counterexamples that are Gettier style involve a separation between the truth maker for the statement in question and the source of justification for the statement.

hard determinism   Hard determinism can be understood as encompassing three theses: (1) Free will is impossible for human beings if determinism is true; (2) Determinism is true; and (3) Given theses 1 and 2, it follows that free will is impossible for human beings.

hedonism   Hedonism is a diverse school of thought which holds that pleasure is the only intrinsic good, and that pain is the only intrinsic evil. Hedonism is often endorsed by consequentialists but is rejected by deontological and virtue-based approaches to ethics.

illusion   Illusions, according to Sigmund Freud, are "fulfillments of the oldest, strongest, and most urgent wishes of mankind." His use of the term thus differs significantly from its common usage. What makes a belief an illusion is not that it is false—Freud thinks there can be true illusions—but that it is acquired and maintained despite lacking proper support.

incompatibilism   This is the thesis that free will and moral responsibility are impossible if determinism is true. Incompatibilists tend to believe that determinism precludes the kinds of open alternatives that are necessary for free will. Incompatibilism is accepted by libertarians, skeptics, and hard determinists.

infallible faculty   A faculty is infallible just in case it is not subject to error.

intentional states   Intentional states are mental states that represent or are "about" something (e.g., Mary saw the cat; Johnny wanted a sandwich). Propositional attitudes are a subclass of intentional states in which the agent bears an attitudinal relation (prototypically a belief or a desire) to a proposition (e.g., Sanjay believed that the swimming pool was open all afternoon).

interpretationism   This is the view that there is no fact of the matter which beliefs a person actually holds at a given time. Rather, belief ascriptions are a matter of third-person interpretation.

is/ought fallacy   Often referred to as the naturalistic fallacy, the is/ought fallacy is when one attempts to argue from descriptive premises (i.e., premises about what *is* the case) to a normative conclusion (i.e., a conclusion about what *ought* to be the case). There is considerable debate among philosophers about whether such reasoning is always a fallacy.

justified belief   A justified belief is one that is well supported by available reasons or evidence. Standard sources of justification include perception, sound reasoning, reliable testimony, and introspection.

libertarianism   Libertarianism can be understood as encompassing three theses: (1) Free will is impossible for human beings if determinism is true; (2) Human beings are capable of possessing free will; and (3) Given theses 1 and 2, it follows that determinism is false. Agent causation is a distinct type of libertarianism.

materialism   Materialism is the doctrine that only material objects exist. This contrasts with idealism, which states that only the mental world exists, and dualism, which states that both the material and the mental exist. See *physicalism*.

matters of fact   For Hume, matters of fact, along with relations of ideas, are one of the two kinds of things we can know. Matters of fact are propositions we can discover only by look-

ing at the world. Because the contrary of every matter of fact is logically possible, we have to look at the world to make sure the matter of fact is the case. Matters of fact amplify our knowledge, which makes them interesting to Hume. For example, "The sun will rise tomorrow" is a matter of fact. It brings together the sun with the notion of rising tomorrow, though these two things are not necessarily connected.

maxim   For Kant, a maxim is a subjective volitional principle of the following form: "In circumstance *C*, I will to do action *A* in order to bring about end *E*." They are subjective insofar as they are about individual subjects or agents, and they are volitional insofar as they describe what those agents have a volition to do.

middle term   The middle term is what makes possible the connection between an attribute and a thing, the cause that produces the connection between the two. In *Posterior Analytics*, Book II, Chapter 2, Aristotle writes: "[T]he object of our inquiry is always the 'middle': we inquire, because we have not perceived it...."

monad   In Leibniz's metaphysics, monads are the basic constituents of the world. They are simple substances that are neither divisible nor extended. They cannot be destroyed by natural means. They are not subject to change from external forces, but each changes in accordance with an internal principle.

moral responsibility   The specific type of responsibility that is required for praise and blame. It is the kind of responsibility that is considered by some to justify, among other things, reward and punishment. Free will is generally taken to be required for moral responsibility.

natural theology   Natural theology is the enterprise of providing support for religious beliefs, such as the existence of God or claims about God's nature, only on the basis of human reason and without the aid of divine revelation. Natural theology is contrasted with revealed theology.

naturalism, methodological   Methodological naturalism is the view that emphasizes the empirical methods of the sciences as the only reliable methods of inquiry.

necessary condition   The phrase "X is a necessary condition for Y" means that if X does not obtain then neither can Y. For example, "being divisible by 2 is a necessary condition for being an even number" means that if a number is not divisible by 2, then it is not even.

necessary truth   A truth is necessary if and only if it cannot possibly be false.

numerical identity   Two things are numerically identical if and only if they are one and the same thing. Numerical identity is a one-to-one relation, which every thing has with itself. This notion becomes important when we discuss the persistence of objects over time. When we ask if something is the same object despite undergoing property changes, we are inquiring about numerical identity.

occasionalism This is the view that mental and physical states do not interact, but correspond to one another. This correspondence is assured by God. For example, he makes it the case that when the body is cut there is a corresponding pain.

ontological arguments Ontological arguments are a family of arguments for the existence of God on the basis of necessary and *a priori* premises (i.e., premises not based on sense experience). The most famous version of ontological argument was presented by St. Anselm of Canterbury.

ontology Ontology is the study of what exists.

Pascal's Wager Pascal's Wager is a particular form of pragmatic argument for belief in the existence of God. Even though one may not be capable of knowing for sure that God exists, the consequences of not believing in God's existence if he does exist are so dire that one should wager that he does exist.

personal identity This phrase is used to pick out a cluster of issues revolving around the question of what makes a person the same person across different times. The identity in question is typically understood as numerical identity: what conditions are required for two people at different times to be one and the same person.

phenomenal consciousness Phenomenal consciousness is a property of mental states when there is something it's like for the subject to be in those states. Primary examples of phenomenally conscious states are perceptual states, like seeing a red apple, or bodily states, like pains.

physicalism Physicalism is usually used as synonymous with *materialism*, the doctrine that everything that exists is ultimately physical. Physicalism thus stands in opposition to substance dualism.

possible worlds Possible worlds are worlds that could be the case. In another possible world, you might have a different hair color, a different gender, or a different gravitational status. Just how far a possible world might vary from the actual would is a matter of interesting debate. The actual world, the one we in fact live in, is one of many possible worlds, one of the many worlds that could have been.

pre-established harmony This is the view that the correspondence between mental and physical states was set up by God at the beginning of the universe. Leibniz, the first proponent of this theory, claimed that the mental and the physical processes of the universe were like two clocks synchronized by God. See also *occasionalism.*

process reliabilism Process reliabilism is the idea that a belief is justified if and only if it is the output of a reliable belief-forming process. We do not need to know that it is reliable. It must simply be the output of a reliable process. A reliable process is generally understood as a process where the number of true outputs is sufficiently greater than the number of false outputs.

propositional attitudes Propositional attitudes are relational mental states like belief and desire which take a "that" clause as their object (e.g., Mary believed *that* the horse could run).

psychologically continuous Two persons are psychologically continuous if they share many of the same psychological states like desires, memories, and personality traits. Some philosophers claim that psychological continuity is the essential factor in questions about personal identity.

qualia Qualia are the qualitative or phenomenal aspects of our conscious experiences, for example, redness or bitterness. See also *phenomenal consciousness.*

qualitative identity Two things are qualitatively identical if and only if they share all the same qualities (or properties), that is, if they are exactly similar. For example, two pencils mass produced from the same factory might be qualitatively identical.

reason explanations These are explanations that explain behavior by referring to people's propositional attitudes (e.g., their beliefs and desires), not their mental dispositions, character traits, or extenuating physical situations or conditions. Reason explanations portray people's behavior as rational.

reducible A property, substance, or system of natural laws is reducible to some other thing or system if it can be fully explained in terms of that other thing or system. It is irreducible if it cannot be fully explained in terms of any other thing or system.

relations of ideas For Hume, relations of ideas, along with matters of fact, are one of the two kinds of things we can know. Relations of ideas are propositions we can discover by thinking alone. They are intuitively or demonstratively certain. For example, "Three times five is equal to half of thirty" relates the idea of "three times five" to the idea of "half of thirty." We do not have to observe anything in the world to get from the former idea to the latter idea. The latter idea seems to drop out of the first one. This is exactly what makes relations of ideas uninteresting for Hume. They do not amplify our knowledge.

religious diversity It is important to differentiate two different versions of religious diversity. Descriptive religious diversity merely points out that there are numerous, and often competing, religious claims. Evaluative religious diversity, on the other hand, makes the stronger claim not only that there are competing religious claims but also that these competing claims are equally good or true.

revealed theology Revealed theology is the enterprise of making and defending claims about the existence, nature, or actions of God which are based on revelation. Revealed theology is contrasted with natural theology.

self-binding Self-binding is a process used in the present to block action on future desires. The most famous literary example of this comes from Homer's description of Odysseus tying himself to the mast of his ship to avoid being seduced by the songs of the sirens.

situationism   Situationism holds that human behavior is determined by features of the situation rather than features of the person. Thus understood, situationism poses a challenge to some philosophical claims about moral virtue.

skeptical argument   A skeptical argument is an argument that draws into question whether something is known or denies that it is known. For example, Doug claims that he knows that there is a chair in front of him because he sees it. But Bonny points out that he cannot rule out the possibility that there is a hologram producing the chair appearance. Bonny has raised a skeptical argument.

skepticism (about free will)   This is the view that free will is impossible for human beings.. Skeptics also tend to hold that true moral responsibility is impossible for people.

skepticism (Academic)   This is the view that we have no knowledge in some domain. The most commonly discussed form of skepticism claims that we have no knowledge of the world external to our minds.

skepticism (Pyrrhonian)   This is the view that we should refrain from making a judgment about whether we have knowledge in some domain. When matters are disputed or uncertain, we should not believe one way or the other.

split brain   This is the result of a surgery which severs the corpus callosum, the bundle of neural fibers that connects the two hemispheres of the brain. Split-brain patients tend to function normally in everyday life but exhibit surprising responses in laboratory conditions. Split-brain patients seem to provide evidence for the claim that there is no single subject of consciousness.

substance   Substance is that in which the properties of a thing inhere. Substance is a metaphysical concept with a long history; many have argued that the concept is indefinable and incoherent.

sufficient condition   The phrase "X is a sufficient condition for Y" means that if X obtains, then Y obtains. For example, "being an even number is a sufficient condition for being a whole number" means that if a number is even, then it is a whole number.

synchronic unity   Synchronic unity is the unity of things that occur simultaneously.

theory of mind, folk   The folk theory of mind is the ordinary ability to produce explanations of others' behavior by attributing mental states.

theory theory   The theory theory claims that normal development of mature cognitive capacities can be understood on the model of scientific theory formation. Just as scientists develop theories about the world and modify those theories in the face of new evidence, so even very young children do the same in trying to understand and explain their world. The theory theory has been applied to many specific domains, for example, to the acquisition of a mature theory of mind.

tripartite analysis of knowledge   The tripartite analysis of knowledge maintains that S knows that P if and only if S has justified true belief that P. The tripartite account of knowledge has roots in the philosophy of Plato, but it was widely taken to be decisively refuted by examples posed by Edmund Gettier. See also *Gettier-style counterexamples*.

utilitarianism   Historically the most well-developed form of consequentialism, utilitarianism holds that the good to be maximized by one's actions is utility, where utility is understood to be the presence of pleasure and the absence of pain. Act utilitarians hold that individual actions are right if and only if they promote the best overall utility. Rule utilitarianism holds that actions are right if and only if they are permitted by those rules that maximize utility.

verbal disagreement   A verbal disagreement occurs when two or more parties disagree about something merely in virtue of assigning different meanings to the words they use. The disagreement is said to be more than merely a verbal disagreement if, upon inquiring further into the nature of the disagreement, the parties discover that neither party's response to the guiding question can be resolved in virtue of a misunderstanding of the question, or in virtue of a distinct understanding of the question.

virtue ethics   Virtue ethics is a loose family of views in normative ethics that places a priority on virtues of character.

virtues   Virtues are moral character traits that make their possessor better off.

warrant   On Alvin Plantinga's view, warrant is the property enough of which makes true belief into knowledge.

About the Editors

Fritz Allhoff, Ph.D., is an Associate Professor in the Department of Philosophy at Western Michigan University and a Senior Research Fellow in the Centre for Applied Philosophy and Public Ethics at the Australian National University. Fritz has had visiting positions at the University of Michigan, the University of Pittsburgh, and the University of Oxford. He works primarily in applied ethics, ethical theory, and philosophy of biology. His latest book is *Terrorism, Ticking Time-Bombs, and Torture* (2012) from the University of Chicago Press.

James R. Beebe, Ph.D., is an Associate Professor of Philosophy at the State University of New York at Buffalo, where he is also a member of the Center for Cognitive Science and the Director of the Experimental Epistemology Research Group. His research interests within mainstream epistemology include naturalistic epistemology, the nature and extent of skeptical challenges to our everyday knowledge, and the nature of *a priori* knowledge. His experimental work centers on the study of epistemic cognition, that is, the ways in which people make judgments about knowledge, rationality, and evidence.

Alexandra Bradner, Ph.D., is an Assistant Professor of Philosophy at Denison University who works in general philosophy of science, history and philosophy of biology, and epistemology. Her work on the pragmatics of explanation has appeared in *Cognitive Processing* and *Teaching Philosophy*. She is currently conducting an experimental study on Thomson's violinist with Jeanine Schroer. Alexandra thinks there is no upper limit on the number of times you have to explain to philosophers that experimental philosophy is not about polling the folk and inducing your philosophical theory from their responses.

Emily Esch, Ph.D., is an Assistant Professor of Philosophy at College of Saint Benedict and Saint John's University in Minnesota. Her work is primarily in the philosophy of mind and epistemology. In philosophy of mind, she has focused especially on the nature of consciousness, and her work in epistemology has explored the differences between "knowledge that" and "know-how."

Ron Mallon, Ph.D., is an Associate Professor of Philosophy and Director of the Philosophy-Neuroscience-Psychology Program at Washington University, St. Louis. His research is in social philosophy, philosophy of cognitive psychology, and moral psychology. He has co-directed two NEH Summer Institutes on Experimental Philosophy; has been a chair of the Society for Philosophy and Psychology Meeting; and has been the recipient of a Laurence S. Rockefeller Visiting Fellowship at Princeton's University Center for Human Values and an American Council of Learned Societies Fellowship.

Eric Mandelbaum, Ph.D., has been the James Martin Research Fellow at the Faculty of Philosophy and Future of Humanity Institute at the University of Oxford. In 2011, he took up an ACLS New Faculty Fellowship at Yale University's Departments of Cognitive Science and Philosophy, and he is now the Mind/Brain/Behavior Postdoctoral Fellow at Harvard University. He was awarded the Cognitive Science Society's inaugural Robert J. Glushko Prize for Outstanding Doctoral Theses in Cognitive Science in 2011. His work focuses on cognitive architecture, belief acquisition, belief storage, judgments of responsibility, and implicit racism.

Stephen G. Morris, Ph.D., is an Assistant Professor in the Department of Political Science, Economics, and Philosophy at the College of Staten Island (CUNY). Prior to this, he served as an Assistant Professor of Philosophy at Missouri Western State University, where he received a Distinguished Professor Award in 2008 and the James V. Mehl Scholarship Award in 2009. Stephen's primary research interests include free will, meta-ethics, applied ethics, and the philosophy of science. His papers have appeared in *Philosophy and Phenomenological Research*, *Philosophy of Science*, and *Philosophical Psychology*.

Shaun Nichols, Ph.D., is Professor of Philosophy at the University of Arizona. He is the author of *Sentimental Rules: On the Natural Foundations of Moral Judgment* and co-author (with Stephen Stich) of *Mindreading*. He is editor of *The Architecture of the Imagination* and co-editor of *Experimental Philosophy* (with Joshua Knobe). He has also published over fifty articles in academic journals, both in philosophy and psychology. At the University of Arizona he directs a research group on experimental philosophy, which attempts to uncover the psychological factors that influence how we think about philosophical matters.

Mark Phelan, Ph.D., is an Assistant Professor of Philosophy at Lawrence University. He received his doctorate from the University of North Carolina, Chapel Hill, and was a Postdoctoral Fellow and Lecturer at Yale University from 2009 to 2011. Mark's primary research interests are in the philosophies of language, mind, and cognitive science. He has published in *Philosophical Studies*, *Mind and Language*, and *Pacific Philosophical Quarterly*, among other journals.

Michael J. Shaffer, Ph.D., is an Associate Professor in the Department of Philosophy at St. Cloud State University. He has been a Fellow of the Rotman Institute of Science and Values at the University of Western Ontario, a Fellow of the Center for

Formal Epistemology at Carnegie-Mellon University, a Lakatos Fellow at the London School of Economics, and an NEH Fellow at the University of Utah. His primary research interests are in epistemology, logic, and the philosophy of science.

Tamler Sommers, Ph.D, is an Assistant Professor in the Department of Philosophy at the University of Houston. His research concerns issues in ethics, meta-ethics, and the philosophy of punishment. He is the author of two books, *Relative Justice* (Princeton, 2011) and *A Very Bad Wizard: Morality behind the Curtain* (McSweeney's, 2009). Other recent publications include "Experimental Philosophy and Free Will" (*Philosophy Compass*), "The Two Faces of Revenge: Moral Responsibility and the Culture of Honor" (*Biology and Philosophy*), "More Work for Hard Incompatibilism" (*Philosophy and Phenomenological Research*), and "The Objective Attitude" (*Philosophical Quarterly*).

Kevin Timpe, Ph.D., is an Assistant Professor in the Department of Philosophy at Northwest Nazarene University. He has held visiting fellowships at Oxford University and the Center for Philosophy of Religion at the University of Notre Dame. Kevin's primary research interests are in the metaphysics of free will, philosophy of religion, and virtue theory. He is the author of two books, *Free Will: Sourcehood and Its Alternatives* and *Free Will in Philosophical Theology* (both with Continuum Press) and over a dozen journal articles. He is the editor of two books, *Arguing about Religion* (Routledge) and the forthcoming *Virtues and Their Vices* (Oxford University Press, with Craig Boyd).

Anand J. Vaidya, Ph.D., is Associate Professor of Philosophy at San Jose State University in Silicon Valley, California. His primary areas of research are epistemology, especially modality and methodology, and philosophy of mind, especially rationality and intuition. Anand has co-edited a series of books on business ethics and the history of philosophy as well as published papers on the epistemology of modality and the methodology of experimental philosophy. At present, he is doing research on the philosophy of economics and the capabilities approach to justice.

Chris Weigel, Ph.D., is Associate Professor of Philosophy at Utah Valley University. Her interests include moral psychology, philosophy of mind, philosophy of psychology, and free will. She is a co-editor of *Living Ethics*. After attending the 2009 National Endowment for the Humanities Summer Seminar on experimental philosophy, she began using experiments to examine the role of psychological distance on intuitions about free will.

Josh Weisberg, Ph.D., is an Assistant Professor of Philosophy at the University of Houston. He received his doctorate from the City University of New York Graduate Center in 2007. His research is in the philosophy of mind, with a focus on consciousness. His work has appeared in philosophical journals such as *Analysis, Philosophical Studies, Philosophical Psychology, Synthese*, and *Journal of Consciousness Studies*, as well as in the ground-breaking volume *What Philosophy Can Tell You about Your Cat* (Open Court, 2008). He went into philosophy to avoid taking math in college.

Jennifer (Jen) Cole Wright, Ph.D., is an Assistant Professor in the Department of Psychology (and an Affiliate with the Department of Philosophy) at the College of Charleston. Having earned graduate degrees in both psychology and philosophy, she has published in journals across several domains, including *Journal of Experimental Social Psychology, Cognition, Mind & Language,* and *Philosophical Studies.* Her main research interests are in the area of moral psychology across the life span and she studies everyone from young children to adults.